Foreign & Commonwealth Office

GW01085609

The Diplomatic Service List 2003

THIRTY-EIGHTH EDITION

London: TSO

Published by The Stationery Office and available from:

Online
www.tso.co.uk/bookshop

Mail, Telephone, Fax & E-mail
TSO
PO Box 29. Norwich NR3 IGN
Telephone orders/General enquiries: 0870 600 5522
Fax orders: 0870 600 5533
E-mail: book.orders@tso.co.uk
Textphone 0870 240 3701

TSO Shops
123 Kingsway. London WC2B 6PQ
020 7242 6393 Fax 020 7242 6394
68 69 Bull Street, Birmingham B4 6AD
0121 236 9696 Fax 0121 236 9699
9-21 Princess Street, Manchester M60 8AS
0161834 7201 Fax 0161 833 0634
16 Arthur Street Belfast BT 1 4GD
028 9023 8451 Fax 028 9023 5401
18 19High Street,Cardiff CF1 2BZ
029 2039 5548 Fax 029 2038 4347
71 Lothian Road, Edinburgh EH3 9AZ
0870 606 5566 Fax 0870 606 5588

TSO Accredited Agents
(see Yellow Pages)

and through good booksellers

Published with the permission of the Foreign and Commonwealth Office on behalf of the Controller of Her Majesty's Stationery Office.

Whilst every attempt has been made to ensure that the information in this directory is up-to-date at the time of publication, the publisher cannot accept responsibility for any inaccuracies.

ISBN 0 11 591775 6

Preface

Her Majesty's Diplomatic Service provides the staffs of British Diplomatic and Consular posts overseas in Commonwealth and Foreign countries, as well as in the Foreign & Commonwealth Office in London.

The organisation of the Service and the careers of its members are described in this List, which will be published each year. It is based on information available in August 2002 but includes details of some later changes.

The Diplomatic Service was established on 1 January, 1965, by the merger of the former Foreign, Commonwealth and Trade Commissioner Services. Subsequently, it incorporated the staffs of the Colonial Office in London, which merged with the Commonwealth Relations Office on 1 August, 1966, to form the Commonwealth Office.

The Foreign Office and Commonwealth Office continued as separate Departments of State responsible to separate Secretaries of State until 17 October, 1968. On that day they combined to form the Foreign and Commonwealth Office responsible to one Secretary of State. The Permanent Under-Secretary of the Office and the Head of the Diplomatic Service is Sir Michael Jay, KCMG.

Representatives of Commonwealth countries and foreign states serving in London are shown in a separate publication, the London Diplomatic List, published by The Stationery Office every six months.

Every effort has been made to ensure that the information given in this edition is correct at the time of going to press. Amendments and new entries to the Diplomatic Service List should be sent to the Editor to arrive no later than Friday, 22nd August 2003:-

> Lisa T. Gamandi (Editor)
> Foreign and Commonwealth Office
> Publications Section
> Room WH. MZ. 11,
> King Charles St,
> LONDON SW1A 2AH.

November 2002.

Table of Contents

Part I

Part II

BRITISH REPRESENTATION OVERSEAS (AUTUMN 2002)

Part III

CHRONOLOGICAL LISTS FROM 1982 of SECRETARIES OF STATE, MINISTERS OF STATE, PERMANENT UNDER-SECRETARIES, AMBASSADORS, HIGH COMMISSIONERS, PERMANENT REPRESENTATIVES TO INTERNATIONAL ORGANISATIONS AND GOVERNORS AND COMMANDERS-IN-CHIEF OF OVERSEAS TERRITORIES

Part IV

BIOGRAPHICAL NOTES AND LISTS OF STAFF

Home Departments

List of Ministers, Senior Officers and
Home Departments in the
Foreign and Commonwealth Office

Part I: Home Departments

Accommodation

Ministers, Senior Officers and most geographical departments are accommodated in the Main Building, Downing Street, London SW1. Departments are also accommodated in other buildings.

Foreign and Commonwealth Office, Downing Street (West) SW1A 2AL	020 7008 1500
Foreign and Commonwealth Office, Downing Street (East) SW1A 2AL	020 7008 1500
Foreign and Commonwealth Office, Whitehall SW1A 2AP	020 7008 1500
Foreign and Commonwealth Office, King Charles St, SW1A 2AH	020 7008 1500
Apollo House, 36 Wellesley Road, Croydon, CR9 3 RR	020 8686 5622
3 Carlton Gardens SW1Y 5AA	020 7008 1500
Vauxhall Cross 85 Albert Embankment, SE1 7TP	020 7008 4440
Cromwell House, Dean Stanley Street, SW1P 3JG	020 7276 7676
94 Victoria Street, SW1E 5JL	020 7917 7000
Hanslope Park, Hanslope, Milton Keynes MK19 7BH	01908 510444
Old Admiralty Building, Whitehall, London, SW1A 2AF	020 7008 1500
British Trade International, Kingsgate House, 66-74 Victoria Street. London SW1E 6SW	020 7215 5000

TELEPHONE ENQUIRIES
If the number, department or building is not known, callers should ring 020 7270 3000 and ask to be connected to the Central Enquiry point.

TELEGRAPHIC ADDRESS
PRODROME LONDON

TELEX 297711 (a/b PRDRME G)

Internet World Wide Web Address: www.fco.gov.uk

The Foreign & Commonwealth Office provides, through its staff in the UK and through its diplomatic missions abroad, the means of communication between the British Government and other governments and international governmental organisations on all matters falling within the field of international relations. It is responsible for alerting the British Government to the implications of developments overseas; for promoting British interests overseas; for protecting British citizens abroad; for explaining British policies to, and cultivating relationships with, governments overseas; for the discharge of British responsibilities to the overseas territories; for entry clearance (through UKvisas, with the Home Office); and for promoting British business overseas (jointly with the Department of Trade and Industry through British Trade International).

MINISTERS AND THEIR STAFFS

Secretary of State for Foreign & Commonwealth Affairs

The Rt Hon Jack Straw MP
Principal Private Secretary: Simon McDonald
Private Secretaries: Jonathan Sinclair, Patrick Davies
Diary Enquiries: 020 7008 2079
GTN: 7008 2079
Clerical Enquiries: 020 7008 2057
GTN: 7008 2057
Special Advisers: Ed Owen, Michael Williams
Telephone: 020 7008 2112/2117
GTN: 7008 2112/2117

Minister of State for Europe

Denis MacShane MP
Senior Private Secretary: James Morrison
Private Secretary: Sarah Lyons
Telephone: 020 7008 3366
GTN: 7008 3366
Assistant Private Secretary: Lisa Glover
Telephone: 020 7008 3371
GTN: 7008 3371

Minister of State for International Trade and Investment (also DTI)

Baroness Symons of Vernham Dean
Private Secretary: Nick Allen
Telephone: 020 7008 2090
GTN: 7008 2090
Assistant Private Secretaries: Jennifer Townson, Bradley Jones
Telephone: 020 7008 2091/2092
GTN: 7008 2091/2092

Parliamentary Under-Secretary of State

Michael O'Brien MP
Private Secretary: Nick Astbury
Telephone: 020 7008 2129
GTN: 7008 2129
Assistant Private Secretaries: Kara Owen, Claire Lawley (UK Visas)
Telephone: 020 7008 2126/2128
GTN: 7008 2126/2128

Parliamentary Under-Secretary of State

Bill Rammell MP
Private Secretary: David Dunn
Assistant Private Secretary: Sian Price
Telephone: 020 7008 8032
GTN: 7008 8032
Diary Secretary: Jan Abbott
Telephone: 020 7008 8031
GTN: 7008 8031
Correspondence Clerks: Emma Dean, Debbie Ward
Telephone: 020 7008 8252/8038
GTN: 7008 8252/8038

Parliamentary Under-Secretary of State

Baroness Amos
Private Secretary: Tom Fletcher
Telephone: 020 7008 2173
GTN: 7008 2173
Assistant Private Secretary: Kay Stokoe

Diary Secretary: Jessica Seaward
Correspondence Clerks: Shelley Williams-Walker, Stuart Taylor
Telephone: 020 7008 3374
GTN: 7008 3374

SENIOR OFFICERS AND THEIR STAFFS

Permanent Under-Secretary of State & Head of the Diplomatic Service

Sir Michael Jay KCMG
Private Secretary: Menna Rawlings
Telephone: 020 7008 2142
GTN: 7008 2142
Assistant Private Secretaries: Martin Duffy, Andrea McGlone
Telephone: 020 7008 2146
GTN: 7008 2146
Diary Secretary: Sarah Ballett
Telephone: 020 7008 2145
GTN: 7008 2145
Email: PSPUS@fco.gov.uk

Group Chief Executive British Trade International

Sir David Wright GCMG LVO
Telephone: 020 7008 2142
GTN: 7008 2142
Private Secretary: Gavin Scott
Telephone: 020 7215 4300
GTN: 215 4300

Director Generals

Peter Collecott CMG (*Corporate Affairs*)
Peter Ricketts CMG (*Political*)
Michael Arthur CMG (*EU & Economic*)
William Ehrman CMG (*Defence/Intelligence*)
Graham Fry (*Public Services*)
Michael Wood CMG (*Legal Adviser*)

Directors

James Bevan (*Director, Africa*)
Richard D Wilkinson CVO (*Director, Americas/Overseas Territories*).
Edward Oakden (*Director, International Security*).
Linda Duffield (*Director, Wider Europe*).
Kim Darroch CMG (*Director, European Union*).
Stephen Sage (*Chief Executive, FCO Services*).
Philippa Drew (*Director, Global Issues*).
James Bevan (*Director South East Europe/Gibraltar*).
Edward Chaplin OBE (*Director, Middle East/North Africa*)
Simon Fraser (*Director, Strategy /Innovation*)
Rosalind Marsden (*Director, Asia Pacific*).
Alan Charlton CMG (*Director, Personnel*).
Dickie Stagg CMG (*Director, Information*).
Simon Gass CMG CVO (*Director, Resources*).

Special Representatives

Alan Goulty CMG (*UK Special Representative for Sudan*)
Tom Phillips CMG (*UK Special Representative for Afghanistan*)
Lord David Hannay GCMG (*UK Special Representative for Cyprus*)

Sir Brian Fall KCMG (*UK Special Representative for Georgia*)

DEPARTMENTS IN THE FOREIGN AND COMMONWEALTH OFFICE

Afghanistan Unit
The Mission of the Afghanistan Unit is to help Afghanistan achieve stability, security and prosperity, to the benefit of the Afghan people, the United Kingdom and the world community.

Whitehall,
LONDON SW1A 2AH
Enquiries: 020 7008 2865/2995
GTN: 7008 2865/2995
UK Special Representative: Tom Phillips CMG
Superintending Director: Rosalind Marsden
Head of Unit: Jan Thompson
Deputy Head of Unit: Dominic Jermey

African Department (Equatorial)
Political and economic relations with Nigeria, Ghana, Sierra Leone, The Gambia, Kenya, Tanzania, Uganda, Ethiopia, Eritrea, Somalia, Djibouti, Liberia, Senegal, Guinea, Mali, Burkina Faso, Cote d'Ivoire, Togo, Benin, Niger, Chad, Cameroon, Gabon, Congo, Democratic Republic of Congo, Burundi, Rwanda, Central African Republic, Equatorial Guinea, Guinea Bissau, Cape Verde, ECOWAS and EAC, Africa Union.

King Charles Street,
LONDON SW1A 2AH
Enquiries: 020 7008 2903
GTN: 7008 2903
Superintending Director: James Bevan
Head of Department: Frank Baker OBE
Deputy Heads of Department: Nigel Bowie, Philip Hall

African Department (Southern)
Political and economic relations with Angola, Botswana, The Comoros, Lesotho, Madagascar, Malawi, Mauritius, Mozambique, Namibia, São Tomé and Principe, Seychelles, South Africa, Swaziland, Zambia and Zimbabwe; Southern African Development Community (SADC).

King Charles Street,
LONDON SW1A 2AH
Enquiries: 020 7008 2535
GTN: 7008 2535
Superintending Director: James Bevan
Head of Department: Dr Andrew Pocock
Deputy Head: Janet Douglas

Aviation, Maritime & Energy Department
Civil aviation and bilateral air services agreements; ICAO; Aerospace industry and civil aircraft exports; Law of the Sea; Maritime Delimitation; Shipping; Fisheries; IMO; Channel Tunnel; Inland Transport; global and multilateral energy policy and collaboration; fossil fuels; nuclear, new and renewable energy technologies; electricity.

King Charles Street,
LONDON SW1A 2AH

Enquiries: 020 7008 2625
GTN: 7008 2625
Superintending Director: Philippa Drew
Head of Department: Christopher Segar
Deputy Head of Department: Nick Griffiths

British Trade International
British Trade International has lead responsibility within Government for trade and investment development and promotion. It is responsible to both FCO and DTI Ministers, bringing together the work of both departments in those areas.
Within British Trade International, trade and outward investment activities on behalf of British business are delivered by Trade Partners UK. Inward investment promotion activity is delivered by Invest UK, which aims to attract, retain and add value to foreign direct investment in the UK

Kingsgate House,
66-74 Victoria Street,
LONDON SW1E 6SW
Enquiries: 020 7215 5000
GTN: 215 5000
Joint Board Chairman: Baroness Symons of Vernham Dean
Group Chief Executive: Sir Stephen Brown KCVO
Deputy Chief Executive: David Hall

TRADE PARTNERS UK

Central Services Group
Group Director: David Hall

Regional Group
Group Director: Ian Jones

International Group
Group Director: Quinton Quayle

Business Group
Group Director: David Warren

Strategy and Communications Group
Group Director: John Reynolds

INVEST UK
Chief Executive: William Pedder

Central and North West European Department
Political and bilateral economic relations with Bulgaria, the Czech Republic, Estonia, Latvia, Lithuania, Hungary, Poland, Romania, Slovakia, Slovenia, Switzerland, Liechtenstein, Iceland and Norway.

Downing Street West,
LONDON SW1A 2AL
Enquiries: Bulgaria, Norway, Switzerland, Iceland and Liechtenstein 020 7008 3608
GTN: 7008 3608
Enquiries: Baltic States and Romania 020 7008 2363
GTN: 7008 2363
Enquiries: Czech Republic, Slovenia and Slovakia 020 7008 3429
GTN: 7008 3429

Enquiries: Hungary and Poland 020 7008 3805
GTN: 7008 3805
Superintending Director: Linda Duffield
Head of Department: Sir John Ramsden Bt
Deputy Head of Department: Charles Garrett

China Hong Kong Department

Relations between the United Kingdom and China, including the Hong Kong Special Administrative Region.

FCO,
Whitehall,
LONDON SW1A 2AP
Enquiries: 020 7008 3074
GTN: 7008 3074
Superintending Director: Rosalind Marsden
Head of Department: Andrew Seaton
Deputy Head of Department: Rod Wye

Common Foreign and Security Policy Department

Co-ordination of foreign policy among EU member states and implementation of Common Foreign and Security Policy.

Downing Street East,
LONDON SW1A 2AH
Enquiries: 020 7008 2807
GTN: 7008 2807
Political Director: Peter Ricketts CMG
Superintending Director: Kim Darroch CMG
Head of Department: Tim Barrow LVO MBE
Deputy Head of Department: Martin Shearman

Commonwealth Co-ordination Department

Policy, procedures and practices relating to the Commonwealth as a whole. Commonwealth Heads of Government Meetings. Commonwealth Ministerial Action Group meetings. Liaison with the Commonwealth Secretariat, Commonwealth Foundation, and a wide range of pan-Commonwealth NGO's professional associations, organisations and societies. Commonwealth constitutional questions.

Downing Street East,
LONDON SW1A 2AL
Enquiries: 020 7008 2962
GTN: 7008 2962
Superintending Director: Philippa Drew
Head of Department: Asif Ahmad
Deputy Head of Department: Tony Humphries OBE

Consular Division

Consular Policy, Supervision of Consular Services. Protection and assistance for British nationals abroad, including financial assistance, relief and repatriation, prisoners, child abduction, forced marriage. Human rights and community liaison. Worldwide travel advice, nationality matters, FCO passport policy and co-ordination of Posts' passport operations, birth and death registration and marriages abroad. Legalisation of documents in the UK and overseas; Notarial acts, taking of evidence (civil) and service of process (civil), estates of deceased persons abroad; setting of

Consular Fees, liaison with the Home Office on extradition matters. Claims for compensation from other Governments in respect of loss, injury or damage suffered overseas by individuals or companies; electoral Registration Overseas.

Old Admirality Building,
LONDON SW1A 2PA
Enquiries: 020 7008 0218
GTN: 7008 0218
Superintending Director: Dickie Stagg CMG
Head of Division: James Watt CVO
Deputy Heads of Division: David Clegg MVO, Richard Morris

Counter Terrorism Policy Department

Counter-terrorism policy, bilaterally and in international fora. Crisis management.

King Charles Street,
LONDON SW1A 2AH
Enquiries: 020 7008 2077
GTN: 7008 2077
Superintending Directors: Edward Oakden, Peter Ricketts CMG
Head of Department: Robert Macaire

Diplomatic Service Families Association

Works with the Administration on 'best practice family-friendly policy'. Promotes the interests and welfare of UK diplomatic families, spouses and partners, at home and abroad, in issues including career development, child education, special needs and disabilities, matters affecting foreign-born spouses/partners, and other welfare and social matters.

FCO,
Old Admiralty Building,
LONDON SW1A 2PA
Enquiries: 020 7008 0286
GTN: 7008 0286
DSFA Chairman: Emilie Salvesen
Vice Chairman and Community Liaison Officer Co-ordinator: Fiona Davies
Executive Secretary: Christine Easter

Directorate for Strategy and Innovation

The Directorate for Strategy and Innovation helps the FCO to set clear strategic goals and to pursue them in innovative and effective ways under stronger, more open corporate leadership.

King Charles Street
LONDON SW1A 2AH
Enquiries: 020 7008 3377
GTN: 7008 3377
Director: Simon Fraser
Team Leaders: Nick Kay (*Strategic Policy Advice*), Andrew Key (*Delivery Strategy*), John Kraus (*Internal Communication Strategy*)

Drugs & International Crime Department

Co-ordination of Government policies to counter the international drugs trade, both bilateral and in international fora; foreign policy implications; foreign policy relating to wider organised crime.

King Charles Street
LONDON SW1A 2AH
Enquiries: 020 7008 1834/1835
GTN: 7008 1834/1835
Superintending Director: Edward Oakden
*Head of Department and Special Representative
for International Drugs Issues:* Michael Ryder
Deputy Head of Department: Guy Warrington

Eastern Adriatic Department

Relations with Croatia, Serbia and Montenegro
(including Kosovo), Bosnia and Herzegovina,
Macedonia and Albania.

Downing Street West,
LONDON SW1A 2AL
Enquiries: 020 7008 2756/2372/3433/3459
GTN: 7008 2756/2372/3433/3459
Superintending Director: James Bevan
Head of Department: Stephen Wordsworth LVO
Deputy Head of Department: Andrew Levi

Eastern Department

Policy on Russia, Ukraine, the South Caucasus
(Armenia, Azerbaijan, Georgia), Central Asia
(Kazakhstan, Kyrgyzstan, Tajikistan,
Turkmenistan, Uzbekistan), Moldova, Belarus and
Caspian energy issues.

Downing Street West,
LONDON SW1A 2AL
Enquiries: 020 7008 2427/2423/3831
GTN: 7008 2427/2423/3831
Superintending Director: Linda Duffield
Head of Department: Simon Butt
Deputy Head of Department: Dominic Schroeder

Economic Policy Department

Analysis of global economic trends. Country and
regional economic analysis for the Americas, Asia,
Australasia, Middle East, Africa, CIS and south-
east Europe. Economic analysis of commodities
markets. Emerging market issues, including
financial sector reform. Globalisation.
Development issues, including debt relief,
migration, health, ICTs and export credits. UK
G7/8 Sherpa Secretariat. Policy on the G7/8.Policy
on and liaison with international economic
organisations (IMF, IBRD, OECD, EBRD, UN
Economic Commission for Europe, Davos World
Economic Forum). Commonwealth Finance
Ministers Meeting. Financial sector relations,
including Financial Action Task Force, mutual
legal assistance, money laundering, bribery and
corruption, financial fraud, asset confiscation and
international tax issues. Investment policy,
investment protection and promotion agreements,
relations with CBI, TUC and business, corporate
social responsibility.

FCO,
Whitehall,
LONDON SW1A 2AP
Enquiries: 020 7008 2735
GTN: 7008 2735
Deputy Under Secretary: Michael Arthur
Chief Economist and Head of Department: Creon

Butler
Deputy Head of Department: Harold Freeman
(*IFIs, Non-European Economies, Globalisation,
Development Issues*).
Deputy Head of Department: Graham Minter (*G8,
OECD, Economic Crime and Tax, Investment and
Business Relations*).

Environment Policy Department

International environment policy; environmental
dimensions of sustainable development and
globalisation; EU environment policy; climate
change; biodiversity; environmental security.
Details at www.fco.gov.uk/environment.

FCO,
King Charles Street,
LONDON SW1A 2AH
Enquiries: 020 7008 4131/4112
GTN: 7008 4131/4112
Superintending Director: Philippa Drew
Head of Department: John Ashton
Deputy Head of Department: Louise de Sousa

Estate Strategy Unit

Formulation and implementation of strategy for the
FCO's estate in the UK and overseas.

Apollo House,
36 Wellesley Road,
CROYDON CR0 9YA
Enquiries: 020 8253 6377/6378
GTN: 3822 6377/6378
Superintending Director: Peter Collecott, CMG
Head of Unit: Julian Metcalfe
Deputy Head of Unit: Jeremy Neate

European Union Department (Bilateral)

Political and economic relations with Andorra,
Austria, Belgium, Denmark, Finland, France,
Germany, Greece, the Holy See, Italy,
Luxembourg, Monaco, the Netherlands, Portugal,
San Marino, Spain, Sweden, non-devolved
Northern Ireland matters affecting relations with
Ireland and other countries; and post-Holocaust
issues.

Downing Street (East),
LONDON,
SW1A 2AL
Director EU: Kim Darroch CMG
Head of Department: Karen Pierce CVO
Deputy Head of Department: James Kidner

European Union Department (External)

Relations between the European Union and third
countries; international trade and development
matters; enlargement of the Union.

Downing Street East,
LONDON SW1A 2AL
Enquiries: 020 7008 3770/2293
GTN: 7008 3770/2293
Superintending Director: Kim Darroch CMG
Head of Department: Simon Featherstone
Deputy Heads of Department: Alex Ellis, Paul
Johnston

European Union Department (Internal)
The internal economic and institutional policies of
the European Union.

Downing Street East,
LONDON SW1A 2AL
Enquiries: 020 7008 3388/3391
GTN: 7008 3388/3391
Superintending Director: Kim Darroch CMG
Head of Department: Nick Baird
Deputy Heads of Department: Richard Jones, Mara
Goldstein
Head of Convention Unit: Catherine Royle

Financial Compliance Unit
Whitehall,
LONDON SW1A 2AH
Enquiries: 020 7008 8275
GTN: 7008 8275
Superintending Director: Simon Gass CMG CVO
Head of Unit: David Major

FCO Association
Old Admirality Building,
LONDON SW1A 2PA
Enquiries: 020 7008 0967
GTN: 7008 0967
Chairman: David Burns CMG
Hon Secretary: Maureen Howley MBE

FCO Services
FCO Services provides the main support services
for the FCO at home and overseas.

Chief Executive: Stephen Sage

CONFERENCE AND VISITS GROUP
King Charles Street,
LONDON SW1A 2AH
Head of Group: James Clark
Deputy Head of Group: Richard Lyne

CONSULTANCY GROUP
Old Admiralty Building,
LONDON SW1A 2PA
Head of Group: Vivien Life

ESTATE GROUP
Apollo House,
36 Wellesley Road,
CROYDON CRO 9YA
Head of Group: John Elgie
Deputy Head of Group: Nigel Morris

FINANCE GROUP
Hanslope Park
Hanslope
MILTON KEYNES MK19 7BH
Head of Group: Kerry Simmonds

HUMAN RESOURCE GROUP
Hanslope Park
Hanslope
MILTON KEYNES MK19 7BH
Head of Group: Elaine Kennedy

INFORMATION MANAGEMENT GROUP
King Charles Street,
LONDON SW1A 2AH
Head of Group: Roger French

LANGUAGE GROUP (DIPLOMATIC SERVICE
LANGUAGE CENTRE)
Old Admiralty Building,
LONDON SW1A 2PA
Head of Group: Dr Vanessa L Davies

STRATEGIC PLANNING BRANCH
Hanslope Park, Hanslope, MILTON KEYNES
MK19 7BH
Old Admiralty Building, LONDON SW1A 2PA
Head of Branch: Joy Herring

SUPPORT GROUP
Hanslope Park,
Hanslope,
MILTON KEYNES MK19 7BH
Head of Group: Michael Carr
Deputy Head of Group: Paul Bell

TECHNICAL GROUP IMPLEMENTATION
Hanslope Park,
Hanslope,
MILTON KEYNES MK19 7BH
Head of Group: Michael Blake

TECHNICAL GROUP (SUPPORT)
Hanslope Park,
Hanslope,
MILTON KEYNES MK19 7BH
Head of Group: Patrick Cullen

Human Rights Policy Department
The FCO point of advice on human rights policy
questions in all international organisations,
including obligations and commitments at the UN,
Council of Europe, OSCE and Commonwealth.
Responsible, in co-operation with geographical
departments, for: developing and co-ordinating
HMG's human rights policy and ensuring
consistency of application in the UK's overseas
bilateral relations; liaison with Department for
International Development on human rights aspects
of bilateral and multilateral development policy;
liaison with Whitehall departments, ensuring that
the development of domestic policy takes account
of HMG's international human rights obligations
and objectives; supervision of UK and Overseas
Territory periodic reports under international treaty
obligations; FCO point of contact and liaison for
NGOs and other bodies on general (i.e. non-
country specific) human rights matters. Manages
FCO's Human Rights Project Fund and produces
the Human Rights Annual Report.

King Charles Street,
LONDON SW1A 2AH
Enquiries: 020 7008 2501
GTN: 7008 2501
Superintending Director: Philippa Drew
Head of Department: Jon Benjamin
Deputy Head of Department: Barbara Woodward

Internal Audit Department (FCO/DFID Department)
King Charles Street,
LONDON SW1A 2AH
Enquiries: 020 7008 8028 FCO
GTN: 3535 0788 DFID
Superintending Directors: Simon Gass CMG CVO (FCO), Richard Manning (DFID).
Head of Department: Jon Hews
Audit Manager (FCO/DFID): Trevor Jarvis
Audit Manager DFID: Mike Noronha

I T Strategy Unit
Responsible for ITC investment policy and budgets and co-ordination with central government Departments on ICT issues.

Old Admiralty Building,
Whitehall,
LONDON SW1A 2PA
Enquiries: 020 7008 0524
GTN: 7008 0524
Superintending Deputy Under-Secretary: Peter Collecott CMG
Head of Unit: Nick Westcott
Deputy Head of Unit: Nick Clouting

Latin America and Caribbean Department
Political and economic bilateral relations with all Latin American and independent Caribbean countries, and Latin American and Caribbean regional organisations.

FCO,
King Charles Street,
LONDON SW1A 2AH
Enquiries: 020 7008 2481
GTN: 7008 2481
Email: LACD.FCO@gtnet.gov.uk
Superintending Director: Richard D Wilkinson CVO
Head of Department: John Dew
Deputy Heads of Department: Trevor Moore, Syd Maddicott

Legal Advisers
Advice on international, EU and UK law and practice in connection with HMG's foreign relations, including treaties and international litigation, and with the work of the FCO generally. Legal advice concerning the governance of UK overseas territories.

King Charles Street
LONDON SW1A 2AH
Enquiries: 020 7008 3080/3081
GTN: 7008 3080/3081
Legal Adviser: Michael Wood CMG
Deputy Legal Advisers: Ian Hendry CMG, Elizabeth Wilmshurst CMG
Legal Counsellors: Catherine Adams, Diana Brookes, John Grainger, Huw Llewellyn, Nigel Parker, Christopher Whomersley

Middle East Department
Relations with Bahrain, Iran, Iraq, Kuwait, Oman, Qatar, Republic of Yemen, Saudi Arabia, United Arab Emirates.

Downing Street West,
LONDON SW1A 2AL
Enquiries: 020 7008 2996
GTN: 7008 2996
Superintending Director: Edward Chaplin OBE
Head of Department: Charles Gray
Deputy Head of Department: Barry Lowen

Near East & North Africa Department
Political and bilateral economic relations with Algeria, Egypt, the West Bank and Gaza Strip, Israel, Jordan, Lebanon, Mauritania, Libya, Morocco, Sudan, Syria and Tunisia. Arab/Israel relations. EU Mediterranean relations.

Downing Street West and King Charles Street,
LONDON SW1A 2AL
Enquiries: 020 7008 3751
GTN: 7008 3751
Superintending Director: Edward Chaplin OBE
Head of Department: Nicholas Archer
Deputy Head of Department: Rosemary Waugh

Non-Proliferation Department
Nuclear non-proliferation issues, including the Nuclear Non-Proliferation Treaty, CTBT, IAEA and Nuclear Suppliers Group. Missile proliferation issues and MTCR. Chemical and Biological Weapons Conventions, Australia Group and CW/BW proliferation issues. UNMOVIC. Policy on conventional arms sales, small arms and exports of Dual-Use Goods. UN Arms Register. Wassenaar Arrangement. Arms Control and Disarmament Research Unit.

Downing Street West,
LONDON SW1A 2AH
Enquiries: 020 7008 2261/2751
GTN: 7008 2261/2751
Superintending Director: Edward Oakden
Head of Department: Tim Dowse
Deputy Heads of Department: Patrick Lamb, Andrew Turner

North America Department
Relations with Canada and the United States.

FCO,
Whitehall,
LONDON SW1A 2AH
Enquiries: 020 7008 2663/2667
GTN: 7008 2663/2667
Superintending Director: Richard D Wilkinson CVO
Head of Department: Nicholas Armour
Head of Canada Section: Rab MacKenzie
Head of US Section: David Hunt

North East Asia and Pacific Department
Relations with Japan, Democratic People's Republic of Korea, Republic of Korea, Mongolia, Australia, New Zealand, Samoa, Fiji, Kiribati, Republic of the Marshall Islands, Federated States of Micronesia, Nauru, Palau, Papua New Guinea, Solomon Islands, Tonga, Tuvalu, Vanuatu and French and US territories in the South Pacific.

King Charles Street,
LONDON SW1A 2AH

Enquiries: 020 7008 2960/3296/3264/2952
GTN: 7008 2960/3296/3264/2952
Superintending Director: Rosalind Marsden
Head of Department: Simon Smith
Deputy Head of Department: Hugo Shorter

Organisation for Security & Co-operation in Europe (OSCE) & the Council of Europe Department
UK Policy on the Organisation for Security & Co-operation in Europe and on the Council of Europe.

Whitehall,
LONDON SW1A 2AH
Enquiries: 020 7008 2426
GTN: 7008 2426
Superintending Director: Linda Duffield
Head of Department: Peter January
Deputy Head of Department: Anneli Conroy

Overseas Territories Department
HMG's responsibilities for the Overseas Territories of Anguilla, Bermuda, the British Antarctic Territory, the British Indian Ocean Territory, the British Virgin Islands, the Cayman Islands, the Falkland Islands, Montserrat, Pitcairn, South Georgia and the South Sandwich Islands, St Helena and its dependencies, Ascension and Tristan da Cunha and the Turks and Caicos Islands. Co-ordination of policy on the Overseas Territories and organisation of the Overseas Consultative Council; liaison on subjects of common interest to the Overseas Territories; interpretation of Colonial Regulations; South Atlantic matters and HMG's responsibilities under the Antarctic Treaty.

King Charles Street,
LONDON SW1A 2AH
Enquiries: 020 7008 2643
GTN: 7008 2643
Superintending Director: Richard D Wilkinson cvo
Head of Department: Alan Huckle
Deputy Head of Department: Roy Osborne

Parliamentary Relations & Devolution Department
Advice and guidance to FCO Ministers and officials on parliamentary procedures. Monitoring of all parliamentary business of interest to the FCO. Contact with Select Committees of both Houses of Parliament. Liaison with the British Group of the Inter-Parliamentary Union. Liaison with the Parliamentary Commissioner for Administration. Responsibility for FCO relations with the devolved administrations and legislatures in Scotland, Wales and Northern Ireland.

King Charles Street,
LONDON SW1A 2AH
Enquiries: 020 7008 2236/2235/2234
GTN: 7008 2236/2235/2234
Email: prd.fco@gtnet.gov.uk
Superintending Director: Dickie Stagg cmg
Head of Department: Matthew Hamlyn
Deputy Head of Department: Nick Allen
Parliamentary Clerk: Charles Hill

Personnel Command
Recruitment, development, motivation, deployment and support of staff.

Old Admirality Building,
LONDON SW1A 2PA
Superintending Director: Alan Charlton cmg

MEDICAL AND WELFARE
Health, safety and welfare of staff at home and overseas.

Joint FCO/DFID Department,
Old Admirality Building,LONDON SW1A 2PA
Superintending Directors: Alan Charlton cmg, Richard Manning (DFID).
Assistant Director: Tony Millson
Principal Welfare Officer and Deputy: Ruth Wills
Clinical Service Manager: Andrew McDermott

PERFORMANCE AND DEVELOPMENT
All aspects of staff performance management including core competences, staff appraisal and assessment, promotion competitions and Assessment and Development Centres.
Assistant Director: Gerry Reffo

PERSONNEL MANAGEMENT
Career planning, individual personnel movements, appointments, probation, promotions, secondments, loans, recruitment and transfers to and from other services.
Assistant Director Personnel - Delegate Grades: Simon Pease
Assistant Director (Senior Management Structure): Nigel Haywood
Heads of Personnel Management Units: Andy Heyn, Judi Garstang, Nat Dawbarn, Marilia Astle

RECRUITMENT
Head: Alison Cookson-Hall

INTERCHANGE
Head: Debbie Clare

PERSONNEL POLICY
Policy aspects of personnel, management questions including implementation of employment legislation and relations with the trade union side, organisation and structure of the FCO's personnel, conduct and discipline, diversity and equal opportunities. Human resource planning, personnel statistics, sick absence and diplomatic status.
Assistant Director: Judith Slater

PERSONNEL SERVICES
Pay, allowances, conditions of service, superannuation.
Assistant Director: David Powell
Head of Pay, Superannuation: Brian Bennett
Head of Allowances Section: John Brook

LOCAL STAFF MANAGEMENT UNIT
Director: Alan Charlton cmg
Assistant Director and Head of Unit: Steve Plater

PROSPER (ADVICE ON
RETIREMENT/OUTPLACEMENT)
Assistant Directors: Tom Malcomson, Ivor
Rawlinson

TRAINING
Assitant Director: Richard Tauwhare
Deputy Heads of Training Wing: Alison Crocket,
Karen Smith

Press Office (formerly News Department)
Advises the Secretary of State and departments of
the FCO on questions of presentation relating to
the British Government's foreign policy. It is the
authorised contact between the FCO and the
British media.

Downing Street West,
LONDON SW1A 2AH
Enquiries: 020 7008 3100
GTN: 7008 3100
Superintending Director: Dickie Stagg CMG
Head of Department: John Williams
Deputy Head of Department: Andrew Patrick

Prism Programme
Prism is the FCO's business change management
programme. Prism will provide the Office with a
global on-line management information system
(covering personnel, pay, finance and
procurement), which will enable better decision
making.

Old Admiralty Building
Whitehall
LONDON SW1A 2PA
Superintending Director: Simon Gass CMG CVO
Programme Manager (Business): Fiona Moore
Deputy Programme Manager: Giles Whitaker

Protocol Division
Diplomatic Missions: Policy on handling of
appointments, privileges, immunities and security
of the Diplomatic Corps and International
Organisations in Britain. Diplomatic and
International Organisations lists. Organisation of
ceremonial events, and policy and advice on
protocol and precedence. Honours Secretariat:
FCO aspects of honours policy. Diplomatic Service
and Overseas Honours Lists, British honorary
awards, Foreign and Commonwealth honours for
British citizens. Investitures, presentation of
insignia. Royal Households Secretariat: Co-
ordination between the FCO and Royal
Households, especially on overseas visits by the
Royal Family. Royal Visits Committee.

Old Admiralty Building
Whitehall
LONDON SW1A 2PA
*Head of Division and Vice Marshal of the
Diplomatic Corps:* Charles de Chassiron
*Deputy Head of Division and Assistant Marshal of
the Diplomatic Corps:* Chris Osborne
Superintending Deputy Under Secretary: Peter
Collecott, CMG

Public Diplomacy Policy Department
Strategic guidance on public diplomacy to Foreign
and Commonwealth Office Commands and Posts
overseas. Management of public diplomacy
resources including: the London Correspondents'
Service; sponsored visits by journalists; press, TV
and radio material; publications about Britain; the
FCO website; the FCO Information Centre; FCO
Open Days and Policy on Expositions.
Administration of the Grants in Aid to the BBC
World Service. Responsibility for the Wilton Park
Executive Agency.

King Charles Street,
LONDON SW1A 2AH
Enquiries: 020 7008 1618
GTN: 7008 1618
Superintending Director: Dickie Stagg CMG
Head of Department: John Buck
Deputy Heads of Department: Carole Sweeney,
Caroline Matthews

Purchasing Directorate
Advice and guidance to FCO departments and
posts overseas on best practice in the purchase of
goods and services; sponsorship and selling into
wider markets; operational environmental issues.

Old Admiralty Building,
LONDON SW1A 2PA
Enquiries: 020 7008 0924
GTN: 7008 0924
Superintending Director: Simon Gass CMG CVO
Head of Purchasing Directorate: Michael Gower
Deputy Head of Purchasing Directorate: Charles
Sime

Quality & Efficiency Unit
Effectiveness and value for money reviews,
Business Audit, Efficiency Techniques and Targets,
Benchmarking, Internal Market, Civil Service
Reform, Service First, Liaison with and training for
Management Officers, FCO Complaints Line.

Old Admiralty Building,
LONDON SW1A 2PA
Enquiries: 020 7008 1057
GTN: 7008 1057
Superintending Director: Simon Gass CMG, CVO
Head of Unit: Karen Jackson
Deputy Head of Unit: Chris Green
Head of Value for Money Section: Anne Jarrett
Head of Management Officer Section: Bob Calder

Records and Historical Department
Open government, data protection, freedom of
information; records custody, access and release;
registry policy and training; treaty information and
publication; historical advice; publication of
Documents on British Policy Overseas.

Old Admirality Building,
LONDON SW1A 2PA
Hanslope Park,
MILTON KEYNES MK19 7BH
Enquiries: 020 7008 1129
GTN: 7008 1129
Superintending Director: Peter Collecott CMG

Head: Heather Yasamee
Deputy Head: Richard Bevins

Research Analysts
Contributes to the formulation of overseas policy through the provision of assessments and advice based on specialist experience.

King Charles Street,
Whitehall,
LONDON SW1A 2AH
Enquiries: 020 7008 5942
GTN: 7008 5942
Director: Simon Fraser
Head of Research Analysts: Simon Buckle
Heads of Research Groups: Dr Clare Thomas (*African Research Group*), Dr Jeremy Hobbs (*Americas Research Group*), Laurence Broyd (*Central European & Eastern Adriatic Research Group*), Janet Gunn (*Eastern Research Group*), Dr Babu Rahman (*Global Issues Research Group*), Greg Shapland (*Middle East & North Africa Research Group*), Mike Cowin (*North Asia/Pacific Research Group*), Dr Andrew Hall (*South & South East Asia Research Group*), Ted Hallett (*Western & Southern European Research Group*).

Resource Accounting Department
Preparation of Appropriation and Resource Accounts. Payment of salaries, travel accounts and invoices. Debtor control, maintenance and development of Fixed Asset Register and Management Accounts. Funding of FCO posts. FMAS, Dynamics and other financial training.

Old Admiralty Building,
LONDON SW1A 2PA
Enquiries: 020 7008 1063
GTN: 7008 1063
Hanslope Park,
MILTON KEYNES MK19 7BH
Enquiries: 01908 515531
GTN: 3905 5531
Superintending Director and Principal Finance Officer: Simon Gass CMG CVO
Head of Department and Chief Accountant: Mike Brown

Resource Budgeting Department
Resource planning, budgeting and allocation, expenditure monitoring and performance measurement, fees and charging.

Old Admiralty Building,
LONDON SW1A 2PA
Enquiries: 020 7008 1085
GTN: 7008 1085
Superintending Director: Simon Gass CMG CVO
Head of Department: Martin Williamson
Deputy Head of Department: Matthew Owen

Science and Technology Unit
Management of S&T work overseas by embassies.

King Charles Street
LONDON SW1A 2AH
Enquiries: 020 7008 4113

GTN: 7008 4113
Superintending Director: Philippa Drew
Acting Head of Unit: Fiona Clouder Richards

Security Policy Department
NATO and EU security and defence policy issues; the foreign policy implications of British defence policy as regards Transatlantic and European defence, including nuclear weapons issues; nuclear and conventional arms control and disarmament; missile defence issues; UN disarmament fora; armaments policy and defence equipment procurement including collaborative projects; conflict prevention; UK defence attachés.

Downing Street East,
LONDON SW1A 2AH
Enquiries: 020 7008 3761
GTN: 7008 3761
Superintending Director: Edward Oakden
Head of Department: (vacant)
Deputy Heads of Department: Robert Deane, Kate Smith

Security Strategy Unit
Formulation of FCO security policy and co-ordination of physical, technical and personnel counter measures, and security education training.

Old Admiralty Building,
LONDON SW1A 2PA
Enquiries: 020 7008 1166
GTN: 7008 1166
Superintending Director: Peter Collecott CMG
Head of Unit: Judith Macgregor LVO
Deputy Head of Unit: Michael Balmer

South Asian Department
Relations with India, Pakistan, Bangladesh, Sri Lanka, Nepal, Bhutan, the Maldives.

Whitehall,
LONDON SW1A 2AL
Enquiries: 020 7008 2388
GTN: 7008 2388
Superintending Director: Rosalind Marsden
Head of Department: Stephen Smith
Deputy Head of Department: Iain Lindsay

South East Asian Department
Political and economic relations with Brunei, Burma, Cambodia, East Timor, Indonesia, Laos, Malaysia, Philippines, Singapore, Thailand and Vietnam; ASEAN and ASEM.

FCO,
Whitehall,
LONDON SW1A 2AH
Enquiries: 020 7008 2600
GTN: 7008 2600
Superintending Director: Rosalind Marsden
Head of Department: John Jenkins LVO
Deputy Head of Department: Richard Powell

Southern European Department
Political and bilateral relations with Cyprus, Malta and Turkey. UK policy towards the UN-sponsored discussions on the future of Cyprus. External

relations and some aspects of internal administration of Gibraltar.

King Charles Street,
LONDON SW1A 2AH
Enquiries: 020 7008 2975
GTN: 7008 2975
Superintending Directors: Linda Duffield (*Cyprus, Malta and Turkey*), James Bevan (*Gibraltar*).
Head of Department: Geoff Gillham
Deputy Head of Department (Eastern Mediterranean): Rob Fenn
Deputy Head of Department (Gibraltar): Simon Martin

Trade Union Side (of the Diplomatic Service Whitely Council)
Representing the interests of all FCO staff, on terms and conditions of service and employer/employee relations.

FCO,
King Charles Street,
LONDON SW1A 2AH
Enquiries: 020 7008 0064
GTN: 7008 0064
TUS Chair: Stephen Watson
TUS Deputy Chairs: Jill Barrett, Robert Streeton
TUS Vice Chairs: Pauline Abrams, Rod Baker, Michael Carbine, Sandra Davis, Patrick Holdich, John Hudson-Peat
TUS Secretary: Ann Herd
TUS Assistant Secretary: Elaine Spencer

UK visas (Joint FCO/Home Office Unit)
Management of the visa operation at British missions overseas in accordance with UK Immigration Rules. Liaison with other interested departments on matters arising from immigration legislation and policy. Replies to letters from MPs and members of the public on individual visa cases.

Correspondence Address: King Charles Street.
LONDON SW1A 2AH
Office Address: 89 Albert Embankment, LONDON SE1 7TP
Enquiries: 020 7008 8438
GTN: 7008 8438
Superintending Directors: Dickie Stagg CMG (*FCO*), Peter Wrench (*Home Office*).
Head of Unit: Robin Barnett
Deputy Heads of Unit: Tony Mercer (*Operations*), Keith Moss (*Policy*), Paul Sherar (*Modernisation*)

United Nations Department
Policy towards the United Nations, particularly the Security Council, General Assembly and ECOSOC; United Nations peace-keeping operations; sanctions; conflict prevention; International humanitarian law (including Geneva Conventions); Red Cross/Crescent issues; International Criminal Tribunals for former Yugoslavia and Rwanda; International Criminal Court; war crimes; humanitarian mine action; migration/refugee policy; general aspects of policy towards the UN specialised agencies.

King Charles Street,
LONDON SW1A 2AH
Enquiries: 020 7008 3583/3581
GTN: 7008 3583/3581
Superintending Director: Philippa Drew
Head of Department: Stephen Pattison
War Crimes Co-ordinator: Alan Weeks
Deputy Head of Department: Sarah MacIntosh

Whitehall Liaison Department
General co-ordination duties and responsibility for liaison with the Cabinet Office and other Government Departments.

Downing Street West,
LONDON SW1A 2AH
Enquiries: 020 7008 2350
GTN: 7008 2350
Vauxhall Cross,
85 Albert Embankment,
LONDON SE1 7TP
Superintending Deputy Under Secretary: Stephen J L Wright CMG
Head of Department: Matthew Kidd
Deputy Head of Department: Paul Fox

Wilton Park
Wilton Park Conferences, lasting up to three and a half days, examine current international challenges, especially EU issues, security policy, European and Atlantic relations; Russia, Central Europe, the Caspian, and North East and Central Asia; areas of conflict in the developing world and global economic policies. Conference participants are experts on the conference topic drawn from different professions and from all over the world. Wiston House is also available for conferences organised by other institutions.

Wilton Park,
Wiston House,
STEYNING,
West Sussex BN44 3DZ
Telephone: 01903 817772
Fax: 01903 816373
Email: lorraine.jones@wiltonpark.org.uk
Web: http://www.wiltonpark.org.uk
Chief Executive: Colin Jennings

Lists of British Representatives in Commonwealth and Foreign Countries and in the Republic of Ireland

British Missions Overseas (addresses and contact Numbers of Missions and Consulates etc.)

PART II. Embassies, High Commissions, Deputy High Commissions and Consular Posts.

AFGHANISTAN

Kabul
British Embassy
Ambassador: Mr R P Nash, LVO
Deputy Head of Mission: Mr R J Laxton
Counsellor (Political): Mr W J C Meath-Baker
First Secretary (Political): Ms F M Morrison
First Secretary (Management): Mr S Smith

ALBANIA

Tirana
British Embassy
Rruga Skenderbeg 12
Tirana
Telephone: (00) (355) (42) 34973/4/5
Facsimile: (00) (355) (42) 47697
Office Hours (GMT): Mon - Thur: 06 30 - 15 00
Fri: 06 30 - 12 30
Ambassador: Dr David Landsman, OBE
Deputy Head of Mission and Consul: Mr G Scott
British Council Director: Mr Michael Moore
First Secretary (Political): Mr N J Barnes
Defence Attaché (Resides at Tirana):
Lieutenant Colonel P G Cox, OBE
*Third Secretary Management Officer and Vice
Consul:* Mr D Brierley
Third Secretary (Political): Mr T Brown
Third Secretary (Immigration): Mr H Ryan
Attaché: Mrs L Towner-Evans

ALGERIA

Algiers
British Embassy
6 Avenue Souidani Boudjemaa,
BP08 Alger-Gare 16000, Algiers
Telephone: (00) (213) (21) 23 00 68
Facsimile: (00) (213) (21) 23 00 67 and 23 07 51
        23 01 83 Chancery
Airtech: (00) (213) (21) 23 00 69
Office Hours (GMT): Sun - Thur: 07 00 - 14 00
Ambassador: Mr G S Hand
Deputy Head of Mission: Mr D.L Brett
Defence Attaché (Resides in London):
Commander R P Woods, RN
Second Secretary (Management Officer/Consul):
Mrs A M Fowle
Third Secretary (Immigration): Mr D A Burrows
General Registry: Ms R J Jordan
Honorary Chaplain: (Vacant)

ANDORRA

British Embassy
Ambassador (resides at Madrid): Mr P J Torry
Consul-General (resides at Barcelona):
Mr D Thomson
e-mail: bcon@cyberbcn.com
N.B Consular and Commercial Enquiries should be
addressed to Barcelona
British Honorary Consulate
Casa Jacint Pons, 3/2
La Massana
Principality of Andorra
Telephone: (00) (376) 839 840
Facsimile: (00) (376) 839 840
e-mail: britconand@mypic.ad
Honorary Consul: Mr Hugh Garner

ANGOLA

Luanda
British Embassy
Rua Diogo Cao, 4
Caixa Postal 1244, Luanda
Telephone: (00) (244) (2) 334582, 334583,
392991, 387681
Facsimile: (00) (244) (2) 333331 (U/C)
Satellite fax: 00 871 144 5140 (Airtech)
e-mail: postmaster.luanda@fco.gov.uk
Office hours (GMT): Mon & Fri 07 00 - 13 00
Tue-Thur 07 00 - 11 30 and 13 00 - 16 00
Ambassador: Mr J Thompson, MBE
Consul and Deputy Head of Mission:
Mr R P Denny
Defence Attaché:
Lieutenant Colonel A A Gilbert, MBE
Defence Attaché Assistant: Staff Sergeant T Stead
Second Secretary (Political): Mr J Astill-Brown
Second Secretary (Commercial): Mr S Graham
Third Secretary (Management) and Vice-Consul:
Ms L Sayle
Registrar: Ms K D H Sowerby

ANTIGUA & BARBUDA

St. John's
British High Commission
P.O. Box 483, Price Waterhouse Coopers Centre,
11, Old Parham Road, St. John's Antigua
Telephone: (00) (1) (268) 462 0008/9, 463 0010
Facsimile: (00) (1) (268) 562 2124
Airtech: (00) (1) (268) 462 2806

Office Hours (GMT): Mon-Thurs: 12 00 - 16 30
and 17 00 - 20 00 Fri: 12 00 - 17 00 (only)
*High Commissioner: Mr John White
Resident British Commissioner:
Miss Jean Sharpe, OBE
*Deputy Resident British Commissioner:
Mr Paul Lawrence
Deputy High Commissioner: Mr Rob Holland
*Defence Adviser: Captain Steve C Ramm, RN
*Counsellor (Regional Affairs):
Mr Nick J L Martin
*First Secretary (Chancery): Mr Graham Honey
*First Secretary (Management/Consular):
Ms Ros Day
*Second Secretary (Chancery): Mr Phil Marshall
*Second Secretary (Chancery/Information):
Mr Nick J Pyle, MBE
*Third Secretary (Consular/Immigration):
Mr Mark Harrison
*Resides at Bridgetown

ARGENTINA

Buenos Aires
British Embassy
Dr. Luis Agote 2412/52, 1425 Capital Federal,
Buenos Aires
Telephone: (00) (54) (11) 4808 2200 Switchboard
4808 **** Direct Extension Access
Facsimile: (00) (54) (11) 4808 2274 Management
              4808 2283 Commercial
              4808 2228 Political and Public
              Diplomacy
              4808 2316 Chancery
              4808 2221 Defence Section
              4808 2235 Consular
Airtech: 4808 2211 Chancery
Office Hours (GMT): Mon-Thurs: 12 45 - 17 00
and 18 00 - 21 30 (Mar-Dec)
Fri:12 45 - 18 00
Mon-Fri: 12 45 - 18 30 (Jan- Feb)
Ambassador (Ext 2202):
Sir Robin Christopher KBE, CMG
Minister and Deputy Head of Mission (Ext 2204):
Mr Steve Williams
Counsellor: (Ext. 2209): Mr John Lewis
Defence, Naval and Military Attaché (Ext 2218):
Colonel Peter A Reynolds, RM
Air Attaché (Ext 2218): Group Captain Tim P
Brewer, OBE, RAF
*First Secretary (Head of Political/Economic
Section) (Ext 2205):* Mr Owen Jenkins
First Secretary (Commercial) (Ext 2251):
Mr Dave Prodger
First Secretary (Political) (Ext 2312):
Mrs Emily Fisher
*Cultural Attaché (British Council Director)
(Tel: 4311 9814 Ext 140):* Mr Paul Dick
First Secretary (Ext 2251): Mr Mike Cavanagh
*Consul and First Secretary (Management) (Ext
2255):* Miss Christine E McEwen
*First Secretary (Technical Works Officer) (Ext
2291):* Mr David Holmes
Second Secretary (Political) (Ext 2207):
Ms Freya Jackson

Second Secretary (Political) (Ext 2275):
Mr Thom Reilly
Second Secretary (Commercial) (Ext 2268):
Ms Paula Walsh
Second Secretary (Technical) (Ext 2215):
Mr Stuart Moss
Vice-Consul (Ext 2294): Ms Lydia Fossaluzza
*Assistant Cultural Attaché (Deputy Director British
Council) (Tel: 4311 9814 Ext 142):*
Ms Lena Milosevic
Third Secretary (Political) (Ext 2210):
Mr Matthew Withers
Third Secretary (Commercial) (Ext 2292):
Mrs Wendy De Luca

Mendoza
Honorary Consulate
Emilio Civit 778,
Mendoza
Telephone: (00) (54) (261) 4238529/4238514
Facsimile: (00) (54) (261) 4238565
Office Hours: Mon-Fri 08 30 – 13 00 and 17 00 –
20 30
Honorary Consul: Mr Carlos Alberto Pulenta

Córdoba
Honorary Consulate
Chacabuco 716,
Córdoba
Telephone: (00) (54) (351) 4208293
Facsimile: (00) (54) (351) 4208201/4208259
Office Hours: Mon-Fri 09 00 – 13 00 and 16.30 –
20 30
Honorary Consul: Mr Fulvio Pagani

Santa Fe
Honorary Consulate
Av Pte J D Perón 8101,
Rosario
Telephone/Fax: (00) (54) (341) 4590206
Office Hours: Mon-Fri 09 00 – 13 00 and 14 30 –
17 30
Honorary Consul: Mr Alberto C Gollan

ARMENIA

Yerevan
British Embassy
28 Charents Street, Yerevan
Telephone: (00) 3741 543822/543832
Facsimile: (00) 3741 543820 (Unclassified)
(00) 3741 543817 (Airtech)
e-mail: britemb@arminco.com
Commercial/General/Other Enquiries
dfidhead@netsys.am DFID
Officer's firstname.lastname@fco.gov.uk
Office Hours (GMT) 05 00 – 09 00 and 10 00 -
13 30
Ambassador: Miss Thorda Abbott-Watt
Deputy Head of Mission: Mr Roy Wilson
Third Secretary (Management and Vice Consul):
Ms Stephanie L Bee, MBE
Third Secretary (Political/PPAS):
Ms Sarah L Murrell
Defence Attaché (resides at Tbilisi):
Wing Commander Andrew W Kerr, RAF

TMO's (reside at Ankara): Mr Chris Fox/Mr David Kingdom
Cultural Attaché: Dr Roger Budd (Designate)
Attaché: Mr Chris Skinn

AUSTRALIA

Canberra
British High Commission
Commonwealth Avenue, Yarralumla,
Canberra, ACT 2600
Telephone: (00) (61) (2) 6270 6666
Facsimile: (00) (61) (2) 6273 3236 General
              6273 4360 Economic
              6270 6653 Chancery
e-mail: bhc.canberra@uk.emb.gov.au
Consular Section:
Level 10, S A P House,
Canberra Centre, Canberra, ACT 2601
Telephone: (00) (61) (2) 1902 941 555 Passports/
Entry Clearances
0394 145 517 " "
Facsimile: (00) (61) (2) 1902 941 600
e-mail: bhc.consular@uk.emb.gov.au
Office Hours (GMT): Apr-Oct 22 45 - 02 30 and
03 30 - 07 00,
Nov-Mar 21 45 - 01 30 and 02 30 - 06 00
High Commissioner: Sir Alastair Goodlad, KCMG
Deputy High Commissioner: Mr Robert Court
Counsellor (Multilateral): Mr Andrew Dean
Defence and Naval Adviser and Head BDLS:
Commodore Graham J Wiltshire, RN
Military and Air Adviser:
Group Captain Steven S Duffill, RAF
First Secretary (Political): Mrs Jean Harrod, MBE
First Secretary (External Affairs): Mr Jeff Harrod
First Secretary (Management): Mr Alan Gee
*First Secretary (Defence/Research) Head of the
British Defence Research and Supply Staff:*
Dr David Watson
First Secretary (Defence Equipment Cooperation):
Mr Roger Matthews
First Secretary (Information/Economic):
Ms Imogen Wiles
First Secretary: Mr Martin Short
First Secretary: Dr Robert Vickery
First Secretary (Technical Management):
Mr Rod Bronson
First Secretary (Technical Security):
Mr Mark Lewington
First Secretary (TWO): Mr Brien Hooker
Second Secretary (Consular): Mr Stan Blake
Third Secretary (External Affairs):
Mr Danny Woodier
Third Secretary (Passports): Mr Darren Cogger

Adelaide
British Consulate
Level 22, 25 Grenfell Street,
Adelaide SA 5000
Telephone: (00) (61) (8) 8212 7280
Facsimile: (00) (61) (8) 8212 7282
Airtech: (00) (61) (8) 8212 7283
e-mail: bcadel@camtech.net.au
Consul: Mr V S Warrington

Brisbane
British Consulate-General
Level 26, Waterfront Place,
1 Eagle Street, Brisbane, Queensland, 4000
Telephone: (00) (61) (7) 3223 3200
              General/Consular 3223 3206/7
              Commercial Section
Facsimile: (00) (61) (7) 3236 2576
e-mail: bcgbris1@uk.emb.gov.au
(All information, visa and routine passport work is
centralised in Canberra).
Office Hours (GMT): 23 00 - 07 00
Consul-General: Mr D H Cairns
Deputy Consul General: Ms C A Saunders
Vice Consul/Management Officer:
Mrs M M Hunt, MBE

Melbourne
British Consulate-General 17th Floor,
90 Collins Street, Melbourne, Victoria 3000
Telephone: (00) (61) (03) (9650) 3699
              Commercial 4155
              Consular
Facsimile: (00) (61) (03) (9650) 2990
Office Hours (GMT): Apr-Oct 23 00 - 07 30
Nov-Mar 22 00 - 06 30
Consul-General: Mr A D Sprake
Deputy *Consul-General:* Mr R F Terry
Vice-Consul: Mr P J Mudie

Perth
British Consulate-General
Level 26, Allendale Square,
77 St. George's Terrace,
Perth, Western Australia 6000
Telephone: (00) (61) (8) 9224 4700
Facsimile: (00) (61) (8) 9224 4720 Consular
              9221 1944 Management
              9221 1586 Commercial
              9421 1959 Airtech
e-mail: bcgperth@mail.uk.emb.gov.au
Issue of all general information about the UK, UK
visas/entry clearances, and passports, centralised at
Canberra
Office Hours (GMT): 0100-05 00, 0600-0900
(Public counter 0100-0600)
Consul-General: Mr H Dunnachie
Deputy *Consul-General:* Mr J Makin
Vice-Consul: Mr R J Andrews

Sydney
British Consulate-General and Directorate of Trade
and Investment Promotion
Level 16, The Gateway,
1 Macquarie Place, Sydney NSW, 2000
Telephone: (00) (61) (2) 9247 7521 (8 lines)
Facsimile: (00) (61) (2) 9233 1826 Commercial
              9251 6201 Consular, Management,
e-mail: bcgsyd2@mail.uk.emb.gov.au
(Commercial)
bcgsyd1@mail.uk.emb.gov.au
(Press and Public Affairs/Consular)
Offices Hours (GMT): Apr-Oct 23 00 - 02 30 and
03 30 - 07 00
Nov-Mar 22 00 - 01 30 and 02 30 - 06 00
Consul-General: Mr P Beckingham

*Director of Trade & Investment Promotion &
Deputy Consul General:* Mr Chris Glynn
Vice-Consul (Commercial): Mrs A Ross McDowell
Management Officer: Mrs Heather Halliwell
Consular/Admin Officer: Mr Les Tod
Press and Public Affairs Manager: Mr R Swift

Tasmania
British Honorary Consulate
1a Brisbane St
Hobart TAS 7000
Telephone: (00) (61) (3) 6230 3400
Facsimile: (00) (61) (3) 6231 1139
e-mail: djmotors@onaustralia.com.au
Office Hours (GMT): Apr - Oct: 23 00 - 07 30
Nov - Mar: 22 00 - 06 30
Honorary Consul: Mr Michael Johns

AUSTRIA

Vienna
British Embassy
Jaurèsgasse 12, 1030 Vienna
Telephone: (00) (43) (1) 716 130
Facsimile: (00) (43) (1) 71613 2999 Chancery
            71613 6900 Commercial
            71613 2900 Management
Airtech: (00) (43) (1) 71613 2310
e-mail: britem@netway.at

Consular Section
Jaurèsgasse 10, 1030 Vienna
Telephone: (00) (43) (1) 71613 5151 or 00 43 1
71613 followed by individual extension number
Facsimile: (00) (43) (1) 71613 5900
(All mail should be addressed to the British
Embassy)
Office Hours (GMT): Winter: Mon - Fri 08 00 - 12
00 and 13 00 - 16 00
Summer: Mon - Fri 07 00 - 11 00 and 12 00 -
15 00
Ambassador (2202): Mr Antony Ford, CMG
*Counsellor, Consul-General, Dep. Head of
Mission: (2204):* Dr Piers Baker
Counsellor (Chancery) (2211):
Mr George B J P Busby, OBE
Counsellor (Labour) (resides at Berlin):
Miss ElaineTrewartha
Defence Attaché (2216):
Lieutenant Colonel Julian A Bourne
First Secretary (Management) and Consul (2261):
Mr Eric M Jones
First Secretary (Technical Works) (2264):
Mr John Sweeney
First Secretary (Commercial) (6148): Mr John Hall
First Secretary (FLO) (2318):
Mr Steven T Muchall
Second Secretary (2219): Mr Michael B Deane
Second Secretary (EU Affairs) (2343):
Mr Andrew Ayre
Second Secretary (Chancery) (2220):
Mr Steve A Hunt
Second Secretary (Chancery) (2224):
Miss Clare Glackin
Second Secretary (2210): Mr Ian Purvis
Second Secretary (DLO) (2256):
Mr David N Hollingbery

Second Secretary (ILO) (2225): Mr Martin J Reeve
Attaché and Vice-Consul (ECO) (5330): (Vacant)
Third Secretary (Management) (2260):
Mr Andy W Partridge
Third Secretary (2272): Mr Philip G Kendall
Vice-Consul (5332): Miss Paula Hoppe

**Vienna United Kingdom Mission to The United
Nations in Vienna, see Missions & Delegations
Vienna United Kingdom Delegation to the
Organisation for Security and Cooperation in
Europe (OSCE), see Missions & Delegations**

Bregenz
British Consulate
Bundesstrasse 110
A-6923 Lauterach/Bregenz
Telephone: (00) (43) (5574) 78586
Facsimile: (00) (43) (5574) 70928
Office Hours (GMT): Winter 08 00 - 11 00
Summer 07 00 - 10 00
Honorary Consul: Dipl-Ing P Senger-Weiss

Graz
British Consulate
Schmiedgasse 12, A-8010 Graz
Telephone: (00) (43) (316) 8216 1621
Facsimile: (00) (43) (316) 8216 1645
Office Hours (GMT): Mon –Thurs 08 00 - 11 00
and 13 30 15 00 and Fri 08 00 - 11 00
Honorary Consul: Mr K D Bruhl, OBE
Honorary Vice-Consul: Ms Eva Bruhl
Secretary: Ms Alexandra Macher

Innsbruck
British Consulate
Kaiserjagerstrasse 1/Top B9
A-6020 Innsbruck
Telephone: (00) (43) (512) 588320
Facsimile: (00) (43) (512) 5799738
Office Hours (GMT): Winter 08 00 - 11 00,
Summer 07 00 - 10 00
Honorary Consul: Ing Hellmut Buchroithner
Honorary Vice-Consul: Dr Ivo Rungg
Secretary: Ms Claudia Loidl

Salzburg
British Consulate
Alter Markt 4, A-5020 Salzburg
Telephone: (00) (43) (662) 848133
Facsimile: (00) (43) (662) 845563
Office Hours (GMT): Winter 08 00 - 11 00,
Summer 07 00 - 10 00
Honorary Consul: Mr M M Kaindl
Honorary Pro-Consul: Mrs Helga Danmayr

AZERBAIJAN

Baku
British Embassy
2 Izmir Street, Baku 370065
Telephone: (00) (99 412) 975188/89/90,924813
Facsimile: (00) (99 412) 922739, 972474
(Commercial Section)
Airtech: (00) (99 412) 975893
e-mail: office@britemb.baku.az
office@ukemb.baku.az (Commercial Section)
Website: www.britishembassy.az

Office Hours (GMT): Summer: Mon - Fri: 04 00 - 1200
Winter: Mon - Fri: 05 00 - 13 00
Ambassador: Mr Andrew Tucker
Deputy Head of Mission: Ms Sylvia Parnell
Defence Attaché (resides at Tbilisi):
Wing Commander Andrew W Kerr, RAF
Cultural Attaché (British Council):
Ms Margaret S Jack
First Secretary (Political): Mr Andrew McCosh
Second Secretary (Commercial): Miss Doris Davis
Second Secretary (Political): Miss Fem M Horine
Vice-Consul: Miss Christine L Richardson
Third Secretary (Management): Miss Carol Wright
Third Secretary (Political): Mr David Proudfoot
Attaché: Miss Amanda Jones

BAHAMAS

Nassau
British High Commission
Ansbacher House (3rd Floor),
East Street, P.O. Box N7516, Nassau
Telephone: (00) (1) (242) 325 7471
Facsimile: (00) (1) (242) 323 3871
Airtech: (00) (1) (242) 325 7474
Office Hours (GMT): 13 30 - 18 00, 19 00 - 21 30
High Commissioner: Mr Peter Heigl
Deputy High Commissioner: Mr Dave Wells
Defence Adviser (resides at Kingston):
Colonel Rob A Hyde-Bales
First Secretary (resides at Kingston):
Mr Malcolm Bragg
Commercial/Press & Public Affairs Officer:
Mrs Helen Wells
Second Secretary (resides at Kingston):
Mr Keith Wiggins

BAHRAIN

Bahrain
British Embassy
21 Government Avenue, Manama 306,
P.O. Box 114, Bahrain
Telephone: (00) (973) 534404
Telegrams: PRODROME, BAHRAIN
Facsimile: (00) (973) 531273 Chancery,
         Information, Defence
         536109 Commercial
         533307 Consular, Management
         531472 Visa
e-mail: britemb@batelco.com.bh
Website: www.ukembassy.gov.bh
Office Hours (GMT): Sat - Wed 04 30 - 11 30
Ambassador and Consul-General: Mr P W Ford
*Deputy Head of Mission and Head of Political
Section:* Mr S C H Wilson
Defence Attaché: Commander N P Smith, RN
First Secretary (Political): Mr P V Kennedy
Second Secretary (Commercial): Ms I Mulvaney
Second Secretary (Consul/ECM/MO): Mr G Fisher
Airline Liaison Officer: Mr A Martin
Third Secretary (Political, Press & Public Affairs):
Mrs T Clayton
Third Secretary (ECO): Mrs J Allan

BANGLADESH

Dhaka
British High Commission
United Nations Road, Baridhara Dhaka
Postal address: P.O. Box 6079, Dhaka-1212
Telephone: (00) (880) (2) 8822705 (5 lines)
followed by individual extension number
8821273 DHC Direct line
Facsimile: (00) (880) (2) 8826181 High
         Commissioner's Office
         8816135 Chancery
         8823437 Management
         8823666 Immigration
         8822819 Consular
e-mail: ukcomsec@bol-online.com (Commercial
Section)
Dhaka.Commercial@fco.gov.uk (Commercial
Section)
Dhaka.Consular@fco.gov.uk (Consular)
Dhaka.Immigration@fco.gov.uk (Immigration)
Dhaka.Management@fco.gov.uk (Management)
Dhaka.Press@fco.gov.uk (Press and Public Affairs)
Website: www.ukinbangladesh.org
Office Hours (GMT): Sun to Wed 02:00 – 10:00
and Thur 02:00 – 08:00
High Commissioner (2201): Dr David Carter, CVO
*Deputy High Commissioner & Commercial
Counsellor (2203):* Mr Robert Gibson
Defence Adviser (resides in New Delhi):
Brigadier Ian Rees
First Secretary (Medical Officer):
Dr Jacqueline Howell
*First Secretary (Senior Management Officer)
(2230):* Mr Barry Greenlee
First Secretary (Immigration/Consular) (2300):
Mr Michael John Holloway
*First Secretary (Drug Liaison) (resides in
Mumbai):* Mr Chris Noon
*Second Secretary (Commercial/Press & Public
Affairs) (2209):* Mr Kristian Sharpless
Second Secretary (Commercial) (2313):
Mr Andrew McAllister
Second Secretary (Political) (2210): Mr Alan Shaw
Second Secretary (Management) (2231):
Mrs Sally Oulmi
Second Secretary (Airline Liaison Officer) (2212):
Mr Ian Angell
Second Secretary (Immigration) (2301):
Ms Meena Joshi
Second Secretary (Immigration) (2349):
Mr Nick Bostin
Second Secretary (Immigration) (2302):
Mrs Claire Shaw
Vice Consul (2303): Mr Daryl Crooks
Registrar (2217): Mr Simon Mitchell

Dhaka
Department for International Development
(DFIDB)
Address and Telephone as for British High
Commission
Facsimile: (00) (880) (2) 882 3474
Head of DFID Bangladesh: Mr Paul Ackroyd
Deputy Head: Dr Mehtab Currey
Head of Management Unit: Mr Peter Troy

First Secretary (Management Unit):
Mrs Jean Forrest
Management Officer: Mr Tom Cushnan
Estate Manager: Mr Graham Bond
Senior Economic Adviser: Reaz Islam
Senior Social Development Adviser:
Richard Montgomery
Enterprise Development Adviser:
Mr Frank Matsaert
Governance and Institutions Adviser:
Mr Chris Murgatroyd
Governance and Institutions Adviser:
Ms Sandra Nicoll
Economic Adviser: Mr Bo Sundstrom
Governance and Institutions Adviser:
Mrs Joanna McGowan
Justice Sector Co-ordinator: Ms Bea Parkes
Social Development Adviser:
Mahmuda Rahman Khan
Social Development Adviser: Amita Dey
Programme Manager: Mr Alistair Fernie
Deputy Programme Manager: Mr Liam Docherty
Senior Health and Population Adviser:
Mr Frank Atherton
Senior Education Adviser: Dr Terri Kelly
Education Adviser: Ms Louise Banham
Health Sector Manager (SHAPLA): Mr John Leigh
Health Sector Manager (NGU): Mr Alec Mercer
Education Manager: Rokeya Khanam
Deputy Programme Manager: Mr Joe Reid
Programme Officer: Mr Yoland Bewick
Senior Rural Livelihood Adviser: Mr Donal Brown
Natural Resources Economic Adviser:
Mr Tim Robertson
Engineering Adviser: Mr Peregrine Swann
Regional Livelihoods Co-ordinator:
Ms Clare Hamilton Shakya
Rural Livelihoods Programme Adviser:
Mr Duncan King
Engineering Manager: Mr Colin Benham
Water and Sanitation Manager: Mr Rodney Dyer
Rural Livelihoods Programme Adviser:
Ms Leigh Stubblefield
Disaster Programme Manager: Dilruba Haider
Deputy Programme Manager: Ms Lesley Reid
Programme Officer: Ms Paula Barrett

BARBADOS

Bridgetown
British High Commission
Lower Collymore Rock (P.O. Box 676),
Bridgetown
Telephone: (00) (1) (246) 430 7800
Facsimile: (00) (1) (246) 430 7851 Chancery
430 7860 Management/Consular
430 7826 Commercial/Information
e-mail: britishhc@sunbeach.net
Office Hours (GMT): 12 00 – 20 00 Monday to
Thursday
12 00 – 17 00 Friday
High Commissioner: Mr John White
Also High Commissioner (Non Resident) To
Antigua and Barbuda, Commonwealth of
Dominica, Grenada

St Kitts and Nevis, St Lucia and St Vincent and the
Grenadines.
Deputy High Commissioner: Mr Rob Holland
Defence Adviser: Captain Steve C Ramm, RN
Counsellor (Regional Affairs): Mr Nick J L Martin
First Secretary (Chancery): Mr Graham Honey
First Secretary (Management/Consular):
Ms Ros Day
Second Secretary (Chancery/Information):
Mr Nick J Pyle, MBE
Second Secretary (Chancery): Mr Phil Marshall
Second Secretary: Mr Stuart R Brough
*Second Secretary (Technical Works) (Resides
Washington):* Mr Ian Sweeney
Third Secretary (Management/ Consular):
Mr Jim Collins
Third Secretary: Mr Tony W White
Third Secretary (Consular): Mr Mark Harrison
Third Secretary: Miss Vicky A Stock
Third Secretary (Regional Affairs): Mr Dan J Cook
Head of Commercial Section:
Mr Hadford S Howell, MBE

Overseas Territories Advisers
First Secretary (Financial Services Adviser):
Mr Kevin Mann
First Secretary (Legal Adviser):
Ms Susan J Dickson

**Department for International Development
Caribbean**
Chelsea House, Chelsea Road
(P.O. Box 167), St Michael
Telephone: (00) (1) (246) 430 7900
Facsimile: (00) (1) (246) 430 7959
Office Hours (GMT): 12 00 – 20 00
Head of DFID (C): Ms Joanne Alston
Senior Natural Resources Adviser: Mr Dick Beales
Programme Manager: Mr Bob Smith
Economist: Ms Weyinmi Omamuli
Economic Adviser: Mr Andrew Hall
Deputy Programme Manager: Ms Kate English
Office Manager: Ms Jane Armstrong
Deputy Programme Manager: Mrs Gaynor Whitley
Senior Education Adviser: Mr Roger Cunningham
Senior Governance Adviser: Mr Bill Baker
Deputy Programme Manager:
Ms Nicole Thompson
Senior Social Development Adviser:
Ms Ann Keeling
Enterprise Development Adviser: Ms Sarah Barlow
Natural Resources Adviser: Mr Graham Chaplin
Private Sector Development Adviser:
Mr Kevin Quinlan
Governance Adviser: Ms Kathy Higgins
Programme Officer: Mr Gordon Purvis
Programme Officer: Mr Rob Bateson
Programme Officer: Ms Lana Wade

BELARUS

Minsk (SP)
British Embassy
37 Karl Marx Street, 220030 Minsk, Belarus
Telephone: (00) (375) (172) 105920 (Switchboard)
292310 (Visa and Consular – Recorded
Information)

Facsimile: (00) (375) (172) 292306 (General)
292311 (Visa Section)
Airtech: 292315
e-mail: pia@bepost.belpak.minsk.by (Information only)
postmaster@minsk.mail.fco.gov.uk (General)
Office Hours (GMT): Summer: Mon-Thurs 06 00 - 10 00 and 11 00 - 14 30; Fri 06 00 - 12 00
Winter: Mon-Thurs 07 00 - 11 00 and 12 00 - 15 30; Fri 07 00 - 13 00
Ambassador and Consul General: Mr Iain C Kelly
Deputy Head of Mission: Mr Martin Fenner
Defence Attaché (resides at Moscow):
Captain Simon R Lister, OBE, RN
Assistant Defence Attaché (resides at Moscow):
Squadron Leader Sean O'Brien, RAF
Second Secretary (Technical Works) (resides in Vienna): Mr Carl Gray
Second Secretary (Technical. Management.) (resides in Warsaw): Mr Jim Dunn
Third Secretary (Immigration) and Vice Consul:
Mr Julian Pearson
Attaché: Mr Steve Haines

BELGIUM

Brussels
British Embassy
Rue D'Arlon 85,
B-1040 Brussels
Telephone: (00) (32) (2) 287 6211
Facsimile: (00) (32) (2) 287 6355 Political
6270 Consular
6240 Commercial
6360 Press and Public Affairs
e-mail: firstname.surname@fco.gov.uk
Website: www.british-embassy.be
Ambassador: Mr G Hewitt, CMG
Deputy Head of Mission, Consul-General and Counsellor (Commercial and Economic):
Mr M J Rous
Counsellor (Political): Ms C A Macqueen
Defence Attaché:
Group Captain J D Bullen, OBE, RAF
Cultural Counsellor (British Council): Mr M Rose
First Secretary (Political): Mr J McManus
First Secretary (Political): Mr P S R Norman
First Secretary (Political): Miss J W Bird
First Secretary (Labour Attaché) (Hague):
Mr P E D Drummond
First Secretary (Commercial): Mr D J Currie
First Secretary (Technical): Mr I Willsher
Second Secretary (EU/Economic): Ms S Cullum
Second Secretary (PPA/Political): Ms L Joyce
Second Secretary (Consul): Miss C F Armstrong
Second Secretary (Technical): Mr R Bruton
Second Secretary (Technical): Mr S Willliams
Third Secretary (Political): Mr M O'Reilly

**Brussels United Kingdom Delegation to NATO,
see Missions & Delegations
Brussels United Kingdom Delegation to the
WEU, see Missions & Delegations
Brussels Office of the United Kingdom
Permanent Representative to the European
Union, see Missions & Delegations**

Brussels
British Embassy
Joint Management Office
Rue d'Arlon 85, 1040 Brussels
Telephone: (00) (32) (2) 287 6211
Facsimile: (00) (32) (2) 287 6320
Counsellor: Mr P Newall
First Secretary: Ms J Sweid
Second Secretary: Mr D L Walker
Third Secretary: Miss G Adams

Antwerp
British Consulate-General
C/o Immobilien Hugo Ceusters
Frankrijklei 31 33
B-2000 Antwerp
Telephone: (00) (32) (3) 213 2125
Facsimile: (00) (32) (3) 213 2991
Office Hours: Wednesdays 14 30 – 16 30
Thursdays 10 00 – 12 30
Honorary Consul-General: Baron P Buysse, CBE
Pro-Consul: Mrs A M Marinus

Liège
British Honorary-Consulate
Quai de Maestricht 14, 4000 Liège
Telephone: (00) (32) (4) 232 9797
Facsimile: (00) (32) (4) 223 1109
Office Hours: Mon-Fri: 8.00 - 12.00
Honorary Consul: Marie-Dominique Laurence
Paule Simonet

BELIZE

Belmopan (SP)
British High Commission
P. O. Box 91 Belmopan, Belize or B.F.P.O 12
Telephone: (00) (501) 822 2146
Facsimile: (00) (501) 822 2761
Airtech: (00) (501) 822 3694
e-mail: brithicom@btl.net
High Commissioner: Mr Philip J Priestley, CBE
Deputy High Commissioner: Mr Martin Fidler
Defence Adviser (resides in Kingston):
Colonel Rob A Hyde-Bales
Second Secretary (resides in Miami):
Mr Brendan Foreman
Second Secretary (Consular/Management):
Mr Carl Mackerras
Second Secretary (Development):
Mrs Sonia Warner
Third Secretary (Chancery): Mr Simon Mustard

BENIN

Cotonou
British Embassy (all staff resident in Nigeria)
Ambassador: Mr Philip Thomas, CMG
Counsellor: Mr D Wyatt
Consul: Mrs J Finnamore-Crorkin
Second Secretary (Commercial): Ms S Pickering
Vice-Consul: Mr T Sanmoogan

BOLIVIA

La Paz (SP)
British Embassy

Avenida Arce No.2732
Casilla 697
Telephone: (00) (591) (2) 2 433424 (connects to 9 lines)
Facsimile: (00) (591) (2) 2 431073
Airtech: (00) (591) (2) 2 432301
Duty Officer: (00) (591) 772 92311
e-mail: (Embassy): ppa@mail.megalink.com
　　　　(DFID): dfid@zuper.net
Office Hours (GMT): Mon - Thur 12 30 - 16 30
and 17 30 - 21 00 Fri 12 30 - 17 30
Ambassador: Mr William Sinton, OBE
Deputy Head of Mission and HM Consul:
Mr Philip Hogarth
Development Attaché (Head of Development Cooperation-DFID): Ms Rosalind Eyben
Defence Attaché (resides in Santiago):
Colonel Mark Rollo-Walker, OBE
First Secretary: Mr Ray Tyler
Development Attaché (Rural Livelihoods, Health-DFID): Ms Sophie Pongracz
Development Attaché (Health-DFID):
Dr Jason Lane
Cultural Attaché (Director of British Council):
Mr Eric Lawrie
Third Secretary (Management/Consular/Visa):
Mr Peter Cartwright
Third Secretary (Technical Management) (resides in Brasil): Mr Alan Barnes
Commercial Officer: Mr Eduardo Suarez

BOSNIA AND HERZEGOVINA

Sarajevo
British Embassy
8,Tina Ujevica, Sarajevo, Bosnia and Herzegovina
Telephone: (00 387 33) 444 429 Chancery;
　　　　　　Management
　　　　　　204 781/2/3 Commercial, KHF;
　　　　　　Consular/Visa
Facsimile: (00 387 33) 666 131 Chancery;
　　　　　　Management
　　　　　　204 780 Commercial; KHF;
　　　　　　Consular/Visa
Airtech: 663 492
e-mail:
PoliticalEnquiries@sarajevo.mail.fco.gov.uk
CommercialEnquiries@sarajevo.mail.fco.gov.uk
KHFEnquiries@sarajevo.mail.fco.gov.uk
ConsularEnquiries@sarajevo.mail.fco.gov.uk
VisaEnquiries@sarajevo.mail.fco.gov.uk
britemb@bih.net.ba
Office Hours (GMT): April-October: Mon-Thur 06
30 – 15 00; Fri 06 30 – 13 30
November-March: Mon-Thur 07 30 – 16 00; Fri 07
30 – 14 30
Ambassador: Mr Ian Cliff, OBE
Deputy Head of Mission: Mr Daniel Fearn
First Secretary (Commercial): Mr Tim Hanson
First Secretary (Chancery): Mr Alistair Sommerlad
First Secretary (British Council Director):
Ms C Newton
First Secretary (Management and Consul):
Mr John Ellis
Second Secretary (KHF): Mr Alan Holmes

Second Secretary (Political/PPA):
Ms Fiona McIlwham
Second Secretary (Political): Ms Sarah Raine
Vice-Consul: Mr Mark Patterson

Banja Luka
British Embassy Office
8 Simeuna Dzaka, Banja Luka,
Bosnia and Herzegovina
Tel/Fax: (00 387 51) 212 395/216 842
Mobile: (00 387 66) 512 698
e-mail: beo-bl@inecco.net
Head of Office: Mr Roy Wilson

BOTSWANA

Gaborone
British High Commission
Private Bag 0023, Gaborone
Telephone: (00) (267) 3 52841
Facsimile: (00) (267) 3 56105
Airtech: (00) (267) 3 52650
e-mail: bhc@botsnet.bw
Office Hours (GMT): Mon - Thur: 06 00 - 10 30
and 11 30 - 14 30
Fri: 06 00 - 11 00
High Commissioner: Mr D B Merry, CMG
Deputy High Commissioner: Mr J L Smith
Defence Adviser (resides at Harare):
Colonel J S Field, CBE
Second Secretary (Development/Regional Affairs):
Mr J L Riley
Third Secretary (Consular and Management):
Mr M J Redden

BRAZIL

Brasília
British Embassy
Setor de Embaixadas Sul, Quadra 801,
Conjunto K,
CEP 70.408-900, Brasilia DF or Avenida das Nacões,
Caixa Postal 07-0586, 70359 Brasilia -DF
Telephone: (00) (55) (61) 225 2710
Facsimile: (00) (55) (61) 225 1777
Airtech: (00) (55) (61) 225 2710 ext 2343
e-mail: britemb@terra.com.br
Website: www.reinounido.org.br
Office Hours (GMT) Mon - Thurs: 11 30 - 20 30
(UK Summer)
Fri: 11 30 - 15 30
Mon - Thurs: 10 30 - 19 30 (UK Winter)
Fri: 10 30 - 14 30
Ambassador: Mr Roger B Bone, CMG
Deputy Head of Mission: Mr Andrew K Soper
Defence, Military and Air Attaché:
Colonel J Michael Bowles, MBE
Naval Attaché: Captain Stephen J Timms, OBE, RN
First Secretary (Economic & Commercial):
Mr Nicholas D Low
First Secretary (Management) and Consul:
Mr Stephen M Weinrabe
First Secretary: Mr Francis A Dick
First Secretary (Technical Co-operation):
Mr Stewart S Mills
Second Secretary: Miss Lisa Whanstall

Second Secretary: Miss Harriet L Mathews
Third Secretary (Technical Management):
Mr Richard H Wildman
Third Secretary (Management) and Vice-Consul:
Miss Kate L Goulden

Belém – PA
British Consulate
Av. Governador Malcher, 815 Ed Palladium Center
Conj. 410/411,
Belém – Para,
CEP 66.035-900,
Caixa Postal 98
Telephone: (00) (55) (91) 222 5074, 223 0990
Facsimile: (00) (55) (91) 212 0274
Honorary Consul: Dr A M dos Santos

Manáus - AM
British Consulate
Swedish Match da Amazonia S.A
Rua Poraque 240
Distrito Industrial
Manaus – Am
CEP 69075 –180
Telephone: (00) (55) (92) 613 1819
Facsimile: (00) (55) (92) 613 1420
Honorary Consul: Mr V J Brown

Rio de Janeiro - RJ
British Consulate-General
Praia do Flamengo, 284/2 andar,
Rio de Janeiro - RJ, CEP 22210-030
Telephone: (00) (55) (21) 2555 9600 (Switchboard)
9640 (Consular Section)
Facsimile: (00) (55) (21) 2555
           9672 (Management)
           9604 (Chancery)
           9679 (Commercial)
           9671 (Consular)
Airtech: (00) (55) (21) 2555 9608
e-mail: britconrio@openlink.com.br (General)
consular.section@fco.gov.uk (Consular Section)
Office Hours (GMT): Mon - Fri: March -
November: 11 30 - 20 00
December - February: 10 00 - 19 00
Consul-General: Mr Paul Yaghmourian
Deputy Consul-General and Consul (Commercial):
Mr Philip John Ambrose
Vice-Consul (Commercial): Mr Gery Juleff
Vice-Consul (Management): Mr Stuart Smith
Vice-Consul (Consular/Immigration):
Mr Andrew Snook
Pro-Consul: Mrs Sara Pereira
Pro-Consul: Ms Marina Zelenoy

Belo Horizonte - MG
British Consulate
Rua dos Inconfidentes, 1075, Sala 1302
Belo Horizonte – MG – 30140 120
Savassi
Telephone: (00) (31) 3261 2072
Facsimile: (00) (31) 3261 0226
e-mail: britcon.bhe@terra.com.br
Honorary Consul: Mr Roger A Gough, MBE
Commercial Officer: Mr Rogerio Pacheco, MBE

Fortaleza - CE
British Consulate
c/o Grupo Edson Queiroz, Praca da Imprensa s/n,
Aldeota, Fortaleza - CE, CEP 60135-900
Telephone: (00) (55) (85) 466 8580/8582
Facsimile: (00) (55) (85) 261-8763
e-mail: annette@edsonqueiroz.com.br
Honorary Consul: Mrs Annette T Reeves de Castro

Recife - PE
Av. Conselheiro Aguiar, 2941/3°,
Boa Viagem,
Recife-PE, CEP 51020-020
Telephone: (00) (55) (81) 3465-0230
Facsimile: (00) (55) (81) 3465-0247
e-mail: recife@britishconsulate-org.br
Honorary Consul: Mr Alan E Fiore
Commercial Officer: Mr Chris Cobb

Salvador - BA
British Consulate
Av. Estados Unidos, No 18-B
8 Andar-Comercio, Ed-Estados Unidos
CEP 40010 - 020, Salvador - BA
Telephone: (00) (55) (71) 243-7399
Facsimile: (00) (55) (71) 242-7293/243-7856
e-mail: adcos@allways.com.br
Honorary Consul: Mr Nigel Lee

São Paulo - SP
British Consulate-General
Centro Brasileiro Britanico
Rua Ferreira de Araujo, 2nd Floor
Pinheiros
05428-002-São Paulo-SP
Brazil
Telephone: (00) (55) (11) 3094 2700
Facsimile: (00) (55) (11) 3094 2717 (Commercial)
           3094 2750 (Management)
Airtech: (00) (55) (11) 3816 4887
e-mail: consulad@uol.com.br
Website: www.Gra.bretahanha.org.br
Office Hours (GMT): Mon - Thurs: 11 30 - 19 45,
Fri 11 30 - 19 30 (UK Summer)
Mon - Thurs: 10 30 - 18 45, Fri 10 30 - 18 30 (UK
Winter)
*Consul-General & Director of Trade & Investment
Brazil:* Mr Bernard Everett, CVO
*Deputy Consul-General and Deputy Director of
Trade & Investment:* Mr Patrick Ashworth
Vice-Consul (Consular/Management):
Mr David Paginton
Vice-Consul (Commercial): Mr Tim Dearden
Vice-Consul (Commercial): Ms Gale Jenkinson
Vice-Consul (Customs): Mr David Sterling
Pro-Consul (Consular/Management):
Ms Lisa Evely

Curitiba - PR
British Trade Office and British Consulate
Rusa Presidente Faria, 51, 2 andar,
CJ.705 - Curitiba, PR CEP 80020-290
Telephone: (00) (55) (41) 322-1202
Facsimile: (00) (55) (41) 322-3537
e-mail: consuladobritanico@mais.sul.com.br
Commercial Officer and Honorary Consul:
Mr Peter ter Poorten

Porto Alegre - RS
British Consulate
Edificio Montreal, Rua Itapeva,
110 Conjunto 505, Passo D'Areia
91350-080 Porto Alegre - RS
Telephone: (00) (55) (51) 341-0720
Facsimile: (00) (55) (51) 341-0720
Honorary Consul: Mr Geoffrey Powell

Porto Alegre - RS
British Commercial Office
Rua Antenor Lemos 57 Cj 403,
Bairro Menino Deus, 90850-100,
Porto Alegre -RS
Telephone: (00) (55) (51) 232 141
Facsimile: (00) (55) (51) 231 6094
e-mail: britconpoa@portoweb.con.br
Commercial Officer: Mrs Denise Pellin

Rio Grande - RS
British Consulate
Wilson Sons, Rua Riachuelo, 201 terreo,
CEP 96200-390, Rio Grande - RS
Porto Alegre - RS
Telephone: (00) (55) (53) 233-7700
Facsimile: (00) (55) (53) 233-7701
(00) (55) (53) 231 1530
e-mail: rjg@wilson.com.br
Honorary Consul: Mr Richard Grantham

Santos - SP
British Consulate
Rua Tuiuti 58, 2 andar, Caixa Postal 204,
11101-220-220, Santos
Telephone: (00) (55) (13) 3211 2300, Direct: (55)
(13) 3219 4659
Mobile: (55) (13) 9972 1622
Facsimile: (00) (55) (13) 3210 3840
(55) (13) 3219 5250
e-mail: daw@wilson.com.br
Honorary Consul: Mr David A Walton

BRUNEI

Bandar Seri Begawan
British High Commission
PO Box 2197
Bandar Seri Begawan 8674
Telephone: (00) (673) (2) 222231/223121
Chancery & Commercial
226001 Management & Consular
Facsimile: (00) (673) (2) 234315
Airtech: (00) (673) (2) 226002
e-mail: brithc@brunet.bn
Office Hours (GMT): Mon to Thurs 00 30 - 04 45
and 06 00 - 09 00
Fri 00 30 - 04 30
High Commissioner: Mr Andrew J F Caie
Deputy High Commissioner: Mr Edward Bousfield
Defence Adviser: Captain Paddy H Watson, RN
First Secretary (Defence Cooperation):
Mr Colin Britteon
Second Secretary (Chancery/Information):
Miss Sue Elliott, MBE
Third Secretary (Commercial/Economic):
Mr Brian Price

Third Secretary (Management/Consular):
Mr Simon Hart
Attaché: Mrs Val Porter
Attaché: Miss Sian Bloxham

BULGARIA

Sofia
British Embassy
9 Moskovska Street, Sofia
FTN: 8521
Telephone: (00) (359) (2) 933 9222
Facsimile: 933 9219 (Chancery)
9250 (Management)
9289 (Defence)
9279 (Commercial)
9263 (Visa/Consular)
9233 (Know How Fund)
9270 (Airtech)
942 4344 (British Council)
e-mail: Officer's firstname.surname@fco.gov.uk
Website: www.british-embassy.bg
Office Hours (GMT): Mon to Thurs 06 30 – 15 30
Fri 06 30 – 11 00
Ambassador: Mr Ian Soutar (2203)
Deputy Head of Mission: Mr Tim Colley (2204)
Defence Attaché: Colonel Richard Ciaglinski
(2214)
First Secretary (Political): Mr John Davies (2206)
Cultural Attaché (British Council Director):
Mr Ian Stewart
First Secretary (Commercial):
Mr Dennis Leith (2228)
Second Secretary (Management):
Mr Tony Williams (2238)
Second Secretary (Political/Press):
Mrs Christine Winterburn (2207)
Second Secretary (DLO): Mr Lee Williams (2281)
Second Secretary (ILO): Mr Adrian Bernard (2304)
Second Secretary (Consul and ECM):
Miss Hilary Arthur (2260)
Assistant Defence Attaché: Lieutenant Commander
Mark Warlow RN (2211)
*Assistant Cultural Attaché (British Council Deputy
Director):* Ms Lisa McManus
Head of Know How Fund: Mrs Toni Grancharova
(2226)
Third Secretary (Political): Mr Karl Tluczek
(2223)
Attaché (Immigration and Vice Consul):
Mr Mark Griffith (2261)
Attaché (Immigration and Vice Consul):
Mr Gary McCall (2262)
Attaché (Immigration): Mr Cris Ashworth (2259)
Chaplain: Rev Steve Hughes

Varna
British Consulate
40 Graf Igantiev Street
PO Box 229
Telephone: (00) (359) (52) 6655 555
Facsimile: 6655 755
e-mail: bozhilov@unimasters.bg
Honorary Consul: Mr Nikolai Bozhilov

BURKINA FASO

Ouagadougou

British Embassy (all staff reside at Abidjan)
Ambassador: Mr J F Gordon, CMG
First Secretary (Commercial), Consul and Deputy Head of Mission: Mr M J K Rickerd, MVO
Second Secretary (Political/Information):
Ms K Miller, MBE
Second Secretary (Management) and Vice-Consul:
Mr D Summers
Second Secretary (Commercial/Political):
Mr C Frean
Third Secretary & Vice- Consul (Passports & Visas): Mr M McGuinness
Third Secretary (Chancery): Ms N McBratney

British Honorary Consulate
Hotel Yibi
10 BP 13593
Ouagadougou
Burkina Faso
Telephone: (00) (226) 30 73 23
Facsimile: (00) (226) 30 59 00
e-mail: ypi@cenatrin.bf
Honorary Consul: Mr A R Turner

BURMA (Union of Myanmar)

Rangoon

Rangoon (Yangon)
British Embassy
80 Strand Road (P.O. Box 638), Rangoon
Telephone: (00) (95) (1) 295300, 295309, 370863, 370864, 370865, 370867, (out of hours: 295309)
Facsimile: (00) (95) (1) 370866
Airtech: (00) (95) (1) 254657/254659
Office Hours (GMT): 01 30 - 10 00
Except Wed 01 30 - 06 30
Ambassador: Mrs Victoria J Bowman
Deputy Head of Mission and HM Consul:
Mr Martin Garrett
Cultural Attaché, British Council Director (Tel: 256290 ext:312): Mr Marcus Milton
Second Secretary: Miss Anne Macro
Second Secretary (Management) and Vice-Consul:
Mr Nick J Enescott
Third Secretary: Mr Nigel Blackwood
Attaché: Miss Karen Sowerby

BURUNDI

Bujumbura

British Embassy (all staff resident in Kigali)
Ambassador: Mrs S E Hogwood, MBE
Deputy Head of Mission: Ms J A Curry-Jones
Defence Attaché (resides at Kampala):
Lieutenant Colonel C J A Wilton

CAMBODIA

Phnom Penh

British Embassy
29 Street 75, Phnom Penh
Telephone: (00) (855 23) 427124, 428295
Facsimile: (00) (855 23) 427125
e-mail: BRITEMB@bigpond.com.kh

Consular@phnompenh.mail.fco.gov.uk
Office Hours (GMT): Mon - Thurs: 01 00 - 10 00
Fri: 01 00 - 06 00
Ambassador: Mr S J Bridges
Second Secretary and Deputy Head of Mission:
Mr I Felton
Attaché: Mr A Bell

DFID Cambodia

c/o British Embassy
Phnom Penh
Telephone: (00) (855 23) 427124, 428295
Facsimile: (00) (855 23) 430290
e-mail: c-khieu@dfid.gov.uk
Head of Office: Dr D Arghiros
Rural Livelihoods Adviser: Mr C Price

CAMEROON

Yaoundé

British High Commission
Avenue Winston Churchill,
BP 547, Yaoundé
Telephone: (00) (237) 2 22 05 45/2 22 07 96
Facsimile: (00) (237) 2 22 01 48
Airtech: (00) (237) 2 22 91 55
Duty Officer Mobile: (00) (237) 7 713 053
e-mail: BHC.yaounde@fco.gov.uk
Office Hours (GMT): Mon: 06 30 - 13 30
Tue - Fri: 06 30 – 13 00
High Commissioner: Mr Richard Wildash, LVO
Deputy High Commissioner: Mr David Williams
Second Secretary: Mrs Pam Tarif
Vice-Consul (Consular/Management):
Mr Nadeem JanJua

Douala

British Consulate
Standard Chartered Bank Cameroon SA,
Boulevard de la Liberté
BP 1784, Douala, Cameroon
Telephone: (00) (237) 3 42 21 77/3 42 81 45
Facsimile: (00) (237) 3 42 88 96
Office Hours (GMT): Mon: 06 30 - 13 30
Tues-Fri: 06 30 – 13 00
Commercial Officer: Mrs Valerie de Tailly

CANADA

Ottawa

British High Commission
80 Elgin Street, Ottawa, Ontario K1P 5K7
Telephone: (00) (1) (613) 237 1530
Voicemail & Direct Lines: (00) (1) (613) 237 1542
- (key in extension shown by name)
Facsimile: (00) (1) (613) 237 7980
                  232 0738 Management
                  232 2533 Visa
                  237 5211 Economic
                  237 6537 Passport
                  567 8045 Political
e-mail: BHC@fco.gov.uk
management@fco.gov.uk
information@fco.gov.uk
chancery@fco.gov.uk
consular@fco.gov.uk
trade-econ@fco.gov.uk

Website: www.britain-in-canada.org
Office Hours (GMT): 13 00 - 21 00
High Commissioner: Sir Andrew Burns KCMG
Deputy High Commissioner (343):
Mr R J Codrington
Counsellor (Trade/Economic) (324):
Mr N R Chrimes
Counsellor (380): Mr R A Foulsham
*Counsellor (Cultural Affairs) (British Council
Director) (318):* Mr P Chenery
Defence and Military Adviser (369):
Brigadier C J R Day
Naval and Air Adviser (384):
Captain D M Booth DSC RN
*First Secretary (Head of Political/Information
Section) (274):* Mr C O'Connor
First Secretary (Management) (326): Mr R Sharp
*First Secretary (Head of Media & Public Affairs)
(262):* Mr P O'Brien
First Secretary (214): Mr B Lowater
Second Secretary (Economic) (247):
Mr A Richmond
Second Secretary (Trade) (282): Mr M Dolan
Assistant Naval Adviser B.D.L.S. (234):
Sqn Ldr Chris McKiernan
Second Secretary (Consular) (320): Mr C Smart
Second Secretary (Political) (228): Mr A Campbell
Third Secretary (Economic) (331): Mr G Crockard

Montreal
British Consulate-General
Suite 4200, 1000 De La Gauchetiere West,
Montreal, Quebec
Canada
H3B 4W5
Telephone: (00) (1) (514) 866-5863
Direct Line - see individual officers
Facsimile: (00) (1) (514) 866-0202
Airtech: (00) (1) (514) 866 4867
Office Hours (GMT): 14 00 - 22 00
Consul-General (233): Ms Sarah Gillett, MVO
Deputy Consul-General (230): Mr Philip Hagger
Consul (Commercial) (225): Mrs Debbie J Fern

**Montreal United Kingdom Representative on
the Council of the International Civil Aviation
Organisation, see Missions & Delegations**

Toronto
British Consulate-General
British Trade & Investment Office
777 Bay Street, Suite 2800, College Park,
Toronto, Ontario M5G 2G2
Telephone: (00) (1) 416 593-1290
Facsimile: (00) (1) 416 593-1229
Airtech: (00) (1) 416 593-1425
e-mail: britcon2@gta.igs.net
Office Hours (GMT): 12 30 - 21 00
Consul-General: Mr Geoffrey Berg, MVO
Deputy Consul-General (2236): Mr Stanley Calder
Consul (Inward Investment) (2234):
Mr John Williams
Consul (Commercial) (2231): Ms Sheila Towe
Vice-Consul/Management Officer (2227):
Miss Jo Bowyer

Vancouver
British Consulate-General
1111 Melville Street, Suite 800,
Vancouver, British Colombia, V6E 4V6
Telephone: (00) (1) (604) 683-4421
Direct Lines - see individual officers
Facsimile: (00) (1) (604) 681-0693
Airtech: (00) (1) (604) 683-7768
Office Hours (GMT): 16 30 - 00 30
Consul-General (1-2205): Mr Ian Kydd
Deputy Consul-General (1-2208):
Mr David Roberts

Calgary
British Trade Office
Suite 1500, Bow Valley Square IV
250-6th Avenue S.W
Calgary, Alberta T2P 3H7
Telephone: (00) (1) (403) 705-1755
Facsimile: (00) (1) (403) 264-1262
Office Hours (GMT): 15 30 – 23 30
Director: Mr Clark Grue
Commercial Assistant: Ms Tara Meinhardt

Halifax/Dartmouth
British Consulate
1, Canal Street, P.O. Box 605,
Dartmouth, Nova Scotia B2Y 3Y9
Telephone: (00) (1) (902) 461-1381
Facsimile: (00) (1) (902) 465-2578
Honorary Consul: Mr A A Smithers

St. John's
British Consulate
113 Topsail Road, St. John's,
Newfoundland A1E 2A9
Telephone: (00) (1) (709) 579 2002
Facsimile: (00) (1) (709) 579 0475
Honorary Consul: Mr F D Smith

Winnipeg
British Consulate
229, Athlone Drive, Winnipeg,
Manitoba, R3J 3L6
Telephone: (00) (1) (204) 896 1380
Facsimile: (00) (1) (204) 269 3025
Honorary Consul: Mr R M Hill

Quebec City
British Consulate
Le Complexe St-Amable
700 - 1150 Claire-Fontaine, Quebec City
Quebec, G1R 5G4
Telephone: (00) (1) (418) 521 3000
Facsimile: (00) (1) (418) 521 3099
Honorary Consul: Mr R Drouin

CAPE VERDE

Praia
British Embassy (all staff resident in Dakar)
Ambassador: Mr Alan Burner
Deputy Head of Mission and Consul:
Mr Simon Bond
Third Secretary and Vice-Consul: (Vacant)
Attaché (Immigration): Ms Christine Johnson

Sao Vincente
British Honorary Consulate
Shell Cabo Verde, Avenue Amilcar Cabral CP4,
Mindelo, Sao Vincente
Telephone: (00) (238) 32 66 25/26/27
Facsimile: (00) (238) 32 66 29
e-mail: antonio.a.canuto@scv.simis.com
Honorary Consul: Mr Antonio Canuto

CENTRAL AFRICAN REPUBLIC

Bangui
British Embassy (all staff reside at Yaoundé)
Ambassador and Consul-General:
Mr Richard Wildash, LVO
First Secretary and Consul: Mr David Williams

CHAD

Ndjamena
British Embassy (all staff reside at Yaoundé)
Ambassador: Mr Richard Wildash, LVO
First Secretary and Consul: Mr David Williams

Ndjamena
British Consulate
BP1060
Ndjamena
Tel/Fax: (00) (235) 52 39 70
Mobile: (00) (235) 841 11 02
e-mail: econsit@hotmail.com
Honorary Consul: Mrs Ermanna Delacroix

CHILE

Santiago
British Embassy
Av. El Bosque 0125, Casilla 72-D
or Casilla 16552, Santiago
Telephone: (00) (56) (2) 370 4100
Facsimile: (00) (56) (2) 370 4180 Commercial
             4170 Consulate
             4160 Management
             335 5988 Information
             4140 Chancery
             235 7375 British Council
e-mail: chancery@fco.gov.uk
commercial@fco.gov.uk
consulate@fco.gov.uk
defence@fco.gov.uk
Web page: www.britemb.cl
Office Hours (GMT): (October - March): 12 00 -
20 30 (March - October) 14 00 - 22.30
Ambassador: Mr G Faulkner
*Counsellor, Consul-General and Deputy Head of
Mission:* Mr P Whiteway (Ext 4112)
Counsellor: Mr N M Jacobsen (Ext 4123)
Defence Attaché: Colonel R M J Rollo-Walker, OBE
(Ext 4120)
First Secretary (Commercial): Mr P Taylor
(Ext 4174)
Cultural Attaché (British Council Director):
Mr J W Knagg OBE
First Secretary (Political): Mr Jo Alba
Second Secretary and Consul:
Miss D E Gordon, MBE (Ext 4138)

Second Secretary (Commercial): Mr S Wadvani
(Ext 4175)
Second Secretary: Mr N Holborn (Ext 4114)
Third Secretary: Miss M G Knapp

Valparaíso
British Consulate
Blanco 1199 Piso 5
Casilla 68 – V
Valparaíso, Chile
Telephone/ Facsimile: (00) (56) (32) 213063
e-mail: con.britainico@entelchile.net
Honorary Consul: Mr Iain Hardy

Punta Arenas
British Consulate
Cataratas del Niagara 01325, Punta Arenas
Casilla 22-D
Telephone: (00) (56) (61) 211535
e-mail: reesking@terra.cl
Honorary Consul: Mr J C Rees

CHINA

Beijing
British Embassy
11 Guang Hua Lu, Jian Guo Men Wai,
Beijing 100600
Telephone: (00) (86) (10) 6532 1961 (plus
extension if known)
6532 6895 (plus extension if known)
Facsimile: (00) (86) (10) 6532 1937
             6532 0901 (Development Section)
e-mail: Commercial Section:
commercialmail@peking.mail.fco.gov.uk
Commercial Library:
library@peking.mail.fco.gov.uk
Science and Technology:
bescitec@peking.mail.fco.gov.uk
Development Section:
dfid@peking.mail.fco.gov.uk
Office Hours (GMT): 03 00 - 04 00 and 05 30 -
09 00

Consular & Visa Section
21st Floor
Kerry Centre
1, Guang Hua Lu
Beijing 100600
Telephone: (00) (86) (10) 8529 6600, 6075, 6084
(office hours)
(00) (86) (10) 6532 1961, 6750 (out of hours):
(00) (86) (10) 8529 6600 (24 hour recorded
information service)
Facsimile: (00) (86) (10) 8529 6081 (Consular)
             (00) (86) (10) 8529 6080 (Visa)
Telegrams: RTI:PEVIS ROU:PV CIR:PVA
e-mail: consularmail@peking.mail.fco.gov.uk
visamail@peking.mail.fco.gov.uk
Office Hours (GMT): 00 30 – 04 00 and 05 00 –
08 30

Cultural and Education Section
4th Floor Landmark Building, Tower 1,
8 North Dongsanhuan Road, Chaoyang District,
Beijing 100004
Telephone: (00) (86) (10) 6590 6903
Facsimile: (00) (86) (10) 6590 0977

e-mail: enquiry@britishcouncil.org.cn
Ambassador: Mr C O Hum, CMG
Minister, Consul-General and Deputy Head of Mission: Mr N J Cox
Counsellor (Political/Economic): Ms C Nettleton
Counsellor (Commercial): Mr C Haswell
Counsellor (Cultural) (British Council Director) (ext 219): Mr M O'Sullivan
Counsellor (Public Affairs): Mr N P Westgarth
Defence, Military and Air Attaché:
Brigadier J G Kerr, OBE, QGM
Naval Attaché: Captain A A Ainslie, RN
First Secretary (Political): Mr D Ellis
First Secretary (Political): Ms T Redshaw
First Secretary (Political): Mr M Pettigrew
First Secretary (Political): Mr W D Morgan
First Secretary (Commercial): Mr S Buckley
First Secretary (Commercial): Mr G Hoar
First Secretary (Commercial): Mr K Brown
First Secretary (Commercial/Science and Technology): Mr P Wusterman
First Secretary (Cultural and Scientific) (British Council): Mr K R Davies
First Secretary (Education) (British Council): Mr A G Slaven
First Secretary (Education) (British Council): Mr A Disbury
First Secretary (Cultural) (British Council): Mr D Knox
First Secretary (Assistant Director) (British Council): Ms M Day
First Secretary (Cultural): Mr P Clementson
First Secretary (Bilateral): Mr B Fender
First Secretary: Ms S A McLean
First Secretary (Economic): Mr N Bridge
First Secretary (Economic): Ms S Peters
First Secretary (Management): Mr P Robinson
First Secretary (Consul): Mr I Wilson
First Secretary (Development): Ms F McConnon
First Secretary (Development): Ms J Haycock
First Secretary (Development): Ms S Milner
First Secretary (Development): Ms P de Waal
First Secretary (Development): Ms C Martin
First Secretary (Development): Ms J Popkins
First Secretary (Technical Management): Mr P Kelly
First Secretary (Technical Works Officer): Mr C Gray
First Secretary (Nurse): Ms J Senior
Second Secretary (Economic): Miss G Cull
Second Secretary (Commercial): Mr B Ladd
Second Secretary (Commercial): Mr G Tebble
Second Secretary (Commercial): Mrs T Evans
Second Secretary (Commercial): Mr D Spires
Second Secretary (Information): Mr A Pinfeld
Second Secretary (Cultural) (British Council) (ext 232): Ms V Grant
Second Secretary (Cultural -Scientific) (British Council) (ext 228): Mrs L Watkins
Second Secretary (Cultural) (British Council): (Vacant)
Second Secretary (Cultural) (British Council): Mr S Forbes
Second Secretary (Immigration): Mr G S Flett
Second Secretary (Immigration): Ms S Morrell

Second Secretary (Immigration-Airport Liaison): Mr R Montgomery
Second Secretary (Management): Mr T O'Connell
Second Secretary (Management): Mr M Page
Second Secretary (Technical Management): Mr R Parker
Second Secretary (Development): Mrs V Malloo
Second Secretary (Security): Mr C Gingell
Third Secretary (Vice-Consul): Mr J Murphy
Third Secretary (Immigration): Mr I Howell
Third Secretary (Immigration): Mr A Mapperley
Third Secretary (Immigration): Mrs G Lowson
Third Secretary (Immigration): Mr G Stein
Third Secretary (Immigration): Mrs S Stilgoe
Third Secretary (Immigration): Mr C Glen
Third Secretary (Immigration): Miss K Dyball
Third Secretary (Immigration): Mr S Thomas
Third Secretary (Immigration): Ms W Shepherd
Third Secretary (Technical Works): Mr G Caldwell
Third Secretary (Visits): Mrs E Evans

Shanghai
British Consulate-General
Suite 301, Shanghai Centre
1376 Nan Jing Xi Lu,
Shanghai 200040
Telephone: (00) (86) (21) 6279 7650
Facsimile: (00) (86) (21) 6279 7651 (General)
6279 7388 (Commercial)
e-mail: britishconsulate@shanghai.mail.fco.gov.uk
firstname.lastname@fco.gov.uk
Website: www.britishconsulate.sh.cn
Office Hours (GMT): 00 30 - 09 00 (Mon - Thu)
Office Hours (GMT): 00 30 - 07 30 (Fri)

Visa Section
Suite 751, Shanghai Centre
1376 Nan Jing Xi Lu
Shanghai 200040
Telephone: (00) (86) (21) 6279 8130
Facsimile: (00) (86) (21) 6279 8254
e-mail: visa@shanghai.mail.fco.gov.uk
Office Hours (GMT): 00 30 - 09 00 (Mon - Thu)
Office Hours (GMT): 00 30 - 07 30 (Fri)

British Council
1 Floor Pidemco Tower
318 Fu Zhou Lu
Shanghai 200001
Telephone: (00) (86) (21) 6391 2626
Facsimile: (00) (86) (21) 6391 2121
e-mail: bc.shanghai@britishcouncil.org.cn
firstname.lastname@britishcouncil.org.cn
Website: www.britishcouncil.org.cn
Office Hours (GMT): 00 30 - 09 00
Consul-General: Mr Paul Sizeland
Deputy Consul-General: Mr Steve Codd
Head of Commercial: Mr Trevor Lewis
Consul (Commercial): Mr Bob Shead
Consul (Commercial): Mr Barry Nicholson
Consul (Economic/Press & Public Affairs): Mr John Edwards
Consul (Commercial): Mr Douglas Barrett
Consul (Director Cultural and Education): Ms Joanna Burke
Consul (Cultural and Education): Mr Jim Hollington

Consul (Education): Ms Sarah Deverill
Consul (Education): Mr Richard Everitt
Consul (Entry Clearance Manager):
Mrs Suzanne Ivins
Vice-Consul (Management): Mr Eliot Groves
Vice-Consul (Visa): Miss Claire Murray
Vice-Consul (Visa): Miss Norah Finlay
Pro Consul (Consular): Mrs Emma Nicholson

Guangzhou
British Consulate-General
2nd Floor Guangdong International Hotel
(Visa/Consular/Management Sections)
7th Floor Guangdong International Hotel
(Commercial/Political/Economic Sections)
339 Huanshi Dong Lu
Guangzhou 510098
Telephone: (00) (86) (20) 8335 1354 General
          8333 1316 British Council
Facsimile: (00) (86) (20) 8331 2799
           Management/Consular
           8333 6485 Commercial
           8332 7509 Visa
           8335 1321 British Council
e-mail: guangbcg@gitic.com.cn (Consulate)
bc.guangzhou@britishcouncil.org.cn (British
Council)
Office Hours (GMT): Mon-Fri: 01 00 - 04 30 &
05 30 - 09 00
Consul General: Mr Stephen Lillie
Deputy Consul General: Mr Sanjay Wadvani
Consul (Political/Economic):
Mr Nick Whittingham
Consul (Commercial): Mr Haden Spicer
Consul (Commercial): Miss Joanne Carey
Consul (Consular/Management): Mr Gary Nicholls
Consul (Visas): Miss Sandra Stowe
Consul (Cultural and Education):
Ms Christine Skinner
Vice-Consul (Visa): Mr John Kennedy
Vice-Consul (Visa): Mr Daniel Jones
Vice-Consul (Visa): Mr Mark Gee
Vice-Consul (Visa): Mr Simon Burton
Attaché: Miss Sarah Pratt

Chongqing
British Consulate-General
Suite 2801, Metropolitan Tower,
68 Zourong Road
Chongqing
40010 People's Republic of China
Telephone: (00) (86) (23) 6381 0321
Facsimile: (00) (86) (23) 6381 0322
Airtech: (00) (86) (23) 6381 0320
e-mail: bcgchq@public.cta.cq.cn
Office Hours (GMT): Mon - Fri 01 00 - 04 00 and
05 00 - 09 00
Consul General: Miss Carma Elliot
Consul: Mr Scott Strain

Hong Kong Special Administrative Region
British Consulate General
No. 1 Supreme Court Road, Central, Hong Kong,
(PO Box 528)
Telephone: (00) (852) 2901 3000
Facsimile: (00) (852) 2901 3066 Commercial
           3007 Management

3008 Press and Public Affairs
3204 Consular
3347 Visa
3420 Fiscal & Drugs Liaison Office
3143 BC Passport
3195 Passport
3295 Airport Liaison Office
e-mail: political@britishconsulate.org.hk Political
and Economic
commercial@britishconsulate.org.hk Commercial
management@britishconsulate.org.hk Management
press@britishconsulate.org.hk Press and Public
Affairs
consular@britishconsulate.org.hk Consular
visa@britishconsulate.org.hk Visa
passport@britshconsulate.org.hk Passport
Website: www.britishconsulate.org.hk
Office Hours (GMT): Mon - Fri: 00 30 - 09 15
Consul-General: Sir James Hodge, KCVO, CMG
Deputy Head of Mission and Director of Trade:
Mr Greg Dorey, CVO
Deputy Consul-General (Political/Economic):
Ms Barbara Ellington, OBE
*Deputy Consul-General (Security and Regional
Affairs):* Mr Malcolm Davies
Consul (Management): Mr Michael Hannant
Consul (Trade Commissioner):
Miss Jean Sharpe, OBE
Consul (Trade Commissioner, Projects):
Mr Nick Khosla
Consul: Mr Bill Ridout
Fiscal & Drugs Liaison Officer:
Mr Ken Newhouse
Consul (Press and Public Affairs):
Mr Trevor Adams
Consul (Passports): Mr John Geoghegan
Airline Liaison Officer: Mrs Sandra Tilley
Consul (Political/Economic): Mr Tim Summers
Vice-Consul (Management): Mr Mark Forrester
Vice-Consul (Assistant Trade Commissioner):
Mr Malcolm Whatley
Vice-Consul (Technical Management):
Mr Andrew Friis
Vice-Consul (IT Management): Mr Paul Francis
Vice-Consul (Security Management):
Mr Mike Sanders
Vice Consul (Political/Economic): Mr Warren Pain
Vice-Consul (Economic/Finance): Ms Kirsty Paton
Vice-Consul (Political/Economic):
Ms Sophie Gregg
Vice-Consul (Political/Economic):
Mr Michael Blake
Vice-Consul (Security and Regional Affairs):
Mrs Deborah Forrester
Vice Consul (Visas): Mr Colin Green
Vice-Consul (Passports): Mrs Clarice Whiteside
Vice-Consul (Consular): Mr L B T Jackson
*Vice-Consul (Executive Assistant to the Consul
General):* Miss Gill Remmington

Invest - UK Regional Office
British Consulate General, No 1 Supreme Court
Road,
Central, Hong Kong, (PO Box 528)
Telephone: (00) (852) 2901 3367
Facsimile: (00) (852) 2901 3155

e-mail: investukasia@fco.gov.uk
Website: www.invest.uk.com/asiapacific
Regional Director: Mr Paul Grey

FCO Procurement Group Hong Kong
2/F, 3 Supreme Court Road, Central, Hong Kong
Telephone: (00) (852) 2901 3488
Facsimile: (00) (852) 2901 3477
e-mail: salesgphk@hongkong.mail.fco.gov.uk
Office Hours (GMT): Mon-Fri 00 15 - 09 30
General Manager: Mr C J Davis

Macau
British Consulate General
No. 1 Supreme Court Rd, Central, Hong Kong
PO Box 528
Telephone: (00) (852) 2901 3000
Facsimile: (00) (852) 2901 3066
Consul General (Resides at Hong Kong):
Sir James Hodge, KCVO, CMG
Deputy Consul-General (Resides at Hong Kong):
Ms B M Ellington, OBE
Consul (Resides at Hong Kong): Mr B Ridout
Vice-Consul (Commercial) (Resides at Hong Kong): Mr M G Whatley
Vice Consul (Resides at Hong Kong):
Mr L B T Jackson
Honorary Consul/General Manager:
Mr Edward J Machin

Est. Cheok Van R/C 13
Ed. hao Yuen
House Number 13
Coloane, Macau
Telephone: (00) (853) 882797
Facsimile: (00) (853) 850083

COLOMBIA

Bogotá
British Embassy
Edificio ING Barings
Carrera 9 No 76 - 49 Piso 9
Bogotá
Telephone: (00) (57) (1) 317 6690, 6310, 6321
Facsimile: (00) (57) (1) 317 6265 Management Section
317 6523 Commercial Section
317 6298 Political Section
317 6401 Visa/Consular Section
Faxlok: 317 6534
e-mail: britain@cable.net.co
Office Hours (GMT): Mon-Thurs: 13 30 - 17 30 and 18 30 - 2130
Fri: 13 30 - 1830
Ambassador: Mr Tom Duggin
Deputy Head of Mission: Mr Russell Thomson
Counsellor: Mr Nicholas Busvine
Counsellor (Cultural: British Council Director) (Tel: 618 0118 ext 146): Mr Joe Docherty
Defence Attaché: Colonel Mike E Wilcox
First Secretary: Mr Ray Tyler
First Secretary: Mr David Wright
First Secretary: Mr David Miller
First Secretary (Commercial): Mr Mel Cumming
First Secretary: Mr Stephen Reynolds
First Secretary (Management): Mr David Gardner

Second Secretary: Mr Robert Tinline
Second Secretary: Miss Moira Allen
Second Secretary (Immigration/Consular):
Mr Chris Wigginton
Second Secretary: Mr Andy Bonsey
Second Secretary: Mr Mark O'Hagan
Second Secretary: Mr Hank Cole
Second Secretary: Mr Mark Sprawson
Second Secretary (Education: British Council) (Tel: 618 0175/218 7518): Mr John Bryant MBE
Second Secretary (Cultural: British Council) (Tel: 618 0118): Mr Richard Shackleton
Third Secretary (Management): Ms Jan Nicol
Third Secretary (Management): Miss Cindy Parker
Third Secretary (Immigration): Mrs Anesha Bayley
Third Secretary (Immigration): Miss Dawn Farr
Third Secretary: Mr David Brough

Cali
British Consulate
Calle 25 No 1N - 65 (Air Mail Box 1326)
Cali
Telephone/Facsimile: (00) (57) (2) 896 1235
e-mail: Britaincali@uniweb.net.co
Honorary-Consul: (Vacant)
Honorary Vice-Consul: Mr Peter Laurence
Consular Assistant: Ms Helen de Frappier

Medellín
British Consulate
Calle 49 No 46A Sur - 103, (Air Mail Box 3372)
Envigado, Medellín
Telephone: (00) (57) (4) 331 8625
Facsimile: (00) (57) (4) 331 0046
e-mail: Embajadabr@geo.net.co
Honorary-Consul: Mr Fernando Osorio
Consular Assistant: Ms Maria Mercedes Botero

COMOROS

Moroni
British Embassy (all staff resident in Madagascar)
Ambassador: Mr B Donaldson
Deputy Head of Mission: Ms R M Owens

Moroni
British Consulate - vacant

(THE DEMOCRATIC REPUBLIC OF) CONGO

Kinshasa
British Embassy
83 Avenue du Roi Baudouin,
Kinshasa
Telephone: (00) (243) 98169100, 98169111, 98169200
Facsimile: (00) (243) 8846102
Duty Officer: (00) (243) 9906129
DHM: (00) (243) 9951429
e-mail: ambrit@ic.cd
Office Hours (GMT): Mon -Thur 06 30 - 13 30; Fri 06 30 - 13 00
Ambassador: Mr Jim Atkinson
Consul and Deputy Head of Mission: Mr Ken Price
Defence Attaché:
Lieutenant Colonel C Tim B Brown

Second Secretary: Miss Rachel Brass
Third Secretary (Consular/Management):
Mr Mark Douglas-Hiley
Attaché (Immigration): Vacant

(THE REPUBLIC OF) CONGO

Brazzaville
British Embassy (all staff reside in Kinshasa)
Ambassador: Mr Jim Atkinson
Consul and Deputy Head of Mission: Mr Ken Price
Defence Attaché:
Lieutenant Colonel C Tim B Brown

Brazzaville
Ets LISA (à côté de DHL)
Avenue Fosch, Brazzaville
Telephone: (00) (242) 620893
Facsimile: (00) (242) 838543
e-mail: yorick@congonet.cg
Honorary Consul: Mr Dominique Picard, MBE

COSTA RICA (SP)

San José
British Embassy
Apartado 815, Edificio Centro Colon,
(11th Floor), San José 1007
Telephone: (00) (506) 258 2025
Facsimile: (00) (506) 233 9938
e-mail: britemb@racsa.co.cr
Office Hours (GMT) Mon-Thurs 14 00 - 22 00
Fri 14 00 - 19 00
Ambassador and Consul-General: Ms G S Butler
Deputy Head of Mission: Mr O Willock
Second Secretary (Resides in Panama City):
Mr A J Davenport

COTE D'IVOIRE

Abidjan
British Embassy
3rd Floor, Immeuble "Les Harmonies",
Angle Boulevard Carde et Avenue Dr Jamot,
Plateau, Abidjan
Postal Address: 01 BP 2581, Abidjan 01
Telephone: (00) (225) 20226850, 20226851,
20221092, 20226852, 20218209
Visa Section: (00) (225) 20217032
Facsimile: (00) (225) 20223221 Chancery
                    20220092 Commercial
                    20220438 Visa Section
Airtech: (00) (225) 20217036
e-mail: britemb.a@aviso.co
Website: www.britaincdi.com
Office Hours (GMT): Mon - Thur 08 30 - 13 00
and 13 30 - 16 00
Fri 08 30 - 13 30
Ambassador: Mr J F Gordon, CMG
*First Secretary (Commercial), Consul and Deputy
Head of Mission:* Mr M J K Rickerd, MVO
Defence Attaché (resides Accra): Lieutenant
Colonel S K E Clarke, OBE
Second Secretary (Political/ Information):
Ms K Miller, MBE
Second Secretary (Management): Mr D Summers

Second Secretary (Commercial/Political):
Mr C Frean
Third Secretary Vice-Consul (Visas & Passports):
Mr M McGuinness
Third Secretary (Chancery): Ms N McBratney

**Abidjan UK Representation at the African
Development Bank see Missions & Delegations**

CROATIA

Zagreb
British Embassy
Ul Ivana Lucica 4, Zagreb
Telephone: (00) (385) (1) 600 9100 (Switchboard)
615 6621/6623/6624/6625 (Visa & Consular)
Facsimile: (00) (385) (1) 600 9111
                    615 6628/6629 (Visa & Consular)
                    466 4379 (Political Section)
                    455 6304 (Commercial)
                    466 4090 (Development Section)
e-mail: british-embassy@zg.tel.hr
commercial.section@zg.tel.hr
Office Hours (GMT): Summer: 06 30 - 15 00
Mon-Thur
06 30 - 12 00 Fri
Winter: 07 30 - 16 00 Mon-Thur
07 30 - 13 00 Fri
Ambassador: Mr N R Jarrold
Deputy Head of Mission: Mr E Mason
Defence Attaché:
Lieutenant Colonel R M Thornely
First Secretary (Commercial): Mr J T Fraser
First Secretary (Political): Mr G Lungley
Second Secretary (Immigration/Consular):
Ms F Maxton
Second Secretary (Development): Mr R A O Jones
Second Secretary (Management): Mr P Robbins
Second Secretary (Immigration Liaison):
Mr T Attwood
Third Secretary (Political/PPA): Ms F Sinclair
Third Secretary (Political): Mr C J Youd
Third Secretary (Vice-Consul): Ms F MacLeod
Third Secretary (Immigration): Ms J Duxbury
Assistant Defence Attaché: Sergeant S M Marshall

Split
British Consulate
Obala Hrvatskog Narodnog Preporoda 10/III,
21000 Split
Telephone: (00) (385) (21) 341 464
Facsimile: (00) (385) (21) 362 905
e-mail: british-consulat-st@st.tel.hr
Office Hours (GMT): Summer: 06 30 - 13 30
Mon-Thur
06 30 - 11 00 Fri
July, August 05 30 - 12 30 Mon-Fri
Winter: 07 30 - 14 30 Mon-Thur
07 30 - 12 00 Fri
Honorary Consul: Captain A Roje
Pro Consul: Mrs S Kalebota

Dubrovnik
British Consulate
Buniceva Poljana 3, 20000 Dubrovnik
Telephone/Facsimile: (00) (385) (20) 324 597
e-mail: honcons.dubrovnik@inet.hr

Office Hours (GMT): Summer: 08 00 - 11 00 Mon,
Tue, Thur & Fri
Winter: 09 00 - 12 00 Mon, Tue, Thur & Fri
Honorary Consul: Mrs S Marojica, MBE

CUBA

Havana
British Embassy
Calle 34 No. 702/4 entre 7ma Avenida y 17,
Miramar, Havana
Telephone: (00) (53) (7) 204-1771 Switchboard
Facsimile: (00) (53) (7) 204-8104
Management/Consular/Immigration
204-1049 Commercial/Information
204-9214 Chancery
e-mail: embrit@ceniai.inf.cu (Embassy)
britcoun@ip.etecsa.cu (British Council)
Office Hours (GMT): Summer: 12 00 - 19 30
Winter: 13 00 - 20 30
Ambassador: Mr P Hare, LVO
First Secretary and Deputy Head of Mission:
Mr J D W Saville
Defence Attaché (resides at Caracas):
Captain E F Searle, RN
First Secretary (Commercial/Economic):
Mr C S George
First Secretary (Management) and Consul:
Mr B H Garside
*First Secretary (Science/Culture, British Council
Director):* Mr M White
First Secretary (resides at Kingston): Mr M Bragg
Second Secretary (Political/Information):
Ms K G L M Ward
Second Secretary (resides at Kingston):
Mr K Wiggins
Second Secretary (resides at Mexico City):
Mr P Haley
Attaché (Chief Security Officer):
Mr J P Vowles, MBE
Third Secretary (Commercial/Immigration):
Ms A Carrick
Third Secretary (Aid/Political): Ms N Terrett
Attaché: Miss P A Langridge
Attaché: Ms K Robinson
Attaché (Works): Mr D Snooks

CYPRUS

Nicosia
British High Commission
Alexander Pallis Street (PO Box 21978), 1587
Nicosia or BFPO 567
Telephone: (00) (357) (22) 861100
Facsimile: (00) (357) (22) 861125 Information
861315 Chancery
861175 Management
861200 Consular:
861150 Commercial
Airtech: 861287
e-mail: infobhc@cylink.com.cy
Office Hours (GMT): Mon - Fri 05 30 - 12 30
High Commissioner: Mr Lyn Parker
Counsellor and Deputy High Commissioner:
Mr Philip Barton, OBE
Defence Adviser: Colonel James Anderson

Counsellor (Political): Mr Paul Ritchie, OBE
British Council Director: Mr Peter Skeeton
First Secretary (Consular): Mr Gordon MacLeod
(tel: 22861360)
First Secretary (Commercial): Mr Lawson Ross
(tel: 22861340)
First Secretary (Chancery): Mr Mick Bispham
(tel: 22861250)
First Secretary (Chancery): Mr Charlie Beckford
(tel: 22861220)
First Secretary (Management): Mr Roger Davies
(tel: 22861350)
Second Secretary (Chancery): Mr Alex Miller
(tel: 22861251)
Second Secretary (Political): Ms Jill Morris
(tel: 22861230)
Second Secretary (Chancery): Mr Steve Bazzoni
(tel: 22861252)
Second Secretary (Chancery): Mr Troy Arnold
(tel: 22861231)
Second Secretary (Chancery/Information):
Mr Stuart Summers (tel: 22862380)
Second Secretary (Political/Military):
Ms Siân Jones (tel: 22861339)
Second Secretary (resides in Tel Aviv):
Mr Simon Gudgeon
Attaché (Consular): Mr Daniel Baker
(tel: 22861362)
Attaché (Consular): Ms Rosaleen Wotton
(tel: 22861363)
Attaché (Consular): Mr Ian Swann (tel: 22861361)
Attaché (Chancery): Mr Ian Hirchfield
(tel: 22861331)

Zygi
British East Mediterranean Relay Station
PO Box 54912, Limassol
Telephone: (00) (357) (24) 332511, 332341
Facsimile: (00) (357) (24) 332595, 332180
Office Hours (GMT): Mon - Fri 05 50 - 12 40
*First Secretary (Management) (Resides in
Nicosia):* Mr Roger Davies

CZECH REPUBLIC

Prague
British Embassy
Chancery, Consular/Visa, Economic/Know How
Fund
Information and Management Section, Defence
Section
Thunovska 14,
118 00 Prague 1
Telephone: (00) (420) (2) 5740 2111
Facsimile: (00) (420) (2) 5740 2296
e-mail: info@britain.cz
Airtech: (00) (420) (2) 5740 2249

Commercial Section
Palac Myslbek
Na Prikope 21
117 19 Prague 1
Telephone: (00) (420) (2) 2224 0021/2/3
Facsimile: (00) (420) (2) 2224 3625
e-mail: commerce@fco.gov.uk

British Council
Narodni 10,
125 01 Prague 1
Telephone: (00) (420) (2) 2199 1111
Facsimile: (00) (420) (2) 2493 3847
Telex: 122097 (a/b BCCZ C)
e-mail: forename.surname@britcoun.cz
Office Hours (GMT): end Oct - end Mar 07 30 - 16 00
Ambassador: Anne Pringle
Counsellor and Deputy Head of Mission (ext 2253): Mr Michael Tatham
Defence Attaché (ext 2261):
Colonel David A Wynne Davies
Cultural Attaché (British Council Director):
Mr Paul Doherty
First Secretary (Commercial): Mr Martin Day
First Secretary (EU/Economic) (ext 2315):
Mrs Judith Gardiner
First Secretary (Management/Consul) (ext 2226):
Mr Dick Coleman
First Secretary (Political/External) (ext 2258):
Mr Paul Coggles
First Secretary (TWO) (resides in Vienna):
Mr John Sweeney
British Council Assistant Director:
Ms Elizabeth White
Assistant Defence Attaché (ext 2240):
Squadron Leader Simon C Buckingham RAF
Second Secretary (Political/Press & Public Affairs) (ext 2245): Miss Eleanor Petch
Second Secretary (Commercial): Mr Andrew Wells
Second Secretary/DLO (resides in Vienna):
Mr David Hollingbury
Second Secretary/TMO (resides in Vienna):
Mr Ian Purvis
Third Secretary and Vice-Consul (ext 2205):
Mr Nick Burns
Third Secretary (Commercial):
Miss Kate Batty-Smith
Third Secretary (Political) (ext 2259):
Mr James Armstrong
Third Secretary (Political/EU) (ext 2237):
Mr Alan Caughey
Third Secretary (Management) (ext 2223):
Mrs Julie Jackson

DENMARK

Copenhagen
British Embassy
Kastelsvej 36/38/40, DK-2100 Copenhagen Ø
Telephone: (00) (45) 35 44 52 00
Facsimile: (00) (45) 35 44 52 93 Information
        Section
        52 14 Political Section
        52 46 Commercial Department
        52 53 Consular
        52 59 Management
e-mail: www.brit-emb@post6.tele.dk
Office Hours (GMT): end Mar - end Oct 07 00 - 15 00 and end Oct - end Mar 08 00 - 16 00

Consular/Visa Section:
Consular: end Mar - end Oct 07 00 - 10 30 and 11 30 - 13 00

end Oct - end Mar 08 00 - 11 30 and 12 30 - 14 00
Visa: end Mar - end Oct 07 00 - 10 00
end Oct - end Mar 08 00 - 11 00
Commercial: end Mar - end Oct 06 30 - 10 30 and 11 30 - 14 30
end Oct - end Mar 07 30 - 11 30 and 12 30 - 15 30

British Council (Cultural Section)
Director: Dr Michael Sorensen-Jones
Gammel Mønt 12. 3. 1117 Copenhagen K
Telephone: (00) (45) 33 36 94 00
(Tel. Hours: 09 00 - 12 00, 13 00 - 15 30)
Educational Enquiries:
Telephone: (00) (45) 33 36 94 04
(Tel. Hours: 12 30 - 15 30)
e-mail: british.council@britishcouncil.dk
Ambassador: Mr P S Astley, LVO
Counsellor and Deputy Head of Mission:
Ms E C Robson
Counsellor: Mr T S A Folliss
Defence Attaché: Commander R P B Ayers RN
First Secretary (Commercial): Mr F J Martin
First Secretary (Political): Mr Peter Cook
First Secretary (Management) & Consul:
Mr J T Fraser
Second Secretary (Political): Mr A Mace
Second Secretary (Political): Miss G G Sharp
Second Secretary (Technical/Management):
Mr A Jones
Third Secretary (Political): Mr A Fehintola
Attaché (AMO/Vice-Consul): Miss B Pitts, MVO
Vice-Consul: Mrs J T Christoffersen
Vice-Consul: Mrs S Oxfeldt Jensen

Aabenraa
British Consulate
Turistchef
c/o Turistbureauet
H.P. Hanssens Gade 5
6200 Aabenraa
Telephone: (00) (45) 74 62 35 00
Facsimile: (00) (45) 74 63 07 44
e-mail: aabtur@post3.tele.dk
Office Hours (GMT): 06 30 - 14 30
Honorary Consul: Mr William Klinker (Danish)

Aalborg
British Consulate
Hasserisvej 112
Postboks 23
9100 Aalborg
Telephone: 98 11 34 99
Facsimile: 98 11 56 99
e-mail: jbh.as@mail.dk
Office Hours (GMT): 05 30 - 13 30
Honorary Consul: Mr Jørgen Bladt (Danish)

Aarhus
British Consulate
c/o SCANAD A/S
Skolegade 19B, 8100 Aarhus C
Telephone: 87 30 77 77
87 30 77 15 (Assistant direct)
Facsimile: 87 30 77 07
e-mail: ch@scanad.dk
Office Hours (GMT): 06 30 - 14 30
Honorary Consul: Mr Claus R Herluf (Danish)

Esbjerg
British Consulate
Kanalen 1, 6700 Esbjerg
Telephone: 79 11 19 00
Facsimile: 79 11 19 01
e-mail: britishconsulate@danbor.dk or
iw@danbor.dk
Office Hours (GMT): 06 30 - 14 00
Honorary Consul: Mr Gert Kragelund (Danish)

Fredericia
British Consulate
Vesthavnen, P O Box 235
7000 Fredericia
Telephone: 75 92 20 00
Facsimile: 76 20 29 80
e-mail: pia raun rasmussen@rahbek.dk
Office Hours (GMT): 06 00 - 14 30
Honorary Consul: Mr Morten Rahbek Hansen
(Danish)

Herning
British Consulate
N C Invest A/S
Nr. Lindevej 35, 7400 Herning
Telephone: 97 22 02 88
Facsimile: 97 21 44 10
Office Hours (GMT): 06 30 - 14 30
Honorary Consul: Mr Niels C Jensen (Danish)

Odense
British Consulate
Albanitorv 4, Postboks 308
5100 Odense C
Telephone: 66 14 47 14
Facsimile: 66 14 61 30
Office Hours (GMT): 06 00 - 14 00
Honorary Consul: Mr Frits Niegel, MBE (Danish)

Rønne (Bornholm) - closed

Tórshavn (Faroe Islands)
British Consulate
P/F Damfar, P O Box 1154
Niels Finsensgøta 5,
FR-110 Tórshavn,
Faroe Islands
Telephone: 298 35 99 77
Facsimile: 298 35 99 80
e-mail: damfar@post.olivant.fo
Office Hours (GMT): 09 00 - 17 00
Honorary Consul: Mr Tummas H Dam

DJIBOUTI
British Embassy (All staff resident at Addis Ababa)
Ambassador: Mr M A Wickstead
First Secretary (Management and Consul):
Miss A Marriott, MBE
Second Secretary: Mr O Richards

British Consulate
PO Box 169, Rue de Djibouti
Djibouti
Telephone (00) (253) 25 09 17
Facsimile: (00) (253) 35 78 15
e-mail: british.consulate@intnet.dj
Honorary Consul (Resident in Djibouti):
Mr A Martinet

DOMINICA, COMMONWEALTH OF

Roseau
British High Commission
Lower Collymore Rock (PO Box 676),
Bridgetown, Barbados
Telephone: (00) (1) (246) 430 7800
Facsimile: (00) (1) (246) 430 7851 Chancery
      (246) 430 7860 Management/Consular
      (246) 430 7826 Commercial/
      Information
e-mail: britishhc@sunbeach.net
Office Hours (GMT) 12 00 – 16 30 and 17 30 – 20
00
High Commissioner: Mr John White
Deputy High Commissioner: Mr Rob Holland
Defence Adviser: Captain Steve C Ramm, RN
Counsellor (Regional Affairs):
Mr Nick J L Martin
First Secretary (Chancery): Mr Graham Honey
First Secretary (Management/Consular):
Ms Ros Day
High Commissioner's Special Representative:
Mr Nick J Pyle, MBE
Second Secretary (Chancery): Mr Phil Marshall
Third Secretary (Consular/Immigration):
Mr Mark Harrison
*Resides at Bridgetown

Roseau
British Consulate
Office of the Honorary British Consul
c/o Courts (Dominica) Ltd
PO Box 2269, Roseau
Commonwealth of Dominica
Telephone: Office: (1 767) 448 7655 or 448 0166
Facsimile: (1 767) 448 7817
e-mail: smaynard@courts.co.dm
Honorary Consul: Mr Simon Maynard

DOMINICAN REPUBLIC

Santo Domingo
British Embassy
Ave 27 de Febrero No 233,
Edificio Corominas Pepín,
Santo Domingo, Dominican Republic
Telephone: (00) (1) (809) 472 7111
472 7905 (Commercial)
472 7373/7671 (Consular)
Facsimile: (00) (1) (809) 472 7190
      (Chancery/Commerial)
      472 7574 (Consular/Management)
Airtech: (00) (1) (809) 472 7475
e-mail: brit.emb.sadom@codetel.net.do
Office Hours (GMT): Mon-Thurs 12 30 - 21 00
Fri 12 30 - 17:30
Ambassador: Mr Andrew Ashcroft
Deputy Head of Mission: Mr Kevin Shaughnessy

Puerto Plata
British Consulate
Calle Beller No.51,
Puerto Plata, R.D.
Telephone: (00) (1) (809) 586-4244, 586-8464
Facsimile: (00) (1) (809) 586-3096
Honorary Consul: Mrs Cindy Salem

EAST TIMOR
(DEMOCRATIC REPUBLIC OF)

Dili

British Embassy
Pantai Kelapa (Avenida de Portugal)
Dili, East Timor
Postal Address: PO Box 194, The Post Office, Dili,
East Timor
Telephone: (00) (61) 417 841 046 (HM
Ambassador)
408 010 991 (DHM)
Facsimile: (00) (670) 390 312 652
Airtech: (00) (870) 600 132 620
e-mail: dili.fco@gtnet.gov.uk
Office Hours (GMT): Mon-Fri 23 30 - 03 30 and
04 30 - 08 45
Ambassador: Mr Hamish St. Clair Daniel, MBE
Deputy Head of Mission: Mr Andy Bowes
Defence Attaché (resides at Jakarta):
Colonel Alan J Roberts

ECUADOR

Quito (SP)

British Embassy
Citiplaza Building,
Naciones Unidas Ave and República de El
Salvador 14th Floor
(Consular Section 12th Floor)
Telephone: (00) (593) (2) 2 970 800 / 970 801
Facsimile: (00) (593) (2) 2 970 807 Consular
             2 970 809 Commercial
             2 970 810 Management
             2 970 811 Chancery
Airtech: 2 970 812
P.O. Box: 17 – 17 - 830
e-mail: britembq@interactive.net.ec
Office Hours (GMT): Mon – Thur 13 30 - 17 30
and 18 30 - 22 00
Fri 13 30 - 18 30
Ambassador: Mr Ian Gerken, LVO
Consul and Deputy Head of Mission:
Mr Patrick Mullee
Defence Attaché (resides at Caracas):
Captain Edward F Searle, RN
Second Secretary (TC/Chancery):
Mr Robin J Shackell
Second Secretary: Mr Brian Corbett
Third Secretary (Management):
Miss Rachel Brazier
Third Secretary (Vice-Consul): Miss Clare Spencer
Vice-Consul: Mr Uwe Roepke

Guayaquil

British Consulate
c/o Agripac
General Córdova 623 y Padre Solano,
PO Box 09-10-8598, Guayaquil
Telephone: (00) (593) (4) 2 560400, ext 318
Facsimile: (00) (593) (4) 2 562641
e-mail: carmstro@agripac.com.ec or
rtorres@agripac.com.ec
Office Hours (GMT): 14 30 - 18 00 and 20 00 -
23 00
Honorary Consul: Mr Colin R Armstrong, OBE
Honorary Vice Consul: Mrs Rocio Torres

Guayaquil

British Embassy - Trade Office
Torres del Norte Building,
Torre A, 5th Floor, Office 503
Kennedy Norte, Av. Miguel H. Alcivar, Manzana
506,
Telephone: (00) (593) (4) 2 687112
Facsimile: (00) (593) (4) 2 687113
e-mail: britembg@interactive.net.ec
Office Hours (GMT): Mon-Thur: 13 30 - 17 30
and 18 30 - 22 00
Fri: 13 30 - 18 30
Commercial Officer: Miss Irene Lertora
Commercial Assistant: Miss Monica Ingarévalo

Galápagos

British Consulate
c/o Etica Office, Barrio Estrada,
Puerto Ayora, Isla Santa Cruz, Galápagos
Telephone: (00) (593) (5) 526157 / 526159
Facsimile: (00) (593) (5) 526591
e-mail: dbalfour@eticapa.com.ec
Office Hours (GMT): 13 00 - 17 00 and 19 00 -
23 00
Honorary Consul: Mr David Balfour

EGYPT

Cairo

British Embassy
7, Ahmed Ragheb Street, Garden City, Cairo
Telephone: (00) (20) (2) 794 0850, 794 0852/8
Facsimile: 796 1458 Political,
             794 3065 Consular & Information
             794 0859 Commercial
             796 3222 Management
             795 1235 Visa
Airtech: 794 0850 (ext. 215)
e-mail: info@britishembassy.org.eg
Website: www.britishembassy.org.eg
Office Hours (GMT): Sunday - Wednesday:
Chancery, Commercial sections work: 06 30 –
14 00
Defence: 06 00 – 14 00 (including lunch)
Consular, Visa, Management: 06 00 – 13 30
Office Hours (GMT): Thursday:
Chancery, Commercial: 06 30 – 12 30
Defence: 06 00 – 12 30
Consular, Visa, Managament: 06 00 – 12 00
Ambassador: Mr John Sawers, CMG
Counsellor and Deputy of Mission:
Mr Michael Gifford
Defence and Military Attaché:
Colonel The Honorable Alistair J C Campbell
Cultural Counsellor (British Council Director):
Dr John Grote, OBE
Counsellor (Regional Affairs): Mr Graham J Ley
Naval and Air Attaché:
Commander Philip W Holihead RN
First Secretary (Commercial): Mr Simon Fisher
*First Secretary & Head of Political & Economic
Section:* Mrs Jacqueline L Perkins
*First Secretary (Cultural) & British Council
Deputy Director:* Ms Gill Caldicott
First Secretary and Consul: Mr Gordon Brown
First Secretary (Cultural): Mr Paul Morris

First Secretary (Regional Affairs):
Mr Kareem Chaudhry
First Secretary (Technical Works Officer):
Mr Ronald Clarke
First Secretary (Management): Mr Shaun Flaherty
Second Secretary (Aid): Mr Ian Ruff
Second Secretary (Commercial):
Mr Stephen Townsend
Second Secretary (Technical Management):
Mr Simon Lochmuller
Second Secretary (Immigration):
Mr James Marshall
Second Secretary (Press and Public Affairs):
Mr Irfan Siddiq
Second Secretary (Cultural):
Miss Samantha Harvey
Third Secretary (Political): Mr Patrick Tobin
Third Secretary (Commercial): Ms Sheridan Grice
Deputy Management Officer: Mr Gordon Horne
Attaché and Vice-Consul: Ms Jo Pendered
Attaché and Vice-Consul: Miss Stephanie Webb
Attaché and Vice-Consul: Mrs Debbie Hare
Attaché: Mr Robert McCallum
Attaché: Mr Michael Whyte
Attaché: Mr Keith Squibb
Attaché: Mr Roger Clark
Attaché: Mrs Susan K Turunc
Attaché: Ms Caroline Begley
Attaché: Mr Colin Murray
Attaché: Mrs Ruth Whelan
Attaché: Ms Rebecca Jones

Alexandria (SP)
British Consulate-General
3 Mina Street, Kafr Abdou, Roushdi,
Ramley Alexandria, 21529
Telephone: (00) (20) (3) 5467001, 5467002
Facsimile: (00) (20) (3) 5467177
Office Hours (GMT): Sun - Wed: 05 30 - 12 30
Thur: 05 30 - 12 00
Consul-General: Mr Mark Stevens
*First Secretary (Cultural Affairs and Director
British Council):* (Vacant)

Suez
British Consulate
HS Supply Co.
9 El-Galaa Street, Suez
Telephone: (00) (20) (62) 334102 (Consulate &
Office), 320727 (Home)
Telex: 66112 DRHSS UN
Facsimile: (00) (20) (62) 320729
Honorary Consul: Dr Hussein Samir

Luxor
British Honorary Consular Agent
Gaddis Hotel
Khaled Ibn El Walid St.
Luxor
Telephone: (00) (20) (95) 382838 (Consulate &
Office), 374814 (Home)
Facsimile: (00) (20) (95) 380814, 382837
Mobile: 012 2327612, 012 3517441
Honorary Consular Agent: Mr Ehab Gaddis

EL SALVADOR

San Salvador
British Embassy
Edificio Inter-Inversiones, Paseo General Escalón
4828, PO Box 1591, San Salvador
Telephone: (00) (503) 263 6527, 263 6529, 263
6520
Facsimile: (00) (503) 263 6516
e-mail: BritEmb.SanSalv@fco.gov.uk
Office Hours (GMT): Mon-Thur 14 00 - 19 00, 20
00 - 22 30
Fri 14 00 - 19 00
Ambassador and Consul-General:
Mr Patrick Morgan
Deputy Head of Mission and Vice-Consul:
Mr Keith Allen
*First Secretary (Commercial) and Director Of
Trade Promotion for Central America (resides at
San Jose):* Mr Christopher J Edge
Defence Attaché (resides at Guatemala City):
Colonel Ian C D Blair-Pilling OBE
DLO (resides at Panama City): Andy Davenport

EQUATORIAL GUINEA

Malabo
British Embassy (all staff reside at Yaounde)
Ambassador and Consul-General: Mr Richard
Wildash, LVO
First Secretary and Consul: Mr David Williams

ERITREA

Asmara
British Embassy
Emperor Yohannes Avenue
House no 24
PO Box 5584 Asmara, Eritrea
Telephone: (00) (291) 1 12 01 45
Facsimile: (00) (291) 1 12 01 04
Airtech: (00) (291) 1 20 28 39
e-mail: alembca@gemel.com.er
Office Hours (GMT): Mon-Thurs 05 00 – 10 30
and 11 30 – 13 30
Fri 05 00 – 10 30
Ambasssador: Mr M T Murray
Defence Attaché (Resident Nairobi):
Colonel R J Barnes
*Third Secretary (Management/Immigration/Vice-
Consul and Deputy Head of Mission):*
Mrs A L Taylor

ESTONIA (SP)

Tallinn
British Embassy
Wismari 6
Tallinn 10136
Estonia
Telephone: (00) (372) 667 4700
Facsimile: (00) (372) 667 4755
(Political/HMA/DHM)
667 4724 (Commercial/DFID
Programme Office)
667 4756 (Management/Defence)
667 4725 (Consular/Visa)

e-mail: information@britishembassy.ee
Website: www.britishembassy.ee
Office Hours (GMT): Summer 06 00 - 14 00,
Winter 07 00 - 15 00
Ambassador: Mrs Sarah Squire
Deputy Head of Mission: Miss Ceinwen Jones
Defence Attaché (resides at Helsinki):
Lieutenant Colonel Patrick W Clarke
First Secretary (British Council Director) (resides at Riga): Mr Chris Edwards
First Secretary (Political): Mr William Evans
Second Secretary (Technical Management) (resides at Helsinki): Mr Paul Jackson, MBE
Third Secretary (Management) and Consul:
Mr John Devine
Third Secretary (Politcal): Mr Richard Dewell
Third Secretary (Regional Affairs):
Mr Simon Shaw
Commercial and Press Officer:
Mrs Neve Hobemägi
Vice-Consul and ECO: Mr Lionel Khoo
Attaché and Archivist: Mr Alex Stalker-Booth

ETHIOPIA

Addis Ababa
British Embassy
Fikre Mariam Abatechan Street, Addis Ababa
Postal address: Post Office Box 858
Telephone: (00) (251) 1 612354
Facsimile: (00) (251) 1 610588
1 614154 Consular and Visa Section
e-mail: britishembassy.addisababa@fco.gov.uk
Office Hours (GMT): Mon-Thurs 05 00 - 13 30
Fri 05 00 - 10 00
Consular /Visa Section Public Opening Hours:
Mon-Fri 05 30 - 09 00
Ambassador: Mr Myles Wickstead
First Secretary and Deputy Head of Mission:
Ms Di Skingle
First Secretary (Management) and Consul:
Miss Allison M Marriott, MBE
Second Secretary (Aid): Dr Nick Taylor
British Military Liaison Officer:
Lieutenant Colonel Charles Comyn
Cultural Attaché (British Council Director):
Ms Rosemary Arnott, OBE
Assistant Cultural Attaché (British Council):
Mr Simon Winetroube
Second Secretary (Political): Mr Owen Richards
Second Secretary (Political/Information):
Miss Laura Williams
Attaché and Vice-Consul: Mr Ian Crammen

FIJI ISLANDS

Suva
British High Commission
Victoria House
Gladstone Road
Suva
Fiji Islands (PO Box 1355)
Telephone: (00) (679) 3311033
Facsimile: (00) (679) 3301406 (General)
              3307497 (Chancery)
Airtech: (00) (679) 3305035

e-mail: Public Affairs: ukinfo@bhc.org.fj
Commercial Office: uktrade@bhc.org.fj
Consular & Management Sections:
ukconsular@bhc.org.fj
e-mail for individual officers – insert:
firstname.surname + @fco.gov.uk
Website: http://www.ukinthepacific.bhc.org.fj
Office Hours (GMT): Sun -Wed 20 15 - 01 00 and
02 00 - 05 00
Thurs 20 15 - 01 00
High Commissioner, also Pitcairn Alternate Representative for the South Pacific Commission; non-resident: Mr Charles F Mochan (Ext 120)
High Commissioner to Nauru, Kiribati and Tuvalu: Deputy High Commissioner. Also non-resident Ambassador to Micronesia, Marshall Islands and Palau; Deputy High: Mr Christopher Haslam
(Mr Ian Powell w.e.f March 03) (ext 122)
Commissioner to Nauru, Kiribati and Tuvalu: Defence Adviser (resides at Wellington):
Colonel Alec A Peebles
First Secretary (Development):
Mr James Medhurst (ext 121)
Second Secretary (Political, Press & Public Affairs); Deputy Head of Mission and Consul to Micronesia: Mr Stephen Tarry (ext110)
Marshall Islands and Palau: Third Secretary (Management/Consular/Immigration):
Mr Andrew George (Ext 105)

FINLAND

Helsinki
British Embassy
Itainen Puistotie 17, 00140
Helsinki
Telephone: (00) (358) (9) 2286 5100
Telefax: Political Section (00) (358) (9) 2286 5284
All other Sections (00) (358) (9) 2286 5262,5272
e-mail: info@ukembassy.fi
Office Hours (GMT): Sep-Apr: 07 00 - 15 00
Apr-Aug: 06 30 - 14 00
Ambassador: Mr Matthew Kirk
Counsellor and Deputy Head of Mission:
Mr R A Cambridge
Counsellor (Political): Mr T I Priest
Defence Attaché: Lieutenant Colonel P W Clarke
First Secretary (Political/EU): Mr D Borland
First Secretary (Commercial): Mr M Towsey
First Secretary (Inward Investment) (Resident in Stockholm): Mr M Cronin
First Secretary (Management and Consul):
Mr R C Woodward
Second Secretary (Commercial): Mr S Rebecchi
Second Secretary (Political/Information):
Miss V Harrison
Second Secretary (Management/Technical):
Mr P M Jackson, MBE
Third Secretary/Vice-Consul/ Assistant Mangement Officer: Mr S M Anderson
Attaché: Miss S Burden
Chaplain: Rev. R Moreton

Jyväskylä
British Consulate
Valmet Corporation, Corporate Head Office

Rautpohjankatu, PO Box 587
40101 Jyväskylä
Telephone: (00) (358) (204) 82150
Telefax: (00) (358) (204) 826526
Honorary Consul: Mr H Siltanen (Finnish)
Kotka
British Consulate
Port Authority of Kotka, Laivurinkatu 7,
48100 Kotka
Telephone: (00) (358) (5) 234 4281
Telefax: (00) (358) (5) 218 1375
Honorary Consul: Mr L I Arminen (Finnish)

Kuopio
British Consulate
Kolari, Heikinheimo,Palsola and Reinikainen, Oy
Kauppakatu 39 A
70100 Kuopio
Telephone: (00) (358) (17) 265 7777
Telefax: (00) (358) (17) 261 1085
Honorary Consul: Mr H A Palsola (Finnish)

Åland Islands
British Consulate
Köpmansgatan 12
22100 Mariehamn, Aland Islands
Telephone: (00) (358) (18) 13591,47720
Telefax: (00) (358) (18) 13196
Honorary Consul: Mr B H Olofsson (Finnish)

Oulu
British Consulate
Stora Enso Fine Paper Oy
PO Box 196, 90101 Oulu
Telephone: (00) (358) (204) 63373
Telefax: (00) (358) (204) 633649
Honorary Consul: Mr J Vanhainen (Finnish)

Pori
British Consulate
United Sawmills Ltd, PO Box 66, Antinkatu 2,
28101 Pori
Telephone: (00) (358) (204) 164002, 164000
Telefax: (00) (358) (204) 16132
Honorary Consul: Mr K J Anttilainen (Finnish)

Tampere
British Consulate
Pirkanmaan Työvoima-ja
Elinkeinokeskus
Kauppakatu 4
PO Box 467
33101 Tampere
Telephone: (00) (358) (3) 256 5701
Telefax: (00) (358) (3) 256 5739
Honorary Consul: Mrs R K Varpe (Finnish)

Turku
British Consulate
Turun Kauppakamari, Puolalankatu 1,
20100 Turku
Telephone: (00) (358) (2) 274 3410
Telefax: (00) (358) (2) 274 3440
Honorary Consul: Mr Jari Lähteenmäki (Finnish)

Vaasa
British Consulate
Kotipizza Oy

Hovioikeudenpuistikko 11,
65100 Vaasa
Telephone: (00) (358) (6) 2822 000
Telefax: (00) (358) (6) 2822 055
Honorary Consul: Mr R Grönblom (Finnish)

FRANCE

Paris
British Embassy
35 rue du Faubourg St. Honoré, 75383 Paris Cedex
08
Telephone: (00) (331) 44 51 31 00
Facsimile: (00) (331) 44 51 34 83 Ambassadors
                    Office/Chancery
                    32 88 Management
                    34 01 Commercial
                    32 34 Press and Public Affairs
                    34 85 Political/Economic
                    34 40 Defence/ Technology
                    31 27 Consular
                    31 28 Visa
Telephone: (00) (331) 49 55 73 00 British Council
Facsimile: (00) (331) 47 05 77 02 British Council
Website: http://www.amb-grandebretagne.fr
Office Hours (GMT): Summer 08 30 - 12 00 and
13 30 - 17 00
Winter 09 30 - 13 00 and 14 30 - 18 00
Ambassador: Sir John Holmes, KBE, CVO, CMG
Minister: Mr Giles Paxman, LVO
Defence and Air Attaché:
Air Commodore Chris J Blencowe, RAF
Naval Attaché: Captain Allan A S Adair, RN
Military Attaché: Brigadier Roy E Ratazzi, CBE
Counsellor (Political): Mr Simon J Fraser
Counsellor: Mr William Sandover
Counsellor (Finance and Economic):
Mr David Frost
Counsellor (Trade, Promotion and Investment):
Mr Stephen E Bradley
Counsellor (Management): Mr Ian R Whitehead
Counsellor (Cultural) (British Council Director):
Mr John Tod
Counsellor (Technology): Mr Rupert Huxter
First Secretary and Consul-General:
Mr Stuart Gregson
First Secretary (Political): Mr Jeremy Legge
First Secretary (Political/Internal):
Mr Angus Lapsley
First Secretary (Political): Mr Paul Arkwright
First Secretary (Political): Mr Philip Boulton
First Secretary (Economic): Mr David I Bendor
First Secretary (Commercial): Mr Philip Shaw
First Secretary (Economic):
Ms Joanna Kuenssberg
First Secretary (International Finance):
Mr Christopher D Steele
*Cultural Attaché (British Council Deputy
Director):* Mr David Kirwan
First Secretary (Agriculture): Mr David C Barnes
First Secretary (Science and Technology):
Mr Andrew P Holt
First Secretary (PPA): Mr Richard de R Morgan
First Secretary/Defence Equipment:
Mr Mark Bason

First Secretary /Defence Procurement:
Mr Robin C B Little
First Secretary (Management): Mr Peter Duffy
First Secretary and Consul: Mr Brian West
First Secretary (Labour and Social Affairs):
Ms Helen Pilkington
First Secretary (Management): Mr Brian Farnham
Second Secretary (Political): Mr Peter Hill
Second Secretary (Political):
Miss Alexandra Martens
Second Secretary (Commercial):
Mr John Greengrass, MBE
Second Secretary (Technology):
Mr Alistair W J Kerr
Second Secretary (Technical Management Officer):
Mr Alexander Bennett
Second Secretary (Labour and Social Affairs):
Ms Claire Etches
Second Secretary (PPA): Mrs Phillipa Thompson
Second Secretary: Mr Joe F Griffin
Private Secretary: Mr Nicolas Hailey
Third Secretary (Management): Mr Mark D Korad
Third Secretary (Passports): Mr Ian Gallacher
Visits Officer: Mrs Bridget O'Kelly / Mrs Marina
Pettigrew
Third Secretary (Commercial): Mrs Sarah J Morris

**Paris British Consulate General (see entry
under Paris below)**
**Paris United Kingdom Delegation to OECD, see
Missions & Delegations**
**Paris United Kingdom Delegation to UNESCO,
see Missions & Delegations**

**Strasbourg United Kingdom Delegation to
Council of Europe, see Missions & Delegations**

Biarritz
British Consulate
"Askenian"
7 Boulevard Tauzin
64200 Biarritz
Telephone: (00) (335) 59 24 21 40
Facsimile: (00) (335) 59 22 33 27
Honorary Consul: Mr Robert Hope, MBE

Bordeaux
British Consulate-General
353 Boulevard du President Wilson,
33073 Bordeaux Cedex
Telephone: (00) (335) 57 22 21 10
Facsimile: (00) (335) 56 08 33 12
e-mail: postmaster.bordeaux@fco.gov.uk
Office Hours (GMT): Summer: 07 00 - 10 30 and
12 00 - 15 30
Winter: 08 00 - 11 30 and 13 00 - 16 30
Consul-General: Mr Thomas Kennedy
Consul (Commercial): Mr Alastair Roberts, MBE
Vice-Consul: Mr Paul Dixon

Toulouse
Hon British Consul
Victoria Center
20 Chemin de Laporte
31300 Toulouse
Telephone: (00) (335) 61 15 02 02
Facsimile: (00) (335) 61 15 08 92
Honorary Consul: Mr Roger Virnuls, MBE

Lille
British Consulate-General
11 Square Dutilleul, 59800 Lille
Telephone: (00) (33) 3 20 12 82 72
Facsimile: (00) (33) 3 20 54 88 16
Airtech: (00) (33) 3 20 54 46 15
Office Hours (GMT): Summer 07 30 - 10 30 and
12 00 - 15 00
Winter 08 30 - 11 30 and 13 00 - 16 00
Consul-General: Miss Monica Harper
Vice-Consul (Commercial): Mr David Hinchliffe
Vice-Consul (Commercial): Mr John Gleave
Vice-Consul: Mrs Carol Vorobieff, MBE

Amiens
c/o Ecole Superieure de Commerce
18 Place Saint Michel, 80000 Amiens
Telephone: (00) (33) 3 22 72 08 48
Facsimile: (00) (33) 3 22 82 23 01
Office Hours (GMT): Summer 06 30 - 10 30 and
12 00 - 16 00
Winter 07 30 - 11 30 and 13 00 - 17 00
Honorary British Consul: Mr Roger Davis

Boulogne-sur-Mer
British Consulate
c/o Cabinet Barron et Brun, 28 rue Saint Jean
62200 Boulogne-sur-Mer
Telephone: (00) (33) 3 21 87 16 80
Facsimile: (00) (33) 3 21 91 30 30
Office Hours (GMT): Summer 06 00 - 10 00 and
12 00 - 16 00
Winter 07 00 - 11 00 and 13 00 - 17 00
Honorary Consul: Mr Gerard Barron, MBE

Calais
British Consulate
c/o P&O Stena Line, 20 rue du Havre,
62100 Calais
Telephone: (00) (33) 3 21 96 33 76
Facsimile: (00) (33) 3 21 19 43 69
Office Hours (GMT): Summer 06 30 - 16 00
Winter 07 30 - 17 00
Honorary Consul: Mr Jean-Michel Inglis, MBE

Dunkirk
British Consulate
c/o Lemaire Freres & Fils
30 rue l'Hermitte
Immeuble "Les Trois Ponts"
PO Box 2/100
59376 Dunkerque
Telephone: (00) (33) 3 28 66 11 98
Facsimile: (00) (33) 3 28 59 09 99
Office Hours (GMT): Summer 06 30-10 00 and
1200-1600
Winter 07 30-11 00 and 1300-1700
Honorary Consul: Mr Christopher R Baker, MBE

Lyon
British Consulate-General
24 rue Childebert, 69002 Lyon
Telephone: (00) 4 72 77 81 70
Facsimile: (00) 4 72 77 81 79
Airtech: (00) 4 78 38 27 77
Office Hours (GMT): Summer 07 00 - 10 30 and
12 00 - 15 30

Winter 08 00 - 11 30 and 13 00 - 16 30
Consul-General: Mr Jonathon Noakes
Consul (Commercial): Mr Graham B Romaine
Vice-consul (Commercial): Mrs Françoise Holl
Vice-consul: Mrs Jeannie Labaye

Marseille (SP)
British Consulate-General
24 Avenue de Prado, 13006 Marseilles
Telephone: (00) (33) (4) 91 15 72 10
Facsimile: (00) (33) (4) 91 37 47 06
Airtech: (00) (33) (4) 91 57 16 38
e-mail: postmaster.marseille@fco.gov.uk
Office Hours (GMT): Summer 07 00 - 10 30 and
11:30 - 15 00
Winter 08 00 - 11 30 and 12 30 - 16 00
Consul-General (also for Monaco):
Mr Simon Lever
Consul (Commercial): Mr Jo J Patanchon, MBE
Vice-Consul: Mrs Donna Faure

Nice
British Consulate
26 Avenue Notre Dame
4th Floor
06000 Nice
Telephone: (00) (33) (4) 93 62 13 56
Facsimile: (00) (33) (4) 93 62 08 24
Honorary Consul: Ms Simone J Paissoni

Perpignan
British Consulate
Honorary British Consul: (Vacant)

Montpellier (HC)
British Consulate
271 Le Capitole Bat A, 64 Rue Alcyone,
34000 Montpellier
Telephone/Facsimile: (00) (33) (4) 67 15 52 07
Honorary British Consul: Mr Norman J Paget

Paris
British Consulate-General
18bis rue d'Anjou 75008 Paris
(All mail should be sent to the British Embassy,
Paris)
Telephone: (00) (331) 44 51 31 00
Facsimile: (00) (331) 44 51 31 27
                (00) (331) 44 51 31 28 (Visas)
Office Hours (GMT): 07 30 - 11 00 and 12 30 -
16 00 (Summer)
08 30 - 12 00 and 13 30 - 17 00 (Winter)
Consul-General: Mr Stuart W Gregson
Consul: Mr Brian West
Vice Consul: Mr Steven J Donnelly, MBE
Vice Consul (Passport Officer): Mr Ian Gallacher
Vice Consul (Immigration): Mr Michael Kearney
Vice Consul (Immigration): Ms Suzanne Groves
Vice Consul (Immigration):
Mr Frederick Cracknell
Vice Consul: Mr Simon M Taylor
Vice Consul: Mr Mark Pettrigrew

Cherbourg
British Consulate
P&O European Ferries, Gare Maritime
Transmanche,
BP 46

50652 Cherbourg Cedex
Telephone: 02 33 88 65 60
Facsimile: 02 33 88 67 07
Honorary Consul: Mr Gerard R Caron, MBE

French Guiana (Cayenne)
16 avenue Président Monnerville, BP 211
97324 Cayenne
Telephone: (00) (594) 311034
Facsimile: (00) (594) 304094
Honorary Consul: Mr Joseph G Nouh-Chaia, MBE

French Polynesia (Papeete)
British Consulate
Propriété Boubée, Route Pinae Tane,
Pirae - Tahiti
BP 1064 Papeete, 98114 Tahiti
Telephone: (00) (689) 424355 Home
419841 Office
Facsimile: 412700
Honorary Consul: Mr Robert J Withers

Nantes
British Consulate
16 Boulevard Guist'Hau
BP 22026
44020 Nantes
Telephone: 02 51 72 72 60
Facsimile: 02 40 47 36 92
Office Hours (GMT): 07 00 - 10 15 and 12 00 -
15 00
Honorary Consul: Mrs Angela M Stokes

St Malo-Dinard
British Consulate – 'La Hulotte'
8 bd des Marechaux
35800 Dinard
Telephone: 02 99 46 26 64
Facsimile: 02 99 16 09 26
Honorary Consul: Mr Ronald Frankel, MBE

Le Havre
British Consulate
c/o P&O European Ferries
Terminal de la Citadelle – B.P. 439
76057 Le Havre Cedex
Telephone: 02 35 19 78 88
Facsimile: 02 35 19 78 98
Honorary Consul: Mme Nadine H Corbel

Lorient
British Consulate
c/o Plastimo
15 Rue Ingénieur Verrière
56325 Lorient Cedex
Telephone: (00) (2) 97 87 36 20
Facsimile: (00) (2) 97 87 36 49
Honorary Consul: Mr Anthony M Le Saffre

Saumur
Chateau de Chaintre
49400 Dampiers Sur Loire
Telephone: (00) 2 41 52 90 54
Facsimile: (00) 2 41 52 99 92
Consular Agent: Mr Khrisna C Leister

Martinique (Fort de France)

British Consulate
Route du Phare, 97200 Fort de France,
Martinique FWI
Telephone: (00) (596) 618892
Facsimile: (00) (596) 613389
Honorary Consul: Mme Alison J Ernoult

Guadeloupe

British Consulate
23 Rue Sadi Carnot
197110 Pointe-à-Pitre
Telephone: (00) (590) 825757
Facsimile: (00) (590) 828933
Honorary Consul: Mr David A Wood
La Réunion
British Consulate
Honorary Consul: (Vacant)

New Caledonia

British Consulate
BP 362, 98845 Noumea Cedex,
Nouvelle Caledonie
Telephone: (00) (687) 282153
Facsimile: (00) (687) 285144
Honorary Consul: Mrs Hilary Shekleton

Tours

British Consulate
7 Route des Rosiers
37510 Savonnières
Telephone/Facsimile: 02 47 43 50 58
Honorary Consul: Mr Brian J Cordery, OBE

GABON

Libreville

British Embassy (except where shown all staff
reside at Yaoundé)
Ambassador and Consul-General: Mr Richard
Wildash, LVO
First Secretary and Consul: Mr David Williams
Defence Attaché (resides at Kinshasa):
Lieutenant Colonel C Tim B Brown
British Consulate
c/o Brossette, BP 486,
Libreville
Telephone: (00) (241) 76 22 00/74 20 41
Facsimile: (00) (241) 76 57 89
Mobile: (00) (241) 75 86 36
Honorary Consul: Mr David Harwood, MBE

GAMBIA, THE

Banjul

British High Commission
48 Atlantic Road, Fajara (PO Box 507), Banjul
Telephone: (00) (220) 495133, 495134
Facsimile: (00) (220) 496134
Airtech: (00) (220) 494505
e-mail: bhcbanjul@gamtel.gm
Office Hours (GMT): Mon-Thurs 08 00 - 15 00
and Fri 08 00 - 13 00
High Commissioner: Mr J Perrott
Deputy High Commissioner: Mr R Rimmer
Defence Attaché (resides at Rabat):
Lieutenant Colonel G D Duthoit

Third Secretary (Management/Consular):
Mr C Barratt
Third Secretary (Immigration): Mrs C Dogan
DFID Office
c/o Britsh High Commission
Banjul
Telephone: (00) (220) 497537
Facsimile: (00) (220) 494127
e-mail: mmdfid@qanet.gm
Head of DFID Office: Mrs M Morrison

GEORGIA

Tbilisi

British Embassy
Sheraton Metechi Palace Hotel,
380003 Tbilisi
Telephone: (00) (995 32) 955497, 998447, 988796
Facsimile: (00) (995 32) 001065
Airtech: (00) (995 32) 775030
e-mail: british.embassy@caucasus.net
Office Hours (GMT): Mon-Fri 04 00 - 12 00
Ambassador: Ms D Barnes-Jones
Deputy Head of Mission: Mr D S McLaren
Defence Attaché: Wing Commander A W Kerr, RAF
First Secretary (Cultural): Mrs J Bakowski
Second Secretary (Political): Mr M J Seaman
*Second Secretary (Technical Management) (based
in Ankara):* Mr C Fox
Third Secretary (Management/Vice Consul):
Mr P W Ford
Attaché (Immigration): Ms K Moss
Defence Assistant: Staff Sergeant T Storer

GERMANY

Berlin

British Embassy
Wilhelmstrasse 70
10117 Berlin
Telephone: (00) (49) (30) 20457-0
Facsimile: (00) (49) (30) 20457-571 (Ambassador)
                                      20457-572 (DHM's
                                      Office)
                                      20457-573 (Political)
                                      20457-574 (Media)
                                      20457-594 (Public
                                      Relations)
                                      20457-575 (EU &
                                      Economics)
                                      20457-576 (Labour &
                                      Social Affairs &
                                      Environment)
                                      20457-577 (Commercial)
                                      20457-578
                                      (Management)
                                      20457-579 (Consular)
                                      20457-581 (Defence)
                                      20457-582 (Defence
                                      Supply)
                                      20457-347 (Agriculture)
                                      20457-346 (Research &
                                      Technology)
Website: http://www.britischebotschaft.de
Office Hours (GMT): 08 00 - 12 00 and 13 00 -
16 30

Please note that the British Embassy - Bonn Office has been closed. The Agriculture and Research & Technology sections have now rejoined the Embassy in Berlin, however, the Fiscal Liaison Office will remain in Bonn. Please see FLO contact details after staff list below.

Ambassador: Sir Paul Lever, KCMG (101)
Deputy Head of Mission and Head of Political & Public Affairs: Mr Jeremy Cresswell, CVO (151)
Counsellor (Research & Technology):
Mr Julian Farrel (Resides Munich)
Defence Attaché: Brigadier Bob Pridham, OBE (401)
Counsellor and Head of Defence Supply Section:
Mr Trevor Strong (421)
Counsellor and Head of EU and Economic Section: Mr Leigh Turner (301)
Counsellor (Labour): Miss Elaine Trewartha (310)
Counsellor (Global Issues): Mr David Woods (451)
First Secretary (Political External):
Mr Nick Alexander (223)
First Secretary (Economic): Mr Mike Bolton (321)
First Secretary (Environment): Ms Catrione Garrett (341)
First Secretary (Political External):
Mr Nigel Ingram (222)
First Secretary (Tech Management): Mr Bob Jones (521)
First Secretary (Research And Technology):
Ms Helen Hughes-McKay (338)
First Secretary and Head of Media:
Mr Alp Mehmet, MVO (251)
Air Attaché: Group Captain John Moloney, RAF (405)
First Secretary (Political Internal):
Mr Hugh Powell (211)
First Secretary and Head of Public Relations:
Ms Patricia Ramsey (223)
First Secretary (European Union):
Ms Susannah Simon (331)
Military Attaché: Colonel Jack Sheldon (407)
First Secretary (Agriculture): Mr Gareth Steel (335)
First Secretary (Fiscal Liaison Officer):
Mr Mike Stevens (241)
First Secretary and Head of Management:
Mr Ramsey Tonkin (501)
Naval Attaché: Captain Dickon Wilkinson, RN (403)
First Secretary (Political External):
Mr Paul Williams (221)
First Secretary and Head of Commercial Section:
Mr Ian Worthington, OBE (451)
Second Secretary (Political): Miss Stella Burch (224)
Assistant Defence Attaché: Major Nigel Dunkley, MBE (407)
Second Secretary (European Union):
Mrs Sophie Goodrick (332)
Second Secretary (PS/Ambassador): Mr Nic Hailey (102)
Second Secretary (Defence Supply):
Mr Terry Hughes (423)
Second Secretary (Drugs Liaison Officer):
Mr Chris Humphrey (407)
Second Secretary (Political Internal):
Mr Andrew Massey (212)

Second Secretary (Tech Management):
Mr Denis Price (522)
Second Secretary (Management/Consular):
Miss Helen Roscoe (531)
Third Secretary (Consular/Management):
Mrs Trudy Curry (541)
Third Secretary (Management):
Mr Les Jones (551)

Fiscal Liaison Office
Kaiser-Friedrich Strasse 19
53113 Bonn
Telephone: (00) (49) (228) 24 99 211/212
Facsimile: (00) (49) (228) 24 99 222
Office Hours (GMT): 08 00 – 12 00 and 13 00 – 16 30
Fiscal Liaison Officer: Mr Steve Pope

Leipzig
British Trade Office
Gohliser Str 7
0-04105 Leipzig
Telephone: (00) (49) 0341 564 9672, 564 9674
Facsimile: (00) (49) 0341 564 9673
Commercial Officer: Frau K Rath
Commercial Assistant: Frau Pia Mann

Düsseldorf
British Consulate-General
Yorckstrasse 19, 40476 Düsseldorf
(Mail from United Kingdom only can be sent to Box 2002, BFPO 105)
Telephone: (00) (49) (211) 9448-0 (Switchboard) + (see officers individual extensions below)
Direct Lines: 9448 170 Passport Section
9448 289 Visa Section
9448 222 Commercial Section
9448 245 Press and Public Affairs
Facsimile: (00) (49) (211) 48 63 59 Commercial & Investment Sections
48 81 90 Press, Passport, Consular and Management
48 86 03 Visa Section
Airtech: 94 48 242
e-mail:
Consular.Section@duesseldorf.mail.fco.gov.uk (Passport Section)
Visa.Section@duesseldorf.mail.fco.gov.uk (Visa Section)
Commercial.Section@duesseldorf.mail.fco.gov.uk (Commercial Section)
Website: www.british-consulate-general.de
www.british-passports.de (for British nationals resident in Germany)
www.british-visas.de
www.britische-handelsfoerderung.de (trade promotion in Germany)
www.investuk.de (Investment promotion in Germany)
Office Hours (GMT): Winter: Mon-Thurs 07 30 - 11 30 and 12 30 - 16 00
Fri 07 30 - 11 30 and 12 30 - 15 30
Summer: Mon-Thurs 06 30 - 10 30 and 11 30 - 15 00
Fri 06 30 - 10 30 and 11 30 - 14 30

Consul-General and Director of Trade and
Investment in Germany (201):
Mr W Boyd McCleary
Deputy Consul-General and Deputy Director for
Trade and Investment in Germany (202):
Mr Richard D Folland
Consul (Commercial/Investment) (203):
Mr Bill Kelly
Consul (Management) (231): Mr John K Hague
Consul (Commercial/CCU) (206):
Mr Ralph C Morton
Consul (Consular/Immigration) (260):
Ms Creena M Lavery
Vice-Consul (Commercial) (208): Mr Ed Noble
Vice-Consul (Immigration) (264):
Mr Tony R Salter
Vice-Consul (Consular/ Passports) (226):
Mr Sean M Rooney
Vice-Consul (Immigration) (267):
Ms Tracey Caulfield
Vice-Consul (Consular) (255): Mr David Kelly
Pro-Consul (Passports) (234): Mr Howard J Bevan
Commercial Officer (CCU) (219):
Mrs Sylvia A Tunmore
Commercial Officer (209): Ms Annette Klerks
Commercial Officer (213): Mr Peter Foster
Inward Investment (205): Mr Christian Fehling
Inward Investment (182): Mr Georg H Rehberg
Press and Public Affairs (223): Mrs Laura Heidgen

Frankfurt
British Consulate-General
Triton Haus
Bockenheimer Landstrasse 42,
60323 Frankfurt-am-Main
Telephone: (00) (49) (69) 1700020
Facsimile: (00) (49) (69) 729553
Office Hours (GMT): Winter: 07 30 - 12 00 and 13
00 - 16 00
Summer: 06 30 - 11 00 and 12 00 – 15 00
Consul-General: Mr W N C Paterson
Consul (Financial): Mr J A A Arrowsmith
Consul (Consular/Management):
Mrs C A Schumann
Vice-Consul: Mr C Shepherd
Commercial Officer: Herr R Schneider
Commercial Officer: Frau S Schnurbusch
Press and Public Affairs Officer: Dr W Dobler
Attaché: Mr A Dean
Attaché: Mr D Connelly
(Visa and Passport work is centralised in
Dusseldorf.)

Hamburg
British Consulate-General
Harvestehuder Weg 8a, 20148 Hamburg
Telephone: (00) (49) (40) 448 0320
Facsimile: (00) (49) (40) 410 7259
Airtech: (00) (49) (40) 448 032 31
Office Hours (GMT): Summer: 06 30 - 10 30 and
11 30 - 15 00
Winter: 07 30 - 11 30 and 12 30 - 16 00
Consul-General: Mr Douglas McAdam
Consul: Mr Anthony J Hackett
Vice-Consul (Consular): Mrs Mary Sanderson
Commercial Officer: Herr Thomas Siems

Commercial Officer: Mr John Holway
Commercial Officer: Herr Bernd Klein
Press & Public Affairs Officer: Ms Jo Dawes
(Visa and Passport work is centralised in
Dusseldorf.)

Bremen
British Consulate
Herrlichkeiten 6, Postfach 10 38 60, 28199 Bremen
Telephone: (00) (49) (421) 590708
Facsimile: (00) (49) (421) 5907109
Office Hours (GMT): Summer: 06 30 - 10 30 and
12 30 - 13 30
Winter: 07 30 - 11 30 and 13 30 - 14 30
Honorary Consul: Herr H-C Enge

Hanover
British Consulate
Hannover Ruchversicherungs AG
Karl-Wiechart-Allee 50
30625 Hannover
Telephone: (00) (511) 3883808
Facsimile: (00) (511) 5604690
Office Hours (GMT): 06 30 - 10 00 and 10 30 -
12 00
Honorary Consul: Herr W Zeller

Kiel
British Consulate
United Canal Agency GmbH
Schleuse, Maklerstrasse 11-14, 24159 Kiel
Telephone: (00) (49) 431 331971
Facsimile: (00) (49) 431 3053746
Telex: 299829 (a/b UBCK D)
Office (GMT): 06 30 - 11 00 and 12 00 - 15 00
Honorary Consul: Herr J Petersen

Munich
British Consulate-General
Bürkleinstrasse 10,
D - 80538 München
(Mail from United Kingdom only should be
addressed:
British Consulate-General, Munich,
PO Box 2010, BFPO 105)
Telephone: (00) (49) (89) 211090
Facsimile: 21109 166 Consul-General
             21109 166 Press &Public Affairs
             21109 166 Research & Technology
             Section
             21109 155 Commercial Section
             21109 155 Investment Section
             21109 144 Management Section
             21109 144 Consular Section
Office Hours (GMT): Winter: 07 30 - 11 00 and
12 00 - 16 00
Summer: 06 30 - 10 00 and 11 00 – 15 00
Consul-General/Counsellor: R&T: Mr J Farrel
Consul: Mr G Deane
Consul Commercial: Mr H Taylor
Consul (Consular/Management): Mrs M Timsit
Vice-Consul (Consular): Mrs C Ruhstorfer
Press & Public Affairs Officer:
Mrs B I Dammert/Ms D Wiesehofer
Vice-Consul (Commercial): Mr C Pattinson
Commercial Officer: Dr A Ritter Heinrich
Inward Investment Officer: Ms Heike Bieber

Research & Technology Officer: Ms M Kistenfeger
(Visa and Passport work is centralised in
Dusseldorf.)

Nuremburg
British Consulate
M Schmitt & Sohn GmbH &Co
Hadermuhle 9-15
D - 90402 Nuremburg
Telephone: (00) (49) (911) 2404-303
Facsimile: (00) (49) (911) 2404-111
Honorary Consul: Dr J Schmitt

Stuttgart
British Consulate-General
Breite Strasse 2, 70173
Telephone: (00) (49) (711) 16 26 9-0
Facsimile: (00) (49) (711) 16 26 9-30
Office Hours (GMT): As Frankfurt
Consul-General: Mr Mark P Twigg
Commercial Officer/Pro-Consul: Herr W R Seidler
Commercial Officer: Frau A Seidler
Pro-Consul: Mrs M Braun

GHANA

Accra
British High Commission
Osu Link, off Gamel Abdul Nasser Avenue
(PO Box 296), Accra
Telephone: (00) (233) (21) 7010650, 221665
(24 hours)
　　　　　7010721 Immigration Section
Facsimile: (00) (233) (21) 7010655
　　　　　783552 Chancery
　　　　　221715 Immigration Section
Airtech: (00) (233) (21) 242936
e-mail: High.Commission@fco.gov.uk
Office Hours (GMT): 07 45 - 14 45
Immigration Section Public Hours 07 45 - 10 45
Consular Section Public Hours 07 30 - 13 30
High Commissioner: Mr Rod Pullen
Deputy High Commissioner: Mr Robert Gwynn
Counsellor (Regional Affairs): Mr Michael Wood
Defence Adviser:
Lieutenant Colonel Steen K E Clarke, OBE
First Secretary (Development): Mr Tony Gardner
First Secretary (Commercial): Mr Kevin Lynch
Second Secretary (Immigration/Consular):
Mrs Caroline Cross
Second Secretary (Development):
Mr Desmond Woode
*Second Secretary (Political, Press and Public
Affairs):* Mr Gregory Quinn
Second Secretary (Management): Mr Seif Usher
Second Secretary (Airline Liason Officer):
Mr Derek McDougal Swanson
Second Secretary (Immigration): Ms Debra Poulier
Second Secretary: Mr Andrew Eelbeck
Third Secretary (Commercial): Mrs Carol Turvill
Third Secretary (Chancery): Mr Jonathan Saunders
Third Secretary (Immigration): Mr Jim Beach
Third Secretary (Immigration): Mr Brendan Gill
Third Secretary (Immigration): Mr Alan Green
Third Secretary (Immigration): Mr Althea Ramsey
Third Secretary (Immigration): Mrs Tracey Singh
Third Secretary (Immigration): Mr Stuart Turvill

Third Secretary (Immigration): Mr Simon Winter

GREECE

Athens
British Embassy
1 Ploutarcou Street, 106 75 Athens
Telephone: (00) (30) 10 727 2600
Night (RSO): (00) (30) 10 723 7727
　　　　　724 1331
Facsimile: (00) (30) 10 727 2734 Political &
　　　　　Commercial Section
　　　　　2720 Consular Section
　　　　　2876 Management Section
　　　　　2723 Chancery
　　　　　2743 Press and Public Affairs
　　　　　2725 Residence
Airech: (00) (30) 10 722 7122
e-mail: britania@hol.gr
Website: http://www.british-embassy.gr
Office Hours (GMT): 06 00 - 13 00
Ambassador: Mr David C A Madden, CMG
*Counsellor, Consul-General and Deputy Head of
Mission:* Mr Peter J Millett
Counsellor: Mr Nicholas J Foster
Defence, Naval and Air Attaché:
Commodore John L Milnes, RN
Military Attaché:
Colonel Simon W L Strickland, OBE
Counsellor (Cultural): Mr Chris Hickey
First Secretary (Economic):
Mr David S Gordon-MacLeod
*First Secretary (Political, Press and Public
Affairs):* Mrs Francesca J G Flessati
First Secretary (External):
Mr Krishna Shanmuganathan
First Secretary (Defence Supply): Mr John Bewley
First Secretary (Management):
Mr Michael D Morley
First Secretary (Commercial):
Mr Graeme G Thomas
First Secretary and Consul: Mr David J Holder
First Secretary (Cultural Affairs): (Vacant)
Second Secretary and Vice-Consul:
Mr Simon Batty
Second Secretary (Political/Information):
Ms Emma C Mills
Second Secretary: Mr Paul Weldon
Third Secretary (Economic):
Miss Margaret M Belof
Third Secretary (Management):
Mr Nigel S Chadwick
Third Secretary and Vice-Consul:
Miss Christine Waterhouse

Corfu
British Consulate
2 Alexandras Avenue, 491 00 Corfu
Telephone: (00) (30) (661) 30055
Facsimile: (00) (30) (661) 37995
Consul: Mr Anthony (Tony) Arnold
Heraklion (Crete)
British Consulate
16 Papa-Alexandrou Street
712 02 Heraklion
Telephone: (00) (30) (81) 224012

Facsimile: (00) (30) (81) 243935
e-mail: crete@british-consulate.gr
Consul: Mrs Marion R Tzanaki, MBE

Kos
British Vice-Consulate
8, Annetas Laoumtzi Street,
853 00 Kos
Telephone: (00) (30) (242) 21549
Facsimile: (00) (30) (242) 25948
Honorary Vice-Consul:
Mr Konstantinos Kourounis

Patras
British Vice-Consulate
Votsi 2
262 21 Patras
Telephone: (00) (30) (61) 277329
Facsimile: (00) (30) (61) 225334
Honorary Vice-Consul:
Mrs Marie Jeanne Morphy-Karatza, MBE

Rhodes
British Consulate
Pavlou Mela 3
PO Box 47
851 00 Rhodes
Telephone: (00) (30) (241) 27247 or 22005
Facsimile: (00) (30) (241) 22615
e-mail: rhodes@british-consulate.gr
Honorary Consul:
Mr Dimitrios E Demetriades, MBE

Thessaloniki
British Consulate
8th Floor, 8 Venizelou Street,
Eleftheria Square, PO Box 10332
541 10 Thessaloniki
Telephone: (00) (30) (31) 278006 or 269984
e-mail: salonika@british-consulate.gr
Honorary Consul: Mr George K Doucas, MBE

Thessaloniki
British Embassy Commercial Liaison Office
c/o The British Council
9 Ethnikis Amynis Street, PO Box 50007
540 13 Thessaloniki
Telephone: (00) (30) (31) 267114, 266711
Facsimile: (00) (30) (31) 267114, 282498
e-mail: sarah.edwards@britcoun.gr
*Head of British Embassy Commercial Liaison
Office:* Mrs Sarah Edwards-Economidi

Syros
British Vice-Consulate
8 Akti Petrou Ralli,
Hermoupolis
841 00 Syros
Telephone: (00) (30) (281) 82232 or 88922
Facsimile: (00) (30) (281) 83293
Honorary Vice-Consul:
Mrs Virginia Parissi-Thermou

Zakynthos
British Vice-Consulate
5 Foskolos Street
291 00 Zakynthos
Telephone: (00) (30) (695) 22906 or 48030

Facsimile: (00) (30) (695) 23769
Honorary Vice-Consul:
Mrs Evridiki (Vicky) Vitsou-Kotsoni

GRENADA

St George's
British High Commission, Netherlands Building,
Grand Anse, St George's, Grenada
Telephone: (00) (1) (473) 440 3536, 440 3222
Facsimile: (00) (1) (473) 440 4939
e-mail: bhcgrenada@caribsurf.com
Office Hours (GMT): Mon - Thurs: 12 00 - 17 00
and 17 30 - 20 00
Fri: 12 00 - 17 00
* *High Commissioner:* Mr John White
Resident British Commissioner: Mr Vic Wallis
* *Deputy High Commissioner:* Mr Rob Holland
* *Defence Adviser:* Captain Steve C Ramm, RN
* *Counsellor (Regional Affairs):*
Mr Nick J L Martin
* *First Secretary (Chancery):* Mr Graham Honey
* *First Secretary (Management/Consular):*
Ms Ros Day
* *Second Secretary (Chancery/Information):*
Mr Nick J Pyle, MBE
** *Second Secretary (Technical Works):*
Mr Mark Jones
* *Second Secretary (Chancery):* Mr Phil Marshall
* *Third Secretary:* Mr Tony W White
* *Third Secretary (Consular/Immigration):*
Mr Mark Harrison
*Resides at Bridgetown
**Resides at Mexico City

GUATEMALA

Guatemala City
British Embassy
Avenida La Reforma 16-00, Zona 10,
Edificio Torre Internacional, Nivel 11
Telephone: (00) (502) 367 5425 to 29
Facsimile: (00) (502) 367 5430
e-mail: embassy@terra.com.gt
Office Hours (GMT): Mon-Thurs 14 30 - 18 30
and 19 30 - 23 00
Fri 14 30 - 18 30
Ambassador: Mr Richard D Lavers
*First Secretary, Consul and Deputy Head of
Mission:* Mr Kevin A Garvey
Defence Attaché: Colonel Ian C D Blair-Pilling, OBE
Second Secretary (Management and Consular):
Mr Colin Gracey
Assistant Defence Attaché: Flt Sgt Glenn Walker
Third Secretary (Acccounts and Registry):
Mr Tony Mesarowicz

GUINEA

Conakry
British Embassy (Resident at the BHC, Freetown)
Ambassador: Mr David Alan Jones
Defence Attaché: Lieutenant Colonel J J P Poraj-
Wilczynski
Third Secretary (Management):
Ms M J D Convery

Conakry
British Consulate-General
BP 834 Conakry, Republic of Guinea
Telephone: (00) (224) 45 58 07 / 45 60 20 (Office)
(224) 45 29 59 (Home)
Facsimile: (00) (224) 45 60 20
Satellite Phone: 00 874 762 471260
Satellite Fax: 00 874 762 471262
e-mail: britcon.oury@biasy.net
(Resident in Conakry)
Consul: Mr L Hartley
Commercial Officer/Press Assistant:
Mr G G Tounkara
Consular/Management Assistant: Mrs O Barry

GUINEA-BISSAU

Bissau
British Embassy (all staff resident in Dakar)
Ambassador (non-resident): Mr Alan Burner
Deputy Head of Mission and Consul:
Mr Simon Bond
Third Secretary and Vice-Consul: (Vacant)
Attaché (Immigration): Ms Christine Johnson

Bissau
British Honorary Consulate
Mavegro Int., CP100, Bissau
Telephone: (00) (245) 20 12 24/20 12 16 (Office)
(00) (245) 20 16 07 (Home)
Facsimile: (00) (245) 20 12 65
Honorary Consul: Mr Jan Van Maanen

GUYANA

Georgetown
British High Commission
44 Main Street, (PO Box 10849), Georgetown
Telephone: (00) (592) (22)65881/2/3/4
Facsimile: 53555

Development/Commercial/Management
50671 Consular and Immigration
37321 Chancery
68818 (Airtech)
e-mail:
firstname.surname@georgetown.mail.fco.gov.uk
Office Hours (GMT): 11 30 - 18 30
High Commissioner: Mr S J Hiscock
Deputy High Commissioner: Mr S N Crossman
Defence Adviser (resides at Bridgetown):
Captain S C Ramm, RN
Second Secretary (Management): Ms A M Fairley
Second Secretary (Development): Mr J McCreadie
Second Secretary (Chancery) (resides at Caracas):
Mr D Stewart
Third Secretary (Immigration / Consular):
Mr I G Angus
Third Secretary (Technical Management) (resides at Bridgetown): Mr A W White

HAITI

Port-au-Prince
British Embassy
Ambassador: (resides Santo Domingo):
Mr Andrew R Ashcroft

Second Secretary and Consul: (resides Santo Domingo): Mr Kevin Shaughnessy

Port-au Prince
British Consulate
Hotel Montana (PO Box 1302), Port-au-Prince
Telephone: (00) (509) 257 3969
Facsimile: (00) (509) 257 4048
Office Hours (GMT): 13 00 - 18 00
Vice-Consul: Mrs Allison Insley-Madsen

HOLY SEE
British Embassy
91 Via dei Condotti, I-00187, Rome
Telephone: (00) (39) (06) 699 23561
Facsimile: (00) (39) (06) 6994 0684
Office Hours (GMT): Oct-Mar 08 00 - 12 00 and
13 00 - 16 00
Apr-June and Sep 07 00 - 11 00 and 12 00-15 00
Jul-Aug 06 00 - 12 00
Ambassador: Mrs K F Colvin
First Secretary and Deputy Head of Mission:
Mrs M de Valencia

HONDURAS

Tegucigalpa
British Embassy
Edificio Financiero BANEXPO
3er Piso
Boulevard San Juan Bosco
Colonia Payaqui
PO Box 290, Tegucigalpa
Telephone: (00) (504) 232 0612, 232 5144
Facsimile: (00) (504) 232 5480
Airtech: (00) (504) 232 0612 - Ext. 2025
Office Hours (GMT): Mon-Thurs 14 00 - 19 00
and 20 00 - 22 30 and Fri 14 00 - 19 00
Ambassador and Consul-General:
Miss Kay Coombs
Second Secretary and Deputy Head of Mission:
Mr Neal Carlin
Defence Attaché (resides at Guatemala City):
Colonel Ian C D Blair-Pilling, OBE
*First Secretary (Commercial) and Director of
Trade Promotion for Central America (resides at
San José):* Mr Christopher Edge
Second Secretary (resides at Panama City):
Mr Andrew Davenport

San Pedro Sula
British Consulate
Avenida Circunvalación, 2-3 Calle, No. 11
Apartado Postal No. 63
San Pedro Sula, Cortés
Honduras
Telephone: (00) (504) 7374; 550-2288
Facsimile: (00) (504) 550-7009
Office Hours (GMT): 08 30 - 11 30
14 00 – 1600 (local time) – Monday to Friday
inclusive
Honorary Consul: Mr Edgardo Dumas

HUNGARY

Budapest
British Embassy

Harmincad Utca 6, Budapest 1051
Telephone: (00) (36) (1) 266 2888
Facsimile: (00) (36) (1) 266 0907
Management/PPA/KHF Sections
429 6360 Consular/Visa/Commercial Sections
429 6301 Political Section
Airtech: (00) (36) (1) 429 6299
e-mail: info@britemb.hu.
Website: http://www.britishembassy.hu
Office Hours (GMT): Summer 07 00 - 15 00,
Winter 08 00 - 16 00
Ambassador: Mr Nigel Thorpe, cvo
Counsellor and Deputy Head of Mission:
Mr Gordon Reid
Counsellor: Dr Dudley Ankerson
Defence Attaché: Colonel Jonathan S B Frere, mbe
Cultural Attaché (British Council Director):
Dr John Richards
First Secretary (Commercial):
Miss Debbie Goldthorpe, lvo
First Secretary (Political/Economic):
Mr Robert Dear
First Secretary (Management/Consul):
Mr Bernard Halliwell, mbe
First Secretary (Political): Mr Mark Morgan
First Secretary (Cultural): Mr John Mitchell
First Secretary (Cultural): Mr Nigel Bellingham
Assistant Defence Attaché:
Squadron Leader Alan Fisher, raf
Second Secretary (Know How Fund/Political):
Mr Jason Moore
Second Secretary (Commercial): Mr Colin Parish
Second Secretary (Political): Mr Stephen Burdes
Second Secretary (Political): Miss Katy Ransome
Second Secretary (Technical Management):
Mr John Walker
Second Secretary (Technical Management):
Mr Terry Wiltshire
Second Secretary (Airline Liaison):
Mr Robin Humphris
Second Secretary: Mr Andy Hewett
Second Secretary: Mr Jason Clarke
Third Secretary (Management): Mr Richard Homer
Third Secretary (Press and Public Diplomacy):
Miss Joanne Penfold
Attaché and Vice-Consul: Mr Brian Simpson

Pécs

British Consulate
Megye Utca. 21
Pécs 7621
Tel/Fax: (00) (36) (72) 210 091
Office Hours (GMT) 08 00- 11 00 Monday to
Friday
Honorary Consul: Dr Zsolt Páva

ICELAND

Reykjavik
British Embassy
Laufasvegur 31, 101 Reykjavik
Postal Address: PO Box 460, 121 Reykjavik
Telephone: (00) (354) 550 5100
Facsimile: (00) (354) 550 5105
Airtech: (00) (354) 550 5104
e-mail: britemb@centrum.is

Office Hours (GMT): Mon-Thurs 08 30 - 16 00,
Fri 08 30 - 15 30
Ambassador and Consul-General:
Mr John Culver, lvo
Deputy Head of Mission and Consul:
Mr Peter Evans
Commercial Officer: Mrs Elsa Einarsdottir
*First Secretary Inward Investment (resides in
Stockholm):* Mr Martin Cronin

Akureyri
British Vice-Consulate
Central Hospital (Fjordungssjukrahusid a Akureyri)
v/Eyrarlandsveg PO Box 380
IS-602 Akureyri
Telephone: (00) (463) 0102
Facsimile: (00) (462) 4621
Office Hours (GMT): 09 00 - 12 00 and 13 00 -
17 00
Honorary Vice-Consul: Mr Halldor Jonsson

INDIA

New Delhi
British High Commission
Chanakyapuri, New Delhi 110021
Telephone: (00) (91) (11) 687 2161
Facsimile: (00) (91) (11) 687 2882 Management
                Dept
                687 0068 Political Dept
                687 0062 Economic & Commercial
                Dept
                687 0065 Press & Public Affairs
                687 0060 Visa Dept
                611 4603 Defence Dept
Airtech: 611 4601
e-mail: postmaster.NewDelhi@fco.gov.uk
Office Hours (GMT): Mon-Fri: 03 30 - 07 30 and
08 30 - 11 30
High Commissioner: Sir Rob Young, kcmg
Minister and Deputy High Commissioner:
Mr Mark Runacres
Defence and Military Adviser: Brigadier Ian Rees
Counsellor (Political): Mr Dominic Martin
Counsellor (Economic and Commercial):
Mr John Dennis
Counsellor: Mr Kevin Sloan
Counsellor (Management):
Mr Norman King, lvo, obe
Naval and Air Adviser:
Group Captain Nick Spiller, raf
First Secretary (Medical Officer):
Dr John Llewellyn
First Secretary (Press & Public Affairs):
Mr Gerry McCrudden, mbe
First Secretary (Commercial):
Mr Peter Stephenson
First Secretary (Economic): Mr John Burton
First Secretary (Political): Mr David Quarrey
First Secretary (Internal): Mr Peter Holland
First Secretary (Science & Technology):
Mr Simon Hosking
First Secretary (Environment & Trade Policy):
Dr David McMahon
First Secretary (Immigration/Consular):
Mr Chris Dix

First Secretary (Estate Manager):
Mr Andrew Lelliot
First Secretary (Management):
Mr Michael Holmes MVO
First Secretary (ALO Regional Manager):
Ms Janet Battersby
First Secretary (Defence Supply):
Mr James Catchpole
First Secretary (Technical Management):
Mr Barry Vargas
First Secretary (Technical Works): Mr Ian Jack
First Secretary (Consular): Mrs Angela Slater
First Secretary (Nursing Officer): Joy Riley
Assistant Defence Adviser:
Lieutenant Commander Ian Jackson, RN
Second Secretary (Political): Mr Jonathan Sinclair
Second Secretary (Political): Miss Alex Mititelu
Second Secretary (Technical Management):
Mr Terence Watson
Second Secretary (Immigration): Mr Tom Burke
Second Secretary (Immigration): Mr Steve Burns
Second Secretary (Commercial): Mr David Slater
Second Secretary (Commercial): Mr Neil Brigden
Second Secretary (Management):
Mr Christopher Stacey
Second Secretary (Security Officer):
Mr Rick Williams
Second Secretary (Airline Liaison Officer):
Mr David Westgate
Third Secretary (Economic & Commercial):
Mr Danny Wells
Third Secretary (Commercial): Mr Alistair Elder
Third Secretary (Political): Mr Eric Taylor
Third Secretary (Political): Mr John Bradshaw
Third Secretary (Political): Mr Simon Williams
Third Secretary (Consular): Vacant
Attaché (Pensions Liaison Officer):
Ms Helen Ibbott

New Delhi
DFID (Department For International Development)
India
B-28 Tara Crescent
Qutab Institutional Area
New Delhi 110 016
Telephone: (00) (91) (11) 6529123
Facsimile: (00) (91) (11) 6529296
Minister (Development) & Head, DFIDI:
Mr Robert Graham-Harrison
Deputy Head DFIDI: Mr Rick Woodham
First Secretary (Economic): Mr John Burton
First Secretary (Environment): Dr Yusaf Samiullah
First Secretary (Social Development): Dr D J Pain
First Secretary (Development): Mr Peter Rose
First Secretary (Governance): Mr Roderick Evans
First Secretary (Governance): Ms Paula Hayes
First Secretary (Development): Ms S Taylor
First Secretary (Development): Mr Peter Zoller
First Secretary (Economic): Mr Shan Mitra
First Secretary (Education): Ms Marshal Elliot
First Secretary (Social Development):
Mr A De Haan
First Secretary (Management): Mr Niall Coffey
First Secretary (Contracts/Procurement):
Mr Will Starbuck
First Secretary (Health): Mr Desmond Whyms

First Secretary (Health): Mr Tim Martineau
First Secretary (Engineering): Mr Peter Davies
First Secretary (Power Policy): Mr Geoff Hayton
First Secretary (Water & Sanitation):
Mr Nigel Kirby
First Secretary (Forestry): Mr Kevin Crockford
First Secretary (Rural Livelihoods):
Mr Simon Croxton
First Secretary (Engineering and Finance):
Mr Simon Kenny
Second Secretary (Development):
Mrs Linda Campbell
Second Secretary (Development):
Mrs Kate Alexander
Second Secretary (Development): Ms Anna Walters
Second Secretary (Development): Mr Steve Burton
Second Secretary (Development):
Mr Ian Alexander

British Council Division
17 Kasturba Gandhi Marg, New Delhi 110001
Telephone: (00) (91) (11) 3711401
Facsimile: (00) (91) (11) 3710717
e-mail: delhi.enquiry@in.britishcouncil.org
Minister (Cultural Affairs): Mr Edmund Marsden
Counsellor (Human Resource Development):
Dr Morna Nance
First Secretary (Resources Management):
Ms Grace Conacher
First Secretary (Education Promotion):
Mr John Nance
First Secretary (Educational Services):
Mr Nick Humphries

Mumbai (Bombay)
Office of the British Deputy High Commissioner
Maker Chambers IV, 222 Jamnalal Bajaj Road,
(PO Box 11714) Nariman Point, Mumbai 400 021
Telephone: (00) (91) (22) 283 0517, 283 2330, 283 3602
Facsimile: (00) (91) (22) 202 7940
e-mail: postmaster@bombay.mail.fco.gov.uk
Office Hours (GMT): 02 30 - 07 30 and 08 30 - 10 30
Deputy High Commissioner:
Mr Howard Parkinson, CVO
First Secretary (Commercial): Mr Merrick Lowes
First Secretary (British Council Director):
Mr Paul Smith
First Secretary (Consular/Management):
Mr David Allan
Second Secretary (Drug Liaison Officer):
Mr Chris Noon
Second Secretary (Inward Investment):
Mr Steve Firstbrook
Second Secretary (Commercial): Ms Claire Tuhey
Second Secretary (Immigration):
Mr Charles Molloy
Second Secretary (Immigration): Mr Rafi Husain
Second Secretary (Airline Liaison Officer):
Mr Simon Rose
Third Secretary (Management): Mr Andy McFarlin
Attaché (Consular): Mr Ian Reakes

Ahmedabad
British Trade Office
4th Floor, 404 Kaivanna Building

Near Ambawadi Circle
Panchwati
Ahmedabad 380 006
Telephone: (00) (91) (79) 6467138
Facismile: (00) (91) (79) 6403537
e-mail: btoabad@icenet.net
Commercial Information Officer: Milind Godbole

Pune
British Library
917/1 Fergusson College Road
Shivaji Nagar
Pune 411 004
Telephone:
Facsimile: (00) (91) (20) 5671580
e-mail: bicpune@vsnl.com
Commercial Officer: Mr Shantanu Parvati

Goa
British Consular Office
302 Manguirish Building
3rd Floor, 18 June Road
Opp. Gulf Supermarket
Panaji 403001, Goa
Telephone: (00) (91) (832) 228571
Facsimile: (00) (91) (832) 232828
e-mail: bcagoa@goatelecom.com
British Consular Officer: Mrs Shilpa Caldeira

Kolkata (Calcutta)
Office of the British Deputy High Commissioner
1A Ho Chi Minh Sarani, Kolkata, 700 071
Telephone: (00) (91) (33) 288 5172/3/4/5/6
5172 after office hours
Facsimile: (00) (91) (33) 288 3435
Airtech: 5010
e-mail: postmaster@calcutta.mail.fco.gov.uk
Office Hours (GMT): 03 30 - 07 30 and 08 30 -
11 30
Deputy High Commissioner: Dr John Mitchiner
Second Secretary (Commercial): Mr Harvey Bell
Third Secretary (Consular): Mr Bernie Andrews

Chennai (Madras)
Office of the British Deputy High Commissioner in
Southern India
24 Anderson Road, Chennai 600 006
Telephone: (00) (91) (44) 8273136, 8273137,
8257422, 8257433
Facsimile: (00) (91) (44) 8269004 Commercial
                8203790 Management/PPA
                8275130 Visa
e-mail: bdhcchen@vsnl.com
Office Hours (GMT): 03 00 - 07 30 and 08 00 -
10 30
Deputy High Commissioner: Mr Michael Herridge
First Secretary (British Council Director):
Ms Eunice Crook
Second Secretary (Commercial): Mr David Abbott
Second Secretary (Immigration): Mr Geoff Wood
*Second Secretary (Airline Liason Officer) (Resides
at Mumbai):* Mr Simon Rose
Third Secretary (Management/Consular):
Mr Stephen Bailey
Attaché (Immigration): Miss Gillian Mearns
Attaché (Immigration): Mr Simon Dadd
Attaché (Immigration): Mr Shashikant Patel

Attaché (Immigration): Mrs Rita Casserly
Attaché (Immigration): Mr. Michael Murtagh
Attaché (Immigration): Mrs Susan Edghill

Bangalore
British Trade Office
7/4, Thapar Niketan
Brunton Road, Bangalore 560 025
Telephone: (00) (91) (80) 5586687, 5588661/3
Facsimile: (00) (91) (80) 5586690
e-mail: bto.bangalore@fco.gov.uk
Second Secretary (Commercial): Mr Kelvin Green

Hyderabad
British Trade Office
H-3-6-322, Chamber 104, 1st Floor
Mahavir House, Basheer bagh
Hyderabad 300 029
Telephone: (00) (91) (40) 6669147/8
Facsimile: (00) (91) (40) 6669149
e-mail: btohyd@hd2.dot.net.in
Senior Trade Promotion Adviser:
Mr M C Srinagesh

INDONESIA

Jakarta
British Embassy
Jalan M H Thamrin 75, Jakarta 10310
Telephone: (00) (62) (21) 315 6264 (Switchboard)
314 4229 (Auto attendant - see individual
extension numbers)
Facsimile: (00) (62) (21) 314 1824 Development
                315 4061 Commercial
                390 7493 Management
                392 6263 Chancery/Economic
                390 2726 Defence
Office Hours (GMT): Mon - Thur 00 45 - 09 00
and Fri 00 45 - 05 45

British Consulate General
Deutsche Bank Building, (19th Floor)
J1 Imam Bonjol 80
Jakarta 10310
Telephone: (00) (62) (21) 390 7484 - 87
Facsimile: (00) (62) (21) 316 0858
Office Hours (GMT): Mon - Thur 00 45 - 09 00
and Fri 00 45 - 05 45
Ambassador (4201): Mr Richard Gozney, CMG
*Deputy Head of Mission and Consul-General
(4203):* Mr Anthony Godson
Counsellor (Commercial/Development) (4232):
Mr Andrew George
Counsellor (Political) (4205): Mr John Fisher
Defence Attaché (4215): Colonel Alan J Roberts
First Secretary (Political/Economic) (4245):
(Vacant)
First Secretary (Commercial) (4239):
Mr Mark Walmsley
First Secretary (Management) (4263):
Mr Mike Tomkins
First Secretary (Development) (4252):
Mr Jim Carpy
DFID – Governance Adviser (4295):
Mr Ben Dickinson
DFID – Social Development Adviser (4260):
Ms Elizabeth Carriere

DFID – Forestry Adviser (4220): Mr Yvan Biot
Second Secretary (Consular): Mr Alan Marshall
Second Secretary (Political) (4208):
Mr Simon Tonge
Second Secretary (Political/Economic) (4284):
Mr Suman Ziaullah
Third Secretary (Political) (4241):
Miss Naomi Kyriacopoulos
Third Secretary (Immigration): Mr Dave Lovell
Third Secretary and Vice-Consul:
Mr Alasdair Hamilton
Third Secretary (Commercial) (4236):
Mr Bikash Dawahoo
Third Secretary (Management/Press) (4267):
Miss Nicola James
Third Secretary (Estate) (4266):
Mr Asif Choudhury

Medan
British Consulate
Jl Kap. Pattimura 459
PO Box 1286,
Medan 20153
Telephone: (00) (62) (61) 821 0559
Facsimile: (00) (62) (61) 821 0991
e-mail: psbaskett@attglobal.net
Office Hours (GMT): Mon-Fri 01 00 - 05 00
Honorary Consul: Mr Pat Baskett

Surabaya
British Consulate
c/o Lamipak Primula Indonesia
26, Jl. Sawunggaling, Gilang, Taman,
Sidoarjo 61257, Indonesia
Telephone: (00) (62) (31) 7881418 (hunting)
7884348 (direct)
Facsimile: (00) (62) (31) 7881419
e-mail: bcsurabaya@cbn.net.id
Office Hours (GMT): 01 30 - 09 00
Honorary Consul: Mr Adrian Spencer
Honorary Vice Consul: Mrs Beverley Spencer

Bali
British Consulate
Jalan Mertasari No. 2,
Sanur
Denpasar 80227
Bali
Telephone: 0361 270 601
Facsimile: 0361 270 572
e-mail: bcbali@dps.centrin.net.id
Office Hours (GMT): 01 30 - 09 00
Honorary Consul: Mr Mark Wilson

IRAN

Tehran
British Embassy
143 Ferdowsi Avenue, Tehran 11344
(PO Box No 11365-4474)
Telephone: (00) (98) (21) 6705011/19 (8 lines)
Facsimile: (00) (98) (21) 6708021 Commercial
6700720 Visa
6710761 Management/Consular
Office Hours (GMT): Sun – Thurs 04 00 - 11 00
Ambassador: Mr Richard Dalton CMG

Counsellor and Deputy Head of Mission:
Mr Neil Crompton
First Secretary (Commercial): Mr Eric Jenkinson
*First Secretary (Education/British Council
Director):* Mr Michael Sargent, OBE
First Secretary (Management) and Consul:
Mr Paul Seaby
Second Secretary (Press and Public Affairs):
Mr Andrew Greenstock
Second Secretary (Commercial): Mr Steve Smith
Second Secretary (Political): Mr Simon Shercliff
Second Secretary (Immigration): Mr Gavin Baptie
Third Secretary (Management) and Vice-Consul:
Mr Doug Tunn
Third Secretary (Immigration):
Ms Barbara Moser-Andon
Third Secretary (Immigration): Ms Marie Donnelly
Third Secretary (Immigration): Mr Paul Kingford
Third Secretary (Immigration): Mr Martin Waspe

IRELAND

Dublin
British Embassy
29 Merrion Road, Ballsbridge, Dublin 4
Telephone: (00 353) (1) 205 3700 (Main
Switchboard)
205 3757 (Commercial)
205 3792 (Defence)
205 3700 (Passport/Visa)
205 3742 (Press & Public Affairs)
Facsimile: (00 353) (1) 205 3731 (Chancery)
205 3880 (Commercial)
205 3885 (Management)
205 3890 (Consular/Passport/Visa)
205 3893 (Press & Public Affairs)
205 3878 (Defence)
e-mail: bembassy@internet-ireland.ie
trade@dublin.mail.fco.gov.uk (Commercial
Section)
Website: www.britishembassy.ie
Office Hours (GMT): Mon-Thur 09.00-
12.45/14.00-17.15
Fri 09.00-12.45/14.00-17.00
Ambassador: Sir Ivor Roberts KCMG (Mr Stewart
Eldon, CMG, OBE w.e.f April 03)
Counsellor and Deputy Head of Mission:
Mr John Rankin
Counsellor (Commercial): Mr Martin McIntosh OBE
Defence Attaché: Colonel Paul Cummings
First Secretary (EU/Economic): Ms Sarah Tiffin
First Secretary (Political): Mr Patrick Reilly
First Secretary (Management): Mr Ian Stevens
Second Secretary (Press & Public Affairs):
Mr Andrew Pike
Second Secretary (Commercial):
Mr Steve Richards
Second Secretary (EU/Economic): Mr Tom Hoskin
Second Secretary (Management):
Mr Robbie Robinson
Third Secretary (Management):
Ms Gillian Edwards
Third Secretary (Chancery): Ms Sharon Brant
Third Secretary (Passports/Visa): Mr Tim Freeman
Attaché: Ms Margaret Rixon
Attaché (Defence): Mr Christensen Ruhle

ISRAEL

Tel Aviv
British Embassy
192 Hayarkon Street, Tel Aviv 63405
Telephone: (00) (972) (3) 7251222
Facsimile: (00) (972) (3) 524 3313 Commercial
                527 1572 Chancery
                527 8574 Management
                510 1167 Consular
Office Hours (GMT): Mon - Thur 06 00 - 14 00
Fri 06 00 - 11 30 (Sept-Mar)
Mon - Thur 07 00 - 15 00
Fri 07 00 - 12 30 (April-Aug)
Ambassador: Mr Sherard Cowper-Coles, CMG LVO
(tel 7251245)
*Counsellor, Consul-General and Deputy Head of
Mission:* Mr Peter L Carter (7251246)
Counsellor: Mr Andrew Gibbs (7251261)
Defence and Military Attaché:
Colonel Tom M Fitzalan Howard, OBE (7251256)
Naval and Air Attaché:
Wing Commander Stephen Cummings RAF
(7251257)
Cultural Attaché (British Council Director):
Mr Kevin Lewis
First Secretary (Commercial): Mr Ian Morrison
(7251231)
First Secretary (Chancery): Mr Neil Wigan
(7251248)
First Secretary (Management): Mr Rick Lee
(7251260)
Second Secretary and Consul: Mr Michael
Hancock (7251222)
Second Secretary (Chancery): Mr Tim Smart
(7251266)
Second Secretary (Technical Management):
Mr Simon Gudgeon (7251265)
Assistant Cultural Attaché (British Council):
Mr Keith Lawrence
Third Secretary and Vice-Consul:
Mr Paul T Stokes (7251222)
Third Secretary (Chancery): Mr Mark Kelly
(7252219)

Tel Aviv
British Consulate-General
Migdalor Building (6th Floor)
1 Ben Yehuda Street, Tel Aviv 63801
Telephone: (00) (972) (3) 7251222
Facsimile: (00) (972) (3) 5101167
Office Hours (GMT): Mon - Thur 05 30 - 13 00
Fri 05 30 - 11 30 (Sept to Mar)
Mon - Thur 06 30 - 14 30
Fri 06 30 - 12 00 (Apr to Aug)
Consul-General: Mr Peter Carter
Consul: Mr Michael Hancock
Vice-Consul: Mr Paul T Stokes

Eilat
British Consulate
c/o Aqua Sport
Coral Beach
P.O. Box 300
Eilat 88102
Telephone: (00) (972) (7) 6326287
Honorary Consul: Mrs Dafna Budden

ITALY

Rome
British Embassy
Via XX Settembre 80a, 00187 Roma
Telephone: (00) (39) 06 4220 0001
06 478141 British Council
Facsimile: (00) (39) 06 487 3324 Information
                06 4220 2333 Chancery
                06 4890 4285, 4201 1507 E&C Dept
                06 4220 2335 Management
                06 4220 2334 Consular
                06 4220 2283 Defence
Airtech: 06 4220 2257
Website: www.UKinItalia.it
Office Hours (GMT): Sept-July: Mon-Fri 08 00 -
16 00
Aug: Mon-Fri 08 00 - 14 00
Ambassador: Sir John Shepherd, KCVO, CMG
Deputy Head of Mission and Minister:
Mr Scott Wightman
Defence and Military Attaché:
Brigadier Allan L Mallinson
Naval Attaché: Captain John Hollidge, RN
Air Attaché: Group Captain David H White, RAF
Counsellor (Political): Mr Adrian M Fulcher
Counsellor (Economic & Commercial):
Mr Martin A Hatfull
Counsellor (British Council Director):
Mr Richard H Alford, OBE
First Secretary (Political, Press & Public Affairs):
Mr Andrew Jackson
First Secretary (Economic): Mr James Bryce
First Secretary (Management):
Mr Peter J Phelan, OBE
First Secretary (Agriculture & Environment):
Mr James P Howie
*First Secretary (Social /Science &Technology
Affairs):* Mr Robert L Embleton
First Secretary (Consul): Mr Alan J Mayland
First Secretary (Political): Mr Andrew Whiteside
First Secretary (Political): Mr Nicholas D Hopton
Second Secretary (Political): Mr Peter A Rudge
Second Secretary (Management):
Mr David P Goodall
Second Secretary (Energy/Commercial):
Mr John R Thurlow
Second Secretary: Mr Graham J Dempsey
Second Secretary: Mr Simon Grunwell
Third Secretary: Mr Alexander E Madisons
Third Secretary (Political):
Miss Emma C Lockwood, MVO
Third Secretary (Vice-Consul):
Miss Deborah M Williams
Vice-Consul: Mrs Angela T Sweeney, MBE

**Rome   United Kingdom Representation to the
United Nations Food and Agriculture Agencies
in Rome, see Missions & Delegations**

Florence
British Consulate
Lungarno Corsini 2,
50123 Florence
Telephone: (00) (39) 055 284133 (including
Airtech)   (00) (39) 055 289556 (Commercial)
Facsimile: (00) (39) 055 219112

e-mail: Consular.Florence@fco.gov.uk
Commercial.Florence@fco.gov.uk
Office Hours (GMT): Apr-Oct 07 00 - 11 00 and
12 00 - 15 00
Nov-Mar 08 00 - 12 00 and 13 00 - 16 00
*Consul (also Consul-General for the Republic of
San Marino):* Mrs Moira A Macfarlane
Vice-Consul: Ms Jane H de C Ireland, MBE
Pro-Consul: Ms Diane L Johnson

Milan (SP)
British Consulate-General
Via San Paolo 7, 20121 Milan
Telephone: (00) (39) 02 723001
Facsimile: (00) (39) 02 72020153 Commercial
86465081 Consular and Management
8692405 Information
(Visa and Passport work is centralized in Rome)
Office Hours (GMT): Apr – Oct 07 00 - 11 00 and
12 00 - 15 00
Nov – Mar 08 00 - 12 00 and 13 00 - 16 00
*Director General for British Trade Development in
Italy and Consul-General:*
Mr Richard J Northern, MBE
Deputy Consul-General and Consul (Commercial):
Mr Brendan Doyle
Consul (Consular/Management): Mr Alan Reuter
Consul (Commercial/Press/PR): Mr Ian Shand, LVO
Vice-Consul: Mrs Elizabeth Crosley
Pro-Consul: Mrs Julia Billingsley

Genoa
British Consulate
c/o Coeclerici Armatori S.p.A
Via di Francia, 28 16149 Genoa
Telephone: (00) (39) 010 416828
Facsimile: (00) (39) 010 416958
Office Hours (GMT): Apr-Oct: Mon - Thur 07 30 –
10 30
Nov-Mar: Mon - Thur 08 30 – 11 30
Honorary Consul: Mr Alexander Edmonds

Turin
British Consulate
The British Council, Via Saluzzo, 60 10125 Turin
Telephone: (00) (39) 011 6509202
Facsimile: (00) (39) 011 6695982
e-mail: bcturin@yahoo.com
Office Hours (GMT): Apr - Oct Mon & Thur: 07
00 - 10 00
Nov - Mar Mon & Thur: 08 00 - 11 00
Honorary Consul: Mr Tim R Priesack

Venice
British Consulate
Accademia, Dorsoduro, 1051,
30123 Venice
Telephone: (00) (39) 041 5227207
Facsimile: (00) (39) 041 5222617
e-mail: britconvenice@tin.it
Office Hours (GMT): Apr-Oct Mon – Fri 08 00 –
11 00
Nov-Mar Mon – Fri 09 00 – 12 00
Honorary Consul: Mr Ivor N Coward
Pro-Consul: Mrs Lita Santin

Trieste
British Consulate
Via Dante Alighieri, 7
34122 Trieste
Telephone: (00) (39) 040 3478303
Facsimile: (00) (39) 040 3478311
Office Hours (GMT): Tue 10 00 - 12 00 and Fri 14
30 - 16 30
Honorary Consul: Prof. John Dodds

Cagliari
British Consulate
Viale Colombo,160 Quartu S.E.
09045 Cagliari
Telephone: (00) (39) 070 813412
Facsimile: (00) (39) 070 862293
Honorary Consul: Mr Andrew Graham, MBE

Naples
British Consulate
Via dei Mille 40, 80121 Naples
UK Postal Address: Consulate, BFPO 8 London
Telephone: (00) (39) (081) 423 8911
Facsimile: (00) (39) (081) 422 434
422 419 (Commercial Section)
e-mail: info.naples@fco.gov.uk
Office Hours (GMT): Summer: 07 00 - 13 00
Winter: 08 00 - 12 00 and 13 00 - 16 00
Consul: Mr Michael Burgoyne, MBE
Commercial Officer: Mr Giuseppe Saraceno
Political &Public Diplomacy: Mr Gerardo Kaiser
Vice Consul: Mr Brian McKeever

Bari
British Consulate
David H Gavan and Sons Shipping SrL,
Via Dalmazia 127, 70121 Bari
Telephone: (00) (39) (080) 554 3668
Facsimile: (00) (39) (080) 554 2977
e-mail: davidhg@tin.it
Honorary Consul: Mr David Gavan, MBE

Catania
British Consulate
Via G Verdi 53,
95129 Catania
Telephone: (00) (39) 095 715 1864
Facsimile: (00) (39) 095 715 1503
e-mail: british@tau.it
Honorary Consul: Mr Richard Brown

Brindisi
British Consulate
Temporarily Closed – Refer To Naples
Honorary Consul: (Vacant)

Palermo
British Consulate
S Tagliavia & Co, Via Cavour 117,
90133 Palermo
Telephone: (00) (39) 091 326412
Facsimile: (00) (39) 091 584240
e-mail: luigi@tagliavia.it
Honorary Consul: Mr Luigi Tagliavia

JAMAICA

Kingston

British High Commission
PO Box 575, Trafalgar Road, Kingston 10
Telephone: (001) (876) 510 0700
Telegrams: UKREPKIN JA
Facsimile: (001) (876) 510 0737
          (Management/Commercial)
          511 5303 (Chancery)
          510 0738 (Immigration/Consular)
Airtech: (00) (1) (876) 510 0711
e-mail: bhckingston@cwjamaica.com
bhckingstone@mail.infochan.com
Office Hours (GMT): Mon - Thu: 13 00 - 18 00
and 19 00 - 21 30
Fri: 13 00 - 18 00
High Commissioner: Mr Peter J Mathers, LVO
Deputy High Commissioner: Mr Phil Sinkinson
Defence Adviser: Colonel Rob A Hyde-Bales
First Secretary (Management): Mr Roger Patten
First Secretary (Chancery): Mr Malcolm Bragg
Second Secretary (Chancery): Mr Keith A Wiggins
Second Secretary (Chancery): Mr Stewart Lister
Second Secretary (Chancery): Mr Tony Ridout
Second Secretary (Chancery): Mr Gavin Tench
Second Secretary (Development):
Mr Gordan Saggers
Second Secretary (Immigration/Consular):
Mr Mike Goodwin
*Third Secretary (Chancery/Press and Public
Affairs):* Ms Mags Fenner
Third Secretary (Immigration): Mr Andrew Fennell
Third Secretary (Immigration): Miss Tina Harrup
Third Secretary (DSS): Mr Wiseman

Montego Bay

Telephone/Facsimile: (00) (1) (876) 912 9117
(Home) (00) (1) (876) 999 9693 (Office Hours)
Honorary Consul: Mr John Terry

JAPAN

Tokyo

British Embassy
No 1 Ichiban-cho, Chiyoda-ku, Tokyo 102-8381
Telephone: (00) (81) (3) 5211-1100
Facsimile: (00) (81) (3) 5275-3164 (All sections
except those listed below)
          5211-1111 (Ambassador's Office)
          5211-1345 (Minister's Office)
          5211-1270 (Energy Section)
          3265-5580 (Commercial Section)
          5275-0346 (Consular & Visa Section)
          5211-1254 (Defence Section)
          5211-1121 (Financial Section)
          5211-1344 (Political Section)
          3230-0624 (Press & Public Affairs)
          3230-4800 (Science & Technology
          Section)
Office Hours (GMT): 00.00 – 03.30/05.00 – 08.30
e-mail:
General Enquiries
embassy.tokyo@fco.gov.uk
Consular and Visa Section
c&vsection.tokyo@fco.gov.uk
Commercial Section

commercial-section.tokyo@fco.gov.uk
Defence Section
defence.tokyo@fco.gov.uk
Energy Section
energy.tokyo@fco.gov.uk
Inward Investment Section
investukjapan.tokyo@fco.gov.uk
Management Section
management.tokyo@fco.gov.uk
Political Section
political.tokyo@fco.gov.uk
Press and Public Affairs Section
ppas.tokyo@fco.gov.uk
Trade Policy Section
trade-policy.tokyo@fco.gov.uk
Science and Technology Section
science.tokyo@fco.gov.uk
Embassy Website: www.uknow.or.jp
Airtech: 5211-1266
Ambassador: Sir Stephen J Gomersall, KCMG
Minister: Mr Stuart Jack, CVO
Defence Attaché: Captain Jim A Boyd, RN
Counsellor (Political Affairs):
Mr Patrick W Sprunt
Counsellor (Management) & Consul-General:
Mr Robin R Hoggard
*Counsellor (Cultural and Director, British
Council):* Mr Terry Toney
Counsellor (Science & Technology):
Dr Mike G Norton
Counsellor (Financial): Mr Peter Green
Counsellor (Energy): Mr Bob Rayner
Counsellor (Political): Mr Colin Roberts
Counsellor (Commercial): Ms Jane Owen
*Counsellor (Trade Policy)/Director, Inward
Investment:* Mr Alastar Morgan
First Secretary (Political): Mr Chris Trott
First Secretary (Press & Public Affairs):
Mrs Sue Kinoshita
First Secretary (Commercial): Mrs Karen Stanton
First Secretary (Inward Investment):
Mr Richard C B Jones
First Secretary (Deputy Director, British Council):
Mr Mike Winter
First Secretary (Science & Technology):
Mr Brian Ferrar
First Secretary (Trade Policy): Mr Tom Goodwin
First Secretary (Science & Technology):
Ms Philippa Rogers
First Secretary (Commercial):
Mrs Camilla Roberts
First Secretary & Consul: Mr Alan Sutton
First Secretary (Management): Ms Gill Lever
Second Secretary (Political): Ms Mara Myers
Second Secretary (Commercial):
Ms Marie-Claire Joyce
Second Secretary (Political): Mr Simon N Brown
Second Secretary (Global Policy): Dr John Murton
Second Secretary (Financial): Mr Andrew King
Second Secretary (Political): Mr Gary Leslie
Second Secretary (Commercial): Mr Simon Wood
Second Secretary (Technical Management):
Mr Robin South
Third Secretary & Vice Consul: Mr Iain Ferguson
Third Secretary & Vice Consul:
Mrs Katherine Hickey

Third Secretary (Political): Ms Lisanne Heaslip
Third Secretary (Press and Public Affairs):
Mr Clare Allbless
Third Secretary (PS to Ambassador):
Mrs Sarah Murton
Third Secretary (Management): Mr Shaun Clarke

British Consulate-General
No 1 Ichibancho, Chiyoda-ku Tokyo 102-8381
Telephone: (00) (81) (3) 5211-1100
Facsimile: (00) (81) (3) 5275-0346
Office Hours (GMT): 00:00 - 03:30/05:00 - 08:30
Consul-General: Mr Robin R Hoggard
Consul: Mr Alan Sutton
Vice-Consul: Mr Iain Ferguson
Vice-Consul: Mrs Katherine Hickey

British Council:
2 Kagurazaka 1-chome Shinjyuku-ku Tokyo 162-8381
Telephone: (00) (81) (3) 3235-8031
Facsimile: (00) (81) (3) 3235-8040
e-mail: bctokyo@britishcouncil.or.jp
Website: www.uknow.or.jp
Office Hours (GMT): Monday-Friday 0000-0800
Director: Mr Terry Toney
Assistant Director: Mr Mike Winter

Sapporo
British Consulate
c/o Sapporo Nissan Motor Co Ltd
17-1-23 O-dori Nishi Chuo-ku
Sapporo-shi, Hokkaido 060-0042
Telephone: (00) (81) (11) 613 1123
Facsimile: (00) (81) (11) 613 4210
Office Hours (GMT): 0000-0820
Honorary Consul: Mr Y Kaneko

Osaka
British Consulate-General
Seiko Osaka Building, 19F, 3-5-1 Bakuro-machi,
Chuo-ku, Osaka 541-0059
Telephone: (00) (81) (6) 6120 5600
Consular enquiries (00) (81) (6) 6120 5601
Facsimile: (00) (81) (6) 6281 1731
e-mail: bcgosaka@gol.com
Consul-General & Director of Trade Promotion:
Mr N K Hook, MVO
Deputy Consul General and Consul, Inward Investment: Mr D Smith
Consul (Commercial): Mr D Chapman
Consul: Ms D Lloyd

Nagoya
British Consulate
Nishiki Park Building 17F
2-4-3 Nishiki, Naka-ku
Nagoya 460-0003, Japan
Telephone: (00) (81) (52) 223 5031
Facsimile: (00) (81) (52) 223 5035
Consul: Mr S Wooten

Fukuoka
Honorary British Consulate
c/o The Nishi-Nippon Bank Ltd,
1-3-6 Hakata-Ekimae,
Hakata-ku, Fukuoka City
Telephone: (00) (81) (92) 476-2154

Facsimile: (00) (81) (92) 476-2619
Office Hours (GMT): Mon - to Fri 03 00 - 07 00
Honorary Consul: Mr S Koga

British Trade Promotion Office
Hakata Riverain 11F
3-1 Shimokawabatamachi
Hakata-ku
Fukuoka 817-0027
Telephone: (00) (81) (92) 262 0405
Facsimile: (00) (81) (92) 262 0374
Office Hours (GMT): Mon - to Fri 03 00 - 07 00
Head of British Trade Promotion Office:
Mr R Cowin
Commercial and Inward Investment Assistant:
Mr K Fujii

Hiroshima
British Consulate
c/o Hiroshima Bank Ltd, 3-8,
1-Chome Kamiyacho,
Naka-ku, Hiroshima
Telephone: (00) (81) (82) 247 5151
Facsimile: (00) (81) (82) 240-5759
Honorary Consul: Mr O Hashiguchi

JERUSALEM

Jerusalem
British Consulate-General
19 Nashashibi Street, Sheikh Jarrah Quarter,
PO Box 19690 East Jerusalem, 97200
Telephone: (00) (972) (2) 541 4100 (Chancery,
Commercial, Information, Management and Visa)
(2) 671 7724 (Consular)
(2) 532 8459/540 0451 (Development)
(2) 626 4392 (British Council)
Facsimile: (00) (972) (2) 532 5629 (Chancery)
(2) 532 2368 (Management and
Commercial)
(2) 672 9820 (Consular)
(2) 628 3021 (British Council)
(2) 541 4157 (Visa)
e-mail: britain@palnet.com
Website: http://www.britishconsulate.org
Office Hours (GMT): Sept - Mar: Mon – Thurs
05 30 – 13 30 and Fri 05 30 – 11 30
Apr - Sept: Mon – Thurs 06 30 – 14 30 and Fri
06 30 – 12 30
Consul-General: Mr Geoffrey Adams
Deputy Consul General:
Mrs Valerie Brownridge, MVO (541 4108)
Consul (Political): Mr Tom Hurd (541 4103)
Consul (Political): Mr Andrew Whittaker
(541 4109)
Vice-Consul (Management):
Mrs Angela Mackenzie (541 4130)
Vice-Consul (Consular/Immigration):
Ms Dawn Naughton (541 4129)
Vice-Consul (Political): Mr Rob Carrick
(541 4115)
Vice-Consul (Political): Mr Jayd Davies
(541 4119)
Vice-Consul (Political): Ms Lucy Rashbrook
(541 4133)
Vice-Consul (Development): Mr Peter Cardy
(532 8459)

Attaché: Miss J McGregor (541 4112)
Attaché: Miss Jane Farrar (541 4105)
Cultural Attaché (British Council Director):
Ms Sarah Ewans (626 4392)
Assistant Cultural Attaché (British Council Deputy Director): Mr D Codling (626 4392)

West Jerusalem:
British Consulate-General
Tower House,
Kikar Remez, Jerusalem 93541
Telephone: (00) (972) (2) 6717724
Facsimile: (00) (972) (2) 6729820
e-mail: britain2@palnet.com
Office Hours (GMT): Sept - Mar: Mon - Fri 07 00
- 10 00
Apr - Sept: Mon - Fri 08 00 - 11 00

Gaza:
British Information and Services Office
1st Floor, Al-Riyad Tower,
Jerusalem Street,
Al-Rimal South, Gaza
Telephone: (00 972 0) 8 283 7704/14/24
Facsimile: (00 972 0) 8 283 7734
e-mail: bisogaza@palnet.com
Office Hours (GMT) Sept - Mar: Sun – Wed 05 30
– 13 30, Thurs 05 30 – 11 30
Apr - Sept: Sun – Wed 06 30 – 14 30, Thurs 06 30
– 11 30

JORDAN

Amman
British Embassy
(PO Box 87) Abdoun, 11118 Amman
Telephone: (00) (962) (6) 5923100
Facsimile: (00) (962) (6) 5923759
Telex: 22209 (a/b 22209 PRODRUM JO)
e-mail: becommercial@nets.com.jo (commercial)
Website: www.britain.org.jo (Information)
Office Hours (GMT): Sun - Mon 06 00 - 13 30
Tue - Thur 06 00 - 13 00
Ambassador: Mr C N R Prentice
Counsellor, Consul-General and Deputy Head of Mission: Mr M D Aron
Counsellor: Mr R H Williams
Defence, Naval and Military Attaché:
Colonel C R Romberg
Air Attaché: Wing Commander S J Orwell, RAF
First Secretary (Chancery): Mr J Goodman
Consul and First Secretary (Management):
Mr R K Dixon
First Secretary (Commercial): Mrs D A Dixon
Second Secretary (Political/Economic/Development): Ms J Chappell
Second Secretary (Political): Miss V J Helmer
Third Secretary (Political): Mr J Layfield
Third Secretary: Mr L Fennell
Entry Clearance Officer: Ms J Singleton
Vice-Consul: Mrs N Humphreys
Assistant Management Officer: Ms J Evans
Accountant: Mrs S El Ouassi

KAZAKHSTAN

Almaty
British Embassy
U1 Furmanova 173, Almaty,
Republic of Kazakhstan
Telephone: (00) (73272) 506191, 506192, 506229
Facsimile: (00) (73272) 506260
Opening hours (GMT): winter 0300-10 00
summer Monday to Friday 0200-1030
e-mail: british-embassy@kaznet.kz
Visa/Consular Section
158 Panfilova Street, Almaty
Telephone: (00) (73272) 508280
Facsimile: (00) (73272) 507432
e-mail: visa-british-embassy@nursat.kz
Opening Hours: Mon-Fri 08.30 – 11.00
Ambassador: Mr J L Sharp
Defence Attaché:
Lieutenant Colonel G J Sheeley, AFC
Cultural Attaché (British Council Director):
Mr J Kennedy
Deputy Head of Mission: Mr A Dinsley
British Council Deputy Director: Mr J Gore
Second Secretary (Commercial): Ms J Stevens
Third Secretary and Vice-Consul: Mr P Edwards
Third Secretary (Political/Aid): Mr M Waller
Management Officer: Mr S M Brown
Defence Assistant: Mr M Headley

KENYA

Nairobi
British High Commission
Upper Hill Road, Nairobi, PO Box 30465, Nairobi
Commercial Department: PO Box 30133, Nairobi
Consular Department: PO Box 48543, Nairobi
Telephone: (00) (254) (2) 714699 (15 Lines)
Facsimile: (00) (254) (2) 719942 Consular
       714760 Chancery
       719082 Commercial
       719664 UK Permanent Mission to
       UNEP and UNCHS HABITAT
       719486 Management
       719112 DFID EA
       719110 Visa
Airtech: 719107 Chancery
e-mail: consular@nairobi.mail.fco.gov.uk
(Consular)
visa@nairobi.mail.fco.gov.uk (Visa)
commercial@nairobi.mail.fco.gov.uk
(Commercial)
information@nairobi.mail.fco.gov.uk (Press & Public Affairs)
management@nairobi.mail.fco.gov.uk
(Management)
Office Hours (GMT): Mon - Thur 07 45 - 12 30
and 13 30 - 16 30
Fri 07 45- 13 00
High Commissioner: Mr E Clay, CMG
Deputy High Commissioner: Mr C P D Harvey
Counsellor: Mr I P Simmons
Defence Adviser: Colonel J R Barnes
First Secretary (Commercial): Mr J Chandler
First Secretary (Political): Mr H Evans
First Secretary (Management): Mrs S Gregory

First Secretary (United Nations): Mr J P T Bell
First Secretary (Consular): Mr D C Levoir
First Secretary (Development): Mr D Bell
First Secretary: Mr M Denton
Second Secretary (Political/Economic):
Mr T Fletcher
Second Secretary (Immigration/ECM):
Miss J Montgomery-Ribbon
Second Secretary (Chancery): Miss J D Miles, MBE
Second Secretary (Commercial): Mr C D R Smart
Second Secretary (Development): Mr A Reid
Second Secretary (Works): Mr D J Gillies
Second Secretary: Mr T Bilimoria
Second Secretary (Management): Mr S Burns
Second Secretary: Mr K Knight
Third Secretary: Mr T Oxley
Third Secretary (Information/Press):
Mr R J Drabble
Third Secretary (Communications): Mr J Mortimer
Third Secretary (Communications):
Mr S M Grinling
Third Secretary (Management/Accounts):
Mr R Mardlin
Third Secretary (Immigration): Mr S Groves
Third Secretary (Immigration): Mr J Lambert
Third Secretary (Immigration): Mr M C Gregory

**Department for International Development
Eastern Africa**
c/o British High Commission
Upper Hill Rd
PO Box 30465, Nairobi
Telephone: (00) (254) (2) 717609 (15 lines)
Facsimile: (00) (254) (2) 719112
Office Hours (GMT): Mon – Thur: 07 45 - 12 30
and 13 30 - 16 30
Fri: 07 45 - 13 00
Head of Development Division: Mr Matthew Wyatt
First Secretary/Senior Education Adviser:
Mr A Penny
First Secretary/Senior Natural Resources Adviser:
Mr M C Leach
*First Secretary/Development/Head of DFIDEA
Kenya:* Mr D Bell
First Secretary/Senior Engineering Adviser:
Mr A Smallwood
First Secretary/Senior Economist: Mr N Dyer
Second Secretary Personnel/Office Manager:
Mr G Dixon
Second Secretary/Development: Mr A Reid
Second Secretary/Health & Population Adviser:
Ms M C Donagh
*Second Secretary/Senior Social Development
Adviser:* Dr R Hogg
Second Secretary/Governance Adviser:
Ms K de Jong
Third Secretary/ IT Manager: Mr A Galbraith
Senior Programme Officer, Kenya:
Ms T Bebbington, MBE
Assistant Office Manager: Ms N Gateru
Assistant Engineering Adviser: Mr L Simon
Regional IT Systems Supervisor: Mr I Rivers
IT Systems Manager, Kenya: Mr J Nyoike
Enterprise Development Adviser: Ms C Masinde
Small Grants Scheme Co-ordinator: Ms S Harley
Training Liaison Officer: Ms A Dearing

Special Projects: Mrs S Unsworth

**Nairobi United Kingdom for Human
Settlements (Habitat), see Missions &
Delegations**

**Nairobi United Nations Environment
Programme, see Missions & Delegations**

Mombasa
Honorary British Consular Representative
Cotts House (First Floor)
Moi Avenue
PO Box 85593, Mombasa
Telephone: (00) (254) (11) 313609
Facsimile: (00) (254) (11) 312416
e-mail: seaforth@africaonline.co.ke
Honorary British Consular Representative:
Mr J W L Knight
*Assistant British Honorary Consular
Representative:* Mr J Attenborough

Assistant Honorary Consular Representative in
Mombasa
c/o Mission to Seamen,
Mogadishu Road,
PO Box 80424, Mombasa
Telephone: (00) (254) (11) 230027/8, 316502/3,
316486, 316285
Facsimile: (00) (254) (11) 230001

KIRIBATI (REPUBLIC OF)

Tarawa
British High Commission Office
PO Box 5
Bairiki
Tarawa, Kiribati
Telephone: (00) (686) 22501
Facsimile: (00) (686) 22505
e-mail: ukrep@tskl.net.ki
Britainkiribati@tskl.net.ki
Office Hours (GMT): Sun-Wed 20 15 – 01 00 and
02 00 – 05 00, Thur 20 15 – 01 00
*High Commissioner: Mr Charles F Mochan
*Deputy High Commissioner:
Mr Christopher Haslam
Resident Deputy High Commissioner:
Mr Vernon Scarborough
*Resides at Suva

**KOREA (THE DEMOCRATIC PEOPLE'S
REPUBLIC OF)**

Pyongyang
British Embassy
Munsu Dong
Pyongyang
Democratic People's Republic of Korea
Telephone: (International): (00) (850) 2 381 7980-4
(5 lines)
Facsimile: (International): (00) (850) 2 381 7985
Telephone: (Within DPRK): 382 7980-2 (3 lines)
Facsimile: (Within DPRK): 382 7983
Chargé d'Affaires and Consul-General:
Dr J E (Jim) Hoare
First Secretary: Mr John Dunne
Management Officer and Consul: Mr Jim Warren

KOREA (REPUBLIC OF)

Seoul
British Embassy
Taepyeongno 40
4 Jeong-dong, Jung-gu
Seoul 100-120
Republic of Korea
Telephone: (00) (82) (2) 3210 5500
Facsimile: (00) (82) (2) 725 1738
        722 7270 (Airtech)
        736 6241 Commercial Section
        3210 5653 Consular Section
        3210 5528 Defence Section
        733 8368 Defence Supplies
        738 2797 Economic Section and
        Science/Technology/Environment
        Section
        735 7473 Political Section
        720 4928 Press and Public Affairs
        Section
        736 3174 Residence
e-mail: bembassy@britain.or.k
postmaster.seoul@fco.gov.uk
Website: www.britain.or.kr
Office Hours (GMT): Mon - Fri 00 00 - 08 30
Ambassador: (5510/5511):
Mr Charles Humfrey, CMG
Deputy Head of Mission and Consul General:
(5517): Mr Christopher Robbins
Counsellor (Regional Affairs): (5535):
Mr Colin Partridge
Counsellor and British Council Director: (3702
0600 ext 0677): Mr Mark Baumfield
Defence and Military Attaché: (5524):
Brigadier John C L King, MBE
Naval and Air Attaché: (5525):
Group Captain Colin R C Greaves, OBE, RAF
First Secretary (Defence Supplies): (5520):
Mr David Bullas
First Secretary (Science/Technology/Environment):
(5590): Dr Jim Thomson
First Secretary (Political): (5530):
Dr Antony Stokes
First Secretary (Commercial): (5620):
Mr David Brown
First Secretary (Management and Consul): (5655):
Mr Mike Hentley
First Secretary (Education/British Council Deputy
Director): Mr Brendan Barker
Second Secretary (Political/Public Affairs): (5560):
Mr Adrian Chapman
Second Secretary (Investment): (5610):
Mr Jonathan Dart
Second Secretary (Political): (5531):
Mr Chris Gotch
Second Secretary (Economic): (5600):
Mr Guy Harrison
Second Secretary (Commercial): (5621):
Ms Jacqueline Mullen
Second Secretary (Regional Affairs):
Mr Michael Richardson
Assistant Cultural Attaché (British Council):
Mr Fred O'Hanlon
Second Secretary (Technical Works Office) (resides
at Tokyo): Mr John Warrener

Second Secretary (Management/Consular):
(5560/5656): Mr Colin Gracey
Third Secretary (Technical Management Officer)
(resides Tokyo): Mr Hugh Smith
Attaché (language training): Mr Phil Ellis
Attaché (language training): Mr Chris Sims

Pusan
Honorary Consul's Office
12th Floor
Yuchang Building, 25-2,
Chungang-Dong, 4 -Ga
Chung-Gu,
Pusan, 600-014
PO Box No 75
Telephone: (00) (82) (051) 463 0041 and 463 4630
Facsimile: (00) (82) (051) 462 5933
Honorary Consul: Mr S E Wang, CBE
Honorary Vice-Consul: Mr H Guack

KUWAIT

British Embassy
Arabian Gulf Street
Postal Address: PO Box 2, Safat, 13001 Kuwait,
Commercial Section Address: PO Box 300, Safat,
13003, Kuwait
Telephone: (00) (965) 240 3334/5/6
Facsimile: 240 7395 Commercial
        242 6799 Chancery/Defence
        242 5778 Consular/Visa
        240 7633 Management
e-mail: general@britishembassy-kuwait.org
Office Hours (GMT): Sat - Wed: 04 30 - 11 30
Ambassador: Mr Christopher E J Wilton
Counsellor and Deputy Head of Mission:
Mr Robin Lamb
Defence Attaché: Colonel Steve Thomas
First Secretary (Political): Mr Alexander Creswell
First Secretary (Management) and Consul:
Mr John Francis
First Secretary (Commercial): Mr Bernard Wilson
First Secretary (Defence Supply): Mr Keith Harper
First Secretary (British Council): Mr John Gildea
Second Secretary (Political/Press & Public
Affairs): Mr Mark Ellam
Third Secretary (Commercial): Mr Yemi Odanye
Vice-Consul and Third Secretary (Management):
Mr Neil Frape
Third Secretary: Mr Kurt Sutherland
Third Secretary: Mr Bernard Ley

KYRGYZSTAN

Bishkek
British Embassy
Ambassador (resides at Almaty): Mr J L Sharp
Defence Attaché (resides at Almaty):
Lieutenant Colonel G J Sheeley, AFC
Cultural Attaché (resides at Almaty):
Ms L Cowcher
Deputy Head of Mission (resides at Almaty):
Mr A Dinsley
Second Secretary (Commercial) (resides at
Almaty): Ms J Stevens
Third Secretary (Political/Aid) (resides at Almaty):
Mr M Waller

Third Secretary and Vice-Consul (resides at Almaty): Mr P Edwards

British Consulate
Tacis Banking Project Office
195A Abdimumonova St
Bishkek
Republic of Kyrgyzstan
Telephone: (00) (7 3312) 660869
Facsimile: (00) (7 3312) 660869
Honorary Consul: Mr L Johnson

LAOS

Vientiane
British Embassy
(All staff reside at Bangkok)
PO Box 6626, Vientiane, Laos, PDR
Telephone: (00) (856) (21) 413606
Facsimile: (00) (856) (21) 413607
Ambassador: Mr L B Smith, CMG
Counsellor: Mr P B West
Counsellor (Commercial): Mr D Wyatt
First Secretary (Political): Mr T C Carter
Consul and First Secretary (Management):
Mr D J Fisher
First Secretary: Mr J Hector
Second Secretary (Immigration):
Mrs J F Lacey-Smith
Third Secretary: Mr P McKenzie

British Trade Office
Office Hours (GMT): Mon – Fri 0100 – 0500 and
0600 – 0930
Head of British Trade Office: Dr R Cooper

LATVIA

Riga (SP)
British Embassy
5 J. Alunana iela,, Riga,
LV 1010, Latvia
Telephone: (00) (371) 777 4700
Facsimile: (00) (371) 777 4707
           Chancery/Commercial/Information
           777 4724 Management/Consular
Airtech: (00) (371) 777 4741
e-mail: british.embassy@apollo.lv
Website: www.britain.lv
Office Hours (GMT): 07 00 - 11 00 and 12 00 -
15 00
Ambassador: Mr H A P Tesoriere
Deputy Head of Mission and Consul:
Mr Nick Carter
Defence Attaché:
Lieutenant Colonel Andrew S Tuggey
First Secretary (British Council Director):
Mr Chris Edwords
First Secretary (resides in Vilnius):
Mr Martin Thursfield
Second Secretary (Commercial): Mrs Jean Quinn
Third Secretary: Ms H Teasdale
*Third Secretary/Vice-Consul and Management
Officer:* Vacant
Third Secretary (resides in Helsinki):
Mr Paul Jackson
Attaché: Mr Garth Robinson

Attaché: FS Joe Stansfield
Technical Works Officer: Mr Andrew Moore

LEBANON

Beirut
British Embassy
Serail Hill
Beirut Centre-Ville
PO Box 11-471 Beirut, Lebanon
Telephone: (00) (961) (1) 990400
(00) (961) (4) 417007 (24 hrs)
Facsimile: (00) (961) (1) 990420
Mobile: (00) (961) (3) 412448
e-mail: britemb@cyberia.net.lb
Website: www.britishembassy.org.lb
Office Hours (GMT): Mon-Thurs: 06 30 – 15 15
and Fri: 06 30 – 11 30
Ambassador: Mr Richard Kinchen
Deputy Head of Mission: Mr Adrian Bedford
Defence Attaché: Lieutenant Colonel Desmond J A
Bergin, OBE
*First Secretary (Education Culture) (British
Council Director):* Mr Kenneth Churchill, MBE
Second Secretary (Commercial):
Ms Karen Williams
Second Secretary (Management):
Miss Denise Davey
Second Secretary (Chancery) (resides in Nicosia):
Mr Mick Bispham
Vice-Consul: Miss Nicolette Smith
Third Secretary (Chancery): Mr Darren James
Attaché: Ms Cathy Dennis
Honorary Consul (Mount Lebanon):
Mr William Zard, MBE

Tripoli
British Consulate
Daar Al Ain, Tripoli
Telephone: (00) (961) (6) 621320
Honorary Consul: Mr Anwar Arida, MBE

LESOTHO

Maseru
British High Commission
PO Box 521 Maseru 100
Telephone: (+) (266) 22313961
Facsimile: (+) (266) 22310120
Airtech: (+) (266) 22310387
e-mail: hcmaseru@lesoff.co.za
Website: www.bhc.org.ls
Office Hours (GMT): Mon - Thur 06 00 - 11.00,
11 45 - 14 30; Fri 06 00-11.00
High Commissioner: Mr Frank Martin
Deputy High Commissioner: Mr Mark Watchorn
Defence Adviser (Resides at Pretoria):
Brigadier M R Raworth
Third Secretary (Consular/Management):
Mr Andrew Osborn

LIBERIA

Monrovia
British Embassy
(All staff resident at Abidjan)
Ambassador: Mr J F Gordon, CMG

Second Secretary (Political/ Information):
Ms K Miller, MBE
Second Secretary (Management): Mr D Summers
Second Secretary (Commercial/Political):
Mr C Frean
Third Secretary (Visa and Passports) and Vice Consul: Mr M McGuinness
Third Secretary (Chancery): Ms N McBratney

Office of the Honorary British Consul
UMARCO (Liberia) Corp.
UN Drive, Bushrod Island
PO Box 10-1196
Monrovia, Liberia
Telephone: (00) (231) 22 60 56
Facsimile: (00) (231) 22 60 61
Office Hours: 08 00 - 16 00 Mon – Fri
Honorary British Consul: Mr E R Chalkley

LIBYA

Tripoli
British Embassy
PO Box 4206,
Tripoli, Libya
Telephone: (00) (218) (21) 340 3644/5 (Chancery)
335 1084 (Consular/Visa/Management)
Facsimile: (00) (218) (21) 340 3648 (Chancery)
335 1425 (Consular/Visa/Management)
Airtech: 340 3650
Office Hours (GMT): Sun - Thur: 07 00 - 14 00
Ambassador: Mr Anthony M Layden
Deputy Head of Mission and Consul General:
Dr Noel J Guckian, OBE
First Secretary (Management & Immigration):
Mr John W C Heffer
First Secretary (Commercial): Mr G P Glover
First Secretary (Education & British Council Director): Mr Tony D Jones
Second Secretary (Political): Ms Bridget Brind
Second Secretary (Commercial):
Ms Jacqueline Lawson-Smith
Third Secretary (Management) and Vice Consul:
Mr Steve Auld
Third Secretary (Immigration): Mr Jim Davidson
Third Secretary (Immigration):
Mr Gordon Summers
Attaché: Ms Lesley Brewer
Attaché: Ms Jill Mundy

LIECHTENSTEIN

Vaduz
Ambassador (resides at Berne):
Mr B S T Eastwood, CMG
Consul-General (resides at Berne):
Mr D G Roberts

LITHUANIA

Vilnius
British Embassy
2 Antakalnio, 2055 Vilnius
Telephone: (00) (370) 2 22 20 70, 2 22 70 71
Direct lines: (00) (370) 2 66 10 23 Ambassador
(00) (370) 2 66 10 17 Deputy Head of Mission
(00) (370) 2 66 10 13 First Secretary (Political)

(00) (370) 2 66 10 21 Third Secretary
(Political/Economic/Public Affairs
(00) (370) 2 66 10 15 Commercial Section
(00) (370) 2 66 10 19 Press/Public Affairs Section
(00) (370) 98 37 097 Duty Officer contact number
Facsimile: (00) (370) 2 72 75 79
Airtech: (00) (370) 2 66 10 20
Website www.britain.lt
Office Hours (GMT): Mon - Thur 0630 - 1000 and
1100 - 1500
Fridays 0630 - 1000 and 1100 - 1400
Ambassador: Mr Jeremy Hill
Deputy Head of Mission and Consul:
Mr Brian Davidson
Defence Attaché:
Lieutenant Colonel Peter R P Swanson, MBE
First Secretary (Political): Mr Martin Thursfield
First Secretary (British Council) (Resides at Riga):
Mr Chris Edwards
Third Secretary (Political): Mr David Buckley
Third Secretary (Political/Economic/Public Affairs): Mr Nicholas Collier
Third Secretary (Management) and Vice-Consul:
Mr Ryan Griffin
Assistant Defence Attaché: CPO(W) Paul Hutton
Attaché: Miss Judith Hitchings
MOD Attaché to Lithuanian Ministry of Defence:
Mr Graham Roberts

LUXEMBOURG

Luxembourg
British Embassy
14 Boulevard Roosevelt, L-2450 Luxembourg
Telephone: (00) (352) 22 98 64/65/66
Facsimile: (00) (352) 22 98 67 (Office)
(00) (352) 22 98 68 (Residence)
Airtech: (00) (352) 22 98 64 (Ext. 2231)
e-mail: britemb@pt.lu
Web Page: webplaza.pt.lu/public/britemb
Office Hours (GMT): Summer 07 00 - 11 00 and
12 00 - 15 00
Winter 08 00 - 12 00 and 13 00 - 16 00
Ambassador and Consul-General:
Mr Gordon Wetherell
Counsellor (Commercial) (resides at Brussels):
Mr Stephen Smith
First Secretary, Consul and Deputy Head of Mission: Mr David Herbert
Defence Attaché (Resides at Brussels):
Group Captain Jeff D Bullen, OBE, RAF
Cultural Attaché (British Council Director) (resides at Brussels): Mr Martin Rose
First Secretary (Labour) (resides at The Hague):
Mr Peter Drummond
First Secretary (Commercial) (resides at Brussels):
Mr Jim Curry
Third Secretary (Management) and Vice-Consul:
Mr Adam Perks

MACEDONIA

Skopje
British Embassy
Dimitrija Chupovski 26
4th Floor

Skopje 9100
Telephone: (00) (389) (2) 116 772, 109 941
Facsimile: (00) (389) (2) 117 555
e-mail: beskopje@mt.net.mk
Office Hours (GMT): Summer:- Mon-Thurs: 06 00
- 14 30; Fri till: 11 00
Winter:- Mon-Thurs: 07 00 - 15 30; Fri till: 12 00
Ambassador: Mr C G Edgar
Deputy Head of Mission: Mr R W Potter
Defence Attaché: Lieutenant Colonel S M Rees
First Secretary (KHF): Mrs R Mustard
First Secretary (Culture and Education):
Mr A Hudley
*Second Secretary (Management/Consular/
Chancery):* Mr R Contractor
Second Secretary (Political): Mrs H Bridge
Third Secretary (Management/Consular):
Mr J Mitchell

Bitola
Honorary British Consulate
Dobrovoje Radosavljevic No.3
Telephone: (00) (389) (47) 360 32 (Work)
(00) (389) (47) 254 945 (Home)
(00) (389) (47) 228 765 (British /Macedonian
Friendship Association)
Facsimile: (00) (389) (47) 222 080
Honorary Consul: Mrs Lijala Spirovska

MADAGASCAR

Antananarivo
British Embassy
Lot II 164 Ter,
Alarobia – Amboniloha, BP 167,
Antananarivo 101
Telephone: (00) (261) (20) 22 49378/79/80
Facsimile: (00) (261) (20) 22 49381
e-mail: ukembant@simicro.mg
Office Hours (GMT): Mon-Wed: 04 30 - 09 00 and
09 30 - 13 00
Thur-Fri: 04 30 - 10 00
Ambassador: Mr B Donaldson
Deputy Head of Mission: Ms D Partridge
Defence Attaché (resides at London):
Lieutenant Colonel G M Thomas, MBE
Commercial Officer: Mr Tsiry Wilkinson

Toamasina
British Consulate
Seal Tamatave
Telephone: (00) (261) (20) 5332548/5332569
Facsimile: (00) (261) (20) 5333937
e-mail: sealtmm@bow.dts.mg
Honorary Consul: Mr M Gonthier

MALAWI

Lilongwe
British High Commission
PO Box 30042, Lilongwe 3
Telephone: (00) (265) 1 772-400
Facsimile: (00) (265) 1 772-657
Airtech: (00) (265) 1 772-153
e-mail: bhclilongwe@fco.gov.uk
Office Hours (GMT): Mon - Thur 05 30 - 10 00
and 1130 - 14 30

Fri 05 30 - 10 30
High Commissioner: Mr Norman Ling
Defence Adviser (resides at Harare):
Colonel John S Field, CBE
First Secretary (Regional Medical Adviser):
Dr Howard Friend
Second Secretary (Management/Consular):
Mrs Julie Bell
*Second Secretary (Political/Press & Public
Affairs):* Mr Michael Nevin
Third Secretary (Consular/Commercial):
Mr Shaun Earl

**Department for International Development
(DFID) Malawi**
*Head of DFID (Malawi) and Deputy High
Commissioner:* Mr Michael Wood
Deputy Head of DFID (Malawi): Mr John Reid
Natural Resources Adviser: Dr Harry Potter
Health and Population Adviser: Ms Susan Mshana
Health and Population Adviser: Ms Anne Austen
Education Adviser: Mr Keith Gristock
Governance Adviser: (Vacant)
Infrastructure Adviser: Mr Jim Craigie
Infrastructure Adviser: Mr Joe Mumar
Economics Adviser: Mr Karl Livingstone
Social Development Adviser: Ms Andrea Cook
Social Development Adviser: Mr Peter Evans

MALAYSIA

Kuala Lumpur
British High Commission
185 Jalan Ampang, 50450 Kuala Lumpur,
or PO Box 11030, 50732 Kuala Lumpur
Telephone: (00) (60) (3) 2170 2200 Switchboard
2170 2 + officer's three digit extension number
FTN: (8) 611 2 + officer's three digit extension
number
Facsimile: (00) (60) (3) 2170 2370 Management
2170 2303 Political
2170 2285 Commercial
2170 2360 Consular
2170 2325 Public Diplomacy
2170 2309 Defence
Airtech: (00) (60) (3) 2170 2304
e-mail: political.kualalumpur@fco.gov.uk
(Political/Economic)
press.kualalumpur@fco.gov.uk
(Public Diplomacy)
information KULUM@fco.gov.uk
(Public Diplomacy – Internal)
scholarships.kl@fco.gov.uk
(Scholarships)
trade.kualalumpur@fco.gov.uk
(Commercial)
defence.kualalumpur@fco.gov.uk
(Defence)
consular.kualalumpur@fco.gov.uk
(Consular/Entry Clearance)
webmaster.kualalumpur@fco.gov.uk
(IT)
Website: www.britain.org.my
Office Hours (GMT): Mon - Fri 24 00 - 04 30 and
05 15 - 08 30

High Commissioner (PA: 224):
Mr Bruce E Cleghorn, CMG
Deputy High Commissioner (238; PA: 244):
Mr Mark Canning
Counsellor (Commercial) (PA: 307):
Mr Michael Horne, OBE
Counsellor (Political) (PA: 222):
Mr Richard Moore
Defence Adviser (226; PA: 206):
Colonel Roger J Little
First Secretary (Political) (202): Mr John Marshall
First Secretary (Defence Supply) (242; PA: 206):
Mr Rob Lingham
First Secretary (Commercial) (232):
Mr Steven Green
First Secretary (Management) (258):
Mrs Di Hansen
First Secretary (resides at Bangkok):
Mr John Hector
Assistant Defence Adviser (228):
Lieutenant Commander Adam Joyner, RN
Second Secretary (Economic) (245):
Mr Jeremy Pilmore-Bedford
Second Secretary (Political) (301):
Dr Michelle Haslem
Second Secretary (Technical Management) (225):
Mr Ian Attwood
Second Secretary (Immigration Attaché) (207;
Asst: 308): Mr Paul Feeney
Second Secretary (Political/Public Diplomacy)
(209): Mr Rob Noble
Second Secretary (Commercial) (210):
Mr Neil Floyd
Second Secretary (Consular) (204):
Ms Julie Johnson
Third Secretary (Commercial) (223):
Mrs Marion Guthrie
Third Secretary (Management) (254):
Miss Margaret Gallacher

Johor
Office of the Honorary British Representative
Lucas Automotive Sdn Bhd, PLO 17,
Senai Industrial Estate,
KB 105, 81400 Senai, Johor, Malaysia
Telephone: (00) (60) (7) 5991301/2/3/4 Ext 111
Facsimile: (00) (60) (7) 5994301
e-mail: john.w.bradbury@trw.com
Honorary British Representative:
Mr John Bradbury, MBE

Kota Kinabalu (Sabah)
Office of the Honorary British Representative
c/o Pekah Sdn Bhd
WDT No 46
88862 Kota Kinabalu
Sabah, Malaysia
Telephone: (00) (60) (88) 253333
Facsimile: (00) (60) (88) 267666
e-mail: pmole@pc.jaring.my
Honorary British Representative: Mr Peter Mole

Kuching (Sarawak)
Office of the Honorary British Representative
1st and 2nd Floors
183 C/D/E Fortune Land Business Centre
Jalan Rock

Kuching, Sarawak, East Malaysia
Tel/Fax: (00) (60) (82) 250950
e-mail: valm@pc.jaring.my
Honorary British Representative:
Mrs Valerie Mashman

Miri (Sarawak)
Office of the Honorary British Representative
NJV Sarawak Shell Berhad,
98100 Lutong, Miri
Sarawak, East Malaysia
Telephone: (00) (60) (85) 475865/452736
Facsimile: (00) (60) (85) 653877
e-mail: sroddy@pc.jaring.my
Honorary British Representative: Mr Simon Roddy

Penang
Office of the Honorary British Representative
c/o Plantation Agencies Sdn Bhd,
3rd Floor, Standard Chartered Bank Chambers
Beach Street, 10300 Penang, Malaysia
10790 Penang, Malaysia
Telephone: (00) (60) (4) 2625333
Facsimile: (00) (60) (4) 2622018
e-mail: pasb@mailworld.net
Honorary British Representative:
Mr John West, MBE

MALDIVES

Malé
British High Commission
(All staff resident in Colombo except where
otherwise stated)
High Commissioner: Mr Stephen N Evans, OBE
Deputy High Commissioner: Mr M H P Hill
Defence Adviser:
Lieutenant Colonel Mark H De W Weldon
Cultural Attaché (British Council Director):
Ms S M Maingay
First Secretary (Economic and Commercial):
Mr A Madeley
Second Secretary (Management): Mr R Morris
Second Secretary (Chancery): Miss A Kemp
Second Secretary (Immigration/Consular):
Mr J Kenny
Second Secretary (Immigration): Mr R P Tate
Second Secretary (resides at Mumbai): Mr C Noon
Second Secretary (Development): Mr M Dawson
Deputy Cultural Attaché (British Council):
Ms J Morgan
Third Secretary (Management): Mr E Groves
Attaché (Immigration): Mr A Dick
Attaché (Immigration): Mr M Redden
Attaché (Immigration/Consular): Mr D Love

MALI

Bamako
British Embassy
Rue 132, Porte 902
Badalabougou - Ouest
Tel/Fax (Office): (00) (223) 23 34 12
e-mail: info@britembmali.org
Ambassador: Mr G N Loten

MALTA

Valletta
British High Commission
Whitehall Mansions
Ta'Xbiex Seafront
Ta'Xbiex
MSD 11
Malta GC
Telephone: (00) (356) 21 233134-7
Facsimile: (00) (356) 21 242001 Consular/
Management
        21 233184 Chancery
        21 251684 Consular & Visa Section
e-mail: bhc@vol.net.mt
(Information Section)
bhccomm@vol.net.mt
(Commercial Section)
Visa/Consular.Valletta@fco.gov.uk
(Visa & Consular Section)
Website: www.britain.com.mt
Office Hours (GMT): Winter: Mon - Thur 07 00 -
15 45; Fri 07 00 - 12 15
Summer: Mon - Fri 05 30 - 11 30
(Individual e-mail: First name.Last
name@Valletta.mail.fco.gov.uk
High Commissioner: Mr Vincent Fean
*Deputy High Commissioner and First Secretary
(Commercial/Economic):* Mr John Hillman
Defence Adviser (resides in Rome):
Captain John Hollidge, RN
First Secretary (Political): Mr Nigel Eager
Second Secretary (Management/Consular):
Ms Jenny Fenton
Third Secretary (Political/Information/Cultural):
Mr Iain Willis
Third Secretary (Consular/Immigration):
Mr Neil Porter

MARSHALL ISLANDS

Majuro
British Embassy
Ambassador (resides at Suva): Mr Christopher
Haslam (Mr Ian Powell w.e.f March 03)

MAURITANIA

Nouakchott
British Embassy
(All staff resident in Rabat)
Ambassador: Mr Haydon Warren-Gash
Counsellor and Deputy Head of Mission:
Mr Rupert Joy
Defence Attaché:
Lieutenant Colonel Graham D Duthoit
Third Secretary (Political/Information):
Mr Matthew Hedges
Nouakchott
B9, 2069 Nouakchott
Telephone: (00) (222) 2 51 756
Facsimile: (00) (222) 2 92 053
Honorary Consul: Mrs N Abeiderrahmane, MBE

MAURITIUS

Port Louis
British High Commission
Les Cascades Building, Edith Cavell Street,
Port Louis, PO Box 1063
Telephone: (00) (230) 202 9400
Facsimile: (00) (230) 202 9408
e-mail: bhc@intnet.mu
bhc@intnet.mu (Consular and Immigration
Section)

Commercial Section:
Les Cascades Building,
Edith Cavell Street, Port Louis, PO Box 1063
Telephone: (00) (230) 202 9400
Facsimile: (00) (230) 202 9408

Consular and Immigration Section:
Les Cascades Building
Edith Cavell St
Port Louis, PO Box 1063
Telephone: (00) (230) 202 9400
Facsimile: (00) (230) 202 9407
e-mail: bhc@intnet.mu
Office Hours (GMT): Mon - Thur 03 45 - 11 45
Fri 03 45 - 09 30
High Commissioner: Mr David R Snoxell
*Deputy High Commissioner and First Secretary
(Commercial):* Mr Richard J Austen
Defence Adviser (resides at Nairobi):
Colonel J Ralph Barnes
British Council Director: Ms Rosalind Burford
Second Secretary (Chancery): Ms Ginny Silva
Third Secretary (Immigration/Consular):
Mrs Sandra Belfitt
Third Secretary (Immigration): Mr Gerald Smith
Third Secretary (Management): Mr Faruk Miah

Rodrigues
British Honorary Consulate
Craft Aid,
Camp du Roi,
Rodrigues, Mauritius
Telephone: (00) (230) 831 1766
Facsimile: (00) (230) 831 2276
e-mail: pdraper@intnet.mu
Opening Hours: (local time) Mon – Fri: 07 00 –
16 00
Sat: 08 00 – 12 00
Honorary Consul: Mr Paul Draper, MBE

MEXICO

Mexico City
British Embassy
Rio Lerma 71, Col Cuauhtémoc,
06500 Mexico City
Telephone: (00) (52) (55) 5 242 8500
Facsimile: (00) (52) (55) 5 242 8517
e-mail: ukinmex@att.net.mx
Website: www.embajadabritanica.com.mx
Office Hours (GMT): Mon - Fri 14 30 - 21 30
(Winter)
Mon - Fri 15 30 - 22 30 (Summer)
Ambassador: Mrs Denise M Holt, CMG

*Deputy Head of Mission, Minister-Counsellor and
Consul-General:* Mr Ian Hughes
*Counsellor (Cultural) (British Council Director)
(263 1900 ext. 1992):* Mr Alan Curry
Defence Attaché (resides at Guatemala City):
Colonel Ian C D Blair-Pilling, OBE
First Secretary (Political and Economic):
Mr James Thornton
First Secretary (Cultural) (British Council):
Mr Simon Milner
First Secretary (Commercial): Mr Mark A G Kent
*First Secretary (Political/Information/Press &
Public Affairs):* Ms Catherine Firth
First Secretary (Management): Ms Lynda E Brettle
Second Secretary and Consul: Ms Valerie Lucien
Second Secretary (Technical Management):
Mr Ian Taylor
Second Secretary (Commercial): Mr David Lelliott
Second Secretary (Commercial):
Mr Andrew J F Ford, MVO
Second Secretary (Economic/Political):
Mrs Lynn Page
Second Secretary (Works) (Resides at Miami):
Mr Mark H Jones
Third Secretary (Management): Mr Alex S Page
Attaché: Ms Sheila Colby
Attaché: Mrs Nikki de Ramos
Attaché: Mr Allan Wilson

Mexico City
British Consulate
Embassy, Consular Section
Rio Usumacinta 30, Col Cuauhtémoc,
06500, Mexico DF
Telephone: As for Embassy
Facsimile: (00) (52) (55) 5242 8523
e-mail: consular.section@fco.gov.uk
Consul: Mr Valerie Lucien
Vice-Consul: Ms Jeanne E Grant

Acapulco
Honorary British Consulate
Centro Internacional Acapulco
Casa Consular
Costera Miguel Aleman,
39851, Acapulco, Guerrero
Telephone: (00) (52) (744) 484 173
Facsimile: (00) (52) (744) 412 533 (ask for tone)
Honorary Consul: Mrs Lorraine E Bajos

Cancun
Honorary British Consulate
The Royal Sands
Blvd Kulkukan,Km 13.5
Zona Hotelera
77500 Cancun, Quintana Roo
Telephone: (00) (52) (998) 881 0100
Facsimile: (00) (52) (998) 888 229
Honorary Consul: Mr Mark Carney

Ciudad Juárez
Honorary British Consulate
Calle Fresno 185, Campestre Juárez,
32460 Ciudad Juárez, Chihuahua
Telephone: (00) (52) (656) 616 7791/617 5088
Facsimile: (00) (52) (656) 887 351
Honorary Consul: Mr Rex Maingot

Guadalajara
British Trade Office
Aurelio Aceves 225, Local 40
Col. Vallarta Poniente
Guadalajara, Jal. 44110
Telephone: (00) (52) (333) 630 43 57/630
4385/630 4359
Facsimile: (00) (52) (333) 616 2159
Commercial Officer: Mr Eduardo Vega

Guadalajara
Honorary British Consulate
Jesus de Rojas No. 20
Colonia Los Pinos
Zapopan
Jalisco CP 45120
Telephone/Facsimile: (00) (52) (33) 3343 2296
Honorary Consul: Mr Simon Cohen, MBE

Monterrey
British Consulate
Ave. Ricardo Margain Zozaya 240
Colonia Valle del Campestre
C P 66225
San Pedro Garza Garcia
Nuevo Leon
Telephone: (00) (52) (818) 356 5359
Facsimile: (00) (52) (818) 356 5379
Consul: Mr Karl Burrows
Commercial Officer: Mr Horacio Licon

Oaxaca
Hotel Xestal
Blvd. Chahue
Lote 37, Mza. 4 Sector R
Bahias de Huatulco, Oaxaca
Telephone: (00) (52) (958) 587 2372 (leave a
message)
Facsimile (00) (52) (958) 587 2373
Consular Correspondent: Mr Wolfgang Wilczek

Tijuana
Honorary British Consulate
Blvd Salinas No 1500, Fracc Aviación Tijuana,
22420 Tijuana, BCN
Telephone: (00) (52) (664) 686 5320/681 7323
Facsimile: (00) (52) (664) 681 8402
Honorary Consul: Mr Eric M Baloyan

Veracruz
Honorary British Consulate
Independencia No 1349-1
Zona Centro (PO Box 724), 91700 Veracruz,
Telephone: (00) (52) (229) 9311255
Facsimile: (00) (52) (229) 931285, (ask for tone)
Honorary Consul: Mr Luis Carbajal

MICRONESIA

Pohnpei
British Embassy
Ambassador (resides at Suva):
Mr Christopher Haslam (Mr Ian Powell w.e.f
March 03)

MOLDOVA

Chisinau
British Embassy
ASITO Building, office 320
57/1 Banulescu-Bodoni St.
Chisinau 2005, Moldova
Telephone: (00) (3732) 238 991 (General Enquiries)
232 712 (Ambassador)
233 018 (DHM)
238 476 (DFID)
Facsimile: (00) (3732) 238 992
238 478
Mobile: (00) (373) 910 4088/910 4443
Ambassador and Consul General
(e-mail: bernardwhiteside@be.moldline.net):
Mr Bernard G Whiteside, MBE
Deputy Head of Mission: Mr Tony Kay
Defence Attaché (resides at Bucharest):
Colonel Andrew T Bruce, MBE

MONACO (HC)

British Consulate
33 Boulevard Princesse Charlotte,
BP 265, MC 98005 Monaco CEDEX
Telephone: (00) (377) 93 50 99 54
Facsimile: (00) (377) 97 70 72 00
Consul-General (resides at Marseille): Mr I Davies
Honorary British Consul: Mr E J F Blair

MONGOLIA

Ulaanbaatar
British Embassy
30 Enkh Taivny Gudamzh (PO Box 703),
Ulaanbaatar 13, Mongolia
Telephone: (00) (976) (11) 458133
FTN Telephone: 8728 1000
Facsimile: (00) (976) (11) 458036
FTN Facsimile: 8728 2034
e-mail: britemb@magicnet.mn
Office Hours (GMT): Winter: Mon – Thurs 00 30 - 05 00 and 06 00 - 09 00
Fri 00 30 - 05 30
Summer: Mon – Thurs 01 30 - 06 00 and 07 00 - 10 00
Fri 01 30 - 06 30
Ambassador: Mr Phil Rouse, MBE
Deputy Head of Mission: Mr Simon Brier
Vice Consul and *Management Officer:*
Mrs Lucy Brier
Defence Attaché (resides in Beijing):
Brigadier Gordon Kerr, OBE, QGM

MOROCCO

Rabat
British Embassy
17 Boulevard de la Tour Hassan (BP 45), Rabat
Telephone: (00) (212) (37) 23 86 00
Facsimile: (00) (212) (37) 70 45 31
(Management/Consular)
26 08 39 (Chancery)
Airtech: 72 99 62
e-mail: britemb.@mtds.com

Office Hours (GMT): Winter: Mon - Thurs 08 00 - 16 30; Fri 08 00 - 13 00
Summer: Mon - Thurs 08 00 - 14 00
Fri 08 00 - 13 00
Ambassador: Mr Haydon Warren-Gash
Deputy Head of Mission: Mr Rupert Joy
Defence Attaché:
Lieutenant Colonel Graham D Duthoit
Cultural Attaché (British Council Director):
Mr Steve McNulty
First Secretary and Consul: Miss Liz Dow
Second Secretary (Political/Information):
Mr Matthew Hedges
Second Secretary (Commercial/Economic):
Mr Steve Moore
Vice Consul: Mrs Ann-Marie Teeuwissen
Attaché (Registry/Communications):
Mr Alan Roberts
Attaché (Chancery): Miss Gill Evans
Attaché (Military): Staff Sergeant Ian Kennedy

Tangier
British Consulate
41 Boulevard Mohamed V, (BP 1203) Tangier
Telephone: (00) (212) (39) 94 15 57, 94 18 78
Facsimile: (00) (212) (39) 94 22 84
e-mail: uktanger@mtds.com
Office Hours (GMT): Winter: Monday to Thursday 08 00 - 16 30
Summer: Monday to Thursday 08 00 - 14 00;
Friday 08 00 - 13 00
Consul: Miss S L Sweet, MBE

Casablanca
British Consulate-General
43 Boulevard d'Anfa
(BP 13.762)
Casablanca 01
Telephone: (00) (212) 22 43 77 00
Facsimile: (00) (212) 22 43 77 04
Visa Section Fax: (00) (212) 22 43 77 03
Airtech: (00) (212) 22 43 77 05
e-mail: british.consulate@casanet.net.ma
Office Hours (GMT): Winter: Mon – Thur 08 00 - 16 30; Fri 08 00 - 13 00
Summer: Mon – Thur 08 00 - 14 00; Fri 08 00 - 13 00
Consul-General and Director, British Trade Promotion: Mr Denis Healy
Consul (Commercial): Mr Simon Williams
Vice-Consul (Commercial): Mr Driss Amal
Vice-Consul/Management Officer: Mr Ian Fox
Vice-Consul (Immigration): Mrs Kamla Taylor
Vice-Consul (Immigration): Mr Danny De Silva

Agadir
British Consulate
Complet Tours
Immeuble Oumlil
No. 26 3rd Floor
Avenue Hassan II
Agadir, Morocco
Telephone: (00) (212) 48 823401,823402
Facsimile: (00) (212) 48 823403
Honorary Consul: Ms Lesley Sanchez

Marrakech
British Consulate
55 Boulevard Zerktouni, Residence Taib,
Marrakech
Telephone: (00) (212) (44) 435095
Facsimile: (00) (212) (44) 439217
Honorary Consul: Mr Mohamed Zkhiri

MOZAMBIQUE

Maputo
British High Commission
Av Vladimir I Lenine 310, Caixa Postal 55,
Maputo
Telephone: (00) (2581) 320111/2/5/6/7
Facsimile: (00) (2581) 321666
Airtech: (00) (2581) 329194
e-mail: info.maputo@fco.gov.uk
Office Hours (GMT): Mon - Thur 06 00 - 10 30-
12 00 - 15 00; Fri 06 00 - 11 00
High Commissioner: Mr Bob Dewar
Deputy High Commissioner and Consul:
Mr Peter Butcher
Defence Adviser (resides at Harare):
Colonel John Field, CBE
First Secretary (British Council Director):
Mr Simon Ingram-Hill
Second Secretary (Management/Consular):
Mr Chris Bowden
Third Secretary (Commercial):
Mr Jonathan Bamber
*Third Secretary (Vice-Consul/Press and Public
Affairs):* Mrs Sarah Cassidy

**Department for International Development
(DFID) Mozambique**
Head of Office: Mr Eamon Cassidy
First Secretary (Rural Livelihoods):
Ms Julia Compton
First Secretary (Health and Education):
Dr Allison Beattie
First Secretary (Economic): Dr Nick Highton
First Secretary (Social Development):
Mr Robin Milton
First Secretary (Governance Adviser):
Ms Caroline Rickatson
Second Secretary (Deputy Programme Adviser):
Mr Tom Jamieson
Second Secretary (Management): Mr John Hawkes

Beira
British Honorary Consulate
Rua Paiva Couceiro 175,
Beira CP 1401
Telephone: (00) (258) 3 311 763
Facsimile: (00) (258) 3 312 318
Honorary Consul: Mr Colin Cronin

NAMIBIA

Windhoek
British High Commission
116 Robert Mugabe Avenue,
Windhoek
Postal Address: PO Box 22202,
Telephone: (00) (264) (61) 274800
Facsimile: (00) (264) (61) 228895

Airtech: (00) (264) (61) 239004
e-mail: bhc@mweb.com.na
Consular@windhoek.mail.fco.gov.uk
Visa@windhoek.mail.fco.gov.uk
Commercial@windhoek.mail.fco.gov.uk
Opening Hours: (April - September GMT+2) Mon-
Thurs 06 00 – 11 00; 12 00 – 15 00
Fri 06 00 – 10 00
(September - April GMT+1) Mon-Thurs 07 00 –
12 00; 13 00 – 16 00
Fri 07 00 – 11 00
High Commissioner: Mr Alasdair MacDermott
Deputy Head of Mission: Mr Neal Hammond
Defence Adviser (Resides at Pretoria):
Wing Commander T A (Tony) Harper, RAF
Third Secretary: Mr Jim Couzens
Attaché: Ms Margaret Horsley

British Council
1-5 Peter Muller Street
Windhoek West
Windhoek
Postal Address: PO Box 13392
Telephone: (00) (264) (61) 226776
Facsimile: (00) (264) (61) 227530
e-mail: general.enquiries@bc-namibia.bcouncil.org
Website: www.britcoun.org/namibia
Opening Hours: same as British High Commission
Director: Ms P Mahlalela

**Department for International Development
(DFID) Field Office**
11th Floor,
Sanlam Centre,
Independence Avenue,
Windhoek
Postal Address: 20689
Telephone: (00) (264) (61) 256294/5; 256251/17
Facsimile: (00) (264) (61) 256296
Opening Hours: same as British High Commision
Head of DFID Field Office/Programme
Administrator: Ms Rachel Malone
(e-mail: r-malone@dfid.gov.uk)

NAURU

Nauru
British High Commission
(All staff resident at Suva)
High Commissioner: Mr Charles F Mochan
*Deputy High Commissioner and First Secretary
(Consular):* Mr Christopher Haslam (Mr Ian
Powell w.e.f March 03)

NEPAL

Kathmandu
British Embassy
Lainchaur Kathmandu (PO Box 106)
Telephone: (00) (977) (1) 410583, 411281, 411590,
414588
Facsimile: (00) (977) (1) 411789, 416723
e-mail: britemb@wlink.com.np
Office Hours (GMT): Mon - Thur: 02 30 - 06 45
and 07 45 - 11 15; Fri: 02 30 - 06 45 and 07 45 -
09 30
Ambassador: Mr K G Bloomfield

First Secretary and Deputy Head of Mission:
Mr D Ward
Defence Attaché: Colonel P R Sharland
*First Secretary (Development) (Head of DFID
Nepal):* Ms S Wardell
*First Secretary (Cultural) (British Council
Director):* Ms B Wickham
Assistant Defence Attaché:
Lieutenant Colonel B D Spencer
First Secretary (Resident in New Delhi): Mr P Free
Head of Management: Mrs V A Chamberlain
Third Secretary (Chancery): Mr J Goddard
Vice-Consul: Ms J Ferguson
*Second Secretary, HM Consul/ECM, (Head,
Consular & Immigration Services):* Mr J C Chick
Attaché: Ms R Howes
Attaché: Ms A Garrity
Political Attaché and Information Officer:
Mr D B Thapa
Commercial Attaché: Mr P G Karmacharya

**Department For International Development,
Nepal (DFIDN)**
Telephone: (00) (977) (1) 542980/542981
Facsimile: (00) (977) (1) 542979
First Secretary (Head of DFID Nepal):
Mr D Wood
First Secretary (Deputy Head of DFID Nepal):
Mr A Harper
*First Secretary (Government and Institution
Adviser):* Mr S Sharples
First Secretary (Economic Adviser): Mr C Jackson
First Secretary (Rural Livelihoods Adviser):
Ms Helen Wedgwood
First Secretary (Health Adviser): Dr M O'Dwyer
First Secretary (Engineering Adviser):
Mr M Harvey
First Secretary (Social Development Adviser):
Ms F Winter
First Secretary (Senior Education Adviser):
(Vacant)
Second Secretary (Head of Finance):
Mr M McGill
Second Secretary - Deputy Programme Manager:
Mrs S McGill
Conflict Adviser (on contract): Mr M Segal

British Council
Lainchaur, PO Box 640,
Kathmandu
Telephone: (00) (977) (1) 410798, 413003
Facsimile: (00) (977) (1) 410545
Office Hours: Mon - Thurs: 08 00 - 17 00 (Office)
Fri: 08 00 - 13 00 (Office)
Winter: Mon - Fri: 10 00 - 18 00 (Library)
Director (British Council and Cultural Attaché):
Ms B Wickham
Assistant Director (British Council): Mr C Early

NETHERLANDS

The Hague
British Embassy
Lange Voorhout 10, 2514 ED, The Hague
Telephone: (00) (31) (70) 427 0427
Facsimile: (00) (31) (70) 427 0345 General
0346 Commercial Section

0347 Ambassador's Office, DHM and Political
Section
Website: www.britain.nl
Office Hours (GMT): Mon - Fri 08 00 - 16 30
Ambassador: Sir C R Budd, KCMG
Deputy Head of Mission: Ms J Darby
Counsellor (Commercial and Economic):
Ms P Phillips
Counsellor: Mr W L Jackson-Houlston, OBE
Defence Attaché: Captain N A M Butler, RN
First Secretary and Head of Political Section:
Mr A Price
First Secretary (Chemical Weapons): Mr G D Cole
First Secretary (Labour): Mr P E Drummond
First Secretary (Press & Public Affairs):
Mr W Evans
First Secretary (Commercial): Mr A J Hennessy
First Secretary (Management): Mr M K Oliver
Second Secretary (Labour): Mr A Kirk
Second Secretary (Chemical Weapons):
Mr J P Murphy
Second Secretary (Economic): Mrs C Lufkin
Second Secretary (Political): Ms J Cooper
Second Secretary (Political): Mr D Tindell
Attaché: Mr K Ditcham
Attaché: Mr P Harris
Attaché: Mr G Bertie
Attaché: Mr M T Bonfield
Attaché: Mr K Field

Amsterdam (SP)
British Consulate-General
Koningslaan 44,
(PO Box 75488, 1070 AL Amsterdam)
Telephone: (00) (31) (20) 676 43 43 (6 lines) for
extensions see individual officers
Facsimile: (00) (31) (20) 676 10 69
                  675 83 81 Consular Section
Airtech: (00) (31) (20) 676 4343 (Option 1,
2252#)
Telex: 15117 (a/b UKAMS NL)
e-mail: PassportEnquiries.amsterdam@fco.gov.uk
VisaEnquiries.amsterdam@fco.gov.uk
Office Hours (GMT): Mon-Fri 08 00 - 16 00
Consul-General (2209): Mr Peter Barklamb
Vice-Consul (Management) (2210):
Ms Vanessa Jennison
Vice-Consul (Consular) (2222):
Mr Malcolm Mason, MBE
Vice-Consul (Immigration) (2216): Mr Barry Wilde

Willemstad (Curacao)
British Consulate
Jan Sofat 38
(PO Box 3803)
Curacao
Netherlands Antilles
Telephone: (00) (599) (9) 747 3322
Facsimile: (00) (599) (9) 747 3330
e-mail: britconcur@attglobal.net
(British Consulate)
owersa@curinfo.an
(Honorary Consul)
Office Hours (GMT): 12 00 - 16 00
Honorary Consul (see address above):
Mr Antony W Owers

Philipsburg (St Maarten)
(Netherlands Antilles)
British Vice-Consulate
(Temporarily closed)

NEW ZEALAND

Wellington
British High Commission
44 Hill Street, Wellington 1
Mailing Address: British High Commission,
PO Box 1812, Wellington
Telephone: (00) (64) (4) 924 2888
Facsimile: (00) (64) (4) 473 4982 Economic/Trade
            Policy Section
            924 2810 Passports
            924 2822 Immigration
            924 2831 Chancery
            924 2809 Management
Airtech: 495 0836
e-mail: bhc.wel@xtra.co.nz
Website: www.britain.org.nz
Office Hours (GMT): 20 45 - 05 00
High Commissioner (Ext 2874): Mr R T Fell, CVO
Deputy High Commissioner (Ext 2859):
Mr M Bourke
Defence Adviser (Ext 2875): Colonel A A Peebles
*First Secretary (Economic/Trade Policy) (Ext
2842):* Mr P D Noon
*First Secretary (Political/Press/Public Affairs) (Ext
2861):* Mrs K S Wolstenholme
*First Secretary (British Council Director) (Ext
2853):* Mr P N Atkins
First Secretary (Political/External) (Ext 2881):
Mr R J Dean
*First Secretary (Senior Technical Management
Officer) (resides at Canberra):* Mr R Bronson
Second Secretary (Management) (Ext 2871):
Miss A Bouch
Second Secretary (Political) (Ext 2862):
Mr J D Wolstenholme
Second Secretary (Consular) (Ext 2899):
Mr W S Robertson
Third Secretary (Consular) (Ext 2891):
Ms C B Livingstone

Auckland
British Consulate-General
Level 17 NZI House, 151 Queen Street,
Auckland 1
Mailing Address: British Consulate-General,
Private Bag 92014, Auckland 1
Telephone: (00) (64) (9) 303 2973
Facsimile: (00) (64) (9) 303 1836
e-mail: postmaster.auckland@fco.gov.uk
Website: www.brittrade.org.nz
Office Hours (GMT): 20 45 - 05 00
Consular, Visa and Passport work is centralised in
Wellington
*Consul-General and Director of Trade
Development:* Mr S E Turner
Deputy Consul-General: Mr W G D Johnson, MBE
Trade Promotion Manager: Mrs F Griffith
Trade Promotion Manager: Mrs B Harris
Trade Promotion Manager: Mr B Murray
Pro-Consul (Management): Ms D Clay

Christchurch
British Trade Office and Consulate
PO Box 13292, Christchurch 8031
Telephone: (00) (64) (3) 337 9933
Facsimile: (00) (64) (3) 337 9938
Office Hours (GMT): 21 00 - 05 00
Trade Representative and Honorary Consul:
Mr I D Howell, OBE

Office of the Honorary British Consul
Muri Beach
PO Box 552
Rarotonga
Cook Islands
Telephone: (00) (682) 21080 (Office)
20444 (Home)
Facsimile: (00) (682) 21087
e-mail: mitchell@oyster.net.nz
Honorary British Consul: Mr M C Mitchell

NICARAGUA

Managua
British Embassy
Plaza Churchill, Reparto "Los Robles",
Managua, Apartado A-169
Telephone: (00) (505) (2) 780014, 780887, 674050
Facsimile: (00) (505) (2) 784085
Airtech: (00) (505) (2) 678271
e-mail: britemb@ibw.com.ni
Office Hours (GMT): 13 30 - 20 30
Consular 15 00 - 18 00
Ambassador and Consul-General:
Mr Timothy Brownbill
*Second Secretary, Vice Consul and Deputy Head of
Mission:* Mr Gary Scroby
*First Secretary (Commercial) and Director of
Trade Promotion, Central America (resides at San
José):* Mr Christopher Edge
Defence Attaché (resides at Guatemala City):
Colonel Ian Blair-Pilling, OBE
Second Secretary (resides at Panama City):
Mr Andrew Davenport

**Department for International Development,
Central American Regional Office**
Casa 17A, Reparto 'Los Robles'
Managua
Telephone: (00) (505) (0) 88 38769
Head of DFID (CARO) and Development Adviser:
Ms Georgia Taylor
Regional Health Adviser: Miss Luana Reale

NIGER

Niamey
British Embassy
(All staff resident in Abidjan)
Ambassador and Consul-General:
Mr J F Gordon, CMG
First Secretary (Commercial) & Consul:
Mr M J K Rickerd, MVO
Second Secretary (Political/Information):
Ms K Miller, MBE
Second Secretary (Commercial/Political):
Mr C Frean

Third Secretary, (Visas/Passports) and Vice-Consul: Mr M McGuinness
Third Secretary (Management) and Vice Consul: Mr D Summers

British Consulate
BP11926, Niamey, Niger
Telephone: (00) (227) 72 46 76 or 75 24 59
Facsimile: (00) (227) 74 46 76
Honorary Consul: Mr B Niandou

NIGERIA

Abuja
British High Commission
Shehu Shangari Way (North),
Maitama, Abuja
Telephone: (00) (234) (9) 413 2010, 2011, 2796, 2880, 2883, 2887, 9817 (Chancery and Defence Sections)
Facsimile: (00) (234) (9) 413 3552 (Chancery and Defence Sections)
Airtech: (00) (234) (9) 413 2010
e-mail: Chancery@abujx.mail.fco.gov.uk
Defence@abujx.mail.fco.gov.uk
Commercial@abuja.mail.fco.gov.uk
Consular@abuja.mail.fco.gov.uk
Management@abuja.mail.fco.gov.uk
VisaEnquiries@abuja.mail.fco.gov.uk
Office Hours (GMT): 07 00 - 14 00

Commercial, Management, Consular and Visa Sections:
Dangote House, Aguyi Ironsi Street,
Maitama, Abuja
Telephone: (00) (234) (9) 413 4559-4564,
0899,.0900, 3885-7, 3889
Facsimile: (00) (234) (9) 413 4565 (Visa Section)
(00) (234) (9) 413 3888 (Management, Commercial and Consular Sections)

Development Section
Telephone/Facsimile: (00) (234) (9) 413 0715
e-mail: wendyjphillips@compuserve.com
British Council
Telephone: (00) (234) (9) 413 0901
Facsimile: (00) (234) (9) 413 0902
e-mail: Abuja@bc-abuja.bcouncil.org
High Commissioner (also Ambassador non –resident to the Republic of Benin):
Mr Philip Thomas, CMG
Deputy High Commissioner: Mr Charles Bird
Defence Adviser: Colonel John R Lemon
Counsellor (Developmental): Mr Eamonn Taylor
First Secretary (Political): Mr Ian Baharie
First Secretary (Political): Ms Gillian Dare
First Secretary (Management): Mr Rob D Elliott
First Secretary (Development):
Mrs Wendy Phillips
First Secretary (Cultural and Aid):
Mr David Roberts
Second Secretary (Economic): Mrs Karen Bell
Second Secretary (Political): Mr Arthur Snell
Second Secretary (Political): Mr Colin Wells
Second Secretary (Immigration): Mr Simon Rose
Second Secretary (Works): Mr John Neale
Third Secretary (Political): Mr Paul Edwards

Third Secretary (Management) & Vice Consul:
Mr Declan Byrne
Third Secretary (Management):
Mr Keith Rowlands
Third Secretary (Immigration):
Ms Sheila Underwood
Third Secretary (Immigration): Mrs Dawn Neale
Third Secretary (Immigration):
Mr Kingsley Magee
Third Secretary (Immigration):
Mr Dominic O'Callaghan
Third Secretary (Immigration): Mrs Arti Rose

Lagos
Chancery Building
British Deputy High Commission
11 Walter Carrington Crescent
Victoria Island
(Private Mail Bag 12136)
Telephone: (00) (234) (1) 2619531, 2619537, 2619541, 2619543, 2619588, 2619592, 2619598
Facsimile: (00) (234) (1) 2614021
Office Hours (GMT): 0700 – 1400
Consular and Visa Sections
11 Walter Carrington Crescent
Victoria Island
Telephone: (00) (234) (1) 2625930-7
Facsimile: (00) (234) (1) 2625940 Consular
(00) (234) (1) 2625941 Visa
Office Hours (GMT): 0630 – 1330
Deputy High Commissioner: Mr D Wyatt
Deputy Head of Mission and First Secretary (Management): Mr P McCoy
First Secretary (Commercial): Mr I M Birks
First Secretary (Immigration): Mr R Gemmell, OBE
First Secretary (Medical): (Vacant)
First Secretary (Technical Management):
Mr A Bagnall
Second Secretary (Political): Mr C Tennant
Second Secretary (Political/Press): Mr J D Sharp
Second Secretary (Management):
Mr A J Kirkpatrick
Second Secretary (Commercial): Ms S E Pickering
Second Secretary (Consular):
Mrs J Finnamore-Crorkin
Second Secretary (Immigration): Mr K Simpson
Second Secretary (Immigration): Mr K Chaplin
Second Secretary (Immigration): Mr A McCann
Second Secretary (Nurse): Mrs Y Gibney
Second Secretary (Technical Management):
Mr J M Lawrie
Third Secretary (Management): Mr G R Williams
Third Secretary (Management): Mr K Curran
Third Secretary (Management): Mr P A Smith
Third Secretary (Consular): Mr T Sanmoogan

Kano
2 Tsauna Close
Off Amadu Bello Way
PO Box 11872
Kano
Telephone: (00) (234) (64) 631 686
Facsimile: (00) (234) (64) 632 590
e-mail: bhc.kan@skannet.com
Honorary Consul: Mr Harold Blackburne, OBE

Kaduna
British Commercial/Liaison Office
3 Independence Way, Kaduna
Telephone: (00) (234) (62) 233380/1
Facsimile: (00) (234) (62) 237267
e-mail: bhc.kad@skannet.com

Port Harcourt
British Commercial/Liaison Office
Plot 300, Olu Obasanjo Road, Port Harcourt,
Rivers State
Telephone: (00) (234) (84) 237173, 335104
Facsimile: (00) (234) (84) 237172

Ibadan
British Liaison Office
Rotimi Williams Avenue, Bodija, Ibadan
Telephone: (00) (234) (22) 810 4953

Lagos
British Council Division (Lagos and Enugu)
11 Kingsway Road, Ikoyi, Lagos
Telephone: (00) (234) (1) 2692193, 2690646
Facsimile: (00) (234) (1) 2690646, 2692193
Telex: 22071 (a/b 22071 BRICO NG)
Office Hours (GMT): 06 30 - 13 30
Counsellor (Cultural and Aid): Ms C Stephens
First Secretary (Cultural and Aid): Mr N Townson
First Secretary (Aid/Management): Mr A Campbell
First Secretary (Book Aid): Ms K Sanders

British Council Division (Enugu, Ibadan, Kaduna and Kanu)
Teachers House, Ogui Road, Enugu
Telephone: (00) (234) (42) 255577, 255677,
258456
Facsimile: (00) (234) (42) 250158
53 Magazine Road, PMB 5314, Jericho, Ibadan
Telephone: (00) (234) (22) 2410299, 2410678
Facsimile: (00) (234) (22) 2410796
Yakubu Gwan Way, Kaduna
Telephone: (00) (234) (62) 236033-5
Facsimile: (00) (234) (62) 236330
10 Emir's Place Road, Kano
Telephone: (00) (234) (64) 646652, 643489
Director's Direct Line: (00) (234) (64) 643861
Facsimile: (00) (234) (64) 632500
First Secretary (Cultural and Aid, Kano):
Mr P Morison

NORWAY

Oslo
British Embassy
Thomas Heftyesgate 8, 0244 Oslo
Telephone: (00) (47) 23 13 27 00
Facsimile: (00) (47) 23 13 27 41 Management
                27 89 Chancery
                27 38 Consular/Visa Section
                27 05 Economic/Commercial Section
                27 27 Information Section
                2797 Defence
Office Hours (GMT): Summer 06 30 - 14 00,
Winter 07 30 - 15 00
Ambassador (2701): Mrs A M Leslie
*Counsellor, Consul-General, Deputy Head of
Mission (2707):* Mr T I Hay-Campell, LVO

Counsellor (2716): Mr A J G Insall, LVO
Defence Attaché (2711):
Lieutenant Colonel S J Hughes, RM
*First Secretary (Economic and Commercial)
(2752):* Dr L Bristow-Smith
First Secretary (Management/Consul) (2751):
Mr J Steeples
*Second Secretary (Economic and Commercial)
(2759):* Mr S J Cartwright
Second Secretary (Information) (2718):
Mr C H J Davies
Second Secretary (2719): Mrs C Evans
Second Secretary (Chancery) (2708):
Mr R Drabble
Vice Consul (2778): Mr M Scales

Bergen
British Consulate
PO Box 7255, 5020 Bergen
VISITING ADDRESS:
Carl Konowsgate 34, 5161 Laksevåg
Telephone: (00) (47) 55 94 47 05
Telefax: (00) (47) 55 34 34 28
Honorary Consul: Mr R C Hestness (Norwegian)

Harstad - Closed

Kristiansand (S)
British Consulate
Post Box 8207, Vågsbygd, 4676 Kristiansand (S)
VISITING ADDRESS:
Lumberveien 49, 4621 Kristiansand (S)
Telephone: (00) (47) 38 01 94 50
Facsimile: (00) (47) 38 01 91 69
Honorary Consul: Mr T Wiese-Hansen
(Norwegian)

Kristiansund (N)
British Consulate
Post Box 148, 6501 Kristiansund N
VISITING ADDRESS:
Vågeveien 7, 6509 Kristiansund N
Telephone: (00) (47) 71 67 53 33
Telefax: (00) (47) 71 67 53 52
Honorary Consul: Mr J Loennechen, MBE
(Norwegian)

Stavanger
British Consulate
PO Box 28, 4001 Stavanger
VISITING ADDRESS:
Prinsensgate, 12 4008 Stavanger
Telephone: (00) (47) 51 52 97 13
Facsimile: (00) (47) 51 53 83 01
Honorary Consul: Mr T Falck, Jnr (Norwegian)

Tromsø
British Consulate
c/o Mack's Ølbryggeri, 9291, Tromsø
VISITING ADDRESS:
c/o Mack's Ølbryggeri, Storgaten 5-13, 9291
Tromsø
Telephone: (00) (47) 77 62 45 00
Facsimile: (00) (47) 77 65 78 35
Honorary Consul: Mr H Bredrup (Norwegian)

Trondheim
British Consulate

Post Box 2521, 7413 Trondheim
VISITING ADDRESS:
Beddingen 8, 7037, Trondheim
Telephone: (00) (47) 73 60 02 00
Facsimile: (00) (47) 73 60 02 50
Honorary Consul: Mrs B Kjeldsberg (Norwegian)

Ålesund
British Consulate
Post Box 1301, 6001 Ålesund
VISITING ADDRESS:
Farstadgården, St Olav's Plass, 6001 Ålesund
Telephone: (00) (47) 70 12 44 60
Facsimile: (00) (47) 70 12 85 30
Honorary Consul: Mr S A Farstad (Norwegian)

Bodø
British Consulate
Post box 1019, 8001 Bod›
VISITING ADDRESS:
Parkveien 43, 8003 Bod›
Telephone: (00) (47) 75 50 67 14
Facsimile: (00) (47) 75 50 67 01
Honarary *Consul:* Mr A Neilsen-Nygaard
(Norwegian)

OMAN

Muscat
British Embassy
PO Box 300, Muscat, Postal Code 113,
Sultanate of Oman
Telephone: (00) (968) 693077
            693086 (Commercial)
            693112 (Commercial)
            693094 (Defence)
Facsimile: (00) (968) 693087 (General)
            693179 (Chancery)
            693088 (Commercial)
            693091 (Consular)
            693089 (Defence)
e-mail: becomu@omantel.net.om
Website: www.britishembassyoman.org
Office Hours (GMT): Sat - Wed 03 30 - 10 30
Ambassador: Mr Stuart Laing
Counsellor and Deputy Head of Mission:
Mr Hugh Philpott
Defence and Military Attaché:
Colonel Hugh Willing, RM
Naval and Air Attaché:
Commander Bob Thomas, RN
First Secretary (Political): Mr Craig Drysdale
First Secretary (Management) and Consul:
Mr Michael Snell, MVO
First Secretary (Commercial): Mr Malcolm Ives
Second Secretary (Chancery/Information):
Mr Alex Brown
Third Secretary (Commercial): Mrs Janine Philpott
British Vice-Consul: Mrs Susan Ives
BERS Liaison Officer: Mrs Lisa Patter

PAKISTAN

Islamabad
British High Commission
Diplomatic Enclave, Ramna 5,
PO Box 1122, Islamabad.

Telephone: (00) (92) (51) 2822131/5, 2206071/5
Auto Direct Dial: (00) (92) (51) 2820941/47 + Ext
(only from a digital phone)
Direct Lines: (00) (92) (51) 2822996 High
Commissioner
(00) (92) (51) 2206056 Counsellor (Political)
Facsimile: (00) (92) (51) 2201109 Chancery
            2825299 Defence
            2823439 Management
            2826217 Commercial
            2279355 Commercial
            2206069 Immigration
            2824728 Immigration
            2279356 Consular
            2279351 Accommodation/TWG
            2277159 Clinic
            2823017 Development
            2271198 DLO
            2279350 DIFD
            2201172 PLO
Secure Facsimile: (00) (92) (51) 2822989
(Cryptek), 2279358 (Airtech)
Telegrams: Prodrome, Islamabad
e-mail: bhctrade@isb.comsats.net.pk
(Commercial Section)
bhcmedia@isb.comsats.net.pk
(Media and Public Affairs)
bhcdefence@isb.comsats.net.pk
(Defence Section)
Office Hours (GMT): High Commission: Mon –
Thurs 03 00 – 11 00, Fri 03 00 – 07 00
Immigration/Consular Sections: Mon – Fri 02 30 –
09 30
High Commissioner: Mr Hilary Synnott, CMG
Deputy High Commissioner: Mr Julian Evans
Counsellor (Political): Mr Matthew Gould
Counsellor (Political): Mr David Cox
Counsellor (Regional Affairs): Mr Tim Clayden
Defence and Military Adviser:
Brigadier Johnny Torrens-Spence
Naval and Air Adviser: Captain Andrew Welch, RN
First Secretary (Political): Mr Nick Cannon
First Secretary (Political): Mr Harvey Woods
First Secretary (Political): Vacant
First Secretary (Immigration/Consular):
Mr Colin Mulcahy
First Secretary (Management): Mr Nick Starkey
First Secretary (Works): Mr J Denoon
First Secretary (Technical Manager):
Mr P Mawston
Head of Development Section: Mr G Aicken
*First Secretary (Health, Population and Women in
Development Adviser):* Vacant
First Secretary (Senior Governance Advisor):
Ms J Charlton
First Secretary (MWD, Nursing Officer):
Ms E McManus
Second Secretary (Political): Mr Adrian Scott
Second Secretary (Political): Mr Trevor Parker
Second Secretary (Political/External): Vacant
Second Secretary (Political): Ms Caroline Jarrett
Second Secretary (Political): Mr Brendon Hughes
Second Secretary (Development): Vacant
Second Secretary (Estates Manager):
Mr David Walters, MVO

Second Secretary (Technical Management):
Ms Debbie Cuthbertson
Second Secretary (Commercial): Mr David Oswald
Second Secretary (Drugs): Mr Eric Lane
Second Secretary (Works): Mr Gary Holmes
Second Secretary (Works): Mr Tony Mason
Second Secretary (Immigration):
Mr Haroon Suleman
Second Secretary (Management): Ms Sally Biskin
Second Secretary (Consular): Mr Mark Kettle, MBE
Second Secretary (Media & Public Affairs):
Ms Rachel Jamieson
Third Secretary (Political): Mr Colin Hicks
Third Secretary (Political): Mr Duncan Holtorp
Third Secretary (Political): Ms Philippa Carnall
Third Secretary (Estates): Mr Donal Ahearn
Third Secretary (Management): Ms Jean Tranter
Third Secretary (Management/Finance):
Mr Neil Scrambler
Third Secretary (Consular): Ms Lara Bryden

Lahore
British Trade Office
65 Mozang Road
PO Box 1679, Lahore
Telephone: (00) (92) (042) 6316589 –90
Facsimile: (00) (92) (042) 6316591
Office Hours (GMT): Mon – Thurs 03 30 – 11 30,
Fri 03 30 – 07 30
Lahore Trade Promotion Adviser:
Mr Imran Masood Chaudhry

Karachi
British Deputy High Commission
Shahrah-e-Iran, Clifton, Karachi 75600
Telephone: (Landline): (92) (21) 5872431-6,
5874300, 5863534
(51) 5862389 (Commercial)
(51) 5874316 (DLO)
Facsimile: (92) (21) 5874014 General
                   5862316 Chancery
                   5874328 Visa
e-mail: bdhc@crestarnet.net
Office Hours (GMT): Mon – Thu 0330 - 1100
Fri 0330 - 0730
Deputy High Commissioner: Mr David D Pearey
Deputy Head of Mission: Mr Roger M S Sykes
First Secretary (Management):
Mr Mick J Mitchell, MVO
Second Secretary: Mr Barry S Watson
Second Secretary (Visa): Ms Amanda Ivemy
Third Secretary (Visa): Mr Simon Regan
Third Secretary (Visa): Ms Collette Goddard
Third Secretary (Visa): Mr Dave Temperley
Third Secretary (Visa): Ms Lesley Nicol
Third Secretary (Visa): Mr Valentine Madojemu
Third Secretary (Visa): Mr David Greenfield
Third Secretary (Commercial/Aid):
Mr Mustaq A Birader
Third Secretary (Consular): Mr Stephen B Smart
Security Officer: Mr Brian Davison

PALAU

Koror
British Embassy

Ambassador (resides at Suva):
Mr Christopher Haslam (Mr Ian Powell w.e.f
March 03)

PANAMA

Panama City
British Embassy
Swiss Tower, Calle 53
(Apartado 889) Zona 1,
Panama City, Republic of Panama
Telephone: (00) (507) 269 0866 (5 lines)
Facsimile: (00) (507) 223 0730
Airtech: (00) (507) 264 6846
e-mail: britemb@cwp.net.pa
Office Hours (GMT): Mon - Thurs 12 30 - 18 00
and 19 00 - 21 30
Fri 12 30 - 17 30
Ambassador and Consul-General:
Mr J I Malcolm, OBE
Deputy Head of Mission and Second Secretary:
Mr A Newlands
Second Secretary: Mr A Davenport
Defence Attaché (resides at Caracas):
Captain E F Searle, RN
Second Secretary (Technical) (resides at Caracas):
Mr K Gibbs
Second Secretary (Technical) (resides at Caracas):
Mr C Tully

PAPUA NEW GUINEA

Port Moresby (SP)
British High Commission
PO Box 212, Waigani NCD 131,
Papua New Guinea
Telephone: (00) (675) 3251643, 3251645,
3251659, 3251677
Facsimile: (00) (675) 3253547
Airtech: (00) (675) 3253953
e-mail: bhcpng@datec.com.pg
Office Hours: Mon-Thurs: 07 45 – 16 20 (Local)
Fri: 07 45 – 12 10 (Local)
The High Commission will continue to be open
over lunch
High Commissioner (ext 1207/9):
Mr Simon Scadden
Deputy High Commissioner (ext.1208):
Mr Christopher Thompson
Defence Adviser (resides at Canberra):
Group Captain Steven Duffill, RAF

PARAGUAY

Asunción
British Embassy
Avda. Boggiani 5848
C/R I6 Boquerón
Asunción
Telephone: (00) (595) (21) 612611
Facsimile: (00) (595) (21) 605007
Airtech: (00) (595) (21) 612611 ext. 2131
e-mail: brembasu@rieder.net.py
Office Hours (GMT): 12 00 - 19 00
Ambassador and Consul-General: Mr A J J Cantor
First Secretary and Deputy Head of Mission:
Mr N R Martin

Defence Attaché (resides at Buenos Aires):
Group Captain T P Brewer, OBE, RAF
Commercial Officer: Mr J Cano
Deputy Commercial Officer: Ms D Diaz de Espada
Aid/Information Officer: Mrs S Melamed
Management Officer/Accountant: Ms J Spalding

PERU

Lima
British Embassy
Torre Parque Mar (Piso 22)
Avenida Jose Larco, 1301
Miraflores
Lima
Telephone: (00) (51) (1) 617-3000 Main
                      617-3030 Commercial
                      617-3050 Consular/Visa
                      617-3060 British Council
                      617-3070 DFID
Facsimile: (00) (51) (1) 617-3100 Main
                      617-3001 Chancery
                      617-3020 Management
                      617-3040 Commercial
                      617-3055 Consular/Visa
                      617-3065 British Council
                      617-3080 DFID
Airtech: (00) (51) (1) 617-3008
e-mail: britemb@terra.com.pe (General)
britcom@terra.com.pe (Commercial)
consvisa.lima@fco.gov.uk (Consular/Visa)
Office Hours (GMT): Summer (Dec - Apr approx):
Mon and Fri 1300 - 1830; Tues, Wed and Thurs
1300 – 2130
Winter (Apr - Nov approx): Mon - Thurs 1300 -
2130; Fri 1300 - 1830
Ambassador: Mr Roger Dudley Hart, CMG
Deputy Head of Mission: Mr Ian Davies
Defence Attaché (Resides at Bogota):
Colonel Mike Wilcox
Cultural Attaché (British Council Director):
Mr Frank Fitzpatrick
First Secretary: (Vacant)
First Secretary (Commercial): Mr Martin Lamport
First Secretary (Development): Mr Mark Lewis
First Secretary (Health Sector): (Vacant)
First Secretary (Management) and HM Consul:
Mr Neil Storey
*Second Secretary (Works) (resides at Buenos
Aires):* Mr David Holmes
Second Secretary: Mr David James Grey
Third Secretary (Chancery):
Mr Graeme Bannatyne
*Third Secretary (Management) (resides at
Brasilia):* Mr Alan Barnes
*Third Secretary (Management/Immigration) and
Vice-Consul:* Mr Scott Simpson
Vice-Consul/Immigration: Mrs Nicola Standen

Arequipa
British Consulate
Tacna y Arica 156, Arequipa
Telephone: (00) (51) (54) 241 340
Facsimile: (00) (51) (54) 236 125
Office Hours (GMT): Mon - Fri 13 30 - 17 30 and
20 00 - 23 30

Honorary Consul: Mr J R G Roberts, MBE

Cusco
British Consulate
Av. Pardo 895
PO Box 606, Cusco
Telephone: (00) (51) (84) 22-6671/23-9974
Facsimile: (00) (51) (84) 23-6706
Office Hours (GMT): 16 00 - 17 00
Honorary Consul: Mr B Walker

Iquitos
British Consulate
Putumayo 182a,
Iquitos
Telephone: (00) (51) (94) 22 2732
Facsimile: (00) (51) (94) 22 3607
Office Hours (GMT): 16 00 – 1700
Honorary Consul: Mr P Duffy

Piura
British Consulate
Huancavelica 223, Piura
Telephone: (00) (51) (74) 333 300/326 233
Facsimile: (00) (51) (74) 327 009
Office Hours (GMT): 14 00 - 18 00/ 21 00 -23 59
Honorary Consul: Mr H E Stewart

Trujillo
British Consulate
Jesus de Nazareth No 312, Trujillo
Telephone: (00) (51) (44) 23 55 48
Facsimile: (00) (51) (44) 25 58 18
Office Hours (GMT): 14 00 - 22 00
Honorary Consul: Mr W Barber

PHILIPPINES

Manila
British Embassy
15th-17th Floors LV Locsin Building,
6752 Ayala Avenue cor Makati Avenue,
1226 Makati, (PO Box 2927 MCPO)
Telephone: (00) (63) (2) 816 7116 Switchboard
816 7271/2, 816 7348/9 Visa & Consular Sections
580 xxxx (direct inward dial; use extensions shown
beside name)
Facsimile: (00) (63) (2) 813 7755 Chancery
                      819 7206 Management
                      815 4809 Information
                      810 2745 Visa
                      840 1361 Consular
                      815 6233 Commercial
Airtech: 894 3367
Telex: 63282 (a/b 63282 PRODME PN)
e-mail: Information Section: uk@info.com.ph
Commercial Section: uktrade@info.com.ph
Office Hours (GMT): Mon – Thurs: 00 00 - 08 30,
Fri 00 00 - 06 00
Consular/Visa Office Hours: 00 00 - 05 00
Ambassador: Mr Paul Dimond (8300)
Deputy Head of Mission: Mr David Campbell
(8301)
Defence Attaché: Colonel Martin K Stretch (8302)
First Secretary (Commercial):
Mr Eammon Staunton (8303)

First Secretary (Cultural) (British Council Director): Ms Gill Westaway (914 1011 ext 20)
HM Consul: Mr Ian C Sargeant (8306)
First Secretary (Management):
Mr George K Hodgson (8307)
Second Secretary (Commercial):
Mr Geoff Wain (8305)
Second Secretary (Political):
Ms Katy Parker (8309)
Second Secretary (Immigration):
Mr Sharad R Ladva (8321)
Third Secretary (Immigration):
Mrs Angela Trott-Charpentier (8315)
Third Secretary (Immigration):
Mrs Kathleen Wain (8316)
Third Secretary (Immigration):
Mr Nigel Greetham (8319)
Third Secretary (Political):
Mr Daniel Painter (8311)
Attaché: Mr Gary Walker (8310)
Attaché: Mrs Charlotte L Rickward (8314)
Attaché: Ms Sheila Tunley (8313)
Attaché: Mr James Hopkins (8308)
Attaché: CPO Dennis Finch (8312)

Manila UK representation at the Asian Development Bank, see Missions & Delegations

Cebu
British Consulate
Villa Terrace, Greenhills Road,
Casuntingan, Mandaue City, Cebu
Telephone: (00) (63) (32) 3460 525
Facsimile: (00) (63) (32) 3460 269
e-mail: moke@gsilink.com
Honorary Consul: Mrs Moya P Jackson

POLAND

Warsaw
British Embassy
Aleje Roz No 1, 00-556 Warsaw
Telephone: (00) (48) (22) 628 1001-5, 625 6262
Facsimiles: (00) (48) (22) 621 7161
622 7659 (Management)
622 7698 (Chancery)
e-mail: britemb@it.com.pl

Commercial, Visa and Consular Sections:
Warsaw Corporate Centre, 2nd Floor,
Emilii Plater 28, 00-688 Warsaw
Telephone: (00) (48) (22) 625
3030/3032/3099/3163/3248/3293
Facsimile: (00) (48) (22) 625 3472
e-mail: ukembwcc@it.com.pl (Commercial)
Consular&Visa@Warsaw.mail.fco.gov.uk
Office Hours (GMT): Summer 06 30 - 14 30
Winter 07 30 - 15 30
Ambassador (ext 4211):
The Honorable Michael Pakenham, CMG
Counsellor and Deputy Head of Mission (ext 4214): Mr Tim Simmons
Counsellor (ext 4279): Mr Guy Spindler
Director of Trade Promotion/Consul-General (625 3413): Mr Michael Davenport, MBE
Counsellor (Cultural) (695 5900 ext 20):
Ms Susan Maingay

Defence and Air Attaché (ext 4246):
Group Capain Tim J Williams, AFC, RAF
Naval and Military Attaché (ext 4241):
Lieutenant Colonel Ian F Watts
First Secretary (Political) (ext 4259):
Mr Dominic Meiklejohn
First Secretary (Management) (ext 4227):
Mr Paul Chatt
First Secretary (Commercial) (622 7146):
Mr John Anderson
First Secretary (Commercial) (625 3030 ext 343):
Mr Howard Lattin-Rawstrone
First Secretary (Education) (695 5900 ext 50):
Mr Robin Rickard
Second Secretary (Political) (ext 4240):
Miss Anna Jackson
Second Secretary (Consul/Commercial) (622 6275): Mr Niall Cullens
Second Secretary (KHF) (ext 4258):
Mr Gilbert Hyde
Second Secretary (Political) (ext 4218):
Miss Alexandra Davison
Second Secretary (LELO) (ext 4256):
Mr George Rakowski
Second Secretary (ext 4203): Mr Jim Dunn
Third Secretary (Political) (ext 4217):
Miss Sara Hunt
Third Secretary (Information) (ext 4278):
Ms Alicia Clyde
Attaché and Vice-Consul (625 3030 ext 325):
Mr Simon Atkinson
Attaché (ext 4253): Mr Scott Melling
Attaché (ext 4211): Miss Nicola Grant

Katowice
British Consulate
ul PCK 10, 40-057 Katowice
Telephone: (00) (48) (32) 206 9801
Facsimile: (00) (48) (32) 205 4646
e-mail: honcon@silesia.top.pl
Office Hours: 09 00 – 15 00
Honorary Consul: Mr Alan Stretton

Poznan
British Consulate
ul Wroclawska 6, 61-837 Poznan
Telephone: (00) (48) (61) 851 72 90 Hotel Poznan
Telephone: (00) (48) (61) 833 19 61
Facsimile: (00) (48) (61) 853 29 19
e-mail: ukcons@protea.pl
info@protea.pl
walkowiak.w@orbis.pl
Office Hours: 09 00 – 15 00
Honorary Consul: Mr Wlodzimierz Walkowiak

Gdansk
British Consulate
ul Grunwaldzka 102, 80-224 Gdansk
Telephone: (00) (48) (58) 341 4365
Facsimile: (00) (48) (58) 344 1608
e-mail: consul@abcc.com.pl
Office Hours: 09 00 - 15 00
Honorary Consul: Mr Andrzej Kanthak

Szczecin
British Consulate
ul. Starego Wiarusa 32

71-206 Szczecin
Telephone: (00) (48) (91) 487 0302
Facsimile: (00) (48) (91) 487 3697
e-mail: gacszz@fnet.pl
Office Hours: 09 00 – 15 00
Honorary Consul: Mr Ryszard Karger

Wroclaw
British Consulate
ul. Olawska 2, 50-123 Wroclaw
Telephone/Facsimile: (00) (48) (71) 344 8961
e-mail: consulate@kmc.com.pl
Office Hours: 09 00 – 15 00
Honorary Consul: Mr Marek Grzegorzewicz

Kraków
British Consulate
ul. Sw.Anny 9
31-008 Kraków
Telephone: (00) (48) (12) 421 7030
Facsimile: (00) (48) (12) 422 4264
e-mail: ukconsul@bci.krakow.pl
Office Hours: 09 00 – 15 00
Honorary Consul: Mr Kazimierz Karasinski

Lublin
British Consulate
ul. Beskidzka 9
20-869 Lublin
Telephone: (00) (48) (81) 742 0101
Facsimile: (00) (48) (81) 742 9130
e-mail: ukconsul@uren.com.pl
Office Hours: 09 00 – 15 00
Honorary Consul: Mr Jan Danilczuk

PORTUGAL

Lisbon
British Embassy
Rua de São Bernardo 33, 1249-082 Lisboa
Telephone: (00) (351) (21) 392 4000
Facsimile: 4178 Chancery
         4184 Defence
         4185 Information
         4186 Commercial
         4187 Management
         4188 Consular
e-mail: Chancery@Lisbon.mail.fco.gov.uk
Commercial@Lisbon.mail.fco.gov.uk
Consular@Lisbon.mail.fco.gov.uk
Management@Lisbon.mail.fco.gov.uk
Political2@Lisbon.mail.fco.gov.uk
PPA@Lisbon.mail.fco.gov.uk
Website: www.uk-embassy.pt
Office Hours (GMT): Summer 08 00 - 12 00 and
13 30 - 16 30
Winter 09 00 - 13 00 and 14 30 - 17 30
Ambassador: Dame M G D Evans, DBE, CMG
Deputy Head of Mission: Mr R M Publicover
Counsellor (Political): Mr K D Evetts, OBE
Defence Attaché: Commander A J Bull, RN
Counsellor (Cultural) (British Council Director):
Mr R Ness
First Secretary (Head of Political Section):
Miss F Patterson
First Secretary (Cultural):
Mrs R Woodward-Carrick

First Secretary (Commercial): Mr M Turner
First Secretary and Consul: Mr J Blakemore
Second Secretary (Political/EU): Mr C Keller
Second Secretary (Commercial): Mr M Stead
Second Secretary (Management): Mr I Haywood
Second Secretary: Mr M Cox
Third Secretary (Press & Public Affairs):
Mrs S Tyler-Haywood
Third Secretary and Vice-Consul: Mr S Askham
Attaché (PA to Ambassador): Miss A Marshall

Oporto
British Consulate
Avenida da Boavista 3072,
4100-120 Oporto
Telephone: (00) (351) (22) 618 4789
Facsimile: (00) (351) (22) 610 0438
e-mail: All.oporto@fco.gov.uk
Consul: Mr Louis Taylor
Pro-Consul: Mrs Z M N Gomes

Portimão
British Consulate
Largo Francisco A Mauricio 7-1,
8500 Portimão
Telephone: (00) (351) (282) 417 800/4
Facsimile: (00) (351) (282) 417 806
e-mail: portimao.lisbon@fco.gov.uk
Honorary Consul: Mr R Nuttall

Funchal (Madeira)
Honorary British Consulate
Avenida de Zarco 2, CP 417,
9000 - 956 Funchal, Madeira
Telephone: (00) (351) (291) 221 221
Facsimile: (00) (351) (291) 233 789
e-mail: brit.confunchal@mail.eunet.pt
Honorary Consul: Mr C H Gedge

Ribeira Grande (Azores)
Honorary British Consulate
Quinta do Bom Jesus, Rua das Almas,
23, Pico da Pedra,
9600 Ribeira Grande, São Miguel,

Azores
Telephone: (00) (351) (296) 498 115
Facsimile: (00) (351) (296) 498 330
Honorary Consul: Mr J A de Vaz Carreiro
Consul (resides at Hong Kong): Mr M J Lowes

QATAR

Doha
British Embassy
PO Box 3, Doha, Qatar
Telephone: (00) (974) 4421991
Facsimile: (00) (974) 4438692
Telegrams: PRODOME DOHA
e-mail: Defence Section: defatdoh@qatar.net.qa
Commercial Section bembcomm@qatar.net.qa
Office Hours (GMT): Sat & Wed 04 30 - 11 30

Visa Section:
Ground Floor, AKC Building,
Al Saad Street
Telephone: (00) (974) 4364189
Facsimile: (00) (974) 4364139

Commercial Section:
8th Floor, Toyota Towers
Telephone: (00) (974) 4353543
Facsimile: (00) (974) 4356131
Ambassador: Mr David R MacLennan
*First Secretary (Commercial) and Deputy Head of
Mission:* Mr Mike Purves
Defence Attaché:
Wing Commander Paul Cottell, RAF
Second Secretary (Commercial):
Mr Peter Harrington
Second Secretary (Defence Sales): Mr Steve May
Second Secretary (Chancery/Information):
Mr Brian G Forsyth
Second Secretary (Management) and Vice-Consul:
Mrs Sarah V Davidson
Third Secretary (Immigration): Mrs Sarah Taylor
Third Secretary (Commercial): Mrs Marie Forsyth
Generalist (Registry): Mr Andy Dallas
Military Assistant to Defence Attaché:
Sgt Pete Mould

British Council
PO Box 2992, Doha
Telephone: (00) (974) 4426185
Facsimile: (00) (974) 4423315

ROMANIA

Bucharest
British Embassy
24 Strada Jules Michelet, 70154 Bucharest
Telephone: (00) (40) (21) 201 7200
Facsimile: (00) (40) (21) 201 7299 (Chancery)
7315 (Management)
7311 (Trade Development)
7317 (Consular)
Airtech: (00) (40) (21) 201 7225
Office Hours (GMT): Apr - Oct: Mon - Thurs: 05
30 - 14 00; Fri 05 30 - 10 30
Nov - Mar: Mon - Thurs: 06 30 - 15 00; Fri 06 30 -
11 30
Ambassador: Mr Quinton Quayle
Counsellor & Deputy Head of Mission:
Mr Andrew Pearce
Defence Attaché: Colonel Andrew T Bruce, MBE
Cultural Attaché (British Council Director):
Mr Stephan Roman
First Secretary (Head of Political/EU/Economic):
Ms Susan Laffey
First Secretary (Political): Mr Gideon Beale
First Secretary (DFID): Mr Bob Napier
First Secretary (Trade Development):
Mr James Halley
First Secretary: Mr Michael White
Deputy Defence Attaché:
Squadron Leader Keith A Marshall, RAF
British Council Deputy Director: Ms Karen Giblin
Second Secretary (Management):
Mr Kevin McCole
Second Secretary and Consul: Mr James Cameron
Second Secretary (Political/Information):
Mrs Margaret McCole
Second Secretary (Works) (resides at Budapest):
Ms Sandra Agnew
Second Secretary: Mr Tom Burns

Third Secretary (Management): Mrs Claire Healy
Third Secretary (Trade Development):
Mr Ian Marsden
Vice-Consul: Mr Gerard Healy
Vice-Consul: Mrs Anne Cheong
Assistant Defence Attaché: Mr Jim Osborne
Attaché (resides at Budapest): Mr Terry Wiltshire
Attaché (Works): Mr George Manson
Chaplain: The Revd James Ramsey

RUSSIAN FEDERATION

Moscow
British Embassy
Smolenskaya Naberezhnaya 10
Moscow 121099
Telephone: (00) (7) (095) 956 7200 (main
Switchboard)
Faxlok: 956 7364
Facsimile: (00) (7) (095) 956 7201 General
7441 Visas
7430 Press and Public Affairs
7254, 7389, 7443 Management
7442 Estates
7264 Defence
7446 Medical Centre
7480 Commercial/Development and
Science
e-mail: moscow@britishembassy.ru
Press & Public Affairs
consular.moscow@fco.gov.uk Consular
Cultural Department/The British Council
Library for Foreign Literature, Nikoloyamskaya 1,
Moscow 109189
Telephone: (00) (7) (095) 782 0200 (Switchboard)
Facsimile: (00) (7) (095) 782 0201
Office Hours (GMT): Winter 06 00 – 10 00; 11 00
– 14 00
Summer 05 00 – 09 00; 10 00 – 13 00
Ambassador: Sir Roderic Lyne, KBE, CMG
Minister and Deputy Head of Mission:
Mr D J Gowan
Defence and Air Attaché:
Air Commodore W Metcalfe, RAF
Counsellor (Political): Mr A C Crombie, OBE
Counsellor (Economic, Commercial and Science):
Ms D Bronnert
Counsellor (Political Affairs): Mr C Newell
Counsellor (Management) and Consul-General:
Mr J Cummins, MBE
Counsellor (Post Security): Mr N Trapé, OBE
*Counsellor (British Council Director) (Cultural
Affairs):* Mr A Greer
Naval Attaché: Captain S R Lister, RN, OBE
Military Attaché: Lieutenant Colonel C A Bulleid
First Secretary (Regional Medical Adviser):
Dr I McDonald
First Secretary (Political): Mr C Lonsdale
First Secretary (Political): Mr J Aves
First Secretary (Political): Mr P Maddinson
First Secretary (Political): Ms K Leach
First Secretary (Development): Mr M Harris
First Secretary (Commercial): Mr D Goodwin
First Secretary (Science and Technology):
Mr S Evans
First Secretary (Economic): Mr A Sharma

First Secretary (Technical Management):
Mr K Reynolds
First Secretary (Estate Management): Mr D Evans
*Cultural Attaché (British Council Deputy
Director):* Mr C Baxter
Cultural Attaché (Deputy Director, Education):
Ms R Addison
Cultural Attaché (Deputy Director, Operations):
(Vacant)
First Secretary (Consular/Immigration):
Mr P Smith
First Secretary (Management): Mr M Walley
*First Secretary (Fiscal, Drugs & Crime Liaison
Officer):* Mr R Gray
First Secretary (Technical Management):
Mr S Huckle
First Secretary (Press and Public Affairs):
Mr R Turner
First Secretary (British Council, Science Officer):
Dr E Bell
First Secretary (British Council Project Officer):
Mr P Norton
Assistant Naval Attaché:
Lieutenant Commander K McTear, RN
Assistant Military Attaché: Major A C J Torrents
Assistant Air Attaché:
Squadron Leader S T O'Brien, RAF
Second Secretary (Economic): Mr R Crowder
Second Secretary (Economic): Ms R Edwards
Second Secretary (External): Mr M Clayton
Second Secretary (Political): Ms R Low
Second Secretary (Commercial): Mr N Latta
Second Secretary (Commercial): Mrs C Cottrell
Second Secretary (Immigration): Mr M Bates
Second Secretary (Immigration): Mrs H Reynolds
Second Secretary (Immigration): Mr L Weldon
Second Secretary (Technical Management):
Mr S Tetlow
Second Secretary (Technical Management):
Mr S Forrester
Second Secretary (Technical Management):
Mr M Thompson
Second Secretary (Technical Management):
Mr C Broadbent
Second Secretary (Development): Mr G Ward
Second Secretary (Development): Mr M Fitzpatrick
Second Secretary (British Council) (Information):
Mr R Kerr
Attaché (Chief Security Officer): Mr R Dalton
Head of Defence Secretariat:
Flight Lieutenant R Corbould, RAF
Third Secretary (Press and Public Affairs):
Mr D Arkley
Third Secretary (Management): Miss L Stephens
Third Secretary (Visits): Mrs G Roberts
Third Secretary (Political Affairs): Mr M Tluczek
Attaché Vice-Consul: Mr N Snee
Attaché (Visas): Mr D Jones
Attaché (Visas): Ms S Manley
Attaché (Visas): Mrs M Helmer
Attaché (Visas): Mrs J Bayliss
Attaché (Visas): Mr T Van Der Eyken
Attaché (Visas): Mr G Jones
Attaché (Visas): Mrs M Morrison
Attaché (Visas): Mr J Akers
Attaché (Visas): Mr D Herbert

NATO Military Liaison Mission
C/o Ulitsa Mytnaya 3
Moscow 117049
Telephone: (00) (7) (095) 775 0270
Facsimile: (00) (7) (095) 775 0280
Head of Mission (accredited to British Embassy):
Major General P Williams, OBE

St Petersburg
British Consulate General
PL Proletarskoy Diktatury 5, Smolninskiy Raion
193124 St Petersburg
Telephone: (00) (7) (812) 320 32 00 Switchboard
320 32 39 Visa Reception
Facsimile: (00) (7) (812) 320 32 11 General
320 32 22 Commercial Section
320 32 33 Visa Section
320 32 44 Chancery (Airtech)
e-mail: bcgspb@peterlink.ru
dfid@peterlink.ru (Development Section)
management@stpetersburg.mail.fco.gov.uk
commercial@stpetersburg.mail.fco.gov.uk
consular@stpetersburg.mail.fco.gov.uk
information@stpetersburg.mail.fco.gov.uk
visa@stpetersburg.mail.fco.gov.uk
Consul-General: Ms B L Hay, CMG, MBE
Deputy Head of Mission/Consul (Commercial):
Mr P O'Connor
Consul (Cultural) (British Council Director):
Ms A Coutts
Consul (Consular/Management): Mr T M Waite
Vice-Consul (Immigration): Mr P M Marsh
Vice-Consul (Immigration): Mr J A Hudson
Attaché: Mr R A Heseltine

British Council
Fontank Reki Nab 46
St Petersburg Tel: (00) (7) (812) 325 6074
Facsimile: (00) (7) (812) 325 6073

Yekaterinburg
British Consulate-General
15a Gogol Street,
620075, Yekaterinburg,
Russian Federation
Telephone: (00) (7) (3432) 564 931
569 201 Visa Section
Facsimile: (00) (7) (3432) 592 901
Airtech: (00) (7) (3432) 777 068
e-mail: commercial.ekaterinburg@fco.gov.uk
brit@sky.ru (General Enquiries/Commercial
Department)
britvisa@sky.ru (Visa Enquiries/Know How Fund)
Website: www.britain.sky.ru
Consul General: Mrs L Cross
Vice Consul: Mr H L Rajguru

Novorossiysk
British Consulate
3a Fabrichnaya Street,
Novorossiysk, PO Box 85
Novorossiysk 353923
Telephone: (00) (7) (8617) 618100
Facsimile: (00) (7) (8617) 618291
e-mail: ecr@laroute.net
Honorary Consul: Mr E C Rumens

Vladivostok
British Consulate
5 Svetlanskaya Street, Vladivostok
Telephone: (00) (7) (4232) 411312
Facsimile: (00) (7) (4232) 410643
e-mail: tiger@ints.vtc.ru
Honorary Consul: Mr A M Fox

RWANDA

Kigali
British Embassy
Parcelle No 1131
Boulevard de l'Umuganda
Kaciryu Sud
BP 576 Kigali
Rwanda
Telephone: (00) (250) 85771, 85773, 84098, 86072
Facsimile: (00) (250) 82044
e-mail: britemb@rwanda1.com
Office Hours (GMT): Mon - Thurs 06 00 - 10.00
and 11 00 - 15 00
Fri 06 00 - 10.00
Ambassador: Mrs S E Hogwood, MBE
Deputy Head of Mission: Mr P Lawrence
Defence Attaché (resides at Kampala):
Lieutenant Colonel C J A Wilton
Third Secretary: Mr T Fisher

Department for International Development
Programme Office (Rwanda)
BP 576 Kigali, Rwanda
Telephone: (00) (250) 85771, 85773, 84098, 86072
Facsimlie: (00) (250) 510588
e-mail: @dfid.gov.uk
Office Hours (GMT): Mon-Thurs 06 00-10 00 and
11 00-15 00
Friday 0600- 10:00
First Secretary Developmental/Head of Office:
Mr Giles Bolton
First Secretary/Education Adviser: (Vacant)
First Secretary/Social Development Adviser:
Mr Gerard Howe
First Secretary/Governanace Adviser:
Mr Rupert Bladon

ST KITTS AND NEVIS

Basseterre
British High Commission
PO Box 483, Price Waterhouse Coopers Centre,
11 Old Parham Rd,
St John's, Antigua
Telephone: (00) (1) (268) 462 0008/9, 463 0010
Facsimile: (00) (1) (268) 562 2124
Office Hours (GMT): 12 00 - 16 30 (Open to the
Public) and 17 00 - 20 00 Fri: 12 00 – 17 00 (only)
*High Commissioner: Mr John White
Resident British Commissioner:
Miss Jean Sharpe, OBE
Deputy *Resident British Commissioner:*
Mr Paul Lawrence
*Deputy High Commissioner: Mr Rob Holland
*Defence Adviser: Captain Steve C Ramm, RN
*Counsellor (Regional Affairs):
Mr Nick J L Martin
*First Secretary: Mr Graham Honey

*First Secretary (Management/Consular):
Ms Ros Day
*Second Secretary (Chancery/Information):
Mr Nick J Pyle, MBE
*Third Secretary: Mr Tony W White
*Third Secretary (Consular/Immigration):
Mr Mark Harrison
*Resides at Bridgetown

British Consulate
Office of the Honorary British Consul
PO Box 559, Basseterre
St Kitts
Telephone: (00) (1 869) 466 8888 Home
Facsimile: (00) (1 869) 466 8889
Honorary Consul: Mr Peter Allcorn

ST LUCIA

Castries
British High Commission
Francis Compton Building,
2nd Floor (P O Box 227), Waterfront
Castries, Saint Lucia
Telephone: (00) (1) (758) 45 22484/5
Facsimile: (00) (1) (758) 45 31543
e-mail: postmaster.castries@fco.gov.uk
britishhc@candw.lc
Airtech: (00) (1) (758) 45 22486
Office Hours (GMT): Mon- Thurs 12 00 - 16 30
and 17 00 - 20 00
Fri 12 00 - 17 00
* High Commissioner: Mr John White
Resident British Commissioner: Mr Douglas Rice
* Deputy High Commissioner: Mr Rob Holland
* Defence Adviser: Captain Steve C Ramm, RN
* Counsellor (Regional Affairs):
Mr Nick J L Martin
* First Secretary (Chancery): Mr Graham Honey
* First Secretary (Management/Consular):
Ms Ros Day
* Second Secretary (Chancery/Information):
Mr Nick J Pyle, MBE
* Second Secretary (Chancery): Mr Phil Marshall
** Second Secretary (Technical Works):
Mr Mark Jones
* Third Secretary: Mr Tony W White
* Third Secretary (Consular/Immigration):
Mr Mark Harrison
*Resides at Bridgetown **Resides at Mexico City

ST VINCENT

Kingstown
British High Commission
Granby Street (PO Box 132),
Kingstown, St Vincent
Telephone: (00) (1) (784) 457 1701
Facsimile: (00) (1) (784) 456 2750
Office Hours (GMT): 12 30 - 20 00
* High Commissioner: Mr John White
Resident Acting High Commissioner:
Mr Terry Knight
* Deputy High Commissioner: Mr Rob Holland
* Defence Adviser: Captain Steve C Ramm, RN
* Counsellor (Regional Affairs):
Mr Nick J L Martin

* *First Secretary (Chancery):* Mr Graham Honey
* *First Secretary (Management/Consular):*
Ms Ros Day
* *Second Secretary (Chancery/Information):*
Mr Nick J Pyle, MBE
* *Second Secretary (Chancery):* Mr Phil Marshall
* *Third Secretary:* Mr Tony W White
Third Secretary (Consular/Immigration):
Mr Mark Harrison
*Resides at Bridgetown

SAMOA

Apia
British High Commission (all staff resident in
Wellington)
Telephone: (00) (64) (4) 472 6049
Facsimile: (00) (64) (4) 473 4982
High Commissioner: Mr R T Fell, CVO
Deputy High Commissioner: Mr M Bourke
First Secretary (External): Mr R Dean
First Secretary (Economic/Trade Policy):
Ms R L Foxwell
*First Secretary (Political/Press and Public
Affairs):* Mrs K S Wolstenholme
Second Secretary (Political):
Mr J D Wolstenholme
Second Secretary (Consular): Mr W S Robertson

Office of the Honorary British Consul
c/o Kruse Enari and Barlow, 2nd Floor, NPF
Building
Beach Rd, Central Apia
PO Box 2029, Apia
Telephone: (00) (685) 21895
Facsimile: (00) (685) 21407
e-mail: barlow@samoa.ws
Honorary British Consul: Mr R M Barlow, MBE

SAN MARINO

San Marino
British Embassy
Via XX Settembre 80/A
00187 Rome
Ambassador (resides at Rome):
Sir John Shepherd, KCVO, CMG

British Consulate-General
Lungarno Corsini 2,
50123 Florence
Telephone: (00) (39) 055 284133 (including
Airtech)
(00) (39) 055 289556 (Commercial)
Facsimile: (00) (39) 055 219112
e-mail: Consular.Florence@fco.gov.uk
Commercial.Florence@fco.gov.uk
Office Hours (GMT): Apr-Oct 07 00 - 11 00 and
12 00 - 15 00
Nov-Mar 08 00 - 12 00 and 13 00 - 16 00
Consul-General: (Resides at Florence):
Mrs Moira A Macfarlane

SÃO TOMÉ AND PRINCIPE

São Tomé
British Embassy

(All staff resident in Luanda)
Ambassador: Ms C Elmes, CMG
Consul: Mr F J Martin
First Secretary: Mr D G Cox
Second Secretary (Aid): Mr E Rich

São Tomé
British Consulate
Residencial Avenida,
Avienda Da Independencia
CP 257, Sao Tomé
Telephone: (00) (239) (12) 21026/7, 22505 (Home)
Facsimile: (00) (239) (12) 21372
Honorary Consul: Mr J Gomes

SAUDI ARABIA

Riyadh
British Embassy
PO Box 94351, Riyadh 11693
Telephone: (00) (966) (1) 488 0077
Facsimile: (00) (966) (1) 488 2373, 488 0623
Management,
488 1209 Consular
Voicemail Numbers: see individual officers
e-mail: Officers firstname.surname followed by
@riyadh.mail.fco.gov.uk
Office Hours (GMT): Sat - Wed 05 00 - 12 00
Ambassador: Sir Derek Plumbly, KCMG
*Counsellor, Deputy Head of Mission and Consul
General (2204):* The Honorable Dominic Asquith
Counsellor (Commercial) (2240):
Mr Philip Parham
Cultural Attaché (British Council Director):
Dr David Burton, OBE
Defence and Military Attaché (2230):
Brigadier John D Deverell
Naval Attaché (2233):
Commander Rupert R D'E Head, RN
Air Attaché (2234):
Wing Commander John A Bartram, RAF
First Secretary (Political) (2217): Mr Nic Coombs
First Secretary (Economic/PPA) (2242):
Mr Nick Abbott
First Secretary (Commercial) (2206):
Mr Gareth O'Brien
First Secretary and Consul (2271): Mr Ken Neill
Second Secretary (Management) (2264):
Mr Steve Mitchell
Second Secretary (Political) (2265):
Mr Derek Cooper
Second Secretary (Political) (2208):
Mr Nicholas Harrocks
Second Secretary (Political) (2330):
Mr Jonathan Luff
Third Secretary and Vice-Consul (2277):
Mrs Janice Banks
Third Secretary and Vice-Consul (2272):
Mr Sean McLean
Attaché (Management) (2261): Mr Peter Bradford
Third Secretary: Mr Sanjay Shah

Jedda
British Consulate-General
PO Box 393, Jedda 21411
Telephone: (00) (966) (2) 622-5550, 5557, 5558
Facsimile: (00) (966) (2) 622-6249

Airtech: (00) (966) (2) 622-5551
e-mail: Officers first name . surname followed by
fco.gov.uk
Office Hours (GMT): Sat-Wed 05 00 - 12 00
Consul-General: Mr Andrew Henderson
*Consul (Commercial) and Deputy Head of
Mission:* Mr Roger Church
Consul (Commercial): Mr Richard Hyde, MBE
Vice-Consul: Mr Ian Hodges
Vice-Consul (Immigration): (Vacant)
Vice Consul (Management): Mr John Barclay

Al Khobar
British Trade Office
PO Box 1868,
Al Khobar 31952
Telephone: (00) (966) (3) 882 5300
Facsimile: (00) (966) (3) 882 5384
e-mail: btokhobar@hotmail.com
officers firstname.surname followed by
@ALKHOBAR.mail.fco.gov.uk
Office Hours (GMT): Sat –Wed: 05 00 - 12 00
Head of British Trade Office: Mr Mike Hurley
Second Secretary (Commercial): Mr Bob Jackson
*Third Secretary (Commercial/Management) and
Vice-Consul:* (Vacant)
Pro-Consul: Mr Abdalla Abdalla
(Visa and Passport work for Eastern Province is the
responsibility of Riyadh)

SENEGAL

Dakar
British Embassy
20 Rue du Docteur Guillet
(Boite Postale 6025), Dakar
Telephone: (00) (221) 823 7392, 823 9971
Facsimile: (00) (221) 823 2766
e-mail: britemb@telecomplus.sn
British Council e-mail:
postmaster@britishcouncil.sn
Office Hours (GMT): Mon - Thurs 08 00 - 16 30,
Fri 08 00 - 12 30
Ambassador: Mr Alan Burner
Deputy Head of Mission and Consul:
Mr Simon Bond
Defence Attaché (Resides at Rabat):
Lieutenant Colonel Simon J A Lloyd
British Council Director: Mr Andrew McNab
Third Secretary and Vice-Consul: (Vacant)
Attaché (Immigration): Ms Christine Johnson

SERBIA AND MONTENEGRO

Belgrade
British Embassy
Resavska 46, 11000 Belgrade
Telephone: (00) (381) (11) 645 055, 3060 900,
3615 660
Facsimile: (00) (381) (11) 659 651
            3061 089 (Chancery)
            3061 072 (Consular/Visa)
            3061 059 (Commercial)
            642 293 (Information)
Airtech: 3061 020
e-mail: britemb@eunet.yu
ukembcom@eunet.yu (Commercial)

ukembbg@eunet.yu (Information)
Website: britemb.org.yu
Office Hours (GMT): Mon - Thur: 07 00 - 15 30;
Fri: 07 00 - 12 00
Ambassador: Mr Charles G Crawford, CMG
Deputy Head of Mission: Ms Sarah H Price
Counsellor: The Hon. Anthony L C Monckton
Defence Attaché:
Colonel Witek E Nowosielski-Slepowron
First Secretary (Commercial): Mr David J Webb
First Secretary (Development): Mr Brian Foy
Second Secreatary (Management and Consul):
Mrs Caroline F Slaymaker
Second Secretary (Chancery): Mr David W Ashley
Second Secretary (Economic): Mr James A Dancer
Second Secretary: Mr Roger Britton
Third Secretary and Vice-Consul:
Mr Julian E Lyon
Third Secretary (Immigration): Mr Philip Jones
Attaché: Mr Frederick M Bennett

Podgorica - Montenegro
British Consulate
National Library "Radosav Ljumovic"
Njegoseva 22
81000 Podgorica
Telephone: (00) (381) (812) 44 495
Facsimile: (00) (381) (812) 44 543 Management
            Section
Office hours (GMT): Mon, Wed & Friday: 07 45 -
15 00
Tue and Thur: 10 45 - 18 00
Honorary Consul: Mr Dragan Vugdelic

Pristina - Kosovo
British Office
Ismail Qemali Nr.6
Dragodan / Arberi
Pristina
Telephone: (00) 381 38 249 559
Facsimile: (00) 381 38 249 799
Office Hours (GMT): Mon - Thur: 07 30 - 16 00
Fri: 07 30 - 15 30
Head of Office: Mr Andrew Lloyd
Deputy Head of Office: Ms Lesley Beaton
Second Secretary (Political): Ms Victoria Whitford
Second Secretary (Political): Ms Rebecca Sutton
Management Officer/Vice Consul: Ms Kay Harris

SEYCHELLES

Victoria
British High Commission
3rd Floor,
Oliaji Trade Centre,
PO Box 161, Victoria, Mahé
Telephone: (00) (248) 225225, 225356
Facsimile: (00) (248) 225127
e-mail: bhcsey@seychelles.net
Office Hours (GMT): Mon - Thurs 04 00 - 12 00
Fri 04 00 – 11 00
High Commissioner: Mr F A Wilson, MBE
Deputy High Commissioner: Ms J Currie
Defence Adviser (Resides in Nairobi):
Colonel J R Barnes
British Council Director (Resides in Port Louis):
Mrs S Ponnappa, OBE

SIERRA LEONE

Freetown
British High Commission
Spur Road, Freetown
Telephone: (00) (232) (22) 232961, 232362,
232563-5
Facsimile: (00) (232) (22) 228169, 232070
Airtech: (00) (232) (22) 231824
e-mail: bhc@sierratel.sl
Office Hours (GMT): Mon-Thurs 08 00 - 16 30
Fri 08 00 - 13 00
High Commissioner: Mr David Alan Jones
Deputy High Commissioner: Ms Andrea Reidy
Counsellor: Mr Sean Holt
Defence Adviser:
Lieutenant Colonel Joe J P Poraj-Wilczynski
First Secretary (Development): Mr Ian Stuart
Second Secretary (PPA): Mr Derek Smith
Third Secretary (Political): Mr David Luttrell
Third Secretary (Management):
Ms Alison Baker-Mavin, BEM
Third Secretary (Immigration/Consular):
Mr Greg Gibson
Third Secretary (Development): Mrs Nancy Stuart
Attaché: Miss Tracey Coleman
Attaché: Staff Sergeant Pete King
Cultural Attaché (British Council Director):
Mr Rajiv Bendre
Deputy Director (British Council):
Ms Honor Flanaghan

SINGAPORE

Singapore
British High Commission
Tanglin Road, Singapore 247919
Commercial Section: Tanglin PO Box 19,
Singapore 247919
Telephone: (00) (65) 6424 4200 (General)
6424 4244 (Commercial)
6424 4270 (Visa/Consular)
Facsimile: (00) (65) 6424 4218 (Chancery)
6424 4250 (Management)
6424 4356 (Commercial)
6424 4264 (Consular)
6424 4230 (Defence)
e-mail: Commercial.singapore@fco.gov.uk
(Firecrest)
Website: www.britain.org.sg
Office Hours (GMT): Mon - Fri 08 30 – 05 00
High Commissioner:
Sir Stephen Brown, KCVO (4202)
*Deputy High Commissioner and Counsellor
(Economic/Commercial):*
Mr Paul D Madden (4300)
Defence Adviser:
Group Captain Martin D Stringer, RAF (4227)
Head of Chancery: Mr Clive Alderton (4204)
First Secretary (Political):
Mr William Brandon (4211)
First Secretary (Management):
Mr Gavin Marshall (4256)
First Secretary (Commercial):
Mrs Rosemary P Clarke, MBE (4302)

First Secretary (Technical):
Mr Richard M Hardy (4224)
First Secretary (Estate): Mr John McLean (4254)
First Secretary (Defence Equipment):
Mr Peter G Wythe, MBE (4225)
Assistant Defence Adviser:
Commander Brian Boxall-Hunt, RN (4229)
Second Secretary (Commercial):
Miss Erica Ackerman (4310)
Second Secretary (Commercial):
Mr Matthew E Oakley (4358)
Second Secretary (Economic/Commercial):
Mr Colin Dick (4323)
Second Secretary (Defence):
Mr Julian H Williams (4209)
Second Secretary (Technical):
Mr Nick Folker (4221)
Second Secretary (Consular/ECM):
Ms Adele Taylor (4360)
Third Secretary (Political):
Mr Dudley Crossland (4206)
Third Secretary (Consular/Visa):
Mr Paul Worster (4274)
Third Secretary (Management):
Mrs Jacqueline Fay (4242)
Third Secretary (Commercial):
Mrs Niki Wright (4303)
Assistant Attaché: Mr Kunle Ogunbanjo (4222)
Assistant Attaché: Miss Heidi Reilly (4213)
Assistant Attaché: Miss Yvonne Ratcliffe (4203)
Assistant Attaché: Mrs Stephanie Keep (4205)
Administrative Officer (Defence):
Mrs Sharn Davison (4235)
Pay and Pensions (Defence):
Staff Sergeant Mark Hincks (4262)
Commercial Officer: Mrs Valsa Panicker (4311)
Commercial Officer: Mr Teo Chong Kee (4309)
Press Public Affairs:
Ms Elisabeth Brodthagen (4305)
Accountant: Mr Alan Yeong, MBE (4261)
Estate Manager: Mr Terlok Singh (4328)
Systems Administrator:
Miss Serene Cheong (4308)

The British Council
30 Napier Road
Singapore 258509
Telephone: (00) (65) 6473 1111
Facsimile: (00) (65) 6472 1010
Cultural and Educational Adviser
(British Council Director):
Mr Les Dangerfield (101)
*Deputy Cultural and Education Adviser (Director,
English Language Centre):* Mr Martin Hope (104)
*Assistant Cultural and Educational Adviser
(British Council Assistant Director):*
Mrs Errim Mahmoud (103)

SLOVAKIA

Bratislava
British Embassy
Panska 16, 811 01 Bratislava
Telephone: (00) (421) (2) 5441
9632/9633/0005/3673
5441 0007 (out of hours)

5441 9240/7623 or 5443 0970
Visa Section
Facsimile: (00) (421) (2) 5441 0002 General
0001 Management/Consular
0003 KHF
0004 Defence Section
7639 Commercial Section
5443 0969 Visa Section
e-mail: bebra@internet.sk
Website: www.britemb.sk
Ambassador: Mr D R Todd
Deputy Head of Mission: Mr J R Setterfield
Defence Attaché:
Lieutenant Colonel N S Southward, OBE
Second Secretary (Commercial): Mr S Digby
Second Secretary (KHF): Mr A Anstead
Second Secretary (Political): Mr G S Pollard
Second Secretary (Management) & HM Consul:
Miss S Perry
Assistant Defence Attaché:
Squadron Leader G Clarke, RAF
Vice Consul/Third Secretary (Management):
Mr S P O'Neil
Third Secretary (Immigration): Mr G J Winter
Third Secretary (Immigration): Ms E Ryan
Third Secretary (Immigration): Mr G Price
Cultural Attaché (British Council Director):
Mr J A D McGrath

SLOVENIA

Ljubljana (SP)
British Embassy
4th Floor Trg Republike 3,
1000 Ljubljana
Telephone: (00) (386) (1) 200 3910 Main
Reception
200 3940 Commercial Section
Facsimile: (00) (386) (1) 425 0174 Chancery
425 9080 Commercial Section
e-mail: info@british-embassy.si
postmaster.ljubljana@fco.gov.uk
Website: www.british-embassy.si
Ambassador (ext 3921): Mr Hugh Mortimer, LVO
Deputy Head of Mission (ext 3922):
Mr Julian Bedingfield
Defence Attaché (3950):
Lieutenant Colonel Lindsay R Wilson
Second Secretary and HM Consul (ext 3914):
Mr David Blogg
Third Secretary (Political) (3928): Mr Neil Abbott
Cultural Attaché (Director, British Council):
Mr Stephen Green

SOLOMON ISLANDS

Honiara
British High Commission
Telekom House, Mendana Avenue,
Honiara, Solomon Islands
Postal Address: PO Box 676
Telephone: (00) (677) 21705, 21706
Facsimile: (00) (677) 21549
e-mail: bhc@welkam.solomon.com.sb
Office Hours (GMT): Mon - Fri 21 00 - 01 00 and
02 00 - 05 00

High Commissioner: Mr B P Baldwin
Deputy High Commissioner: Mr D S Jones

SOMALIA

Mogadishu
British Embassy
Waddada Xasan Geedd Abtoow 7/8
(PO Box 1036), Mogadishu
Telephone: (00) (252) (1) 20288/9, 21472/3
Telex: 3617 (a/b PRODROME SM)
Staff temporarily withdrawn from post

SOUTH AFRICA

Cape Town
British High Commission
91 Parliament Street,
Cape Town 8001
Telephone: (00) (27) (21) 405 2400
Facsimile: (00) (27) (21) 425 1427
e-mail: britain@icon.co.za
Office Hours (GMT): Staff currently working from
BCG building. See below for contact details.

Pretoria
British High Commission
255 Hill Street, Arcadia 0002
Telephone: (00) (27) (12) 483 1200
Facsimile: (00) (27) (12) 483 1302
e-mail: bhc@icon.co.za
Website: http://www.britain.org.za
Office Hours (GMT): Mon-Thurs: 06 00 - 15 00
Fri: 06 00 - 10 30
High Commissioner: Ms Ann Grant
Counsellor and Deputy High Commissioner:
Mr A J Sparkes
Counsellor (Political): Mr P N Shott
Defence and Military Adviser:
Brigadier M R Raworth
Air and Naval Adviser:
Wing Commander T A Harper, RAF
First Secretary: Mr M Frost, OBE
First Secretary: Mr N Fisher
First Secretary (Management): Mr T Connolly, OBE
First Secretary (Technical Works):
Mr P J Sullivan, MBE
First Secretary: Mr A Millar
First Secretary (PPA): Mr N Sheppard
First Secretary (Technical Management):
Mr M A Elvins
Second Secretary: Mr D Thomas
Second Secretary (Management): Mr M P Kay
Second Secretary (Technical Management):
Mr P Cullen
Second Secretary (Technical Management):
Mr N Roper
Second Secretary: Mr R Watters
Second Secretary: Mr J Plank
Second Secretary: Miss D Sheard
Third Secretary: Miss S Campbell

Consular Section
Liberty Life Place, Block B
256 Glyn Street, Hatfield 0083
Postal Address: P O Box 13611
and P O Box 13612,

Hatfield, 0028, Pretoria
Telephone: (00) (27) (12) 4831 402 Visas
4831 401 Passports
Facsimile: (00) (27) (12) 4831 433 Visas
             4831 444 Passports
e-mail: PTA.PassportEnquiries@fco.gov.uk
PTA.VisaEnquiries@fco.gov.uk
Office Hours (GMT): Mon-Thurs: 06 00-14 15
Fri: 06 00-11 30
(* Based at High Commission, Pretoria)
* *Consul General:* Mr A J Sparkes
Consul: Mr P Seaby
Second Secretary (Immigration/ECM):
Mr R T Jones
Second Secretary (ALO): Mr T Moloney
Third Secretary (Consular): Miss J Sibbons
Third Secretary (Immigration): Mrs T B Connolly
Third Secretary (Immigration): Mr M Player
Third Secretary (Immigration): Miss M Coleman
Third Secretary (Immigration): Mr M Wardle
Third Secretary (Immigration): Mrs P Garnham

Pretoria
Department for International Development:
Southern Africa
Suite 208, Infotech Building,
1090 Arcadia Street,
Hatfield 0083, Pretoria, Gauteng
Telephone: (00) (27) (12) 342 3360
Facsimile: (00) (27) (12) 342 3429
Counsellor (Head of Office): Mr S Sharpe
First Secretary (Senior Education Adviser):
Ms B Payne
*First Secretary (Senior Natural Resources
Adviser):* Ms P Chalinder
First Secretary (Senior Governance Adviser):
Dr R Thomas
*First Secretary (Regional Sustainable Livelihoods
Adviser):* Mr A T Barrett
*First Secretary (Programme Manager BLSN and
Deputy Head of Division):* Dr J C Barrett
First Secretary (Economic Adviser): Mr P Barbour
First Secretary (Social Development Adviser):
Miss B Dillon
First Secretary (Enterprise Development Adviser):
Mr H Scott
*First Secretary (Senior Health and Population
Adviser):* Dr D Tracey
First Secretary (Environmental Adviser):
Ms B Arthy
First Secretary (Engineering Adviser):
Mr R Blakelock
First Secretary (HIV/AIDS and Health Adviser):
Mrs A De Cleene
First Secretary (Regional Forestry Adviser):
(Vacant)
First Secretary Programme Manager (RSA):
Mr J McAlpine
First Secretary(Senior Regional Statistics Adviser):
Ms J Bunting
*Second Secretary (Senior Economist Assistant:
BLSN/SADC):* Ms H McLeod
*Second Secretary Deputy Programme Manager
RSA (Governance):* Mr D Fidler
Second Secretary (Programme Manager – BLSN):
Mr M Moir

Deputy Programme Manager:
RSA (SL): Mr R Taylor
Second Secretary (IT Manager): Mr A Bromley
Second Secretary (Finance and Contracts Officer):
Mr D Collingwood
Third Secretary (Programme Officer - BLNS):
Ms P Hoffman

Cape Town
British Consulate General
Postal address: PO Box 500,
Cape Town, 8000
Callers: 15th Floor, Southern Life Centre,
8 Riebeeck Street, Cape Town, 8001
Telephone: (00) (27) (21) 405 2400
             422 7741 Commercial Section
Facsimile: (00) (27) (21) 425 1427
             425 3660 Commercial Section
Airtech: (00) (27) (21) 425 1423
Office Hours (NOT PUBLIC HOURS) (GMT):
Mon-Thurs: 06 00 - 10 30 and 11 15 - 14 30
Fri: 06 00 - 11 30
Consul-General (2428): Mr Peter D Broom
Second Secretary (Political) (2467):
Mr James Barbour
Vice-Consul (Commercial) (2420): Ms Janet Usher
Vice-Consul (Management/Consular) (2421):
Mrs Sarah L Young
Vice-Consul (2432): Mr Iain D Bain
Vice-Consul (2413): Mrs Lisa Woolley

East London
British Consulate
c/o Price Waterhouse Coopers & Lybrand, Suite 7,
Norvia House, 34 Western Avenue,
Vincent 5247
Postal Address:
P O Box 19537, Tecoma,
East London 5214
Telephone: (00) (27) (43) 726 9380
Facsimile: (00) (27) (43) 726 9390
Honorary Consul: Mr John L Fletcher

Port Elizabeth
British Consulate
5th Floor 1st Bowring House
66 Ring Road, Greenacres
Port Elizabeth, 6045
Postal Address: PO Box 35098
Newton Park
Port Elizabeth, 6055
Telephone: (00) (27) (41) 363 8841
Facsimile: (00) (27) (41) 363 8842
Telex: 242326
Telegraphic Address: Britain, Port Elizabeth
Office Hours (GMT): 07 00 - 10 30
Honorary Consul: Mr Harry Marston

Johannesburg
British Trade and Investment
Callers - Dunkeld Corner, 275 Jan Smuts Avenue,
Dunkeld West, 2196
Postal Address:
P O Box 1082, Parklands 2121, Johannesburg
Telephone: (00) (27) (11) 537 7000 Commercial
Services
Facsimile: (00) (27) (11) 537 7257

Public Information Line:
Telephone: (00) (27) (11) 537 7206
Facsimile: (00) (27) (11) 537 7253
Management:
Telephone: (00) (27) (11) 537 7241
Facsimile: (00) (27) (11) 537 7253
Office Hours: Mon- Thurs 06 00 - 14.30 Fri 06 00
- 11.30
Director of Trade and Investment:
Mr Michael Mowla
Deputy Director for Trade and Investment:
Ms J M Leon
Trade Development Adviser: Mrs H McKenzie
Trade Development Adviser: Ms L S Hill
Management Officer: Mr R A Sylvester

British Council
8th Floor, 76 Juta St
Braamfontein
PO Box 30637
Braamfontein 2017
Telephone: (00) (27) (11) 403 3316
Facsimile: (00) (27) (11) 339 3715
Cultural Attaché (British Council Director):
Mr C Gobby

Durban
British Consulate
Suite 1901, 19th Floor, The Marine,
22 Gardiner Street, Durban 4001
Postal Address: P O Box 1404,
Durban, 4000
Telephone: (00) (27) (31) 305 3041
Facsimile: (00) (27) (31) 307 4661
Office Hours (GMT): Mon-Thurs: 06 00 - 15 00
Fri: 06 00 - 11 30
Consul: Mr D Pearce
Vice-Consul: Mrs J M Smith
Vice-Consul (Commercial): Mr W G Tyler
Vice-Consul (Management): Mrs J Busch

SPAIN

Madrid
British Embassy
Calle de Fernando el Santo 16,
28010 Madrid
Telephone: (00) (34) 91 700 82 00
Facsimile: (00) (34) 91 700 83 09 Chancery
                       83 07 Defence
                       83 29 EU/Economic
                       83 11 Commercial
                       82 72 Information
                       82 10 Management
Office Hours (GMT): Winter 07 00-15 30
Summer Mon - Thurs 06 30-13 00
Fri 06 30-12 30
Ambassador: Mr Peter J Torry
Deputy Head of Mission: Mr Edward A Oakden
*Counsellor (Commercial) and Director of Trade
Promotion:* Mr John Hawkins
Counsellor: Ms Rosie Sharpe
Defence and Naval Attaché: Captain Anthony
Croke, RN
Military and Air Attaché:
Group Captain Gavin C Daffarn, RAF

*Counsellor (Cultural Affairs) (British Council
Director):* Mr Peter Sandiford
First Secretary (Head of Public Affairs & Press):
Mr Jon Davies
First Secretary and Consul-General:
Mr Jeffrey Thomas
First Secretary (Management):
Mr Michael H F Legg
First Secretary (Press Officer): (vacant)
First Secretary (Agriculture):
Mr Anthony J Bastian
First Secretary (Political/Economic):
Mr Anthony J Ball
First Secretary (Labour): Mr Giles Dickson
First Secretary (Cultural Affairs): (vacant)
First Secretary (Political/Economic):
Mr Christopher Sainty
First Secretary (Technical Management):
Mr Keith Ager
*First Secretary (Cultural Affairs) (British Council
Deputy Director):* Ms Christine Melia
British Council: Ms Margaret Douglas
Second Secretary: Mr David Sykes
Second Secretary: Mr Michael Keogh
Second Secretary: Mr Mark Cox
Second Secretary (Management):
Ms Karen Roskilly
Second Secretary (Commercial): Mr David J Chun
Second Secretary (Commercial):
Mr Trevor Cayless
Second Secretary (Political/Economic):
Ms Priya Guha
Second Secretary (Technical Management):
Mr Paul Oliver
Senior Economic Officer: Mr William Murray
Third Secretary (Press Attaché):
Ms Caroline Sprod
Third Secretary/Vice-Consul: Mr Steve Morgan
Attaché: Mr Benedict Lyons

Madrid
British Consulate-General
Paseo de Recoletos 7-9, 4ª
28004 Madrid
Telephone: (00) (34) 91 524 9700
Facsimile: (00) (34) 91 524 9730
Office hours (GMT): All year: 07.00-17.00
Consul-General: Mr J Thomas
Vice-Consul: Miss R Choudhury
Vice-Consul: Mr D Wickham
Pro-Consul: Mr B Ormston

Alicante
British Consulate
Plaza Calvo Sotelo 1-2,
Apartado De Correos 564,
03001 Alicante
Telephone: (00) (34) 96 521 60 22
Facsimile: (00) (34) 96 514 05 28
e-mail: enquiries.alicante@fco.gov.uk
Office Hours (GMT): Winter: 06 00-13 30
Summer: 06 00-12 30
Consul: Mr Michael Mcloughlin
Vice-Consul: Mr Amos A Santolaya Diaz, MBE
Vice-Consul: Mr George Outhwaite

Honorary Vice-Consul (resides at Benidorm):
Mr John A Seth-Smith (e-mail: jass@ctv.es)

Andorra
Tel/Fax: (00) (34) 376 83 98 40
e-mail: britcoand@mypic.ad
Honorary Consul: Mr Hugh Garner

Las Palmas (Canary Islands)
British Consulate
Edificio Cataluña,
Calle Luis Morote 6-3
35007 – Las Palmas de Gran Canaria
(Postal address: PO Box 2020, 35080 - Las Palmas
de Gran Canaria)
Telephone: (00) (34) 928 262 508
Facsimile: (00) (34) 928 267 774
e-mail: laspalmasconsulate@ukinspain.com
firstname.surname@fco.gov.uk
Office Hours (GMT): Winter: 08 00-15 30
Summer: 07 00-14 30
Consul: Mr Peter J Nevitt
Vice-Consul: Mrs Anita J Pavillard
Commercial Officer: Mrs Montse Clemente

Málaga
British Consulate
Edificio EUROCOM
C/Mauricio Moro Pareto, 2, 2
29006 Málaga
Telephone: (00) (34) (95) 235 2300
Facsimile: (00) (34) (95) 235 9211
e-mail: postmaster@malaga.mail.fco.gov.uk
Office Hours (GMT): Winter: 07 00-14 30
Summer: 06 00-12 30
Consul: Mr Bruce McIntyre, MBE
Vice-Consul: Mr Patrick Boyce
Vice-Consul: Ms Rosslyn D Crotty
*Commercial Officer (Tel/Fax: (00) (34) 95
4187032):* Mr Joseph Cooper
*Commercial Officer (Tel/Fax: (00) (34) 95
4915874):* Ms Caroline Gray

Santa Cruz de Tenerife
British Consulate
(Canary Islands)
Plaza Weyler 8-1,
Santa Cruz de Tenerife 38003
Telephone: (00) (34) 922 28 68 63, 28 66 53
Facsimile: (00) (34) 922 28 99 03
e-mail: tenerifeconsulate@ukinspain.com
Office Hours (GMT): Winter: 08 30-14 00
Summer: 08 00-13 30
Consul: Mr Keith Hazell
Vice-Consul: Mrs Helen Diaz de Arcaya Keating

Vigo
British Consulate
Plaza de Compostela 23-6 I
(Aptdo 49), 36201 Vigo
Telephone: (00) (34) 986 43 71 33
Facsimile: (00) (34) 986 43 71 33
e-mail: vigoconsulate@ukinspain.com
Office Hours (GMT): 07 00-12 00
Honorary Consul: Mr John M Cogolludo

Barcelona
British Consulate-General
Edificio Torre de Barcelona,
Avenida Diagonal
477-13o, 08036 Barcelona
Telephone: (00) (34) 93 366 6200 (6 lines)
Facsimile: (00) (34) 93 366 6221
e-mail: bcon@cyberbcn.com
Website: www.ukinspain.com
Office Hours GMT: 07 00-16 00 April – June,
September and October
08 00-17 00 November to March
06 30-12 30 July to August
*Consul-General (also Consul-General for Co-
Principality of Andorra):* Mr D Thomson
Consul (Commercial): Ms Y E Cherrie
Director, The British Council: Mr M Frier
Vice-Consul (Consular): Ms R Clavell
Vice-Consul (Commercial): Mr J H V Hankin
Commercial Officer: Ms E Prada
Pro-Consul (Management): Ms J Millet

Bilbao
British Consulate-General
Alameda de Urquijo 2-8, 48008 Bilbao
Telephone: (00) (34) 94 415 76 00, 415 77 11, 415
77 22
Facsimile: (00) (34) 94 416 76 32
Airtech: (00) (34) 94 416 47 51
e-mail bcgbilbo@readysoft.es
Office Hours (GMT): 07 00 - 16 00 (Apr - Jun,
Sept & Oct)
08 00 - 17 00 (Nov - Mar)
06 30 - 12 30 (Jul - Aug)
Consul-General: Mr Ian Lewis
Vice-Consul: Mr Derek Doyle, MBE
Pro-Consul: Mrs Flora Dorronsoro
Commercial Officer: Mr Angel Beti

Santander
British Consulate
Paseo de Pereda 27, 39004 Santander
Telephone: (00) (34) 942 22 00 00
Facsimile: (00) (34) 942 22 29 41
e-mail: mpineiro@nexo.es
Office Hours (GMT): 07 00 - 11 00 and 13 30 - 16
00 (April to mid June, mid Sept to Oct)
08 00 - 12 00 and 14 30 - 17 30 (Nov- March)
06 00 - 12 30 (Mid Jun to mid Sept)
Honorary Consul: Mr Modesto Pineiro, MBE

Palma
British Consulate
Balearic Islands
Plaza Mayor 3D,
07002 Palma de Mallorca,
Balearic Islands, Spain
Telephone: (00) (34) 971 712445, 712085,
716048,718501,712696
Facsimile: (00) (34) 971 717520
e-mail: consulate@palma.mail.fco.gov.uk
Office Hours (GMT): Nov-March: 07 00 - 14 30
Apr-Jun & Sep-Oct: 06 00 - 13 30
Jul-Aug: 06 00 - 12 30
Consul: Mr Michael K Banham
Vice-Consul: Mr Esteban Mas Portell

Ibiza
British Vice-Consulate
Avenida Isidoro Macabich
45-1, Apartado 307,
07800 Ibiza
Telephone: (00) (34) 971 301818, 303816, 301058
Facsimile: (00) (34) 971 30 19 72
e-mail: ibizacons@worldonline.es
Office Hours (GMT): Nov-March: 07 00 - 14 30
Apr-Jun & Sep-Oct: 06 00 - 13 30
Jul-Aug: 06 00 - 12 30
Vice-Consul: Mrs Helen Watson, MBE
Pro-Consul: Miss Raquel de la Osa

Menorca
British Vice-Consulate
St Casa Nova, Cami de Biniatap 30,
07720 Es Castell, Menorca
Telephone: (00) (34) 971 36 33 73
Facsimile: (00) (34) 971 35 46 90
e-mail: deborah@infotelecom.es
Honorary Vice-Consul: Mrs Deborah Hellyer

SRI LANKA

Colombo
British High Commission
190 Galle Road, Kollupitiya
(PO Box 1433),
Colombo 3
Telephone: (00) (94) (1) 437336/43
Facsimile: (00) (94) (1) 430308,
335803 Consular/Visa
e-mail: bhc@eureka.lk
Office Hours (GMT): Mon - Thurs: 02 00 - 11 00;
Fri: 02 30 - 07 30
Visa Hours (GMT): Mon - Thurs: 02 00 - 05 30;
Fri: 02 30 - 04 30
British Council: 49 Alfred House Gardens
(PO Box 753), Colombo 3
Telephone: (00) (94) (1) 581171/2, 587078,
580301,502487, 582449
Facsimile: (00) (94) (1) 587079
e-mail: enquiries@britishcouncil.lk
High Commissioner (also High Commissioner to the Republic of Maldives):
Mr Stephen N Evans, OBE
Deputy High Commissioner: Mr Peter J Hughes
Defence Adviser:
Lieutenant Colonel Mark H De W Weldon
Cultural Attaché (British Council Director): Mr T O'Brien
First Secretary (Commercial and Economic):
Mr D J Waring
Second Secretary (Management): Mr R Morris
Second Secretary (Chancery): Miss A Kemp
Second Secretary (Immigration/Consular):
Mr J Kenny
Second Secretary (Immigration): Mr R Goodall
Second Secretary (resides at Mumbai): Mr C Noon
Second Secretary (Development): Miss P Thorpe
Deputy Cultural Attaché: (British Council):
Ms A Searle
Third Secretary (Management): Mrs R Brett
Attaché (Immigration): Mr S Gordon
Attaché (Immigration/Consular): Mr M Redden

Attaché (Immigration/Consular): Mrs C Botha
Attaché: Mrs S Grimes
Attaché: Ms D White
Attaché: Mr P Nalden
Attaché: Staff Sergeant N Pusey
Attaché: Mr F Denn

SUDAN

Khartoum
British Embassy
Off Sharia Al Baladia, Khartoum East
(PO Box No 801)
Telephone: (00) (249) (11) 777105
Facsimile: (00) (249) (11) 776457
775562 (Consular/Visa)
Airtech: 775492
e-mail: british@sudanmail.net
Office Hours (GMT): Sun - Thur: 04 30 - 11 30
Visa Office Hours (GMT): Sun - Thur: 04 30 - 11 30
Ambassador: Mr William Patey
DHM/Consul General: Mr Ric Girdlestone
First Secretary (British Council):
Mr Paul Doubleday
Second Secretary (Management/Commercial):
Mr Malcolm Collard
Second Secretary (Aid): Mr Graham Wicks
Second Secretary (Political/Information):
Mr Alastair King-Smith
Third Secretary and Vice-Consul: Miss Tiiu Morris
Third Secretary Entry Clearance Officer:
Mr Jonathan Knight

SURINAM

Paramaribo
British Embassy
* *Ambassador:* Mr S J Hiscock
* *Second Secretary (Commercial), Consul and Deputy Head of Mission:* Mr S Crossman
Defence Attaché (Resides at Bridgetown):
Captain S C Ramm, RN
* *Second Secretary (Management):*
Ms A M Fairley
* *Third Secretary (Immigration/Consular):*
Mr A J McFarlin
* Resides at Georgetown

Paramaribo
British Consulate
c/o VSH United Buildings, Van't Hogerhuysstraat, 9-11
PO Box 1860, Paramaribo, Surinam
Telephone: (00) (597) 402558,402870
Facsimile: (00) (597) 403515,403824
e-mail: united@sr.net
Office Hours (GMT): Mon - Fri: 11 00 - 20 15
Honorary Consul: Mr J J Healy, Jr

SWAZILAND

Mbabane (SP)
British High Commission
Callers: 2nd Floor, Lilunga House,
Gilfillan Street
Mbabane

Postal: Private Bag, Mbabane
Telephone: (00) (268) 404 2581/2/3/4
Facsimile: (00) (268) 404 2585
e-mail: enquiries.mbabane@fco.gov.uk
Office Hours (GMT): Mon - Thur: 06 00 - 11 00
and 12 00 - 14 45
Fri: 06 00 - 11 00
High Commissioner: Mr David Reader
Deputy High Commissioner: Ms Liz Ripard
Defence Adviser (resides at Pretoria):
Brigadier Mike R Raworth
Attaché: Mrs Christine Costantini

Department for International Development
Telephone: (00) 268 404 9731/2/3
Facsimile: (00) 268 404 9734

SWEDEN

Stockholm
British Embassy
Skarpögatan 6-8, Box 27819,
115 93 Stockholm
Telephone: (00) (46) (8) 671 3000 Direct Dial - use
extensions below in brackets
Facsimile: (00) (46) (8) 662 9989 Management
671 3104 Chancery/Defence
671 3077 Commercial
661 9766 Consular/Visa
671 3100 Information
Airtech: 671 3137
Office Hours (GMT): Winter: 08 00 -16 00
Summer 06 30 -14 30
Ambassador: (3102) Mr John Grant, CMG
Counsellor (Economic and Commercial) (3050):
Mr John Tucknott, MBE
Counsellor (3112): Mr Andrew Stafford
Defence Attaché (3105):
Wing Commander Phil M Leadbetter, MVO, RAF
Cultural Attaché (British Council Director) (3082):
Mr Jim Potts
First Secretary (Political) (3119):
Miss Alison Blackburne
First Secretary (Political) (3111):
Mr Andrew Brear
First Secretary (Inward Investment) (3067):
Mr Martin Cronin
First Secretary (Management and Consul) (3070):
Mr Peter Langham
First Secretary (Commercial) (3053):
Mr Ian Cormack
Second Secretary (Political/Information) (3108):
Mrs Emma Sundblad
Second Secretary (Political/Economic) (3115):
Ms Claire Jeffrey
*Second Secretary (Media & Public Relations)
(3006):* Mr Damion Potter
Third Secretary (Political) (3191):
Mr Rupert Potter
Vice-Consul (3023): Ms Karen Farley
Entry Clearance Manager (3022):
Mr Henry Hodge
Honorary Chaplain: The V Rev. David Ratcliff

Gothenburg
British Consulate-General
Södra Hamngatan 23,

S 41114 Göthenburg
Telephone: (00) (46) (31) 339 3300
Facsimile: (00) (46) (31) 339 3302
Consul-General: Mr Chris P Greenwood

Malmö
British Consulate
Hyregatan 8,
211 21 Malmö
Telephone: (00) (46) (40) 611 55 25
Facsimile: (00) (46) (40) 611 55 25
Honorary Consul: Mr Anders Wixell (Swedish)

Sundsvall
British Consulate
SCA Graphic
Sundsvall AB,
Ostrand Pulp Mill,
861 81 Timra
Telephone: (00) (46) (60) 16 40 00
Facsimile: (00) (46) (60) 57 49 90
Honorary Consul: Mr Ola Hildingsson (Swedish)

SWITZERLAND

Berne
British Embassy
Thunstrasse 50, 3005 Berne
Telephone: (00) (41) (31) 359 7700
Facsimile: (00) (41) (31) 359 7701 General
359 7769 Political and Information Section
359 7765 Management and Consular Sections
Internet Address: http://www.britain-in-switzerland.ch
Office Hours (GMT): 07 30 - 11 30 and 12 30 -
16 00
Ambassador: Mr B S T Eastwood, CMG*
*Counsellor and Deputy Head of Mission, Director
of Trade Promotions (also Consul-General for the
Principality of Liechtenstein):* Mr D G Roberts
*Counsellor (Science and Technology) (resident at
Bonn):* Ms H Hughes-McKay
Counsellor: Mr H W G Patterson
Defence Attaché:
Lieutenant Colonel R H Bangham
First Secretary (Political): Dr S Harkin
First Secretary (Commercial): Miss A J Pring
*First Secretary (Management) and Consul (also
Consul for the Principality of Liechtenstein):*
Mr A M Bates, MVO
Second Secretary (Investment): Mr B W Hamill
Third Secretary (Political): Mr M G Webber
Third Secretary (Political): Mr I Paterson
Vice Consul (Commercial): Mr B Haessig
Vice Consul (Commercial): Mrs S Valdettaro
Vice Consul (Commercial): Mr P Mueller
Vice-Consul (Science & Technology): Mr B Sander
Pro-Consul: Miss W Page, MBE
* Also Ambassador to the Principality of
Liechtenstein

Geneva
British Consulate General
37-39 Rue de Vermont (6th Floor),
1211 Geneva 20
Telephone: (00) (41) (22) 918 24 00
Facsimile: (00) (41) (22) 918 23 22

Telex: 414195 (a/b 414195 UKGV CH)
Office Hours (GMT): Summer: 06 30 - 10 30 and
12 00 - 15 00
Winter: 07 30 - 11 30 and 13 00 - 16 00
HM Consul General: Mr I A Crees
HM Consul: Mrs V H Rowe
British Vice-Consul: Ms L Sowerby
Vice-Consul (Commercial): Mrs E C Baha
Pro-Consul: Ms J Murray

Geneva
Joint Management Unit
37-39 Rue de Vermont, 1211 Geneva 20
Telephone: (00) (41) (22) 918 23 00
Facsimile: (00) (41) (22) 918 23 10
Telex: 414195 (a/b 414195 UKGV CH
Office Hours (GMT): Summer: 07 00 - 11 00 and
12 30 - 16 00
Winter: 08 00 - 12 00 and 13 30 - 17 00
First Secretary, Joint Management Officer:
Mr I A Crees
Deputy Management Officer: Mr R W Harmer
Assistant Management Officer: Ms L Sowerby

Montreux/Vevey
British Consulate
13 chemin de l'Aubousset,
1806 St Légier, Vaud
Telephone and Facsimile:
          (00) (41) (21) 943 3263
Honorary Consul: Mrs S Darra, MBE

Valais
British Vice-Consulate
Rue des Fontaines,
CH 3974 Mollens - Valais
Telephone: (00) (41) (27) 480 32 10
457 51 11 (Radio Pager)
Facsimile: (00) (41) (27) 480 32 11
Honorary Vice Consul: Mr A Bushnell

Geneva United Kingdom Mission to United Nations, see Missions & Delegations

Geneva United Kingdom Permanent Representation to the Conference on Disarmament, see Missions & Delegations

Zurich
British Vice-Consulate
Hegibachstrasse 47
CH- 8032 Zurich
Telephone: (00) 01 383 65 60
Facsimile: (00) 01 383 65 61
Honorary Consul: Mr A L T McCammon

Lugano
British Vice-Consulate
Via Sorengo 22,Third Floor
PO Box 184
6903 Lugano
Telephone: (00) (41) (91) 950 0606
Facsimile: (00) (41) (91) 950 0609
Office Hours (GMT): 10 00 - 12 00
Honorary Consul: Mr J Takield, OBE

Basel
British Vice-Consulate
Innovation Centre

Gewerbestrasse 14
CH4123
Allschwill
Tel/fax: (00) (41) (61) 483 0977
Mobile: (00) (41) 763 789 987
Honorary Consul: Dr A Chalmers

SYRIA

Damascus
British Embassy
Kotob Building,
11 Mohammad Kurd Ali Street,
Malki, PO Box 37, Damascus
Telephone: (00) (963) (11) 373 9241/2/3/7
Facsimile: (00) (963) (11) 373 1600
Office Hours (GMT): Sun - Wed 06 00 - 13 15;
Thur 06 00 - 12 00
Ambassador: Mr H G Hogger
Counsellor and Deputy Head of Mission:
Mr S H Innes
Defence Attaché: Colonel R C J Martin, OBE
British Council Director: Dr P Brazier
First Secretary (Political): Dr D M Haines
First Secretary (Management) and Consul:
Mr F J McGinley
Second Secretary (Commercial): Mr J A Chadwick
Vice-Consul (Immigration/Consular):
Mr J S Walker
Third Secretary (Political/Information):
Mr M R Bell
Third Secretary (Economic): Miss E J Robertson

Aleppo
British Consulate
PO Box 199
Aleppo
Telephone: (00) (963) (21) 267 2200, 2336771
(Office),
267 5033 (Home)
Facsimile: (00) (963) (21) 267 7640
Office Hours (GMT): 06 00 - 09 00
Honorary Consul: Mr Alexander Akras

British Trade Office
P O Box 5547
Aleppo
Telephone: (00) (963) (21) 268 0502/3
Facsimile: (00) (963) (21) 268 0501
Senior Commercial Officer: Mr Z Abu Baker

TAIWAN
See Annex for details.

TAJIKISTAN

Dushanbe
British Embassy
43 Lutfi Street
Dushanbe, Tajikistan
Telephone: (00) 992 91 901 5079
(00) 870 762 856 221 (Satellite)
Facsimile: (00) 992 91 901 5078
e-mail: dushanbe3@gtnet.gov.uk (Chargé)
Staff resident in Dushanbe
Chargé d'Affaires: Mr M Smith

Deputy Head of Mission: (Temporary position until further notice)
Defence Attaché (resides at Almaty):
Lieutenant Colonel G J Sheeley, AFC

TANZANIA

Dar es Salaam
British High Commission
Umoja House,
Garden Avenue, PO Box 9200
Dar es Salaam
Telephone: (00) (255) (22) 211 0101 Main Switchboard
Facsimile: (00) (255) (22) 211 0120 Chancery
211 0112 Management
211 0296 Consular
211 0297 Visa
211 0080 Commercial
Airtech: 211 0102
e-mail: bhc.dar@dar.mail.fco.gov.uk
Office Hours (GMT): Summer: Mon-Fri 04 30 – 11 30
High Commissioner: Mr R Clarke
Deputy High Commissioner: Mr S Banks
Defence Adviser (resides at Nairobi):
Colonel J R Barnes
British Council Director: Mr T Cowin
Second Secretary (Commercial/Consular):
Mr M Rash
Second Secretary (Management): Ms H M Feather
Second Secretary (Political/Press and Public affairs): Ms S Hussey
Third Secretary (Consular/Immigration):
Ms P Smith
Third Secretary (Immigration): Mr D Mills

Department for International Development Eastern Africa (Tanzania): DFIDEA (T)
British High Commission
Plot 874
Msasani Peninsular
(PO Box 9200)
Dar es Salaam
Telephone: (00) (255) (22) 2600572-8
Facsimile: (00) (255) (22) 2600334
Office Hours (GMT): Mon-Fri 05 00 – 12 30
Head of DFIDEA (T): Ms C Sergeant
Deputy Head of DFIDEA (T): Ms L Campbell
Second Secretary/Senior Programme Officer:
Miss L M Saunderson
Third Secretary/Programme Officer: Mr J Orton
Rural Livelihoods/Private Sector Adviser:
Ms L Ditcatern
Economic Adviser: Ms F Shera
Social Development Adviser: Ms A Albee
Health & Population Adviser: Mr P Smithson
Education Adviser: Mr J Baxter
Engineering Adviser: Mr G Macdonald
Governance Adviser: Mr P Van Heesewijk
Human Resources and Administrative Manager:
Ms M Negri

THAILAND

Bangkok
British Embassy
Wireless Road, Bangkok, 10330
Telephone: (66) (2) 305 8333
Facsimile: (66) (2) 305 8372 or 8380 Chancery
(66) (2) 305 8220 Defence
(66) (2) 255 8619 Commercial/Press and Public Affairs
(66) (2) 255 9278 Management
(66) (2) 255 6051 Consular
(66) (2) 254 9579 Immigration
Airtech: (66) (2) 254 4720
Website: www.britishemb.or.th
Office Hours (GMT): Mon-Thurs: 0100 - 0500 and 0545 - 0930
Fri: 0100 - 0600 (Duty Staff until 0930)
EXTN
Ambassador: Mr L B Smith, CMG 2301
Counsellor and Deputy Head of Mission:
Mr P B West 2266
Counsellor (Commercial): Mr M Hill 2319
Defence Attaché: Colonel A R E Singer, OBE 2222
Counsellor and Permanent Representative to ESCAP: Mr R Campbell 2288
First Secretary (Political): Mr T Carter 2224
Consul & First Secretary (Management):
Mr D J Fisher 2208/2239
First Secretary: Mr J Hector 2232
First Secretary: Mr D Kilby 2226
First Secretary (Technical): Mr K Griggs 2267
Second Secretary (Political):
Mr M R Findlay 2230
Second Secretary (Commercial):
Mr K Cunningham 2294
Second Secretary (Immigration):
Mrs J Lacey-Smith 2245
Second Secretary (Airline Liaison Officer):
Miss D Broderick 2362
Second Secretary (Management):
Mr D M Surman 2317
Second Secretary and Vice Consul:
Mrs A Tokalau 2253
Second Secretary (Technical): Mr P Haigh 2369
Third Secretary (Commercial):
Mr M Woodham 2350
Third Secretary (Economic/Development):
Mr P McKenzie 2291
Third Secretary and Vice-Consul:
Mrs F Lavender-Borisuth 2229
Third Secretary (Immigration): Mrs G Lewis 2363
Third Secretary (Immigration): Mrs D Tok 2352
Third Secretary (Immigration):
Mr N Faulkner 2329

Department for International Development (DFID SEA)
C/O British Embassy
Wireless Road, Bangkok, 10330
Telephone: (66) (2) 305 8333
Facsimile: (66) (2) 253 7124
EXTN
Head of Division: Mr M Mallalieu 2250
Senior Engineering Adviser: (Vacant) 2233
Senior Education Adviser: Mr S Passingham 2295

Senior Governance Adviser: Mr P Owen 2335
Senior Economic Adviser: Mr P Balacs 2227
Senior Natural Resources and Environment
Adviser: Mr S Bland 2261
Senior Social Development Adviser:
Mr R Edwards 2272
Social Development Adviser: Mr A Burke 2214
Health & Population Adviser: Dr D Ghandhi 2325
Senior Programmes Adviser: Mr C Athayde 2202
Programmes Manager: Mr R Leverington 2204
Economist: Mr O Bargawi 2247
Deputy Programme Manager: Mrs K Parsons 2383
Programmes Officer: Ms D Avery 2215
Programmes Officer: Mr J Black 2280

Chiang Mai
British Consulate
British Council Offices,
198 Bumrungraj Rd
Muang, Chiang Mai, 50000
Telephone: (00) (66) (53) 242103, 248706
Facsimile: (00) (66) (53) 244781
Office Hours (GMT): Mon – Thur: 0100 – 0500
and 0545 – 0930
Fri: 0100 – 0600
Honorary Consul: (vacant)

TOGO

Lomé
British Embassy
(All staff resident in Accra)
Ambassador and Consul-General: Dr Rod Pullen
Counsellor and *Deputy Head of Mission:*
Mr Craig Murray
Defence Attaché:
Lieutenant Colonel Steen K E Clarke, OBE
First Secretary (Development): Mr Tony Gardner
First Secretary (Commercial): Mr Kevin Lynch
First Secretary (Political/External):
Mr David Keegan
Second Secretary and Vice-Consul:
Mrs Caroline Cross
Second Secretary (Development):
Mr Desmond Woode
Second Secretary (Political, Press and Public
Affairs): Mr Gregory Quinn
Second Secretary (Management): Mr Seif Usher
Second Secretary (Airline Liaison Officer):
Mr Derek McDougal Swanson
Second Secretary (Immigration): Ms Debra Poulier
Second Secretary: Mr Andrew Eelbeck
Third Secretary (Commercial): Mrs Carol Turvill
Third Secretary (Chancery): Mr Jonathan Saunders
Third Secretary (Immigration): Mr Jim Beach
Third Secretary (Immigration): Mr Brendan Gill
Third Secretary (Immigration): Mr Alan Green
Third Secretary (Immigration): Mr Althea Ramsey
Third Secretary (Immigration): Mrs Tracey Singh
Third Secretary (Immigration): Mr Stuart Turvill
Third Secretary (Immigration): Mr Simon Winter

Lomé
British Consulate
British School of Lomé, BP 20050, Lomé
Telephone: (00) (228) 264606
Facsimile: (00) (228) 264989

e-mail: "For Mrs Jeni Sayer, British Consulate"
Admin@bsl.tg
Office Hours (GMT): Mon - Fri: 09 00 - 11 00
Honorary Consul: Mrs J A Sayer

British Commercial Office
Concession OTAM, Zone Portuaire,
Port de Peche, BP 9224, Lomé-Port, Lomé, Togo
Telephone: (00) (228) 271141, 275054
Facsimile: (00) (228) 274207
Mobile: 042180
e-mail: tom@netcom.tg
Commercial Officer: Captain R A M Jones

TONGA, KINGDOM OF

Nuku'alofa
British High Commission
PO Box 56, Nuku'alofa, Tonga
Telephone: (00) (676) 24285/24395
Facsimile: (00) (676) 24109
Airech: (00) (676) 23922
e-mail: britcomt@kalianet.to
Office Hours (GMT): Sun - Wed: 19 15 - 23 30
and 00 30 - 03 45
Thurs: 19 15 - 00 15
High Commissioner and Consul for American
Samoa: Mr Paul Nessling
Management Officer: Mrs Kathryn Nessling
Defence Adviser (resides at Wellington):
Colonel Alec A Peebles

TRINIDAD AND TOBAGO

Port of Spain
British High Commission
19 St Clair Avenue, St Clair
Port of Spain, Trinidad
Telephone: (00) (1) (868) 622 2748, 622 8960/1/2,
622 9895/6
Facsimile: (00) (1) (868) 622 4555 Management
                      622 9087 Commercial
                      628 3064 Consular
                      628 8715 Chancery
Airtech: (00) (1) (868) 622 4533
e-mail: csbhc@opus.co.tt
Website: www.britain-in-trinidad.org
Office Hours (GMT): Mon - Thurs: 11 30 - 16 00
and 17 00 - 20 00
Fri: 11 30 - 16 30
High Commissioner: Mr P G Harborne
Deputy High Commissioner: Mr C J Edge
Defence Adviser (Resides at Bridgetown):
Captain S C Ramm, RN
Counsellor (Regional Affairs) (Resides at
Bridgetown): Mr N J L Martin
Second Secretary (Management/Consular):
Mrs S Nicholas
Second Secretary (Chancery): Mr T Reader
Second Secretary (Commercial): Mr B Nicholas
Third Secretary (Chancery/Information):
Mr C Hilton

TUNISIA

Tunis
British Embassy
5 Place de la Victoire, Tunis 1000
Telephone: (00) (216) 71 341 444
Facsimile: (00) (216) 71 341 877
Airtech: (00) (216) 71 350 707
e-mail: british.emb@planet.tn
Consular and Visa Sections: 141-143 Avenue de la
Liberté, Tunis 1002
Telephone: (00) (216) 71 793 322 Visa
(216) 71 846 184 Consular
Facsimile: (216) 71 792 644
e-mail: uk.visa@planet.tn
Office Hours (GMT): Mon - Friday 07 00 - 11 00
and 12 00 - 15 00
Ambassador and Consul-General:
Mr Robin A Kealy, CMG
Deputy Head of Mission: Ms Janet C Hancock
Defence Attaché (resides in London):
Commander Roly Woods, RN
Cultural Attaché (British Council Director):
Mr John Whitehead
*Second Secretary (Commercial/Press & Public
Affairs):* Mr Brian J Conley
Second Secretary (Management):
Miss Joanna J Lowis
*Second Secretary (Entry Clearance Manager and
Consul):* Mr John P R Jeffrey
Vice-Consul: Mrs Val Zaoui, MBE
Third Secretary (Immigration): Mr Gary E Benham
Third Secretary (Immigration): Mr Chris Daltrey
Attaché: Mr Robert F McGlennan
Attaché: Mrs Lorraine H McColl

Sfax
Honorary British Consulate
55 Rue Habib Maazoun, 3000,
Sfax 3000, Tunisia
Telephone: (00) (216) (74) 223 971
Facsimile: (00) (216) (74) 299 278
Honorary Consul: Mr Moneef Sellami

TURKEY

Ankara
British Embassy
Sehit Ersan Caddesi 46/A
Cankaya, Ankara
Telephone: (00) (90) (312) 455 3344
455 + extension number
Facsimile: (00) (90) (312) 455 3351
        Commercial/Economic
        455 3353 Consular/Visa
        455 3386 Clinic
        455 3226 Defence
        455 3259 Drugs
        455 3356 Information
        455 3352 Management
        455 3350 Political
        455 3320 HMA
Airtech: 455 3240
e-mail: britembank@fco.gov.uk (check Firecrest
for individuals)
Website: www.britishembassy.org.tr

British Council
Esat Caddesi 41
Kucukesat, Ankara 06660
Telephone: (00) (90) (312) 424 1644
Facsimile: (00) (90) (312) 427 6182
Office Hours (GMT): Summer 05 45 - 10 00 and
11 15 - 14 30
July, August 05 45 - 10 00 and 11 15 - 14 30 (Mon
- Thurs)
05 45 - 10 00 (Fri)
Winter 06 45 - 11 00 and 12 15 - 15 30
Extn
Ambassador: Mr Peter J Westmacott, CMG, LVO 3201
Counsellor and Deputy Head of Mission:
Mr David J Fitton 3203
Defence and Military Attaché:
Brigadier Kim O Winfield 3221
*Counsellor (British Council Director, Cultural
Affairs):* Dr Ray Thomas, OBE
Naval & Air Attaché:
Commander Steve M Pegg, RN 3223
*First Secretary (Head of Economic/Commercial
Section):* Mr Chris Innes-Hopkins 3241
First Secretary (Head of Political Section):
Dr Laurence Bristow 3205
First Secretary (Political): Mr David Craig 3207
First Secretary (Political/Military):
Dr Liane Saunders 3210
First Secretary (Management) and Consul:
Mr Dominic Clissold 3261
*First Secretary (British Council and Cultural
Affairs):* Mr Tony Lockhart
*First Secretary (British Council and Cultural
Affairs):* Ms Sally Goggin
First Secretary (Defence Equipment):
Mr Chris Comper 3225
First Secretary (Drugs): Mr David Parker 3360
First Secretary (Technical Management):
Mr David Kingdom 3214
Second Secretary (Economic):
Mr Stephen McCormick 3244
Second Secretary (Political/Information):
Dr Sangeeta Ahuja 3209
Second Secretary (Drugs): Mr Warren Spivey 3380
Second Secretary (Technical Management):
Mr Chris Fox 3218
Third Secretary (Management):
Mr Richard Whiteley 3262
Vice-Consul: Mrs Trudie Pak 3257

Antalya
British Vice-Consulate
Fevzi Çakmak Cad
1314 Sokak No.6/8
Antalya
Telephone: (00) (90) (242) 244 5313
Facsimile: (00) (90) (242) 243 2095
e-mail: britconant@celik.net.tr
Vice Consul: Mrs Jane Baz

Bodrum
British Consulate
Kibris Sehitleri Caddesi
Konacik Mevkii No 401/B
Bodrum
Telephone: (00) (90) (252) 319 0093-94

Facsimile: (00) (90) (252) 319 0095
e-mail: britconbod2@superonline.com
Honorary Consul: Mrs Fatma Nese Coskunsu

Izmir
British Consulate
1442 Sokak No 49
Alsancak
PK 300 Izmir
Telephone: (00) (90) (232) 463 5151
Facsimile: (00) (90) (232) 465 0858
e-mail: postmaster@izmir.mail.fco.gov.uk (check
Firecrest for individuals)
Consul: Mr Willie Buttigieg

Marmaris
British Consulate
c/o Yesil Marmaris Tourism & Yacht Management
Inc.
Barbaros Caddesi 11, Marina
P O Box 8, 48700 Marmaris
Telephone: (00) (90) (252) 412 6486
Facsimile: (00) (90) (252) 412 5077
e-mail: brithonmar@superonline.com
Honorary Consul: Mr Adnan Dogan Tugay

Mersin
British Consulate
Cakmak Caddesi, 124 Sokak
Mahmut Tece Is Merkezi, A Blok, Kat 4/4
Mersin
Telephone: (00) (90) (324) 232 1248, 237 8687
Facsimile: (00) (90) (324) 232 2991
Honorary Consul: Mr Andre Nofal

Istanbul
British Consulate-General
Mesrutiyet Caddesi No 34,
Tepebasi, Beyoglu,
PK 33 Istanbul 80072
Telephone: (00) (90) (212) 293 7540, 293 7545/9
Facsimile: 245 4989
Visa Section:
Telephone: (00) (90) (212) 252 6436/40
Facsimile: 252 6441 Visa
        245 6354 Consular
        252 8682 British Council
e-mail: brcgist@verisoft.com.tr
comsec@escortnet.com.tr
Office Hours (GMT): Summer: 05 30 - 11 00 and
11 45 - 13 45
Winter: 06 30 - 11 00 and 11 45 - 14 45
Consul-General and Director of Trade Promotion:
Mr Roger Short
Deputy Consul-General: Mr Jim Begbie
*Consul (British Council Director and Cultural
Affairs):* Ms Sue Barnes
Consul (Management): Mr David Morton
Consul (Political Affairs): Mr Owen Traylor
Consul: Mr Paul Free
Consul: Mr Kevin Grist
Consul: Mr Andy Kellaway
Consul (Immigration): Ms Kim Charman
Consul (Immigration): Ms Janice Mills
Consul (Project Liaison Officer): Mr John Collier
Vice-Consul (Technical Works Officer):
Mr Gavin Thomas

Vice-Consul: Mr Shane Campbell, MBE
Vice-Consul (British Council and Cultural Affairs):
Mr Barry Breary
Vice-Consul (Commercial):
Mr Richard di Salvatore, MBE
Vice-Consul (Commercial): Mrs Lynne Smith
Vice-Consul: Mr Peter Clasen
Vice-Consul (Information):
Mrs Najma Bouakaze-Khan
Vice-Consul (Management): Mr Les Rowlands
Vice-Consul (Immigration): Mr Hector Hughes
Vice-Consul (Immigration):
Mrs Alison Jones-Early
Vice-Consul (Immigration): Mr Charlie Cosker
Vice-Consul (Immigration): Mr Paul Hardy
Vice-Consul (Immigration): Mr Steve McBride
Vice-Consul (Immigration): Mr Eddie Scanlon
Vice-Consul (Immigration): Ms Jenni Williams
Vice-Consul: Ms Carole Jarvie

Bursa
British Honorary Consulate
Ressam Sefik Bursali Sokak,
Basak Caddesi No.
Zemin Kat, 16010 Bursa
Telephone: (00) (90) (224) 220 25 34
Facsimile: (00) (90) (224) 220 88 01
Home Telephone: (00) (90) (224) 221 29 84
Honorary Consul: Mr E Kagitcibasi

TURKMENISTAN

Ashgabat
British Embassy
3rd Floor, Office Building
Four Points Ak Altin Hotel,
Ashgabat, Turkmenistan
Telephone: (00) (993) (12) 363462, 363463,
363464, 363466, 363498
Facsimile: (00) (993) (12) 363465
Airtech: (00) (993) (12) 363463 x292
e-mail: beasb@online.tm (General)
beasbtrade@online.tm (Commercial)
beasbppa@online.tm (Press & Public Affairs)
Website: www.britishembassytm.org.uk
Office Hours (GMT): Mon - Thurs: 04 00 - 08 00
and 09 00 - 12 30
Fri: 04 00 - 08 00 and 09 00 - 11 00
Ambassador: Mr Paul Brummell
Deputy Head of Mission: Mr Clive J McGill
Defence Attaché (resides at Moscow):
Lieutenant Colonel Colin A Bulleid
Assistant Defence Attaché (resides at Moscow):
Major Alfonso Torrens
Cultural Attaché (resides at Tashkent):
Mr Neville McBain
Second Secretary: Mr Stuart O'Neill
Third Secretary (Chancery): Mr Justin D Tait
Third Secretary (Management) and Vice-Consul:
Ms Jane E Rowlands

TUVALU

Funafuti
British High Commission
(All staff resident at Suva)
High Commissioner: Mr Charles F Mochan

Deputy High Commissioner and First Secretary (Consular): Mr Christopher Haslam (Mr Ian Powell w.e.f March 03)

UGANDA

Kampala
British High Commission
10/12 Parliament Avenue,
PO Box 7070, Kampala
Telephone: (00) (256) 78 312000
Facsimile: (00) (256) (41) 257304
                78 312281 (Consular /Visa Section)
Airtech: (00) (256) 78 312210
e-mail: bhcinfo@starcom.co.ug. (Press and Public Affairs Section)
bhccomm@starcom.co.ug (Commercial Section)
bhcimm@infocom.co.ug (Consular/Visa Section)
firstname.lastname@fco.gov.uk
Office Hours (GMT): Mon to Thurs: 05 30 - 10 00
and 11 00 - 14 00
Fri: 05 30 - 10 00

British Council
Ground Floor, Rwenzori Courts
Plot 2 Nakasero Road
PO Box 7306
Kampala
Telephone: (00) (256) (41) 234 730/7/9/234 748
Facsimile: (00) (256) (41) 254 853
e-mail: firtsname.lastname@britishcouncil.or.ug
High Commissioner: Mr Adam Wood
Deputy High Commissioner: Mr Chris Skilton
Defence Adviser: Lieutenant Colonel Chris Wilton
First Secretary (Regional Affairs):
Mr Justin Hustwitt
First Secretary (British Council Director):
Mr Philip Goodwin
First Secretary (Management):
Mr Brian Cope, MVO
First Secretary (British Council):
Ms Kate Ewart-Biggs
Second Secretary (Economic): Miss Joanne Cetti
Second Secretary (Political/Press and Public Affairs): Mr Ewan Ormiston
Second Secretary (Entry Clearance Manager):
Mr Stephen Powell
Second Secretary (Political External):
Mr Craig Fulton
Second Secretary (Commercial/Consular):
Ms Sarah Young
Third Secretary (Political): Mr Matthew Caney

Department for International Development Eastern Africa (Uganda)
3rd Floor Rwenzori Courts
Plot 2 Nakasero Road
P O Box 7306, Kampala
Telephone: (00) (256) (41) 348727/9 & 348730/7
Facsimile: (00) (256) (41) 348732, 348735
e-mail: initial-surname@dfid. gov.uk
Head of Office: Mr Mike Hammond
Deputy Head of Office: Ms Janet Al-Utaibi
Education Adviser: Mr Michael Ward
Renewable Natural Resources Adviser:
Dr Alwyn Chilver
Health & Population Adviser: Ms Ros Cooper

Assistant Health Adviser: Ms Angela Spilsbury
Social Development Adviser: Ms Bella Bird
Governance Adviser: Mr Tim Williams
Economic Adviser: Mr Paul Mullard
Economist: Ms Kate Tench
Enterprise Development Adviser: Mr Anthony Way
Emergencies Adviser: Mr Graham Carrington
Programme Officer: Miss Sandra Grant
Governance Officer: Mr Jeremy Armon
Deputy Programme Manager: Ms Alison Cochrane

UKRAINE

Kiev
British Embassy
01025 Kiev Desyatinna 9
Telephone: (00) (380) (44) 462 0011, 462 0012, 462 0014
Facsimile: (00) (380) (44) 462 0013
e-mail: ukembinf@sovam.com
Consular/Visa Section:
01021 Kiev, 6 Mazepy Street (Formerly - Sichnevoho,
Povstannya 6)
Telephone: (00) (380) (44) 290 7317,290 2919,
Facsimile: (00) (380) (44) 290 7947
Office Hours (GMT): Mon – Thurs 06 00 – 14 15
Fri 06 00 – 14 00

British Council:
040704 Kiev
4/12, Hruhoria Skovorody
Telephone: (00) (380) (44) 490 5600
Facsimile: (00) (380) (44) 490 5605
Ambassador: Mr R E Brinkley
Consul-General and Deputy Head of Mission:
Mr D Maclaren
Defence Attaché: Captain R E Drewett, MBE, RN
First Secretary (Political): Miss F MacCallum
First Secretary (Commercial): Mr R C C Cook
First Secretary (Management/Consular):
Mr R B Smith
First Secretary (British Council Director):
Ms L Biglou
Second Secretary (Chancery/Information):
Miss N A Davison
Second Secretary (Development): Mr S Clark
Second Secretary (Immigration): Mrs E Allen
Second Secretary (Assistant Director, British Council): Mr I Law
Assistant Defence Attaché: Major S I Mehers
Third Secretary (Political): Mr S J Brown
Third Secretary (Management): Mrs S Garnham
Third Secretary (Immigration/Vice-Consul):
Miss N Rennie
Third Secretary (Immigration): Mr A M Lake
Third Secretary (Immigration): Miss J Connor
Assistant Defence Attaché: Staff Sergeant P Durkin

UNITED ARAB EMIRATES

Abu Dhabi
British Embassy
PO Box 248, Abu Dhabi,
United Arab Emirates
Telephone: (00) (971) (2) 6326600 (7 lines),
                6321364 (Night Service).

6321660 (Commercial)
Facsimile: (00) (971) (2) 6318138 (Chancery)
6341744 (Commercial)
6345968 (Consular/Management)
6342676 (Visa Section)
6327700 (Airtech)
e-mail: chancery@abudhabi.mail.fco.gov.uk
Website: www.britain-uae.org
Office Hours (GMT): Sat - Wed 03 30 - 10 30
Ambassador: Mr Patrick Nixon, CMG, OBE
(Mr Richard Makepeace w.e.f March 03)
Counsellor and Deputy Head of Mission:
Mr Alistair McKenzie, MBE
First Secretary (Political): Mr Andrew Neil
Defence Attaché: Colonel Anthony Malkin
*Counsellor (Cultural Affairs) (British Council
Director):* Mr Peter Ellwood
First Secretary (Commercial): Mr John Gardner
First Secretary, Defence Sales: Mr Navin Patel, MBE
Second Secretary (Management/Consul/ECM):
Mr Steve Davies
*Second Secretary (Chancery/Press and Public
Affairs):* Mr Jason Smith
Second Secretary (Commercial): Mr Rahat Siddiqi
Third Secretary and Vice-Consul:
Mr Amias Moores
Third Secretary (Chancery/Consular):
Mr Andrew Miller
Third Secretary (ECO): Mrs Anne Hammond

Dubai

British Embassy
PO Box 65, Dubai, United Arab Emirates
Telephone: (00) (971) (4) 3971070
3971893 Commercial Section
Facsimile: (00) (971) (4) 3971095
Commercial Section
3971620 Chancery
3972153 Management/Consular
3977539 Visa
Office Hours (GMT): Sat - Wed 03 30 - 10 30
Consul-General and *Counsellor:* Mr Simon Collis
*First Secretary (Commercial) Consul and Deputy
Head of Mission:* Mr Ted Cole, OBE
First Secretary (Political): Mr David Spencer, MBE
Royal Navy Liaison Officer:
Commander Steve Bennett, RN
Customs Liaison Officer: Mr Chris Hardwick
Cultural Attaché (British Council Director):
Ms Jo Maher
First Secretary (Management/Consul/ECM):
Mr Anthony Mills
Airline Liaison Officer: Mr Steve Hart
Second Secretary (Commercial): Mr Lee Jennings
Second Secretary (Technical): Mr Robert Fletcher
Second Secretary (Press and Public Affairs):
Mr Jon Yarrow
Second Secretary (Economic):
Miss Blaise Metreweli
Third Secretary (Political): Mr Alex Bannerman
Third Secretary (Commercial/Information):
Mr Darren Forbes-Batey
Third Secretary (Immigration): Mr Neale Jones
Third Secretary (Immigration):
Mrs Joan Fontaine-Harvey

Third Secretary (Immigration) and Vice-Consul:
Mrs Suzanne Bastin

UNITED STATES

Washington

British Embassy
3100 Massachusetts Avenue, NW
Washington DC 20008
Telephone: (00) (1) (202) 588 6500 Embassy
7800 Consular
7830 British Council
Facsimile: (00) (1) (202) 588 7870 Chancery
7866 Management
7901 Trade
7850 Consular
Office Hours (GMT): Winter: 14 00 - 22 30
Summer: 13 00 - 21 30
Ambassador: Sir Christopher Meyer, KCMG
Minister: Mr Antony R Brenton
Minister (Economic): Mr Thomas Scholar
*Defence Attaché and Head of British Defence
Staff:* Rear Admiral Antony K Dymock
Minister (Defence Material): Ms Shuna Lindsay
Naval Attaché and Commander British Naval Staff:
Commodore Nicholas H L Harris, MBE, RN
*Military Attaché and Commander British Army
Staff:* Brigadier John J Keeling
*Air Attaché and Commander British Air Force
Staff:* Air Commodore Geoffrey D Simpson, CBE,
AFC, RAF
Counsellor (Political and Public Affairs):
Mr Robert Peirce
Counsellor (Political/Military/Europe):
Mr Peter O Gooderham
Counsellor (Trade & Transport):
Mr Antony J Phillipson
Counsellor: Mr Ian F McCredie, OBE
Counsellor (Management) and Consul-General:
Mr Warren D Townend
Counsellor (External Affairs): Mr Sebastian Wood
*Counsellor (Science Technology, Environment and
Energy):* Dr Peter Hayes
Counsellor: Dr Ruth Martin
Counsellor: Mr Tristram Riley-Smith
Counsellor (NIB): Mr Daniel McNeill
Counsellor (DST): Mr Adrian Baguley
Counsellor (Defence Equipment):
Mr Robert Regan
Counsellor (Head of NSD): Mr David Deardon
Counsellor (Economic): Mr Alex Gibbs
Counsellor: Mr Steve Rowton
Cultural Attaché: Mr Andrew Mackay
First Secretary (Political): Mr John Casson
First Secretary (Chancery): Mr Colin Crooks
First Secretary (Chancery): Mr Carl Newns
First Secretary (Chancery): Mr St John Gould
First Secretary (Chancery): Ms Alison Blake
First Secretary (Chancery): Ms Joanne Adamson
First Secretary (Agricultural): Mr James Hughes
First Secretary (Science and Technology):
Mr Christopher Pook
First Secretary (Economic): Mr Dermot Finch
First Secretary (Trade Policy): Mr Philip Budden
First Secretary (Transport): Mr Simon Knight

First Secretary (Press and Public Affairs):
Mr Peter Reid
First Secretary (Politico/Military):
Mr Marcus Winsley
First Secretary: Mr Alasdair Share
First Secretary (Political): Mr Steve Hill
First Secretary (Management):
Mr Peter J Newman
First Secretary (Technical Management/IT Co-ordination): Mr Keith Edwards
First Secretary (Technical Management):
Mr Simon R Drew
First Secretary: Mr Richard Seddon
First Secretary (Scottish Affairs):
Ms Susan Stewart
First Secretary (Defence Equipment):
Mr Chris Cook
First Secretary (Trade Promotion):
Mr Alan Attryde
First Secretary (Technical Works Officer):
Mr John Miles
First Secretary (Consul): Mr Graeme Wise
First Secretary (Education): Ms Jenny A Scott
First Secretary (NIB): Mr Michael Gould
Attaché (Defence Equipment - Sea/Air):
Mr Tim Whitemore
Attaché (Defence Equipment - Land): Mr Jim Platt
Attaché (Defence Equipment - Legal):
Mr Graham Farnsworth
Attaché (Defence Equipment - Commercial):
Mr Mike Newman
Assistant Naval Attaché:
Captain John H J Gower, RN
Head of BDILS (NA): Colonel Michael K Hill
Assistant Military Attaché:
Colonel Timothy F L Weeks, OBE
Assistant Air Attaché:
Group Captain Andrew J Barrett, RAF
First Secretary (Defence/Trade): Mr Tim Johnson
First Secretary (Defence Supply - Land and Sea Systems): Mr Alan Nisbet
Second Secretary (PS to Ambassador):
Ms Kirsty Paton
Second Secretary (Technical Management):
Mr Jerry Harland
Second Secretary (Management): Mr John Burran
Second Secretary (Transport): Mr Carl Sutcliffe
Second Secretary (Chancery): Mr Peter Jones
Second Secretary (Chancery/External):
Miss Rachel J Laycock
Third Secretary: Mr Ian Allan
Third Secretary (Vice-Consul): Mr Adam Radcliffe
Third Secretary (Technical Management):
Mr Martin Burn
Third Secretary (Technical Management):
Mr Matthew Ormond
Third Secretary (Technical Management):
Mr Barney Griffiths
Head of Defence Administration: Mr Phil Jones

Washington United Kingdom Delegation to the International Monetary Fund and International Bank for Reconstruction and Development, see Missions & Delegations

Washington United Kingdom Representation at the Inter-American Development Bank, see

Missions & Delegations

Atlanta
British Consulate-General
Suite 3400, Georgia Pacific Center
133 Peachtree Street NE,
Atlanta, GA 30303
Telephone: (00) (1) (404) 954 7700
Facsimile: (00) (1) (404) 954 7702
Voicemail Numbers: see individual officers
Office Hours (GMT): 13.00 - 23.00
e-mail: {officers first name.surname} followed by
@fco.gov.uk
Consul-General (Ext 7716): Mr Michael Bates, OBE
Deputy Consul-General and Consul (Trade) (Ext 7720): Mr Steve Collier, MVO, RVM
Vice-Consul (Management/Consular) (Ext 7313):
Ms Linda Nassar
Vice-Consul (Trade) (Ext 7725): Mr Mark Borst
Vice-Consul (Trade) (Ext 7722): Ms Mary Storch
Vice-Consul (Investment) (Ext 7730):
Mr Glen Whitley
Vice-Consul (Investment) (Ext 7731):
Mr Ian Stewart
Vice Consul (Press and Public Affairs) (Ext 7706):
Ms Jo Le Good

Miami
British Consulate
Suite 2800, Brickell Bay Office Tower,
1001, Brickell Bay Drive, Miami
Florida 33131
Telephone: (00) (1) (305) 374 1522
Facsimile: (00) (1) (305) 374 8196
Consul: Mr Simon J Davey, MBE
Vice-Consul (Commercial): Mrs B George-Hoerber
Vice-Consul (Commercial): Mr J Wright
Vice-Consul (Customs): Mr B Foreman
Vice-Consul (OTRCIS): Mr L Covington

Nashville
British Consulate
c/o Nashville Area Chamber of Commerce
211 Commerce Street
Nashville, TN 37201
Telephone: (00) (1) 615 743 3061
Facsimile: (00) (1) 615 256 6982
e-mail: jbutler@nashvillechamber.com
Honorary Consul: Mr J Butler

Orlando
British Vice-Consulate
Suite 2110, SunTrust Center,
200 South Orange Avenue,
Orlando, Fl 32801
Telephone: (00) (1) 407 426 7855 Consular
Facsimile: (00) (1) 407 426 9343
Vice-Consul: Mr H Hunter

Charlotte
British Consulate
Two First Union Center
301 South Tryon St. 7th Floor
Charlotte, NC 28288-0748
Telephone: (00) (1) 704 383 4359
Facsimile: (00) (1) 704 383 6545
e-mail: mteden@carolina.rr.com

Honorary Consul: Mr Michael Teden, OBE

Puerto Rico
British Consulate
Torre Chardón
Suite 1236
350 Chardon Avenue
San Juan, PR 00918
Telephone: (787) 758 9828
Facsimile(787) 758 9809
Vice Consul: Mrs P Martinez

Boston
British Consulate-General
One Memorial Drive, 15th Floor
Suite 1500
Cambridge, MA 02142
USA
Telephone: (00) (1) (617) 245 4500
Facsimile: (00) (1) (617) 621 0220
e-mail: British.Consulate@fco.gov.uk
Postmaster@fco.gov.uk
Officers first name.last name followed by
@fco.gov.uk
Consul-General (4502): Mr G D Fergusson
Deputy Consul-General (4515): Mr M G Plant
Consul (Science & Technology(4547):
Mr M. Sinclair
Vice-Consul (Trade) (4503): Ms M Meyer
Vice-Consul (Trade) (4510): Mr J Shipala
Vice-Consul (Press & Public Affairs) (4513):
Mrs T Evans
Vice-Consul (Management) (4520):
Mrs K M Tunsley
Vice-Consul (Investment) (4507): Ms A Sloan
Vice-Consul (Life Sciences & Healthcare US-wide)
(4530): Ms A Lin

Chicago
British Consulate-General
13th Floor, The Wrigley Building,
400 N Michigan Avenue, Chicago,
Illinois 60611
Telephone: (00) (1) (312) 970 3800
Facsimile: (00) (1) (312) 970 3852
970 3854 Consular and Visa Sections
only
Airtech: (00) (1) (312) 970 3818
Office Hours (GMT): 13 30 - 22 00
HM Consul-General: Mr Robert Culshaw, MVO
Deputy Consul-General: Mr Jonathan Darby
Consul - Trade: Mr Jeff Taylor
Consul - Investment: Mr Rafe Courage
Head of Politics, Press & Public Affairs:
Ms Caroline Cracraft, MBE
Head of Management: Mr Chris Shaw
Trade Officer: Mr Robert Blackburn
Trade Officer: Mrs Reet Robinson
Trade Officer: Mr Fred Levitan
Trade Officer: Mr Richard Knox
Trade Officer: Mr Brian Shapiro
Investment Officer: Mr Kevin Wilson
Investment Officer: Mr Jonathan Wood
Entry Clearance Manager/British Vice-Consul:
Mrs Janet Bershers, MBE

Minneapolis
British Consulate
2600 U.S Bancorp Centre,
800 Nicollet Mall, suite 2600
Minneapolis, MN 55402-7035
Telephone: (00) (1) (612) 338 2525
Facsimile: (00) (1) (612) 339 2386
Office Hours (GMT): 14 30 - 23 00
Honorary Consul: Mr W R McGrann

Kansas City
British Consulate
12109 Aberdeen Road,
Shawnee Mission, KS 66209
Telephone: (00) (1) (913) 469 9786
Facsimile: (00) (1) (913) 469 8597
e-mail: britconkswmo@hotmail.com
Office Hours (GMT): 14 30 - 23 15
Honorary Consul: Mr J Scott Brown

St Louis
British Consulate
2323 Manor Grove Drive #8,
Chesterfield, Missouri 63017
Telephone: (00) (1) (636) 227 1334
Honorary Consul: (Vacant)

Houston
British Consulate-General
Suite 1900, Wells Fargo Plaza,
1000 Louisiana Suite 1900, Houston, Texas 77002
Telephone: (00) (1) (713) 659 6270
659 6275 Commercial Department
Facsimile: (00) (1) (713) 659 7094
Office Hours (GMT): 15 00 - 23 00
Consul-General: Mr I R Murray
Deputy Consul-General and Consul (Commercial):
Mr P Williams
Vice-Consul (Commercial): Mr K Rost
Vice-Consul (Commercial, oil and gas): Mr B Foy
Vice-Consul (Information): Ms H Mann
Consul (Investment): Mr M Hobbs
Vice-Consul (Investment): Miss K Fairweather
Vice-Consul (Science and Technology):
Dr M Akrawi
Vice-Consul (Consular): Miss L Kelly
Management Officer: Ms A Medlin

Denver
British Consulate
Suite 1030, World Trade Center
1675 Broadway
Denver,
Colorado 80202
Telephone: (00) (1) (303) 592 5200 (General)
5205 (Consul – direct)
5212 (Trade Assistant – direct)
Facsimile: (00) (1) (303) 592 5209
e-mail: John.Maguire@britcondenver.com
info@britcondenver.com
Office Hours (GMT): 16 00 - 24 00
Consul (Commercial): Mr John Maguire
Commercial Assistant: Ms Vicky Lea

Dallas
British Consulate
2911 Turtle Creek Blvd.,

Suite 940, Dallas TX75219
Telephone: (00) (1) (214) 521 4090
Facsimile: (00) (1) (214) 521 4807
e-mail: bc@airmail.net
Office Hours (GMT): 15 00 - 23 00
Consul (Commercial): Mr P L Martinez
Vice-Consul (Commercial): Mrs B Schnaufer

New Orleans
British Consulate
10th Floor, 321 St Charles Avenue,
New Orleans, Louisiana, 70130
Telephone: (00) (1) (504) 524 4180
Office Hours (GMT): Sat & Wed 04 30 - 11 30
Honorary Consul: Mr J J Coleman Jr
Consular Assistant: Ms W Roberts

Los Angeles
British Consulate-General
11766 Wilshire Boulevard, Suite 1200,
Los Angeles, California 90025-6538
Telephone: (00) (1) (310) 481 0031 (for officers
direct numbers see below)
          481 2900 Visas only
Facsimile: (00) (1) (310) 481 2960
          481 2961 Visas only
          481 2963 Airtech
e-mail: trade.losangeles@fco.gov.uk
invest.losangeles@fco.gov.uk
pppa.losangeles@fco.gov.uk
visas.losangeles@fco.gov.uk
firstname.lastname@fco.gov.uk
Website: www.BritainUSA.com
Office Hours (GMT): 16 30 - 01 00
Consul-General (310 481 2950):
Mr Peter L Hunt, CMG
*Deputy Consul-General & Consul (Trade) (310
996 3036):* Mr Alan Cobden
Consul (Investment) (310 996 3021):
Ms Lorraine Johnson
*Consul (Consular/Entry Clearance) (310 481
2919):* Mr Paul Stevens
*Vice-Consul (Press, Political & Public Affairs)
(310 996 3028):* Mr Angus Mackay
Vice-Consul (Management) (310 996 3020):
Mrs Nancy Bridi
Vice-Consul (Trade) (310 996 3030):
Mr Carl Gipson
Vice-Consul (Investment) (310 996 3024):
Mr Kevin Aisbitt
Vice-Consul (Trade) (310 996 3031):
Ms Patrice Brayer
Director (British Film Office) (310 481 2933):
Ms Susan Finlayson-Sitch
*Vice-Consul (Consular/Entry Clearance) (310 481
2903):* Ms Anne Morton
Vice-Consul (Entry Clearance) (310 481 2912):
Ms Francesca Dooley
Vice-Consul (Entry Clearance) (310 481 2915):
Mr Des Brewer

Phoenix
British Consulate
15249 North 59th Street
Glendale, Arizona 85306-6000
Telephone: (00) (1) (602) 978 7200
Facsimile: (00) (1) (602) 978 9663

Office Hours (GMT): 16 30 - 01 00
Honorary Consul: Dr Roy Herberger

British Trade and Investment Office
2375 East Camelback Road,
5th Floor, Phoenix, Arizona 85016
Telephone: (00) (1) (602) 387 5092
Facsimile: (00) (1) (602) 387 5001
e-mail: btiophoenix@aol.com
Office Hours (GMT): 15 00 - 23 30
Director: Mr Hank Marshall

Salt Lake City
British Consulate
Eagle Gate Tower, Suite 2100,
60 East South Temple,
Salt Lake City, Utah 84111
Telephone: (00) (1) (801) 297 6922
Facsimile: (00) (1) (801) 297 6940
Office Hours (GMT): 16 00 - 01 00
Honorary Consul: Mr G Frank Joklik

San Diego
British Consulate
7825 Fay Ave, Suite 200
La Jolla, California 92037
Telephone: (00) (1) (858) 459 8231
Facsimile: (00) (1) (858) 459 9250
Office hours (GMT): 15.00-01 00
Honorary Consul: Mr William Black

New York
British Consulate-General
(incorporating British Trade and Investment
Offices)
845 Third Avenue, New York, N.Y. 10022
Telephone: (00) (1) (212) 745 0495 Trade
0300 Investment
Facsimile: (00) (1) (212) 745 0456 Trade and
          Investment
          754 3062 Consular/Visa
Airtech: (00) (1) (212) 745 0296
*Consul-General and Director-General of Trade
and Investment:* Mr Thomas G Harris, CMG
*Deputy Consul General, Political, Press & Public
Affairs and Deputy Head of Mission:*
Mr Duncan J R Taylor
*Deputy Consul-General and Director of Trade;
USA:* Mr Mike Cohen
*Deputy Consul-General and Director of
Investment:* Mr Alastair Newton
Consul (Management): Mr Andrew Dimbleby
Consul (Investment): Ms Helen Gates
*Consul (Press and Public Affairs, Northern
Ireland):* Mr Paul Johnston
Consul (Trade): Mr Clive V Thompson
Consul (Trade): Mr Colin Brazier
*Consul and Director of Entry Clearance Issuing
Posts:* Mr Patrick Owens, MBE
Vice-Consul (Consular): Mrs Jacqueline Cerdan
Vice-Consul (Immigration): Mr Stephen Thompson
Vice-Consul (Immigration): Mr Martin Southey
Vice-Consul (Political): Dr Ray Raymond, MBE
Vice-Consul (Trade): Mr Charles Picarelli
Vice-Consul (Trade): Mr Robert F Lomnicki
Vice-Consul (Trade): Mr Robert Cassidy
Vice-Consul (Trade): Mr Michael Formosa

Vice-Consul (Trade): Ms Christina Lynton
Vice-Consul (Investment): Ms Kerry Appleton
Vice-Consul (Investment): Mr Ian Baines
Vice-Consul (National Market Research Co-ordinator): Mrs Francine J Conran
Vice-Consul (Fairs and Promotions):
Ms Annie Wildey
Vice-Consul (Commercial Publicity):
Mr Dominic Varle
Visits Officer (For all British Government Offices in New York): Ms Louise Redmond, MBE

New York (SP)
British Information Services
845 Third Avenue, New York, NY 10022
Telephone: (00) (1) (212) 745 0200
Public Inquiries: (00) (1) (212) 745 0277
Facsimile: (00) (1) (212) 745 0359
e-mail: public.enquiries@newyork.mail.fco.gov.uk
Office Hours (GMT): Summer: 13 00 - 21 30
Winter: 14 00 - 22 30
Counsellor (Political &Public Affairs) and Head of BIS (resides at Washington): Mr Robert N Peirce
Director, BIS and Consul (Press & Public Affairs):
Mrs Judy Legg
Vice-Consul (Reference & Library): (Vacant)
Vice-Consul (Radio & Television): (Vacant)
Vice-Consul (Internet): (Vacant)

New York United Kingdom Mission to United Nations, see Missions & Delegations

Philadelphia
British Consulate
33rd Floor, 1818 Market St
Philadelphia, PA 19103
Telephone: (00) (1) (215) 557 7665
Facsimile: (00) (1) (215) 557 6608
Honorary Consul: Mr O St C Franklin

Pittsburgh
British Consulate
Buchanan Ingersoll
301 Grant Street
One Oxford Center, 20th Floor
Pittsburgh, PA 15219-1410
Telephone: (00) (1) (412) 562 8872
Facsimile: (00) (1) (412) 391 0910
Honorary Consul: Mr W Newlin

Pacific Islands
(American Samoa)
British Consulate (US Territories South of the Equator)
Consul (resides at Nuku'alofa): Mr Paul Nessling

San Francisco
British Consulate-General
Suite 850, 1 Sansome Street,
San Francisco, California 94104
Telephone: (00) (1) (415) 617 1300
Facsimile: (00) (1) (415) 434 2018 Group 3
Website: www.britainusa.com/sf
Office Hours (GMT): 16 30 - 01 00
Consul-General: Mr D R Thomas, CMG
Deputy Consul-General and Consul (Commercial):
Mr G G Simpson
Consul (Investment): Mr J Lindfield, MBE

Vice-Consul (Information): Ms E Stevenson
Vice-Consul (Commercial): Mr B Frieder
Vice-Consul (Commercial): Mrs A Eisler
Vice-Consul (Investment): Mr M Corson
Vice-Consul (Management/Consular):
Mrs K S Thomas
Vice-Consul (Commercial): (Vacant)
Vice-Consul (Commercial): Ms M S Katari

Anchorage (Alaska)
British Consulate
College of Arts and Sciences
University of Alaska Anchorage
3211 Providence Drive
Anchorage, AK 99508
Telephone: (00) (1) (907) 786 4848
Facsimile: (00) (1) (907) 786 4647
e-mail: afdh1@uaa.alaska.edu
Honorary Consul: Dr Diddy R M Hitchins

Portland (Oregon)
British Consulate
1300 SW Fifth Avenue
Suite 2300
Portland, OR 97201
Telephone (Direct Line): (00) (1) (503) 778 5337
227 5669 Consulate
Facsimile: (00) (1) (503) 778 5299
e-mail: iainlevie@dwt.com
Honorary Consul: Mr I Levie

San Jose (California)
British Consulate
1139 Karlstad Drive
Sunnyvale
San Jose, CA 94089
Telephone: (00) (1) (408) 747 7140 x1200 or x1400 (Assistant)
Facsimile: (00) (1) (408) 747 7198
e-mail: belder@genus.com
Honorary Consul: Dr W R Elder

Seattle
British Consulate
900 Fourth Avenue,
Suite 3001,Seattle, WA 98164
Telephone: (00) (1) (206) 622 9255
Facsimile: (00) (1) (206) 622 4728
Office Hours (GMT): 16 30 - 01 30
Consul (Commercial) (ext. 4178): Mr D Broom
Vice-Consul (Commercial) (ext. 4183):
Mr R Alvarez
Vice-Consul (Commercial) (ext. 4183):
Mr D Baron

Nashville (Tennessee)
British Consulate
PO Box 50135
6107 Robin Hill Rd
Nashville Tennessee 37205
Telephone: (00) (1) (615) 356 8049
Facsimile: (00) (1) (615) 354 0879
e-mail: Jbutle69@mail.idt.net
Honorary Consul: Mr J Butler

UPPER VOLTA See BURKINA FASO

URUGUAY
Montevideo (SP)
British Embassy
Calle Marco Bruto 1073, 11300 Montevideo, PO Box 16024
Telephone: (00) (598) (2) 622 3630, 622 3650
Facsimile: (00) (598) (2) 622 7815
Office Hours (GMT): Mid Mar - Mid Dec: 12 00 - 16 00 and 17 00 - 20 15
Mid Dec - Mid Mar: 11 00 - 17 00
e-mail: officers first name.surname @MONTEVIDEO.mail.fco.gov.uk
Embassy e-mail address:
bemonte@internet.com.uy
For officers residing in Buenos Aires refer to e-mail addresses in Argentina.
Ambassador: Mr John Everard
Deputy Head of Mission, First Secretary and Consul: Mr James Waterton
Defence Attaché (resides at Buenos Aires): Group Captain T P Brewer, OBE, RAF
First Secretary (resides at Buenos Aires): Mr Michael Cavanagh
Second Secretary (Management) and Vice-Consul: Mr Gerald S Evans
Second Secretary (TMO) (resides at Buenos Aires): Mr Stuart Moss

UZBEKISTAN

Tashkent
British Embassy
Ul. Gulyamova 67, Tashkent 700000, Uzbekistan
Telephone: (00) (99871) 1206451,1206288,1207852,1207853,1207854
Facsimile: (00) (99871) 1206549 (General) 1206430 (Consular/Visa)
e-mail: brit@emb.uz
Office Hours (GMT)
Winter: 04 00-07 30 and 08 30-12 00 (GMT + 5 hours)
Summer: 05 00-08 30 and 09 30-13 00 (GMT + 4 hours)
Ambassador: Mr Craig J Murray
Deputy Head of Mission: Ms Karen Moran
Defence Attaché: Lieutenant Colonel Nick Ridout
British Council Deputy Director: Mr M Seviour
Third Secretary (Political/PPA): Mr Chris Hirst
Third Secretary (Vice Consul/MO/ECO): Mr Dave Muir
Attaché/ECO: Ms Jackie Bates
British Council Director: Mr Neville McBain

VANUATU

Port Vila
British High Commission
KPMG House, Rue Pasteur, Port Vila, Vanuatu
PO Box 567, Port Vila, Vanuatu
Telephone: (00) (678) 23100 (3 lines)
25550 (1 line) DFID (Pacific) Vila
Facsimile: (00) (678) 27153 (Airtech)
23651 (General)
25280 DFID (Pacific) Vila

e-mail: bhcvila@vanuatu.com.vu
n-duggin@dfid.gov.uk
dfidpacific@vanuatu.com.vu
firstname.surname@vila.mail.fco.gov.uk
Office Hours (GMT): Mon, Tue, Thu & Fri: 20 30 - 00.45 and 02 00 - 05 30
Wed: 20 30 - 00 45
High Commissioner: Mr Michael T Hill
Deputy High Commissioner: Mr Joel Watson
DFID Programme Support Officer: Mr Nick Duggin

VENEZUELA

Caracas
British Embassy
Edificio Torre Las Mercedes (Piso 3), Avenida La Estancia, Chuao, Caracas 1061
Postal Address: Embajada Britanica, Apartado 1246,Caracas 1010-A
Telephone: (00) (58) (21) (2) 993 41 11, 993 42 24 03 39 Commercial Section
02 64 Management Section
Facsimile: (00) (58) (21) (2) 993 99 89
Commercial, Information, Management
03 15 Chancery
Airtech: (00) (58) (21) (2) 993 0376
e-mail: britishembassy@internet.ve
Website: www.britain.org.ve
Office Hours (GMT): Mon-Thur: 12 00 - 1630 and 17 30 - 20 30
Fri: 12 00 -17 30
Consular Section Hours (GMT): Mon -Fri 12 30 - 16 00
Ambassador: Mr E J Hughes
Deputy Head of Mission: Mr S M Fisher
Counsellor: Mr R J Knowlton
Defence Attaché: Captain E F Searle RN
Cultural Attaché (British Council Director)
(Tel: 952 9965/9757): Mr J C Greenwood
First Secretary: Mr A Buckingham
First Secretary (Commercial): Mr S J Seaman MBE
Second Secretary (Management) and Consul: Mrs S I Campbell
Second Secretary (Political): Mr A Tate
Second Secretary: Mr R A Williams
Second Secretary (Technical): Mr A Linnell
Second Secretary (Commercial): Mr C J Campbell
Third Secretary (Management/Consular): Mrs J M De Larrabure
Third Secretary (Technical): Mr K Gibbs
Attaché: Mr D P Morgan
Attaché: Mrs J P Micallef
Attaché: Mrs S V Diaz

Maracaibo
British Consulate
Avenida 2G, #67-49, Sector La Lago, Urbanizacion Virginia (diagonal al Club Creole)
Telephone: (00) (58) (2) (61) 915589/921355/925557
Facsimile: (00) (58) (2) (61) 913487
Office Hours (GMT): 12 00 - 16 30
Honorary Consul: (Vacant)

Margarita
British Consulate

Av. Principal No B-14, (Callejón) Urb. Playas del Angel
Pampatar, Distrito Maneiro, Island of Margarita
Telephone/Facsimile: (00) (58) (2) (95) 262 46 65/ 0149951267
e-mail: dw@enlared.net
Honorary Consul: Mr D M Weller

Mérida
British Consulate
Avenida Las Americas
Edificio Don Chabelo, Apto PH-4,
(Freate a la Urb.Humboldt), Merida 5101
Telephone: (00) (58) (2) (74) 266 20 22
Facsimile: (00) (58) (2) (74) 266 33 69
Honorary Consul: Dr R G Kirby

Valencia
Agropecuaria Flora C.A
Calle 143, No 100-227
Callejon La Cieba, Urbanizacion La Cieba
Valencia, Estado Carabobo, Venezuela
Telephone: (00) (58) (2) 41 82 38 401
Facsimile: (00) (58) (2) 41 82 34 742
e-mail: agroflora@compuserve.com
Office Hours: Mon, Wed, Fri 09 00 - 11 30
Honorary Consul: Mr D Martin

San Cristobal
British Consulate
Anglo Venezuelan Engineering & Controls
CA AVECO Britania House
Av. Rotaria, Esq.Av Parque Exposición,
La Concordia, San Cristobal
Telephone: (00) (58) (2) 76 471644/460434
Facsimile: (00) (58) (2) 76 470544
Honorary Consul: Mr R Burnison

VIETNAM

Hanoi
British Embassy
Central Building, 31 Hai Ba Trung
Telephone: 00 84 4 936 0500
00 84 90340 4919 Duty officer mobile
Facsimile: 00 84 4 936 0561
            Chancery/Commercial
            936 0562 Consular/Management
e-mail: behanoi@fpt.vn
Website: www.uk-vietnam.org
Office Hours (GMT): Mon-Fri 01.30 – 05.30 and 06.30 – 09.30

DFID
Central Building, 7th Floor
Telephone: (00) (84) (4) 936 0555
Facsimile: (00) (84) (4) 936 0556
Office Hours (GMT): Mon-Thur 01.00 – 05.00 and 06.00 – 09.30; Fri 01.00 – 06.30
British Council:
40 Cat Linh Street, Hanoi
Telephone: (00) (84) (4) 8436780/2
Facsimile: (00) (84) (4) 8434962
e-mail: bchanoi@britishcouncil.org.vn
Office Hours (GMT): Mon - Fri 01.30 – 05.00 and 06.30 – 10.00
Ambassador: Mr Warwick Morris

Deputy Head of Mission and Consul:
Mr Mac McLachlan
British Council Director and Cultural Attaché (ext 114): Mr David Cordingley
British Council Assistant Director and Cultural Attaché (ext 107): Ms Kate Owen
British Council Deputy Director and Cultural Attaché (ext 112): Mr Paul Zetter
Defence Attaché (resides at Kuala Lumpur): Colonel Roger J Little
First Secretary (Development): Mr Alan Johnson
First Secretary (Development): Ms Cathy Welch
First Secretary (Development): Mr Simon Lucas
First Secretary (Development): Ms Jane Rintoul
First Secretary (Defence Supply - resides at KL): Mr Rob Lingham
Second Secretary (Commercial): Mr Rob Lally
Second Secretary (Chancery, Press and Information): Mr Jonathan Dunn
Second Secretary (Management):
Mr Tim D C Fisher
Vice Consul, Third Secretary (ECO):
Ms Elaine M Henry
Third Secretary (Chancery): Mr Richard Ridout
Attaché: Ms Sylvia Allen
Attaché: Ms Anne-Marie Meconi

Ho Chi Minh City (SP)
British Consulate General
25 Le Duan,
District 1, Ho Chi Minh City,Vietnam
Telephone: (00) (84) (8) 8298433
(00) (84) 91392 0991 (Duty officer mobile)
Facsimile: (00) (84) (8) 8295257 (Visa/Consular)
            8221971 (Commercial/Information)
e-mail: bcghcmc@hcm.vnn.vn
Website: www.uk-vietnam.org
Office Hours (GMT): Mon - Fri 01 00 – 05 00 and 06 30 – 09 30

British Council:
25 Le Duan,
District 1, Ho Chi Minh City, Vietnam
Telephone: (00) (84) (8) 8232862 (Main Office)
8256403 (Teaching Centre)
Facsimile: (00) (84) (8) 8232861 (Main Office)
            8222105 (Teaching Centre)
e-mail: bchcmc@britishcouncil.org.vn
Office Hours (GMT): Mon-Fri: 01 30 - 05 00;
06 30 - 10 00
Consul-General: Mr Adrian C Stephens
Second Secretary (Commercial): Mr Phil Wyithe
British Council Director and Cultural Consul (Tel: 825 6402): Ms Angela Knights
Vice-Consul/Management Officer:
Ms Charlotte Rimmer

YEMEN

Sanaa
British Embassy
129 Haddah Road, Sanaa
Postal address: PO Box 1287
Telephone: (00) (967) (1) 264081/82/83/84
Facsimile: (00) (967) (1) 263059
Office Hours (GMT): Sat - Wed: 04 30 - 11 30
Ambassador and Consul General: Ms Frances Guy

Deputy Head of Mission and Consul:
Ms J Lawson-Smith
Defence Attaché (resides at Riyadh):
Brigadier J D Deverell
British Council Director: Mr A T N Chadwick
Second Secretary (Political/Aid/Information):
(Vacant)
Second Secretary (Management) and HM Consul:
Mr R Hunter
Second Secretary (Political/Aid): Mr C R Heatly
Third Secretary (Immigration): Mr G Sykes
Third Secretary/Vice Consul: Ms J Crabtree

Aden
British Consulate-General
20 Miswat Road
Postal address: P O Box 6304, Khormaksar, Aden
Telephone: (00) (967) (2) 232712-4
Facsimile: (00) (967) (2) 231256
Office Hours (GMT): Sat - Wed: 04 30 - 11 30
Vice-Consul (Commercial): Mr M Rajamanar

Hodeidah
British Consulate
Sanaa Road, KM7,
P O Box 3337, Hodeidah
Telephone: (00) (967) (3) 238130/131, 238958
Facsimile: (00) (967) (3) 211533
                238269
Office Hours (GMT): Mon - Wed: 08 00 - 13 00
Honorary Consul: Mr Abdul Gabbar Thabet

YUGOSLAVIA - SEE SERBIA AND MONTENEGRO

ZAMBIA

Lusaka
British High Commission
5210 Independence Avenue
P.O.Box 50050
15101 Ridgeway, Lusaka
Telephone: (00) (260) (1) 251133
Facsimile: (00) (260) (1) 253798
                Management/Press and Public
                Affairs/Development)
                251923 Commercial
                252842 Visa/Consular
e-mail: brithc@zamnet.zm
Office Hours (GMT): Mon - Thur: 06 00 - 11 00
and 12 00 - 14 30
Fri: 06 00 - 11 00
High Commissioner: Mr T J David
Deputy High Commissioner: Ms J Painting, MBE
Head of DFID Zambia: Ms H Mealins
Defence Adviser (Resides in London):
Lieutenant Colonel G M Thomas, MBE
Second Secretary (Management): Mrs C Cullen
Second Secretary (Political/Press/Public Affairs):
Mr Ian Mason
Deputy Head of DIFD Zambia: Mr Steve Graham
Second Secretary: Mr Alex Holey
Second Secretary (Consular/Commercial/ECM):
Mrs Lyn Shaw
Third Secretary (Immigration): Mr O Everitt

ZIMBABWE

Harare
British High Commission
Corner House, 7th Floor
Samora Machel Avenue/Leopold Takawira Street
(PO Box 4490), Harare
Telephone: (00) (263) (4) 772990,774700
Facsimile: (00) (263) (4) 774617
Airtech: (00) (263) (4) 774703
e-mail: british.info@fco.gov.uk
(Press & Public Affairs)
british.management@fco.gov.uk
(Management Section)
british.passports@fco.gov.uk
(Consular/Visa Section)
british.trade.harare@fco.gov.uk
(Commercial Section)
Website: www.britainzw.org
Office Hours (GMT): 06 00 - 10 30 and 11 30 -
14 30 (Mon-Thu),
06 00 - 12 00 (Fri)
High Commissioner: Mr J B Donnelly, CMG
Deputy High Commissioner: Ms D Corner
Counsellor: Mr A Stones
Defence Adviser: Colonel J S Field, CBE
*First Secretary (Medical Officer) (resides in
Lilongwe):* Dr H Friend
First Secretary (Commercial): Mr D Seddon
First Secretary (Management): Mr R D Hazlewood
Second Secretary (Political): Mr R S Lindsay
Second Secretary (Consular/Immigration):
Mr J Liddell
Second Secretary: Mr J A St J Fisher
Third Secretary (Management): Mrs S C Howard
Third Secretary (Political/Press & Public Affairs):
Mrs T Wicke
Third Secretary (Consular/Immigration):
Mr W N Pagett
Assistant to Defence Adviser: WO. D A Hardinges

**Department for International Development:
Zimbabwe**
Corner House, 6th Floor Samora Machel
Avenue/Leopold Takawira Street
PO Box 1030 Harare
Telephone: (00) (263) (4) 774719-28
Facsimile: (00) (263) (4) 775695
Office Hours (GMT): 06 00 – 14 30 (Mon-Fri)
Head of DFID Zimbabwe: Mrs G Wright
Senior Social Development Adviser: Mr E Hanley
Regional Food Security Adviser: Mr J Hansell, OBE
Regional Private Sector Adviser: Mr D Spence
(until Oct 02)
Regional Health & Population Adviser:
Dr C Presern (until Dec 02)
Economic Adviser: Ms V Plater
Health and HIV Adviser: Ms M Temin
Head of Management (SAIC): Mrs P Barber
Deputy Programme Manager (SAIC):
Mrs C Hungwe
**See also DFIDCA country programme offices
Lilongwe, Lusaka and Maputo.**
e-mail: initial-surname@dfid.gov.uk
(eg: J-Winter@dfid.gov.uk)

PART II: MISSIONS AND DELEGATIONS

*UNITED KINGDOM MISSION TO THE UNITED NATIONS

New York
One Dag Hammarskjold Plaza, 28th Floor,
885 Second Avenue, New York, N.Y. 10017
Telephone: (00) (1) (212) 745 9250
Facsimile: (00) (1) (212) 745 9316
Airtech: (00) (1) (212) 745 9272
Postal address: PO Box 5238 New York, NY
10150-5238
e-mail: UK@UN.INT
Office Hours (GMT): Summer 13 00 - 22 00
Winter 14 00 - 2300
*United Kingdom Permanent Representative to the
United Nations and United Kingdom
Representative on the Security Council (with
personal rank of Ambassador):*
Sir Jeremy Greenstock, KCMG
*Deputy Permanent Representative to the United
Nations (with personal rank of Ambassador):*
Mr Adam Thomson
Counsellor and Head of Chancery:
Mr Alistair Harrison, CVO
*Counsellor (Economic, Social and Humanitarian
Affairs):* Mr Mark Runacres
Counsellor (Political): Mr Eugene Curley, OBE
Counsellor (Legal Adviser): Mr Iain MacLeod
Counsellor (ACABQ): Mr Nick Thorne, CMG
Counsellor (Finance): Dr Richard Moon
Military Adviser to UK Permanent Representative:
Colonel Nicholas Seymour
Deputy Military Adviser: Mr Peter Hunter
First Secretary (Chancery): Ms Anna Clunes
First Secretary (Chancery): Mr Dominic Fortescue
First Secretary (Chancery/Press):
Ms Catherine Mackenzie
First Secretary (Economic): Ms Sarah MacIntosh
First Secretary (Chancery): Mr Mike Anderson
First Secretary (Social Development Adviser):
Ms Pat Holden
First Secretary (Chancery):
Miss Vanessa Howe-Jones
First Secretary (Human Rights): Mr Jolyon Welsh
First Secretary (Finance): Mr Bill Longhurst
First Secretary (Environment): Ms Alice Walpole
First Secretary (Chancery): Mr Carne Ross
First Secretary (Management):
Ms Madeleine Campbell
First Secretary (Humanitarian Affairs):
Mr Tom Kelly
Assistant Legal Adviser: Ms Alice Burnett
Second Secretary (Chancery): Ms Charlotte Cutler
Second Secretary (Chancery): Ms Rosemary Davis
Second Secretary (Management):
Mr Melvin Bell, MBE
Second Secretary (Chancery): Ms Sarah Broughton
Second Secretary (Finance): Mr David Turnbull
Second Secretary (Chancery): Miss Tina Falzarano
Second Secretary (Chancery): Miss Kathy Mackay
Second Secretary (Chancery):
Mr Gerard McGurk, MBE

Second Secretary (Social Affairs):
Mr Matthew Johnson
Third Secretary (Economic): Ms Beverley Simpson
Third Secretary (Library): Ms Jane Crellin

UNITED KINGDOM MISSION TO THE OFFICE OF THE UNITED NATIONS AND OTHER INTERNATIONAL ORGANISATIONS AT GENEVA

Geneva
37-39 rue de Vermont, 1211 Geneva 20
Telephone: (00) (41) (22) 918 23 00
Facsimile: (00) (41) (22) 918 23 33 Main No
            24 35 Chancery
            24 44 Spec Agencies
            23 77 WTO/Economic
            23 10 Joint Management Unit
Telex: 414195 (a/b 414195 UKGV CH)
Office Hours (GMT): Summer: 07 00 - 11 00 and
12 30 - 16 00
Winter: 08 00 - 12 00 and 13 30 - 17 00
*United Kingdom Permanent Representative (holds
personal rank of Ambassador):*
Mr S W J Fuller, CMG
Minister and Deputy Permanent Representative:
Mr N M McMillan, CMG
*First Secretary (Head of Chancery, Human
Rights):* Mr K Lyne
First Secretary (UN, Press Officer):
Mrs S E March
First Secretary (Legal Adviser): Mrs S McCrory
First Secretary (Specialised Agencies):
Ms H R Nellthorp
First Secretary (WTO): Mr A G Sims
First Secretary (Humanitarian): Mrs J Caley
First Secretary (Management): Mr I A Crees
First Secretary (UNCTAD, ECE): Mrs E Fuller
First Secretary (Humanitarian): Mr M Middlemiss
Second Secretary (WTO): Mr R E Twyman
Second Secretary (WTO): Miss J Lomas
Second Secretary (Specialised Agencies):
Mr J M Bradley
Second Secretary (ECE, UNCTAD):
Mr R Fairweather
Second Secretary (Humanitarian, Human Rights):
Mr P Bentall
Second Secretary (Management): Mr R W Harmer
Second Secretary (Political): Mr N E Joseph

**Geneva Joint Management Office, UK
Government Offices, see main list of posts**

UNITED KINGDOM DELEGATION TO THE UNITED NATIONS EDUCATIONAL, SCIENTIFIC AND CULTURAL ORGANISATION (UNESCO)

Paris
1 Rue Miollis
75732 Paris
Cedex 15
Telephone: (00) (331) 45 68 27 84

Facsimile: (00) (331) 47 83 27 77
United Kingdom Permanent Delegate (holds
personal rank of Ambassador): Mr D L Stanton
United Kingdom Deputy Permanent Delegate:
Ms C Atkinson
Third Secretary: Mrs H J Izon

UNITED KINGDOM MISSION TO THE UNITED NATIONS IN VIENNA

Vienna

Jaurèsgasse 12, 1030 Vienna
Telephone: (00) (43) (1) 716 130 or (43) (1) 71613
+ extension
Facsimile: (00) (43) (1) 71613 4900
e-mail: ukmisv@netway.at
Office Hours (GMT): Winter: Mon - Fri 08 00 -
12 00 and 13 30 - 16 30
Summer: Mon - Fri 07 00 - 11 00 and 12 30 -
15 30
United Kingdom Permanent Representative (with
personal rank of Ambassador) (4237):
Mr Peter R Jenkins
First Secretary and United Kingdom Deputy
Permanent Representative (4234):
Mr Mark Etherton
First Secretary (IAEA) (4240): Miss Alison Giles
First Secretary (IAEA) (4232): Mr Tim Andrews
First Secretary (CTBTO) (4296): Ms Tracy Roberts
Second Secretary (UN/UNIDO) (4297):
Mr Graham Clough
Second Secretary (CTBTO/UN/IAEA) (4298):
Mr Llewellyn Skidmore

Joint Management

First Secretary (Management) (2261):
Mr Eric Jones
Third Secretary (Management) (2260):
Mr Andy Partridge

UNITED KINGDOM PERMANENT REPRESENTATION TO THE CONFERENCE ON DISARMAMENT

Geneva

37-39 rue de Vermont, 1211 Geneva 20
Telephone: (00) (41) (22) 918 23 00
Facsimile: (00) (41) (22) 918 23 44
Telex: 414195 (a/b 414195 UKGV CH)
Office Hours (GMT): Summer: 07 00 - 11 00 and
12 30 - 16 00,
Winter: 08 00 - 12 00 and 13 30 - 17 00
United Kingdom Permanent Representative: (holds
personal rank of Ambassador): Mr D S Broucher
Deputy Permanent Representative: Mr I Donaldson
First Secretary (Legal Adviser): Mrs S McCrory
Second Secretary: Mr J Wattam
Second Secretary: Mr N E Joseph

Geneva Joint Management Office, UK Government Offices, see main list of posts

UNITED KINGDOM DELEGATION TO THE ORGANISATION FOR SECURITY AND COOPERATION IN EUROPE (OSCE) IN VIENNA

Vienna

Jaurèsgasse 12, 1030 Vienna
Telephone: (00) (43) (1) 716130
71613 + extension (for direct lines and voicemail)
Facsimile: (00) (43) (1) 71613 3900
Telegraphic address: UKDEL Vienna
e-mail: ukdel@netway.at
Office Hours (GMT): Summer: Mon - Fri 07 00 -
16 00
Winter: Mon - Fri 08 00 - 17 00
Head of Delegation (Personal rank of
Ambassador) (PA 3302):
Mr John R de Fonblanque, CMG
Counsellor and Deputy Head of Delegation (PA
3304): Mr Ian A M Bond
Counsellor (Arms control) (PA 3318):
Mr Andrew Brentnall
Military Adviser (PA 3318):
Colonel George A Young
First Secretary (Political) (3319):
Ms Kate Knight-Sands
First Secretary (Political) (3318):
Mr Eric Penton-Voak
First Secretary (Arms Control) (PA 3336):
Mr Henry Bradley
Second Secretary (Political) (3306):
Mr Stuart Adam
Second Secretary (Political) (3307):
Mr David Townsend
Third Secretary (3320): Mr Grant Pritchard

Joint Management Office

First Secretary (Management) (2261):
Mr Eric Jones
Third Secretary (Management) (2260):
Mr Andy Partridge

UNITED KINGDOM DELEGATION TO THE NORTH ATLANTIC TREATY ORGANISATION

Brussels

OTAN/NATO, Autoroute Bruxelles - Zaventem,
Evere
1110 Brussels
Telephone: (00) (32) (2) 707 7211
Facsimile: (00) (32) (2) 707 7596
e-mail: ukdelnato@csi.com
United Kingdom Permanent Representative on the
North Atlantic Council (holds personal rank of
Ambassador): Dr Emyr Jones Parry, KCMG
Minister, United Kingdom Deputy Permanent
Representative: Dr J Freeman
United Kingdom Military Representative:
Lieutenant General K O'Donoghue, CBE
Deputy United Kingdom Military
Representative/COS: Commodore J G H Tighe, RN
Counsellor (Political): Mr P Arkwright
Counsellor (Defence): Mr N Brind
Counsellor (Budget and Infrastructure): Dr F Price
First Secretary (Political): Mr P Moody

First Secretary (European Defence):
Mr P V Devine
First Secretary (Defence Equipment):
Mr J Mattiussi
First Secretary (Nuclear Cooperation):
Mr J Dickinson
Staff Officer Plans & Policy:
Captain I K Goddard, RN
First Secretary (Defence Plans and Policy):
Mr G Muir
Staff Officer (Operations):
Lieutenant Colonel G A Gelder, RM
Staff Officer (Operations/Plans):
Lieutenant Colonel R Smith
First Secretary (Infrastructure and Military Budget): Mr R Ladd-Jones
Staff Officer Intelligence:
Wing Commander P Edwards, RAF
Staff Officer (Resources and Arms Control):
Lieutenant Colonel J Lyne-Pirkis
First Secretary (Infrastructure and Military Budgets): Ms H Hakiwumi
Second Secretary (Political): Miss S Crombie
Second Secretary (Operations and Exercises):
Mrs T Collingridge
Second Secretary (Management): Mrs S Pavis
Second Secretary: Mr L Cameron
Attaché (Political): Mr E Manley
Attaché (Defence): Mr A Collingridge
Attaché (Defence): Mr S Gallacher
Attaché (Budget and Infrastructure):
Mr N Wapshere
Staff Officer (CISCP):
Lieutenant Colonel M S Reid
Staff Officer (Cooperation):
Wing Commander J Squelch, RAF

UNITED KINGDOM DELEGATION TO THE WESTERN EUROPEAN UNION

Brussels
c/o UK Permanent Representation to the EU,
Avenue d'Auderghem 10
1040 Bruxelles
Telephone: (00) (32) (2) 287 8346
Facsimile: (00) (32) (2) 287 8396
United Kingdom Permanent Representative -
(holds personal rank of Ambassador):
Mr David Richmond
Military Delegate:
Lieutenant General Kevin O'Donoghue, CBE
Deputy UK Military Representative:
Air Commodore John Thomas, RAF
Deputy Permanent Representative - First Secretary
(Pol/Mil Affairs): Ms Jennifer Anderson
First Secretary (Defence): Mr Sandy Johnston
Staff Officer EU1: Lieutenant Colonel Ian Raley
Staff Officer EU2:
Wing Commander (Rtd) Barry Horton
Staff Officer EU4: Wing Commander Q D'Arcy
Third Secretary (WEAG/WEAO):
Mr Scott Gallacher
Assistant Military Delegate: Sergeant Chris Vear

Brussels Joint Management Office for the four Missions, see main list of posts

UNITED KINGDOM DELEGATION TO THE ORGANISATION FOR ECONOMIC CO-OPERATION AND DEVELOPMENT

Paris
19 Rue de Franqueville, 75116 Paris
Telephone: (00) (331) 45 24 98 28
Facsimile: (00) (331) 45 24 98 37
Office Hours (GMT): Nov-Mar 08 30 - 17 00,
Apr-Oct 07 30 - 16 00
United Kingdom Permanent Representative (holds personal rank of Ambassador):
Mr Christopher D Crabbie, CMG
Deputy United Kingdom Permanent Representative and Counsellor (Economic and Financial):
Mr David Moran
Counsellor (Management): Mr Ian Whitehead
First Secretary (Energy & Environment):
Mr A Shaun Cleary
First Secretary (Economic): Mr Martyn K Roper
First Secretary (Trade & Investment):
Mr Jonathan Knott
First Secretary (Employment, Education & Social Affairs, Science & Technology, Public Management): Ms Jo Newstead

OFFICE OF THE UNITED KINGDOM PERMANENT REPRESENTATIVE TO THE EUROPEAN UNION

Brussels
Ave d'Auderghem 10, 1040 Brussels
Telephone: (00) (32) (2) 287 8211
Facsimile: (00) (32) (2) 287 8398 (2 lines)
Telex: 24312 (a/b 24312 UKEC BR B)
e-mail: ukrep@fco.gov.uk
Website: http://ukrep.fco.gov.uk
United Kingdom Permanent Representative (holds personal rank of Ambassador):
Sir Nigel Sheinwald, KCMG
Deputy UK Permanent Representative: Mr W Stow
Interim Political Security Committee Representative: Mr D Richmond
Counsellor (Political & Institutional): Mr M Aron
Counsellor (Agriculture): Ms K Williams
Counsellor (External Relations): Mr D Chilcott
Counsellor (JHA): Mr N Baird
Counsellor (Industry): Mr A Vinall
Counsellor (Economics and Finance): Mr N Ilett
Counsellor (Social Affairs, Environment, Regional Policy): Mr S Morgan
Counsellor (Legal Adviser): Ms S Brooks
Counsellor (Development): Mr A Wood
First Secretary (External Relations):
Mr R Drummond
First Secretary (External Relations):
Mr K O'Flaherty
First Secretary (External Relations):
Mr A J H Cowell
First Secretary (External Relations): Ms H Corbett
First Secretary (Trade Policy): Mr T Smith
First Secretary (Institutions): Mr P Wilson
First Secretary (Commercial): Ms J Martin
First Secretary (Transport): Mr D Tripp
First Secretary (Research and Telecoms):
Mr N Leake

First Secretary (Energy): Mr I Holt
First Secretary (Industry and Competition):
Mr J Fiennes
First Secretary (Internal Market): Mr S Gill
First Secretary (Consumer Affairs and Industry):
Ms B Schwarz
First Secretary (Economics and Finance):
Mr S James
First Secretary (Press and Information):
Mr D Pruce
First Secretary (Budget): Mrs F Jones
First Secretary (JHA): Ms S Langrish
First Secretary (Legal): Mr P McKell
First Secretary (Justice and Home Affairs):
Mr A Jones
First Secretary (Justice and Home Affairs):
Mr N Bradley
First Secretary (Customs and Finance):
Ms L Clare
First Secretary (Agriculture): Dr K Riggs
First Secretary (Fisheries): Dr D Bates
First Secretary: Mr C Hay
First Secretary (Agriculture and Food):
Mr R Norton
First Secretary: Ms C Wilson
First Secretary (Political): Mr S McGregor
First Secretary (Social Affairs): Mr A Dalgleish
First Secretary (Environment): Mr M Nesbit
First Secretary (Social Affairs): Mr J Kittmer
First Secretary (Regional Policy): Ms A Rose
First Secretary (Management): Mr P May
Second Secretary (EU Staffing): Mr M Hancock
Second Secretary (Institutions): Mr S Furssedonn
Second Secretary (Agriculture and Forestry):
Mr S Stannard
Second Secretary (Agriculture): Mr K Morrison
Second Secretary (JHA): Ms E Gibbons
Second Secretary (Industry): Ms K L Siddall
Second Secretary (Transport): Mr S Johnston
Second Secretary (Budget): Ms L Ryan
Second Secretary (Trade Policy): Ms L Boyles
Second Secretary (External Relations):
Ms C Van der Walt
Second Secretary (Health): Ms L Stewart
Second Secretary (Management): Mr D Harrison
Third Secretary (External Relations):
Mrs R Pearson
Third Secretary (External Relations): Ms K Hill

Strasbourg
(Office only open when the EUROPEAN
PARLIAMENT is in session in Strasbourg)
Offices 561/562 IPE 1 Building, Strasbourg
Telephone: (00) (333) 88 17 68 15
Facsimile: (00) (333) 88 35 41 30
First Secretary (Institutions): Mr P Wilson
Second Secretary (Institutions): Mr S Furssedonn

**Brussels Joint Management Office for the four
Missions, see main list of posts**

**UNITED KINGDOM DELEGATION TO THE
COUNCIL OF EUROPE**

Strasbourg
18 rue Gottfried, 67000-Strasbourg
Telephone: (00) (333) (88) 35 00 78

Facsimile: (00) (333) (88) 36 74 39
*United Kingdom Permanent Representative to
Council of Europe (holds personal rank of
Ambassador):* Mr A Carter, CMG (Mr Stephen F
Howarth w.e.f March 03)
*Deputy United Kingdom Permanent
Representative:* Mr M M Hall
Second Secretary: Mr T F Robins
Third Secretary (Chancery/Management):
Mr J A Webster

**UNITED KINGDOM DELEGATION TO THE
INTERNATIONAL MONETARY FUND AND
INTERNATIONAL BANK FOR
RECONSTRUCTION AND DEVELOPMENT**

Washington
Room 11-120, International Monetary Fund,
700 19th Street, NW, Washington, DC 20431
Telephone: (00) (1) (202) 623 4562
Facsimile: (00) (1) (202) 623 4965
*United Kingdom Executive Director of the
International Monetary Fund and World Bank:* -
e-mail: tscholar@imf.org Mr T Scholar
Alternate Executive Director of the World Bank: -
e-mail: rstevenson@imf.org Ms R Stevenson
*Alternate Executive Director of the International
Monetary Fund:* - e-mail: mbrooke@imf.org
Mr M Brooke
Assistant (IMF/IBRD): - e-mail: njoicey@imf.org
Mr N Joicey
Assistant (IMF/IBRD): - e-mail:
bkelmanson@imf.org Mr B Kelmanson
Assistant (IMF/IBRD): - e-mail: bmellor@imf.org
Mr B Mellor
Assistant (IMF/IBRD): - e-mail: dmerotto@imf.org
Mr D Merotto
Assistant (IMF/IBRD): - e-mail: astuart@imf.org
Ms A Stuart
Assistant (IMF/IBRD): - e-mail: dtaylor@imf.org
Mr D Taylor

**UNITED NATIONS CENTRE FOR HUMAN
SETTLEMENTS (HABITAT)**

Nairobi
*United Kingdom Permanent Representative to the
United Nations Centre for Human Settlements
(Habitat):* Mr E Clay, CMG
Alternate Permanent Representative:
Mr A V G Tucker
*Deputy United Kingdom Permanent
Representative:* Mr J P T Bell

**UNITED NATIONS ENVIRONMENT
PROGRAMME**

Nairobi
*United Kingdom Permanent Representative to the
United Nations Environment Programme:*
Mr E Clay, CMG
Alternate Permanent Representative:
Mr A V G Tucker
*Deputy United Kingdom Permanent
Representative:* Mr J P T Bell

UNITED KINGDOM REPRESENTATION AT THE AFRICAN DEVELOPMENT BANK

Abidjan

Rue Joseph Anoma, Abidjan
Postal Address: 01 BP 1387, Abidjan 01
Telephone: (00) 20 40 23, 20 43 43
Telex numbers: 22203/2202/27717/23263
Executive Director: Mr M Bauer (German)
Alternate Executive Director:
Mr W Bronkhurst (Dutch)
Assistant to the Executive Director:
Mr P R Williams (British)

UNITED KINGDOM REPRESENTATION AT THE ASIAN DEVELOPMENT BANK

Manila

6 ADB Avenue, Mandaluyong City, Metro Manila,
Philippines
Postal address: PO Box 789, 0980 Manila,
Philippines
Telephone: (00) (63) (2) 632 4444, 632 6079
Facsimile: (00) (63) (2) 636 2444, 636 2056
Executive Director: Uwe Henrich
Alternative Director: Mr Frank Black

UNITED KINGDOM REPRESENTATION AT THE INTER-AMERICAN DEVELOPMENT BANK

Washington

1300 New York Avenue, N W Washington, DC
20577
Telephone: (00) (1) (202) 623
1059/1058/1773/1179
Facsimile: (00) (1) (202) 623 3610
Cable address: Intambanc, Washington, DC
Telex numbers: 64141, 44240
Executive Director: Mr Y Ueda (Japanese)
Alternate Executive Director: Mr Kurosawa
(Japanese)
Senior Counsellor: Mr M Power (British)
Counsellor: Mr Andrej Kavcic (Slovenia)

UNITED KINGDOM REPRESENTATION TO THE UNITED NATIONS AGENCIES FOR FOOD AND AGRICULTURE IN ROME

Rome

Viale Aventino, 36/1. 00153 Roma
Telephone: (00) (39) 06 578 1535, 574 4438
Facsimile: (00) (39) 06 572 85010
Minister (UN Agencies and Aid Affairs) &
Permanent Representative: Mr Anthony Beattie
First Secretary (Humanitarian Affairs):
Mr Michael Ellis
First Secretary (Development) Senior Livelihoods
Adviser: Dr Peter Reid
First Secretary (Development) Livelihoods Adviser:
Jo Yuon
Associate Professional Officer (partly based in
UKREP and partly in FAO): Emma Fernandez
Technical Systems Administrator: Fiona Pryce
PA to Anthony Beattie: Nicolette Ciorba

UNITED KINGDOM REPRESENTATIVE ON THE COUNCIL OF THE INTERNATIONAL CIVIL AVIATION ORGANISATION

Montreal

Suite 1415, 999 University Sreet,
Montreal, Quebec
Canada
H3C 5J9
Telephone: (00) (514) 954 8302/3
Direct Line – see individual officers
Facsimile: (00) (514) 954 8001
Airtech: (00) (1) (514) 866 4867 (Located in
British Consulate-General Offices)
Office Hours (GMT) 14 00 – 22 00
United Kingdom Representative:
Mr Douglas S Evans (00) (1) (514) 954 8326
Deputy United Kingdom Representative:
Mr Richard W Allison (00) (1) (514) 954 8327

ORGANISATION FOR THE PROHIBITION OF CHEMICAL WEAPONS

The Hague

United Kingdom Permanent Representative:
Sir C R Budd, KCMG
First Secretary: Mr D G Cole
First Secretary: Mr M E Rack

GOVERNORS AND COMMANDERS-IN-CHIEF ETC. OF THE UK OVERSEAS TERRITORIES

Anguilla

Government House, Anguilla Telephone: Office:
Governor/EA: (00) (1) (264) 497 2621/2622
Deputy Governor: (00) (1) (264) 497 3312/3313
Staff Officer: (00) (1) (264) 497 3315
Residence: (00) (1) (264) 497 2292 (Tel/Fax)
Facsimile: (00) (1) (264) 497 3314 (Unclassified)
(00) (1) (264) 497 3151 (Airtech)
e-mail: govthse@anguillanet.com
Office Hours (GMT): 12 00 – 16 00, 17 00 20 00
Governor: Mr Peter Johnstone
Deputy Governor: Mr Mark Capes
Staff Officer: Ms Jackie Barlow
Defence Adviser (resides at Bridgetown):
Captain Steve C Ramm, RN
Executive Assistant to the Governor:
Miss Sarah Reid

Bermuda

Government House, Hamilton
Telephone: (00) (1) (441) 292 3600
Deputy Governor's Office: (00) (1) (441) 292 2587
Calls from UK: (00) (1) (441) 292 3600
Government House
2587 Deputy Governor's Office
Facsimile: (00) (1) (441) 295 3823
e-mail Address: depgov@ibl.bm
Office Hours (GMT): Summer: 11 45 - 16 00 and
17 15 - 20 00
Winter: 12 45 - 17 00 and 18 15 - 21 00
Governor:
(e-mail: governor@gov.bm): Sir John Vereker, KCB

Deputy Governor:
(e-mail: deputygovernor@gov.bm):
Mr Tim Gurney
Registrar: (e-mail: registrar@gov.bm):
Mr Malcolm Ostler

British Antarctic Territory
Foreign and Commonwealth Office,
Overseas Territories Department
Telephone: 020 7008 2742
Commissioner: Mr Alan E Huckle (non-resident)
Administrator: Dr M G Richardson (non-resident)

British Indian Ocean Territory
Foreign and Commonwealth Office,
Overseas Territories Department
Telephone: 020 7008 2890
Commissioner: Mr Alan E Huckle (non-resident)
Administrator: Mr Charles A Hamilton (non-resident)

Diego Garcia, c/o BFPO Ships
Facsimile: (00) 246 370 3943
Commissioner's Representative:
Commander Adam Peters, RN. JP

British Virgin Islands (SP)
Government House,
Road Town, Tortola,
British Virgin Islands
Telephone: (00) (1) (284) 494 2345/494 2370/494
3520 Office
494 2721/494 3400 Residence
Facsimile: (00) (1) (284) 468 4490 Office
494 8871 Residence
Airtech: (00) (1) (284) 494 5582
e-mail: officer's first name.surname followed by
@fco.gov.uk
Website: http://www.bvi.gov.vg
Office Hours (GMT): 12 30 - 20 30
Governor: Mr Tom Macan
First Secretary and Head of Governor's Office:
Mr Malcolm B Kirk
*Third Secretary and Private Secretary (External
Affairs):* Mr Stuart V Smith
Defence Adviser (resides at Bridgetown):
Captain Steve C Ramm, RN
Personal Assistant: Mrs Claire Means

Office of the Deputy Governor
Government Administration Building
Road Town, Tortola
Telephone: (00) (1) (284) 468 0346
Facsimile: (00) (1) (284) 494 6481
Deputy Governor: Mr Elton Georges, OBE
Royal Virgin Island Police Force
Telephone: (00) (1) (284) 494 3822 (24 hrs)
Immigration Department
Telephone: (00) (1) (284) 494 3471

Cayman Islands (SP)
4th Floor, Government Administration Building,
Elgin Avenue
George Town, Grand Cayman,
Cayman Islands
Telephone: (00) (1) (345) 949 7900 Switchboard
5776 PA direct
0980 Staff Officer

Facsimile: (00) (1) (345) 945 4131 Governor's
Office
Airtech: 949 6556
945 5537 Social Secretary
e-mail: staffoff@candw.ky
Office Hours (GMT): 13 30-17 30 and 19 00 -
22 00
Governor: Mr Bruce H Dinwiddy
Chief Secretary: Mr James M Ryan, MBE, JP
Deputy Chief Secretary: Mr Donnie Ebanks, MBE
Defence Adviser (Resides at Kingston):
Colonel Rob A Hyde-Bales
*Second Secretary and Staff Officer to the
Governor:* Mr Kevin L Mowbray
Secretary to the Governor: Mrs Fiona Mowbray

Government Information Services
Telephone: (00) (1) (345) 949 8092
Facsimile: (00) (1) (345) 949 5936/946 0664

Immigration Department
Telephone: (00) (1) (345) 949 8344
Enquiries within the UK: Cayman Islands
Government Office,
6 Arlington Street, London SW1A 1RE
Telephone: 020 7491 7772
Facsimile: 020 7491 7944
Representative: Mrs Jennifer P Dilbert

Falkland Islands
Government House, Stanley,
Falkland Islands
Telephone: (00) (500) 27433 Office
22210 Residence
Facsimile: (00) (500) 27434
e-mail: gov.house@horizon.co.fk
Office Hours (GMT): Winter: 11 00-15 15 and
16 30-19 30
Summer: 12 00-16 15 and 17 30-20 30
Governor: Mr Howard J S Pearce, CVO
First Secretary: Mr Russ T Jarvis

South Georgia and the South Sandwich Islands
Government House, Stanley
Falkland Islands
Telephone: (00) (500) 27433 Office
22210 Residence
Facsimile: (00) (500) 27434
e-mail: gov.house@horizon.co.fk
OfficeHours (GMT): Winter 11 00 - 15 15 and
16 30 - 19 30
Summer 12 00 - 16 15 and 17 30 - 20 30
Commissioner (Resides in Falkland Islands):
Mr Howard J S Pearce, CVO
Assistant Commissioner and Director of Fisheries:
Mr Russ T Jarvis

Gibraltar
Office of the Governor
The Convent, Main Street
Gibraltar
Telephone: (00) (350) 45440 (Switchboard)
47828 (PA to the Governor)
Facsimile: (00) (350) 47823 (Unclassified)
47830 (Airtech)
e-mail: convent@gibnet.gi
Office Hours (GMT) 08 00 - 16 15 (Winter); 07 30
- 13 30 (Summer)

Governor and Commander-in-Chief:
Mr David R C Durie, CMG
Deputy Governor: Mr David G Blunt, CVO
Assistant Deputy Governor: Mr Ian F Powell, OBE
Second Secretary (Convent Liaison Officer):
Mr Lawrence J Weldon, MVO
Second Secretary (EU Affairs):
Ms Alison F MacMillan
Third Secretary (Political): Mr Timothy J Freeman
Third Secretary (Management Officer):
Ms Lauren Johnstone

Consular/Visa inquiries:
Civil Status and Registration Office
Telephone: (00) (350) 51727/59839/59840
Facsimile: (00) (350) 42706

Commercial inquiries:
Department of Trade and Industry:
Telephone: (00) (350) 52052
Facsimile: (00) (350) 71406

Montserrat
Lancaster House
Olveston
Telephone: (00) (1) (664) 491 2688/9 Office
       6124 Governor's Residence
Facsimile: (00) (1) (664) 491 8867
Airtech: 4553
e-mail: govoff@candw.ag
monmedia@candw.ag Information section
Office Hours (GMT): 12 00 - 16 00 and 17 00 -
20 00
Governor: Mr A J Longrigg, CMG
First Secretary and Head of Governor's Office:
Mr D F Graham
Personal Assistant to the Governor: Miss D Baker
Defence Adviser (resides at Bridgetown):
Captain S C Ramm, RN
Third Secretary and Staff Officer: Mr G J Patton

Pitcairn Henderson Ducie and Oeno Islands
British High Commission,
Wellington, New Zealand
Governor: Mr R T Fell, CVO
(non-resident)
Pitcairn Islands Administration, Private Box
105696
Auckland, New Zealand
Commissioner (non resident): Mr L Salt
Telephone: (00) (9) (64) 366 0186
e-mail: pitcairn@iconz.co.nz
Website: http://www.government.pn

St Helena
Governor's Office
The Castle, Jamestown
St Helena Island,
South Atlantic Ocean
Telephone: (00) (290) 2555 Office
       4444 Residence
Facsimile: (00) (290) 2598 Office
       4418 Residence
Airtech: 2476
e-mail: OCS@helanta.sh
joany@sainthelena.gov.sh

Office Hours (GMT): 08 30 – 12 30 and 13 00 –
16 00 (Mon – Fri)
Governor and Commander-in Chief:
Mr David J Hollamby
Chief Secretary's Office
The Castle, Jamestown
St Helena Island, South Atlantic Island
Telephone: (00) (290) 4552 Residence
       2525 Office
Facsimile: (00) (290) 2598 Office
e-mail: OCS@helanta.sh
sandrab@sainthelena.gov.sh
Office Hours (GMT): 08 30 – 12 30 and 13 00 –
16 00 (Mon – Fri)
Chief *Secretary:* Mr John Styles

Ascension Island (Dependency of St Helena)
The Administrator's Office, Georgetown
Ascension Island,
South Atlantic Ocean, ASCN IZZ
Telephone: (00) 247 6311 Office
       4525 Home
Facsimile: (00) 247 6152
Airtech: (00) 247 6892
e-mail: administrator@atlantis.co.ac
Website: http://www.ascension-island.gov.ac
Office Hours (GMT): 08 30 - 12 30 and 13 30 -
16 30 (Mon-Fri)
*Governor and Commander-in-Chief (Resides in St
Helena):* Mr David J Hollamby
Administrator: Mr Geoffrey Fairhurst

Tristan da Cunha (Dependency of St Helena)
The Administrator's Office
Edinburgh of the Seven Seas
Tristan da Cunha, South Atlantic Ocean
e-mail: hmg@cunha.demon.co.uk
Office Hours (GMT): 08 30 - 12 30 and 13 00 -
16 30 (Mon-Fri)
*Governor and Commander-in-Chief (Resides in St
Helena):* Mr D J Hollamby
Administrator: Mr B P Baldwin

Turks and Caicos Islands
Waterloo, Government House,
Grand Turk, Turks and Caicos Islands
Telephone: (00) (1) (649) 946 2309
Facsimile: (00) (1) (649) 946 2903
Airtech: (00) (1) (649) 946 2766
e-mail: govhouse@tciway.tc
Governor: Mr M T Jones
First Secretary: Mr D J Peate, OBE
Second Secretary and Assistant to Governor:
Mr D V E Vickers
Personal Assistant: Mrs J White
Chief Secretary's Office
Government Secretariat, Grand Turk
Telephone: (00) (1) (649) 946 2702
Facsimile: (00) (1) (649) 946 2886
Chief Secretary: Mrs C Astwood, MBE
Defence Adviser (resides at Kingston):
Colonel R A Hyde-Bales
Office Hours (GMT): Winter: 13 00-17 30 and 19
00-21 30 (Mon-Thu),
13 00-17 30 and 19 00-21 00 (Fri)
Summer: 12 00-16 30 and 18 00-20 30 (Mon-Thu),
12 00-16 30 and 18 00-20 00 (Fri)

SMALL POSTS

SOVEREIGN
Abidjan
Algiers
Almaty
Antananarivo
Ashgabat
Asuncion
Baku
Banjul
Belmopan
Bratislava
Castries
Dakar
Dili
Freetown
Gaborone
Georgetown (Guyana)
Guatemala City
Holy See (Vatican)
Honiara
Kigali
Kingstown, St Vincent
Kinshasa
La Paz
Luxembourg
Ljubljana
Managua
Maseru
Mbabane
Minsk
Montevideo
Nassau
Nuku'alofa
Panama City
Phnom Penh
Port Moresby
Port of Spain
Port Vila
Quito
Rangoon
Reykjavik
Riga
St George's (Grenada)
San José
Santo Domingo
San Salvador
Skopje
Strasbourg
Suva
Tallinn
Tashkent
Tbilisi
Tegucigalpa
Tirana
Ulaanbaatar
Victoria
Vilnius
Windhoek
Yerevan

SUBORDINATE
Al Khobar
Alexandria
Amsterdam
Atlanta
Auckland
Barcelona
Bilbao
Bordeaux
Boston
Brisbane
Cape Town
Casablanca
Chiang Mai
Chicago
Dallas
Durban
Frankfurt
Guangzhou (Canton)
Hamburg
Ho Chi Minh City
Houston
Kolkata (Calcutta)
Kuching
Lille
Los Angeles
Lyon
Marseille
Melbourne
Miami
Milan
Montreal
Munich
Naples
Oporto
Palma
Perth
San Francisco
Seattle
Stuttgart
Sydney
Toronto
Vancouver
Yekaterinburg
Zurich

OVERSEAS TERRITORY
Anguilla
Georgetown, Ascension Island
Gibraltar
Grand Cayman, Cayman Islands
Grand Turk, Turks and Caicos Islands
Hamilton, Bermuda
Plymouth, Montserrat
Stanley, Falkland Islands
Jamestown, St Helena
Tortola, British Virgin Islands
Tristan Da Cunha

ANNEX: NON GOVERNMENTAL TRADE OFFICES

TAIWAN
Her Majesty' s Government do not recognise Taiwan as a sovereign state and consequently have no diplomatic relations with it. However, there are non- governmental trade and cultural offices at the following addresses:

Taipei
British Trade and Cultural Office
8-10th Floor Fu Key Building
99 Jen Ai Road, Section 2,Taipei 100
Telephone: (00) (886) (2) 2192 7000
            2192 + extension (Direct Line)
Facsimile: (00) (886) (2) 2394 8673(Commercial)
            2397 3559 (Inward Investment)
            2393 1985 (Visa Handling Unit)
            2397 3609 (Management)
Airtech: 2322 3265
e-mail: firstname.lastname@fco.gov.uk
Internet Website: www.btco.org.tw
Office Hours (GMT): 01 00 - 04 30 and 05 30 - 09 00
Director General: Mr Derek Marsh, cvo (ext 7009)
Deputy Director General:
Mr Rod Bunten (ext 7001)
Head of Commercial Section:
Ms Pam Balkin (ext 7006)
Head of Inward Investment Section:
Mr Bob Manning (ext 7066)
Head of Political and Economic Section:
Ms Kate White (ext 7055)
Head of Management Section:
Mr Peter Karmy (ext 7002)
Head of Visa Handling Unit:
Mr Alan Dillon (ext 7040)
Science and Technology Officer:
Mr Andrew Garth (ext 7089)
Press and Public Affairs Officer:
Ms Maggie Yeh (ext 7015)

Education and Cultural Section
British Trade and Cultural Office
7th Floor Fu Key Building
99 Jen Ai Road, Section 2,Taipei 100
Telephone: (00) (886) (2) 2192 7050
Facsimile: (00) (886) (2) 2341 5749
e-mail: firstname.lastname@britishcouncil.org.tw
Website: www.britishcouncil.org.tw
*Director, Educational and Cultural Operations
(British Council Director, Taipei):*
Mr Geoffrey Evans (ext 7077)

Kaohsiung
British Trade and Cultural Office (Kaohsiung Section)
Unit D, 7th Floor, Fu Bon Commercial Building
95 Ming-Tsu 2nd Road, Kaohsiung 800
Telephone: (00) (886) 7238 1034/5
Facsimile: (00) (886) 7238 1032
Commercial Officer: Ms Anne Lai

Education and Cultural Section
Unit D, 7th Floor, Fu Bon Commercial Building
95 Ming-Tsu 2nd Road, Kaohsiung 800

Telephone: (00) (886) 7235 1715
Facsimile: (00) (886) 7238 0411
Branch Manager: Ms Fay Chen

Guide to places and countries
Embassies, High Commissions, Deputy High Commissions and Consular Posts – Part 1

Note: There is no HMG representation in Bhutan.
It is therefore omitted from the List.

Aabenraa, Denmark
Aalborg, Denmark
Aarhus, Denmark
Abidjan, Côte d'Ivoire
Abuja, Nigeria
Abu Dhabi, United Arab
Emirates
Acapulco, Mexico
Accra, Ghana
Addis Ababa, Ethiopia
Adelaide, Australia
Aden, Yemen
Agadir, Morocco
Ahmedabad, India
Akureyri, Iceland
Aleppo, Syria
Ålesund, Norway
Alexandria, Egypt
Algiers, Algeria
Alicante, Spain
Al Khobar, Saudi Arabia
Almaty, Kazakhstan
Amiens, France
Amman, Jordan
Amsterdam, Netherlands
Anchorage, United States
Anguilla, See UK Overseas
Territories
Ankara, Turkey
Antalya, Turkey
Antananarivo, Madagascar
Antwerp, Belgium
Apia, Samoa
Arequipa, Peru
Ascension Island, See UK
Overseas Territories
Ashgabat, Turkmenistan
Asmara, Eritrea
Asunción, Paraguay
Athens, Greece
Atlanta, United States
Auckland, New Zealand
Bahrain, Bahrain
Baku, Azerbaijan
Bali, Indonesia
Bamako, Mali
Bandar Seri Begawan,
Brunei
Bangalore, India
Bangkok, Thailand
Banja Luka, Bosnia and
Herzegovina
Banjul, The Gambia
Barcelona, Spain
Bari, Italy
Basel, Switzerland
Basseterre, St Kitts and Nevis
Beijing, China
Beira, Mozambique

Beirut, Lebanon
Belém, Brazil
Belgrade, Serbia and
Montenegro
Belmopan, Belize
Belo Horizonte, Brazil
Bergen, Norway
Berlin, Germany
Berne, Switzerland
Biarritz, France
Bilbao, Spain
Bishkek, Kyrgyzstan
Bissau, Guinea Bissau
Bitola, Macedonia
Bodrum, Turkey
Bogotá, Colombia
Bonn, Germany
Bordeaux, France
Boston, United States
Boulogne-sur-Mer, France
Brasilia, Brazil
Bratislava, Slovakia
Brazzaville, Congo
Bregenz, Austria
Bremen, Germany
Bridgetown, Barbados
Brindisi, Italy
Brisbane, Australia
Brussels, Belgium
Bucharest, Romania
Budapest, Hungary
Buenos Aires, Argentina
Bursa, Turkey
Cagliari, Italy
Cairo, Egypt
Calais, France
Calgary, Canada
Cali, Colombia
Canberra, Australia
Cancun, Mexico
Cape Town, South Africa
Caracas, Venezuela
Casablanca, Morocco
Castries, St Lucia
Catania, Italy
Cayenne, French Guiana
Cebu, Philippines
Charlotte, United States
Chennai (Madras), India
Cherbourg, France
Chiang Mai, Thailand
Chicago, United States
Chisinau, Moldova
Chongqing, China
Christchurch, New Zealand
Ciudad Juárez, Mexico
Colombo, Sri Lanka
Conakry, Guinea
Copenhagen, Denmark

Córdoba, Argentina
Corfu, Greece
Cotonou, Benin
Cuenca, Ecuador
Curitiba, Brazil
Cusco, Peru
Dakar, Senegal
Dallas, United States
Damascus, Syria
Dar es Salaam, Tanzania
Denver, United States
Dili, East Timor (Democratic
Republic of)
Dhaka, Bangladesh
Djibouti, Djibouti
Doha, Qatar
Douala, Cameroon
Dubai, United Arab Emirates
Dublin, Irish Republic
Dubrovnik, Croatia
Dunkirk, France
Dushanbe, Tajikistan
Durban, South Africa
Düsseldorf, Germany
East London, South Africa
Eilat, Israel
Esbjerg, Denmark
Florence, Italy
Fort de France
(Martinique)
Fortaleza, Brazil
Frankfurt, Germany
Fredericia, Denmark
Freetown, Sierra Leone
Fukuoka, Japan
Funchal (Madeira), Portugal
Gaborone, Botswana
Galápagos, Ecuador
Gävle, Sweden
Gdansk, Poland
Geneva, Switzerland
Genoa, Italy
Georgetown, Guyana
Gothenburg, Sweden
Graz, Austria
Guadalajara, Mexico
Guadeloupe, France
Guangzhou, China
Guatemala City, Guatemala
Guayaquil, Ecuador
Halifax, Canada
Hamburg, Germany
Hanoi, Vietnam
Hanover, Germany
Harare, Zimbabwe
Harstad, Norway
Havana, Cuba
Havre (Le), France
Helsinki, Finland

Heraklion, Crete (Greece)
Herning, Denmark
Hiroshima, Japan
Ho Chi Minh City, Vietnam
Hobart, Australia
Hong Kong, China
Honiara, Solomon Islands
Houston, United States
Hyderabad, India
Ibadan, Nigeria
Ibiza, Spain
Innsbruck, Austria
Iquitos, Peru
Islamabad, Pakistan
Istanbul, Turkey
Izmir, Turkey
Jakarta, Indonesia
Jedda, Saudi Arabia
Jerusalem, Jerusalem
Johannesburg, South Africa
Johor, Malaysia
Jyväskylä, Finland
Kabul, Afghanistan
Kaduna, Nigeria
Kampala, Uganda
Kano, Nigeria
Kansas City, United States
Karachi, Pakistan
Kathmandu, Nepal
Katowice, Poland
Khartoum, Sudan
Kiel, Germany
Kiev, Ukraine
Kigali, Rwanda
Kingston, Jamaica
Kingstown, St Vincent and the
   Grenadines
Kinshasa, Democratic Republic
   of Congo
Kolkata (Calcutta), India
Kos, Greece
Kota Kinabalu, Malaysia
Kotka, Finland
Kraków, Poland
Kristiansand, Norway
Kristiansund, Norway
Kuala Lumpur, Malaysia
Kuching, Malaysia
Kuopio, Finland
Kuwait, Kuwait
Lagos, Nigeria
Lahore, Pakistan
La Paz, Bolivia
Las Palmas Spain (Grand
   Canary)
Le Havre, France
Leipzig, Germany
Libreville, Gabon
Liège, Belgium
Lille, France
Lilongwe, Malawi
Lima, Peru
Lisbon Portugal
Ljubljana, Slovenia
Lomé, Togo
Lorient, France

Los Angeles, United States
Luanda, Angola
Lublin, Poland
Lugano, Switzerland
Lusaka, Zambia
Luxembourg, Luxembourg
Luxor, Egypt
Lyon, France
Macau, China
Madrid, Spain
Málaga, Spain
Malé, Maldives
Malmö, Sweden
Managua, Nicaragua
Manáus, Brazil
Manila, Philippines
Maputo, Mozambique
Macaibo, Venezuela
Margarita, Venezuela
Mariehamn, Finland
Marmaris, Turkey
Marrakech, Morocco
Marseille, France
Martinique, France
Maseru, Lesotho
Mbabane, Swaziland
Medan, Indonesia
Medellin, Colombia
Melbourne, Australia
Mendoza, Argentina
Menorca, Spain
Mérida, Mexico
Mérida, Venezuela
Mersin, Turkey
Minneapolis, United States
Mexico City, Mexico
Miami, United States
Milan, Italy
Minsk, Belarus
Miri, Malaysia
Mogadishu, Somalia
Mombasa, Kenya
Monaco, Monaco
Monrovia, Liberia
Montego Bay, Jamaica
Monterrey, Mexico
Montevideo, Uruguay
Montpellier, France
Montreal, Canada
Montreux, Switzerland
Moroni, Comoros
Moscow, Russian Federation
Mumbai (Bombay), India
Munich, Germany
Muri Beach, Cook Islands
Muscat, Oman
Nagoya, Japan
Nairobi, Kenya
Nantes, France
Naples, Italy
Nashville, United States
Nassau, Bahamas
Ndjamena, Chad
New Caledonia, France
New Delhi, India
New Orleans, United States

New York, United States
Niamey, Niger
Nice, France
Nicosia, Cyprus
Norfolk, United States
Nouakchott, Mauritania
Novorossiysk, Russia
Nuku'alofa, Tonga
Nuremburg, Germany
Oaxaca, Mexico
Odense, Denmark
Oporto, Portugal
Orlando, United States
Osaka, Japan
Oslo, Norway
Ottawa, Canada
Ouagadougou, Burkina Faso
Oulu, Finland
Palermo, Italy
Palma, Spain
Panama City, Panama
Papeete, France (French
   Polynesia)
Paramaribo, Surinam
Paris, France
Patras, Greece
Pécs, Hungary
Perpignan, France
Perth, Australia
Philadelphia, United States
Phoenix, United States
Phnom Penh, Cambodia
Penang, Malaysia
Pittsburgh, United States
Piura, Peru
Plymouth, Montserrat
Podgorica - Montenegro,
   Serbia and Montenegro
Pointe- à-Pitre, France
   (Guadeloupe)
Pori, Finland
Ponta Delgada, Portugal
   (Azores)
Port-au-Prince, Haiti
Port Elizabeth, South Africa
Port Harcourt, Nigeria
Portimão, Portugal
Portland (Oregon), United
   States
Port Louis, Mauritius
Port Moresby, Papua New
   Guinea
Port of Spain, Trinidad and
   Tobago
Port Vila, Vanuatu
Porto Alegre, Brazil
Poznan, Poland
Prague, Czech Republic
Praia, Cape Verde
Pretoria, South Africa
Pristina - Kosovo, Serbia and
   Montenegro
Puerto Plata, Dominican
   Republic
Puerto Rico, United States
Punta Arenas, Chile

Pusan, Korea (Republic of)
Pyongyang, Korea (Democratic
Republic of)
Quebec City, Canada
Quito, Ecuador
Rabat, Morocco
Rangoon, Burma (Union of
Myanmar)
Recife, Brazil
Réunion, France
Reykjavik, Iceland
Rhodes, Greece
Riga, Latvia
Rio de Janeiro, Brazil
Rio Grande (do Sul), Brazil
Riyadh, Saudi Arabia
Rodrigues, Mauritius
Rome, Italy
Roseau, Dominica
St George's, Grenada
St John's, Antigua and Barbuda
St John's, Canada
St Louis, United States
St Malo-Dinard, France
St Petersburg, Russian
Federation
Salonika, Greece
Salt Lake City, United States
Salvador, Brazil
Salzburg, Austria
Sanaa, Yemen
San Cristobal, Venezuela
San Diego, United States
San Francisco, United States
San Jose (California), United
States
San José, Costa Rica
San Pedro Sula, Honduras
San Salvador, El Salvador
Santa Cruz de Tenerife, Spain
(Canary Islands)
Santa Fe, Argentina
Santander, Spain
Santiago, Chile
Santo Domingo, Dominican
Republic
Santos, Brazil
São Paulo, Brazil
São Tomé, São Tomé and
Principe
Sao Vincente, Cape Verde
Sapporo, Japan
Sarajevo, Bosnia and
Herzegovina
Saumur, France
Seattle, United States
Seoul, Korea (Republic of)
Sfax, Tunisia
Shanghai, China
Singapore, Singapore
Skopje, Macedonia
Sofia, Bulgaria
Split, Croatia
Stavanger, Norway
Stockholm, Sweden
Stuttgart, Germany

Suez, Egypt
Sundsvall, Sweden
Surabaya, Indonesia
Suva, Fiji
Sydney, Australia
Syros, Greece
Szczecin, Poland
Taipei, Taiwan (China)
Tallinn, Estonia
Tampere (Tammerfors), Finland
Tangier, Morocco
Tarawa, Kiribati (Republic of)
Tashkent, Uzbekistan
Tasmania, Australia
Tbilisi, Georgia
Tegucigalpa, Honduras
Tehran, Iran
Tel Aviv, Israel
The Hague, Netherlands
Tijuana, Mexico
Tirana, Albania
Toamasina, Madagascar
Tokyo, Japan
Toronto, Canada
Tørshavn, Denmark (Faroes)
Tortola, British Virgin Islands
Toulouse, France
Tours, France
Trieste, Italy
Tripoli, Lebanon
Tripoli, Libya
Tromso, Norway
Trondheim, Norway
Trujillo, Peru
Tunis, Tunisia
Turin, Italy
Turku, Finland
Ulaanbaatar, Mongolia
Vaasa (Vasa), Finland
Varna, Bulgaria
Vaduz, Liechtenstein
Valais, Switzerland
Valencia, Venezuela
Valletta, Malta
Valparaíso, Chile
Vancouver, Canada
Venice, Italy
Veracruz, Mexico
Victoria, Seychelles
Vienna, Austria
Vientiane, Laos
Vigo, Spain
Vilnius, Lithuania
Vladivostok, Russia
Warsaw, Poland
Washington, United States
Wellington, New Zealand
Willemstad, Netherlands
Antilles
Windhoek, Namibia
Winnipeg, Canada
Wroclaw, Poland
Yaoundé, Cameroon
Yekaterinburg, Russian
Federation
Yerevan, Armenia

Zagreb, Croatia
Zakynthos, Greece
Zurich, Switzerland

Chronological Lists from 1982 onwards
of Secretaries of State,
Ministers of State,
Permanent Under-Secretaries of State,
British Ambassadors etc.,
High Commissioners,
Permanent Representatives
to International Organizations and
Governors and Commanders-in-chief
of Dependent territories

Reference should be made to the Foreign Office and Commonwealth Relations Office Lists of 1965, to the Colonial Office List of 1966 and to the Diplomatic Service List 2002 and earlier Lists for previous lists of officers holding these appointments.

Part III: Chronological Lists

The Foreign and Commonwealth Office was formed in October 1968 by the merger of the former Foreign Office and the Commonwealth Office

SECRETARIES OF STATE FOR FOREIGN AND COMMONWEALTH AFFAIRS 1982-2002

1982   Apr5 The Rt Hon. Francis Pym, MC, MP (later Lord Pym)
1983   June11 The Rt Hon. Sir Geoffrey Howe, PC, QC, MP (later Baron Howe of Aberavon)
1989   July25 The Rt Hon. John Major, MP
1989   Oct26 The Rt Hon. Douglas Hurd, CBE, MP (later Baron Hurd of Westwell)
1995   July6 The Rt Hon. Malcolm Rifkind, QC, MP
1997   May2 The Rt Hon. Robin Cook, MP
2001   June8 The Rt Hon. Jack Straw, PC, MP

MINISTERS OF STATE FOR FOREIGN AND COMMONWEALTH AFFAIRS 1982-2002

1982   April5 The Lord Belstead
1982   April5 Cranley Onslow, MP
1983   June14 Malcolm Rifkind, MP
1983   June14 The Rt Hon. Baroness Young
1983   June14 Richard Luce (later the Rt Hon. Sir Richard Luce, MP)
1983   June14 The Rt Hon. Timothy Raison, MP
1984   Sept11 Timothy Renton, MP (later the Rt Hon. Baron Renton)
1986   Jan13 Mrs Lynda Chalker, MP (later the Rt Hon. Baroness Chalker)
1986   Sept8 Christopher Patten, MP (later the Rt Hon. Christopher Patten)
1987   June16 The Lord Glenarthur
1987   June16 David Mellor, QC, MP (later the Rt Hon. David Mellor)
1988   July16 The Rt Hon. William Waldegrave, MP (later Baron Waldegrave)
1989   July25 The Hon. Francis Maude, MP (later the Rt Hon. Francis Maude MP)
1989   July25 The Lord Brabazon
1989   July25 The Hon. Timothy Sainsbury, MP (later the Rt.Hon Timothy Sainsbury)
1990   July23 Tristan Garel-Jones, MP (later the Rt Hon. Tristan Garel-Jones, MP)
1990   July23 The Rt Hon. The Earl of Caithness
1990   July23 The Hon. Mark Lennox-Boyd, MP (later the Hon. Sir Mark Lennox-Boyd)
1990   Nov1 The Hon. Douglas Hogg, QC, MP (later the Rt Hon. Douglas Hogg, QC, MP)

1992   The Rt Hon. Alastair Goodlad, MP
1994   July20, David Davis MP (later the Rt Hon. David Davis MP)
1995   July5, The Rt Hon. Sir Nicholas Bonsor(Bt), MP
1995   July5, The Rt Hon. Jeremy Hanley, MP (later the Rt.Hon Sir Jeremy Hanley)
1997   May5, Derek Fatchett, MP (later the Rt Hon. Derek Fatchett, MP)
1997   May5, Tony Lloyd, MP
1997   May5, Doug Henderson, MP
1998   July28, Ms Joyce Quin, MP (later the Rt Hon. Joyce Quin, MP)
1999   May17, Geoff Hoon, MP
1999   July29, Peter Hain, MP
1999   July29, John Battle, MP
1999   July29, Baroness Scotland
1999   Oct12, Keith Vaz, MP
2001   Jan25, Brian Wilson, MP
2001   June11, Peter Hain, MP
2001   June11, Baroness Symons
2001   June11, Ben Bradshaw, MP
2001   June11, Denis MacShane, MP
2001   June11, Baroness Amos
2002   May30, Mike O'Brien, MP
2002   Oct 28, Bill Rammell, MP

PERMANENT UNDER-SECRETARIES OF STATE FOR FOREIGN AND COMMONWEALTH AFFAIRS AND HEAD OF HM DIPLOMATIC SERVICE 1982-2002

1982   April8, Sir Antony (Arthur) Acland, KCMG KCVO (later KG GCMG GCVO)
1986   June23, Sir Patrick (Richard Henry) Wright, GCMG (later Baron Wright of Richmond)
1991   June28, Sir David (Howe) Gillmore, KCMG (later Baron Gillmore)(Dec'd 20th March 1999)
1994   Aug1, Sir (Arthur) John Coles, KCMG (later GCMG)
1997   Nov13, Sir John (Olav) Kerr, GCMG
2002   Jan14, Sir Michael (Hastings) Jay, KCMG

CHRONOLOGICAL LIST OF BRITISH REPRESENTATIVES ABROAD INCLUDING COMMONWEALTH COUNTRIES 1982-2002

Afghanistan
1984   Charles David Stephen Drace-Francis, Chargé d'Affaires a.i. July18
1987   Ian Warren Mackley, Chargé d'Affaires a.i. Jan8
        Staff temporarily withdrawn from post February 1989
1994   Sir Nicholas Barrington, amb. ex. and plen. Feb22
2002   Ronald Peter Nash, amb. ex. and plen. May16

Albania
1992   Sir Patrick Stanislaus Fairweather, amb. ex. and plen. July20
1996   Harcourt Andrew Pretorius Tesoriere, amb.ex. and plen. Jan21
1998   Stephen Nash amb. ex. and plen. May15
1999   Dr Peter January amb. ex. and plen. March1
2001   Dr David Maurice Landsman OBE, amb. ex. and plen. July16

Algeria
1984   Alan (later Sir A) Gordon Munro, amb. ex. and plen. Jan21
1987   Patrick Howard Caines Eyers amb. ex. and plen. April12
1990   Christopher Charles Richard Battiscombe amb. ex. and plen. March6
1994   Christopher Donald Crabbie amb. ex. and plen Aug2
1996   Peter James Marshall, amb. ex. and plen Jan6
1997   (Jean) Francois Gordon, amb. ex. and plen. Nov4
1999   William Baldie Sinton OBE, amb. ex. and plen. July16
2001   Richard John Smale Edis, amb. ex. and plen. Sept15
2002   Graham Stewart Hand, amb. ex. and plen. July1

Andorra
1994   Anthony David Brighty amb. ex. and plen. Aug25
1998   Peter Torry amb. ex. and plen. Sep2

Angola (Republic of)
1983   Marrack Irvine Goulding, amb. ex. and plen. June29
1985   Patrick Stanislaus Fairweather, amb. ex. and plen. Oct2
1987   Michael John Carlisle Glaze, amb. ex. and plen. Nov18
1990   John Gerrard Flynn, amb. ex. and plen. May9
1993   Anthony Richard Thomas, amb. ex. and plen. April8
1995   Roger Dudley Hart, amb. ex. and plen. July24
1998   Caroline Elmes, amb. ex. and plen. Sept14
2002   John Thompson, amb. ex. and plen. Feb21

Antigua and Barbuda
HIGH COMMISSIONERS
1982   Viscount (John William) Dunrossil. Sept25
1983   Giles (later Sir G) Lionel Bullard. Aug6
1986   Kevin Francis Xavier Burns. Oct19
1991   Emrys Thomas Davies. Feb15
1994   Richard Thomas. Oct7
1998   Gordon Meldrum Baker Aug3
2001   (Charles) John Branford White. Aug11

The Argentine Republic
Diplomatic and Consular relations with the Argentine Republic were broken off with effect from 2 April 1982. Consular Relations were resumed on 19 October 1989 and Diplomatic Relations on 15th February 1990.

1989   Alan Charles Hunt Consul General. Oct19
1989   Alan Charles Hunt Chargé d'Affaires a.i. and Consul General. Feb15
1990   The Hon Humphrey John Hamilton Maud, amb. ex. and plen. July15
1993   Sir Peter Hall, amb. ex. and plen. Sept8
1997   William Marsden, amb. ex. and plen. July27
2000   (Duncan) Robin Carmichael Christopher, amb. ex. and plen. Nov17

Armenia
1992   Sir Brian James Proetel Fall, amb. ex. and plen. July15
1995   David Ivimey Miller, amb. ex. and plen. July31
1997   John Edward Mitchiner, amb. ex. and plen. April1
1999   Timothy Aidan Jones, amb. ex. and plen. Nov13
2002   Thorhilda Mary Vivia Abbott-Watt, amb. ex. and plen. Dec15

Australia
HIGH COMMISSIONERS
1984   Sir John Henry Gladstone Leahy. Oct13
1988   (Arthur) John (later Sir J) Coles. March22
1991   Brian (later Sir B) Leon Barder. April11
1994   Roger (later Sir R) John Carrick. July27
1997   Alexander Claud Stuart Allan. Nov16
1999   Sir Alastair Goodlad KCMG. May25.

Austria (Republic of)
1982   Michael O'Donel Bjarne Alexander, amb. ex. and plen. Jan25
1986   Robert James O'Neill, amb. ex. and plen. Sept2
1989   Brian Lee Crowe, amb. ex. and plen. May31
1992   Terence Courtney Wood, amb. ex. and plen. April30
1996   Anthony (later Sir A) St John Howard Figgis, amb. ex. and plen. Sept29
2000   Antony Ford, amb. ex. and plen. Sept1

Azerbaijan
1992   Sir Brian James Proetel Fall, amb. ex. and plen. July14
1993   Thomas Nesbitt Young, amb. ex. and plen. Sept1
1997   Roger Thomas, amb. ex. and plen. July1
2000   Andrew Victor Gunn Tucker, amb. ex. and plen. Nov1

Bahamas
HIGH COMMISSIONERS
1983   Peter William Heap. May23
1986   Colin Garth Mays. Oct16
1991   Michael John Gore. July16
1992   Brian Attewell. Sept16
1996   Peter Michael Heppell Young. May1
1999   Peter Richard Heigl. July15

Bahrain
1984   Francis Sidney Edward Trew, amb. ex. and plen. Dec5
1988   John Alan Shepherd, amb. ex. and plen. April4
1992   Hugh James Oliver Redvers Tunnell, amb. ex. and plen. Feb16
1996   David Ian Lewty, amb. ex. and plen. Jan13
1999   Peter Ford, amb. ex. and plen. April18

Bangladesh (People's Republic of)
HIGH COMMISSIONERS
1983   Terence George (later Sir T) Streeton. Dec20
1989   Colin (later Sir C) Henry Imray. Oct21
1993   Peter James Fowler. Sept21
1996   David Critchlow Walker. Sept15
2000   David Carter. Jan19

Barbados
HIGH COMMISSIONERS
1982   Viscount (John William) Dunrossil. Sept25
1983   Giles (later Sir G) Lionel Bullard. Aug6
1986   Kevin Francis Xavier Burns. Oct19
1991   Emrys Thomas Davies. Jan13
1994   Richard Thomas. Oct7
1998   Gordon Meldrum Baker. Mar8
2001   (Charles) John Branford White. Aug11

Belarus
1992   Sir Brian James Proetel Fall, amb. ex. and plen. July27
1993   John Vivian Everard, amb. ex. and plen. Oct12
1996   Jessica Mary Pearce, amb. ex. and plen. Jan22
1999   Iain Kelly, amb. ex. and plen. April6

Belgium
1982   John (later Sir J) Edward Jackson, amb. ex. and plen. April30
1985   Peter (later Sir P) Charles Petrie, amb. ex. and plen. July7
1989   Robert James O'Neill, amb. ex. and plen. May10
1992   Sir John Walter David Gray, amb. ex. and plen. June18
1996   David Hugh Colvin, amb. ex. and plen. Oct6
2001   Gavin Wallace Hewitt, amb. ex. and plen. Feb2

Belize
HIGH COMMISSIONERS
1984   John Michael Crosby. Oct19
1987   Peter Alexander Bremner Thomson. Nov10
1991   David Patrick Robert Mackilligin. Feb13
1995   Gordon Meldrum Baker. March30
1998   Timothy James David. April15

2001   Philip John Priestley. July16

Republic of Benin
1983   William Erskine Hamilton Whyte, amb. ex. and plen. Aug18
1986   Martin (later Sir M) Kenneth Ewans, amb. ex. and plen. Aug8
1988   Brian (later Sir B) Leon Barder, amb. ex. and plen. Sept23
1991   (Alastair) Christopher (later Sir C) Donald Summerhayes MacRae, amb. ex. and plen. June17
1994   (John) Thorold Masefield, amb. ex. and plen. May14
1997   Graham (later Sir G) Stuart Burton, amb. ex. and plen. May2
2001   Philip Lloyd Thomas, amb. ex. and plen. March5

Bolivia
1985   Alan White, amb. ex. and plen. March9
1987   Colum John Sharkey, amb. ex. and plen. Aug19
1989   Michael Francis Daly, amb. ex. and plen. June4
1991   Richard Michael Jackson, amb. ex. and plen. May15
1995   David Frederick Charles Ridgway, amb. ex. and plen. June1
1998   Graham Leslie Minter, amb. ex. and plen. Aug15
2001   William Baldie Sinton, amb. ex. and plen. Oct15

Bosnia and Herzegovina
1994   Robert William Barnett, amb. ex. and plen. April26
1995   Bryan Hopkinson, amb. ex. and plen. March30

When Yugoslavia broke up "The Republic of Bosnia and Herzegovina" emerged as a new country. At Dayton in 1995 it was agreed that the country should be renamed "Bosnia and Herzegovina". This took effect in 1996

1996   Charles Graham Crawford, amb. ex. and plen. July2
1998   Graham Stewart Hand, amb. ex. and plen. July25
2001   Ian Cameron Cliff, amb. ex. and plen. Oct19

Botswana
HIGH COMMISSIONERS
1986   Peter Albert Raftery. Feb21
1989   Brian Smith. Feb18
1991   John Coates Edwards. Nov19
1994   David Colin Baskcomb Beaumont. Dec19
1998   John Wilde. May17
2001   David Byron Merry. Aug18

Brazil
1984 John Burns Ure, amb. ex. and plen. Feb26
1987 Michael John Newington amb. ex. and plen. Dec15
1992 Peter William (later Sir P) Heap, amb. ex. and plen. Aug4
1995 Donald Keith Haskell, amb. ex. and plen. May15.
1999 Roger Bridgland Bone, amb. ex. and plen. May20.

Brunei
HIGH COMMISSIONERS
1983 (Robert) Francis Cornish. Aug5
1986 Roger Westbrook. Sept8
1991 Adrian John Sindall. April9
1994 Ivan (later Sir I)Roy Callan. July7
1998 Stuart Laing. July27
2002 Andrew John Forbes Caie. Jan16

Bulgaria (Republic of)
1983 John Michael Owen Snodgrass, amb. ex. and plen. Sept6
1986 John Harold Fawcett, amb. ex. and plen. Aug30
1989 Richard Thomas, amb. ex. and plen. May5
1994 Roger Guy Short, amb. ex. and plen. Sept29
1998 Richard Stagg, amb. ex. and plen. July 8
2001 (Samuel) Ian Soutar, amb. ex. and plen. Dec3

Burkina Faso
(Country re-named on 3August 1984)
1983 John Michael Wilson, amb. ex. and plen. July12
1988 Veronica Evelyn Sutherland, amb. ex. and plen. Jan26
1990 Margaret Irene Rothwell, amb. ex. and plen. Dec17
1997 Haydon Boyd Warren-Gash, amb. ex. and plen. Oct7
2001 Jean Francois Gordon, amb. ex. and plen. June7

Burma (Union of Myanmar)
1982 Nicholas Maed Fenn, amb. ex. and plen. Oct20
1986 Martin Robert Morland, amb. ex. and plen. Oct19
1990 Julian Dana Nimmo Hartland-Swann, amb. ex. and plen. May5
1995 Robert Anthony Eagleson Gordon, amb. ex. and plen. Sept6
1999 John Jenkins, amb. ex. and plen. April26
2002 Victoria Jane Bowman, amb. ex. and plen. Dec16

Republic of Burundi
1984 Nicholas Peter Bayne, amb. ex. and plen. Feb7
1985 Patrick Howard Caines Eyers, amb. ex. and plen. Sept23
1987 Robert Linklater Burke Cormack, amb. ex. and plen. June11
1994 Edward Clay, amb. ex. and plen. Sept19
1995 Kaye Wight Oliver, amb. ex. and plen. Dec11

1998 Graeme Neil Loten. amb. ex. and plen. May11
2001 Susan Elizabeth Hogwood. amb. ex. and plen. July26

Cambodia
1994 Paul Reddicliffe, amb. ex. and plen. June24
1997 Christopher George Edgar, amb. ex. and plen. July29
2000 Stephen John Bridges, amb. ex. and plen. Dec17

Republic of Cameroon
AMBASSADORS
1984 Michael John Carlisle Glaze, amb. ex. and plen. July7
1987 Martin Reith, amb. ex. and plen. Oct15
1991 William Ernest Quantrill, amb. ex. and plen. April16
1995 Nicholas Melvyn McCarthy, amb. ex. and plen. April11
In 1995 Cameroon joined the Commonwealth.

HIGH COMMISSIONERS
1998 George Peter Richard Boon. Feb8
2002 Richard James Wildash. June21

Canada
HIGH COMMISSIONERS
1984 Sir Derek (Malcolm) Day. Aug1
1987 Sir Alan Bedford Urwick. Dec4
1989 Brian James Proetel Fall. Oct5
1992 Nicholas (later Sir N) Peter Bayne. April7
1996 Anthony (later Sir A) Michael Goodenough. Mar6
2000 Sir Robert Andrew Burns. July7

Cape Verde (Republic of)
1982 (Peter) Laurence O'Keeffe, amb. ex. and plen. Sept15
1986 John Esmond Campbell Macrae, amb. ex. and plen. June17
1990 Roger Campbell Beetham, amb. ex. and plen. Oct18
1993 Alan Edwin Furness, amb. ex. and plen. Oct13
1997 David Raymond Snoxell, amb. ex. and plen. April 26
2000 Edward Alan Burner, amb. ex. and plen. Aug10

Central African Republic
1982 Bryan Sparrow, amb. ex. and plen. Jan28
1985 Michael John Carlisle Glaze, amb. ex. and plen. Feb9
1987 (vacant)
1988 Martin Reith, amb. ex. and plen. July2
1991 William Ernest Quantrill, amb. ex. and plen.
1998 George Peter Richard Boon, amb. ex. and plen. Feb8
2002 Richard James Wildash, amb. ex. and plen. June21

Chad (Republic of)
1982 (Alistair) Christopher Donald Summerhayes MacRae, amb. ex. and plen. Feb2
1985 Michael Francis Daly, amb. ex. and plen. March20

1987   Maeve Geraldine Fort, amb. ex. and plen.
        March7
1990   Charlotte Susanna Rycroft, amb. ex. and
        plen. March19
1991   William Ernest Quantrill, amb. ex. and plen.
        June
1994   John Thorold Masefield, amb. ex. and plen.
        May14
1995   Nicholas Melvyn McCarthy, amb. ex. and
        plen. April11
1998   George Peter Richard Boon, amb. ex. and
        plen. Feb8
2002   Richard James Wildash, amb. ex. and plen.
        June21

Chile
1982   John Kyrle Hickman, amb. ex. and plen.
        June13
1987   Alan White, amb. ex. and plen. July31
1990   Richard Alvin Neilson, amb. ex. and plen.
        Aug31
1993   Frank Basil Wheeler, amb. ex. and plen.
        Oct27
1997   Madelaine (later Dame M) Glynne Dervel
        Evans, amb. ex. and plen. June8
2000   Leo Gregory Faulkner, amb. ex. and plen.
        April1

China (People's Republic of)
1984   Sir Richard Mark Evans, amb. ex. and plen.
        Jan19
1988   Alan (later Sir A) Ewen Donald, amb. ex.
        and plen. May14
1991   Sir Robin John Taylor McLaren, amb. ex.
        and plen. June5
1994   Sir Leonard Vincent Appleyard, amb. ex.
        and plen. Sept8
1997   Anthony (later Sir A) Charles Galsworthy,
        amb. ex. and plen. May21
2002   Christoper Owen Hum, amb. ex. and plen.
        March19

Colombia
1982   John (later Sir J) Adam Robson, amb. ex.
        and plen. May29
1987   Richard Alvin Neilson, amb. ex. and plen.
        Feb5
1990   Keith (later Sir K) Elliott Hedley Morris,
        amb. ex. and plen. Sept26
1994   (Arthur) Leycester (later Sir Leycester)
        Scott Coltman, amb. ex. and plen. Nov1
1998   Jeremy Walter Thorp, amb. ex. and plen.
        May,31
2001   Thomas Joseph Duggin, amb. ex. and plen.
        Aug16

Comoros (Federal Islamic Republic of)
1984   James Nicholas Allan, amb. ex. and plen.
        June7
1986   Richard Borman Crowson, amb. ex. and
        plen. Aug29
1989   Michael Edward Howell, amb. ex. and plen.
        Sept27
1991   Dennis Oltrieve Amy, amb. ex. and plen.
        May14
1992   Peter John Smith, amb. ex. and plen. Oct20

1996   Robert Scott Dewar, amb. ex. and plen.
        April14
1999   Charlie Mochan, amb. ex. and plen.
        March30
2002   Brian Donaldson, amb. ex. and plen. Oct17

Democratic Republic of The Congo
1983   Nicholas Peter Bayne, amb. ex. and plen.
        Nov23
1985   Patrick Howard Caines Eyers, amb. ex. and
        plen. Feb24
1987   Robert Linklater Burke Cormack, amb. ex.
        and plen. June11
1991   Roger Westbrook, amb. ex. and plen. July30
1996   Marcus Laurence Hulbert Hope, amb. ex.
        and plen. Jan21
1998   Doug Scrafton CMG, amb. ex. and plen.
        June15
2000   James Oswald Atkinson, amb. ex. and plen.
        May3

Costa Rica
1983   Peter Wayne Summerscale, amb. ex. and
        plen. Jan24
1986   Michael Francis Daly, amb. ex. and plen.
        June6
1989   William Marsden, amb. ex. and plen.
        April14
1992   Mary Louise Croll, amb. ex. and plen. July5
1995   Richard Michael Jackson, amb. ex. and
        plen. Sept1
1997   Alan Stanley Green, amb. ex. and plen.
        Sept10
1999   Peter Joseph Spiceley, amb. ex. and plen.
        Jan5
2002   Georgina Susan Butler, amb. ex. and plen.
        Mar8

Côte d'Ivoire (Ivory Coast)
1983   John Michael Wilson, amb. ex. and plen.
        Feb2
1987   Veronica (later Dame V) Evelyn Sutherland,
        amb. ex. and plen. June27
1990   Margaret Irene Rothwell, amb. ex. and plen.
        Dec17
1997   Haydon Boyd Warren-Gash, amb. ex. and
        plen. Oct7
2001   Jean Francois Gordon, amb. ex. and plen.
        June7

Croatia
1992   Bryan Sparrow, amb. ex. and plen. July23
1994   Gavin Wallace Hewitt, amb. ex. and plen.
        June16
1997   Colin Andrew Munro, amb. ex. and plen.
        Aug8
2000   Nicholas Jarrold, amb. ex. and plen. Nov10

Cuba
1984   (Patrick) Robin (later Sir R) Fearn, amb. ex.
        and plen. Feb29
1986   Andrew Eustace Palmer, amb. ex. and plen.
        July15
1989   (Anthony) David Brighty, amb. ex. and
        plen. Jan22
1991   (Arthur) Leycester (later Sir Leycester)
        Scott Coltman, amb. ex. and plen. March3

1994   Philip Alexander McLean, amb. ex. and
       plen. Nov25
1998   David Frederick Charles Ridgway, amb. ex.
       and plen. July27
2001   Paul Webster Hare, amb. ex. and plen. July11

Cyprus (Republic of)
HIGH COMMISSIONERS
1982   (William) John Antony Wilberforce. May10
1988   The Hon. Humphrey Maud. Sept7
1990   David (later Sir David) John Michael Dain.
       July4
1994   David Christopher Andrew Madden. May14
1999   Edward Clay. March12
2001   Lyn Parker. Sept16

Czech Republic
1985   Stephen Jeremy Barrett, amb. ex. and plen.
       March8
1988   (Peter) Laurence O'Keeffe, amb. ex. and
       plen. Nov1
1991   (Anthony) David Brighty, amb. ex. and
       plen. July21
1994   Sir Michael St Edmund Burton, amb. ex.
       and plen. Sept19
1997   David Stuart Broucher, amb. ex. and plen.
       Oct1
2001   Anne Fyfe Pringle, amb. ex. and plen. Nov8

Denmark
1983   James Mellon, amb. ex. and plen. May7
1986   Peter William Unwin, amb. ex. and plen.
       July9
1989   Nigel Christopher Ransome Williams, amb.
       ex. and plen. Jan4
1993   Hugh James Arbuthnott, amb. ex. and plen.
       June6
1996   Andrew Philip Foley Bache, amb. ex. and
       plen. Nov8
1999   Philip Astley, amb. ex. and plen. June4

Djibouti
1985   David Everard Tatham, amb. ex. and plen.
       Jan14
1988   Mark Anthony Marshall, amb. ex. and plen.
       Jan18
1993   (Robert) Douglas Gordon, amb. ex. and
       plen. March20
1994   Duncan Robin Carmichael Christopher,
       amb. ex. and plen. April1
1997   Gordon Geoffrey Wetherell, amb. ex. and
       plen. Sept11
2000   Myles Antony Wickstead, amb. ex. and
       plen. Nov9

Dominica
HIGH COMMISSIONERS
1982   Viscount (John William) Dunrossil. Sept25
1983   Giles (later Sir G) Lionel Bullard. Aug6
1986   Kevin Francis Xavier Burns. Oct19
1991   Emmrys Thomas Davies. Feb20
1994   Richard Thomas. Oct7
1998   Gordon Meldrum Baker. March8
2001   (Charles) John Branford White. Aug11

Dominican Republic
1983   Roy George Marlow, amb. ex. and plen.
       July1
1985   Michael John Newington, amb. ex. and
       plen. July7
1988   Giles Eden FitzHerbert, amb. ex. and plen.
       May11
1993   John Gerrard Flynn, amb. ex. and plen.
       April4
1995   Dick Thomson, amb. ex. and plen. Sept.15
1998   David Gordon Ward, amb. ex. and plen.
       Sept18
2002   Andrew Richard Ashcroft, amb. ex. and
       plen. July30

East Timor
BRITISH REPRESENTATIVES
New British Mission (Dili) was formally opened in
January 2000
2000   Dominic James Robert Jermey, Brit. Rep.
       Jan5
2000   Jane Elizabeth Mary Penfold, Brit. Rep.
       Nov21

On the 20th May 2002 East Timor became
independent. The British Mission is now an Embassy.

2002   Hamish St Clair Daniel, amb. ex. and plen.
       May20

Ecuador
1985   Michael William Atkinson, amb. ex. and
       plen. June28
1989   Frank Basil Wheeler, amb. ex. and plen.
       Aug18
1993   Richard Douglas Lavers, amb. ex. and
       plen.Nov18.
1997   John William Forbes-Meyler, amb. ex. and
       plen. June27
2000   Ian Gerken, amb. ex. and plen. Feb4.

Egypt (Arab Republic of)
1985   Sir Alan Bedford Urwick, amb. ex. and
       plen. Feb15
1987   (William) James (later Sir J) Adams, amb.
       ex. and plen. Dec14
1992   Christopher William Long, amb. ex. and
       plen. April26
1995   David Elliott Spiby Blatherwick, amb. ex.
       and plen. April25
1999   Graham (later Sir G) Boyce, amb. ex. and
       plen. Feb10
2001   (Robert) John Sawers, amb. ex. and plen.
       Sept19

El Salvador
1982   Colum John Sharkey, amb. ex. and plen.
       Feb11
1984   Bryan Oliver White, amb. ex. and plen.
       Dec5
1987   David Joy, amb. ex. and plen. Sept8
1989   Peter John Streams, amb. ex. and plen.
       Sept13
1991   Michael Henry Connor, amb. ex. and plen.
       Nov25
1995   Ian Gerken, amb. ex. and plen. July1
1999   Patrick Morgan, amb. ex. and plen. July5

Republic of Equatorial Guinea
1982   Bryan Sparrow, amb. ex. and plen. Feb11
1985   Michael John Carlisle Glaze, amb. ex. and plen. April25
1987   Martin Reith, amb. ex. and plen. Nov26
1991   William Ernest Quantrill, amb. ex. and plen.
1998   George Peter Richard Boon, amb. ex. and plen. Feb8
2002   Richard James Wildash, amb. ex. and plen. June21

Eritrea (Republic of)
1994   Duncan Robin Carmichael Christopher, amb. ex. and plen. April29
1997   Gordon Geoffrey Wetherell, amb. ex. and plen. Sept11
2000   Myles Antony Wickstead, amb. ex. and plen. Nov9
2002   Michael Thomas Murray, amb. ex. and plen. Mar17

Estonia (Republic of)
1991   Brian Buik Low, amb. ex. and plen. Oct8
1994   Charles Richard Lucien de Chassiron, amb ex. and plen. Oct15
1997   Timothy James Craddock, amb. ex. and plen. Sept20
2000   Sarah Squire, amb. ex. and plen. Sept6

Ethiopia
1982   Brian Leon Barder, amb. ex. and plen. Sept21
1986   Harold (later Sir H) Berners Walker, amb. ex. and plen. April29
1990   Michael John Carlisle Glaze, amb. ex. and plen. March21
1994   Duncan Robin Carmichael Christopher, amb. ex. and plen. April18
1997   Gordon Geoffrey Wetherell, amb. ex. and plen. Sept11
2000   Myles Antony Wickstead, amb. ex. and plen. Nov9

Fiji
HIGH COMMISSIONERS
1982   Roger Arnold Rowlandson Barltrop. July30

AMBASSADORS
†1988 Roger Arnold Rowlandson Barltrop, amb. ex. and plen. March1
1989   (Alexander Basil) Peter Smart, amb. ex. and plen. Aug19
1992   Timothy James David, amb. ex. and plen. March14

†From 1March 1988, the British High Commission became the British Embassy

1995   Michael John Peart, amb. ex. and plen. April14.
1997   Michael Alan Charles Dibben, amb. ex. and plen. Dec3
2000   Michael Anthony Price, amb. ex. and plen. Oct16
2002   Charles Francis Mochan, amb. ex. and plen.

Finland
1983   Alan Brooke Turner, amb. ex. and plen. Jan25

1986   (Hubert Anthony) Justin Staples, amb. ex. and plen. Feb25
1989   (George) Neil Smith. Nov21
1995   David Allan Burns, amb. ex. and plen. March9.
1997   Gavin Wallace Hewitt, amb. ex. and plen. Sept15
2001   Alyson Judith Kirtley Bailes, amb. ex. and plen. Jan5
2002   Matthew John Lushington Kirk, amb. ex. and plen. July24

France
1982   Sir (Major) John Emsley Fretwell, amb. ex. and plen. March4
1987   Sir Ewen Alastair John Fergusson, amb. ex. and plen. June22
1993   Sir Christopher Leslie George Mallaby, amb. ex. and plen. Jan29
1996   Sir Michael Hastings Jay, amb. ex. and plen. July10
2001   Sir John Eaton Holmes, amb. ex. and plen. Oct16

Gabon (Republic of)
1982   Alan Hartley Grey, amb. ex. and plen. April25
1985   Ronald Henry Thomas Bates amb. ex. and plen. Feb18
1986   Mark Aubrey Goodfellow, amb. ex. and plen. Feb3
1990   Philip John Priestley, amb. ex. and plen. Nov22
1994   William Ernest Quantrill, amb. ex. and plen. Aug12
1995   Nicholas Melvyn McCarthy, amb. ex. and plen. April11
1998   George Peter Richard Boon, amb. ex. and plen. Feb8
2002   Richard James Wildash, amb. ex. and plen. June21

The Gambia
HIGH COMMISSIONERS
1984   John Donald Garner. Nov6
1988   Alec Ibbott. Feb20
1990   Alan John Pover. Oct12
1994   Michael John Hardie. Jan7
1995   John Wilde. Feb13
1998   Tony Millson. March13
2000   John Gayford Perrott. April1

Georgia
1992   Sir Brian James Proetel Fall, amb. ex. and plen. June22
1995   Stephen Thomas Nash, amb. ex. and plen. Oct15
1998   Richard Thomas Jenkins, amb. ex. and plen. Jan27
2001   Deborah Elizabeth Vavasseur Barnes Jones, amb. ex. and plen. Apr6

Germany (Federal Republic of)
1984   Sir Julian Leonard Bullard, amb. ex. and plen. Sept1
1988   Sir Christopher Leslie George Mallaby, amb. ex. and plen. March20

1993   Nigel Hugh Robert Allen Broomfield, amb.
        ex. and plen. Jan17
1997   Sir Christopher Meyer, amb. ex. and plen.
        March5
1997   Sir Paul Lever, amb. ex. and plen. Dec31

German Democratic Republic
1984   Timothy John Everard, amb. ex. and plen.
        Aug21
1988   Nigel Hugh Robert Allen Broomfield, amb.
        ex. and plen. May10
1990   Patrick Howard Eyers, amb. ex. and plen.
        Jan26
On 3 October 1990 the German Democratic
Republic ceased to exist.

Ghana
HIGH COMMISSIONERS
1983   Kevin Francis Xavier Burns. May30
1986   Arthur Hope Wyatt. Oct24
1989   Anthony Michael Goodenough. Oct16
1992   David Critchlow Walker. June14
1996   Ian Warren Mackley. July21
2000   Roderick Allen Pullen. Oct11

Greece
1982   Peregrine (later Sir P) Alexander Rhodes,
        amb. ex. and plen. May28
1985   Sir Jeremy Cashel Thomas, amb. ex. and
        plen. June6
1989   Sir (Henry) David Alastair Capel Miers,
        amb. ex. and plen. May24
1993   (Richard) Oliver Miles, amb. ex. and plen.
        July19
1996   Michael (later Sir M) John Llewellyn
        Smith, amb. ex. and plen. April4
1998   David Madden CMG, amb. ex. and plen.
        Dec,8

Grenada
HIGH COMMISSIONERS
1982   Viscount (John William) Dunrossil. Sept25
1983   Giles (later Sir G) Lionel Bullard. Aug6
1986   Kevin Francis Xavier Burns. Oct19
1991   Emrys Thomas Davies. Feb5
1994   Richard Thomas. Oct7
1998   Gordon Meldrum Baker. March8
2001   (Charles) John Branford White. Aug11

Guatemala
1987   Bernard Jonathan Everett, amb. ex. and
        plen. June25
1991   Justin Patrick Pearse Nason, amb. ex. and
        plen. March22
1995   Peter Marcus Newton, amb. ex. and plen.
        March28
1998   Andrew John Forbes Caie, amb. ex. and
        plen. July21
2001   Richard Douglas Lavers, amb. ex. and plen.
        Oct25

Guinea (Republic of)
1982   (Peter) Laurence O'Keeffe, amb. ex. and
        plen. Sept15
1986   John Esmond Campbell Macrae, amb. ex.
        and plen. May6
1990   Roger Campbell Beetham, amb. ex. and
        plen. Nov29

1994   Alan Edwin Furness, amb. ex. and plen.
        April21
1997   David Raymond Snoxell, amb. ex. and plen.
        April4
2000   Edward Alan Burner, amb. ex. and plen.
        Aug10
2000   David Alan Jones, amb. ex. and plen. May4

Guinea Bissau
1982   (Peter) Laurence O'Keeffe, amb. ex. and
        plen. Sept15
1986   John Esmond Campbell Macrae, amb. ex.
        and plen. May30
1990   Roger Campbell Beetham, amb. ex. and
        plen. April12
1994   Alan Edwin Furness, amb. ex. and plen.
        Jan18
1997   David Raymond Snoxell, amb. ex. and plen.
        April4
2000   Edward Alan Burner, amb. ex. and plen.
        Aug10

Guyana
HIGH COMMISSIONERS
1982   (William) Kenneth Slatcher. Aug28
1985   John Dudley Massingham. April6
1987   David Purvis Small, July16
1990   (Robert) Douglas Gordon, Oct24
1993   David John Johnson, March22
1998   Edward Glover, Nov19
2002   Stephen John Hiscock, Aug29

Haiti
1982   Barry Granger Smallman, amb. ex. and
        plen. Jan8
1984   (Harold) Martin Smith Reid, amb. ex. and
        plen. March9
1987   Alan Jeffrey Payne, amb. ex. and plen.
        Oct15
1989   Derek Francis Milton, amb. ex. and plen.
        June29
1995   Anthony Richard Thomas, amb. ex and
        plen. Oct15
1998   David Gordon Ward, amb. ex. and plen.
        Sept18
2002   Andrew Richard Ashcroft, amb. ex. and
        plen.

Holy See
1982   Sir Mark Evelyn Heath, amb. ex. and plen.
        March4
1985   David Neil Lane, amb. ex. and plen. May16
1988   John Kenneth Elliott Broadley, amb. ex. and
        plen. May18
1991   Andrew Eustace Palmer, amb. ex. and plen.
        Aug21
1995   Maureen Elizabeth MacGlashan, amb. ex.
        and plen. May27.
1998   Mark Edward Pellew, amb. ex. and plen.
        Jan1
2002   Kathryn Frances Colvin, amb. ex. and plen.
        July16

Honduras
1984   Bryan Oliver White, amb. ex. and plen.
        Nov20
1987   David Joy, amb. ex. and plen. July17

1989 Peter John Streams, amb. ex. and plen.
      July30
1992 Patrick Morgan, amb. ex. and plen. Jan30
1995 Peter Rodney Holmes, amb. ex. and plen.
      Aug3
1998 David Allan Osborne, amb. ex. and plen.
      July31
2002 Kay Coombs, amb. ex. and plen. Sept2

Hungary (Republic of)
1983 Peter William Unwin, amb. ex. and plen.
      July5
1986 Leonard Vincent Appleyard, amb. ex. and
      plen. July30
1989 John (later Sir J) Allan Birch, amb. ex. and
      plen. Aug21
1995 Christopher William Long, amb. ex. and
      plen. June2.
1998 Nigel James Thorpe, amb. ex. and plen.
      Aprl7

Iceland (Republic of)
1983 Richard Thomas, amb. ex. and plen. April30
1986 Mark Fenger Chapman, amb. ex. and plen.
      Oct8
1989 Richard (later Sir R) Radford Best, amb. ex.
      and plen. March15
1991 Patrick Francis Wogan, amb. ex. and plen.
      Sept16
1993 Michael Stuart Hone, amb. ex. and plen.
      June21
1996 James Rae McCulloch, amb. ex. and plen.
      May12
2001 John Howard Culver, amb. ex. and plen.
      Jan15

India
HIGH COMMISSIONERS
1982 Robert (later Sir R) Lucian Wade-Gery.
      July31
1986 Sir (Arthur) David Saunders Goodall.
      April2
1991 Sir Nicholas Maxted Fenn. Nov13
1996 The Hon. David Alwyn Gore-Booth. Mar9
1999 Sir (John) Rob(ertson) Young. Jan18

Indonesia
1984 Alan Ewen Donald, amb. ex. and plen.
      May16
1988 (William) Kelvin Kennedy White, amb. ex.
      and plen. March9
1990 Roger John Carrick, amb. ex. and plen.
      Aug3
1994 Graham Stuart Burton, amb. ex. and plen.
      Aug18
1997 (Duncan) Robin Carmichael Christopher,
      amb. ex. and plen. April13
2000 (Richard) Hugh Turton Gozney, amb. ex.
      and plen. Aug16

Iran
1988 Gordon Andrew Pirie, Chargé d'Affaires a.i.
      Dec4
1989 Nicholas Walker Browne, Chargé d'Affaires
      a.i. Feb1
1990 David Norman Reddaway, Chargé
      d'Affaires a.i. Oct28

1993 Jeffrey Russell James, Chargé d'Affaires a.i.
      Aug16
1997 Nicholas Walker Browne, Chargé d'Affaires
      a.i. Nov13
1999 Nicholas Walker Browne, amb. ex. and
      plen. May
1999 Richard Anthony Neil Crompton, Chargé
      d'Affaires a.i. May24
2002 Richard John Dalton, amb. ex.and plen. Dec

Iraq
1982 John (later Sir J) Campbell Moberly, amb.
      ex. and plen. Oct29
1985 Terence Josph Clark, amb. ex. and plen.
      March18
1990 Harold (later Sir H) Berners Walker amb.
      ex. and plen. Feb9
1991 Embassy Staff Withdrawn.
Diplomatic relations with Iraq were broken off
      with effect from 6 February 1991.

Ireland
1983 Alan (later Sir A) Clowes Goodison, amb.
      ex. and plen. June17
1986 Nicholas (later Sir N) Maxted Fenn, amb.
      ex. and plen. Dec7
1991 David Elliott Spiby Blatherwick, amb. ex.
      and plen. Sept10
1995 Veronica (later Dame V) Evelyn Sutherland,
      amb. ex. and plen. March29
1999 Ivor (later Sir I) Anthony Roberts, amb. ex.
      and plen. Feb20
2003 Stewart Graham Eldon, amb. ex. and plen.
      Apr14

Israel
1984 (Clifford) William Squire, amb. ex. and
      plen. Sept11
1988 Mark Elliott, amb. ex. and plen. June19
1992 Robert Andrew Burns, amb. ex. and plen.
      July12
1995 David Geoffrey Manning, amb. ex. and
      plen. Nov11
1998 Francis Cornish, amb. ex. and plen. Sept7
2001 Sherard Louis Cowper-Coles, amb. ex. and
      plen. Sept16

Italy
1983 The Lord Bridges, amb. ex. and plen. March1
1987 Sir Derek Morison David Thomas amb. ex.
      and plen. Dec3
1989 Sir Stephen Loftus Egerton, amb. ex. and
      plen. Nov14
1992 Sir Patrick Stanislaus Fairweather, amb. ex.
      and plen. July5
1996 Thomas Leigh Richardson, amb. ex. and
      plen. July10
2000 John (later Sir J) Alan Shepherd, amb. ex.
      and plen. July26

Ivory Coast see Côte d'Ivoire

Jamaica
HIGH COMMISSIONERS
1982 Barry Granger Smallman. Jan8
1984 (Harold) Martin Smith Reid. March9
1987 Alan Jeffrey Payne. June23
1989 Derek Francis Milton. April13

1995 Anthony Richard Thomas. Oct1
1999 Anthony Smith. March29
2002 Peter James Mathers. July4

Japan
1984 Sir (Charles) Sydney Rycroft Giffard, amb. ex. and plen. March1
1986 Sir John Stainton Whitehead, amb. ex. and plen. Nov12
1992 Sir John Dixon Ikl Boyd, amb. ex. and plen. July7
1995 David John Wright, amb. ex. and plen. Jan1
1999 Stephen John Gomersall, amb. ex. and plen. May28

Jordan
1984 (Arthur) John Coles, amb. ex. and plen. Nov4
1988 Anthony Reeve, amb. ex. and plen. Feb3
1991 Patrick Howard Caines Eyers, amb. ex. and plen. April27
1993 Peter Robert Mossom Hinchcliffe, amb. ex. and plen. Oct19
1997 Christopher Charles Battiscombe, amb. ex. and plen. April14
2000 Edward Graham Mellish Chaplin, amb. ex. and plen. May16
2002 Christopher Norman Russell Prentice, amb. ex. and plen. June1

Kazakhstan
1992 Sir Brian James Proetel Fall, amb. ex. and plen. Sept14
1993 No'l Stephen Andrew Jones, amb. ex. and plen. Oct26
1996 Douglas Baxter McAdam, amb. ex. and plen. March7
1999 Richard George Lewington. Feb7
2002 James Lyall Sharp. Oct

Kenya
HIGH COMMISSIONERS
1982 Sir (Walter) Leonard Allinson. Sept20
1986 John (later Sir J) Rodney Johnson, June15
1990 (William) Roger (later Sir R) Tomkys, Oct19
1992 Sir Kieran Prendergast, Oct19
1995 Simon Nicholas Peter Hemans. April14
1997 Jeffrey Russell James, July7
2001 Edward Clay. Dec16

Kiribati (Republic of)
HIGH COMMISSIONERS
1983 Charles Thompson. Sept26
1990 Derek Leslie White. Jan17
1993 Frank McDermott. April14
1994 Timothy James David. Sept1
1995 Michael John Peart. April14
1997 Michael Alan Charles Dibben. Dec3
2000 Michael Anthony Price. Oct16
2002 Charles Francis Mochan.

Korea (Democratic People's Republic of)
New British Embassy (Pyongyang) was formally opened in July 2001

2001 Dr James Edward Hoare, Chargé d'Affaires Feb

Korea (Republic of)
1983 (John) Nicholas Teague Spreckley, amb. ex. and plen. May4
1986 Lawrence John Middleton, amb. ex. and plen. Oct7
1990 David John Wright, amb. ex. and plen. April9
1994 Thomas George Harris, amb. ex. and plen. March19
1997 Sir Stephen David Reid Brown, amb. ex. and plen. April4
2000 Charles Thomas William Humfrey CMG, amb. ex. and plen. July1

Kuwait
1982 (Michael) Ramsay Melhuish, amb. ex. and plen. Sept5
1985 Sir Peter James Scott Moon, amb. ex. and plen. Feb17
1987 Peter Robert Mossom Hinchcliffe, amb. ex. and plen. May30
1990 Michael (later Sir M) Charles Swift Weston amb. ex. and plen. March18
1992 William Hugh Fullerton, amb. ex. and plen. Aug3
1996 Graham Hugh Boyce, amb. ex. and plen. March17
1998 Richard Muir CMG, amb. ex. and plen. Dec14
2002 Christopher Edward John Wilton, amb. ex. and plen. Aug16

Kyrgyzstan
1992 Sir Brian James Proetel Fall, amb. ex. and plen. Oct26
1994 No'l Stephen Andrew Jones, amb. ex. and plen. Feb2
1996 Douglas Baxter McAdam, amb. ex. and plen. March7
1999 Richard George Lewington. Feb7
2002 James Lyall Sharp. Oct

Laos
1982 (William) Bernard Josph Dobbs, amb. ex. and plen. March22
1985 (Hubert Anthony) Justin Staples. April25
1986 Derek Tonkin, amb. ex. and plen. June4
1990 (Michael) Ramsey Melhuish, amb. ex. and plen. Jan24
1992 (Charles) Christian Wilfrid Adams, amb. ex. and plen. March14
1997 Sir James William Hodge, amb. ex. and plen. Sept6
2000 Lloyd Barnaby Smith, amb. ex. and plen. March1

Latvia
1992 Richard Christopher Samuel, amb. ex. and plen. Feb2
1993 Richard Peter Ralph, amb. ex. and plen. Aug8
1996 Nicholas Robert Jarrold, amb. ex. and plen. Feb1
1999 Stephen Thomas Nash CMG, amb. ex. and plen. July16
2002 (Harcourt) Andrew Pretorius Tesoriere, amb. ex. and plen. March28.

Lebanon
1983 (Henry) David (later Sir D) Alastair Capel Miers, amb. ex. and plen. Nov11
1985 John (later Sir J)Walton David Gray, amb. ex. and plen. Nov28
1988 Allan John Ramsay, amb. ex. and plen. June16
1990 David Everard Tatham, amb. ex. and plen. April28
1992 Maeve (later Dame M) Geraldine Fort, amb. ex. and plen. July31
1996 David Ross MacLennan amb. ex. and plen. Oct9
2000 Richard Kinchen amb. ex. and plen. Dec16

Lesotho (Kingdom of)
HIGH COMMISSIONERS
1984 Peter Edward Rosling. March5
1988 John Coates Edwards. May31
1992 James Roy Cowling. Feb1
1996 Peter John Smith. April1
1998 Kaye Oliver. Dec15
2002 Francis James Martin. April19

Liberia (Republic of)
1985 Alec Ibbott, amb. ex. and plen. April19
1988 Michael Edward John Gore, amb. ex. and plen. Feb2
1990 Margaret Irene Rothwell, amb. ex. and plen. Dec17
1997 Haydon Boyd Warren-Gash, amb. ex. and plen. Oct7
2001 Jean Francois Gordon, amb. ex. and plen. June7

Libya
1984 (Richard) Oliver Miles, amb. ex. and plen. Jan5

Diplomatic and Consular relations with Libya were broken off with effect from 30 April 1984

1999 Richard John Dalton CMG, amb. ex. and plen. Nov30
2002 Anthony Michael Layden, amb. ex. and plen. Oct

Liechtenstein
1991 Christopher William Long, amb. ex. and plen. Dec12
1992 David Beattie, amb. ex. and plen. May21
1997 Christopher Hulse, amb. ex. and plen. April1
2001 Basil Stephen Talbot Eastwood, amb. ex. and plen. Aug15

Lithuania
1991 Michael John Peart, amb. ex. and plen. Oct8
1995 Thomas Townley Macan, amb. ex. and plen. Jan1
1995 Christopher William Robbins, amb. ex. and plen. July28
2001 Peter Jeremy Oldham Hill, amb. ex. and plen. Sept16

Luxembourg
1982 The Hon. Humphrey John Hamilton Maud, amb. ex. and plen. Sept20

1985 (Richard) Oliver Miles, amb. ex. and plen. Feb26
1988 Juliet Jeanne d'Auvergne Campbell, amb. ex. and plen. Feb24
1991 The Hon. Michael Pakenham, amb. ex. and plen. Oct19
1994 John Nicholas Elam, amb. ex. and plen. May23
1998 William Ehrman, amb. ex. and plen. Sept13
2000 Gordon Geoffrey Wetherell, amb. ex. and plen. Sept5

Macedonia
1993 Tony Millson, amb. ex. and plen. Dec23
1997 Woodman Mark Lowes Dickinson, amb. ex. and plen. April14
2001 Christopher George Edgar, amb. ex. and plen. Sept28

Madagascar (Republic of)
1984 (David) Malcolm McBain, amb. ex. and plen. Oct2
1987 Anthony Victor Hayday, amb. ex. and plen. Dec28
1990 Dennis Oldrieve Amy, amb. ex. and plen. April26
1993 Peter John Smith, amb. ex. and plen. Jan2
1996 Robert Scott Dewar, amb. ex. and plen. April14
1999 Charles Francis Mochan, amb. ex. and plen. July2
2002 Brian Donaldson, amb. ex. and plen. Oct17

Malawi
HIGH COMMISSIONERS
1983 (Arthur) Henry Brind. May25
1987 Denis Gordon Osborne. Aug17
1990 (William) Nigel Wenban-Smith. Nov3
1993 John Francis Ryde Martin Oct1
1998 George Finlayson, May15
2001 Norman Arthur Ling, Sept23

Malaysia
HIGH COMMISSIONERS
1983 David (later Sir D, later Lord Gillmore) Howe Gillmore. Sept17
1986 (John) Nicholas (later Sir N) Teague Spreckley Oct31
1992 Duncan Slater. March10
1994 David Joseph Moss. Aug15
1998 Graham Fry. June23
2001 Bruce Elliot Cleghorn. Nov17

†Maldives (Republic of)
†From 9July 1982 the British Embassy became a High Commission

HIGH COMMISSIONERS
1982 John (later Sir J) William Nicholas. July9
1984 John Anthony Benedict Stewart. Nov11
1987 David Arthur Stewart Gladstone. June29
1991 Edward John Field. Dec30
1996 David Everard Tatham, Mar31
1999 Linda Joy Duffield. Jan18
2002 Stephen Nicholas Evans. July16

Mali (Republic of)
1982 (Peter) Laurence O'Keeffe, amb. ex. and plen. Sept15
1986 John Esmond Campbell Macrae, amb. ex. and plen. March21
1990 Roger Campbell Beetham, amb. ex. and plen. Nov6
1993 Alan Edwin Furness, amb. ex. and plen. Sept3
1997 David Raymond Snoxell, amb. ex. and plen. April4
2000 Edward Alan Burner, amb. ex. and plen. Aug10
2001 Graeme Neil Loten, amb. ex. and plen. Oct1

Malta
HIGH COMMISSIONERS
1982 Charles Leonard Booth. Oct9
1985 Stanley Frederick St Clair Duncan. May3
1988 Brian Hitch. Jan10
1991 Peter (later Sir P) Gordon Wallis. Oct29
1995 Graham Robertson Archer. Jan3
1999 Howard John Pearce. June14
2002 Vincent Fean. Sept16

Marshall Islands (Republic of)
1992 Derek Leslie White, amb. ex. and plen. July22
1996 Vernon Marcus Scarborough, amb. ex. and plen. July23
2000 Christopher Haslam, amb. ex. and plen. Jan15
2003 Ian Francis Powell, amb. ex. and plen. March1

Mauritania (Islamic Republic of)
1982 (Peter) Laurence O'Keeffe, amb. ex. and plen. Oct5
1986 John Esmond Campbell Macrae, amb. ex. and plen. April24
1993 Sir Allan John Ramsey, amb. ex. and plen. April26
1996 William Hugh Fullerton, amb. ex. and plen. April17
1999 Anthony Layden, amb. ex. and plen. March16
2002 Haydon Boyd Warren-Gash, amb. ex. and plen. July11

Mauritius
HIGH COMMISSIONERS
1985 Richard Borman Crowson. Dec11
1989 Michael Edward Howell. Aug12
1993 John Clive Harrison. May5
1997 James Daly. May30
2000 David Snoxell. Sept21

Mexico
1983 Cynlais (later Sir C) Morgan James, amb. ex. and plen. Nov7
1986 John (later Sir J) Albert Leigh Morgan, amb. ex. and plen. May21
1989 Michael (later Sir M) Keith Orlebar Simpson-Orlebar, amb. ex. and plen. July27
1992 Sir Roger Blaise Ramsay Hervey, amb. ex. and plen. March2

1994 Adrian John Beamish, amb. ex. and plen. Oct2
1998 Adrian Charles Thorpe CMG, amb. ex. and plen. Oct30
2002 Denise Mary Holt, amb. ex. and plen. June15

Micronesia (Federated States of)
1992 Derek Leslie White, amb. ex. and plen. July22
1996 Vernon Marcus Scarborough, amb. ex. and plen. July23
2000 Christopher Haslam, amb. ex. and plen. Jan15
2003 Ian Francis Powell, amb. ex. and plen. March1

Moldova (Republic of)
1992 Sir Brian James Proetel Fall, Aug28
1995 Sir Andrew Marley Wood. July12
1999 Richard Peter Ralph. Aug27
2002 Bernard Gerrard Whiteside. April16

Mongolian People's Republic
1982 James Rupert Paterson, amb. ex. and plen. April1
1984 Allan Geoffrey Roy Butler, amb. ex. and plen. Oct11
1987 Guy William Pulbrook Hart, amb. ex. and plen. March19
1989 David Keith Sprague, amb. ex. and plen. April20
1991 Anthony Bernard Nicholas Morey, amb. ex. and plen. May29
1994 Ian Christopher Sloane, amb. ex. and plen. Jan18
1997 John Clive Durham, amb. ex. and plen. March1
1999 Kay Coombs, amb. ex. and plen. July30
2001 Philip Terence Rouse, amb. ex. and plen. Dec15

Morocco
1982 (Sydney) John Guy Cambridge, amb. ex. and plen. Dec1
1985 Ronald Archer Campbell Byatt, amb. ex. and plen. Jan28
1987 John William Richmond Shakespeare amb. ex. and plen. Nov15
1990 John Esmond Campbell Macrae, amb. ex. and plen. June12
1992 Sir Allan John Ramsey, amb. ex. and plen. Dec21
1996 William Hugh Fullerton, amb. ex. and plen. April17
1999 Anthony Layden, amb. ex. and plen. March16
2002 Haydon Boyd Warren-Gash, amb. ex. and plen. July11

Mozambique (Republic of)
1984 Eric Victor Vines, amb. ex. and plen. Feb6
1986 James Nicholas Allan, amb. ex. and plen. Feb21
1989 Maeve (later Dame M) Geraldine Fort, amb. ex. and plen. Sept10

1992   Richard John Smale Edis, amb. ex. and
        plen. Aug10
1996   Bernard Jonathan Everett, amb. ex. and
        plen. Jan1
2000   Robert Scott Dewar, amb. ex. and plen. Aug4

Namibia
HIGH COMMISSIONERS
1990   Francis Neville Richards. June4
1992   Henry George Hogger. Oct3
1996   Glyn Davies. Feb1
1999   Brian Donaldson. Jan17
2002   Alasdair Tormod MacDermott, April16

Nauru
HIGH COMMISSIONERS
1982   Roger Arnold Rowlandson Barltrop. July30
1990   (Alexander Basil) Peter Smart. March15
1995   Michael John Peart. April14
1997   Michael Alan Charles Dibben. Dec3
2000   Michael Anthony Price. Oct16
2002   Charles Francis Mochan.

Nepal
1983   Anthony (later Sir A) Gerald Hurrell, amb.
        ex. and plen. Nov2
1987   Richard Eagleson Gordon Burges Watson,
        amb. ex. and plen. March1
1990   Timothy John Burr George, amb. ex. and
        plen. Oct16
1995   Lloyd Barnay Smith, amb. ex. and plen.
        Dec9
1999   Ronald Nash, amb. ex. and plen. March26
2002   Keith George Bloomfield, amb. ex. and
        plen. June27

Netherlands
1984   John (later Sir J) William Denys Margetson,
        amb. ex. and plen. Nov30
1988   Michael Romilly Heald Jenkins, amb. ex.
        and plen. Jan23
1993   Sir (Henry) David Alastair Miers, amb. ex.
        and plen. July1
1996   Dame Rosemary Jane Spencer, 1999, amb.
        ex. and plen. Nov15
2001   Colin (later Sir C) Richard Budd, amb. ex.
        and plen. Apr4

New Zealand
HIGH COMMISSIONERS
1984   Terence Daniel O'Leary. July24
1987   Ronald Archer Campbell Byatt. Dec15
1990   David Joseph Moss. Sept27
1994   Robert Alston. Aug1
1998   Martin Williams OBE. Apr15
2001   Richard Taylor Fell. Dec10

Nicaragua
1983   Peter Wayne Summerscale, amb. ex. and
        plen. Jan24
1986   Michael Francis Daly, amb. ex. and plen.
        July14
1989   William Marsden, amb. ex. and plen.
        April19
1991   Roger Hugh Brown, amb. ex. and plen.
        Dec3
1992   John Howard Culver, amb. ex. and plen.
        Nov25

1997   Roy Paul Osborne, amb. ex. and plen.
        July15
2000   Harry Wiles, amb. ex. and plen. Sept
2002   Timothy Patrick Brownbill, amb. ex. and
        plen. Nov1

Niger (Republic of)
1983   John Michael Willson, amb. ex. and plen.
        Feb2
1987   Veronica (later Dame V) Evelyn Sutherland,
        amb. ex. and plen. Oct16
1990   Margaret Irene Rothwell, amb. ex. and plen.
        July10
1997   Haydon Boyd Warren-Gash, amb. ex. and
        plen. Oct7
2001   Jean Francois Gordon, amb. ex. and plen.
        June7

Nigeria (Federal Republic of)
HIGH COMMISSIONERS
1983   William Erskine Hamilton Whyte. Aug18
1986   Sir Martin Kenneth Ewans. Feb28
1988   Brian (later Sir B) Leon Barder. July27
1991   (Alistair) Christopher (Donald
        Summerhaves) MacRea. March7
1994   (John) Thorold Masefield. May14
1997   Graham (later Sir G) Stuart Burton. May2
2001   Philip Lloyd Thomas. March5

Norway
1983   William (later Sir W) Bentley, amb. ex. and
        plen. Sept18
1987   John Adam (later Sir J) Robson, amb. ex.
        and plen. March9
1990   David John Edward Ratford, amb. ex. and
        plen. May7
1994   Mark Elliott CMG, amb. ex. and plen. June4
1998   Richard (later Sir R) Dales CMG, amb. ex.
        and plen. July3
2002   Alison Mariot Leslie, amb. ex. and plen.
        Sept5

Oman
1986   Robert John Alston, amb. ex. and plen.
        June3
1990   Terence Joseph (later Sir T) Clark, amb. ex.
        and plen. Jan29
1994   Richard John Sutherland Muir, amb. ex. and
        plen. June5
1999   Sir Ivan Callan amb. ex. and plen. Feb15
2002   (John) Stuart Laing, amb. ex. and plen.
        April12

†Pakistan
AMBASSADORS
1984   Richard Alwyne Fyjis-Walker, amb. ex. and
        plen. Oct12
1987   Nicolas John (later Sir N) Barrington, amb.
        ex. and plen. July20

HIGH COMMISSIONERS
†1989   Nicholas (later Sir N) John Barrington. Oct1
1994   Sir (Alastair) Christopher Donald
        Summerhayes MacRae, May31
1997   David (later Sir D) John Michael Dain,
        May5
2000   Hilary Nicholas Hugh Synnott. Oct15

†From 30January 1972, the British High
Commission became the British Embassy, then
from 1October 1989 it reverted to the British
High Commission

Palau (Republic of)
1996   Vernon Marcus Scarborough, amb. ex. and
       plen. July23
2000   Christopher Haslam, amb. ex. and plen.
       Jan15
2003   Ian Francis Powell, amb. ex. and plen.
       March1

Panama (Republic of)
1983   Terence Harry Steggle, amb. ex. and plen.
       May18
1986   Margaret Bryan, amb. ex. and plen. April9
1990   John Grant MacDonald, amb. ex. and plen.
       Jan6
1992   Thomas Herbert Malcomson, amb. ex. and
       plen. Jan31
1996   William Baldie Sinton OBE, amb. ex. and
       plen. Jan19
1999   Robert Harold Davies, amb. ex. and plen.
       Mar15
2002   James Ian Malcolm, amb. ex. and plen.
       Mar16

Papua New Guinea
HIGH COMMISSIONERS
1982   Arthur John Collins. Jan18
1986   Michael Edward Howell. Jan27
1989   (Edward) John Sharland. June11
1991   John Westgarth Guy. July12
1994   Brian Buik Low. Dec12
1997   Charles Drace-Francis. Dec16
2000   Simon Mansfield Scaddan. March1

Paraguay
1984   Bernard Coleman, amb. ex. and plen. Jan19
1986   John Grant MacDonald, amb. ex. and plen.
       May3
1989   Terence Harry Steggle, amb. ex. and plen.
       May31
1991   Michael Alan Charles Dibben, amb. ex. and
       plen. March2
1995   Graham John Campbell Pirnie, amb. ex. and
       plen. Aug31
1998   Andrew Neil George, amb. ex. and plen.
       Oct15
2001   Anthony John James Cantor, amb. ex. and
       plen. Nov16

Peru
1983   John William Richmond Shakespeare, amb.
       ex. and plen. Oct30
1987   Adrian John Beamish, amb. ex. and plen.
       Dec16
1990   (Donald) Keith Haskell, amb. ex. and plen.
       Feb11
1995   John Illman, amb. ex. and plen. May5
1999   Roger Hart, amb. ex. and plen. June4

Philippines
1985   Robin John Taylor McLaren, amb. ex. and
       plen. May15
1987   Keith Gordon MacInnes, amb. ex. and plen.
       April27

1992   Alan Everard Montgomery, amb. ex. and
       plen. July11
1995   Adrian Charles Thorpe, amb. ex. and plen.
       July8
1998   Alan Stanley Collins CMG, amb. ex. and
       plen. Dec31
2002   Paul Stephen Dimond, amb. ex. and plen.
       April1

Poland (Republic of)
1983   John Albert Leigh Morgan, amb. ex. and
       plen. May16
1986   Brian (later Sir B)Leon Barder, amb. ex.
       and plen. May27
1988   Stephen (later Sir S) Jeremy Barrett, amb.
       ex. and plen. Aug20
1991   Michael John Llewellyn Smith, amb. ex.
       and plen. Sept20
1996   Christoper Owen Hum, amb. ex. and plen.
       May6
1998   John Macgregor, amb. ex. and plen. Sept7
2001   The Hon Michael Aidan Pakenham, amb.
       ex. and plen. Jan5

Portugal
1986   Michael Keith Orlebar Simpson-Orlebar,
       amb. ex. and plen. March15
1989   Hugh James Arbuthnott, amb. ex. and plen.
       Aug23
1993   (John) Stephen (later Sir S) Wall, amb. ex.
       and plen. May31
1995   Roger Westbrook, amb. ex. and plen. July24
1999   John (later Sir John) Holmes, amb. ex. and
       plen. June14
2001   Dame (Madelaine) Glynne Dervel Evans,
       amb. ex. and plen. Sept16

Qatar
1984   Julian Fortay Walker, amb. ex. and plen.
       Oct10
1987   Patrick Michael Nixon, amb. ex. and plen.
       June11
1990   Graham Hugh Boyce, amb. ex. and plen.
       Feb27
1993   Patrick Francis Michael Wogan, amb. ex.
       and plen. Oct23
1997   David Alan Wright OBE, amb. ex. and plen.
       June4
2002   David Ross MacLennan, amb. ex. and plen.
       June15

Romania
1983   Philip McKearney, amb. ex. and plen. Oct19
1986   Hugh James Arbuthnott, amb. ex. and plen.
       Nov14
1989   Michael William Atkinson, amb. ex. and
       plen. Sept4
1992   Andrew Philip Foley Bache, amb. ex. and
       plen. April15
1996   Christopher Donald Crabbie, amb. ex. and
       plen. June30
1999   Richard Peter Ralph, amb. ex. and plen.
       Aug27
2002   Quinton Mark Quayle, amb. ex. and plen.
       Nov2

Russian Federation
1992 Sir Brian James Proetel Fall, amb. ex. and plen. June3
1995 Sir Andrew Marley Wood, amb. ex. and plen. July12
2000 Sir Roderic Michael Lyne, amb. ex. and plen. Jan14

Rwanda (Republic of)
1984 Nicholas Peter Bayne, amb. ex. and plen. Feb7
1985 Patrick Howard Caines Eyers, amb. ex. and plen. Aug20
1987 Robert Linklater Burke Cormack, amb. ex. and plen. June11
1991 Roger Westbrook, amb. ex. and plen. July30
1994 Edward Clay, amb. ex. and plen. Jan10
1995 Kaye Wight Oliver, amb. ex. and plen. Dec11
1998 Graeme Neil Loten, amb. ex. and plen. May11
2001 Susan Elizabeth Hogwood. amb. ex. and plen. July26

Saint Kitts and Nevis
HIGH COMMISSIONERS
1983 Giles (later Sir G) Lionel Bullard. Sept19
1986 Kevin Francis Xavier Burns. Oct19
1991 Emrys Thomas Davies. Feb13
1994 Richard Thomas. Oct7
1998 Gordon Meldrum Baker. March8
2001 (Charles) John Branford White. Aug11

St Lucia
HIGH COMMISSIONERS
1982 Viscount (John William) Dunrossil. Sept25
1983 Giles (later Sir G) Lionel Bullard. Aug6
1986 Kevin Francis Xavier Burns. Oct19
1991 Emrys Thomas Davies. Feb13
1994 Richard Thomas. Oct7
1998 Gordon Meldrum Baker. March8
2001 (Charles) John Branford White. Aug11

St Vincent and the Grenadines
HIGH COMMISSIONERS
1982 Viscount (John William) Dunrossil. Sept25
1983 Giles (later Sir G) Lionel Bullard. Aug6
1986 Kevin Francis Xavier Burns. Oct19
1991 Emrys Thomas Davies. Feb11
1994 Richard Thomas. Oct7
1998 Gordon Meldrum Baker. March8
2001 (Charles) John Branford White. Aug11

Samoa
HIGH COMMISSIONERS
1984 Terence Daniel O'Leary. July24
1987 Ronald Archer Campbell Byatt. Dec15
1991 David Joseph Moss. Aug6
1994 Robert Alston. Aug1
1998 Martin Williams. Apr15
2001 Richard Taylor Fell. Dec10

São Tomé and Principe
1983 Marrack Irvine Goulding, amb. ex. and plen. Oct24
1986 Patrick Staislaus Fairweather, amb. ex. and plen. June9
1988 Michael John Carlisle Glaze, amb. ex. and plen. March25

1990 John Gerrard Flynn, amb. ex. and plen. May22
1993 Anthony Richard Thomas, amb. ex. and plen. April27
1996 Roger Dudley Hart, amb. ex. and plen. Sept18
1999 Caroline Elmes, amb. ex. and plen. Sept14

Saudi Arabia
1984 Sir Patrick Richard Henry Wright, amb. ex. and plen. Sept4
1986 Stephen (later Sir S) Loftus Egerton, amb. ex. and plen. April20
1989 Alan (later Sir A) Gordon Munro, amb. ex. and plen. Aug16
1993 The Hon. David Alwyn Gore-Booth, amb. ex. and plen. April4
1996 Andrew (later Sir A) Fleming Green, amb. ex. and plen. March27
2000 Derek (later Sir D) John Plumbly, amb. ex. and plen. June15

Senegal (Republic of)
1982 (Peter) Laurence O'Keeffe, amb. ex. and plen. Sept15
1985 John Esmond Campbell Macrae, amb. ex. and plen. Dec18
1990 Roger Campbell Beetham, amb. ex. and plen. July7
1993 Alan Edwin Furness, amb. ex. and plen. Aug24
1997 David Raymond Snoxell, amb. ex. and plen. April4
2000 Edward Alan Burner, amb. ex. and plen. Aug10

Serbia and Montenegro (formerly Yugoslavia)
2001 Charles Graham Crawford, CMG, amb. ex. and plen. Jan12

Seychelles
HIGH COMMISSIONERS
1983 Colin Garth Mays. Oct1
1986 (Alexander Basil) Peter Smart. Sept30
1989 Guy William Pulbrook Hart. June22
1992 Edward John Sharland. Jan24
1995 Peter Alexander Bremner Thomson. Feb17
1997 John William Yapp. Nov1
2002 Fraser Andrew Wilson. May7

Sierra Leone
HIGH COMMISSIONERS
1984 Richard Dennis Clift. Sept7
1986 Derek William Partridge. June6
1991 David Keith Sprague. May30
1993 Ian McCluney. Sept23
1997 Peter Alfred Penfold. March10
2000 David Alan Jones. May4

Singapore (Republic of)
HIGH COMMISSIONERS
1982 Sir Peter James Scott Moon. June14
1985 Sir (William Erskine) Hamilton Whyte. March16
1987 Michael Edmund Pike. (later Sir M) July13
1991 Gordon Aldridge Duggan. Jan12
1997 Alan Charles Hunt. Aug8
2001 Sir Stephen David Reid Brown. March1

Slovakia (Republic of)
1993   David Brighty, amb. ex. and plen.
1994   Michael Charles Bates, amb. ex. and plen. July1
1995   Peter Gale Harborne, amb. ex. and plen. Feb20
1998   David Edward Lyscom, amb. ex. and plen. Oct15
2001   Damian Roderic Todd, amb. ex. and plen. Nov16

Slovenia (Republic of)
1992   Gordon Mackenzie Johnston, amb. ex. and plen. Aug25
1997   David Andrew Lloyd, amb. ex. and plen. Feb21
2001   Hugh Roger Mortimer, amb. ex. and plen. Jan1

Solomon Islands
HIGH COMMISSIONERS
1982   George Norman Stansfield. June15
1986   John Bramble Noss. March17
1988   (David) Junor Young. Oct10
1991   Raymond Francis Jones. May12
1995   Brian Norman Connelly. Dec31
1998   Alan Waters. Sept1.
2001   Brian Paul Baldwin. May16

Somali Democratic Republic
1983   William Hugh Fullerton, amb. ex. and plen. Sept26
1987   Jeremy Richard Lovering Grosvenor Varcoe, amb. ex. and plen. Feb15
1989   Ian McCluney, amb. ex. and plen. July9

South Africa (Republic of)
HIGH COMMISSIONERS
1994   Sir Anthony Reeve. June1
1996   Maeve (later Dame Maeve) Geraldine Fort. Nov11
2000   Ann Grant. Oct1

AMBASSADORS
†1982 Ewen Alastair John Fergusson, amb. ex. and plen. April29
†1984 Patrick (later Sir P) Hamilton Moberly, amb. ex. and plen. Oct8
†1987 Robin (later Sir R) William Renwick, amb. ex. and plen. July24
†1991 Anthony (later Sir A) Reeve, amb. ex. and plen. July1

†From 10 May 1961, the British High Commission became the British Embassy, then from 1June 1994 it reverted to the British High Commission.

Soviet Union now see Russian Federation
1982   Sir Iain Johnstone Macbeth Sutherland, amb. ex. and plen. Sept16
1985   Sir Bryan George Cartledge, amb. ex. and plen. July18
1988   Sir Rodric Quentin Braithwaite, amb. ex. and plen. Sept20

Spain
1984   Lord Nicholas Charles Gordon Lennox, amb. ex. and plen. July2

1989   (Patrick) Robin (later Sir R) Fearn, amb. ex. and plen. Nov23
1994   Anthony David Brighty, amb. ex. and plen. Sept1
1998   Peter Torry, amb. ex. and plen. Sept2

Sri Lanka (Republic of)
HIGH COMMISSIONERS
1984   John Antony Benedict Stewart. Nov11
1987   David Arthur Stuart Gladstone. June29
1991   Edward John Field. Nov22
1996   David Everard Tatham. Mar21
1999   Linda Duffield, Jan18
2002   Stephen Nicholas Evans, July16

Sudan (Republic of)
1984   Sir Alexander John Dickson Stirling, amb. ex. and plen. Sept1
1986   John Lewis Beaven, amb. ex. and plen. Dec3
1990   Allan John Ramsay, amb. ex. and plen. June23
1991   Peter John Streams, amb. ex. and plen. Nov29
1995   Alan Fletcher Goulty, amb. ex. and plen. March23
1999   Richard Edward Makepeace, amb. ex. and plen. July13
2002   William Charters Patey, amb. ex. and plen. Sept1

Surinam (Republic of)
1982   (William) Kenneth Slatcher. Aug28
1985   John Dudley Massingham, amb. ex. and plen. July3
1987   David Purvis Small, amb. ex. and plen. July16
1991   (Robert) Douglas Gordon, amb. ex. and plen. April27
1993   David John Johnson, amb. ex. and plen. Feb19
1998   Edward Glover, Nov19
2002   Stephen John Hiscock, Aug29

Swaziland
HIGH COMMISSIONERS
1983   Martin Reith. July29
1987   John Gerrard Flynn. May26
1990   Brian Watkins. May20
1993   Richard Hugh Turton Gozney. Aug8
1996   John Frederick Boble. Feb29
1999   Neil Kenneth Hook, Oct4
2001   David (George) Reader, Sept26

Sweden
1984   Sir Richard Edmund Clement Fownes Parsons, amb. ex. and plen. July26
1987   Sir John Burns Ure, amb. ex. and plen. Dec7
1991   Robert Linklater Burke Cormack, amb. ex. and plen. June17
1995   Roger Bridgland Bone, amb. ex. and plen. Sept1
1999   John Douglas Kelso Grant CMG, amb. ex. and plen. April6

Switzerland
1982   John Ernest Powell-Jones, amb. ex. and
       plen. May24
1985   John Rowland Rich, amb. ex. and plen.
       May2
1988   Christopher William Long, amb. ex. and
       plen. July25
1992   David Beattie, amb. ex. and plen. May5
1997   Christopher Hulse, amb. ex. and plen. April
2001   Basil Stephen Talbot Eastwood, amb. ex.
       and plen. Aug15

Syria
The Syrian Republic severed Diplomatic and
Consular Relations with the United Kingdom on
6June 1967 until 28May 1973

1982   The Hon. Ivor Thomas Mark Lucas, amb.
       ex. and plen. Jan27
1984   (William) Roger Tomkys, amb. ex. and
       plen. Nov13

Diplomatic and Consular relations with the Syrian
Arab Republic were broken off with effect from
31October 1986. They were resumed on
28November 1990

1991   Andrew (later Sir A)Fleming Green, amb.
       ex. and plen. Feb17
1994   Adrian John Sindall, amb. ex. and plen.
       May28
1996   Basil Stephen Talbot Eastwood, amb. ex.
       and plen. Sept30
2000   Henry George Hogger, amb. ex. and plen.
       June12

Tajikistan (the Republic of)
1994   Alexander Paul A'Court Bergne, amb. ex.
       and plen. Jan27
1995   Barbara Logan Hay, amb. ex. and plen. May15
1999   Christopher Ingham, amb. ex. and plen. Feb3
2002   Michael Forbes Smith, amb. ex. and plen.
       May26

Tanzania (United Republic of)
HIGH COMMISSIONERS
Diplomatic Relations were broken off with
Tanzania from 15December 1965 to 4July 1968

1982   John Anthony Sankey. June23
1986   Colin (later Sir C) Henry Imray. Jan6
1989   (John) Thorold Masefield. July22
1992   Roger Westbrook. Sept30
1995   Alan Everard Montgomery. July15
1998   Bruce Harry Dinwiddy. April22
2001   Richard Ian Clarke. Aug2

Thailand
1986   Derek Tonkin, amb. ex. and plen. Feb18
1989   (Michael) Ramsay Melhuish amb. ex. and
       plen. Nov7
1992   Charles Christian Wilfrid Adams, amb. ex.
       and plen. March14
1996   James (later Sir J) William Hodge, amb. ex.
       and plen. Sept6
2000   Lloyd Barnaby Smith, amb. ex. and plen.
       March1

Togo
1983   Kevin Francis Xavier Burns, amb. ex. and
       plen. May30
1986   Arthur Hope Wyatt, amb. ex. and plen. Oct24
1989   Anthony Michael Goodenough, amb. ex.
       and plen. Dec5
1992   David Crithlow Walker, amb. ex. and plen.
       June16
1996   Ian Warren Mackley CMG, amb. ex. and plen.
       Jul7
2000   Roderick Allen Pullen, amb. ex. and plen.
       Oct 11

Tonga
HIGH COMMISSIONERS
1984   Gerald Francis Joseph Rance. Jan4
1987   Andrew Paul Fabian. March7
1990   William Lawson Cordiner. April3
1994   Andrew James Morris. Nov8
1998   Brian Connelly. Aug20
2002   Paul William Downs Nessling. Jan14

Trinidad and Tobago
HIGH COMMISSIONERS
1985   Martin (later Sir M) Seymour Berthoud.
       April11
1991   Brian Smith. Nov11
1996   Leo Gregory Faulkner. July3
1999   Richard Gale Harborne. July15

Tunisia (Republic of)
1984   (William) James Adams, amb. ex. and plen.
       Aug21
1987   Stephen Peter Day, amb. ex. and plen. Dec17
1992   Michael Logan Tait, amb. ex. and plen. July9
1995   Richard John Smale Edis, amb. ex. and
       plen. Dec4
1999   Ivor Rawlinson, amb. ex. and plen. Feb15
2002   Robin Andrew Kealy, ex. and plen. Jan15

Turkey
1983   (Robert) Mark (later Sir M) Russell, amb.
       ex. and plen. Feb28
1986   Timothy (later Sir T) Lewis Achilles Daunt,
       amb. ex. and plen. Nov1
1992   Peter John Goulden, amb. ex. and plen. Oct23
1995   Sir (Walter) Kieran Prendergast, amb. ex.
       and plen. March23
1997   David Brian Carleton Logan, amb. ex. and
       plen. March28
2002   Peter John Westmacott, amb. ex. and plen.
       Jan15

Turkmenistan
1993   Sir Brian James Proetel Fall, amb. ex. and
       plen. Jan31
1995   Neil Kenneth Hook, amb. ex. and plen. Sept15
1998   Fraser Wilson MBE, amb. ex. and plen. July6
2002   Paul Brummell, amb. ex. and plen. Feb16

Tuvalu
HIGH COMMISSIONERS
1982   Roger Arnold Rowlandson Barltrop. July30
1989   (Alexander Basil) Peter Smart. Nov29
1995   Michael John Peart. April14
1997   Michael Alan Charles Dibben. Dec3
2000   Michael Anthony Price. Oct16
2002   Charles Francis Mochan.

Uganda

HIGH COMMISSIONERS
Diplomatic Relations were broken off on 28July 1976 until 21April 1979

1983 Colin McLean. Sept14
1986 Derek (later Sir D) Maxwell March. June29
1989 Charles Augustine Kaye Cullimore. Dec21
1993 Edward Clay. Oct1
1997 Michael Edgar Cook. April10
2000 Tom Richard Vaughan Phillips. May15
2002 Adam Wood. Oct14

Ukraine

1992 David Arthur Stewart Gladstone, Chargé d'Affaires. Jan17
1992 Simon Nicholas Peter Hemans, amb. ex. and plen. June4
1995 Roy Stephen Reeve, amb. ex. and plen. June5
1999 Roland Hedley Smith, amb. ex. and plen. May16
2002 Robert Edward Brinkley, amb. ex. and plen. Aug3

United Arab Emirates

1986 Michael Logan Tait, amb. ex. and plen. April27
1990 Graham Stuart Burton, amb. ex. and plen. Feb6
1994 Anthony Davis Harris, amb. ex. and plen. June25
1998 Patrick Michael Nixon, amb. ex. and plen. Nov1
2003 Richard Edward Makepeace, amb. ex. and plen. March

United States

1982 Sir (John) Oliver Wright. Sept2
1986 Sir Antony Arthur Acland, amb. ex. and plen. Aug28
1991 Sir Robin William Renwick, amb. ex. and plen. Aug20
1995 Sir John Olav Kerr, amb. ex. and plen. Aug15
1997 Sir Christopher Meyer, amb. ex. and plen. Oct31

Upper Volta (Republic of) (now see Burkina Faso)

1983 John Michael Willson, amb. ex. and plen. July12

Uruguay (Oriental Republic of)

1983 Charles William Wallace, amb. ex. and plen. Oct12
1986 Eric Victor Vines, amb. ex. and plen. March14
1989 Colum John Sharkey, amb. ex. and plen. July14
1991 Donald Alexander Lamont, amb. ex. and plen. July14
1994 Robert Andrew Michie Hendrie, amb. ex. and plen. Sept1
1998 Andrew Murray, amb. ex. and plen. May23
2001 John Vivian Everard. ex. and plen. Sept4

Uzbekistan

1992 Sir Brian James Proetel Fall, amb. ex. and plen. Oct21
1993 Alexander Paul A'Court Bergne, amb. ex. and plen. Oct29
1995 Barbara Logan Hay, amb. ex. and plen. May15
1999 Christopher Ingham, amb. ex. and plen. Feb3
2002 Craig John Murray, amb. ex. and plen. Sept16

Vanuatu (Republic of)

HIGH COMMISSIONERS
1982 Richard Bostock Dorman. April25
1985 Malcolm Lars Creek. Aug27
1988 John Thompson. March25
1992 Thomas Joseph Duggin. Jan15
1997 Malcolm Geoffrey Hilson.
2000 Michael Thomas Hill. Nov16

Vatican City (see Holy See)

Venezuela

1982 Hugh Michael Carless, amb. ex. and plen. June26
1985 Michael John Newington, amb. ex. and plen. April28
1988 Giles Eden FitzHerbert, amb. ex. and plen. Jan18
1993 John Gerrard Flynn, amb. ex. and plen. April4
1997 Richard Denys Wilkinson, amb. ex. and plen. May2
2000 Dr Edgar John Hughes, amb. ex. and plen. July22

South Vietnam (Republic of)

(Vietnam was formally unified in July 1976)

Vietnam (Socialist Republic of)

1982 Michael Edmund Pike, amb. ex. and plen. Dec17
1985 Richard Gilbert Tallboys, amb. ex. and plen. June12
1987 Emrys Thomas Davies, amb. ex. and plen. May27
1990 Peter Keegan Williams, amb. ex. and plen. Oct27
1997 David William Fall, amb. ex. and plen. Apr25
2000 Warwick Morris, amb. ex. and plen. June16

Yemen (Republic of)

1984 David Everard Tatham, amb. ex. and plen. Sept19
1987 Mark Anthony Marshall, amb. ex. and plen. Nov23
1993 (Robert) Douglas Gordon, amb. ex. and plen. March20
1995 Douglas Scrafton amb. ex. and plen. March4
1997 Victor Joseph Henderson CMG, amb. ex. and plen. Oct19
2001 Frances Mary Guy, amb. ex. and plen. Mar9

Yemen (People's Democratic Republic of)

1983   Peter Keegan Williams, amb. ex. and plen.
       Feb23
1986   Arthur Stirling-Maxwell Marshall, amb. ex.
       and plen. Jan4
1989   (Robert) Douglas Gordon, amb. ex. and
       plen. Jan29

The People's Democratic Republic of Yemen and
the Yemen Arab Republic merged on 22May 1990
to become the Republic of Yemen

Yugoslavia (Federal Republic of) (now see Serbia and Montenegro)

1996   Ivor (later Sir I) Antony Roberts, amb. ex.
       and plen. May6
1997   Joseph Brian Donnelly, amb. ex. and plen.
       Nov17

Diplomatic Relations with The Federal Republic of
Yugoslavia were broken off with effect from 26
March 1999 and were restored on 17 November
2000.

2000   David Maurice Landsman, OBE, Chargé
       d'Affaires Nov17

Zambia (Republic of)

HIGH COMMISSIONERS
1984   (William) Kelvin Kennedy White. Sept10
1988   John Michael Wilson. Jan21
1990   Peter Robert Mossom Hinchcliffe. May19
1994   Patrick Michael Nixon. Feb1
1998   Thomas Nesbitt Young. Jan3
2002   Timothy James David. May16

Zimbabwe (Republic of)

HIGH COMMISSIONERS
1983   Martin Kenneth Ewans. April9
1985   (Michael) Ramsay Melhuish. Feb20
1989   (Walter) Kieran (later Sir K) Prendergast.
       Aug10
1992   Richard Nigel Dales. Sept21
1995   Martin John Williams. Nov28
1998   Peter Longworth. Apr7
2001   Joseph Brian Donnelly. June30

CHRONOLOGICAL LIST OF BRITISH REPRESENTATIVES TO INTERNATIONAL ORGANISATIONS 1982-2002

UNITED KINGDOM MISSION TO THE UNITED NATIONS

New York

1982   Sir John Adam Thomson, Perm. Rep. and
       Rep. on the Security Council with personal
       rank of amb. Aug17
1987   Sir Crispin Charles Cervantes Tickell, Perm.
       Rep. and Rep. on the Security Council with
       personal rank of amb. May29
1990   Sir David Hugh Alexander Hannay Perm.
       Rep. and Rep. on the Security Council with
       personal rank of amb. Sept7
1995   Sir (Philip) John Weston, Perm. Rep. and
       Rep. on the Security Council with personal
       rank of amb. July15

1998   Sir Jeremy Quentin Greenstock, Perm. Rep.
       and Rep. on the Security Council with
       personal rank of amb. Aug8

UNITED KINGDOM MISSON TO THE OFFICE OF THE UNITED NATIONS AND OTHER INTERNATIONAL ORGANISATIONS AT GENEVA

1983   Dame Anne Marion Warburton, Perm. Rep.
       with personal rank of amb. May16
1985   John Anthony Sankey, Perm. Rep. with
       personal rank of amb. Dec17
1990   Martin Robert Morland, Perm. Rep. with
       personal rank of amb. July13
1993   Nigel Christopher Ransome Williams,
       Perm. Rep. with personal rank of amb.
       Sept15
1997   Roderic Michael Lyne, Perm. Rep. with
       personal rank of amb. May1
2000   Simon William Fuller, Perm. Rep. with
       personal rank of amb. Jan16

UNITED KINGDOM DELEGATION TO THE CONFERENCE ON DISARMAMENT (formerly the UK Delegation to the Conference of the 18-Nation Committee on Disarmament)

Geneva

1982   (Ronald) Ian Talbot Cromartie, Leader of
       Del. with personal rank of amb. Oct1
1987   Tessa Audrey Hilda Solesby, Leader of Del.
       with personal rank of amb. Oct10
1992   Sir Michael Charles Swift Weston, Leader
       of Del. with personal rank of amb. April6
1997   (Samuel) Ian Soutar, Leader of Del. with
       personal rank of amb. Aug8
2001   David Stuart Broucher, Leader of Del. with
       personal rank of amb. Oct1

UNITED KINGDOM DELEGATION TO THE NORTH ATLANTIC TREATY ORGANISATION

Brussels

1982   Sir John Alexander Noble Graham, Perm.
       Rep. on the North Atlantic Council with
       personal rank of amb. Feb15
1986   Michael (later Sir M) O'Donel Bjarne
       Alexander, Perm. Rep. on the North Atlantic
       Council with personal rank of amb. Aug30
1992   Sir (Philip) John Weston, Perm. Rep. on the
       North Atlantic Council with personal rank
       of amb. Jan25
1995   Peter John Goulden, Perm. Rep. on the
       North Atlantic Council with personal rank
       of amb. April1
2000   David (later Sir D) Geoffrey Manning,
       Perm. Rep. on the North Atlantic Council
       with personal rank of amb. Dec
2001   Dr Emyr Jones Parry, Perm. Rep. on the
       North Atlantic Council with personal rank
       of amb. Sept16

UNITED KINGDOM DELEGATION TO THE WESTERN EUROPEAN COUNCIL

Brussels

1993 Sir (Philip) John Weston, Perm. Rep. on the Permanent Council of the Western European Union with personal rank of amb. Jan1

UNITED KINGDOM DELEGATION TO THE ORGANISATION FOR ECONOMIC CO-OPERATION AND DEVELOPMENT

Paris

1982 Kenneth James Uffen, Perm. Rep. with personal rank of amb. May2

1985 Nicholas Peter Bayne, Perm. Rep. with personal rank of amb. Oct1

1988 John Walton David Gray, Perm. Rep. with personal rank of amb. July11

1992 Keith Gordon MacInnes, Perm. Rep. with the personal rank of amb. July1

1995 Peter William Medlicott Vereker, Perm. Rep. with the personal rank of amb. Sept1

1999 Christopher Crabbie Perm. Rep. with the personal rank of amb. June11

OFFICE OF THE UNITED KINGDOM PERMANENT REPRESENTATIVE TO THE EUROPEAN UNION (formerly UK Delegation to the European Communities)

Brussels

1985 David (later Sir D) Hugh Alexander Hannay, Perm. Rep. with personal rank of amb. Oct14

1990 John (later Sir J) Olav Kerr, Perm. Rep. with personal rank of amb. Sept2

1995 John (later Sir S) Stephen Wall, Perm. Rep. with personal rank of amb. Aug15

2000 Nigel (later Sir N) Elton Sheinwald, Perm. Rep. with personal rank of amb. Aug31

UNITED KINGDOM DELEGATION TO THE COUNCIL OF EUROPE

Strasbourg

1983 Christopher Duncan Lush, Perm. Rep. with personal rank of amb. Jan6

1986 Colin McLean, Perm. Rep. with personal rank of amb. Aug6

1990 No'l Hedley Marshall, Perm. Rep. with personal rank of amb. Sept6

1993 Roger Campbell Beetham, Perm. Rep. with personal rank of amb. Aug1

1997 Andrew Carter, Perm. Rep. with personal rank of amb. Aug1

2003 Stephen Frederick Howarth, Perm. Rep. with personal rank of amb. March1

UNITED KINGDOM MISSION TO THE INTERNATIONAL ATOMIC ENERGY AGENCY, THE UNITED NATIONS INDUSTRIAL DEVELOPMENT ORGANISATION AND THE UNITED NATIONS (VIENNA) (formerly UK Mission to the IAEA and to UN Organisations at Vienna)

Vienna

1982 Michael Joseph Wilmshurst, Perm. Rep. with personal rank of amb. Aug16

1987 Gerald Edmund Clark, Perm. Rep. with personal rank of amb. June3

1992 Christopher Hulse, Perm. Rep. with personal rank of amb. Nov26

1997 John Patrick George Freeman, Perm. Rep. with personal rank of amb. May2

2001 Peter Redmond Jenkins, Perm. Rep. with personal rank of amb. Aug9

UNITED KINGDOM DELEGATION TO THE CONFERENCE ON SECURITY AND COOPERATION IN EUROPE (OSCE) IN VIENNA

Vienna

1989 (John) Michael Edes, Perm. Rep. with personal rank of amb. March6

1990 Paul Lever, Head of Del. with personal rank of amb. May7

1992 Terence Courtney Wood, Head of Del. with personal rank of amb. April4

1993 Simon William John Fuller, Head of Del. with personal rank of amb. Sept1

1999 John Robert de Fonblanque, Head of Del. with personal rank of amb. June16

CHRONOLOGICAL LIST OF GOVERNORS AND COMMANDERS-IN-CHIEF ETC. OF OVERSEAS TERRITORIES 1982-2002 (MEMBERS HM DIPLOMATIC SERVICE ONLY)

Anguilla

1982 Charles Henry Godden

1985 Alistair Turner Baillie

1990 Brian George John Canty

1992 Alan William Shave

1995 Alan Norman Hoole

1997 Robert Malcolm Harris

2000 Peter Johnstone

Bermuda

1982 Sir Richard Neil Posnett

1984 Viscount Dunrossil

1988 Major General Sir Desmond Langley

1992 The Rt Hon The Lord Waddington

1997 Thorold Masefield

2002 Sir John Vereker

British Indian Ocean Territory

1983 William Nigel Wenban-Smith

1986 William Marsden

1988 Richard John Smale Edis

1991 Thomas George Harris

1994 David Ross MacLennan

1996 Bruce Dinwiddy

1999 John White

2001   Alan Edden Huckle

British Virgin Islands
1987   John Mark Ambrose Herdman
1992   Peter Alfred Penfold
1995   David Patrick Robert Mackilligin
1998   Francis Joseph Savage
2000   Thomas Townley Macan

Cayman Islands
1992   Michael Edward John Gore
1995   John Wynne Owen
1999   Peter Smith
2002   Bruce Harry Dinwiddy

Falkland Islands/British Antarctic Islands
1986   Gordon Wesley Jewkes
1989   William Hugh Fullerton
1993   David Edward Tatham
1996   Richard Peter Ralph
1999   Donald Lamont
2002   Howard John Stredder Pearce

Gibraltar
1992   Sir Hugo White
1997   The Rt Hon Sir Richard Luce
2000   David Robert Campbell Durie

Montserrat
1985   Arthur Christopher Watson
1987   Christopher John Turner
1990   David Pendleton Taylor
1993   Francis Joseph Savage
1997   Anthony John Abbott
2001   Anthony James Longrigg

Pitcairn, Henderson, Ducie and Oeno Islands
1985   Terrence Daniel O'Leary
1988   Robert Archer Campbell Byatt
1991   David Joseph Moss
1994   Robert John Alston
1998   Martin Williams
2001   Richard Taylor Fell

St Helena (incl. Ascension and Tristan da Cunha)
1982   John Dudley Massingham
1989   Robert Frederick Stimson
1991   Alan Norman Hoole
1995   David Leslie Smallman
1999   David James Hollamby

Turks and Caicos Islands
1982   Christopher John Turner
1987   Michael John Bradley
1993   Martin Bourke
1996   John Philip Kelly
2000   Mervyn Thomas Jones

CHRONOLOGICAL LIST OF NON GOVERNMENTAL TRADE OFFICES (ANNEX) 1992-2002

Taipei
1992   Philip Morrice
1995   Alan Stanley Collins, CMG
1999   David Coates
2000   Derek Richard Marsh, CVO

**Biographical Notes and
List of Staff**

ABBREVIATIONS

m	married
ptnr	partner
d	daughter
s	son
Diss	Dissolved
Dec'd	Deceased
AUSS	Assistant Under Secretary of State
BOTB	British Overseas Trade Board
CDA	Career Development Attachment
CDE	Conference on Confidence and Security- Building Measures and Disarmament in Europe
CENTO	Central Treaty Organisations
CFE	Negotiations on Conventional Armed Forces in Europe
CO	Cabinet Office
COI	Central Office of Information
CRO	Commonwealth Relations Office
CSBM	Negotiations on Confidence-and Security Building Measures
CSC	Civil Service Commission
CSCE	Conference on Security and Co-operation in Europe
CSD	Civil Service Department
CSO	Chief Security Officer
CSSB	Civil Service Selection Board
DoE	Department of Environment
DETR	Department for Environment, Transport and the Regions
DHC	Deputy High Commissioner
DoI	Department of Industry
DfID	Department for International Development
DS	Diplomatic Service
DSAO	Diplomatic Service Administration Office
DSS	Department of Social Security
DoT	Department of Trade
DTI	Department of Trade and Industry
DUSS	Deputy Under Secretary of State
ECGD	Export Credits Guarantee Department
ECSC	European Coal and Steel Community
ENA	Ecole Nationale d'Administration (Paris)
FCO	Foreign and Commonwealth Office
FO	Foreign Office
HCS	Home Civil Service
HMOCS	Her Majesty's Overseas Civil Service
HO	Home Office
IISS	International Institute for Strategic Studies
JSDC	Joint Services Defence College
MBFR	Mutual Reduction of Forces and Armaments (Vienna)
MECAS	Middle East Centre for Arab Studies
MoD	Ministry of Defence
MPBW	Ministry of Public Buildings and Works
MPNI	Ministry of Pensions and National Insurance
MPO	Management and Personnel Office
NATO	North Atlantic Treaty Organisation
OEEC	Organisation for European Economic Co-operation
OFTEL	Office of Telecommunications
OMCS	Office of the Minister for the Civil Service
POMEF	Political Office Middle East Forces
PRO	Principal Research Officer
RCDS	Royal College of Defence Studies
SEATO	South East Asia Treaty Organisation
SO	Security Officer
SOAS	School of Oriental and African Studies
SOWC	Senior Officers War Course
SRO	Senior Research Officer
SUPL	Special Unpaid Leave
UN	United Nations
UNHCR	United Nations High Commission for Refugees
WO	War Office

Part IV: Biographical List

Statement concerning the present appointments and some other particulars of the careers of established members of Her Majesty's Diplomatic Service.

A

Abbott, Anthony John, CMG (2001), OBE (1997), MBE (1986); Auckland since June 2001; born 09/09/41; FO 1959; Khorramshahr 1963; Helsinki 1966; FCO 1969; Lusaka 1972; Second Secretary and Consul Santiago 1976; FCO 1981; On loan to DOT 1982; First Secretary and Consul Lisbon 1983; First Secretary (Commercial) Calcutta 1987; First Secretary FCO 1991; Consul-General Perth 1993; Governor Plymouth 1997; m 1962 Margaret Stuart Green (3s 1963, 1965, 1970; 1d 1968).

Abbott, Belinda-Jayne (née Simmons); FCO since May 2001; born 12/09/65; FCO 1988; Buenos Aires 1990; Phnom Penh 1996; Band B3; m 2000 Peter Douglas Abbott.

Abbott, David; Second Secretary (Commercial) Madras since September 2001; born 06/06/64; FCO 1983; Singapore 1985; Africa/ME Floater 1989; Kaduna 1991; Abuja 1993; FCO 1994; Band C4; m 1990 Nor Hayati Binte Ibrahim (1d 1992; 1s 1993).

Abbott, Neil Middleton; Third Secretary Ljubljana since 1999; born 21/06/65; FCO 1987; Riyadh 1990; FCO 1994; Third Secretary (Chancery/Consular) Abu Dhabi 1996; Band B3; m 1990 Janet Probyn (1s 1992; 1d 1995).

Abbott, Nicholas Robert John; First Secretary (Economic) Riyadh since September 2000; born 25/04/63; FCO 1985; Language Training 1986; Third Secretary (Chancery/Information) Riyadh 1988; Brussels-Stagiare 1991; Third Secretary (Economic) Paris 1992; Second Secretary (Commercial) Doha 1995; FCO 1998; m 1989 Marcelle Ghislaine Julienne Delvaux (2d 1995, 1996).

Abbott-Watt, Thorhilda Mary Vivia; HM Ambassador Yerevan since December 2002; FCO 1974; SUPL 1977; FCO 1978; Latin American Floater 1979; Paris 1981; Brussels (UKREP) 1984; Second Secretary FCO 1986; Second Secretary Bonn 1988; First Secretary FCO 1991; First Secretary (Commercial/Know How Fund) Kiev 1995; FCO/Home Office Joint Clearance Office 1999.

Abel, Martin Jeremy; First Secretary (Management/Consul) Istanbul since December 2001; born 30/04/51; MPBW 1969; FCO 1971; Paris 1974; Madras 1976; FCO 1978; Luxembourg 1979; Peking 1982; FCO 1984; Istanbul 1988; Wellington 1993; FCO 1997; m (1) 1974 Lynne Diane Bailey (1d 1978; 1s 1980); (diss); (2) 1992 Nilufer Fasiha Kantarci (1d 1984).

Abrahams, David William; Second Secretary FCO since August 1983; born 14/07/53; FCO 1974; Geneva 1978; Brussels 1981; Band C4; m 1978 Susan Joy Denise Gibson (3d 1987,1988, 1990).

Ackerman, Erica Alexandra (née Smith); Second Secretary (Commercial) Singapore since November 2001; born 09/04/63; FCO 1983; Caracas 1985; SUPL 1989; FCO 1995; Third Secretary (Aid/Commercial) Manila 1998; SUPL 1999; Band C4; m 1989 Robert Joseph Ackerman (dec'd 1992).

Adam, Stuart William; Vienna since June 2000; born 20/03/71; FCO 1990; Bonn 1992; Peking 1995; Band B3; m Lesley Elizabeth (1d 2000).

Adams, Catherine Elizabeth; Assistant Legal Adviser FCO since February 2000; born 29/11/65; Assistant Legal Adviser FCO 1994; First Secretary (Legal) Brussels (UKREP) 1997; Band D7.

Adams, Geoffrey Doyne; Consul-General Jerusalem since May 2001; born 11/06/57; FCO 1979; Language Training 1980; Third later Second Secretary Jedda 1982; First Secretary ENA Paris 1985; FCO 1986; Private Secretary to the PUS 1987; First Secretary (Head of Political Section) Pretoria/Cape Town 1991; FCO 1994; On loan to (European Secrerariat) Cabinet Office 1996; Counsellor and DHM Cairo 1998; m 1999 Mary Emma Baxter.

Adams, Gillian; Brussels (JMO) since June 1998; born 10/06/65; MOD 1982; FCO 1984; Nicosia 1986; Africa/Middle East Floater 1989; FCO 1993; Language Training 1997; Band B3.

Adams, Trevor Malcolm; Second Secretary (Commercial) Bangkok since September 2002; born 16/04/51; FCO 1971; Paris 1973; Middle East Floater 1976; Bucharest 1977; JAO New

York 1979; FCO 1982; Vientiane 1984; Rangoon 1985; HM Consul Casablanca 1988; FCO 1993; First Secretary (Press and Public Affairs) Hong Kong 1998; m 1979 Linda Jane Burgess (1d 1985).

Adamson, Donald Snaith; FCO since January 2000; born 03/04/49; Ministry of Social Security 1967; FCO 1968; Khartoum 1971; Brussels (EC) 1972; Wellington 1975; Dacca 1978; loan to ODA 1981; FCO 1983; Cape Town 1985; FCO 1988; Second Secretary (Consular) Islamabad 1992; Second Secretary FCO 1993; Abuja 1996; m 1970 June Alice Manson Hall (1s 1973; 1d 1977).

Adamson, Joanne; On secondment to UNWRA since January 1999; born 09/07/67; FCO 1989; Language Training Cairo 1991; Third later Second Secretary (Chancery/Comm) Jerusalem 1992.

Addiscott, Emily Margaret (née Dallas); SUPL since April 1997; born 27/05/72; FCO 1991; SUPL 1994; Kiev 1996; Band A2; m 1993 Fraser John Addiscott (2d 1997, 1999).

Addiscott, Fraser John; SUPL since January 2001; born 04/09/71; FCO 1990; Vice Consul Helsinki 1994; Third Secretary (Management) Kiev 1996; Third Secretary (Political) Singapore 1997; Band C4; m 1993 Emily Margaret Dallas (2d 1997, 1999).

Ager, Keith; FCO since July 1991; born 25/06/48; FO 1965; Bonn 1975; FCO 1977; Lilongwe 1979; Montevideo 1982; FCO 1982; FCO 1985; Rome 1988; Band C4; m 1969 Ann Simmons (2d 1974, 1978).

Ager, Martyn Eric; FCO since August 1993; born 17/06/55; FCO 1972; Moscow 1982; FCO 1985; Amman 1990; Band C4; m 1981 Kathryn Margaret Pierson (2s 1984, 1992; 1d 1986; twins, 1s, 1d 1994).

Agnew, Gail Eileen; Second Secretary FCO since November 1988; born 21/01/48; FCO 1966; Lisbon 1970; Peking 1973; Bonn 1974; Vientiane 1977; FCO 1980; Nicosia 1982; Budapest 1985.

Ahmad, Asif Anwar; Head of Commonwealth Coordination Department FCO since April 2002; born 21/01/56; DTI Business Link 1996; First Secretary FCO 1999; m (1) (diss 1991); m (2) 1993 Zubeda Khamboo (1d 1975; 3s 1980, 1982, 1984).

Albright, John Rowland; First Secretary (Commercial) Singapore since March 1996; born 14/07/44; DHSS 1962; DSAO 1966; Havana 1968; Brussels (EC) 1969; Moscow 1972; FCO 1973; Nairobi 1976; Muscat 1979; FCO 1981; Second Secretary (Commercial) Manila 1985; First Secretary (Commercial/Aid) Colombo 1989; First Secretary FCO 1993; m (1) 1969 Gillian Susan Long (1d 1972; 1s 1974) m (2) 1993 Maria Alma Samaniego.

Alcock, Caroline; Third Secretary Bahrain since August 1996; born 08/12/70; Full-Time Language

Training 1993; FCO 1993; Band B3; m 1996 Amr Waguih.

Alcock, Michael Leslie, MBE (1986); FCO since April 1999; born 07/08/50; Ministry of Labour 1967; DSAO (later FCO) 1968; Bangkok 1971; Port of Spain 1975; Tehran 1977; FCO 1979; Second Secretary (Chancery) and Vice-Consul Addis Ababa 1984; Second later First Secretary (Comm/Econ) New Delhi 1987; First Secretary FCO 1991; First Secretary (Aid/Commercial) Kathmandu 1994; m 1971 Barbara Ann Couch (2s 1972, 1976).

Alderton, Clive; Head of Chancery Singapore since September 1998; born 09/05/67; FCO 1986; Vice-Consul Warsaw 1988; Third Secretary (External Relations) Brussels (UKREP) 1990; Second later First Secretary FCO 1993; m 1990 Catriona Mitchell Canning (1d 1998, 1s 2000).

Aldridge, Terence John; FCO since February 2000; born 11/09/56; FCO 1980; Darwin 1982; FCO 1984; Tel Aviv 1987; FCO 1988; Rome 1997; Band C5; m 1988 Janet Lorna Shore (1d 1991, 1s 1994).

Alessandri, Madeleine Kay (née Hateley); FCO since June 2000; born 06/03/65; FCO 1988; Second Secretary (Chancery/Info) Vienna 1990; Second later First Secretary FCO 1993; Consul (Economic) Frankfurt 1996; Language Training 1999; Band D6; m 1990 Enrico Alessandri (1d 1993, 1s 1998).

Aliaga, Deborah Joy; Third Secretary (Political) Lisbon since September 2002; born 08/07/60; FCO 1979; Bonn 1980; La Paz 1983; Resigned 1986; Reinstated FCO 1987; Third Secretary (Man/VC/ECO) La Paz 1997; Full-Time Language Training (Portugese) 2002; Band B3; m 1989 Kenny Aliaga (1d 1996; 1s 2000).

Allan, Duncan Brierton; Principal Research Officer FCO since August 1996; born 22/11/61; FCO 1989; Moscow 1992; m 1994 Joanne Clare Youde.

Allan, Jane Alison (née Higgs); SUPL since June 1998; born 09/03/63; FCO 1981; HCS 1981; Washington 1984; FCO 1987; SUPL 1989; Peking 1990; SUPL 1991; FCO 1996; Band A2; m 1987 Ian Allan.

Allan, Justine Rachel Anne; Floater Duties since July 1999; born 15/07/69; FCO 1990; Cape Town/Pretoria 1992; Band B3.

Allan, Keith Rennie; FCO since August 2000; born 25/08/68; MOD 1986; FCO 1988; Gaborone 1990; Floater Duties 1993; FCO 1996; Deputy Head of Mission Tashkent 1997; Band C5; m 1996 Martha Harriette Medendorp (1s 2000).

Allan, Lynne Fleming; SUPL since March 2002; born 22/10/68; FCO 1989; Moscow 1993; FCO 1995; Ankara 1998; Band B3; m 1999 Marat Ucer (1s 2001).

Allan, Moira; Second Secretary Bogotá since March 2000; born 27/05/61; FCO 1983; Prague

1985; FCO 1987; Mexico City 1989; Santiago 1993; FCO 1996; Band C4.

Allan, Nicholas Edward; First Secretary FCO since March 2002; born 03/08/65; FCO 1990; Brussels (UKREP) 1993; Africa/Middle East Floater Duties 1994; Language Training 1995; Third Secretary (Political) Brussels 1996; Third later Second Secretary FCO 1999; Assistant Private Secretary to Peter Hain later Brian Wilson and Baroness Symons 2001; Band D6; m 2001 Elizabeth Rosemary Waugh.

Allan, Richard Joseph; FCO since April 1995; born 03/10/48; FO (later FCO) 1966; Berlin 1970; Kathmandu 1973; FCO 1977; Milan 1980; FCO 1982; Canberra 1984; Colombo 1987; Islamabad 1990; Band B3; m (1) Jeanette Marshall (1s 1974); (2) 1985 Margaret Janette Smylie.

Allbless, Clare Brickley; Third Secretary (PPA) Tokyo since October 2000; born 04/05/71; FCO 1997; Band B3; m Dan Lindfield

Allen, Jonathan Guy; Nicosia since August 1999; born 05/03/74; FCO 1997; Band D6.

Allen, Keith; Deputy High Commissioner San Salvador since June 2000; born 05/09/72; FCO 1992; New Delhi 1996; Full-Time Language Training 2000; Band B3.

Allen, Mark John Spurgeon, CMG (2002); Counsellor FCO since February 1994; born 03/07/50; Third Secretary FCO 1973; Language Training MECAS 1974; Third later Second Secretary Abu Dhabi 1975; Second Secretary FCO 1977; Second later First Secretary Cairo 1978; FCO 1981; First Secretary (Economic) Belgrade 1982; First Secretary FCO 1986; Counsellor FCO 1990; m 1976 Margaret Mary Watson (1s 1978, 1d 1980).

Allen, Rory James Colclough; First Secretary FCO since December 1992; born 05/09/48; FCO 1972; Second Secretary Jakarta 1974; First Secretary FCO 1978; Language Training Hong Kong 1981; Bangkok 1982; First Secretary FCO 1985; First Secretary (Political) Rome 1991; Band D6; m 1982 Hazel Rose Dawe (1s 1983).

Allen, Ross Christopher Edward; FCO since September 2001; born 30/11/78; Band C4.

Allen, Ruth Alexandra; FCO since September 2000; born 31/08/76; Band C4.

Allen, Sylvia Ann; Hanoi since December 1999; born 08/08/60; FCO 1984; La Paz 1986; Tunis 1990; Floater Duties 1995; Band A2.

Alloway, Terence Michael; FCO since October 1998; born 18/05/59; FCO 1980; Budapest 1982; Tel Aviv 1983; FCO 1986; SE Asia Floater 1987; FCO 1988; Kuwait 1992; Full-Time Language Training 1994; FCO 1994; Third later Second Secretary (Chancery) Geneva (UKDIS) 1995; Band D6; m 1991 Christine Ann Carr.

Ambrose, Philip John; Consul-General (Commercial) Rio de Janeiro since June 2002;

born 03/11/59; FCO 1978; Brussels (UKREP) 1980; Jedda 1983; Riyadh 1986; South-East Asia Floater 1987; FCO 1992; Deputy Head of Mission and Vice-Consul Kinshasa 1995.

Amin, Jacqueline Harris; FCO since October 1989; born 02/06/62; FCO 1984; Port Stanley 1985; Luanda 1986; Band A2; m 1989 Paul John Harms.

Amos, Rex; FCO since November 1999; born 24/09/72; Band B3; m 1999 Jacqueline Palin.

Anderson, Annabel Mary; Paris since December 1998; born 15/07/50; FCO 1995; Band A2; m 1974

Anderson, Henry Ian; First Secretary FCO since September 2001; born 20/08/52; HO 1974; Dhaka 1983; Second Secretary FCO 1987; Vice-Consul Munich 1989; Second Secretary FCO 1994; First Secretary Budapest 1997; Band D6; m 1976 Janice Irene Leeman (1s 1984; 1d 1987).

Anderson, Jennifer Elizabeth; First Secretary (Political/Military) Brussels (UKREP) since June 2001; born 16/11/68; Second later First Secretary FCO 1997; m 1997 Stephen Ashworth.

Anderson, John; First Secretary (Commercial) Warsaw since January 2002; born 25/08/49; FCO 1966; Abu Dhabi 1970; Peking 1974; Lagos 1975; FCO 1978; HM Consul Istanbul 1982; Second later First Secretary (Comm) Paris 1987; First Secretary FCO 1991; First Secretary (Management) Harare 1995; FCO 1998; m 1970 Jacqueline Thorburn (2d 1981, 1990; 1s 1983).

Anderson, Lorraine Michelle; FCO since May 1994; born 29/12/63; FCO 1989; Damascus 1992; Band A2; m (1) 1988 Lawrence Malcolm Reginald Simpson (diss 1994), (2) 1999 Neil Barrowman (1s 2000).

Anderson, Michael James; First Secretary (Political) New York (UKMIS) since July 2000; born 03/04/61; FCO 1984; Language Training 1986; Second Secretary (Scientific/Econ) Moscow 1988; First Secretary FCO 1989; First Secretary Geneva (UKDIS) 1992; FCO 1997; T/D Doha 2000; Band D6; m 1987 Julie Ann Dickens (2s 1992, 1994; 1d 1996).

Anderson, Paul James; FCO since August 2001; born 25/09/78; Band C4.

Anderson, Philip Brian; FCO since October 2001; born 18/07/73; HCS 1993; FCO 1997; Nicosia 1999; Band A2; m 1997 Jennie Linda Willis (1s 1996).

Anderson, Steven Martin; Third Secretary (Management/VC) Helsinki since December 2000; born 29/12/70; FCO Home Civil Service 1991; Dubai 1997; Moscow 1998; Band B3; ptnr, Eevamaija Sofia Laitinen.

Andrews, Francesca Therese; FCO since July 1989; born 23/02/54; FCO 1973; Cape Town/Pretoria 1975; Moscow 1978; FCO 1980;

Brussels (UKDEL) 1982; Port of Spain 1986; Band A2.

Andrews, Moira Fraser, TD (1992); Legal Counsellor FCO since June 2000; born 22/03/59; DTI 1995; Assistant Legal Adviser FCO 1998; m 1989 Ian Andrews (1s 1989; 1d 1992).

Andrews, Paul Philip; FCO since June 1998; born 24/09/68; FCO 1988; Hong Kong 1993; Seoul 1996; Band B3.

Andrews, Timothy John; First Secretary (IAEA) Vienna (UKMIS) since September 2001; born 01/08/55; FCO 1976; Dacca 1979; Stuttgart 1982; Bonn 1984; FCO 1987; Second Secretary (Chancery/Info) Lusaka 1990; Deputy Head of Mission Port Louis 1994; First Secretary FCO 1997; m 1987 Carolyn Mary Moffat (1d 1989, 1s 1991).

Angell, Ben Thomas; Second Secretary Ankara since August 2002; born 27/12/76; FCO 2000; Band C4.

Angell, Neil Christopher; Third Secretary (Political) Lima since April 1999; born 31/10/66; Mexico City 1987; FCO 1989; Budapest 1991; Moscow 1991; Bangkok 1991; T/D Bangkok 1994; FCO 1995; Band B3; m 1995 Suntraree Charoenwattana (1s 1997).

Angrave, Gillian Linda; FCO since October 1994; born 16/04/45; Manila 1976; FCO 1976; Lima 1980; Guatemala City 1981; Santiago 1982; FCO 1985; Mexico City 1987; Budapest 1991; Band B3.

Ankerson, Dr Dudley Charles; Counsellor FCO since April 2002; born 04/09/48; Second Secretary FCO 1976; Second Secretary Buenos Aires 1978; First Secretary FCO 1981; First Secretary Mexico City 1985; First Secretary FCO 1988; FCO 1991; First Secretary FCO on secondment to the Private Sector 1991; Counsellor Madrid 1993; FCO 1997; Counsellor Budapest 1998; m 1973 Silvia Ernestina Galicia (1d 1985, 1s 1986).

Anstead, Alan Roger Hugh; Bratislava since August 2000; born 06/02/62; FCO 1980; Moscow 1983; Monrovia 1985; Hamburg 1989; FCO 1991; On loan to the DTI 1993; Deputy Head of Mission Riga 1996; Band C4; m 1986 Paula Marita Nikkanen (1s 1991).

Anthony, Helen Louise; FCO since June 1988; born 06/12/67; Band A2.

Anthony, Ian Nicholas; First Secretary FCO since April 1997; born 18/01/60; FCO 1985; Second later First Secretary Lisbon 1988; First Secretary FCO 1990; First Secretary (Political) Brasilia 1993; Band D6.

Anthony-Rigsby, Lisa; SUPL since September 2001; born 01/04/65; FCO 1998; Full-Time Language Training 2000; Band A2.

Arbon, Helen Marie; Second Secretary Chisinau since October 2001; born 21/04/70; FCO 1988; Jakarta 1991; World-wide Floater 1995; T/D

Montevideo 1998; SUPL 1998; FCO 1999; SUPL 1999; Band B3; m 1998 Adolfo Pando Molina.

Archer, Marie-Louise; Second Secretary New Delhi since September 2002; born 27/10/61; FCO 1984; Resigned 1986; FCO 1987; Reinstated 1987; Third Secretary (Immigration) Karachi 1991; Third Secretary FCO 1995; DHM Managua 1996; Language Training 1996; Band B3.

Archer, Nicholas Stewart, MVO (2001); Head of Near East and North Africa Dept FCO since May 2002; born 24/12/60; FCO 1983; Third later Second Secretary (Chancery) Amman 1986; Second later First Secretary FCO 1989; PS/Minister of State 1992; First Secretary (Commercial) Oslo 1995; Language Training 1995; on loan to St James's Palace 1997; m 1999 Erica Margaret Power.

Arkley, David Ballantine; Third Secretary (PPA) Moscow since October 2000; born 10/10/66; FCO 1986; Moscow 1988; Floater Duties 1990; MO/Vice Consul São Paulo 1992; FCO 1995; Third Secretary (Press and Public Affairs) Washington 1997; Band B3; m 1992 Melissa Lea Buchanan.

Arkwright, Paul Thomas; Counsellor (Political) September 2001; born 02/03/62; FCO 1986; Second Secretary (Chancery) BMG Berlin 1988; First Secretary FCO 1991; First Secretary (Chancery) New York (UKMIS) 1993; Attachement to Quai d'Orsay 1997; First Secretary (Chancery) Paris 1998; m 1997 Patricia Anne Holland (1d 1999).

Armour, Nicholas Hilary Stuart; Head Of North America Department FCO since November 2000; born 12/06/51; Third Secretary FCO 1974; Language Training MECAS 1975; FCO 1976; Third later Second Secretary Beirut 1977; First Secretary FCO 1980; Head of Chancery Athens 1984; First Secretary FCO 1989; Counsellor and Deputy Head of Mission Muscat 1991; Counsellor on loan to the DTI 1994; Consul-General/Counsellor Dubai 1997; m 1982 Georgina Elizabeth Fortescue (2d 1985, 1987).

Armstrong, Catherine Fraser; HM Consul Brussels since September 2000; born 16/07/53; FCO 1971; Paris 1974; Gaborone 1977; FCO 1980; Manila 1985; Athens 1989; FCO 1990; Full-Time Language Training 1994; Second Secretary (Consular/Management) Caracas 1995; Second Secretary FCO 1997; m 1981 Clive Paul Ranson (diss 1986).

Arnold, Troy Zachary Moncur; Second Secretary (Economic) Nicosia since October 2000; born 19/12/72; Second Secretary FCO 1997; Language Training 1999; Band C4.

Aron, Michael Douglas; Counsellor (Political) Brussels (UKREP) since July 2002; born 22/03/59; FCO 1984; Conference Support Officer New York (UKMIS) 1985; Second later First Secretary FCO 1986; on Secondment to European Commission 1986; First Secretary Brasilia 1988;

First Secretary FCO 1991; First Secretary
(Political) New York (UKMIS) 1993; First
Secretary later Counsellor FCO 1996; Deputy
Head of Mission Amman 1999; m 1986 Rachel
Ann Golding Barker (2d 1986, 1996, 2s 1990,
1994).

Aron, Peter James; Counsellor FCO since
December 2000; born 27/02/46; FO (later FCO)
1965; Bonn 1968; Second later First Secretary
FCO 1971; First Secretary (Chancery) Singapore
1984; First Secretary (Chancery) Washington
1986; First Secretary FCO 1990; Counsellor
(Regional Affairs) Seoul 1997; m 1968 Penelope
Joan Sebley (2d 1969, 1971; 2s 1976, 1988).

Aron, Dr Rachel Ann Golding (née Barker); FCO
since April 2001; born 18/07/51; First Secretary
FCO 1984; Head of Chancery Brasilia 1988;
SUPL 1990; First Secretary FCO 1992; First
Secretary (Political) New York (UKMIS) 1993;
SUPL 1996; Counsellor on loan to RAS as CSSB
Chairman 1997; SUPL (Amman) 1999; m 1986
Michael Douglas Aron (2d 1986, 1996, 2s 1990
1994).

Arroyo, James Jose-Maria; First Secretary FCO
since June 2002; born 25/03/67; FCO 1990; Full-
Time Language Training 1991; Full-Time
Language Training Cairo 1992; Second Secretary
(Political) Amman 1993; Cairo 1996; Consul
(Political) Jerusalem 1999; Band D6; m 1992
Kerry Ann Louise Ford (1d 2001).

Arthur, Hilary Jane; Sofia since September 2001;
born 28/01/61; FCO 1984; Karachi 1987; Vice
Consul (Consular) Düsseldorf 1991; Frankfurt
1993; T/D Islamabad 1994; FCO 1995; Second
Secretary (Development) Lusaka 1998; Band C4.

Arthur, Michael Anthony, CMG (1992); Minister
Washington since June 1999; born 28/08/50;
Second later First Secretary FCO 1978; New York
1972; FCO 1972; FCO 1973; Second Secretary
Brussels (UKREP) 1974; Second Secretary
Kinshasa 1976; PS to Lord Privy Seal 1980; PS to
Minister of State 1982; First Secretary (Chancery)
Bonn 1984; Counsellor FCO 1988; Counsellor
(Political) Paris 1993; Director (Resources) and
Chief Inspector 1997; m 1974 Plaxy Gillian
Beatrice Corke (2d 1978, 1980; 2s 1982, 1985).

Ash, Elizabeth; On secondment to Buckingham
Palace since July 1996; born 31/07/52; FCO 1975;
New Delhi 1976; Geneva (UKMIS) 1978; Peking
1980; FCO 1982; Kingston 1983; FCO 1987; East
Berlin 1988; FCO 1990; Band B3.

Ashcroft, Andrew Richard; HM Ambassador
Santo Domingo since July 2002; born 28/05/61;
FCO 1980; Muscat 1982; Tel Aviv 1987; Second
Secretary 1989; FCO 1991; First Secretary Harare
1996; FCO 1999.

Ashdown, Julie Anne; Second Secretary (Aid)
Quito since June 1996; born 31/08/57; FCO 1976;
Amman 1978; Asunción 1982; Brasilia 1983; FCO
1985; Belgrade 1990; Second Secretary FCO
1993.

Ashford, Leslie David; Second Secretary
(Consular) Harare since January 2002; born
07/09/50; Royal Air Force 1967-1996; FCO 1996;
T/D Abu Dhabi 2000; T/D Khartoum 2000; Band
C4; m 1971 Francetta Xavier Marie (1d 1973, 1s
1979).

Ashton, John; Counsellor FCO since May 1998;
born 07/11/56; FCO 1978; Language Training
Hong Kong 1980; Third later Second Secretary
Peking 1981; FCO 1984; First Secretary on loan to
the Cabinet Office 1986; Rome 1988; First
Secretary later Counsellor Deputy Political
Adviser Hong Kong 1993; On secondment as
Visiting Fellow, Green College Oxford 1997; m
1983 Kao Fengning (1s 1986).

Ashworth, Patrick; Deputy Consul-General and
Deputy Director of Trade Promotion São Paulo
since January 2001; born 02/11/50; FCO 1968;
Dar es Salaam 1971; Castries 1975; Moscow
1978; FCO 1980; Valletta 1983; Vice-Consul
(Commercial) São Paulo 1987; Second Secretary
FCO 1992; Second Secretary (UNCED) Brasilia
1992; First Secretary (Press and Public Affairs)
The Hague 1995; Band D6; m 1973 Pauline Mary
Harrison (1d 1982, 1s 1986).

Askham, Denise Ann (née Vaughan); SUPL since
January 1999; born 15/10/64; FCO 1983; Bonn
1985; Washington 1988; Vienna (UKDEL) CSCE
1988; Berne 1991; SUPL 1995; FCO 1995; FCO
1998; Band B3; m 1998 Stephen David Askham
(1d 1997, 1s 2000).

Askham, Stephen David; Lisbon since October
2000; born 20/05/60; RAF 1976-1984; FCO 1984;
Bonn 1991; FCO 1994; FCO 1994; Bahrain 1999;
FTLT 2000; Band B3; m 1988 Denise Ann
Vaughan (1d 1997, 1s 2000).

Aspden, Susan Elizabeth; Stockholm since
September 2002; born 20/01/57; FCO 1980; Rabat
1981; Jakarta 1983; Havana 1987; FCO 1989; On
loan to DTI 1996; Band C4.

Aspery, Kevin; Hong Kong since September
1999; born 05/04/52; Army 1968-1992; Havana
1993; Moscow (MNEB) 1997; Colombo 1998; m
Penelope Jane (1d 1973, 2s 1975, 1977).

Asquith, Hon Dominic Anthony Gerard; Deputy
Head of Mission Riyadh since October 2001; born
07/02/57; FCO 1983; Second Secretary and Head
of Interests Section Damascus 1986; First
Secretary (Chancery) Muscat 1987; First Secretary
FCO 1989; PS/Minister of State 1990; Washington
1992; Minister and Deputy Head of Mission
Buenos Aires 1997; m 1988 Louise Cotton (2d
1989, 1990; 2s 1992, 1994).

Astbury, Nicholas Paul; First Secretary FCO since
April 1999; born 13/08/71; FCO 1994; Second
Secretary (Chancery) Colombo 1995; m 1995
Elayna Joanne Gutteridge (1s 1999).

Astill-Brown, Jeremy; Second Secretary
(Political/Development) Luanda since September
1999; born 14/03/67; FCO 1987; Kampala 1990;

Addis Ababa 1993; FCO 1997; Band B3; m 1991 Marie-Loiuse (Marisa) Alegria Gunner.

Astle, Marilia Silva; FCO since April 1998; born 14/04/68; FCO 1991; Vice-Consul later Press & Public Affairs Lisbon 1994; Band C4; m 2000 Jonathan Jones.

Astley, Philip Sinton, LVO (1979); HM Ambassador Copenhagen since August 1999; born 18/08/43; British Council 1965-73; First Secretary FCO 1973; First Secretary Copenhagen 1976; First Secretary and Head of Chancery East Berlin 1980; First Secretary FCO 1982; Counsellor, Home Inspectorate 1984; Head of Management Review Staff 1985; Counsellor (Econ/Comm/Aid) and Consul-General Islamabad 1986; Deputy Head of Mission Copenhagen 1990; Counsellor FCO 1994; AUSS (Protocol) and Vice Marshal of the Diplomatic Corps 1996; m 1966 Susanne Poulsen (2d 1969, 1972).

Atkin, Patricia Lois; Port Louis since March 1975; born 21/04/44; FCO 1974; Band B3.

Atkinson, Christine; Deputy Permanent Delegate Paris (UKDEL) UNESCO since June 2001; born 05/07/57; British Museum 1979; COI 1986; FCO 1990; APS/Minister of State 1996; PS/PUSS DFID 1997.

Atkinson, James Oswald; HM Ambassador to Democratic Republic of Congo and non-resident Ambassador to Republic of Congo (Brazzaville) since May 2000; born 20/10/44; Board of Trade 1964; DSA 1966; Commonwealth Office (later FCO) 1967; Nicosia 1969; Gaborone 1972; Second Secretary (Commercial) Damascus 1976; FCO 1980; First Secretary (Commercial) Athens 1984; First Secretary (Chancery/Inf) Jakarta 1988; First Secretary FCO 1990; Deputy Head of Mission Kampala 1993; FCO 1997; m 1980 Annemiek van Werkum (1d 1981).

Atkinson, Jane; Port Louis since June 1999; born 20/07/60; MOD 1978-87; FCO 1987; Quito 1988; Floater Duties 1992; FCO 1996; Band B3.

Atkinson, Kim Louise (née Kemp); Warsaw since September 1999; born 04/04/74; FCO 1992; Islamabad 1996; Band A2; m 1999 Simon Manington Atkinson.

Atkinson, Simon Manington; ECO/Vice Consul Warsaw since March 2000; born 11/05/71; FCO 1989; Oslo 1992; Pro-Consul Islamabad 1995; FCO 1995; Band B3; m 1999 Kim Kemp.

Attryde, Alan Robert James; First Secretary (Commercial) July 2000; born 21/08/47; Ministry of Labour 1966; DSAO 1967; Middle East Floater 1970; Washington 1971; Jakarta 1974; FCO 1978; Cairo 1980; on loan to DTI 1985; Second Secretary 1985; Consul (Commercial) Shanghai 1987; FCO 1987; Second Secretary (Man/Cons) Caracas 1990; Full-time Language Training 1992; First Secretary (Commercial) Al Khobar 1993; FCO 1997; T/D as First Secretary (Management) Washington 1999; Band C5; m 1992 Ana Maria Diaz Molina.

Attwood, Ian; Kuala Lumpur since March 2000; born 14/04/62; FCO 1983; Hong Kong 1991; FCO 1992; Bangkok 1993; FCO 1996; Band C4; m 1987 Tina Louise (1d 1989; 1s 1991).

Augustine-Aina, Felicity; Islamabad since March 2000; born 10/07/57; MAFF FCO 1989; Lagos 1991; FCO 1994; Dublin 1998; SUPL 1999; Band B3; m 1992 Henry Abayomi Aina.

Auld, Steven James; Third Secretary (Management) and Vice Consul Tripoli since January 2001; born 09/07/71; FCO 1990; Moscow 1993; Nuku'alofa 1995; FCO 1996; Band B3; m 2001 Andrea Baity.

Austen, Richard James, MBE (1996); Deputy High Commissioer Port Louis since September 2001; born 25/05/55; Inland Revenue 1972-77; SUPL 1974-77; FCO 1981; Dar es Salaam 1983; Third Secretary (Consular) Ottawa 1987; Second Secretary FCO 1990; Deputy High Commissioner Banjul 1993; First Secretary FCO 1996.

Austin, David John Robert, OBE (1999); Deputy Head of Mission Zagreb since August 1999; born 07/10/63; FCO 1986; Third later Second Secretary Dhaka 1989; FCO 1992; First Secretary (Political/Information) Belgrade 1993; On secondment as Political Adviser to Carl Bildt, ICFY/OHR 1995; FCO 1997; m 1990 Emma Jane Carey (1d 1995, 1s 1997).

Austin, Rebecca-Jane Victoria (née Hall); SUPL since March 1996; born 27/02/68; FCO 1990; Port Louis 1993; FCO 1994; Band B3; m 1994 J Mark Austin (1d 1996).

Austin, Vanessa Anne; Nairobi since July 2000; born 04/08/71; FCO 1994; Cairo 1996; Band A2.

Avery, Robert Rember; First Secretary (Management) Oslo since September 1994; born 31/01/46; DSAO 1965; Port of Spain 1968; Colombo 1972; FCO 1975; Amman 1978; Helsinki 1980; FCO 1982; Second Secretary (Commercial) Kuala Lumpur 1987; Second Secretary FCO 1991; m 1967 Christine Ruth Floate (1s 1968, 1d 1971).

Axworthy, Michael George Andrew; SUPL since July 2000; born 26/09/62; FCO 1986; Third later Second Secretary Valletta 1988; Second Secretary FCO 1991; Second Secretary (Political/Military) Bonn 1993; Second Secretary (Economic) Bonn 1996; First Secretary FCO 1998; m 1996 Sally Hinds (1d 1999).

Axworthy, Sally Jane; SUPL since June 2000; born 01/09/64; FCO 1986; Language Training 1988; Second Secretary Kiev 1989; Third Secretary Moscow 1989; First Secretary FCO 1993; First Secretary Bonn 1994; FCO 1998; m 1996 Michael G A Axworthy (1d 1999).

Ayre, Andrew; Second Secretary Vienna since November 2001; born 30/04/66; FCO 1986; Warsaw 1988; Rio de Janeiro 1990; FCO 1991; Nicosia 1994; SUPL 1997; Third Secretary Tel

Aviv 1998; Band B3; m 1990 Bettina
Mooseberger.

Ayres, Robert Charles; Second later First
Secretary FCO since February 1990; born
12/12/41; CRO 1958; Seconded to Department of
Technical Co-operation 1961; CRO 1963; DSAO
1965; Tripoli 1967; Lahore 1969; Islamabad 1971;
FCO 1972; Brussels (NATO) 1975; Second
Secretary FCO 1978; Second Secretary (Admin)
Brussels (JAO) 1985; m 1978 Elizabeth Anne
Kirkland (1d 1979).

B

Babbage, Ann Michelle; FCO since May 1995;
born 18/05/72; Band A2.

Bach, Alison Helen (née Clewes); Brussels since
December 2001; born 04/11/65; ODA 1987; FCO
1990; Manila 1992; FCO 1994; SUPL 1996; T/D
Sarajevo 1996; Bonn 1997; Reykjavik 2000; Band
A2; m 1997 Anthony Gordon James Bach (1s
1998).

Backhouse, Nigel Anthony Richard, MVO (1986);
Counsellor FCO since September 2001; born
19/01/56; FCO 1982; Second Secretary Kabul
1984; Second later First Secretary Kathmandu
1985; FCO 1986; First Secretary (Chancery)
Madrid 1989; FCO 1992; Counsellor Paris 1998;
m (1) 1979 Kathleen Helen Gordon (diss 1988)
(2s 1983, 1985); (2) 1996 Sharon Lindsay
Rathbone (1d 1998; 1s 2001).

Bagnall, Andrew William; Second Secretary
Nairobi since June 1994; born 28/02/48; GPO
1964-70; FCO 1970; Pretoria 1982; Second
Secretary FCO 1985; Attaché Caracas 1987; m
1981 Margaret Christine Bromwich (1s 1981, 1d
1985).

Baharie, Ian Walter; First Secretary (Political)
Abuja since March 1999; born 03/05/61; Second
later First Secretary FCO 1987; FCO 1982;
Language Training SOAS 1983; Third later
Second Secretary (Chancery) Cairo 1985; First
Secretary Abu Dhabi 1991; First Secretary FCO
1994; Consul Jerusalem 1996; Band D6; m 1991
Bonaventura Agatha Jasperina Buhre (3d 1991,
1998, 2001).

Bailey, Ian Peter; FCO since December 1998; born
21/08/57; DTI 1985; FCO 1987; Language
Training 1988; Third Secretary (Political) Muscat
1990; Second Secretary (Commercial) Seoul 1995;
Band C5; m 1990 Teresa Weronika Maria
Frosztega (1s 1998).

Bailey, Michael; Third Secretary FCO since
January 1991; born 24/02/41; FO 1965; Singapore
1967; FCO 1969; Khartoum 1971; FCO 1973; St
Helena 1974; FCO 1976; Muscat 1977; FCO
1980; Peking 1981; FCO 1983; Rangoon 1984;
FCO 1986; Third Secretary Rome 1988; Band C4;
m 1967 Wendy Nichol Pocklington (2s 1969,
1970).

Bailey, Rosemarie Anne (née Edwards); FCO
since December 1997; born 20/04/59; FCO 1979;

Tokyo 1983; FCO 1986; SUPL 1988; Vice-Consul
Singapore 1992; SUPL 1996; Band C4; m 1982
Mark Adrian Stephen Bailey (1s 1996).

Bailey, Stephen; Madras since January 2000; born
13/04/53; FCO 1971; Mexico City 1975;
Gaborone 1977; Sana'a 1981; FCO 1983;
Wellington 1987; Budapest 1990; FCO 1995;
Band B3; m 1975 Carol Joan Sterritt (1d 1980).

Baines, Paul Vincent; Second Secretary (Consular)
New Delhi since June 2002; born 22/07/47;
Registrar General's Office 1966; Inland Revenue
1966; DSAO (later FCO) 1967; Blantyre 1971;
Algiers 1973; Warsaw 1976; FCO 1978; Lusaka
1981; FCO 1984; Second Secretary (Admin)
Riyadh 1988; Consul Tokyo 1992; FCO 1996;
Zomba 1997; m 1969 Edith Lauraine Baxter Price.

Baird, Jamie Peter; FCO since December 1997;
born 25/08/72; Band A2.

Baird, Nicholas Graham Faraday; Head of
European Union Department (Internal) FCO since
February 2002; born 15/05/62; FCO 1984; Third
later Second Secretary Kuwait 1986; Second later
First Secretary (Econ/Finance) Brussels (UKREP)
1989; Private Secretary to the Parliamentary
Under Secretary of State FCO 1993; Counsellor
and Deputy Head of Mission Muscat 1997;
Counsellor (Justice/Home Affairs) Brussels
(UKREP) 1998; m 1985 Caroline Jane Ivett (1s
1989, 2d 1990, 1992).

Baker, Catherine Margaret; FCO since January
1998; born 11/09/68; FCO 1991; Third Secretary
(Chancery/Information) Tel Aviv 1994; Band B3.

Baker, Denise; Belgrade since April 1994; born
27/09/67; FCO 1987; Brussels 1991; Band A2.

Baker, Francis Raymond, OBE (1997); Private
Secretary to the Minister of State July 1998; born
27/01/61; FCO 1981; Panama City 1983; Third
later Second Secretary Buenos Aires 1986; Second
Secretary FCO 1991; First Secretary
(Political/Military) Ankara 1993; First Secretary
on secondment to State Department Washington
1996; First Secretary FCO 1997; m 1983 Maria
Pilar Fernandez (1d 1989; 1s 1991).

Baker, Nigel Marcus; on loan to St James's Palace
since June 2000; born 09/09/66; Third Secretary
FCO 1989; Third later Second Secretary (Econ)
Prague 1992; Second Secretary later DHM
Bratislava 1993; Resigned 1995; First Secretary
FCO 1998; Reinstated 1998; m 1997 Alexandra
Cechova.

Baker, Piers Howard Burton; Deputy Head of
Mission Vienna since January 2001; born
23/07/56; Second Secretary FCO 1983; First
Secretary (Chancery) Brussels 1985; First
Secretary FCO 1988; First Secretary Brussels
(UKREP) 1993; First Secretary FCO 1996; m
1979 Maria Eugenia Vilaincour (1s 1984).

Baker, Rodney Kelvin Mornington; FCO since
November 1996; born 24/03/49; FO (later FCO)
1966; Warsaw 1974; FCO 1975; Athens 1977;

Ankara 1978; FCO 1981; Third Secretary Tokyo 1984; FCO 1986; Third Secretary Madrid 1989; FCO 1992; Düsseldorf 1994; Band D6; m 1971 Christine Mary Holt (2d 1979, 1983).

Baker, Russell Nicholas John; First Secretary (Commercial) Dublin since June 1996; born 06/10/53; FCO 1977; Prague 1979; Language Training 1979; Private Secretary to HMA Bonn 1982; Second Secretary FCO 1986; APS to Minister of State 1987; Second Secretary (Political/Info/Comm) Lima 1990; First Secretary FCO 1994; m 1996 Silvia Chavez Montoya.

Baker-Mavin, Alison Bertha (née Baker), BEM (1991); SUPL since March 2001; born 09/05/62; FCO 1989; Algiers 1991; Banjul 1995; Third Secretary (Management/Commercial) Freetown 1998; Band B3; m 1997 G J Mavin.

Baldwin, Brian Paul; High Commissioner Honiara since May 2001; born 07/12/44; Ministry of Transport 1964; Board of Trade 1965; FCO 1967; Johannesburg 1970; Belgrade 1973; FCO 1976; Vice-Consul (Pol) Johannesburg 1979; Second later First Secretary FCO 1983; First Secretary (Commercial) Muscat 1988; Deputy Head of Mission Port Moresby 1993; Tristan da Cunha Administrator 1998; m Elizabeth Mary Evans (3s 1969, 1970, 1973; 1d 1971).

Baldwin, Peter Graham; FCO since April 1998; born 28/08/43; Paymaster General's Office 1962; CRO 1963; Lusaka 1964; Calcutta 1967; Vienna (BE) 1971; Second Secretary Brussels (UKREP) 1973; FCO 1977; Algiers 1981; Second Secretary FCO 1983; Second Secretary (Immigration/Consular) Colombo 1987; Second Secretary (Consular) Jakarta 1991; Second Secretary (Immigration) Islamabad 1995; m 1968 Patricia Joyce Carter (2d 1970, 1972;1s 1980).

Bale, Carolie Margaret; FCO since June 1991; born 25/07/57; FCO 1980; Geneva (UKMIS) 1981; Moscow 1983; Port Stanley 1986; Sofia 1987; Gaborone 1989; Band A2.

Balfour, Alison Hannah; Amman since March 2002; born 13/05/61; Scottish Office 1980-87; FCO 1987; Mexico City 1989; Nicosia 1992; Rome 1995; FCO 1999; Band B3.

Ball, Anthony James; First Secretary (Political) Madrid since July 1999; born 18/12/68; FCO 1989; Full-Time Language Training 1991; FCO 1993; Second Secretary (Economic) Kuwait 1994; FCO 1996; Band D6; m 1995 Celia Garcia-Marugan Mino (1s 2001).

Ballet, Sarah Elizabeth; FCO since August 2000; born 31/10/71; FCO 1990; Washington 1994; Washington 1997; SUPL 1997; Band B3.

Balmer, Michael Anthony; FCO since September 2000; born 21/07/51; MOD (Navy) 1969; FCO 1971; Geneva (UKMIS) 1973; Moscow 1975; LA Floater 1977; Jedda 1979; Second Secretary (Commercial) Warsaw 1981; Second later First Secretary FCO 1984; Language Training 1987; First Secretary (Commercial) Athens 1988; First

Secretary FCO 1992; Deputy Consul-General Düsseldorf and Deputy Director-General (Trade and Investment Promotion) Germany 1996; Band D7; m 1982 Helen Charmian Burgoine (2d 1984, 1987).

Bamber, Jonathan James; Third Secretary (Commercial) Maputo since August 2001; born 24/09/65; FCO 1994; ECO later Vice-Consul Bangkok 1997; FTLT 2000; Band B3; m 2001 Sarah Louise Cooke.

Bamber, Sarah Ann; Second Secretary FCO since March 2001; born 06/01/74; FCO 1996; Second Secretary New York (UKMIS) 1998; Band C4.

Bamford, Victoria Jane; SUPL since February 2001; born 23/12/67; FCO 1989; Moscow 1992; FCO 1995; Nicosia 1996; FCO 1999; Band B3.

Banham, Michael Kent; Consul Palma since September 2001; born 20/09/44; FO 1963; Rawalpindi 1967; Quito 1970; FCO 1974; Tripoli 1976; Nairobi 1980; FCO 1983; Second Secretary (Commercial) Bombay 1987; Second Secretary (Management/Consular) Lima 1990; First Secretary (Management) Riyadh 1994; First Secretary (Management) Cairo 1998; m (1) 1965 Christine Scott (1s 1969; 1d 1971) (diss); (2) 1995 Marie Louise Smith.

Banks, Alison Elizabeth; FCO since April 2000; born 10/01/870; FCO 1992; Canberra 1994; Peking 1998; Band B3.

Banks, Jacinta Mary Catharine (née Cookson); Islamabad since December 1996; born 25/11/57; FCO 1977; Paris 1980; Bombay 1983; FCO 1987; Nicosia 1990; Damascus 1994; Band B3; m 1982 Jamie Paul Banks (1d 1992).

Banks, Jamie Paul; Deputy Head, Asia Pacific, Invest UK March 2001; born 09/06/57; FCO 1977; Paris (UKDEL OECD) 1980; Bombay 1983; FCO 1987; Nicosia 1990; Second Secretary (Commercial) Damascus 1994; Second Secretary (Development) Islamabad 1996; FCO 2000; Band C5; m 1982 Jacinta Mary Catharine Cookson (1d 1992).

Banks, Simon John; Deputy High Commissioner Dar es Salaam since August 1999; born 05/04/66; FCO 1988; Third later Second Secretary (Economic) Warsaw 1990; Language Training 1990; on secondment to DGIA EC Commission Brussels 1993; First Secretary FCO 1996; m 1989 The Hon Rowena Joynson-Hicks (3s 1994, 1996, 1999).

Bannatyne, William Graeme; Lima since May 2000; born 05/03/67; FCO 1988; Canberra 1990; Sofia 1993; FCO 1993; FCO 1995; Full-Time Language Training 2000; Band B3; m 1990 Caterina Prestigiacomo (1d 1995).

Banner, Nick; First Secretary (Information) Brussels since January 2002; born 28/02/74; FCO 1999; First Secretary FCO 2000; Band D6; m 1999 Emma Reisz.

Bannerman, Alexander Campbell; T/D Sana'a since July 2002; born 29/09/67; FCO 1988; Nicosia 1993; FCO 1995; Dubai 1998; Band B3; m 1998 Fiona Vari MacKillop.

Bannister, Irene Marshall; SUPL since August 1993; born 14/03/67; FCO 1988; Lusaka 1990; Band A2.

Baptie, Gavin William; Second Secretary (Immigration) Tehran since November 2000; born 07/11/70; Home Office 1993; FCO 1998; Band C4; m 2000 Caroline Jane Houston.

Barber, Caroline Jane; SUPL since May 1993; born 05/08/856; FCO 1978; Geneva (UKMIS) 1980; Jakarta 1983; FCO 1985; Second Secretary (Chancery/Info) Addis Ababa 1990; Full-Time Language Training 1990; m 1990 Andrew John Barber (2d 1991, 1993).

Barclay, John Hamish; Jedda since June 2000; born 11/09/64; Royal Air Force 1983-92; Department of Transport 1993-95; FCO 1995; Abu Dhabi 1997; Band A2.

Barclay, Philip Jeremy; FCO since January 1999; born 14/10/67; Band C4; m 1996 Emma Robinson.

Barker, Caroline Susan; FCO since July 1999; born 15/09/69; Language Training 1993; Second Secretary (KHF) Bratislava 1994; Second Secretary FCO 1995; SUPL 1997.

Barker, Philip John; Berlin since December 1998; born 18/11/70; FCO 1989; m 1998 Elizabeth Margaret Jean Hindle.

Barker, Rowland Gifford Palgrave; FCO since September 2000; born 06/06/75; Band C4.

Barklamb, Peter Richard; Consul (Head of Post) later Consul-General Amsterdam since November 1998; born 18/07/51; FCO 1970; Delhi 1973; Islamabad 1975; Geneva 1976; Brussels 1978; FCO 1981; Warsaw 1984; Second Secretary (Commercial/Aid) Bridgetown 1989; Second Secretary (Commercial) Riyadh 1991; FCO 1994; Band C5; m 1974 Jane Bosworth (2d 1979, 1981; 1s 1984).

Barlow, Andrew Watson; FCO since October 1987; born 23/12/54; UKAEA 1977; FCO 1978; UKAEA 1981; Private Secretary to Chairman 1983-84; Band D6.

Barlow, Jacqueline; Anguilla since February 2002; born 21/07/47; Berne 1969; FCO 1969; Baghdad 1971; Islamabad 1972; Moscow 1973; Phnom Penh and Hanoi 1975; FCO 1976; Moscow 1977; Floater Duties 1980; FCO 1984; Tokyo 1987; FCO 1990; Vice-Consul Shanghai 1994; Third Secretary (Commercial) Kuwait 1997.

Barlow, Richard David; FCO since September 2000; born 17/01/75; Band C4; ptnr, Silvia Claudia Da Graça.

Barnard, Michael Trevelyan; FCO since October 1995; born 15/12/61; FCO 1986; Dar es Salaam 1989; Bratislava 1993; Band B3; m 1993 Tracy Dawn Clifford.

Barnes, Catherine Eleanor; Human Rights Officer Jakarta since January 1998; born 12/06/68; FCO 1995; Band B3.

Barnes, Nicholas John; First Secretary (Political) Tirana since May 2002; born 25/11/72; FCO 2000; Band D6.

Barnes, Stewart George; First Secretary FCO since February 1991; born 08/07/48; FCO 1967; Tel Aviv 1973; Second Secretary FCO 1980; SUPL 1980; Second later First Secretary Vienna 1987; Band C5; m 1975 Jennifer Mary Windebank (1s 1977; 1d 1979).

Barnes Jones, Deborah Elizabeth Vavasseur (née Barnes); HM Ambassador Tbilisi since April 2001; born 06/10/56; FCO 1980; Moscow 1983; First Secretary on loan to Cabinet Office 1985; Resigned 1986; First Secretary (Chancery) Tel Aviv 1988; Reinstated 1988; First Secretary FCO 1992; Deputy Head of Mission Montevideo 1996; m 1986 Frederick Richard Jones (2d (twins) 1991).

Barnett, Robert William; Counsellor (Review of FCO Science and Technology) since September 1999; born 25/05/54; FCO 1977; Language Training SOAS 1979; Language Student Kamakura 1980; Tokyo 1981; Second later First Secretary FCO 1983; First Secretary (Economic) Bonn 1988; seconded to the State Economics Ministry, Dresden 1992; First Secretary FCO 1993; HM Ambassador Sarajevo 1994; Counsellor (Science Technology and Environment) Bonn 1995; m 1979 Caroline Sara Weale (2s 1982, 1984).

Barnett, Robin Anthony; Head of Joint Entry Clearance Unit later UKVisas (FCO/HO) since January 2002; born 08/03/58; FCO 1980; Third later Second Secretary Warsaw 1982; Second later First Secretary FCO 1985; First Secretary Vienna (UKDEL) 1990; First Secretary New York (UKMIS) 1991; First Secretary FCO 1996; Deputy Head of Mission Warsaw 1998; m (1) 1989 Debra Marianne Bunt (diss 1999) (1step s 1987, 1 s 1990), (2) Tesca Maria Osman (1 step d 1990, 1 step s 1990).

Barnsley, Pamela Margaret; SUPL since November 1999; born 02/06/57; FCO 1982; Second Secretary (Chancery) Brasilia 1983; First Secretary (Comm/Econ) Peking 1987; Trade Commissioner BTC Hong Kong 1989; SUPL 1990; First Secretary FCO 1995; Band D6; m 1986 Perry Neil Keller (1d 1999).

Barr, Richard Barclay; Second Secretary (Press and Public Affairs) July 1997; born 03/05/55; FCO 1975; Freetown 1977; FCO 1980; Prague 1981; Düsseldorf 1983; Accra 1988; FCO 1992; Second Secretary 1994; Full-Time Language Training 1997; m 1977 Jane Anne Greengrass (1s 1978).

Barras, Ian Alexander; FCO since March 1998; born 27/04/50; FCO 1976; Geneva 1979; Peking 1981; Douala 1984; FCO 1986; Athens 1989; FCO

1990; Washington 1991; Third Secretary (Information/Visits) Islamabad 1994; Band B3.

Barratt, Colin Ernest; Third Secretary (Management/Vice-Consul) Banjul since June 1999; born 02/03/62; FCO 1995; Band B3.

Barrett, Douglas Wilson; Second Secretary (Commercial) Shanghai since February 2001; born 28/01/56; HCS 1976; FCO 1978; Brussels (UKREP) 1980; Havana 1983; Latin America Floater 1986; Islamabad 1988; T/D Manila 1992; FCO 1993; T/D Geneva (UKDEL) 1993; Second Secretary/Management Officer/HM Consul Bombay 1996; m 2000 Gayle Viegas.

Barrett, Janet Ceclyn; FCO since May 2000; born 19/12/67; HCS 1988; FCO 1994; Geneva (UKMIS) 1997; Band A2.

Barrett, Jill Mary; Assistant Legal Adviser FCO since 1997; born 06/07/58; Assistant Legal Adviser FCO 1989; First Secretary (Legal) New York (UKMIS) 1994.

Barrett, Richard Martin Donne, OBE (1993); Counsellor FCO since October 1998; born 14/06/49; MOD 1975-81; First Secretary FCO 1982; First Secretary Ankara 1983; First Secretary FCO 1986; First Secretary New York (UKMIS) 1988; First Secretary later Counsellor FCO 1992; Counsellor Amman 1997; m 1973 Irene Hogg (1d 1976; 2s 1980, 1981).

Barrie, Patricia Ann (née Gallagher); FCO since October 1998; born 17/04/65; FCO 1988; Athens 1991; Montevideo 1993; Band A2; m 1993 Alexander Barrie (1d 1995; 1s 1998).

Barron, Elaine Marie; FCO since June 1993; born 30/01/63; FCO 1984; Istanbul 1988; Luxembourg 1991; Phnom Penh 1992; Band B3.

Barros, Lesley Susan; Riyadh since August 2000; born 02/05/60; FCO 1980; Brussels 1981; Havana 1982; Brasilia 1984; FCO 1987; Paris 1990; Tokyo 1993; Gibraltar 1996; Band B3; m 1989 José Barros Filho (2d 1991, 1994)

Barrow, Christine Louise; Lagos since May 1996; born 07/09/71; FCO 1991; Band B3; m 1996 David P J Hills

Barrow, Sarah Jane (née Green); on loan to DTI since March 1995; born 08/06/64; FCO 1982; Paris (UKDEL OECD) 1985; San Jose 1988; FCO 1991; Band B3; m 1989 Diego Leonardo Barrow Clevas (1s 1991)

Barrow, Timothy Earle, LVO (1994); First Secretary Brussels (UKREP) since June 1996; born 15/02/64; FCO 1986; Language Training 1988; Second Secretary (Chancery) Moscow 1990; First Secretary FCO 1993.

Barrs, Neville Stuart; FCO since March 1987; born 20/05/55; FCO 1971; Nairobi 1978; FCO 1980; Dubai 1983; Band C4; m (1) 1978 Alison Chambers; m (2) 1983 Susan Rosemary Walker (1s 1985; 1d 1987).

Barson, Jacqueline Anne, MBE (1995); Olympic Attaché Sydney since September 1999; born 26/05/59; FCO 1979; Prague 1981; Abu Dhabi 1982; Belgrade 1982; Brunei 1985; Geneva (UKMIS) 1986; FCO 1990; Brussels 1992; Copenhagen 1992; Athens 1993; Ottawa 1994; Band C5.

Barter, Craig Alan Roger; FCO since July 2001; born 24/07/69; HCS 1990; FCO 1996; Tehran 1999; Band A2; m 2000 Lilis Purhaniah

Barton, Helen Mary; SUPL since October 1999; born 05/12/65; FCO 1991; Second Secretary (Political) The Hague 1996; m 1996 Alastair Matthew Wright.

Barton, Philip Robert, OBE (1997); Deputy High Commissioner Nicosia since July 2000; born 18/08/63; FCO 1986; Third later Second Secretary Caracas 1987; First Secretary on loan to the Cabinet Office 1991; First Secretary FCO 1993; First Secretary (Political) New Delhi 1994; On loan as Private Secretary to the Prime Minister at No. 10 1997; m (1) 1995 Sabine Friederike Schnittger (diss) (2) 1999 Amanda Joy Bowen

Barton-Appiah, Delsie; Brussels (UKREP) since January 2002; born 18/11/76; FCO 2000; Band A2.

Bassnett, Stephen Andrew, MBE (1983); First Secretary FCO since July 1999; born 24/01/49; Army 1967-86; FCO 1986; First Secretary (Chancery) Cairo 1991; First Secretary FCO 1993; First Secretary (Political) Bahrain 1997; Band D6; m 1980 Judith Christine Anne Whitty.

Bastin, Suzanne Sarah (née Baxter); Dubai since September 2000; born 03/07/69; Home Office 1989; Home Office 1994; Bombay 1994; Peking 1996; FCO 2000; Band B3; m 1998 David Richard Bastin

Bateman, Peter; Counsellor (Commercial) Tokyo since March 1998; born 23/12/55; FCO 1984; Language Training Tokyo 1986; Second later First Secretary Tokyo 1987; First Secretary FCO 1991; First Secretary (Commercial) Berlin 1993; FCO 1997; m 1985 Andrea Subercaseaux-Peters (2s 1987, 1990;1d 1992).

Bates, Anthony Michael, MVO (1994); First Secretary (Management) and Consul Berne since August 2001; born 12/11/58; FCO 1978; Islamabad 1980; Wellington 1982; FCO 1987; Private Secretary Bonn 1990; Language Training 1990; Cayman Islands 1993; Second Secretary FCO 1996; Band C5; m 1985 Colette Ann Stewart (2d 1988, 1992).

Bates, Michael Charles, OBE (1994); Consul-General Atlanta since April 2001; born 09/04/48; DSAO later FCO 1966; Delhi 1971; Third Secretary Moscow 1974; Second Secretary FCO 1977; Second later First Secretary Singapore 1979; First Secretary (Inf/Chancery) Brussels 1983; On loan to No.10 Downing Street 1987; First Secretary FCO 1990; First Secretary Riga 1991; Chargé d'Affaires later HM Ambassador

Bratislava 1993; First Secretary FCO 1995; Deputy High Commissioner Bombay 1996; m 1971 Janice Kwan Foh Yin (1d 1977; 1s 1978)

Bates, Nicholas Hilary; Counsellor FCO since August 2001; born 05/02/49; Third later Second Secretary FCO 1973; Language Training 1976; FCO 1977; First Secretary Geneva (UKMIS) 1979; FCO 1983; Cairo 1984; First Secretary FCO 1988; First Secretary (Chancery) Muscat 1989; First Secretary FCO 1993; Counsellor (Regional Affairs) Kingston 1996; FCO 1997; Counsellor (Regional Affairs) Kampala 1998; m 1971 Rosemary Jane Seaton (3d 1973, 1975, 1976)

Batson, Philip David; Second later First Secretary FCO since October 1997; born 26/06/68; FCO 1987; Bombay 1991; Third Secretary Paris 1995.

Battson, Andrew John; SUPL since December 2000; born 08/05/66; FCO 1984; Bombay 1991; Bonn 1995; Port of Spain 1997; Band C4; m 1993 Andrea Jaun.

Batty, Simon Robert; Second Secretary Athens since September 2000; born 30/09/62; FCO 1982; New Delhi 1985; FCO 1989; Cairo 1990; Second Secretary FCO 1993; Second Secretary Bogotá 1997; Band C4; m 1991 Sharon Morris (1d 1996, 1s 1998).

Batty-Smith, Katharine Amelia Louise; Prague since December 1999; born 19/08/64; FCO 1984; Budapest 1986; Brasilia 1988; Floater Duties 1992; On loan to DTI 1994; Vice-Consul Sana'a 1997; Band B3.

Bavinton, Sharon Jayne (née Vince); FCO since January 1999; born 17/12/58; FCO 1979; New York (UKMIS) 1981; FCO 1983; Canberra 1984; FCO 1987; Abu Dhabi 1989; FCO 1993; Overseas Inspectorate 1995; Band B3; m 1982 Russell Alexander Bavinton (diss 1992).

Baxendale, James Lloyd; First Secretary FCO since December 2001; born 23/02/67; FCO 1991; Language Training 1993; Language Training Cairo 1994; Second Secretary FCO 1995; First Secretary (Political) Amman 1997; First Secretary (Political) Brussels 1999; Band D6; m 1996 Valerie Nathalie Bouchet (1s 2001)

Baxter, Alison Jane; Canberra since July 1993; born 15/05/67; FCO 1990; Islamabad 1992; Band B3.

Baxter Amade, Vicki Louise; FCO since September 2000; born 18/03/63; FCO 1982; T/D Luxembourg 1983; Lisbon 1984; Maputo 1987; FCO 1990; Khartoum 1993; Canberra 1996; Band B3; m 1990 Amade Chababe Amade (diss 2000) (1s 1992).

Bayliss, Jill Elizabeth (née Hooper); Moscow since May 1998; born 03/08/68; FCO 1989; Colombo 1995; Band B3; m 1994 (Buster) IHW Bayliss.

Beach, Louise Eleanor (née Horwood); FCO since July 1995; born 27/03/68; FCO 1989; New York (UKMIS) 1991; Nicosia 1993; PA/DHM Athens 1995; Second Secretary (Political) The Hague 1996; FCO 1998; Band A2; m 1998 Charles Beach.

Beal, Gordon Kenneth; FCO since September 1988; born 21/10/53; MAFF 1978; FCO 1980; Port of Spain 1981; Paris 1983; Kuwait 1986; Band A2.

Beale, Gideon David; First Secretary Bucharest since August 2002; born 09/07/62; FCO 1986; Third Secretary/Vice-Consul Athens 1990; Second Secretary FCO 1994; First Secretary (Political) Lagos later Abuja 1995; First Secretary FCO 1999; Band D6.

Beats, Lesley; FCO since July 1998; born 01/04/65; Prague 1989; Brussels (UKREP) 1991; Phnom Penh 1994; Brussels (UKREP) 1996; FCO 1998; Band B3.

Beattie, Phoebe; Brussels since April 1998; born 25/11/59; FCO 1984; Bangkok 1985; Stanley 1988; Floater Duties 1989; FCO 1993; Jakarta 1994; Band B3.

Beaumont, David Colin Baskcomb; High Commissioner Gaborone since November 1994; born 16/08/42; CRO 1961; Nairobi 1965; Bahrain 1967; Second Secretary 1969; FCO 1970; Second Secretary (Commercial) Accra 1974; First Secretary FCO 1977; First Secretary (Aid) Kathmandu 1981; First Secretary and Head of Chancery Addis Ababa 1983; First Secretary later Counsellor FCO 1986; m 1965 Barbara Morris (1d 1970; 2s 1972, 1973).

Beaven, Keith Andrew; First Secretary FCO since August 1997; born 07/01/61; FCO 1983; Third later Second Secretary (Chancery) Mexico City 1986; First Secretary FCO 1988; First Secretary (Political) Pretoria 1993; Band D6; m 1986 Jane Marion Wells (1s 1996, 1d 1999)

Beckett, Alison Joan; Second Secretary (Political) Bucharest since March 1999; born 01/07/61; FCO 1989; Third Secretary (Management/Cons) Kiev 1992; Paris (UKDEL OECD) 1996; Band C4.

Beckford, Charles Francis Houghton; First Secretary (Political) Nicosia since October 1999; born 04/11/63; FCO 1991; First Secretary (Political) Islamabad 1993; First Secretary FCO 1995; Band D6; m 1993 Clare Elizabeth Stourton (twin s 1997, 1d 1999).

Beckingham, Peter; Consul-General Sydney since August 1999; born 16/03/49; BOTB 1974; Director New York (BIS) 1979; First Secretary FCO 1983; First Secretary (Commercial) Stockholm 1988; First Secretary later Head of Political Section Canberra 1992; Director Joint Export Promotion Directorate (FCO/DTI) 1996; m 1975 Jill Mary Trotman (2d 1980, 1982).

Bedford, Adrian Frederick; First Secretary and Deputy Head of Mission Beirut since December 1999; born 30/10/56; Land Registry 1975; FCO 1976; Islamabad 1978; Hanoi 1981; Johannesburg 1982; FCO 1985; Bogota 1988; Second later First

Secretary FCO 1992; Tehran 1996; Band D6; m 1995 Alexandra Pamela Cole.

Bedford, Andrew Kenneth; Lagos since May 1995; born 18/02/71; Band B3; m 1994 Samantha Louise Stevens

Bedingfield, Julian Peter; Deputy Head of Mission Ljubljana since December 1999; born 23/07/45; FO 1964; Language Training 1968; Scientific Attaché Moscow 1969; Düsseldorf 1971; FCO 1971; Bonn 1973; Second Secretary (Commercial) Dacca 1975; Ulaanbaatar 1977; FCO 1978; Second Secretary (Admin) and Consul Berne 1982; Second Secretary (Chancery/Inf) Rabat 1986; Second later First Secretary FCO 1992; First Secretary Brussels UKDEL NATO 1994; First Secretary and DHM Ljubljana 1999; m 1975 Margery Mary Jones Davies (2d 1979, 1984; 1s 1982).

Bee, Stephanie Louise, MBE; Third Secretary and Vice-Consul Yerevan since June 2001; born 27/01/67; FCO 1986; Warsaw 1988; Brussels (UKDEL) 1988; Moscow 1992; FCO 1995; Hong Kong 1998; Band B3.

Beer, Nicholas James Gilbert; Counsellor (Regional Affairs) Buenos Aires since June 1999; born 06/12/47; Second Secretary FCO 1976; Nairobi 1977; FCO 1979; First Secretary Madrid 1982; First Secretary FCO 1986; First Secretary later Counsellor (Political) The Hague 1992; FCO 1996; m 1975 Diana Eva Brooke (diss 1996) (1d 1977, 1s 1980).

Beer, Nicola Geraldine (née Calvert); Second Secretary Dubai since January 2002; born 21/06/67; FCO 1985; Nicosia 1988; Resigned 1990; Reinstated 1996; Band C4; m 1999 Andrew John Beer (1d 2000).

Beeson, Richard John; Full-time Language Training since June 1996; born 07/06/54; FCO 1973; East Berlin 1975; Damascus 1976; FCO 1977; Brussels (UKREP) 1978; Peking 1980; FCO 1983; Tripoli 1984; FCO 1986; Singapore 1988; Third Secretary (Management) and Vice Consul Hamburg 1991; Second Secretary FCO 1994; m (1) 1978 Kim Margaret Cotter; (2) 1989 Elizabeth Ann Allin.

Begbie, James Alexander; Deputy Consul General Istanbul since May 1999; born 10/12/53; FCO 1973; Bahrain 1975; Middle Eastern Floater 1979; FCO 1980; Tunis 1983; Shanghai 1986; Third later Second Secretary (Comm) Muscat 1989; FCO 1993; Band B3; m 1980 Janice Isobel Mills (1s 1984, 1d 1985)

Begbie, Janice Isobel (née Mills); Istanbul since October 1999; born 18/04/51; FCO 1971; Lusaka 1973; FCO 1975; Middle East Floater 1977; FCO 1980; SUPL 1983; Muscat 1989; SUPL 1993; FCO 1994; Second Secretary 1996; SUPL 1999; m 1980 James Alexander Begbie (1s 1984, 1d 1985).

Belcher, Patrick Fred; Beijing since April 2002; born 25/08/48; Royal Air Force 1965-90; LCD 1990-92; Prague 1992; Moscow 1994; World-wide

Floater Duties 1996; Hong Kong 1998; Band B3; m 1971 Ann Carr (1s 1977).

Belfitt, Sandra Jane; Port Louis since April 2002; born 14/03/65; HM Customs and Excise 1986-93; FCO 1996; Brasilia 1997; Band A2; m 1984 Andrew Belfitt (1d 1990, 1s 1993)

Belgrove, David Raymond; Ottawa since April 1998; born 18/01/62; FCO 1982; Prague 1984; Kuwait 1986; FCO 1991; Third Secretary (Consular/Economic) Calcutta 1994; Band C4; m 1985 Mette Ofstad (2d 1986, 1989).

Bell, Alan Douglas; Phnom Penh since March 2001; born 26/05/72; FCO 1995; Madrid 1997; Band A2.

Bell, Anne-Marie; Lima since November 1988; born 12/02/68; FCO 1993; Seoul 1996; Band A2.

Bell, Harvey Spencer; Second Secretary (Consular/Management) Calcutta since January 1999; born 07/07/45; Royal Navy 1960-72; FCO 1972; Bonn 1975; Peking 1977; Wellington 1980; FCO 1982; Mogadishu 1985; Milan 1988; FCO 1991; DTI 1993; Lagos 1995; m 1978 Wendy Lydia Frances Ellis.

Bell, Jeremy Paul Turnbull; First Secretary (UN) Nairobi since July 1998; born 04/01/52; FCO 1974; The Hague 1976; Bahrain 1981; Hanoi 1982; FCO 1985; Tokyo 1988; Third Secretary (Management/Cons) Gaborone 1992; Second Secretary FCO 1996; Band C5; m (1) 1978 Jane Dorron Lee (diss 1981) (2) 1991 Setsuko Yamamoto (1d 1995)

Bell, Julie Dawn (née Raines); Second Secretary (Management/Consular) Lilongwe since March 2001; born 12/11/66; FCO 1989; Language Training 1990; Moscow 1991; Budapest 1994; Belgrade 1995; Second Secretary FCO 1997; m 1991 Andrew Michael Bell (2d 1993, 1997).

Bell, Karen Ann (née Norris); Second Secretary (Commercial) Abuja since August 1999; born 22/04/66; FCO 1983; Strasbourg 1986; New Delhi 1988; FCO 1991; Ottawa 1996; Band C5; m 1987 Adrian Bell (2s 1993, 1996).

Bell, Kay Beverley; Colombo since January 2002; born 11/06/57; FCO 1984; Bonn 1986; Floater Duties 1989; New York (UKMIS) 1993; Band A2.

Bell, Laura (née Page); FCO since April 2000; born 06/09/69; FCO 1995; Algiers 1997; Bridgetown 1998; SUPL 1999; Band A2; m 1999 Ian McDonald Bell.

Bell, Mark Robert; Full-Time Language Training Cairo since June 1999; born 04/05/71; FCO 1997; Band B3.

Bell, Melvin, MBE (2002); New York (UKMIS) since November 1999; born 14/05/65; FCO 1984; Madrid 1987; FCO 1990; Third Secretary Mexico City 1993; FCO 1997; Band C4; m 1997 Maria Louisa Toxtle de Bautista.

Bell, Samantha Jane; Athens since April 1999; born 01/10/71; FCO 1997; Band A2.

Bellas, David Livingston; FCO since September 2000; born 06/11/74; Band C4.

Bellerby, Julie; FCO since September 1985; born 26/11/60; Band A1; m 1986 Andrew Patrick Myers.

Bellham, Richard Anthony; FCO since 1998; born 26/01/50; HM Forces (Army) 1968 -74; FCO 1976; Bangkok 1986; FCO 1989; Tokyo 1995; Band C5; m 1987 Chidphan Jaiprasat (1d 1989).

Belof, Margaret Mary; Third Secretary (Economic) Athens since December 1998; born 06/09/61; FCO 1990; Third Secretary Bucharest 1994; Band B3.

Bendor, David Ian; First Secretary (Financial & Economic) Paris since March 1999; born 14/03/66; Economic Advisers FCO 1991-96; T/D Paris 1993; On secondment to IMF (European Division) 1996-98; Band D6.

Benjamin, Jon; FCO since May 2000; born 19/01/63; ODA 1986; Third later Second Secretary Jakarta 1988; First Secretary FCO 1992; Private Secretary to Minister of State FCO 1993; Full-Time Language Training 1995; Ankara 1996; SUPL 1999; Band D7.

Bennett, Alexander; Paris since January 1998; born 04/11/67; FCO 1987; Band C4; m 1997 Deborah Karen Stirzaker (1d 2001).

Bennett, Brian Maurice; Deputy Head of Mission Tunis since May 1997; born 01/04/48; FCO 1971; Prague 1973; Helsinki 1977; Second Secretary FCO 1979; Second Secretary (Comm/Aid) Bridgetown 1983; Second later First Secretary Vienna (UKDEL) MBFR 1986; First Secretary (Chancery/Inf) The Hague 1988; First Secretary FCO 1992; m 1969 Lynne Skipsey (3s 1974, 1978, 1991)

Bennett, Frederick Michael; Belgrade since February 2002; born 07/12/49; Royal Military Police 1967-92; Prague 1992; Floater Duties 1994; Peking 1997; FCO 1997; Band B3; m 1978 Lynne Louise Jane Russell (2d 1979, 1980)

Bennett, Marylyn; Second Secretary (Chancery) Lilongwe since November 1996; born 16/12/48; New Delhi 1972; Monrovia 1974; FCO 1977; South America Floater 1979; FCO 1982; Floater Duties 1983; Panama City 1986; Second Secretary FCO 1988; Deputy Head of Mission Asuncion 1993.

Bennett, Stephen Paul; FCO since October 1997; born 28/10/62; FCO 1982; Nairobi 1986; FCO 1990; SUPL 1993; FCO 1994; Moscow 1995; Band A2; m 1990 Stephanie Cattermole (1 step d 1986, 1s 1991).

Bennett-Dixon, Vanessa May (née Bennett); Paris since July 2001; born 12/01/57; FCO 1975; Nairobi 1978; Havana 1981; Kuwait 1982; Montserrat 1988; Stanley 1992; Hanoi 1994; Luanda 1996; Band A2; m 1987 Ronald William Dixon.

Bensberg, Jacqueline Margaret (née Campbell); Third Secretary (Political) Brussels since November 1998; born 06/06/63; FCO 1983; Cape Town/Pretoria 1985; UKDEL CSCE 1987; Third Secretary UKDEL CFE 1989; FCO 1990; Accra 1994; Accra 1994; FCO 1997; Band B3; m 1991 Mark Bensberg (1d 1999).

Bensberg, Mark; Second Secretary (Political/Press & Public Affairs) Brussels since October 1997; born 19/07/62; FCO 1980; Paris 1982; Africa/ME Floater 1985; Vice-Consul Vienna 1988; FCO 1991; Accra 1994; m 1991 Jacqueline Margaret Campbell (1d 1999).

Berg, Geoffrey, MVO (1976); Consul-General Toronto since January 2002; born 05/07/45; CRO 1963; DSA 1965; LA Floater Duties 1968; Second Secretary 1970; Bucharest 1970; FCO 1971; Second later First Secretary (Inf) Helsinki 1975; FCO 1979; First Secretary (Commercial) Madrid 1984; First Secretary FCO 1988; Counsellor on loan to the DTI 1990; Deputy Head of Mission Mexico City 1993; Deputy Consul General and Director of Trade New York 1997; m 1970 Sheila Maxine Brown (1s 1975)

Berman, Paul Richard; Legal Counsellor Brussels (UKREP) since August 2002; born 23/11/64; Called to the Bar, Gray's Inn 1990; Assistant later Senior Assistant Legal Adviser FCO 1991; Seconded to the International Committee of the Red Cross, Geneva 1996; FCO 1998; Legal Counsellor on loan to the Attorney General's Chambers (LSLO) 2000.

Berry, Susanna Gisela; SUPL since September 1997; born 06/09/62; FCO 1986; Second Secretary Vienna (UKDEL) 1989; Second Secretary (Economic) Vienna 1990; Full-Time Language Training 1992; Full-Time Language Training Cairo 1993; FCO 1994; Band D6; m 1996 Paul Adams (1s 1999)

Bersin, Jacqueline; First Secretary (Management/Consular) Singapore since November 1999; born 13/08/58; FCO 1977; SUPL 1978; Islamabad 1979; SUPL 1980; FCO 1981; Rome 1982; Warsaw 1983; FCO 1985; Port Louis 1988; Montserrat 1993; Second Secretary FCO 1995; Band C5; m 1990 Alan Maurice Bersin

Bertie, Julie Karina (née Finnigan); SUPL since October 1999; born 08/06/71; FCO 1990; Nairobi 1996; Band A2; m 1995 Stewart Valentine Bertie (2d 1998, 2000).

Bertie, Stewart Valentine; Paris since October 1999; born 19/02/66; FCO 1986; Geneva (UKMIS) 1992; FCO 1995; SUPL 1996; Band A2; m 1995 Julie Karina Finnigan (2d 1998,2000).

Best, Christopher Davey; Second later First Secretary FCO since August 1989; born 03/08/47; Army 1966-69; FCO 1969; Muscat 1971; Jedda 1973; FCO 1974; Sana'a 1975; FCO 1976; Hong Kong 1981; Second Secretary Lagos 1986; Band C5; m 1971 Mary Elizabeth Cannon (4d 1977, 1979, 1981, 1982)

Best, Eleanor Marion; Copenhagen since May 2000; born 28/04/63; MOD 1986-89; FCO 1996; Brussels 1997; Band A2.

Bethel, Samantha Claire Risby; Pro Consul Düsseldorf since July 1997; born 25/02/70; FCO 1990; Jakarta 1993; Band A2.

Betterton, Judith Anne; Ankara since September 2002; born 02/08/57; FCO 1983; Warsaw 1984; Lilongwe 1987; Bogota 1989; Canberra 1991; FCO 1994; Amman 1998; Band B3.

Bevan, Howard James; Pro Consul Düsseldorf since August 2000; born 19/11/54; Royal Signals 1970-92; FCO 1995; Brussels (UKREP) 1997; Band A2; m 1973 Christine (1d 1975, 1s 1986).

Bevan, James David; FCO since July 1998; born 13/07/59; FCO 1982; Kinshasa 1984; Second later First Secretary Brussels (UKDEL) 1986; First Secretary FCO 1990; First Secretary Paris 1993; First Secretary (Political) Washington 1994; m 1984 Alison Janet Purdie (3d 1986, 1989, 1998)

Bevan, Terence Richard; First Secretary FCO since May 1992; born 10/04/54; FCO 1970; Bonn 1977; FCO 1980; Second later First Secretary Oslo 1988; Band C5; m 1978 Gillian Margaret Francis (2d 1981, 1984)

Bewley, Sarah Margaret; Second Secretary FCO since May 1999; born 05/08/73; FCO 1995; Kuala Lumpur 1997; Band C4.

Beynon, Debra Jane; FCO since February 2002; born 22/07/62; Department of Transport 1978; Department of Employment 1979; FCO 1983; Berlin BMG 1985; Kingstown 1988; Dhaka 1989; FCO 1993; Second Secretary (Immigration/Consular) Dhaka 1995; Second later First Secretary (Immigration) Islamabad 1998; Band C5; m 1985 Paul Ogwyn Beynon.

Bibby, Sue Wendy; FCO since August 1994; born 12/01/67; MOD 1986; Band A2.

Bicker, David Alan; Anguilla since November 1998; born 25/10/48; Army 1966-88; Brussels (UKDEL) 1989; Cairo 1991; FCO 1994; Tirana 1996; Band B3; m 1974 Molly Patricia (1d 1976; 2s 1978, 1983).

Bickers, Esméá Lillian; FCO since June 2000; born 18/12/54; FCO 1988; Ottawa 1989; FCO 1992; The Hague 1997; Band A2.

Bielby, Richard Stephen; Full-Time Language Training since November 1999; born 18/09/65; FCO (HCS) 1989; FCO 1991; Islamabad 1993; FCO 1997; Band B3.

Biggerstaff, Sarah Jane; SUPL since September 2002; born 04/11/70; FCO 1997; Budapest 1998; FCO 2000; Band A2.

Bilimoria, Tehemton Pirosha; Second Secretary Nairobi since August 2000; born 21/01/46; HM Forces (Army) 1964-70; PO 1970-76; FCO 1979; Washington 1984; FCO 1987; Paris 1992; Band C5; m 1980 Tayariez Dastoor (1d 1984; 1s 1986).

Billing, Victoria Elizabeth; Rangoon since June 1999; born 31/05/75; FCO 1997; SOAS University of London 1998; Band C4.

Billinger, Claire Louise; SUPL since September 2002; born 15/06/72; FCO 1990; Hong Kong 1995; FCO 1996; Vienna 1998; FCO 2001; Band A2.

Binfield, Marella Jane; FCO since May 2002; born 12/01/69; FCO 1995; Warsaw 1996; Band A2.

Binnie, Serena Clare; FCO since October 1990; born 04/09/63; FCO 1986; Montevideo 1989; Band C4.

Binns, Angela Jane; New Delhi since December 1993; born 25/06/69; MOD 1988-90; FCO 1990; Band A2.

Birch, Ann Elizabeth (née Ridge); FCO since January 2000; born 23/10/62; FCO 1990; New Delhi 1992; FCO 1995; Hanoi 1997; Band B3; m 1996 Paul David Birch.

Bird, Charles Philip Glover; First Secretary (Political) Abuja since August 2001; born 08/10/54; Second Secretary FCO 1986; Language Training 1987; Language Training Cairo 1988; Second Secretary (Chancery) Abu Dhabi 1989; Second Secretary Belgrade 1992; Second later First Secretary FCO 1993; First Secretary (Political) Athens 1995; m 1975 Clare St. John (2s 1978, 1980; 1d 1982).

Bird, Christabel Helen; Second later First Secretary FCO since May 1993; born 18/11/53; Tehran 1978; FCO 1979; Caracas 1980; FCO 1982; Second Secretary Geneva (UKMIS) 1989; Consul Geneva 1990; Band C5.

Bird, Juliette Winsome; First Secretary (Political) Brussels since April 2001; born 04/10/63; FCO 1990; New Delhi 1992; Second later First Secretary FCO 1994; Band D6; m 2002 Donald Peter Scargill (1s 2002).

Birks, Ian Martin; Second Secretary (Commercial) New Delhi since August 1997; born 03/06/52; FCO 1971; Canberra 1973; Belgrade 1976; Georgetown 1978; New York 1981; FCO 1984; Islamabad 1988; Second Secretary (Aid) Lagos 1992; Second Secretary FCO 1994; m (1) 1976 Sheridan Elizabeth Grice (diss 1997) (2d 1987, 1991); (2) Anny Bhatti 1997 (1d 1999).

Bish, Michael William; Second Secretary FCO since January 1992; born 03/12/42; CRO 1964; DSAO 1965; Rawalpindi 1966; Bonn 1970; FCO 1972; Brussels (JAO) 1976; Wellington 1979; Second Secretary FCO 1982; Second Secretary (Commercial) Johannesburg 1987; m 1966 Patricia June Bedingfield

Bishop, Peter George; FCO since January 2002; born 23/11/55; Home Civil Service 1984; Bonn 1998; Band B3; m 1983 Fiona Christine Buchanan (2s 1988, 1992).

Biskin, Sally-Ann (née Peters); Second Secretary (Management) Islamabad since June 2001; born 08/02/65; FCO 1983; Brussels 1985; Harare 1988; Lagos 1989; Maputo 1989; Istanbul 1990; FCO 1993; SUPL 1994; FCO 1994; SUPL 1997; FCO 1998; Band C4; m 1991 Cneyt Cem Biskin (diss) (2d 1992, 1994)

Blackburn, Derek; Second later First Secretary FCO since August 1982; born 06/12/44; GPO 1961; FO (later FCO) 1968; Beirut 1969; FCO 1972; Islamabad 1973; FCO 1974; Washington 1979; Band C4; m 1967 Dorothy Margaret Fawcett (1s 1968, 1d 1972).

Blackburne, Alison; First Secretary (Political) Stockholm since April 2000; born 20/06/64; FCO 1987; Third later First Secretary (Chancery) Warsaw 1989; First Secretary FCO 1992; First Secretary New York (UKMIS) 1996; Band D6.

Blacker, Catherine Louise; T/D Islamabad since April 2000; born 15/09/68; FCO 1989; Brussels (UKDEL) 1991; FCO 1997; Band B3.

Blackwell, Christopher Robert; Second Secretary FCO since May 1984; born 11/08/58; FCO 1975; Geneva (UKMIS) 1978; FCO 1981; Aden 1983; Band C4; m 1982 Catherine Rose Gallagher (1d 1987, 1s 1989).

Bladen, John; Second Secretary FCO since February 1987; born 08/07/44; FCO 1971; Bangkok 1973; FCO 1975; Accra 1976; FCO 1979; Kingston 1980; FCO 1983; Second Secretary Harare 1984; m 1969 Nina Shaw (1d 1972).

Blair, Camilla Frances Mary; First Secretary FCO since November 1994; born 23/11/66; FCO 1988; Full-Time Language Training 1990; Third later Second Secretary Prague 1991; m 2000 Colin Roberts.

Blair, Katherine; Full-Time Language Training since August 1997; born 11/02/69; FCO 1988; Tokyo 1989; Colombo 1992; Peking 1993; Band B3.

Blake, Michael David; Head of Technical Group (Implementation) FCO Services since October 2001; born 19/01/55; FCO 1971; HCS 1976; FCO 1978; Washington 1979; Ottawa 1981; FCO 1981; FCO 1984; FCO Services 1999; m 1978 Audrey Layfield (1s 1983).

Blake, Michael John Warwick; Consul (Political/Economic) Hong Kong since December 2000; born 05/03/75; FCO 1997; Full-Time Language Training Peking 1999; Band C4.

Blake, Stanley Clement; Second Secretary (Consular/Immigration) Accra since October 1993; born 14/07/44; FO 1964; UK delegation NATO Paris and Brussels 1966; Amman 1969; FCO 1970; Moscow 1974; Paris 1975; FCO 1978; Tunis 1981; Second Secretary (Admin) and Consul Muscat 1984; Second Secretary 1984; Second Secretary FCO 1988; Second Secretary (Management) Addis Ababa 1991; Second

Secretary FCO 1992; m (1) Marion Lesley Jelly (diss 1972) (1s 1968); (2) 1977 Lindsay Jane Townsend (1s 1981).

Blakemore, John Laurence; First Secretary and Consul Lisbon since December 2000; born 21/01/44; RAF 1961-69; FCO 1969; Mexico City 1972; Caracas 1975; FCO 1978; On loan to DoE 1979; Second Secretary Buenos Aires 1981; Second Secretary (Commercial) Madrid 1982; Second later FirstSecretary 1986; First Secretary (Commercial) Milan 1990; Consul Palma 1994; m 1967 Joan Eileen Black (2s 1972,1974).

Blanchard, William Hume James, OBE (1997); MVO (1993); First Secretary FCO since November 2001; born 08/01/67; FCO 1988; Second Secretary (Information) Budapest 1992; Second Secretary FCO 1995; SUPL 1997; First Secretary (Chancery) Islamabad 1998; Band D6; m 1998 Meriel Beattie (1s 2000).

Blogg, David John; Second Secretary (Management) T/D Ljubljana since April 2002; born 08/09/48; FCO 1971; East Berlin 1973; Khartoum 1974; Dacca 1977; FCO 1979; Calcutta 1981; Baghdad 1982; Jedda 1983; Athens 1986; Second Secretary Tripoli 1989; Second Secretary FCO 1991; Second Secretary (Management/Consular) Sana'a 1993; Second Secretary Ulaanbaatar 1994; Second Secretary FCO 1995; Second Secretary Lima 1996; Consul (Management) St Petersburg 1997; Second Secretary FCO 1998; m 1973 Susan Robinia Meloy.

Bloomfield, Keith George; HM Ambassador Kathmandu since July 2002; born 02/06/47; HCS 1969-80; Brussels (UKREP) 1980; First Secretary FCO 1985; Head of Chancery Cairo 1987; Counsellor, Consul-General and Deputy Head of Mission Algiers 1990; Counsellor (Political/Management) Rome 1994; Minister and Deputy Head of Mission Rome 1996; FCO 1998; m 1976 Geneviève Paule (3d 1979, 1982, 1985).

Blows, Glyn Christopher; FCO since April 1999; born 27/08/70; FCO 1990; Nicosia 1995; Band A2; (1d 2001).

Bloxham, Siân Landis; Bandar Seri Begawan since July 2000; born 11/11/64; HCS 1990; FCO 1996; St Petersburg 1998; Band A2.

Blunt, David Graeme, LVO (1986); Deputy Governor Gibraltar since January 2002; born 19/01/53; FCO 1978; Second later First Secretary Vienna 1979; First Secretary (External Affairs) Peking 1983; FCO 1987; First Secretary (Chancery) Canberra 1989; Counsellor FCO 1994; Deputy Head of Mission and Consul-General Oslo 1997; m 1975 Geirid Bakkeli (3s 1982,1984, 1990).

Blyth, Fraser Alexander; SUPL since May 1999; born 07/06/69; FCO 1990; Sofia 1994; Peking 1996; Band B3; m 1994 Deborah Robertson

Boam, Rachel Christine (née Wickens); PA/Ambassador Berlin since May 2000; born

05/11/68; FCO 1988; New York (UKMIS) 1991; PA/Deputy Head of Mission Athens 1995; FCO 1998; Language Training 1999; SUPL 1999; Band A2; m 1993 Jason Daniel Boam (1s 1999).

Boardman, Clarence Ronald; Deputy High Commissioner Head of Mission Bandar Seri Begawan since July 1995; born 11/12/48; DSAO1/FCO 1965; Algiers 1970; Ottawa 1972; Warsaw 1974; FCO 1977; MECAS 1978; Aden 1979; Riyadh 1982; Second Secretary FCO 1986; Consul (Commercial) Vancouver 1989; m 1973 Marion Lynn Fraser (1s 1991).

Boardman, Sarah Christine; Floater Duties since June 1996; born 17/08/67; FCO 1990; Third Secretary (UN) Geneva (UKMIS) 1993; Band D6.

Boffa, Sandra Jean (née issac); Vienna since November 1999; born 22/08/67; Ministry of Agriculture 1984-90; FCO 1990; Tokyo 1995; FCO 1998; Band A2; m 1992 Anthony Paul Vincent Boffa (1d 1993, 2s 1994, 1998).

Bolton, Ada Winefride; Copenhagen since March 1997; born 26/12/44; Jakarta 1973; Rangoon 1978; FCO 1980; Sanaa 1988; Lagos 1989; Brussels (UKDEL) 1992; FCO 1996; Band A2.

Bond, Clare Elizabeth; Second Secretary FCO since October 2001; born 17/01/75; FCO 1997; Second Secretary (Political) Kuala Lumpur 1999; Band C4.

Bond, Ian Andrew Minton; Counsellor Vienna (UKDEL) OSCE since June 2000; born 19/04/62; FCO 1984; Third later Second Secretary (Political) Brussels (UKDEL NATO) 1987; First Secretary FCO 1990; First Secretary (Political) Moscow 1993; First Secretary FCO 1996; m 1987 Kathryn Joan Ingamells (1d 1989, 1s 1993).

Bond, Simon; Dakar since March 2000; born 23/04/65; Home Office 1988-89; FCO 1989; Port of Spain 1993; Kampala 1997; FCO 1999; Band C4.

Bone, Roger Bridgland, CMG (1996); HM Ambassador Brasilia since September 1999; born 29/07/44; Third Secretary New York (UKMIS) 1966; FCO 1967; Stockholm 1968; Third later Second Secretary FCO 1970; First Secretary Moscow 1973; First Secretary FCO 1975; First Secretary Brussels (UKREP) 1978; Asst Private Secretary to the Secretary of State FCO 1982; Centre of International Affairs, Harvard University 1984; Counsellor and later Head of Chancery Washington 1985; Counsellor FCO 1989; AUSS FCO 1991; HM Ambassador Stockholm 1995; m 1970 Lena Marianne Bergman (1s 1977, 1 d 1980).

Bonnici, Gail Margaret; SUPL since December 1997; born 11/12/60; FCO 1984; Madrid 1985; LA Floater 1988; Valetta 1989; FCO 1991; Riyadh 1992; Buenos Aires 1996; Band A2; m 1990 Martin Mario Bonnici (1s 1991).

Bonsey, Jennifer Elaine; Bucharest since January 2001; born 23/12/46; MOD 1964; FCO 1981;

Paris 1982; Tunis 1985; Brussels (UKREP) 1988; FCO 1989; Singapore 1997; Band B3.

Booker, Jacqueline Alice; FCO since June 1997; born 19/01/62; FCO 1982; Athens 1984; Hanoi 1987; LA Floater 1988; FCO 1992; Dar es Salaam 1995; Band B3.

Booth, Mark James; Hong Kong since November 1998; born 13/03/72; FCO 1991; Geneva (UKMIS) 1995; Band A2.

Booth, Susan Jane (née Corcoran); FCO since March 1996; born 03/08/68; FCO 1986; New York (UNGA) (UKMIS) 1988; Cape Town/Pretoria 1989; Warsaw 1991; Rabat 1993; Band B3; m 1991 Rodney James Booth.

Borland, David; First Secretary Helsinki (EU) since January 2000; born 20/06/60; on loan to DTI Second Secretary FCO 1991; T/D Second Secretary (Political) Maputo 1993; Second Secretary (Political) Caracas 1994; First Secretary (Political/Economic) Mexico City 1995; Band D6.

Borley, Salud Maria Victoria; FCO since August 1998; born 06/05/70; FCO 1989; Caracas 1992; Floater Duties 1996; Band B3.

Bossley, Edward; FCO since November 1999; born 22/09/71; FCO 1991; New York (UKMIS) 1994; Islamabad 1997; Band B3; m 1994 Stefany Elizabeth Rocque (1d 1997).

Bossley, Stefany Elizabeth (née Rocque); FCO since April 1999; born 28/07/66; FCO 1989; World-wide Floater Duties 1992; New York (UKMIS) 1994; Islamabad 1997; Band B3; m 1994 Edward Bossley (1d 1997).

Boswell, Clive Timothy; Washington since December 2001; born 29/08/70; FCO 1996; Brussels (UKREP) 1998; Band A2.

Botha, Caroline Jane; Attaché (Immig/Cons) Colombo since August 2000; born 01/04/70; FCO 1996; Bratislava 1997; Band B3; m 1993 Peter Bortha (1d 1994, 1s 1998).

Bottomley, Patricia Fiona; First Secretary (Political) Rome since September 2000; born 29/03/59; FCO 1983; (Second Secretary) 1985; Second Secretary and Vice Consul Havana 1986; First Secretary (Chancery) Mexico City 1988; First Secretary FCO 1991; Brussels 1994; FCO 1998; Band D6; m 1997 Arno Baecker (1s 1999).

Bouakaze-Khan, Najma (née Khan); Istanbul since December 1999; born 11/06/67; FCO 1987; Addis Ababa 1989; Brussels (UKDEL NATO) 1993; FCO 1996; Full-Time Language Training 1999; Band B3; m 1992 Didier Bouakaze-Khan. (2s 1996, 1999).

Bourke, Martin; Deputy High Commissioner Wellington since May 2000; born 12/03/47; Third Secretary FCO 1970; Brussels 1971; Second Secretary Singapore 1974; Second later First Secretary FCO 1975; First Secretary Lagos 1978; On loan to DOT 1980; FCO 1980; Consul (Comms) Johannesburg 1984; First Secretary FCO

1988; Governor Turks and Caicos Islands 1993; m 1973 Anne Marie Marguerite Hottelet (4s 1974, 1977, 1979, 1983).

Bousfield, Edward; Deputy High Commissioner Bandar Seri Begawan since May 1998; born 09/10/42; FO 1959; Moscow 1964; Geneva (UKMIS) 1965; Rabat 1968; FCO 1970; MECAS 1973; Kuwait 1974; Abu Dhabi 1976; Paris 1978; Second Secretary FCO 1981; Second Secretary (Aid/Comm) Suva 1984; Second Secretary (Management) Lusaka 1987; First Secretary FCO 1990; First Secretary (Development) Lilongwe 1993; m (1) 1975 Madeleine Jean Dart (1s 1979); m (2) 1986 Wan Noor Siha Wan Din.

Bowden, Christopher John; Maputo since June 2001; born 06/07/59; FCO 1977; Copenhagen 1979; Karachi 1982; Bucharest 1983; Paris 1985; FCO 1988; Calcutta 1991; Istanbul 1994; FCO 1998; Band C4; m 1983 Jane Susan Manville (1d 1986).

Bowden, James Nicholas Geoffrey, OBE (2002); First Secretary FCO since October 2000; born 27/05/60; Royal Green Jackets 1979-86; Second Secretary FCO 1986; Language Training 1988; Language Training Cairo 1989; Deputy, later Acting Consul-General Aden 1990; Second later First Secretary (Chancery) Khartoum 1991; First Secretary FCO 1994; Washington 1996; First Secretary (Economic and Commercial) Riyadh 1999; m (1) 1985 Alison Hulme (diss) (1s 1993, 1d 1995); m (2) 1999 Sarah Peaslee (1d 2001).

Bowe, Michael Henry; Second Secretary (Consular) Sarajevo since March 1997; born 08/03/46; FCO 1971; Lagos 1974; New Delhi 1978; FCO 1981; Second Secretary (Commercial) Lilongwe 1982; Second Secretary (Comm) Gaborone 1986; Second Secretary FCO 1990; Second Secretary (Management) and Consul Maputo 1993; m (1) 1970 Ann Frances Ballard (diss 1985) (1d 1976, 1s 1979); m (2) 1985 Sandra Jean Brown Lassale.

Bowes, Andrew Martin; Deputy Head of Mission Dili since June 2002; born 10/08/74; FCO 1997; Third Secretary (Vice-Consul/Press and Public Affairs) Maputo 1999; m 2001 Isabel Filipa Oliveira Goncalves.

Bowes, Jacqueline; FCO since October 1990; born 28/02/60; Inland Revenue 1976-90; Band A2.

Bowie, Nigel John Graydon; First Secretary (Political) Abuja since January 1999; born 31/05/51; FCO 1975; Seoul 1977; Paris 1981; Athens 1983; Second Secretary FCO 1985; Second Secretary (Comm/Econ) Oslo 1988; First Secretary (Comm) Athens 1992; FCO 1997; m 1977 Mildred Alice Sansom (2s 1979, 1984; 1d 1982).

Bowling, Nicola Carron (née Jackson); Second Secretary Kuala Lumpur since April 1998; born 01/12/67; FCO 1991; Third Secretary (Aid/Commercial) Maputo 1994; Band C4; m 1996 David John Robinson Bowling (1s 2000).

Bowman, Victoria Jane (née Robinson); HM Ambassador Rangoon since December 2002; born 12/06/66; FCO 1988; Third later Second Secretary Rangoon 1990; First Secretary FCO 1993; First Secretary (Information/Press) Brussels (UKREP) 1996; SUPL 1999; m 1991 Mark Andrew Bowman.

Bowskill, Robert Colin; Tel Aviv since May 1998; born 21/09/43; Army 1959-77; Police 1977-84; Prague 1984; Lusaka 1987; Warsaw 1989; New Delhi 1991; Bucharest 1995; Band C4; m 1966 Jean Spencer (2s 1967, 1968).

Bowyer, Aileen Jane (née Gemmell); SUPL since January 1994; born 10/09/62; FCO 1983; Belgrade 1985; SUPL 1987; FCO 1990; Kaduna 1990; Band A2; m 1987 Anthony Harvey Bowyer (1d 1992).

Bowyer, Anthony Harvey; FCO since August 2001; born 21/11/62; FCO 1982; Belgrade 1984; Kaduna 1987; FCO 1990; Harare 1994; Dublin 1997; Band C4; m 1987 Aileen Jane Gemmell (1d 1992).

Bowyer, Joanne Louise; Toronto since June 2001; born 30/03/68; FCO 1989; Bogota 1991; Abuja 1994; FCO 1998; Band B3.

Boxer, Peter John; Second Secretary (Political) Nicosia since September 1997; born 24/07/71; FCO 1995; Band C4.

Boyce, Sir Graham Hugh, KCMG (2001), CMG (1991); HM Ambassador Cairo since February 1999; born 06/10/45; Third Secretary FCO 1968; Third later Second Secretary Ottawa 1971; MECAS 1972; First Secretary Tripoli 1974; Head of Chancery 1975; FCO 1977; First Secretary (Economic/Finance) and later Head of Chancery Kuwait 1981; First Secretary FCO 1985; Counsellor and Head of Chancery Stockholm 1987; Counsellor FCO 1993; HM Ambassador Doha 1993; HM Ambassador Kuwait 1996; m 1970 Janet Elizabeth Spencer (1s 1971; 3d 1974, 1980, 1984).

Boyd, Andrew Jonathan Corrie, OBE (1992); Counsellor FCO since June 1999; born 05/05/50; Royal Navy 1968-80; FCO 1980; First Secretary (Econ) Accra 1981; FCO 1984; First Secretary (Chancery) Mexico City 1988; First Secretary FCO 1991; Counsellor Islamabad 1996; m 1979 Ginette Anne Vischer (2s 1985, 1987; 1d 1991).

Boyden, Simon Denis; Second Secretary (Commercial) Moscow since March 1999; born 24/02/68; FCO 1997; Band C4; m 1998 Geraldine Gallagher.

Boyles, Elizabeth; Second Secretary (Trade Policy) Brussels (UKREP) since August 2000; born 28/08/67; DHM San Salvador 1997; FCO 1990; Third Secretary (Political) Brussels 1994; New York (UKMIS) 1996; Band C4; m 1997 Patrick Dens.

Bradbury, Jonathan Edward; Dublin since August 2000; born 16/12/67; HCS 1989-95; Nairobi 1997;

Band A2; m 1994 Rebecca Clare Sebborn (2s 1998, 2000).

Bradford, Peter; Riyadh since September 1999; born 30/01/54; Royal Navy 1971-94; FCO 1994; Paris 1996; Band A2; m 1976 Rosemary Ann Slater (2s 1977, 1983; 1d 1979).

Bradley, Guy; FCO since April 1987; born 03/02/62; FCO 1981; New Delhi 1983; Band C5; m 1987 Andrea Stannard. (1s 1993, 1d 1994).

Bradley, Henry Alexander Jarvie; First Secretary Vienna (UKDEL) OSCE since May 2000; born 23/07/52; HM Customs and Excise 1969; FCO 1971; Brussels (EC) 1975; Budapest 1978; Bahrain 1979; FCO 1982; Munich 1984; Third Secretary (AO/Vice-Consul) Maseru 1987; Second Secretary FCO 1992; Deputy Hign Commissioner Banjul 1996; Band C5; m 1979 Gabriella Maria Schwery.

Bradley, Joseph Maxwell; Second Secretary Geneva (UKMIS) since November 1998; born 14/02/60; FCO 1978; East Berlin 1981; Resigned 1983; Reinstated 1986; Lusaka 1987; Vienna (UKDEL) 1990; FCO 1993; Full-Time Language Training 1995; Third Secretary (Information) Berlin 1995; m 1987 Melanie Rose (2d 1988,1992; 1s 1990).

Bradley, Richard Marriott; Second Secretary (Management) Düsseldorf since November 1997; born 03/08/41; FO 1964; Dacca 1966; FO (later FCO) 1967; Singapore 1969; Kampala 1973; FCO 1976; Pretoria 1977; FCO 1980; Tunis 1983; Jedda 1986; FCO 1988; Prague 1991; Second Secretary Washington 1993; m 1965 Mary Cecilia MacDonald (1s 1968; 1d 1972).

Bradley, Stephen Edward; Deputy Head of Mission Beijing since August 2002; born 04/04/58; FCO 1981; Language Training 1982; Second later First Secretary Tokyo 1983; SUPL 1987; Deputy Political Adviser Hong Kong 1988; SUPL 1993; FCO 1995; Counsellor and Director of Trade Paris 1999; m 1982 Elizabeth Gomersall 1s 1985).

Bradley, Susan Pauline; Pretoria since February 1999; born 16/05/62; FCO 1987; FCO 1996; Band A2.

Bradley, Timothy Gawin, OBE (1991); First Secretary FCO since May 1999; born 03/06/59; FCO 1983; Language Training 1984; Second later First Secretary (Chancery) Kuwait 1986; First Secretary FCO 1989; Belgrade 1996; Band D6; m 1990 Kathleen Scanlon (3s 1993, 1995, 1997).

Bradshaw, John Vincent; New Delhi since November 2000; born 19/08/64; FCO 1999; Band B3; m 1994 Doris Jungling (2s 1994, 1996).

Bradshaw, Philip James; FCO since June 1993; born 11/06/70; FCO 1988; SUPL 1990; Band A2.

Braidford, Lindsey; FCO since February 1988; born 20/04/47; Jedda 1975; Belize 1976; The Hague 1979; Rangoon 1982; Pretoria/Cape Town 1984; Band B3.

Braithwaite, Angela; Moscow since May 1992; born 13/11/70; FCO 1989; Band A2.

Braithwaite, Julian Nicholas; Sarajevo since May 2002; born 25/07/68; Second Secretary FCO 1994; Seconded to ICFY, Zagreb 1995; Second Later First Secretary (Chancery) Belgrade 1996; On loan to No.10 Press Office 1998; Seconded to SHAPE 1999; Prime Minister's Speech Co-ordinator 2000; m 1999 Biljana Njagulj (1d 2000).

Bramley, Sheila Jane; Second Secretary (Commercial) Islamabad since October 1998; born 25/10/63; FCO 1982; Tokyo 1984; Sofia 1987; SE Asia/FE Floater 1989; FCO 1991; Kuala Lumpur 1994; Canberra 1995.

Brammer, Geoffrey Ian; Second Secretary (Management) Bridgetown since July 1998; born 09/06/65; FCO 1985; Kaduna 1987; Nassau 1990; Tehran 1991; FCO 1992; Deputy Head of Mission Ashgabat 1995; Band B3; m 1991 Shelley Diane Chalmers

Brandon, William Roland; First Secretary (Political) Singapore since April 2001; born 07/06/64; FCO 1993; First Secretary (Economic) Vienna 1996; First Secretary FCO 1999; Band D6; m 1991 Polly Jennifer Nyiri (3d (twins) 1996, 1998).

Brannigan, Virginia (née Reynolds); SUPL since July 1999; born 16/01/62; FCO 1985; San Jose 1986; Madrid 1990; FCO 1998; Band A2; m 1992 Stuart Patrick Brannigan.

Brant, Astrid Lorita Sophia; Tunis since December 1992; born 27/02/53; DHSS 1980-91; FCO 1991; Band A2.

Brant, Sharon Linda (née Acheson); Third Secretary (Chancery) Dublin since July 2001; born 15/02/73; FCO 1992; Kuala Lumpur 1995; Kingston 1997; Band B3; m 1996 Andrew Brant.

Braun, David Alan; FCO since February 2000; born 27/02/71; FCO 1991; Madrid 1998; Band B3; m 1998 Susan Jane Robottom.

Brazier, Colin Nigel; Consul (Commercial) New York since September 2000; born 31/10/53; FCO 1973; Warsaw 1976; Singapore 1977; Accra 1980; FCO 1982; Dhaka 1985; Third Secretary (Comm)later Second Secretary (Development) Kingston 1989; Second Secretary FCO 1992; Deputy High Commissioner Georgetown 1997; m 1975 Jane Ann Pearson (1d 1979, 1s 1983).

Brear, Andrew James; First Secretary (Political) Stockholm since March 2000; born 28/01/60; Army 1979-90; Second later First Secretary FCO 1991; First Secretary (Inf) Santiago 1994; First Secretary FCO 1997; Band D6; m 1986 Jane Susan Matthews (1d 1991, 1s 1993).

Breeze, Christopher Mark; First Secretary FCO since October 2001; born 13/08/63; FCO 1985; Second Secretary (Chancery) Nicosia 1988; Second later First Secretary FCO 1991; First Secretary (Trade Policy) New Delhi 1994; First

Secretary (Political) Ankara 1997; Band D6; m 1990 Janet Suzanne Champion (2d 1995, 1998).

Breeze, Susan Jane (née Cockel); FCO since 1996; born 09/03/66; FCO 1989; Language Training 1990; Full-Time Language Training Peking 1991; Third Secretary (Commercial) Peking 1992; On loan to China-Britain Trade Group 1995; T/D Moscow 1996; m 2002 Paul Breeze.

Brennan, Anthony Bradford; Second Secretary (Economic/KHF) Prague since August 1996; born 06/02/66; FCO 1994.

Brenton, Anthony Russell, CMG (2001); Minister Washington since January 2001; born 01/01/50; FCO 1975; MECAS 1977; First Secretary Cairo 1978; FCO 1981; FCO 1982; Presidency Liaison Officer Brussels 1982; First Secretary (Energy) Brussels (UKREP) 1985; On loan to the European Commission 1986; Counsellor FCO 1989; CDA Harvard University 1992; Full-Time Language Training 1993; Counsellor (Economic/Aid/Scientific) Moscow 1994; Director FCO 1998; m (1) 1971 Susan Mary Blacker (diss 1978); (2) 1982 Susan Mary Penrose (1s 1984, 2d 1987,1988).

Brenton, Jonathan Andrew; First Secretary (Economic) Moscow since March 1999; born 24/12/65; FCO 1994; Moscow 1996; Band D6.

Brett, David Lawrence; Consul-General Algiers since November 2001; born 20/09/52; FCO 1978; Tehran 1980; Chicago 1983; FCO 1986; Second Secretary (Chancery) Kingston 1989; Consul-General Alexandria 1992; First Secretary FCO 1996; m 1984 Carol Sue Lane (2s 1986, 1991, 1d 1988).

Brett, Rebecca Louise (née Fenwick); Colombo since September 2000; born 27/11/64; FCO 1984; Washington 1987; The Hague 1990; SUPL 1992; FCO 1994; Abu Dhabi 1996; Band B3; m 1987 Paul Brett (2d 1992, 1996, 1s 1994).

Brett, Russell Michael; FCO since January 1999; born 14/09/69; FCO 1989; Athens 1995; Band B3; m 1999 Simone Walsh (1d 2000).

Brett Rooks, Bedelia, LVO; FCO since August 2001; born 09/12/46; FCO 1969; On loan to SEATO Bangkok 1972; Copenhagen 1975; Rome 1976; Second Secretary FCO 1978; Second Secretary Accra 1983; Brussels (UKREP) 1986; First Secretary FCO 1987; First Secretary (Inf) Berlin (BMG) 1989; First Secretary FCO 1993; First Secretary Brussels 1996.

Brettle-Cockman, Lynda Elizabeth; SUPL since July 2001; born 02/10/62; FCO 1980; Tokyo 1983; SE Asia Floater 1987; Islamabad 1988; SUPL 1992; FCO 1993; Second Secretary (Management) and Consul Caracas 1997; Mexico City 2000; Band C5; m 1994 Michael Anthony Cockman (1d 1994; 1s 2001).

Brewer, Dr Jonathan Andrew; Counsellor FCO since January 2002; born 20/03/55; FCO 1983;

Second later First Secretary Luanda 1986; First Secretary FCO 1988; First Secretary (Chancery) Mexico City 1991; Counsellor FCO 1995; Counsellor (Political Affairs) Moscow 1998; m (1) 1978 Tessa Alexandra Swiney (diss 1990); (2) 1993 Angela Margarita Sosa Teran.

Brewer, Lesley Ann; Tripoli since March 2000; born 29/07/57; FCO 1995; Prague 1997; Band A2.

Brewer, Nicola Mary; Counsellor New Delhi since June 1998; born 14/11/57; FCO 1983; Second Secretary (Chancery) Mexico City 1984; First Secretary FCO 1987; First Secretary (Economic) Paris 1991; SUPL 1994; Counsellor FCO 1995; m 1991 Geoffrey Charles Gillham (1d 1993, 1s 1994).

Bridge, Heather Susan (née Brown); Second Secretary Skopje since April 2000; born 19/04/62; FCO 1985; Band C4; m 1986 Christopher Martin Gibbons Bridge (2d 1990,1992).

Bridge, Karen Maria (née Chadbourne); Dhaka since July 2002; born 03/09/70; FCO 1990; Brussels (UKREP) 1993; FCO 1995; Brussels (UKREP) 1996; FCO 1997; Riyadh 1999; Band A2; m 1992 Peter Charles Benson Bridge (2s 1998, 2000).

Bridge, Richard Philip; Counsellor FCO since July 2001; born 24/03/59; Second Secretary (Inf) Warsaw 1986; FCO 1988; First Secretary (Chancery) Moscow 1989; FCO 1993; Counsellor New Delhi 1998; m 1994 Philippa Anne Leslie-Jones (2s 1995, 1997).

Bridges, Stephen John; HM Ambassador Phnom Penh since December 2000; born 19/06/60; FCO 1980; Africa/ME Floater 1983; Luanda 1984; Third later Second Secretary (Comm) Seoul 1987; Second later First Secretary FCO 1992; First Secretary Kuala Lumpur 1996; m 1990 Yoon Kyung Mi.

Bridgwood, Alistair Charles Jeudwine; FCO since September 2001; born 12/05/73; Band C4; m 2001 Rachel Beale.

Brier, Lucy Jane (née Richardson); Ulaanbaatar since September 2002; born 18/03/69; FCO 1995; Kuala Lumpur 1997; SUPL 2000; Band B3; m 1996 Simon Richard Brier.

Brier, Simon Richard; Deputy Head of Mission Ulaanbaatar since September 2001; born 15/09/67; FCO 1987; Prague 1989; SE Asia/Far East Floater Duties 1991; FCO 1994; Kuala Lumpur 1997; m 1996 Lucy Jane Richardson.

Brierley, David Anthony; Kuwait since March 1996; born 14/10/47; Royal Marines 1965; Budapest 1987; Madrid 1989; FCO 1991; Band B3; m 1993 Denise Mary Jones (1s 1998).

Brigden, Neil Stephen; Second Secretary (Commercial) New Delhi since October 2000; born 07/08/68; Colombo 1989; Bucharest 1992; Sana'a 1995; FCO 1996; Band C4.

Brigenshaw, David Victor; First Secretary FCO since April 1998; born 01/06/56; FCO 1973; Nairobi 1976; FCO 1981; Kuala Lumpur 1983; Third Secretary (Commercial) Quito 1986; Second Secretary FCO 1990; m 1977 Yvonne Lesley Bush.

Briggs, Geoffrey; Second Secretary FCO since July 1997; born 20/02/64; FCO 1988; Third Secretary (Econ/Aid) Cairo 1990; Second Secretary FCO 1992; Tirana 1995; Band C4.

Bright, Colin Charles; FCO since April 1998; born 02/01/48; Second Secretary FCO 1975; First Secretary Bonn 1977; FCO 1979; On loan to the Cabinet Office 1983; Consul New York (BTDO) 1985; Counsellor and Head of Chancery Berne 1989; Consul-General Frankfurt 1993; m (1) 1978 Helen-Ann Michie (diss 1990); (2) 1990 Jane Elizabeth Gurney Pease (1s 1992, 1d 1995).

Brimfield, Valerie; Bucharest since November 1997; born 27/07/49; FCO 1979; Tunis 1980; Tehran 1983; New Delhi 1985; Dhaka 1989; Ottawa 1992; FCO 1995; Tokyo 1996; Band B3.

Brind, Kevin James; Second Secretary FCO since April 1998; born 05/10/59; FCO 1977; Bonn 1980; Khartoum 1982; Moscow 1986; FCO 1987; Canberra 1990; Third Secretary (Development) Kathmandu 1993; Second Secretary, Deputy Head of Mission Ulaanbaatar 1997; m 1983 Jane Louise Burns.

Brinkley, Robert Edward; HM Ambassador Kiev since August 2002; born 21/01/54; FCO 1977; Language Training 1978; Third Secretary UKDEL Comprehensive Test Ban, Geneva 1978; Second Secretary Moscow 1979; First Secretary FCO 1982; First Secretary (Political/Military) Bonn 1988; First Secretary later Counsellor FCO 1992; Counsellor (Political) Moscow 1996; Head of Joint Entry Clearance Unit (FCO/Home Office) 2000; m 1982 Frances Mary Webster (3s 1982, 1984, 1989).

Bristow, Dr Lawrence Stanley Charles; Ankara since June 1999; born 23/11/63; FCO 1990; Full-Time Language Training 1991; Second Secretary (Chancery/Inf) Bucharest 1992; First Secretary FCO 1995; Private Secretary to Minister of State 1996; Full-Time Language Training 1998; m 1998 Fiona McCallum.

Britton, Catherine Mary; First Secretary FCO since July 1988; born 13/04/61; FCO 1983; Dar es Salaam 1985; m 1986 Rhodri James Lewis Britton.

Bromley, Peter Richard Ober; Deputy High Commissioner Port of Spain since January 2000; born 14/10/47; FCO 1966; Kuala Lumpur 1970; Dacca 1973; Georgetown 1976; On loan to DOT 1980; Oslo 1982; Second Secretary (Commercial) Dubai 1984; Second Secretary FCO 1987; Second later First Secretary (Dev) Lilongwe 1989; Deputy High Commissioner Maseru 1993; First Secretary FCO 1995; Band D6; m 1978 Yasmin Amna Majeed (2s 1981, 1984).

Bronnert, Deborah Jane; Counsellor (Commercial) Moscow since July 2002; born 31/01/67; DOE 1989; Royal Commission on Environmantal Pollution 1990; Brussels (UKREP) 1991; DOE 1993; FCO 1994; On secondment to European Commission (Kinnock Cabinet) 1995; FCO 1999; Band D7.

Bronson, Rodney Charles; Canberra since October 1999; born 09/08/46; FCO 1971; Brussels 1974; FCO 1977; Moscow 1977; Copenhagen 1980; Cairo 1984; Second Secretary FCO 1988; Second Secretary Singapore 1991; m 1968 Margaret Ann Williams (2d 1972, 1974).

Brook, John Edwin; FCO since November 1997; born 21/03/45; FO 1964; Moscow 1967; Latin American Floater 1970; Calcutta 1972; Second Secretary FCO 1975; Second Secretary (Commercial) Moscow 1978; Second later First Secretary Berne 1981; First Secretary (Commercial) East Berlin 1984; First Secretary on attachment to JSDC 1988; First Secretary FCO 1989; Consul-General Stuttgart 1993; Full-Time Language Training 1993; m 1981 Moira Elizabeth Lands (1d 1983, 1s 1986).

Brook, Simon Douglas; FCO since February 1989; born 05/02/61; FCO 1982; Geneva 1986; Band B3; m 1995 Lesley June Holmwood.

Brooke, Sandra Jane; SUPL since May 1994; born 21/08/63; FCO 1985; Algiers 1987; FCO 1989; Bahrain 1991; Band A2; m 1991 Jean-Marc Jefferson (1s 1993).

Brookes, Carter, MBE (1990); FCO since December 1992; born 13/12/46; FCO 1971; Saigon 1973; FCO 1974; St Helena 1976; FCO 1978; Singapore 1980; FCO 1983; Moscow 1986; New Delhi 1989; Beirut 1991; Band B3; m 1971 Margaret Jean Stewart (3s 1974, 1976, 1977).

Brookes, Diana Lorraine; Legal Counsellor FCO since December 1999; born 19/04/64; Assistant Legal Adviser FCO 1989; Solicitor 1989; First Secretary (Legal) Brussels (UKREP) 1995; FCO 1998; m 1990 Gerald Blais (1d 1999).

Brookes, Maurice John; Third Secretary (Immigration/Visa) Harare since August 1997; born 14/06/49; FCO 1968; Accra 1971; Aden 1972; Nairobi 1974; Karachi 1976; FCO 1978; Tehran 1981; Kampala 1982; FCO 1982; FCO 1985; Paris 1986; FCO 1989; Warsaw 1989; Abidjan 1993; Band B3.

Brooking, Karen (née Moore); Second Secretary (Political) Copenhagen since September 2002; born 15/07/64; FCO 1987; Peking 1990; FCO 1992; SUPL 1994; FCO 1995; Band C4.

Brooking, Stephen John Allan, OBE (2002); Counsellor (Political) Kabul since August 2002; born 13/03/64; FCO 1986; Second Secretary (Economic) Peking 1989; Second Secretary FCO 1992; First Secretary (Political) Sarajevo 1994; FCO 1995; First Secretary (ESCAP) Bangkok 1998; First Secretary FCO 2001.

Brooks, Helen Katherine; First Secretary FCO since September 1999; born 21/06/67; FCO 1991; On loan to the Hong Kong Government 1994; Hong Kong 1997; SUPL 1998; Band PRO.

Brooks, Shelagh Margaret Jane; FCO since October 2002; FCO 1979; On loan to Hong Kong Government 1987; Legal Counsellor FCO 1991; Brussels (UKREP) 1998.

Broom, David Charles; Second Secretary (Commercial) Kuala Lumpur since May 1996; born 17/09/54; FCO 1973; Islamabad 1975; FCO 1976; Brussels (UKREP) 1977; Baghdad 1981; Home Civil Service 1982; FCO 1983; Rome 1986; FCO 1989; Paris 1989; Second Secretary FCO 1993; m 1976 Diana Josephine Hewer (1s 1978, 1d 1989).

Broom, Peter David; Consul-General Cape Town since July 2000; born 07/08/53; FCO 1970; Oslo 1974; Jedda 1977; Islamabad 1979; FCO 1981; Mbabane 1984; New Delhi 1987; Second Secretary FCO 1989; Consul (Commercial) Brisbane 1991; First Secretary (Commercial), Consul and DHM Yaounde 1997; Band C5; m 1976 Vivienne Louise Pyatt (5d 1979, 1981, 1985, 1988, 1994).

Broomfield, David Norman; Consul (Commercial) Barcelona since July 1998; born 21/05/54; FCO 1973; Banjul 1975; LA Floater 1978; Prague 1980; FCO 1983; Tripoli 1986; Second Secretary (Chancery/Inf) Lusaka 1987; Vice-Consul Naples 1991; First Secretary FCO 1995.

Brosnan, Sheryl (née Landman); Kampala since August 2002; born 05/12/71; FCO 1991; Bangkok 1993; Istanbul 1997; Abidjan 2000; m 1994 Mark Paul Brosnan (2s 1998, 2000).

Broucher, David Stuart; UK Permanent Representative to the Conference on Disarmament in Geneva since October 2001; born 05/10/44; FO 1966; Berlin 1968; Second Secretary on loan to the Cabinet Office 1972; First Secretary 1973; First Secretary Prague 1975; First Secretary (ECOFIN) Brussels (UKREP) 1983; Counsellor (Comm/Aid) Jakarta 1985; Counsellor (Econ) Bonn 1989; Counsellor later AUSS FCO 1994; HM Ambassador Prague 1997; m 1971 Marion M Blackwell (1s 1972).

Brough, Stuart Richard; Second Secretary Bridgetown since May 2002; born 24/06/65; FCO 1989; Band C4; m 1989 Delia Claire Hickman (1s 1992; 1d 1995).

Broughton, Sarah; Second Secretary (Economic/Social) New York (UKMIS) since December 1999; born 12/08/66; FCO 1984; Ottawa 1987; Lilongwe 1990; Floater 1992; FCO 1995; Full-Time Language Training 1999; Band C4.

Brown, Alexander Mark; Ashgabat since December 1997; born 21/07/64; DHSS 1986; FCO 1988; Lagos 1991; FCO 1992; Full-Time Language Training 1993; Hamburg 1994; Band B3; m 1997 A Gehrke

Brown, Alexander Nicholas Seaton; FCO since September 2000; born 31/07/72; Band C4.

Brown, Andrew Paul; FCO since January 2002; born 12/10/68; FCO 1987; New York (UKMIS) 1991; FCO 1994; Third Secretary Seoul 1998; Band B3; m 1998 Joanna Beresford

Brown, Christine Audrey Frances; Attaché (Aid) Dhaka since May 1991; born 22/06/51; FCO 1970; New Delhi 1971; Lagos 1973; Bucharest 1975; Kuala Lumpur 1977; FCO 1981; Floater Duties 1982; FCO 1985; Johannesburg 1988; Band B3.

Brown, Deirdre Rebecca (née Herdman), MBE (2002); FCO since October 1998; born 19/07/66; FCO 1986; Dhaka 1988; FCO 1992; Third Secretary (Political/Economic) Bangkok 1995; Band C4; m 1991 Stephen William Brown (1d 1992, 1s 1994).

Brown, Edward James Murch, MBE (1991); Second Secretary Geneva (UKMIS) since April 1996; born 27/08/59; FCO 1978; Bonn 1980; Prague 1983; Rabat 1985; FCO 1987; Düsseldorf 1992; FCO 1995; m 1980 Hannah Jane Gibbons.

Brown, Gordon Williams; First Secretary and HM Consul Cairo since May 2001; born 17/10/54; Inland Revenue 1975; FCO 1976; Guatemala City 1979; The Hague 1981; SE Asia Floater 1983; Kampala 1985; FCO 1988; Second Secretary (Man and Consul) Havana 1991; Second Secretary (Management) and HM Consul Muscat 1995; British Trade International 1998; m 1985 Rosalind Patricia Harwood (2s 1992, 1993).

Brown, Herbert George, MBE (1981); FCO since February 2001; born 02/01/43; FO 1964; Rawalpindi 1966; Kuala Lumpur 1969; FCO 1973; Barcelona 1975; Maseru 1978; FCO 1981; Second Secretary and Vice-Consul Baghdad 1982; On loan to DTI 1985; First Secretary (Commercial) Rio de Janeiro 1988; First Secretary FCO 1990; HM Consul later HM Consul-General Cape Town 1996; m 1975 Susan Atkin (1d 1977).

Brown, John Mark; Damascus since March 1999; born 15/05/43; RAF 1962-84; Islamabad 1990; Belgrade 1993; Moscow 1996; Band B3; m 1965 Carole Elizabeth Thompson (2d 1966, 1970).

Brown, Linda; Moscow since January 1996; born 24/12/55; FCO 1974; Bonn 1977; Budapest 1980; FCO 1980; Oslo 1982; FCO 1985; Rome 1992; Band B3.

Brown, Richard Anthony; Brussels since April 2002; born 29/10/72; FCO 1996; Band B3.

Brown, Simon Nicholas; Second Secretary Tokyo since October 2000; born 19/07/73; FCO 1997; Full-Time Language Training 1998; Full-Time Language Training Kamakura 1999; Band C4.

Brown, Sir Stephen (David Reid), KCVO (1999); FCO since November 2002; born 26/12/45; HM Forces 1964-76; FCO 1976; First Secretary Nicosia 1977; First Secretary (Commercial) Paris 1980; FCO 1985; Consul-General Melbourne 1989; T/D DTI 1989; Counsellor (Commercial)

Peking 1994; HM Ambassador Seoul 1997; Pre Post Training FCO 2000; High Commissioner Singapore 2001; m 1966 Pamela Gaunt (1s 1965, 1d 1969).

Brown, Stephen Leonard; Tehran since September 2001; born 07/03/56; Army 1974-96; FCO 1998; Riyadh 1999; FCO 2001; Band A2; m 1978 Gaynor Ruth (2d 1974, 1982).

Brown, Stephen Michael; Bahrain since July 2002; born 09/06/63; Household Cavalry 1980-95; Mostar 1997; FCO 1997; Amman 1998; Third Secretary (Management) Almaty 2000; Band A2.

Brown, Stuart James; Kiev since August 2001; born 29/04/75; FCO 1994; Band B3; ptnr, Fiona Brougham.

Brownbill, Timothy Patrick; HM Ambassador Managua since November 2002; born 06/02/60; FCO 1979; Lagos 1982; Madrid 1986; FCO 1989; Resigned 1990 (March), Reinstated 1990 (July); Deputy Head of Mission Vilnius 1992; Language Training 1992; Second Secretary 1994; Second Secretary (Commercial) Havana 1996; On loan to the DTI 2000.

Browne, Dr Carolyn; Brussels (UKREP) since June 2002; born 19/10/58; FCO 1985; Language Training 1987; Second later First Secretary Moscow 1988; FCO 1991; First Secretary New York (UKMIS) 1993; FCO 1997; Counsellor FCO 1999; Full-Time Language Training 2002.

Browne, Nicholas Walker, KBE (2002), CMG (1999); HM Ambassador Tehran since May 1999; born 17/12/47; Third Secretary FCO 1969; Tehran 1971; Second later First Secretary FCO 1975; On loan to the Cabinet Office 1976; First Secretary and Head of Chancery Salisbury 1980; First Secretary FCO 1981; First Secretary (Environment) Brussels (UKREP) 1984; Counsellor FCO 1989; Chargé d'Affaires Tehran 1989; Counsellor (Press and Public Affairs) Washington and Head of BIS New York 1990; Counsellor FCO 1994; Chargé d'Affaires Tehran 1997; m 1969 Diana Marise Aldwinckle (2s 1970, 1980, 2d 1972, 1976).

Brownhut, Naomi Judith; SUPL since May 1995; born 07/06/69; HM Customs and Excise 1988; FCO 1990; Prague 1993; Band A2.

Brownridge, Valerie (née Ewan); Deputy Consul-General Jerusalem since October 1999; born 10/12/56; FCO 1979; Paris (ENA) 1980; Third Secretary Paris 1981; Third Secretary Lagos 1986; Second Secretary FCO 1988; Second Secretary Berlin 1991; First Secretary FCO 1994; Band D6; m 1999 John L.F. Brownridge.

Broyd, Laurence Paul; FCO since February 1999; born 12/11/60; Principal Research Officer FCO 1990; First Secretary (Economic) Moscow 1995; m 1990 Catherine Mary Carslake (1s 1994, 1d 1998).

Bruce, Dawn Susan; Cairo since March 1989; born 18/12/61; FCO 1981; Muscat 1983; Peking 1986; Band B3.

Brummell, Paul; HM Ambassador Ashgabat since February 2002; born 28/08/65; FCO 1987; Third later Second Secretary (Chancery) Islamabad 1989; First Secretary FCO 1993; Full-Time Language Training 1994; First Secretary (Political/Inf) Rome 1995.

Brunton, Janice Louise; Colombo since January 1996; born 19/06/71; FCO 1991; Moscow 1993; Band A2.

Bruton, Robert James; Brussels since August 1999; born 01/01/57; FCO 1980; Band C4.

Bryant, John Edward; First Secretary FCO since 2000; born 04/01/51; FCO 1970; Canberra 1972; Kingston 1975; FCO 1977; Bahrain 1978; Cairo 1979; FCO 1983; Nairobi 1986; FCO 1990; Dubai 1994; m 1972 Joyce Anne Barrie (1d 1975, 2s 1985, 1988).

Bryant, Richard John; FCO since June 1998; born 22/09/53; Department of Energy 1973; DTI 1973; DOT 1975; DTI 1982; FCO 1984; Dhaka 1986; Brussels (UKREP) 1990; Brunei 1993; Floater Duties 1997; T/D Islamabad 1997; Band B3; m 1986 Rosalyn Louise Morris (diss 1991) (1s 1991).

Bryden, Lara-Jean; Islamabad since August 2001; born 15/10/71; Employment Service 1991-96; FCO 1996; Floater Duties 1997; Band B3.

Bryson, Alan Robert; Bangkok since October 1998; born 12/03/70; FCO 1991; Riyadh 1995; Band A2.

Bryson-Richardson, Mark Edward; Full-Time Language Training Cairo since July 2001; born 30/10/76; FCO 1999; Full-Time Language Training 2000; Band C4.

Bubbear, Alan Keith; Second Secretary (Commercial) Helsinki since July 1996; born 14/09/64; FCO 1983; Moscow 1985; SUPL 1988; Johannesburg 1990; FCO 1992; Second Secretary 1994; m 1988 Thérésa Bernice Allen (3d twins 1992, 1995).

Bubbear, Thérésa Bernice (née Allen); Second Secretary (Political) Helsinki since July 1996; born 14/12/62; FCO 1985; Moscow 1987; Johannesburg 1990; FCO 1992 (Second Secretary) FCO 1993; m 1998 Alan Keith Bubbear (3d twins 1992, 1995).

Buchanan, Sarah Louise (née Allen); FCO since March 2000; born 31/07/69; FCO 1991; Vice-Consul Stockholm 1994; Full-Time Language Training 1994; Third Secretary (Political/Press) Tel Aviv 1997; Full-Time Language Training 1997; Band B3; m 1995 Hamish Malcolm Robert Buchanan (1s 1998).

Buck, John Stephen; Head of Public Diplomacy Department FCO since July 2000; born 10/10/53; FCO 1980; Second Secretary Sofia 1982; First

Secretary FCO 1984; Head of Chancery Lisbon 1988; FCO 1992; Counsellor on loan to the Cabinet Office 1994; Counsellor and Deputy Head of Mission Nicosia 1996; m 1980 Jean Claire Webb (1d 1985, 1s 1989).

Buckley, Stephen; First Secretary (Commercial) Peking since July 2000; born 18/06/53; FCO 1972; Export Credit Guarantee Department 1972; Amman 1975; Canberra 1978; FCO 1980; Dakar 1983; Third later Second Secretary (Commercial) Seoul 1987; Second later First Secretary FCO 1992; First Secretary (Commercial) Kuala Lumpur 1996; m 1974 Barbara Frances Yelcich.

Bucknell, Bruce James; FCO since July 1999; born 15/04/62; FCO 1985; Third Secretary Amman 1988; FCO 1992; Secondment to EBRD 1992; HM Consul Milan 1995; Band C4; m 1993 Henrietta Dorrington-Ward (2s 1994, 1996).

Budd, Sir Colin Richard, KCMG (2002), CMG (1991); HM Ambassador The Hague since April 2001; born 31/08/45; Third Secretary FCO 1967; Assistant Private Secretary to Minister without Portfolio FCO 1968-69; Third later Second Secretary Warsaw 1969; Second later First Secretary (Chancery) Islamabad 1972; First Secretary FCO 1976; Head of Chancery The Hague 1980; Assistant Private Secretary to the Secretary of State FCO 1984; Counsellor 1986; On loan to the Cabinet Office 1987; Counsellor and Head of Chancery Bonn 1989; On loan as Chef de Cabinet to Sir Leon Brittan, European Commission 1993; On loan to the Cabinet Office 1996; DUS (EU and Economic) FCO 1997; m 1971 Agnes Antonia Maria Smit (1d 1979, 1s 1986).

Budden, Alexander James; Third Secretary (Development) Zagreb since September 1998; born 18/04/68; FCO 1991; Kathmandu 1994; Band B3; m 1995 Diane Margaret Scott (1d 2000).

Budden, Philip Marcus; First Secretary (Trade/Political) Washington since August 2002; born 12/09/65; Second Secretary FCO 1993; First Secretary Vienna 1999; m 1992 Deborah Allen Tripp (1d 1997).

Buglass, Melvyn James; Management Officer Tunis since June 2002; born 25/09/46; Army 1966-89; Rome 1989; Brussels (UKDEL/NATO) 1992; DSLC 1995; Vice-Consul Beirut 1998; Band B3; m 1973 Sandra Ann Whitehouse (1d 1974, 1s 1975).

Bull, Carol Elizabeth (née Gardener); FCO since February 1993; born 10/08/66; FCO 1988; Athens 1990; Band A2; m 1999 Keith Leslie Bull.

Bull, David Thomas John; On loan to the DTI since June 2000; born 20/02/61; FCO 1982; Rio de Janeiro 1983; Lusaka 1986; FCO 1990; Third Secretary (Consular/Passports) Kingston 1994; Second Secretary (Management) Kathmandu 1997; Band C4; m 1989 Aisling Maccobb (1d 1989).

Bulmer, Sandra Kay (née Ferguson); FCO since June 1998; born 11/11/67; FCO 1986; Vienna 1989; FCO 1991; Ottawa 1995; Band A2; m 1995 Ian Bulmer (1s 1998).

Bundy, Rosalind (née Johnson); Moscow since July 1999; born 25/01/45; Paris 1977; FCO 1977; Tripoli 1980; FCO 1983; Bonn 1985; FCO 1987; Algiers 1993; Ottawa 1995; Band B3; m 1984 David Alan Bundy.

Bunten, Roderick Alexander James; First Secretary (Information) Canberra since August 1997; born 24/11/59; FCO 1984; SOAS 1985; Language Training 1986; On secondment as Assistant Political Adviser to the Hong Kong Government 1987; SUPL 1990; Second Secretary FCO 1991.

Burch, Andrew David; Second Secretary São Paulo since May 2002; born 18/03/57; Department of the Environment 1972; FCO 1976; Nicosia 1980; New Delhi 1982; FCO 1986; Nairobi 1989; Budapest 1994; British Trade International 1998; On loan to DTI 1999; Band C4; m 1982 Sarah Miranda Hodgson Clarke (2s 1989, 1991, 1d 1995).

Burch, Stella Jane; Second Secretary (Bilateral) Berlin since June 2002; born 30/05/76; FCO 2000; Band C4.

Burdekin, Elizabeth Mary; FCO since September 1972; born 16/10/54; Band A2.

Burdes, Stephen Edward; Second Secretary (Political) Budapest since August 2000; born 17/12/71; FCO 1996; Band C4.

Burgin, Allan Lewis; FCO since November 1995; born 22/03/48; Royal Navy 1968-90; Moscow 1990; Paris 1991; Belgrade 1994; Band B3; m 1970 Susan Hewison (2s 1978, 1982).

Burke, Alison Jane (née Wickham); New Delhi since March 1999; born 25/07/65; FCO 1983; Prague 1988; Canberra 1990; SUPL 1991; Bucharest 1992; SUPL 1995; SUPL 1998; FCO 1998; Band A2; m 1992 Thomas John Burke (1d 1995, 1s 1996).

Burke, Thomas John; Second Secretary (Immigration) New Delhi since July 1998; born 12/12/50; Treasury 1968; FCO 1974; Brasilia 1976; Harare 1979; FCO 1979; Islamabad 1983; FCO 1984; Canberra 1987; Vice-Consul Düsseldorf 1991; Vice-Consul and later Second Secretary Bucharest 1992; m 1991 Alison Jane Wickham (1d 1995, 1s 1996).

Burke-Wood, Alison Carmen (née Ferry); Muscat since March 2002; born 07/06/66; FCO 1996; Canberra 1997; Band A2; m 1997 Joseph Burke-Wood.

Burlison, Sharon (née Clarke); Cape Town since May 1999; born 22/07/70; FCO 1993; Harare 1996; Band A2; m 1998 Andrew Burlison.

Burner, Edward Alan; HM Ambassador Dakar since August 2000; born 26/09/44; Commonwealth

Office (later FCO) 1967; Sofia 1970; Bonn 1972; Second Secretary 1973; Second Secretary (Commercial) Bridgetown 1974; Assistant Private Secretary to Minister for Overseas Development 1979; Second later First Secretary FCO 1979; FCO 1981; First Secretary, Head of Chancery and Consul Sofia 1984; On loan to ODA 1987; FCO 1990; Counsellor (Comm) Lagos 1992; Consul-General Munich 1995; FCO 1999; m 1969 Jane Georgine Du Port (2d 1970, 1972, 1s 1977).

Burnett, Alice Margaret; First Secretary (Legal) New York (UKMIS) since July 2000; born 17/10/68; Senior Assistant Legal Adviser, called to the Bar, Middle Temple 1991; FCO 1994; Band D6.

Burnhams, Robin Edward; FCO since January 1997; born 10/12/42; CSC 1960; FCO 1967; Buenos Aires 1970; Moscow 1973; FCO 1974; Kingston 1978; Mbabane 1982; Second Secretary FCO 1984; Second Secretary (Admin) and Consul Caracas 1987; Second Secretary FCO 1990; Second Secretary (Aid) Dar es Salaam 1992; T/D Bosnia Conference, Lancaster House 1996; m 1978 Hilda Charlotte Patricia Phibbs (1d 1985).

Burns, Lynda Edwards; Second Secretary (Political) Athens since April 2002; born 19/07/75; FCO 1999; Full-Time Language Training 2001; Band C4.

Burns, Nicholas John; Third Secretary and Vice-Consul Prague since September 2000; born 20/03/62; FCO 1980; The Hague 1983; Kuala Lumpur 1984; Hanoi 1988; FCO 1989; Third Secretary (Management) Riyadh 1992; FCO 1995; Band B3.

Burns, Sir (Robert) Andrew, KCMG (1997), CMG (1992); British High Commissioner Ottawa since July 2000; born 21/07/43; Third Secretary FO 1965; SOAS 1966; Third later Second Secretary Delhi 1967; Second later First Secretary FCO 1971; First Secretary and Head of Chancery Bucharest 1976; FCO 1978; Private Secretary to Permanent Under-Secretary of State FCO 1979; CDA Harvard University 1982; Counsellor (Information) Washington and Head of British Information Services New York 1983; Counsellor FCO 1986; AUSS (Asia/Far East) FCO 1990; HM Ambassador Tel Aviv 1992; DUSS (non-Europe, Trade and Investment Promotion) FCO 1995; Consul-General Hong Kong and Macau 1997; m 1973 Sarah Cadogan (1 step d 1968, 2s 1975, 1977).

Burns, Sarah Elizabeth; SUPL since September 1998; born 20/04/66; FCO 1988; Third later Second Secretary (Chancery) Vienna 1991; Second Secretary FCO 1995; Band C4.

Burns, Sean Gilbert Peter, MBE (2001); Second Secretary (Management) Nairobi since September 2000; born 19/02/61; FCO 1978; Dar es Salaam 1983; Antigua 1987; FCO 1991; Dhaka 1993; Third Secretary (Management) and Vice Consul Dakar 1997; m 1983 Marina Higgins (1d 1989, 1s 1991).

Burran, John Eric; Washington since February 2001; born 18/05/63; FCO 1982; Bucharest 1987; LA/Caribbean Floater 1989; Islamabad 1992; FCO 1995; On loan to DCMS 1998; Band C4.

Burrell, Demelza Fiona; World-wide Floater Duties since 2000; born 09/12/70; FCO 1994; Madrid 1996; FCO 1999; Band A2.

Burrett, Louise Victoria; SUPL since May 2000; born 16/08/61; FCO 1978; Bridgetown 1981; Dublin 1984; Bombay 1987; FCO 1990; SUPL 1993; On loan to the DTI 1995; SUPL 1997; Second Secretary (Management) Tripoli 1999; Band C4.

Burrows, Christopher Parker; First Secretary (Political) Brussels since April 1998; born 12/09/58; FCO 1980; East Berlin 1982; Africa/Middle East Floater 1985; Second Secretary Bonn 1987; Second Secretary FCO 1989; First Secretary (Political/External) Athens 1993; First Secretary FCO 1996; m 1988 Betty Cordi (2d 1987, 1990, 1s 1992).

Burrows, Karl; Consul Monterrey since July 2000; born 08/05/68; FCO 1988; Floater Duties 1990; Tegucigalpa 1992; FCO 1993; Panama City 1996; Band C4; m (1) 1991 Jane Marie O'Mahoney (diss); (2) 2001 Denise Victoria Vergara (1d 2002).

Burt, Nicola Jayne; Stockholm since July 2001; born 06/02/67; FCO 1986; Moscow 1989; FCO 1992; Tel Aviv 1993; FCO 1996; Kuala Lumpur 1997; FCO 2000; Band A2.

Burton, David Stewart; The Hague since February 2003; born 12/08/77; FCO 2001; Band C4.

Burton, Simon David; FCO since July 1998; born 11/04/73; Band A2.

Busby, George Benedict Joseph Pascal, OBE (1996); Counsellor Vienna since January 2000; born 18/04/60; FCO 1987; Second later First Secretary (Chancery) Bonn 1989; First Secretary FCO 1991; First Secretary Belgrade 1992; First Secretary FCO 1996; m 1988 Frances Hurll (3d 1989, 1994, 2000, 1s 1991).

Busk, Lieutenant Colonel Walter Patrick Anthony; Queen's Messenger 1989; born 20/09/39; HM Forces (Army) 1961-89.

Busvine, Nicholas John Lewis, OBE (1995); Counsellor (Regional Affairs) Bogotá since January 2002; born 13/05/60; FCO 1982; Third later Second Secretary Kuala Lumpur 1985; FCO 1988; First Secretary Maputo 1991; First Secretary FCO 1995; m (1) 1991 Sarah Ann Forgan (diss 1996) (2) 1997 Madeleine Ann Lewis (2d 1999, 2001).

Butcher, Peter Roderick; Maputo since March 2000; born 06/08/47; FCO 1974; Second Secretary Lima 1979; Second Secretary (Commercial) Bombay 1983; First Secretary FCO 1987; Deputy High Commissioner Maseru 1990; First Secretary FCO 1994; On secondment to DFID 1997; Band D6.

Bute, Paul Kenrick; First Secretary FCO since July 1999; born 18/05/73; FCO 1994; Full-Time Language Training 1995; Third later Second Secretary (Chancery) New Delhi 1996.

Butler, Christopher Giles Moffat; Second Secretary Berne since January 1995; born 13/03/40; HM Forces (Army) 1960-77; FCO 1977; Durban 1979; Johannesburg 1980; FCO 1982 later Second Secretary FCO 1985; m 1973 Sandra Ann Barnes (1s 1974, 1d 1978).

Butler, Georgina Susan; HM Ambassador San Jose since February 2002; born 30/11/45; FCO 1968; Paris 1969; Resigned on marriage 1970; Re-employed on contract FCO 1971; Reinstated in service 1972; SUPL (New York and Brussels UKREP) 1975; Seconded to European Commission, Brussels 1982; FCO 1985; Resigned (New Delhi/Brussels UKREP/Washington) 1987; Re-employed FCO 1999; m 1970 Stephen John Leadbetter Wright (diss 2000) (1d 1977, 1s 1979).

Butler, Penelope Margaret; FCO since May 1972; born 14/02/52; Band A2.

Butler, Sally-Anne; SUPL since June 1996; born 30/03/69; FCO 1988; Stanley 1990; Istanbul 1993; Band A2; m 1991 Jonathan Jeffers Butler.

Butt, Simon John; Head of Eastern Department April 2001; born 05/04/58; FCO 1979; Third later Second Secretary Moscow 1982; Second Secretary Rangoon 1984; Second Secretary FCO 1986; First Secretary (External Relations) Brussels (UKREP) 1990; First Secretary FCO 1994; Deputy Head of Mission Kiev 1997.

Butt, Stephen; First Secretary Athens since August 2001; born 07/05/63; FCO 1981; Cairo 1986; Athens 1991; Third Secretary FCO 1992; Second Secretary (Chancery) Islamabad 1997; FCO 2000; Band C5.

Butterfield, Sarah Jane; FCO since March 1992; born 01/07/72; Band A2.

Butterworth, Pamela Cynthia Anne, MBE (1987); FCO 1988 later Second Secretary FCO since December 1995; born 24/04/43; Geneva 1964; Hong Kong 1967; FCO 1969; Peking 1971; FCO 1973; New York 1976; FCO 1978; Washington 1986; Band C4.

Bye, Adam William; First Secretary (Chancery) New York (UKMIS) since June 2002; born 06/11/72; Customs and Excise 1994; FCO 1996; Second Secretary on Attachment to the European Commission 1997; FCO 1998; First Secretary FCO 1999; On loan to Cabinet Office 2000.

Byford, Rebecca (née Mills); Washington since November 1999; born 30/08/69; FCO 1991; Athens 1995; FCO 1996; Band A2; m 1999 David Byford.

Byrd, Margaret (née Allen); Lagos since October 1998; born 19/06/61; FCO 1987; Nairobi 1990; SUPL 1993; Washington 1994; Band B3; m 1993 Roger Anthony Byrd.

Byrde, Petronella Leoni Diana; First Secretary (Consular) Cairo since February 1998; born 20/10/48; DSAO (later FCO) 1967; Gaborone 1971; Dacca 1974; FCO 1977; Second Secretary 1979; Tokyo 1981; First Secretary (Commercial) Colombo 1986; First Secretary FCO 1990; First Secretary (Aid/Economic) Kampala 1994.

Byroo, Jacqueline Sandra; Kampala since July 2001; born 30/04/63; FCO 1982; Brussels (UKREP) 1987; FCO 1989; Vienna (UKREP) 1991; Copenhagen 1993; Kingston 1999; Band A2.

C

Caie, Andrew John Forbes; High Commissioner Bandar Seri Begawan since January 2002; born 25/07/47; FCO 1969; SRO (DS Gr.7) FCO 1972; Second Secretary Manila 1976; PRO (DS Gr.5) FCO 1980, First Secretary FCO 1983; First Secretary Head of Chancery and Consul Bogota 1984; First Secretary later Counsellor FCO 1988; Deputy Head of Mission Islamabad 1993; On loan to CSSB 1996; FCO 1997; HM Ambassador Guatemala City 1998; m 1976 Kathie-Anne Williams (1s 1979, 1d 1987).

Cairaschi, Lucien Marius; FCO since October 1985; born 11/02/65; HCS 1984; Band A2.

Cairns, Alison Marie; Tehran since November 2000; born 03/12/72; FCO 1994; Tallinn 1996; Band A2.

Cairns, David Seldon; First Secretary Geneva (UKMIS) since August 2002; born 17/04/69; FCO 1993; Second Secretary Tokyo 1995; FCO 1999; Private Secretary to Baroness Scotland FCO 2000; m 1996 Sharon Anouk Aeberhard (1d 2000).

Cairns, Donald Hunter; British Trade International since June 1998; born 29/10/46; Post Office 1967; FCO 1969; Anguilla 1972; Montevideo 1974; Abu Dhabi 1977; FCO 1980; Second Secretary (Commercial) Bogota 1982; Second Secretary (Admin) and HM Consul Caracas 1984; First Secretary (Commercial) Canberra 1988; Deputy Consul-General (Comm) Melbourne 1990; Counsellor New York (UKMIS) 1992; First Secretary FCO 1992; m 1972 Judy Francis Woods (1s 1977).

Cairns, Gina Stephanie (née Tart), MVO (1992); SUPL since January 2000; born 21/09/65; FCO 1984; Bridgetown 1986; Bonn 1990; FCO 1993; Vice-Consul Amsterdam 1997; Band C4; m 1987 William John Cairns (1s 1995, 1d 1998).

Cairns, Julie Margaret; FCO since September 1997; born 13/03/59; FCO 1977; Bonn 1979; Africa/ME Floater 1982; JAO Brussels 1984; FCO 1986; Gaborone 1990; Second Secretary (Finance) New York (UKMIS) 1993.

Calder, Stanley Shearer; Deputy Consul-General Toronto since May 2001; born 07/02/44; Immigration Service 1965; Islamabad 1972; Second Secretary Lima 1975; FCO 1980; Deputy High Commissioner Belmopan 1982; First

Secretary Peking 1986; First Secretary FCO 1990; First Secretary (Commercial) Caracas 1994; First Secretary (Commercial) Paris 1996; m 1967 Isobel Masson Leith (1s 1968, 1d 1970).

Caldwell, Christine Bernadette; ECO Vienna since May 1999; born 31/07/56; HCS 1973-77; FCO 1977; Ankara 1979; Warsaw 1979; Tripoli 1983; FCO 1984; SUPL 1986; Vice Consul Johannesburg 1991; FCO 1993; SUPL 1995; Band B3; m 1982 Clive David Wright (2d 1986, 1989).

Caley, Joanne; First Secretary (Chancery) Geneva (UKMIS) since April 1999; born 13/08/65; FCO 1991; Second Secretary Maputo 1993; FCO 1996; m 1991 Peter David Morgan (2s 1996, 1998).

Callow, Judith Elizabeth; Athens since May 2001; born 27/12/48; FCO 1970; Tananarive 1971; Geneva (UKMIS) 1973; Belgrade 1974; Abidjan 1975; Brussels (UKREP) 1977; Dakar 1979; Madrid 1983; Paris 1985; Brussels (UKDEL) 1987; Ottawa 1990; FCO 1993; Stockholm 1996; Band B3.

Callun, Rosemary (née Beckmann); FCO since February 1987; born 17/01/54; FCO 1975; Cairo 1976; Bangkok 1978; Prague 1979; Pretoria 1981; Accra 1983; Port Stanley 1985; Harare 1986; Band B3.

Calvert, Andrew Paul; Floater Duties since June 1999; born 17/01/69; HCS Cadre FCO 1989; FCO 1992; Bonn 1994; Band B3; m 1994 Julie Louis (1d 1995).

Cambridge, Roger Alan, MVO (1985); Deputy Head of Mission Helsinki since February 1999; born 12/09/52; FCO 1972; Africa Floater 1975; Stockholm 1977; Dar es Salaam 1979; Second Secretary (Chancery/Inf) Port of Spain 1983; Second later First Secretary FCO 1986; Consul (Commercial) New York (BTIO) 1990; First Secretary New York (UKMIS) 1993; FCO 1996.

Cameron, Hazel; Assistant Legal Adviser FCO since October 2000; born 14/02/75; Solicitor .

Cameron, James; Second Secretary and Consul Bucharest since January 2001; born 21/04/50; Army 1966-90; Peking 1990; FCO 1990; Bucharest 1991; FCO 1993; Taipei 1994; Band C4; m 1977 Angela Jane Arnold (2d 1977, 1979).

Cameron, Lee; Second Secretary Brussels (UKDEL NATO) since October 2000; born 01/09/76; FCO 1999; Band C4.

Campbell, Amanda Joan; SUPL since July 2002; born 24/01/69; FCO 1990; Full-Time Language Training 1999; Floater Duties 2000; Band B3.

Campbell, Christopher John; Second Secretary (Commercial) Caracas since April 1999; born 12/04/63; FCO 1982; Khartoum 1985; Dhaka 1988; Jakarta 1992; FCO 1995; Band C4; m 1989 Sharon Isabel Hale.

Campbell, David Ian; Deputy Head of Mission Manila since March 2000; born 09/07/58; FCO 1981; Budapest 1984; Third later Second Secretary

Georgetown 1985; Second Secretary FCO 1988; First Secretary (Humanitarian) Geneva (UKMIS) 1989; First Secretary FCO 1994; First Secretary (Political) Belgrade 1994.

Campbell, Robert Pius; Counsellor (ESCAP) Bangkok since August 2001; born 19/10/57; FCO 1980; Second Secretary Nairobi 1984; FCO 1985; First Secretary (Economic) Belgrade 1986; First Secretary FCO 1990; First Secretary (Political) Helsinki 1992; First Secretary (Political) Skopje 1994; First Secretary FCO 1997; m (1) 1985 Amanda Jane Guy (diss 1992) (1s 1989) (2) m 1992 Ailsa Irene Robinson (1s 1999).

Campbell, Sharon Isabel (née Hale); SMO/Consul Caracas since May 2000; born 12/02/62; FCO 1983; Warsaw 1985; FCO 1986; Dhaka 1988; Jakarta 1992; FCO 1995 later Second Secretary FCO 1996; SUPL 1999; Caracas 1999; m 1989 Christopher John Campbell.

Campbell, Susan Margaret; Pretoria since January 2000; born 28/07/64; FCO 1984; Harare 1986; FCO 1990; Brasilia 1991; Floater Duties 1993; FCO 1995; Band B3.

Canning, Mark; FCO since December 1998; born 15/12/54; FCO 1974; Freetown 1976; SUPL 1978; FCO 1978; FCO 1981; Georgetown 1982; Chicago 1986; First Secretary FCO 1988; First Secretary (Commercial) Jakarta 1994; m 1988 Leslie Marie Johnson.

Cannon, Nicholas, OBE (2002); First Secretary (Chancery) Islamabad since June 2000; born 29/05/58; FCO 1988; Second Secretary Paris 1990; Second Secretary FCO 1992; Second Secretary (Political/Commercial) Nicosia 1994; Full-Time Language Training 2000; Band D6; m 1982 Alice Cheung (2s 1992,1993).

Cantor, Anthony John James; HM Ambassador Asuncion since November 2001; born 01/02/46; DSAO 1965; Rangoon 1968; Language Training Sheffield University 1971; Tokyo 1972; Second Secretary (Consular) Accra and Vice Consul Lomé 1977; Second Secretary FCO 1980; Consul (Commercial) Osaka 1983; Deputy Head of Mission Hanoi 1990; On loan to Invest in Britain Bureau DTI 1992; First Secretary (Commercial) Tokyo 1994; Consul (Commercial) later Deputy Consul-General Osaka 1995; T/D Hanover 2000; m 1968 Patricia Elizabeth Naughton (2d 1969, 1972, 1s 1980).

Cantwell, Sarah Louise; FCO since October 2001; born 16/01/77; Home Office 2000; Band C4.

Capelin, Melanie Jane; PA/DHC Bridgetown since June 2000; born 19/12/65; FCO 1998; Band A2.

Capes, Mark Andrew; Deputy Governor Anguilla since August 2002; born 19/02/54; FCO 1971; Brussels (UKREP) 1974; Lisbon 1975; Zagreb 1978; FCO 1980; Lagos 1982; Vienna 1986; Second Secretary FCO 1989; Deputy Chief Secretary Providenciales Turks and Caicos Islands 1991; First Secretary (Economic) Wellington

1994; First Secretary FCO 1999; m 1980 Tamara Rossmanith (2d 1985, 1988).

Carbine, Michael Julian; SUPL since March 2000; born 16/01/56; FCO 1975; Budapest 1977; Khartoum 1979; FCO 1982; Budapest 1983; Second Secretary FCO 1986; Second Secretary (Visas) Düsseldorf 1990; Sofia 1995; On secondment to ICL 1998; Band C5; m 1975 Marian Parkinson (1s 1975).

Carew-Hunt, Robert Anthony; Second Secretary FCO since September 1988; born 11/10/49; FO (later FCO) 1968; Bonn 1972; Cairo 1975; FCO 1975; FCO 1979; Second Secretary Bandar Seri Begawan 1986; Band C4.

Carey, Colin Paul; FCO 1990 later Second Secretary FCO since 1994; born 21/09/57; FCO 1974; Bonn 1988; m 1981 Janet Coleman (1d 1984, 2s 1986, 1990).

Carey, Joanne Claire; Second Secretary (Commercial) Guangzhou since September 2000; born 06/02/72; FCO 1991; Islamabad 1995; T/D Peking 1999; Band C4.

Carlin, Neal Daniel; Second Secretary and Deputy Head of Mission Tegucigalpa since August 2000; born 22/03/71; FCO 1990; Geneva (UKMIS) 1994; Vice-Consul Khartoum 1996; T/D Cairo 1999; Full-Time Language Training 2000; Band C4; m 1994 Tracey Alison Rae (1s 2002).

Carnall, Philippa Jane, MBE (1986); FCO since August 2000; born 31/07/57; FCO 1980; Beirut 1983; Damascus 1984; FCO 1986; Hanoi 1988; Washington 1991; FCO 1993; Cairo 1997; Band B3.

Carney, Jonathan Patrick; Bahrain since October 1999; born 23/02/68; DHSS 1986; FCO 1989; Islamabad 1992; Riyadh 1995; Band B3; m 1996 Rhonda Ann Fitzgerald (2d 1997,1999).

Carr, Corrine (née Cannard); SUPL since July 1999; born 28/02/70; FCO 1991; Berne 1994; FCO 1996; Band A2; m 1996 Darren Andrew Carr.

Carr, Peter Douglas; Deputy Management Officer New Delhi since July 2002; born 02/05/47; DSAO (later FCO) 1967; Kaduna 1969; FCO 1970; Delhi 1971; Bogota 1974; FCO 1978; Kuwait 1981; FCO 1984; New York (JAO) 1985; Second Secretary FCO 1988; Second Secretary (Consular) Jakarta 1997; m 1972 Cynthia Jane Begley (1s 1975, 2d 1977, 1983).

Carr-Alloway, Christine Anne (née Carr); FCO since October 1998; born 13/02/60; FCO 1978; Paris 1980; Brussels (UKREP) 1983; FCO 1986; Kuwait 1992; Full-Time Language Training 1994; FCO 1994; Third later Second Secretary Geneva (UKMIS) 1995; Band C4; m 1991 Terry Alloway.

Carrick, Aileen Margaret; Floater Duties since June 1995; born 21/02/69; FCO 1989; Rome 1992; Band B3.

Carrick, Nicholas John, OBE (2002); First Secretary FCO since May 2002; born 01/02/67; FCO 1990; Second Secretary (Political) Berlin 1993; Second later First Secretary FCO 1995; First Secretary Lagos 1999; Band D6.

Carrick, Robert Thomas; Jerusalem since March 2002; born 05/05/64; FCO 1987; Damascus 1994; FCO 1997; SUPL 2000; Band B3; m 1997 Rachel Woodward.

Carroll, Heidi Amanda; FCO since September 2000; born 09/05/68; FCO 1988; Brussels 1992; FCO 1995; Floater Duties 1998; Band B3.

Carson, Christine; Seoul since September 1998; born 18/05/65; FCO 1990; Hong Kong (JLG) 1992; Lima 1995; Band A2.

Carter, Andrew, CMG (1995); UK Representative with the personal rank of Ambassador to the Council of Europe, Strasbourg since 2000; born 04/12/43; FCO 1971; Second Secretary Warsaw 1972; First Secretary 1974; Bonn 1975; FCO 1978; On loan to MOD 1981; FCO 1983; Counsellor CDA Chatham House 1984; Counsellor and Head of Chancery Brussels (UKDEL NATO) 1986; Deputy Govenor Gibraltar 1990; Minister Moscow 1995; Ambassador Moscow 1997; m (1) 1973 Anne Caroline Morgan (diss 1986) (1d 1978); (2) 1988 Catherine Mary Tyler (1d 1989,1s 1993).

Carter, Dr David, CVO (1995); High Commissioner Dhaka since January 2000; born 04/05/45; FCO (Research Cadre) 1970; Second Secretary Accra 1971; FCO/Cabinet Office 1975; First Secretary 1977; First Secretary and Head of Chancery Manila 1980; FCO 1983; Deputy High Commissioner and Head of Chancery Lusaka 1986; Counsellor FCO 1990; Deputy Head of Mission, later Deputy High Commissioner (1994) Cape Town/Pretoria 1992; Minister and Deputy High Commissioner New Delhi 1996; m 1968 Susan Victoria Wright (1d 1975, 1s 1978).

Carter, Dennis Sidney; First Secretary FCO since April 1999; born 12/06/47; Commonwealth Office 1964; DSAO (later FCO) 1966; Bogota 1969; Moscow 1973; FCO 1974; Bonn 1978; Washington 1982; Harare 1984; Second Secretary FCO 1987; Second Secretary (Aid) Addis Ababa 1991; Second Secretary (Comm/Man/Vice Consul) Montevideo 1995; First Secretary (Management Officer) T/D Madrid 1998; m 1968 Catherine Rose (2s 1969,1975).

Carter, Hannah Katharine; FCO since November 1998; born 20/08/74.

Carter, Kevin Robert; T/D Amsterdam and Brussels since January 2000; born 26/08/55; OPCS 1972-76; Dar es Salaam (LE) 1979-82; FCO 1983; Warsaw 1984; Third Secretary (Consular) Valletta 1987; FCO 1989; Second Secretary Peking 1992; Full-Time Language Training 1994; Vice-Consul (Commercial) Düsseldorf 1995; Band C4; m 1976 Sandra Ann McHugh (2d 1985, 1986).

Carter, Nicholas Paul; Deputy Head of Mission Riga since December 1999; born 13/03/46; Commonwealth Office (later FCO) 1966; Belgrade 1970; Bombay 1972; Prague 1976; On loan to Midland Bank (International) 1980; FCO 1981; Second Secretary Bonn 1983; First Secretary (Commercial) Kuala Lumpur 1986; First Secretary FCO 1990; Consul-General Ho Chi Minh City 1994; Attached to the Department for International Development 1997; Band D6; m (1) 1970 (2s 1971,1978, 1d 1974); m (2) 1994 Andrea Helen Abrahams.

Carter, Peter Leslie; Counsellor, Consul-General and Deputy Head of Mission Tel Aviv since May 2001; born 19/11/56; FCO 1984; Second later First Secretary (Chancery) New Delhi 1986; First Secretary FCO 1989; On Secondment as Principal Administrator CFSP Unit, EU Council Secretariat, Brussels 1994; Counsellor FCO 1998; m 1985 Rachelle Hays (1d 1991)

Carter, Thomas Henry; First Secretary (Head of Political Section) Bangkok since October 1999; born 22/11/53; FCO 1976; Paris (ENA) 1978; Paris 1979; Vice-Consul later Second Secretary (Chancery) Bogotá 1983; Second Secretary FCO 1987; First Secretary (Environment) Bonn 1990; T/D Paris 1990; FCO 1995; Full-Time Language Training 1999; m 1997 Carolyn Jayne Davidson (2s 1998, 1999).

Cartmell, Glyn Richard; Third Secretary Addis Ababa since December 2001; born 23/02/69; British Army 1985-92 and 1996; FCO 1996; FCO 1997; Kiev 1997; Royal Air Force 1997; Kampala 1998; Band B3; ptnr, Vanessa Cathy Thom (1s 1992).

Cartwright, Peter John; Management Officer La Paz since December 2001; born 23/03/55; FCO 1975; On loan to Masirah 1978; Athens 1979; Paris 1982; Kabul 1984; FCO 1986; UKDEL NATO 1990; Banjul 1992; FCO 1996; On secondment to Business Link , Shropshire, DTI 1999; Band B3; m 1984 Pamela Jane Edwards (2s 1988, 1992, 1d 1986).

Cartwright, Stephen Mark; Oslo since March 2000; born 23/08/64; FCO 1985; East Berlin 1987; Bombay 1988; FCO 1993; Third Secretary (Aid) Gaborone 1996; Band C4; m 1988 Nicola Bjorg Joyce (1s 1991).

Carty, Helen Elizabeth (née Measures); Floater Duties since June 2001; born 23/06/66; FCO 1992; Johannesburg 1994; Bonn 1998; Jedda 2000; Band B3.

Carwithen, Paul Ivor; Second Secretary FCO since January 1999; born 18/02/64; FCO 1993; Copenhagen 1996; Band C4; m 1992 Ann Davies (2s 1994, 1996).

Cary, Anthony Joyce, CMG (1997); SUPL since September 1999; born 01/07/51; FCO 1973; Third Secretary Berlin (BMG) 1975; Second later First Secretary FCO 1978; Harkness Fellow at Stanford Business School 1980; FCO 1982; PS to Minister of State FCO 1984; First Secretary and Head of Chancery Kuala Lumpur 1986; On loan to EC Commission 1989; Counsellor FCO 1993; Counsellor Washington 1997; m 1975 Clare Louise Katharine Elworthy (3s 1978, 1980, 1983, 1d 1985).

Casey, Claudia; Second Secretary Seoul since July 2002; born 05/10/67; FCO 1996; Third later Second Secretary (Political/Information) Addis Ababa 1998.

Casey, Nigel Philip, MVO (1995); Full-Time Language Training (Russian) since January 2002; born 29/05/69; FCO 1991; Vice-Consul (Political/Aid/Information) Johannesburg 1993; Second later First Secretary Washington 1996; FCO 1998.

Cassidy, Sarah Jane (née Gardner); FCO since January 1998; born 27/12/68; FCO 1986; Bangkok 1989; Lilongwe 1992; SUPL 1996; Band B3; m 1995 Eamon Martin Cassidy

Cassy, Grace Aldren; Second Secretary Islamabad since September 2000; born 04/08/76; FCO 1998; Band C4.

Castillo, Oscar Luis; Kathmandu since December 2001; born 05/08/69; FCO 1990; Islamabad 1993; FCO 1995; Floater Duties 1999; Band A2.

Caton, Michael Malusi; SUPL since 1999; born 18/05/64; DHSS 1986-89; FCO 1989; Third Secretary (Chancery) Canberra 1992; Third Secretary (Chancery) Durban 1995; Band B3; m 1991 Ann Margaret Elliott

Caton, Dr Valerie; Head of Environment Policy Dept FCO since October 2002; born 12/05/52; FCO 1980; Second later First Secretary (EC Affairs) Brussels 1982; First Secretary FCO 1984; First Secretary (Chancery) Paris 1988; Counsellor and Consul-General Stockholm 1993; Counsellor (Financial & Economic) Paris 1997; m 1987 David Mark Harrison (1d 1992, 1s 1994).

Catsaras, Zamir Nicholas; FCO since October 2001; born 19/02/73; Life Guards 1995-01; Band C4; m 1999 Natasha Landell-Mills.

Caughey, Alan Marsh; Third Secretary (Political/EU) Prague since February 2001; born 17/11/71; FCO 1990; Geneva (UKMIS) 1994; Bombay 1997; Band B3.

Caulfield, Tracy Ann; Düsseldorf since September 2001; born 10/03/70; FCO 1988; Vienna (UKMIS) 1990; FCO 1993; Wellington 1994; FCO 1998; Band B3.

Cavagan, John Raymond; Bogotá since May 1993; born 09/10/66; FCO 1990; Band B3.

Cavill, David John; Floater Duties since March 2000; born 13/06/41; HM Forces (Army) 1961-76; HMC and E 1979-84; RUC 1984-89; Moscow 1989; Havana 1990; Bangkok 1991; Floater Duties 1995; Moscow 1996; FCO 1999; Band C4; m 1983 Eve Nicholl.

Cawdron, Thomas Andrew; FCO since April 2002; born 27/05/78; Band C4.

Cayless, Trevor Martin; Second Secretary (Commercial) Madrid since August 2001; born 18/05/66; DHSS 1985; FCO 1986; Third Secretary (Aid) Lusaka 1990; Full-Time Language Training 1993; Frankfurt 1994; Second Secretary FCO 1997; m 1989 Rosemary Anne Whiting (1s 1996, 1d 1999).

Cazalet, Piers William Alexander; Second Secretary (Political/Information) Nicosia since September 1995; born 20/10/66; FCO 1991; Language Training 1994; m Alyana Sharafutdinova (1s 1990, 1d 1995).

Cetti, Joanne Martine; FCO since June 2002; born 18/01/72; Second Secretary FCO 1997; Second Secretary (Economic) Kampala 2000; Band C4.

Chadwick, Janine Linda (née Laurence); Khartoum since November 1999; born 09/04/54; FCO 1983; Brasilia 1987; Vienna (UKMIS) 1991; Reykjavik 1994; FCO 1997; Band A2; m 1985 Peter Guy Chadwick.

Chadwick, John Anthony; Second Secretary (Commercial) Damascus since February 2000; born 16/12/52; FCO 1971; Malta 1973; Manila 1976; FCO 1980; Islamabad 1983; São Paulo 1988; FCO 1992 later Second Secretary FCO 1994; Second Secretary (Commercial) Riyadh 1996; Band C4; m 1976 Jane Saliba (3d 1979, 1983, 1986, 1s 1981).

Chadwick, Nigel Spencer; Athens since September 1999; born 17/09/52; FCO 1971; Berne 1973; Buenos Aires 1977; Dacca 1980; Lima 1981; FCO 1984; Bombay 1988; FCO 1992; Banjul 1996; Band B3.

Chalmers, Kathleen Corbett; SUPL since September 1997; born 19/08/59; Brasilia 1981; FCO 1982; Hanoi 1983; FCO 1986; Rome 1987; SUPL 1990; FCO 1991; Hong Kong 1994; Band A2.

Chalmers, Nicholas John Pender; First Secretary FCO since May 2002; born 04/05/71; FCO 1988; FCO 1993; Second Secretary (Political) Islamabad 1995; First Secretary Pristina 2000; Band D6.

Chamberlain, Valerie Ann (née Crocombe); Kathmandu since April 2002; born 16/07/62; FCO 1980; Washington 1984; Gibraltar 1987; Prague 1989; FCO 1991; Bombay 1998; Mumbai 2001; SUPL 2001; Band B3; m 1997 Martin Chamberlain (1s 2001).

Chambers, Dr David Ian; First Secretary FCO since April 1998; born 04/12/47; Principal Research Officer FCO 1987; First Secretary and Consul Macao BTC Hong Kong 1994; Band D6; m (1) 1978 Merilyn Figueroa (diss 1990); (2) 1991 Tharinee Plobyon.

Chambers, David Michael Anthony; Deputy High Commissioner Victoria since February 1999; born 12/11/61; Inland Revenue 1986; FCO 1993; Lagos

1995; Band B3; m 1990 Tracey Robinson (1s 1994, 1d 1999).

Chandler, Julian; First Secretary (Commercial) Nairobi since December 1998; born 07/07/50; DSAO (later FCO) 1967; Istanbul 1971; Singapore 1976; Kuala Lumpur 1977; FCO 1979; Port Stanley 1982; Assistant Trade Commissioner Hong Kong 1984; First Secretary FCO 1989; Deputy High Commissioner Mbabane 1992; m 1998 Caroline Louise Parkinson (1d 1980, 3s 1982, 1992, 1994).

Chandler, Steven; Third Secretary (Chancery) Stockholm since March 2002; born 27/01/71; Ottawa 1994; FCO 1994; SUPL 1999; T/D Belgrade 2000; Band B3; m 1996 Jenny Wieslander (1s 1997).

Chandler, Steven Clive; SUPL since June 2002; born 16/03/68; DHSS 1986; FCO 1987; Berlin (BMG) 1989; Dhaka 1992; Istanbul 1995; Sarajevo 1997; Third later Second Secretary FCO 1998; Band C4.

Chaplin, Edward Graham Mellish, OBE (1998); Director to Middle East Command FCO since April 2002; born 21/02/51; FCO 1973; MECAS 1974; Third Secretary Muscat 1975; Second Secretary Brussels 1977; Paris (ENA) 1978; Private Secretary to Lord President of the Council 1979; First Secretary FCO 1981; First Secretary and Head of Chancery Tehran 1985; First Secretary FCO 1987; Counsellor FCO on secondment to Price Waterhouse Management Consultants 1990; Deputy Permanent Representative and Head of Chancery Geneva (UKMIS) 1992; Counsellor FCO 1996; HM Ambassador Amman 2000; m 1983 Nicola Helen Fisher (2d 1984, 1989, 1s 1987).

Chapman, Adrian Paul; Second Secretary (Political/Public Affairs) Seoul since June 2001; born 14/08/69; FCO 1988; Brussels (UKREP) 1990; Islamabad 1993; FCO 1996; On loan to DTI 1998; Band C4; m 1999 Fiona Witty (1d 2000).

Chapman, Colin; FCO since September 2000; born 12/01/58; Army 1974-79; FCO 1980; Bonn 1986; FCO 1988; Third Secretary Rome 1991; Second Secretary Ankara 1997; m 1983 Katherine Anne French (1d 1987).

Chapman, Frederick John; FCO since November 1997; born 15/10/44; GPO 1961; FCO 1968; Singapore 1969; FCO 1972; Bahrain 1972; Helsinki 1973; FCO 1975; Nairobi 1979; FCO 1982; Addis Ababa 1983; FCO 1986; Third Secretary Brasilia 1990; FCO 1994; Attaché Vienna 1995; m (1) 1967 Mary Patricia Clarke (diss 1988) (1d 1968, 1s 1973); (2) Maria Schuh (née Hedl).

Chapman, Yvonne Kay; Geneva (UKMIS) since November 1999; born 28/09/62; DETR 1987; FCO 1998; Band A2; (1s 1991).

Chappell, Julie Louise Jo; Second Secretary (Political/Economic) Amman since November

2000; born 02/04/78; FCO 1999; Full-Time
Language Training 2000; Band C4.

Chapple, Katherine Margaret; FCO since October
1990; born 19/09/64; Home Civil Service 1988;
Band A2.

Charlton, Alan, CMG (1996); Director South East
Europe later Director Personnel FCO since
January 2001; born 21/06/52; FCO 1978;
Language Training 1979; Second later First
Secretary Amman 1981; First Secretary FCO
1984; First Secretary (Deputy Political Adviser)
Berlin (BMG) 1986; On loan to the Cabinet Office
1991; Counsellor FCO 1993; Counsellor
(Political) and then Minister and Deputy Head of
Mission Bonn 1996; Minister and Deputy Head of
Mission Berlin 1999; m 1974 Judith Angela
Carryer (2s 1979, 1985, 1d 1981).

Chase, Robert John; Consul-General Milan since
July 1996; born 13/03/43; FO 1965; Third later
Second Secretary Rangoon 1966; FCO 1969; First
Secretary (Info) Rio de Janeiro 1972; FCO 1976;
On secondment to ICI Ltd 1980; First Secretary
FCO 1982; Counsellor (Comm) Moscow 1985;
Counsellor FCO 1988; Consul-General Chicago
1993; m 1966 Gillian Ann Shelton (1d 1968, 1s
1969).

Chassels, Lilias Penman Morton; FCO since May
1993; born 08/05/66; FCO 1988; Addis Ababa
1991; Band A2.

Chatfield, Louise Mary; Mbabane since January
1999; born 28/04/71; FCO 1997; Band A2.

Chatt, Paul Anthony; First Secretary
(Management) Warsaw since January 2000; born
07/04/56; FCO 1975; Ottawa 1977; East Berlin
1979; Khartoum 1981; FCO 1984; Third later
Second Secretary (Aid/Comm) Banjul 1987;
Second Secretary (Man/Cons) Berne 1990; Second
later First Secretary FCO 1995; Band C5; m (1)
1979 Delyth Hudson (diss 1988); (2) 1990 Tracie
Cavell Heatherington (2d 1992, 1993).

Chatterton-Dickson, Robert Maurice French;
First Secretary FCO since September 2000; born
01/02/62; FCO 1990; Second Secretary
(Chancery/Information) Manila 1991; First
Secretary FCO 1994; First Secretary (Press, later
PS/HMA) Washington 1997; m 1995 Teresa
Bargielska Albor (2d 1996, 1997, 1 step d 1982, 1
step s 1984).

Chaudhry, Kareem Arthur; First Secretary
(Regional Affairs) Cairo since May 2001; born
03/03/70; FCO 1994; Dubai 1996; Second
Secretary FCO 1999; Band D6; m 1993 Nicola
Lauraine Kelly (3s 1994, 1998, 2002).

Cherrie, Yvonne Elizabeth; Deputy Consul-
General and Consul (Commercial) Barcelona since
July 2002; born 31/03/62; FCO 1980; Brussels
(UKREP) 1982; Sana'a 1985; Bahrain 1988; FCO
1989; On secondment to Birmingham Chamber of
Commerce 1991; Third Secretary (Commercial)
Berlin 1993; Second later First Secretary

(Pol/PPA) Mexico City 1997; Band C5; m 1996
William Theodore von Minden.

Chesman, Rebecca; Second Secretary
(Commercial) Peking since November 1997; born
31/10/72; FCO 1994; Full-Time Language
Training (Mandarin) 1995; Band C4.

Chick, John Charles; Second Secretary (HM
Consul/ECM) Kathmandu since September 2000;
born 22/10/47; FCO 1971; Baghdad 1973; FCO
1975; Amman 1976; FCO 1979; Darwin 1980;
FCO 1984; Hanoi 1985; FCO 1988; Third
Secretary (Management) and Vice-Consul Quito
1990; Third Secretary (Comm/Chan/P&PA) Dhaka
1995; Second Secretary FCO 1999; m (1) 1971
Denese Irene Smalley (diss); (2) 1989 Tran Thi
Thuy Duong (1s 1989, 1d 1994).

Chilcott, Dominick John; Counsellor Brussels
(UKREP) since July 1998; born 17/11/59; Royal
Navy 1978-79; FCO 1982; Language Training
1984; Third later Second Secretary Ankara 1984;
First Secretary FCO 1988; First Secretary Lisbon
1993; First Secretary FCO 1996; m 1983 Jane
Elizabeth Bromage (1d 1986, 3s 1988, 1991,
1995).

Childs, Marie-Louise; SUPL since April 2002;
born 23/03/66; FCO 1989; Vice-Consul Bangkok
1991; Quito 1995; Band B3; m 1997 Mr S
O'Sullivan.

Chown, Christopher James; FCO since August
1996; born 05/03/67; FCO 1988; Paris 1993; Band
C5; (1s 1994).

Chrimes, Neil Roy; Counsellor (Trade/Economic)
Ottawa since July 2001; born 10/06/54; MAFF
1975; Harkness Fellow MIT 1977; MAFF 1979;
Economic Adviser FCO 1981; IMF Research
Dept. 1987; Senior Economic Adviser FCO 1989;
Deputy Permanent Representative Paris (UKDEL
OECD) 1994; Jakarta 1998; Head of African
Department (Southern) 1999; m 1982 Anne
(Henny) Barnes (1s 1988, 1d 1990).

Christie, Iain Robert; SUPL since October 2000;
born 07/12/65; Called to the Bar (Inner Temple)
1989; Assistant Legal Adviser FCO 1992; Senior
Assistant Legal Adviser FCO 1995; Bridgetown
1998; m Katherine Ann Gillam (2d 1996, 1997).

Christie, Katherine Ann (née Gillam); SUPL since
November 1997; born 25/01/69; FCO 1992; Band
B3; m 1995 Iain Robert Christie (2d 1996, 1998).

Christopher, Sir Duncan Robin Carmichael, KBE
(2000), CMG (1997); HM Ambassador Buenos
Aires since November 2000; born 13/10/44; FCO
1970; Second later First Secretary New Delhi
1972; First Secretary FCO 1976; Head of
Chancery Lusaka 1980; First Secretary FCO 1983;
On loan to Cabinet Office 1985; Counsellor
(Comm) Madrid 1987; Counsellor FCO 1991; HM
Ambassador Addis Ababa 1994; HM Ambassador
Jakarta 1997; m 1980 Merril Stevenson (2d 1989,
1991).

Chubbs, Sylvia Sharon; Budapest since March 2001; born 09/05/58; FCO 1984; Paris 1986; Colombo 1989; Moscow 1993; Brussels (UKREP) 1995; FCO 1998; Band A2.

Chugg, Daniel Patrick; Vice-Consul (Political) Hong Kong since August 2001; born 26/01/73; FCO 1998; Language Training 1999; Language Training Hong Kong 2000; Band C4; m 1999 Alison Fiona Cubie.

Chun, David John; Second Secretary (Commercial) Madrid since August 1999; born 04/04/64; FCO 1985; Lagos 1987; Moscow 1992; FCO 1996; Band C4; m 1987 Grace Fotheringham (1d 1994).

Chun, Grace (née Fotheringham); SUPL since August 1999; born 24/07/66; FCO 1985; Lagos 1987; Moscow 1992; FCO 1996; Band B3; m 1987 David John Chun (1d 1994).

Church, Alistair John Bentley; FCO since July 2002; born 23/08/63; FCO 1992; Kiev 1995; Second Secretary FCO 1998; SUPL 2000; Band C4; m 1990 Michelina Patrizia Forgione (1d 1997).

Church, Bettina Frances; SUPL since June 1997; born 30/04/63; FCO 1983; Gaborone 1984; Geneva (UKMIS) 1987; SUPL 1990; New York (UKMIS) 1991; FCO 1992; Band B3; m 1990 Julian Andrew Church (1s 1995).

Church, Roger Gilbert; Jedda since March 2000; born 01/06/46; FO 1965; Abu Dhabi 1968; Bonn 1970; East Berlin 1973; Lusaka 1974; FCO 1976; Madras 1979; Colombo 1980; Quito 1982; Second Secretary (Commercial) Madras 1983; Second Secretary FCO 1988; Deputy High Commissioner Nassau 1990; Deputy Head of Mission Lima 1994; FCO 1998; Band C5; m 1972 Kathleen Wilson Dryburgh (2s 1974, 1977).

Clare, Debbie Marie; FCO since June 2000; born 21/03/69; FCO 1987; Resigned 1990; Reinstated (FCO) 1994; Berne 1996; Dar es Salaam 1997; Bonn 1998; Lusaka 1999; Band B3.

Claridge, Susan Elisabeth; FCO since November 1998; born 10/05/60; FCO 1984; Brussels (UKREP) 1987; Geneva (UKDIS) 1990; FCO 1993; Bonn 1995; Band B3.

Clark, Angela; Dubai since May 1999; born 22/11/67; FCO 1997; Kuala Lumpur 1998; SUPL 2000; Band A2; m 1998 Christopher Neil Walker (2s 1996, 1999).

Clark, Catherine Elizabeth (née Ferguson); SUPL since May 2000; born 12/06/59; FCO 1979; Singapore 1981; Istanbul 1985; FE/SEA Floater 1988; Brussels (UKDEL NATO) 1991; Band C4; m 1990 Eldred Richard Wraighte Clark (2d 1994, 1996).

Clark, Christopher George; Floater Duties since February 1999; born 15/04/70; FCO 1990; T/D Mostar 1994; Santiago 1995; Band B3.

Clark, Hilary Mary; FCO since April 1985; born 10/04/62; FCO 1980; Brussels (UKREP) 1982; Bonn 1983; Band B3.

Clark, James Frame; Head of Conference and Visits Group August 1999; born 12/03/63; FCO 1988; Second Secretary 1989; FCO 1990; Full-Time Language Training Cairo 1990; Second Secretary (External Affairs) Brussels (UKREP) 1991; Second later First Secretary FCO 1993; On loan to German Foreign Ministry 1997; First Secretary (EU) Bonn 1998; m 1990 Michele Taylor (diss 1998).

Clark, Janet E; FCO since April 1998; born 18/07/67; Band A2.

Clark, Katherine Margaret (née Storey); FCO since June 1985; born 18/03/50; FCO 1971; Muscat 1972; Budapest 1974; FCO 1975; Peking 1977; New York (UKMIS) 1978; Rio de Janeiro 1982; Band B3; m 1987 Richard William Clark.

Clark, Kenneth; FCO since August 1997; born 18/08/49; Post Office Savings Department 1966; DSAO 1967; Kuwait 1971; Moscow 1974; Rio de Janeiro 1975; FCO 1978; New York 1981; Jedda 1983; Second Secretary FCO 1986; Second Secretary (Comm) Gaborone 1989; Second Secretary (Management) and Consul Lima 1994; m 1970 Agnes Pearson Elder (3s 1971, 1974 1978).

Clark, Michael; FCO since September 1996; born 21/09/59; FCO 1979; Georgetown 1983; Stockholm 1986; Kuwait 1988; Montreal 1992; Band D6; m 1983 Jacqueline Anne Wilkins (2s 1985, 1987).

Clark, Paul Nicholas; T/D Bratislava since July 2000; born 26/01/69; FCO 1988; Vienna 1992; Brussels (UKDEL NATO) 1993; Dhaka 1996; Band B3; m 1991 Katherine Walsh (1s 1991).

Clark, Peter; Tehran since January 2000; born 26/03/47; Royal Air Force 1962-87; FCO 1987; Nairobi 1991; FCO 1995; Band B3; (2s 1974, 1977).

Clark, Peter; SUPL since April 2002; born 18/04/54; Principal Research Officer FCO 1982; First Secretary (Chancery) Peking 1988; First Secretary FCO 1992; First Secretary Canberra 1996; FCO 2001; m 1977 Alison Padgett (1d 1982, 1s 1984).

Clark, Sandra Jean; Vice-Consul Düsseldorf since January 1989; born 03/12/67; FCO 1985; Brussels (UKDEL NATO) 1987; Band B3; m 1990 Mark Stephen Parnell.

Clark, Teresa Melanie; FCO since November 1990; born 29/05/70; Band A2.

Clarke, Julie Linda; SUPL since August 2002; born 13/01/64; FCO 1988; Moscow 1990; New York (UKMIS) 1993; Brasilia 1999; Band A2; m 2002 Gary Soper.

Clarke, Pauline Joyce; FCO since August 2002; born 08/10/67; FCO 1987; Dhaka 1989; Floater Duties 1993; FCO 1996; Zagreb 1999; Band C4.

Clarke, Peter Michael; FCO since January 1998; born 23/08/63; FCO 1988; Language Training 1990; Full-Time Language Training Taiwan 1991; Second Secretary (Science/Technology) Peking 1993.

Clarke, Richard Ian; High Commissioner Dar es Salaam since August 2001; born 07/09/55; FCO 1977; Caracas 1978; Second later First Secretary FCO 1983; First Secretary Washington 1987; First Secretary later Counsellor FCO 1991; Deputy Head of Mission Dublin 1996; FCO 1998; m (1) 1978 Ann Menzies (1s 1984) (diss); (2) 1993 Sheenagh Marie O'Connor (2s 1995, 1997).

Clarke, Roger Colin; Cairo since April 2000; born 01/10/52; Armed Forces 1969-92; FCO 1992; Moscow 1993; New Delhi 1996; Band C4; m (1) 1971 Linda (2s 1973) (diss 1998); (2) Maria Louise Wesstrom.

Clarke, Roger Stephen Graver, LVO (1991); Deputy Observer later Deputy High Commissioner Windhoek since March 1989; born 08/05/55; FCO 1977; Third Secretary Kinshasa 1978; Second Secretary Paris 1980; First Secretary FCO 1984; On loan to DTI 1986.

Clarke, Rosemary Protase, MBE (1992); First Secretary (Commercial) Singapore since July 2000; born 13/02/50; FCO 1977; Port Louis 1978; FCO 1982; Manila 1984; Bahrain 1988; Second Secretary FCO 1991; Second Secretary (Immigration) Dhaka 1992; Band C5; m 1982 Daniel Sinassamy (1s 1984, 1d 1987).

Clarke, Sarah (née Hutson); FCO since May 2002; born 28/01/61; FCO 1983; Accra 1985; Ankara 1988; FCO 1991; Islamabad 1993; FCO 1996; Vice-Consul (Political) Jerusalem 1998; Band B3; m 1993 Richard Henry Clarke.

Clarke, Shaun Jerome; Third Secretary (Management) Tokyo since July 2001; born 07/11/67; Home Civil Service 1989-93; FCO 1993; Amman 1996; Valletta 1999; Band B3; m 1996 Karen Angela Evans.

Clasen, Peter; Vice-Consul Istanbul since December 2001; born 02/12/74; FCO 1998; Band C4.

Clay, Edward, CMG (1994); High Commissioner Nairobi since December 2001; born 21/07/45; Third Secretary FO (later FCO) 1968; Nairobi 1970; Second later First Secretary (Chancery) Sofia 1973; FCO 1975; First Secretary (Comm) Budapest 1979; First Secretary FCO 1982; Counsellor and Head of Chancery Nicosia 1985; Counsellor FCO 1989; High Commissioner Kampala 1993 additionally HM Ambassador Burundi and Rwanda 1994; FCO 1997; High Commissioner Nicosia 1999; m 1969 Anne Stroud (3d 1972, 1974, 1978).

Clay, Pamela (née Kendall); SUPL since April 2001; born 26/11/62; FCO 1986; Moscow 1989; FCO 1990; Copenhagen 1992; FCO 1995; Helsinki 1997; The Hague 1998; Band A2; m 1998 Andrew Garry Clay (1d 2000).

Clayden, Dr Timothy, OBE (2000); Counsellor (Political) Islamabad since October 2001; born 28/03/60; Second later First Secretary FCO 1989; First Secretary (Info) Warsaw 1991; FCO 1994; Lagos 1995; First Secretary FCO 1999; Band D6; m 1984 Katharine Susan Jackson.

Clayton, Mark Darrell; Third Secretary (Political) Moscow since August 1998; born 12/06/73; FCO 1997; Band C4.

Clayton, Tamsin Mary Clare; Third Secretary (Political Press and Public Affairs) Bahrain since May 2001; born 25/05/69; FCO 2000; Band B3.

Cleary, Anthony Shaun; First Secretary (Energy) Paris (OECD) since September 1998; born 27/10/65; FCO 1988; Third later Second later First Secretary (Chancery) Pretoria/Cape Town 1990; First Secretary FCO 1994.

Cleaver, Helen Louise; FCO since June 2001; born 11/12/68; FCO 1989; Brussels 1996; FCO 1999; Stockholm 2000; Band A2.

Clegg, Laura Margaret; SUPL since June 2000; born 29/03/65; FCO 1989; Vice-Consul Bucharest 1994; Deputy Head of Mission Antananarivo 1997; Band C4.

Clegg, Leslie David, MVO (1985); Deputy Head of Consular Division since March 2000; born 12/10/49; FO (later FCO) 1967; Banjul (formerly Bathurst) 1971; Wellington 1974; FCO 1977; New Delhi 1980; Second Secretary Lisbon 1984; First Secretary FCO 1988; First Secretary (Commercial) Madrid 1992; First Secretary (Management) Nairobi 1996; FCO 2000; m 1970 Louise Elizabeth Straughan (3d 1973, 1976, 1984).

Cleghorn, Bruce Elliot; High Commissioner Kuala Lumpur since November 2001; born 19/11/46; Second Secretary Geneva (UKDEL CSCE) 1974; Second Secretary FCO 1974; Second Secretary FCO 1975; First Secretary Brussels (NATO) 1976; First Secretary New Delhi 1980; First Secretary FCO 1983; Counsellor Vienna (UKDEL CSCE) 1987; Deputy Head of Delegation Vienna (UKDEL CFE) 1989; Counsellor and Deputy High Commissioner Kuala Lumpur 1992; Head of Non Proliferation Dept FCO 1995; Minister and Deputy Permanent Representative Brussels (UKDEL NATO) 1997; m 1976 Sally Ann Robinson (3s 1978, 1981, 1986).

Cleland, Deborah Julia (née Caldow); Second Secretary FCO since February 1999; born 08/09/67; FCO 1987; Accra 1990; FCO 1992; Oslo 1994; Band C4; m 1993 James Cleland.

Clements, Martin Hugh, OBE (2002); FCO since October 2002; born 26/07/61; FCO 1983; Second Secretary (Chancery) Tehran 1986; FCO 1987; First Secretary (IAEA) Vienna (UKMIS) 1990;

First Secretary FCO 1994; First Secretary Bonn 1998; Counsellor Berlin 1999.

Clements, Micheal Colin; SUPL since September 1992; born 24/08/49; FCO 1974; Second later First Secretary Athens 1976; On loan to the Cabinet Office 1980; FCO 1982; First Secretary and Head of Chancery Singapore 1985; First Secretary FCO 1989; Counsellor and Deputy High Commissioner Nicosia 1990; m 1972 Julia Mary Roebuck.

Clemitson, Lynne Dawn; FCO since July 1991; born 04/05/61; FCO 1979; Washington 1982; Dhaka 1985; Wellington 1988; Band B3; m 1983 Malcolm John Clemitson.

Clephane, James Cavin Alexander, OBE (1996); SUPL since November 1999; born 03/02/54; FCO 1973; Budapest 1976; Seoul 1977; Jakarta 1980; FCO 1983; Third later Second Secretary Muscat 1986; Second later First Secretary Bandar Seri Begawan 1991; First Secretary (Defence Co-operation) Bandar Seri Begawan 1995; On loan to MOD 1998; Band D6; m 1974 Mary Buchanan Dorman.

Cliff, Ian Cameron, OBE (1991); HM Ambassador Sarajevo since October 2001; born 11/09/52; FCO 1979; Language Training 1980; Second later First Secretary Khartoum 1982; First Secretary FCO 1985; First Secretary (Chancery) New York (UKMIS) 1990; Counsellor on loan to DTI 1993; Deputy Head of Mission Vienna 1996; m 1988 Caroline Mary Redman (1s 1989, 1d 1993).

Clissold, Sean Dominic; First Secretary (Management) and Consul Ankara since November 2000; born 06/04/58; FCO 1975; Geneva (UKMIS) 1978; Rabat 1981; Ankara 1983; Lagos 1987; FCO 1990; Third Secretary (Commercial) Istanbul 1993; Second Secretary (Consular) Warsaw 1997; Band C5; m 1986 Belgin Savaci

Clough, Graham Ronald; Second Secretary Vienna (UKMIS) since March 2002; born 13/05/55; FCO 1995; Second Secretary (Political) Dhaka 1998; Band B3; m 1995 Harvinder Kaur Sabharwal.

Cloughton, Stephen Paul; FCO since June 2000; born 04/11/65; FCO 1986; Bangkok 1991; FCO 1994; Skopje 1996; Band B3; m 1997 Karen Dowen.

Clunes, Anna Louise; First Secretary (Chancery) New York (UKMIS) since February 2000; born 12/03/73; FCO 1994; Second Secretary Warsaw (KHF) 1996; Full-Time Language Training 1996; Band D6.

Clydesdale, William Reginald; FCO since January 1997; born 12/08/43; MOD 1960; FCO 1980; Lagos 1985; Third Secretary Sofia 1987; FCO 1990; Washington 1994; Band C5; m 1969 Noreen Foister (2s 1973, 1976).

Coates, David; Director-General of Trade Taipei since April 1999; born 13/11/47; Second later First

Secretary FCO 1974; Language Training Hong Kong 1977; First Secretary (Commercial) Peking 1978; FCO 1981; First Secretary Geneva (UKMIS) 1986; Counsellor Peking 1989; Counsellor FCO 1993; m 1974 Joanna Kay Weil (2d 1976, 1978).

Coates, Sally Ann (née Mawby); Accra since October 1998; born 29/07/60; FCO 1979; Washington 1984; FCO 1987; Tortola 1988; FCO 1992; Georgetown 1992; Mbabane 1993; Beirut 1996; Band A2; m 1995 Alan Roger Coates.

Cobden, Alan; Deputy Consul-General and Consul (Commercial) Los Angeles since September 1998; born 15/07/54; FCO 1970; Canberra 1975; Tehran 1977; African Floater 1978; Bombay 1980; FCO 1983; Third later Second Secretary Sofia 1986; Second Secretary (Agriculture/Environment) Dublin 1989; Second Secretary FCO 1994; m 1982 Karen Anne Fawn (1s 1985, 1d 1987).

Cochrane-Dyet, Fergus John; T/D Conakry since September 2001; born 16/01/65; FCO 1987; Third later Second Secretary (Political) Lagos 1990; Second Secretary Abuja 1993; First Secretary FCO 1994; Head of BIS Tripoli 1996; Deputy Consul-General and Director of Trade and Investment Promotion Sydney 1998; First Secretary (Commercial) Jakarta 1998; m 1987 Susan Emma Aram (3s 1990, 1991, 1996).

Codd, Steven; Deputy Consul-General Shanghai since December 2000; born 19/05/61; FCO 1981; Bagdad 1982; FCO 1985; Beirut 1986; FCO 1988; Hanoi 1990; Lusaka 1993; Second Secretary FCO 1996; First Secretary (Management) Kuala Lumpur 1997; Band C5; m 1993 Ruth Brown Mulligan.

Codrington, Richard John; Deputy High Commissioner Ottawa since May 1999; born 18/12/53; MOD 1975; FCO 1978; Second later First Secretary Dar es Salaam 1980; FCO 1983; New Delhi 1985; First Secretary FCO 1989; On loan to SG Warburg & Co Ltd. 1992; Counsellor on loan to the Department of National Heritage 1994; Counsellor (Trade Promotion and Investment) Paris 1995; m 1985 Julia Elizabeth Nolan (Twin s 1991).

Cogger, Darren Barry; Canberra since November 2001; born 20/05/63; FCO 1984; Athens 1988; Belgrade 1991; New Delhi 1993; FCO 1996; Third Secretary (Management) Kiev 1997; Band B3; m 1986 Johanna Lesley Payne (1d 1989).

Coggles, Paul James; First Secretary (Political) Prague since September 2000; born 24/06/66; FCO 1989; Third Secretary (Chancery) Sofia 1992; Third Secretary FCO 1995; Full-Time Language Training 1996; Second Secretary (Political) Prague 1997; Band C5.

Coglin, Gillian Joanna; First Secretary (Management) Tokyo since June 2002; born 09/08/67; FCO 1989; Bucharest 1991; Bombay

1994; Second Secretary FCO 1997; SUPL 2000; SUPL (Japan) 2001; Band C4.

Colby, Sheila Joan, MBE (2001); Buenos Aires since January 2002; born 07/05/56; FCO 1979; Lima 1980; FCO 1983; Floater Duties 1984; FCO 1988; Kuala Lumpur 1990; Madrid 1993; FCO 1996; Mexico City 1998; Band B3.

Cole, Alexandra Pamela; Second Secretary (Political) Sarajevo since July 2002; born 02/06/70; FCO 1990; Tehran 1996; Full-Time Language Training 2000; SUPL 2001; Band C4; m 1995 Adrian Frederick Bedford.

Cole, Norman Edward, OBE (1985); First Secretary (Commercial) Riyadh since August 1995; born 24/04/43; Crown Estate Office 1962; DSAO (later FCO) 1967; Second Secretary/Vice-Consul Karachi 1969; Ottawa 1973; On loan to DOT 1977; Second Secretary FCO 1980; First Secretary (Commercial) Lusaka 1981; First Secretary FCO 1984; First Secretary (Management) Rome 1987; First Secretary FCO 1992; m 1966 Loretta Scott (2s 1970, 1972, 1d 1975).

Coleman, Julie; Colombo since June 2001; born 13/03/67; Department of Employment 1989-95; FCO 1995; Addis Ababa 1997; Band A2.

Coleman, Richard Alan; First Secretary (Management/Consul) Prague since July 2000; born 01/02/45; CRO (later FCO) 1963; Dacca 1968; FCO 1971; FCO 1972; Salisbury 1972; Freetown 1973; Tehran 1975; FCO 1979; Vientiane 1982; Kingston 1985; Second Secretary FCO 1988; Second Secretary (Consular) Peking 1991; Bridgetown 1995; FCO 1999; Karachi 1999; m (1) 1968 Susan Robertson (diss 1973) (1s 1969); (2) 1973 Celia Frances Burnett (1d 1986).

Coleman, Sandra Marie (née Duffy); Washington since June 1997; born 21/11/60; FCO 1984; Algiers 1985; Jerusalem 1987; Turks and Caicos Islands 1991; Dakar 1993; SUPL 1996; Band A2; m 1995 Scott Stanley Coleman.

Coleman, Tracey; Freetown since March 1999; born 23/01/71; FCO 1990; Ottawa 1992; World-wide Floater Duties 1995; Band A2.

Collard, James Malcolm John; MO Khartoum since August 1999; born 30/07/43; DSAO 1965; Belgrade 1968; Colombo 1971; East Berlin 1975; FCO 1976; Dacca 1979; Zurich 1981; FCO 1985; Rome 1989; Second Secretary (Management) Islamabad 1992; Band C4; m 1971 Margaret Mary Melver (1d 1980, 1s 1982).

Collard, Timothy Michael; First Secretary (Hong Kong) Peking since August 1995; born 21/03/60; FCO 1986; Language Training SOAS 1987; Language Training Hong Kong 1988; Second Secretary (Science and Technology) Peking 1989; First Secretary FCO 1993; m 1985 Patricia Polzer (2s 1987, 1989).

Collecott, Peter Salmon; Director Resources FCO since June 1999; born 08/10/50; Second Secretary

FCO 1977; MECAS 1978, First Secretary 1979; First Secretary (Political) Khartoum 1980; First Secretary (Economic/Commercial/Agricultural) Canberra 1982; FCO 1986; Counsellor (Head of Chancery, later DHM) Jakarta 1989; Counsellor (EU and Economic) Bonn 1994; FCO 1998; m 1982 Judith Patricia Pead.

Colley, Timothy John; Deputy Head of Mission Sofia since July 2000; born 13/03/65; FCO 1989 (Second Secretary 1991); Full-Time Language Training 1991; Second Secretary (Political) Islamabad 1992; First Secretary FCO 1995; Full-Time Language Training 1999; Band D6; m 1993 Janet Mary Rodemark (1s 1997, 2d 1999, 2002).

Collier, Geoffrey Thomas Grey; Second Secretary (Political) Ankara since August 2002; born 27/04/68; FCO 1990; Belgrade 1993; Dakar 1997; FCO 2000; Full-Time Language Training (Turkish) 2002; m 1999 Müge Elif Törüner.

Collier, Nicholas Gavin; Third Secretary (Political/Economic) Vilnius since May 1998; born 10/02/69; FCO 1996; Band C4; m 1999 Simona Gatti.

Collier, Stephen John, MVO (1991), RVM (1979); Deputy Consul-General and Consul (Commercial) Atlanta since October 1999; born 11/01/52; DTI 1968; FCO 1969; Bonn 1972; Aden 1975; Lilongwe 1976; Lagos 1979; FCO 1983; Amman 1985; Second Secretary Windhoek 1989; Second Secretary FCO 1992; First Secretary (Commercial) Lima 1996; m 1987 Erica Mary Cholwill Wilson.

Collingridge, Andrew; Brussels (UKDEL NATO) since January 2002; born 02/11/62; FCO 1985; Lagos 1990; FCO 1994; Bucharest 1998; FCO 2001; Band C4; m 1993 Tanya Suzanne Parsons (2d 1998, 2001).

Collingridge, Tanya Suzanne (née Parsons); Second Secretary (Political/Information) Bucharest since June 1998; born 04/02/65; FCO 1984; Warsaw 1987; Vienna (UKDEL) 1989; Lagos 1991; FCO 1994; Full-Time Language Training 1997; Band C4; m 1993 Andrew Collingridge (2d 1998, 2001).

Collings, Barry Anthony; First Secretary FCO since September 1996; born 14/06/50; RAF 1968-69; FCO 1970; Holy See 1974; Beirut 1975; Berlin 1976; Budapest 1980; Second Secretary 1981; FCO 1983; Islamabad 1985; FCO 1988; First Secretary (Bilateral Relations) Bonn 1991; Consul Munich 1993; Band C5; m 1973 Shirley Gibson (1s 1980, 1d 1984).

Collins, Alan Stanley, CMG; HM Ambassador Manila since December 1998; born 01/04/48; Ministry of Defence 1970; Private Secretary to Vice Chief of the Air Staff 1973-1975; FCO 1981; First Secretary and Head of Chancery Addis Ababa 1986; Counsellor (Commercial) and Deputy Head of Mission Manila 1990; Counsellor FCO 1993; Director of BTCO Taipei 1995; m 1971 Ann Dorothy Roberts (1d 1985, 2s 1988, 1995).

Collins, Helen Laura; Cairo since May 1998; born 15/11/70; FCO 1990; Washington 1994; Band A2.

Collins, James Robert; Bridgetown since November 2001; born 09/11/63; FCO 1986; Strasbourg 1988; Moscow 1990; FCO 1993; Band B3; m 1987 Sheila Marie Barry.

Collinson, Martin; Dubai since January 2002; born 07/09/66; FCO 1987; Band A2; m 1999 Sharon Particia Stillwell (2d 2000).

Collis, Simon Paul; Consul-General Dubai since March 2000; born 23/02/56; On secondment to BP Amoco, 1999; FCO 1978; Language Training 1979; Third later Second Secretary Bahrain 1981; First Secretary FCO 1984; New York (UKMIS) 1986; FCO 1987; First Secretary and Head of Chancery Tunis 1988; FCO 1990; First Secretary (Political) New Delhi 1991; First Secretary FCO 1994; Counsellor and Deputy Head of Mission Amman 1996.

Colloms, Catherine; FCO since 2002; born 18/08/76; FCO 1998; On loan to Coalition Information Centre 2001; T/D (Public Diplomacy) Gibraltar 2002.

Collyer, Neil Patrick; Abuja since August 2000; born 28/05/66; ODA 1985-89; FCO 1991; Pretoria 1996; Lagos 1999; Band B3; m 1997 Sara-Louise Hall.

Collyer, Nicholas Edwin; Second Secretary (Commercial/Consular) Port of Spain since August 1995; born 15/09/52; Forestry Commission 1969; FCO 1971; Moscow 1974; Colombo 1975; Budapest 1979; FCO 1981; Geneva (UKMIS) 1983; FCO 1986; New Delhi 1987; Second Secretary FCO 1989; Second Secretary (Commercial) Seoul 1992; m 1973 Kathryn Dobson (2s 1978, 1983).

Collyer, Sara-Louise (née Hall); Abuja since August 2000; born 28/10/73; FCO 1992; SUPL 1996; Pretoria 1997; Lagos 1999; Band A2; m 1997 Neil Patrick Collyer.

Colvin, Kathryn Frances; HM Ambassador Holy See since July 2002; born 11/09/45; FO (later FCO) 1968; Principal Research Officer FCO 1980; Vice Marshal of the Diplomatic Corps FCO 1999; m 1971 Brian Trevor Colvin.

Conley, Brian John; Second Secretary (Commercial/Information) Tunis since April 1999; born 10/04/67; FCO 1986; Lusaka 1989; Third Secretary (Management) and Vice Consul Auckland 1993; FCO 1994.

Connolly, Patrick Anthony, OBE (2001); First Secretary (Management) Pretoria since September 2001; born 15/02/45; CO 1964; FO 1966; Salisbury 1967; Pretoria 1969; Islamabad 1970; FCO 1973; Vienna 1976; Baghdad 1979; Second Secretary (Aid) New Delhi 1981; FCO 1984; Second Secretary and Vice-Consul Dubai 1986; First Secretary (Commercial) Tel Aviv 1990; FCO 1995; SMO Peking 1998; m 1967 Teresa Bernadette Crinion (twin s 1969, 1s 1973).

Connolly, Peter Terence; Second Secretary (Political) Lisbon since November 1996; born 02/05/65; FCO 1988; Third Secretary Managua 1990; Brussels (UKREP) 1993; Second Secretary FCO 1994.

Connor, Michael Leslie; First Secretary (Commercial) Prague since September 1995; born 15/11/49; FCO 1971; Moscow 1975; Vienna (UKDEL) 1975; Tehran 1977; FCO 1980 (APS to Minister of State 1982; Second Secretary Bonn 1983; Second later First Secretary (Commercial) Abu Dhabi 1987; First Secretary FCO 1991; m 1973 Linda Helen Woolnough (1d 1984).

Conroy, Anne Elizabeth, MVO (1991); First Secretary (Political) Budapest since August 1996; born 30/08/63; FCO 1985; Third later Second Secretary (Chancery) Manila 1988; Second later First Secretary FCO 1992; Full-Time Language Training 1995.

Contractor, Robert; Second Secretary Skopje since November 2001; born 17/05/68; FCO 1989; Floater Duties 1992; FCO 1993; Warsaw 1995; FCO 1997; Band C4.

Conway, Benjamin Simon; FCO since September 2001; born 19/09/78; Band C4.

Conway, Nicholas Peter; FCO since September 2001; born 25/06/78; Band C4.

Cook, Peter Duncan Gifford; Second later First Secretary (Chancery) Copenhagen since June 1997; born 15/08/63; FCO 1982; Georgetown 1985; Doha 1989; Third later Second Secretary FCO 1992; Second Secretary (Political/Information) Bridgetown 1995; m 1993 Maureen Nanette Sharp (2s 1995, 1996).

Cooke, Ann; Hong Kong since March 2000; born 26/02/66; DoT 1982; CCA 1989; FCO 1992; New York (UKMIS) 1996; Band A2; m 1986 Lloyd Norman Cooke (1d 1990).

Coombs, Kay; HM Ambassador Tegucigalpa since September 2002; born 08/07/45; DSAO later FCO 1967; Bonn 1971; Latin American Floater 1973; Second Secretary (Consul) Zagreb 1976; FCO 1979; Second Secretary (Aid/Inf) La Paz 1982; First Secretary (Inf) Rome 1987; First Secretary FCO 1991; First Secretary Peking 1995; HM Ambassador Ulaanbaatar 1999.

Coombs, Nicholas Geoffrey; First Secretary (Political) Riyadh since June 2000; born 14/12/61; FCO 1984; Language Training 1985; Second Secretary (Chancery) Riyadh 1987; Second later First Secretary FCO 1989; First Secretary Amman 1993; First Secretary FCO 1997; Band D6; m 1990 Julie Elizabeth Hardman (2d 1996, 1998).

Cooper, Amanda Jane; Tokyo since June 2002; born 02/03/60; HSE 1987-95; FCO 1995; Vilnius 1996; Shanghai 1999; Band A2.

Cooper, Andrew George Tyndale; Counsellor FCO since May 1999; born 13/12/53; FCO 1983; First Secretary Canberra 1984; FCO 1987; First Secretary (UN/Press) Geneva (UKMIS) 1988;

First Secretary later Counsellor FCO 1992; Stockholm 1995; m 1981 Donna Mary Elizabeth Milford (2s 1988, 1996).

Cooper, Derek John William; Second Secretary (Political) Riyadh since July 2001; born 07/01/68; FCO 1986; Islamabad 1989; FCO 1992; Zagreb 1994; FCO 1998; Band C4; m 1998 Sanja Vilus.

Cooper, Julie Maria (née Ingham); Pretoria since January 1999; born 03/01/65; FCO 1984; Harare 1986; SUPL 1990; Dhaka 1991; SUPL 1994; Gaborone 1997; Cape Town 1997; FCO 1997; Band B3; m 1987 Eric Robert Cooper (diss 1994) (2s 1989, 1990).

Cooper, Rachel Elizabeth; FCO since May 1999; born 03/11/65; FCO 1989; Vice-Consul Copenhagen 1992; Deputy Head of Mission Bratislava 1995.

Cooper, Robert Francis, CMG (1997), MVO (1975); SUPL since April 2002; born 28/08/47; Seconded to Bank of England, 1982; Third Secretary FCO 1970; Sheffield University 1971; Tokyo 1972; Second Secretary 1973; First Secretary 1976; FCO 1977; First Secretary (External Trade) Brussels (UKREP) 1984; Counsellor FCO 1987; Counsellor (Political) Bonn 1993; Minister Bonn 1996; Director FCO 1998; Head of Overseas Defence Section Cabinet Office 1999.

Cope, Brian Roger, MVO (2000); Kampala since January 2000; born 01/03/59; Inland Revenue 1975; FCO 1976; Paris 1979; Bucharest 1982; Islamabad 1984; FCO 1988; Third Secretary Colombo 1991; Second Secretary (Management) Accra 1995; Band C5; m 1982 Heather Margaret Frensham (1d 1990, 1s 1993).

Cope, John Charles; Second Secretary (Management/Consular) Prague since February 1995; born 10/08/46; FO 1964; Paris 1968; Moscow 1971; Delhi 1972; Karachi 1974; FCO 1976; Dakar 1978; Warsaw 1981; FCO 1982; Hanoi 1985; FCO 1987; Second Secretary (Admin/Consular) Kathmandu 1988; Second Secretary FCO 1991.

Copland, Joanne Catherine; Band B3; SUPL since August 2000; born 02/09/71; FCO 1990; Washington 1993; Peking 1996; On loan to the Cabinet Office, 1999.

Copleston, John de Carteret; Counsellor FCO since September 2000; born 26/01/52; FCO 1971; Paris 1975; Third later Second Secretary FCO 1978; Second later First Secretary Islamabad 1980; First Secretary FCO 1983; First Secretary (Chancery) Jakarta 1987; First Secretary FCO 1990; Counsellor Abuja later Lagos 1993; Counsellor FCO 1995; Counsellor (Multilateral) Canberra 1997; m 1987 Jane Marie Francesca Wilcox (4d 1988, 1991, 1993, 1997).

Copley, Caroline Helen (née Hall); SUPL since June 2001; born 19/01/65; FCO 1987; Third later Second Secretary (Chancery) Oslo 1990; Floater Duties 1991; FCO 1992 (First Secretary, 1994);

First Secretary (Political) Paris 1997; SUPL 1999; First Secretary (Political) Paris 2000; Band D6; m 1996 John Richard Copley (1d 1999).

Coppin, Nicholas James; First Secretary FCO since November 1999; born 27/03/71; FCO 1992; Second Secretary (Pol/PPA) Bucharest 1995; First Secretary Skopje 1999.

Corbett, Hannah Kathleen Taylor; Second later First Secretary (External) Brussels (UKREP) since May 1999; born 04/08/74; FCO 1997; On loan to HM Treasury, 1998.

Cordery, Andrew David; Counsellor FCO since June 1999; born 02/05/47; Second Secretary FCO 1974; Nairobi 1975; First Secretary New York (UKMIS) 1977; FCO 1981; First Secretary (Economic) Lusaka 1984; First Secretary Berlin (BM) 1988; First Secretary later Counsellor FCO 1991; Counsellor Oslo 1995; m 1970 Marilyn Jean Smith (2d 1975, 1977).

Cork, Richard John; First Secretary (Commercial) Bucharest since August 1998; born 14/11/42; FO 1960; Kathmandu 1964; Bonn 1968; FCO 1971; Manila 1974; FCO 1976; Ottawa 1977; Vice-Consul (Admin) Karachi 1980; Second later First Secretary (Comm) Bahrain 1984; First Secretary FCO 1988; First Secretary (Commercial) Manila 1990; First Secretary (Management/Consular) Stockholm 1994; m (1) 1964 Joan Dorothy Seabourne (1d 1969); (2) 1976 Annabelle Alvestir y Empleo (1d 1978, 2 step d 1969, 1974).

Cormack, Ian Ronald; First Secretary (Commercial) Stockholm since September 1998; born 20/11/56; FCO 1975; Nairobi 1978; Havana 1980; Latin America Floater 1982; Africa/Middle East Floater 1984; FCO 1986; Shanghai 1988; Third Secretary Stockholm 1991; FCO 1995.

Corner, Diane Louise; Deputy Head of Mission Harare since February 2001; born 29/09/59; On loan to the Cabinet Office, 1991; FCO 1982; Second Secretary (Chancery) Kuala Lumpur 1985; First Secretary FCO 1989; SUPL 1989; Second Secretary FCO 1989; Deputy Head of Mission and First Secretary (Pol) Berlin 1994; FCO 1996; m 1986 Peter Timothy Stocker (3d 1989, 1991, 1994); Nato College, Rome, 2000.

Corrans, Paula Anne; São Paulo since November 1998; born 04/02/70; FCO 1995; Brussels (UKREP) 1997; Band A2.

Correa, Clive Joel; Durban since August 2002; born 05/11/64; FCO 1988; Transferred to Diplomatic Service 1989; Rangoon 1991; Full-Time Language Training 1995; Budapest 1996; FCO 1998; On loan to British Trade International 2000; Band C4; m 1990 Andrea Parker (2d 1993, 1996).

Corrigan, Rosalind Mary; Third Secretary (Chancery) Buenos Aires since May 1994; born 07/12/66; FCO 1991; New York (UKMIS) 1993; Band C4.

Cottrell, Cathy; Second Secretary (Commercial) Moscow since January 1999; born 03/04/63; FCO 1991; Band C4; m 1984 Simon John (2d 1990, 1992).

Coulson, Andrew John, LVO (1984); Counsellor FCO since March 1998; born 17/12/50; FCO 1973; Tel Aviv 1976; Tehran 1978; Second later First Secretary FCO 1980; First Secretary (Inf) Amman 1983; FCO 1986; First Secretary (Chancery) Harare 1989; First Secretary FCO 1991; First Secretary (Political) Muscat 1995; m 1978 Merope Jane Wilkinson (1d 1982, 1s 1986).

Coulson, Graham; Kingston since August 1999; born 11/10/46; Army 1962-86; Vienna 1988; New Delhi 1989; Sofia 1992; Floater Duties 1996; Band B3; m 1971 Maureen Joyce Howard (diss 1994) (1s 1971, 1d 1974).

Coulter, Anthony Julian; First Secretary (Chancery) Baku since January 1999; born 01/11/61; FCO 1984; Second Secretary (Chancery) Ankara 1987; Second Secretary FCO 1990; First Secretary (Political) Amman 1994; FCO 1998; Band D6; m 1997 Munire Gulay Kilic (1d 2000)

Courage, Rafe Philip Graham; Consul Chicago since August 2002; born 20/10/63; FCO 1986; Third Secretary Brussels 1989; Third Secretary Islamabad 1991; Second Secretary FCO 1995; Full-Time Language Training 1997; Second Secretary (Economic/Commercial) Ankara 1998; m 1988 Theresa Jayne Pile (4d 1990, 1992, 1996, 1997).

Court, Robert Vernon; Deputy High Commissioner Canberra since April 2001; born 28/01/58; FCO 1981; Concurrently Third Secretary and Vice-Consul Chad; Second Secretary Bangkok, 1984; First Secretary FCO 1986; Private Secretary to the Minister of State, 1988; First Secretary (Political) Brussels (NATO) 1990; First Secretary (Press/Information) Brussels (UKREP) 1993; On loan to Rio Tinto Plc,1996; SUPL 1997; m 1983 Rebecca Ophelia Sholl (3s 1986, 1988, 1990, 1d 1993).

Couzens, James McGeorge Dale; Third Secretary Windhoek since January 2001; born 19/02/67; FCO 1990; Bridgetown 1995; Third Secretary Tunis 1997; Band B3; m 1993 Susan Ann Phillips (1d 1994, 1s 1996).

Covington, Susan Elsie (née Perin); SUPL since 2000; born 04/11/52; FCO 1987; Vienna (UKDEL) 1989; FCO 1991; Brussels (UKDEL) 1996; Band A2; m 1993 Colin Covington.

Cowan, Anthony Evelyn Comrie; Counsellor FCO since May 2000; born 28/03/53; Third Secretary FCO 1975; Language Training Cambridge 1977; Language Training Hong Kong 1978; Second later First Secretary Peking 1980; First Secretary FCO 1982; First Secretary (Chancery) Brussels 1987; First Secretary FCO 1991; Consul (Political and Economic) Hong Kong 1996.

Coward, Ruth Valerie; The Hague since June 1996; born 18/09/60; FCO 1985; New Delhi 1988; Mexico City 1991; Band B3; m 2000 Barry Willis.

Cowell, (Andrew) (John) Hamish; First Secretary (External Relations) Brussels (UKREP) since July 2001; born 31/01/65; FCO 1987; New York (UKMIS) 1988; Third later Second Secretary Colombo 1989; Douala 1989; First Secretary (Chancery) and Deputy Head of Mission Tehran 1992; First Secretary FCO 1994; Head of Political, Economic and Aid Sections Cairo 1996; FCO 1999.

Cowell, Anita Ann; Jakarta since March 2000; born 07/05/54; FCO 1993; Band A2.

Cowling, Geoffrey Stanley; Full-Time Language Training since May 2002; born 20/09/45; Board of Trade 1964; Colonial Office later Commonwealth Office Later FCO 1966; Vice-Consul and Third Secretary Kabul 1970; Vice-Consul and Third Secretary Port Moresby 1974; Second Secretary (Tech Asst) Lima 1976; FCO 1979 (First Secretary 1982); First Secretary (Economic) Copenhagen 1982; Joint Service Defence College 1987; First Secretary FCO 1988; Deputy Consul-General São Paulo 1991; On loan to Rover International, 1995; FCO 1996; Consul-General Rio de Janeiro 1999; m 1970 Irene Joyce Taylor (1s 1971; 2d 1975, 1980).

Cowper-Coles, Sherard Louis, CMG (1997), LVO (1991); HM Ambassador Tel Aviv since September 2001; born 08/01/55; FCO 1977; Language Training MECAS 1978; Third later Second Secretary Cairo 1980; First Secretary FCO 1983; Private Secretary to the Permanent Under-Secretary, 1985; First Secretary (Chancery) Washington 1987; First Secretary FCO 1991; On secondment to the International Institute of Strategic Studies, 1993; Counsellor FCO 1994; Counsellor (Political) Paris 1997; Private Secretary to the Secretary of State for Foreign and Commonwealth Affairs, 1999; m 1982 Bridget Mary Elliot (4s 1982, 1984, 1987, 1990, 1d 1986).

Cox, David George; First Secretary FCO since April 2000; born 07/12/61; FCO 1984; Third later Second Secretary (Chancery) Canberra 1986; Second later First Secretary (Econ) Islamabad 1989; FCO 1992; First Secretary (Political) Luanda 1995; Band D6.

Cox, David Thomas; On loan to the DTI since December 1998; born 27/04/44; FO (FCO) 1967; Berlin 1970; FCO 1972; Prague 1974; Munich 1976; FCO 1979; Lusaka 1982; Second Secretary (Commercial) Budapest 1986; First Secretary FCO 1990; Copenhagen 1993; m 1975 Claudia Zeillinger (1s 1981, 1d 1989).

Cox, Jeffrey William; FCO since December 1997; born 26/10/43; Second Secretary FCO 1973; First Secretary Vienna 1975; First Secretary FCO 1978; First Secretary Madrid (CSCE Delegation) 1980; Pretoria 1981; First Secretary FCO 1985; First Secretary Berlin (BMG) 1988; First Secretary later Counsellor FCO 1990; Consul Munich 1994; m

1969 Elizabeth Louise Bendle (3d 1971, 1973, 1978).

Cox, Jolyon Nicholas; Second Secretary FCO since September 2001; born 21/09/61; FCO 1979; Bonn 1983; Sana'a 1985; FCO 1988; Second Secretary (Bilateral Relations) Bonn 1993; Second Secretary FCO 1998; Second Secretary (Political) Tehran 2000; Band C4; m 1986 Francesca Ann Hindson (1s 1993).

Cox, Julie Ann, MVO (1996); New Delhi since January 2001; born 10/07/62; FCO 1986; Peking 1988; Jerusalem 1990; Warsaw 1993; FCO 1996; Band B3.

Cox, Nigel John; Minister Peking since January 2000; born 23/04/54; FCO 1975; Language Training Cambridge 1976; Language Training Hong Kong 1977; Second Secretary Peking 1978; Second later First Secretary FCO 1981; Paris (ENA) 1984; First Secretary Paris 1985; First Secretary FCO 1990; Counsellor Peking 1992; Counsellor FCO 1996; m 1992 Olivia Jane Paget.

Cox, Olivia Jane (née Paget); SUPL since December 1999; born 31/07/57; FCO 1978; Mexico City 1980; FCO 1982; Third Secretary (Chancery) Paris 1987; FCO 1990 (Second Secretary 1991); SUPL 1992; FCO 1996; Band C4; m 1992 Nigel John Cox.

Cox, Richard James; Georgetown since September 2002; born 07/08/67; FCO 1991; Addis Ababa 1993; Third Secretary (Management) Hanoi 1997; Band C4.

Crabbie, Christopher Donald, CMG (1995); UK Representative for the Organisation for Economic Co-operation and Development, Paris since October 1999; born 17/01/46; Second Secretary FCO 1973; First Secretary Nairobi 1975; Washington 1979; FCO 1983; Counsellor on loan to HM Treasury, 1985; Counsellor FCO 1987; Counsellor (Financial and European Community) Paris 1990; HM Ambassador Algiers 1994; HM Ambassador Bucharest 1996; m 1992 Frances Patricia Bogan.

Crabtree, Joanne Elizabeth; Sana'a since December 1999; born 26/09/68; FCO 1988; Mexico City 1990; Dubai 1993; Band B3.

Craddock, Timothy James; On loan to DFID since October 2000; born 27/06/56; FCO 1979; Vice-Consul (Information) Istanbul 1981; Second Secretary Ankara 1982; First Secretary FCO 1985; First Secretary Paris (UKDEL) 1990; First Secretary FCO 1995; HM Ambassador Tallinn 1997.

Craig, David Hamilton; First Secretary (Political) Ankara since August 2001; born 05/12/61; Full-Time Language Training 1994; FCO 1989; Language Training 1990; Second Secretary (Chancery) Nicosia 1991; Second later First Secretary FCO 1993; Full-Time Language Training Cairo 1995; Consul Jedda 1996; First Secretary FCO 1999; Band D6; m 1994 Hala el-Kara (2s 1995, 1997, 1d 1999).

Craig, Deborah Louise (née Tyson); SUPL since July 2002; born 01/01/72; FCO 1990; Nicosia 1995; FCO 1998; Islamabad 2000; Band A2; m 1995 Ian Douglas Craig (1d 1999, 1s 2000).

Craig, John Jenkinson; Second Secretary FCO since September 1979; born 08/01/49; FCO 1972; Third Secretary Rome 1978; Band C4; m 1965 Glenys Menai Edmunds (2d 1977, 1984; 2s 1979, 1981).

Craig, Lesley, MBE (1995); Tel Aviv since June 2000; born 13/05/67; FCO 1988; T/D Islamabad 1990; Vice-Consul Kathmandu 1991; Third Secretary (Chancery) Kampala 1994; FCO 1997; Band B3.

Craig, Robyn Jean; Addis Ababa since August 1996; born 09/03/65; FCO 1984; Moscow 1986; Oslo 1987; Rabat 1990; FCO 1993; Band B3.

Cramman, Ian Pallister; Addis Ababa since November 2000; born 11/03/70; FCO 1989; Khartoum 1992; Full-Time Language Training 1994; Düsseldorf 1995; Band B3; m 1997 Ding Yu.

Craven, Stella Susan; Wellington since July 2001; born 24/03/50; WRAF 1967-71; FCO 1972; Suva 1973; FCO 1975; Khartoum 1976; FCO 1977; Resigned 1978; Reinstated 1979; FCO 1979; Islamabad 1981; FCO 1984; Harare 1986; FCO 1989; Band B3.

Crawford, Charles Graham, CMG; HM Ambassador Belgrade since January 2001; born 22/05/54; FCO 1979; Second later First Secretary (Information) Belgrade 1981; First Secretary FCO 1984; First Secretary Cape Town/Pretoria 1987; First Secretary FCO 1991; Counsellor Moscow 1993; HM Ambassador Sarajevo 1996; Harvard University 1998; Director South East Europe 1999; m 1990 Helen Margaret Walsh (2s 1991, 1993,1d 1999).

Crawford, Fabiola Magdalena; Riyadh since April 1996; born 01/04/66; FCO 1987; Vienna (UKDEL) 1988; Damascus 1991; FCO 1994; Band B3.

Crawford, Marilyn Elisabeth; FCO since July 1995; born 16/08/47; FCO 1975; Brussels (UKDEL NATO) 1977; Antigua 1980; FCO 1982; Brussels (UKDEL) 1988; FCO 1991; Paris 1994; Band A2.

Crawford, Michael James; Counsellor FCO since September 2001; born 03/02/54; FCO 1981; Second later First Secretary Cairo 1983; First Secretary Sana'a 1985; First Secretary Riyadh 1986; First Secretary FCO 1990; First Secretary (Political) Warsaw 1992; FCO 1995; Counsellor Islamabad 1999; m 1984 Georgia Anne Moylan (twins, 1s 1d 1986, 1s 1989).

Crees, Ian Alec; HM Consul General and Joint Management Officer Geneva since March 1999; born 31/01/43; Air Ministry 1960; Passport Office 1961; CRO 1963; Nairobi 1963; Nicosia 1966; FCO 1968; Rawalpindi (later Islamabad) 1971;

Vice Consul Strasbourg 1975; FCO 1978; Second Secretary (Political/Aid), Kinshasa, 1980 (also accredited to Congo-Brazzaville, Rwanda and Burundi); Second Secretary (Commercial) Seoul, 1984 (First Secretary, 1988); First Secretary FCO 1989; First Secretary (Comm/DHM) Bombay 1993; FCO, Conference Department (European Council) 1998; T/D Islamabad 1998; m 1963 Betty Winifred Kelder (1d 1965, 1s 1967).

Cresswell, Jeremy Michael, CVO (1996); Deputy Head of Mission and Head of Political and Public Affairs Berlin since June 2001; born 01/10/49; FCO 1972; Third later Second Secretary Brussels 1973; Second Secretary Kuala Lumpur 1977; First Secretary; FCO 1978; Private Secretary to Parliamentary Under-Secretary, then Minister of State 1981-82; Deputy Political Adviser Berlin (BMG) 1982; First Secretary FCO 1986; Counsellor and Head of Chancery Brussels (UKDEL) 1990; Full-Time Language Training 1994; Deputy Head of Mission Prague 1995; Counsellor FCO 1998; m 1974 Ursula Petra Forwick (1d 1978, 1s 1985).

Creswell, Alexander John Peter; First Secretary (Political) Kuwait since July 2001; born 27/07/65; FCO 1993; Second Secretary (Political) Pretoria 1995; Second Secretary FCO 1998; Band D6; m 1995 Katharine Louise Reid.

Critoph, Tracey Marjorie; Bombay since December 1998; born 26/08/64; FCO 1988; Jakarta 1990; Port Louis 1994; FCO 1997; Band A2; m 1997 M J E Fleurot.

Crockard, Gavin; Third Secretary Ottawa since June 2002; born 11/02/68; FCO 1989; Bombay 1991; Pretoria 1995; FCO 1996; Floater Duties 1998; Band B3.

Crocker, Helen; Madrid since September 2000; born 24/10/67; FCO 1999; Band A2.

Crocker, John Michael; On loan to Shell since May 1997; born 27/06/63; FCO 1988; Second Secretary 1989; Full-Time Language Training Cairo 1991; Second Secretary (Chancery) Riyadh 1992; First Secretary FCO 1995.

Crockett, Patricia Anne; Nicosia since November 1993; born 19/11/48; Tokyo 1974; Copenhagen 1977; FCO 1980; Port Louis 1981; FCO 1983; Lusaka 1985; Peking 1989; FCO 1991; Band B3.

Crombie, Anthony Campbell, OBE (1997); Counsellor (Political) Moscow since September 1999; born 18/10/56; COI 1980; FCO 1985; Second later First Secretary Havana 1987; First Secretary FCO 1990; Deputy Head of Mission Belgrade 1994; SUPL 1997; m 1982 Jane Nicholls Talbot (diss 1987).

Crompton, Angela Louise; Maputo since August 2001; born 04/05/64; FCO 1990; Oslo 1991; T/D Islamabad 1994; Brasilia 1995; FCO 1998; Band A2.

Crompton, Richard Anthony Neil; Counsellor and Deputy Head of Mission Tehran since May 1999;

born 25/09/64; FCO 1995; Senior Research Officer, First Secretary FCO 1997; Full-Time Language Training 1998; m 1996 Rosa Zaragoza (1d 2000; 1s 2001).

Cronin, Martin Eugene; First Secretary Stockholm since September 1999; born 22/01/65; DoE 1987; FCO 1988; Vice-Consul/AMO Sana'a 1990; FCO 1993; Second Secretary (Political/Economic/Development) Amman 1994; Band D6.

Crooke, Alastair Warren; Counsellor FCO since March 1995; born 30/06/49; FCO 1974; Third later Second Secretary (Comm) Dublin 1975; First Secretary (Political/Press) Pretoria 1978; First Secretary FCO 1981; Islamabad 1985; First Secretary FCO 1988; Counsellor Brasilia 1991; Counsellor Bogotá 1993; m 1976 Carole Cecilia Flaxman (1s 1979, twin s 1981).

Crooks, Colin James, LVO (1999); Washington since June 2002; born 18/02/69; FCO 1992; Full-Time Language Training (Korean) 1993; Full-Time Language Training (Korean) Seoul 1994; Seoul 1995; First Secretary FCO 1999; m 1996 Kim Young-Kee (1s 1997).

Crooks, Daryl; ECO later Vice-Consul Dhaka since December 1998; born 27/05/68; FCO 1991; Transferred to Diplomatic Service 1999; Band B3; m 1999 Dina R Napao (1d 2000).

Crorkin, Colin Wynn, MBE (1993); First Secretary (Management) later Deputy Head of Mission Lagos since 1997; born 31/01/57; FCO 1975; Rome 1977; Beirut 1980; Brussels (UKREP) 1983; FCO 1984; Kinshasa 1987; Second Secretary BTIO New York 1992; Second later First Secretary FCO 1993; m (1) 1978 Gillian Smith (diss 1991), (2) 1991 Joanne Lynn Finnamore (1s 1985, 1d 1998).

Cross, Caroline Janice, MBE (1991); Second Secretary (Immigration/Consular) Accra since June 2001; born 30/09/64; FCO 1984; Warsaw 1986; Floater Duties 1989; Third Secretary (Chancery/Information) Kampala 1991; Third later Second Secretary FCO 1994; SUPL 1999; Band C4; m 1998 M Higgins.

Cross, Harriett Victoria Saltonstall; FCO since January 2002; born 25/09/74; FCO 1997; Second Secretary (Political) Rabat 1998; Band C4; m 1999 Lieutenant Philip Saltonstall RN

Cross, Linda Mary (née Guild); Third Secretary (Political) New York (UKMIS) since December 1994; born 15/03/56; Rabat 1978; FCO 1978; Prague 1981; Quito 1983; Paris 1985; FCO 1988; Vienna 1991; m 1989 Michael John Cross

Cross, Margaret Christine; SUPL since April 1992; born 13/01/62; FCO 1980; Dhaka 1985; Frankfurt 1989 (Second Secretary 1991); FCO 1991.

Cross, Shelley; SUPL since June 1996; born 19/11/59; FCO 1980; Bonn 1982; Floater Duties 1985; FCO 1989; Third Secretary (Commercial)

Paris 1993; m 1990 Robert Simon George Parker (1d 1992).

Crossland, Dudley Stewart; Third Secretary (Political) Singapore since January 2001; born 02/05/63; FCO 1987; Berne 1989; Brussels (UKREP) 1990; FCO 1993; New Delhi 1995; Band B3; m 1993 Jennifer Patricia Brown (diss 2000).

Crossland, Jennifer Patricia (née Brown); SUPL since August 2001; born 28/08/64; FCO 1988; Brussels (UKREP) 1990; FCO 1993; SUPL 1995; New Delhi 1996; Bangkok 1998; Band A2; m 1993 Dudley Stewart Crossland (diss 2000).

Crossman, Steven Nigel; Deputy High Commissioner Georgetown since April 2001; born 16/11/55; FCO 1975; Muscat 1977; Washington 1978; New Delhi 1984; FCO 1987; Third Secretary (Aid) Dar es Salaam 1990; Hanoi 1995; Deputy High Commissioner Freetown 1999; m 1998 Le Hoang Lan (1s 2000).

Crosthwaite, Maureen; FCO since November 1990; born 04/05/43; FCO 1987; Vienna 1988; Band A2.

Croucher, Lance Hans Frederick, MBE (2000); Second Secretary (Consular/Management) Dar es Salaam since August 1996; born 17/03/40; RAF 1956-83; FCO 1983; Karachi 1985; Pretoria 1988; Third later Second Secretary FCO 1991; Second Secretary (Immigration/Consular) Colombo 1994; m (1) 1965 (1d 1966, 1s 1967), (2) 1981 Hildegard Faller (2d 1986, 1987).

Crowder, Richard Lawrence Robert; Second Secretary (Economic) Moscow since October 1999; born 14/11/73; FCO 1996; Full-Time Language Training (Russian) 1998; Band C4; m 2000 Hilary Jane Louise Scott.

Crowther, Diane Elaine; FCO since November 1981; born 05/09/64; Band A2.

Crowther, Kathryn Valerie Bryden; SUPL since September 1996; born 14/02/47; FCO 1987; Rabat 1989; Gibraltar 1992; FCO 1992; Band A2.

Cruickshank, Diane (née Robinson); New Delhi since January 1998; born 15/07/60; FCO 1981; Bogota 1982; Jakarta 1985; FCO 1988; Lusaka 1990; SUPL 1992; Tehran 1994; Band B3; m 1994 Douglas Graham Cruickshank.

Cullen, Carol Dulceta (née Fisher); Lusaka since April 1999; born 12/11/56; DoE 1975; FCO 1977; Paris 1979; Dublin 1982; FCO 1985; Nairobi 1988; SUPL 1992; FCO 1993; Bridgetown 1996; Band C4; m 1979 Thomas Cullen (1d 1984, 1s 1988).

Cullens, Niall James David; Second Secretary Consul (Commercial) Warsaw since July 2000; born 28/02/65; FCO 1986; Berlin (BMG) 1988; LA/Caribbean Floater 1990; FCO 1993; Rome 1996; Band C4; m 1998 Caroline Anne Stramik.

Culligan, Phillip David; Deputy High Commissioner Nassau since September 1997; born

27/02/61; FCO 1981; Tripoli 1982; Pretoria/Cape Town 1983; Düsseldorf 1986; FCO 1989 (Second Secretary 1992); Budapest 1993; m (1) 1982 Carole Anne Rouse (diss); (2) 1997 Elizabeth Jane Huggins (1d 1999).

Culshaw, Robert Nicholas, MVO (1979); Consul-General Chicago since June 1999; born 22/12/52; FCO (APS to the Secretary of State) 1984; Third Secretary FCO 1974; Language Training MECAS 1975; Language Training 1976; Third Secretary Muscat 1977; Second Secretary Khartoum 1979; First Secretary Rome 1980; First Secretary and Head of Chancery later Counsellor, Consul General and Deputy Head of Mission Athens 1989; Counsellor and Head of News FCO 1993; Minister-Counsellor (Trade and Transport) Washington 1995; m 1977 Elaine Ritchie Clegg (1s 1992).

Culver, John Howard, LVO (2000); HM Ambassador Reykjavik since January 2001; born 17/07/47; Board of Trade 1967; FO later FCO 1968; Latin American Floater 1971; FCO 1973; Third Secretary Moscow 1974; Second Secretary La Paz 1977; Second later First Secretary FCO 1980; First Secretary (Commercial) Rome 1983; Head of Chancery Dhaka 1987; First Secretary FCO 1990; HM Ambassador and Consul-General Managua 1992; Consul-General Naples 1997; T/D Rome 2000; Band D7; m 1973 Margaret Ann Davis (1d 1974, 2s 1978, 1981).

Cummins, John, MBE (1983); Counsellor Moscow since September 2001; born 07/09/46; FCO 1976 (Second Secretary 1978); FO later FCO 1964; Budapest 1969; Luxembourg 1971; Tunis 1973; Consul and Second Secretary (Admin) Santiago 1980; First Secretary Libreville 1985; First Secretary FCO 1988; Full-Time Language Training 1991; First Secretary (Commercial) Prague 1992; First Secretary FCO 1995; m 1969 Gillian Anne Biss (2s 1970, 1972).

Cummins, Rodney Robert; Consul-General Osaka since September 1998; born 19/10/41; On loan to DoT 1977; FO 1959; Prague 1963; Buenos Aires 1964; Vienna 1967; San Francisco 1970; Language Training 1971; Tokyo 1972; Second Secretary (Inf) and Vice-Consul Osaka 1974; FCO 1980; First Secretary (Commercial) Mexico City 1982; Deputy High Commissioner Georgetown 1986; First Secretary FCO 1988; First Secretary (Commercial) Tokyo 1992; m 1964 Sandra Mary Hanmer (2s 1966, 1970; 1d 1967).

Cunningham, Kevin Francis; Second Secretary (Commercial) Bangkok since June 1999; born 08/03/63; Civil Aviation Authority/National Air Traffic Services 1982; Royal Navy 1987; FCO 1992; Gaborone 1995; Band C4; m 1993 Alison Hilary Kathleen Leeland (2d 1995, 1999).

Cunningham, Raymond Peter, MBE (2001); Islamabad since January 2000; born 21/01/45; Army 1963-1989; T/D Helsinki 1989; FCO 1989; Warsaw 1990; Floater Duties 1992; FCO 1994; Floater Duties 1997; Band B3.

Cupac, Dawn (née Womersley); SUPL since July 2002; born 02/02/64; FCO 1992; Belgrade 1995; Vienna 1999; Vienna 2000; SUPL 2000; Band A2; m 1997 Dkordje Cupac.

Curle, Moira Rosemary; FCO since November 1997; born 08/10/68; FCO 1986; Belgrade 1990; Bombay 1994; Band B3; m 1995 Ivor MacNamara.

Curley, Eugene Gerard, OBE (1991); Counsellor New York (UKMIS) since September 2000; born 30/09/55; FCO 1981; Second later First Secretary Mexico City 1984; First Secretary FCO 1986; First Secretary later Counsellor Paris 1993; Counsellor FCO 1998; m 1982 Joanne England (diss 1991); (2) 1993 Jane Margaret Crosland (1d 1996, 1s 2000).

Curley, Jane Margaret (née Crosland); Second Secretary FCO since February 1998; born 24/11/61; FCO 1989; Second Secretary (Political) Copenhagen 1992; SUPL 1993; Band C4; m 1993 Eugene Gerard Curley (1d 1996, 1s 2000).

Curotto, Francine Elene; FCO since November 1999; born 29/08/63; FCO 1990; Copenhagen 1993; FCO 1995; Havana 1997; Band B3.

Curran, David; First Secretary FCO since November 2000; born 08/06/60; FCO 1987; Second later First Secretary Manila 1989; First Secretary (Chancery) New York (UKMIS) 1992; First Secretary FCO 1994; First Secretary (Political) Lusaka 1997; Band D6; m 1989 Lesley Jane Thomas.

Currie, David James; First Secretary (Commercial) Brussels since June 1998; born 21/10/46; CRO (later FCO) 1963; Peking 1969; Helsinki 1971; FCO 1972; Hanoi 1975; Brussels 1976; Manila 1978; Second Secretary FCO 1982; Second Secretary (Commercial) Algiers 1986; Assistant Trade Commissioner, later Trade Commissioner (China Trade) Hong Kong (BTC) 1989; First Secretary FCO 1993; m (1) 1968 Valerie Kirk (1s 1970) (diss 1975); (2) 1977 Joyce Rosalie Deacon (1 step s 1970, 1 foster s 1970)

Currie, Jacqueline Ann; Deputy High Commissioner Victoria since January 2001; born 08/02/67; FCO 1987; Baghdad 1989; FCO 1991; LA Floater 1992; Atlanta 1994; Kigali 1998; Band C4.

Curry, Trudy Gay (née Hibbs); Third Secretary (Consular/Management) Berlin since June 2001; born 09/12/57; FCO 1975; SUPL 1980; Canberra 1981; Brussels 1984; SUPL 1987; FCO 1992; Accra 1994; Doha 1997; Band B3; m (1) 1980 Peter Ian Webb (diss 1983); (2) 1983 Peter Lester Curry (1d 1987, 1s 1990).

Curtis, Penelope Ann; Madrid since November 1996; born 24/06/68; FCO 1990; Mexico City 1992; Band B3.

Cuthbertson, Deborah Ann; Islamabad since November 2000; born 07/04/72; FCO 1991; Band C4.

Cutler, Charlotte Margaret; Second Secretary (Chancery) New York (UKMIS) since February 2001; born 16/10/72; FCO 1998; Band C4.

Cuxford, Stephanie Anne; FCO since August 1982; born 20/07/65; Band A1.

D

Dacey, Alan Treharne; FCO since November 1998; born 10/04/70; FCO 1988; Brussels (UKDEL NATO) 1991; Africa/Middle East Floater Duties 1994; Band B3; m 1999 Salome Marit

Dakin, Nigel John; FCO since June 2002; born 28/02/64; FCO 1996; First Secretary New Delhi 1999; Band D6; m 1987 Amanda Louise Johnson (1d 1995).

Daley Goldsmith, Robyn Jean; FCO since May 2001; born 08/08/69; FCO 1990; World-wide Floater Duties 1993; Third Secretary Bombay 1995; Third later Second Secretary Belmopan 1998; Band C4; m 1995 Simon Geoffrey Goldsmith.

Dallas, Andrew James; Doha since February 1999; born 15/01/71; FCO 1990; Dublin 1995; Band A2; m 2001 Sarah Gordon.

Dallas, Ian Michael; First Secretary Dublin since January 1997; born 13/12/42; Board of Trade 1961; Commonwealth Office 1966; Peking 1969; Lagos 1971; Accra 1973; FCO 1975; Chicago 1978; Second Secretary FCO 1982; Second Secretary (Admin) Lusaka 1985; FCO 1988; Vice-Consul (Comm) Karachi 1989; First Secretary (Comm/Aid) Colombo 1993; m 1968 Angela Margaret Moore (1s 1971, 1d 1976).

Dalton, Raymond Glyn; Moscow since April 1999; born 25/04/45; Royal Air Force 1960-85; MOD Police 1985-88; Warsaw 1988; Pretoria/Cape Town 1990; Santiago 1992; Sofia 1996; Band C4; m 1964 Mary.

Dalton, Richard John, CMG (1996); HM Ambassador Tehran since December 2002; born 10/10/48; Counsellor on CDA at Chatham House 1991; Counsellor on loan to MAFF 1988; Third Secretary FCO 1970; MECAS 1971; Second Secretary Amman 1973; Second later First Secretary New York (UKMIS) 1975; FCO 1979; First Secretary Head of Chancery and Consul Muscat 1983; First Secretary FCO 1987; Counsellor FCO 1992; Consul-General Jerusalem 1993; Counsellor FCO 1998; HM Ambassador Tripoli 1999; m 1972 Elisabeth Keays (2s 1978, 1982; 2d 1973, 1979).

Daltrey, Christopher; Secondment to China - British Trade Group Since October 1997; born 21/09/68; FCO 1988; Rome 1990; FCO 1992; Third Secretary Hong Kong (BTC) 1993; m 1991 Kim Rowena Newson (1s 1992, 2d 1993, 1995).

Daltrey, Kim Rowena (née Newson); SUPL since April 1992; born 05/05/63; FCO 1986; Berne 1988; FCO 1989; Rome 1990; Band A2; m 1991 Christopher Daltrey (1s 1992, 2d 1993, 1995).

Damper, Carol Ann; FCO since February 2000; born 17/12/44; Mogadishu 1975; FCO 1975; Bonn 1977; Belmopan 1979; FCO 1982; Vienna 1984; FCO 1987; Athens 1988; Bucharest 1991; FCO 1993; Sofia 1997; Band B3.

Dancer, James Anthony; Second Secretary (Political) Belgrade since August 2001; born 19/04/75; FCO 1999; Band C4.

Daniel, Hamish St Clair, MBE (1992); HM Ambassador Dili since May 2002; born 22/08/53; FCO 1973; Algiers 1975; Prague 1977; Lisbon 1978; Islamabad 1980; FCO 1982; San Francisco 1985; Second Secretary Khartoum 1989; Second Secretary FCO 1992; Deputy Head of Mission and HM Consul Sana'a 1994; First Secretary (Political/Economic) Jakarta 1997; British Representative Dili 2001; m (1) 1975 Susan Brent (diss) (1d 1981, 1s 1985); (2) 2002 Heather Ann Bull.

Daniels, Malcolm; FCO since September 1986; born 04/09/48; FCO 1965; Singapore 1980; Helsinki 1984; Band C5; m 1976 Jeannette Susan (2s 1977, 1980).

Daniels, Mark Ian; FCO since January 1994; born 30/08/65; FCO 1982; New Delhi 1985; Washington 1989; Band B3; m 1989 Suzanne Jayne Woodworth (2s 1999, 2001).

Daniels, Suzanne Jane (née Woodworth); FCO since April 1989; born 07/05/63; FCO 1983; New Delhi 1985; Band A2; m 1989 Mark Daniels (2s 1999, 2001).

Darby, Jane; Deputy Head of Mission The Hague since January 2002; born 01/04/53; FCO 1984; Bonn 1990; HM Treasury 1994; Cabinet Office 1995; FCO 1996; Full-Time Language Training 2001; m 1984 Michael Reece (1s 1986, 1d 1988).

Darby, Jonathan; Deputy Consul-General Chicago since February 2002; born 28/12/69; FCO 1999; Band D6.

Dare, Gillian Angela; First Secretary (Political) Abuja since March 2002; born 07/07/48; FCO 1999; Band D6.

Darke, John Martin Jamie; First Secretary FCO since June 1999; born 02/05/53; FCO 1975; MECAS 1977; FCO 1979; MBA London Business School 1981, Management Consultant, HAY-MSL 1983; First Secretary FCO 1985; First Secretary (Chancery) Cairo 1988; First Secretary FCO 1991; First Secretary (Political) Dubai 1996; Band D6; m 1980 Diana Taylor (1d 1989, 1s 1991).

Darker, Aidan; Dar es Salaam since July 2002; born 08/10/62; Royal Air Force 1983-1995; FCO 1995; Hong Kong 1996; Bahrain 1999; m 1989 Angela Darker (1s 1999).

Darker, Angela; SUPL since February 1999; born 12/02/68; Royal Air Force 1986-1990; FCO 1995; Hong Kong 1996; m 1989 Aidan Darker (1s 1999).

Darroch, Nigel Kim, CMG; Counsellor FCO since July 1998; born 30/04/54; FCO 1976; Third later Second later First Secretary Tokyo 1980; FCO 1985 (Private Secretary to the Minister of State, January 1987); First Secretary (Economic) Rome 1989; First Secretary later Counsellor Secretary FCO 1993; Counsellor (External Relations) Brussels (UKREP) 1997; m 1978 Vanessa Claire Jackson (1s 1983, 1d 1986).

Dart, Jonathan, MVO; Second Secretary (Inward Investment/Financial Services) Seoul since August 1999; born 14/07/64; FCO 1988; Third Secretary (Science and Technology) Bonn 1991; Third Secretary Pretoria 1994; Full-Time Language Training 1998; Band B3; m 1990 Claire Emma Juffs (2s 1992, 1994; 1d 1998).

Dauris, James Edward; First Secretary (Commercial) Moscow since January 1999; born 15/01/66; FCO 1995; Band D6; m 1995 Helen Parker.

Davenport, Michael Hayward, MBE (1994); Consul-General and Director of Trade Promotion Warsaw since March 2000; born 25/09/61; FCO 1988; Warsaw 1990; FCO 1993; First Secretary (Political) Moscow 1996; m 1992 Lavinia Sophia Elisabeth Braun (1s 1994, 1d 1996).

Davey, Denise; Second Secretary (Management) Beirut since August 2001; born 08/05/69; HCS 1987; FCO 1989; Dubai 1990; Mexico City 1994; FCO 1994; Guatemala City 1995; FCO 1996; Band B3.

Davey, Simon James, MBE (1985); Consul (Commercial) Miami since November 2001; born 01/02/47; Army 1965-68; FCO 1969; Latin American Floater 1972; Havana 1973; Second Secretary (Aid/Commercial) Kathmandu 1976; Second later First Secretary FCO 1980; Consul Durban 1983; First Secretary (Commercial) Prague 1988; First Secretary FCO 1992; First Secretary (Commercial) Bogotá 1995; First Secretary 1999; m 1992 Marcela Eva Dzurikova.

David, Timothy James; High Commissioner Lusaka since May 2002; born 03/06/47; FCO 1974; Second later First Secretary Dar es Salaam 1977; FCO 1980; Loan to ODA 1983; First Secretary Geneva (UKMIS) 1985; First Secretary later Counsellor FCO 1988; HM Ambassador Suva 1992; Deputy High Commissioner Harare 1996; High Commissioner Belmopan 1998; m 1996 Rosemary Kunzel.

Davidson, Barry Alexander; Vice Consul Kathmandu since November 1997; born 01/08/64; HCS 1985; Geneva (UKMIS) 1988; Freetown 1990; FCO 1994; Band B3; m 1985 Elizabeth Helen Oxley (1s 1992, 2d 1994, 1999).

Davidson, Brian John; Deputy Head of Mission Vilnius since September 2001; born 28/04/64; First Secretary on loan to the Cabinet Office 1992; FCO 1985; Language Training 1986; Third later Second Secretary (Chancery/Inf) Peking 1988; First Secretary FCO 1994; First Secretary

(Political) Canberra 1996; Full-Time Language Training 2001.

Davidson, Carolyn Jayne; SUPL since January 2000; born 18/04/64; FCO 1986; Language Training 1987; Language Training Kamakura 1988; Tokyo 1989; Bonn 1993; European Commission 1993; Second later First Secretary FCO 1995; Band D6; m 1997 Thomas Henry Carter (2s 1998, 1999).

Davidson, James Gerard; Tripoli since March 2000; born 20/05/67; MOD 1985; FCO 1988; Budapest 1989; Lagos 1991; FCO 1994; Jerusalem 1997; Band B3.

Davidson, Raymond John Bruce, MBE (1995); Islamabad since August 1999; born 24/12/62; FCO 1995; Paris 1997; Band A2; m 1988 Shivaun Anne (2s 1991, 1994).

Davidson, Sarah Victoria (née Fox); Doha since January 2000; born 08/10/65; FCO 1985; Warsaw 1987; Hamilton 1989; Budapest 1992; FCO 1994; SUPL 1999; Band B3; m 1997 Fraser Reid Davidson (1s 1999; 1d 2002).

Davidson, Susan; SUPL since August 2001; born 13/12/57; FCO 1987; Tokyo 1990; FCO 1992; Bangkok 1996; FCO 1998; Band A2.

Davies, Bethany Louise (née Rowland); SUPL since August 2001; born 11/12/68; FCO 1988; Mexico City 1991; FCO 1993; Band A2; m 1997 Peter George Davies (2s (twins) 2002).

Davies, Caroline Elizabeth; World-wide Floater Duties since October 2000; born 04/06/63; RAF 1983-88; FCO HCS 1991-99; Kuwait 1998; Band B3.

Davies, Deborah Ann (née Kidd); Seoul since December 2000; born 23/09/70; FCO 1992; Islamabad 1996; FCO 1999; Band A2.

Davies, Elved Richard Malcolm; Deputy Consul-General Hong Kong since April 2000; born 19/01/51; Army 1972-75; Third later Second Secretary FCO 1975; Second later First Secretary Jakarta 1977; Language Training 1977; FCO 1980; Athens 1984; FCO 1985; First Secretary (Chancery) Nairobi 1989; FCO 1991; First Secretary later Counsellor Oslo 1991; Counsellor FCO 1995; m 1976 Elizabeth Angela Osborne (1d 1981, 1s 1984).

Davies, Gerald Howard; Consul Brussels since October 1995; born 24/04/48; FCO 1968; Paris 1971; Karachi 1973; Ibadan 1977; FCO 1978; Warsaw 1981; FCO 1984; Melbourne 1986; FCO 1988; Consul and Second Secretary (Man) Muscat 1990; m 1972 Yvonne Arnold (2d 1984, 1988).

Davies, Griselda Christian Macbeth (née Todd); SUPL since October 1999; born 20/02/59; Budapest 1981; FCO 1982; Buenos Aires 1983; FCO 1985; Damascus 1987; FCO 1988; SUPL 1989; FCO 1990; Riga and Vilnius 1993; FCO 1997; Band A2; m 1989 John Howard Davies (1s 2001).

Davies, Ian; Deputy Head of Mission Lima since April 2002; born 01/08/56; FCO 1976; Moscow 1978; SUPL 1980; FCO 1983; Paris 1985; Third later Second Secretary Moscow 1988; Second Secretary FCO 1990; Second Secretary (Com/Con) and Deputy Head of Mission La Paz 1993; Consul-General Marseille 1997; m 1979 Purificacion Bautista Hervias (2d 1985, 1988).

Davies, Jennifer Ann Tudor; Second Secretary FCO since February 1995; born 02/03/50; FCO 1969; Khartoum 1972; Valletta 1974; Singapore 1977; FCO 1979; Buenos Aires 1980; FCO 1982; New Delhi 1984; FCO 1987; Hong Kong 1992; Band C4.

Davies, John Howard; First Secretary (Political) Sofia since October 1999; born 31/01/57; FCO 1980; Riyadh 1983; Second later First Secretary FCO 1985; First Secretary and Head of Interests Section Damascus 1987; First Secretary FCO 1990; First Secretary (Political) Riga and Vilinius 1993; First Secretary FCO 1997; Band D6; m 1989 Griselda Christian Macbeth Todd (1s 2001).

Davies, Jonathan Mark; Counsellor Madrid since November 2000; born 01/12/67; FCO 1990; Language Training Cairo 1992; Second Secretary (Political/Information) Kuwait 1993; On loan to the Cabinet Office 1996.

Davies, Maureen Kerr Stewart (née Paisley); Brussels (UKREP) since August 1994; born 12/06/53; FCO 1984; Washington 1987; Kathmandu 1990; Band A2; m 1988 Maxim Philip Davies

Davies, Nicola Claire (née Dixon); Third Secretary FCO since July 1996; born 10/07/68; FCO 1990; Third Secretary (Political) Singapore 1993; Band C4; m 1996 Jonathan Mark Davies.

Davies, Nicola Jane; SUPL since February 2002; born 18/08/65; RAF 1983-1991; FCO 1995; Gibraltar 1996; Band B3; m 1999 Henry T Gill.

Davies, Patrick James; Private Secretary FCO since August 2000; born 08/05/68; FCO 1993; Full-Time Language Training 1994; Second Secretary (Political/Press) Rabat 1995; First Secretary FCO 1999.

Davies, Paul Ronald; First Secretary FCO since May 2000; born 30/03/53; FCO 1970; African Floater 1974; Dacca 1976; FCO 1979; Tripoli 1982; Kingston 1984; Third Secretary (Commercial) Peking 1988; Second Secretary FCO 1990; Second Secretary (Political/Commercial/Information) Lima 1993; Consul (Commercial/Economic/Press and Public Affairs) Shanghai 1996; Deputy Consul-General Shanghai 1997; m 1976 Fiona Avril Canning (1d 1979, 1s 1981).

Davies, Peter Brian; Counsellor FCO since October 1999; born 30/12/54; Third Secretary FCO 1977; Language Training Hong Kong 1980; Second Secretary FCO 1981; Second later First Secretary Rome 1983; First Secretary FCO 1987; First Secretary and Consul Peking 1988; First

Secretary FCO 1992; Counsellor (Political) Jakarta 1996; m 1981 Charlotte Helena Allman Hall (1d 1984, 1s 1986).

Davies, Roger James; First Secretary (Management) Nicosia since June 2001; born 23/09/47; HCS 1965; FO (later FCO) 1967; Moscow 1970; Kampala 1971; Islamabad 1973; Kathmandu 1974; FCO 1978; Baghdad 1981; Vice-Consul (Comm) Johannesburg 1985; Second Secretary FCO 1987; Second Secretary (Management/Consular) Doha 1991; Deputy Consul-General Melbourne 1994; FCO 1998; m (1) 1974 Catherine Yvonne Moorby (diss 1990) (1s 1982, 1d 1984); (2) 1990 Jean Thérésa Austin

Davies, Samantha Jayne Elizabeth; FCO since June 2002; born 27/11/79; Band A2.

Davies, Tracy Denise (née Chagnot); SUPL since March 2001; FCO 1986; Vancouver 1987; Paris 1988; Rome 1988; FCO 1990; SUPL 1991; FCO 1992; Bangkok 1993; SUPL 1997; FCO 1999; Band B3; m 1990 Mark John Henry Davies (1s 1991; 1d 1994).

Davis, Andrew Cornwall; Santiago since February 1999; born 29/04/68; FCO 1995; HCS 1995-97; ECMM Sarajevo 1997; FCO 1998; Band A2.

Davis, Ashley James; FCO since July 1991; born 23/02/59; FCO 1986; Islamabad 1987; Band B3; m 1988 Roberta Scott (1d 2000).

Davis, Carole May; FCO since August 1994; born 26/03/59; Band A2.

Davis, Doris; Second Secretary (Commercial) Baku since October 1999; born 26/01/47; DSAO 1967; Bagdad 1968; Sofia 1970; FCO 1971; Kuala Lumpur 1972; Peking 1973; Washington 1975; FCO 1978; Cairo 1980; Cape Town/Pretoria 1984; FCO 1988; Washington 1992; Third Secretary (Man) Rangoon 1995; Band C4.

Davis, Joseph Alan; SUPL since November 1996; born 12/11/64; FCO 1982; Nicosia 1990; FCO 1993; Band A2; m (1) 1990 Joanne Marie Bulheller (diss 1994) (2) 1996 Joanne Louise Withers.

Davis, Kevin Roy; SUPL since July 1997; born 02/01/65; FCO 1981; Washington 1989; FCO 1991; Band C4; m 1991 Karen Roberts (1s 1994).

Davis, Rosemary; Second Secretary (Chancery) New York (UKMIS) since August 2001; born 28/01/63; FCO 1987; Language Training 1988; Language Training Cairo 1989; FCO 1990; Brussels (UKREP) 1991; Third Secretary (Chancery) Damascus 1994; FCO 1998; Band D6.

Davis, Stephen Alexander James; Management Officer Abu Dhabi since May 2001; born 24/09/65; FCO 1983; Mexico City 1986; Warsaw 1990; FCO 1993; Third Secretary (Commercial) Accra 1997; m 1986 Maureen Patricia Oates.

Davison, Andrew James; Third Secretary New Delhi since January 2000; born 11/08/70; FCO 1992; Kiev 1997; Band B3; m 1997 Lana Jane Sawa.

Davison, Brian William Edward; Karachi since February 1999; born 06/06/45; Royal Marines 1961; MOD Police 1985; HM Prison Service 1986; Lusaka 1988; Cairo 1992; Lagos 1995; Band B3; m 1966 Sandra June Thompson (2s 1970, 1971).

Davison, John Paul; First Secretary later Counsellor FCO since April 1989; born 25/06/50; FCO 1974; MECAS 1975; Abu Dhabi 1977; Resigned 1978; Reappointed 1985; First Secretary Dubai 1986; m 1978 Elizabeth Jane Clark (2d 1981, 1986, 1s 1983).

Davison, Nicole April; Third Secretary FCO since January 1996; born 06/08/68; FCO 1988; Pretoria/Cape Town 1990; Dhaka 1991; Band B3.

Dawbarn, John Nathaniel Yelverton; First Secretary (Political) Berlin since June 1998; born 03/05/65; FCO 1987; Third later Second Secretary (Chancery/Information) Belgrade 1990; Language Training 1990; Second Secretary FCO 1993 (First Secretary 1994); First Secretary T/D (Political/Information) Belgrade 1995; FCO 1996; m 1989 Katherine Sarah Urry.

Dawber, Mary Welsh (née Campbell); SUPL since April 1997; born 04/04/56; FCO 1996; Band A2; m 1975 Philip Dawber (1d 1976).

Dawber, Philip; Ankara since May 2000; born 01/04/54; Armed Forces 1971-1994; FCO 1995; Band A2; m 1995 Mary Welsh Campbell (1d 1976).

Day, Mark Christopher; Lusaka since January 1999; born 01/05/63; FCO 1994; Hong Kong 1996; Band A2.

Day, Martin Charles; First Secretary (Commercial) Prague since March 2000; born 04/11/65; FCO 1989; Language Training Cairo 1991; Second Secretary (Chancery) Cairo 1992; First Secretary FCO 1995; Band D6.

Day, Rosamund; Bridgetown since September 2001; born 27/06/64; FCO 1983; Bonn 1985; Suva 1987; Africa/ME Floater 1989; FCO 1991; Second Secretary (Management) Colombo 1996; SUPL 1999; Band C5; m 1993 Nicholas John Pyle (2s 1996, 2001; 1d 1999).

de Chassiron, Charles Richard Lucien, CVO (2000); Consul-General Milan since August 1997; born 27/04/48; FCO 1971; Third Secretary Stockholm 1972; First Secretary Maputo 1975; FCO 1978; First Secretary (Commercial) Brasilia 1982; First Secretary later Counsellor FCO 1985; Counsellor (Comm/Econ) Rome 1989; HM Ambassador Tallinn 1994; m 1974 Britt-Marie Sonja Medhammar (1d 1975, 1s 1976).

De Csillery, Patricia Katrina; Full-Time Language Training since March 2001; born 30/04/69; FCO 1993; Second Secretary (Political) New York (UKMIS) 1996; Second Secretary 1998; Band C5; m 1993 Michael de Csillery (1d 2000).

De Fonblanque, John Robert, MBE (1993); Head of UK Delegation to OSCE Vienna since August 1999; born 20/12/43; Third Secretary FCO 1968; Jakarta 1969; Second later First Secretary Brussels (UKDEL) EEC 1972; On loan to the HM Treasury 1977; FCO 1980; Counsellor FCO 1983; Counsellor on loan to the Cabinet Office 1983; Head of Chancery New Delhi 1986; Head of Chancery Brussels (UKREP) 1988; AUSS International Organisations 1994; AUSS Director Europe 1998; m 1984 Margaret Prest (1s 1985).

De Gier, Helen Majorie; Peking since April 1998; born 19/02/59; HCS 1976-84; FCO 1984; Freetown 1986; FCO 1989; Band A2; m 1992 Joseph Eugene O'Carroll.

de Jeune d'Allegeershecque, Susan Jane (née Miller); Deputy Head of Mission Bogotá since October 2002; born 29/04/63; FCO 1985; Brussels (UKREP) 1987 (Second Secretary 1989); FCO 1990; Second Secretary (Economic/Information) Singapore 1992; First Secretary FCO 1995; Deputy Head of Mission Caracas 1999; m 1991 Stephane Herv Marie le Jeune d'Allegeershecque (2s 1993, 1995).

De Larrabure, Jacqueline Mary (née Elliot); FCO since August 2002; born 25/01/64; Lima 1986; LA Floater 1989; San José 1991; FCO 1996; Caracas 1998; Band C4; m 1991 Jos Larrabure Muro (1d 1991).

de Mauny, Alix Claire Evelyne; FCO since September 2001; born 23/12/73; Band C4.

De Pauw, Amanda Jayne (née Rutter); SUPL since May 2002; born 20/03/64; HM Land Registry 1984; FCO 1988; Brussels (UKREP) 1989; Yaoundé 1993; FCO 1996; Ottawa 1999; Band A2; m 1993 Luc Paul Solange Marie De Pauw (2d 1998, 2000).

De Ramos, Nicola Anne (née Smyth); SUPL since September 2002; born 11/08/65; FCO 1988; Bucharest 1989; Quito 1992; Havana 1996; Mexico City 1999; Band A2; m 1994 Bryan Dubal Ramos Montero (2d 1995, 1997).

de Ridder, Kathryn Louise Carmel (née Peacock); Tel Aviv since July 1998; born 16/07/60; FCO 1984; New Delhi 1985; Brussels (UKREP) 1988; FCO 1991; SUPL 1992; Lagos 1994; SUPL 1997; Band B3; m 1992 Wouter de Ridder (1d 1993)

De Sousa, Louise Amanda (née Clark); First Secretary FCO since February 1997; born 23/07/68; FCO 1991; Second Secretary (Political/Information/Aid) Brasilia 1993; m 1994 Allan Rivail de Sousa (1s 1998, 1d 2001).

de Valencia, Michelle (née Lawler); Deputy Head of Mission Holy See since September 2001; born 08/06/64; FCO 1987; Bogotá 1990; Third Secretary (Commercial later Chancery) Stockholm 1993; Second Secretary FCO 1999; Band C4; m 1993 Jairo Alberto Valencia Diaz (1d 1996, 1s 1998).

De Vere Lane, Graham Vaughan, MBE (1991); FCO since July 1993; born 05/05/45; FCO 1968; Singapore 1969; FCO 1971; Lusaka 1973; FCO 1975; Darwin 1976; FCO 1978; Amman 1979; FCO 1983; Khartoum 1984; FCO 1987; Moscow 1988; Pretoria 1990; Band C4; m 1964 Janet Pine (1s 1964, 2d 1967, 1979).

de Villamizar, Bernadette Teresa (née Edwards); FCO since August 2000; born 02/03/63; FCO 1983; Brussels (UKREP) 1985; Shanghai 1987; Rio de Janeiro 1988; FCO 1992; Madrid 1993; Caracas 1996; FCO 1999; SUPL 2000; Band B3; m 1999 Igor Antonio Villamizar Rojas.

de Waal, James Francis; Full-Time Language Training (Spanish) since September 2002; born 18/12/68; FCO 1990; New York (UKMIS) 1992; Second Secretary (Political/Information) Berlin 1994; Full-Time Language Training 1994; FCO 1998; Washington 2002.

Dean, Andrew John; Counsellor (Multilateral) Canberra since September 2000; born 06/02/55; FCO 1982; Second Secretary (UNIDO/UN) Vienna (UKMIS) 1984; Second later First Secretary FCO 1986; First Secretary (Chancery) Hanoi 1990; First Secretary FCO 1992; São Paulo 1997; First Secretary FCO 1999; m 1989 Nicola Moreton (1s 1993).

Dean, Robert John; First Secretary (External) Wellington since November 1999; born 21/05/59; MOD 1977; FCO 1978; Second Secretary Copenhagen 1987; Second later First Secretary FCO 1992; On secondment to MOD 1994; FCO 1995; Band C5; m 1981 Julie Margaret Scott (2d 1986, 1988).

Deane, Geoffrey; HM Consul Munich since July 2001; born 19/02/50; FCO 1976; Nairobi 1980; Second Secretary FCO 1984; First Secretary (Chancery) East Berlin 1988; FCO 1991; First Secretary FCO 1997; Band D6; m Karen Aileen Wallace (4d 1980, 1983, 1986, 1994).

Deane, Michael Boyd; Second Secretary (Economic) Vienna since January 2001; born 01/08/72; Second Secretary FCO 1999; Band C4; m 2001 Natalya Samantha Pilbeam.

Deane, Robert Edward; FCO since 1998; born 28/09/62; HM Treasury 1985; Bonn 1994; Band D6; m 1993 Corinna Osmann (1s 1998).

Deaney, Tina Marie; Floater Duties since June 2002; born 18/04/72; FCO 1991; Islamabad 1995; Prague 1999; Band B3.

Dear, Robert Edward; First Secretary (Political/Economic) Budapest since October 2000; born 19/02/55; FCO 1986; First Secretary 1987; First Secretary FCO 1992; Deputy Head of Mission Havana 1994; m 1982 Caroline Margaret Reuss.

Dearden, Christopher Robert; Vice-Consul Warsaw since January 1997; born 07/12/59; FCO 1978; Wellington 1981; Ankara 1984;

LA/Caribbean Floater 1987; FCO 1989; Athens 1993.

Dearden, Janine Elaine (née Lawrence); SUPL since June 2001; born 18/10/60; FCO 1982; Rome 1983; Nairobi 1985; SUPL 1988; FCO 1989; SUPL 1990; FCO 1998; Band A2; m 1985 Timothy John Dearden (2s 1987, 1989).

Dee, Pauline (née Thompson); SUPL since September 2000; born 11/10/63; FCO 1987; Bridgetown 1989; FCO 1992; Peking 1993; Grand Turk 1996; Sarajevo 1998; Band A2; m 1998 Stewart Dee (1d 1999).

Dee, Stewart; Third Secretary (Political) Gibraltar since November 2000; born 12/08/69; FCO 1988; Bonn 1990; FCO 1993; SUPL 1996; Vice Consul Sarajevo 1998; Band B3; m (1) 1991 Claire Duggan (diss 1996); m (2) 1998 Pauline Thompson (1d 1999).

Delaney, Michael; Colombo since March 1995; born 14/12/67; FCO 1988; Ankara 1989; Lagos 1990; Abuja 1992; Band B3; m 1990 Zeliha Doganavsargil.

Dempster, Sharon Louise; Paris since February 1991; born 13/02/69; FCO 1989; Band A2.

Deneiffe, Paul Michael; Madrid since November 1995; born 21/06/63; FCO 1982; Cairo 1987; FCO 1989; Band C4.

Dening-Smitherman, Major Peter Clemens Henri; Queen's Messenger since 1990; born 12/07/47; HM Forces 1967-90.

Dennis, Catherine Teresa; Beirut since August 2002; born 20/05/70; FCO 1998; Vienna (UKDEL) 1999; Band A2.

Dennis, John David; Counsellor (Economic and Commercial) New Delhi since July 2001; born 06/08/59; FCO 1981; Hong Kong 1983; Peking 1985; Second later First Secretary FCO 1987; First Secretary Kuala Lumpur 1992; On secondment to Standard Chartered Bank 1997; Counsellor on loan to the DTI 1998; m 1989 Jillian Margaret Kemp (2s 1994, 1999).

Denny, Ross Patrick; Deputy Head of Mission Luanda since April 2002; born 13/09/55; RN 1972-79; FCO 1979; Santiago 1980; Doha 1983; Warsaw 1985; FCO 1988; Second Secretary (Political) The Hague 1992; FCO 1997; São Paulo 1998; m (1) 1977 Barbara Harvard (diss 1996) (1d 1979, 1s 1981); (2) 2000 Claudenise De Lima.

Dent, Alastair Ross Moller; Second Secretary (Management) Manila since November 1997; born 07/02/54; FCO 1989 (Second Secretary 1991); DHSS 1972; FCO 1974; Brussels (UKREP) 1976; Moscow 1979; FCO 1981; LA Floater 1984; Mexico City 1986; Second Secretary (Commercial/Information) Gaborone 1993; Deputy High Commissioner Gaborone 1996; m (1) 1977 (diss 1983); (2) 1985 Ligia Esperanza Zeledon Castillo (2s 1988, 1996).

Dent, Shannon Elizabeth; Dubai since April 1985; born 29/03/58; Lusaka 1979; FCO 1979; Peking 1981; Athens 1982; Band A2.

Denwood, Judith Elizabeth; Second Secretary FCO since April 2000; born 21/10/65; FCO 1986; Bridgetown 1988; FCO 1991; Third Secretary FCO 1993; T/D New Delhi, Accra, Damascus 1995; Third Secretary (Management) and Vice-Consul Bahrain 1997; Band C4.

Desloges, Christina Anne (née Sanders); Stanley since August 2000; born 30/11/63; FCO 1984; Lagos 1987; FCO 1991; Harare 1992; Bandar Seri Begawan 1996; Band A2; m 1989 Daniel Albert Joseph Desloges (1d 1990, 1s 1997).

Devine, John Joseph; Third Secretary (Management) and Consul Tallinn since February 2000; born 03/07/70; FCO 1991; Floater Duties 1994; New Delhi 1996; Band B3.

Devine, Paul Graham; FCO since May 1995; born 19/01/51; DHSS 1973; FCO 1981; Bonn 1983; Riyadh 1985; Suva 1988; Düsseldorf 1992; Band B3; m 1993 Losana Lewamoqe Di Lo Tuisawau.

Dew, John Anthony; Head of Latin America and Caribbean Department FCO since January 2000; born 03/05/52; FCO 1973; Third Secretary Caracas 1975; Second later First Secretary FCO 1979; First Secretary Paris (OECD) 1983; First Secretary FCO 1987; Counsellor and Deputy Head of Mission Dublin 1992; Minister Madrid 1996; m 1975 Marion Bewley Kirkwood (3d 1977, 1980, 1984).

Dewar, Robert Scott; High Commissioner Maputo since August 2000; born 10/06/49; FCO 1973; Third later Second Secretary Colombo 1974; First Secretary FCO 1978; First Secretary (Comm) Head of Chancery and Consul Luanda 1981; First Secretary FCO 1984; First Secretary and Head of Chancery Dakar 1988; Deputy High Commissioner Harare 1992; HM Ambassador Antananarivo 1996; FCO 2000; m 1979 Jennifer Mary Ward (1d 1988, 1s 1995).

Diaz, Alison Jean; Mexico City since March 2002; born 24/02/68; FCO 1991; Belgrade 1993; Lima 1995; Vienna (OSCE) 1999; Band A2; m 1998 Juan Carlos Diaz (2s 1998, 2001).

Diaz, Sharon Vanessa (née Gordon); Caracas since August 1999; born 28/09/69; FCO 1998; Band A2; m 1998 Tirso Diaz Garcia.

Dibble, Hilary Anne (née Light); FCO since June 1998; born 17/07/51; FCO 1973; Moscow 1974; FCO 1975; Rome 1976; Kingston 1980; Islamabad 1983; FCO 1987; Moscow 1990; Third later Second Secretary (Consular) Canberra 1993; m 1980 Geoffrey Walter Dibble.

Dick, Colin John; Second Secretary (Economic) Singapore since September 2001; born 22/06/70; FCO 1990; World wide Floater Duties 1994; Third later Second Secretary FCO 1996; Band C4; m 2001 Elaine Hargreaves.

Dick, Paula Jayne; SUPL since August 2002; born 20/06/69; FCO 1988; Amman 1990; Belmopan 1994; Cairo 1998; Band B3.

Dickerson, Nigel Paul; Deputy High Commissioner and Second Secretary (Aid) Windhoek since September 1995; born 25/04/59; FCO 1978; Bonn 1981; Warsaw 1984; FCO 1987 (Second Secretary 1990); Second Secretary (Management) and Consul Santiago 1992; m 1984 Marianne Gaye Tatchell (2d 1992, 1994, 1s 1995).

Dickins, Nicholas William; New York (UKMIS) since May 1997; born 15/11/56; FCO 1985; Tel Aviv 1991; FCO 1994; Band C5; m 1991 Marina Papaspyrou.

Dickinson, Woodman Mark Lowes, OBE (2000); Head of Office Pristina since August 2002; born 16/01/55; FCO 1976; Second Secretary Ankara 1979; First Secretary FCO 1983; First Secretary (Pol/Inf) Dublin 1987; First Secretary FCO 1991; First Secretary on loan to the Bank of England 1994; Full-Time Language Training 1996; HM Ambassador Skopje 1997; SUPL 2001; m (1) 1986 Francesca Infanti (diss 1991); (2) 1995 Christina Houlder.

Dickson, Susan Jane; First Secretary (Overseas Territories Department Legal Adviser) Bridgetown since October 2000; born 30/07/64; Admitted as Solicitor (Scotland) 1989; Assistant later Senior Assistant Legal Adviser FCO 1990; First Secretary (Legal) New York (UKMIS) 1997.

Dickson, William Andrew; FCO since August 1998; born 17/12/50; FCO 1969; SUPL to attend University 1970; FCO 1974; Cairo 1976; Nairobi 1980; Second Secretary (Commercial) Budapest 1982; Second Secretary FCO 1982; Second later First Secretary FCO 1986; First Secretary (IAEA) Vienna 1989; First Secretary (Information) Hong Kong 1994; Band D6; m 1981 Gillian Ann Hague.

Digby, Simon; Consul and Second Secretary (Commercial) Bratislava since May 1999; born 04/08/55; Crown Agents 1977; FCO 1980; Tehran 1982; LA Floater 1986; FCO 1987; Third Secretary (Admin/Cons) Mbabane 1989; FCO 1991; Luanda 1997.

Dillan, Rachel Elizabeth; Amman since September 1985; born 22/08/63; FCO 1983; Band A2.

Dimbleby, Andrew Timothy; Consul (Management) New York since April 2002; born 20/05/59; FCO 1979; Accra 1981; FCO 1985; Pretoria 1986; Language Training 1989; Third Secretary (Commercial/Information/Chancery) Dubai 1989; Second Secretary FCO 1993; Second Secretary (Commercial) Manila 1996; First Secretary New York (UKMIS) 2000; Band C5; m 1981 Susan Margaret Joy Irvine (1s 1988, 2d 1991, 1996).

Dimond, Paul Stephen; HM Ambassador Manila since March 2002; born 30/12/44; FO 1963; DSA 1965; Language Training Tokyo 1966; Osaka 1968 (Consul (Comm) 1970); Second Secretary Tokyo 1972; On loan to DTI 1973; Second Secretary

FCO 1975; First Secretary (Economic) Stockholm 1977; First Secretary FCO 1980; First Secretary (Commercial) Tokyo 1981; First Secretary FCO 1986; On secondment to Smiths Industries plc 1988; Counsellor (Commercial) Tokyo 1989; Deputy Head of Mission The Hague 1994; Consul-General Los Angeles 1997; m 1965 Carolyn Susan Davis-Mees (2s 1968, 1970).

Dinsdale, Ian McLean Taylor; Lagos since May 2002; born 20/10/49; FCO 1969; Nairobi 1972; Colombo 1976; Second Secretary FCO 1979; Second Secretary Santo Domingo 1982; Maseru 1985; Second Secretary Riyadh 1986; Second Secretary FCO 1989; Second Secretary Islamabad 1993; Second Secretary (Consular) Wellington 1997; m 1975 Elizabeth Ann Montaut.

Dinsley, Andrew; Deputy Head of Mission Almaty since August 2000; born 22/08/66; FCO 1990; Kiev 1992; FCO 1996; Band C4; m 2000 Larissa Kolomiyets (1s 1986).

Dinwiddy, Bruce Harry; Governor Cayman Islands since May 2002; born 01/02/46; Counsellor on loan to the Cabinet Office 1986; Second Secretary FCO 1973; First Secretary Vienna (UKDEL MBFR) 1975; FCO 1977; First Secretary and Head of Chancery Cairo 1981; First Secretary FCO 1983; FCO 1988; Counsellor Bonn 1989; Deputy High Commissioner Ottawa 1992; High Commissioner Tanzania 1998; FCO 2001; m 1974 Emma Victoria Llewellyn (1d 1976, 1s 1979).

Dix, Christopher John; First Secretary (Visa/Consular) New Delhi since 1999; born 30/09/64; FCO 1983; Geneva (UKMIS) 1985; Dhaka 1988; Second Secretary FCO 1993; Second Secretary (Commercial) Madrid 1995; Language Training 1995; Band C5; m 1988 Julia Milward (1d 1991, 1s 1994).

Dixon, Debra Audrey (née Churchill); Lusaka since November 1993; born 06/04/58; FCO 1978; Washington 1980; Sana'a 1983; FCO 1986; Düsseldorf 1989; SUPL 1992; Band C4; m 1978 Russell Kenneth Dixon (2d 1985, 1992, 1s 1990).

Dixon, Hazel; Maputo since May 2001; born 19/08/49; HM Forces 1967-77; Ankara 1989; Peking 1992; Moscow 1999; Band B3.

Dixon, Russell Kenneth; First Secretary (Management) Amman since July 2000; born 24/01/58; MOD 1976; FCO 1978; Washington 1980; Sana'a 1983; FCO 1985; Düsseldorf 1989; Second Secretary (Political/Information) Lusaka 1993; SUPL 1993; Band C5; m 1978 Debra Audrey Churchill (2d 1985, 1992; 1s 1990).

Dobson, Sharon Gail, MBE (2002); Third Secretary UKDEL NATO since April 1997; born 04/01/68; FCO 1991; Third Secretary (Chancery) Dakar 1995; Band B3.

Docherty, Claire Elizabeth; SUPL since June 2000; born 30/07/68; FCO 1992; Santiago 1995; Havana 1999; Band A2.

Doe, Marc Gavin; FCO since September 2001; born 09/01/79; Band C4.

Doherty, Emer Maria; T/D Paris since December 1996; born 10/01/69; FCO 1990; Geneva (UKMIS) 1993; Full-Time Language Training 1993; Band C4.

Doherty, Felicity Mary (née Tebboth); Second Secretary FCO since April 1988; born 24/10/52; FCO 1970; Bonn 1975; SUPL 1976; Moscow 1979; FCO 1981; Second Secretary 1983; Second Secretary (Commercial) Lisbon 1986; m 1977 Francis Doherty (diss) (2d 1982, 1984).

Doidge, Mary Ellen; FCO since April 1995; born 21/01/46; On loan to Home Office 1991; Bonn 1971; FCO 1974; Warsaw 1975; Tokyo 1977; FCO 1980; Floater Duties 1982; Moscow 1983; FCO 1985; Brussels (UKDEL NATO) 1988; Band B3.

Doig, Michael David; Second Secretary (Press and Public Affairs) Cape Town since March 1998; born 28/05/54; FCO 1973; Tokyo 1975; Karachi 1979; Vienna 1982; Kaduna 1983; FCO 1987; Third Secretary (Comm/Econ) Ottawa 1990; FCO 1993; m 1983 Mary Walker McKinnie (diss 2000) (1d 1985).

Dolan, Sharon Beverley; ECO Pretoria since September 1999; born 28/11/66; MAFF 1991; FCO 1993; Peking 1994; MO/VC Guangzhou 1998; Band B3.

Donaldson, Brian; HM Ambassador Antananarivo since September 2002; born 06/04/46; APS to the Minister of State 1983; Ministry of Aviation 1963; DSAO (later FCO) 1965; Algiers 1968; La Paz 1971; FCO 1974; Lagos 1975; Luxembourg 1979; Second Secretary FCO 1982; Second later First Secretary (Aid/Comm) Port Louis 1985; First Secretary (Comm) Head of Chancery and Consul Yaoundé 1989; First Secretary (Immigration/Consular) Dhaka 1992; FCO 1992; FCO 1996; High Commissioner Windhoek 1999; m 1969 Elizabeth Claire Sumner (3s 1971, 1973, 1979).

Donaldson, Ian Martin; First Secretary Geneva (UKDEL) since July 1999; born 21/07/66; FCO 1988; Third later Second Secretary (Political) Jakarta 1991; FCO 1995; m 1990 Elspeth Jane Chovil Maguire (2d 1996, 1997).

Donegan, Susan Peta (née McAllister); Rome since June 2002; born 28/05/67; FCO 1985; Paris 1987; LA Floater Duties 1990; Caracas 1992; SUPL 1993; Accra 1994; SUPL 1997; Band B3; m 1993 James Edward Donegan.

Donnelly, Joseph Brian, CMG; High Commissioner Harare since June 2001; born 24/04/45; Second Secretary FCO 1973; First Secretary (ECOSOC) New York (UKMIS) 1975; First Secretary and Head of Chancery Singapore 1979; First Secretary FCO 1982; Counsellor on loan to the Cabinet Office 1985; Counsellor and Consul-General Athens 1988; RCDS Course 1991; Counsellor FCO 1992; Minister and Deputy Permanent Representative Brussels (UKDEL

NATO) 1995; HM Ambassador Belgrade 1997; m (1) 1966 Susanne Gibb (diss 1994) (1d 1970) (2) 1997 Julia Mary Newsome.

Donnelly, Matthew; FCO since November 1999; born 21/11/61; FCO 1981; Algiers 1985; Nassau 1988; FCO 1990; Lagos 1992; Third Secretary (Commercial) Buenos Aires 1996; Band C4; m (1) 1982 Lesley-Ann Jones (diss 1988) (2) 1988 Tracy May Basnett (1s 1989).

Donnelly, Tracy May (née Basnett); SUPL since May 1995; born 26/03/62; FCO 1982; Berne 1983; Algiers 1985; SUPL 1988; T/D Lagos 1994; Band A2; m 1988 Matthew Donnelly (1s 1989).

Dorey, Gregory John; Deputy Consul General/Trade Counsellor Hong Kong since June 2000; born 01/05/56; MOD 1977; On loan at UKDEL NATO 1982; MOD 1984; First Secretary FCO 1986; First Secretary (Chancery) Budapest 1989; First Secretary and PS/Minister of State FCO 1992; Counsellor (Economic) and later Deputy High Commissioner Islamabad 1996; m 1981 Alison Patricia Taylor (1d 1990, 2s 1988, 1994).

Dorrian, Claire Hicks (née Jones); Kampala since August 1999; born 15/07/68; HCS 1987; DS 1989; Stanley 1992; Riyadh 1995; Band B3; m 1992 Stuart Forsyth Dorrian (1s 1996).

Douglas, Janet Elizabeth; First Secretary (Political) Stockholm since April 1996; born 06/01/60; FCO 1985; Language Training 1987; Second later First Secretary (Chancery/Inf) Ankara 1988; First Secretary FCO 1991; First Secretary on loan to the ODA 1993.

Douglas, Paul Leslie; SUPL since June 1999; born 05/11/58; Army 1975-1988; Hanoi 1998; Band A2; m 1993 Tina Marie Field.

Douglas-Hiley, Mark Charles Piers Quentin; Third Secretary (Consular/Management) Kinshasa since November 2001; born 06/11/54; Department of Employment 1972; DHSS 1973; FCO 1974; Castries 1977; FCO 1979; Geneva (UKMIS) 1980; FCO 1983; Lagos 1987; New York (JMO) 1991; FCO 1994; FCO 1997; Sofia 1998; FCO 2000; Band B3.

Douse, Sarah Louise (née Ansell); FCO since March 1998; born 08/04/70; FCO 1990; Rome 1992; Bonn 1995; Band B3; m 2001 Carl Anthony Douse.

Doust, Claire Heather (née Barlow); Lagos since October 2001; born 07/03/72; FCO 1991; Brussels (UKDEL NATO) 1995; Third Secretary (Management) Islamabad 1998; Band B3; m 1998 Stephen Terence Doust.

Doust, Stephen Terence; Islamabad since June 1998; born 04/12/72; FCO 1992; Brussels (UKDEL NATO) 1995; Band A2; m 1998 Claire Heather Barlow.

Douthwaite, Ann Mary, MBE (1991); Canberra since May 1996; born 25/04/40; Düsseldorf 1961; Warsaw 1962; Paris 1963; Moscow 1965; Beirut

1966; FCO 1969; New York (UKMIS) 1970; Muscat 1973; Manila 1976; FCO 1978; Tokyo 1984; Algiers 1987; Jakarta 1991; Band B3.

Dove, John Henry; FCO since October 1997; born 10/03/65; HM Customs and Excise 1989; FCO 1990; Full-Time Language Training 1991; Deputy Head of Mission Tallinn 1992; Moscow 1993; Second Secretary Tashkent 1996.

Dow, Elizabeth Anne; Consul Rabat since January 1999; born 09/03/58; FCO 1976; New Delhi 1978; Brasilia 1982; FCO 1984; New York (CG) 1988; Vice-Consul/MO Jerusalem 1991; FCO 1995.

Downer, James Robert Stephen; FCO since September 1998; born 09/07/68; FCO 1992; Full-Time Language Training 1993; Full-Time Language Training Cairo 1994; Sana'a 1995; Band D6; m 1998 Nicola Marguerite Neary.

Downing, Joanne Watson; FCO since September 2001; born 17/12/71; FCO 1995; Bosnia 1997; Attaché Dakar 1998; Band B3.

Dowse, Timothy Michael; Counsellor FCO since 2001; born 18/12/55; Counsellor, Cabinet Office 1997-1998; FCO 1978; Manila 1980; Second later First Secretary Tel Aviv 1982; First Secretary FCO 1986; Washington 1992; On loan to HM Treasury (Head of Defence, Diplomacy and Intelligence Spending)1998-2000; m 1989 Vivien Frances Life (2d 1991, 1994).

Dowsett, Moira; SUPL since May 1999; born 06/11/61; FCO 1988; Brussels 1991; FCO 1993; Band A2; m 2001 Dominic O'Donnell (2s 1998, 2000).

Drabble, Rufus John; Second Secretary (Political) Oslo since February 2002; born 12/02/70; FCO 1995; Nairobi 1998; Band C4; m 1997 Stella Elizabeth Waldron (1d 2001).

Drace-Francis, Charles David Stephen, CMG (1987); High Commissioner Port Moresby since November 1997; born 15/03/43; Third Secretary FO 1965; Tehran 1967; Second later First Secretary FCO 1971; Assistant Political Adviser Hong Kong 1974; First Secretary Brussels (UKREP) 1978; FCO 1980; Counsellor attached to All Souls Oxford 1983; Counsellor and Chargé d'Affaires a.i. Kabul 1984; Counsellor (Commercial) Lisbon 1987; On loan to British Aerospace 1991; Counsellor FCO 1994; m 1967 Griselda Hyacinthe Waldegrave (2s 1969, 1971, 1d 1979).

Drake, David Allen; Consul (Commercial) New York since July 1996; born 01/09/47; Kuwait 1982 (Second Secretary 1984); RAF 1967-75; FCO 1977; Lagos 1979; Second later First Secretary FCO 1985; First Secretary (Civil Aviation) Bonn 1989; First Secretary (Commercial) Singapore 1991; m 1972 Anne Veronica Paice.

Drake, Howard Ronald; Deputy Consul General New York since September 1997; born 13/08/56; FCO 1975; LA Floater 1979; Los Angeles 1981; Second Secretary 1982; Second Secretary FCO

1983; Second Secretary (Chancery/Info) Santiago 1985; First Secretary FCO 1988; First Secretary (Political/Co-ordination) Singapore 1992; First Secretary FCO 1995; m 1988 Gill Summerfield (1s 1992, 1d 1994).

Drayton, Frank Anthony; FCO British Trade International since April 1997; born 10/12/54; FCO 1974; Islamabad 1976; Cape Town 1979; Munich 1982; FCO 1985; Prague 1989; Vice-Consul Doha 1990; FCO 1994; Band B3; m 1988 Fidelma Bernadette Tuohy.

Drew, Simon Richard; Second Secretary FCO since May 1997; born 07/05/65; FCO 1981; Pretoria/Cape Town 1989; FCO 1992; Ankara 1993; m 1991 Katharine Chappell (1d 1995).

Drew, Thomas; FCO since February 2002; born 26/09/70; FCO 1995; Second Secretary Moscow 1998; First Secretary (Economic) Moscow 2000.

Drew, Timothy James; Riyadh since September 2000; born 02/04/65; FCO 1994; Geneva (UKMIS) 1996; FCO 1999; Band B3; m 1991 Claire Melanie (2d 1998, 2002).

Dring, Sarah Anne Maxwell; First Secretary FCO since March 2000; born 23/11/48; FCO 1987 (Second Secretary 1989); FCO 1974; Sofia 1975; Nicosia 1977; FCO 1979; South East Asia Floater 1983; Algiers 1985; Johannesburg 1991; FCO 1995; First Secretary (Management) Kampala 1997; Band D6.

Drummond, Roderick Ian; Deputy Head of Mission Amman since July 2002; born 07/09/62; FCO 1985; Language Training SOAS 1986; University of Jordan 1987; Second Secretary (Political/Economic) Algiers 1988; First Secretary FCO 1992; Deputy Consul-General (Trade/Investment) Johannesburg 1996; First Secretary (External) Brussels (UKREP) 1998; m 1985 Carolyn Elizabeth Elliott (1s 1986, 2d 1988, 1990).

Drury, Alan Hyslop; FCO since July 1998; born 21/02/52; FCO 1970; Budapest 1973; Dacca 1975; LA Floater 1977; FCO 1980; Second Secretary (Comm) Muscat 1983; Second later First Secretary FCO 1987; Resident Representative St. Georges 1989; Consul (Commercial) Barcelona 1994; m 1980 Joan Lamb (1d 1984, 1s 1986).

Drysdale, Craig Morrison; First Secretary (Political) Muscat since April 2001; born 22/03/56; FCO 1981; Full-Time Language Training 1994; Full-Time Language Training Cairo 1995; First Secretary FCO 1996; Band C5; m 1988 Clare Elizabeth (2d 1993, 1996).

Drysden, Heather; Third Secretary Warsaw (KHF) since June 1997; born 02/06/56; Brussels (NATO) 1977; FCO 1977; Tokyo 1980; FCO 1983; Reykjavik 1984; FCO 1987; Floater Duties 1987; Valletta 1993; Band B3.

Duckett, Keith Dyson; SUPL/Temporary Duties since October 1997; born 11/04/58; FCO 1977; Kuala Lumpur 1979; Maputo 1983; Brasilia 1985;

FCO 1986; Jakarta 1989; Third Secretary (Man) Paris 1993; Second Secretary (Man) Damascus 1995; Band C4; m 1989 Diane Puckridge (1d 1990, 1s 1991).

Duddy, Fiona Lindsay; Stockholm since December 1994; born 30/08/72; FCO 1991; Band A2.

Duff, Janet Nancy; FCO since October 1997; born 03/12/67; FCO 1990; Language Training 1991; Chiang Mai 1992; Vice-Consul Bangkok 1993; Addis Ababa 1996; Band D6.

Duff, Morwenna Marion Finlayson; SUPL since July 1993; born 06/10/65; HCS 1988; FCO 1989; Jakarta 1990; Band A2.

Duffield, Linda Joy; High Commissioner Colombo since May 1999; born 18/04/53; DHSS 1976; Paris (ENA) 1986; First Secretary FCO 1987; First Secretary (Comm) Moscow 1989; First Secretary later Counsellor FCO 1992; Deputy High Commissioner Ottawa 1995.

Duffin, David Robert; FCO since 1996; born 04/11/53; FCO 1972; New Delhi 1979; FCO 1981; Singapore 1987; FCO 1990; Berlin 1995; Band C5; m (1) 1980 Angela Thicke (diss 1984); (2) Carole Susan Matthews (diss 1996).

Duffy, Peter John; First Secretary (Management) Paris since April 2001; born 20/06/50; Ministry of Aviation (later Ministry of Technology) 1966; FCO 1967; Addis Ababa 1971; Maseru 1974; Khartoum 1977; FCO 1978; Yaoundé 1982; Johannesburg 1985; Attaché later Second Secretary Budapest 1989; Second Secretary FCO 1991; Second Secretary Amsterdam 1994; Second later First Secretary (Management) Kingston 1995; m 1971 Juliet Heather Woodward (1s 1972).

Duggin, Thomas Joseph; HM Ambassador Bogotá since August 2001; born 15/09/47; Commonwealth Office (later FCO) 1967; Oslo 1969; Bucharest 1973; Assistant Private Secretary to the PUSS, FCO 1977; Second Secretary Bangkok 1979; First Secretary FCO 1982; First Secretary (Commercial), Consul and Head of Chancery La Paz 1985; First Secretary and Head of Chancery Mexico City 1989; High Commissioner Vila 1992; Counsellor FCO 1995; m (1) 1968 (diss 1983) (2s 1973, 1975); (2) 1983 (diss 1996) (3) 1999 Janette Mortimer (neé David).

Dun, Peter John; On Commercial Secondment since August 2000; born 06/07/47; 93; FCO 1970; Third later Second Secretary Kuala Lumpur 1972; Second later First Secretary FCO 1976; First Secretary (External Relations) Brussels (UKREP) 1980; First Secretary New York (UKMIS) 1983; FCO 1987; Counsellor on secondment to RCDS 1989; Counsellor (Economic) Islamabad 1990; Foreign Policy Adviser to External Affairs Commissioner, EC Brussels 1993; Counsellor FCO 1996; m 1983 Cheng-Kiak Pang (2s 1987, 1989).

Duncan, Colin; Floater Duties since September 1998; born 03/03/70; DSS 1988; FCO 1989; Brussels (UKREP) 1992; Sofia 1995; Band B3.

Duncan, John Stewart, OBE (1993); Counsellor (Commercial) Paris since April 2002; born 17/04/58; FCO 1980; Paris 1982; Khartoum 1985; Second Secretary FCO 1988; On loan to ODA as APS to Minister of State 1991; Chargé d'Affaires Tirana 1992; NATO Defence College, Rome 1992; Brussels (UKDEL WEU/NATO) 1993; First Secretary FCO 1996; On loan at SACEUR since August 1998; m 1984 Anne Marie Jacq (1d 1990, 1s 1994).

Duncan, Rachel Mignonne Bridget (née Blanche); SUPL since June 2002; born 17/01/74; FCO 1997; Vice-Consul (Political) Jerusalem 2000; FCO 2002; Band B3; m 2000 Stuart Duncan.

Duncan, Reginald Arthur; Pyongyang since July 2002; born 23/08/45; HM Forces 1963-1993; FCO 1995; Ankara 1997; Stanley 2000; Band A2; m 1967 Cecily Coleman (2d 1971, 1974).

Duncan-Smith, Louise-Marie Veronica; Sana'a since August 2000; born 16/12/62; FCO 1984; Ottawa 1986; FCO 1989; Banjul 1989; Victoria 1992; Berne 1996; Berne 1999; SUPL 1999; SUPL 2000; Band A2; m 1986 Brian David Smith.

Dunlop, Alexander James Macfarlane; Vienna (UKDEL OSCE) since March 2000; born 14/06/48; FCO 1968; Ottawa 1971; Vientiane 1974; Sana'a 1980; Vienna 1983; FCO 1986; Second later First Secretary (Chancery/Info) Lilongwe 1989; First Secretary FCO 1994; First Secretary (Consular) Nairobi 1996; Band C5; m 1978 Ortrud Wittlinger.

Dunn, Andrew Patrick Rymer; FCO since September 2000; born 14/09/69; Band C4; m 1995 Caroline Nicola Cann (1s 1998).

Dunn, David Hedley; T/D Stockholm since October 2000; born 21/09/68; FCO 1989; Oslo 1992; LA/Caribbean Floater Duties 1995; On secondment to UNEP Nairobi as Second Secretary (Environment), 1998; Band C4.

Dunn, James Michael; Warsaw since June 1999; born 07/01/59; FCO 1980; Washington 1984; FCO 1986; Paris 1990; Third Secretary Lagos 1993; Band C4; m 1993 B C Boyle.

Dunn, Jonathan Michael; Second Secretary (Chancery) Hanoi since October 2000; born 07/03/75; FCO 1997; SOAS University of London 1998; Full-Time Language Training Hanoi 1999; Band C4.

Dunn, Michael George; FCO since November 2000; born 08/11/48; FO (later FCO) 1966; New York 1971; Lima 1974; FCO 1976; Copenhagen 1980; Harare 1983; Caracas 1986; FCO 1989; Quito 1992; Bogotá 1997; m 1983 Mercedes Josefina Fuguet-Sanchez (3d 1987, 1990, 1998).

Dunnachie, (Doreen) Carole (née Cleaver); Abu Dhabi since April 1997; born 20/12/46; FCO 1973; Kinshasa 1974; FCO 1976; Helsinki 1977;

Suva 1980; The Hague 1982; FCO 1984; SUPL
1986; FCO 1989; SUPL 1992; Canberra 1994;
SUPL 1996; Band B3; m 1986 Hugh Dunnachie

Dunnachie, Hugh, MBE (1987); Consul-General
Perth since March 2000; born 07/12/44; MOD
(Navy) 1961-65; DSAO 1965; Singapore (Political
Adviser's office) 1967; Warsaw 1972; Vice-Consul
Cairo 1973; Second Secretary FCO 1976; Second
Secretary (Commercial) The Hague 1980; Consul
and Head of British Interests Tripoli 1984; First
Secretary FCO 1989; Deputy Consul-General
Melbourne 1992; First Secretary
(Economic/Agriculture) Canberra 1994; Deputy
Head of Post and HM Consul Dubai 1996; m (1)
1963 Elizabeth Mosman Baxter (diss 1986) (3d
1964, 1971, 1980; 1s 1965); (2) 1986 (Doreen)
Carole Cleaver.

Dunne, John Richard; Deputy Head of Mission
Pyongyang since May 2002; born 04/10/67; FCO
1992; Third later Second Secretary New York
(UKMIS) 1996; SUPL 2000; First Secretary FCO
2001; Band D6; m 1997 Naomi Anita Scott.

Duranko, Elizabeth Jean (née Paris); SUPL since
August 2000; born 23/01/69; FCO 1993; Geneva
1996; SUPL 1998; Pretoria 1999; Band C4; m
1997 John Eric Duranko (1d 1998).

Dutch, Alastair Keith; Second later First Secretary
FCO since January 1980; born 04/05/52; FCO
1971; Ankara 1974; Moscow 1977; Bombay 1978;
m 1974 Lesley Joan Carol Hearsum (2s 1975,
1983).

Duxbury, Julie Annette; Third Secretary
(Immigration) Zagreb since August 2000; born
05/02/70; FCO 1988; Brussels (UKDEL NATO)
1990; FCO 1993; Full-Time Language Training
1995; Vice-Consul Athens 1996; Dubai 1998;
Band B3.

Dwyer, Michael John; HM Consul/ECM, and later
First Secretary (Director of US ECIPs) New York
since February 1995; born 29/12/55; DOE 1972-
74; FCO 1974; Ottawa 1977; Belmopan 1979;
Islamabad 1982; FCO 1986; Vice-Consul
(Man/Comm/Con) Toronto 1990; Second
Secretary (Commercial) Toronto 1991; m 1982
Karen Leolin Meighan (2s 1983, 1985, 1d 1989).

Dyson, John Alva, MVO (1995); Deputy High
Commissioner T/D Suva since June 2002; born
15/04/49; DSAO (later FCO) 1966; Port of Spain
1970; Geneva 1973; Yaoundé 1976; FCO 1978;
Nuku'alofa 1982; FCO 1985; Second Secretary
(Commercial) Jedda 1987; Vice-Consul
(Management Officer) Cape Town 1991; First
Secretary FCO 1996; T/D Asmara 2001; m 1971
Deirdre Anne George (2s 1974, 1981).

E

Ead, Mark; Nicosia since March 2002; born
20/04/76; FCO 1997; Band A2; m 2001 Victoria
Swan.

Eager, Helen Christine (née Gillings), BEM
(1991); SUPL since May 1998; born 10/06/65;

FCO 1985; SUPL 1986; Baghdad 1988; FCO
1988; FCO 1990; Bangkok 1993; FCO 1997;
Band A2.

Eager, Nigel Dominic; First Secretary (Political)
Valletta since September 1998; born 09/05/62;
FCO 1981; Dublin 1986; Third Secretary/Vice
Consul Baghdad 1988; FCO 1990; Band C5; m (1)
1987 Helen Christine Gillings (diss 1993); (2)
1998 Catherine Thomas.

Eakin, Christopher Howard; SUPL since July
2000; born 01/12/64; FCO 1984; East Berlin 1985;
Paris 1987; FCO 1990; Vienna 1993; Grand
Cayman 1996; Band C4.

Ealand, Jane Elizabeth; FCO since November
1991; born 10/08/67; FCO 1986; New Delhi 1988;
Paris 1990; FCO 1990; Band A2.

Earl, Jane Ann (née Kerr); SUPL since February
2001; born 15/06/68; FCO 1989; Luanda 1991;
Islamabad 1995; SUPL 1998; Brussels 2000; Band
B3; m 1991 Shaun Earl (1d 1997).

Earl, Shaun; Lilongwe since June 2001; born
04/01/70; FCO 1989; Luanda 1991; Third
Secretary Brussels (UKDEL) 1998; Band B3; m
1991 Jane Ann Kerr (1d 1997).

Easson, Hilary; Vienna since September 2000;
born 10/01/68; FCO 1987; Kuwait 1990; Algiers
1991; FCO 1994; Bogotá 1995; FCO 1999; Band
A2.

Easter, Christine Marie; FCO since July 1994;
born 22/11/44; Cape Town 1975; FCO 1975; FCO
1979; Luxembourg 1982; Anguilla 1985; Rangoon
1987; Budapest 1989; Washington 1991; Band B3.

Eastwood, Basil Stephen Talbot, CMG (1999);
HM Ambassador, Berne additionally HM
Ambassador (non-resident) Liechtenstein since
August 2001; born 04/03/44; On loan to Cabinet
Office 1976; Third Secretary FO 1966; MECAS
1967; Jedda 1968; Third later Second Secretary
Colombo 1969; Second later First Secretary Cairo
1972; FCO 1978; Bonn 1980; Counsellor and
Head of Chancery Khartoum 1984; Counsellor
(Econ/Comm) Athens 1987; Counsellor FCO
1991; HM Ambassador Damascus 1996; m 1970
Alison Faith Hutchings (4d 1972, 1973, 1977,
1979).

Eastwood, Helen; SUPL since April 1996; born
10/12/63; FCO 1989; Dubai 1992; Band A2; m
1990 David Allan Eastwood (1d 1996).

Eatwell, Jonathan David; SUPL since July 2001;
born 08/11/67; FCO 1986; Lusaka 1988; FCO
1992; Dhaka 1995; Jakarta 1998; FCO 1998; Band
B3; m 1991 Lisa Ann Brecknell (1d 1997).

Ebeling, Adrian Stanley Arthur; FCO since
November 2000; born 20/01/48; FCO 1984; Paris
1989; FCO 1992; Pretoria 1998; Band C4; m 1979
Laura Phipps (1s 1987).

Edgar, Christopher George; HM Ambassador
Skopje since September 2001; born 21/04/60;
FCO 1981; Moscow 1983; Lagos 1986; FCO

1988; Resigned 1992; Reinstated 1995; First Secretary FCO 1995; HM Ambassador Phnom Penh 1997; Full-Time Language Training 2001; m 1994 Yelena Nagornichnykh (2d 1994, 1998).

Edge, Christopher James; Deputy High Commissioner Port of Spain since January 2002; born 30/08/53; First Secretary (Commercial), San José and Director of Trade Promotion in Cenral America 1999; FCO 1972; Kabul 1975; East Berlin 1977; Rome 1980; Kaduna 1981; FCO 1984; Beirut 1985; Third Secretary (Commercial) Mexico City 1987; Deputy Head of Mission Tegucigalpa 1988; Second later First Secretary (Commercial) Madrid 1992; FCO 1996.

Edghill, Susan Christine (née Cranwell); Chennai since April 2002; born 14/07/58; FCO 1990; Paris 1993; Port Louis 1996; Manila 1998; Band A2; m 1996 Samuel Carlisle Edghill.

Edis, Rachel Pauline; FCO since October 2001; born 24/11/76; Band C4.

Edusei, Charmaine (née Howe); FCO since 1997; born 17/09/59; FCO 1988; Brussels (UKDEL NATO) 1991; FCO 1993; Valletta 1994; Band B3; m 1989 Isaac Edusei (1d 1993).

Edwards, Carole Lilian (née Hellier); Brasilia since April 2002; born 07/07/45; Freetown 1973; FCO 1973; Washington 1975; Belgrade 1978; Prague 1978; FCO 1979; Beirut 1980; Ottawa 1982; Moscow 1985; FCO 1986; Washington 1989; FCO 1992; Band B3.

Edwards, David Vaughan; Tehran since May 2001; born 27/09/43; RAF 1961-89; Budapest 1989; Islamabad 1990; Kingston 1994; Moscow 1996; Riyadh 1998; Band B3; m 1967 Patricia Ann (2d 1968, 1969, 1s 1972).

Edwards, Gillian Rose; Dublin since January 2000; born 07/02/64; FCO 1983; Resigned 1987; Reinstated 1988; FCO 1988; World wide Floater Duties 1991; St Petersburg 1993; FCO 1994; Vice-Consul New York 1996; Band B3; m 1995 David Jonathan Mead.

Edwards, Keith Nigel; Second Secretary FCO since April 1995; born 09/05/53; FCO 1969; Warsaw 1977; Athens 1978; FCO 1981; Hong Kong 1985; FCO 1988; Second Secretary Madrid 1992; m 1975 Wendy Ann Carrington (2d 1980, 1982).

Edwards, Mannetta Beverley (née Leigh); FCO since July 1994; born 14/02/59; FCO 1979; Kuwait 1982; FCO 1986; Brussels (UKDEL NATO) 1991; Band C4; m 1980 Christopher James Edwards (2s 1981, 1986).

Edwards, Paul Martin; Third Secretary (Management and Vice-Consul) Almaty since September 1998; born 11/11/66; FCO 1996; Band B3; m 1990 Jane Baker (1d 1993).

Edwards, Rose Catherine Amy; Second Secretary (Economic) Moscow since February 2001; born 10/11/73; FCO 1998; Full-Time Language Training 1999; Band C4.

Eelbeck, Andrew; FCO since January 2002; born 02/03/59; FCO 1979; Islamabad 1980; Singapore 1982; FCO 1982; FCO 1986; Third Secretary Prague 1988; Third Secretary Pretoria 1992; FCO 1995; Accra 1997; Band C5; m 1994 Miss F Botes (1s 1995).

Ehrman, William Geoffrey, CMG (1998); Director (International Security) FCO since September 2000; born 28/08/50; Third Secretary FCO 1973; Language Training Hong Kong 1975; Third later Second Secretary Peking 1976; First Secretary (ECOSOC) New York (UKMIS) 1979; First Secretary Peking 1983; FCO 1985; On secondment in Hong Kong as Political Adviser to the Governor 1989; Counsellor FCO 1993; Principal Private Secretary to the Secretary of State for Foreign and Commonwealth Affairs 1995; On secondment to Unilever 1997; HM Ambassador Luxembourg 1998; m 1977 Penelope Anne Le Patourel (1s 1981, 3d 1977, 1979, 1986).

El Beleidi, Cecille Maude (née Greaves); Second Secretary (Chancery) Riyadh since March 2000; born 22/11/62; FCO 1982; Kuwait 1985; FCO 1986; Kathmandu 1989; Vice-Consul Casablanca 1992; APS/Baroness Symons FCO 1995; SUPL 1999; Second Secretary (Chancery) Riyadh 1999; Band C4; m 1987 Magdi El Beleidi (1d 1999).

El Ouassi, Sabine; Amman since September 1999; born 29/01/64; HCS 1990-1993; FCO 1994; Riyadh 1995; Band A2; m 1988 Mohamed El Ouassi (2s 1994, 2001).

El Roubi, Julie Anne (née Mooney); Abu Dhabi since December 2000; born 21/04/71; Brussels (UKDEL NATO) 1991; Khartoum 1995; Lagos 1998; Band A2; m (1) 1992 Prince Felix Lewis (diss) (1d 1992); (2) 1999 Murtada Saad El Roubi (1s 2000).

Elder, Alistair Alexander; Third Secretary (Commercial) New Delhi since July 2001; born 14/05/71; FCO 1989; Brussels (UKREP) 1992; FCO 1994; Vice-Consul Tel Aviv 1997; m Charlotte Dawson (2d 1992, 1995).

Elder, Peter Edward; FCO since December 1997; born 14/03/68; FCO 1989; Brussels 1992; New Delhi 1994; FCO 1994; Band B3; m 1994 Rosalind Anita Hall (1d 1997).

Elder, Rosalind Anita (née Hall); SUPL since March 2002; born 19/07/65; FCO 1990; Brussels (UKREP) 1992; New Delhi 1994; FCO 1997; Band A2; m 1994 Peter Edward Elder (1d 1997).

Eldon, Stewart Graham, CMG (1999), OBE (1991); HM Ambassador Dublin since April 2003; born 18/09/53; FCO 1976; New York (UKMIS) 1976; Third later Second Secretary Bonn 1978; First Secretary FCO 1982; Private Secretary to the Minister of State 1983; First Secretary (Chancery) New York (UKMIS) 1986; First Secretary FCO 1990; Counsellor on loan to the Cabinet Office 1991; Fellow, Center for International Affairs, Harvard University 1993; Counsellor (Political) Brussels (UKDEL NATO/WEU) 1994; Director

(Conferences) FCO 1997; Deputy Permanent Representative (with the personal rank of Ambassador) New York (UKMIS) 1998; m 1978 Christine Mary Mason (1d 1982, 1s 1985).

Elliot, Caroline Margaret (Carma); Consul-General Chongqing since March 2000; born 24/08/64; FCO 1987; Peking 1989; Brussels 1991; EC Presidency Liaison Officer Bonn, Paris and Madrid 1995-1996; Second later First Secretary FCO 1996; Band D6.

Elliot, Christopher Lowther; Second Secretary FCO since March 1997; born 26/12/54; DNS 1974; FCO 1975; DOE 1975; Cairo 1979; Bridgetown 1982; FCO 1986; Islamabad 1990; Muscat 1993; m 1975 Julie Lorraine Inman (1s adopted 1975, 1d 1982).

Elliot, Hugh Stephen Murray; Counsellor Paris since July 2002; born 21/08/65; FCO 1989; Third later Second Secretary (Chancery) Madrid 1991; FCO 1996; Buenos Aires 1999; m 1989 Toni Martin-Elena (1s 1993, 1d 1995).

Elliott, Jane Susan; First Secretary FCO since April 2002; born 16/06/55; FCO 1980; Hong Kong 1991; FCO 1997; Consul-General Hong Kong 2000; Band D6.

Elliott, Jonathan Andrew; First Secretary FCO since February 2001; born 03/09/66; FCO 1991; Full-Time Language Training 1993; Tokyo 1995; Second Secretary FCO 1999; Band D6.

Elliott, Robert David; First Secretary (Management) Abuja since November 2000; born 25/11/60; FCO 1980; Prague 1981; Peking 1982; Language Training 1983; Abu Dhabi 1984; Port Louis 1988; FCO 1993; HM Consul Jerusalem 1997; Band C5; m 1998 Victoria Louise Holloway (1s 1998, 1d 2000).

Elliott, Stuart; Athens since October 1999; born 15/04/75; HCS 1994; FCO 1997; Athens 1999; Band A2; m 1999 Margaret Redmond.

Elliott, Susan Jayne, MBE (1991); Second Secretary (Chancery) Bandar Seri Begawan since January 1999; born 13/06/61; FCO 1978; SUPL 1980; Rome 1982; SUPL 1982; Cairo 1984; FCO 1985; Beirut 1988; FCO 1992; Bombay 1992; Band B3; m 1980 John Anthony Tucknott (diss 1992).

Elliott, William, OBE (2002); Second Secretary (Political) Warsaw since October 1995; born 16/03/68; Second Secretary FCO 1993; Language Training 1994.

Ellis, Alexander Wykeham; First Secretary (Economic) Brussels (UKREP) since June 1996; born 05/06/67; FCO 1990; Third later Second Secretary (Political/Economic) Lisbon 1992; m 1996 Maria Teresa Adegas.

Ellis, Amanda Jane; Quito since July 1999; born 07/12/60; FCO 1987; Brussels 1989; FCO 1991; Jakarta 1995; Band A2.

Ellis, Ann; FCO since September 1990; born 19/11/47; Band A2.

Ellis, Hugo; FCO since January 1999; born 13/09/66; FCO 1988; Riyadh 1992; Strasbourg (UKDEL) 1995; Band B3.

Ellis, John Arthur; Sarajevo since June 2002; born 27/03/52; DHSS 1969-71; FCO 1971; Wellington 1974; Khartoum 1976; Dar es Salaam 1979; FCO 1981; Islamabad 1982; Seoul 1986; Second Secretary FCO 1989; Second Secretary (Commercial/Aid) Cairo 1993; Second Secretary FCO 1996; m 1974 Law Kwai Chun (1s 1980, 1d 1983).

Ellis, Philip Donald; First Secretary FCO since October 1997; born 09/05/57; FCO 1978; Brussels (NATO) 1981; Peking 1984; FCO 1987; New Delhi 1990; Vice-Consul São Paulo 1995; m 1981 Gail Teresa Drayton (1s 1997).

Ellis, Richard Anthony; Full-Time Language Training (Greek) since February 2002; born 02/02/77; FCO 2000; Band C4.

Ellwood, Dr Sheelagh Margaret; FCO since October 1998; born 21/02/49; FCO 1988; Assistant Deputy Governor Gibraltar 1995; Senior Principal Research Officer 1998.

Elvins, Christine Patricia (née Pettit); SUPL since February 1999; born 04/06/60; FCO 1979; Bonn 1983; Pretoria 1986; FCO 1987; SUPL 1988; FCO 1993; Band C4; m 1988 Martyn Andrew Elvins.

Elvins, Martyn Andrew; Pretoria since February 1999; born 13/02/58; FCO 1984; Warsaw 1988; Band C4; m 1988 Christine P Pettit.

Elvy, Simon David; Second Secretary (Political) Stockholm since June 1996; born 08/12/61; FCO 1983; Baghdad 1985; Stockholm 1989; FCO 1992; Band B3; m 1985 Lesley Jane (1s 1991).

Embleton, Robert Leitch; First Secretary (Social/Science) Rome since August 1998; born 09/10/42; FO 1960; Leopoldville 1964; Bonn 1968; St Vincent 1969; FCO 1973; Stuttgart 1976; Prague 1979; Second Secretary FCO 1980; Second later First Secretary (Chancery) Washington 1984; Consul (Commercial) Düsseldorf 1989; First Secretary FCO 1993; m 1970 Ursula Biebricher (1d 1975).

Emery, Peter Michael; Tokyo since February 2000; born 25/11/72; FCO 1997; Helsinki 1999; Band A2.

Emery, Simon Richard; FCO since June 1985; born 22/08/57; FCO 1981; Paris (OECD) 1982; Band A2; m 1981 Dorothy Seery.

Enescott, Nicholas John; MO/VC Rangoon since March 2002; born 06/12/51; FCO 1972; Cape Town 1975; Ankara 1977; Tripoli 1980; FCO 1983; Hanoi 1986; Third Secretary (Comm) and Vice-Consul Dakar 1989; Second Secretary (Management) Lilongwe 1991; Second Secretary FCO 1995; ECM Bombay 1998.

Engdahl, Denise Jean (née Sanders); Stockholm since March 2000; born 19/09/60; FCO 1982; Wellington 1983; Colombo 1986; Mbabane 1989; FCO 1993; SUPL 1995; Kingston 1996; Band B3; m 1989 Geran Magnus Engdahl (1s 1991, 1d 1994).

Esling, Paul Francis; Lagos since August 2000; born 16/11/73; FCO 1996; Harare 1998; Band B3; m 1997 Lindsey Jane Esling (1s 2000).

Estlin, Jennifer Frances (née Haxton), MBE (1999); Montserrat since January 1996; born 21/04/44; FCO 1992; Sana'a 1993; Band A2; m 1995 Boyd Estlin (1s 1970).

Etherington, Richard David Ernest; T/D Dubai since November 2001; born 29/11/73; FCO 1999; Band C4.

Etherton, Mark Roy; Deputy Permanent Representative Vienna (UKMIS) since April 1999; born 17/03/58; FCO 1983; Second Secretary (Chancery) Paris 1988; First Secretary (Political/Economic) Warsaw 1991; First Secretary on loan to Cabinet Office 1994; FCO 1996; m 1991 Suzanne Margaret Miskin (2d 1994, 1996).

Evans, Alison Joan; FCO since July 1990; born 30/10/63; FCO 1982; Caracas 1984; African/ME Floater 1988; Band B3.

Evans, Carol Jeanette (née Kendall); SUPL since July 1997; born 10/04/59; FCO 1982; Vienna (UKDEL) 1984; Warsaw 1987; FCO 1988; Band B3; m 1991 Keith Dennis Evans.

Evans, Claire Elizabeth; First Secretary FCO since June 2000; born 02/11/61; FCO 1987; Jakarta 1989; Third Secretary (Commercial) Islamabad 1992; Second Secretary FCO 1996; Band C5.

Evans, Claire Margaret (née Bolland); Second Secretary Oslo since March 2002; born 13/01/70; Second Secretary FCO 1994; Band C4; m 1996 David Howard Evans (2d 1997, 1999; 1s 2001).

Evans, David Hugh; First Secretary (Political) Nairobi since May 2001; born 27/03/59; FCO 1985; Islamabad 1988; FCO 1989; First Secretary (Political) Washington 1995 (on loan to the US State Department); On secondment to the CBI as Senior Policy Adviser 1999; Band D6; m 1988 Nirmala Vinodhini Chrysostom (2d 1996, 2001).

Evans, Elizabeth Ann (née McNab); Third Secretary (Visits, Press and Public Affairs) Peking since November 1999; born 26/07/61; FCO 1998; Band B3; m 1987 Laurance Bolton Evans (1s 1989).

Evans, Gayle Evelyn Louise (née Sperring); SUPL since April 1997; born 01/09/62; FCO 1983; Accra 1984; Moscow 1986; FCO 1987; Floater Duties 1990; SUPL 1991; New York (UKMIS) 1992; FCO 1996; Band B3; m 1991 Julian Ascott Evans (2d 1997, 1999).

Evans, Gerald Stanley; Deputy Head of Mission Asunción since November 1996; born 26/10/51; FCO 1971; Havana 1973; Bonn 1974; FCO 1977;

Jedda 1977; Third Secretary and Vice-Consul Dubai 1979; FCO 1983; Third Secretary (Commercial) Bogotá 1986; Third Secretary (Management) Athens 1990; Second Secretary FCO 1994; m 1991 Graciela Elisa Casetta.

Evans, Gillian; Rabat since September 2000; born 01/09/59; FCO 1981; Berlin (BMG) 1982; Kinshasa 1984; Africa/Asia/ME Floater 1988; Zagreb 1992; Damascus 1996; Band A2.

Evans, Jennifer Louise; FCO since July 2001; born 07/11/78; Band C4; ptnr, Nicholas Cole.

Evans, Jennifer Mary (née Lewis); SUPL since January 1995; born 03/03/59; FCO 1978; Far East Floater 1981; SUPL 1983; Vienna 1984; SUPL 1985; Dhaka 1989; Second Secretary FCO 1993; m 1982 Wayne Evans (3d 1985, 1988, 1994; 1s 1997).

Evans, Julian Ascott; Deputy High Commissioner Islamabad since March 2002; born 05/07/57; FCO 1978; Language Training 1980; Moscow 1982; Zurich 1985; Second Secretary FCO 1987; Second later First Secretary New York (UKMIS) 1991; First Secretary FCO 1996; m 1991 Gayle Evelyn Louise Sperring (2d 1997, 1999).

Evans, Karen-Lane (née Williams); FCO since December 1999; born 09/04/63; FCO 1989; Second Secretary (Chancery) The Hague 1992; Second Secretary FCO 1996; SUPL 1998; Band C4; m 1998 Paul Lawson Evans.

Evans, Laurance Bolton; First Secretary and HMC Peking since April 1999; born 30/03/43; FO 1962; Saigon 1964; Washington 1968; FCO 1970; Brussels (JAO) 1974; Paris 1976; FCO 1979; Vienna 1982; Second Secretary (Development) Amman 1984; Second Secretary (Consular) Dar es Salaam 1988; Second Secretary FCO 1992; Manila 1995; m (1) 1963 Heather Duxbury (dec'd 1986) (2s 1965, 1968); (2) 1987 Elizabeth Ann McNab (1s 1989).

Evans, Dame Madelaine Glynne Dervel, DBE (2000), CMG (1992); HM Ambassador Lisbon since September 2001; born 23/08/44; Second Secretary FCO 1971; Buenos Aires 1972; First Secretary FCO 1975; Private Secretary to PUSS 1976; On loan to UN Secretariat New York 1978; First Secretary New York (UKMIS) 1979; First Secretary later Counsellor FCO 1982; Counsellor and Head of Chancery Brussels 1987; Counsellor FCO 1990-1996; (IISS) 1996; HM Ambassador Santiago 1997; Attachment to ACAD/IND as Detached National Expert 2000.

Evans, Peter Dering; Third later Second Secretary FCO since February 1993; born 09/04/57; FCO 1976; Dhaka 1978; FCO 1980; Barcelona 1985; San Salvador 1988; Third Secretary (Management/Accounts) Caracas 1990; m 1985 Susan Elizabeth Parker (2s 1987, 1989).

Evans, Stephen Nicholas, CMG (2002), OBE (1994); High Commissioner Colombo since July 2002; born 29/06/50; Third Secretary FCO 1974; Language Training SOAS 1975; Second Secretary

FCO 1976; Head of Chancery and Consul Hanoi 1978; FCO 1980; Language Training Bangkok 1982; First Secretary Bangkok 1983; First Secretary FCO 1986; First Secretary (Political) Ankara 1990; Counsellor (Economic/Commercial/Aid) Islamabad 1993; Secondment to United Nations Special Mission to Afghanistan 1996; Counsellor FCO 1997; m 1975 Sharon Ann Holdcroft (2d 1981, 1984; 1s 1986).

Evans, Stephen Paul; Singapore since July 2002; born 28/10/57; HM Forces (Army) 1975; Police Constable 1997; FCO 2000; Band B3; m 1986 Julie Spackman (1s 1988,1d 1990).

Evans, Stephen Shane; FCO since July 2001; born 07/12/54; FCO 1992; Second Secretary Zagreb 1998; Band C4; m 1995 Susan Jane (1d 1987).

Evans, Wayne; First Secretary (Political) The Hague since July 2000; born 29/08/53; FCO 1971; Paris 1974; Maseru 1977; FCO 1979; Baghdad 1981; Vienna 1984; FCO 1987; Second Secretary (Aid) Dhaka 1989; Second later First Secretary FCO 1993; Deputy Head of Mission and Consul (Commercial) Jedda 1996; Band C5; m 1982 Jennifer Mary Lewis (3d 1985, 1988, 1994; 1s 1997).

Evans, William John Eldred; First Secretary (Political) Tallinn since July 2002; born 13/04/71; FCO 1994; Language Training 1996; On loan to OHR Sarajevo 1997; Second Secretary (Political/Military) Sarajevo 1998; Second Secretary FCO 1999; Band D6.

Everard, John Vivian; HM Ambassador Montevideo since September 2001; born 24/11/56; FCO 1979; Third later Second Secretary Peking 1981; Second Secretary Vienna 1983; Resigned 1984; Reinstated 1987; Second later First Secretary FCO 1987; First Secretary (Commercial) Santiago 1990; HM Ambassador Minsk 1993; OSCE Mission to Bosnia-Herzegovina 1995; Counsellor FCO 1996; Counsellor Peking 1998; m 1990 Heather Ann Starkey.

Everard, Thomas James; Tehran since June 2001; born 11/08/75; FCO 1998; Band A2.

Everett, Bernard Jonathan, CVO (1999); Consul General São Paulo and Director of Trade Promotion for Brazil since September 2000; born 17/09/43; Counsellor on loan to DTI 1984; FO 1966; Third later Second Secretary Lisbon 1967; Second later First Secretary FCO 1971; First Secretary FCO 1975; Consul (Pol) Luanda 1975; First Secretary and Head of Chancery Lusaka 1978; Consul (Comm) Rio de Janeiro 1980; First Secretary FCO 1983; HM Ambassador Guatemala City 1987; Consul-General Houston 1991; High Commissioner Maputo 1996; m 1970 Maria Olinda Goncalves de Albuquerque (1d 1974, 2s 1980, 1981; 1d 1976, dec'd 1979).

Everett, Sara Gillian; Deputy Director New York (BIS) since January 1996; born 06/07/55; FCO 1979; Paris (ENA) 1981; Caracas 1983; Second Secretary (Econ) Brussels (UKREP) 1986; Second

Secretary (Econ) Brussels 1987; First Secretary FCO 1991; m 1989 Christopher Ian Montague Jones (1s 1994).

Everitt, Oliver Hunter; FCO since January 2002; born 28/12/71; FCO 1992; Vienna 1995; Third Secretary (Immigration) Lusaka 1999; Band B3.

Everson, Clare Elizabeth; SUPL since November 1999; born 20/12/59; FCO 1981; Karachi 1983; SE Asia Floater 1988; FCO 1990; Deputy High Commissioner Vila 1994; Band D6.

Evetts, Keith Derek, OBE (1989); FCO since September 2002; born 20/05/48; Third Secretary FCO 1973; Language Training 1974; Second Secretary Warsaw 1975; Language Training 1976; First Secretary Maputo 1977; FCO 1980; New York (UKMIS) 1983; Kingston 1986; First Secretary (Chancery) Lisbon 1988; First Secretary later Counsellor FCO 1991; Counsellor Brussels 1995; Counsellor FCO 1998; Counsellor Lisbon 1998; m (1) 1971 Bridget Elizabeth Peachey (diss 1988) (2s 1981, 1982); (2) 1988 Lesley Ann Myers (1s 1989, 2d 1990, 1996).

F

Fairley, Averil Margaret; Second Secretary (Management) Georgetown since March 2001; born 18/06/67; FCO 1986; East Berlin 1988; Hanoi 1990; European Council Unit Edinburgh 1992; Bombay 1993; FCO 1997; Band C4.

Fairweather, Maria Louise (née Latta); SUPL since November 2001; born 25/05/67; MOD 1986; FCO 1988; Berne 1989; FCO 1992; Peking 1993; T/D Kiev 1995; FCO 1996; Band B3; m 1993 Robert John Fairweather.

Fairweather, Robert John; Second Secretary Geneva (UKMIS) since April 2002; born 26/02/67; HMCE 1987-96; FCO 1996; Band C4; m 1993 Marie Louise.

Falconer, Lynne Marie; Lisbon since August 2000; born 27/09/67; HM Forces 1986-1995; FCO 1995; Helsinki 1997; Band A2.

Fall, David William; Estate Modernisation Manager, FCO since September 2000; born 10/03/48; On loan to Cabinet Office 1977; Third Secretary FCO 1971; Language Training Bangkok 1973; First Secretary Bangkok 1976; FCO 1979; First Secretary (Chancery) Pretoria/Cape Town 1981; First Secretary later Counsellor FCO 1985; Deputy Head of Mission and Counsellor (Commercial) Bangkok 1990; Deputy High Commissioner Canberra 1993; HM Ambassador Hanoi 1997; m 1973 Margaret Gwendolyn Richards (3s 1976, 1977, 1980).

Fallon, Helen Clare; ECO/VC Bridgetown since November 1998; born 13/06/68; FCO 1987; Lagos 1990; FCO 1994; Band B3; m 1990 Michael Thomas Fallon (diss 1998) (2s 1991, 1992).

Falzarano, Assuntina; Second Secretary (Chancery) New York (UKMIS) since December 2000; born 10/08/73; FCO 1998; Band C4.

Farish, Sandra Mary (née Olley); Beirut since June 2000; born 07/06/71; FCO 1995; Copenhagen 1996; Band B3; m 1996 Joseph Farish.

Farnham, Brian George; Paris since April 2000; born 16/04/52; FCO 1968; Paris 1974; FCO 1977; Baghdad 1978; FCO 1980; Tokyo 1981; FCO 1984; Hong Kong 1988; Second Secretary FCO 1991; Singapore 1995; FCO 1998; Band C5; m 1982 Emiko Ishida (2d 1985, 1990).

Farnsworth, Lee; La Paz since May 1999; born 28/01/71; FCO 1998; Band A2; m 2001 Audrey Giovanna (née Vergara Rojas).

Farr, Charles Blanford; First Secretary FCO since February 1995; born 15/07/59; Second Secretary FCO 1985; Second Secretary Pretoria 1987; Second Secretary FCO 1990; First Secretary (Chancery) Amman 1992; Band D6.

Farr, Dawn Margaret; Seoul since December 1996; born 05/07/70; FCO 1989; Nicosia 1992; Mostar 1995; Band A2.

Farrand, John Percival Morey; First Secretary (Consul) Havana since July 2002; born 04/06/54; HM Customs and Excise 1971; FCO 1972; Tokyo 1974; Mexico City 1977; Kuala Lumpur 1981; FCO 1985; San Francisco 1988; FCO 1990; Second Secretary FCO 1991; Deputy High Commissioner Nassau 1994; First Secretary (Management) Ottawa 1997; Band C5; m 1979 Sharon Anne Eddie (3d 1980, 1982, 1987).

Farrant, David Cornelius; Second later First Secretary FCO since January 1987; born 05/07/53; FCO 1972; Geneva (UKMIS) 1976; Moscow 1978; FCO 1980; Athens 1984; Band C5; m 1976 Anne Laing (2s 1982, 1987).

Farrare, Jane; Jerusalem since September 2000; born 05/02/72; FCO 1999; Band A2.

Farrell, Sarah; Taipei since April 2000; born 27/06/69; FCO 1991; Lisbon 1995; Istanbul Floater 1998; SUPL 1999; Taipei 1999; FCO 1999; Band A2.

Farrent, Susan Jennifer; Dhaka since September 2000; born 17/01/48; FCO 1986; Monrovia 1987; Port Moresby 1991; Port of Spain 1992; FCO 1995; Bangkok 1996; Band B3.

Farrey, Sonia Louise; FCO since September 2001; born 21/01/77; Band C4.

Farrington, Angela (née Hunt); FCO since April 1985; born 28/09/62; Band A2; m 1987 Danny Farrington.

Farrington, Ian Francis; First Secretary FCO since December 1995; born 21/08/63; FCO 1986; Third later Second Secretary (Econ) Athens 1989; Second later First Secretary FCO 1991; First Secretary Lagos 1993; Band D6.

Farrow, Stephen Alan; Dar es Salaam since August 1997; born 23/07/56; Armed Forces 1972-1996; FCO 1996; Band A2; m 1979 Linda Alexis Jeffrey (1s 1979, 1d 1981).

Faulkner, Leo Gregory; Ambassador Republic of Chile since April 2000; born 21/09/43; FCO 1968; Second later First Secretary Lima 1972; First Secretary Lagos 1976; FCO 1979; First Secretary and Head of Chancery Madrid 1982; Counsellor on loan to DTI 1984; Counsellor (Comm) The Hague 1986; Minister, Consul-General and Deputy Head of Mission Buenos Aires 1990; Counsellor FCO 1993; High Commissioner Port of Spain 1996; Counsellor FCO 1999; m 1970 Fiona Hardie Birkett (3d 1973, 1975, 1978).

Faulkner, Nicholas Anthony; Bonn since July 1994; born 19/05/72; FCO 1991; Band A2.

Faulkner, Richard John; FCO since August 1998; born 20/02/48; FCO 1969; Seoul 1972; Dubai 1975; FCO 1979; Islamabad 1983; Rome 1986; Second Secretary FCO 1989; Second Secretary Washington 1993; m 1973 Francoise Marie Christine Armande Trine (1d 1979).

Fawcett, Christine Anne; Second Secretary FCO since October 1993; born 17/08/50; FCO 1986 (Second Secretary 1989); FCO 1968; Dar es Salaam 1971; Lima 1973; Havana 1976; Freetown 1977; FCO 1979; SEA Floater 1982; Belgrade 1983; Second Secretary (Management/Consular) Port of Spain 1991.

Fay, Jacqueline Ann (née Builder); Third Secretary (Management/Consular) Bratislava since March 1995; born 22/09/61; FCO 1980; Dhaka 1983; Peking 1985; Vice-Consul New York 1987; FCO 1991; SUPL 1991; Band B3; m 1987 Kevin Michael Fay (1s 1990, 1d 1994).

Fean, Vincent; British High Commissioner Valletta since September 2002; born 20/11/52; FCO 1975; MECAS 1977; Third Secretary Baghdad 1978; Second later First Secretary Damascus 1979; Gaborone 1979; FCO 1982; First Secretary Brussels (UKREP) 1985; First Secretary FCO 1990; Counsellor Paris 1992; FCO 1996; On loan to DTI (sub-Saharan Africa, South Asia) 1999; m 1978 Anne Marie Stewart (2d 1979, 1981; 1s 1983).

Fear, Harriet; Third Secretary (Commercial) Prague since November 1997; born 11/08/68; Department of Employment 1986; FCO 1987; Dakar 1989; Africa/Middle East Floater 1992; FCO 1994; T/D Phnom Penh 1994; Band B3.

Fearis, Timothy Rupert; FCO since July 1989; born 05/02/58; FCO 1979; Accra 1982; FCO 1984; Attaché Islamabad 1987; Band B3.

Fearn, Thomas Daniel; Deputy Head of Mission Sarajevo since January 2001; born 16/09/62; FCO 1991; Second Secretary (Political) Budapest 1992; First Secretary FCO 1996; Band D6.

Feasey, Susan Catherine; Floater Duties since October 1998; born 08/05/64; FCO 1983; Vienna (UKMIS) 1985; Dakar 1988; FCO 1990; Riga 1992; FCO 1993; Band B3.

Feather, Helen Mary; Second Secretary (Management) Dar es Salaam since February

2000; born 02/01/63; FCO 1982; Moscow 1985; Gaborone 1988; Latin American/Caribbean Floater 1990; Third Secretary Brussels (UKDEL WEU) 1993; Third Secretary FCO 1994; DTI 1996; Third Secretary (Immigration) Dar es Salaam 1999; Band B3; m 1999 L. Ross Field.

Featherstone, Simon Mark; Counsellor FCO since September 1998; born 24/07/58; FCO 1980; Language Training Hong Kong 1982; Second Secretary (Chancery) Peking 1984; First Secretary FCO 1987; On loan to Cabinet Office 1988; First Secretary (Environment) Brussels (UKREP) 1990; HM Consul-General Shanghai 1994; Counsellor (Political and Economic) Peking 1996; m 1981 Gail Teresa Salisbury (2d 1985, 1992; 1s 1988).

Fehintola, Adebowale Bamidele; Copenhagen since May 2000; born 14/11/67; FCO 1987; Copenhagen 1989; Sana'a 1992; Gaborone 1993; Band B3.

Fell, Richard Taylor, CVO (1996); British High Commissioner Wellington since December 2001; Also British High Commissioner (Non resident) Samoa, Governor (Non resident) of the Pitcairn, Henderson, Ducie and Oeno Islands; born 11/11/48; FCO 1971; Third Secretary Ottawa 1972; Second Secretary Saigon 1974; Second later First Secretary FCO 1975; Vientiane 1975; Brussels (NATO) 1979; Chargé d'Affaires a.i. Hanoi 1979; First Secretary and Head of Chancery Kuala Lumpur 1983; First Secretary FCO 1986; On secondment to Industry 1988; Counsellor (Comm/Econ) Ottawa 1989; Counsellor and Deputy Head of Mission Bangkok 1993; Counsellor FCO 1997; Consul-General T/D Toronto 2000; m 1981 Claire Peta Gates (3s 1983, 1987, 1990).

Felton, Ian; Deputy Head of Mission Phnom Penh since May 2000; born 16/05/66; FCO 1986; Brussels 1987; Floater Duties 1990; FCO 1993; New York (ECOSOC UKMIS) 1995-1999; Band C4.

Fenn, Robert Dominic Russell; Deputy Head of Southern European Department (Emed) FCO since September 2001; born 28/01/62; FCO 1983; Third Secretary (Chancery) The Hague 1985; Second Secretary (Chancery) Lagos 1988; First Secretary FCO 1990; First Secretary New York (UKMIS) 1992; First Secretary (EU/Economic) Rome 1997.

Fennell, Leigh; Amman since March 2000; born 13/12/60; FCO 1982; Darwin 1986; FCO 1988; Third Secretary Accra 1993; FCO 1997; Band C4.

Fenner, Margaret Patricia Jean (née Watson); Kingston since November 1999; born 29/01/66; Wellington 1986; FCO 1988; Warsaw 1988; Lagos 1990; Tehran 1993; Helsinki 1994; FCO 1995; Band B3; m 1989 Martin David Fenner (diss 1994) (1s 1990).

Fenning, Camilla Jane Vance (née Packman); FCO since October 1990 (Second Secretary 1991, First Secretary 1994); born 29/04/64; FCO 1985;

Language Training 1986; Tokyo 1987; m 1988 Richard John Fenning. (1s 1993, 1d 1995).

Fenton, Jennifer Muriel; Second Secretary (Management) Valletta since December 1999; born 30/12/57; Home Civil Service 1976; FCO 1977; Beirut 1980; Floater Duties 1982; Singapore 1984; SUPL 1986; FCO 1987; New Delhi 1989; Mbabane 1993; Second Secretary FCO 1996; (1d 1986)

Ferguson, Christine Julia; FCO since March 1998; born 05/10/57; FCO 1982; Language Training 1983; Second Secretary Cairo 1985; Second later First Secretary FCO 1987; First Secretary Geneva (UKDIS) 1990; m 1990 Michael (later Sir Michael) Charles Swift Weston (1s 1993, 1d 1996).

Ferguson, Iain; Vice-Consul Tokyo since April 1999; born 18/02/70; FCO 1990; Lagos 1995; Band B3; m 1994 Helen Jane Lennie

Ferguson, Jean McCauley; ECO/Vice-Consul Kathmandu since July 1999; born 08/10/55; Department of Employment 1985; Inland Revenue 1988; FCO 1998; Band B3; (1d 1975)

Fergusson, George Duncan; Consul-General Boston since August 1999; born 30/09/55; NIO 1978 (Private Secretary to NIO Minister of State 1982-83); First Secretary Dublin 1988; Transferred to Diplomatic Service 1990; First Secretary FCO 1991; First Secretary (Political/Information) Seoul 1993; First Secretary FCO 1996; Counsellor FCO 1997; m 1981 Margaret Wookey (3d 1982, 1986, 1991, 1s 1984).

Ferrand, Simon Piers; FCO since September 2002; born 05/03/68; FCO 1989; Kinshasa 1991; Paris 1996; BTI 1999; Band B3; m 1995 Bettina Barbara Paustian (2s 1998, 2002).

Fewster, Miles Nicholas, MBE (1991); Second Secretary FCO since August 1999; born 26/08/62; FCO 1982; Khartoum 1985; Riyadh 1989; FCO 1992; Second Secretary (Political) Nairobi 1996; Band C4; m 1986 Alexandria Fusco (3d 1992, 1993, 1998).

Fidler, Martin Alfred; Deputy High Commissioner Belmopan since November 1999; born 10/12/53; DHSS 1972; FCO 1974; Belmopan 1977; Africa/ME Floater 1980; Havana 1981; Third Secretary New York (UKMIS) 1984; FCO 1987; Nuku'alofa 1989; Gibraltar 1992; FCO 1996; Band C4; m 1981 Nicky Williams (2s 1982, 1985).

Field, Robert; Second Secretary FCO since November 1995; born 04/01/53; FCO 1971; Karachi 1975; Far East Floater 1979; Second Secretary (Commercial) Harare 1982; Second Secretary FCO 1987; Second Secretary (Management) Addis Ababa 1992.

Fielder, John; HM Consul Tel Aviv since July 1994; born 27/06/47; HM Forces 1967-73; CO (later Commonwealth Office) 1966; FCO 1974; Accra 1976; Nassau 1977; Prague 1980; SE

Asia/FE Floater 1982; FCO 1987; Second Secretary (Management/Consular) Maputo 1990.

Fielder, Richard John; Second Secretary (Management) Lusaka since June 2002; born 28/03/52; FCO 1971; Tokyo 1974; FCO 1975; Stockholm 1978; Khartoum 1981; FCO 1982; Dhaka 1985; Chicago 1988; Freetown 1990; FCO 1995; Second Secretary Ottawa 1997; m 1988 Samantha Louise Monton (3d 1988, 1993, 1996, 1s 1990).

Finch, Peter Leonard; FCO since November 1997; born 01/01/58; FCO 1975; Geneva (UKMIS) 1978; Tel Aviv 1981; New Delhi 1983; FCO 1986; Tokyo 1991; Manila 1994; Band C4; m 1979 Mitsue Uchida (1d 1990).

Findlay, Matthew Ross; FCO since August 2002; born 02/05/68; FCO 1996; Full-Time Language Training Bangkok 1998; Second Secretary (Political) Bangkok 1999; Band D6.

Fines, Barry John; SUPL since January 2002; born 13/09/69; FCO 1988; New Delhi 1991; FCO 1994; Lagos 1997; FCO 2001; Band A2; m 1997 Monika Graf

Finlay, Norah Ferguson Watson; Shanghai since January 2002; born 13/04/70; FCO 1989; Singapore 1992; Islamabad 1995; Band A2.

Finlayson, Sharon Christine; FCO since June 2002; born 04/05/58; Band A2; m 1976 (2d 1980, 1982).

Finley, Robert William; FCO since April 2002; born 21/08/68; Band D6; m 1997 Claire Walker.

Finnamore Crorkin, Joanne Lynn; Lagos since December 1997; born 22/09/63; Floater Duties 1989; FCO 1982; Moscow 1984; Colombo 1985; Consulate-General New York 1992; SUPL 1992; FCO 1994 (Second Secretary 1996); m 1991 Colin Wynn Crorkin (1d 1998).

Finnerty, Kevin John; First Secretary and Consul Washington since August 1997; born 01/02/49; FCO 1967; Kuwait 1970; Warsaw 1974; FCO 1976; Language Training (Full-Time) 1978; FCO 1979; Mogadishu 1983; Chicago 1985; FCO 1985; Second Secretary FCO 1989; Düsseldorf 1993; Language Training (Full-Time) 1993; m (1) 1970 Sandra Tidy (diss 1982); (2) 1982 Norma Collins

Firmstone, Imogen Joan; Havana since November 2002; born 21/06/74; FCO 1999; Band B3.

Firstbrook, Steven Paul; Second Secretary (Commercial) Mumbai since November 2000; born 22/02/70; FCO 1989; Helsinki 1992; World-Wide Floater Duties 1994; FCO 1996; Band C4.

Firth, Catherine Alison Jane (née Readdie); First Secretary (Political) Mexico City since June 2001; born 17/06/66; FCO 1990; Third Secretary (Chancery) Warsaw 1992; FCO 1994; Vice Consul Caracas 1995; FCO 1998; Full-Time Language Training 2001; Band C5; m 1994 Andrew Charleson Firth

Fish, Rosemary; SUPL since November 1992; born 28/08/49; Ankara 1974; Honiara 1976; Bogotá 1978; FCO 1979; Far East Floater 1980; FCO 1982; On loan to DTI 1984; Rio de Janeiro 1986; FCO 1988; m 1987 Anthony John Stafford (1s 1991, 1d 1993).

Fisher, Deborah Joan; Paris since September 2002; born 04/03/62; SUPL 1996; FCO 1985; Second Secretary (Chancery) Dar es Salaam 1988; First Secretary FCO 1991; FCO 1997; m 1992 William James Lodge.

Fisher, Deryck John; First Secretary (Management) Bangkok since May 2000; born 26/07/46; Inland Revenue 1961; Department of Technical Co-operation/ODA 1964; FCO 1973; Kinshasa 1975; Islamabad 1978; Second Secretary FCO 1980; Second Secretary (Consular) Accra 1983; First Secretary (Admin/Consul) Copenhagen 1987; First Secretary FCO 1991; First Secretary (Management) Dhaka 1996; Band D6; m 1973 Lynda Elizabeth Robinson (2d 1974, 1975; 3s 1976, 1979, 1983).

Fisher, Emily Caroline Gay (née Shapland); First Secretary (Political) Buenos Aires since October 2000; born 05/05/72; FCO 1997; Lusaka 1998; Band D6; m 1998 Roland Barnabas Fisher.

Fisher, Gary John; Third Secretary (MO/VC) Bahrain since March 2000; born 27/12/69; FCO 1989; Peking 1992; Third Secretary Düsseldorf 1996; Band B3; m 1992 Claire Louise White (1s 1998).

Fisher, John; Counsellor (Political) Jakarta since October 1999; born 03/08/48; Third later Second Secretary FCO 1974; Language student SOAS 1975 and Bursar 1976; Second Secretary (Inf) Ankara 1976; First Secretary FCO 1979; Vienna (UKMIS) IAEA 1982; First Secretary FCO 1986; Counsellor Santiago 1993; Counsellor FCO 1997; m 1970 Lynette Joyce Corinne Growcott (1d 1978, 1s 1980).

Fisher, Julian Alexander St.John; Second Secretary Harare since September 2001; born 12/02/70; FCO 1998; Second Secretary (Political/Economic) Nairobi 2000; Band C4; m 1998 Alex Gillian Wood.

Fisher, Kate; SUPL since January 1996; born 12/11/70; FCO 1991; Lusaka 1993; Band A2.

Fisher, Miles Lyndon; SUPL since March 1999; born 28/11/61; FCO 1981; Vienna 1995.

Fisher, Simon John; First Secretary (Commercial) Cairo since January 2002; born 08/06/59; FCO 1983; Athens 1985; Language Training Kamakura 1989; Tokyo 1990; Osaka 1992; Second later First Secretary FCO 1996; Deputy Head of Mission and Consul General Hanoi 1999; SUPL 2000 Band D6.

Fisher, Steven Mark; Deputy Head of Mission Caracas since July 2002; born 07/02/65; FCO 1993; Second Secretary (Economic/Commercial) Singapore 1995; FCO 1998; Band D6; m 1990 Linda Westwood (3s 1993, 1995, 1997).

Fisher, Thérésa Ellen; Manila since May 1987; born 05/06/60; FCO 1977; Geneva (UKMIS) 1982; Belgrade 1984; Band A2; m 1985 Ali Gecim.

Fisher, Timothy Dirk Colomb; Third later Second Secretary (Aid) Jakarta since August 1991; born 23/08/47; FCO 1975; Moscow 1976; FCO 1977; Port Moresby 1978; Nairobi 1981; FCO 1985; Colombo 1987; m 1992 Patricia-Jane Van Der Vooren (1d 1993, 1s 1994).

Fisher, Timothy Sinnett; Third Secretary (Political) Kigali since September 2000; born 15/07/71; FCO 1998; Band B3; m 2000 Joanna Dinnen.

Fishman, Jason; Peking since November 1997; born 05/10/69; FCO 1990; Berlin 1994; Band A2.

Fishwick, Nicholas Bernard Frank; First Secretary FCO since September 1997; born 23/02/58; FCO 1983; Language Training 1986; First Secretary (Inf) Lagos 1988; First Secretary FCO 1991; Consul (Political Affairs) Istanbul 1994; Band D6; m 1987 Susan Thérésa Rouane Mendel (2s 1987, 1995, 1d 1989).

Fitch, Diana May (née Francis); Seoul since August 2002; born 26/12/53; SE Asia Floater 1984; FCO 1975; Dar es Salaam 1976; Tortola 1977; FCO 1981; Singapore 1986; FCO 1988; Second Secretary Honiara 1995; FCO 1998; m Geoffrey William Fitch (1s 1988, 1d 1993).

Fitchett, Robert Duncan; FCO since September 1998; born 10/06/61; FCO 1983; Dakar 1984; Second Secretary (Chancery) Bonn 1988; First Secretary FCO 1990; First Secretary on loan to the Cabinet Office 1993; Paris 1994; m 1985 Adèle Thérèsa Hajjar (1s 1987, 2d 1988, 1993).

Fitton, David John; Deputy Head of Mission Ankara since January 2001; born 10/01/55; FCO 1980; Language Training Kamakura 1982; Second later First Secretary (Economics) Tokyo 1983; FCO 1986; First Secretary (Chancery) New Delhi 1990; First Secretary FCO 1994; Head of Chancery Tokyo 1996; m 1989 Hisae Iijima (1d 1996, 1s 1999)

Fitton-Brown, Edmund Walter; Counsellor (Political) Helsinki since October 2002; born 05/10/62; FCO 1984; Third later Second Secretary Helsinki 1987; Second Secretary FCO 1989 (First Secretary 1991); Language Training Cairo 1991; First Secretary FCO 1992; First Secretary (Political) Cairo 1993; First Secretary FCO 1996; First Secretary (Political) Kuwait 1998; FCO 2001; m 1995 Julie Ann Herring (1d 1996, 1s 1998).

FitzGerald, Jillian (née Lane); Second Secretary (Management) Rome since May 2002; born 29/01/69; FCO 1989; Bonn 1992; Islamabad 1995; SUPL 1997; FCO 1998; Band B3; m 1998 Paul Edward FitzGerald (1s 1997).

Fitzgerald-Prono, Antonia (née Fitzgerald); FCO since September 1999; born 13/06/71; FCO 1990; Brasilia 1991; Brussels (UKDel WEU) 1995; Paris 1996; SUPL 1999; m 1999 Raphael Jacques Gerard Prono (1s 1999).

Flaherty, Shaun David; First Secretary (Management) Cairo since June 2001; born 29/01/66; FCO 1984; Washington 1987; Ankara 1990; Lagos 1992; FCO 1996; Band C5.

Flear, Timothy Charles Fitzranulf, MVO (1989); FCO since May 2000; born 22/01/58; FCO 1980; Third Secretary (Comm/Inf) Dubai 1982; Resigned and reinstated 1985; FCO 1985; Third later Second Secretary Kuala Lumpur 1987; Second Secretary FCO 1991 (APS/Minister of State 1993); First Secretary (Economic) later First Secretary (Investment) subsequently First Secretary (Political) Seoul 1996; ptnr, Christopher Curtain.

Fleming De Luca, Wendy Alexandra; Third Secretary (Commercial) Buenos Aires since May 1999; born 11/05/70; FCO 1991; Jakarta 1995; Band B3; m 1995 Dino De Luca.

Flessati, Francesca Josephine Giovanna; First Secretary (Political) Athens since April 1999; born 27/10/58; FCO 1990; Language Training 1991; Third Secretary (Aid) Moscow 1992; FCO 1996; m 1985 Nicholas John Foster.

Fletcher, Elaine Karen; Rabat since February 1996; born 05/01/63; FCO 1984; Budapest 1987; East Berlin 1988; Suva 1989; Floater Duties 1992; FCO 1993; Band A2.

Fletcher, Patricia Anne (née Jones); FCO since February 2000; born 12/05/70; FCO 1989; Bonn 1991; FCO 1993; Brasilia 1994; SUPL 1999; Band B3; m 1993 Richard Fletcher (1s 1996).

Fletcher, Patricia May; Second Secretary (Management) Beirut since January 2000; born 08/09/42; FCO 1983; Berlin (BMG) 1984; Tortola 1986; FCO 1988; Brussels (UKDEL) 1990; FCO 1991; Munich 1994; Tel Aviv 1997; Band C4; m 1974 Herbert Fletcher (dec'd 1986) (1s 1978).

Fletcher, Thomas Stuart Francis; FCO since September 1997; born 27/03/75; Band D6.

Flint, David Leonard; Liason Officer Gibraltar since April 2001; born 21/10/56; FCO 1975; Budapest 1979; Jedda 1980; FCO 1984; Athens 1986; Lagos 1990; Second Secretary FCO 1994; Deputy High Commissioner Gaborone 1997; m 1984 Mary Anne Elizabeth Goodale (3s twins 1986, 1988).

Flint, John David; Antigua since May 2001; born 05/11/69; FCO 1996; Third Secretary (Political/PPA) Tallinn 1998; Band B3; m 1998 Sally Brazier

Flisher, Nigel Frederick; Second Secretary (Immigration) Moscow since May 1996; born 20/04/53; FCO 1971; Singapore 1974; Vientiane 1978; Colombo 1979; FCO 1982; Islamabad 1984; Third Secretary (Passports/Visas) Dublin 1988; FCO 1991; Second Secretary 1994; m 1977 Valerie Tay Kim Heok (1d 1978, 1s 1980)

Floyd, Linda Vivienne (née Colvin); SUPL since August 2000; born 17/03/65; FCO 1987; New Delhi 1989; SUPL 1991; Georgetown 1994; SUPL 1997; FCO 1999; Band A2; m 1990 Neil Floyd (1d 1991, 2s 1993, 1995).

Floyd, Neil; FCO since July 1997; born 20/05/67; FCO 1987; New Delhi 1989; Warsaw 1991; Georgetown 1993; Band C4; m 1990 Linda Vivienne Colvin (1d 1991, 2s 1993, 1995).

Foakes, Joanne Sarah; SUPL since August 2001; born 09/03/57; Called to the Bar, Inner Temple 1979; FCO 1984; Deputy Principal Crown Counsel Hong Kong 1991; Assistant Legal Adviser FCO 1994; SUPL 1995; Legal Counsellor 1997.

Foley, Victoria Beth Louise; FCO since December 1986; born 23/06/60; FCO 1978; Budapest 1982; Paris 1984; Band A2.

Folker, Nicholas Mark; Singapore since October 2000; born 20/05/67; FCO 1989; Band C4; m 1998 Laura Elizabeth Samm (1d 2000).

Folland, Richard Dudley; Deputy Consul General Düsseldorf since August 2000; born 10/03/61; FCO 1981; Moscow 1983; Third Secretary (Comms/Information) Gaborone 1985; FCO 1988; Second Secretary (Political/Inf) Stockholm 1991; First Secretary FCO 1996; On secondment to British Aerospace 1998; m 1985 Gwen Alison Evans (2s 1989, 1993).

Folliss, Tarquin Simon Archer; Counsellor Copenhagen since September 2001; born 23/10/57; HM Forces 1981-86; Second Secretary FCO 1986; Second later First Secretary (Chancery) Jakarta 1989; First Secretary FCO 1992; First Secretary Bucharest 1995; First Secretary FCO 1998; Band D6; m 1991 Anne Mary Segar (1d 1996, 2s 1998, 1999).

Fontaine-Harvey, Joan; Dubai since May 2000; born 03/10/67; FCO 1990; Band B3; m 1999 Christopher Antonio Harvey.

Foote, Daniel Edward; Third Secretary (Deputy Management Officer) Freetown since August 2001; born 11/02/46; Royal Navy 1965-90; Moscow 1991; Lagos 1992; Abuja 1994; FCO 1996; Pretoria 1997; Band B3; m 1967 Carol Elizabeth Combe (2d 1970, 1971).

Forbes, Lachlan Pelly Ferrar; FCO since January 2001; born 24/04/70; Second Secretary FCO 1996; Second Secretary (Political) Nairobi 1998; Band C4; m 1999 Melanie Fiona Knights (1s 2000).

Forbes, Matthew Keith; Deputy High Commissioner Maseru since July 1999; born 19/04/66; FCO 1987; Peking 1989; Colombo 1990; FCO 1995; Band C4; m 1988 Lydia Mary Bagg (2s 1989, 1991, 1d 1994).

Forbes, Melanie Fiona (née Knights); FCO since May 2001; born 03/03/64; FCO 1996; Second Secretary (Political) Nairobi 1999; Band C4; m 1999 Lachlan Pelly Ferrar Forbes (1s 2000).

Forbes Batey, Darren Francis; Third Secretary (Management) Dublin since August 1996; born 09/01/66; FCO 1984; Rabat 1987; Kampala 1990; FCO 1993; Band B3; m 1993 Sarah Frances Trevelyan.

Ford, Andrew James Ford, MVO (1995); Second Secretary (Commercial) Mexico City since February 2000; born 21/06/64; FCO 1987; Third Secretary (Chancery/Information/Consular) Georgetown 1990; Third Secretary (Political) Pretoria/Cape Town 1993; Second Secretary FCO 1996; m 1994 Claudeli Edna Dos Santos Silva (2 step d 1985, 1987).

Ford, Antony, CMG (1997); HM Ambassador Vienna since September 2000; born 01/10/44; Commonwealth Office 1967; Third later Second Secretary Bonn 1968; Kuala Lumpur 1971; First Secretary FCO 1973; First Secretary (Commercial) Washington 1977; First Secretary FCO 1981; Counsellor East Berlin 1984; Counsellor FCO 1987; Consul-General San Francisco 1990; Attached to RAS as CSSB Chairman 1994; Minister Berlin 1996; On secondment to Andersen Consulting 1999; m 1970 Linda Gordon Joy (1970, 1s 1976).

Ford, Kerry May; SUPL since March 2001; born 04/05/67; Home Office 1990-1993; FCO 1994; The Hague (T/D) 1996; Hanoi (T/D) 1996; Hong Kong 1997; FCO 2000; Band A2; m 2001 Stuart Moss.

Ford, Peter William; HM Ambassador Bahrain since April 1999; born 27/06/47; MECAS 1971; Second later First Secretary Cairo 1974; University of Harvard 1990; Third Secretary FCO 1970; Beirut 1973; First Secretary FCO 1977; ENA Paris 1980; First Secretary Paris 1981; First Secretary FCO 1985; Counsellor (Comm) Riyadh 1987; Counsellor Singapore 1991; Counsellor FCO 1994; m (1) 1975 Aurora Raquel Garcia Mingo (diss 1991), (2) 1992 Alganesh Haile Beyene.

Forrester, Mark Adrian; Second Secretary (Management) Hong Kong since November 1999; born 29/06/59; FCO 1978; Geneva (UKMIS) 1980; Santiago 1983; Third Secretary FCO 1986; Dhaka 1989; Third Secretary (Management/Consular) Nuku'alofa 1992; Second Secretary FCO 1995; m 1982 Deborah Cannell (1d 1987, 1s 1990).

Forrester, Sally Joanne (née Watmough); FCO since September 2000; born 22/05/64; FCO 1984; Belgrade 1987; FCO 1989; Buenos Aires 1990; FCO 1992; Vienna 1994; SUPL 1997; Band A2; m 1993 Guy Hamilton Forrester (1d 1995, 1s 1998).

Forrester, Stuart Russell; Moscow since October 2000; born 10/02/62; FCO 1983; Washington 1990; FCO 1994; Band C4; m 1990 Deborah Channon.

Forryan, Anne May; SUPL since November 1999; born 03/08/66; FCO 1990; Düsseldorf 1993; Vice-Consul Madrid 1996; Madrid 1997; SUPL

1997; Band B3; m 1996 Joaquin Rodriguez-Toubes Muniz.

Forsyth, Brian Gilbert; Doha since August 1999; born 27/02/65; FCO 1984; Bucharest 1987; Dhaka 1989; FCO 1992; Third Secretary Cairo 1996; Band B3; m 1987 Marie Boyle (1s 1989, 1d 1992).

Forsyth, Marie (née Boyle); SUPL since January 2000; born 26/04/66; FCO 1984; Mexico City 1986; SUPL 1987; Dhaka 1990; FCO 1993; Cairo 1996; Band B3; m 1987 Brian Gilbert Forsyth (1s 1989, 1d 1992).

Fortescue, Dominic James Lewis; First Secretary New York (UKMIS) since July 2000; born 09/10/66; FCO 1991; Second Secretary (Political) Pretoria 1993; Cape Town 1995; Second later First Secretary FCO 1996; Band D6; m 1990 Miriam Cathleen Rolls (1s 2001).

Fossaluzza, Lydia; Buenos Aires since September 1999; born 12/03/64; FCO 1996; Band A2.

Foster, Hazel; FCO since May 1998; born 10/04/69; World Wide Floater duties 1996; FCO 1989; Ankara 1991; Band A2.

Foster, John Michael; FCO since 1997; born 07/05/55; FCO 1989; New Delhi 1991; Third Secretary Tel Aviv 1994; Band B3; m 1986 Julie Bearfoot.

Foster, Julie Maria (née Bearfoot); Second Secretary FCO since July 1998; born 19/12/59; FCO 1978; Brussels (UKDEL NATO) 1981; Doha 1983; FCO 1987; Third Secretary New Delhi 1991; Tel Aviv 1994; On loan to the DTI 1997; Band C4; m 1986 John Michael Foster.

Foster, Nicholas John; Counsellor Athens since September 1998; born 03/09/57; Second Secretary FCO 1984; Second later First Secretary (Chancery) Nicosia 1986; First Secretary FCO 1989; First Secretary (Chancery) Moscow 1992; First Secretary FCO 1995; m 1985 Francesca Josephine Giovanna Flessati.

Foster, Sarah Louise; Tokyo since January 2000; born 04/11/73; UKMIS later UKDEL Vienna 1995; FCO 1992; Band B3.

Foster, Victoria Evelyn; FCO since January 1997; born 28/12/72; FCO 1990; Geneva (UKMIS) 1994; Band A2.

Foulcer, Monique Antoinette (née Twigg); FCO since December 2000; born 22/07/64; DTI 1985; FCO 1987; Kinshasa 1989; Third Secretary (Chancery) Geneva (UKDIS) 1992; FCO 1995; SUPL 1997; Second Secretary (Political) Paris 1998; SUPL 1999; Band C5; m 1995 Kevin Andrew Foulcer.

Foulds, Sarah Ann; SUPL since September 1998; born 10/08/57; FCO 1979; PRO (Band D6) 1987; First Secretary FCO 1992; First Secretary Geneva (UKMIS) 1995; m (1) 1981 (diss 1995) (1d 1985, 1s 1988), m (2) 1999 Peter Van Wulfften Palthe (3 step d).

Foulsham, Richard Andrew; Counsellor Ottawa since February 2001; born 24/09/50; Second Secretary FCO 1982; First Secretary Badar Seri Begawan 1984; First Secretary (Chancery) Lagos 1986; First Secretary FCO 1990; Counsellor (Political) Rome 1995; Counsellor FCO 1999; m 1982 Deirdre Elizabeth Strathairn (1d 1984, 1s 1986).

Fowle, Angela Mary (née Hatcher); Second Secretary (Management) and Consul Algiers since September 2001; born 25/04/44; SUPL 1990; SUPL 1993; FO 1964; Bangkok 1966; Moscow 1968; Athens 1969; FCO 1972; Santiago 1974; FCO 1976; Geneva (UKMIS) 1980; FCO 1983; Düsseldorf 1986; FCO 1989; FCO 1995; Belgrade 1998; T/D Second Secretary (Management) Madrid 1999; Belgrade 2000; Band C4; m 1978 Leslie Thomas Fowle (1s 1983).

Fowler, Joanna; Madrid since February 1999; born 12/04/43; FCO 1976; Tehran 1977; Rangoon 1979; FCO 1982; Belgrade 1983; Abu Dhabi 1985; FCO 1989; Islamabad 1994; Band B3.

Fowler, Rosalind Mary Elizabeth; First Secretary FCO since July 1994; born 27/09/65; FCO 1987; Language Training 1988; Language Training Hong Kong 1989; Second Secretary (Inf) Hong Kong 1990; Language Training 1993; Band D6.

Fox, Alexander Norman Robson; FCO since September 2001; born 20/09/77; Band C4.

Fox, Christopher Roderick Henry; Ankara since July 2000; born 19/09/70; FCO 1991; Band C4.

Fox, Ian David; Secondment to London Chamber of Commerce since March 1995; born 02/06/66; FCO 1987; Peking 1988; Floater Duties 1991; FCO 1993; Band B3; m 1993 Alison Elizabeth Margaret Bain.

Fox, John Frederick; Full-Time Language Training (Mandarin) since January 2002; born 09/04/75; FCO 1997; Brussels 1999; SUPL 1999; FCO 2000; Band C4.

Fox, Michael Roger; FCO since October 1997; born 09/07/58; FCO 1988; Consul Geneva 1993; Band C4; m 1993 Charlotte Jane Gray.

Fox, Paul Leonard; FCO since April 1999; born 24/07/62; FCO 1987; New Delhi 1990; Baku 1994; Bangkok 1996; Band D7; m 1991 Vicki Ann Rathbun (3d 1997, 1998, 2002).

Foxwell, Rachael Louise; First Secretary (Economic/Commercial) Wellington since June 1999; born 29/10/59; Africa/Middle East Floater 1984; FCO 1982; Harare 1985; Third later Second Secretary Hanoi 1988; Second Secretary FCO 1991; Tunis 1992; (1d 1991).

Francis, Catherine Joan; Jakarta since December 1997; born 01/04/50; Brussels 1972; FCO 1972; Kuala Lumpur 1976; FCO 1980; Bonn 1980; Helsinki 1985; FCO 1987; Riyadh 1989; FCO 1991; Sofia 1993; Band B3; m 1991 John Treharne Francis.

Francis, John Alexander; HM Consul Kuwait since September 1999; born 14/12/42; FO 1962; Beirut 1964; Athens 1964; Stockholm 1965; Seoul 1968; Malta 1971; FCO 1972; Paris 1972; Dacca 1975; Prague 1979; Kaduna 1981; Second Secretary FCO 1983; Consul Bangkok 1988; First Secretary (Management) Ankara 1992; First Secretary (Management/Consular) Seoul 1996; m 1981 Grace Engelen.

Francis, Julie Mary; FCO since August 1990; born 21/02/50; Kabul 1976; FCO 1976; FCO 1978; Sofia 1979; Brussels (UKDEL NATO) 1981; FCO 1984; Kathmandu 1987; Band A2.

Franklin, Elizabeth Fay (née Bolton); SUPL since March 1995; born 25/11/60; FCO 1981; Khartoum 1985; Valletta 1988; Dhaka 1992; Band B3; m 1994 John William Franklin.

Franklin, Joanna Mary Clare; SUPL since November 2000; born 12/08/60; FCO 1978; Peking 1981; FCO 1982; Cairo 1986; Yaoundé 1989; FCO 1990; Beirut 1994; FCO 1997; Canberra 1998; Band C4; m 1988 Habib Elie Gouel.

Franklin, Sarah Louise; FCO since April 2001; born 02/04/66; FCO 1985; Geneva (UKMIS) 1989; FCO 1991; Warsaw 1997; Band B3.

Franklin-Brown, Alexander, MBE (2002); FCO since February 1991; born 30/03/72; Band A2.

Fransella, Cortland Lucas; Counsellor FCO since September 1995; born 09/09/48; Third Secretary FCO 1970; Language Training Hong Kong 1971; Assistant Trade Commissioner Hong Kong 1973; Second later First Secretary FCO 1975; Kuala Lumpur 1980; Santiago 1982; FCO 1986; Counsellor (Political) Rome 1991; m 1977 Laura Ruth Propper (2s 1979, 1981).

Frape, Neil Jeremy; Kuwait since July 2000; born 16/11/63; FCO 1984; Addis Ababa 1986; Paris 1990; FCO 1992; Language Training (FT) 1995; Vice-Consul (Press and Public Affairs) Istanbul 1996; Band B3; m 1987 Christine Mary Allen (1d 1989, 1s 1992).

Frary, Helen Elizabeth; Third Secretary (United Nations) Geneva (UKMIS) since July 1995; born 23/02/69; FCO 1988; New Delhi 1991; Band B3.

Fraser, James Terence; First Secretary (Management) and HM Consul Copenhagen since December 1997; born 12/04/49; GPO 1966; FCO 1967; Nicosia 1971; Johannesburg 1972; Prague 1974; Africa Floater 1975; FCO 1978; Vice-Consul (Information) Düsseldorf 1981; Language Training 1983; Commercial Attaché Baghdad 1984; FCO 1988 Deputy Head of Political and Information Section later Head of Consular Section Ottawa 1993; m 1988 Nada Babic (1s 1992, 1d 1995).

Fraser, Shelley; FCO since February 1991; born 21/03/70; Band A2.

Fraser, Simon James; Director for Strategy and Innovation FCO since May 2002; born 03/06/58;

FCO 1979; Third later Second Secretary Baghdad 1982; Second Secretary (Chancery) Damascus 1984; First Secretary FCO 1986; (Private Secretary to Minister of State) 1989; First Secretary (Economic) Paris 1994; Counsellor on secondment to the EU Commission 1996; SUPL 1997; Counsellor (Political) Paris 1999; (1d 1993).

Fraser Darling, Richard Ogilby Leslie, OBE (2001); First Secretary later Counsellor FCO since August 1988; born 02/03/49; Third Secretary FCO 1971; Language Training Helsinki 1973; Third later Second Secretary Helsinki 1974; First Secretary FCO 1978; Washington 1984; m 1991 Nicola Kirkup.

Frean, Christopher William; FCO since July 2002; born 31/07/64; HCS 1988; FCO 1990; Abidjan 1992; Karachi 1995; FCO 1997; Third Secretary (Commercial/Political) Abidjan 1999; Band B3; m 1994 Aya Esperance Gbakatchetche (2d 1995, 1996).

Freel, Philip John; Third Secretary (Management) December 1995; born 24/12/55; On loan to CAD Hanslope Park 1986; FCO 1974; Paris 1976; Mogadishu 1979; Lisbon 1980; Addis Ababa 1983; FCO 1985; Lagos 1987; Rome 1991; FCO 1992; m 1977 Joan Winifred Hill (1d 1979, 1s 1986).

Freeman, Judith Louise; Geneva (UKMIS) since January 2000; born 24/03/61; FCO 1984; Berne 1985; East Berlin 1989; Floater Duties 1991; FCO 1994; Luxembourg 1996; T/D Berlin 1999; Band A2.

Freeman, Timothy John; Third Secretary (Passports/Visas) Dublin since March 2001; born 24/04/65; FCO 1989; Paris 1992; Honiara 1996; Third Secretary (Aid/Chancery) Gibraltar 1997; Band B3.

Freeman, Wendy Paula; Second Secretary (Commercial) Beirut since April 2001; born 09/03/61; FCO 1980; Bonn 1982; Africa/ME Floater 1985; Abidjan 1988; FCO 1992; Kingston 1997; SUPL 1999; Band C4.

French, Roger; Head of Information Management Group FCO since October 2001; born 03/06/47; FCO 1965; Havana 1970; Vice-Consul Madrid 1971; San Juan 1973; FCO 1977; Second later First Secretary (Chancery) Washington 1980; First Secretary (Commercial) Muscat 1985; Deputy Head North America Dept FCO 1988; Deputy Consul-General Milan 1992; Counsellor (Management) and Consul General Washington 1997; Acting Deputy High Commissioner Abuja 2001; m 1969 Angela Joyce Cooper (1d 1974, 1s 1980).

Friel, Nicola; Floater Duties since November 1998; born 08/03/70; FCO 1989; Washington 1992; Moscow 1995; Band B3.

Friis, Andrew Stuart; FCO since March 2002; born 04/04/60; Metropolitan Police 1981; FCO 1982; Kuwait 1986; FCO 1988; Hong Kong 1997;

Band C5; m 1989 Maria Carina Lumatan Reyes (1s 1991, 1d 1994).

Friston, Paula Jane; Washington since September 2002; born 27/01/69; FCO 1992; Washington 1996; Algiers 1999; FCO 2001; Band B3.

Frizzel, Squadron Leader John Stewart; Queen's Messenger 1989; born 12/07/46; HM Forces 1966-89.

Frost, David George Hamilton; Counsellor (EU/Economic) Paris since April 2001; born 21/02/65; FCO 1987; Third Secretary Nicosia 1989; Resigned 1990, reinstated 1992; First Secretary Brussels (UKREP) 1993; First Secretary New York (UKMIS) 1996; FCO 1998; m 1993 Jacqueline Elizabeth Dias (1d 1998).

Frost, Michael Reginald, OBE (2001); First Secretary (Political) Pretoria since June 2000; born 02/12/52; FCO 1971; Prague 1974; Dar es Salaam 1976; Peking 1979; FCO 1982; Washington 1984; Consul (Political/Inf) Cape Town 1986; First Secretary (Aid/Comm) Kampala 1991; First Secretary FCO 1994; First Secretary (Political) Lagos 1996; Band D6; m 1973 Marie Thérésa McAllen.

Frost, Simon Jaye; FCO since March 1996; born 24/05/70; FCO 1990; World-Wide Floater Duties 1993; T/D Mostar 1995; Band B3.

Frost, Steven Alan; Second Secretary Stockholm since February 1999; born 21/09/64; FCO 1987; Islamabad 1992; FCO 1996; Band C4; m 1993 Angela Elaine Morrissey.

Fry, Graham Holbrook; DUS (Wider World) FCO since October 2001; born 20/12/49; FCO 1972; Third later Second Secretary Tokyo 1974; First Secretary on loan to DOI 1979; FCO 1981; First Secretary Paris 1983; FCO 1987; Counsellor (Chancery) Tokyo 1989; Counsellor FCO 1993; AUSS (Northern Asia and the Pacific) 1995; High Commissioner Kuala Lumpur 1998; m (1) 1977 Meiko Iida (diss), (2) 1994 Toyoko Ando.

Fuguet Debarr, Margaret (née Debarr); FCO since March 1993; born 02/01/48; Inland Revenue 1964; FCO 1967; Brussels (UKDEL EC) 1970; FCO 1972; Copenhagen 1974; FCO 1977; Harare 1982; FCO 1985; Dublin 1990; Band B3; m 1976 Juan Inocencio Fuguet Sanchez (1s 1977).

Fulcher, Michael Adrian; Counsellor Rome since October 1999; born 15/10/58; FCO 1982; Second later First Secretary Athens 1985; First Secretary FCO 1989; First Secretary (Political) Sofia 1993; First Secretary FCO 1996; m 1983 Helen Parkinson (1s 1987, 1d 1988).

Full, Ian Francis; Suva since January 1994; born 16/08/54; FCO 1972; Paris 1975; San José 1978; Jedda 1981; FCO 1986; Islamabad 1989; Band B3.

Fuller, Eleanor Mary (née Breedon); First Secretary Geneva (UKMIS) since January 2000; born 31/12/53; FCO 1975; ENA Course, Paris 1977 and 1978; Resigned 1980, reinstated 1981; FCO 1981; On loan to the ODA 1983; SUPL 1986; Second later First Secretary FCO 1990; SUPL 1993; UNRWA Vienna 1994-1996; First Secretary Vienna (UKDEL) 1998; m 1984 Simon William John Fuller (3s 1986, 1988, 1991).

Fuller, Martin John; FO (later FCO) since May 1965; born 26/01/41; Principal Research Officer, Senior Principal Research Officer in 1990.

Fuller, Rebecca Margaret, MBE (1998); Brussels (UKDEL) since October 1998; born 25/01/59; FCO 1995; Sarajevo 1996; Band A2; m 1996 Peter Richard Miller.

Fuller, Robert; FCO since September 2001; born 19/09/74; Band C4; ptnr, Angela Richmond.

Fuller, Simon William John, CMG (1994); Permanent Representative Geneva (UKMIS) since January 2000; born 27/11/43; Third Secretary FCO 1968; Second Secretary Singapore 1969; Kinshasa 1971; First Secretary seconded to Cabinet Office 1973; FCO 1976; First Secretary New York (UKMIS) 1977; First Secretary FCO 1980; Counsellor, Deputy Head of Personnel Operations Department, FCO 1984; Counsellor, Head of Chancery and Consul-General, Tel Aviv 1986; Counsellor FCO 1990; Permanent Representative UKDEL CSCE, Vienna 1993; m 1984 Eleanor Mary Breedon (3s 1986, 1988, 1991).

Fulton, Craig John; Second Secretary (Regional Affairs) Kampala since April 2002; born 30/10/67; FCO 1987; Singapore 1990; Islamabad 1992; FCO 1996; Band B3; m 1992 Claire Elizabeth Evans.

Fussey, Lorraine Helen; SUPL since October 2000; born 30/01/67; FCO 1989; Bombay 1991; Tel Aviv 1995; FCO 1998; Band C4; m 1996 Alastair Walton Totty (2s 1997, 2001).

G

Gallacher, Ian Charles; Third Secretary (Consular) Paris since October 2001; born 02/05/63; FCO 1983; Paris 1988; Peking 1990; FCO 1993; Band B3; m 1987 Diane Warren.

Gallacher, Margaret; Kuala Lumpur since July 2001; born 05/12/63; MOD 1986-1996; FCO 1996; Anguilla 1997; Band B3.

Gallagher, Francis Xavier, OBE (1986); Deputy Head of Mission Copenhagen since August 1995; born 28/03/46; Third Secretary FCO 1971; MECAS 1972; Second Secretary 1972; Second Secretary Beirut 1974; Second later First Secretary FCO 1975; Copenhagen 1979; First Secretary and Head of Chancery, Beirut 1984; First Secretary FCO 1987; Counsellor, Head of Chancery, Khartoum 1989; Counsellor and Deputy Head of Mission, Kuwait 1992; m 1981 Marie-France Martine Guiller.

Gallagher, Tracy Anne; First Secretary FCO since September 1998; born 22/01/58; FCO 1981; Language Training 1982; Third later Second Secretary (Comm) later First Secretary (Econ), Moscow 1983; First Secretary FCO 1988; First Secretary (Chancery) Dublin 1991; SUPL 1994; m 1986 Ian Robert Whitting (2d 1990, 1994).

Galvez, Elizabeth Ann (née Sketchley); On secondment since January 2001; born 24/12/51; FCO 1970; SUPL to attend University 1970; FCO 1973; Helsinki 1974; Geneva (UKMIS) 1977; Second Secretary Tegucigalpa 1981; FCO 1981; Second Secretary FCO 1985; SUPL 1987; FCO 1988; First Secretary Vienna (UKDEL) 1989; First Secretary FCO 1994; Deputy Head of Mission Bucharest 1997; Language Training (FT) 1997; m 1985 Roberto Arturo Galvez Montes (1d 1987).

Gamble, Adrian Mark; First Secretary FCO since August 2001; born 30/03/61; FCO 1991; Second Secretary (EC Affairs) Brussels 1993; First Secretary FCO 1995; First Secretary (Political) Rome 1998; Band D6; m 1990 Jane Brison (2s 1991, 1993, 1d 1995).

Ganderton, Jennifer Louise; SUPL since September 1999; born 15/06/70; Inland Revenue 1988; MOD 1988; FCO 1989; Stockholm 1992; World-Wide Floater 1995; Band B3.

Ganney, Sharon Ann (née Feeney); Vice-Consul (Management) Rio de Janeiro since March 2002; born 11/10/70; FCO 1989; Warsaw 1992; Hamilton 1994; FCO 1996; T/D Doha 1997; Vice-Consul St Petersburg 1998; Band B3; m 1998 Mark William Ganney.

Garden, Alyson Margaret; FCO since September 1999; born 21/03/69; FCO 1988; Canberra 1991; FCO 1994; Warsaw 1996; Band B3.

Gardener, Carol Elizabeth; FCO since February 1993; born 10/08/66; FCO 1988; Athens 1990; Band A2.

Gardiner, Judith Margaret (née Farnworth); Second Secretary (Chancery/Press and Public Affairs) Kiev since March 1996; born 25/04/66; FCO 1991; Senior Research Officer 1992; m 1994 Christopher Gardiner

Gardner, David Martin; First Secretary (Management) Bogotá since February 2001; born 11/11/60; FCO 1978; Mexico City 1981; Tegucigalpa 1984; FCO 1988; Third Secretary (Chancery) Warsaw 1991; Vice-Consul Paris 1993; Second Secretary (Commercial) Mexico City 1996; Band C5; m 1983 Ana Luisa Dominguez Ortiz (1s 1992, 1d 1994).

Gardner, John Ewart; First Secretary (Commercial) Abu Dhabi since November 2000; born 28/02/53; FCO 1971; Abu Dhabi 1974; Kinshasa 1978; Wellington 1981; FCO 1984; Lagos 1986; Los Angeles 1989; FCO 1992; Second Secretary 1994; Deputy Head of Mission and Consul La Paz 1996; Band C5; m 1975 Alexandra Marie Donald.

Gardner, Julie Ann (née Taylor); SUPL since June 1999; born 15/02/67; FCO 1988; Peking 1990; Buenos Aires 1993; Karachi 1997; Band A2; m 1997 Stuart William Gardner (1d 1999).

Gardner, Stuart William; Brussels since August 2001; born 10/03/70; FCO 1989; Buenos Aires

1993; Karachi 1999; Band B3; m 1997 Julie Taylor.

Garn, Carl Raymond; FCO since September 2000; born 17/10/56; Cabinet Office 1977; CSD 1979; FCO 1981; Dacca 1982; SEA Floater 1985; Vice-Consul Istanbul 1986; FCO 1990; Deputy Head of Mission Tallinn 1993; Tortola 1996; Band C4; m 1987 Lisa Elaine Walter (1d 1995, 1s 1997).

Garner-Winship, Stephen Peter; First Secretary FCO since September 1994; born 26/10/56; FCO 1989; Consul Rio de Janeiro 1991; First Secretary (Political) Lisbon 1993; Band D6; m 1978 Mary Carmel (1s 1979, 1d 1982).

Garnham, Penelope Jane (née White); Pretoria since September 2000; born 13/07/71; FCO 1989; Kingston 1992; Dubai 1996; Band B3; m 1993 Glen Joseph Garnham (1d 1999; 1s 2002).

Garnham, Sandra Jayne (née Hibbert); Islamabad since April 1998; born 15/09/68; FCO 1989; Rome 1992; FCO 1996; Band B3; m 1992 Clive Julian Marcus Westbrook Garnham.

Garrett, Charles Edmund; First Secretary Berne since July 1997; born 16/04/63; FCO 1987; Language Training 1988; Language Training Hong Kong 1989; Second Secretary Nicosia 1990; Second Secretary Hong Kong (UKREP JLG) 1991; First Secretary FCO 1993; m 1991 Véronique Frances Edmonde Barnes (2d 1992, 1993, 3s 1995, 1999, 2000).

Garrett, Martin, MVO (1996); Deputy Head of Mission Rangoon since March 2002; born 21/02/54; FCO 1974; Governor's Office Honiara 1976; Paris 1979; BERS Masirah 1981; Tripoli 1982; FCO 1984; Stockholm 1990; Second Secretary (Commercial/Aid) Hanoi 1994; Bangkok 1996; Second Secretary FCO 1997.

Garrity, Alison; Kathmandu since January 2001; born 19/10/71; FCO 1999; Band A2.

Garside, Bernhard Herbert; Second later First Secretary (Management) and HM Consul, Havana since April 1999; born 21/01/62; FCO 1983; Masirah 1986; Dubai 1987; Lagos 1990; FCO 1994; Band C5; m 1989 Jennifer Susan Yard (2d 1992, 1998, 1s 1996).

Garth, Andrew John; Taipei since October 1999; born 28/09/69; FCO 1988; Warsaw 1990; South/South East Asia Floater Duties 1992; FCO 1996; On loan to the DTI 1998; Band B3.

Garvey, Kevin Andrew; First Secretary (Deputy Head of Mission) and HM Consul Guatemala City since December 2001; born 10/08/60; FCO 1978; Bangkok 1981; Hanoi 1985; Latin America Floater 1986; FCO 1988; Phnom Penh 1992; Second Secretary Turks and Caicos Islands 1993; On loan to the British Trade International 1999.

Gaskin, Rupert John Addison; Second Secretary FCO since May 2001; born 19/06/74; FCO 1997; Second Secretary (Political) Cairo 1999; Band C4.

Gass, Simon Lawrance, CMG (1998), CVO (1999); Director (Resources) FCO since September 2001; born 02/11/56; FCO 1977; Lagos 1979; Second later First Secretary Athens 1984; First Secretary FCO 1987; APS to the Secretary of State 1990; Rome 1993; FCO 1995; Deputy High Commissioner Pretoria 1998; m 1980 Marianne Enid Stott (2s 1986, 1989, 1d 1995).

Gates, Helen Deborah; Consul New York since August 2002; born 31/01/67; FCO 1990; Third Secretary (Political) Berlin 1993; World-Wide Floater Duties 1996; FCO 1997; Second Secretary Geneva (UKDIS) 1999; T/D Johannesburg 2001.

Gatward, William Henry Richard; FCO since 1999; born 01/03/73; Band C4; ptnr, Lynne Morrice.

Gault, Jean Jos, MBE (1999); FCO since January 1995; born 15/10/45; FCO 1970; Madrid 1971; Warsaw 1974; Rome 1975; FCO 1977; Caracas 1980; Paris 1983; The Hague 1986; FCO 1988; Copenhagen 1992; Band B3.

Gay, Andrew Michael; First Secretary Bogotá since September 2002; born 04/03/70; First Secretary FCO 1998; Band D6.

Gebicka, Anna Maria Teresa; Prague since July 2001; born 27/01/64; FCO 1990; Tokyo 1992; Caracas 1995; FCO 1999; T/D Stanley 1999; Band B3.

Gecim, Thérésa Ellen; SUPL since July 1993; born 05/06/60; FCO 1977; Geneva (UKMIS) 1982; Belgrade 1984; Manila 1987; FCO 1990; Band B3; m 1985 Ali Gecim (1d 1993, 1s 1995).

Geddes, Jonathan Paul; FCO since June 2001; born 03/09/65; FCO 1985; Rome 1987; Madras 1990; FCO 1994; Dhaka 1998; Band C5; m 1996 Susan Jane Fleming.

Geddes, Susan Jane (née Fleming); SUPL since June 2000; born 02/08/64; FCO 1984; Brussels (UKREP) 1985; Nassau 1988; FCO 1990; Dhaka 1998; Band B3; m 1996 Jonathan Paul Geddes.

Gedny, Philippa; SUPL since August 2000; born 09/08/59; FCO 1977; Bonn 1979; Montevideo 1982; Antigua 1985; FCO 1987; APS to the PUS 1988; Lisbon 1992; Dubai 1995; FCO 1998; Band C4; (1d 1999).

Gee, Alan Francis; First Secretary (Management) Canberra since October 2000; born 02/12/43; FO 1960; Tokyo 1967; Blantyre 1970; Nicosia 1973; FCO 1975; JAO Brussels 1978; Lagos 1981; Second Secretary FCO 1984; Second Secretary (Admin) Sofia 1988; Second later First Secretary FCO 1992; First Secretary (Management) Brasilia 1997; m 1970 Wendy Rugman (1s 1973).

Gee, Mark Leonard; Guangzhou since July 2002; born 27/06/70; FCO 1991; Moscow 1995; Pretoria 1999; Band B3; (1d 2000).

Geere, Francis George; First Secretary and Deputy Head of Mission Abidjan since June 1997; born 20/03/44; FO 1961; Rawalpindi 1965; DSAO

1965; Dacca 1966; Khartoum 1968; Bombay 1969; FCO 1973; MECAS 1975; Second Secretary and Consul Jedda 1976; Second Secretary (Inf) Berne 1980; Second Secretary FCO 1985; First Secretary (Comm) and Consul Kinshasa 1988; First Secretary (Comm) and Deputy Head of Mission Doha 1992; First Secretary FCO 1995; m (1) 1968 Julie Christine Lawrence (diss) (1s 1969, 1d 1971); (2) 1980 Rosalind Jessie Richards (diss) (1s 1984, 1d 1989); (3) 1997 Paula Rosalind Francesca Lincoln.

Gelling, William John; FCO since September 2001; born 30/12/77; Band C4.

Gemmell, Roderick, OBE (2002); First Secretary (Consular/Immigration) later Director of Entry Clearance Lagos since March 1998; born 19/08/50; POSB 1966; DSAO (later FCO) 1967; Bahrain 1971; Washington 1972; The Hague 1975; FCO 1979; Mbabane 1982; Stockholm 1984; Second Secretary (Comm/Econ) Ankara 1987; Second Secretary FCO 1991; First Secretary (Management) Kampala 1994; m 1975 Janet Bruce Mitchell (1d 1981).

George, Andrew Neil; HM Ambassador Asunción since October 1998; born 09/10/52; Third Secretary FCO 1974; Second later First Secretary FCO 1980; First Secretary Canberra 1984; First Secretary and Head of Chancery Bangkok 1988; First Secretary FCO 1992; m 1977 Watanalak Chaovieng (1d 1979; 1s 1982).

George, Christopher Stephen; First Secretary (Commercial/Economic) Havana since June 2001; born 08/05/62; Home Office 1982; FCO 1991; Band D6; m 1993 Susan Vince (1s 1999).

Gerken, Ian, LVO (1992); HM Ambassador Quito since January 2000; born 01/12/43; FO 1962; Budapest 1965; Buenos Aires 1966; FCO 1968; Vice-Consul Caracas 1971; FCO 1975; Second Secretary 1978; Second later First Secretary Lima 1979; First Secretary FCO 1985; Deputy High Commissioner and Head of Chancery Valletta 1988; Counsellor FCO 1992; HM Ambassador San Salvador 1995; m 1976 Susana Drucker (1 step d, 2s 1980, 1982).

German, Robert Charles; First Secretary FCO since November 1999; born 17/01/58; FCO 1978; Masirah 1985; FCO 1986; Third Secretary Kuala Lumpur 1990; Third Secretary FCO 1993; Second Secretary Tel Aviv 1997; m 1982 Penelope Jane Cooper (2s 1986, 1989, 1d 1996).

Gibbins, Ian Paul; Second Secretary Brussels since November 1995; born 27/06/47; GPO 1963; FCO 1969; Washington 1975; FCO 1977; Brussels 1981; Third Secretary Prague 1984; Second Secretary Bonn 1990; Second Secretary FCO 1992; m 1975 Rose Elizabeth Devlin (2s 1978, 1980; 1d 1983).

Gibbs, Andrew Patrick Somerset, OBE (1992); Counsellor Tel Aviv since July 2002; born 08/12/51; Third later Second Secretary FCO 1977; Vice-Consul later Consul (Econ) Rio de Janeiro

1979; First Secretary FCO 1981; Language
Training 1983; First Secretary Moscow 1984; First
Secretary FCO 1985; First Secretary (Inf) Pretoria
1987; First Secretary FCO 1989; SUPL 1991; First
Secretary FCO 1993; Counsellor Lisbon 1994;
Counsellor FCO 1998; m 1981 Roselind Cecilia
Robey (2d 1982, 1986; 2s 1983, 1990).

Gibbs, Kristian Mark; Caracas since March 2000;
born 12/05/74; FCO 1997; Band C4.

Gibbs, Timothy; FCO since September 1981; born
20/10/48; FO (later FCO) 1967; Beirut 1974; FCO
1976; Paris 1978; Band C4; m 1978 Catherine
MacDougall.

Gibson, John Stuart; Second Secretary
(Consular/Management) Kathmandu since
September 1994; born 15/03/48; Commonwealth
Office 1967; FCO 1969; Moscow 1970; Bonn
1972; Berne 1974; Helsinki 1975; FCO 1977;
Cairo 1979; Riyadh 1983; Düsseldorf 1984; Dhaka
1987; Second Secretary FCO 1991; m 1972 Grete
Sandberg (2d 1975, 1977).

Gibson, Pamela Ann (née O'Hanlon), MBE
(2000); FCO since April 1996; born 27/09/56;
FCO 1975; Geneva (UKMIS) 1978; Kuwait 1981;
FCO 1983; Copenhagen 1984; SUPL 1987; FCO
1990; Nairobi 1995; Band A2; m 1987 Graeme
Robert Gibson (dec'd 1996).

Gibson, Robert Winnington; Deputy Head of
Mission Dhaka since January 2002; born 07/02/56;
FCO 1978; Jedda 1981; Second Secretary UKREP
Brussels 1984; Second Secretary (Chancery/Inf)
Port of Spain 1986; Second later First Secretary
FCO 1989; First Secretary (Political) UKDEL
OECD Paris 1995; FCO 1999.

Gifford, Michael John; Deputy Head of Mission
Cairo since January 2001; born 02/04/61; Third
Secretary (Commercial); FCO 1981; Language
Training 1982; Abu Dhabi 1983; Second Secretary
(Chancery) Oslo 1988; On loan to European
Commission Brussels 1990; Second later First
Secretary FCO 1991; First Secretary (Economic)
Riyadh 1993; First Secretary FCO 1996; m 1986
Patricia Anne Owen (1d 1989, 1s 1991).

Gilbert, Juliet; New York (UKMIS) since
September 1999; born 20/02/69; FCO 1998; Band
A2.

Gilbert, Mary Jean; Auckland since April 2002;
born 17/01/52; New Zealand Army 1979-1994;
FCO 1995; Jakarta 1999; Band B3.

Giles, Alison Mary; First Secretary (IAEA)
Vienna (UKMIS) since August 1998; born
15/09/64; FCO 1988; Third later Second Secretary
Pretoria 1990; Second Secretary FCO 1993; Band
D6.

Gill, Anne Frances; FCO since September 2001;
born 06/07/63; FCO 1988; East Berlin 1989; FCO
1990; Brussels (UKREP) 1992; Rangoon 1995;
Tehran 1999; Band B3.

Gillett, Sarah, MVO (1986); Consul General
Montreal since February 2002; born 21/07/56;

FCO 1976; SUPL 1978; FCO 1982; Washington
1984; Third later Second Secretary Paris 1987;
Second Secretary on secondment to ODA 1990;
Vice-Consul Los Angeles 1992; First Secretary
FCO 1994; First Secretary (Political) Brasilia
1996.

Gillham, Geoffrey Charles; Head of Southern
European Department FCO since April 2001; born
01/06/54; FCO 1981; Second Secretary Caracas
1983; On loan to the Cabinet Office 1986; FCO
1988; First Secretary (Chancery) Madrid 1989;
First Secretary (Economic) Paris (UKDEL OECD)
1991; First Secretary later Counsellor FCO 1995;
Counsellor New Delhi 1998; m 1991 Dr Nicola
Mary Brewer (1d 1993, 1s 1994).

Gillon, Angela May; FO (later FCO) since
September 1964; born 27/09/41; Principal
Research Officer, Senior Principal Research
Officer 1990; m 1966 Raanan Gillon (1d 1977).

Gilmore, Julie Louise; FCO since September
1986; born 10/12/63; FCO 1981; Bridgetown
1984; Band B3; m 1983 Brian Gilmore.

Gimblett, Jonathan James; First Secretary
(Political) Washington since August 1998; born
03/03/65; FCO 1988; Third later Second Secretary
Paris (OECD) 1989; First Secretary FCO 1993;
Chargé d'Affaires Tirana 1993; m 1987 Elizabeth
Marie Bauer.

Gingell, Colin John; Peking since September
2001; born 05/03/45; Royal Marines 1966-88;
Warsaw 1988; Madrid 1989; Bonn 1992; Kiev
1993; Khartoum 1995; Tehran 1999; Band C4; m
1964 Sandra Hall.

Girdlestone, John Patrick; Deputy Head of
Mission Lima since January 1998; born 26/09/46;
FO 1964; Khartoum 1968; Mexico City 1971;
Cairo 1974; FCO 1976; MECAS 1978; Doha
1979; Madrid 1983; Second Secretary and Consul
Al Khobar 1986; Chairman, Diplomatic Service
Trade Union Side 1991; Second Secretary FCO
1991; First Secretary (Commercial) Abu Dhabi
1994; m 1975 Djihan Labib Nakhla (1d 1976).

Glackin, Clare Siobhan; Second Secretary
(Chancery) Vienna since July 2002; born 13/12/70;
FCO 1999; Band C4.

Gladwin, Rob William; Third Secretary (Science
and Technology) Paris (OECD) since January
1998; born 21/03/64; Home Office 1987; FCO
1989; Geneva (UKMIS) 1992; Third Secretary
Tehran 1996; Band B3; m 1992 Edwige Denis
Danielle Foltte (1s 1998).

Glass, Colin, MBE; Deputy High Commissioner
Freetown since June 1995; born 06/02/55; FCO
1973; Paris 1975; Luanda 1977; Warsaw 1978;
Luanda 1981; Stockholm 1985; FCO 1988; Vice-
Consul Bahrain 1991; m 1981 Ruth Kathleen
Elizabeth Pearce (1s 1986, 1d 1989).

Glover, Edward Charles, MVO (1976); High
Commissioner Georgetown and Ambassador
Paramaribo since December 1998; born 04/03/43;

Postgraduate University Research 1968-69; Board of Trade 1962; FO 1966; Third Secretary Canberra 1971; Second Secretary Washington 1973; Second later First Secretary FCO 1978; First Secretary FCO (Seconded Guinness Peat) 1980; First Secretary FCO 1983; BMG Berlin 1985; First Secretary later Counsellor FCO 1989; Brussels 1994; m 1971 Audrey Frances (née Lush) (2d 1973, 1976; 2s 1980, 1983).

Glover, Graham Dingwall; First Secretary (Commercial) Tripoli since December 2001; born 14/08/68; FCO 1988; Peking 1989; FCO 1992; Warsaw 1993; On loan to DfID Guyana 1998; Band B3; m 1992 Joanne Whittle.

Glover, Joanne (née Whittle); SUPL since January 1999; born 20/04/67; FCO 1986; Peking 1989; FCO 1992; Warsaw 1993; FCO 1996; Kingston 1996; Band B3; m 1992 Graham Dingwall Glover.

Glynn, Christopher Barry; Deputy Consul-General Sydney since August 2001; born 23/12/49; FO (later FCO) 1967; Bonn 1971; Abidjan 1973; FCO 1975; Alexandria 1978; FCO 1982; Canning House 1983; Vice-Consul (Commercial) São Paulo 1985; Second Secretary (Commercial) later First Secretary/Consul Lisbon 1988; First Secretary FCO 1992; First Secretary (Commercial) Manila 1994; Deputy Consul General and Deputy Director of Trade Promotion São Paulo 1997; m 1988 Dr Wilma Sarino Ballat.

Glynn, Vanessa Jane; First Secretary Brussels (UKREP) since July 1996; born 05/08/60; FCO 1983; SUPL 1985; Second Secretary FCO 1987; Second Secretary (E Trade) Brussels (UKREP) 1988; SUPL 1990; First Secretary 1990; m 1984 Colin Thomas Imrie (1d 1985).

Goddard, Colette (née Boyd); Lagos since July 2002; born 09/05/65; FCO 1995; Singapore 1997; Karachi 2000; Band B3; m 1997 Paul Anthony Goddard (1s 1995).

Goddard, Jonathan; Third Secretary (Chancery) Kathmandu since March 2000; born 21/12/66; Home Office 1994; FCO 1997; Band B3; m 1996 Hayley Morgan (2s 1998, 2000).

Godfrey, Ian David; Third Secretary Islamabad since November 1993; born 02/10/60; FCO 1980; Washington 1987; FCO 1989; m 1994 C Hochreiter (1s 1994).

Godson, Anthony; Counsellor later Deputy Head of Mission and Consul General Jakarta since October 1998; born 01/02/48; FCO 1966; Bucharest 1970; Third Secretary Jakarta 1972; Private Secretary to the High Commissioner Canberra 1976; FCO 1979; Second Secretary 1980; Second later First Secretary New York (UKMIS) 1983; First Secretary FCO 1988; Deputy Head of Mission Bucharest 1990; First Secretary Geneva (UKMIS) 1991; m 1977 Marian Jane Margaret Hurst.

Goksin, Jill Elaine (née Cooke); Vienna since March 2002; born 15/09/58; FCO 1982; Belgrade 1983; FCO 1986; Gaborone 1987; Istanbul 1989;

FCO 1989; Colombo 1992; FCO 1996; Addis Ababa 1997; Band A2; m 1994 Cenk Bulent Goksin (2d 1996, 1997).

Gola, Elizabeth Ann; ECO Manila since October 2000; born 04/07/61; FCO 1996; Havana 1998; Band B3.

Golding, Terence Michael; Second Secretary Singapore since April 1996; born 26/07/49; FCO 1969; Washington 1973; Berne 1975; São Paulo 1978; FCO 1981; Budapest 1986; Kaduna 1988; FCO 1990; later Second Secretary 1992; m 1978 Irene Elizabeth Blackett.

Goldsmith, Simon Geoffrey; Third Secretary (On secondment to DFID) Belmopan since March 1998; born 23/01/69; FCO 1990; Paris 1992; Bombay 1994; Band B3; m 1995 Robyn Jean Daley.

Goldthorpe, Debra Kay, LVO (1999); First Secretary (Commercial) Budapest since November 2000; born 30/01/58; FCO 1977; Africa Floater 1981; New York 1982; Second Secretary FCO 1985; Second Secretary Budapest 1989; Language Training 1989; First Secretary FCO 1993; HM Consul Durban 1996; Band D6; m 1989 Roger William Lamping.

Golland, Roger James Adam, OBE (1993); Counsellor FCO since January 2001; born 08/05/55; FCO 1978; Third later Second Secretary Ankara 1979; FCO 1982; Language Training 1983; First Secretary Budapest 1984; FCO 1986; First Secretary Buenos Aires 1989; First Secretary FCO 1992; Counsellor (Political) Brussels 1998; m 1978 Jane Lynnette Brandrick (2s 1985, 1987).

Gomersall, Stephen John, KCMG (2000), CMG (1997); HM Ambassador Tokyo since July 1999; born 17/01/48; FCO 1970; Language Student Sheffield and Tokyo 1971; Third later First Secretary Tokyo 1972; FCO 1977; Private Secretary to Lord Privy Seal 1979; First Secretary Washington 1982; Counsellor (Economic) Tokyo 1986; Counsellor FCO 1990; Minister New York (UKMIS) 1994; m 1975 Lydia Veronica Parry (2s 1978, 1980; 1d 1982).

Goodall, Clare; New Delhi since June 2001; born 08/05/61; FCO 1982; Lima 1983; FCO 1986; Islamabad 1988; Paris 1991; SUPL 1991; SUPL 1993; Belgrade 1998; SUPL 1999; FCO 2000; Band A2; m 1987 David Spires (1s 1986, 1d 1990).

Goodall, David Paul; Second Secretary (Management) Rome since May 1998; born 16/04/57; FCO 1976; Wellington 1978; Seoul 1981; SEA Floater 1985; FCO 1987; Third Secretary (Commercial) Accra 1990; (Second Secretary 1994); Second Secretary FCO 1994; m 1996 Diane Bainbridge.

Goodall, Diane (née Bainbridge); Rome since December 1998; born 07/10/58; FCO 1985; Ankara 1987; Accra 1991; FCO 1995; Band B3; m 1996 David Paul Goodall.

Gooderham, Peter Olaf; Counsellor (Political) Washington since June 1999; born 29/07/54; FCO 1983; Second later First Secretary (Chancery) Brussels (UKDEL NATO) 1985; First Secretary FCO 1987; First Secretary (Economic) Riyadh 1990; First Secretary FCO 1993; New York (UKMIS) 1996; m 1985 Carol Anne Ward.

Gooding, Mark; Full-Time Language Training Peking since September 2001; born 17/12/74; FCO 1999; SUPL 2000; Band C4.

Goodman, James Henry Adam; First Secretary (Political) Amman since January 2002; born 31/12/65; FCO 1993; Full-Time Language Training 1995; Full-Time Language Training Cairo 1996; Second Secretary (Political) Riyadh 1997; Second Secretary FCO 1999; Band D6; m 1992 Andrea Dawn Wells (3s 1994, 1996, 1998).

Goodman, Sean Adrian; FCO since December 1990; born 19/03/64; FCO 1983; Riyadh 1989; Band B3; m 1991 Sara Ashley Palmer (1d 1998).

Goodrick, Clair Isabella; Zagreb since March 1999; born 16/09/71; FCO 1993; Pretoria 1996; Band A2.

Goodrick, Sophie Louise; on secondment Berlin since July 2000; born 28/02/70; FCO 1997; Full-Time Language Training 2000; Band C4.

Goodwin, Andrew John; Consul/Management Officer Tehran since July 2002; born 22/03/59; FCO 1978; Hong Kong 1980; Dhaka 1982; Africa/ME Floater 1984; Aden 1987; Lagos 1992; FCO 1993 (Second Secretary 1995); Deputy Head of Mission and Consul Ulaanbaatar 1998; m 1997 (Carol) Louise Mottershead.

Goodwin, David Howard; First Secretary (Commercial) Moscow since April 2002; born 16/08/46; FO (later FCO) 1964; Budapest 1969; Kinshasa 1970; Montevideo 1973; FCO 1975; Moscow 1978; San Francisco 1980; FCO 1983; Second Secretary (Immigration) New Delhi 1987; Second later First Secretary FCO 1990; First Secretary (Commercial) The Hague 1996; T/D Deputy Project Director Expo 2000 Hanover 2000; Band C5; m 1968 Dorothea Thompson (2d 1970, 1976).

Goodwin, Michael Roy; Second Secretary (Immigration/Consular) Kingston since January 2001; born 17/03/60; FCO 1981; Victoria 1983; Dublin 1987; FCO 1987; Third Secretary (Aid) Banjul 1990; FCO 1992; Ottawa 1995; Band C4; m 1983 Kerry Linda Graney (2d 1986, 1992).

Goodworth, Adrian Francis Norton; SUPL since January 2001; born 06/07/53; FCO 1982; Third Secretary Seoul 1984; Third later Second Secretary Brussels (UKREP) 1988; FCO 1990; Second Secretary (Commercial) Jakarta 1992; First Secretary (Commercial) Caracas 1996; m (1) 1981 Caroline Ruth Steele (diss 1985), (2) 1987 Valerie Ann Chipcase (diss) (1s 1990, 1d 1992), (3) 1996 Susanti Djuhana (1s 1997).

Gordon, Alison Jill; FCO since April 2002; born 02/02/72; Band D6.

Gordon, Claire Sandra; New York (UKMIS) since October 2001; born 19/11/76; FCO 1998; Lima 1999.

Gordon, Diane Eily, MBE; Santiago since February 1999; born 26/08/43; Lagos 1965; Ankara 1968; FCO 1970; Buenos Aires 1971; FCO 1974; Madrid 1978; FCO 1983; Bridgetown 1985; Bogotá 1989; Second Secretary 1992; Second Secretary FCO 1994.

Gordon, Emma Louise; FCO since April 2002; born 25/05/74; Band C4.

Gordon, Jean Francois, CMG (1999); HM Ambassador Abidjan and HM Ambassador non-resident to Liberia, Niger and Burkina Faso since June 2001; born 16/04/53; FCO 1979; Second later First Secretary Luanda 1981; First Secretary Geneva (UKDIS) 1983; First Secretary FCO 1988; First Secretary (Political) Nairobi 1990; First Secretary FCO 1992; HM Ambassador Algiers 1996; seconded to Royal College of Defence Studies 2000; m Elaine Margaret Daniel (2d 1984, 1988).

Gordon, Robert Anthony Eagleson, OBE (1983), CMG (1999); Counsellor FCO since June 1999; born 09/02/52; FCO 1973; Language Student 1974; Third later Second Secretary Warsaw 1975; Second later First Secretary (Head of Chancery) Santiago 1978; First Secretary FCO 1983; First Secretary (Economic) Paris (UKDEL OECD) 1987; Deputy Head of Mission Warsaw 1992; HM Ambassador Rangoon 1995; m 1978 Pamela Jane Taylor (2d 1980, 1981; 2s 1985, 1988).

Gordon-MacLeod, David Scott; First Secretary (Economic) Athens since July 1998; born 04/05/48; ODA 1973; Mbabane 1978; Second later First Secretary FCO 1983; First Secretary and Head of Chancery Maputo 1987; First Secretary FCO 1991; Deputy Head of Mission Bogotá 1994; Full-Time Language Training 1994; m 1988 Adrienne Felicia Maria Atkins (2d 1989, 1992, 2s 1994, 1996).

Gotch, Chris; Second Secretary (Political) Seoul since September 1997; born 28/11/69; FCO 1996.

Gould, Clive Anthony; First Secretary Washington since May 1999; born 28/06/44; GPO 1960; FO 1968; Attaché Brussels 1970; FCO 1972; Vienna 1973; Third Secretary FCO 1976; Budapest 1979; Third Secretary FCO 1982; Hong Kong 1983; Second Secretary FCO 1986; Second Secretary Berlin 1990; FCO 1993; m 1969 Barbara Sheila Austin (1s 1972).

Gould, David Christopher; FCO then FCO Services since November 1990; born 31/12/55; FCO 1976; Washington 1982; FCO 1985; On loan to Cabinet Office 1987; Band C5; m 1977 Susan Kensett (2d 1975, 1980).

Gould, John Richard William; Second Secretary FCO since April 2002; born 28/11/73; FCO 1997; Second Secretary Sarajevo 2000; Band C4.

Gould, Matthew Steven, MBE (1998); T/D Islamabad since June 2002; born 20/08/71; FCO 1993; Manila 1994; FCO 1997.

Gould, St.John Byrhtnoth; First Secretary (Political) Washington since July 2000; born 12/08/68; FCO 1995; Band C5; m 1993 Siân Elizabeth Edwards.

Gould, Tina Louise; FCO since January 1991; born 07/06/70; Band A2.

Goulden, Katherine Lucy; Brasilia since January 1998; born 20/06/67; FCO 1991; Third Secretary (Aid/Chancery) Port Louis 1994; Band B3.

Goulty, Alan Fletcher, CMG (1998); UK Special Representative to Sudan since February 2002; born 02/07/47; Third Secretary FCO 1968; MECAS 1969; Third later Second Secretary Beirut 1971; Khartoum 1972; Second later First Secretary FCO 1975; On loan to Cabinet Office 1977; Washington 1981; First Secretary later Counsellor FCO 1985; Deputy Head of Mission Cairo 1990; HM Ambassador Khartoum 1995; Director Middle East 2000; m (1) 1968 Jennifer Wendy Ellison (1s 1970); (2) 1983 Lillian Craig Harris.

Gowan, David John; Minister and Deputy Head of Mission Moscow since November 2000; born 11/02/49; Ministry of Defence 1970; Home Civil Service 1973; Second Secretary FCO 1975; Second later First Secretary (Comm) Moscow 1977; First Secretary FCO 1981; Head of Chancery and Consul Brasilia 1985; On loan to the Cabinet Office 1988; FCO 1989; Counsellor on loan to the Cabinet Office 1990; Counsellor (Commercial and Know How Fund) Moscow 1992; Counsellor and Deputy Head of Mission Helsinki 1995; Counsellor FCO 1999; On loan at St Antony's College Oxford 1999; Full-Time Language Training 2000; m 1975 Marna Irene Williams (2s 1978, 1982).

Gowen-Smith, Stephen Donald; FCO since August 2000; born 10/12/59; FCO 1984; Vice-Consul Geneva 1997; Band C4; m 1981 Janet Elizabeth (1s 1987, 1d 1991).

Gozney, Richard Hugh Turton, CMG (1993); HM Ambassador Jakarta since August 2000; born 21/07/51; FCO 1973; Third Secretary Jakarta 1974; Second later First Secretary Buenos Aires 1978; First Secretary FCO 1981; Head of Chancery Madrid 1984; APS later PPS to Secretary of State FCO 1989; High Commissioner Mbabane 1993; Counsellor FCO 1996; On loan to Cabinet Office (Chief of Assessment Staff) 1998; m 1982 Diana Edwina Baird (2s 1987, 1990).

Gracey, Colin; Guatemala City since June 2002; born 25/03/47; FCO 1965; Anguilla 1969; Lima 1971; Bombay 1974; FCO 1976; La Paz 1979; FCO 1983; Geneva (UKMIS) 1986; Islamabad 1989; FCO 1992; Third later Second Secretary (Commercial) Caracas 1996; Consul (Commercial)

Ho Chi Minh City 1999; Band C4; m 1972 Mercedes Ines Rosenthal (1d 1973, 1s 1977).

Graham, Alison Forbes; FCO since January 1994; born 24/08/59; FCO 1980; East Berlin 1982; FCO 1984; Ottawa 1987; Paris 1990; Band A2.

Graham, David Frank; First Secretary (Head of Governor's Office) Montserrat since July 2000; born 27/06/59; FCO 1978; Vice-Consul (Commercial) Munich 1982; LA Floater 1985; Third later Second Secretary (Economic) Warsaw 1987; FCO 1991; Second Secretary (Commercial) Berlin 1992; First Secretary (Commercial) Seoul 1997; m 1990 Anne Marie D'Souza.

Graham, Iain George; FCO since June 2001; born 01/03/70; FCO 1989; Cairo 1991; Anguilla 1995; Islamabad 1998; Band B3.

Graham, Steven; Second Secretary (Commercial) Luanda since May 2001; born 08/07/68; FCO 1989; Islamabad 1993; Vice-Consul (Commercial) Rio de Janeiro 1996; Full-Time Language Training 1996; Band B3; m (1) 1991 Pauline Lannie (diss 1995), (2) 2000 Luisa Maria Satiago.

Grainger, David Quentin; Kampala since September 1996; born 02/02/69; FCO 1990; Lusaka 1992; Band B3.

Grainger, John Andrew; Legal Counsellor New York (UKMIS) since August 1997; born 27/08/57; called to the Bar (Lincoln's Inn) 1981; Assistant Legal Adviser FCO 1984; First Secretary (Legal Adviser) BMG (later BM) Berlin 1989; Assistant Legal Adviser FCO 1991; Legal Counsellor FCO 1994; m 1998 Katherine Veronica Bregou.

Grainger, Susan Carol; Dublin since April 1997; born 17/06/67; FCO 1987; New York (UKMIS) 1989; Montserrat 1992; FCO 1996; Band A2; m 1991 Angus James Robert Steele.

Grant, Ann; High Commissioner Cape Town since October 2000; born 13/08/48; FCI 1971; Calcutta 1973; FCO 1975; On loan to the Department of Energy 1976; First Secretary FCO 1979; Head of Chancery and Consul Maputo 1981; FCO 1984; First Secretary (Energy) Brussels (UKREP) 1987; resigned 1989; Communications Director OXFAM 1989-1991; reinstated FCO 1991; Counsellor (ECOSOC) New York (UKMIS) 1992; Counsellor FCO 1996; Director FCO 1999.

Grant, John Douglas Kelso, CMG (1999); HM Ambassador Stockholm since August 1999; born 17/10/54; FCO 1976; Stockholm 1977; Language Training 1980; Moscow 1982; FCO 1984; Resigned 1985; Reinstated 1986; First Secretary FCO 1986; First Secretary (Press) Brussels (UKREP) 1989; First Secretary on loan to the Cabinet Office 1993; Brussels (UKREP) 1994; Principal Private Secretary to the Secretary of State for Foreign and Commonwealth Affairs 1997; m 1983 Anna Lindvall (1d 1987).

Gray, Douglas Macdonald; Counsellor FCO since September 1997; born 13/03/54; FCO 1975; Far

East Floater 1978; Istanbul 1980; Second Secretary Yaoundé 1983; Second Secretary FCO 1986; First Secretary (Commercial) Seoul 1989; Deputy Head of Mission and Consul Quito 1994; m 1980 Alison Ann Hunter (1d 1985).

Gray, John Charles Rodger; Head of Middle East Department FCO since March 2002; born 12/03/53; Third Secretary FCO 1974; Language Training 1975; Third later Second Secretary Warsaw 1976; FCO 1979; First Secretary FCO 1981; First Secretary Paris (UKDEL OECD) 1983; On loan to Cabinet Office 1987; First Secretary FCO 1989; Deputy Head of Mission Jakarta 1993; On secondment to Harvard University 1996; Washington 1997; FCO 2001; m 1988 Anne-Marie Lucienne Suzanne de Dax d'Axat (3s 1995, 1997, 2000).

Gray, Trudi Elisabeth Mary; Bogotá since July 2001; born 19/07/47; FCO 1978; Buenos Aires 1979; Prague 1982; Port Stanley 1984; Nassau 1985; Lima 1988; Lisbon 1992; FCO 1995; Seoul 1997; Band A2.

Greatrex, Avril; Second Secretary FCO since February 1995; born 17/04/47; DSAO (later FCO) 1967; Kuwait 1971; Lagos 1973; Latin America Floater 1976; FCO 1979; Second Secretary (Management) and Vice Consul Buenos Aires 1991.

Green, Andrew Philip; Third later Second Secretary FCO since August 1992; born 12/05/58; FCO 1975; Moscow 1982; FCO 1984; Third Secretary Tokyo 1989; m 1982 Susan Mary Merry.

Green, Colin Harvey; Hong Kong since March 2001; born 22/05/69; FCO 1989; New York (UKMIS) 1992; Abidjan 1995; Band B3; m 1997.

Green, Frances Moira; Moscow since February 2002; born 29/04/48; Washington 1975; Georgetown 1977; The Hague 1981; FCO 1984; Maseru 1987; FCO 1991; Brussels (UKREP) 1993; Valletta 1997; Band A2.

Green, Helen; FCO since March 1996; born 05/09/71; FCO 1990; Madrid 1992; Band A2.

Green, John Edward; World-Wide Floater Duties since May 1994; born 15/02/65; FCO 1983; Tehran 1991; Band C4; m 1994 Caroline Ann Hockings (1s, 1d (twins) 1999).

Green, Keith William; First Secretary FCO since August 2001; born 14/02/64; FCO 1990; Second Secretary (Chancery) Buenos Aires 1992; Second Secretary FCO 1995; First Secretary Sarajevo 1998; Band D6.

Green, Kelvin Edward; Second Secretary Bangalore since January 2001; born 19/01/63; Inland Revenue 1981; FCO 1982; Washington 1984; Kampala 1987; Lilongwe 1990; FCO 1993; Second Secretary (Commercial/Consular) Dar es Salaam 1997; Band C4; m 1984 Gillian Mary Lewis (2d 1991, 1993).

Green, Muriel Ruth (née Bailey); On loan to the Cabinet Office since February 1999; born

13/06/49; WRAF 1971-75; FCO 1975; Mexico City 1976; Islamabad 1982; FCO 1984; SUPL 1992; FCO 1993; Band A2; m 1981 William Charles Green (1s 1984).

Green, Noël Frank; First Secretary FCO since June 1996; born 08/01/49; FCO 1968; Jedda 1971; Brussels (BE) 1974; Private Secretary to the Ambassador Brussels (UKDEL NATO) 1975; Second Secretary 1977; FCO 1977; Second Secretary (Commercial) Lagos 1981; Second Secretary (Admin) Moscow 1985; First Secretary FCO 1987; First Secretary (Management/Consular) Stockholm 1990; First Secretary (Commercial) Kuala Lumpur 1995; m 1984 Kerstin Anita Maria Höijer.

Green, Richard Charles Benedict; First Secretary FCO since November 1990; born 02/05/49; FCO 1971; Kuwait 1975; FCO 1977; Ankara 1978; FCO 1979; Second Secretary Beirut 1980; Second Secretary FCO 1982; Second Secretary (Chancery) Pretoria 1985; Second later First Secretary (Chancery) Bangkok 1988; Band C5.

Green, Steven John; First Secretary (Commercial) Kuala Lumpur since August 2000; born 17/05/55; HM Customs and Excise 1972-74; FCO 1974; Peking 1976; Stockholm 1978; SUPL (Exeter University) 1980; FCO 1983; Third Secretary Lilongwe 1985; Third Secretary Geneva (UKDIS) 1989; Second Secretary FCO 1992; Full-Time Language Training 1995; Second Secretary (Commercial) Paris 1996; m 1978 Ulla Marianne Nilsson (1s 1980; twin d 1986).

Greene, Bernadette Theresa; T/D Port of Spain since April 2001; born 17/04/66; FCO 1988; Geneva (UKDEL) 1991; Maseru 1994; T/D Bosnia 1996; FCO 1997; on loan to DTI 2000; Band B3.

Greengrass, John Kenneth, MBE (1999); Second Secretary (Commercial) Paris since June 2000; born 19/07/53; Ministry of Housing and Local Government 1970; FCO 1971; Brussels (UKREP) 1975; Washington 1978; Islamabad 1981; FCO 1983; Lagos 1986; Second Secretary Kuala Lumpur 1989; Second Secretary FCO 1993; Second Secretary (Consular) New Delhi 1996; Band C4; m 1975 Marian Cecilia Williams (3d 1981, 1983, 1986).

Greenland, Samuel John; Second Secretary (Political) Kiev since January 1999; born 28/05/74; FCO 1997; Band C4.

Greenlee, James Barry; First Secretary (Management) Dhaka since March 2000; born 21/12/45; FO (later FCO) 1963; Vienna 1969; Tokyo 1971; FCO 1974; Calcutta 1979; Second Secretary (Admin) and Consul Budapest 1983; Second Secretary (Commercial) Lagos 1986; Second Secretary FCO 1989; First Secretary (Management) and Consul Seoul 1993; First Secretary (Management) Warsaw 1996; Band D6; m 1971 Amanda Jane Todd (2d 1979, 1981).

Greenslade, Natalie Samantha Juliet; FCO since March 2000; born 28/06/72; FCO 1993; Tokyo 1994; Floater Duties 1998; Band B3.

Greensmith, Lynn (née Baxter); Geneva (UKDEL) since December 1996; born 24/01/72; FCO 1995; Band A2; m 1997 David John Greensmith.

Greenstock, Andrew John; Second Secretary (DFID/Public Diplomacy) Tehran since July 2001; born 26/10/72; Second Secretary FCO 1998; Full-Time Language Training 2000; Band C4; m 1999 Katherine Emma Gardner.

Greenstock, Sir Jeremy (Quentin), CMG (1991), KCMG (1998); United Kingdom Permanent Representative to the United Nations at New York and the United Kingdom Permanent Representative on the Security Council since July 1998; born 27/07/43; Second Secretary FCO 1969; MECAS 1970; Second later First Secretary Dubai 1972; First Secretary (Private Secretary to the Ambassador) Washington 1974; FCO 1978; Counsellor (Comm) Jedda (later Riyadh) 1983; Head of Chancery Paris 1987; Deputy Political Director and AUSS (Western and Southern Europe) FCO 1990; Minister (Political) Washington 1994; DUS (Middle East/Eastern Europe) 1995; DUS (Political Director) 1996; m 1969 Anne Ashford Hodges (2d 1970, 1975; 1s 1973).

Greenwood, Christopher Paul; Consul-General Göthenburg since September 1999; born 22/04/53; FCO 1973; Islamabad 1975; Moscow 1977; Manila 1980; APS to Secretary of State 1982; FCO 1982; Los Angeles 1985; Third later Second Secretary Budapest 1988; Second Secretary 1989; Second Secretary FCO 1992; Full-Time Language Training 1994; Second later First Secretary (Comm) Berne 1995; m 1976 Dorothy Gwendolyn Margaret Hughes (1s 1983; 1d 1988).

Greenwood, Jeremy David; Attaché Yerevan since August 2000; born 01/10/70; FCO 1991; New York (UKMIS) 1995; Band A2.

Greenwood, Rachael; Full-Time Language Training Tokyo since August 1995; born 04/03/68; FCO 1993; Language Training 1994; Band B3.

Gregg, Sophie Catherine; Consul (Political/Economic) Hong Kong since October 2000; born 17/04/72; FCO 1998; Full-Time Language Training 1999; Band C4.

Gregson, Stuart Willens; Consul-General Paris since April 2000; born 26/04/50; FO (later FCO) 1966; Cairo 1971; Yaoundé 1973; Islamabad 1976; FCO 1978; Gaborone 1982; Vice-Consul Johannesburg 1983; Second Secretary FCO 1987; First Secretary 1989; First Secretary (Information) Rome 1991; First Secretary FCO 1996; Full-Time Language Training 2000; Band D6; m 1976 Anne-Christine Wasser (1d 1976; 1s 1979).

Greig, Rosalind Philippa; FCO since October 1996; born 16/04/66; FCO 1989; Third Secretary Bangkok 1992; SUPL 1995; T/D Moscow 1996; Band B3; m 1997.

Grennan, Gemma Brigid Anne; FCO since September 1986; born 04/07/43; FO 1962; Vientiane 1967; Singapore 1969; Brussels 1971; Special leave 1973; Addis Ababa 1974; FCO 1977; Islamabad 1981; FCO 1983; Ottawa 1984; Band C4; m 1973 Christopher Roy Heaven (1s 1981).

Grice, Sheridan Elizabeth; Third Secretary (Commercial) Cairo since June 1999; born 14/07/54; FCO 1973; Canberra 1974; Belgrade 1976; SUPL 1976; Georgetown 1978; New York (UKMIS) 1981; FCO 1984; SUPL 1987; Islamabad 1988; Lagos 1992; Third Secretary FCO 1994; SUPL 1997; (2d 1987).

Griffin, Joseph Francis; FCO since June 2002; born 14/03/73; FCO 1996; Second Secretary Paris 1999; Band D6.

Griffin, Ryan John; Vilnius since July 1999; born 09/04/72; FCO 1991; Rome 1994; Band A2.

Griffiths, Glyn Justyn; Hong Kong since March 2002; born 11/07/61; FCO 1980; Darwin 1990; FCO 1993; Bonn 1996; FCO 1998; Band C4; m 1989 Susan Caroline Dover (1s 1995, 1d 1998).

Griffiths, Major David Allison; Queen's Messenger since 1990; born 28/07/43; HM Forces 1966-90.

Griffiths, Nicholas Mark; First Secretary UKDEL OECD since June 1996; born 20/11/58; FCO 1985; Moscow 1988; FCO 1990.

Griffiths, Trudy Maureen; Brussels (UKDEL NATO) since July 1999; born 10/09/70; FCO 1991; Warsaw 1993; Lusaka 1996; Band A2.

Griggs, Kenneth John; FCO since August 2002; born 02/09/61; FCO 1984; Washington 1985; FCO 1988; Athens 1989; FCO 1992; BTC Hong Kong 1993; FCO 1996; Bangkok 1999; Band C4; m 1986 Leisa Jayne (3d 1988, 1991, 1992).

Grime, Ann Kathleen (née Jenkins); Budapest since December 1998; born 18/06/51; FCO 1975; Muscat 1976; FCO 1978; Moscow 1979; Brussels (UKREP) 1981; Resigned 1983; Reinstated 1988; Bucharest 1988; Islamabad 1989; Luxembourg 1990; FCO 1990; Colombo 1993; FCO 1997; Band B3; m 1983 Stephen Howard Grime.

Grimes, Eleanor Claire; First Secretary FCO since September 1997; born 22/08/63; Band D6; m 1998 Major Sean Robert Armstrong (1d 1999; 1s 2001).

Grimes, Susan (née Metcalfe); SUPL since March 2002; born 02/10/65; DHSS 1984; FCO 1987; Copenhagen 1990; FCO 1993; Nairobi 1994; Colombo 1998; Band A2; m 1989 Jason Richard Grimes (1d 1993, twin s 1996).

Grinling, Scott MacKenzie; Third Secretary FCO since January 1998; born 29/10/49; FCO 1991; m 1974 Anita Fitzhugh.

Gristock, Frances Lorraine (née Alexander); SUPL since September 1998; born 21/07/59; FCO 1981; SE Asia Floater 1983; FCO 1985; Third Secretary Quito 1986; FCO 1990; SUPL 1991; Second Secretary (Commercial/Consular) Victoria 1992; m 1986 Keith Gristock (1s 1994).

Grover-Minto, Helen Katherine (née Grover); Harare since April 1999; born 18/04/65; FCO 1986; Addis Ababa 1988; FCO 1991; Lagos later Abuja later Lagos 1992; FCO 1995; Band B3; m 1991 John Minto.

Groves, Eliot Sion; Management Officer Shanghai since July 2002; born 17/07/69; FCO 1988; New York (UKMIS) 1994; Colombo 1997; New York 2000; Band B3; m 1996 Christine Ann Reynolds.

Growcott, Michael William; FCO since March 1998; born 15/11/48; FCO 1968; Kampala 1972; Peking 1974; Pretoria 1975; FCO 1978; Assistant to Governor Port Stanley 1979; Second Secretary (Inf/Aid/Econ) Kuala Lumpur 1982; Second Secretary FCO 1986; Chairman Diplomatic Service Whitley Council Trade Union Side 1987; First Secretary (Management) Brussels 1990; Resident Acting High Commissioner Castries 1994; m 1971 Avril Heather Kemp (2d 1972, 1976; 1s 1974).

Guckian, Dr Noël Joseph, OBE (2001); Deputy Head of Mission Damascus since July 2002; born 06/03/55; FCO 1980; Consul (Commercial) Jedda 1984; Second Secretary FCO 1987; Second later First Secretary FCO 1988; Paris 1988; Deputy Head of Mission Muscat 1994; FCO 1997; Head of British Interests Section later Chargé d'Affaires and then DHM Tripoli 1998; m 1990 Lorna Ruth Warren (3d 1992, 1994, 2001; 1s 1997).

Guckian, Lorna Ruth (née Warren); SUPL since July 1994; born 18/06/63; FCO 1983; Port Stanley 1986; Düsseldorf 1987; Africa/ME Floater 1989; FCO 1990; Kuwait 1991; FCO 1992; Band B3; m 1990 Dr Noël Joseph Guckian (3d 1992, 1994, 2001; 1s 1997).

Gudgeon, Jonathan Roy; FCO since May 1995; born 09/05/64; GPO 1980-1984; FCO 1984; Moscow 1988; Vienna 1992; Band C5; m 1988 Lisa Anne Forte (2s 1992, 1993).

Gudgeon, Simon Peter; Tel Aviv since July 1999; born 08/02/66; FCO 1982; Lagos 1987; Moscow 1992; FCO 1996; Band C4; m 1994 C J Stewart (1s 1999; 1d 2001).

Guha, Priya Victoria; Second Secretary (EU) Madrid since September 1999; born 21/09/73; FCO 1996; Band C4.

Gunn, Janet Frederica (née Podolier); FCO since June 1997; born 04/10/48; Research Counsellor FCO 1970; SUPL 1976; FCO 1978; Moscow 1984; FCO 1985; Deputy Head of Mission Sofia 1994; (1s 1976).

Gunnett, Martin John; Second Secretary Peking since August 1995; born 01/04/50; FO 1967; Darwin 1976; FCO 1978; Belgrade 1987; Second

Secretary Prague 1990; Second Secretary FCO 1994; m 1973 Linda Leah (1d 1979, 1s 1981).

Gurney, Tim; Deputy Governor Bermuda since September 1998; born 28/04/55; FCO 1973; Istanbul 1976; Karachi 1979; Montreal 1982; Second Secretary FCO 1985; Second Secretary (Chancery/Inf) Accra 1989; Deputy Director and Consul (Inf) New York (BIS) 1991; First Secretary FCO 1996; m 1976 Denise Elizabeth Harker (1d 1984; 1s 1986).

Guthrie, Marion (née Whalley); Yaoundé since June 1999; born 04/03/69; FCO 1988; Paris 1990; Islamabad 1992; Belgrade 1994; FCO 1996; Band B3; m 1998 Robin Guthrie.

Guy, Frances Mary; HM Ambassador Sana'a since March 2001; born 01/02/59; FCO 1985; Language Training 1987; Second Secretary (Chancery) Khartoum 1988; First Secretary FCO 1991; First Secretary and Head of Political Section Bangkok 1995; Deputy Head of Mission Addis Ababa 1997; m 1989 Guy Charles Maurice Raybaudo (2d 1991, 1996, 1s 1993).

Guymont, Sarah Jean (née Crouch); SUPL since October 2001; born 08/08/52; FCO 1975; Islamabad 1976; FCO 1977; Moscow 1978; resigned 1980; reinstated FCO 1982; Africa/ME Floater 1983; FCO 1987; Dar es Salaam 1989; SUPL Cairo 1992; Cairo 1993; SUPL 1996; Washington 1997; Band B3; m 1991 Frederick James Guymont.

Gwynn, Diana Caroline (née Hamblyn); SUPL since February 1997; born 15/08/64; DOE 1986-89; FCO 1989; Third Secretary (Political/Information) Nairobi 1992; SUPL 1995; Third later Second Secretary FCO 1996; m 1988 Robert Charles Patrick Gwynn (1d 1995; 1s 1997).

Gwynn, Robert Charles Patrick (known as Robin); Deputy High Commissioner Accra since January 2002; born 17/03/63; Department of Employment 1986-88; FCO 1988; Second Secretary (Chancery/Information) Nairobi 1992; First Secretary FCO 1995; Private Secretary to the Minister of State 2000; m 1988 Diana Caroline Hamblyn (1d 1995; 1s 1997).

H

Hackett, Anthony John; HM Consul Hamburg since July 2001; born 19/12/55; FCO 1975; Muscat 1977; Karachi 1981; FCO 1981; FCO 1985; Manila 1988; Oslo 1992; FCO 1996; On loan to the DTI 1999; m 1983 Nilofer Akbar (1d 1986).

Haddock, Michael Kenneth; First Secretary (Information) Moscow since November 1997; born 25/09/50; FCO 1973; Geneva (UKDEL) 1978; Moscow 1981; Kuwait 1983; Second Secretary Damascus 1986; Second Secretary (Commercial) Prague 1988; First Secretary (Commercial) Abu Dhabi 1991; First Secretary FCO 1995; m 1972 Irene Doughty (1d 1979; 1s 1984).

Hadley, William Gerard; FCO since July 2002; born 06/11/70; Customs and Excise 1989; MOD 1990; FCO 1991; Brussels (UKREP) 1994; FCO 1996; Full-Time Language Training 1997; Vice-Consul Paris 1998; Band B3; m 1996 Jacqueline Lillian Smart.

Hafele, Alec Graham; Bucharest since 1999; born 10/05/50; FCO 1995; Band B3; m 1976 Brigitte Ann.

Hagart, Peter Richard; Consul (Commercial) Auckland since May 1994; born 11/07/48; Department of Agriculture and Fisheries for Scotland 1966; FCO 1969; Bucharest 1972; Quito 1974; Bonn 1975; FCO 1977; FE Floater 1980; Hanoi 1982; Second Secretary (Admin) and Vice-Consul Brasilia 1983; Second Secretary FCO 1986; Second later First Secretary (Commercial) Bombay 1990; Consul and Deputy Head of Mission Rangoon 1992.

Hagger, Philip Paul; Consul Montreal since October 2001; born 05/09/50; FCO 1970; Singapore 1973; FCO 1974; Washington 1975; Nicosia 1978; Casablanca 1981; Lagos 1982; Second Secretary FCO 1987; Second Secretary (Commercial) Riyadh 1989; Second Secretary (Consul) Caracas 1992; Second Secretary The Hague 1994; Second Secretary FCO 1995; Second Secretary (Commercial) Perth 1997; m (1) 1971 Janet Mary Milnes (dec'd 1975) (1s 1972); (2) 1976 Julie Elizabeth Eastaugh (diss 1988) (1d 1977); (3) 1990 Linda Mary Parmegiani (2s 1993, 1996).

Haggie, Paul; Counsellor FCO since October 2001; born 30/08/49; Third Secretary FCO 1974; Second later First Secretary Bangkok 1976; FCO 1980; First Secretary (Economic) Islamabad 1982; First Secretary FCO 1986; First Secretary (Chancery) Pretoria 1989; First Secretary FCO 1993; Counsellor on loan to the Cabinet Office 1994; Counsellor FCO 1995; Counsellor Bangkok (ESCAP) 1998; m 1979 Deborah Frazer (1s 1984; 1d 1986).

Hague, John Keir; First Secretary FCO since December 1995; born 26/03/47; CO (later FCO) 1966; Dakar 1970; Kuala Lumpur 1973; Munich 1975; Moscow 1977; FCO 1979; Houston 1983; Second Secretary Islamabad 1985; Second Secretary FCO 1989; Second Secretary (Commercial) Seoul 1992; m 1969 Julie Anne Knight (2d 1972, 1975).

Haig-Thomas, Hugo Alistair Christian; Second Secretary (Economic) Berlin since November 1996; born 21/05/47; FCO 1974; MECAS 1975; Language Training Amman 1976; Sana'a 1977; Vice-Consul Düsseldorf 1980; FCO 1982; Second Secretary on loan to ODA 1982; Second Secretary (Deputy Economic Adviser) BMG Berlin 1986; Second Secretary (Chancery) Copenhagen 1989; Second Secretary (Press and Information) Bonn 1992.

Haigh, Trevor Denton; Lusaka since February 1997; born 07/08/44; FCO 1982; Hong Kong 1985; FCO 1988; Moscow 1990; FCO 1993; m 1977 Freda Mary Porritt.

Hailey, Nicholas James; Private Secretary to the Ambassador Berlin since April 2002; born 27/01/75; Seconded to Ecole Nationale D'Administration, FCO 1997; Paris 1999; Band C4.

Haines, Dr David Michael; First Secretary (Political) Damascus since September 2000; born 06/04/63; FCO 1989; Full-Time Language Training 1991; Full-Time Language Training Cairo 1992; First Secretary (Political) Tunis 1993; Consul (Political) Jerusalem 1994; First Secretary FCO 1996; Band D6; m 1993 Susan Caroline Goodman (1d 1994; 1s 1996).

Haines, Stephen Andrew; Minsk since August 1999; born 12/06/64; FCO 1997; Band A2.

Haley, Anthony Peter; Mexico City since April 1997; born 14/03/59; RAF 1979; FCO 1988; New Delhi 1991; Third Secretary FCO 1994; m 1979 Elaine Cuthbertson (3s 1979, 1982, 1985).

Halksworth, Matthew Kenneth; FCO since June 2002; born 21/02/75; Band A2.

Hall, Andrew Rotely, OBE (1994); FCO since January 1995; born 03/05/50; FCO 1980; First Secretary New Delhi 1984; First Secretary FCO 1987; Deputy Head of Mission and Consul Kathmandu 1991; Senior Principal Research Officer 1996; m 1973 Kathleen Dorothy Wright (2d 1973, 1978).

Hall, Caroline Jane (née Oakley); Second Secretary (Immigration) Moscow since October 1998; born 16/09/64; FCO 1984; Santiago 1987; Floater Duties 1990; SUPL 1992; Karachi 1993; FCO 1996; Band C4; m 1992 James William Hall.

Hall, Harriet; FCO since September 1999; born 24/12/69; FCO 1992; Full-Time Language Training 1994; Full-Time Language Training Peking 1995; Second Secretary (Political) Peking 1996.

Hall, James William David; First Secretary Pristina since April 2002; born 01/03/65; FCO 1987; Third later Second Secretary (Economic) Lusaka 1989; Second Secretary (Commercial) New Delhi 1991; Second Secretary FCO 1994; First Secretary Vienna 1999; ptnr, Jacqueline Ann Loveridge.

Hall, John George; First Secretary (Commercial) Vienna since May 2002; born 07/08/51; FCO 1971; Pretoria/Cape Town 1976; The Hague 1979; Nairobi 1982; FCO 1986; Second Secretary (Aid) Dar es Salaam 1989; Second Secretary FCO 1993; First Secretary Hamburg 1996; Consul (Commercial) Düsseldorf 1998; m (1) 1974 Alison Margaret Eden (2s 1976, 1979); (2) 1990 Margaret Elizabeth Bell (1d 1991).

Hall, Margaret Ann; FCO since December 1991; born 01/04/48; FCO 1975 PRO on CDA at SOAS 1991; m 1974 Govind Anant Walawalkar (dec'd 2001).

Hall, Martin Vivian; Second later First Secretary FCO since February 1991; born 10/11/50; FCO 1970; Singapore 1972; FCO 1974; Paris 1975; FCO 1977; Second Secretary (Chancery) Lagos 1989; Second Secretary (Commercial) Baghdad 1990; Band C5; m 1972 Mary Rawkins (2s 1976, 1980; 1d 1987).

Hall, Mary Eleanor (née Ford); Gibraltar since July 2000; born 26/09/53; FCO 1978; Aden 1979; Geneva (UKMIS) 1980; Paris 1983; Ankara 1985; Warsaw 1988; Belgrade 1990; Lagos 1992; FCO 1995; Cape Town 1997; Band B3; m 1983 Peter Henry Hall.

Hall, Michael Morden; Deputy UK Permanent Representative to the Council of Europe Strasbourg since September 1998; born 26/03/42; Central Office of Information 1969-73; FCO 1973; British Election Commission Rhodesia 1979-80; First Secretary (Chancery/Information) The Hague 1984; First Secretary FCO 1988; Consul (Commercial) Frankfurt 1991; First Secretary FCO 1996; (1s 1974; 1d 1977).

Hall, Rebecca; Second Secretary (Political) Vienna (EU) since June 1999; born 29/09/72; FCO 1994; FCO 1996; Brussels (UKREP) 1997; m 2000 Robert Page.

Hall, Russell David; Santiago since August 2000; born 12/03/64; FCO 1984; Sofia 1996; Band A2; m 1985 Karen Hipkiss (1s 1985; 2d 1988, 1993).

Hall, Simon David; Second Secretary Kabul since April 2002; born 20/03/76; FCO 2000; Band C4.

Hall, Simon Lee; Second later First Secretary FCO since May 2000; born 29/04/63; FCO 1982; Rome 1984; Hanoi 1986; Africa/Middle East Floater 1987; FCO 1990; Seconded to DTI 1991; Ottawa 1993; Kingston 1996; Band C5.

Hall, Thomas Mark; FCO since December 1985; born 15/09/47; HM Inspector of Taxes 1964; Commonwealth Office (later FCO) 1967; Tokyo 1970; FCO 1973; Milan 1979; Algiers 1981; Athens 1984; Band B3.

Hall Hall, Alexandra Mary; SUPL since July 2001; born 01/02/64; FCO 1986; Second Secretary 1989; Full-Time Language Training Bangkok 1989; First Secretary FCO 1993; On loan to the Cabinet Office 1995; Washington 1999.

Hall-Hughes, Rita; On loan to Office of Fair Trading since February 1979; born 31/10/52; FCO 1972; Warsaw 1975; FCO 1976; Band A2.

Hallett, Edward Charles; Senior Principal Research Officer FCO since 1995; born 15/07/47; FCO 1971; Bonn 1972; FCO 1975; PRO (Band D6) 1979; Dublin 1984; FCO 1985; On loan to NIO 1988; FCO 1990; T/D Dublin 1996, 1997, 1998; m 1972 Audrey Marie Tobin.

Halley, James Henry; First Secretary (Commercial) Bucharest since March 2002; born 27/05/53; FCO 1970; The Hague 1973; San José 1976; Vienna 1978; FCO 1980; Third later Second Secretary Seoul 1983; Second Secretary (Consular/Admin) Sana'a 1987; Second Secretary FCO 1989; Consul (Information) Milan 1991; Consul/Management Officer and later Consul (Commercial) Chicago 1995; m 1972 Patricia Catherine Bennett (1d 1977; 1s 1983).

Halliwell, Bernard, MBE (1981); First Secretary (Management)/Consul Budapest since November 1999; born 31/01/45; Ulaanbaatar, Geneva and Beirut 1973-74; FO 1963; Salisbury 1967; Bahrain Residency 1969; Muscat 1970; FCO 1974; FCO 1975; Addis Ababa 1975; Hong Kong 1977; Peking 1978; Second Secretary (Chancery/Information) later (Admin/Cons) Bridgetown 1981; Second Secretary FCO 1985; First Secretary (Management) Bangkok 1988; First Secretary (Trade Promotion) Washington 1992; FCO 1996; Language Training 1999; m 1981 Vanessa Diane Brierley (3s 1984, 1986, 1989).

Hallsworth, Valerie; FCO since November 1988; born 09/11/48; Band A2; m 1999 Yousif Rahhal.

Hallworth, Lisa; Istanbul since May 2000; born 29/06/65; FCO 1987; Madrid 1989; Geneva (UKMIS) 1991; FCO 1994; Band A2.

Halpin, Michael Christopher; Floater Duties since November 2000; born 04/09/75; FCO 1999; Band A2.

Hamblett, Christine; Tel Aviv since February 1995; born 08/12/60; FCO 1990; Rome 1992; Band A2.

Hamill, Brian William; Second Secretary (Investment) Berne since September 2001; born 08/01/63; FCO 1981; Manila 1983; Masirah 1983; Budapest 1988; FCO 1989; Paris 1992; Third Secretary (Commercial) Berlin 1996; Second Secretary (Commercial) Düsseldorf 1998; Band C4; m 1987 Katrina Lacson Puentevella (1d 1991).

Hamilton, Alasdair Alexander; Jakarta since June 1999; born 13/04/71; FCO 1990; Kuala Lumpur 1993; Port Moresby 1997; Freetown 1998; Band B3; m 1998 Erie Alu (1s 1999).

Hamilton, Charles Allan; Deputy Consul General Montreal since May 1997; born 05/12/48; DSAO 1968; Vice-Consul Düsseldorf 1970; Third Secretary Prague 1973; Vice-Consul Phnom Penh 1974; Third later Second Secretary Cairo 1975; FCO 1979; Second Secretary Addis Ababa 1981; DHC and Head of Chancery Port Louis 1984; FCO 1988; Deputy Head of Mission Yaoundé 1992; m Mary Indiana Lazare.

Hamilton, Jacqueline Ann (née Hopkins); Oslo since March 1997; born 10/06/43; Kampala 1983; Amman 1986; SUPL 1989; FCO 1992; Brussels 1994; Band A2; m 1967 William Hamilton (1s 1968; 1d 1971).

Hamilton, John; Calcutta since July 2002; born 28/09/68; FCO 1988; Brussels (UKDEL NATO) 1990; Windhoek 1993; FCO 1996; Third Secretary (Political) Abuja 1998; Band B3; m 1998 Maxine Jones (1d 1999).

Hamilton, Josephine Anne Temple, MBE (1989); FCO since February 1996; born 15/06/45; FCO 1972; Georgetown 1974; FCO 1976; Ankara 1978; FCO 1982; Kingston 1986; FCO 1989; Rome 1993; Band B3.

Hamilton, Roger Patrick; Counsellor FCO since June 2000; born 27/05/48; FCO 1971 (Second Secretary 1976); First Secretary Jakarta 1978; First Secretary Tokyo 1982; FCO 1983; On loan to Hong Kong Government 1984; FCO 1986; First Secretary (Chancery) Copenhagen 1989; Counsellor FCO 1993; Counsellor Santiago 1997; m 1976 Linda Anne Watson.

Hampson, Fiona Patricia; Munich since August 2002; born 13/12/67; FCO 1987; Santiago 1992; SUPL 1997; FCO 2001; Band A2; (1s 1996).

Hancock, Janet Catherine; Deputy Head of Mission Tunis since July 2000; born 05/01/49; FCO 1970; SRO 1975; PRO 1983; First Secretary FCO 1995; Full-Time Language Training 2000; Band D7; m 1973 Roger A Hancock (diss 1980).

Hancock, Michael John; Second Secretary Chancery Brussels (UKREP) since July 1998; born 21/10/62; FCO 1982; Bonn 1984; Belgrade 1987; Islamabad 1989; FCO 1991; Deputy Head of Mission Tbilisi 1995; Vice-Consul Rome 1995; Band C4; m (1) 1983 Elizabeth Alison Ormrod (diss 1999) (2s 1989, 1991, 1d 1987); (2) 1999 Rusudan Gachechiladze (2s 1992, 2001).

Hancock, Nicola Jane; FCO since September 1995; born 30/07/66; FCO 1989; Rome 1992; Band B3; m 1993 Mark Westwood.

Hancon, John Anthony; FCO since July 1991; born 05/01/48; GPO 1965; FCO 1969; Kuala Lumpur 1971; FCO 1973; Paris 1976; FCO 1978; Sofia 1982; FCO 1984; Nicosia 1988; Band C4; m 1970 Anne Lesley Hawke (1d 1975; 1s 1980).

Hand, Graham Stewart; HM Ambassador Algiers since July 2002; born 03/11/48; HM Forces 1967-80; FCO 1980; Second later First Secretary Dakar 1982; First Secretary FCO 1984; First Secretary and Head of Chancery Helsinki 1987; Language Training 1987; Counsellor FCO 1992; Deputy High Commissioner Lagos 1994; on loan to the Royal College of Defence Studies 1997; Ambassador Bosnia Herzegovina 1998; m 1973 Anne Mary Seton Campbell (1s 1979; 1d 1984).

Hand, Jessica Mary (née Pearce); First Secretary FCO since March 1999; born 01/09/57; FCO 1985; Second Secretary (Chancery) Dakar 1987; First Secretary FCO 1990; Full-Time Language Training 1994; HM Ambassador Minsk 1996; m 1999 Robert Wayne Hand.

Handley, Timothy Sean; FCO since October 1994; born 08/02/51; HCS 1969; FCO 1971; Abu Dhabi 1973; Stockholm 1976; Warsaw 1979; FCO 1981; Georgetown 1985; FCO 1986; Düsseldorf 1988; Tel Aviv 1991; Band B3; m 1985 Julie Anne Russell (1s 1986; 1d 1989).

Handyside, Nancy Patricia; Brussels (UKREP) since May 1999; born 27/08/51; Islamabad 1984; Kampala 1988; Khartoum 1991; Sana'a 1995; Bucharest 1998; Band A2.

Hannah, Craig John; FCO since November 1999; born 02/06/63; Department of Employment 1980; FCO 1983; Accra 1984; Sofia 1987; FCO 1990; Kuala Lumpur 1994; Vienna 1998; Band B3.

Hannah, Jane Patricia; LA/Caribbean Floater Duties since March 1995; born 23/09/70; FCO 1989; Athens 1991; Band A2.

Hans, Ravinder; Buenos Aires since November 1997; born 17/03/73; FCO 1996; Band A2.

Hansen, Caroline (née Thearle); SUPL since October 1999; born 17/02/66; FCO 1984; Copenhagen 1987; SUPL 1990; Bangkok 1992; SUPL 1995; Dhaka 1996; Band B3; m 1989 Jakob Hansen.

Hansen, Diane (née Davies); First Secretary (Management) Kuala Lumpur since July 2000; born 23/07/45; Lagos 1974; FCO 1974; Athens 1977; FCO 1980; Copenhagen 1987; Port Moresby 1991; FCO 1993; Wellington 1996; Full-Time Language Training 1999; Band C5; m 1988 Jan B Hansen.

Hanshaw, Danielle May; FCO since 2001; born 11/02/71; MOD 1991-98; FCO 1998; Jakarta 2001; Band A2.

Hanson, Timothy Myles; First Secretary (Commercial) Sarajevo since June 2001; born 27/06/65; FCO 1984; Third Secretary (Chancery) Muscat 1987; Third Secretary (Aid) New Delhi 1991; Second Secretary FCO 1994; Second Secretary (Commercial) Kuala Lumpur 1997.

Harborne, Peter Gale; High Commissioner Port of Spain since 1999; born 29/06/45; DHSS 1966; FCO 1972; Ottawa 1974; Mexico City 1975; Resigned 1979; Reinstated 1981; First Secretary FCO 1981; First Secretary and Head of Chancery Helsinki 1983; Counsellor and Head of Chancery Budapest 1988; FCO Overseas Inspectorate 1991-94; HM Ambassador Bratislava 1995-98; m 1976 Tessa Elizabeth Henri (2s 1980, 1981).

Hardie, Alison; Lima since June 2002; born 31/03/65; FCO 1988; Washington 1990; FCO 1992; Canberra 1994; FCO 1997; Floater Duties 1998; Yaoundé 2000; Band A2.

Hardman, Peter James William; T/D Shanghai since February 2000; born 28/10/56; FCO 1974; SE Asia Floater 1978; Bombay 1979; Perth 1983; Bangkok 1986; Second Secretary on loan to ODA 1988; Language Training 1990; Second Secretary Sofia 1991; First Secretary (Commercial) Bangkok 1996; Band C5; m 1982 Joelle Helene Schneider (1d 1984).

Hardy, Richard Martin; Singapore since July 2001; born 07/10/50; FCO 1967; Brussels 1976; FCO 1978; Buenos Aires 1979; FCO 1982; Bridgetown 1986; Second Secretary FCO 1989; Paris 1993; FCO 1997; Band C5; m (1) 1975

Amanda Smith (diss 1981); (2) 1982 Astrid Posse (diss 1996); (3) 2001 Alison Jane Fossey.

Hare, Paul Webster, LVO (1985); HM Ambassador Havana since July 2001; born 20/07/51; FCO 1978; Second Secretary/PS to HMA Brussels (UKREP) 1979; First Secretary Lisbon 1981; Head of Chancery 1983; FCO 1985; Consul (Investment) and Deputy Director Investment USA BTIO New York 1988; Deputy Head of Mission and later Counsellor (Commercial/Economic) Caracas 1994; Counsellor FCO 1997; m 1978 Lynda Carol Henderson (3d 1979, 1982, 1994; 3s 1984, 1988, 1991).

Hargreaves, Elaine; FCO since July 1998; born 29/10/71; FCO 1991; Harare 1995; Band B3.

Hargreaves, Roger John; First Secretary FCO since September 1999; born 08/12/50; FCO 1968; Hong Kong 1973; FCO 1975; Sana'a 1976; FCO 1977; Second Secretary Hong Kong 1985; Second later First Secretary FCO 1990; First Secretary (Political) Wellington 1996; Band C5; m Andrea Margaret Kent (1s 1989; 1d 1992).

Harkin, Simon David; First Secretary (PPA) Berne since September 2001; born 04/10/58; FCO 1989; New York (UKMIS) 1990; FCO 1991; Second Secretary (Political) Harare 1992; First Secretary FCO 1996; Full-Time Language Training 2000.

Harland, Jeremy; Washington since September 1999; born 08/04/63; FCO 1983; Moscow 1988; Bridgetown 1992; FCO 1992; FCO 1996; Band C4.

Harle, Roger William; FCO since August 1988; born 04/02/59; FCO 1982; Darwin 1986; Band C4.

Harmer, Roger William; Geneva (Joint Management Office) since July 1998; born 05/01/53; FCO 1972; Bucharest 1974; La Paz 1976; Maseru 1978; FCO 1980; Third Secretary Muscat 1983; Ottawa 1986; FCO 1989; Riga 1992; Second Secretary FCO 1993; m 1976 Cristobalina López Munoz (1d 1977).

Harper, Maurice Bertrand; HM Consul Bucharest since October 1996; born 03/12/46; FCO 1974; Bangkok 1976; East Berlin 1980; FCO 1981; Bombay 1984; Port Louis 1988; Second Secretary FCO 1993; m (1) 1977 Susan Hayward (1s 1979); m (2) 1986 Veera Printer (1d 1987).

Harper, Monica Celia; Consul-General Lille since September 1998; born 18/08/44; FCO 1967; SEATO (Bangkok) 1969; ENA Paris 1972; BMG Berlin 1974; Second Secretary Bonn 1977; FCO 1979; Second Secretary Mexico City 1982; First Secretary Brussels (UKDEL NATO) 1984; First Secretary FCO 1989; Deputy Head of Mission Luxembourg 1994.

Harries, David George, MBE (1990), OBE (1998); Second Secretary (Consular) BCG New York since October 2001; born 10/03/60; FCO 1980; BGWRS Darwin 1982; FCO 1984; Islamabad 1986; Beirut 1988; FCO 1988; FCO

1991; Third Secretary (Consular/Management) Freetown 1993; Third Secretary (Commercial/Development) Maputo 1998; Band C4; m 1993 Carol Chammas (1d 2002).

Harrington, Clare Elizabeth; FCO since August 1980; born 30/08/61; Band A2.

Harrington, Peter; Second Secretary (Commercial) Doha since August 2001; born 29/09/62; FCO 1981; Baghdad 1984; Stockholm 1988; Georgetown 1990; FCO 1994; On loan to DTI 1995; Madras 1997; Band C4; m (1) 1984 Angela Elizabeth Dent (diss); (2) 1993 Veronica Ann Clementson (1s 1993; 1d 1995).

Harris, Joan; FCO since July 1995; born 27/12/49; FCO 1975; Dakar 1976; Budapest 1978; Oslo 1981; FCO 1983; Paris 1987; FCO 1990; Third Secretary (Science and Technology) Moscow 1992; Band B3.

Harris, Karina Lynn; World Wide Floater Duties since July 2001; born 28/02/62; FCO 1983; Cairo 1984; Tokyo 1988; FCO 1990; Vienna (UKMIS) 1993; Rabat 1997; T/D Jerusalem 2000; Band A2.

Harris, Kay; Pristina since January 2002; born 25/11/72; FCO 1992; Islamabad 1998; Band B3.

Harris, Martin Fergus; On loan to DfID as First Secretary (KHF), Moscow, since November 1999; born 17/05/69; FCO 1991; (CFE) UKDEL Vienna 1992; FCO 1997; Full-Time Language Training 1998; m 1993 Linda Margaret Maclachlan (1d 2001).

Harris, Peter Harold Charles; Counsellor Warsaw since May 1998; born 25/01/50; Second later First Secretary (Social and Agriculture) Lisbon 1981; FCO 1981; FCO 1984; First Secretary Moscow 1985; FCO 1988; First Secretary Santiago 1990; FCO 1993; m 1976 Maria Judith Ocazionez (4s 1980, 1982, 1984, 1993).

Harris, Thomas George, CMG (1995); Consul-General New York and Director-General Trade & Investment USA since June 1999; born 06/02/45; BOT 1966; Third Secretary Tokyo 1969; DOT 1971; Cabinet Office 1976; DTI 1979; Counsellor (Commercial) Washington 1983; Counsellor and Head of Chancery Lagos 1988; Deputy High Commissioner 1990; Counsellor FCO and Commissioner British Indian Ocean Territories 1991; HM Ambassador Seoul 1994; m 1967 Mei-Ling (3s 1969, 1970, 1984).

Harrison, Anthony Julian; Second Secretary FCO since May 1981; born 19/03/53; FCO 1975; Pretoria 1978; Band C4; m 1978 Sharon Readman (1d 1986; 1s 1990).

Harrison, Caroline Margaret; First Secretary FCO since August 1999; born 08/09/66; FCO 1989; First Secretary Helsinki 1997; Band C5.

Harrison, Charles Dale; Second Secretary (Management) Brussels (UKREP) since July 1998; born 23/02/55; MOD 1971; FCO 1976; Accra 1978; Mbabane 1982; FCO 1985; Rome 1988;

Islamabad 1991; FCO 1994; Band C4; m 1978
Lorraine Josie Richards (1d 1987; 1s 1990).

Harrison, Guy Andrew; First Secretary
(Commercial) Brussels since June 2002; born
30/05/64; FCO 1986; Language Training and later
Third Secretary (Political) Seoul 1987; Munich
1992; Hanoi 1993; FCO 1995; Second Secretary
(Economic) Seoul 1998; Band C4; m 1996 Ann
Van Dyck (1d 1999).

Harrison, Mark Simon; Auckland since August
2001; born 08/07/68; FCO 1989; Montevideo
1991; SUPL 1992; Jedda 1994; Nairobi 1996;
Abidjan 2000; Band C4; m 1992 Roxane Miller
(1s 2000).

Harrison, Paula Leslie; FCO since September
2000; born 05/09/78; Band C4.

Harrison, Robert James; FCO since April 2002;
born 10/09/76; Band C4; ptnr, Andrea Robinson.

Harrison, Stephen Thomas, MBE (2001); On
attachment to Buckingham Palace since June
2001; born 14/08/64; FCO 1986; Language
Training SOAS 1987; Language Training Cairo
1988; Third Secretary (Chancery) Bahrain 1989;
Full-Time Language Training (Russian) 1993;
Moscow 1994; HM Consul-General Ekaterinburg
1998; FCO 2000; Band D6; m 1995 Philippa
Capper (1d 1993; 1s 1998).

Harrison, Victoria Jane; Second Secretary
(Political) Helsinki since August 2000; born
31/10/74; FCO 1997; Full-Time Language
Training 1999; Band C4.

Harrison, William Alistair, CVO (1996);
Counsellor and Head of Chancery New York
(UKMIS) since February 2000; born 14/11/54;
FCO 1977; Third later Second Secretary Warsaw
1979; Second later First Secretary FCO 1982;
Private Secretary to the Parliamentary Under
Secretary 1984; First Secretary New York
(UKMIS) 1987; First Secretary FCO 1992; Deputy
Head of Mission Warsaw 1995; On loan to
European Commission as Foreign Policy Adviser
1998; m (1) 1981 Thérésa Mary Morrison (diss
1991); (2) 1996 Sarah Judith Wood (1d 1999).

Harrocks, Nicholas James Laurent; SUPL since
September 2002; born 16/04/73; FCO 1996;
(Economic Relations Dept.); Full-Time Language
Training 1998; Second Secretary (Political)
Riyadh 1999.

Harrod, Jean (née Geary); First Secretary
(Political) Canberra since October 2000; born
28/04/54; FCO 1972; Geneva (CSCE) 1973; East
Berlin 1975; Port Louis 1977; Peking 1980; SUPL
1983; FCO 1986; Third later Second Secretary
(Chancery) Brussels (UKREP) 1992; Second
Secretary and Consul Jakarta 1994; FCO 1997; m
1974 Jeffrey Harrod.

Harrod, Jeffrey; First Secretary (External Affairs)
Canberra since October 2000; born 01/04/54; FCO
1970; Geneva (CSCE) 1973; East Berlin 1975;
Port Louis 1977; Vice-Consul (Commercial) and

later Second Secretary Peking 1980; Consul
(Commercial) Shanghai 1984; Second later First
Secretary FCO 1986; First Secretary (Commercial)
Brussels (UKREP) 1990; First Secretary
(Political/Economic) Jakarta 1994; m 1974 Jean
Geary.

Harrower, Hazel; Tehran since July 1997; born
18/12/64; FCO 1985; Bucharest 1988; Seoul 1989;
FCO 1994; Band B3.

Harrup, Christine Mary; Kingston since
December 2000; born 18/04/49; Baghdad 1974;
FCO 1974; Lagos 1977; FCO 1978; Dublin 1981;
FCO 1985; Addis Ababa 1987; Colombo 1992;
Budapest 1994; Kiev 1999; Band B3.

Harsent, Susan Elizabeth; Shanghai since April
1998; born 16/06/49; FCO 1970; Bonn 1972; FCO
1975; Suva 1976; FCO 1978; Tel Aviv 1982; FCO
1984; Brussels (UKREP) 1989; Band B3.

Harston, Stewart Ian; FCO since January 1994;
born 03/11/63; Singapore 1990; Band C4; m (1)
1990 Marianne Stallard (diss); (2) 1994 BG
Carvello (2s 1995, 1998).

Hart, Graham Donald; New Delhi since March
1994; born 25/10/46; FCO 1975; Tokyo 1977;
Monrovia 1982; FCO 1985; JMO New York 1988;
FCO 1992; Band B3.

Hart, Jeremy Michael; First Secretary (Political)
Valletta since September 2002; born 24/02/57;
FCO 1975; Paris 1978; FCO 1980; Second
Secretary (Vice-Consul) Athens 1986; First
Secretary FCO 1990; Band C5; m (1) 1979 Alison
Jane Morrell (diss 1993) (1d 1984); (2) 1995
Penelope Helen Margaret Smyth (2d 1996, 1999).

Hart, Roger Dudley, CMG (1998); HM
Ambassador Lima since September 1999; born
29/12/43; Third Secretary FO 1965; Third later
Second Secretary Berlin 1967; Bahrain 1970;
Second later First Secretary FCO 1972; First
Secretary (Aid) Nairobi 1975; First Secretary
Lisbon 1978; First Secretary FCO 1983; CDA at
RCDS 1985; Consul-General Rio de Janeiro 1986;
Deputy Head of Mission Mexico City 1990;
Counsellor FCO 1993; HM Ambassador Luanda
1995; m 1968 Maria de los Angeles de Santiago
Jimnez (2s 1969, 1970).

Hart, Simon Charles; Bandar Seri Begawan since
June 2000; born 13/12/57; FCO 1975; Brussels
1978; Tehran 1981; LA Floater 1983; Bogotá
1985; FCO 1989; Third Secretary Panama City
1993; Brasilia 1997; Band B3; m 1987 Amparo
Meza (2s 1993, 1995; 1d 1996).

Harte, Josephine Moira (née Campbell); Brussels
since February 2000; born 17/11/67; FCO 1988;
Prague 1990; FCO 1992; Full-Time Language
Training 1994; Vice-Consul Berlin 1995; SUPL
1999; Band B3; m 1996 Derek Thomas Harte.

Hartley, James Leslie; Conakry since April 2002;
born 18/08/49; St Helena 1975; FCO 1977;
Lusaka 1978; FCO 1980; LA Floater 1983;
Khartoum 1985; Second Secretary and Head of

Chancery Ulaanbaatar 1989; Second Secretary FCO 1992; Deputy Head of Mission Phnom Penh 1994; First Secretary and Consul Kuwait 1997; Deputy Head of Mission Algiers 1999; Band C5; m 1984 Ann Lesley Oakley.

Harvey, Christopher Paul Duncan; Deputy High Commissioner Nairobi since April 2000; born 21/07/56; FCO 1986; (Second Secretary 1986); Second Secretary Suva 1988; First Secretary (Chancery) Brussels 1990; First Secretary FCO 1995; UK Special Representative for Peace in Sierra Leone 1999; m 1989 Anasaini Vesinawa Kamakorewa (1 step d 1987; 1 step s 1988).

Harvey, David; FCO since October 2001; born 10/11/57; FCO 1977; Dublin 1980; Kinshasa 1982; East Berlin 1986; FCO 1988; Guatemala City 1992; Second Secretary (WTO) Geneva (UKMIS) 1997; m 1983 Bernadette Louise McMahon (1s 1987; 1d 1990).

Harvey, Lindsay; Washington since September 2001; born 31/03/59; FCO 1984; Tehran 1986; Budapest 1987; Bridgetown 1988; SUPL 1993; FCO 1993; Grand Cayman 1997; Band B3.

Haslam, Christopher Peter de Landre; Deputy High Commissioner Suva and HM Ambassador (non resident) to Micronesia, Palau and Marshall Islands since January 2000; born 22/03/43; Admiralty and Ministry of Defence (Navy) 1960; DSAO 1966; Jakarta 1969; Sofia 1973; FCO 1974; Canberra 1978; Lagos 1981; Second Secretary FCO 1986; First Secretary (Commercial) Copenhagen 1989; First Secretary FCO 1993; First Secretary (Commercial) Colombo 1996; Band D6; m 1969 Lana Whitley (2s 1971, 1973).

Haslem, Michelle; Second Secretary (Political) Kuala Lumpur since September 2001; born 18/02/74; FCO 1999; Band C4.

Haswell, Charles Chetwynd Douglas; On loan to British Invisibles since June 1998; born 18/02/56; FCO 1979; Language Training Hong Kong 1981; Peking 1982; Third later Second Secretary (Chancery) Ottawa 1986; Second later First Secretary FCO 1989; First Secretary (Political) Vienna (UKDEL) 1994; First Secretary FCO 1996; m 1991 Sarah Caroline Folkes (1s 1994; 1d 1995).

Hatfield, Samuel Andrew Roland; FCO since November 2000; born 15/01/63; FCO 1992; First Secretary (Political) Lagos 1995; First Secretary FCO 1996; SUPL 1999; Band D6; m 1995 Rachel Althea Rodney Pollaers (3d 1995, 1997, 2000).

Hatfull, Martin Alan; Counsellor (Economic and Commercial) Rome since July 1998; born 07/06/57; FCO 1980; Language Training 1982; Second later First Secretary Tokyo 1983; First Secretary FCO 1987; First Secretary Brussels (UKREP) 1991; First Secretary later Counsellor FCO 1995; m 1980 Phyllis Morshead (2s 1984, 1987).

Haveron, Monica; Tel Aviv since November 2001; born 29/06/67; FCO 1987; Nicosia 1990; FCO

1993; Valletta 1995; FCO 1998; World Wide Floater 2000; Band A2.

Hawkes, Julie Anne (née Carr); SUPL since November 1996; born 05/07/64; FCO 1990; Budapest 1992; FCO 1996; Band A2; m 1996 Edward Clifford Hawkes.

Hawkins, Carl McArthur; FCO since August 2001; born 25/09/50; FCO 1967; HCS 1974; FCO 1977; Third Secretary Bangkok 1989; Second Secretary FCO 1992; First Secretary Singapore 1998; m 1987 Yuko Shibuya (1d 1988).

Hawkins, John Mark; Counsellor (Commercial) Madrid and Director of Trade and Investment Promotion for Spain since March 2000; born 30/04/60; FCO 1982; Third later Second Secretary (Chancery) Pretoria/Cape Town 1984; First Secretary FCO 1989; First Secretary (Commercial) New Delhi 1993; First Secretary later Counsellor FCO 1997; m 1991 Rosemarie Anne Kleynhans (2s 1993, 1996).

Hay, Barbara Logan, CMG (1998), MBE (1991); Consul-General St Petersburg since August 2000; born 20/01/53; FCO 1971; Language Training 1974; Moscow 1975; Johannesburg 1978; Second Secretary FCO 1980; Vice-Consul (Commercial) Montreal 1985; First Secretary (Information) Moscow 1988; HM Consul-General St Petersburg 1991; First Secretary FCO 1992; Language Training 1994; HM Ambassador Tashkent and non-resident Dushanbe 1995; Language Training 1999.

Hay, Charles John, MVO (1996); First Secretary (Economic/Finance) Brussels (UKREP) since November 1999; born 22/09/65; HM Forces (Army) 1987-93; FCO 1993; Second Secretary (Political/Information) Prague 1995; First Secretary FCO 1998; Band D6; m (1) 1992 Caroline Jane Windsor (diss 1997); (2) 2001 Pascale Sutherland.

Hay-Campbell, (Thomas) Ian, LVO (1994); Deputy Head of Mission Oslo since September 2001; born 19/05/45; BBC 1972-84; First Secretary FCO 1984; First Secretary Head of Chancery and Consul Kinshasa 1987; First Secretary FCO 1990; Full-Time Language Training 1993; First Secretary (Press and Public Affairs Unit) Moscow 1994; Deputy High Commissioner Harare 1998; Full-Time Language Training 2001; m 1970 Margaret Lorraine Hoadley (4s 1973, 1974, 1977, 1979).

Haydon, Joanna Mary; FCO since October 1999; born 14/03/69; FCO 1992; Vice-Consul Bangkok 1995; Full-Time Language Training Bangkok 1995; Band B3; m 1998 Peter L Spoor.

Hayes, Julie Patricia; SUPL since August 2001; born 22/07/59; FCO 1988; Hanoi 1991; FCO 1993; Harare 1996; FCO 1999; Band B3.

Haywood, Ian; Lisbon since February 1998; born 02/10/59; FCO 1978; Kampala 1981; Düsseldorf 1985; FCO 1989; Peking 1994; Full-Time

Language Training 1997; m (1) 1984 Angela Jane
Kennedy (diss 1988); (2) 1991 June Sandra Tyler.

Haywood, Nigel Robert; Assistant Director,
Personnel FCO since June 2000; born 17/03/55;
HM Forces (Army) 1977-80; FCO 1983; Second
later First Secretary Budapest 1985; First
Secretary FCO 1989; Deputy Consul-General
Johannesburg 1992; Counsellor and Deputy Head
of Delegation UKDEL OSCE Vienna 1996; m
1979 Mary Louise Smith (3s 1984, 1985, 1991).

Hazlewood, Roger Derek; First Secretary
(Management) Harare since January 2001; born
10/01/50; FCO 1968; Georgetown 1971; Bonn
1975; Paris 1977; FCO 1980; Cairo 1983; Brussels
(UKREP) 1987; FCO 1990; Second Secretary
1991; Full-Time Language Training 1993; Second
Secretary (Commercial) Warsaw 1994; Second
Secretary (Management) Dhaka 1997; m 1971
Yvonne Helen Betty Johnston McPhee (3s 1973,
1976, 1978).

Head, Ian; FCO since April 1993; born 21/10/46;
Home Civil Service 1987; Bonn 1990; Band C4;
m 1992 S. Bigonesse-Caron

Healy, Denis Terence; Consul-General Casablanca
since February 2002; born 18/11/43; FO 1963;
DSAO 1965; Belgrade 1967; FCO 1970; Port of
Spain 1974; Second Secretary 1975; Vice-Consul
Douala 1976; FCO 1979; Second Secretary
(Chancery/Aid) Bridgetown 1983; First Secretary
(Commercial) Brussels (UKREP) 1985; First
Secretary FCO 1990; First Secretary (Commercial)
Ankara 1991; First Secretary FCO 1996; First
Secretary (Commercial) Tokyo 2000.

Healy, Dora Claire Sarah; First Secretary
(Political) Nairobi since September 1995; born
30/08/52; Principal Research Officer FCO 1982;
Language Training 1986; Second later First
Secretary (Chancery/Information) Addis Ababa
1987; FCO 1991; m 1983 Nicholas Guttmann (2d
1976, 1983; 1s 1985).

Healy, Martin Frederick; FCO since October
2000; born 21/10/55; FCO 1972; Moscow 1978;
FCO 1979; Third Secretary Pretoria 1984; FCO
1987; Hong Kong 1990; Second Secretary FCO
1993; Second Secretary Nairobi 1997; m 1977
Jane Catherine Stacey (2d 1981, 1983).

Hearn, Natalie Louise; ECO/VC Düsseldorf since
September 1998; born 13/07/72; FCO 1992;
Peking 1995; Band B3.

Heaslip, Lisanne Marie; Tokyo since September
2000; born 16/01/69; FCO 1988; Belgrade 1998;
FCO 1999; Band B3.

Heath, Gillian Carol; Suva since April 2001; born
21/08/45; FCO 1969; Islamabad 1970; Kampala
1971; San Salvador 1973; Panama 1973; Kuala
Lumpur 1975; Brunei 1976; FCO 1978; Havana
1980; Dar es Salaam 1981; Singapore 1984;
Washington 1988; FCO 1989; Algiers 1990; FCO
1994; Cairo 1996; T/D Canberra 2000; Band B3.

Heatly, Charles Robert; Second Secretary
(Political/Economic) Amman since June 1997;
born 07/08/70; FCO 1993; Full-Time Language
Training Cairo 1995.

Hebden, Ian Mark; Washington since January
2001; born 25/03/60; Royal Navy 1976-1987;
FCO 1987; Bonn 1990; Harare 1992; FCO 1996;
Brussels (UKREP) 1997; Band A2; (1d 2002).

Heffer, John William Charles; First Secretary
(Management) Tripoli since June 2000; born
31/07/52; FCO 1971; Kampala 1973; FCO 1974;
Victoria 1975; Bogotá 1977; Peking 1980; FCO
1981; Warsaw 1983; FCO 1984; Valletta 1988;
Pretoria 1991; FCO 1994; (Second Secretary
1995); Band C4; m 1975 Lynne Ida Brown (2s
1977, 1980).

Hefford, Brian; FCO since October 1997; born
10/08/48; FCO 1969; Karachi 1972; Paris 1976;
FCO 1979; Islamabad 1983; FCO 1986; Colombo
1989; Second Secretary Bangkok 1994; m 1971
Susan Mary Gorman (1s 1975 (dec'd 1991)).

Heigl, Peter Richard; High Commissioner Nassau
since July 1999; born 21/02/43; First Secretary
(Commercial) Riyadh 1984 later Consul
(Commercial) Jedda; On secondment to FCO as
Second Secretary (Commercial) Kuala Lumpur
1974; Ministry of Power 1963; Ministry of
Technology 1968; DTI 1971; Accra 1975; First
Secretary FCO 1981; First Secretary FCO 1989;
First Secretary, Consul-General and Deputy Head
of Mission Khartoum 1991; First Secretary,
Deputy Head of Mission Kathmandu 1994;
Language Training 1994; m 1965 Sally Lupton (3s
1971, 1973, 1977; 1d 1982).

Helke, Jill Beynon (née Barker-Harland); SUPL
since April 1999; born 10/04/56; FCO 1978;
Language Training Hong Kong 1981; Peking
1983; Second Secretary New York (UKMIS) 1986;
SUPL 1990; First Secretary FCO 1990; New York
(UKMIS) 1992; Geneva (UKMIS UN) 1993;
SUPL 1993; m 1987 Heinz Michael Rudolf
Juergen Helke (1s 1988; 1d 1990).

Hellen, Gary David; Nicosia since May 1999;
born 24/06/70; FCO 1990; Zagreb (ECMIS) 1992;
FCO 1993; Dhaka 1995; Band A2.

Helmer, Victoria Jane; Second Secretary
(Political) Amman since October 2001; born
19/10/75; FCO 1998; Full-Time Language
Training 1999; Full-Time Language Training Cairo
2000; Band C4.

Hemingway, Janette (née Hunt); Abidjan since
February 1997; born 17/08/59; FCO 1984; Vienna
(UKDEL) 1986; FCO 1990; Dhaka 1993; Band
B3; m 1988 William Piers Hemingway.

Hemingway, William Piers; SUPL since May
1999; born 10/11/60; FCO 1979; Kuala Lumpur
1981; Luanda 1985; Vienna 1987; Dhaka 1993;
Abidjan 1997; Band B3; m 1988 Janette Hunt.

Hemmings, Kathryn Louise; SUPL since
November 1999; born 20/08/70; FCO 1991; New

York (UKMIS) 1993; FCO 1996; Nairobi 1999; Band A2.

Henderson, Andrew David Forbes; Consul-General Jedda since April 2000; born 12/07/52; FCO 1971; Latin America Floater 1975; Rio de Janeiro 1977; Second Secretary (Chancery) Oslo 1980; APS/Minister of State FCO 1985; Consul New York (CG) 1987; First Secretary Washington 1988; Consul and Deputy Head of Mission Luanda 1992; Cairo 1994; Head of Parliamentary Relations Department FCO 1998; m 1987 Julia Margaret King (2d 1988, 1990).

Henderson, Christopher George; Third Secretary FCO since 1999; born 23/04/66; Metropolitan Police Office (Civil Staff) 1987; FCO 1990; Lilongwe 1993; FCO 1996; BTCO Taipei 1997; Jedda 1997; Bridgetown 1997; Amman 1997; Madras 1997; St Petersburg 1997; Kinshasa 1998; Banjul 1998; Accra 1998; Bahrain 1998; Lagos 1998; Pristina 1999; Naples 1999; Band B3.

Henderson, Lesley; SUPL since October 2000; born 21/11/67; FCO 1987; Paris 1989; FCO 1991; Turks and Caicos Islands 1993; FCO 1996; Floater Duties 1998; Band A2.

Henderson, Matthew Magnus Murray; First Secretary FCO since March 1996; born 19/07/60; Second Secretary FCO 1986; Second later First Secretary BTC Hong Kong 1988; First Secretary FCO 1990; First Secretary (External/Press) Peking 1992; Band D6.

Henderson, William Robert, LVO (1988); First Secretary FCO since February 1996; born 07/11/47; DSAO later FCO 1965; Moscow 1970; Sana'a 1971; Lima 1972; Rio de Janeiro 1973; FCO 1976; MECAS 1977; Dubai 1978; (Second Secretary 1980); FCO 1983; First Secretary (Information) Madrid 1985; First Secretary FCO 1989; Deputy Head of Mission Abu Dhabi 1992; m 1969 Carol Mary Smith (1d 1973; 1s 1976).

Hendry, Carol Anne Walls; FCO since October 2002; born 07/12/66; FCO 1985; Brussels (UKREP) 1987; Tokyo 1990; World Wide Floater Duties 1993; FCO 1995; On loan to the DTI 1999; FCO 2001; SUPL 2002; Band C4; ptnr, Roy Ireland (1s 2002).

Hendry, Ian Duncan, CMG (1996); Deputy Legal Adviser FCO since October 1999; born 02/04/48; Assistant Legal Adviser FCO 1971; First Secretary (Legal Adviser) BMG Berlin 1982; Assistant Legal Adviser, later Legal Counsellor FCO 1986; Counsellor (Legal Adviser) Brussels (UKREP) 1991; Legal Counsellor FCO 1995; m (1) 1973 Elizabeth Anne Southall (1d 1975; 1s 1977); (2) 1991 Sally Annabel Hill.

Hennessy, Alexandra Mary (née Wintour); T/D The Hague since May 2000; born 25/03/66; Office of Fair Trading 1985; FCO 1987; New York (UKMIS) 1988; Vienna 1991; FCO 1995; SUPL 1996; Band A2; m 1993 Anthony John Hennessy (1d 1996).

Hennessy, Anthony John; First Secretary (Commercial) The Hague since June 2000; born 01/02/55; FCO 1980; Singapore 1981; FCO 1985; Second Secretary (Commercial) Riyadh 1987; Second Secretary (UN/UNIDO) Vienna (UKMIS) 1991; First Secretary FCO 1995; Band C5; m 1993 Alexandra Mary Wintour (1d 1996).

Henry, Elaine Monica; FCO since April 2001; born 11/09/69; FCO 1989; New Delhi 1993; Maputo 1997; FCO 1999; T/D La Paz 2000; Band B3; (1d 1991).

Hentley, Michael Joseph; First Secretary and Consul Seoul since May 1999; born 13/07/46; CRO 1964; DSAO 1965; Benghazi 1969; Moscow 1972; Lagos 1973; Kaduna 1976; FCO 1978; Second Secretary (Commercial) Port of Spain 1982; Second Secretary FCO 1985; First Secretary (COCOM) Paris 1987; Deputy Head of Mission Dakar 1992; First Secretary FCO 1995; m 1969 Janice Paterson (1s 1971; 2d 1973, 1979).

Herbert, David; Deputy Head of Mission Luxembourg since June 1998; born 13/07/47; CO 1966; Algiers 1969; Baghdad 1970; Tananarivo 1971; FCO 1974; Second Secretary Luxembourg 1977; Second Secretary (Commercial) Prague 1981; First Secretary FCO 1985; Consul (Commercial) Montreal 1988; First Secretary (Political/Economic) Abuja 1993; First Secretary FCO 1995; m 1970 Maureen Violet Edmundson (2d 1976, 1978).

Herd, Theresa Ann; Deputy Head of Mission Kinshasa since August 1999; born 24/10/54; FCO 1972; Resigned 1974; Reinstated 1980; Lilongwe 1981; FCO 1984; Pretoria 1986; Cape Town 1987; LA/Caribbean Floater 1989; FCO 1991; Full-Time Language Training 1994; Luanda 1995; Second Secretary FCO 1996; Full-Time Language Training 1999; Band C4.

Herridge, Michael Eric James; Deputy High Commissioner Madras since February 1999; born 23/09/46; DSAO 1966; FCO 1968; Prague 1969; Düsseldorf 1969; Nairobi 1972; FCO 1975; Lagos 1979; Second later First Secretary New York (UKMIS) 1982; First Secretary FCO 1986; First Secretary (Management) Madrid 1990; FCO 1995; m 1968 Margaret Elizabeth Bramble (1d 1971).

Herring, Julie Ann; SUPL since August 1994; born 10/04/65; FCO 1984; Helsinki 1987; FCO 1989; SUPL 1993; Cairo 1994; Band B3.

Heseltine, Lavinia Pauline; Lagos since April 2002; FCO 1974; Brussels 1975; Moscow 1979; Canberra 1981; Khartoum 1984; Lagos 1988; Dhaka 1992; SUPL 1995; FCO 1998; Peking 2000; Band B3; m 1990 Barry Heseltine.

Heseltine, Robert Andrew; ECO Casablanca since December 2002; born 18/11/73; MAFF 1996-97; FCO 1997; St Petersburg 2000; Full-Time Language Training (French) 2002; Band B3.

Hetherington, Martin Duncan; T/D Second Secretary (Political) Islamabad since February 2002; born 22/02/74; DETR 1997; FCO 1998.

Hewer, Susan Jane; Floater Duties since April 2001; born 18/09/61; FCO 1980; Washington 1982; New Delhi 1985; FCO 1985; Strasbourg (UKDEL) 1989; Kuwait 1991; FCO 1995; New York (UKMIS) 1997; Band B3.

Hewitt, Gavin Wallace, CMG (1995); HM Ambassador Brussels since February 2001; born 19/10/44; Ministry of Transport 1967; On secondment as Third later Second Secretary from Ministry of Transport (later Department of the Environment) to Brussels (EEC) 1970; FCO 1972; First Secretary Canberra 1973; First Secretary FCO 1978; First Secretary and Head of Chancery Belgrade 1981; Counsellor attached to the BBC (for Review of External Services) 1984; Counsellor on loan to the HCS 1984; Deputy Permanent Representative (Head of Chancery) Geneva (UKMIS) 1987; Counsellor FCO 1992; HM Ambassador Zagreb 1994; HM Ambassador Helsinki 1997; m 1973 Heather Mary Clayton (2d 1975, 1979; 2s 1977, 1982).

Hewitt, Norman; FCO since January 1989; born 12/09/46; FCO 1981; Washington 1985; Band C4; m 1968 Catherine Georgina Sahadeo (1s 1975; 2d 1970, 1983).

Heyn, Andrew Richard; First Secretary (Political) Lisbon since February 1996; born 14/01/62; DTI 1985-89; Second Secretary FCO 1989; Second Secretary (Chancery) Caracas 1991; First Secretary FCO 1994; m 1988 Jane Carmel (1d 1994).

Hickey, Patricia Helen; FCO since September 1997; FCO 1975; Bangkok 1977; FCO 1979; Canberra 1981; FCO 1984; New York 1986; Berlin 1988; FCO 1991; Hong Kong 1995; Band C5.

Hickey, Stephen Benedict; FCO since September 2001; born 07/06/79; Band C4.

Hicking, Nicola Jane (née Boyles); Montevideo since 1999; born 28/07/63; FCO 1983; Brasilia 1985; Lagos 1987; FCO 1988; Band A2; m 1992 Robert Hicking (2s 1994, 1996).

Hicks, Colin Michael, MBE (2002); Islamabad since January 2001; born 04/03/74; MAFF 1993-96; FCO 1996; Dublin 1997; Band B3; m 1998 (1s 1999).

Hickson, Philip John; FCO since November 1997; born 21/03/65; FCO 1984; Kingston 1986; Floater Duties 1990; Tehran 1993; New Delhi 1996; Band B3; m 1992 Amanda Ruth Woolham (2s 1993, 1995).

Higginbottom, Sandra Patricia (née Wright); Lagos since October 2000; born 03/03/65; FCO 1984; Brussels 1986; Dhaka 1989; FCO 1992; Tunis 1997; Band B3; m (1) 1989 Robert Freeman Walker (diss); (2) 1997 Andrew Higginbottom (1s 1996).

Higgins, Gillian (née Newbury); FCO since 2000; born 23/03/63; FCO 1987; Budapest 1989; FCO 1991; Grand Cayman 1995; Band A2; m 1995 Russell Mark Higgins (1d 1997).

Higgins, Robert Geoffrey; FCO since November 1985(Second Secretary 1989); born 23/03/48; FCO 1968; The Hague 1971; Phnom Penh 1974; Caribbean Floater 1975; Dacca 1977; FCO 1978; Far East Floater 1980; Bridgetown 1982.

Higham, Andrew Bolton; FCO since July 1997; born 28/10/59; FCO 1982; Singapore 1986; FCO 1988; Government Secretary Hong Kong 1993; Band C4; m 1989 Veronica Jane Nazareth (1d 1990; 1s 1993).

Hildersley, Sarah Jane; SUPL since January 2002; born 30/05/68; FCO 1987; Brussels (UKDEL NATO) 1988; FCO 1989; Third Secretary (Management) JMO Brussels 1990; Floater Duties 1991; FCO 1994; Deputy Head of Mission Santo Domingo 1998; Band C4; (1s 1996).

Hill, Charles Edward; First Secretary FCO since September 2000; born 31/03/63; FCO 1990; Third Secretary (Chancery) Doha 1993; Deputy Head of Mission Almaty 1997; Band C5; m 1996 Suzanne Victoria Stock.

Hill, Duncan N; MO/Consul Shanghai since September 2000; born 08/12/68; FCO 1989; Berlin 1991; Full-Time Language Training 1994; Rio de Janeiro 1995; FCO 1997; Band C4; m 1992 Lisa Pegram.

Hill, Jeremy John Leonard; Second Secretary (Commercial) Seoul since November 1998; born 03/05/57; FCO 1975; SOAS 1978; Tokyo 1979; Jakarta 1982; FCO 1986; Harare 1990; Second Secretary FCO 1994; Second Secretary 1994; Sana'a 1996; m 1985 Roossnadia Peni Hestiani Roesno (1s 1990; 1d 1992).

Hill, Kristina Maria; Third Secretary (External Relations) Brussels (UKREP) since June 2000; born 10/04/72; FCO 1999; Band B3.

Hill, Lauren Sarah; Johannesburg since May 1999; born 14/02/73; FCO 1992; Conference Officer Brussels (UKREP) 1995; World Wide Floater Duties 1997; Band B3.

Hill, Martin Henry Paul; Counsellor (Commercial) Bangkok since February 2002; born 17/05/61; Ministry of Agriculture, Fisheries and Food 1983; Privy Council Office 1985; MAFF 1986; Bonn 1993; FCO 1996; Deputy High Commissioner Colombo 1998; Band D6; m Kim Lydyard (3d 1992, 1993, 1996).

Hill, Michael Thomas; High Commissioner Vila since November 2000; born 02/01/45; FO 1963; New York (UKMIS) 1966; Vientiane 1969; Kaduna 1970; FCO 1974; T/D Sana'a 1975; Second Secretary, DHM and Vice-Consul Ulaanbaatar 1978; Second Secretary (Cons/Immig/Aid) Port of Spain 1981; Second later First Secretary FCO 1985; Assistant to Deputy Governor Gibraltar 1988; First Secretary (Aid) Nairobi 1993; First Secretary FCO 1997; m

1977 Elizabeth Louise Carden (3s 1981, 1988, 1990; 1d 1983).

Hill, Peter Jeremy Oldham; HM Ambassador Vilnius since November 2001; born 17/04/54; FCO 1982; First Secretary (Legal Adviser) Bonn 1987; On loan to the Law Officers' Department 1991; Legal Counsellor Brussels (UKREP) 1995; Counsellor FCO 1999; m 1981 Katharine Hearn (1d 1987; 1s 1989).

Hill, Sarah; First Secretary FCO since August 2000; born 18/09/72; FCO 1995; Third Secretary (Aid) Belgrade 1996; Second Secretary (Political) Buenos Aires 1997; Band C4.

Hill, Simon Robert; SUPL since October 2000; born 18/03/67; FCO 1994; Brussels 1996; FCO 1999; Band B3; m 1998 Carina Megia Abarca.

Hill, Steven John; First Secretary (Political) Washington since August 2001; born 07/04/62; FCO 1984; Second Secretary (UNIDO/UN) Vienna (UKMIS) 1988; Second later First Secretary FCO 1990; First Secretary New York (UKMIS) 1996; First Secretary FCO 1999; Band D6; m 1998 Geraldine Steele (2d 1995, 2001; 1s 1998).

Hill, Suzanne Victoria (née Stock); Second Secretary FCO since August 2000; born 01/12/65; Home Office 1988-91; FCO 1991; T/D Accra 1993; Doha 1994; Third Secretary (Political/Aid) Almaty 1997; SUPL 1999; Band C4; m 1996 Charles Edward Hill.

Hilley, Marie Thérésa (née Donnelly); Tehran since May 2001; born 21/05/61; FCO 1996; Kathmandu 1997; Band A2.

Hillman, John; Deputy High Commissioner Valletta since June 2002; born 30/05/48; FO (later FCO) 1967; Dhaka 1971; Budapest 1974; Calcutta 1975; Second Secretary (Commercial) Dublin 1979; Second Secretary FCO 1983; First Secretary and Consul Cairo 1988; Deputy Consul-General Sydney 1991; First Secretary FCO 1997; m 1978 Pushp Kanta Sahney (1d 1981).

Hilson, Marian Joan; SUPL since May 1997; born 05/02/44; FCO 1988; New Delhi 1990; FCO 1993; Band B3; m 1965 Malcolm Geoffrey Hilson (2s 1966, 1968).

Hilton, Christopher Charles Donald; FCO since November 2002; born 07/11/69; FCO 1988; Budapest 1991; World Wide Floater Duties 1994; FCO 1997; Third Secretary (Chancery) Port of Spain 1999; Band B3.

Hilton, Margaret; FCO since September 1995; born 09/08/53; FCO 1990; Strasbourg 1993; Band A2.

Hilton, Michael Anthony; First Secretary (Commercial) Tehran since December 1992; born 07/03/50; FCO 1973; Department of Employment 1973; Manchester Business School 1975; Frankfurt 1977; FCO 1979; Second Secretary Ulaanbaatar 1981; Second later First Secretary FCO 1983; First Secretary (Dev/Comm)

Kathmandu 1987; Hanoi 1990; m 1976 Janet Elizabeth Tyler.

Himmer, Melanie (née Read-Ward); SUPL since December 1997; born 16/05/68; FCO 1989; Warsaw 1991; Tashkent 1994; Band B3; m 1993 Alan Keith Himmer.

Hinchley, Carol Ruth; Second Secretary (Chancery) Wellington since August 1994; born 09/04/59; FCO 1981; Gaborone 1983; Stockholm 1987; Second Secretary FCO 1991.

Hinchon, David Alan; Third Secretary (Political) Almaty since September 2002; born 15/04/67; FCO 2000; Band B3; ptnr, Anna Taylor (2s 1997, 1999).

Hines, Trevor John; British Trade International (London) since October 2000; born 10/11/60; FCO 1979; Floater Duties 1982; Third Secretary (Consular) Jedda 1984; Riyadh 1985; FCO 1987; Third Secretary (Man/Cons) Belmopan 1990; Second Secretary (Commercial) Mexico 1995; Secondment to industry, May 2000; Band C4; m 1985 Sandra Bradley (1s 1992; 1d 1994).

Hirst, Harold Christopher; Tashkent since August 2000; born 26/12/66; FCO 1984; DHSS 1984; Maseru 1987; Peking 1991; FCO 1994; Hong Kong 1995; Band B3.

Hiscock, Stephen John; High Commissioner Georgetown and Ambassador Paramaribo since August 2002; born 16/06/46; Inland Revenue 1963; FO 1965; Kuala Lumpur 1968; Lusaka 1972; FCO 1976; Second Secretary 1977; Islamabad 1978; First Secretary (Comm/Inf) Seoul 1982; First Secretary FCO 1986; Deputy High Commissioner Georgetown 1988; First Secretary FCO 1993; Consul-General Brisbane 1997; m (1) (diss 1982) (2s 1967, 1971); (2) 1983 Denise Mary Forster (1d 1986; 2s 1989, 1991).

Hitchens, Timothy Mark; On secondment to Buckingham Palace since January 1999; born 07/05/62; FCO 1983; Language Training Tokyo 1985; Second Secretary Tokyo 1986; Second later First Secretary FCO 1989; Private Secretary to the Minister of State 1991; First Secretary (Political/Info) Islamabad 1994; FCO 1997; m 1985 Sara Kubra Husain (1d 1991; 1s 1993).

Ho, David Tat Lun; Brussels (UKDEL NATO) since November 1999; born 05/05/61; Home Civil Service 1989-1998; FCO 1998; Band A2.

Hoar, Gareth Keith; Consul (Economic) Guangzhou since October 1999; born 23/06/65; FCO 1984; Peking 1986; Santiago 1989; Washington 1991; FCO 1994; Language Training Guangzhou 1998; m 2000 Rebecca Xie.

Hoare, James Edward; Chargé d'Affaires and Consul-General Pyongyang since February 2001; born 16/04/43; Research Analyst FCO 1969; Principal Research Officer 1975; Head of Chancery/Consul Seoul 1981; FCO 1985; Head of Chancery/Consul-General Peking 1988; Seconded to International Institute of Strategic Studies 1992;

Senior Principal Research Officer FCO 1993; Research Counsellor 1998; m (1) 1965 Jane Maureen Fletcher (diss) (2s 1968, 1972); (2) 1978 Susan Pares (1d 1978).

Hobart, Edward Andrew Beauchamp; First Secretary FCO since May 1998; born 30/11/71; FCO 1993; Third later Second Secretary Havana 1995; Band D6; m 1999 Suzanna Louise Massey.

Hobbs, Jeremy Alexander; Principal Research Officer FCO since September 1999; born 08/02/61; Senior Research Officer FCO 1991; Second Secretary (Political/Technical Co-operation) Bogotá 1995; Band D6; m 1983 Ana Maria Erndira (1s 1990; 1d 1994).

Hodge, Sir James William, KCVO (1996), CMG (1996); Consul-General Hong Kong since July 2000; born 24/12/43; Third Secretary Commonwealth Office 1966; Tokyo 1967; Second Secretary (Information) Tokyo 1970; First Secretary FCO 1972; First Secretary (Development) later (Chancery) Lagos 1975; FCO 1978; First Secretary (Economic) later Counsellor (Commercial) Tokyo 1981; Counsellor and Head of Chancery Copenhagen 1986; Counsellor FCO 1990; On loan at RCDS 1994; Minister, Deputy Head of Mission and HM Consul-General Peking 1995; HM Ambassador Bangkok 1996; m 1970 Frances Margaret Coyne (3d 1973, 1975, 1979).

Hodges, Ian Foyle; Vice-Consul Jedda since April 2001; born 30/10/67; FCO 1987; Budapest 1989; Paris 1990; Third Secretary FCO 1994; Third Secretary (Consular) Karachi 1994; FCO 1994; Third Secretary (Management) and Vice-Consul Tehran 1997; m 1991 Patricia Paule Andre Seguin (1s 1992; 1d 1993).

Hodges, Jeremy Andrew; Full-Time Language Training since May 1998; born 16/07/67; FCO 1988; Floater Duties 1990; Peking 1992; Karachi 1994; m 1992 Adele Bushnell.

Hodgetts, Susan Jacqueline; Second later First Secretary FCO since January 1995; born 07/11/48; DSAO (later FCO) 1967; Lagos 1970; Kathmandu 1973; Warsaw 1973; Madrid 1975; Montevideo 1975; FCO 1978; Bridgetown 1981; FCO 1985; Vice-Consul Bucharest 1990; HM Consul Algiers 1993; Band D6.

Hodgson, Allen Richard; Second Secretary FCO since October 2001; born 08/02/60; FCO 1977; Geneva (UKMIS) 1991; FCO 1995; Second Secretary (Regional Affairs) Cairo 1998; Band C4; m 1989 Sally Maureen Cole-Hamilton (1d 1993; 1s 1997).

Hodgson, George Kenneth; First Secretary Manila since February 2001; born 15/02/49; FCO 1969; Lagos 1971; Belgrade 1974; Berlin CG 1975; Reykjavik 1976; Karachi 1977; FCO 1979; DHSS 1980-84; FCO 1984; Colombo 1985; Luxembourg 1989; Second Secretary FCO 1992; Ulaanbaatar 1995; Nicosia 1997; m 1971 Jill Taylor (1s 1975; 2d 1978, 1980).

Hogarth, Philip; Deputy Head of Mission/Consul La Paz since March 2000; born 10/05/55; FCO 1976; Damascus 1978; Accra 1982; FCO 1984; Tokyo 1988; Paris 1991; Second Secretary FCO 1995; Band C4; m 1978 Monique Marie Therese Morand.

Hoggard, Robin Richard; Counsellor (Management/Con) Tokyo since November 1998; born 26/11/56; FCO 1982; Language Training SOAS 1983; Kamakura 1984; Second later First Secretary (Commercial) Tokyo 1985; later First Secretary (Economic); First Secretary FCO 1989; On loan to DTI 1991; First Secretary (Political) Brussels (UKDEL NATO/UKDEL WEU) 1994; m 1988 Tonoko Komuro (1s 1995).

Hogger, Henry George; HM Ambassador Damascus since June 2000; born 09/11/48; Third Secretary FCO 1969; MECAS 1971; Second Secretary Caracas 1972; Aden 1972; Second later First Secretary Kuwait 1975; FCO 1978; First Secretary, Head of Chancery and Consul Abu Dhabi 1982; FCO 1986; Counsellor and Head of Chancery Amman 1989; High Commissioner Windhoek 1992; Counsellor FCO 1996; m 1972 Fiona Jane McNabb (2d 1979, 1982; 2s 1984).

Hogwood, Jonathan Felix; Second Secretary British Trade International since June 1998; born 24/07/52; FCO 1971; Warsaw 1974; Islamabad 1975; Luanda 1978; FCO 1981; Dhaka 1986; Tokyo 1989; FCO 1992; SUPL 1995; Second Secretary (Commercial) Nairobi 1996; m 1978 Susan Elizabeth Farmer.

Hogwood, Susan Elizabeth (née Farmer), MBE (1981); HM Ambassador Kigali since July 2001; born 27/05/52; FCO 1971; Islamabad 1974; SUPL 1978; Second Secretary FCO 1982; Second Secretary (Aid) Dhaka 1986; Second later First Secretary (Consular) Tokyo 1989; First Secretary FCO 1992; First Secretary (Humanitarian) Nairobi 1994; FCO 1998; m 1978 Jonathan Felix Hogwood.

Holder, Donald John; HM Consul Athens since October 2000; born 16/08/50; FCO 1976; Bonn 1978; Islamabad 1981; FCO 1984; Auckland 1985; BMG Berlin 1987; FCO 1988; Second Secretary (Commercial) Bahrain 1990; Language Training 1994; Second Secretary (Info/Visits) Warsaw 1995; Consul (Immigration/Passports) Düsseldorf 1996.

Holdich, Patrick Godfrey Hungerford; First Secretary (Chancery) Ottawa since December 1992; born 19/09/56; Senior Research Officer FCO 1985; Principal Research Officer 1990; m 1987 Ailsa Elizabeth Beaton (diss 1992).

Holifield, Martin; Sarajevo since September 2002; born 08/09/61; FCO 1979; Islamabad 1986; FCO 1989; Kuwait 1991; FCO 1995; Luanda 1997; FCO 2001; Band B3; m (1) 1985 Morag Catherine Fraser (diss 1995); (2) 1996 Anna Maria Sandelin (1s 1998; 1d 2001).

Hollamby, David James; Governor St Helena, Ascension Island and Tristan da Cunha since June 1999; born 19/05/45; CO 1961; DSAO 1964; Beirut 1967; Latin America Floater 1970; Asuncion 1972; Second Secretary FCO 1975; Vice-Consul (Commercial) BTDO New York 1978; Consul (Commercial) Dallas 1983; First Secretary FCO 1986; First Secretary Rome 1990; First Secretary FCO 1994; m 1971 Maria Helena Guzman (2 step s 1961, 1964).

Holland, Denise Ann; On loan to DTI since July 2000; born 13/04/63; FCO 1986; Washington 1989; JLG Hong Kong 1991; FCO 1994; British Trade International 1997; Band C4; m 2000 Anthony James Dudgeon.

Holland, Henry Robert Cumber; First Secretary FCO since September 1997; born 25/11/57; FCO 1984; Second Secretary (Chancery) Nairobi 1986; First Secretary FCO 1989; First Secretary (Political/Information) Canberra 1993; m 1983 Anne Elizabeth Wardle (2s 1987,1990; 1d 1988).

Holland, Patricia Anne (Tricia); On loan to the EU Commission since September 2002; born 02/04/64; FCO 1986; Third Secretary (Chancery) Prague 1988; Second later First Secretary FCO 1989; First Secretary (Finance) New York (UKMIS) 1993; SUPL 1997; First Secretary (EU Affairs) Paris 1998; SUPL 2001; m 1997 Paul Thomas Arkwright (1d 1999).

Holland, Stephen Peter; First Secretary (Internal) New Delhi since December 2000; born 31/08/65; FCO 1999; Band D6; m Judith Kent.

Holland, Tracey Joanne; SUPL since March 1996; born 16/07/66; FCO 1990; Language Training 1991; Full-Time Language Training Tokyo 1992; FCO 1993; Band B3.

Hollis, Anthonia; FCO since October 1994; born 02/01/66; FCO 1987; Bonn 1992; Band A2.

Hollis, Ian Malcolm; Lisbon since July 1997; born 16/12/70; FCO 1989; Bonn 1994; Band A2; m 1997.

Holloway, Michael John; First Secretary Dhaka since July 2002; born 14/01/57; FCO 1976; Dubai 1978; Bucharest 1979; Africa/Middle East Floater 1981; Mexico City 1983; FCO 1984; Barcelona 1988; FCO 1991; Second Secretary (Political/Information/Aid) Mexico City 1994; Deputy Consul-General Rio de Janeiro 1998.

Hollywood, Jane Christina Emma; FCO since June 2002; born 07/03/66; FCO 1991; Second Secretary (Political) The Hague 1998; Band C4.

Holmes, Alan Thomas; Second Secretary Sarajevo since October 2000; born 25/09/53; FCO 1977; Brussels (UKDEL NATO) 1980; FCO 1982; Bridgetown 1986; Cairo 1989; FCO 1992; Full-Time Language Training 1996; Moscow 1997; FCO 1998; Band C4; m 1980 Helen Hook.

Holmes, Helen (née Hook); Second Secretary FCO since December 1998; born 26/05/51; FCO 1969; Department of Employment and Productivity 1969; Bangkok 1973; Lagos 1975; FCO 1976; SUPL 1980; FCO 1982; Bridgetown 1986; Cairo 1989; FCO 1992; Moscow 1998; m 1980 Alan Thomas Holmes.

Holmes, John Dominic; Full-Time Language Training since January 1999; born 18/08/59; Inland Revenue 1977; FCO 1978; Paris 1984; FCO 1987; Warsaw 1989; The Hague 1991; FCO 1994; Band B3.

Holmes, Sir John Eaton, KBE (1999), CVO (1998), CMG (1997); HM Ambassador Paris since October 2001; born 29/04/51; Third Secretary FCO 1973; Language Training 1975; Third Secretary Moscow 1976; Second later First Secretary FCO 1978; First Secretary (Economic) Paris 1984; First Secretary FCO 1987; Counsellor 1989; On secondment to the De La Rue Company 1989; Counsellor and Head of Chancery (later Counsellor (Econ/Comm)) New Delhi 1991; Head of European Union Department (External) FCO 1995; Private Secretary to the Prime Minister for Overseas Affairs 1996; Principal Private Secretary to the Prime Minister 1997; HM Ambassador Lisbon 1999; m 1976 Margaret Penelope Morris (3d 1981, 1982, 1985).

Holmes, Michael, MVO (1991); First Secretary (Management) New Delhi since October 2001; born 03/04/54; FCO 1973; Belmopan 1975; Rio de Janeiro 1978; Baghdad 1981; FCO 1985; Third Secretary Harare 1988; Second Secretary (Cons/Comm) Melbourne 1992; Second Secretary later Consul (Comm) Casablanca 1994; FCO 1998; m 1980 Jennifer Margaret Lesley Pike (1d 1982; 1s 1985).

Holmes, Paul Barry; FCO since 1997; born 15/11/54; FCO 1972; Warsaw 1978; Bonn 1980; FCO 1982; Third Secretary Accra 1986; Addis Ababa 1990; FCO 1993; Hong Kong 1995; FCO 1997; Band C5; m (1) 1975 Elaine Down (diss) (2s 1981, 1983); (2) 1988 Sarah Penelope Briggs (1d 1989; 1s 1991).

Holmes, Timothy Charles; Deputy Head of Mission and Consul-General The Hague since October 1997; born 26/04/51; Third Secretary FCO 1974; Language Training SOAS 1975; Language Training Tokyo 1976; Second later First Secretary Tokyo 1977; On loan to the DOT 1981; First Secretary FCO 1983; First Secretary (Chancery) Islamabad 1986; First Secretary FCO 1990; Deputy Head of Mission and Counsellor (Commercial/Economic) Seoul 1994; m 1973 Anna-Carin Magnusson (1s 1977; 1d 1988).

Holt, Denise Mary (née Mills), CMG (2002); HM Ambassador Mexico City since August 2002; born 01/10/49; Research Analyst FCO 1970; First Secretary (Political) Dublin 1984; SUPL 1987; FCO 1988; SUPL 1990; First Secretary (Political) Brasilia 1991; Deputy Head of Eastern Department FCO 1993; SUPL 1994; Deputy Director Personnel Management FCO 1996; Counsellor and Deputy Head of Mission Dublin

1998; Director (Personnel Command) FCO 1999; m 1987 David Holt (1s 1987).

Holt, Sean Christopher Eric, OBE (1999); Counsellor Freetown since November 2001; born 18/12/49; HM Armed Forces (Army) 1968-78; FCO 1978; Second Secretary Havana 1979; First Secretary FCO 1980; Athens 1982; First Secretary FCO 1984; First Secretary (Chancery) Khartoum 1987; First Secretary FCO 1990; First Secretary (Political) Accra 1991; First Secretary FCO 1994; Counsellor Bogotá 1995; Counsellor Luanda 1999; m (1) 1973 Jennifer Patricia Trevaskis (diss 1987) (1s 1974; 1d 1976); (2) 1987 Joyce Amanda Anderson (diss 1994); (3) 1999 Johanna Antonia Maria Rutten.

Holtum, Roger Adrian; Third Secretary Lilongwe since August 1993; born 02/10/51; FCO 1972; Port of Spain 1975; Tel Aviv 1978; FCO 1981; Dhaka 1983; Helsinki 1986; FCO 1989; Third Secretary (Aid/Commercial) Kampala 1991; Band B3; m 1983 Nina Lange (1d 1984; 1s 1986).

Homer, Richard David; Budapest since January 2001; born 24/12/72; FCO 1992; Stockholm 1995; Washington 1997; FCO 1997; Band B3.

Hood, Laura Elizabeth; FCO since November 1989; born 27/04/63; FCO 1983; Bucharest 1985; Port of Spain 1987; Band A2.

Hook, Neil Kenneth, MVO (1983); Consul-General Osaka since October 2001; born 24/04/45; FCO 1968; Moscow 1971; FCO 1972; Language Training Sheffield University 1974; Tokyo 1975; Second Secretary (Aid) Dhaka 1980; First Secretary FCO 1984; On loan to DTI 1986; First Secretary (Commercial) Tokyo 1987; First Secretary FCO 1992; HM Ambassador Ashgabat 1995; High Commissioner Mbabane 1999; m 1973 Pauline Ann Hamilton (1d 1975; 1s 1977).

Hopkins, Kathleen Elizabeth; Paris since December 1999; FCO 1994; Vienna 1996; Language Training 1999; Band A2.

Hopkinson, Celia Lois; FCO since September 1995; born 09/10/59; FCO 1979; New York (UKMIS) 1982; Sofia 1984; Paris 1986; FCO 1988; Lusaka 1992; Band B3.

Hopkinson, Moira Elizabeth; FCO since April 1994; born 28/08/59; FCO 1980; Copenhagen 1982; Peking 1985; Islamabad 1986; FCO 1990; Beirut 1992; Band B3.

Hopton, Nicholas Dunster; First Secretary (Political) Rome since October 2000; born 08/10/65; FCO 1989; Second Secretary (Political/Information) Rabat 1991; First Secretary FCO 1995; m 1993 Maria Alejandra Echenique (1s 2002).

Horine, Fern Marion; Second Secretary (Political) Baku since August 2000; born 28/07/69; FCO 1987; Vienna (UKDEL) 1990; FCO 1995; On loan to the DTI 1998; Band C4.

Horne, Gordon; FCO since September 1994; born 05/12/66; FCO 1986; Riyadh 1988; New York (UKMIS) 1992; Band B3; m 1989 Susan Lisa Berry.

Horne, Michael John, OBE (1996); Counsellor (Commercial) Kuala Lumpur since June 2000; born 29/05/44; FO 1961; Bucharest 1965; Bangkok 1967; Accra 1971; FCO 1975; Second Secretary (Commercial) Kuala Lumpur 1978; Second later First Secretary Libreville 1981; On loan to No 10 Downing Street 1985; Consul (Information) and Deputy Director, later Director New York (BIS) 1987; FCO 1992; On loan to the World War II Commemorations Team, MOD, 1994; Counsellor on loan to the Cabinet Office (Office of Deputy Prime Minister) 1995; Consul-General Perth 1997; m 1965 Deborah Elaine Hopkinson (1s 1966; 1d 1971).

Horner, Katharine Sarah Julia; First Secretary (Political) (Internal) Moscow since July 1997; born 15/08/52; FCO 1980; Moscow 1985; Senior Research Officer FCO 1987; PRO 1996.

Horner, Simon; Second Secretary (Finance) New York (UKMIS) since June 2002; born 10/12/69; DHSS 1987; FCO 1988; Nassau 1991; Floater Duties 1993; FCO 1995; Canberra 1998; Band B3; m 1995 Katherine Jean Gallager.

Horton-Jones, Sarah Caroline; Second Secretary FCO since July 1998; born 13/10/68; Lord Chancellor's Department 1991-93; FCO 1993.

Hosie, Angela June (née Binns); SUPL since July 1999; born 25/06/69; MOD 1988-1990; FCO 1990; New Delhi 1994; Accra 1997; Band C4; m 1993 Colin Hosie (1s 1995).

Hosking, Simon Paul; First Secretary (Science and Technology) New Delhi since January 2001; born 15/06/71; FCO 1993; Second Secretary Santiago 1997; First Secretary FCO 1999; Band D6; m 1995 Allison Jane Christou (2d 1998, 1999; 1s 2001).

House, Gregory Stewart; Floater Duties since May 1999; born 03/06/68; FCO 1988; Lilongwe 1991; Lagos 1995; Band B3.

Houston, Sharon (Sher) Linda; Islamabad since July 1998; born 14/06/68; FCO 1989; Bridgetown 1991; Brussels (UKREP) 1995; Band B3; m 1993 Steve Giovanni Campbell (diss 1997) (1s 1996).

Howard, Alayne Anne (née Whitehouse); First Secretary FCOS since April 2000; born 04/06/63; FCO 1982; New Delhi 1985; Third Secretary (Consular) Bridgetown 1989; SUPL 1992; Second Secretary FCO 1993; Second Secretary (Immigration) Islamabad 1996; FCOS 1997; Band C5; m 1984 Paul Howard (2s 1987, 1988).

Howard, (Charles Andrew) Paul; Second Secretary FCOS since November 1999; born 23/09/60; FCO 1983; New Delhi 1985; Third Secretary Bridgetown 1989; FCO 1992; Third Secretary (Consular) Islamabad 1996; FCOS 1997; Band C4; m 1984 Alayne Anne Whitehouse (2s 1987, 1988).

Howard, Sarah Catherine (née Sullivan); Harare since December 1998; born 05/11/68; FCO 1987; Kingston 1989; Tehran 1993; FCO 1995; Band B3; m 1989 Simon James Howard.

Howarth, Stephen Frederick; UK Representative with the Personal rank of Ambassador, to the Council of Europe at Strasbourg since March 2003; born 25/02/47; FCO 1966; Vice-Consul Rabat 1971; Third later Second Secretary Washington 1975; Second later First Secretary FCO 1980; Seconded ENA Paris 1982; Deputy Head of Mission Dakar 1984; First Secretary FCO 1984; First Secretary FCO 1988; Counsellor and Deputy Head of PUSD 1990; Head of Consular Department later Division 1992; Minister Paris 1997; m 1966 Jennifer Mary Chrissop (2d 1966, 1970; 1s 1974).

Howden, Yvonne Catherine Helen; Prague since April 2000; born 06/03/73; FCO 1997; Luanda 1998; FCO 1999; Band A2.

Howe-Jones, Vanessa Jane; First Secretary (Political) New York (UKMIS) since September 2001; born 23/06/65; FCO 1991; Full-Time Language Training 1992; Second Secretary Budapest (KHF) 1993; First Secretary FCO 1996; T/D Brussels (UKREP) 2000.

Howel, Iwan Gruffydd; Peking since June 1999; born 05/01/68; FCO 1988; Washington 1991; Brasilia 1994; Band B3.

Howells, Julie (née Satchell); SUPL since July 2001; born 03/06/64; FCO 1982; Brussels (UKDEL NATO) 1986; Seoul 1991; Dar es Salaam 1996; Band B3; m 1991 David Howells.

Howitt, Derrick; Istanbul since May 1999; born 14/02/43; Royal Navy 1958-83; Moscow 1983; Paris 1985; Singapore 1988; Colombo 1991; Floater Duties 1995; Band B3; m 1966 Averil E Rose (1d 1968; 1s 1972).

Howlett, David John; FCO since June 1982; born 17/01/55; Principal Research Officer m 1979 Bridget Mary de Boer.

Howlett, Keith Raymond; FCO since 1998; born 29/03/50; FCO 1968; Moscow 1980; FCO 1982; Tokyo 1986; Second Secretary FCO 1989; Second Secretary Caracas 1994; m 1984 Claudine Cecile Odette Stedman (diss 1998); (2) 1998 Natasha Mota Hurtado (1 step d 1996).

Huckle, Alan Edden; Counsellor, Head of OSCE/Council of Europe Department FCO since August 1998; born 15/06/48; Civil Service Department 1971; On loan to Northern Ireland Office 1974; Civil Service Department 1975; On loan to Northern Ireland Office 1978; First Secretary FCO 1980; Executive Director British Information Services New York 1983; Head of Chancery Manila 1987; First Secretary FCO 1990; Counsellor and Deputy Head of Delegation Vienna (UKDEL CSCE) 1992; Head of Dependent Territories Regional Secretariat Bridgetown 1996; m 1973 Helen Myra Gibson (1s 1981; 1d 1985).

Huckle, Steven Allan; First Secretary Moscow since August 2000; born 24/10/64; FCO 1981; Brussels (UKREP) 1989; FCO 1992; Sofia 1994; FCO 1997; Band C5; m 1987 Alison Elaine Porter (1s 1990; 1d 1991).

Hudman, Anne (née Lister); Third Secretary (Commercial) Vienna Embassy since February 1999; born 01/09/62; FCO 1987; Helsinki 1989; FCO 1992; Bonn 1993; St Petersburg 1996; Band B3; m 1991 Roger Grenville Hudman.

Hudson, James Alexander; St Petersburg since December 2000; born 14/01/72; FCO 1994; Havana 1996; FCO 1998; Tirana 1999; T/D Skopje 2000; T/D Budapest 2000; Band B3; m 1996 Sally Barrett (diss 1997) (1d 1995).

Hudson, Julie Marie; Gaborone since August 1988; born 25/05/65; FCO 1984; Riyadh 1986; Band A2.

Huggins, Elaine Anne; Lisbon since July 1998; born 04/05/59; WRAC 1978-82; MOD 1983-86; FCO 1997; Band A2; m Michael James Huggins.

Huggins, Elizabeth June; SUPL since May 1998; born 25/06/70; DSS 1987; FCO 1989; Copenhagen 1992; FCO 1993; Budapest 1995; Band A2; m 1997 Phillip David Culligan (1d 1999).

Hughes, Beverley Elizabeth (née Lewis); SUPL since January 1998; born 22/07/66; FCO 1985; HCS 1985; Karachi 1987; Africa/Middle East Floater 1991; FCO 1994; Band B3; m 1997 Peter John Hughes

Hughes, Brendan Christopher; Second Secretary (Political) Islamabad since October 1999; born 31/10/71; FCO 1996; Band C4.

Hughes, Edgar John; HM Ambassador Caracas since May 2000; born 27/07/47; FCO 1973; On secondment to Cabinet Office 1979; First Secretary CSCE Madrid 1981; FCO 1982; First Secretary and Head of Chancery Santiago 1983; First Secretary (Information) Washington 1985; First Secretary later Counsellor FCO 1989; Deputy Head of Mission Oslo 1993; Change Manager FCO 1997; On secondment to BAe Systems 1999; m 1982 Lynne Evans (2s 1984, 1988).

Hughes, Ian Noël; Deputy Head of Mission Mexico City since July 2000; born 05/12/51; FCO 1971; Latin America Floater 1974; Kabul 1976; Warsaw 1980; FCO 1982; Second Secretary and Vice-Consul Tegucigalpa 1985; First Secretary (Political) Berne 1988; First Secretary (Press/Information) New Delhi 1993; First Secretary FCO 1993; First Secretary FCO 1997; m 1978 Teresa June Tinguely (2s 1979, 1981; 1d 1984).

Hughes, Peter John; Deputy Head of Mission Colombo since December 2001; born 14/09/53; FCO 1976; Islamabad 1978; Rome 1980; Warsaw 1983; FCO 1985; (Second Secretary 1987); Vice-Consul (Commercial) Sydney 1989; Second later First Secretary FCO 1994; Acting High

Commissioner Castries 1998; m (1) 1978
Jacqueline Alexander (diss 1987); (2) 1997
Beverley Elizabeth Lewis.

Hulands, Michael Robert; FCO since February
2000; born 29/11/53; FCO 1970; Singapore 1976;
Tel Aviv 1978; FCO 1981; Third Secretary
Bangkok 1983; Addis Ababa 1986; FCO 1990;
Second Secretary Bonn 1995; FCO 1998; North
American IT Advisor Washington 1999; m 1979
Normah Binti Maznun (2d 1981, 1986).

Hulbert, Neil Peter; Oslo since August 2001; born
21/06/63; FCO 1995; Berlin 1997; Band A2.

Hum, Christopher Owen, CMG (1996); HM
Ambassador Beijing since March 2002; born
27/01/46; FO 1967; Hong Kong 1968; Peking
1971; Second later First Secretary/Private
Secretary to Permanent Representative Brussels
(UKREP) 1973; FCO 1975; First Secretary Peking
1979; First Secretary (Chancery) Paris 1981; First
Secretary FCO 1983; Counsellor and Deputy Head
of Falkland Islands Department FCO 1985;
Counsellor FCO 1986; Counsellor and Head of
Chancery New York (UKMIS) 1989; AUSS
(Northern Asia and the Pacific) FCO 1992; HM
Ambassador Warsaw 1996; Chief Clerk 1998; m
1970 Julia Mary Park (1d 1974; 1s 1976).

Humfrey, Charles Thomas William, CMG (1999);
HM Ambassador Seoul since August 2000; born
01/12/47; Third Secretary FCO 1969; Language
Student Sheffield University 1970; Tokyo 1971;
(Second Secretary 1972, First Secretary 1976);
FCO 1976; Private Secretary to Minister of State
1979; New York (UKMIS) 1981; First Secretary
FCO 1985; Counsellor Ankara 1988; Tokyo 1990;
Counsellor FCO 1994; Minister Tokyo 1995; m
1971 Enid Wyn Thomas (2s 1975, 1983; 1d 1977).

Humphreys, Lucy Ann Marie; Beijing since June
2001; born 17/06/72; FCO 1993; New York
(UKMIS) 1996; SUPL 1999; FCO 2000; Band A2.

Humphreys, Nita (née Saha); FCO since
December 1998; born 23/12/69; FCO 1990; SUPL
1998; Band B3; m 1997 Phillip David Humphreys
(1d 1998).

Humphries, Eric Henri Edward; Dhaka since
March 1995; born 11/10/59; FCO 1978; Islamabad
1982; Nairobi 1984; Victoria 1987; FCO 1990;
Zagreb 1992; FCO 1993; Band B3; m 1982 Sara
Dorothy Watts (1d 1984).

Hunt, Peter Lawrence, CMG (2001); Consul-
General Los Angeles since October 2001; born
10/06/45; FO 1962; DSAO 1965; Africa Floater
Duties 1967; Brussels 1969; Managua 1970; FCO
1973; Second Secretary (Commercial) Caracas
1978; First Secretary FCO 1982; Head of
Chancery Montevideo 1987; FCO 1990; Deputy
Head of Mission Santiago 1993; Consul-General
Istanbul 1997; m 1971 Anne Langhorne Carson
(2d 1972, 1976; 2s 1974, 1984).

Hunt, Sara Jennifer; Third Secretary (Political)
Warsaw since October 1999; born 29/10/67; FCO
1987; Bonn 1990; Latin America/Caribbean

Floater 1993; Full-Time Language Training 1993;
FCO 1995; Band B3.

Hunt, Stephen Anthony; Second Secretary
(Political) Vienna since January 1999; born
03/09/57; MOD 1977; FCO 1978; Lisbon 1981;
Prague 1984; Gaborone 1986; Moscow 1988; FCO
1990; La Paz 1994; Full-Time Language Training
1997; Band C4; m 1984 Eileen Crossan (2s 1994,
1s 1996).

Hunt, Stephen Paul; First Secretary FCO Services
since 1998; born 13/01/61; FCO 1993; Brussels
1994; FCO 1997.

Hunter, David Eric; FCO since September 2001;
born 08/12/71; FCO 1989; Third Secretary
(Political) Kiev 1998; Band B3; m 2000 Peta
Leigh Brennan.

Hunter, Paulette Elaine; Nairobi since August
2001; born 17/10/65; FCO 1985; Lagos 1987;
Peking 1990; Bridgetown 1993; FCO 1997; T/D
Islamabad 1997; Band B3.

Hunter, Robert; Second Secretary (Management)
and Consul Sana'a since September 2000; born
10/08/47; HM Forces 1964-70; Merchant Navy
1973-74; FCO 1974; Darwin 1975; Beirut 1976;
Peking 1977; FCO 1979; Lilongwe 1980; Jedda
1981; FCO 1984; Pretoria 1985; FCO 1988; Vice-
Consul (Consular/Management) Suva 1989; Full-
Time Language Training 1994; Deputy Head of
Mission Antananarivo 1995; Second Secretary
FCO 1997; Full-Time Language Training 2000;
Band C5; m 1981 Carol Mary Chorley.

Hunter, Sally; Karachi since January 1985; born
10/12/65; FCO 1985; Band A2.

Hunter, Wendy; FCO since September 1987; born
09/11/67; Band B3.

Huntington, Janet Elizabeth (née Bull); First
Secretary FCO since July 2001; born 22/09/63;
FCO 1986; Third later Second Secretary
(Chancery) Managua 1988; Second Secretary
(Chancery) Lisbon 1990; Second later First
Secretary FCO 1993; First Secretary (Political)
Caracas 1995; First Secretary (Trade Policy) New
Delhi 1997; Band D6; m 1995 Daniel Peter
Huntington (2d 1997, 1999).

Hurd, Thomas Robert Benedict; Consul (Political)
Jerusalem since March 2002; born 22/09/64; FCO
1992; Language Training 1994; First Secretary
(Political) Warsaw 1995; First Secretary Amman
1998; Band D6; m 1994 Katherine Siân Aubrey
(2s 1996, 1998; 1d 1997).

Hustwitt, Justin John; First Secretary (Regional
Affairs) Kampala since April 2001; born 08/09/67;
FCO 1991; Full-Time Language Training 1992;
Language Training Cairo 1993; Second Secretary
(Political) Cairo 1994; Second Secretary
(Commercial) Riyadh 1995; First Secretary FCO
1997; Band D6.

Hutchings, Nicholas Alexander; FCO since April
2002; born 29/02/80; Band C4.

Hutchison, Jacqueline Margaret (née Wigzell); SUPL since August 2002; born 12/05/65; FCO 1987; Third Secretary (Commercial) Berlin 1990; Third Secretary Port of Spain 1993; Third later Second Secretary FCO 1997; Band C4; m 1993 Ian James Hutchison (1s 1995; 2d 2000).

Hyde, Richard Damian; Second Secretary (Commercial) Jedda since October 2001; born 18/09/69; FCO 1989; Hamilton 1991; Vice-Consul Paris 1995; Band C4; m 1994 Jacqueline Pearl Sadio.

Hyland, Mark; Sarajevo since October 2000; born 03/07/69; HCS 1986; FCO 1990; Brussels (UKDEL NATO) 1993; T/D New York (UKMIS) 1995; Belgrade 1996; SUPL 1999; Band A2; m 1992 Deborah Jane Tomlinson.

Hyland, Susan Margaret; Private Secretary to the Permanent Under Secretary FCO since June 2001; born 30/10/64; Second Secretary FCO 1990; New York (UKMIS) 1992; Second Secretary (Political) Oslo 1992; Second Secretary UKDEL OECD 1993; ENA Paris 1994; First Secretary FCO 1996; First Secretary (Political) Moscow 2000; Band D7.

Hyne, Sarah Jean; New York (UKMIS) since August 2001; born 20/04/74; PA to Deputy Heads of Economic Policy 1999; FCO 1999; Band A2.

I

Ingamells, John Mawgan; SUPL since December 1999; born 08/06/61; FCO 1984; Language Training Seoul 1985; Third Secretary (Chancery) Seoul 1987; Third Secretary (Commercial) later Second Secretary (Information) Buenos Aires 1990; Second later First Secretary FCO 1994; On secondment to Fidelity Investments 1999; m 1990 Nicola Jane Dobb (2s 1991, 1993).

Inglehearn, Catherine Mary; Third Secretary Ljubljana since April 1996; born 15/05/65; FCO 1990; Rome 1992; Band B3.

Ingold, Andrew Henrik; FCO since September 1994; born 30/07/53; Customs and Excise 1972; FCO 1973; Valletta 1975; Monrovia 1978; Paris 1982; FCO 1984; Bombay 1987; Vice-Consul Abu Dhabi 1990; Band B3.

Ingram, Rachel Victoria; World Wide Floater Duties since December 1998; born 25/04/69; FCO 1994; Berne 1996; Band C4.

Inkster, Nigel Norman; Counsellor FCO since January 1998; born 11/04/52; Third Secretary FCO 1975; Third later Second Secretary FCO 1976; Language Student/Third Secretary Kuala Lumpur 1976; Second later First Secretary Bangkok 1979; FCO 1982; First Secretary and Consul Peking 1983; Buenos Aires 1985; First Secretary FCO 1989; Counsellor Athens 1992; Counsellor BTC Hong Kong 1994; m 1977 Leong Chui Fun (1d 1980; 1s 1981).

Innes, Stuart Harcourt; Deputy Head of Mission Damascus since May 1999; born 30/10/55; FCO 1980; Doha 1983; Second Secretary Cairo 1986; First Secretary FCO 1989; Deputy Permanent Representative New York (UKMIS) 1993; m 1983 Susan Jane Wood (1s 1987; 1d 1989).

Innes-Hopkins, Christopher Randolph; First Secretary (Commercial) Ankara since June 2001; born 26/11/53; On secondment to the European Union 1997; FCO 1976; Georgetown 1979; Paris 1982; First Secretary FCO 1985; Second Secretary Tunis 1988; Deputy Consul-General Jerusalem 1993; First Secretary FCO 1999; m 1983 Soraya Nizamodin Dookie (1s 1986; 1d 1993).

Insall, Anthony John Godwin, LVO (1986); Counsellor Oslo since April 1999; born 27/06/49; FCO 1973; Third later Second Secretary (Information) Lagos 1975; Second later First Secretary FCO 1977; Language Training Hong Kong 1982; First Secretary FCO 1983; First Secretary and Consul Peking 1985; First Secretary FCO 1988; Counsellor Kuala Lumpur 1992; Counsellor FCO 1995; m 1979 Leonie Bridget Meryon (3s 1980, 1982, 1984).

Insall, Christopher Wharton; FCO since October 1984; born 31/12/45; FCO 1966; Jedda 1970; FCO 1971; Paris 1981; Band B3; m 1982 Lynn Melrose Irvine.

Irens, Jules Marie Nigel; FCO since March 2002; born 11/08/68; Band D6.

Ives, Malcolm Albert; First Secretary (Commercial) Accra since November 1997; born 10/03/47; MPNI 1964; FO (later FCO) 1966; Dacca 1969; FCO 1971; Sana'a 1973; Addis Ababa 1974; Warsaw 1976; FCO 1978; São Paulo 1981; Jakarta 1985; Second Secretary (Development) Amman 1987; Second Secretary FCO 1991; On loan to the DTI 1992; Second Secretary (Commercial) Riyadh 1994; m 1973 Susan Robertson (3s 1969, 1974, 1976).

Ives, Susan; SUPL since October 1997; born 08/02/44; FCO 1992; Riyadh 1994; FCO 1997; Band A2; m 1973 Malcolm Albert Ives (3s 1969, 1974, 1976).

Ivey, Peter Robert; Düsseldorf since September 2001; born 25/05/58; FCO 1982; Bahrain 1983; Language Training 1987; Second Secretary (Information/Chancery) Helsinki 1988; On loan to the London Chamber of Commerce 1992; On loan to the DTI 1993; Full-Time Language Training 1995; First Secretary (Commercial) Zagreb 1996; Band C5; m 1998 Sally Helen Elizabeth Hill (2s 1998, 2000).

Ivey, Sally Helen Elizabeth (née Hill); SUPL since September 1998; born 25/10/65; FCO 1987; New Delhi 1988; FCO 1990; World Wide Floater Duties 1992; Full-Time Language Training 1995; Zagreb 1996; Band A2; m 1998 Peter Robert Ivey (2s 1998, 2000).

Ivins, Suzanne Gillian (née Parker); Second Secretary (Immigration) Shanghai since December 2000; born 05/02/65; FCO 1983; Tokyo 1985; FCO 1988; Third Secretary (Consular) Ottawa 1992; Third Secretary Ho Chi Minh City 1996; Band C4; m 1988 James Browell Ivins (1d 1994).

Ivory, Jason; New Delhi since July 2000; born 04/08/70; Madrid 1991; Bombay 1994; FCO 1998; Band B3; m 1992 Susannah Ruth Knowles (1s 1994; 1d 1995).

Izzard, Richard Brian George; Full-Time Language Training since April 2000; born 04/01/69; Metropolitan Police 1987; FCO 1988; Sofia 1990; Accra 1992; World Wide Floater Duties 1993; FCO 1997; Luanda 2000; Band B3.

J

Jack, Stuart Duncan Macdonald, CVO (1994); Minister Tokyo since April 1999; born 08/06/49; FCO 1972; Third later Second later First Secretary Tokyo 1974; FCO 1979; First Secretary and Press Attaché Moscow 1981; First Secretary FCO 1984; Bank of England 1984; First Secretary (Economic) Tokyo 1985; Counsellor FCO 1989; HM Consul-General St Petersburg 1992; FCO 1996; m 1977 Mariko Nobechi (2d 1980, 1982; 1s 1986).

Jackson, Andrew Michael; Second Secretary FCO since July 1991; born 06/11/58; FCO 1984; Third Secretary (Chancery) Bonn 1987; Band C4; m 1987 Susan Elizabeth Welsh (2d 1989, 1992).

Jackson, Anna Elizabeth; Second Secretary (EU) Warsaw since May 2001; born 08/06/78; FCO 1999; Band C4.

Jackson, Elizabeth Anne (née Irwin); SUPL First Secretary FCO since February 1992; born 08/08/55; FCO 1977; Moscow 1980; Second later First Secretary Brussels (UKDEL NATO) 1982; First Secretary FCO 1985; First Secretary FCO 1986; m 1981 Richard Charles Edward Jackson (2s 1986, 1988; 1d 1990).

Jackson, Freya; Second Secretary Buenos Aires since June 2000; born 10/04/74; FCO 1997; Support Officer New York (UKMIS) 1999; Full-Time Language Training 2000; Band C4.

Jackson, Helen; SUPL since September 1999; born 27/01/62; FCO 1981; Stockholm 1983; Port of Spain 1986; Moscow 1990; Bridgetown 1993; FCO 1998; Band A2; (1d 1998).

Jackson, Lee Barry Thomas; Vice-Consul (Consular) Hong Kong since January 2000; born 02/07/65; FCO 1996; Full-Time Language Training Hong Kong 1997; Band B3; m 1995 Vanda Morais-Jackson (diss 1999).

Jackson, Linda Margaret; On loan to Cabinet Office since September 2000; born 21/12/46; FO 1965; Prague 1968; Santiago 1969; Moscow 1972; FCO 1973; Vienna (UKDEL) 1976; Peking 1978; FCO 1979; Paris 1981; FCO 1984; Brussels 1986; FCO 1989; Band B3.

Jackson, Paul Michael, MBE (2000); Helsinki since July 1999; born 05/04/63; HCS 1982; FCO 1983; Islamabad 1985; FCO 1987; Washington 1991; FCO 1994; Belgrade 1997; Band C4; m 1984 Cheryl Barrington (1d 1986; 1s 1988).

Jackson, Robert Frederick; Assistant Trade Commissioner BTC Hong Kong since June 1995; born 08/02/57; FCO 1975; Prague 1978; Bandar Seri Begawan 1979; Gaborone 1981; Sana'a 1987; FCO 1990; Band C4; m (1) 1977 Rosalind Barbara Sackett (diss) (2d 1983, 1986); (2) 1995 Maria Mouskovias.

Jackson-Houlston, William Lester, OBE (1994); Counsellor The Hague since August 1999; born 06/10/52; FCO 1979; Second Secretary Brussels (UKREP) 1980; Second later First Secretary FCO 1981; Buenos Aires (BIS) 1982; FCO 1986; First Secretary Belgrade 1990; First Secretary FCO 1993; m 1985 Susana Olivia Fitzpatrick (twins, 1s and 1d 1989).

Jacobs, Lisa Claire; Peking since November 1995; born 21/03/65; FCO 1986; Moscow 1988; Riyadh 1990; FCO 1993; Band B3.

Jacobsen, Neil Marius; First Secretary (Regional Affairs) Santiago since May 2000; born 16/06/57; Second Secretary FCO 1984; Second later First Secretary (Economics) Athens 1986; First Secretary FCO 1989; First Secretary (Political) Madrid 1992; First Secretary FCO 1996; Band D6; m 1982 Susan Clark (1d 1984; 2s 1988, 1990).

Jacobson, Charles Eugene; On loan to Oldham Chamber of Commerce since October 1999; born 17/09/64; FCO 1988; Third Secretary (Chancery) Tel Aviv 1991; Manila 1995; FCO 1995; Band B3; m 1993 Sarah Madeline Henry (1s 1997; 1d 1999).

Jagoe, Neale David; FCO since January 2002; born 11/06/68; Royal Hong Kong Police 1990-96; Second Secretary FCO 1996; Second Secretary (Political/Information) Manila 1997; Band D6; m 1992 Margarita Hanio (1d 1992).

James, Neill; Sana'a since August 2001; born 06/07/71; FCO 1991; Dhaka 1994; Manila 1998; Band A2; m 1997 Rangsiya Promsrisuk (1 step s, 1990, 1s 1999).

James, Nia Llewelyn (née Hughes); FCO since November 1997; born 26/04/74; Band B3; m 1999 Christopher John James.

James, Nicola Patricia; Jakarta since April 2002; born 29/09/60; FCO 1980; Peking 1983; Kuala Lumpur 1985; Bandar Seri Begawan 1988; FCO 1993; Band B3.

James, Stephen Anthony; Second Secretary (Management) Tokyo since April 1996; born 01/09/51; Customs and Excise 1968; FCO 1971; Saigon 1973; Peking 1975; Warsaw 1976; Manila 1977; Berne 1981; FCO 1984; Islamabad 1987; Third Secretary (Aid/Commercial) Mbabane 1990; Second Secretary FCO 1994; m 1979 Nikki Jean Smith (2d 1980, 1982; 1s 1984).

Jamieson, Rachel Janet; Islamabad since November 1999; born 31/05/68; FCO 1993; Full-Time Language Training 1995; Bucharest 1996; Band B3.

January, Dr Peter; Head of OSCE/CoE Department FCO since July 2001; born 13/01/52; FCO 1983; First Secretary (Commercial) Budapest 1985; First Secretary FCO 1988; Consul and

Deputy Head of Mission Maputo 1991; First Secretary later Counsellor FCO 1993; HM Ambassador Tirana 1999.

Jardine, Martine; Madrid since July 1993; born 27/09/70; FCO 1990; Band A2.

Jarrett, Anne; FCO since March 2001; born 26/01/60; FCO 1978; Moscow 1981; Africa/Middle East Floater 1984; Brussels (UKDEL NATO) 1986; Second Secretary FCO 1989; Second Secretary (Political) Peking 1993; First Secretary (Economic) Bucharest 1997; Full-Time Language Training 1997; Band D6.

Jarrett, Caroline Julia Rachel; Second Secretary (Political) Islamabad since August 2002; born 07/09/76; FCO 1999; Band C4.

Jarrold, Nicholas Robert; HM Ambassador Zagreb since August 2000; born 02/03/46; Third Secretary FCO 1968; Third later Second Secretary The Hague 1969; Dakar 1972; First Secretary FCO 1975; Nairobi 1979; (Head of Chancery 1983); FCO 1983; Counsellor and Deputy Head of Mission Havana 1989; CDA at St Antony's College Oxford University 1991; Counsellor (Commercial/Economic) Brussels 1992; HM Ambassador Riga 1996; m 1972 Anne Catherine Whitworth (2s 1976, 1979).

Jarvie, Carole Marina; ECO Istanbul since June 2000; born 26/09/54; FCO 1984; The Hague 1986; Canberra 1989; Brussels (UKDEL) 1992; FCO 1998; Band B3.

Jarvis, Russell Thomas; Deputy Head of Mission Stanley since January 1997; born 27/09/47; Commonwealth Office (later FCO) 1964; Sofia 1969; Sana'a 1972; EC Brussels 1972; Islamabad 1973; FCO 1975; Dar es Salaam 1978; (Second Secretary 1979); Vice-Consul (Commercial) BTDO New York 1982; First Secretary FCO 1986; First Secretary (Management) BTC Hong Kong 1990; First Secretary FCO 1994; m 1969 Joan Ann Wyard (2s 1971, 1986; 1d 1973).

Jay, Sir Michael Hastings, KCMG (1997), CMG (1992); Permanent Under Secretary of State and Head of the Diplomatic Service since January 2002; born 19/06/46; ODM 1969; UKDEL IMF/IBRD Washington 1973; ODM 1975; First Secretary (Development) New Delhi 1978; First Secretary FCO 1981; Private Secretary to Permanent Under Secretary of State FCO 1982; Counsellor on loan to Cabinet Office 1985; Counsellor (Finance/Commercial) Paris 1987; AUSS (European Community) FCO 1990; HM Ambassador Paris 1996; m 1975 Sylvia Mylroie.

Jebb, Christopher Quayle Gladwyn; Second Secretary FCO since March 1996; born 02/10/50; FCO 1970; Caribbean Floater 1973; Vientiane 1975; Düsseldorf 1978; FCO 1980; Tristan da Cunha 1982; Istanbul 1984; FCO 1987; Second Secretary (Head of Chancery) Asunción 1988; Second Secretary (Commercial/Information) Kingston 1991; Mexico City 1992; m 1975 Maria Aida Hoyos (1d 1979; 1s 1981).

Jeenes, Kelley Elizabeth; Nairobi since August 1995; born 23/02/71; FCO 1992; Band A2.

Jeffery, Claire Rachel; Second Secretary (Political) Stockholm since July 2002; born 20/04/73; FCO 1997; Band C4.

Jeffrey, Frieda King (née Rolland); Bridgetown since April 2000; born 17/10/63; FCO 1988; Brussels (UKREP) 1990; Manila 1993; FCO 1996; Uganda 1997; Band A2; m 1997 Bruce Jeffrey.

Jeffrey, John Peacock Reid; Second Secretary FCO since February 1996; born 04/04/53; FCO 1971; Jakarta 1974; Singapore 1975; Africa Floater 1977; FCO 1980; Mexico City 1982; Bucharest 1986; Second Secretary FCO 1988; Second Secretary (Commercial/Consular/Management) Montevideo 1992; m 1980 Arlene Elizabeth Watson (1s 1991).

Jeffreys, Stella Ann; FCO since December 1999; born 16/11/62; FCO 1990; Dar es Salaam 1992; Hanoi 1996; Band A2.

Jenkins, John, LVO (1989); HM Ambassador Rangoon since April 1999; born 26/01/55; Second Secretary FCO 1980; Second later First Secretary Abu Dhabi 1983; First Secretary FCO 1986; First Secretary and Head of Chancery Kuala Lumpur 1989; First Secretary FCO 1992; Deputy Head of Mission Kuwait 1995; SOAS, University of London 1998; m 1982 Nancy Caroline Pomfret.

Jenkins, Owen John; First Secretary (Political) Buenos Aires since June 2002; born 21/08/69; FCO 1991; Full-Time Language Training 1993; Third later Second Secretary (Political/Information) Ankara 1994; FCO 1998; m 1998 Catherine Margaret Baker.

Jenkins, Paul David; Yaoundé since May 2000; born 22/06/51; FCO 1968; Bonn 1972; Prague 1974; FCO 1974; Monrovia 1976; Kaduna 1978; FCO 1981; Nairobi 1984; Gaborone 1986; Second Secretary FCO 1990; Second Secretary (Commercial) Lagos 1992; First Secretary (Commercial) Islamabad 1996; m (1) 1972 Jennifer Whitmarsh (diss) (2s 1976, 1979); (2) 1987 Elaine Vera Walsh (neé Avery).

Jenkins, Peter Redmond; UK Permanent Representative with Personal rank of Ambassador Vienna since August 2001; born 02/03/50; FCO 1973; Third later Second Secretary UNIDO/IAEA Vienna 1975; First Secretary FCO 1978; First Secretary and PS to HM Ambassador Washington 1982; First Secretary FCO 1984; First Secretary (Economic) Paris 1987; Minister/Counsellor, Consul-General and Deputy Head of Mission Brasilia 1992; Minister and Deputy Permanent Representative Geneva (UKMIS) 1996; m 1990 Angelina Chee-Hong Yang (1d 1992; 1s 1994).

Jenkinson, Eric; High Commissioner Banjul since November 2002; born 13/03/50; FO 1967; EC Brussels 1971; Islamabad 1973; Second Secretary (Commercial) Jedda 1978; Second Secretary FCO 1982; First Secretary (Economic) Bonn 1986; Consul and Deputy Head of Mission Bahrain

1992; First Secretary FCO 1995; First Secretary
Tehran 1999; m 1973 Kathleen Forster (2s 1980,
1981).

Jenkinson, Gale Louise; São Paulo since March
2000; born 24/11/63; FCO 1984; Islamabad 1986;
Ottawa 1989; FCO 1992; Third Secretary
(Management) and Vice-Consul Doha 1996; Band
C4; m 1990 Tony Takashi Baba (1d 1992).

Jennings, Kay (née Henderson); Nicosia since
October 2001; born 27/02/72; FCO 1993; Band
A2; m 2000 Richard Llewellyn Jennings

Jennison, Vanessa Sandford; Vice-Consul
Amsterdam since April 2000; born 25/02/64; FCO
1988; Third Secretary Geneva (UKMIS) 1990;
FCO 1993; Vice-Consul Paris 1995; SUPL 1998;
m 1989 Geoffrey John Peck (2s 1993, 1997).

Jermey, Dominic James Robert, OBE (2001);
FCO since October 2000; born 26/04/67; FCO
1993; Full-Time Language Training 1994; Second
Secretary (Political/Information) Islamabad 1995;
First Secretary Afghanistan 1998; T/D Skopje
1999; T/D Dili 2000; Band D6.

Joad, Kate Louise; Second Secretary FCO since
July 1999; born 18/03/69; FCO 1990; Tokyo 1992;
Floater Duties 1996; T/D Pretoria 1999; Band C4.

Johns, Allison Marie; Damascus since August
2000; born 20/11/66; FCO 1988; Washington
1991; Bonn 1993; FCO 1997; Band A2.

Johnsen, Emma Louise (née Williams); SUPL
since September 1998; born 23/02/66; FCO 1990;
Geneva (UKMIS) 1993; FCO 1996; Band B3; m
1992 Per-Arne Johnsen.

Johnson, Alison Jane (née Sindon); FCO since
March 1999; born 16/11/63; FCO 1983; Mexico
City 1985; Asunción 1988; FCO 1991; Sofia 1995;
SUPL 1997; Band B3; m 1997 Clive Andrew
Johnson.

Johnson, Christine; Dakar since August 2001;
born 12/04/73; FCO 1997; Budapest 1998; Full-
Time Language Training 2001; Band A2.

Johnson, George Michael; Dhaka since April
1999; born 10/01/43; Post Office 1960; FO 1961;
Kinshasa 1965; Moscow 1967; Paris 1968; FCO
1971; Lagos 1973; Sofia 1976; FCO 1979;
(Second Secretary 1980); Vice-Consul
(Commercial) Toronto 1984; First Secretary
(Admin) Brasilia 1988; First Secretary FCO 1994;
Harare 1995; m 1971 Anne Marion Little (diss)
(1s 1971); (2) 1992 Cecilia Da Conceicao Dos
Santos Rodrigues.

Johnson, Helen (née Matthews); SUPL since
September 2000; born 27/03/62; FCO 1981;
Dhaka 1984; Tunis 1985; Moscow 1985; Berne
1988; FCO 1991; Islamabad 1994; San José 1998;
Band B3; m (1) 1987 R B L Marzouk (diss 1999)
(1s 1994); (2) 2000 Ridha Ben Larbi.

Johnson, Julie Michelle; Second Secretary
(Consular) Kuala Lumpur since September 2000;
born 12/11/63; FCO 1983; Port Stanley 1985;

FCO 1986; Vienna 1987; Hong Kong 1990; FCO
1991; FCO 1993; Bombay 1993; Third Secretary
(Management) and Vice-Consul Guatemala City
1996; Band C4.

Johnson, Katrina; SUPL since June 2001; born
10/03/66; FCO 1985; Paris 1987; FCO 1990;
SUPL 1992; Third Secretary (Institutions) Brussels
(UKREP) 1993; On loan to the ODA/DFID 1996;
SUPL 1998; Second Secretary (Economic/Trade
Policy) New Delhi 1999; Band D6; m 1994
Richard Adam Noble (2s 1996, 1998).

Johnson, Matthew Alfred; Second Secretary
(Social Policy Issues) New York (UKMIS) since
May 2000; born 11/06/70; FCO 1988; Cape
Town/Pretoria 1990; FCO 1993; Osaka 1994; FCO
1996; On loan to No 10 Downing Street 1999;
Band C4; m 1993 Heidi Suzanne Burton (1s 1997;
1d 1999).

Johnson, Sandra Lissenden; FCO since July 1999;
born 13/02/43; FCO 1970; Washington 1971;
Resigned 1973; Reinstated 1982; UKDEL CSCE
Madrid 1982; Moscow 1983; Rangoon 1984; FCO
1987; Helsinki 1992; Nairobi 1995; Seconded to
the Cabinet Office 1998 – 99; Band B3.

Johnson, Simon William; Third Secretary (Visits)
Peking since July 1996; born 26/05/64; FCO 1983;
Budapest 1987; Istanbul 1989; FCO 1993.

Johnson, Stuart James; Second Secretary FCO
since January 2002; born 08/05/72; Second
Secretary FCO 1998; Second Secretary (Pol/Mil)
Banja Luka on secondment to MOD 2000; Band
C4.

Johnson, Tamsin Jane; Addis Ababa since
February 1991; born 15/01/70; FCO 1989; Band
A2.

Johnson, Walter George Devon, MBE (1982);
Deputy Consul-General Auckland since July 1998;
born 28/06/44; FO 1963; Mexico City 1965; Sofia
1968; FCO 1969; Wellington 1970; Bogotá 1973;
FCO 1975; Brussels (UKDEL NATO) 1978;
Caracas 1981; Second Secretary, Bursar Wiston
House 1983; Second Secretary (Commercial)
Abidjan 1987; Second later First Secretary
(Management) JMO New York 1990; First
Secretary FCO 1995; m 1989 Margaret Murray-
Lee (2d 1969, 1972).

Johnston, Elizabeth Ann (née Barker); SUPL
since October 1987; born 02/12/57; FCO 1978;
Belgrade 1980; FCO 1982; Pretoria/Cape Town
1983; FCO 1986; Band A2; m 1987 Paul Neville
Johnston.

Johnston, Paul Charles; Counsellor FCO since
November 2002; born 29/05/68; MOD 1990-93;
FCO 1993; Private Secretary to Lord Owen
(International Conference on Former FCO
Yugoslavia) 1994; Second Secretary (PS/HMA)
Paris 1995; Second Secretary (Political) Paris
1997; FCO 1999; Deputy Head of European
Union Department (External) FCO 2001; Band
D6.

Johnstone, James; Hong Kong since July 1998; born 16/03/44; Army 1962-88; New York 1988; Peking 1991; Geneva (UKMIS) 1992; T/D Moscow 1995; Moscow 1996; Band B3; m (1) 1967 Patricia Anne Strong (1d 1968; 2s 1969, 1974) (diss 1983); (2) 1986 Rachel Baliti (1s 1991).

Johnstone, Lauren Clair (née Blagburn); Gibraltar since July 1997; born 21/07/70; FCO 1989; Scottish Office 1992; SUPL 1992; FCO 1993; Band B3; m 1992 Andrew Johnstone (diss 1999); (1s 2001).

Johnstone, Peter; Governor Anguilla since January 2000; born 30/07/44; FO 1962; Berne 1965; Benin City 1966; Budapest 1968; Maseru 1969; FCO 1973; Second Secretary 1975; Second Secretary (Chancery) Dacca 1977; First Secretary (Local Rank) Dublin 1979; First Secretary FCO 1983; First Secretary (Commercial) Harare 1986; Consul-General Edmonton 1989; First Secretary FCO 1991; Counsellor (Commercial/Development) Jakarta 1995; m 1969 Diane Claxton (1s 1971; 1d 1977).

Jones, Alison; World Wide Floater Duties since 1999; born 19/12/72; DSS 1995; FCO 1998; Band A2.

Jones, Amanda Louise; Baku since January 2001; born 16/03/69; FCO 1997; Kigali 1998; Band A2.

Jones, Andrew; FCO since August 2000; born 02/03/67; FCO 1988; Hong Kong 1997; Band C4; m 1989 Lisa Roberts (1d 1993; 2s 1997, 2000).

Jones, Andrew Martin; Copenhagen since March 2000; born 14/12/59; FCO 1980; Darwin 1981; FCO 1984; Singapore 1986; FCO 1989; Third Secretary Amman 1993; FCO 1997; Band C4; m 1985 Amanda Wainer (1s 1988; 1d 1990).

Jones, Annabel Nicole (née Russ); FCO since November 1994; born 26/10/60; FCO 1981; Floater Duties 1983; Washington 1986; FCO 1988; (Second Secretary 1990); SUPL 1994; m 1989 Gareth Richard Jones.

Jones, Caitlin Olga; Guatemala City since August 1999; born 03/06/67; FCO 1990; Nicosia 1993; Brussels (UKDEL) 1996; Band C4.

Jones, Catherine Helen Courtier, MBE (1999); SUPL since August 2000; born 13/09/56; FCO 1976; Moscow 1979; Latin America Floater 1982; Bogotá 1984 (Second Secretary 1985) Second Secretary FCO 1989; Deputy Head of Mission Tirana 1997.

Jones, Ceinwen Jane; Deputy Head of Mission Tallinn since June 1999; born 02/05/50; FCO 1976; Bangkok 1977; Moscow 1979; Geneva (UKDIS) 1981; FCO 1984; Banjul 1990; FCO 1992; Brussels (UKREP) 1995; Band B3.

Jones, David Alan; High Commissioner Freetown and also non resident HM Ambassador to Republic of Guinea since May 2000; born 26/10/53; Second Secretary on loan to MOD 1981; Lord Chancellor's Department 1970; FCO 1971; Tehran 1975; Islamabad 1978; Second Secretary FCO 1983; First Secretary (Commercial) Cairo 1986; First Secretary FCO 1989; Deputy Head of Mission/Consul Luanda 1993; Full-Time Training 1993; Deputy High Commissioner Dar es Salaam 1996; m (1) 1975 Jennifer Anne Wright (diss 1992); (2) 1994 Daphne Patricia Foley (1d 2001).

Jones, David Stephen; Deputy High Commissioner Honiara since June 1998; born 19/09/51; Public Records Office 1970-73; FCO 1976; Port of Spain 1978; Peking 1981; Africa/Middle East Floater 1982; FCO 1984; Brasilia 1988; Tripoli 1991; Second Secretary on loan to the DTI 1994 Second Secretary FCO 1995; m (1) 1973 Jane Martin (diss 1978) (2) 1997 Carole Banstead.

Jones, Eric Malcolm; First Secretary (Management) Vienna since November 2001; born 07/10/45; Passport Office Liverpool 1963; DSAO 1966; Middle East Floater 1969; Düsseldorf 1970; Vice-Consul Peking 1973; FCO 1974; Third Secretary (Commercial) Kuwait 1976; Second Secretary FCO 1980; Second Secretary (Aid) later Second Secretary (Chancery) Dhaka 1982; Second Secretary (Commercial) later First Secretary (Development) Lilongwe 1985; First Secretary FCO 1990; First Secretary (Development) Jakarta 1994; First Secretary FCO 1998; m 1988 Sylvia Margáret Hayhurst (1s 1989).

Jones, Frank; First Secretary (Commercial) Athens since May 2001; born 07/09/48; FO (later FCO) 1967; Kaduna 1970; Brussels (NATO) 1974; Sana'a 1977; FCO 1978; Ottawa 1982; FCO 1984; Second Secretary (Visa) Paris 1989; Second Secretary (Commercial) Kuala Lumpur 1994; FCO 1997; Band C5; m 1982 Elizabeth Mary Lendrum (1d 1985; 1s 1991).

Jones, Jennifer Ann (née Wright); Second Secretary FCO since January 1990; born 07/08/49; DSAO (later FCO) 1967; Delhi 1970; Kathmandu 1970; Lisbon 1972; Tripoli 1972; Tehran 1975; Islamabad 1978; FCO 1981; Cairo 1986.

Jones, Joan Elizabeth, BEM (1991); Kampala since July 1996; born 06/11/43; FCO 1988; Belmopan 1991; Band A2.

Jones, Katherine; Second Secretary New Delhi since September 2002; born 07/08/65; Home Office 1990-92; FCO 1992; SUPL 1998; FCO 2001; Band C4; m 1999 Richard Joseph David Perry (1d 1998).

Jones, Leslie Norman; Berlin since June 2000; born 26/05/48; Army 1964-88; Cairo 1988; Moscow 1991; Budapest 1993; FCO 1995; Language Training 1999; Band B3; m 1972 Dorothy Alma Tanner (1s 1977; 1d 1978).

Jones, Llinos Dawn; Santiago since October 1997; born 27/03/68; FCO 1988; Kuwait 1989; Warsaw 1990; New York (UKMIS) 1992; Bandar Seri Begawan 1993; Band A2.

Jones, Neale Robert; Dubai since June 1999; born 20/02/63; FCO 1986; Islamabad 1989; Istanbul

1992; Band B3; m (1) 1992 Catherine Ingham (diss 1999) (2s 1993, 1995); (2) 2000 Ebru Jones (1 step d 1996; 1d 2000).

Jones, Peter; Second Secretary (Political) Washington since September 1997; born 23/07/57; FCO 1976; Port Stanley 1979; Madrid 1981; Kathmandu 1984; FCO 1986; Peking 1988; Luxembourg 1992; Third later Second Secretary FCO 1995; m 1979 Elaine Frances Scott.

Jones, Peter Edward; FCO since July 1998; born 28/08/61; FCO 1985; Second later First Secretary Vienna (UKDEL) 1989; First Secretary FCO 1992; First Secretary (Politico-Military) Bonn 1994; m 1998 Sumita Biswas.

Jones, Phillip Roy; FCO since May 1985; born 18/02/50; FO (later FCO) 1966; Washington 1976; FCO 1979; Attaché Muscat 1982; Band C4; m (1) 1972 Lesley Pamela Goody (diss 1981) (2s 1973, 1978; 1d 1975); (2) 1982 Karen Patricia Lyle (1s 1985; 1d 1987).

Jones, Ralph Mahood; FCO since July 2002; born 04/05/69; FCO 1989; Riyadh 1992; T/D New Delhi 1995; Karachi 1996; T/D Kuwait 1997; World Wide Floater Duties 1999; Band B3.

Jones, Randolph Thomas; Second Secretary (Immigration) Pretoria since June 2000; born 12/09/56; FCO 1976; Islamabad 1978; Colombo 1982; FCO 1985; Port of Spain 1989; Peking 1989; Copenhagen 1993; Second Secretary FCO 1997; Band C4; m 1980 Kathryn Rosemary Smith (2s 1984, 1987).

Jones, Rebecca Louise; Cairo since May 2000; born 18/10/74; FCO 1998; Band A2.

Jones, Richard Alexander Owen; Second Secretary Zagreb since September 2001; born 19/04/71; FCO 1990; World Wide Floater Duties 1993; Third Secretary (Vice-Consul) Tashkent 1997; Band B3; m 2000 Madina H Sagindirova.

Jones, Richard Christopher Bentley; First Secretary FCO since June 1992; born 22/03/53; Second Secretary FCO 1978; PS to HM Ambassador Tokyo 1980; First Secretary FCO 1984; First Secretary and Head of Chancery Suva 1988.

Jones, Richard Hugh Francis; First Secretary FCO since September 1998; born 28/09/62; FCO 1983; Third later Second Secretary Abu Dhabi 1986; Second later First Secretary FCO 1989; First Secretary (External Relations) Brussels (UKREP) 1994.

Jones, Robert Edward; Second Secretary FCO since October 1994; born 30/05/47; FCO 1966; Singapore 1973; FCO 1974; Belgrade 1978; FCO 1981; Prague 1985; FCO 1988; (Second Secretary 1989); Attaché Budapest 1993; m 1972 Linda Joan Edith Watts (1d 1974; 1s 1977).

Jones, Siân; Second Secretary (Pol/Mil) Nicosia since December 2000; born 08/11/74; FCO 1999; Band C4.

Jones, Timothy Aidan; HM Ambassador Yerevan since November 1999; born 05/09/62; FCO 1984; Language Training 1986; T/D Vienna (UKDEL CSCE) 1987; Second Secretary (Chancery) The Hague 1988; First Secretary FCO 1992; T/D Mostar (EUAM) 1994; Full-Time Language Training 1995; Deputy Head of Mission Tehran 1996; m 2001 Christin Marschall.

Jones Parry, Emyr, CMG (1992); Permanent Representative Brussels (UKDEL NATO) since September 2001; born 21/09/47; FCO 1973; Second later First Secretary (Political) later First Secretary (Economic) Ottawa 1974; FCO 1979; First Secretary (Energy) later First Secretary (Institutions) Brussels (UKREP) 1982; Counsellor on SUPL Brussels (EC) 1987; Counsellor FCO 1989; Deputy Head of Mission Madrid 1993; Deputy Political Director 1996; Director EU 1997; Political Director 1998; m 1971 Lynn Noble (2s 1977, 1979).

Joseph, Nicholas Eli; Second Secretary Geneva (UKMIS) since January 2002; born 12/01/71; FCO 2000; Band C4.

Joshi, Bharat Suresh; Second Secretary FCO since August 2001; born 23/08/69; FCO 1995; Third Secretary later Deputy High Commissioner Banjul 1999; Band C4; m 1997 Bhakti Oza (2d 2000, 2002).

Joy, Rupert Hamilton Neville; Deputy Head of Mission Rabat since January 2000; born 05/09/63; FCO 1990; Full-Time Language Training 1991; Full-Time Language Training Cairo 1992; Second Secretary (Comm/Econ/Pol) Sana'a 1994; Second later First Secretary (Political) Riyadh 1995; First Secretary FCO 1996; Band D6.

Joyce, Lucy Rebecca; Second Secretary (Political) Brussels since January 2000; born 11/12/69; FCO 1992; Third Secretary (Economic/Management) Sofia 1995; Band C4.

Joyce, Marie-Claire; SUPL since August 2001; born 04/05/69; FCO 1995; Third Secretary (Commercial) later Second Secretary (Political) Tokyo 1998; Band C4; (1d 2001).

Joynson-Squire, Richard James; Second Secretary FCO since April 2002; born 11/09/74; FCO 1996; Full-Time Language Training 1998; Second Secretary (Political/External) Islamabad 1999; Band C4; m 1998 Rolla Khadduri.

Judd, Claire (née Rowswell); FCO since October 1988; born 13/01/55; Quito 1979; FCO 1979; Brussels (UKREP) 1981; Moscow 1984; FCO 1985; Mexico City 1986; Band B3; m 1996 David Judd.

Judge, Christopher John; Washington since August 2001; born 19/05/64; FCO 1980; Second Secretary Moscow 1996; FCO 2000; Band C5; m 1995 Fiona Jane (1s 2000).

Juleff, Andrew John Gerent; Second Secretary (Commercial) Rio de Janeiro since May 2000; born 03/05/60; FCO 1986; Third Secretary

(Aid/Comm) Kampala 1989; Vice-Consul CG New York 1991; Second Secretary FCO 1994; Band C4.

Jupp, Sheridan Arlene; SUPL since January 2002; born 02/01/57; FCO 1990; Stockholm 1993; Band A2.

K

Kahlow, Bonita; SUPL since August 2001; born 23/01/66; FCO 1989; Rome 1993; FCO 1996; Rome 1998; Band A2.

Kana-Rupal, Sadhana (née Rupal); FCO since January 1995; born 31/05/66; Band A2; m 1996 Animesh Kana.

Kane, Jacqueline; SUPL since August 2002; born 25/03/67; FCO 1987; Athens 1990; FCO 1993; New Delhi 1994; FCO 1998; Band B3.

Kariuki, James; New York (UKMIS) since September 2002; born 06/05/71; FCO 1993; On secondment to UN Special Commission (UNSCOM) Baghdad 1994; Second Secretary (Political/Economic) Caracas 1995.

Karmy, Peter John; Head of Management Section Taipei since June 2001; born 01/07/47; FO (later FCO) 1967; Benghazi 1969; San José 1970; Seoul 1973; Kuwait 1976; FCO 1977; Sofia 1980; FCO 1984; Second Secretary (Admin) and Consul Manila 1985; Second Secretary and Consul (later Second Secretary Commercial) Ankara 1989; Second Secretary FCO 1993; Bogotá 1998; m 1977 Eui Jong Han (2d 1979, 1981).

Kavanagh, Karen Jane (née Williams); Bombay since May 1997; born 28/04/70; FCO 1991; Brussels (UKDEL NATO) 1994; Band B3; m 1996 Neil Richard Kavanagh.

Kavanagh, Neil Richard; Bombay since May 1997; born 28/03/72; FCO 1992; Brussels (UKDEL NATO) 1995; Band B3; m 1996 Karen Jane Williams.

Kay, Anthony Paul; Bucharest since April 1999; born 29/06/72; FCO 1992; Hong Kong 1995; Band B3.

Kay, Martin Paul; Pretoria since February 1999; born 21/03/68; FCO 1987; New York (UKMIS) 1989; Suva 1991; FCO 1994; Band B3.

Kay, Nicholas Peter; First Secretary FCO since 2000; born 08/03/58; First Secretary FCO 1994; First Secretary and Deputy Head of Mission Havana 1997; m 1986 Susan Wallace (1s 1987; 2d 1988, 1991).

Kazer, Kathleen; FCO since September 1970 (Senior Principal Research Officer 1998); born 01/06/47.

Kealy, Robin Andrew, CMG (1991); HM Ambassador and Consul-General Tunis since February 2002; born 07/10/44; Third Secretary FO 1967; MECAS 1968; Tripoli 1970; Second later First Secretary Kuwait 1972; First Secretary FCO 1975; Political Advisor Belmopan 1978; Head of

Chancery Port of Spain 1978; First Secretary (Commercial) Prague 1982; First Secretary later Counsellor FCO 1986; Counsellor, Consul-General and Deputy Head of Mission Baghdad 1987; Counsellor, Director of Trade Promotion and Investment Paris 1990; Head of AMD FCO 1995; Consul-General Jerusalem 1997; m 1987 Annabel Jane Hood (2s 1989, 1992).

Keefe, Denis Edward Peter Paul; Deputy Head of Mission Prague since August 1998; born 29/06/58; FCO 1982; Second Secretary (Chancery) Prague 1984; Language Training 1984; First Secretary FCO 1988; First Secretary (Political) Nairobi 1992; First Secretary later Counsellor FCO 1996; m 1983 Catherine Ann Mary Wooding (3d 1985, 1993, 1996; 3s 1987, 1989, 1991).

Keegan, David Barclay; First Secretary FCO since May 2002; born 04/04/63; FCO 1986; Vice-Consul (Economic) Rio de Janeiro 1989; Second Secretary FCO 1991; Washington 1995; First Secretary (Political) Accra 1999; Band D6; m 1987 Susan Amanda Line (1s 1994; 1d 1996).

Keeling, Alison Heather; Private Secretary to the Political Director FCO since January 2002; born 29/08/72; FCO 1996; Geneva (UKMIS) 1997; Beirut 1998; Band C4; m 2002 Reuben Thorpe.

Keen, Gillian; Bangkok since September 2001; born 18/02/61; Home Office 1979; Cabinet Office 1987; FCO 1992; Hanoi 1993; Tokyo 1997; Band A2; m 1987 Raymond Keen.

Keep, Stephanie Marie (née Holmes); Geneva (UKDEL) since September 2002; born 28/12/56; FCO 1997; Singapore 1999; Band A2; m 1999 Richard L Keep.

Kehoe, Elizabeth Anne (née McEwan); Third Secretary Maseru since July 1995; born 29/04/52; FCO 1972; Suva 1975; Brussels (EEC) 1977; Budapest 1979; Montserrat 1981; FCO 1985; Anguilla 1986; FCO 1988; m 1991 Anthony Kehoe (1s 1991)

Keith, Deborah Jeanne; Full-Time Language Training since February 2000; born 01/07/68; FCO 1988; Tokyo 1990; Floater Duties 1993; SUPL 1995; FCO 1996; Band C4; m 1999 Steven Rennie Fern.

Keller, Ciaran Joseph; SUPL since August 2002; born 02/02/77; FCO 1998; New York (UKMIS) 1999; Full-Time Language Training Lisbon 2000; Second Secretary (Political/EU) Lisbon 2000; Band C4.

Kelly, Iain Charles MacDonald; HM Ambassador Minsk since May 1999; born 05/03/49; FCO 1974; Language Training 1975; Moscow 1976; Kuala Lumpur 1979; FCO 1982; (Second Secretary 1984); Istanbul 1986; FCO 1988; Los Angeles 1990; First Secretary (Commercial) Moscow 1992; Consul Amsterdam 1995; m 1981 Linda Clare McGovern (2s 1984, 1988).

Kelly, Mark; Third Secretary (Chancery) Tel Aviv since May 2001; born 17/09/71; GCO 1990;

Amman 1994; World Wide Floater Duties 1996; Panama 1999; FCO 2000; Band B3.

Kelly, Paul John, MBE (1984); Beijing since March 1999; born 11/03/64; FCO 1982; Pretoria 1987; FCO 1989; Nicosia 1994; FCO 1996; Band C4; m 1993 V L Stone.

Kelly, Robert Anthony; Second Secretary FCO since September 2000; born 10/12/59; FCO 1986; Third later Second Secretary Hong Kong 1990; Second Secretary FCO 1994; Second Secretary and Vice-Consul Athens 1996; Band C4; m 1986 Heather Erica Christina Smith (1s 1992; 1d 1993).

Kelly, William Charles; Consul (Commercial) Düsseldorf since March 2002; born 05/01/61; FCO 1980; Jedda 1982; Lisbon 1985; Warsaw 1988; FCO 1990; Private Secretary to the Ambassador Bonn 1993; Third Secretary (Commercial) Paris 1996; FCO 1999; Band C4; m 1983 Carol Ann Villis (4s 1985, 1987, 1990, 1992; 1d 2000).

Kendall, Louise Margaret (née Wood); SUPL since March 2000; born 16/01/63; FCO 1981; Prague 1984; Tel Aviv 1986; FCO 1988; Language Training 1991; Third Secretary (Commercial) Budapest 1992; Vienna 1996; Band B3; m 1988 Philip Gary Kendall (1d 1992).

Kendall, Philip Gary; FCO since July 2002; born 28/04/65; FCO 1984; Tel Aviv 1986; FCO 1988; Budapest 1992; SUPL 1996; Vienna 1998; Band A2; m 1988 Louise Margaret Kendall (1d 1992).

Keningale, Jacqueline; SUPL since October 1999; born 18/02/66; FCO 1986; Moscow 1987; SUPL 1990; Jedda 1992; FCO 1994; Damascus 1996; Band B3; m 1990 Paul Bevan Downing.

Kennedy, Alison Cranston; Seconded to DfID 1999; born 21/08/62; FCO 1983; Third Secretary (Aid) Khartoum 1987; Vice-Consul Abidjan 1991; FCO 1991; SUPL 1993; Second Secretary FCO 1994; On loan to DfID 1997.

Kennedy, Megan Jordan; FCO since 1996; born 01/04/69; FCO 1989; Moscow 1990; Washington 1993; Band B3.

Kennedy, Paul Vincent; First Secretary (Political) Bahrain since June 1999; born 18/04/57; FCO 1989; Second Secretary (Chancery) Riyadh 1991; FCO 1995; Band D6; m 1984 Najia Ben Salah (1d 1990).

Kennedy, Thomas John; Consul-General Bordeaux since February 2002; born 03/02/57; FCO 1992; Second Secretary (Aid/Information) Buenos Aires 1994; First Secretary FCO 1997; m 1985 Clare Marie Ritchie (1s 2000).

Kenny, John David; Colombo since October 1999; born 07/06/55; FCO 1973; Vienna 1976; Georgetown 1978; East Berlin 1982; FCO 1984; Cairo 1987; Third Secretary Dublin 1991; FCO 1995; Band C4; m 1979 Pamela Bernadette Baptiste (1s 1981; 1d 1985).

Kent, Andrew Magnus; First Secretary FCO since January 2001; born 30/11/65; FCO 1989; Second

Secretary (Commercial) Tehran 1992; Second Secretary FCO 1995; Consul Jedda 1999; Band D6; m 1991 Sarah Louise Mills (1s 1994).

Kent, Mark Andrew Geoffrey; Full-Time Language Training since April 2000; born 14/01/66; FCO 1987; Third later Second Secretary (Chancery/Information) Brasilia 1989; Brussels (UKREP) 1993; First Secretary FCO 1998; Band D6; m 1991 Martine Delogne (1s 1992; 1d 1995).

Kent, Sarah Louise (née Mills); FCO since April 1996; born 28/01/65; FCO 1983; Prague 1987; FCO 1989; SUPL 1992; Band B3; m 1991 Andrew Magnus Kent (1s 1994).

Kenwrick-Piercy, Theodore Maurice; Counsellor FCO since December 1998; born 16/01/48; Third later Second Secretary FCO 1971; Second later First Secretary (Press) Brussels (UKREP) 1974; FCO 1977; Nicosia 1982; First Secretary FCO 1986; First Secretary (Chancery) The Hague 1988; First Secretary FCO 1992; Counsellor Athens 1994; m 1976 Elisabeth Kenwrick-Cox (1s 1981; 1d 1983).

Keogh, David John; Khartoum since October 1988; born 24/06/56; FCO 1979; Ankara 1980; Abu Dhabi 1981; FCO 1983; Islamabad 1984; FCO 1988; Band B3; m 1987 Carolyn Ann Connolly (diss 1990).

Kernohan, Neil Alexander, MBE (1997); FCO since February 2000; born 20/09/65; FCO 1989; Riyadh 1992; T/D Vice-Consul Sana'a 1994; Vice-Consul and Third Secretary (Management) BIS Tripoli 1995; Third Secretary (IAEA/UN) Vienna (UKMIS) 1997; Band B3.

Kerr, Christine; Nicosia since July 2002; born 07/04/60; FCO 1989; Cape Town/Pretoria 1991; Moscow 1994; FCO 1996; Lilongwe 1998; Band A2; m 1991 Andrew Tuck (diss 1996) (1d 1994).

Kerr, Douglas James; First Secretary (Commercial) Lima since April 1999; born 04/11/58; FCO 1980; Bucharest 1982; Kampala 1984; Tel Aviv 1988; FCO 1991.

Kerr, Michael John; Second Secretary (Management) Prague since September 1998; born 12/08/49; RAF 1969-73; FCO 1973; Islamabad 1975; FCO 1977; Dakar 1979; FCO 1983; Cairo 1985; Osaka 1989; Second Secretary FCO 1992; Jedda 1995; m 1975 Linda Ruth Campbell (2s 1982, 1984; 1d 1989).

Kerrison, Irene; Moscow since March 1999; born 09/02/65; FCO 1986; Peking 1988; FCO 1990; Nassau 1991; FCO 1995; Language Training 1998-99; Band B3.

Kerry, Catherine; Tortola since July 1998; born 31/07/65; FCO 1988; Lagos 1991; Band A2.

Kershaw, Alexander Richard; SUPL since May 2002; born 15/01/67; FCO 1991; Language Training 1993; Second Secretary FCO 1995; First Secretary (UN) Geneva (UKMIS) 1997; First Secretary FCO 2000; Band D6; m 1994 Suzanne Michelle Jones (2s 1996, 1999).

Kershaw, Roger; FCO since September 2001; born 18/03/58; FCO 1982; Language Training 1983; Second Secretary (Commercial) Tehran 1984; First Secretary FCO 1987; First Secretary (Economic) Bonn 1992; First Secretary FCO 1996; Deputy High Commissioner Lagos 2000; m 1983 Annick Marie Jeanne Réné Gourley (2d 1986, 1988; 1s 1993).

Kettle, Mark Brian, MBE (2002); Third Secretary (Consular) Islamabad since February 1999; born 22/10/66; FCO 1985; Vienna (UKMIS) 1990; FCO 1993; Muscat 1995; Band A2; m 1995 Justine Carey.

Khoo, Lionel John; Bandar Seri Begawan since March 1996; born 30/04/68; Northern Ireland Office 1991; FCO 1994; Band A2.

Kidd, John Christopher William; Counsellor (Political) Bonn later Berlin since September 1998; born 04/02/57; FCO 1978; Third later Second Secretary Nicosia 1980; Second Secretary and PS to HM Ambassador Paris 1984 ; (First Secretary 1985); First Secretary FCO 1986; Deputy Head of Mission Addis Ababa 1990; FCO 1993; Counsellor on secondment to European Commission 1996; m 1995 Carine Celia Ann Maitland (1 step d 1983; 1 step s 1986; twin d 1996).

Kidner, James Hippisley; First Secretary (Political) Sofia since October 1996; born 26/02/61; FCO 1985; Second Secretary Kuala Lumpur 1987; First Secretary FCO 1990; On attachment to Privy Council Office as PS to Leader of the House of Commons 1992; First Secretary FCO 1993; m 1987 Sally Baillie-Hamilton (2d 1996, 1998).

Kilby, David James; First Secretary (Political) and Deputy Permanent Representative ESCAP Bangkok since April 2001; born 05/11/66; FCO 2000; Band D6; m 1997 Alison Jean McKenna.

Kilford, Yvonne; World Wide Floater Duties since April 1997; born 08/01/70; FCO 1988; Brussels (UKREP) 1993; Band A2.

Kiloh, Eleanor Anne; Second Secretary (Political) Jakarta since March 2002; born 20/04/77; FCO 1999; Band C4.

Kilroy, Sarah-Jill Lennard; First Secretary FCO since November 1998; born 19/04/56; FCO 1981; Third Secretary Montevideo 1982; Brussels (UKREP) 1983; Second Secretary FCO 1983; First Secretary FCO 1985; Budapest 1994; Band D6; m 1987 Mark Kilroy (1s 1989; 1d 1992).

Kilvington, Sally Louise; FCO since July 1995; born 20/02/67; FCO 1989; Santiago 1991; Band A2.

Kinchen, Richard, MVO (1976); HM Ambassador Beirut since December 2000; born 12/02/48; (temporary secondment to British Commission on Rhodesian Opinion 1972); Third Secretary FCO 1970; MECAS 1972; Kuwait 1973; Second Secretary FCO 1974; Second later First Secretary

Luxembourg 1975; First Secretary (Economic) Paris 1977; FCO 1980; PS/Parliamentary Under-Secretary of State 1982; First Secretary and Head of Chancery Rabat 1984; Counsellor (Finance) New York (UKMIS) 1988; Head of Dependent Territories Secretariat Bridgetown 1993; m 1972 Cheryl Vivienne Abayasekera (1s 1976; 3d 1973 (dec'd 1980), 1979, 1982).

King, Albert Norman, OBE, LVO (1983); First Secretary (Management) Lagos since September 1994; born 29/03/43; Customs and Excise 1963; Government Actuary's Department 1963; CRO 1964; DSA 1965; Ibadan 1967; BMG Berlin 1971; Second Secretary (Commercial) Singapore 1973; Second Secretary (Commercial) Muscat 1976; First Secretary Dacca 1980; First Secretary FCO 1984; First Secretary (Admin) Vienna 1987; First Secretary FCO 1992; m 1969 Dympna Mary Farren (1s 1971; 2d 1973, 1979).

King, Alison Jane; FCO since January 1998; born 11/06/66; FCO 1984; Brussels (UKREP) 1987; Mexico City 1989; Band C4.

King, Julian Beresford; First Secretary (External) Brussels (UKREP) since August 1998; born 22/08/64; FCO 1985; Third later Second Secretary Paris 1987; (ENA and PS/HMA); EC Presidency Liason Officer Luxembourg and The Hague 1991; Second later First Secretary FCO 1992; Private Secretary to Permanent Under-Secretary of State FCO 1995; m 1992 Lotte Viwdelov Knudsen.

King, Larry; FCO since March 1998; born 01/07/62; FCO 1982; Amman 1985; FCO 1988; Band C4; m 1988 Elaine Margaret Neeve (1d 1996).

King-Smith, Alastair; Khartoum since November 1999; born 27/09/74; FCO 1996; Full-Time Language Training 1997; Cairo 1998; Band C4.

Kingdom, David George; Ankara since August 2000; born 19/08/46; FCO 1986; Third Secretary Brussels 1992; First Secretary FCO 1994; Band C5; m 1968 Janice (2s 1972, 1981).

Kingston, Iain Conger; Second Secretary FCO since 1995; born 30/05/50; DOE (PSA) 1975; FCO 1976; Cairo 1979; Lilongwe 1983; FCO 1985; Houston 1988; Maseru 1991; Band B3; m 1978 Georgia Georgiou (2s 1982, 1983).

Kinoshita, Susan Margaret (née Copnell); First Secretary (Press and Public Affairs) Tokyo since August 1999; born 28/07/61; FCO 1983; Language Training Tokyo 1985; Tokyo 1986; FCO 1989; SUPL 1991; FCO 1992; SUPL 1993; Osaka 1996; Band D6; m 1989 Makoto Kinoshita (1d 1991; 1s 1993).

Kirby, Diane (née Tallon); Gibraltar since March 1993; born 25/01/67; FCO 1986; Muscat 1988; Band A2; m 1988 Sean William Kirby.

Kirby, Gordon; First Secretary (Commercial/Economic) Zagreb since April 1999; born 22/02/43; GPO 1960; Ministry of Technology 1968; FCO 1970; Amman 1972; MECAS 1975;

Arabic language training at Army School of Languages 1976; Vice-Consul Beirut 1976; Vice-Consul Jedda 1977; Serbo-Croatian language training 1981; Second Secretary (Commercial) Belgrade 1982; FCO 1985; First Secretary and Deputy Head of Mission Sana'a 1989; First Secretary FCO 1994; FCO 1996; m 1972 Kathleen Margaret Dawn (2d 1978, 1982).

Kirk, Andrew Philip; Second Secretary (Development) The Hague since September 1999; born 26/02/54; FCO 1972; Yaoundé 1975; Havana 1979; FCO 1981; Vice-Consul Lisbon 1985; Aid Attaché Nairobi 1987; Second Secretary FCO 1991; BTIO New York 1994; Vice-Consul (Investment) San Francisco 1997; FCO 1997; Band C4; m 1978 Cheryl Jeanne Nichols (2d 1983, 1987).

Kirk, Anna Theresa (née Macey); Counsellor on loan to Civil Service Selection Board as Resident Chair since September 1999; born 01/06/59; FCO 1982; Third later Second Secretary Oslo 1984; Language Training 1984; First Secretary FCO 1988; First Secretary (Political) Paris 1992; First Secretary FCO 1997; m 1989 Matthew John Lushington Kirk (2d 1995, 1998).

Kirk, Malcolm; Staff Officer Tortola since June 2000; born 10/04/59; FCO 1978; Nassau 1980; Dakar 1981; FCO 1984; Havana 1985; FCO 1987; Paris 1990; Deputy Head of Mission Tegucigalpa 1993; FCO 1997; Band C4; m 1982 Linda Patricia Greenwood (1 step s 1980; 1s 1983).

Kirk, Matthew John Lushington; HM Ambassador Helsinki since August 2002; born 10/10/60; FCO 1982; Third later Second Secretary (Political/Information) Belgrade 1984; Language Training 1984; Second later First Secretary FCO 1988; ENA Paris 1992; First Secretary (Political/Military) Paris 1993; Counsellor FCO 1997; Counsellor on loan to Cabinet Office 1998; Counsellor FCO 1999; m 1989 Anna Thérèse Macey (2d 1995, 1998).

Kirk, Susan Mary; Rabat since September 2002; born 28/04/46; FCO 1994; Nairobi 1996; Floater Duties 2000; Band A2; m 1969 (1s 1975).

Kirkpatrick, Andrew John; Second Secretary (Management) Lagos since January 1999; born 01/06/63; FCO 1988; Third Secretary (Chancery) Budapest 1990; Third Secretary FCO 1992; Third Secretary (Immigration) Islamabad 1995; Third Secretary FCO 1998; Band C5; m 1992 Sara Elizabeth Pickering.

Kitsell, Corinne Angela; FCO since August 1998; born 18/10/69; FCO 1992; T/D New York (UKMIS) 1994; T/D Beijing 1995; Vice-Consul Beirut 1996; Band C4.

Knapp, Maria Grace; Santiago since July 2002; born 03/04/70; On loan to HM Customs and Excise at Caracas 1996; FCO 1989; Madrid 1992; FCO 1995; FCO 1999; Band B3.

Knewstubb, Rosemary Ann (née Urch); Brussels (UKREP) since July 2002; born 26/10/68; FCO

1992; Ottawa 1995; Bucharest 1999; Band A2; m 1996 Mark Andrew Knewstubb.

Knight, Terence Ronald; Resident British Commissioner Kingstown since August 2002; born 03/09/51; FCO 1973; Rabat 1976; Lima 1978; Islamabad 1981; FCO 1983; Oslo 1986; Third later Second Secretary (Chancery) Port of Spain 1989; Second Secretary FCO 1993; First Secretary (Management) Washington 1997; m 1971 Jane Willcocks (2d 1975, 1980; 2s 1977, 1982).

Knott, Graeme Jonathan; First Secretary (Trade and Investment) UKDEL OECD Paris since September 2000; born 02/11/66; FCO 1988; Third later Second Secretary (Chancery) Havana 1991; First Secretary FCO 1995; First Secretary Mexico City 1996; Full-Time Language Training 2000; Band D6.

Knott, Paul Robert; Second Secretary (Commercial) Brussels (UKREP) since February 2001; born 30/06/70; FCO 1989; Bucharest 1992; Dubai 1993; Third Secretary (Chancery) Tashkent 1997; Full-time Russian language training 1997; Second Secretary (Political) Kiev 2000; Band C4.

Knowlton, Richard Jonathan; Counsellor Caracas since March 2002; born 25/03/50; Third later Second Secretary FCO 1973; Language Student FCO and Finland 1977; Second later First Secretary Helsinki 1978; First Secretary FCO 1981; Harare 1984; FCO 1989; First Secretary (Chancery/Economic) Dubai 1991; First Secretary later Counsellor FCO 1995; Counsellor (Regional Affairs) Bridgetown 1997; Counsellor FCO 2000; m 1995 Evelina Ravarino.

Korad, Mark David; Paris since August 1998; born 19/06/69; FCO 1991; Bucharest 1994; Band B3; m 1996 Corina Ioana Mantu.

Kotak, Sheetal Arun; FCO since September 1993; born 27/08/69; FCO 1988; Madrid 1991; Band B3.

Kraus, John Arthur; Second Secretary (Political) Bonn since May 1995; born 07/05/66; FCO 1993; m 1995 Judith Mary Smakman (1s 1996).

Kruger, Gabrielle Lisa; FCO since September 2001; born 22/02/76; Band C4.

Kuenssberg, Joanna Kate; First Secretary (EU Economic) Paris since January 2001; born 06/02/73; Attachment, Foreign Ministry, Budapest 1999; Attachment, Quai d'Orsay, Paris 2000; Second Secretary FCO 1997; FCO 1997; m 1997 Finbarr O'Sullivan

Kydd, Ian Douglas; Consul-General Vancouver since March 1998; born 01/11/47; First Secretary on loan to No 10 Downing Street 1981; DSAO (later FCO) 1966; CO 1966; New Delhi 1970; Second Secretary (Radio/TV) BIS New York 1975; FCO 1979; Language Training 1983; First Secretary (Chancery) Lagos 1984; First Secretary (Economic/Commercial) Ottawa 1988; First Secretary FCO 1993; Counsellor (Management) Moscow 1995; m 1968 Elizabeth Louise Pontius (1s 1971; 1d 1973).

Kyle, Michael Anthony; Counsellor FCO since February 1998; born 20/07/48; FCO 1970; Third later Second Secretary Saigon 1972; Second later First Secretary FCO 1975; Washington 1978; FCO 1981; First Secretary (Political/Economic) Accra 1984; First Secretary (Chancery) Dar es Salaam 1988; First Secretary later Counsellor FCO 1991; Counsellor Berlin 1995; m 1976 Wendy Suzanne Sloan (1d 1979; 1s 1981).

Kyles, Raymond William; Deputy Head of News Department FCO since October 2000; born 10/03/56; FCO 1980; Geneva (UKMIS) 1982; Second Secretary Brussels (UKREP) 1985; First Secretary FCO 1987; First Secretary (Chancery) Pretoria 1991; First Secretary FCO 1996; Deputy Permanent Representative Paris (OECD) 1998; m 1981 Christine Jane Thompson.

L

Lacey-Smith, Jane Frances; T/D Manila since July 2000; born 20/09/63; FCO 1984; East Berlin 1985; Dublin 1987; Algiers 1990; Vice-Consul/Management Frankfurt 1997; Bangkok 1999; Band C4; m 1995 Martin Frederick Smith.

Ladd, Michael John; FCO since 1992; born 23/10/54; FCO 1971; Washington 1980; FCO 1983; Baghdad 1986; Vienna 1990; Band D6; m 1979 Christine Jane Tate (1s 1983; 1d 1986).

Ladva, Sharad Raiya; Manila since July 1998; born 12/07/60; FCO 1978; Belmopan 1985; Yaoundé 1989; FCO 1993; T/D Riga 1994; Zagreb 1998; Band B3; m 1988 Ellen Louis Santana (1s 1991).

Laffey, Susan; First Secretary (Political) Bucharest since January 2001; born 09/10/61; FCO 1985; Senior Research Officer (DS Band C4) 1987; East Berlin 1987; Second Secretary (Chancery) Bucharest 1989; FCO 1992; UKDEL OSCE Budapest 1994; Principal Research Analyst FCO 1995; FCO 1996; UKDEL OSCE Vienna 1996; T/D Zagreb 1998; Band D6.

Laing, (John) Stuart; HM Ambassador Muscat since April 2002; born 22/07/48; Third Secretary FCO 1970; MECAS 1971; Third later Second Secretary Jedda 1973; Second later First Secretary Brussels (UKREP) 1975; FCO 1978; First Secretary and Head of Chancery Cairo 1983; First Secretary FCO 1987; Deputy Head of Mission Prague 1989; Counsellor and Deputy Head of Mission Riyadh 1992; Counsellor FCO 1995; High Commissioner Brunei 1998; m 1972 Sibella Dorman (1s 1974; 2d 1979, 1985).

Laing, Paul James; First Secretary FCO since December 1992; born 01/12/53; HM Customs and Excise 1974-80; FCO 1980; APS to Parliamentary Under Secretary of State 1982; New Delhi 1983; Second later First Secretary FCO 1985; BMG later BEBO Berlin 1990; Band D6; m 1982 Dawn Myerscough (3d 1986, 1988, 1990; 1s 1992).

Laird, Alison Margaret; FCO since September 2000; born 05/12/75; Band C4.

Lake, Robin Duncan; Third Secretary New York (UKMIS) since January 2002; born 15/12/70; FCO 1989; Berlin 1991; Ottawa 1994; FCO 1997; Third Secretary (Immigration) Tehran 1998; Band B3.

Lamb, Robin David; Counsellor and Deputy Head of Mission Kuwait since October 2001; born 25/11/48; PRO (Band D6); Counsellor, on loan to the DTI 1999; Research Officer (DS Band C4); FCO 1971; Language Training MECAS 1974; FCO 1977; Second Secretary Jedda 1979; Principal Research Officer FCO 1982; First Secretary (Economic) Riyadh 1985; FCO 1988; First Secretary (Head of Political Section) Cairo 1993; FCO 1996; m 1977 Susan Jane Moxon (1d 1982; 2s 1986, 1996).

Lambert, Jason Edward; Nairobi since October 1999; born 27/09/71; FCO 1990; Brussels 1994; FCO 1997; Band B3; m 1997 Lucy Anne Edwards.

Lambert, Lucy Anne (née Edwards); Nairobi since July 2000; born 05/05/71; FCO 1993; Brussels (UKREP) 1995; FCO 1997; SUPL 1999; Band A2; m 1997 Jason Edward Lambert.

Lamont, Donald Alexander; Governor Stanley and Commissioner for South Georgia and Sandwich Islands since May 1999; born 13/01/47; Second later First Secretary FCO 1974; First Secretary (UNIDO/IAEA) Vienna 1977; First Secretary (Commercial) Moscow 1980; First Secretary FCO 1982; Counsellor and Head of Chancery BMG (later BM) Berlin 1988; Counsellor on attachment to IISS 1988; HM Ambassador Montevideo 1991; Head of Republic of Ireland Department 1994; Chief of Staff, OHR Sarajevo 1997; m 1981 Lynda Margaret Campbell (1d 1983; 1s 1986).

Lampert, Sarah Jane; SUPL since September 1999; born 08/11/65; FCO 1988; Language Training 1990; Third later Second Secretary (Chancery) Sofia 1991; First Secretary FCO 1995; SUPL 1996; First Secretary FCO 1997; Band D6; m 1993 Andrew William Kenningham (2d 1996, 1998).

Lamport, Martin Henry; First Secretary (Commercial) Lima since July 2002; born 22/11/52; HM Forces 1972; FCO 1975; SUPL 1976; FCO 1979; Tripoli 1980; Caracas 1983; FCO 1987; Third Secretary (Institutions) Brussels (UKREP) 1990; Deputy High Commissioner Belmopan 1993; FCO 1996; Deputy Head of Mission Sana'a 1999; Band C5; m 1990 Catherine Priscilla Maxwell (3d 1992, 1994, 1996).

Lamport, Stephen Mark Jeffrey; SUPL since December 1996; born 27/11/51; New York (UKMIS) 1974; Third later Second Secretary Tehran 1975; Third Secretary FCO 1975; First Secretary FCO 1980; Private Secretary to Minister of State 1981; First Secretary (Chancery) Rome 1984; First Secretary later Counsellor FCO 1988; On loan to the Prince of Wales' Office as Deputy Private Secretary 1993; m 1979 Angela Vivien Paula Hervey (2s 1983, 1985; 1d 1990).

Lancaster, Ian Francis Millar; Counsellor FCO since January 1995; born 23/09/47; Second Secretary FCO 1974; Second later First Secretary and Consul Hanoi 1975; First Secretary FCO 1977; Prague 1978; First Secretary FCO 1981; First Secretary (Chancery) Brussels 1983; First Secretary FCO 1987; First Secretary (Chancery) later Counsellor Ankara 1991; m 1972 Simone Daniel (1d 1978; 1s 1981).

Lance, Andrew Robert; Senior Principal Research Officer FCO since September 1993; born 13/08/43; FO 1962; SUPL 1962; DSAO 1965; Prague 1969; Second Secretary (Chancery) The Hague 1972; FCO 1976; First Secretary (Commercial) East Berlin 1977; FCO 1981; Transferred to Research Cadre 1990; m 1966 Sandra Rosemarie Jackson (1d 1967).

Landsman, Dr David Maurice, OBE (2000); HM Ambassador Tirana since July 2001; born 23/08/63; FCO 1989; Second Secretary (Economic) Athens 1991; FCO 1994; Deputy Head of Mission Belgrade 1997; FCO 1999; Head of British Embassy Office Banja Luka and concurrently First Secretary (Regional Affairs) Budapest 1999; Chargé d'Affaires Belgrade 2000; m 1990 Catherine Louise Holden (1s 1992).

Lane, Bari Albert; First Secretary (Management) Paris since December 1992; born 06/05/48; Ministry of Technology 1965; Vice-Consul Aden 1970; Warsaw 1973; Bombay 1974; FCO 1975; Second Secretary (Admin) Peking 1978; Vice-Consul (Commercial) Sydney 1980; Second later First Secretary FCO 1985; FO, DSAO and FCO 1966; m 1971 Jacqueline Mary Chatt.

Lang, Susan Margaret; Bonn since March 1984; born 30/04/48; Beirut 1970; Brussels 1972; FCO 1978; Dublin 1979; East Berlin 1982; Band B3.

Langham, Elizabeth Jane (née Webb); SUPL since July 2001; born 04/08/61; FCO 1984; Moscow 1986; Washington 1988; FCO 1991; SUPL 1992; Bahrain 1995; SUPL 1996; Second Secretary Stockholm 1997; m 1989 Peter Andrew Langham (2d 1992, 1994).

Langham, Peter Andrew; Second Secretary Stockholm since April 1998; born 26/09/64; FCO 1983; Moscow 1985; Hamilton 1988; Washington 1990; FCO 1991; Bahrain 1994; m 1989 Elizabeth Jane Webb (2d 1992, 1994).

Langman, Nicholas John Andrew; First Secretary FCO since September 1998; born 01/11/60; FCO 1983; Second Secretary Montevideo 1986; Second later First Secretary New York (UKMIS) 1988; First Secretary FCO 1991; Paris 1994; Band D6; m 1992 Sarah Jane Pearcey (2d 1994, 1995).

Langridge, Pauline Anne; Havana since August 2000; born 17/08/63; FCO 1988; Madrid 1990; Guatemala 1993; FCO 1995; Band A2.

Langrish, Sally (née Monk); First Secretary (JHA) Brussels (UKREP) since September 2001; born 05/08/68; Called to the Bar Middle Temple 1991; Treasury Solicitors Department 1993; Assistant Legal Advisor FCO 1995; First Secretary (Legal) Brussels (UKREP) 2000; Band D7; m 1996 Richard Michael John Langrish.

Lapsley, Angus Charles William; First Secretary (Political/Internal) Paris since April 2001; born 16/03/70; Second Secretary Department of Health 1991; Second Secretary Brussels (UKREP) 1994; Private Secretary Department of Health 1995; Private Secretary No 10 Downing Street 1996; First Secretary Head IGC Unit EUD(I) 1999; Band D6; m 1999 Georgina Maria Power.

Larden, Kendra Jane; Peking since April 2000; born 07/03/71; FCO 1991; Paris 1993; Muscat 1996; Band A2.

Larkins, Christopher Paul; FCO since March 2000; born 02/10/63; FCO 1986; Warsaw 1991; FCO 1994; Hong Kong 1996; Band A2.

Larmouth, Helen Dorothy; Lilongwe since December 1994; born 22/08/63; FCO 1989; Washington 1992; Band A2.

Larner, Jeremy Francis; Deputy Director General BTCO Taipei since 1999; born 12/11/49; Inland Revenue 1967; FCO 1968; Cairo 1971; Abu Dhabi 1972; Benghazi 1972; Seoul 1975; Moscow 1975; Manila 1976; Monrovia 1977; FCO 1980; Third later Second Secretary (Commercial) Tunis 1983; Second Secretary (Commercial) Port Louis 1989; Second later First Secretary FCO 1992; Deputy Head of Mission and HM Consul Rangoon 1995; Band D6; m 1975 Sally Dewhurst (2s 1978, 1980).

Lassman, Louise (née Mason); FCO since April 2000; born 30/08/63; FCO 1986; Gibraltar 1993; Hong Kong 1996; Band B3; m 1993 Nigel Abraham Lassman.

Latham, Sarah Jane; FCO since July 2002; born 24/06/70; FCO 1996; Ankara 1998; Band B3; m 2002 Firat Ucer.

Latta, Nicholas Karim; Second Secretary (Commercial) Moscow since May 2002; born 02/09/71; FCO 1995; Full-Time Language Training 1996; Full-Time Language Training Cairo 1997; Second Secretary Muscat 1998; Band C4; m 1997 Susanna Mary Davis (1d 2000, 1s 2002).

Latter, Edwin John Scott; First Secretary FCO since August 1997; born 16/02/68; FCO 1991; Vice-Consul Istanbul 1994; Band D6; m 1994 Rosemary Helen Fabre (1d 1996).

Lattin-Rawstrone, Howard; First Secretary (Commercial) Warsaw since August 1999; born 23/03/55; FCO 1975; Buenos Aires 1977; Maputo 1981; Brussels 1982; FCO 1984; Cairo 1988; Second Secretary (Commercial/Aid) Cairo 1991; Second Secretary Lilongwe 1993; FCO 1997; m (1) 1980 Sylvia Christine Waller (diss 1987); (2) 1987 Caroline Sarah Lattin (2 adopted d 1976, 1978; 1s 1987).

Lavender, Fiona Jayne; Bangkok since January 2000; born 12/06/70; FCO 1991; Tokyo 1992; La Paz 1996; Band B3.

Lavers, Richard Douglas; HM Ambassador Guatemala City since October 2001; born 10/05/47; Third Secretary FCO 1969; Buenos Aires 1970; Second later First Secretary Wellington 1973; FCO 1976; First Secretary (Political/Economic) Brussels 1981; On secondment to Guinness Mahon 1985; First Secretary FCO 1987; NATO Defence College Rome 1989; HM Ambassador Quito 1993; Deputy Head of Mission and Consul-General Santiago 1993; Counsellor FCO 1997; Head of Research Analysts FCO 1999; m 1986 Brigitte Anne Julia Maria Moers (2s 1988, 1989).

Lavery, Creena Christina Maureen; Consul (Consular/Immigration) Düsseldorf since September 2000; born 17/05/62; FCO 1991; Brussels (UKDEL NATO) 1993; Presidency Liason Officer Luxembourg 1997; Bonn 1999; Band C4.

Lavery, Derek John; Baku since July 2002; born 01/06/68; FCO 1987; Islamabad 1989; Bonn 1993; FCO 1996; Band B3; m 1992 Claire Ruth Haines.

Lavocat, Amanda Joyce (née Thomas); Dakar since August 2000; born 21/12/67; DHSS 1986; FCO 1987; Pretoria 1989; Algiers 1992; FCO 1994; Istanbul 1997; Band B3; m 1993 Frederic Paul Francis Lavocat (1s 1995).

Lawley, Claire Angela; FCO since 2001; born 14/06/62; FCO 1984; Rome 1985; SUPL 1988; Resigned 1989; Reinstated 1994; FCO 1994; Ottawa 1996; Vice-Consul New Delhi 1999; Band B3; (1s 1988).

Lawrence, Joanne Louise (née Watson); T/D Kabul since August 2002; born 30/04/68; FCO 1986; Wellington 1988; SUPL 1992; Stanley 1995; Islamabad 1998; FCO 2001; Band C4; m 1991 Martin Lawrence (2d 1993, 1999).

Lawrence, Paul David; Kigali since May 2000; born 10/04/68; FCO 1989; New York (UKMIS) 1993; World Wide Floater Duties 1997; Band B3.

Lawrie, James Malcolm, MBE (1985); Second Secretary Lagos since November 2000; born 01/06/44; FCO 1970; Jedda 1972; FCO 1973; Islamabad 1975; FCO 1977; Kuwait 1979; FCO 1983; Third Secretary Peking 1984; FCO 1986; Accra 1990; FCO 1993; Cairo 1995; FCO 1998; Band C4; m (1) 1971 Anne Margaret Martin (diss) (3s 1974, 1977, 1982); (2) 2000 Sheila Boxer.

Laxton, Rowan James; Deputy Head of Mission Kabul since September 2002; born 19/02/61; FCO 1993; First Secretary (Chancery) Islamabad 1997; FCO 2000; Band D6; m 2000 Sonya L Laxton.

Laycock, Rachel Jane; Second Secretary (Chancery) Washington since May 2000; born 20/05/71; FCO 1994; Band C4; m 2000 Owen Pengelly.

Layden, Anthony Michael; HM Ambassador Tripoli since October 2002; born 27/07/46; Third Secretary FCO 1968; MECAS 1969; Second Secretary Jedda 1971; Second later First Secretary Rome 1973; FCO 1977; First Secretary FCO 1982; First Secretary and Head of Chancery Jedda 1982; Head of Chancery Muscat 1987; Counsellor (Commercial/Economic) Copenhagen 1991; Counsellor FCO 1995; HM Ambassador Rabat 1999; m 1969 Josephine Mary McGhee (3s 1973, 1974, 1977; 1d 1982).

Layfield, Jonathan Timothy Whitton; Amman since December 2001; born 09/06/67; FCO 1997; Band B3; m 1997 Rebecca Anne (1s 2001).

Leach, Patricia Kathleen; Brussels (UKREP) since February 1983; born 15/01/53; DOI 1973-76; East Berlin 1978; FCO 1978; New York (UKMIS) 1981; Band A2.

Leake, Nicholas Howard; First Secretary (Industry) Brussels (UKREP) since September 2000; born 15/01/72; FCO 1994; Second Secretary (KHF) Budapest 1996.

LeBlond, Charmaine Mary; FCO since June 1998; born 24/02/43.

Leck, George; FCO since July 1991; born 06/04/56; FCO 1979; Ankara 1980; Africa/Middle East Floater 1984; Latin America/Caribbean Floater 1986; Islamabad 1987; Band B3.

Lee, Adrian Jonathan; FCO since 2000; born 24/10/68; FCO 1989; Full-Time Language Training Cairo 1991; Third Secretary (Commercial later Political) Riyadh 1992; British Vice-Consul and Management Officer São Paulo 1996; Band C4.

Lee, Julie Yvonne (née Watts); Peking since November 1998; born 22/12/67; FCO 1987; New York (UKMIS) 1988; Budapest 1991; Banjul 1993; FCO 1994; Band A2.

Lee, Richard John Clifton; SMO Tel Aviv since September 2002; born 26/09/51; FCO 1971; Copenhagen 1973; Addis Ababa 1976; Moscow 1979; FCO 1982; Accra 1984; Lusaka 1987; FCO 1989; Second Secretary (Commercial) Kuwait 1992; Jakarta 1994; Second Secretary FCO 1999; m 1973 Lesley Eleanor McConnell (1d 1980; 1s 1982).

Lee, Thomas David; SUPL since July 2002; born 09/05/63; FCO 1983; Nicosia 1987; Third later Second Secretary FCO 1990; Band C4.

Lee-Gorton, Victoria (née Lee); Full-Time Language Training since May 2001; born 05/03/70; FCO 1990; Full-Time Language Training 1992; Third Secretary Maputo 1993; Third Secretary EU Presidency Liason Officer Rome/Dublin/The Hague 1995; Third later Second Secretary FCO 1997; Band C4; m 1992 Christopher John Gorton (1d 2001).

Lees, Andrea Margaret; FCO since June 1989; born 19/07/68; Band A2.

Lees, Diana Jane; Second Secretary FCO since May 1996; born 08/03/44; FCO 1977; New Delhi 1978; Moscow 1981; Bonn 1983; FCO 1985; Valletta 1989; Sana'a 1993; Band C5.

Legg, Judy; Director New York since May 2002; born 29/04/67; FCO 1991; Full-Time Language Training 1992; Second Secretary 1993; Moscow 1994; First Secretary FCO 1995; SUPL 2000; Band D6; m 1994 Graham Barry Stanley (1d 1998).

Legg, Michael Henry Frank; First Secretary (Management) Madrid since 1999; born 11/03/43; On loan to DOT 1978; CRO 1961; DSAO 1965; Beira 1967; Delhi 1968; Belgrade 1972; FCO 1976; Second Secretary (Commercial) Madras 1980; Consul (Commercial) Milan 1984; First Secretary FCO 1989; First Secretary Mexico 1991; First Secretary FCO 1996; Band D6; m 1972 Chantal Violette Gonthier (2s 1976, 1979).

Legg, Rufus Alexander; Second Secretary FCO since October 2000; born 13/03/68; FCO 1990; Third Secretary Port Moresby 1993; Third later Second Secretary and Deputy Head of Mission Tegucigalpa 1997; Band C4.

Leggatt, Alison Elaine; FCO since October 1995; born 06/12/43; FO 1965; Bonn 1967; Munich 1969; Frankfurt 1969; Islamabad 1972; FCO 1973; Bridgetown 1974; FCO 1976; FCO 1977; Washington 1977; Helsinki 1979; FCO 1981; Caracas 1985; FCO 1988; The Hague 1993; Band A2.

Legge, Jeremy John; First Secretary (Political) Paris since August 2001; born 19/05/61; Second Secretary FCO 1985; Second Secretary Lusaka 1987; Second later First Secretary FCO 1989; First secretary on loan to the Cabinet Office 1989; Vienna (UKMIS) 1994; First Secretary FCO 1998; Band D6; m 1990 Melanie King (3s 1991, 1992, 1994).

Leigh, David John; Second later First Secretary FCO since August 1987; born 03/07/48; Post Office 1964; FCO 1969; Lagos 1974; FCO 1975; Third Secretary Tokyo 1978; FCO 1981; Third Secretary Sofia 1984.

Leigh Phippard, Dr Helen Thérèse; FCO since December 1990; born 08/11/64; Band SRO; m 1990 Anthony David Phippard.

Leister, Helen Grace (née McCarthy); Ottawa since August 2000; born 01/02/64; FCO 1983; Paris 1985; Luxembourg 1988; Paris 1991; Kiev 1994; FCO 1996; Ottawa 1999; SUPL 2000; Band B3; m 1991 Alan Leister.

Leith, Dennis, RVM (1975); First Secretary (Commercial) Sofia since September 1998; born 10/12/48; FCO 1967; Moscow 1971; Mexico City 1972; Sofia 1975; FCO 1976; Guatemala City 1979; Vienna 1982; Second Secretary FCO 1984; Second Secretary (Commercial) Bahrain 1987; On secondment to the London Chamber of Commerce 1991; Consul-General Ho Chi Minh City 1992; Second Secretary FCO 1995; m 1971 Barbara Mary Hum (1s 1974; 1d 1979).

Lelliott, David Patrick; Second Secretary (Commercial) Mexico City since June 2000; born

13/09/66; FCO 1993; Third Secretary Doha 1996; Band C4.

Leon, Judith Mary; Deputy Consul-General Johannesburg since June 2001; born 17/07/63; Home Office 1984; FCO 1987; New York 1989; Bangkok 1992; FCO 1994; Second Secretary 1995; Second Secretary (Commercial) Bombay 1997.

Leslie, Alison Mariot (née Sanderson); HM Ambassador Oslo since August 2002; born 25/06/54; FCO 1977; Singapore 1978; Bonn 1982; FCO 1986; Quai d'Orsay Paris 1990; Head of ESED 1992; Scottish Office 1993-95; Head of Policy Planning Staff FCO 1996; Deputy Head of Mission Rome 1998; m 1978 Andrew David Leslie (2d 1987, 1990).

Leslie, Thomas Gary; Tokyo since September 1999; born 27/04/69; FCO 1989; Karachi 1991; FCO 1993; Tokyo 1994; Kamakura 1998; Band B3; m 2001 Angela Burns.

Leslie-Jones, Philippa Anne; First Secretary FCO since January 1994; born 19/07/59; FCO 1984; Second Secretary Warsaw 1986; First Secretary FCO 1989; First Secretary (Chancery) Moscow 1991; m 1994 Richard Philip Bridge (2s 1995, 1997).

Levenson, Brenda Susan; Second Secretary FCO since April 1982; born 26/05/44; FO 1962; UKDEL to the Council of Europe Strasbourg 1965; Kampala 1968; FCO 1972; Warsaw 1975; Dar es Salaam 1976; FCO 1979; Second Secretary Belmopan 1981.

Lever, Giles; Tokyo since August 2001; born 20/03/68; FCO 1990; Third later Second Secretary (Political) Hanoi 1993; First Secretary FCO 1997; Full-Time Language Training 2000.

Lever, Simon Jeffrey; Marseilles since September 2001; born 04/01/63; FCO 1983; Doha 1985; SE Asia/FE Floater 1988; Full-Time Language Training 1989; Language Training Hong Kong 1990; Peking 1991; On loan to the DTI 1996; HM Consul Chiang Mai 1998; Peking 2000; Band C5; m 1993 Krisana Khumnuan.

Lever, Sir Paul, KCMG (1998), CMG (1991); HM Ambassador Berlin since October 2000; born 31/03/44; Third Secretary FCO 1966; Third later Second Secretary Helsinki 1967; Brussels (UKDEL NATO) 1971; First Secretary FCO 1973; Assistant Private Secretary to Secretary of State 1978; SUPL with EC Commission Brussels 1981; Head of United Nations Department FCO 1985; Head of Defence, later Security Policy Department 1986; Head of Delegation UKDEL CFE/CSBM Vienna (with personal rank of Ambassador) 1990; AUSS (Defence) FCO 1992; Deputy Secretary, Cabinet Office and Chairman of the Joint Intelligence Committee 1994; DUS (Economic and EU Director) FCO 1996; HM Ambassador Bonn 1997; m 1990 Patricia Anne Ramsey.

Levey, Joanna Claire (née Brewis); SUPL since November 2002; born 22/09/60; FCO 1981;

Kuwait 1983; Luanda 1986; FCO 1989; Copenhagen 1990; FCO 1992; Band A2; m 1997 Robert Edward Levey (1d 2000).

Levi, Andrew Peter Robert; Seconded to Office of the Special Co-ordinator Stability Pact since September 1999; born 04/03/63; FCO 1987; Second Secretary 1989; Second Secretary (Chancery) Bonn 1990; First Secretary FCO 1993; On secondment to the EC September 1996; Band D7.

Levoir, Derek Charles; First Secretary (Consular) Nairobi since September 1999; born 08/08/46; DSAO 1965; Latin America Floater 1969; Rome 1971; FCO 1974; Second Secretary 1976; Asunción 1978; Lisbon 1982; Vice-Consul Naples 1986; FCO 1991; m 1973 Liana Annita Ugo (2d 1975, 1976).

Lewington, Richard George; HM Ambassador Almaty and HM Ambassador (non-resident) Bishkek since July 1999; born 13/04/48; Attached to Army School of Languages 1971; DSAO (later FCO) 1968; Ulaanbaatar 1972; Second Secretary (Chancery/Information) Lima 1976; FCO 1980; Second Secretary (Commercial) Moscow 1982; Second later First Secretary FCO 1983; First Secretary (Commercial) Tel Aviv 1986; First Secretary FCO 1990; EU Monitoring Mission Yugoslavia 1991; Deputy High Commissioner Valletta 1995; m 1972 Sylviane Paulette Marie Cholet (1s 1982; 1d 1984).

Lewis, Alan Edward; Counsellor Ottawa since April 1992; born 18/02/44; Second Secretary FCO 1971; Language Training Tokyo 1972; Second later First Secretary Tokyo 1973; FCO 1975; First Secretary (Economic) Pretoria 1985; First Secretary FCO 1989; m 1966 Linda Mary Goffrey (1s 1979; 1s 1d (twins) 1981).

Lewis, Claire Samantha; New Delhi since March 1998; born 03/06/66; FCO 1990; Madras 1993; Band B3; m 2000 Ian David Booth.

Lewis, Ian Roger; Consul-General Bilbao since September 1998; born 29/10/43; Ministry of Overseas Development 1964; Commonwealth Office DSAO and FCO 1966; Warsaw 1968; Nicosia 1969; Dacca 1972; FCO 1975; LA Floater 1978; FCO 1979; Paris 1981; Athens 1982; HM Consul and Second Secretary (Admin) Santiago 1984; FCO 1984; Second Secretary FCO 1989; Deputy Head of Mission Tegucigalpa 1992; Second Secretary (Commercial) Bahrain 1994; m 1978 Marina Rosa Diez.

Lewis, Dr John Ewart Thomas; Counsellor (Regional Affairs) Buenos Aires since October 2002; born 05/11/55; FCO 1987; First Secretary (Chancery) Bonn 1991; Consul (Economic) Frankfurt 1993; First Secretary FCO 1996; Band D6.

Lewis, Joy Suzanne (née Spalding); SUPL since September 2002; born 01/08/60; FCO 1980; Rio de Janeiro 1983; Buenos Aires 1986; FCO 1988; SUPL 1991; FCO 1998; Band C4.

Lewis, Marion Rachel (née Douche); SUPL since November 1996; born 19/03/69; FCO 1991; Band B3; m 1994 Peter Robert Lewis (2s 1997, 1999; 1d 2001).

Lewis, Peter Robert; First Secretary FCO since October 1999; born 16/08/68; Second Secretary FCO 1994; Second Secretary Berlin 1997; Band D6; m 1994 Marion Rachel Douche (2s 1997, 1999; 1d 2001).

Lewis, Sin; Brussels (UKDEL NATO) since February 1988; born 23/12/65; FCO 1986; Band A2.

Lewis, Trevor James; Second Secretary (Commercial) Shanghai since April 2000; born 08/10/60; FCO 1979; Brussels (UKREP) 1982; Accra 1984; FCO 1988; Washington 1991; Third Secretary (Commercial/Information) Dubai 1994; FCO 1997; Band C4; m 1993 Claire Louise Hawthorne.

Ley, Christopher John; Resource Management Officer, Wider Europe Command; born 14/01/46; FO 1964; Sofia 1968; Rawalpindi/Islamabad 1970; Chicago 1973; Ottawa 1974; FCO 1976; Madrid 1980; Bombay 1983; Second Secretary FCO 1984; Second Secretary (Admin) Rome 1989; Second Secretary (Management) Moscow 1994; First Secretary FCO 1998; m 1969 Joan Marie Lager (2s 1971, 1972).

Ley, Graham John; First Secretary (Regional Affairs) Cairo since September 1999; born 31/05/61; FCO 1984; Second Secretary Cairo 1987; Second later First Secretary FCO 1989; First Secretary (Chancery) Nicosia 1994; First Secretary FCO 1998; Band D6; m 1988 Carol Anne Buchan (1d 1991; 1s 1995).

Liddell, James; Harare since October 1998; born 20/06/45; FCO 1970; Buenos Aires 1973; Blantyre 1975; FCO 1977; Seoul 1980; Suva 1984; Second Secretary FCO 1988; Consul (Commercial) Perth 1992; m 1978 Jillian Stella Coventry.

Liddle, Johanna Mary; FCO since April 2002; born 13/09/71; Band D6.

Life, Vivien Frances; Counsellor FCO since April 1999; born 30/05/57; Civil Service Dept. 1979; HM Treasury 1981; FCO 1988; First Secretary Washington 1992; First Secretary FCO 1996; m 1989 Timothy Michael Dowse (2d 1991, 1994).

Lillie, Stephen; Consul-General Guangzhou since October 1999; born 04/02/66; FCO 1988; Full-Time Language Training 1989; Full-Time Language Training Hong Kong 1990; Second later First Secretary (Economic/Political) Peking 1992; FCO 1996; m 1991 Denise Chit Lo (2s 1997, 1999).

Lillington, Leisa; FCO since April 1995; born 23/01/65; Home Office 1985; FCO 1991; Vienna (UKDEL) 1992; Band A2.

Linacre, Joanne Tracy; Peking since September 1987; born 22/10/64; DHSS 1981; FCO 1985; Band A2.

Lindfield, John Richard, MBE (1999); Consul (Investment) San Francisco since July 1999; born 12/05/59; FCO 1978; DHSS 1978; Cairo 1981; Floater Duties 1984; Karachi 1985; FCO 1989; Second Secretary 1994; Vice-Consul (Commercial) Cape Town 1995; m 1985 Judith Christine Brown (2s 1988, 1990).

Lindley, Graham; Kampala since May 2000; born 18/03/46; Royal Navy 1964; HOPD 1982; Bucharest 1988; Prague 1990; Brussels 1992; Hong Kong 1996; Band B3; m 1967 Anita Wood (1s 1969; 1d 1976).

Lindsay, Bridget Clare (née O'Riordan); Second Secretary British Trade International since January 2001; born 13/08/59; FCO 1980; Warsaw 1982; Tokyo 1984; SUPL 1986; Canberra 1987; FCO 1989; SUPL 1991; FCO 1992; SUPL 1994; SUPL 1995; Tokyo 1995; m 1983 Iain Ferrier Lindsay (1s 1991).

Lindsay, Dawn Novelle; On loan to DfID since September 1998; born 06/06/62; FCO 1985; Lagos 1988; FCO 1991; Minsk 1994; Band B3.

Lindsay, Iain Ferrier, OBE (2002); FCO since September 1999; born 09/03/59; FCO 1980; Warsaw 1982; Tokyo 1983; Third later Second Secretary (Political) Canberra 1986; Second Secretary FCO 1989; First Secretary (Political) Tokyo 1994; m 1983 Bridget Clare O'Riordan (1s 1991).

Lindsay, Kathryn Hilary (née Buchanan); Dakar since February 1995; born 07/07/70; FCO 1989; Brussels (UKREP) 1992; Band A2; m 1994 Douglas Tennant Lindsay.

Lindsay, Richard Stephen; Second Secretary Harare since August 1998; born 18/02/69; Second Secretary FCO 1996; m 1997 Xanthe Critchett (1s 1998; 1d 2000).

Ling, Norman Arthur; High Commissioner Lilongwe since September 2001; born 12/08/52; Second Secretary FCO 1978; Second Secretary Tripoli 1980; Second later First Secretary Tehran 1981; First Secretary FCO 1984; Deputy Consul-General Johannesburg 1988; Full-Time Language Training 1992; Deputy Head of Mission Ankara 1993; Counsellor FCO 1997; m 1979 Selma Osman.

Lingwood, Dave Michael; Second Secretary and Deputy Head of Mission Yerevan since August 2000; born 10/05/68; FCO 1989; Cairo 1991; Bonn 1994; FCO 1997; Band C4.

Link, Joan Irene (née Wilmot), LVO (1992); Counsellor FCO since August 1996; born 03/03/53; FCO 1974; Third Secretary Bonn 1975; Third later Second Secretary FCO 1977; Second later First Secretary Geneva (UKDIS) 1980; First Secretary FCO 1983; First Secretary (Information) Bonn 1990; First Secretary FCO 1994; (2s 1977, 1985).

Linnell, Aidan John; FCO since March 2002; born 13/04/60; FCO 1982; Canberra 1987; FCO 1989;

Third Secretary Bonn 1993; FCO 1996; Second Secretary Caracas 1998; Band C4; m 2000 Zenaida Degadillo.

Lintner, Francesca Jane; FCO since March 1995; born 05/04/72; Band A2.

Lion, Stephanie Ann (née Smith); SUPL since August 2000; born 16/02/65; FCO 1986; Madrid 1988; SUPL 1989; FCO 1992; Berne 1994; FCO 1997; Band A2; m 1997 Dominique Lion (1d 1999).

Lisbey, Lisa Marie (née Harrison); New Delhi since August 2000; born 23/02/69; Customs and Excise 1992-95; FCO 1995; Belmopan 1996; Band A2; m 1999 Nestor Lisbey (1s 2001).

Little, Alison Jane; FCO since August 1997; born 03/04/68; FCO (HCS) 1986; FCO (DS) 1988; Lusaka 1990; FCO 1992; Maseru 1993; Tunis 1994; Band B3.

Little, Jennifer Margaret; FCO since July 1989; born 21/06/47; Senior Research Officer FCO 1970-72.

Little, Margaret Cambridge; FCO since May 1989; born 05/03/49; FCO 1973; Warsaw 1974; Tehran 1976; Rome 1979; Hanoi 1979; FCO 1982; Colombo 1986; Band B3.

Livesey, Timothy Peter Nicholas; On secondment to No. 10 Downing Street (Press Office) since August 2000; born 29/06/59; FCO 1987; FCO 1988; Rabat 1988; Second later First Secretary (Aid) Lagos 1989; FCO 1993; Head of Press and Public Affairs Section Paris Embassy 1996; m 1986 Catherine Eaglestone (3d 1990, 1996, 1999; 2s 1992, 1997).

Livingston, Carolyn B; Abidjan since May 1999; born 04/11/48; FCO 1997; Band B3; (1d 1974).

Livingston, Catherine Mary (née Bramley); Hong Kong since October 1996; born 22/06/56; FCO 1975; Cairo 1977; Resigned 1980; Reinstated 1982; FCO 1982; Rome 1984; Muscat 1986; SUPL 1990; SUPL 1991; FCO 1991; FCO 1995; Band B3; m 1985 Richard Ian Livingston (1s 1990; 1d 1992).

Livingstone, Scott, OBE (2002), MBE (Mil) (1995); First Secretary FCO since January 2000; born 28/11/65; First Secretary (Legal) Geneva (UKMIS and UKDIS) 1994; First Secretary FCO 1996; First Secretary (Political) Islamabad 1998; Band D6; m 1996 Lorna Jane Pettipher (2d 1998, 2000).

Llewellyn, Huw; Legal Counsellor, FCO since 1999; born 21/05/59; Assistant Legal Adviser FCO 1988; m 1990 Fiona Jane Boote (2d 1994, 1995).

Lloyd, Andrew, MBE (1995); Head of Post Pristina since July 2000; born 22/10/64; FCO 1982; Washington 1984; Kaduna 1987; FCO 1990; Second Secretary 1992; Second Secretary (Economic) Seoul 1993; Second later First Secretary (Political/Press) New York (UKMIS) 1995; m 1987 Sandra Leigh Craven (1s 1990).

Lloyd, Diane Elizabeth; Osaka since January 2000; born 27/02/68; FCO 1987; Full-Time Language Training 1989; Warsaw 1989; Full-Time Language Training Tokyo 1990; Vice-Consul Tokyo 1991; Rabat 1995; T/D Japan 1999; Band B3; m 1994 Souichiroh Saito (née Urushibara).

Lloyd, Susan Jacqueline; St John's since July 2002; born 28/02/70; FCO 1989; Harare 1991; Montevideo 1998; Band B3.

Lochmuller, Simon; Cairo since June 1998; born 26/07/70; FCO 1986; Bonn 1993; FCO 1996; Band C4; m 1998 Verena Mackenzie (1d 1995).

Lock, Jennifer Hazel; Second Secretary (Immigration) Islamabad since July 1998; born 09/07/59; FCO 1978; Jakarta 1982; Stockholm 1985; FCO 1988; Tunis 1991; Third Secretary (Management/Consular) Almaty 1994; Band C4.

Lockwood, Emma Constance, MVO (2000); Third Secretary (Political) Rome since December 1999; born 01/01/71; FCO 1996; Language Training 1999; Band B3.

Lodge, Katherine Rosemary; SUPL since August 1994; born 03/08/59; FCO 1984; Language Training Tokyo 1985; Third Secretary Tokyo 1986; FCO 1990; Second Secretary 1992.

Logan, Jane; T/D Ottawa since February 2000; born 11/10/64; FCO 1984; Pretoria 1986; Port of Spain 1989; FCO 1992; Istanbul 1994; Band A2.

Logan, Marilla Joy Fiona (née Tandy); First Secretary FCO since April 1998; born 12/09/53; FCO 1974; Moscow 1977; FCO 1978; Düsseldorf 1980; FCO 1983; Second Secretary Kuala Lumpur 1992; FCO 1996; m 1986 Allan Robert Logan (1s 1994).

Lomas, Joanne; Second Secretary (WTO) Geneva (UKMIS) since July 2001; born 07/09/70; FCO 1993; Full-Time Language Training 1995; Third Secretary (Political/Information) Damascus 1997; Secondment to UNSCOM Baghdad 1997; Band C4.

London, David Charles George; First Secretary FCO since June 2000; born 24/01/66; FCO 1994; Second Secretary (Political) Bonn 1996; First Secretary (Political) Buenos Aires 1997; Band D6; m 1996 Monique Day (1s 1998).

Longbottom, Julia Margaret; First Secretary (Political) The Hague since September 1998; born 13/07/63; Attachment, European Commission 1988; FCO 1986; Language Training 1988; Second Secretary (Chancery) Tokyo 1990; First Secretary FCO 1994; m 1990 Richard James Sciver (2d 1992, 1993; 1s 1995).

Longdon, Catherine Mary; FCO since November 1990; born 15/12/64; Band B3.

Longhurst, William Jesse; First Secretary (Finance) New York (UKMIS) since June 2001; born 07/02/67; On loan to the DTI 1998; FCO 1990; Second Secretary 1992; Seoul 1992; First Secretary (Commercial) Tokyo 1995; m 1991 Eriko Niimi (2d 1991, 1993).

Longrigg, Anthony James, CMG (1992); Governor Plymouth since May 2001; born 21/04/44; FCO 1972; Second later First Secretary (Political) Moscow 1975; FCO 1978; First Secretary and Head of Chancery Brasilia 1981; First Secretary FCO 1985; Counsellor (Internal) Moscow 1987; Counsellor (Economic/EC) Madrid 1991; Counsellor FCO 1995; Minister Moscow 1997; m 1968 Jane Rosa Cowlin (3d 1970, 1973, 1977).

Lonsdale, Charles John; First Secretary (Political) Moscow since October 1998; born 05/07/65; FCO 1987; Vienna CSCF 1988; FCO 1989; Third later Second Secretary Budapest 1990; On loan to the Cabinet Office 1993; First Secretary FCO 1995; Full-Time Language Training Moscow 1998.

Lorimer, Eamonn Barrington; On loan to DTI since April 2002; born 11/12/64; Home Civil Service 1985-88; Washington 1989; FCO 1993; Valletta 1994; FCO 1997; Band B3.

Loten, Graeme Neil; HM Ambassador Bamako, Mali since October 2001; born 10/03/59; FCO 1981; Brussels (UKDEL NATO) 1983; Khartoum 1986; Second Secretary (Economic/Agriculture) The Hague 1988; Second Secretary Almaty 1993; Full-Time Language Training 1993; FCO 1997.

Lott, Ann Veronica (née Lewis); Second Secretary FCO since November 1996; born 22/11/55; FCO 1978; Algiers 1979; Montevideo 1982; FCO 1984; Latin America Floater 1987; FCO 1988; Canberra 1989; SUPL 1992; m 1989 Justin Karl Lott (1d 1993).

Louth, Michael; FCO since July 1999; born 21/05/63; FCO 1981; Lagos 1984; East Berlin 1988; FCO 1989; Third Secretary (Management/Commercial) Ljubljana 1992; Vienna 1994; Port of Spain 1996; m 1992 Carmen Elena Fuentes (1s 1994; 1d 1998).

Love, Darren Mark; Floater Duties since February 2001; born 26/02/68; FCO 1988; Warsaw 1989; Accra 1991; FCO 1993; Colombo 1997; Band B3.

Love, Stephanie Cynthia; FCO since January 1993; born 24/07/45; Rio de Janeiro 1969; Bogotá 1969; Antigua 1971; Cairo 1971; Manila 1973; New York (UKMIS) 1975; FCO 1978; Bahrain 1979; FCO 1984; Budapest 1986; Islamabad 1988; FCO 1990; Lisbon 1991; Band B3.

Loveday-Baugh, Christine; FCO since August 2001; born 15/08/59; FCO 1984; Muscat 1986; Kingston 1989; FCO 1991; Rome 1994; New York (UKMIS) 1999; Band A2; m 1992 C. Anthony Baugh.

Lovett, Simon Joseph, MBE (2000); HM Consul Riyadh since August 1997; born 11/08/57; DHSS 1977; FCO 1981; Bombay 1983; Ottawa 1987; Second Secretary FCO 1990; Second Secretary (Information/Political) Oslo 1993; m 1985 Amita Rani Sarwal (1s 1986).

Low, Nicholas David; Brasilia since November 1999; born 14/12/57; Metropolitan Police 1982-92; FCO 1993; T/D Rabat 1994; Santiago 1995; Full-Time Language Training 1999; Band D6.

Lowen, Barry Robert; FCO since June 2001; born 09/01/64; FCO 1986; Language Training Cairo 1987; Third later Second Secretary (Chancery) Kuwait 1989; First Secretary FCO 1993; First Secretary (Economic) New York (UKMIS) 1997; Band D7; m 1989 Karin Rhiannon Blizard.

Lowes, Merrick John; First Secretary (Commercial) Mumbai since June 2001; born 14/11/44; RAF 1962-74; FCO 1975; Vienna 1978; Maseru 1981; Vice-Consul Naples 1983; Second Secretary FCO 1986; First Secretary on loan to the Office of Fair Trading 1989; First Secretary (Commercial) Damascus 1991; Trade Commissioner Hong Kong and Consul Macao 1994; Deputy Consul-General Johannesburg and Head of Southern Africa Regional Commercial Hub 1998; m 1970 (Christine) Wendy Ralley (1s 1975; 1d 1978).

Loweth, Alan Robert; First Secretary later Counsellor FCO since May 1995; born 12/12/52; FCO 1973; Language Training 1977; Copenhagen 1978; FCO 1981; Language Training 1984; Second Secretary Moscow 1985; First Secretary FCO 1988; First Secretary Warsaw 1991; m 1986 Linda Susan Parr.

Lowis, Joanna Jill; Second Secretary (Management) Tunis since March 1999; born 02/08/42; Warsaw 1965; Düsseldorf 1966; FCO 1969; Wellington 1972; UKDEL OECD Paris 1974; FCO 1977; Pretoria/Cape Town 1978; FCO 1981; Kathmandu 1984; FCO 1988; Third Secretary (Consular) Ottawa 1989; Second Secretary FCO 1992; Islamabad 1995.

Lownds, Matthew John; First Secretary FCO since February 2000; born 06/08/65; FCO 1987; Dublin 1989; Düsseldorf 1990; Luanda 1992; Second Secretary FCO 1995; Second Secretary (Political) UKDEL OSCE Vienna 1996; Band D6; m 1996 Rebecca Louise Allen (1s 1997; 1d 1999).

Lucas, Stephen John; FCO since July 2000; born 30/06/62; DTI 1986-90; FCO 1990; Third Secretary (Press/Information) Paris 1992; HM Consul Mexico City 1996; m 1994 Claudia Bautista Alfonso (1s 1998)

Lucey, Janette Margaret (née Mansley); Canberra since May 1997; born 14/07/64; FCO 1983; New Delhi 1985; Luanda 1989; Suva 1992; Band A2; m 1994 James Courtney Lucey.

Lucien, Valerie Linda; Consul-General Mexico City since May 2000; born 12/08/47; FCO 1977; Lagos 1978; Brussels (UKREP) 1981; Africa/Middle East Floater 1984; FCO 1987; Third Secretary Kingston 1990; Third Secretary (Cultural/Information) Valletta 1993; Second Secretary FCO 1996; Band C4.

Luff, Jonathan James; Second Secretary (Political) Riyadh since September 2001; born 19/04/73;

FCO 1998; Full-Time Language Training 1999; Full-Time Language Training Cairo 2000; Band C4.

Lufkin, Christine Anne (née Wilson), MVO; Second Secretary (Economic) The Hague since November 2000; born 05/01/66; FCO 1988; Washington 1990; Kuwait 1994; Second Secretary FCO 1997; SUPL 2000; m 1996 David Jonathan Peter Lufkin (1d 1999).

Lumsden-Bedingfeld, Ann; FCO since August 1997; born 11/08/62; FCO 1985; East Berlin 1987; FCO 1989; Colombo 1990; FCO 1993; Floater Duties 1995; Band A2.

Lungley, Gareth Geoffrey; First Secretary Zagreb since October 2002; born 08/01/71; FCO 1994; Full-Time Language Training 1996; Second Secretary (Commercial) Tehran 1997; Second Secretary FCO 1999; Band D6; m 1997 Suzanne Clare Smith (1s 2001).

Lunt, Iain Andrew; FCO since September 2001; born 11/05/77; Band C4.

Lusher, David; First Secretary (Management) Tripoli since September 2002; born 27/12/55; DOE 1973; FCO 1975; Belgrade 1977; Seoul 1978; Accra 1982; FCO 1984; Islamabad 1987; Vice-Consul Milan 1991; Second Secretary FCO 1994; Second Secretary (UN/UNIDO) UKMIS Vienna 1998; m 1978 Soon-Ja Chung (1s 1983).

Lusty, Gregor Malcolm; FCO since October 2001; born 12/03/69; FCO 1991; Full-Time Language Training Cairo 1993; Third Secretary (Chancery) Amman 1994; Kinshasa 1998; Second Secretary on loan to the DTI 1999.

Luttrell, David Charles; Freetown since August 2001; born 03/06/72; FCO 1999; Band B3.

Lyall, Michael David; Moscow since January 2002; born 09/09/43; Royal Navy 1961-89; Moscow 1991; Warsaw 1992; Geneva (UKMIS) 1993; Moscow 1996; Peking 1998; Band B3; m 1967 Janet Haugh (1s 1969).

Lyall Grant, Mark Justin; Director (Africa) FCO since July 2000; born 29/05/56; FCO 1980; Second Secretary Islamabad 1982; First Secretary FCO 1985; First Secretary (Chancery) Paris 1990; First Secretary FCO 1993; Counsellor on loan to the Cabinet Office 1994; Deputy High Commissioner Pretoria 1996; FCO 1998; m 1986 Sheila Jean Tresise (1s 1989; 1d 1991).

Lyall Grant, Sheila Jean (née Tresise); FCO since 1999; born 16/12/60; FCO 1980; Islamabad 1982; FCO 1985; Vice-Consul Paris 1990; FCO 1993; SUPL 1997; Band C4; m 1986 Mark Justin Lyall Grant (1s 1989; 1d 1991).

Lycett, Nadine Claire; FCO since July 2000; born 19/04/65; FCO 1984; Brussels (UKDEL NATO) 1986; FCO 1988; Washington 1992; Ankara 1997; Band A2.

Lygo, Clifford George; FCO since September 1982; born 02/02/51; FCO 1967; Rome 1976;

FCO 1979; Khartoum 1980; Band B3; m 1976
Sandra Francida Wilson (2d 1978, 1983).

Lyne, Kevin Douglas; First Secretary (Chancery)
Geneva (UKMIS) since August 1998; born
06/11/61; Research Officer FCO 1988; Senior
Research Officer FCO 1989; Second Secretary
(Chancery) Santiago 1991; Principal Research
Officer FCO 1995; First Secretary FCO 1996; m
1988 Anne Francoise Dabbadie (2d 1989, 1995).

Lyne, Richard John; Deputy Head of Conference
and Visits Group FCO since September 2000; born
20/11/48; FCO 1970; Belgrade 1972; Algiers
1974; Damascus 1977; FCO 1980; On loan to DTI
1981; Second Secretary (Commercial) New Delhi
1984; Second later First Secretary
(Chancery/Information) Stockholm 1988; First
Secretary FCO 1992; Deputy High Commissioner
Port of Spain 1996; m 1977 Jennifer Anne
Whitworth (1d 1982; 1s 1985).

Lyne, Sir Roderic Michael John, CMG (1992),
KBE (1999); HM Ambassador Moscow since
January 2000; born 31/03/48; FCO 1970; Attached
to Army School of Languages 1971 Moscow
1972; Second Secretary Dakar 1974; FCO 1976;
Assistant Private Secretary to Secretary of State
1979; First Secretary New York (UKMIS) 1982;
Chatham House (CDA) 1986; Counsellor (Head of
Chancery) Moscow 1987; Counsellor FCO 1990;
On loan to No 10 Downing Street as PS/Prime
Minister 1993; On loan to British Gas 1996; UK
Permanent Representative Geneva 1997; m 1969
Amanda Mary Smith (2s 1971, 1974; 1d 1981).

Lyon, Julian Edmund; Third Secretary and Vice-
Consul Yerevan since April 1999; born 20/10/65;
FCO 1990; Transferred to Diplomatic Service
1999; Band B3.

Lysaght, Stephen Peter; FCO since 1999; born
17/05/70; FCO 1989; Washington 1992; Moscow
1995; Band B3.

Lyscom, David Edward; FCO since January 2002;
born 08/08/51; FCO 1972; Third later Second
Secretary Vienna 1973; Second Secretary Ottawa
1977; Second later First Secretary FCO 1979; First
Secretary 1980; First Secretary Bonn 1984; First
Secretary (Economic) Riyadh 1988; First
Secretary FCO 1990; Counsellor (Science and
Technology) Bonn 1991; Counsellor FCO 1996;
HM Ambassador Bratislava 1998; m 1973 Nicole
Jane Ward (2d 1983, 1987; 1s 1985).

Lyster-Binns, Benjamin Edward Noël; Second
Secretary FCO since 1998; born 19/10/65; FCO
1989; Third Secretary (Chancery/Information)
Muscat Lilongwe 1991; Band B3; (1s 2002).

M

Macadie, Jeremy James; Deputy Head of Mission
Algiers since October 1997; born 10/07/52; FCO
1972; Dakar 1975; Addis Ababa 1980; FCO 1981;
Sana'a 1984; Antananarivo 1986; FCO 1991;
Assistant Private Secretary to Minister of State for
Europe 1995; Band B3; m 1975 Chantal Andrea
Jacqueline Copiatti (1d 1978).

Macaire, Robert Nigel Paul; Head of Counter-
Terrorism Policy Dept FCO since June 2002; born
19/02/66; MOD 1987-90; FCO 1990; Second
Secretary (Know How Fund) Bucharest 1992;
FCO 1995; First Secretary Washington 1998; m
1996 Alice MacKenzie (2d 1997, 1999).

Macan, Thomas Townley; Governor of the British
Virgin Islands since October 2002; born 14/11/46;
FCO 1969; Third later Second Secretary Bonn
1971; Second later First Secretary Brasilia 1974;
FCO 1978; First Secretary (Press and Information)
Bonn 1981; First Secretary later Counsellor FCO
1986; Counsellor and Deputy Head of Mission
Lisbon 1990; HM Ambassador Vilnius 1995; On
loan to the BOC Group 1998; Minister New Delhi
1999; m 1976 Janet Ellen Martin (1s 1981; 1d
1984).

Macartney, Glen Patrick Charles; Second later
First Secretary FCO since February 1975; born
24/09/49; Third Secretary FCO 1971; Language
Training Sheffield University 1972; Third later
Second Secretary Tokyo 1973.

MacCallum, Fiona, MBE (1997); First Secretary
(Political) Kiev since August 2000; born 25/06/62;
FCO 1986; Moscow 1989; FCO 1992; Second
Secretary Riga 1995; Band C5.

MacDermott, Alastair Tormod; High
Commissioner Windhoek since April 2002; born
17/09/45; FO (later FCO) 1966; Kabul 1971;
Accra 1973; FCO 1973; FCO 1977; Language
Training Tokyo 1978; Second Secretary Tokyo
1979; Colombo 1983; First Secretary
(Information) Tokyo 1986; First Secretary FCO
1991; First Secretary (Commercial) Ankara 1995;
Full-Time Language Training 1995; m (1) 1968
Helen Gordon (diss 1992) (2d 1969, 1971); (2)
1994 Gudrun Geiling.

MacDonald, Catriona MacLeod; FCO since
November 2000; born 18/04/64; FCO 1988;
Belgrade 1990; FCO 1992; Berlin 1993; FCO
1996; Vienna 1997; Band A2.

MacDonald, Michelle; SUPL since February
2002; born 18/09/78; FCO 2000; Band A2.

MacDougall, David; SUPL since June 2002; born
07/07/73; FCO 1991; Helsinki 1995; Tel Aviv
1997; T/D Kinshasa 1999; Guatemala City 1999;
Band B3.

Macgregor, John Malcolm, CVO (1992); Director
Wider Europe FCO since October 2000; born
03/10/46; FCO 1973; Second later First Secretary
New Delhi 1975; First Secretary FCO 1979;
Private Secretary to Minister of State 1981;
Counsellor and Head of Chancery Prague 1986;
Counsellor and Head of Chancery Paris 1990;
Counsellor FCO 1993; Consul-General Düsseldorf
1995; HM Ambassador Warsaw 1998; m 1982
Judith Anne Brown (1d 1984; 3s 1986, 1987,
1990).

Macgregor, Judith Anne (née Brown), LVO
(1992); Counsellor FCO since March 2001; born
17/06/52; FCO 1976; First Secretary

(Chancery/Information) Belgrade 1978; FCO 1981; SUPL 1986; First Secretary (Political/Information) Prague 1989; SUPL 1990; First Secretary (Chancery) Paris 1992; First Secretary FCO 1993; SUPL 1993; SUPL 1995; m 1982 John Malcolm Macgregor (1d 1984; 3s 1986, 1987, 1990).

Macintosh, Anne; SUPL since October 1997; born 15/04/61; FCO 1980; Rome 1982; Havana 1985; FCO 1988; Third later Second Secretary (Commercial) Buenos Aires 1991; m 1993 Gustavo Javier Barreiro (1d 1996).

Macintosh, Kenneth Gilbert; FCO since October 1990; born 29/03/72; Band A2.

MacIntosh, Sarah; FCO since May 2002; born 07/08/69; FCO 1991; Third Secretary (AEA/UN) Vienna (UKMIS) 1994; Second Secretary (Economic/EU) Madrid 1996; First Secretary FCO 1997; New York (UKMIS) 2000.

Mackay, Gavin Anderson, MBE (1994); Second Secretary Nicosia since September 1989; born 01/11/49; FCO 1973; Wellington 1975; Suva 1978; Dhaka 1981; FCO 1983; Dubai 1986; (Second Secretary 1988); m 1975 Glenys Pickup (1d 1977; 2s 1980, 1984).

Mackay, Katherine Wendy; Second Secretary New York (UKMIS) since April 2000; born 06/07/72; FCO 1996; Band C4.

MacKenna, Roderic Hamish; Tbilisi since July 2002; born 15/08/58; FCO 2000; Band B3; m 1991 Ayoma Indrani Nethsingha (2d 1992, 1993).

MacKenzie, Angela Susan (née Wright); Jerusalem since July 2001; born 17/01/67; FCO 1985; Lilongwe 1989; SUPL 1993; FCO 1995; SUPL 1997; Band B3; m (1) 1988 Mohammed Ouassine (diss 1992); (2) 1997 Graham John MacKenzie.

MacKenzie, Catherine Louise Hay; New York (UKMIS) since March 2000; born 09/08/66; FCO 1989; Language Training 1991; Second Secretary 1992; Language Training Tokyo 1992; Second Secretary (Chancery) Tokyo 1993; Band D6; m 1992 John Page.

Mackenzie, Dorothy (née Byers); SUPL since January 1999; born 01/03/56; FCO 1974; The Hague 1976; Lusaka 1979; FCO 1982; Ottawa 1985; SUPL 1990; Singapore 1991; FCO 1993; Band C4; m 1978 Robert Mackenzie (1d 1987).

MacKenzie, Hilary (née Grace); Vice-Consul Helsinki since March 1996; born 01/03/59; FCO 1980; Islamabad 1982; Oslo 1984; Bombay 1987; Amsterdam 1989; FCO 1992; Band B3; m 1989 Ian James McKenzie.

MacKenzie, Ian Johnston; Moscow since March 1998; born 30/08/42; RAF 1958-86; Budapest 1988; Washington 1990; Bonn 1993; World Wide Floater Duties 1996; Band B3; m 1984 Inge Schmitz.

MacKenzie, Kenneth John Alexander; First Secretary FCO since July 2001; born 09/09/49; FCO 1973; Brussels 1975; Second later First Secretary FCO 1978; Buenos Aires 1981; First Secretary FCO 1982; First Secretary (Economic) Bucharest 1985; First Secretary FCO 1988; First Secretary Vienna 1992; First Secretary FCO 1995; Consul Munich 1997; Band D6; m 1980 Alison Mary Linda Sandford (1d 1983; 1s 1987).

Mackenzie, Robert; First Secretary (Commercial) Muscat since July 1998; born 05/03/54; Dept of National Savings 1973; FCO 1974; The Hague 1976; Lusaka 1979; FCO 1982; Ottawa 1985; Second Secretary (Commercial) Mexico City 1988; Second Secretary FCO 1988; Second Secretary (Commercial) Singapore 1990; Second Secretary FCO 1993; m 1978 Dorothy Byers (1d 1987).

MacKerras, Carl Anthony; Vice-Consul Copenhagen since August 1997; born 13/11/69; Land Registry 1988-90; FCO 1990; St Petersburg 1995; m 1997 Vera Ermolova (2d 1997, 2000).

Mackie, Anne Bernadette; Geneva (UKMIS) since October 1999; born 24/10/59; FCO 1983; Cairo 1985; Lagos 1988; SUPL 1990; FCO 1991; Hong Kong 1995; FCO 1997; Band A2; (1s 1990).

Mackrell, William Michael; Bonn since June 1992; born 11/08/47; Band B3.

Maclean, Andrew Mark; FCO since April 2002; born 25/11/72; Band D6.

MacLennan, David Ross; HM Ambassador Doha since June 2002; born 12/02/45; FO 1963; DSAO 1965; MECAS 1966; Aden 1969; Second later First Secretary FCO 1972; Civil Service College 1972; First Secretary UKDEL OECD Paris 1975; First Secretary, Head of Chancery and Consul Abu Dhabi 1979; First Secretary FCO 1982; On secondment to European Commission 1984; Counsellor (Commercial) Kuwait 1985; Counsellor and Head of Chancery Nicosia 1989; HM Consul-General Jerusalem 1990; Counsellor FCO 1994; HM Ambassador Beirut 1996; m 1964 Margaret Lytollis (2d 1964, 1966).

MacLeod, Fiona; T/D Belmopan since May 1996; born 19/10/70; FCO 1992; Seoul 1994; Band A2.

MacLeod, Frances Ann; FCO since August 1991; born 04/12/59; FCO 1983; Warsaw 1985; Maputo 1988; Band B3; m 1989 James Robert McDougall.

MacLeod, Gordon Stewart; Nicosia since February 2002; born 15/02/52; FCO 1971; Ankara 1973; Washington 1977; Dacca 1979; FCO 1982; Valletta 1985; Third later Second Secretary New Delhi 1988; Second Secretary FCO 1992; Consul (Commercial and Information) Casablanca 1998; m 1978 Susan Raggatt (2d 1981, 1984).

MacLeod, Iain; Counsellor (Legal Adviser) New York (UKMIS) since August 2001; born 15/03/62; Assistant Legal Adviser FCO 1987; First Secretary (Assistant Legal Adviser) Brussels (UKREP) 1991; FCO 1995; Legal Secretariat to the Law

Offices 1997; FCO 2000; m 1988 Dr Alison Mary Murchison (2d 1991, 1995; 2s 1993, 1997).

MacLeod, Siân Christina, OBE (2002); First Secretary (Political) The Hague since July 1996; born 31/05/62; FCO 1986; Language Training 1987; Second Secretary (Chancery) Moscow 1988; Second later First Secretary FCO 1992; m 1987 Richard Anthony Robinson (2d 1991, 1994; 1s 1998).

MacMillan, Alison Flora; Second Secretary (EU) Gibraltar since October 1996; born 22/08/61; FCO 1982; Mexico City 1983; Washington 1987; SUPL 1989; FCO 1990; Third Secretary Vice-Consul and Deputy Head of Mission Managua 1993; m 1997 Julian Thomas Lee (1s 1997; 1d 1999).

Macphail, John Patrick Nicholson; British Trade International FCO since June 1998; born 21/05/48; FCO 1968; Middle East Floater 1971; Moscow 1973; Georgetown 1974; FCO 1976; Budapest 1979; Mexico City 1980; Brussels (UKDEL NATO) 1983; Second Secretary FCO 1985; Second Secretary (Commercial) Lagos 1989; Second Secretary (Commercial) Kuala Lumpur 1993; SUPL 1996; m (1) 1981 Joy Chambers (diss 1989) (1d 1983 dec'd 1989); (2) 1992 Carolyn Inness Turner (1s 1998).

Macpherson, John Bannerman; Counsellor FCO since November 1996; born 23/06/51; Third later Second Secretary FCO 1975; Language Training MECAS 1977; Second Secretary Khartoum 1979; Second later First Secretary Sana'a 1980; FCO 1983; Language Training 1985; First Secretary Sofia 1987; First Secretary FCO 1990; Counsellor Cairo 1993; m 1985 Monica Jane Lancashire (2s 1986, 1988; 1d 1992).

Macpherson, Kara Isobel; Second Secretary FCO since September 1998; born 03/08/60; FCO 1981; Islamabad 1983; Prague 1986; Africa/Middle East Floater 1988; FCO 1992; FCO 1994; T/D Khartoum 1994; T/D New York (UKMIS) 1996; FCO 1997; Band B3.

MacQueen, Christine Ann; Counsellor Brussels since July 2002; born 24/05/59; FCO 1982; Second Secretary (Economic) Brasilia 1984; Second later First Secretary FCO 1987; New York 1989; First Secretary and UNESCO Observer Paris 1990; First Secretary later Counsellor FCO 1995; m 1992 Bruno Pascal Castola (1d 1992; 1s 1994).

MacSween, Norman James; Counsellor FCO since October 1998; born 22/01/48; FCO 1970; Third later Second Secretary Nairobi 1972; FCO 1975; Language Training SOAS 1976; and Shiraz 1977; First Secretary Tehran 1977; FCO 1979; First Secretary (Chancery) Bonn 1983; First Secretary FCO 1987; First Secretary later Counsellor Stockholm 1991; Counsellor Moscow 1995; m 1983 Julia Jane Reid (1s 1988; 1d 1990).

Madden, David Christopher Andrew, CMG (1996); HM Ambassador Athens since May 1999; born 25/07/46; Third Secretary FCO 1970; Third later Second Secretary BMG Berlin 1972; First Secretary on loan to Cabinet Office 1975; First Secretary Moscow 1978; First Secretary and Head of Chancery Athens 1981; FCO 1984; Counsellor, Head of Chancery and Consul-General Belgrade 1987; Counsellor FCO 1990; High Commissioner Nicosia 1994; m 1970 Penelope Anthea Johnston (1s 1972; 2d 1974, 1975).

Madden, Paul Damien; Deputy High Commissioner and Counsellor (Commercial/Economic) Singapore since November 2000; born 25/04/59; DTI 1980; PS/PUSS 1984; Language Training/Kamakura 1987; First Secretary Tokyo 1988; First Secretary FCO 1992; First Secretary Washington 1996; m 1989 Sarah Pauline Thomas (2s 1991, 1992; 1d 1996).

Maddicott, David Sydney; First Secretary (Head of Pol/Info Section) Ottawa since August 1997; born 27/03/53; On attachment to the Canadian Government 1996; First Secretary FCO 1994; Full-Time Language Training 1996; m 1980 Elizabeth Wynne (4s 1980, 1984, 1990, 1993; 1d 1982).

Maddinson, Paul Francis; First Secretary (Political) Moscow since November 2001; born 16/05/72; FCO 1995; Second Secretary (Political) Nairobi 1996; Second Secretary FCO 1998; Full-Time Language Training 2000; Band D6; m 1996 Rebecca Anne Jackson (1s 2000; 1d 2002).

Madisons, Alexander Emil; Third Secretary Rome since October 1999; born 09/11/62; FCO 1983; Peking 1990; Belgrade 1994; FCO 1997; Band C4.

Madojemu, Valentine Isi; FCO since November 1998; born 27/03/58; Band B3; m 1989 Rita (1s 1992; 1d 1997).

Maguire, John; HM Consul Denver since January 2000; born 04/06/49; FCO 1968; Moscow 1971; Belmopan 1972; New Delhi 1974; Tokyo 1978; FCO 1982; Alexandria 1985; Consul (Commercial) Perth 1988; FCO 1992; Deputy Head of Mission, Consul and First Secretary (Commercial) Doha 1995; FCO 1999; Band C5; m 1978 Mette Lucie Konow Monsen.

Maguire, Natalie (née Rule); Bahrain since June 2001; born 22/05/62; FCO 2000; Band A2; m 1981 Robin Maguire.

Maher, Heather Kirsten Maria; Kiev since November 2000; born 12/01/70; FCO 1988; Bangkok 1990; FCO 1993; Athens 1994; Kuwait 1995; FCO 1999; Harare 1999; Abidjan 2000; Band A2.

Major, Pamela Ann; First Secretary later Counsellor FCO since February 1996; born 04/03/59; FCO 1982; Language Training SOAS 1983; Second Secretary (Chancery) Peking 1986; First Secretary FCO 1988; First Secretary Moscow 1993; m 1992 Robert Leigh Turner (1s 1992; 1d 1994).

Makepeace, Richard Edward; HM Ambassador
Abu Dhabi since March 2003; born 24/06/53;
FCO 1976; Language Training MECAS 1977;
Third later Second Secretary Muscat 1979; Second
later First Secretary (Chancery) Prague 1981; FCO
1985; Private Secretary to the Parliamentary
Under-Secretary of State 1986; First Secretary
Brussels (UKREP) 1989; Counsellor FCO 1993;
Cairo 1995; HM Ambassador Khartoum 1999; m
1980 Rupmani Catherine Pradhan.

Makin, John; Second Secretary (Commercial)
Perth since March 2001; born 13/01/64; DHSS
1984; FCO 1985; Kaduna 1987; Düsseldorf 1990;
Floater Duties 1992; FCO 1996; Jakarta 1999;
Band C4.

Makriyiannis, Lorraine Elizabeth (née Colhoun);
SUPL since May 1999; born 10/06/69; FCO 1991;
Sofia 1993; Nicosia 1995; Band A2; m 1995
Michael Makriyiannis.

Malcolm, James Ian, OBE (1995); HM
Ambassador Panama City since March 2002; born
29/03/46; MPBW 1964; FO 1966; Brussels
(UKDEL NATO) 1969; Rangoon 1972; FCO
1974; Nairobi 1977; Damascus 1980; Second
Secretary (Commercial) Luanda 1983; Second
Secretary FCO 1985; First Secretary
(Political/Economic) Jakarta 1987; First Secretary
FCO 1994; Deputy High Commissioner Kingston
1997; m 1967 Sheila Nicholson Moore (1s 1976;
1d 1980).

Malik, Runa; ECO Dhaka since September 2000;
born 23/06/74; FCO 1996.

Malin, Carl Spencer; SUPL since March 2002;
born 07/07/69; FCO 1987; Ottawa 1989; FCO
1992; Floater Duties 1993; FCO 1995; Vice-
Consul Lagos 1996; Band C4; m 1995 Kerstin
Ruge.

Malin, Keith Ian; Counsellor FCO since
November 1999; born 11/12/53; FCO 1976; Third
Secretary (Developing Countries) Brussels
(UKREP) 1978; Second later First Secretary FCO
1979; First Secretary on secondment to HCS 1983;
First Secretary (UN/Press) Geneva (UKMIS)
1984; FCO 1986; First Secretary
(Chancery/Economic) Sofia 1990; First Secretary
later Counsellor FCO 1993; Counsellor Peking
1996; m 1977 Gaynor Dudley Jones (2s 1985,
1992).

Mallion, Richard Julian; Addis Ababa since
January 2001; born 23/12/68; FCO 1999; Band
A2.

Malone, Philip; First Secretary FCO since May
1999; born 03/12/61; FCO 1981; Buenos Aires
1983; Guatemala City 1986; FCO 1989; Third
Secretary (Commercial/Information) Luxembourg
1992; Second Secretary (Chancery) Bandar Seri
Begawan 1995; m 1999 Sarah Tan Yee Whey.

Mamet, Emma Kate (née Miller); Third Secretary
(Economic) Ottawa since March 1999; born
06/08/70; FCO 1991; Third Secretary (Chancery)

Geneva (UKMIS) 1994; Port Louis 1995; Band
B3; m 2000 Anthony Roger Mamet.

Man, Kam Lon; Islamabad since March 2000;
born 16/06/72; FCO 1996; Band A2.

Manley, Ernest George; Brussels (UKDEL NATO)
since June 1999; born 15/02/51; FCO 1970; Aden
1973; Milan 1975; East Berlin 1978; FCO 1980;
Kuala Lumpur 1983; Consul Milan 1986; FCO
1990; Band C4; m 1973 Mary Catherine Whelan
(1s 1975).

Manley, Philip Ernest; FCO since September
1999; born 17/06/44; GPO 1960; FCO 1969;
Washington 1971; FCO 1974; Amman 1975; FCO
1976; Attaché Moscow 1978; FCO 1980; Third
Secretary Lagos 1981; FCO 1984; Second
Secretary Bonn 1987; Second Secretary FCO
1990; (First Secretary 1993); Moscow 1996; Band
D6; m 1967 Christine Anne Kellett (1s 1970; 1d
1972).

Manley, Simon John; FCO since September 2002;
born 18/09/67; FCO 1990; On secondment to the
European Commission 1993; Second later First
Secretary (Political) New York (UKMIS) 1993; On
secondment to the EU Council Secretariat Brussels
1998; m 1996 Maria Isabel Fernandez-Utges (2d
2000, 2001).

Manley, Suzanne Marie Theresa; Moscow since
April 2001; born 12/12/64; FCO 1987; La Paz
1990; T/D Havana 1993; Santiago 1994; FCO
1998; T/D Buenos Aires 1998; Band B3.

Manning, Sir David Geoffrey, KCMG (2001),
CMG (1992); Foreign Policy Adviser to the Prime
Minister September 2001; born 05/12/49; Third
Secretary FCO 1972; Language Training 1973;
Third later Second Secretary Warsaw 1974;
Second later First Secretary New Delhi 1977; FCO
1980; First Secretary Paris 1984; Counsellor on
loan to the Cabinet Office 1988; Political
Counsellor Moscow 1990; Head of Eastern
Department FCO 1993; Head of Policy Planning
FCO 1994; UK Member of ICFY Contact Group
for Bosnia 1994; HM Ambassador Tel Aviv 1995;
Deputy Under-Secretary FCO 1998; Permanent
Representative Brussels (UKDEL NATO) 2000; m
1973 Catherine Parkinson.

Mansfield, Clive; Plymouth since July 1997; born
08/04/54; FCO 1973; Beirut 1975; Bombay 1976;
Mexico City 1979; Rome 1981; FCO 1984;
Islamabad 1987; FCO 1988; Band B3; m (1) 1980
Gail Denise Purvis (diss 1989); (2) Hilda Margaret
Eddie.

March, Shirley Elizabeth; First Secretary (UNPR)
Geneva (UKMIS) since June 2000; born 04/02/61;
FCO 1984; Second Secretary (EC Affairs)
Brussels 1988; First Secretary FCO 1990; Band
D6; m 1984 Paul Louis March (2s 1990, 1992).

Marchant, Trixie Jane (née Farmer); FCO since
February 1991 (Second Secretary 1993); born
01/03/65; FCO 1987; Geneva 1989; Band C4; m
1989 Andrew John Marchant (1s 1998).

Marden, Nicholas; Counsellor Tel Aviv since January 1998; born 02/05/50; Army 1971-74; Third later Second Secretary FCO 1974; Second Secretary Nicosia 1977; First Secretary FCO 1980; Warsaw 1982; FCO 1985; First Secretary Paris 1988; First Secretary FCO 1993; m 1977 Melanie Gaye Glover (2d 1980, 1982).

Mardlin, Robert Andrew; Nairobi since October 1999; born 13/01/65; FCO 1984; Lima 1986; Sofia 1990; Dhaka 1992; FCO 1996; Band B3; m 1988 Amanda Karen Morall.

Marmion, Elisabeth Claire (née Terry); Hong Kong since May 1999; born 09/07/72; FCO 1995; Band A2; m 1999 Nicholas Paul Marmion.

Marren, Marrena Ruby; Muscat since September 2002; born 15/01/68; FCO 1987; Paris 1989; Prague 1992; FCO 1994; Geneva 1994; Brussels (UKREP) 1998; Band B3.

Marriott, Allison Mary, MBE (1997); SUPL since July 2002; born 31/03/66; FCO 1987; Vice-Consul Amman 1990; Third Secretary Brussels (UKDEL) 1993; Copenhagen 1996; Second Secretary FCO 1997; First Secretary (Management) Addis Ababa 2000; Band C5.

Marriott, Anne Stewart Murray (née Corbett), MBE (2002); FCO since February 2001; born 29/10/57; FCO 1979; Brasilia 1982; FCO 1984; Abu Dhabi 1985; Bangkok 1988; FCO 1992; Amman 1997; Band B3; m 1988 Paul James Marriott.

Marsden, Ian Thomas; Third Secretary (Commercial) Bucharest since March 2002; born 05/10/69; Department of Social Security 1989; FCO 1990; Colombo 1993; FCO 1996; Sarajevo 1997; On loan to the DTI 1998; T/D Pristina 1999; Band B3.

Marsden, Rosalind Mary; Director Asia - Pacific since December 1999; born 27/10/50; Third Secretary FCO 1974; Language Training SOAS 1975; Third, Second and later First Secretary Tokyo 1976; First Secretary FCO 1980; First Secretary (Economic) Bonn 1985; First Secretary FCO 1989; Counsellor on secondment to the National Westminster Bank 1991; Head of Chancery Tokyo 1993; Counsellor FCO 1996.

Marsh, Derek Richard, CVO (1999); Director-General of British Trade and Cultural Office Taipei since July 2002; born 17/09/46; MOD 1968; DTI 1988; Deputy Head of Mission and Consul-General Seoul 1997; Seconded to the FCO 1997; m 1969 Frances Anne Roberts (1s 1972; 1d 1975).

Marsh, Elaine (née Skinner); Third Secretary Valletta since August 2002; born 06/01/57; FCO 1976; Port of Spain 1978; Bucharest 1982; Valletta 1984; FCO 1987; New Delhi 1989; Third Secretary (Consular) Dar es Salaam 1992; Third Secretary FCO 1994; Washington 1998; Band B3; m 1985 Andrew Peter Marsh (diss 1989) (1s 1988).

Marshall, Alan John; Second Secretary (Consular) Jakarta since April 2001; born 11/09/52; FCO 1971; Cairo 1973; Lilongwe 1975; Salisbury 1978; Sana'a 1980; FCO 1981; Islamabad 1983; Lisbon 1987; Luanda 1990; Second Secretary FCO 1993; Lisbon 1996; Consul Lisbon 1998; Band C4; (1s 1979; 1d 1986).

Marshall, Angela Rosemary; Brussels (UKREP) since July 2002; born 22/08/60; FCO 1988; Maseru 1991; Kiev 1994; FCO 1997; Full-Time Language Training 2000; Lisbon 2000; Band B3.

Marshall, Bernard Alan; Second Secretary (Commercial) T/D Tripoli since July 2001; born 23/03/48; FCO 1968; Bombay 1971; Islamabad 1971; Moscow 1973; Anguilla 1974; Bonn 1976; Vice-Consul (Commercial) FCO 1978 (Second Secretary 1979); Melbourne 1982; Second Secretary FCO 1986; First Secretary (Commercial) Bucharest 1989; First Secretary FCO 1993; Full-Time Language Training 1995; Consul Munich 1995; Sarajevo 1997; First Secretary FCO 1998; T/D Tehran 1999; Band C5.

Marshall, Brian; Second Secretary FCO since April 1985; born 13/12/51; On loan to HCS 1974; FCO 1971; FCO 1977; Second Secretary Muscat 1984; Band C4; m 1973 Susan Joyce Bishop (2d 1976, 1980).

Marshall, Francis James; Deputy Head of Mission Rangoon since 1999; born 10/08/46; CRO 1963; Commonwealth Office (later FCO) 1965; Mogadishu 1969; Singapore 1971; FCO 1974; Port Louis 1977; Tripoli 1981; Addis Ababa 1983; FCO 1984; Vice-Consul Toronto 1987; Second Secretary (Management) JMO Brussels 1991; SUPL 1994; m 1971 Clare Wray (1s 1972; 1d 1976).

Marshall, Jonathan Neil; FCO since July 1999; born 26/08/70; FCO 1992; Athens 1994; Band D6; m 1997 Maria Kontou (1s 1999).

Marshall, Michael Gavin; SMO Singapore since May 2002; born 13/09/60; FCO 1980; Moscow 1982; Baghdad 1983; Floater Duties 1988; FCO 1990; Second Secretary (Consul) St Petersburg 1992; Seoul 1995; Second later acting First Secretary FCO 1998; m 1993 Amanda Louise O'Connor (1d 1997; 1s 1999).

Marshall, Robert; First Secretary FCO since November 1986; born 21/08/44; First Secretary FCO 1975; First Secretary (Information) Rome 1977; First Secretary FCO 1980; First Secretary (Chancery) Lagos 1986; Band C5; m (1) 1971 Patricia Daly (dec'd 1995); (2) 1996 Susan Alexandra Caroline James.

Marshall, Robert John; First Secretary Kuala Lumpur since January 2000; born 19/06/65; FCO 1988; Second Secretary Tokyo 1992; First Secretary FCO 1995; Band D6.

Martens, Alexandra Mary; Second Secretary Paris since May 2000; born 20/10/57; FCO 1978; Johannesburg 1980; FCO 1981; FCO 1987; Paris 1987; Vienna 1989; FCO 1991; Band C4.

Martin, Alexander Benedict Lowry; Second Secretary FCO since November 2001; born 16/09/70; FCO 1996; Second Secretary (Economic) Jakarta 1999; Band C4; m 1999 Nicola Barbara Hill.

Martin, Angus Charles Trench; World Wide Floater Duties since November 2001; born 27/12/71; FCO 1991; World Wide Floater Duties 1995; T/D Geneva (UKMIS) 1998; FCO 1999; Band B3.

Martin, Christopher Nichols; FCO since July 1981; born 04/05/62; Band B3.

Martin, Craig Keith; Washington since July 1988; born 16/11/69; Band B3; m 1998 Natalie Jayne Wren.

Martin, Dominic David William; Counsellor (Political) New Delhi since May 2001; born 25/11/64; FCO 1987; Third later Second Secretary (Chancery) New Delhi 1989; First Secretary FCO 1992; First Secretary (Head of Political and Economic Section) Buenos Aires 1996; FCO 2000; m 1996 Emily Rose Walter (3d 1996, 1998, 2001).

Martin, Frances Edith Josephine; Second Secretary Montreal since September 1996; born 20/02/48; MOD 1965; Montevideo 1973; FCO 1973; Peking 1976; Tehran 1977; Moscow 1979; FCO 1981; Washington 1987; Athens 1990; FCO 1993.

Martin, Francis James; High Commissioner Maseru since April 2002; born 03/05/49; DSAO later FCO 1968; Reykjavik 1971; Stuttgart 1973; FCO 1976; Second Secretary 1978; Vice-Consul (Political/Information) Cape Town 1979; Second later First Secretary (Institutions) Brussels (UKREP) 1983; Deputy High Commissioner Freetown 1988; FCO 1988; First Secretary FCO 1991; On loan to the DTI 1992; Deputy Head of Mission Luanda 1995; Full-Time Language Training 1995; First Secretary (Commercial) Copenhagen 1998; m 1970 Aileen Margaret Shovlin (2s 1973, 1975; 2d 1976, 1978).

Martin, Neil Richard; First Secretary and Deputy Head of Mission Asunción since May 2000; born 14/03/67; FCO 1987; Tunis 1989; Sofia 1991; Ho Chi Minh City 1994; On secondment to China Britain Trade Group 1996; FCO 1997; Band C4.

Martin, Nicholas Jonathan Leigh; Counsellor Regional Affairs Bridgetown since February 2000; born 29/01/48; First Secretary FCO 1979; First Secretary (Chancery) Nairobi 1981; First Secretary FCO 1984; First Secretary (Chancery) Rome 1987; First Secretary FCO 1991; Counsellor Jakarta 1993; Counsellor FCO 1996; m 1980 Anna Louise Reekie (1s 1983; 2d 1985, 1987).

Martin, Simon Charles; First Secretary (Commercial) Budapest since November 1996; born 15/05/63; FCO 1984; Language Training 1986; Third later Second Secretary and Vice-Consul Rangoon 1987; Second later First Secretary FCO 1990; Full-Time Language

Training 1995; m 1988 Sharon Margaret Joel (1s 1996; 1d 1998).

Martinez, Paul Lawrence; Consul Dallas since September 1999; born 06/11/53; FCO 1972; Paris 1975; Dublin 1975; Kingston 1977; Chicago 1981; FCO 1984; Second Secretary (Chancery/Information) Lima 1986; Second Secretary FCO 1990; Second Secretary and HM Consul Mexico City 1993; First Secretary FCO 1996; m 1978 Ann Elizabeth Stokes (2d 1982, 1985).

Maryan-Green, Kerri-Lyn (née Miller); FCO since September 1996; born 11/11/64; FCO 1987; Shanghai 1989; Port Louis 1990; SUPL 1994; Band B3; m 1992 James Richard Maryan-Green (2d 1993, 1998).

Masefield, (John) Thorold, CMG (1986); Governor Hamilton since May 1997; born 01/10/39; First Secretary UKDEL Disarmament Conference Geneva 1970; CRO 1962-64; Private Secretary to Permanent Under-Secretary of State 1963; Kuala Lumpur 1964; Second Secretary Warsaw 1966; FO (later FCO) 1967; First Secretary FCO 1974; Counsellor and Head of Chancery and Consul-General Islamabad 1979; Counsellor FCO 1982; CDA Harvard 1987; Attached to OMCS (CSSB) 1988; High Commissioner Dar es Salaam 1989; AUS (South and South-East Asia) 1992; High Commissioner Lagos 1994; m 1962 Jennifer Mary Trowell (2s 1964, 1970; 1d 1966).

Mason, Colette Hazel, MBE (1999); SUPL since September 2001; born 15/07/65; FCO 1987; Mogadishu 1989; Port of Spain 1991; FCO 1994; Peking 1996; Vice-Consul Maseru 1998; Band B3.

Mason, Edward Charles; Deputy Head of Mission Zagreb since September 2002; born 11/05/68; FCO 1990; Third later Second Secretary Oslo 1992; Second later First Secretary FCO 1995; Full-Time Language Training (Croatian) 2001.

Mason, Ian David; Second Secretary (Political/Press/Public Affairs) Lusaka since May 2001; born 26/10/67; FCO 1987; Mogadishu 1989; Floater Duties 1991; Phnom Penh 1993; FCO 1994; Third Secretary (Chancery) Buenos Aires 1997; Band C4; m 1992 Judith Caroline Elizabeth Owens (1s 1994; 2d 1996, 1998).

Mason, James Muir Angel; FCO since July 1989; born 13/08/69; Band A2.

Mason, Judith Caroline Elizabeth (née Owens); SUPL since July 1994; born 11/08/64; FCO 1984; Washington 1986; Warsaw 1988; Floater Duties 1990; Phnom Penh 1993; Band A2; m 1992 Ian David Mason (1s 1994; 2d 1996, 1998).

Massam, David Robert; FCO since July 2000; born 02/10/70; Second Secretary FCO 1996; Second Secretary (IAIE) Vienna (UKMIS) 1998; Band C4; m 1996 Elisabeth Katharine Jenkinson (1d 1999).

Massey, Andrew Fraser; Bonn since August 1998; born 24/07/63; FCO 1984; Bangkok 1987; Jedda 1989; FCO 1994; Band C4; m 1996 Patricia Elizabeth Parsons (1d 1997; 2s 2000, 2002).

Massingham, Andrea Sharron; BTCO Taipei since June 1999; born 10/03/71; FCO 1990; Brussels (UKDEL NATO) 1992; SUPL 1992; Kathmandu 1995; FCO 1995; Band B3.

Mastin-Lee, Christopher Ernest; Legal Counsellor FCO since April 1995; born 11/08/56; Assistant Legal Counsellor FCO 1990; m 1988 Katherine Louise Heron (2s 1994, 1996; 1d 1998).

Mathers, Peter James, LVO (1995); High Commissioner Kingston since July 2002; born 02/04/46; HM Forces 1968-71; Tehran (Commercial) 1973; FCO 1971; SOAS 1972-73; Bonn (Chancery) 1976; FCO 1978; Copenhagen (Chancery and Information) 1981; Tehran 1986; (Commercial); FCO 1987; On secondment to UN Offices Vienna 1988; FCO 1991; Deputy High Commissioner Bridgetown 1995; Counsellor (Commercial and Economic) Stockholm 1998; m 1983 Elisabeth Hoeller (1s 1984; 1d 1986).

Mathewson, Iain Arthur Gray; Counsellor FCO since August 1996; born 16/03/52; HM Customs and Excise 1974-77; DHSS 1977-80; FCO 1980; First Secretary New York (UKMIS) 1981; Warsaw 1985; FCO 1985; First Secretary FCO 1989; Counsellor Prague 1993; m 1983 Jennifer Bloch (1s 1984; 1d 1986).

Mattey, Eric; FCO since April 2000; born 26/03/49; FCO 1968; Bucharest 1971; Rabat 1973; Moscow 1975; FCO 1977; Vienna 1980; Port Louis 1983; Second Secretary FCO 1985; Second later First Secretary (Commercial) Kuala Lumpur 1990; Consul Oporto 1995; Band D6; m 1970 Janet Walker (1s 1971; 1d 1974).

Matthews, Andrew John; FCO since May 1992; born 28/04/55; FCO 1974; Bonn 1976; Singapore 1979; Dublin 1982; FCO 1982; FCO 1985; Colombo 1988; Paris 1992; Band B3; m (1) 1976 Carole Susan Thomson (diss 1986) (1d 1976; 1s 1978); (2) 1988 Denise Ann Mary Carroll (1d 1992).

Matthews, Harriet Lucy; Second Secretary Brasilia since August 1999; born 22/12/73; On secondment Brazilian Diplomatic Academy (Instituto Rio Branco) 1999; FCO 1997; Band C4.

Matthews, Mark Julian; First Secretary FCO since September 2000; born 24/08/68; FCO 1990; Third Secretary (Defence) Brussels (UKDEL NATO) 1992; Full-Time Language Training (Arabic) 1996; Second Secretary (Political/Press and Public Affairs) Abu Dhabi 1997; m 1997 Shauna Rudge (1s 1998).

Maxton, Fiona; Zagreb since July 2000; born 19/12/67; FCO 1985; Bonn 1988; Third Secretary (Management) Rabat 1989; Third Secretary FCO 1993; Vice-Consul Kiev 1997; Band C4.

Maxwell, Letitia Kelso; T/D Brussels (UKREP) since January 2002; born 12/02/42; FCO 1977; Helsinki 1979; Doha 1981; FCO 1984; Copenhagen 1989; FCO 1992; Brussels (UKDEL NATO) 1995; FCO 1998; Band B3.

May, Philip; First Secretary (Management) Brussels (UKREP) since July 2001; born 12/11/60; Ottawa 1982; Moscow 1985; Islamabad 1986; FCO 1988; Resigned/Reinstated 1990; Tehran 1992; BTC Hong Kong 1994; Second Secretary FCO 1997; DSTUS Chairman 1998; Band C5; m 1985 Susan Ann Checketts (2d 1989, 1990).

May, Susan Ann (née Checketts); FCO since February 1997; born 18/08/56; FCO 1978; Peking 1980; Ottawa 1982; Moscow 1985; Islamabad 1986; SUPL 1989; Band B3; m 1985 Philip May (2d 1989, 1990).

Mayhew, Michael John Ernest; Deputy Head of Mission Bridgetown since July 1998; born 06/11/46; DSAO (later FCO) 1966; Mexico City 1969; Algiers 1972; Tokyo 1974; FCO 1975; Prague 1978; Second Secretary (Information) Oslo 1981; Second Secretary FCO 1985; First Secretary (Commercial/Development) Bangkok 1987; First Secretary (Commercial) The Hague 1990; First Secretary FCO 1993; m 1976 Elizabeth Carol Owen (1d 1987).

Mayland, Alan John; Consul Rome since March 1999; born 05/11/46; FO 1965; Warsaw 1968; Cairo 1970; Brussels 1971; Calcutta 1974; Budapest 1975; FCO 1976; Paris 1981; Ottawa 1982; Second Secretary FCO 1986; Second Secretary (Admin) Colombo 1989; Bucharest 1993.

Mayne, Julie Ann; World Wide Floater Duties since January 1999; born 03/04/58; FCO 1989; Caracas 1992; Quito 1996; Band B3.

McAdam, Douglas Baxter; Consul-General Hamburg since November 1999; born 25/06/44; FO 1961; Ulaanbaatar 1966; Vice-Consul Luanda 1969; Delhi 1972; FCO 1975; Second Secretary Ulaanbaatar 1978; Vice-Consul (Commercial) Rio de Janeiro 1979; Second later First Secretary and Head of Chancery Vienna (UKDEL) 1983; FCO 1986; First Secretary (Consular/Immigration) Lagos 1990; First Secretary FCO 1994; HM Ambassador Almaty 1996; m 1965 Susan Clare Jarvis (1s 1970; 1d 1975).

McAdam, Susan Clare (née Jarvis); SUPL since February 1996; born 04/10/42; FO 1961; Resigned 1965; Reinstated 1984; Vienna 1984; FCO 1986; Lagos 1990; Second Secretary FCO 1995; m 1965 Douglas Baxter McAdam (1s 1970; 1d 1975).

McAllister, Andrew Thornton; Second Secretary (Commercial) Dhaka since June 2001; born 30/11/67; FCO 1988; Karachi 1990; Seoul 1993; FCO 1998; Band C4; m 1995 Han Boon AE.

McAllister, Dominic James; FCO since July 2001; born 12/02/64; FCO 1990; Full-Time Language Training 1992; Full-Time Language Training Cairo 1993; Third Secretary (Cypher/Information)

Riyadh 1994; Second Secretary (Management) Taipei 1998; m 1993 Hei Yee Chan (2d 1996, 1997).

McAllister, Lesley (née Dorris); Peking since March 2001; born 04/04/72; FCO 1999; Band A2; m 2000 Gordon McAllister.

McAree, Kevin Thomas; SUPL since December 2001; born 27/06/52; FCO 1971; Honiara 1974; FCO 1974; Caracas 1974; Moscow 1977; Georgetown 1979; FCO 1983; Munich 1988; FCO 1989; Istanbul 1993; Brussels (UKDEL) 1997; Band B3; m 1975 Susan Margaret Humphrey.

McAree, Patrick Sean; FCO since March 1991(Second Secretary 1994); born 30/12/53; FCO 1971; Cairo 1975; Calcutta 1978; FCO 1982; Tehran 1984; Düsseldorf 1988; Band C5; m 1975 Maureen Alexander.

McBride, Christophe Charles Rene; Second Secretary FCO since March 2001; born 20/03/75; FCO 1997; Second Secretary (Political) Abuja 1998; Band C4; m 2001 Caroline Jane Davies.

McCafferty, Marie Claire; Wellington since May 1998; born 17/05/65; FCO 1988; Bonn 1990; Nairobi 1993; FCO 1996; Band A2.

McCall, Gary; ECO Sofia since October 2000; born 08/02/69; FCO 1987; Bridgetown 1989; Dhaka 1993; Karachi 1997; Band B3; m (1) 1990 Patricia Ann Chin (diss 1993); (2) 1993 Sharon Anne Thomas (diss) (1s 1994); ptnr, Puticha NaNongkai (1d 1998).

McCallum, Robert Campbell; Cairo since July 2001; born 04/11/45; Moscow 1989; New York (UKMIS) 1991; Kiev 1993; Moscow 1997; T/D Tripoli 2000; T/D Moscow 2001; Band B3.

McCallum, Ruth Elizabeth (née Thomson); FCO since April 1995; born 12/11/63; FCO 1985; Moscow 1988; FCO 1989; Ankara 1991; Band C4; m 1997 Martin Douglas McCallum.

McCann, Alec; Lisbon since April 1994; born 04/11/70; FCO 1988; Rome 1991; Band A2.

McCann, Gerry; FCO since February 1996; born 24/09/68; FCO 1988; Bangkok 1990; Africa/Middle East Floater 1994; Band B3.

McCarthy, Susan Margaret (née Hutton); Tortola since June 1994; born 01/04/59; FCO 1984; Khartoum 1985; Georgetown 1989; Band A2; m 1990 Jonathon Paul McCarthy (1d 1992; 1s 1996).

McCarthy, Tina Ann; FCO since December 1998; born 25/01/66; FCO 1984; Peking 1987; FCO 1988; Dar es Salaam 1990; FCO 1993; Budapest 1995; Band B3.

McCleary, William Boyd; Director General Trade and Investment Promotion and Consul-General Düsseldorf since November 2000; born 30/03/49; HCS 1972; First Secretary (Agriculture later Chancery) Bonn 1975; First Secretary FCO 1981; First Secretary, Head of Chancery and Consul Seoul 1985; First Secretary FCO 1988; Counsellor, Deputy Head of Mission and Director of Trade

Promotion Ankara 1990; Counsellor (Economic) Ottawa 1993; Head, Estate Strategy Unit FCO 1997; m (1) 1977 Susan Elizabeth Williams (diss 1999) (2d 1983, 1985); (2) 2000 Jenny Collier.

McCluskie, Matthew William; Warsaw since November 1997; born 06/05/65; FCO 1984; Bonn 1986; Prague 1988; Tunis 1990; FCO 1992; Band B3.

McColl, Lorraine Helen, RVM (1992); Tunis since September 2000; born 20/08/57; FCO 1989; Bonn 1990; Ottawa 1993; Berlin 1996; Band B3; m 1992 Alan McElroy (1d 1996).

McColl, Sally Ann; FCO since February 1990; born 27/11/64; FCO 1983; Brussels (UKREP) 1987; Band A2.

McColm, Sean; FCO since March 1998; born 10/07/72; FCO 1990; Copenhagen 1994; Dhaka 1997; Band B3.

McCombe, Iain Stewart; FCO since July 1988; born 22/11/69; Band A2.

McConnell, Gillian Anne; FCO since January 1988; born 10/05/68; Band A1.

McCooey, Geraldine Mary; Second Secretary FCO since November 2001; born 25/05/73; FCO 1996; Second Secretary (Economic) Nicosia 1998; Full-Time Language Training 2000; Band C4.

McCormack, Elizabeth (née McKenna); Doha since May 2002; born 28/06/66; Office of Electricity Regulation 1991; FCO 1996; Brussels (UKDEL NATO) 1997; Vienna 1999; Band A2; m 1986 Columbus McCormack (2s 1988, 1996).

McCormick, Stephen; Second Secretary (Economic) Ankara since July 2002; born 05/09/67; FCO 1990; Istanbul 1993; Bangkok 1993; Tokyo 1997; Tbilisi 1997; FCO 2001; Band B3; m 1996 Sevda Unalan (1d 1999).

McCosh, Andrew David; First Secretary (Political) Baku since June 2002; born 06/01/72; FCO 1994; Vice-Consul (Political) Istanbul 1997; FCO 1999; Band C4.

McCoy, Peter Owen David; Deputy Head of Mission Lagos since January 2002; born 28/04/52; FCO 1971; New Delhi 1974; Kaduna 1977; FCO 1981; Maseru 1984; AO/Vice-Consul/Comm Montreal 1987; (later Second Secretary); Second Secretary FCO 1990; Vice-Consul (Commercial) Los Angeles 1992; Assistant Trade Commissioner (China Trade) BTC Hong Kong 1993; First Secretary (Commercial) Bombay 1996; m 1975 Sally Ann Lord (2d 1976, 1978; 1s 1982).

McCreadie, Katrina; FCO since August 2001; born 19/05/73; Band A2.

McCredie, Ian Forbes, OBE (1984); Counsellor Washington since January 1999; born 28/12/50; Third Secretary FCO 1975; Third later Second Secretary (Economic) Lusaka 1976; FCO 1979; First Secretary (Economic/Commercial) Tehran 1981; FCO 1983; Copenhagen 1985; First Secretary FCO 1989; Counsellor New York

(UKMIS) 1992; Counsellor FCO 1997; m (1)
1976 Katherine Lucy Frank (1s 1981; 1d 1983)
(diss 1998); (2) 1998 Katherine Suzanne Heiny (1s
2000).

McCrory, Susan Margaret Therese; Assistant
Legal Adviser FCO since 1996; born 17/12/64;
Solicitor Legal Adviser MAFF 1992; m 1990
Ignacio de Castro (1s 1998).

McCrudden, Patrick Gerald, MBE (1993); First
Secretary (Press and Public Affairs) New Delhi
since May 2000; born 22/04/50; FCO 1969;
Saigon 1971; Mexico City 1974; Bahrain 1976;
FCO 1977; Tristan da Cunha 1980; Brussels 1981;
Pretoria 1982; Second Secretary FCO 1985;
Second Secretary (Chancery) Bridgetown 1988;
First Secretary (Somalia/Humanitarian) and
Deputy Permanent Representative UNEP/UNCHS
Nairobi 1991; First Secretary FCO 1995; Director
BIS and Deputy Consul General New York 1997;
Band D6; m 1973 (diss 1989) (1s 1974; 2d 1974,
1976).

McCulloch, Susan Geddes; Kampala since July
1997; born 29/06/70; FCO 1989; Berne 1992;
Helsinki 1996; Band B3.

McDermott, Andrew Muir Miller; Second later
First Secretary FCO since October 1991; born
24/12/43; Ministry of Transport 1959; MOD
(Navy) 1961; FO 1964; Phnom Penh 1965;
Pretoria/Cape Town 1969; Dacca 1971; Yaoundé
1974; FCO 1975; MECAS 1977; Kuwait 1978;
Second Secretary FCO 1983; Second Secretary
(Admin) and Consul Berne 1986; m 1979
Catherine Michelle Brunet.

McDonald, David Christopher; Washington since
June 1990; born 12/05/64; FCO 1984; Band B3.

McDonald, Simon Gerard; Private Secretary to
the Secretary of State for Foreign and
Commonwealth Affairs June 2001; born 09/03/61;
FCO 1982; Language Training SOAS 1983; Third
later Second Secretary Jedda (later Riyadh) 1985;
Second Secretary (Economic) Bonn 1988; First
Secretary FCO 1990; Private Secretary to
Permanent Under-Secretary 1993; First Secretary
(Chancery) Washington 1995; Counsellor and
Deputy Head of Mission and Consul-General
Riyadh 1998; m 1989 The Hon. Olivia Mary
Wright (2s 1990, 1994; 2d 1992, 1996).

McDuff, Nicholas Frederic; Second Secretary
FCO since March 1995; born 22/07/50; On loan to
the DTI 1990; MOD (Navy) 1967; FCO 1970;
Brussels (UKDEL NATO) 1972; Muscat 1972;
BMG Berlin 1975; Karachi 1978; Islamabad 1980;
FCO 1982; Athens 1983; Brussels (UKDEL
NATO) 1984; Bandar Seri Begawan 1987; Second
Secretary Casablanca 1992; m 1978 Jennifer Mary
Cain (3s 1981, 1985, 1986).

McEvoy, Edward James; First Secretary Manila
since July 1997; born 06/02/46; CRO (later FO)
1962; Belgrade 1968; Mbabane 1970; FCO 1972;
Aden 1975; Luxembourg 1977; Addis Ababa
1979; On loan to Home Office 1982; Second

Secretary (Immigration) Dhaka 1985; Second
Secretary (Commercial) Manila 1989; Vice-Consul
(Commercial) Cape Town 1990; FCO 1995; m
1967 Patricia Gibbs (diss 1991) (1s 1972).

McEwen, Christine Elizabeth; HM Consul and
First Secretary (Management) Buenos Aires since
April 2001; born 04/10/58; FCO 1978; BMG
Berlin 1981; Peking 1984; Bombay 1987; FCO
1990; Rome 1994; Deputy Head of Mission
Guatemala City 1997; FCO 2000; Band C5.

McFarlane, David Andrew; T/D Beijing since
August 2002; born 20/10/77; FCO 1999; Band C4.

McFarlane, Jacqueline (née Stewart); SUPL since
June 2001; born 01/11/67; FCO 1986; Manila
1988; FCO 1992; Damascus 1994; Islamabad
1997; Band B3; m 1988 Neil Ross McFarlane (1s
2001).

McFarlane, Neil Ross; Mumbai since January
2001; born 26/03/69; FCO 1991; Damascus 1994;
Islamabad 1997; Band B3; m 1988 Jacqueline
Stewart (1s 2001).

McFarlin, Andrew John; Mumbai since February
2002; born 30/08/70; FCO 1990; Vienna 1993;
Floater Duties 1996; Georgetown 1998; Band B3;
m 1999 Juanita Adrian.

McGee, Annie (née Brown); Full-Time Language
Training (Spanish) since May 2002; born
14/10/68; HCS FCO 1987; FCO 1994; Tunis
1996; FCO 1999; Band A2; m 1996 W M V
McGee (1s 1999).

McGill, Clive John; Deputy Head of Mission
Ashgabat since April 1999; born 09/10/58; FCO
1978; Belmopan 1982; Stockholm 1985; FCO
1988; Karachi 1991; Baku 1995; Band C4; m (1)
1983 Thelma Garcia; (2) 1988 Angela Raw.

McGinley, Francis John; First Secretary
(Management) Damascus since August 2001; born
12/01/49; FCO 1971; Brussels (NATO) 1974;
Nairobi 1977; FCO 1980; Banjul 1982; Second
Secretary (Information) Oslo 1984; Second
Secretary FCO 1989; Second Secretary
(Commercial) Zagreb 1992; First Secretary
(Management/Consular/Immigration) Kiev 1995;
Full-Time Language Training 2001; m 1994
Neriman Kreso.

McGlone, Andrea Lynne (née Webb); Vice-Consul
Riyadh since February 1999; born 27/03/66; FCO
1985; The Hague 1987; FCO 1990; Harare 1995;
Band B3; m 1993 Kevin McGlone (2d 1994,
1997).

McGlone, Jane Mary; Brussels (UKREP) since
September 1988; born 07/12/61; FCO 1987; Band
A2.

McGregor, Julie; Jerusalem since June 2001; born
23/06/80; FCO 1999; Band A2.

McGregor, Peter; HM Consul Tel Aviv since
1998; born 30/05/50; FCO 1970; Jedda 1972;
Lusaka 1976; FCO 1979; Damascus 1982; Port of
Spain 1986; New Delhi 1989; Second Secretary

FCO 1992; Second Secretary Peking 1994; m (1) 1972 Vanessa Avril Utteridge (dec'd 1989) (1s 1980); (2) 1991 Alexandra Davenport Gillies (1d 1991).

McGregor-Bell, Sharon Ann (née McGregor); FCO since December 2001; born 23/06/71; FCO 1990; Brussels 1993; FCO 1996; SUPL 1998; Tel Aviv 1999; Band A2; m 1995 Kevan Watson Bell.

McGuinness, Cheryl Vinetta (née Lynch); Abidjan since June 1994; born 04/11/66; FCO 1988; Peking 1991; Band A2; m 1996 Mark John McGuinness.

McGuinness, Mark Andrew; Abidjan since May 1999; born 25/08/67; FCO 1988; Islamabad 1990; FCO 1992; Doha 1996; Band B3.

McGuinness, Patrick Joseph, OBE (1997); First Secretary FCO since September 1999; born 27/04/63; FCO 1985; Language Training 1986; Second Secretary (Chancery) Sana'a 1988; Second Secretary FCO 1991; First Secretary (Political) Abu Dhabi 1994; First Secretary Cairo 1996; Band D6; m 1994 Susannah Imogen Mills (1d 2001).

McGurgan, Kevin; FCO since August 2000; born 31/05/71; FCO 1990; Floater Duties 1992; Brussels (UKREP) 1994; Sarajevo 1996; Third later Second Secretary (Chancery) New York (UKMIS) 1997; Band D6; m 1997 Victoria Ann Harrison.

McGurgan, Victoria Ann (née Harrison); SUPL since February 2002; born 13/08/71; FCO 1994; New York (UKMIS) 1997; FCO 2000; Band A2; m 1997 Kevin McGurgan.

McGurk, Gerard, MBE (2000); Second Secretary (Chancery) New York (UKMIS) since August 2000; born 22/12/70; FCO 1988; Athens 1991; Floater Duties 1994; Deputy Head of Mission and Vice-Consul Skopje 1996; Band B3; m 1998 Sonja Kurcieva.

McHugh, Susan Mary; Second later First Secretary FCO since November 1994; born 12/02/44; On loan to SEATO Bangkok 1974; FCO 1971; New Delhi 1977; SUPL 1980; Victoria (Seychelles) 1981; Second Secretary FCO 1983; Second Secretary Nicosia 1994; Band C5.

McIntosh, Elaine; FCO since November 1993; born 02/09/68; FCO 1988; Luxembourg 1991; Band A2; m 1990 Angus Lyon McIntosh.

McIntosh, Margaret Claire; FCO since August 2001; born 31/05/63; FCO 1995; Brussels (UKREP) 1997; World Wide Floater Duties 1999; Band B3.

McIntosh, Martin Howard, OBE (1994); · Counsellor (Commercial) Dublin since April 2001; born 26/12/47; FO (later FCO) 1966; Tokyo 1970; Jakarta 1970; Moscow 1972; Beirut 1973; FCO 1976; Madrid 1979; Second Secretary Bogotá 1982; Second later First Secretary (Commercial) Nairobi 1984; First Secretary FCO 1989; First Secretary (Commercial) Buenos Aires 1990; First Secretary (Commercial) Mexico City 1994; On

loan to the DTI 1997; m 1970 Erika Wagner (2d 1983, 1985).

McIver, Damian John; First Secretary FCO since April 1999; born 02/11/61; FCO 1986; HM Customs and Excise 1986; Third Secretary (Political) Belgrade 1987; Second Secretary FCO 1991; Political Adviser ECMIS Zagreb 1992; FCO 1993; Second Secretary (KHF) Bucharest 1995; First Secretary (Political) Belgrade 1998; Band D6; m 1998 Raluca Vasiliu.

McKee, Tracey Anne; Kigali since December 2000; born 03/06/77; FCO 2000; Band A2.

McKell, Paul Leo; Brussels (UKREP) since September 2001; born 01/09/66; Assistant Legal Adviser FCO 1997; m 2001 Elizabeth C Hanlon.

McKelvey, Diane Elizabeth; FCO since July 2001; born 06/07/67; FCO 1989; Third Secretary (Political) Copenhagen 1992; FCO 1994; Second Secretary (Political/Press and Public Affairs) Lusaka 1998.

McKen, Dawn; FCO since January 2000; born 23/07/66; FCO 1995; Second Secretary (Political) Moscow 1996; Band D6.

McKendrick, Ian; Floater Duties since January 1998; born 04/10/70; FCO 1991; BTC Hong Kong 1995; Band B3.

McKenzie, Alistair William, MBE (1980); Counsellor and Deputy Head of Mission Abu Dhabi since July 2001; born 19/02/45; DSAO 1965; Budapest 1967; Singapore 1969; Brasilia 1972; FCO 1975; San Salvador 1978; San Jose 1980; Commercial Attaché Madrid 1982; (Second Secretary 1983); Second Secretary FCO 1984; Deputy High Commissioner and Head of Chancery Banjul 1986; Consul-General Bilbao 1990; First Secretary (Immigration/Consular) Lagos 1995; British Trade International 1998; m 1968 Margaret Emily Young (2s 1970, 1974).

McKenzie, Philip; Third Secretary (Political/Economic) Bangkok since September 2001; born 26/04/65; FCO 1986; Lusaka 1987; San José 1991; FCO 1993; BTC Hong Kong 1996; Band B3.

McKenzie Smith, Justin James; First Secretary FCO since October 1999; born 04/02/69; FCO 1994; Full-Time Language Training 1995; Second Secretary (Political) Moscow 1996.

McKeogh, Fiona (née Sutherland), MBE (1993); New York (UKMIS) since September 1999; born 17/09/59; FCO 1983; Bonn 1984; Cape Town 1987; Brussels (UKREP) 1989; SUPL 1993; FCO 1993; FCO 1995; Moscow 1997; Band B3; m 1992 Paul Nicolas McKeogh.

McKeown, Patricia; Banjul since April 1992; born 13/05/69; FCO 1987; Geneva (UKDIS) 1989; Band A2.

McKerrow, Elizabeth Mary (née Foot); FCO since August 1991; born 18/01/67; FCO 1986;

Buenos Aires 1990; Band B3; m 1991 Ian Bernard Harry McKerrow (1s 1998; 1d 2000).

McKie, Margaret Stevenson; Brussels (UKREP) since May 2001; born 07/08/62; FCO 1988; Prague 1991; Cairo 1993; FCO 1996; Floater Duties 1998; Full-Time Language Training 2001; Band A2.

McKinlay, Ian Leonard; Second Secretary (Management) Geneva since August 2002; born 17/09/58; FCO 1978; Geneva (UKMIS) 1980; Tehran 1983; FCO 1986; Addis Ababa 1989; Dakar 1992; FCO 1997; m 1984 Ann Hugoline Cameron (1s 1989; 2d 1991, 1993).

McKnight, Elisabeth Eithne; Brussels (UKREP) since November 1985; born 02/08/41; FCO 1973; Dacca 1974; FCO 1975; Mbabane 1976; FCO 1978; Grand Turk 1980; New York (UKMIS) 1983; Band B3.

McLachlan, Malcolm Orde; Deputy Head of Mission Hanoi since September 2001; born 10/09/63; FCO 1981; Karachi 1984; Guatemala City 1988; FCO 1993; Second later First Secretary (Political) Nairobi 1998; m 1989 Maricruz Mendia Moynes (1d 1995).

McLaren, Donald Stuart; Deputy Head of Mission Tbilisi since June 2001; born 01/08/44; FCO 1971; Jakarta 1973; FCO 1975; St Helena 1976; FCO 1977; Pretoria 1979; FCO 1982; Third Secretary Darwin 1984; FCO 1986; Accra 1988; Third Secretary (Commercial) Kuala Lumpur 1992; Consul Kuching 1995; FCO 1999; Band C4; m 1968 Glenys Catherine Bryant (1d 1971; 2s 1973, 1979).

McLaren, Marilynn, MBE (1993); SUPL since January 1998; born 20/07/47; Scottish Office 1963; Dacca 1981; FCO 1981; Tehran 1985; Lisbon 1987; FCO 1989; Tehran 1990; Washington 1994; Band B3.

McLean, Siân Alexis; First Secretary (Economic) Peking since July 2001; born 12/09/69; FCO 1993; Full-Time Language Training Peking 1996; Consul (Economic) Hong Kong 1997; Band D6.

McMahon, Brian Patrick; British Trade International since November 1999; born 26/03/46; CRO and DSAO 1963; Prague 1968; Bonn 1969; Kabul 1972; FCO 1975; Islamabad 1978; Geneva (UKMIS) 1981; Second Secretary FCO 1984; Second Secretary (Immigration/Consular) Colombo 1990; HM Consul Rome 1994; FCO 1999; m 1967 Eileen Conroy (1d 1970; 1s 1975).

McMahon, Dr David John Hugh; First Secretary (Environment and Trade Policy) New Delhi since June 2001; born 04/05/65; FCO 1991; Second Secretary (Political/Information) Dhaka 1993; FCO 1997; Band D6; m 1994 Kay Taylor Lacey.

McMahon, Ian Irvine; Counsellor FCO since October 2001; born 08/06/55; Army 1973-83; Second Secretary FCO 1983; Second later First Secretary (Chancery) Islamabad 1985; First Secretary FCO 1987; First Secretary (Chancery) New Delhi 1989; First Secretary later Counsellor FCO 1992; Counsellor Copenhagen 1997; m 1979 Anne Elizabeth Baker (diss 2002) (1d 1981).

McMahon, Keith David, MBE (1998); FCO since August 1998; born 10/03/68; FCO 1988; Lusaka 1990; SE Asia/Middle East Floater Duties 1993; Deputy Head of Mission Yerevan 1995; Band C4; m 2000 Melissa Schwartz.

McManus, John Andrew; First Secretary (Political) Brussels since January 2001; born 20/05/55; FCO 1977; Paris 1980; Algiers 1983; FCO 1985; Language Training 1987; (Second Secretary 1987); Second Secretary Moscow 1988; Second Secretary Brussels (UKREP) 1992; Second later First Secretary (Information) Berne 1993; FCO 1997; Band D6.

McMinn, Wendy Lily Alexandra; Canberra since April 2001; born 07/07/71; MOD 1991; FCO 1999; Band A2.

McNair, Richard Andrew; FCO since April 1995; born 18/02/59; FCO 1979; Lagos 1980; FCO 1982; Ankara 1984; FCO 1987; Cairo 1991; Band C4; m 1978 Julie Elaine Stephen (1d 1981; 1s 1983).

McNeill, Alasdair Morrell; FCO since February 1999; born 13/11/67; FCO 1988; Istanbul 1992; FCO 1995; Moscow 1997; Band B3; m 1994 Elizabeth Hall (1s 2000).

McNeill, Christine Mary; Deputy High Commissioner Mbabane since January 1999; born 12/03/62; FCO 1979; Cairo 1983; Suva 1987; Second Secretary FCO 1992; Madras 1995; m 1982 Scott Robertson McNeill (1d 1994; 1s 1998).

McPhail, Dr Alastair David; second later First Secretary (Political/Military) Ankara since November 1996; born 02/03/61; FCO 1994; Language Training 1995; m 1989 Pamela Joanne Davies (2s 1992, 1994).

McPhail, Pamela Joanne (née Davies); SUPL since September 1996; born 03/12/62; FCO 1990; Third Secretary (Public Affairs) Moscow 1992; FCO 1995; Band B3; m 1989 Alastair David McPhail (2s 1992, 1994).

McQuibban, Peter James; FCO since April 2002; born 07/11/55; First Secretary on loan to the Cabinet Office 1992; Third later Second Secretary FCO 1981; Second Secretary (Economic) Brasilia 1982; First Secretary FCO 1985; First Secretary (Political) Warsaw 1988; First Secretary FCO 1992; SUPL 1995; First Secretary on sabatical at Copenhagen University since September 1995; Band D6; m (1) 1982 Susan Jennifer Magdalen Hitch (diss 1996); (2) 1996 Annegrette Felter Rasmussen (1d 1996).

McQuilton, Patricia Bernadette (née Edwards); Nicosia since November 1998; born 15/03/69; Home Civil Service 1988; FCO 1996; Band A2; m 1999 Craig McQuilton.

McVey, Andrea; SUPL since August 1997; born 28/01/64; FCO 1988; Paris 1991; Luxembourg 1993; FCO 1996; Band A2.

Mealor, Michelle Louise; Riyadh since September 1991; born 08/04/68; FCO 1988; SUPL 1990; Band A2.

Means, Claire Stewart (née Hunter); Tortola since October 2001; born 02/03/69; FCO 1990; Kuala Lumpur 1993; SUPL 1994; New York (UKMIS) 1997; Band A2; m 1994 Thomas E Means.

Mearns, Stuart; Paris since July 1995; born 21/11/58; FCO 1982; Khartoum 1985; FCO 1989; Band C4; m 1983 Andrea Chapman (2s 1993, 1996).

Meath Baker, William John Clovis, OBE (2002); Counsellor Kabul since January 2002; born 11/05/59; FCO 1985; Second later First Secretary (Chancery and Information) and Consul Kabul 1988; First Secretary and Consul Prague 1989; FCO 1989; First Secretary FCO 1993; Consul (Political) Istanbul 1997; First Secretary FCO 2000; Band D6; m 1985 Elizabeth Diana Woodham-Smith (4d 1988, 1990, 1992, 1995).

Meconi, Anne-Marie; Hanoi since October 1999; born 14/01/61; Transferred from the Scottish Office 1997; FCO 1997; Band A2.

Mee, Jeffery Bryan; Second Secretary FCO since September 1997; born 08/07/56; Passport Office 1975; FCO 1976; Kathmandu 1978; FCO 1980; Khartoum 1982; Peking 1985; FCO 1987; Vancouver 1987; Vice-Consul Vienna 1991; Lisbon 1994; (1s 1990; 1d 1993).

Mehmet, Alper, MVO (1990); First Secretary (Information) Bonn since January 1999; born 28/08/48; Immigration Service 1970; Lagos 1979; FCO 1983; (Second Secretary 1986); Bucharest 1986; Second Secretary (Head of Chancery) Reykjavik 1989; FCO 1993; m 1968 Elaine Susan Tarrant (2d 1969, 1971).

Meiklejohn, Dominic Francis; Second later First Secretary (EU/Public Affairs) Warsaw since June 1993; born 14/11/67; HM Customs and Excise 1989-90; FCO 1990; Full-Time Language Training 1993; Band D6; m 1997 Anna Iwona Reichel.

Melbourne, Sean; Baku since September 2002; born 09/12/68; FCO 1988; Maputo 1990; Tashkent 1994; FCO 1998; Band C4; m 1997 Elmira Vakkasova.

Melling, Scott Richard; Third Secretary (Management) Warsaw since December 2000; born 10/05/72; FCO 1990; Madrid 1994; FCO 1997; World Wide Floater Duties 1998; FCO 1999; Band B3; (1d 2002).

Mellor, John; Sana'a since August 2002; born 09/02/52; Department of National Savings 1968; FCO 1971; Belgrade 1973; Middle East Floater 1975; Dar es Salaam 1977; FCO 1979; Strasbourg 1980; FCO 1982; Washington 1987; Ankara 1990; FCO 1993; Jakarta 1997; Band B3; m 1987 Mary Bridget Ann McGettigan.

Meredith, Richard Evan; First Secretary FCO since August 1998; born 31/01/61; FCO 1983; Third Secretary Bridgetown 1985; Second Secretary Managua 1987; Second later First Secretary FCO 1989; Bonn 1995; Band D6; m 1986 Louisa Jane Oriel (2d 1992, 1995).

Merry, David Byron, CMG (2000); High Commissioner Gaborone since August 2001; born 16/09/45; Ministry of Aviation 1961; CRO (later Commonwealth Office, later FCO) 1965; Bangkok 1969; Second Secretary (Information) Budapest 1974; Second later First Secretary FCO 1977; First Secretary (Civil Air Attaché) Bonn 1981; Head of Chancery East Berlin 1985; First Secretary FCO 1989; Deputy Head of Mission Manila 1993; Deputy High Commissioner Karachi 1997; FCO 2000; m 1967 Patricia Ann Ellis (2d 1969, 1972; 1s 1971).

Mesarowicz, Anthony David; Guatemala City since May 1999; born 28/07/70; FCO 1991; Paris 1995; Band A2.

Metcalfe, Caryl Aileen; FCO since January 1987; FCO 1977; Baghdad 1978; Stockholm 1980; FCO 1983; Lilongwe 1985; New Delhi 1988; Band B3; m 1991 Duncan Richard Mackinnon.

Metcalfe, Julian Ross; First Secretary FCO since July 1997; born 24/02/56; Economic Adviser FCO 1983; First Secretary Cairo 1987; First Secretary FCO 1991; Full-Time Language Training 1994; Deputy Head of Mission Zagreb 1995; m 1985 Rachel Mai Jones (1d 1997).

Metreweli, Blaise Florence; Second Secretary (Economic) Dubai since September 2000; born 30/07/77; FCO 1999; Band C4.

Meyer, Sir Christopher John Rome, KCMG (1998), CMG (1988); HM Ambassador Washington since October 1997; born 22/02/44; Third Secretary FO 1966; Third later Second Secretary Moscow 1968; Madrid 1970; First Secretary FCO 1973; Brussels (UKREP) 1978; Counsellor and Head of Chancery Moscow 1982; Counsellor FCO 1984; Harvard University 1988; Minister Washington 1989; Chief Press Secretary to the Prime Minister 1994; Full-Time Language Training 1996; HM Ambassador Bonn 1997; m (1) 1976 Francoise Elizabeth Hedges (2s 1978, 1984); (2) 1997 Catherine Laylle (2 step s 1985, 1987).

Miah, Faruk; Management Officer Port Louis since February 2002; born 18/12/70; FCO 1990; Singapore 1994; Dar es Salaam 1997; FCO 1998; Band B3; m 1993 Nilufa Yasmin (1d 1996).

Micallef, Janice Pauline (née Roughley); Caracas since May 2000; born 15/01/66; FCO 1993; New Delhi 1996; SUPL 1999; Band A2; m 1996 Mark Antoine Micallef (2d 1999, 2002).

Michael, Alan Rhys; Consul-General Casablanca since January 1999; born 02/01/48; FCO 1971; MECAS 1973; Jedda 1975; Jedda/Riyadh 1976; FCO 1978; Second Secretary Geneva (UKMIS) 1982; First Secretary (Commercial) Kuwait 1986;

First Secretary FCO 1988; Brussels (UKREP) 1994; m 1973 Anita Ruth Ford (1s 1973; 1d 1977).

Middel, Julie; On loan to the DTI since November 1996; born 26/04/58; DHSS 1976; FCO 1979; Copenhagen 1982; Floater Duties 1985; Sofia 1986; Brussels 1987; SUPL 1990; FCO 1990; FCO 1994; Karachi 1994; Band B3; m 1988 Wolfgang Middel.

Middlemiss, Matthew, MBE (1991); First Secretary (Humanitarian) Geneva (UKMIS) since July 2001; born 11/01/62; First Secretary FCO 1998; Band D6; m 2001 Phyllida Alison Cheyne.

Middleton, David Farquharson; Counsellor FCO since August 2001; born 21/11/53; FCO 1982; Language Training Kamakura 1984; First Secretary Tokyo 1985; First Secretary FCO 1988; First Secretary Lusaka 1991; First Secretary FCO 1994; Counsellor Amman 1998; m 1984 Georgina Mary Housman (1s 1987; 2d 1989, 1992).

Miles, Joanne Denise, MBE (1993); Second Secretary (Political) Nairobi since August 1999; born 10/06/57; FCO 1980; Prague 1982; FCO 1984; Bandar Seri Begawan 1986; Guatemala City 1988; San José 1991; FCO 1992; Caracas 1994; FCO 1997; Band C4.

Miles, John; First Secretary Washington since October 2000; born 30/10/46; Nepal 1972; Germany 1974; Home Civil Service 1978; Hong Kong 1980; New Delhi 1984; FCO 1988; Moscow 1995; Band D6; m 1968 Lynda Patricia Frances McNair (1d 1972; 1s 1974).

Millar, Andrew James; First Secretary (Economic/Political) Pretoria since September 2000; born 13/07/65; Office of Gas Supply 1994; FCO E/Advs 1996; FCO 1999; Band D6; m 1996 Catherine Jo Russell Davis.

Millar, Lindsey; The Hague since February 1997; born 18/06/67; Scottish Office 1984-90; FCO 1991; Berlin 1993; Band A2.

Miller, Andrew John; Second Secretary Muscat since July 2002; born 29/05/66; FCO 1985; Munich 1991; FCO 1995; Abu Dhabi 1998; Band C4; m 1991 Coral Annabel (1d 1997; 1s 1999).

Miller, Anne Virginia; FCO since February 1997; born 16/01/72; FCO 1991; Brussels (UKDEL NATO) 1995; Band A2.

Miller, David; First Secretary (Chancery) Bogotá since May 2000; born 19/05/66; Second Secretary FCO 1997; Band D6; m 1993 Carmen Delgado.

Miller, David Roland; Resident Acting High Commissioner Grenada since May 1998; born 01/11/52; FCO 1972; Bucharest 1975; Tripoli 1976; Rome 1979; FCO 1982; Kuala Lumpur 1985; Second Secretary FCO 1989; Deputy High Commissioner Vila 1990; Second later First Secretary FCO 1994; m 1976 Gillian Mary Cornthwaite (2s 1980, 1983).

Miller, Jamie Jonathan, MBE (1999); First Secretary (Political) Freetown since November

2000; born 01/05/72; FCO 1996; Second Secretary (Chancery) Islamabad 1998; Band D6.

Miller, Julian Peter; FCO since October 1998; FCO 1987; Language Training Kamakura 1989; Language Training 1989; Tokyo 1990; San José 1994; m 1993 Yasuko Yanai (2s 1995, 1998).

Miller, Julie; Buenos Aires since April 1995; born 21/11/70; FCO 1988; Jakarta 1991; FCO 1994; Band B3.

Miller, Nicholas Michael; Hamburg since June 1997; born 10/10/62; FCO 1982; Bangkok 1984; Peking 1987; FCO 1990; Tehran 1993; Full-Time Language Training 1996; m 1995 Raquel Evangelina Varela (2d 1994, 1999).

Miller, Pablo; FCO since August 2002; born 27/02/60; FCO 1990; First Secretary (Political) Abuja later Lagos 1992; First Secretary FCO 1995; First Secretary Tallinn 1997; Band D6; m 1989 Elke Schmidt (3d 1991, 1994, 1996).

Miller, Penelope Helen; Second Secretary (Commercial) Tokyo since December 1998; born 18/03/70; FCO 1995; Language Training Kamakura 1997; Band C4.

Miller, Peter Charles William; First Secretary (Political) Abuja since December 1992; born 27/08/46; FCO 1964; Madrid 1987; FCO 1989; m (1) 1970 Jennifer O'Toole (diss 1984) (1s 1971; 1d 1973); (2) 1985 Jean Ward (3s 1974, 1976, 1977; 1d 1994).

Miller, Shirley; Vienna since June 2002; born 06/12/56; FCO 1976; Reykjavik 1981; Geneva (UKDIS) 1984; Port Stanley 1987; FCO 1988; Brussels (UKREP) 1992; Helsinki 1995; FCO 1998; Band A2; m 1997 Martin Corcoran.

Millett, Peter Joseph; FCO since October 2001; born 23/01/55; FCO 1974; LA Floater 1976; Caracas 1978; Doha 1981; Second Secretary FCO 1985; First Secretary (Energy) Brussels (UKREP) 1989; Counsellor FCO 1993; Deputy Head of Mission Athens 1997; m 1981 June Harnett (3d 1984, 1987, 1991).

Millington, Claire; FCO since January 1999; Band B3.

Mills, Anthony; Second later First Secretary (Management/HM Consul) Dubai since July 1999; born 29/05/43; Inland Revenue 1966; FCO 1970; Addis Ababa 1973; Brussels (UKREP) 1975; Prague 1977; Dacca 1979; FCO 1981; Third Secretary (Management) Freetown 1982; Third later Second Secretary FCO 1986; Second Secretary (Management) Karachi 1990; Second Secretary (Management) Lagos 1995; m 1978 Christine Mary Napp (2s 1979, 1982).

Mills, Anwen Eluned (née Rees); SUPL since April 1999; born 22/07/64; FCO 1991; T/D New York (UKMIS) 1992; Resigned 1993; Reinstated 1994; Cape Town 1995; Band A2; m 1993 (William) Gary Mills (1s 1997).

Mills, Beverley; Washington since July 1999; born 09/05/69; FCO 1990; Brussels 1995; FCO 1997; Band A2.

Mills, David Paul; T/D Dar es Salaam since January 2000; born 02/10/67; FCO 1987; Cairo 1989; FCO 1992; Addis Ababa 1993; HO 1999; Band B3.

Mills, Emma, MBE (2001); Second Secretary (Political/Information) Athens since March 2001; born 27/02/69; FCO 1988; Baghdad 1990; Peking 1991; Bogotá 1994; FCO 1997; Pristina 1999; Band C4.

Mills, Hilary Clare; FCO since January 1998; born 05/06/46; Dakar 1978; FCO 1978; Rio de Janeiro 1980; Brasilia 1982; Moscow 1984; FCO 1985; Bonn 1987; FCO 1991; Copenhagen 1994; Band C4.

Millson, Tony; Head of Medical and Welfare FCO since June 2001; born 25/11/51; FCO 1970; MECAS 1973; Third Secretary (Commercial) Tripoli 1974; Third later Second Secretary (Development) Amman 1976; FCO 1980; Second Secretary BMG Berlin 1983; First Secretary FCO 1986; Head of Chancery Kuwait 1988; First Secretary FCO 1991; HM Ambassador Skopje 1993; Counsellor FCO 1997; High Commissioner Banjul 1998; T/D Abuja 2000.

Milne, Carole Lesley; SUPL since August 2001; born 01/10/66; FCO HCS 1989; FCO 1994; Executive Assistant Lusaka 1996; Staff Officer Montserrat 1998; FCO 1999; Band B3.

Milne, Hilary Taylor; SUPL since August 2001; born 07/06/65; FCO 1984; Rome 1985; Freetown 1988; FCO 1990; FCO 1991; Windhoek 1994; Moscow 1998; Band B3; m 2001 John Burton.

Milton, Kirstie Jane (née Levitt); FCO since July 1997; born 04/07/69; FCO 1988; Cairo 1991; FCO 1992; The Hague 1995; Band A2; m 2000 Jonathan Milton.

Minshall, Heidi Jane; First Secretary FCO since May 1997; born 02/03/67; FCO 1990; Full-Time Language Training Cairo 1993; Second Secretary (Political/Information) Abu Dhabi 1995.

Minshull, Simon Peter; Vice-Consul Bridgetown since March 1999; born 21/11/68; FCO 1988; Moscow 1990; Islamabad 1992; FCO 1996; Band B3; m 1991 Hrefna Dis Luthersdottir (2d 1991, 1994).

Minter, Graham Leslie, LVO (1983); HM Ambassador La Paz since August 1999; born 04/01/50; FCO 1968; Anguilla 1971; Latin America Floater 1973; Asunción 1975; FCO 1978; First Secretary (Economic) Mexico City 1979; First Secretary FCO 1984; First Secretary (Economic/Agriculture) Canberra 1990; First Secretary later Counsellor FCO 1994; m 1975 P Anne Scott (1s 1978).

Mirtle, Catherine Grace; Paris since July 1993; born 08/01/69; FCO 1989; Band A2.

Mistry, Hemlata; FCO since April 1994; born 07/06/62; FCO Home Civil Service 1988; FCO 1990; Floater Duties 1992; Band B3.

Mitchell, Andrew Jonathan; Deputy Head of Mission Kathmandu since May 1999; born 07/03/67; FCO 1991; Second Secretary (Political) Bonn 1993; First Secretary FCO 1996; m 1996 Helen Sarah Anne Magee (2s 1998, 2000).

Mitchell, Carole, RVM (1990); Sarajevo since August 2000; born 07/06/57; Scottish Office 1975; FCO 1987; Reykjavik 1988; The Hague 1991; Geneva (UKDIS) 1994; FCO 1999; Band A2.

Mitchell, Helen Sarah Anne (née Magee); SUPL (c/o Kathmandu) since May 1999; born 18/10/67; FCO 1990; Second Secretary (EU) Bonn 1993; First Secretary FCO 1997; m 1996 Andrew Jonathan Mitchell (2s 1998, 2000).

Mitchell, John Steven; Riyadh since June 1999; born 28/11/67; FCO 1985; Tokyo 1988; Stockholm 1990; T/D Riga 1991; FCO 1992; Dhaka 1995.

Mitchell, Jonathan Kenneth Milton; First Secretary Bucharest since June 1998; born 18/12/59; Second Secretary FCO 1987; Second later First Secretary (Information) Amman 1989; First Secretary FCO 1990; First Secretary (Chancery) Harare 1991; First Secretary FCO 1994; Band D6; m 1986 Joyce Ann Henderson (2d 1990, 1993).

Mitchell, Margaret Rose (née Howie); Third Secretary FCO since 1997; born 07/03/66; FCO 1985; Tokyo 1988; Stockholm 1990; FCO 1993; Rome 1994.

Mitchell, Michael James, MVO (1989); Second Secretary (Management) Colombo since September 2002; born 07/08/54; HM Customs & Excise 1980; FCO 1985; Third Secretary (Aid) Kampala 1986; Third Secretary (Chancery) Singapore 1989; Deputy Head of Mission Guatemala City 1993; Full-Time Language Training 1993; Second Secretary FCO 1997; First Secretary (Management) Karachi 1999; Band C5; m 1982 Dominique Steggle (1d 1994).

Mitchell, Robert; Second Secretary FCO since September 1983; born 20/10/43; GPO 1967; FCO 1969; Islamabad 1972; Milan 1975; FCO 1978; Second Secretary (Admin) Kabul 1981; m 1981 Janet Frances Booth.

Mitchell, Sheilah Dawn (née Bramley); SUPL since February 1998; born 15/04/59; FCO 1979; Brussels (UKDEL NATO) 1980; Maputo 1982; Floater Duties 1987; FCO 1990; Third Secretary (Management)/Vice-Consul Jerusalem 1994; Band B3; m 1994 Alan Stuart Mitchell.

Mitchell, Simon Andrew; FCO since October 1999; born 27/11/64; PSA DoE 1987; The Court Service 1995; Band A2.

Mitchiner, Dr John Edward; Deputy High Commissioner Calcutta since 1999; born 12/09/51; FCO 1980; Third later Second Secretary Istanbul 1982; Second Secretary FCO 1985; Second

Secretary (Development) New Delhi 1987; Second later First Secretary (Political) Berne 1991; First Secretary FCO 1995; HM Ambassador Yerevan 1997; m 1983 Elizabeth Mary Ford.

Mitchison, Pamela Denise; SUPL since December 1997; born 28/12/58; FCO 1978; Far East Floater 1981; Moscow 1982; Paris 1985; Second Secretary FCO 1988; APS Minister of State 1989; First Secretary (Chancery) Washington 1991; First Secretary FCO 1995; SUPL 1996; First Secretary FCO 1997; m 1996 Ian Richard Whitehead (1d 1996).

Mititelu, Alexandra Marie; Second Secretary (Political) New Delhi since March 2002; born 15/09/76; FCO 1999; Full-Time Language Training 2001; Band C4.

Mochan, Charles Francis; High Commissioner Suva since November 2002; born 06/08/48; MOD (Navy) 1966; FCO 1967; Port Elizabeth 1970; Kingston 1972; FCO 1974; Second Secretary 1975; Seoul 1977; FCO 1980; Second later First Secretary (Commercial) Helsinki 1981; First Secretary FCO 1984; Deputy High Commissioner and Head of Chancery Port Louis 1988; First Secretary FCO 1991; Consul-General Casablanca 1995; HM Ambassador Antananarivo 1999; m 1970 Ilse Sybilla Carleon Cruttwell (1d 1971; 1s 1974).

Monckton, The Honourable Anthony Leopold Colyer; Counsellor Belgrade since March 2001; born 25/09/60; HM Forces 1979-87; Second Secretary FCO 1987; Second later First Secretary Geneva (UKDEL) 1990; First Secretary FCO 1992; First Secretary (Political) Zagreb 1996; British Embassy Banja Luka Office 1998; First Secretary FCO 1999; Band D6; m 1985 Philippa Susan Wingfield (1s 1988; 1d 1989).

Montagnon, Giles; FCO since September 2001; born 08/12/77; Band C4.

Moody, Patrick Thomas Robert; First Secretary (Political) Brussels (UKDEL NATO) since September 1998; born 17/03/66; FCO 1988; Third later Second Secretary (Political/Information) Mexico City 1990; First Secretary FCO 1994; m 1996 Atalanta Sturdy (1s 1998; 1d 2000).

Moon, Dorian Lawrence; FCO since March 1993; born 02/01/59; HCS 1985; BEMRS Cyprus 1986; HCS 1989; FCO 1990; Moscow 1992; Band A2; m 1989 Joanne Ashley (1d 1989; 1s 1991).

Moon, Michael Yelland; Second Secretary Bandar Seri Begawan since April 1996; born 19/08/59; FCO 1977; Brussels (UKREP) 1979; Khartoum 1982; Africa/Middle East Floater 1986; FCO 1990; Third Secretary (Aid/Information) Mbabane 1993; Consul Brussels 1995.

Moon, Dr Richard John; New York (UKMIS) since March 1999; born 03/01/59; FCO 1983; Second Secretary Jakarta 1985; First Secretary FCO 1988; First Secretary (Political) Rome 1993; FCO 1997; m 1987 Sandra Sheila Francis Eddis (1s 1990; 1d 1993).

Moon, Sandra Sheila Francis (née Eddis), MVO (1984); SUPL since January 1994; born 11/03/56; FCO 1980; Washington 1982; Jakarta 1984; FCO 1988; Band C4; m 1987 Richard John Moon (1s 1990; 1d 1993).

Mooney, Laura; World Wide Floater Duties since April 2001; born 30/04/73; MOD 1989-96; FCO 1996; Wellington 1997; Band B3.

Moonlight, Julie Anne (née Thorpe); SUPL since April 1997; born 12/08/68; FCO 1986; Paris 1989; FCO 1992; Washington 1994; Band A2; m 1991 Philip Lindsay Moonlight.

Moore, Charles Jonathan Rupert; Second Secretary (UN/UNIDO) Geneva (UKMIS) since August 1998; born 14/04/63; FCO 1982; Harare 1984; Gaborone 1987; Masirah 1987; FCO 1991; Third Secretary (Commercial) Jakarta 1995; Band C4; m 1988 Deborah Mary Ford (1s 1989; 1d 1992).

Moore, David; Madrid since September 1996; born 18/06/59; HO 1977; FCO 1978; Moscow 1980; Wellington 1982; FCO 1986; Vice-Consul Osaka 1990; FCO 1992; Second Secretary 1994; Full-Time Language Training 1996; m (1) 1981 Annette May Gardner (diss) (1d 1982; 1s 1985); (2) 1996 Janice Ann Bell.

Moore, Deborah Mary (née Ford); SUPL since August 1998; born 15/04/63; FCO 1982; Muscat 1985; SUPL 1988; FCO 1991; SUPL 1993; Jakarta 1995; Band B3; m 1988 Charles Jonathan Rupert Moore (1s 1989; 1d 1992).

Moore, Fiona Charlotte; Counsellor FCO since January 2000; born 15/08/59; FCO 1981; Third later Second Secretary Warsaw 1983; Second later First Secretary FCO 1987; First Secretary (Chancery) Athens 1991; First Secretary FCO 1995; CDA, Imperial College London 1995;

Moore, Geraldine Fiona; FCO since July 1976; born 06/06/54; Band B3.

Moore, Janice Ann (née Bell); Kiev since March 2002; born 06/10/64; FCO 1984; Accountant Nairobi 1986; Vice-Consul Budapest 1989; Resigned 1991; Reinstated (FCO) 1992; Second Secretary 1994; Second Secretary Madrid 1996; Band C5; m 1996 David Moore.

Moore, Jason Richard Alexander; Second Secretary (Press and Public Affairs/Programmes) Budapest since September 2000; born 06/04/73; FCO 1998; Full-Time Language Training 1999; m 2000 Rebecca Marie Letts

Moore, Richard Peter; Counsellor (Political) Kuala Lumpur since November 2001; born 09/05/63; Second Secretary FCO 1987; Second Secretary Ankara 1990; Consul (Information) Istanbul 1991; First Secretary FCO 1992; Islamabad 1995; First Secretary FCO 1999; m 1985 Margaret Martin (1s 1989; 1d 1992).

Moore, Sarah Jane; Assistant Legal Adviser FCO since January 1995; born 20/09/66; Band D7.

Moore, Stephen Lawrence; Second Secretary (Economic/Commercial) Rabat since February 2002; born 22/07/68; On loan to DTI 1999; Paris 1991; FCO 1993; Islamabad 1994; FCO 1997; Band C4; m 1992 Carolyn Andrea (1d 1998).

Moore, Trevor Charles; First Secretary (CTBT) Vienna (UKMIS) since April 1997; born 19/01/58; FCO 1980; Belgrade 1982; Vice-Consul New York 1986; Second Secretary Washington 1987; Second later First Secretary FCO 1989; m 1991 Diane Elizabeth Burns (3s 1994, 1997, 1999).

Moores, Amias Steven; Third Secretary and Vice-Consul Abu Dhabi since April 2001; born 31/03/71; FCO 1990; Geneva (UKMIS) 1994; FCO 1997; Abu Dhabi 1997; Band B3; m 2000 Lindsey Cave.

Moorhead, Michelle Anne; Tel Aviv since August 2002; born 02/02/70; FCO 1988; Washington 1991; Accra 1995; FCO 1998; SUPL 2000; FCO 2001; Band B3; m 1990 Ian William Moorhead (1s 2000; 1d 2002).

Moran, David John; Deputy Permanent Representative UKDEL OECD Paris since January 2001; born 22/08/59; ODA 1985; DTI 1985; Second Secretary (Programmes Adviser) British Development Division in Eastern Africa Nairobi 1988; First Secretary ODA/FCO 1991; First Secretary (Know How Fund) Moscow 1993; First Secretary FCO 1996; m 1993 Carol Ann Marquis.

Moran, Karen (née Pinkney); Deputy Head of Mission Tashkent since July 2000; born 02/03/65; National Savings Department 1984; FCO 1984; Washington 1986; Seoul 1989; FCO 1993; Third Secretary (Management) Hong Kong 1996; Band C4; m 1986 Sean Moran (diss 1995).

Moran, Lindy Jane (née Preston); SUPL since July 2000; born 09/10/58; FCO 1981; Caracas 1982; Grand Turk 1986; FCO 1989; Warsaw 1990; Nairobi 1992; Band B3; m 1995 Eamon Andrew Moran.

Moran, Sean; World Wide Floater Duties since August 1998; born 06/03/64; Inland Revenue 1984; FCO 1984; Washington 1986; Seoul 1989; FCO 1993; On secondment to DTI 1996; Band B3; m 1986 Karen Pinkney (diss 1995).

Morgan, Angela Merril; Second Secretary (Consular) Bangkok since July 2001; born 14/03/68; FCO 1989; Warsaw 1991; FCO 1992; Riga 1993; FCO 1994; New Delhi 1995; FCO 1996; Third Secretary (Political) Suva 1997; Suva 2000; SUPL 2000; Band B3; m 2001 Sainivalati Tokalau (1d 2000).

Morgan, Charles Edward William; FCO since September 2001; born 24/08/73; Band C4.

Morgan, Deborah Edith; FCO since July 1985; born 31/05/64; Band A1.

Morgan, Linda; FCO since June 2002; born 09/07/72; Band A2; ptnr, Stephen Watson.

Morgan, Mark Scott Thomas, MBE (1997); First Secretary Budapest since July 2001; born 26/04/58; FCO 1976; Geneva 1984; FCO 1986; Second Secretary and Vice-Consul Aden 1988; Second Secretary FCO 1990; Second later First Secretary Valletta 1994; First Secretary FCO 1998; Band C5; m 1998 Samantha Thompson.

Morgan, Patrick; HM Ambassador San Salvador since September 1999; born 31/01/44; Board of Trade 1963; CRO 1964; FO 1965; Bonn 1967; Kuwait 1969; La Paz 1972; On loan to DTI 1972; FCO 1975; Second Secretary Washington 1979; First Secretary (Chancery/Economic) Jakarta 1983; First Secretary FCO 1987; HM Ambassador Tegucigalpa 1992; Counsellor and Deputy Head of Mission Abu Dhabi 1995; FCO 1998; m 1966 Marlene Collins Beaton (2s 1967, 1968; 2d 1973, 1982).

Morgan, Richard de Riemer; First Secretary (PPA) Paris since September 2000; born 09/05/61; FCO 1984; Language Training Tokyo 1986; Second Secretary (Commercial) Tokyo 1987; First Secretary FCO 1991; First Secretary (Political/Aid) Pretoria 1995; m 1987 Susan Carolyn McGaw (1s 1992; 1d 1994).

Morgan, Steven Leonard; Second Secretary (Chancery) Bogotá since September 2002; born 14/01/65; Department of Employment 1983; FCO 1984; Budapest 1986; FCO 1987; Paris 1988; Guatemala City 1990; Mexico City 1993; FCO 1994; Madrid 1999; Band C4; m 1995 Maria del Carmen Toledo Municio.

Morgan, Stuart John; FCO since December 1990; born 02/12/63; FCO 1983; Khartoum 1988; Band B3; m 1993 Milla Heidi Susan Chapman (1s 2000).

Morgan, William Donovan; Second later First Secretary (Political) Peking since October 2000; born 02/06/71; Second Secretary FCO 1996; Full-Time Language Training 1998; Full-Time Language Training Peking 1999; Band D6; m 1992 Lucy Bullock (2s 1992, 1995).

Morley, David John; First Secretary (Information) Brussels (UKDEL NATO) since June 1999; born 23/10/54; MAFF 1972; FCO 1973; Geneva (UKMIS) 1975; Port Stanley 1978; Kuala Lumpur 1980; FCO 1981; Kaduna 1984; FCO 1988; Second Secretary (Management) Moscow 1991; Second Secretary FCO 1994; Deputy High Commissioner Mbabane 1995; Band C5; m 1978 Jacqueline Ann Wells.

Morley, Ian Robert; Zagreb since October 2000; born 24/07/71; FCO 1992; New York (UKMIS) 1996; Luanda 1999; Band A2.

Morley, Jacqueline Ann (née Wells), MBE (1991); Brussels (UKDEL NATO) since February 2000; born 20/07/55; FCO 1973; New York (UKMIS) 1974; Geneva (UKMIS) 1975; Port Stanley 1978; SUPL 1980; FCO 1981; Kuala Lumpur 1981; SUPL Kaduna 1984; Kaduna 1987; FCO 1988; Moscow 1991; FCO 1994; SUPL 1995; SUPL

1999; FCO 1999; Band B3; m 1978 David John Morley.

Morley, Michael Donald; First Secretary (Management) Athens since January 1999; born 18/02/53; FCO 1973; Moscow 1975; Kuala Lumpur 1977; Latin America Floater 1981; Beirut 1983; FCO 1984; La Paz 1987 (Second Secretary 1990); Second Secretary (Commercial) Santiago 1991; FCO 1995; m 1983 Carmen Gloria Del Prado (2s 1987, 1989).

Morley, Stuart Richard, OBE (2002); First Secretary FCO since April 1999; born 26/01/59; Second Secretary FCO 1988; Second later First Secretary (Chancery/Information) San José 1989; First Secretary (Chancery) Bridgetown 1990; First Secretary FCO 1992; First Secretary (Chemical Weapons) The Hague 1996; Band D6; m 1987 Janet Henry (3d 1990, 1993, 1998; 1s 1996).

Morrell, Susan Mary; Peking since September 2001; born 07/11/50; FCO 1977; New York (UKMIS) 1978; Budapest 1981; Khartoum 1982; Islamabad 1985; Moscow 1988; FCO 1992; Sofia 1996; Band C4.

Morris, Richard Charles; Second Secretary (Political) Bridgetown since November 1996; born 01/11/67; Third Secretary (Political) Ottawa 1993; New York (UKMIS) 1993; m 1992 Alison Jane Waring (1d 1996; 1s 1998).

Morris, Richard Peter; Second Secretary (Management) Colombo since October 1999; born 08/09/64; FCO 1983; Dhaka 1985; Bucharest 1988; FCO 1991; Vice-Consul Rome 1995; Full-Time Language Training 1995; m 1990 Diane Jacqueline Harvey.

Morris, Rose Marie June Townson (née Bennett); FCO since May 1979; born 21/11/45; FCO 1970; Singapore 1971; Beirut 1973; FCO 1976; Lagos 1977; Band B3; m 1980 Jeremy Robin David Morris.

Morris, Sara Joanne; FCO since May 1995; born 19/10/62; FCO 1983; Mexico City 1987; FCO 1991; Floater Duties 1993; Band A2.

Morris, Timothy Colin; Counsellor (Trade and Investment) Tokyo since June 1998; born 17/09/58; FCO 1981; SOAS 1982; Language Training Tokyo 1983; Second Secretary (Commercial) Tokyo 1984; First Secretary FCO 1987; On loan to DTI 1989; First Secretary (Head of Political Section) Madrid 1991; First Secretary FCO 1996; m 1996 Patricia Isabel Tena Garcia (3s 1998, 1999, 2001).

Morris, Warwick; HM Ambassador Hanoi since June 2000; born 10/08/48; FCO 1969; Paris 1972; Language Training Seoul 1975; (Second Secretary 1977); FCO 1979; (PS to Deputy PUS 1979-80); First Secretary 1982; First Secretary (Commercial) Mexico City 1984; First Secretary and Head of Chancery Seoul 1988; First Secretary later Counsellor FCO 1991; New Delhi 1995; Career Development Attachment Royal College of

Defence Studies 1999; m 1972 Pamela Jean Mitchell (1s 1976; 2d 1978, 1982).

Morrison, Alan; Ottawa since September 1997; born 04/01/70; FCO 1989; Islamabad 1992; FCO 1995; Band A2; m 1997 Lynne Jean Gregory.

Morrison, Fiona Margaret; First Secretary (Political) Kabul since September 2002; born 23/01/67; FCO 1989; Third Secretary (Chancery) Brussels (UKDEL) 1991; FCO 1994; Third Secretary (Commercial) Oslo 1995; Third Secretary (Chancery/PPA) Kingston 1996; Second Secretary FCO 2000; Band D6.

Morrison, Ian Kenneth; First Secretary (Commercial) Tel Aviv since July 1999; born 27/12/54; Inland Revenue 1974; FCO 1977; Budapest 1979; Islamabad 1981; Madrid 1983; FCO 1986; Third Secretary Accra 1988; Vice-Consul (Political/Information) Cape Town 1991; FCO 1996; Band C4; m (1) 1978 Gillian Winifred Turk (diss) (1d 1982); (2) 1994 Jean MacAlpine Kerr (2s 1995, 1998).

Morrison, Jonathan James Howard; FCO since 1999 (Private Secretary to Minister for Europe 2000 -); born 31/12/67; Home Office 1989-91; Third later Second later First Secretary Brussels (UKREP) 1994; Band D6; m 1994 Helen Louisa Pope (2d 1996, 1998).

Morrison, Melanie Kathryn (née Girling); Moscow since January 2002; born 18/03/62; FCO 1995; Wellington 1997; Band A2; m 1997 John Morrison.

Morrison, Thérésa Mary; Vienna (UKDEL) since January 2000; born 07/01/55; Copenhagen 1976; Warsaw 1978; FCO 1982; Resigned 1985; Reinstated 1991; Montevideo 1992; FCO 1993; FCO 1998; Budapest 1998; Band A2; m 1981 William Alastair Harrison (diss 1991).

Morrissey, Gillian Lesley (née Worrall); FCO since February 1990; born 02/02/60; FCO 1979; Helsinki 1981; Doha 1984; Bonn 1988; Band C4; m 1984 Patrick John Morrissey (1d 1993).

Mortimer, Hugh Roger, LVO (1992); HM Ambassador Ljubljana since January 2001; born 19/09/49; Royal College of Defence Studies (RCDS) 1996; FCO 1973; Rome 1975; Singapore 1978; FCO 1981; Second later First Secretary New York (UKMIS) 1983; First Secretary FCO 1987; On attachment to the Auswärtiges Amt 1990; First Secretary (Chancery) Berlin 1991; Counsellor FCO 1994; Deputy Head of Mission Ankara 1997; m 1974 Zosia Cecylia Rzepecka (2d 1976 (dec'd 1993), 1980).

Morton, David Stanley Thomas; First Secretary (Management) Copenhagen since January 2002; born 06/12/45; FO 1963; Cairo 1967; Kinshasa 1967; Wellington 1969; Brussels (UKREP) 1972; FCO 1975; Beirut 1977; Washington 1979; Dacca 1982; Second Secretary FCO 1985; Second Secretary (Commercial) Baghdad 1990; Second Secretary (Commercial) Nairobi 1991; Second Secretary FCO 1995; Consul (Management)

Istanbul 1998; m (1) 1972 Judith Anne Amies (diss 1983) (1s 1973); (2) 1987 Beverley Anne Sheppard (2s 1988, 1991).

Morton, Ralph Christopher; Consul (Commercial/CCU) Düsseldorf since July 2001; born 13/12/55; FCO 1979; Khartoum 1982; Brussels (UKDEL NATO) 1984; Third later Second Secretary (Chancery) East Berlin 1987; Second Secretary FCO 1991; Second Secretary (Commercial/Consular) Kampala 1992; Second Secretary (Commercial) Johannesburg 1995; Second Secretary FCO 1996; Second Secretary (Political) Vienna Embassy 1998.

Moseley, Simon Arthur; Peking since 2002; born 11/02/72; FCO 1989; Band C4; m 1999 Aleesha.

Moser-Andon, Barbara; Tehran since November 2000; born 04/08/47; FCO 1991; Damascus 1993; FCO 1996; Kathmandu 1997; Band B3.

Moss, Keith Cyril; Consul-General Paris since January 1995; born 11/06/46; FO 1965; Moscow 1968; Tokyo 1969; Budapest 1973; FCO 1974; Paris 1977; Vice-Consul Douala 1981; Second Secretary FCO 1983; Second later First Secretary (Chancery) Vienna (UKMIS) 1987; First Secretary FCO 1991; m 1969 Lynn Butler (2s 1971, 1975).

Moss, Kylie Joanne; T/D Kinshasa since April 2002; born 22/10/71; FCO 1990; Amman 1993; Tbilisi 1999; Band A2.

Moss, Stuart; Second Secretary (Technical) Buenos Aires since March 2001; born 14/06/67; FCO 1987; Washington 1994; FCO 1996; Band C4; m 2001 Kerry May Ford.

Moss-Norbury, Nicholas Adam; FCO since July 2000; born 12/05/72; FCO 1991; Third Secretary Peking 1997; Band C4.

Mott, Alan Lawrence; FCO since August 1991; born 05/10/65; FCO 1984; Washington 1989; Band C4; m 1988 Tina Michaela.

Mowbray, Fiona (née Roberts); Grand Cayman since June 1999; born 08/11/63; FCO 1983; Washington 1984; Addis Ababa 1986; Nassau 1990; Ankara 1991; SUPL 1994; FCO 1996; Band A2; m 1986 Kevin Lewis Mowbray (1s 1993).

Mowbray, Joy Diana (née Smith); SUPL since June 2000; born 01/07/71; FCO 1990; Muscat 1992; Floater Duties 1999; Band A2; m 1995 David Jonathan Mowbray.

Mowbray, Kevin Lewis; Grand Cayman since June 2000; born 05/04/59; FCO 1977; Brussels (UKREP) 1979; Africa/Middle East Floater 1982; FCO 1984; Addis Ababa 1986; Nassau 1990; Second Secretary (Chancery/Consular) Ankara 1991; FCO 1996; SUPL 1999; m 1986 Fiona Roberts (1s 1993).

Muir, David John; Third Secretary (Vice-Consul) Tashkent since December 2000; born 22/05/58; FCO 1995; Floater Duties 1996; Attaché Tashkent 1999; Band B3; m 1999 Deborah Okey.

Mulcahy, Colin Paul Peter, OBE (2000); First Secretary (Consular) Islamabad since July 2000; born 21/06/44; CRO 1963; Freetown 1966; DSAO (later FCO) 1968; Attaché (Consular) Bombay 1972; Second Secretary (Chancery) Wellington 1976; Second Secretary FCO 1981; Second Secretary (Commercial) Damascus 1984; Vice-Consul later Consul (Commercial) Toronto 1985; First Secretary (Management) and Consul Khartoum 1989; Consul Warsaw 1992; First Secretary FCO 1993; First Secretary (Consular/Immigration) New Delhi 1996; m 1969 Josephine Ann Molly Smyth (2s 1973, 1976).

Muldoon, Julie Aileen; Accra since May 1986; born 04/05/61; FCO 1984; Band A2.

Mullee, Patrick; Deputy Head of Mission Quito since August 2000; born 08/10/54; FCO 1974; Prague 1976; Caracas 1977; Africa Floater 1980; Latin America Floater 1983; FCO 1985; Third later Second Secretary San José 1988; Second Secretary (Chancery/Information) Bridgetown 1991; Second later First Secretary FCO 1995; Full-Time Language Training 2000; Band C5; m 1987 Joanna Louise Johnson (2d 1989, 1994).

Mullender, Andrea; FCO since October 1999; born 16/08/73; Band A2.

Mulvaney, Isabella Maria; FCO since October 1994; born 18/03/68; FCO 1986; Brussels (UKDEL) 1988; Karachi 1991; Band B3.

Mulvein, Helen Jane; Assistant Legal Adviser FCO since April 2000; born 04/12/70.

Muncie, Heather; SUPL since March 2001; born 19/08/67; FCO 1992; Jakarta 1994; Paris 1998; Band A2.

Mundy, Jill (née Dalgleish); Tripoli since February 2000; born 29/04/42; DTI 1987; FCO 1989; Jerusalem 1992; New Delhi 1997; Band B3; m 1967 Timothy Wingfield Mundy (diss 1992) (2d 1968, 1970).

Munks, Robert John; FCO since January 1997; born 14/02/72; Band C4.

Munro, Catriona Mairi; FCO since October 1994; born 06/03/65; FCO 1988; Brussels 1991; Band A2.

Munro, Colin Andrew; HM Ambassador Zagreb since August 1997; born 24/10/46; Inland Revenue 1968; Third Secretary FCO 1969; Bonn 1971; Second later First Secretary Kuala Lumpur 1973; FCO 1977; Private Secretary to Minister of State 1979; First Secretary and Head of Chancery Bucharest 1981; First Secretary FCO 1983; Counsellor East Berlin 1987; HM Consul-General Frankfurt 1990; Counsellor FCO 1993; m 1967 Ehrengard Maria Heinrich (2s 1967, 1978).

Murdoch, Charles Edward; FCO since April 2002; born 02/11/66; Band D6; m 2001 Jocelyn Drew.

Murphy, John Matthew; Vice-Consul Beijing since December 1999; born 10/03/70; HCS 1990-93; Moscow 1995; Band B3.

Murphy, Jonathan Philip; Second Secretary (Chemical Weapons) The Hague since April 2001; born 20/01/77; FCO 1999; Band C4.

Murphy, Sandra; Resident Acting High Commissioner St John's since October 1999; born 09/04/50; FCO 1968; Brussels (UKREP) 1972; Resigned 1975; Reinstated 1978; FCO 1978; Harare 1981; Second Secretary FCO 1984; Second Secretary (Aid) Kingston 1987; Second Secretary (Commercial) Addis Ababa 1991; Second Secretary (Commercial) Caracas 1993; First Secretary FCO 1996.

Murray, Craig John; HM Ambassador Tashkent since August 2002; born 17/10/58; FCO 1984; Second Secretary (Commercial) Lagos 1986; First Secretary FCO 1990; Full-Time Language Training 1993; First Secretary (Political/Economic) Warsaw 1994; FCO 1998; Deputy High Commissioner Accra 1999; m 1984 Fiona Anne.

Murray, Gillian; Vienna since July 1995; born 18/09/69; FCO 1990; Paris 1992; Language Training 1995; Band A2.

Murray, Iain Richard, OBE (1991); Consul-General Houston since January 2001; born 13/08/44; SUPL at University 1965; CRO 1963; Commonwealth Office (later FCO) 1968; Accra 1970; Second Secretary Addis Ababa 1972; Vice-Consul (Commercial) Rio de Janeiro 1975; Consul Oporto 1979; First Secretary on loan to No. 10 Downing Street 1983; First Secretary FCO 1985; Chargé d'Affaires San Salvador 1987; First Secretary FCO 1992; Counsellor (Commercial/Economic) Kuala Lumpur 1994; Consul-General and Director of Trade Promotion in Brazil São Paulo 1997; m (1) 1967 Victoria Crew Gee (diss 1983) (1d 1969; 1s 1971); (2) 1993 Norma Agnes Wisden (née Hummel).

Murray, June; Ankara since May 1998; born 09/06/50; FCO 1986; Tegucigalpa 1988; Johannesburg 1990; Moscow 1992; FCO 1995; Band B3.

Murray, Michael Thomas; HM Ambassador Asmara since March 2002; born 13/10/45; FO DSAO 1964; Prague 1967; Vienna 1971; Vice-Consul (Commercial) Frankfurt 1973; Second Secretary (Development) Khartoum 1977; FCO 1980; First Secretary and Head of Chancery Banjul 1983; First Secretary FCO 1987; First Secretary (Development/Economic) Lusaka 1995; On loan to DfID at Lusaka 1998; Deputy Consul-General Chicago 1999; Band D6; m 1968 Else Birgitta Margareta Paues (1s 1974; 1d 1981).

Murray, Winston Anthony; Bahrain since May 1994; born 04/07/64; FCO 1985; OFT 1985; Bonn 1991; Band A2; m 1990 Judith Muponda.

Murtagh, Michael Louis; Chennai since October 2001; born 12/02/53; RAF Flt Lt 1981-97;

Defence Attaché's Office, Moscow 1995-97; Moscow, New Embassy Project 1997-2000; FCO 2000; Band B3; m 1988 Diana Morford (2s 1980, 1983).

Murton, John Evan; Full-Time Language Training Tokyo since October 1998; born 18/03/72; FCO 1997; Band C4.

Musgrave, David William; First Secretary FCO since October 1998; born 12/05/53; FCO 1983; Second later First Secretary Copenhagen 1985; First Secretary FCO 1989; First Secretary (Political/Information) Lagos 1994; First Secretary (Political) Abuja 1995; m 1978 Madeleine Nnomo Assembe (2d 1979, 1991; 1s 1981).

Myers, Sally; Athens since October 1999; born 13/08/68; FCO 1998; Band A2.

Myers, Sharon Theresa; Copenhagen since January 2001; born 19/04/65; FCO 1987; Moscow 1988; Bogotá 1991; FCO 1995; Band B3; m 1993 Manuel Bolano (2s 1996, 2002).

N

Nailard, Allison Mary (née Abbott); FCO since August 1999; born 03/07/73; Band A2; m 1999 Michael Nailard.

Nalden, Philip Nigel; Colombo since August 1999; born 30/03/45; Army (CRMP) 1963-88; Moscow 1988; Lagos 1989; Peking 1993; Dhaka 1994; FCO 1997; Belgrade 1998; Band B3; m 1982 Heather McIntosh.

Napthen, Florence Wilson; FCO since November 2000; born 25/10/61; Crown Office, Edinburgh 1978; FCO 1986; Wellington 1988; FCO 1991; Washington 1993; Addis Ababa 1996; Band B3; m 1990 Stephen Kenneth Napthen (1s 1997).

Nash, Ronald Peter, LVO (1984), MVO (1983); HM Ambassador Kabul since May 2002; born 18/09/46; FCO 1970; Second later First Secretary Moscow 1974; First Secretary Vienna (UKDEL) 1976; FCO 1979; New Delhi 1983; First Secretary FCO 1986; Counsellor and Head of Chancery Vienna 1988; Deputy High Commissioner Colombo 1992; Counsellor FCO 1996; HM Ambassador Kathmandu 1999; m 1976 Annie Olsen (3s 1979, 1981, 1983).

Naughton, Dawn Karen; Jerusalem since November 2000; born 22/08/69; FCO 1988; Brussels (UKDEL) 1990; Maputo 1993; Lagos 1997; Band B3; m 1993 Steven John Horsup.

Neale, Dawn Teresa; ECO Abuja since August 2002; born 13/08/60; FCO 1996; Abuja 1998; FCO 2002; Band A2; m 1995 John Harry Albert (1s 2001).

Needham, David Brent; Floater Duties since April 2002; born 22/02/51; Royal Marines 1968-91; Moscow 1992; Kingston 1996; Brussels (UKDEL NATO) 1999; Band B3; m 1992 Karen Dawn Ackers (2s 1993, 1995).

Neely, Maxine Lorna (née Hunter); SUPL since September 2001; born 09/12/64; FCO 1988;

Washington 1989; Bangkok 1992; FCO 1995; Tokyo 1997; British Trade International 1999; Band B3; m 2000 Peter Gordon Neely.

Neil, Andrew Alasdair; First Secretary (Political) Abu Dhabi since April 2001; born 11/06/68; FCO 1991; Second Secretary (Political) Nairobi 1994; Second Secretary FCO 1996; Band D6; m 1998 Amanda Lewis (2s twins 2000).

Neil, William John; Jedda since January 2002; born 23/05/67; T/D Sofia (CSCE Conference) and East Berlin 1989; FCO 1988; Brussels (UKREP) 1990; Brussels (UKDEL NATO) 1990; Baku 1993; Bombay 1995; Vice-Consul (Visas) Shanghai 1999; Band B3.

Neill, Kenneth Andrew; HM Consul Riyadh since July 2001; born 06/11/44; FO 1961; Tripoli 1967; Vientiane 1970; Moscow 1970; FCO 1974; Hanoi 1977; Karachi 1979; Second Secretary (Chancery/Information) Lilongwe 1982; Second Secretary FCO 1986; Second later First Secretary Honiara 1988; First Secretary (Commercial/Consular) Lusaka 1992; First Secretary FCO 1996; Deputy Head of Mission T/D Yaoundé 2000; m 1977 Julie C Brown (2s 1981, 1991; 2d 1987, 1993).

Neilson, James George Lovie; Ankara since November 2000; born 27/07/44; Army 1965-88; Geneva 1988; Moscow 1991; Budapest 1992; Pretoria 1994; Peking 1997; Band B3; m 1967 Lorraine (1d 1968; 1s 1971).

Nellthorp, Helen Rosemary; First Secretary (Specialised Agencies) Geneva (UKMIS) since September 2001; born 10/05/62; FCO 1980; Athens 1984; Floater Duties 1987; Third Secretary (Commercial) Washington 1989; Second Secretary (Commercial) Prague 1991; Second Secretary FCO 1994.

Nelson, Diana June (née Gordon); FCO since September 1997; born 17/06/58; FCO 1981; Paris 1984; Algiers 1987; Second Secretary FCO 1989; SUPL 1991; FCO 1992; SUPL 1995; m 1985 Miles Christopher Nelson (2d 1991, 1993).

Nelson, Emma Sutherland; SUPL since September 1997; born 20/03/71; FCO 1990; Band B3.

Nelson, Matthew Charles; Full-Time Language Training since January 2002; born 19/06/74; FCO 2000; Band C4.

Nelson, Philip Raymond; First Secretary later Counsellor FCO since April 1994; born 07/04/50; FCO 1972; Third later Second Secretary (Commercial) Budapest 1974; Second later First Secretary Paris 1976; FCO 1979; Rome 1980; First Secretary FCO 1983; First Secretary (Chancery) Manila 1989; First Secretary Budapest 1991; Band D6; m (1) 1971 Cynthia Elson (diss 1978); (2) 1992 Lyndsay Ann Halper (2s twins 1992).

Nessling, Paul William Downs; High Commissioner Nuku'alofa since January 2002; born 26/09/45; Chicago 1971 (From BOT);

Bahrain 1975 (from DOI); Second Secretary FCO 1979; Lisbon 1981; Warsaw 1982; T/D Aden 1984; First Secretary (Aid) Nairobi 1984; FCO 1987; First Secretary (Commercial) Harare 1989; First Secretary (Commercial) Muscat 1993; First Secretary Sarajevo 1996; FCO 1997; Deputy High Commissioner Lusaka 1998; m 1975 Kathryn Freeman.

Nethersole, Jonathan Sebastian; World Wide Floater Duties since 1998; born 07/11/69; FCO 1988; Pretoria 1990; Sana'a 1993; FCO 1995; Band B3.

Nettleton, Catherine Elizabeth, OBE (1999); Counsellor (Political/Economic) Peking since October 2000; born 13/03/60; FCO 1983; Language Training 1984; Peking 1987; Second Secretary 1988; Second Secretary FCO 1989; First Secretary (Political/Economic) Mexico City 1991; First Secretary FCO 1995; Counsellor FCO 1999.

Nevin, Michael Patrick; Second Secretary (Chancery) Lilongwe since December 1999; born 13/01/69; FCO 1993; Osaka 1996; Band B3; m 1997 Sawako (1 step d 1989; 1s 1998).

Newall, Peter; Counsellor, Head of Joint Management Office Brussels since October 1999; born 20/03/47; DSAO (later FCO) 1966; Tehran 1970; Delhi 1972; FCO 1976; Second Secretary (Commercial) Belgrade 1979; First Secretary (Commercial) Kuwait 1982; FCO 1986; HM Consul Marseilles 1989; First Secretary (Management) Geneva (UKMIS) 1990; FCO 1995; m 1969 Marina Joy McHugh (2d 1972, 1973; 1s 1976).

Newell, Clive Dare; Counsellor Moscow since October 2001; born 22/12/53; FCO 1976; Third Secretary (Commercial) later Second Secretary Tehran 1979; FCO 1980; Second later First Secretary Kabul 1982; FCO 1984; First Secretary Addis Ababa 1986; FCO 1990; First Secretary on secondment to Ministry of Defence 1992; FCO 1993; First Secretary on loan to Cabinet Office 1993; Counsellor (Political) Ankara 1994; Counsellor FCO 1998; m 1997 Gamze Ozen (1s 1999; 1d 2002).

Newlands, Andrew; Deputy Head of Mission Panama City since April 2000; born 10/02/68; DHSS 1984; FCO 1988; Bonn 1990; FCO 1992; Manila 1993; T/D Hong Kong 1996; FCO 1997; m 1989 Eileen Mitchell (1s 1993; 1d 1996).

Newman, George William; FCO since March 1983 (Second Secretary 1991); born 16/06/54; FCO 1972; Munich 1976; FCO 1978; Moscow 1981; Band C4; m 1975 Elaine Haron Turner (1s 1983; 1d 1987).

Newman, James Michael; Third Secretary (Political) Harare since September 2002; born 31/03/70; Metropolitan Police 1989; FCO 1990; Cairo 1992; Cape Town 1996; FCO 1999; Band B3; m 2000 Sarah Louise.

Newman, Kevin Paul; Bangkok since September 2002; born 31/07/73; Home Office 1994; FCO 1995; Abuja 1998; T/D Harare 2001-02; Band B3.

Newman, Pauline Agnes; FCO since September 1978; born 07/04/48; FO 1966; Addis Ababa 1969; Sofia 1971; Islamabad 1972; FCO 1973; Tokyo 1975; Band B3.

Newman, Peter James; First Secretary (Management) Washington since September 2001; born 29/05/46; FO 1963; Muscat 1968; Bahrain Residency 1970; Tokyo 1971; FCO 1975; Dacca 1978; Second Secretary UKDEL MBFR Vienna 1980; Second Secretary (Economic) Oslo 1983; First Secretary FCO 1987; Deputy High Commissioner and Head of Chancery Gaborone 1989; First Secretary (Commercial) Nicosia 1992; First Secretary FCO 1996; Deputy Head of Mission Abuja 1998; m 1966 Kathryn Yvonne Alcock (1d 1969; 1s 1972).

Newns, Carl Edwin Francis; First Secretary (Chancery) Washington since March 2000; born 30/06/68; FCO 1989; Third later Second Secretary (Political) The Hague 1992; First Secretary FCO 1996; Private Secretary to the Parliamentary Under-Secretary of State 1997; Band D6; m 1999 Christina Klaassen.

Newson, Gavin Erskine Walter; Second Secretary FCO since April 2001; born 20/07/71; FCO 1996; Second Secretary (Financial/Economic) Tokyo 1998; Band C4.

Newton, Alan Peter; FCO since April 1998; born 21/06/46; Inland Revenue 1963; DSAO 1965; Accra 1969; Tel Aviv 1969; San José 1973; Dacca 1976; FCO 1980; Montevideo 1983; Copenhagen 1987; Second Secretary FCO 1989; Second Secretary (Management) Manila 1994; m 1976 Mayra Rosa Antonia Camacho.

Newton, Alastair Dan Barr; Head of IUK USA New York since July 2002; born 08/01/54; FCO 1985; Second later First Secretary Kinshasa 1986; First Secretary FCO 1989; First Secretary Paris (UKDEL) 1992; On secondment to Lehman Bros as Economic Adviser 2000; m 1988 Vivienne Jane Ivanich (2d 1979, 1980).

Nicholas, Barry Stewart; Second Secretary (Commercial) Port of Spain since April 1999; born 01/11/62; FCO 1981; East Berlin 1984; Dubai 1986; Warsaw 1988; FCO 1991; Cairo 1995; m 1989 Susan Jane Parker (1s 1992; 1d 2002).

Nicholas, Susan Jane (née Parker); SUPL since January 1999; born 17/09/62; FCO 1981; Warsaw 1984; Bonn 1987; Düsseldorf 1988; Warsaw 1989; (Second Secretary 1991); FCO 1993; SUPL 1995; Cairo 1996; m 1989 Barry Stuart Nicholas (1s 1992; 1d 2002).

Nicholas, Suzanne Elizabeth; FCO since March 2000; born 14/08/70; FCO 1995; Second Secretary (Political) Warsaw 1999; Band C4.

Nicholls, Gary Patrick; HM Consul Guangzhou since August 2000; born 04/10/68; FCO 1988;

Tokyo 1990; Islamabad 1993; FCO 1998; Band C4; m 1993 Helen Marie Glanfield (diss 1998) (1s 1994; 1d 1997).

Nichols, John Roland; On secondment to British Invisibles since September 2000; born 13/11/51; Third later Second Secretary FCO 1977; Second later First Secretary Budapest 1979; FCO 1982; First Secretary (Commercial) Brasilia 1985; First Secretary FCO 1989; Counsellor and Deputy High Commissioner Dhaka 1993; Consul-General Geneva 1995; Deputy Head of Mission and Director of Trade Promotion Berne 1997; m 1983 Angela Suzanne Davies (1s 1987; 1d 1989).

Nichols, Martin Christopher; FCO since August 1994; born 04/05/62; FCO 1981; Tel Aviv 1984; FCO 1987; Darwin 1988; FCO 1990; New Delhi 1991; Band B3; m 1983 Julie Marie Wilkins (2s 1983, 1988; 1d 1992).

Nicholson, Karen Jayne (née Baudains); On loan to the DTI since July 1998; born 29/09/55; FCO 1977; Mexico City 1979; South East Asia Floater Duties 1983; Second Secretary FCO 1985; Second later First Secretary (Commercial) Lisbon 1992; m 1994 David Joseph Nicholson.

Nicolopulo, Evangelo Paul; First Secretary (Political) Copenhagen since June 1995; born 14/01/50; FCO 1969; Lourenco Marques 1972; Saigon 1973; FCO 1974; Kingston 1977; Madrid (CSCE) 1980; Alexandria 1982; Second Secretary FCO 1985; Vice-Consul (Commercial) Montreal 1988; First Secretary FCO 1993; m 1981 Kareen Elizabeth Sun.

Nithavrianakis, Elizabeth Rosemary (née Hingston-Jones); T/D Riyadh since June 2001; born 27/06/63; FCO 1983; Peking 1985; Kuala Lumpur 1986; Moscow 1990; FCO 1990; FCO 1992; Band B3; m 1992 Michael Stephen Nithavrianakis (1s 1996; 1d 2000).

Nithavrianakis, Michael Stephen, MVO (2000); First Secretary (Commercial) Riyadh since October 2000; born 30/04/67; FCO 1984; Kuala Lumpur 1987; Moscow 1990; FCO 1992; Second Secretary (Chancery) Accra 1997; Band C5; m 1992 Elizabeth Rosemary Hingston-Jones (1s 1996; 1d 2000).

Nixon, Patrick Michael, CMG (1989), OBE (1984); HM Ambassador Abu Dhabi since November 1998; born 01/08/44; Third Secretary FO 1965; MECAS 1966; Cairo 1968; (Second Secretary 1969); Lima 1970; Second later First Secretary FCO 1973; First Secretary and Head of Chancery Tripoli 1977; Director and Consul (Information) BIS New York 1980; First Secretary later Counsellor FCO 1983; HM Ambassador and Consul-General Doha 1987; Counsellor FCO 1990; High Commissioner Lusaka 1994; FCO 1997; m 1968 Elizabeth Rose Carlton (4s 1970, 1971, 1975, 1978).

Noakes, Jonathan Arnott; Consul-General Lyon since April 2001; born 04/01/44; FO 1965; Third Secretary Ankara 1966; FO 1967; Second

Secretary FCO 1971; First Secretary FCO 1974; First Secretary (Economic) Oslo 1981; First Secretary FCO 1985; Deputy High Commissioner Bridgetown 1991; First Secretary FCO 1995; m 1973 Nicola Jane Macaulay Langley.

Noakes, Stephen Martin, OBE (1993); First Secretary FCO since August 2000; born 06/02/57; Home Civil Service 1979-88; Second Secretary FCO 1988; First Secretary (Chancery) Luanda 1990; First Secretary FCO 1993; First Secretary New York (UKMIS) 1996; Band D6; m 1989 Hazel Clarke.

Nobes, Paula Louise; Deputy Head of Mission Baku since September 2002; born 01/08/69; FCO 1988; Language Training 1990; Third Secretary (Chancery) Belgrade 1991; APS Lord Owen, Peace Conference Geneva 1993; Kiev 1994; Zagreb 1995; Second Secretary FCO 1998; Band C4.

Noble, Andrew James, LVO (1995); Deputy Head of Mission Athens since August 2001; born 22/04/60; FCO 1982; Third Secretary (Chancery/Information) Bucharest 1983; On attachment to Auswärtiges Amt, Bonn 1986; Second Secretary (Chancery) Bonn 1987; First Secretary FCO 1989; First Secretary (Political) and Head of Political Section Pretoria/Cape Town 1994; FCO 1998; m 1992 Helen Natalie Pugh (2s 1995, 1996).

Noble, Helen Natalie (née Pugh); SUPL since May 1994; born 17/07/66; Second Secretary on loan to the ODA 1993; FCO 1988; On secondment to Auswärtiges Amt 1989; Third later Second Secretary Bonn 1990; Second Secretary FCO 1992; m 1992 Andrew James Noble (2s 1995, 1996).

Noble, Richard Adam; Head of Research Analysts FCO since June 2001; born 09/06/62; Third later Second Secretary (Chancery) Moscow 1987; FCO 1987; Second later First Secretary FCO 1989; First Secretary The Hague 1993; FCO 1995; First Secretary (Political) New Delhi 1998; m 1994 Katrina Johnson (2s 1996, 1998).

Noble, Robert Antony; Second Secretary (Political) Kuala Lumpur since September 2002; born 24/08/66; FCO 1984; Lisbon 1986; Islamabad 1989; FCO 1992; Rio de Janeiro 1995; FCO 1999; Band C4; m 1997 Elisabeth Patrice Wilkinson.

Noël, Louisa Veronica; Bangkok since October 1999; born 24/04/62; FCO 1988; Kuala Lumpur 1989; Amman 1993; FCO 1996; Band B3.

Nolan, Julia Elizabeth; SUPL since June 1997; born 02/01/59; FCO 1983; Bangkok 1984; SUPL 1986; New Delhi 1987; Second Secretary FCO 1989; First Secretary FCO 1993; SUPL 1994; First Secretary (Political) Paris 1995; m 1985 Richard John Codrington (Twin s 1991).

Noon, Paul David; First Secretary (Trade) Wellington since September 2001; born 01/06/68; FCO 1989; Damascus 1991; Bonn 1995; FCO

1998; Band C5; m 1990 Karren Lesley Robson (1d 1993; 1s 1998).

Norburn, Jonathan Edward; Second Secretary FCO since March 2002; born 16/08/76; FCO 1999; Second Secretary (Chancery) Bridgetown 2001; Band C4.

Norman, Duncan Charles, MBE (2000); FCO since May 2000; born 12/10/71; FCO 1990; Riyadh 1994; Yerevan 1998; m 1997 Kerry Jones (1d 2000).

Norman, Paul Stephen Raymond; First Secretary (Political) Brussels since July 2002; born 04/05/56; FCO 1992; Consul Hong Kong 1995; First Secretary FCO 2000; Band D6; m 1989 Felicity Shan Abram (1s 1991; 2d 1993, 1998).

Norman, Sarah Caroline; SUPL since September 1994; born 16/12/70; FCO 1990; New Delhi 1991; FCO 1992; Band B3.

Norris, Peter James; FCO since September 2000; born 22/12/55; FCO 1982; First Secretary Lagos 1985; FCO 1988; Deputy Head of Mission and Consul Guatemala City 1990; First Secretary FCO 1993; First Secretary (Political) Jakarta 1997; Band D6; m 1982 Dilvinder Kaur Dhaliwal (2d 1986, 1990; 2s (twins) 1993).

Norsworthy, Sean Francis; FCO since January 1996; born 18/04/68; FCO 1987; Islamabad 1989; Tunis 1992; Band A2.

Northern, Richard James, MBE (1982); Consul-General Milan since September 2001; born 02/11/54; FCO 1976; Language Training 1978; MECAS 1978; Riyadh 1980; Second later First Secretary (Chancery) Rome 1983; First Secretary FCO 1987; First Secretary (Economic/Commercial) Ottawa 1992; Deputy Consul-General and Deputy Director Trade/Investment Toronto 1994; Counsellor (Commercial/Economic) Riyadh 1997; Counsellor FCO 2000; m 1981 Linda Denise Gadd (2s 1983, 1986; 1d 1992).

Norton, Mark Rolffe; Deputy High Commissioner Georgetown since April 2000; born 03/01/55; Customs and Excise 1974; Immigration Service 1983; On secondment to Kaduna 1987; FCO 1992; On secondment to ICFY/Observer Mission to Serbia and Montenegro 1994; Addis Ababa 1995; Ottawa 1996; Copenhagen 1996; m 1995 Gelila Assefa Wedajo (2d 1996, 1998).

Norton, Redmond; Deputy Head of Mission Montevideo since October 1999; born 30/04/46; Board of Trade 1962; FCO 1969; Rio de Janeiro 1972; Caracas 1975; Dacca 1977; FCO 1980; Second Secretary (Admin) Tripoli 1984; Second Secretary Quito 1985; Second later First Secretary (Commercial) Helsinki 1988; First Secretary FCO 1992; Consul (Commercial) Houston 1994; Band D6; m 1969 Jean McGarrigle (1d 1974; 1s 1979).

Nye, Alison Claire (née Edwards); SUPL since March 2001; born 18/12/64; FCO 1983; SUPL 1985; Vienna 1986; Algiers 1987; Karachi 1990;

FCO 1993; Third later Second Secretary (Development) Lilongwe 1997; SUPL 1999; Second Secretary (Development) Lilongwe 2000; Band B3; m 1985 Richard Paul Nye (1s 1999).

Nye, Richard Paul; SUPL since March 2001; born 29/02/64; FCO 1982; Vienna 1984; Algiers 1987; Karachi 1990; FCO 1994; Second Secretary Lilongwe 1997; Band C4; m 1985 Alison Claire Edwards (1s 1999).

O

O'Brien, Gareth David; First Secretary (Commercial) Riyadh since November 2001; born 27/07/65; FCO 1982; Copenhagen 1985; Warsaw 1988; Africa/Middle East Floater 1990; FCO 1991; Belmopan 1995; Consul (Commercial) Jedda 1998; Band C5; m 1991 Lisa Margaret Donagher (2s 1997, 1999).

O'Brien, Julie Ann Valentine; Kuwait since June 1999; born 20/03/61; FCO 1994; Moscow 1996.

O'Brien, Lisa Margaret (née Donagher); SUPL since June 1997; born 30/10/66; FCO 1984; BMG Berlin 1986; Floater Duties 1989; FCO 1991; Belmopan 1995; Band B3; m 1991 Gareth David O'Brien (2s 1997, 1999).

O'Brien, Patrick Thaddeus Dominic, MBE (1995); Head of Media and Public Affairs Ottawa since August 2002; born 03/11/49; Post Office 1966; FCO 1968; Lagos 1971; Georgetown 1975; FCO 1978; JAO Brussels 1982; Abidjan 1984; Second Secretary FCO 1988; Brussels 1993; First Secretary and Deputy Head of Mission Dakar 1998; Madrid 2001; m 1970 Maureen Mortimer (3d 1970, 1971, 1979; 1s 1973).

O'Callaghan, John Matthew; First Secretary FCO since September 2001; born 27/04/66; FCO 1990; Second Secretary (Information) Santiago 1992; Second Secretary FCO 1994; First Secretary (Political) Moscow 1998; Band D6; m 1996 Sophie Dauchez (2d 1998, 2001).

O'Connell, Philip; FCO since March 2000; born 14/11/66; FCO 1985; Nairobi 1990; FCO 1991; Damascus 1997; Band B3; m 1998 Nesrene Masroun.

O'Connell, Ruairí; FCO since November 2001; born 22/02/77; Band C4.

O'Connell, Terence; Peking since May 2000; born 19/09/58; MOD 1976; FCO 1978; Stockholm 1980; Tripoli 1983; Santiago 1984; FCO 1984; Bombay 1987; FCO 1990; Full-Time Language Training 1995; Mexico City 1996; Full-Time Language Training 2000; Band C4; m 1991 Valerie Anna-Maria Gonsalves.

O'Connor, Christopher Paul; First Secretary (Political) Ottawa since August 1999; born 18/12/68; Third later Second Secretary FCO 1993; Full-Time Language Training Cairo 1995; Riyadh 1996.

O'Connor, Lorraine; FCO since November 1994; born 13/02/66; Band A2.

O'Connor, Paul Vincent; Deputy Head of Mission and Consul (Commercial) St Petersburg since August 1999; born 29/06/56; FCO 1975; Jedda 1977; Washington 1980; Floater Duties 1983; FCO 1985; Istanbul 1987; Second Secretary (Aid/Commercial) Maseru 1991; On loan to the DTI 1995; Language Training 1998; m 1985 Georgina Louise Jayne (2s 1987, 1989; 1d 1991).

O'Connor, Sheila Mary; Third Secretary (Chancery/Development) Kathmandu since January 1997; born 28/12/60; FCO 1982; Brussels (UKREP) 1983; Yaoundé 1986; Rangoon 1989; Prague 1991; FCO 1993; OSCE Sarajevo 1996.

O'Conor, Fionnuala Katharine; FCO since February 1994; born 10/04/69; Band C4.

O'Donnell, Patricia (née Daubeney); Third Secretary (Press and Public Affairs) Moscow since August 1997; born 22/12/68; FCO 1991; Warsaw 1994; Band C4; m 1993 Simon Tristan O'Donnell.

O'Donnell, Sara Jane (née Sharp); SUPL since September 2001; born 24/12/67; FCO 1991; Third Secretary Brussels (UKDEL WEU) 1994; Yaoundé 1996; m 1996 Francis Joseph O'Donnell.

O'Flaherty, Kenneth James; First Secretary (External Relations) Brussels (UKREP) since July 2000; born 04/03/72; FCO 1996; Secondment to French Foreign Ministry 1998; Second Secretary (Political) Paris 1999; m 1997 Maria de los Reyes Lopez Garcia (diss 2000) (1d 1998).

O'Flaherty, Stephen John; First Secretary later Counsellor FCO since August 1992; born 15/05/51; Third Secretary FCO 1975; Language Training India 1977; Second Secretary New Delhi 1978; First Secretary FCO 1980; Prague 1981; First Secretary FCO 1984; First Secretary (Chancery) Vienna 1988; m 1975 Sarah Louise Gray (2d 1979, 1987; 1s 1983).

O'Hara, Violet Brown McGregor (née Steele); FCO since 1999; born 22/09/42; FO 1961; Singapore 1964; Tokyo 1964; Kinshasa 1967; FCO 1970; Strasbourg 1971; Jakarta 1975; Hanoi 1978; FCO 1980; Second later First Secretary (Commercial) Washington 1985; Consul (Commercial) Rio de Janeiro 1990; Consul Dallas 1995; m 1986 Basil Austin Samuel O'Hara (dec'd 2000).

O'Keeffe, Deanna Maureen; FCO since October 1991; born 24/09/61; FCO 1980; Vienna 1989; Band A2.

O'Kelly, Bridget Jane (née Hoare); SUPL since October 2000; born 07/12/67; FCO 1993; Bahrain 1996; SUPL 1997; Third Secretary (Visits) Paris 1999; Band B3; m 1995 Richard Edward Henry O'Kelly (1s 1997).

O'Mahony, Angela Millar (née Lindsay); SUPL since June 2000; born 17/08/66; FCO 1989; Paris 1991; Kampala 1994; FCO 1996; Stockholm 1996; Band B3; m 1994 Daniel Lawrence O'Mahony.

O'Neill, Douglas Matthew; Seconded to Benefits Agency October 1999; born 13/06/69; FCO 1990; Dublin 1994; Floater Duties 1998; Band A2.

O'Neill, Michael Angus; Counsellor (Economic) New York (UKMIS) since July 2002; born 25/05/65; MOD 1988; Second Secretary UKDEL NATO/WEU 1991; FCO 1994; First Secretary (Political) Washington 1998; m 1991 Claire Bannerman (1d 1994; 3s 1996, 1998, 2001).

O'Rourke, Peter Vincent; FCO since April 2000; born 26/09/60; FCO 1980; Maputo 1981; Lisbon 1984; Rabat 1987; FCO 1990; Yaoundé 1993; Third later Second Secretary (Management) Beirut 1997; Band C4; m 1999 Louise Karen.

O'Shaughnessy, Jonathan Edward; Islamabad since October 2000; born 07/10/71; FCO 1991; Bonn 1995; Band A2; m 1997.

Oakden, Edward Anthony; Director (International Security) FCO since November 2002; born 03/11/59; FCO 1981; Third later Second Secretary (Chancery) Baghdad 1984; Second Secretary (Chancery) Khartoum 1985; First Secretary and Private Secretary to HM Ambassador Washington 1988; First Secretary FCO 1992; Private Secretary to Prime Minister (Overseas/Defence) 1995; Counsellor FCO 1997; Counsellor Madrid 1998; Deputy Head of Mission and Minister Madrid 2000; Acting Head of Non-Proliferation Dept FCO 2002; m 1989 (diss) (1d 1995).

Oakley, Matthew Edward, MVO (1999); Second Secretary (Commercial) Singapore since June 2000; born 19/07/65; FCO 1983; Athens 1985; Jedda 1988; Riyadh 1990; Third Secretary FCO 1992; Third Secretary (Political) Cape Town 1996; Band C4.

Oertle-Hurt, Jane Michelle; Africa/Middle East Floater since April 1994; born 13/09/65; HCS 1987-89; Rome 1990; Band B3; m 1995 Horst Dietrich Oertle.

Ogg, Fiona; Lagos since August 1999; born 25/07/70; FCO 1989; Warsaw 1992; Paris 1994; FCO 1996; Band B3.

Oliver, Geoffrey Harold; World Wide Floater Duties since September 1993; born 11/06/48; HM Forces 1965-88; Moscow 1989; Madrid 1991; Band B3.

Oliver, Kaye Wight, CMG (2001), OBE (1994); High Commissioner Maseru since March 1999; born 10/08/43; Customs and Excise 1962; FCO 1965; DSAO (later FCO) 1966; Kuala Lumpur 1970; Second Secretary FCO 1974; Lilongwe 1978; Paris 1981; First Secretary Nairobi 1983; First Secretary, Head of Chancery and Consul Yaoundé 1984; First Secretary FCO 1987; First Secretary, Consul and Deputy Head of Mission, later Chargé d'Affaires Kinshasa (also Chargé d'Affaires non-resident to Burundi and Rwanda) 1990; On loan to the ODA 1994; HM Ambassador Kigali (also Ambassador non-resident to Burundi) 1995; Adviser on Burundi to ex-President Nyerere Dar-es-Salaam 1998.

Oliver, Matthew Keith; Second Secretary (Management) The Hague since February 1999; born 16/08/51; Blantyre 1973; Washington 1975; Belgrade 1978; FCO 1979; Bombay 1980; Tehran 1980; Warsaw 1983; FCO 1984; Auckland 1986; Istanbul 1989; Second Secretary FCO 1993; Baku 1996; m 1993 Hatice Iker Urgen (dec'd 1999).

Oliver, Paul John; Madrid since July 2000; born 11/02/74; FCO (Hanslope Park) 1996; Band C4.

Oman, Magnus Paul; On loan to DTI since November 1999; born 05/08/68; FCO 1989; Valletta 1991; Doha 1994; FCO 1998; Band B3; m 1998 Ms S Broderick.

Onn, Anthony Wilfred; Belgrade since August 1993; born 16/04/44; Royal Navy 1959-84; Sofia 1987; Bonn 1989; Band B3.

Ord-Smith, Robin Jeremy, MVO (1998); Seconded to BAe Systems Japan since October 2001; born 08/10/65; FCO 1989; Vice-Consul Bucharest 1991; Third Secretary (Political/Information) Kuala Lumpur 1994; Second Secretary (State Visit) Kuala Lumpur 1998; Second Secretary FCO 1999; Seconded to Auswärtiges Amt 1999; Full-Time Language Training 2000; Band D6; m 1995 Tania Jane Vallis (2s 1996, 1998).

Ormiston, Ewan Kenneth; Kampala since August 1999; born 27/08/68; FCO 1989; Brussels 1992; Luanda 1995; Third Secretary Lima 1996; Band B3; m 1994 Gillian Keating.

Ormiston, Gillian (née Keating); SUPL since 1999; born 01/06/66; FCO 1988; Brussels (UKREP) 1991; Luanda 1995; SUPL 1996; Band A2; m 1994 Ewan Kenneth Ormiston.

Ormond, Matthew John; Washington since January 2001; born 23/04/73; FCO 1991; Band C4.

Orr, Gwendolen; FCO since September 1996; born 16/12/73; FCO 1996; Band C4.

Orr, Iain Campbell; Counsellor and Deputy High Commissioner Accra since March 1998; born 06/12/42; Third later Second Secretary FCO 1968; Hong Kong 1969; Second later First Secretary Peking 1972; FCO 1974; Assistant Political Adviser Hong Kong 1978; Dublin 1981; First Secretary FCO 1984; Consul-General Shanghai 1987; Counsellor and Deputy High Commissioner Wellington 1991; FCO 1994; m 1978 Susan Elizabeth Gunter (1d 1983; 1s 1984).

Osborn, Andrew Robert; Third Secretary (Consular/Management) Maseru since August 2001; born 13/02/64; FCO 1982; Lagos 1987; Budapest 1990; Moscow 1992; FCO 1994; Vice-Consul Dar-es-Salaam 1997; Band B3; m 1988 Karyn Lindsay Heraty.

Osborn, Karyn Lindsay (née Heraty); SUPL since July 1997; born 12/02/66; FCO 1986; Lagos 1988; Budapest 1990; Moscow 1992; FCO 1994; Band B3; m 1988 Andrew Robert Osborn.

Osborn, Sally Mary; SUPL since November 1988; born 26/01/57; FCO 1976; Dacca 1978; Amsterdam 1982; Second Secretary FCO 1984; Second Secretary (Information/Chancery) Lisbon 1988; m 1988 Neil Gordon Haddock (1s 1990).

Osborne, Christopher Wyndham; Deputy Head of Mission Luanda since March 1998; born 18/06/46; CO 1964; Commonwealth Office (later FCO) 1966; Lusaka 1968; Kampala 1970; Bridgetown 1973; FCO 1976; Second Secretary Dacca 1979; Second Secretary (Commercial) Caracas 1982; First Secretary FCO 1986; First Secretary (Information) BTC Hong Kong 1989; First Secretary FCO 1994; First Secretary T/D BTC Hong Kong 1996; m 1967 Gillian Mary (3s 1967, 1974, 1979).

Osborne, David Allan; HM Ambassador Tegucigalpa since July 1998; born 31/08/42; Department of Technical Co-operation 1961; CRO 1961; CRO 1963; Accra 1963; DSAO 1966; Guatemala 1968; (Second Secretary 1970); Second Secretary (Information) Bonn 1973; Second Secretary Valletta 1974; Central London Polytechnic 1977; First Secretary FCO 1978; First Secretary, Head of Chancery and Consul San José also accredited to Nicaragua and El Salvador 1980-84; First Secretary FCO 1984; Deputy Consul-General São Paulo 1988; European Union Monitor Yugoslavia 1991; First Secretary FCO 1992; T/D First Secretary (Political) Santiago 1994; First Secretary FCO 1995; Chargé d'Affaires Managua 1997; m 1966 Joan Marion Duck (1s 1970; 2d 1971, 1973).

Osborne, Roy Paul; HM Ambassador Managua since July 1997; born 13/07/51; FCO 1970; Oslo 1972; Islamabad 1974; Vice-Consul Rome 1978; Second Secretary FCO 1981; Second Secretary (Commercial/Development), later First Secretary, Head of Chancery and Consul Yaoundé 1985; First Secretary (Chancery/Information) Madrid 1989; First Secretary FCO 1993; m 1977 Vivienne Claire Gentry (2d 1983, 1984).

Ostler, Malcolm Thomas; Hamilton since May 2002; born 20/09/66; FCO 1988; Bonn 1997; Band B3.

Oswald, David; Second Secretary (Commercial) Islamabad since December 2001; born 15/06/46; FO 1965; Amman 1968; Zomba 1970; Blantyre 1971; Tokyo 1973; FCO 1976; Gaborone 1978; FCO 1982; Jedda 1986; Second Secretary FCO 1990; Second Secretary (Management) Dhaka 1993; Consul (Commercial/Economic) Shanghai 1997; m 1972 Jane Avril Bennett Edmunds (2d 1974, 1977).

Oulmi, Sally Teresa (née Cashman); Second Secretary (Management) Dhaka since November 1996; born 04/10/52; FCO 1974; Brussels (UKREP) 1975; Abidjan 1979; Strasbourg 1983; FCO 1986; Ottawa 1987; Stockholm 1990; FCO 1993; Band C4; m 1976 Hocine (Frank) Oulmi (2s 1993, 1994).

Owen, Amy Grace; Vice-Consul Hong Kong since October 2002; born 29/08/75; FCO 1999; Full-Time Language Training 2000; Full-Time Language Training Peking 2001; Band C4.

Owen, Caroline Jane; Dhaka since December 1998; born 29/10/66; FCO 1986; Washington 1990; FCO 1992; Bombay 1994; Band A2.

Owen, Gareth Wynn; FCO since September 2001; born 24/11/69; FCO 1989; Prague 1992; FCO 1993; Warsaw 1994; Lusaka 1996; Baku 1999; Band B3.

Owen, Helen Patricia; FCO since August 1987; born 09/04/49; Sana'a 1974; FCO 1974; FCO 1976; Bandar Seri Begawan 1981; Manila 1982; Madrid 1984; Band B3.

Owen, Jane Caroline; Counsellor (Commercial) Tokyo since May 2002; born 15/04/63; FCO 1987; Language Training (Japanese) 1988; Second Secretary (Commercial) Tokyo 1989; First Secretary DTI Exports to Japan Unit 1993; FCO 1996; Deputy Head of Mission Hanoi 1998; SUPL 1999; Deputy High Commissioner Hanoi 2000; m 1998 David Donnelly.

Owen, Kara Justine (née Palmer); Vice-Consul Hong Kong since December 1996; born 27/05/71; FCO 1993; Band C4; m 1995 Craig Sterling Owen.

Owen, Richard Lloyd; Counsellor FCO since January 1998; born 21/04/48; Second Secretary FCO 1975; Language Training 1976; Language Training MECAS 1977; First Secretary Abu Dhabi 1978; Beirut 1980; FCO 1981; San José 1983; BMG Berlin 1986; First Secretary FCO 1988; Counsellor Copenhagen 1993; m 1985 Eva Maria Steller (2d 1986, 1988).

Owens, Patrick Eldred, MBE (1998); HM Consul New York since July 2001; born 20/04/53; FCO 1972; Muscat 1974; Bucharest 1977; Algiers 1979; FCO 1981; Jakarta 1984; Riyadh 1988; (Second Secretary 1990); Second Secretary FCO 1994; First Secretary (Information) Madrid 1997; m 1978 Merle de Ceuninck van Capelle (1d 1980; 2s 1982, 1985).

Owens, Ruth Mary; FCO since August 2002; born 28/03/67; FCO 1987; Nairobi 1989; FCO 1992; Moscow 1995; Antananarivo 1999; Band B3.

Oxley, Anthony, BEM; Nairobi since July 1999; born 09/09/42; Royal Navy 1961-83; Baghdad 1983; Bucharest 1984; Montevideo 1986; East Berlin 1987; New York (UKMIS) 1989; Prague 1991; Belgrade 1993; Band C4; m 1964 Wenda Romaine Coper (1s 1966; 1d 1968).

P

Packer, Deborah (née Wilde); Tokyo since August 2000; born 10/05/66; FCO 1985; NEDO 1986; Tokyo 1994; Bridgetown 1997; Band A2; m 1990 Philip Anthony Packer (1s 1995).

Page, Alexander Simon; Third Secretary (Management) Mexico City since December 1999;

born 20/10/64; FCO 1987; Warsaw 1989; Dhaka 1989; FCO 1993; Valletta 1996; Band B3; m 1989 Isabella Lynn Marshall (1s 1996).

Page, Andrew John Walter; First Secretary (Chancery) Paris since September 2000; born 17/09/65; FCO 1990; Full-Time Language Training 1991; Second Secretary Kiev 1992; Second Secretary FCO 1996.

Page, Brian Ronald; Second Secretary (Consular/Immigration) Accra since February 1997; born 05/03/49; FCO 1968; Helsinki 1971; Doha 1973; Cape Town 1976; FCO 1978; Muscat 1979; Singapore 1983; FCO 1986; (Second Secretary 1988); Dubai 1992; m 1973 Susan Frances Vinall (2s 1975, 1979).

Page, Derek Alan; Second Secretary Taipei since November 1994; born 29/09/50; FCO 1975; Pretoria 1977; Bombay 1979; FCO 1981; Frankfurt 1984; Montevideo 1987; FCO 1990; (Second Secretary 1992); m 1972 Inger Merete Ebbesvik (2s 1977, 1981).

Page, Isabella Lynn (née Marshall); Third Secretary (Political/Information) Valletta since May 1996; born 06/01/64; FCO 1981; Kuala Lumpur 1984; Prague 1987; Warsaw 1989; SUPL 1989; Dhaka 1990; FCO 1993; m 1989 Alexander Simon Page (1s 1996).

Page, Martin; Second Secretary (Management) Peking since January 1999; born 16/11/51; MOD 1969; FCO 1970; Beirut 1973; Lima 1976; FCO 1976; Warsaw 1979; FCO 1982; Vila 1983; Dar es Salaam 1987; Second Secretary FCO 1990; Second Secretary (Management) New Delhi 1993; Second Secretary FCO 1997; Band C4; m 1975 Christine Mary Ogilvy (1s 1979; 1d 1984).

Page, Simon David; SUPL since July 1999; born 22/02/67; FCO 1990; Language Training 1991; Language Training Peking 1992; Second Secretary (JLG) Hong Kong 1994; Band D6.

Page, Simon Graham; Second Secretary FCO since September 2001; born 22/11/61; FCO 1979; Kuala Lumpur 1983; Floater Duties 1987; Dublin 1988; FCO 1990; Third Secretary (Chancery) New Delhi 1992; FCO 1996; Second Secretary (Political) Riyadh 1998; Band C4; m 1985 Sharon Ann Murphy (2s 1990, 1995; 1d 2000).

Pagett, Christopher Robert Geoffrey, OBE (1990); Counsellor FCO since September 2000; born 13/06/52; Third Secretary FCO 1975; Second Secretary Havana 1978; Second later First Secretary (Economic) Lusaka 1979; First Secretary FCO 1984; First Secretary (Chancery) Maputo 1988; First Secretary FCO 1991; Counsellor New York (UKMIS) 1997; m (1) 1974 Anne-Marie Roberts; (2) 1988 Diane Brown (1s 1993).

Pagett, Ian William; Warsaw since October 1993; born 19/09/69; FCO 1988; Khartoum 1989; FCO 1992; Band A2.

Pagett, Wayne Norman; Third Secretary (Consular/Immigration) Harare since March 2001; born 26/03/67; FCO 1988; New Delhi 1990; Tel Aviv 1994; FCO 1997; Band B3; m 1990 Kay Louise Clements (1d 1994).

Paginton, David Alan; HM Consul Buenos Aires since January 1998; born 01/04/51; Board of Inland Revenue 1968; FCO 1971; Istanbul 1973; Brussels (UKREP) 1976; Sofia 1979; FCO 1981; São Paulo 1984; Islamabad 1988; FCO 1991; Second Secretary (Commercial) Dar es Salaam 1994; m 1986 Marcia Rosana Antonio (1s 1986; 1d 1987).

Pain, Warren David; Vice-Consul (Political/Economic) Hong Kong since February 2000; born 17/05/71; FCO 1992; Peking 1995; World Wide All-Rounder 1998; m 2000 Armine Ghevondyan.

Painter, Anthony Clifford; Paris since August 1996; born 20/03/59; FCO 1994; Band A2; m 1984 Lisa Nelson (1d 1984).

Painting, Julia, MBE (1993); Deputy Head of Mission Lusaka since October 2001; born 24/04/60; FCO 1981; Prague 1983; Africa/Middle East Floater 1985; South East Asia Floater 1987; FCO 1989; Tallinn 1991; FCO 1992; Milan 1994; HM Consul Naples 1995; Second Secretary FCO 1997; First Secretary FCO 1998.

Pakenham, The Hon Michael (Aidan); HM Ambassador Warsaw since January 2001; born 03/11/43; Third Secretary FO 1966; Third later Second Secretary Warsaw 1967; Second Secretary FCO 1970; Assistant Private Secretary later Private Secretary to the Chancellor of the Duchy of Lancaster 1971; On secondment to Cabinet Office 1972; First Secretary 1972; First Secretary New Delhi 1974; Geneva (UKDEL CSCE) 1974; Washington 1978; Counsellor FCO 1983; Counsellor (External Relations) Brussels (UKREP) 1987; HM Ambassador and Consul-General Luxembourg 1991; Minister Paris 1994; On loan to the Cabinet Office 1997; m 1980 Meta Landreth Doak (2d 1981, 1985).

Pakes, Stuart Murray; Islamabad since August 1998; born 08/05/49; FO 1967; FCO 1968; Aden 1970; Reykjavik 1973; Anguilla 1973; East Berlin 1976; FCO 1977; Madrid 1981; Cairo 1984; FCO 1987; (Second Secretary 1989); Second Secretary (Immigration/Consular) Accra 1990; Second Secretary (Commercial) Abu Dhabi 1994; m 1972 Linda Anne Rawlings (2d 1977, 1981; 1s 1984).

Palmer, Andrew David; World Wide Floater Duties since February 2000; born 21/01/76; FCO (HCS) 1994; Transferred to Diplomatic Service 2000; Band B3.

Palmer, Sara (née Abbots-Darbyshire); Vice-Consul Geneva since July 1993; born 16/11/64; FCO 1983; Geneva (UKMIS) 1985; Montevideo 1988; SUPL Geneva 1991; FCO 1991; Band B3; m 1991 Christopher John Palmer.

Pankhurst, Donia Lee; Geneva (UKMIS) since October 1998; born 27/05/65; House of Commons 1991-97; FCO 1997; Band A2.

Parfitt, Alan Frank, MBE (1997); SUPL since October 1998; born 06/08/66; Senior Research Officer FCO 1989; Vienna (UKDEL) 1994.

Parham, Philip John; Counsellor (Commercial) Riyadh since September 2000; born 14/08/60; FCO 1993; Private Secretary to the Parliamentary Under-Secretary of State 1995; First Secretary (Chancery) Washington 1996; m 1985 Kasia Giedroyc (2d 1986, 1994; 5s 1988, 1989, 1990, 1992, 1996).

Parish, Colin; Second Secretary FCO since November 1995; born 27/11/43; Royal Navy 1961-70; FCO 1970; Phnom Penh 1973; Accra 1974; SUPL 1978; FCO 1982; Belgrade 1986; Consul (Commercial) Jedda 1990; m (1) 1966 Carole Grace (diss 1978); (2) 1978 Fairroligh Janet Lee Syme (2s 1985, 1989).

Parish, Paul Edward; FCO since March 2002; born 10/08/63; FCO 1983; Vienna 1986; FCO 1989; SUPL 1992; Second Secretary FCO 1995; Second Secretary (Bilateral) Bonn 1998; Second Secretary Berlin 1999; Band C4.

Parker, Cindy; T/D Third Secretary Tashkent since March 2000; born 01/02/72; FCO 1997; Band B3.

Parker, David John; FCO since November 1989; born 02/06/57; FCO 1978; Mexico City 1987; Band C4; m 1987 Mary Elizabeth Garner.

Parker, Lyn; British High Commissioner Nicosia since September 2001; born 25/11/52; FCO 1978; Second later First Secretary Athens 1980; FCO 1984; Counsellor on loan to the Cabinet Office 1989; Counsellor and Head of Chancery New Delhi 1992; Counsellor (Political) Brussels (UKREP) 1995; Counsellor FCO 1999; m 1991 Jane Elizabeth Walker (2d 1993, 1996).

Parker, Nigel Denis; Legal Counsellor FCO since February 2001; born 25/08/61; Called to the Bar, Middle Temple 1985; Assistant Legal Adviser FCO 1988; Legal Adviser Bridgetown 1995; Assistant Legal Adviser FCO 1998.

Parker, Nigel Graham; Geneva (UKMIS) since April 2000; born 13/09/56; FCO 1982; Kingston 1985; FCO 1988; Budapest 1990; Band C4; m 1983 Paula Northwood (1s 1987, 1d 1991).

Parker, Rod; Peking since June 2000; born 14/11/60; FCO 1996; Band C4; m 1981 Bernadette Corr (2d 1987, 1991).

Parker, Susan Caroline; FCO since June 1993; born 01/07/63; FCO 1985; Brussels (UKREP) 1987; FCO 1988; Vienna 1990; Band A2.

Parker, Valerie Ann; Jakarta since February 1999; born 21/02/42; FCO 1990; SUPL 1992; FCO 1997; SUPL 1998; Band A2; m 1965 David John Parker (1d 1966; 1s 1968).

Parker-Brennan, Michael; FCO since August 1999; born 30/05/52; Royal Corps of Transport 1967-92; Helsinki 1992; FCO 1992; Bucharest 1993; Pretoria 1996; Moscow 1997; Band B3; m (1) 1982 Catherine Mary Parker (diss); (2) 1988 Carmen Dorina.

Parkins, David Alan; FCO since August 1997; born 07/05/64; GPO 1980-84; FCO 1984; Third Secretary Nairobi 1989; FCO 1993; Third Secretary Bucharest 1994; Band C4; m 1991 Diane Reed (2s 1992, 1994).

Parkinson, Guy Paul; Floater Duties since July 2000; born 05/06/70; FCO 1989; Budapest 1992; Moscow 1995; Band B3; m 2002 Romina Rodriguez.

Parkinson, Howard, CVO (1998); Deputy High Commissioner Mumbai since January 2001; born 29/03/48; BOT 1967; FCO 1969; LA Floater 1972; Tegucigalpa 1974; Buenos Aires 1975; Second Secretary 1977; Maputo 1978; Second later First Secretary FCO 1981; First Secretary (Commercial) Lisbon 1985; First Secretary on loan to British Gas 1989; First Secretary FCO 1991; Consul-General and Counsellor (Management) Washington 1994; Counsellor (Commercial) Kuala Lumpur 1997; m 1974 Linda Wood (1d 1979; 1s 1982).

Parmley, Jane Helen (née Buchanan); Lagos since October 1984; born 18/08/63; FCO 1982; Band A2; m 1987 Nigel William Kenneth Parmley.

Parsons, Alexander Colin; Second Secretary FCO since June 2001; born 26/03/73; FCO 1997; Second Secretary (Political) Santiago 1999; Band C4.

Parton, Charles William, OBE (1995); First Secretary FCO since September 1994; born 23/03/56; FCO 1979; Language Training Hong Kong 1982; Second Secretary FCO 1983; First Secretary (Economic) Peking 1985; First Secretary FCO 1987; First Secretary Joint Liaison Group Hong Kong 1990; Band D6; m 1983 Charmian Constance Denman (1d 1987; 1s 1990).

Partridge, Andrew Warren; Third Secretary Vienna since July 2000; born 26/04/68; FCO 1986; Islamabad 1989; Moscow 1992; FCO 1995; SUPL 1997; Band B3; m 1988 Margaret Robertson (1s 1996; 1d 1998).

Partridge, Colin Douglas; Counsellor Seoul since June 2000; born 12/12/55; FCO 1978; Third later Second Secretary (Chancery) New Delhi 1980; Second later First Secretary FCO 1983; Language Training 1986; Head of Chancery and Consul Hanoi 1987; First Secretary FCO 1989; First Secretary Hong Kong 1994; Language Training 1998; m (1) 1983 Gita Sahgal (diss 1989); (2) 1993 Helena June Beattie (1d 1996).

Partridge, Diane Freda; Deputy Head of Mission Antananarivo since June 2002; born 29/11/44; OECD Paris 1966; Yaoundé 1969; Lagos 1970; Rio de Janeiro 1971; FCO 1972; Antananarivo 1974; FCO 1976; Buenos Aires 1977; FCO 1979;

Brasilia 1981; FCO 1985; Third Secretary (Aid)
Belmopan 1989; Third Secretary ATTC Taipei
1993; FCO 1995; Second Secretary (Commercial)
Luanda 1999; T/D Durban 2001; Band C4.

Partridge, Margaret (née Robertson), MBE
(1995); SUPL since May 2000; born 03/03/66;
FCO 1986; Islamabad 1989; Vice-Consul Moscow
1992; FCO 1995; Vice-Consul Muscat 1997; Band
B3; m 1988 Andrew Warren Partridge (1s 1996;
1d 1998).

Pasquill, Derek James; Vice-Consul Abu Dhabi
since July 1997; born 11/01/59; HCS 1984; FCO
1986; Kampala 1988; Maseru 1990; FCO 1993.

Patel, Shofiya; Dushanbe since September 2002;
born 03/02/69; DSS 1988; FCO 1990; Canberra
1992; FCO 1995; Riga 1996; Floater Duties 2000;
Band B3.

Paterson, Fiona; First Secretary (Political) Lisbon
since November 1999; born 06/04/51; FCO 1977;
Bogotá 1979; Ottawa 1983; Second Secretary
FCO 1987; Second Secretary
(Chancery/Information) Bangkok 1989; Second
later First Secretary (Information) Paris 1990; First
Secretary FCO 1994; Band D6.

Paterson, Ian Robert; Second Secretary (Political)
Nairobi since April 2002; born 22/09/62; FCO
Communications 1986; FCO 1996; Third
Secretary (Political) Berne 1998; Band C4; m
Diane (2d 1992, 1997).

Paterson, Lynne Kathryn; Wellington since
September 2001; born 22/05/63; FCO 1999; Band
A2.

Paterson, Nicola (née Brydon); SUPL since
August 1996; born 11/12/69; MOD 1989; FCO
1990; Nairobi 1992; FCO 1995; Band B3; m 1992
Duncan Alexander Paterson.

Paterson, Robert Ralston; FCO since January
2000; born 31/01/74; Band C4.

Paterson, William Neil Carlton; Consul-General
Frankfurt since April 2001; born 19/10/50; FCO
1978; Sofia 1980; FCO 1981; Düsseldorf 1983;
Second Secretary (Commercial/Aid) Yaoundé
1986; Second Secretary FCO 1989; Consul
(Commercial) Montreal 1992; Consul-General
Stuttgart 1997; m 1975 Margaret Christine
Schmidt-Feuerheerd (1s 1976; 3d 1978, 1981,
1983).

Patey, William Charters; HM Ambassador
Khartoum since September 2002; born 11/07/53;
FCO 1975; MECAS 1977; Abu Dhabi 1978;
Second Secretary (Commercial) Tripoli 1981; First
Secretary FCO 1984; First Secretary (Chancery)
Canberra 1988; First Secretary later Counsellor
FCO 1992; Deputy Head of Mission Riyadh 1995;
FCO 1998; m 1978 Vanessa Carol Morrell (2s
1987, 1991).

Paton, Kirsty Isobel; Private Secretary to the
Ambassador Washington since January 2002; born
02/02/77; FCO 1999; Vice-Consul (Political and
Economic) Hong Kong 2000; Band C4.

Patrick, Andrew Silas; Assistant Private Secretary
to Secretary of State FCO since January 1998;
born 28/02/66; FCO 1988; Third later Second
Secretary (Chancery) Nicosia 1991; First Secretary
T/D Brussels (UKDEL) 1995; FCO 1996; Band
D7.

Patten, Roger; First Secretary (Management)
Kingston since September 2000; born 24/07/43;
CRO 1963; Bombay 1966; Pretoria/Cape Town
1970; Warsaw 1973; FCO 1974; San Juan 1976;
FCO 1978; Prague 1980; Düsseldorf 1982; Second
Secretary FCO 1987; Second Secretary FCO 1989;
Nicosia 1989; Second Secretary (Consular/Visa)
Rabat 1991; Second Secretary Addis Ababa 1995;
m 1966 Anna Jones (2s 1967, 1970).

Patterson, Ernest Mark; Addis Ababa since
September 1996; born 22/02/69; Vienna 1989;
FCO 1989; Band A2.

Patterson, Hugh William Grant; Counsellor Berne
since April 2000; born 17/10/50; FCO 1979; First
Secretary BMG Berlin 1980; First Secretary FCO
1984; First Secretary (Head of Chancery) and
Consul Guatemala City 1987; First Secretary FCO
1990; First Secretary later Counsellor Caracas
1992; Counsellor FCO 1995; m 1981 Philippa
Anne Colbatch Clark (1d 1986; 1s 1997).

Pattison, Stephen Dexter; Director of Trade
Promotion and Consul-General Warsaw since
February 1997; born 24/12/53; FCO 1981; Nicosia
1983; FCO 1986; First Secretary (Chancery)
Washington 1989; FCO 1994; m 1987 Helen
Andrea Chaoushis 1987 (1d 1993).

Patton, Geoffrey Joseph Laurence; Plymouth,
Montserrat since August 2000; born 26/04/62;
MOD 1985-86; FCO 1986; Warsaw 1989; Floater
Duties 1991; Floater Training 1991; Colombo
1994; FCO 1998; T/D Bombay 2000; Band B3.

Paver, James Edward Luke, MVO (1994); Second
Secretary (Political) Brussels (UKDEL) since
September 1998; born 02/10/63; FCO 1991; Third
Secretary (Press and Public Affairs) Moscow
1994; Second Secretary FCO 1997; m 1992
Rebecca Jane Ash (3d 1993, 1995, 1997).

Pavis, Susan Mary (née Hartland); Brussels
(UKDEL NATO) since August 1999; born
16/04/64; FCO 1983; Washington 1986; Riyadh
1988; FCO 1991; Vice-Consul Singapore 1995;
Band C4; m (1) 1985 Neil Cronin (diss 1994) (1s
1993); (2) 2002 Christopher Pavis.

Paxman, Timothy Giles, LVO (1989); Minister
Paris since June 2002; born 15/11/51; Department
of Environment/Transport 1974; First Secretary
Brussels (UKREP) 1980; FCO 1985; First
Secretary and Head of Chancery Singapore 1989;
Counsellor on loan to the Cabinet Office 1992;
Counsellor (Commercial/Economic) Rome 1994;
Full-Time Language Training 1994; Counsellor
(Political) Brussels (UKREP) 1999; m 1980
Segolene Claude Marie (3d 1982, 1984, 1988).

Peacock, Paula Geraldine (née Hackett); Vice-
Consul Prague since June 1997; born 01/01/65;

FCO 1990; Third Secretary Nairobi 1993; Full-Time Language Training 1996; Band B3; m 1997 David Lawrence Peacock.

Peake, Philippa Jane; SUPL since December 2000; born 30/03/64; FCO 1990; Moscow 1993; UKDEL NATO 1996; FCO 1999; Band A2; m 1997 Dominic Alister Stephens.

Pearce, Andrew John; First Secretary (Economic) Pretoria since October 1996; born 07/10/60; FCO 1983; Language Training 1984; Third later Second Secretary Bangkok 1986; First Secretary FCO 1988; First Secretary (Chancery) Tel Aviv 1992; m 1986 Pornpun Pathumvivantana.

Pearce, David Avery; HM Consul Durban since April 2000; born 17/02/52; FCO 1971; New York (UKMIS) 1973; Rome 1976; FCO 1979; Dhaka 1982; FCO 1986; Paris 1987 (Second Secretary 1987); Second Secretary and Deputy Head of Mission Libreville 1990; Consul Douala 1991; Deputy Head of Mission and Consul-General Sana'a and Aden 1996; m (1) 1973 Anne Matthews (dec'd 1986) (1d 1980; 1s 1984); (2) 1988 Virginia Martin (2d 1991, 1995; 1s 1993).

Pearce, Howard John Stredder, CVO (1993); Governor Stanley and Commissioner for South Georgia and Sandwich Islands since October 2002; born 13/04/49; FCO 1972; Buenos Aires 1975; First Secretary FCO 1978; First Secretary and Head of Chancery Nairobi 1983; First Secretary later Counsellor FCO 1987; Language Training 1990; Deputy Head of Mission Budapest 1991; On loan at Harvard University 1994; Head of Central European Department 1996; British High Commissioner Valletta 1999.

Pearey, David Dacre; Deputy High Commissioner Karachi since July 2000; born 15/07/48; Ankara 1979 (on secondment from MOD); First Secretary FCO 1983; First Secretary and Head of Chancery Kampala 1987; First Secretary later Counsellor FCO 1990; Counsellor (Commercial/Economic) Lagos 1995; m 1996 Susan Anne Knowles (1d 2000).

Pearey, (Dorothy) Jane, MBE (1980); FCO since September 1999; born 31/05/45; OECD Paris 1969; Moscow 1972; FCO 1973; Belgrade 1977; FCO 1980; New York (UKMIS) 1983; Seconded to NATO 1984; Seconded to 21st Century Trust 1988; FCO 1989; (Second Secretary 1991); Second Secretary (Aid) Harare 1995; On secondment to DfID (Harare) 1998.

Pearson, Frances; Buenos Aires since May 1998; born 17/07/54; FCO 1987; Washington 1988; Brussels (UKREP) 1991; Moscow 1994; FCO 1996; Band A2.

Pearson, John Anthony; SUPL since September 2001; born 28/04/68; FCO 1990; Madrid 1992; FCO 1994; Brasilia 1996; FCO 2000; Band D6.

Pearson, Julian Christopher; Tirana since December 2001; born 08/07/69; FCO 1990; Third Secretary Prague 1992; Third Secretary Kinshasa 1995; Minsk 1998; FCO 1998.

Pearson, Nigel John; Islamabad since July 1998; born 04/03/69; FCO 1987; Peking 1992; Band C5.

Pearson, Ruth Alexandra (née Stephens); SUPL since March 2000; born 30/01/71; FCO 1993; Full-Time Language Training 1995; Budapest 1996; Second Secretary (Political) Brussels (UKREP) 1999; Band C4; m 1996 Simon Mark Pearson.

Peart, Christopher John Stuttle; Moscow since January 2002; born 23/08/75; FCO 1998; Band A2.

Pease, Simon Robert Hellier; Assistant Director, Personnel Management FCO since September 2001; born 20/02/52; FCO 1972; Ibadan 1975; SUPL 1978; FCO 1981 (Second Secretary 1982); Second later First Secretary UKDEL CDE Stockholm 1984; First Secretary FCO 1986; First Secretary and Head of Chancery Rabat 1988; First Secretary later Counsellor FCO 1992; Deputy Head of Mission and Consul-General Tel Aviv 1997; m 1975 Catherine Elizabeth Bayley (1d 1981; 1s 1983).

Peate, David James, OBE (1989); First Secretary Turks and Caicos Islands since July 2001; born 02/07/44; FO 1964; DSAO 1965; Delhi 1967; Warsaw 1971; Second Secretary Lomé 1972; FCO 1975; Melbourne 1978; FCO 1983; First Secretary Brussels 1984; First Secretary (Commercial) East Berlin 1989; First Secretary FCO 1993; Deputy Consul-General Milan 1996; m 1971 Siri Jean Jessica Elizabeth Zetter (2d 1973, 1990; 2s 1975, 1986).

Peers, Gary Clive; FCO since June 1997; born 06/12/58; FCO 1985; Third Secretary Bonn 1990; Third Secretary Pretoria 1995; Band C4; m 1979 Pamela Jane Tailby (1d 1981; 2s 1983, 1985).

Peirce, Robert Nigel; Counsellor Washington since October 1999; born 18/03/55; FCO 1977; Language Training Cambridge 1978; Language Training Hong Kong 1979; Second later First Secretary (Chancery) Peking 1980; First Secretary FCO 1983; On loan to Cabinet Office 1985; On secondment to Hong Kong Government as Deputy Political Adviser 1986; Assistant Private Secretary to the Secretary of State 1988; First Secretary (Chancery) New York (UKMIS) 1990; Political Adviser Hong Kong 1993; On secondment to the Royal College of Defence Studies 1998; m (1) 1978 Christina Anne Skipworth Davis (1s 1986; 1d 1988); (2) 2000 Robin Lynn Raphel (2 step d 1986, 1990).

Pemberton, Robert John; FCO since May 1989; born 11/06/63; FCO 1982; Lagos 1985; Band B3; m 1988 Rhonda Karen Leps (1d 1991).

Pendered, Joanne Michelle; Dili since January 2001; born 02/11/65; FCO 1984; Bombay 1987; Santiago 1990; FCO 1992; Third Secretary (Management) Athens 1996; Cape Town 1999; Band B3.

Penfold, Jane Elizabeth Mary (née Govier); FCO since June 2002; born 21/03/62; FCO 1984;

Language Training 1986; Third Secretary (Commercial) Peking 1987; Vice-Consul (Management) Istanbul 1990; Presidency Liaison Officer Luxembourg 1990 (Second Secretary 1991); T/D Bangkok 1991; Second Secretary FCO 1992; Full-Time Language Training 1994; Second Secretary (Political) Sofia 1995; FCO 1998; First Secretary Dili 2000; m 1997 Nigel John Penfold.

Pengelly, Rachel Jane (née Laycock); Second Secretary (Chancery/External) Washington since May 2000; born 20/05/71; FCO 1994; Band C4; m 2000 Owen Pengelly.

Penrith, Alan Paul; On loan to the DTI since January 1999; born 24/05/58; Inland Revenue 1977; FCO 1978; Mexico City 1980; Yaoundé 1983; FCO 1985; Third later Second Secretary (Political/Information) Ottawa 1988; Assistant to Governor British Virgin Islands 1993; Second later First Secretary FCO 1996; m 1982 Karen Cooper (2s 1987, 1991).

Penton-Voak, Martin Eric; First Secretary Vienna (UKDEL) since May 2001; born 09/11/65; Third later Second Secretary FCO 1991; Moscow 1995; First Secretary FCO 1998; Band D6; m 1994 Lucy Katrina Howarth.

Percy, Michael Vivian; FCO since July 2002; born 09/08/50; DSAO (later FCO) 1968; Paris 1972; Brasilia 1975; Budapest 1977; FCO 1980; Quito 1983; Warsaw 1987; FCO 1989 (Second Secretary 1991); Deputy Head of Mission Riga 1993; Second Secretary FCO 1994; Second Secretary British Trade International 1998; Band C5; m 1972 Susan Roslyn Penrose (2d 1974, 1981; 1s 1977).

Perkins, Jacqueline Louise (née Gage); SUPL since July 2001; born 03/10/64; FCO 1989; Second Secretary 1990; Language Training Cairo 1991; Second Secretary (Chancery/Information) Abu Dhabi 1992; First Secretary FCO 1995; SUPL 1996; First Secretary Cairo 1999; m 1991 Stuart Blair Perkins (1s 1996).

Perks, Adam Cecil; Second Secretary (Immigration) Moscow since September 2002; born 03/05/66; FCO (HCS) 1984; FCO 1987; Kuwait 1988; Third Secretary (Consular) Ottawa 1991; FCO 1991; Third Secretary FCO 1994; Vice-Consul Luxembourg 1998; m 1990 Nicola Rose Wardle (2s 1992, 1996; 1d 1998).

Perrin, Geoffrey Gordon; Second later First Secretary FCO since October 1978; born 12/08/49; FCO 1971; Geneva 1975; Band C5; m 1977 Heather Beryl Robson (2s 1979, 1984).

Perrott, John Gayford; High Commissioner Banjul since April 2000; born 05/07/43; CRO 1962; Karachi 1966; Ankara 1970; Calcutta 1972; Second Secretary (Consular/Admin) Calcutta 1974; Second Secretary FCO 1976; Second later First Secretary Kathmandu 1979; Consul (Commercial) Istanbul 1984; First Secretary FCO 1988; Chief Secretary St Helena 1993; FCO 1997; m 1964 Joan Wendy Lewis (1d 1964; 1s 1966).

Perry, Christopher Ian; Lagos since June 2002; born 27/05/70; FCO 1990; Brussels (UKREP) 1993; Paris 1995; New Delhi 1999; Band B3; m (1) 1992 Charlotte Dawson (diss 1995) (1d 1992); (2) 1995 Lesa Jayne Elliot (3d 1996, 1997, 1998).

Perry, Geoffrey Colin; First Secretary FCO since August 1996; born 13/01/51; Third Secretary FCO 1973; Language Training Cambridge University 1975; Language Training/Second Secretary Kuala Lumpur 1976 and Singapore 1977; Second later First Secretary FCO 1977; Trade Commissioner Hong Kong 1981; First Secretary FCO 1986; First Secretary (UN/Press) Geneva (UKMIS) 1992; Band D6; m 1975 Barbara Elisabeth Gysin (née Kaestlin) (2d 1977, 1979).

Perry, Susan; Vice-Consul Shanghai since April 1997; born 07/03/44; HCS 1965; FCO 1977; Havana 1979; Tunis 1980; Warsaw 1983; Kathmandu 1986; FCO 1990; Kampala 1993; Band B3.

Perry, Thomas Ian; Jerusalem since May 1998; born 29/03/55; MOD 1972; FCO 1974; New York (UKMIS) 1976; Africa/Middle East Floater 1979; T/D Dubai 1979; Jakarta 1981; FCO 1983; The Hague 1986; FCO 1988; T/D Dar es Salaam 1990; T/D Warsaw 1990; Islamabad 1991; FCO 1996; Band B3; m 1982 Jeannie Bell (2s 1992, 1995).

Persighetti, Stephen Victor; Second Secretary (Political/Aid) Cape Town since January 1996; born 31/03/56; FCO 1975; Moscow 1977; Beirut 1978; Tokyo 1981; Floater Duties 1983; On loan to ODA 1985; Third Secretary (Aid) Jakarta 1988; Second Secretary FCO 1991; Band C5; m 1992 Rozany Deen.

Pert, David John; Kiev since March 2001; born 21/01/68; Royal Navy 1987-94; FCO 1994; Third Secretary (Political) Sofia 1996; m 1990 Christine Walsh (2s 1991, 1994).

Petch, Eleanor; Prague since August 2001; born 26/01/77; FCO 1998; Full-Time Language Training 2000; Band C4.

Peters, Mark Crispin; Second Secretary (Chancery) Oslo since August 1996; born 07/06/64; Royal Engineers 1987-94; FCO 1994.

Petherbridge, Richard Sydney; FCO since January 1996; born 23/08/55; DHSS 1975; FCO 1980; Nicosia 1982; Seoul 1985; FCO 1987; Prague 1990; Riyadh 1992; Band A2; m 1982 Pauline Joan Mulvey (1s 1984; 1d 1986).

Pethick, Mark Julian; Deputy Head of Mission Minsk since September 1997; born 03/04/68; FCO 1990; Karachi 1993; Band C4.

Phillips, Alison Jane (née Francis), OBE (1991); SUPL since January 2001; born 18/04/56; FCO 1974; New York (UKMIS) 1981; Second Secretary FCO 1982; First Secretary Paris 1986; First Secretary FCO 1990; Band D6; m 1978 Richard Charles Jonathan Phillips, QC.

Phillips, Duncan Keith; FCO since July 1989; born 07/03/69; Band A2.

Phillips, Harjit Kaur (née Jagpal); Moscow since April 1998; born 08/10/68; FCO 1988; Lagos 1991; Abuja 1993; SUPL 1995; Band A2; m 1996 Robin David Phillips.

Phillips, Linda Ann; Washington since November 2000; born 17/01/56; FCO 1995; Accra 1997; Band A2.

Phillips, Patricia Ruth; SUPL since December 2000; born 11/03/62; MAFF 1984; Washington 1992; First Secretary FCO 1997; Band C4.

Phillips, Quentin James Kitson; First Secretary FCO since September 2000; born 20/10/63; FCO 1986; Second Secretary (Information) Budapest 1989; Second later First Secretary FCO 1992; First Secretary (Political) Moscow 1995; First Secretary FCO 1996; First Secretary (Political) Kiev 1997; Band D6; m 1989 Gillian Lynne Murray (2d 1993, 1996; 1s 1999).

Phillips, Russell James; Abuja since September 1998; born 24/02/64; FCO 1983; Georgetown 1985; Khartoum 1988; FCO 1991; Bombay 1995; Band C4.

Phillips, Tom Richard Vaughan, CMG; High Commissioner Uganda since May 2000; born 21/06/50; DHSS 1977; FCO 1983; First Secretary Harare 1985; First Secretary FCO 1988; Counsellor, Consul-General and Deputy Head of Mission Tel Aviv 1990; Counsellor (External) Washington 1993; Counsellor FCO 1997; m 1986 Anne Renee Marie de la Motte (2s 1987, 1989).

Philpott, Hugh Stanley; Deputy Head of Mission Muscat since October 2001; born 24/01/61; FCO 1980; Oslo 1982; Budapest 1985; Language Training 1987; Third Secretary (Commercial) Baghdad 1988; FCO 1990 (Second Secretary 1992); Second Secretary (Political/Military) Washington 1993; On loan to DfID 1997; First Secretary FCO 1999; Band D6; m 1984 Janine Frederica Rule (1d 1998).

Philpott, Janine Frederica; FCO since January 1998; born 30/01/60; FCO 1980; Brussels (UKDEL NATO) 1982; Budapest 1985; FCO 1986; Baghdad 1988; FCO 1990; Third Secretary (Press) Washington 1993; Band B3; m 1984 Hugh Stanley Philpott (1d 1998).

Pickering, Helen Mary; FCO since June 2001; born 10/07/64; FCO 1986; Moscow 1988; Algiers 1989; Geneva 1990; FCO 1993; Second Secretary (EU) Warsaw 1997; Band D6; m 1996 James Owen.

Pickering, Sara Elizabeth; Second Secretary (Commercial) Lagos since December 1998; born 22/04/67; FCO 1988; Vice-Consul Budapest 1991; FCO 1992; Islamabad 1995; Band C4; m 1992 Andrew John Kirkpatrick.

Pickett, Jane Louise (née Houghton), MBE (1994); FCO since November 1995; born 05/12/64; FCO 1984; Santiago 1987; FCO 1991; Bogotá 1993; Band C4; m 1998 Peter Derek Pickett.

Pickup, Lawrence; Deputy Head of Mission Khartoum since May 2000; born 10/09/52; FCO 1976; Dar es Salaam 1980; Dubai 1982; Floater Duties 1986; On loan to the DTI 1989; FCO/DTI 1991; Consul Warsaw 1993; Deputy Head of Mission Phnom Penh 1997; Band D6.

Pierce, Anne Nicholson (née Creighton); SUPL since January 1995; born 20/07/65; ODA 1984-89; FCO 1989; SUPL 1991; Riyadh 1992; FCO 1993; Band A2; m 1991 Timothy Karl Pierce (2d 1995, 1999).

Pierce, Karen Elizabeth; Head of Eastern Adriatic Dept FCO since November 2002; born 23/09/59; FCO 1981; Language Training 1984; Tokyo 1985; FCO 1987; Private Secretary to the Ambassador Washington 1991 (First Secretary 1994); FCO 1996; Counsellor FCO 2001; m 1987 Charles Fergusson Roxburgh (2s 1991, 1997).

Pigott, Carsten Orthöfer; Counsellor FCO since 1998; born 31/05/53; FCO 1972; Lagos 1975; Language Training MECAS 1977; Language Training 1978; Third Secretary (Commercial) Khartoum 1979; Second Secretary (Commercial) Tripoli 1982; Second Secretary FCO 1984; First Secretary (Chancery) Peking 1987; First Secretary FCO 1991; Deputy Head of Mission Addis Ababa 1993; First Secretary (Chancery) New Delhi 1997; m 1976 Susan Kathlyn Pugh (1d 1981; 1s 1983).

Pike, Andrew Kerry; Second Secretary (Chancery and Information) Dublin since July 1998; born 06/06/64; Dept of Transport 1982; FCO 1984; Sana'a 1985; Warsaw 1990; FCO 1993; Band C4.

Pilmore-Bedford, Jeremy Patrick; Second Secretary (Economic) Kuala Lumpur since September 2001; born 22/08/67; FCO 1990; Singapore 1993; Third Secretary (Aid) Moscow 1995; Full-Time Language Training 1995; FCO 1998; Band C4; m Amanda Joanne West (1d 1997; 1s 1999).

Pinnock, Stuart Graham; SUPL since September 2000; born 19/05/63; FCO 1981; Paris 1984; Lagos 1986; FCO 1989; SUPL 1993; FCO 1995 (Second Secretary 1997); On loan to the DTI 1998.

Pinsent, Guy Hume; FCO since September 2000; born 07/03/76; Band C4.

Pinson, David Richard; Full-Time Language Training since April 2002; born 07/05/77; FCO 2000; Band C4.

Pinto, Alison Louise (née Johnson); FCO since October 1997; FCO 1989; Vice-Consul Tokyo 1992; Third Secretary (Chancery) Berlin 1995; Band D6; m 2001 Andrew Pinto.

Pisa, Adrian; FCO since September 2001; born 13/03/72; Band C4.

Pitts, Barbara Anne, MVO (1989); Copenhagen since October 2000; born 26/01/54; Lagos 1975; FCO 1975; Moscow 1977; FCO 1979; Nairobi 1981; FCO 1984; Kuala Lumpur 1987; FCO 1990; New Delhi 1997; Band B3.

Plank, John; Second Secretary (Political) Pretoria since February 2000; born 03/10/64; FCO 1986; Band C4; m 1997 Corinne Lambshead (1s 2001).

Plant, Michael Geoffrey; Deputy Consul-General Boston since May 2000; born 12/10/46; Post Office 1964; DSAO 1966; Moscow 1969; Rabat 1970; Peking 1973; Brussels (JAO) 1975; FCO 1978; Banjul 1980; Los Angeles 1984; Second Secretary FCO 1987; Second Secretary (Commercial/Consular) Al Khobar 1990; First Secretary (Management) Yerevan, Tbilisi and Ashgabat 1995; FCO 1998; Band C5; m 1971 Hayfa Theodora Massouh (2d 1972, 1975).

Plater, Stephen James; First Secretary FCO since February 1995; born 23/01/54; FCO 1976; Second Secretary Tokyo 1978; Second later First Secretary FCO 1982; First Secretary and Head of Chancery Vienna (UKDEL MBFR) 1987; First Secretary Vienna (UKDEL CACN) 1989; First Secretary (Commercial) Tokyo 1990; m 1980 Keiko Kurata (1d 1990).

Platt, David Watson; New Delhi since October 2001; born 09/04/54; Inland Revenue 1972; FCO 1973; Beirut 1977; Brasilia 1980; Sofia 1981; FCO 1983; Dhaka 1985; Bridgetown 1988; FCO 1992; Dubai 1997; Band B3.

Platt, Janet Elizabeth (née Howells); SUPL since July 2001; born 26/03/61; Brussels (NATO) 1982; Washington 1985; FCO 1987; Anguilla 1988; FCO 1991; Brussels (UKREP) 1992; Band A2; m 1988 Philip Charles Platt (2s 1987, 1990; 1d 1997).

Plumb, Michael Barry George; Management Officer Kuala Lumpur since June 2002; born 16/05/45; DSAO 1965; Kampala 1968; Lahore 1971; FCO 1975; Washington 1977; Canberra 1979; Baghdad 1982; FCO 1986; Jakarta 1990; FCO 1995; Deputy High Commissioner Port Moresby 1997; T/D Jakarta 2001; m 1968 Linda Wills Gledhill (1s 1972; 1d 1975).

Plumbly, Sir Derek John, KCMG (2001), CMG (1991); HM Ambassador Riyadh since September 2000; born 15/05/48; Reporting Officer New York 1972; FCO 1972; MECAS 1973; FCO 1973; Second later First Secretary Jedda 1975; First Secretary Cairo 1977; FCO 1980; First Secretary (Commercial) Washington 1984; Counsellor and Head of Chancery Riyadh 1988; Counsellor and Head of Chancery New York (UKMIS) 1992; AUS FCO 1996; m 1979 Nadia Youssef Gohar (1d 1983; 2s 1985, 1987).

Pocock, Andrew John; Head of African Department (Southern) FCO since May 2001; born 23/08/55; FCO 1981; Second later First Secretary (Commercial) Lagos 1983; First Secretary FCO 1986; First Secretary (Chancery) Washington 1988; First Secretary FCO 1992; Counsellor on loan to the Royal College of Defence Studies 1996; Deputy High Commissioner Canberra 1997; m (1) 1976 Dayalini Pathmanathan (diss); (2) 1995 Julie Eyre-Wilson.

Polatajko, Mark Alexander; New Delhi since August 1998; born 16/10/70; FCO 1991; Cairo 1995; Band B3.

Poll, Christopher John; Deputy High Commissioner Vila since November 1997; born 29/06/57; Army 1972-84; FCO 1984; Brussels (UKREP) 1988; FCO 1991; Canberra 1994; Band C4; m 1988 Gillian Anne Smith (1d 1994; 1s 1998).

Poll, Gillian Anne (née Smith); SUPL since 1994; born 30/04/58; HCS 1976; FCO 1985; Brussels 1987; Brussels (UKREP) 1990; FCO 1991; Band A2; m 1988 Christopher John Poll (1d 1994; 1s 1998).

Pollard, Guy Sephton; Third later Second Secretary (Political) Bratislava since October 1998; born 03/06/71; FCO 1991; Islamabad 1995; Band C4; ptnr, Catherine Louise Nicol (1d 2000).

Pond, John; Brussels (UKDEL NATO) since January 1997; born 22/05/52; Armed Forces 1969-92; FCO 1995; Band A2; m 1973 Catherine Herbert (1s 1971).

Ponsonby, Gareth James; FCO since May 2000; born 25/05/70; FCO 1991; Islamabad 1996; Band B3; m 1995 Natalie Lalanie Beverley Yeo (1d 2000).

Poole, Christopher George Robert; T/D Second Secretary (Political) Freetown since March 2000; born 19/04/52; FCO 1970; Algiers 1973; Brasilia 1974; Rio de Janeiro 1976; Freetown 1978; Paris 1981; Kinshasa 1984; FCO 1988; Third later Second Secretary Antananarivo 1991; Vice-Consul (Commercial/Information) São Paulo 1995; FCO 1998; Band C5; m 1977 Maria Madalena Gomes Ferreira.

Poole, Christopher James, MBE (1987); T/D Deputy Head of Mission Tirana since July 2002; born 24/12/46; CRO 1964; FCO 1968; Georgetown 1969; Africa Floater 1969; St Lucia 1971; Bridgetown 1973; FCO 1976; Munich 1979; FCO 1982; Second Secretary Beirut 1985; Second Secretary Luxembourg 1987; EC Monitor Mission Former Yugoslavia 1992; Deputy Head of Mission Zagreb 1993; Deputy Head of Mission Jerusalem 1995; First Secretary FCO 1996; First Secretary (Commercial) Sarajevo 1998; SUPL 2001; m (1) 1973 Lillian Hodgson (diss) (2d 1979, 1980); (2) 1987 Marilyn Kathleen Povey (diss 1996); (3) 1996 Lynne Diana Merrin.

Pooley, Nigel Arthur; On secondment to Oxfam since September 2000; born 12/11/61; FCO 1991; Third later Second Secretary (Chancery) Vienna 1994; First Secretary FCO 1998; m 1985 Helena Falle (3s 1986, 1991, 1994; 1d 1988).

Porter, Gillian Sarah; New York (UKMIS) since July 2000; born 07/04/66; FCO 1988; Moscow 1991; Manila 1993; Band A2.

Porter, Neil David; Valletta since July 1999; born 14/04/63; FCO 1982; Riyadh 1985; Budapest 1989; FCO 1992; Third Secretary Johannesburg

1996; Band B3; m 1986 Gajetana Dominica Maria de Wit (1s 1988; 1d 1989).

Portman, Giles Matthew; Second Secretary (Political/Information) Prague since April 1998; born 25/05/71; Department of Transport 1994; FCO 1995; Band D6.

Poston, James, CBE (2002); FCO since October 1999; born 19/06/45; Third Secretary FCO 1970; Concurrently Third Secretary and Vice-Consul HM Embassy to Chad; Second Secretary and Private Secretary to Head of UKDEL EC Brussels 1971; First Secretary Tel Aviv 1973; FCO 1978; First Secretary (Commercial) Lagos 1982; FCO 1985; Counsellor and Head of Chancery Pretoria 1988; Counsellor FCO 1992; Consul-General Boston 1995; m (1) 1976 Anna Caroline Bos (diss 1980); (2) Rosemary Fullerton (2d 1987, 1988; 1s 1991).

Potter, Richard William; First Secretary Skopje since December 1999; born 22/05/60; FCO 1983; Third later Second Secretary Riyadh 1985; Second Secretary FCO 1988; First Secretary (Information) Nicosia 1990; First Secretary FCO 1994; First Secretary Sarajevo 1995; FCO 1998; Band D6.

Potter, Rupert James; Third Secretary (Political) Stockholm since April 1999; born 14/11/68; FCO 1992; Amman 1995; Band B3; m 1995 Juliette Wilcox (1s 1998).

Powell, David Herbert; Assistant Director (Personnel Services) FCO since September 2002; born 29/04/52; MOD 1974; FCO 1984; First Secretary Tokyo 1988; First Secretary FCO 1992; Counsellor on loan to Cabinet Office 1995; Political Counsellor UKDEL NATO/WEU Brussels 1997; m 1984 Gillian Mary Croft (1d 1994).

Powell, Hugh Eric; First Secretary Political (Internal) Berlin since April 2000; born 16/02/67; FCO 1991; Second Secretary Paris 1993; First Secretary FCO 1998; Full-Time Language Training 2000; Band D6; m 1993 Catherine Claire Young (2s 1996, 1997).

Powell, Ian Francis, OBE (1995); First Secretary Gibraltar since September 1998; born 30/12/47; Commonwealth Office (later FCO) 1966; Freetown 1970; Havana 1973; FCO 1975; Stockholm 1978; Dublin 1981 (Second Secretary 1983); Second Secretary FCO 1986 (First Secretary 1988); First Secretary (Management/HM Consul) Kingston 1989; Deputy Head of Mission Sana'a 1994; First Secretary FCO 1995; m 1969 Priscilla Ann Fenton (2d 1974, 1980).

Powell, Leslie; Warsaw since March 1996; born 15/05/66; FCO 1994; Band A2.

Powell, Martin; Second Secretary Singapore since January 1988; born 21/10/46; FCO 1969; Warsaw 1973; FCO 1974; Brussels 1982; FCO 1985; m (1) 1972 Susan Kay Bower (diss); (2) 1982 Patricia Helen Scruby (1s 1987).

Powell, Richard Stephen; FCO since October 1998; born 19/10/59; FCO 1981; Third later Second Secretary Helsinki 1983; First Secretary FCO 1988; First Secretary (Science) Tokyo 1992; CDA Imperial College London 1996.

Power, Anne Maria; FCO since January 1999; born 14/08/65; FCO 1989; Strasbourg UKDEL 1992; Consulate-General Geneva 1993; Strasbourg UKDEL 1993; SUPL 1996; Band C4.

Power, Carmel Angela; Copenhagen since September 2001; born 30/10/63; FCO 1990; Third Secretary (Political) Vienna (UKDEL) 1992; Vice-Consul (Commercial) Damascus 1995; FCO 1997; Band D6.

Prentice, Christopher Norman Russell; HM Ambassador Amman since June 2002; born 05/09/54; FCO 1977; Language Training MECAS 1978; Third later Second Secretary Kuwait 1980; First Secretary on loan to Cabinet Office 1983; First Secretary Washington 1985; First Secretary FCO 1989; Deputy Head of Mission Budapest 1994; Counsellor FCO 1998; m 1978 Marie-Josephine (Nina) King (2s 1981, 1988; 2d 1982, 1985).

Preston, James David; On loan to the DTI since September 1999; born 21/04/68; FCO 1987; Helsinki 1994; FCO 1997; Band C4; m 1992 Kim Dickinson (1s 1995).

Preston, Joseph Raymond; On loan to BTI (Institute of Export) since September 1999; born 01/06/61; FCO 1980; Dhaka 1983; Kathmandu 1985; Nicosia 1989; FCO 1993; Third Secretary (Commercial) Islamabad 1995; FCO 1999; Band C4; m 1993 Sandra Elizabeth Cook.

Preston, Sandra Elizabeth (née Cook); FCO since August 1999; born 12/06/64; FCO 1987; Nicosia 1990; FCO 1992; Islamabad 1996; Band A2; m 1993 Joseph Raymond Preston.

Preston, William Edward Johnston; First Secretary Nicosia since January 1996; born 07/07/47; FCO 1965; Ankara 1969; Kinshasa 1972; FCO 1974; Rabat 1976; Oslo 1979; Second Secretary (Admin) Moscow 1983; Second Secretary FCO 1985; Second Secretary (Commercial) Port of Spain 1988; First Secretary (Commercial) Bucharest 1992; m 1969 Anne Kathleen Smith (1s 1974).

Price, Denis Charles; Berlin since January 2002; born 20/04/52; Royal Electrical and Mechanical Engineers 1973-95; FCO 2000; Band C4; m 1977 Jane Ann (1s 1978).

Price, Kenneth George; Deputy Head of Mission Kinshasa since September 2001; born 12/04/65; FCO 1983; Bonn 1985; Accra 1988; FCO 1991; Third Secretary (Political/Aid) Almaty 1994; World Wide Floater Duties 1997; Second Secretary FCO 1998; Band C4.

Price, Michael Anthony, LVO (1991); HM Ambassador Suva since October 2000 also High Commissioner (non-resident) Kiribati, Nauru and

Tuvalu; born 13/08/44; Board of Trade 1964; DSAO 1966; Commonwealth Office 1967; New Delhi 1969; Second Secretary (Chancery) Freetown 1972; FCO 1973; Second later First Secretary (Aviation and Defence) Paris 1974; Consul (Commercial) Montreal 1979; JSDC Greenwich 1983; First Secretary FCO 1984; First Secretary (Press and Public Affairs) Washington 1988; Counsellor (Management) and HM Consul-General Tokyo 1993; Counsellor on loan to No 10 Downing Street 1994; Counsellor (Management) Paris 1995; m 1968 Elizabeth Anne Cook (1d 1972; 1s 1974).

Price, Sarah Helena; Head of British Interests Section Belgrade since October 2000; born 04/06/66; FCO 1990; Second Secretary Helsinki (UKDEL CSCE) 1992; Second Secretary (Economic/KHF) Prague 1993; First Secretary FCO 1996; Secondment to the EU Secretariat of the Finnish Ministry for Foreign Affairs 1999; Full-Time Language Training 2000; Band D6.

Price, Siân Rhyannon; FCO since January 2000; born 17/02/76; Band B3.

Price, Tristan Robert Julian; SUPL since August 1999; born 24/11/66; Economic Assistant 1993; Economic Adviser 1995; m 1988 Judith Ann Torrance (1d 1996; 1s 1998).

Priest, Timothy Ian; Counsellor (Political) Helsinki since June 1999; born 27/10/47; FCO 1972; Vienna 1975; First Secretary (Chancery) Helsinki 1981; FCO 1985; First Secretary (Chancery/Information) Athens 1989; Counsellor FCO 1993; m Teresa Jean Bagnall (2d 1975, 1980; 2s 1978, 1987).

Priestley, Carol Ann (née Edwards); Second Secretary FCO since May 1993; born 11/11/53; FCO 1974; Paris 1976; Düsseldorf 1979; Kathmandu 1980; FCO 1982; Dhaka 1985; Auckland 1989; m 1976 Lawrence Minton Priestley.

Priestley, Philip John, CBE (1996); High Commissioner Belmopan since July 2001; born 29/08/46; FCO 1969; Third Secretary Sofia 1971; Third later Second Secretary Kinshasa 1973; First Secretary FCO 1976; Head of Chancery Wellington 1979; First Secretary FCO 1984; Counsellor (Commercial) Manila 1987; HM Ambassador Libreville 1990; CDA Harvard University 1991; Consul-General Geneva 1992; Head, North America Department FCO 1996; m 1972 Christine Rainforth (1d 1976; 1s 1978).

Prime, Ashley Walter John; FCO since March 2001; born 06/08/59; FCO 1978; Bonn 1980; Kingston 1983; Peking 1986; FCO 1989; Milan 1993; Full-Time Language Training 1993; Rome 1995; Deputy Consul-General Guangzhou 1996; Full-Time Language Training 1996; On loan to the DTI 1999; Band C4; m 1997 Silvia Ardizzone (1s 1999).

Pring, Alison June; First Secretary (Commercial) Berne since October 1999; born 18/06/61; SUPL 1983; FCO 1983; FCO 1984; Third Secretary Brussels 1986; Third later Second Secretary Caracas 1989; Second Secretary FCO 1991; Full-Time Language Training 1995; Second Secretary (Commercial) and Deputy Head of Mission St Petersburg 1996; Band C5.

Pring, Mary; FCO since January 1999; born 29/06/60; FCO 1991; Full-Time Language Training 1993; Language Training Cairo 1994; Jerusalem 1995; Band B3.

Pringle, Anne Fyfe; HM Ambassador Prague since November 2001; born 13/01/55; FCO 1977; Moscow 1980; San Francisco 1983; Second Secretary Brussels (UKREP) 1986; Second later First Secretary FCO 1987; First Secretary on secondment to European Political Cooperation Secretariat 1991; First Secretary later Counsellor FCO 1994; Full-Time Language Training 2001; m 1987 Bleddyn Glynne Leyshon Phillips.

Pringle, Julia Margaret Georgina; Bogotá since December 1998; born 28/03/48; FCO 1966-71; Metropolitan Police 1971; FCO 1991; SUPL 1993; Band A2; m 1971 Raymond Elliot Pringle (1d 1981).

Pringle, Raymond Elliott; First Secretary (Commercial) Copenhagen since October 2001; born 28/11/51; Department of Employment 1968-69; FCO 1970; Brussels (UKREP) 1972; Quito 1975; FCO 1978; Bilbao 1981; Barcelona 1983; Second Secretary (Chancery/Information) Lilongwe 1986; Second later First Secretary FCO 1989; Deputy Consul-General and Consul (Commercial) San Francisco 1993; First Secretary (Management) Washington 1999; SUPL 1999; m 1971 Julia Margaret Georgina Wright (1d 1981).

Pritchard, Grant; Third Secretary Vienna (OSCE) since September 2000; born 02/06/70; FCO 1990; Peking 1994; Third Secretary (Management) and Vice-Consul Kuwait 1997; m 1996 Rebecca Louise Williams.

Pritchard, Rebecca Louise (née Williams); Berne since January 2000; born 17/08/71; FCO 1989; Geneva (UKMIS) 1991; Peking 1994; PA/HMA Kuwait 1997; Band A2; m 1996 Grant Pritchard.

Proctor, Jacqueline (née Jones); Geneva (UKDis) since July 1996; born 03/10/71; FCO 1991; Athens 1993; SUPL 1996; Band A2; m 1996 Matthew Joel Proctor.

Proctor, Matthew Joel; Kampala since December 1999; born 16/07/71; FCO 1991; SUPL 1993; Geneva (UKMIS) 1996; Band B3; m 1996 Jaqueline Jones.

Prodger, David Wilce; First Secretary (Commercial) Buenos Aires since March 2002; born 28/09/66; FCO 1999; Band D6; m 1993 Tiffany Darwent (2s 1997, 2000).

Proudfoot, David Owen; Baku since August 2002; born 15/04/71; HCS 1991; FCO 1995; Sarajevo 1998; FCO 2001; Band B3.

Prouten, Matthew David, MBE (1996); Full-Time Language Training since November 2000; born 10/03/69; FCO 1988; Tokyo 1992; FCO 1996; Third Secretary (Political) Vilnius 1997; FCO 2000; Band B3; m 1994 Akino Matsumoto (1s 1997; 1d 2000).

Pruce, Daniel Robert; First Secretary (Information) Brussels (UKREP) since September 1999; born 24/07/66; FCO 1990; Brussels (UKREP) 1993; FCO 1996; Band C4.

Pryce, Andrew William; FCO since November 1997; born 09/02/70; FCO 1988; Washington 1991; FCO 1993; Karachi 1994; Band B3; m 1993 Corienne Marie Madden.

Publicover, Ralph Martin; Deputy Head of Mission Lisbon since January 1999; born 02/05/52; FCO 1976; Language Training MECAS 1977; Second later First Secretary Dubai 1979; First Secretary (Economic) Ottawa 1981; First Secretary on loan to Cabinet Office 1985; FCO 1987; First Secretary (Chancery) Washington 1989; First Secretary FCO 1992; Bucharest 1994; Full-Time Language Training 1994; m 1973 Rosemary Sheward (2d 1979, 1988; 1s 1983).

Pugh, David Evan; FCO since July 2000; born 26/04/51; FCO 1982; Pretoria 1983; FCO 1985; Cairo 1988; FCO 1991; Tokyo 1992; FCO 1995; Vienna 1997; Band C5; m (1) 1976 Bethan Jones (diss 1989) (4d 1980, 1982, 1984, 1986); (2) 1992 Sally Anne Jones.

Pullen, Brian Peter; Consul-General Lyon since September 1996; born 02/05/41; GPO 1960; FO 1961; Jedda 1963; Brussels 1965; Belgrade 1967; Freetown 1970; FCO 1974; Second Secretary (Admin/Consular) Algiers 1977; Consul Bordeaux 1980; Second later First Secretary (Economic) Paris 1982; First Secretary FCO 1988; First Secretary Copenhagen 1993; m 1965 Annie Bernes (2s 1967, 1969).

Pullen, Roderick Allen; High Commissioner Accra since October 2000; born 11/04/49; MOD 1975; Second Secretary Brussels (UKDEL NATO) 1978; MOD 1980; First Secretary Madrid (UKDEL CSCE) 1981; FCO 1982; DHC Suva 1984; First Secretary FCO 1988; Counsellor (Technology) Paris 1990; Deputy High Commissioner Nairobi 1994; Deputy High Commissioner Lagos 1997; FCO 2000; m 1971 Karen Lesley Sketchley (1d 1975; 4s 1978, 1989, twins 1994).

Pullen, Russell Lewis, MBE (2002); First Secretary FCO since April 1986; born 10/01/54; Second Secretary FCO 1975; Band C5; m 1979 Gillian May Wright (1s 1985; 1d 1988).

Purdy, Samantha Louise, MVO (1996); First Secretary FCO since July 1999; born 22/08/71; FCO 1992; Full-Time Language Training 1994; Full-Time Language Training Bangkok 1995; Second Secretary (Political/Information) Bangkok 1996.

Purves, Michael; First Secretary (Commercial) and Deputy Head of Mission Doha since September 2000; born 03/11/57; FCO 1975; New Delhi 1978; ME Floater 1982; Mogadishu 1983; FCO 1986; Third later Second Secretary (Economic/Aid) Kuala Lumpur 1989; Second Secretary (Management) Colombo 1992; First Secretary FCO 1996; m 1985 Ruth Joan Goodwin (1d 1986; 1s 1990).

Puryer, Stuart John; FCO since July 1996; born 03/06/67; FCO 1987; Copenhagen 1990; Ljubljana 1993; Band C4.

Pyle, Nicholas John, MBE (1999); Second Secretary Bridgetown since February 2000; born 09/12/60; FCO 1981; Geneva (UKMIS) 1984; Kabul 1986; Jedda 1990; FCO 1992 (Second Secretary 1995); Second Secretary (Immigration) Colombo 1996; Band C4; m 1993 Rosamund Day (2s 1995, 2001; 1d 1999).

Pyper, Alan; Berlin since June 2001; born 13/06/62; DSS 1990-97; FCO 1999; Band A2; m 1995 Patrocinia Haban.

Q

Quarrey, David; First Secretary (Political) New Delhi since September 2000; born 06/01/66; FCO 1994; Second Secretary (Political) Harare 1995.

Quayle, Quinton Mark; HM Ambassador Bucharest since November 2002; born 05/06/55; FCO 1977; Language Training 1978; Third Secretary (Chancery) Bangkok 1979 (Second Secretary 1981); FCO 1983 (First Secretary 1984); ENA Paris 1986; First Secretary Paris 1987; First Secretary FCO 1991; First Secretary seconded to Price Waterhouse 1993; Counsellor FCO 1994; Deputy Head of Mission Jakarta 1996; International Group Director Trade Partners UK 1999; Director British Time International 1999; m 1979 Alison Marshall (2s 1982, 1985).

Quinn, James Gregory; Second Secretary (Political/PPA) Accra since August 2000; born 16/06/71; Language Training 1999; Second Secretary FCO 1999; Band C4; m 1995 Wendy Dackombe.

Quinn, Jean Margaret (née Leiper); Second Secretary (Commercial) Riga since February 2000; born 21/03/53; FCO 1975; Abidjan 1978; Brasilia 1982; Second Secretary FCO 1984; SUPL 1990; FCO 1994; Second Secretary (Commercial/ECM) Tunis 1996; Band C4; m 1985 Peter Nugent Quinn (1d 1987; 1s 1989).

Quinn, Lorraine; Helsinki since July 2000; born 25/06/66; FCO 1991; Bonn 1993; Gibraltar 1997; Band B3; m (1) 1986 Martin Quinn (diss 2000) (1s 1988); (2) 2000 Stephen Andrew Pettigrew.

R

Raab, Dominic; Assistant Legal Adviser FCO since October 2000; born 25/02/74.

Raby, Charlotte Jane; FCO since May 2002; born 05/05/72; HCS FCO 1992; FCO 1996; Peking 1998; Band A2.

Rack, Martin Elliott; Second Secretary FCO since May 2001; born 30/12/73; FCO 1997; Second Secretary (Political) The Hague 1999; Band C4.

Radcliffe, Adam, MBE (2002); FCO since October 1996; born 10/06/67; FCO 1988; Geneva (UKMIS) 1990; Istanbul 1993; Band A2; m 1992 Julie Anne Nichols.

Rae, Karen (née Hooper); Second Secretary (Commercial) Prague since November 1997; born 28/05/60; FCO 1980; Port Stanley 1983; Berne 1984; Cairo 1987; FCO 1990; Third Secretary (Consular) Islamabad 1993; Language Training 1997; Band C4; m 1984 Thomas Park Rae (1d 1993).

Raine, John Andrew; First Secretary Pristina since March 2002; born 12/07/62; FCO 1984; Language Training 1986; Second Secretary (Information) Kuwait 1988; First Secretary FCO 1991; First Secretary (Political) Damascus 1994; First Secretary Riyadh 1997; FCO 2000; Band D6.

Raine, Sarah Emily; Second Secretary (Political) Sarajevo since March 2002; born 16/07/76; FCO 1999; Full-Time Language Training 2001; Band C4.

Rajguru, Harish L; SUPL since July 2002; born 23/04/61; HCS cadre of the FCO 1989; FCO 1990; Sofia 1992; Kiev 1994; FCO 1996; Floater Duties 1999; Ekaterinburg 2001; Band B3.

Rakestraw, Mark Andrew; Vice-Consul Lisbon since August 1997; born 30/11/67; FCO 1988; Athens 1990; FCO 1993; Full-Time Language Training 1996; Band C4.

Ralph, Richard Peter, CMG (1997), CVO (1991); HM Ambassador Bucharest since August 1999; born 27/04/46; Third Secretary FCO 1969; Third later Second Secretary Vientiane 1970; Second later First Secretary (Information) Lisbon 1974; First Secretary FCO 1977; First Secretary and Head of Chancery Harare 1981; First Secretary later Counsellor FCO 1985; Counsellor Washington 1989; HM Ambassador Riga 1993; HM Governor Stanley 1996; m 1970 Margaret Elisabeth Coulthurst (diss 2001) (1s 1970; 1d 1974).

Rampe, Christopher Mark; FCO since June 1999; born 15/01/61; FCO 1988; Second Secretary Accra 1995; Band C4; m 1993 Cecily Jacqueline Newby.

Ramsay, Paul Andrew, MBE (1988); First Secretary (Management) Singapore since January 1997; born 10/10/55; FCO 1975; East Berlin 1977; Istanbul 1979; Brussels (UKDEL NATO) 1981; Tehran 1984; FCO 1987 (Second Secretary 1990); Second Secretary Madrid 1992; m 1980 Carey-Jane Lambert (1d 1987; 2s 1989, 1993).

Ramscar, Michael Charles; Counsellor FCO since December 2000; born 26/02/48; Second Secretary FCO 1975; Second Secretary (Economic) Lagos 1977; First Secretary (Economic) Brasilia 1979; First Secretary FCO 1982; Madrid 1986; San José 1989; First Secretary FCO 1991; Counsellor

Madrid 1997; m 1970 Janis Lemon (2s 1976, 1981).

Ramsden, Sir John (Charles Josslyn), Bt; Head of Central and North West European Department FCO since June 1999; born 19/08/50; FCO 1975; Third later Second Secretary Dakar 1976; First Secretary Vienna (UKDEL MBFR) 1979; First Secretary, Head of Chancery and Consul Hanoi 1980; First Secretary FCO 1982; First Secretary FCO 1988; On loan to HM Treasury 1988; Counsellor and Deputy Head of Mission East Berlin later British Embassy Berlin Office 1990; Counsellor FCO 1993; Deputy Head of Mission Geneva (UKMIS) 1996; m 1985 Jane Bevan (2d 1987, 1989).

Ramsey, Patricia Anne; Second later First Secretary (Political) Berlin since September 1998; born 09/01/48; FO 1967; Brussels (UKDEL EEC) 1969; Rio de Janeiro 1972; FCO 1974; Athens 1980; Geneva (UKMIS) 1983; FCO 1986; Paris 1987; SUPL 1991; FCO 1992; SUPL 1997; Band C4; m 1990 Paul Lever.

Rangarajan, Francis Vijay Narasimhan; FCO since November 1999; born 22/09/69; FCO IGC Unit, EUD(I) 1995; Second later First Secretary (Trade Policy and Antici) Brussels (UKREP) 1997; Private Secretary to Permanent Under-Secretary of State 1999; m 2000 Rosie Francis Cox.

Rankin, John James; Counsellor and Deputy Head of Mission Dublin since September 1999; born 12/03/57; Assistant, later Senior Legal Adviser FCO 1988; Legal Adviser Geneva (UKMIS & UKDIS) 1991; Legal Counsellor FCO 1995; First Secretary FCO 1996; First Secretary Dublin 1998; m 1987 Lesley Marshall (2d 1989, 1991; 1s 1993).

Ranson, Catherine Fraser (née Armstrong); Athens since February 1989; born 16/07/53; FCO 1971; Paris 1974; Gaborone 1977; FCO 1980; Manila 1985; Band B3; m 1981 Clive Paul Ranson.

Rapp, Stephen Robert; Vice-Consul Lahore since July 2001; born 09/03/52; FCO 1986; Home Office 1986; Accra 1988; Hanoi 1992; FCO 1994; Vice-Consul Jedda 1996; Ekaterinburg 1999; Band B3; m 1978 Judy Elizabeth Flewett.

Ratcliffe, Deborah; T/D Islamabad since January 2001; born 06/04/62; FCO 1980; Geneva (UKMIS) 1982; Harare 1985; Manila 1988; FCO 1991; Vice-Consul Hanoi 1995; Third Secretary (Management) Kingston 1997; Band C4.

Ratcliffe, Yvonne; Singapore since August 2000; born 18/06/62; FCO 1988; Athens 1989; Peking 1992; FCO 1994; Prague 1996; T/D Khartoum 1999; Band B3.

Raven, Martin Clark; Counsellor Stockholm since August 1998; born 10/03/54; FCO 1976; Third Secretary Lagos 1978; Third later Second Secretary New Delhi 1979; FCO 1979; Second later First Secretary FCO 1983; First Secretary New York (UKMIS) 1988; First Secretary FCO

1993; Counsellor FCO 1996; m 1978 Philippa Michaela Morrice Ruddick (2s 1982, 1984).

Rawbone, Jane Lynn; Canberra since April 2000; born 21/03/53; FCO 1976; Vienna (UKDEL MBFR) 1977; Helsinki 1980; FCO 1982; Mexico City 1984; New York (UKMIS) 1988; Madrid 1991; FCO 1993; Kuala Lumpur 1996; Band B3.

Rawlins, Helen Catherine; Second Secretary (Consular) Kampala since May 1998; born 31/07/64; FCO 1986; Bonn 1988; Manila 1991; Second Secretary FCO 1994.

Rawlinson, Colin James; Consul-General Vancouver since November 2002; born 21/02/46; FCO 1967; Reykjavik 1968; Nicosia 1971; Hamburg 1973; Second Secretary FCO 1976; Copenhagen 1979; Second Secretary (Commercial) New Delhi 1981; First Secretary FCO 1984; New York (UKMIS) 1993; FCO 1994; Consul-General Bordeaux 1998; m 1966 The Hon Catharine Julia Trend (2d 1967, 1969).

Rawlinson, Ivor Jon, OBE (1988); FCO since March 2002; born 24/01/42; FO 1964; Warsaw 1966; Bridgetown 1969; Second Secretary FCO 1971; Assistant Private Secretary to Minister of State FCO 1973; Second Secretary (Economic) Paris 1974; First Secretary FCO 1978; First Secretary (Commercial) Mexico City 1980; Consul Florence 1984; First Secretary later Counsellor FCO 1988; Consul-General Montreal 1993; Royal College of Defence Studies 1993; HM Ambassador Tunis 1999-2002; m 1976 Catherine Paule Caudal (1s 1980; 2d 1977, 1983).

Rawlinson, Timothy Simeon; First Secretary FCO since May 2000; born 12/01/62; Second Secretary FCO 1988; Second later First Secretary (Information) Lagos 1991; First Secretary FCO 1993; First Secretary (Political) Stockholm 1996; Band D6; m 1998 Janet Mary Cooper.

Rayner, Robert Alan; Counsellor (Atomic Energy) Tokyo since January 2001; born 14/12/50; FCO 1968; Islamabad 1972; Language Training 1974; Tokyo 1975; DOT 1979; FCO 1981; Second Secretary (Chancery/Information) and Vice-Consul Lima 1984; FCO 1987; Consul (Commercial) Osaka 1989; First Secretary (Press and Public Affairs) Tokyo 1995; First Secretary FCO 1999; m 1984 Dawn Carol Ashton (1d 1991).

Rea, Elizabeth Rose, MBE (1993); FCO since May 1996; born 31/10/54; FCO 1976; Luxembourg 1978; Lima 1981; Washington 1984; FCO 1987; Brussels (UKREP) 1992; Band B3.

Read, Rachel Frances; FCO since August 1996; born 23/10/65; FCO 1989; Cairo 1991; Sofia 1994; Band A2.

Reader, David George; High Commissioner Mbabane since September 2001; born 01/10/47; CRO, DSAO and FCO 1964; Warsaw 1969; Paris 1972; Bucharest 1974; FCO 1976; Kinshasa 1979; Kathmandu 1982; Second Secretary FCO 1984; Vice-Consul (Commercial) Brisbane 1987; First Secretary (Management) and Consul Belgrade

1992; First Secretary FCO 1996; First Secretary Cairo 1998; m 1969 Elaine McKnight (1s 1975; 1d 1980).

Rebecchi, Silvano Marco Raffaele; Second Secretary (Commercial) Helsinki since August 2000; born 14/08/52; Department of Education and Science 1972; FCO 1975; Baghdad 1977; Valletta 1981; Dhaka 1984; FCO 1986; Paris 1990; Cairo 1992; Amman 1992; Second Secretary FCO 1996; Full-Time Language Training 2000; m 1984 Eileen Zammit (2s 1985, 1987).

Reddaway, David Norman, CMG (1993), MBE (1980); UK Special Representative for Afghanistan, with personal rank of Ambassador and Visiting Fellow at Harvard University since August 2002; born 26/04/53; FCO 1975; Language Training SOAS 1976; Third later Second Secretary (Commercial) Tehran 1977; Language Training Iran 1977; Second later First Secretary (Chancery) Tehran 1978; First Secretary (Chancery) Madrid 1982; First Secretary FCO 1985; Private Secretary to Minister of State 1986; First Secretary (Chancery) New Delhi 1988; Chargé d'Affaires a.i. Tehran 1990 (Counsellor 1991); Minister and Deputy Head of Mission Buenos Aires 1993; FCO 1997; Director, Public Services 1999; m 1981 Roshan Taliyeh Firouz (2s 1983, 1996; 1d 1987).

Redden, Michael James; Management Office Gaborone since January 2002; born 22/02/70; DHSS 1987; FCO 1990; Khartoum 1994; FCO 1997; Colombo 1998; Band B3; m 1995 Nicola Jane Elizabeth Sharp (1d 1997).

Reddicliffe, Paul, OBE; FCO since August 1997; born 17/03/45; Senior Principal Research Officer FCO 1977; First Secretary Canberra 1985; First Secretary FCO 1989; HM Ambassador Phnom Penh 1994; Band D7; m 1974 Wee Siok Boi (2s 1977, 1979).

Redshaw, Tina Susan; First Secretary (Political) Beijing since July 2000; born 25/01/61; FCO 1999; Band D6; (1d 2001).

Reed, Pamela Karen (née Williams); FCO since August 1999; born 10/05/70; HCS 1989; FCO 1994; Brasilia later São Paulo 1997; Band A2; m 1997 Antony Jason Reed.

Reeve, Charles Michael Campbell; First Secretary (Political) Zagreb since April 2001; born 12/07/71; Second Secretary FCO 1997; Second Secretary (Political/Military) Banja Luka 1999; Band D6.

Reeve, Richard Robert; Counsellor FCO since June 2000; born 28/07/48; FCO 1971; Third later Second Secretary Singapore 1973; Language Training Cambridge University 1975; Language Training Hong Kong 1976; Trade Commissioner Hong Kong 1977; First Secretary FCO 1981; First Secretary Hong Kong 1983; First Secretary FCO 1987; Counsellor Berne 1996; m 1971 Monique Marie-Louise Moggio (2s 1974, 1977).

Reeves, Ceinwen Mary; FCO since September 2001; born 09/06/57; SUPL 1976; FCO 1976;

FCO 1979; Bonn 1982; Lilongwe 1984; Paris 1987; FCO 1989; Vice-Consul Sofia 1993; Second Secretary (Commercial) Beijing 1995; FCO 1998; SUPL 2000; m 1990 Peter Clive Wilkinson (diss 1994).

Regan, Michael John; Counsellor FCO since September 1998; born 17/08/55; FCO 1983; Second later First Secretary Kabul 1986; FCO 1988; First Secretary (Chancery/Economic) Dubai 1989; First Secretary FCO 1991; Bangkok 1995; m 1986 Carolyn Gaye Black (2s 1987, 1989).

Rehal, Opinder Kumar; Canberra since April 1992; born 15/09/48; FCO 1979; Bonn 1982; FCO 1985; Islamabad 1989; FCO 1990; Band C5; m 1974 Jagdeep Nandra (1s 1975 (dec'd 1990); 1d 1978).

Reid, Gordon Bryden; Deputy Head of Mission Budapest since July 1998; born 09/05/56; FCO 1980; Second Secretary Budapest 1982; First Secretary FCO 1985; First Secretary (Chancery) Santiago 1988; First Secretary (Chancery) Islamabad 1990; First Secretary FCO 1994; m 1979 Marinella Ferro (2s 1982, 1988; 1d 1984).

Reid, Norma Fraser; Third Secretary (Consular) Nicosia since March 1997; born 19/08/43; Saigon 1968; Rome 1970; Bucharest 1971; FCO 1973; HCS 1975; Latin America Floater 1977; Peking 1979; FCO 1980; Moscow 1983; FCO 1984; Rome 1986; FCO 1988; Bucharest 1993.

Reid, Thomas Samuel; T/D Second Secretary Harare since January 2002; born 28/12/76; FCO 2000; Band C4.

Reidy, Andrea Jane; Deputy High Commissioner Freetown since September 2000; born 24/11/58; FCO 1995; Second Secretary (KHF) Bratislava 1997; (1d 1981).

Reilly, Julian; FCO since June 2000; born 03/02/71; FCO 1993; Full-Time Language Training 1994; Full-Time Language Training Cairo 1995; Second Secretary (Chancery) Khartoum 1996.

Reilly, Michael David; Head of Cultural Relations Department FCO since May 2000; born 01/03/55; FCO 1978; Language Training Seoul 1979; First Secretary FCO 1984; First Secretary Paris (UKDEL OECD) 1988; First Secretary (Political) and Consul Seoul 1991; First Secretary FCO 1994; Deputy Head of Mission Manila 1996; m 1981 Won-Kyong Kang (1d 1987; 1s 1992).

Reilly, Michael Patrick; FCO since December 1997; born 30/07/66; FCO 1984; Bonn 1987; Bombay 1990; FCO 1991; Third Secretary (Development) Lilongwe 1994; Band C4; m 1991 Andrea Louise Bradley.

Reilly, Patrick; First Secretary (Political) Dublin since January 2002; born 03/11/70; FCO 1995; Second Secretary (Political) Cape Town 1997; FCO 2000; Band C4.

Reilly, Peter Marius Julian Prowse; Second Secretary FCO since October 1996; born 03/02/71;

FCO 1993; Full-Time Language Training 1994; Full-Time Language Training Cairo 1995; Second Secretary (Chancery) Khartoum 1996.

Reilly, Richard John; Peking since March 2002; born 17/09/73; FCO 1999; Band A2; m 2001 Angela Forsyth.

Reilly, Thomas Saul Anthony; Second Secretary (Political) Buenos Aires since July 2001; born 17/11/70; Second Secretary FCO 1998; Band C4.

Remmington, Gillian Elizabeth; Hong Kong since December 2000; born 26/02/56; FCO 1984; Quito 1985; Berne 1988; World Wide Floater Duties 1991; FCO 1993; Nicosia 1997; Band B3.

Renfrew, Laura; Abidjan since August 1995; born 16/03/62; FCO 1984; Moscow 1986; FCO 1988; Damascus 1989; FCO 1992; Full-Time Language Training 1995; Band B3.

Rennie, Brian William; FCO since December 1989; born 06/02/40; FO 1964; Bangkok 1965; FO (later FCO) 1967; St Helena 1969; FCO 1971; Tehran 1972; FCO 1975; Darwin 1976; FCO 1978; Warsaw 1979; FCO 1981; Attaché Havana 1982; FCO 1985; Rangoon 1986; Band C4; m 1963 Annie Daurge (2s 1964, 1971; 1d 1967).

Rennie, Nadia Jane; Kiev since May 2000; born 30/09/71; FCO 1990; Brussels (UKDEL NATO) 1994; Band B3.

Reuter, Alan; Consul Milan since February 2000; born 05/07/51; FCO 1970; Bucharest 1972; Kaduna 1974; Frankfurt 1978; Gaborone 1980; FCO 1982; Tel Aviv 1986; Third Secretary (Commercial) Kuala Lumpur 1988; Second Secretary FCO 1992; Second Secretary (Consular/Immigration) Lagos 1995; Nairobi 1998; FCO 1999; Band C4; m (1) 1973 Christine Caton; (2) 1982 Brenda Yvonne Mary Neumann (1s 1983; 1d 1985).

Revington, Thomas Mark Bowen; Second Secretary FCO since January 2002; born 19/09/73; FCO 1997; Vice-Consul (Political) Istanbul 1999; Band C4.

Rey, Rosemary; SUPL since April 1996; born 14/03/55; FCO 1974; Cayman Islands 1976; FCO 1978; Gibraltar 1979; Bogotá 1981; FCO 1986; Bogotá 1988; Caracas 1990; Band B3; m 1983 Alvaro Rey Romero (2s 1991, 1995).

Reynolds, Colin; Assistant Private Secretary to Minister of State FCO since October 1999; born 03/07/71; FCO 1990; Nicosia 1992; Africa/Middle East Floater 1995; Second Secretary FCO 1998.

Reynolds, Gillian Marjorie; FCO since October 1993; born 16/10/50; FCO 1976; New Delhi 1977; Budapest 1979; Mbabane 1981; FCO 1984; Singapore 1987; Peking 1991; Band B3.

Reynolds, Heather (née Turnbull); FCO since December 1991; born 30/05/54; FCO 1973; Moscow 1975; FCO 1976; Brasilia 1977; Bridgetown 1980; SUPL 1983; Kuala Lumpur

1984; FCO 1986; Prague 1988; SUPL 1990; Band B3; m 1982 Keith James Reynolds (1s 1990).

Reynolds, Keith James; Moscow since August 1999; born 02/08/44; FCO 1969; Bridgetown 1980; Kuala Lumpur 1982; FCO 1986; Second Secretary Prague 1988; Second Secretary FCO 1990; Second Secretary New Delhi 1993; Second Secretary FCO 1997; Band C5; m 1982 Heather Turnbull (1s 1990).

Reynolds, Leslie Roy; Dublin since May 1997; born 22/09/59; DTI 1978; Passport Office 1979; FCO 1984; HO 1984; Wellington 1986; Islamabad 1988; FCO 1992; Band B3; m 1982 Tracey Sapsford.

Reynolds, Martin Alexander Baillie; Second Secretary (Economic/Commercial) Singapore since September 1998; born 05/06/69; FCO 1997; Band D6.

Reynolds, Victoria Caroline; FCO since February 2001; born 07/06/69; FCO 1988; Lagos/Abuja 1992; FCO 1994; Mexico City 1996; Tallinn 1997; Band B3.

Rhodes, Ian Peter; Second Secretary FCO since September 1998; born 12/04/60; Second Secretary FCO 1986; Nicosia 1995; Band C4.

Rice, Douglas; Resident Acting High Commissioner Castries since May 2001; born 28/01/46; FO 1964; Jedda 1968; Paris 1970; Sana'a 1972; Sofia 1973; FCO 1974; Full-Time Language Training 1977; Doha 1978; Düsseldorf 1982; Second Secretary (Consular/Passports) Singapore 1983; Second later First Secretary FCO 1986; First Secretary (Press and Public Affairs) Madrid 1993; FCO 1998; m (1) 1969 Christine Elizabeth Chisholm (1d 1973; 1s 1977); (2) 1995 Allison Denise Hay.

Rice, John Gordon; Deputy Head of Mission Lilongwe since October 1997; born 06/01/46; Home Office 1962; Commonwealth Office DSAO and FCO 1967; Ankara 1969; Paris 1972; FCO 1976; Seoul 1978; Assistant Trade Commissioner (Second Secretary) Hong Kong 1980; FCO 1985 (Parliamentary Clerk); First Secretary (Commercial) and Head of Chancery Doha 1988; Deputy High Commissioner Windhoek 1992; First Secretary FCO 1995; m 1972 Gail Marjorie Pearce (2s 1975, 1979; 1d 1976).

Richards, Claire Michelle; FCO since December 2000; born 09/12/72; FCO 1991; Bangkok 1997; Band A2.

Richards, Sir Francis Neville, KCMG (2002), CMG (1994), CVO (1991); Head of GCHQ Cheltenham August 1998; born 18/11/45; Army 1967-69; Third Secretary FCO 1969; Moscow 1971; Second later First Secretary Vienna (UKDEL MBFR) 1973; First Secretary FCO 1976; Counsellor (Commercial/Economic) New Delhi 1985; Counsellor FCO 1988; High Commissioner Windhoek 1990; Minister Moscow 1992; AUS (Central and Eastern Europe) FCO 1995; Director (Europe) 1996; DUSS (Defence and Intelligence)

1998; m 1971 Gillian Brûce Nevill (1s 1975; 1d 1977).

Richards, Ian; Consul (Commercial) Shanghai since November 1996; born 07/10/62; FCO 1993; Full-Time Language Training 1994; Band C4.

Richards, Miranda Jane; Mexico City since June 1996; born 20/01/69; FCO 1994; Band A2.

Richards, Owen Jeremy; On loan to the DTI since September 2000; born 28/06/66; FCO 1988; Bombay 1991; Third Secretary (ECE/UNCTAD) Geneva (UKMIS) 1995; Band C4.

Richards, Rodney, MBE (1986); FCO since April 1991; born 27/08/48; FO 1967; Geneva 1970; Phnom Penh 1972; Islamabad 1973; FCO 1975; Saigon 1975; Jakarta 1976; FCO 1978; Nairobi 1983; Kampala 1986; Band A2.

Richards, Steven Thomas; Second Secretary (Commercial) Dublin since July 2000; born 29/01/58; FCO 1978; New Delhi 1980; Beirut 1982; Europe Floater 1985; FCO 1987; FCO 1988; Warsaw 1988; Vice-Consul Moscow 1990; FCO 1993 (Second Secretary 1994); Second Secretary (Management/Consular) Valletta 1996; Band C4; m 1989 Tracey Lee Barnett (1d 1995).

Richardson, Christine Lynn; Baku since June 1998; born 04/10/67; FCO 1987; Brussels (UKREP) 1989; Africa/Middle East Floater 1992; On loan to DTI 1997; Band B3.

Richardson, Michael John; Second Secretary (Regional Affairs) Seoul since November 2001; born 16/05/66; FCO 1985; Warsaw 1988; FCO 1991; Attaché Cairo 1993; FCO 1996; Band C4; m 1989 Audrey Zena Fairall (1s 1994).

Richman, Menna Frances; First Secretary Tel Aviv since September 1998; born 16/09/67; FCO 1989; Third later Second Secretary (Institutions) Brussels (UKREP) 1991; Second Secretary (Economic/Environment) Nairobi 1993; FCO 1997; SUPL 1998; m 1990 Stephen Charles Richman.

Richmond, Alan Thomas; Second Secretary (Economic) Ottawa since July 1999; born 22/04/55; Department of Education 1973; FCO 1975; Maputo 1977; Lima 1981; FCO 1983; Islamabad 1985; Singapore 1988; FCO 1991; Full-Time Language Training 1994; Abidjan 1995; Band C4; m 1976 Iseabal MacLean Graham (1d 1986).

Richmond, David Frank; Political and Security Committee Representative Brussels (UKREP) since March 2000 (and Permanent Representative to the Council of the WEU since January 2001); born 09/07/54; FCO 1976; Language Training MECAS 1977; Third later Second Secretary Baghdad 1979; Second later First Secretary FCO 1982; First Secretary (External Trade) Brussels (UKREP) 1987; Deputy Head of NENAD FCO 1991; Head of Economic Relations Department 1994; Head of Chancery New York (UKMIS)

1996; m 1990 Caroline Florence Pascale Matagne (1s 1992; 1d 1994).

Rickerd, Martin John Kilburn, MVO (1985); Deputy Head of Mission Abidjan since August 2000; born 17/08/54; FCO 1972; Brussels (UKDEL NATO) 1975; Wellington 1978; Assistant Private Secretary to Parliamentary Under Secretary of State 1980; Bridgetown 1982; Consul (Information) Milan 1986; First Secretary FCO 1991; Head of Chancery Singapore 1995; On secondment to the Standard Chartered Bank 1998; FCO 2000; Band D6; m 1976 Charmain Gwendoline Napier (2s 1986, 1988).

Ricketts, Peter Forbes, CMG (1999); Political Director and Deputy Under-Secretary FCO since September 2001; born 30/09/52; FCO 1974; New York 1974; Third Secretary Singapore 1975; FCO 1975; Second Secretary Brussels (UKDEL NATO) 1978; First Secretary FCO 1982; APS to Secretary of State 1983; First Secretary (Chancery) Washington 1986; First Secretary later Counsellor FCO 1989; Counsellor (EC/Finance) Paris 1994; Deputy Political Director FCO 1997; Director International Security FCO 1999; On loan to the Cabinet Office as Chairman of the Joint Intelligence Committee 2000; m 1980 Suzanne Julia Horlington (1s 1982; 1d 1987).

Rickitt, Clare Louise; First Secretary FCO since August 1996; born 20/09/64; FCO 1991; Full-Time Language Training 1992; Second Secretary (Economic Trade Policy) Brasilia 1993.

Rickward, Charlotte Lucy; Manila since June 2000; born 12/05/72; FCO 1997; Band A2; m 1994 Jarlath Ambrose.

Ridley, Michelle; Grand Turk since August 2002; born 22/01/63; DHSS 1986-87; FCO 1987; Kaduna 1990; Peking 1993; New York (UKMIS) 1997; Band A2.

Ridout, Anthony Robert; Second Secretary (Political) Kingston since June 2001; born 31/03/66; FCO 1986; New Delhi 1989; Paris 1992; FCO 1995; Second Secretary Cairo 1996; Second Secretary FCO 1998; Band C4; m 1989 Karen Marie Hendy (1d 1991).

Ridout, Richard William; Third Secretary (Political) Hanoi since July 2002; born 19/11/67; FCO 1986; Moscow 1990; FCO 1993; Third Secretary Riyadh 1994; FCO 1998; Band B3; m 1992 Sarah Beth Evans (1d 1996).

Ridout, William Anthony Frederick; HM Consul Hong Kong since July 2001; born 27/04/50; MOD 1970; FCO 1974; Islamabad 1976; Stuttgart 1979; FCO 1982; Bridgetown 1982; Bombay 1984; Second Secretary (Commercial) East Berlin 1988; Consul Milan 1990; FCO 1995; Deputy Head of Mission Khartoum 1997; First Secretary (Commercial) Tripoli 1999; m (1) 1971 Muriel Jessica Stewart Benigan (diss); (2) 1980 Frances Mary Bond (diss); (3) 1996 Louise Victoria Burrett.

Riley, John Lawrence; Third Secretary (Aid) Gaborone since July 1999; born 13/08/61; FCO 1982; Cairo 1984; Ankara 1986; FCO 1986; Hanoi 1991; FCO 1992; New Delhi 1995; m (1) 1982 Caroline Peacock (diss); m (2) 1990 Ayce Birergin.

Rimmer, Ronald Stanley; Deputy High Commissioner Banjul since December 2001; born 24/02/54; Royal Air Force 1972-95; FCO 1995; Lagos 1998; Band C4.

Ringham, Christine Mary; SUPL since February 2000; born 11/12/61; FCO 1988; Brussels (UKDEL) 1991; Prague 1995; FCO 1998; Band A2; m 1998 Kevin P Ringham.

Ripard, Elizabeth Anne (née Auld); Deputy High Commissioner Mbabane since March 2002; born 27/06/57; FCO 1976; Madrid 1979; SE Asia Floater 1982; San José 1984; FCO 1988; Third Secretary Valletta 1991; Third later Second Secretary FCO 1994; Second Secretary Abidjan 1998; Language Training 1998; m 1992 Nicholas Charles Ripard (diss).

Ritchie, Joseph Battle; FCO since January 1998; born 13/07/44; RAF 1961-91; Band A2; m Paula May (1d 1975; 1s 1980).

Ritchie, Paul John, OBE (1994); Counsellor Nicosia since July 1999; born 26/03/62; FCO 1983; Second Secretary (Chancery) Nicosia 1986; Second later First Secretary FCO 1988; First Secretary New York (UKMIS) 1991; First Secretary FCO 1996; m 1991 Jane Risely (1d 1997; 1s 2002).

Rixon, Margaret Carol; Dublin since May 1999; born 16/02/57; FCO 1976; Castries 1978; Washington 1980; Peking 1982; FCO 1983; Vienna (UKMIS) 1984; East Berlin 1987; Kingston 1988; FCO 1991; Band B3.

Road-Night, Susan Catherine; Mexico City since October 1995; born 13/03/67; FCO 1991; Kiev 1992; Full-Time Language Training 1995; Band A2.

Robbins, Christopher William; Deputy Head of Mission and Consul-General Seoul since November 2001; born 16/06/46; First Secretary FCO 1984; First Secretary (Chancery) New Delhi 1987; First Secretary FCO 1990; Counsellor on loan to the DTI 1991; Counsellor (Commercial) The Hague, later also Consul-General Amsterdam 1994; HM Ambassador Lithuania 1998.

Roberts, Amanda Claire; FCO since May 2000; born 06/09/67; FCO 1989; Santiago 1996 (Second Secretary 1997); Band C4.

Roberts, Catherine Mary; Washington since December 1997; born 05/10/68; FCO 1995; Band A2.

Roberts, Colin; Counsellor (Political) Tokyo since January 2001; born 31/07/59; Called to the Bar 1986; FCO 1989; Second Secretary (Economic) later First Secretary (Political) Tokyo 1990; First Secretary FCO 1995; First Secretary

(Political/Military) Paris 1997; Counsellor FCO 1998; m 2000 Camilla Frances Mary Blair.

Roberts, David Eric; Vancouver since June 1999; born 15/08/54; Customs and Excise 1971; FCO 1973; Lagos 1977; Doha 1979; FCO 1983; Washington 1986; Helsinki 1989; On loan to London Chamber of Commerce 1993; HM Consul Jedda 1995; m 1979 Kim Louise Fyleman (3d 1990, 1992, 1993).

Roberts, David George; Deputy Head of Mission, Director of Trade and Investment and Consul-General for Switzerland and Liechtenstein at the British Embassy in Berne since August 2000; born 11/04/55; FCO 1976; Third later Second Secretary (Chancery) Jakarta 1977; Second Secretary (Chancery) Havana 1981; First Secretary FCO 1984; First Secretary (Economic) Madrid 1988; First Secretary (Financial/EC) Paris 1991; First Secretary FCO 1994; FCO 1994; Deputy Head of Mission Santiago 1996; Full-Time Language Training 2000; m 1985 Rosemarie Rita Kunz (1d 1990; 1s 1992).

Roberts, Gillian (née Phenna); Moscow since June 2002; born 03/12/68; FCO 1986; Cape Town/Pretoria 1988; Buenos Aires 1992; FCO 1995; Third Secretary (Passports) Paris Embassy 1998; Band B3; m 1993 Michael John Roberts.

Roberts, Ian; FCO since November 1993; born 26/10/66; FCO 1987; Buenos Aires 1991; Band A2.

Roberts, Sir Ivor Anthony, KCMG (2000), CMG (1995); HM Ambassador Dublin since February 1999; born 24/09/46; Third Secretary FCO 1968; MECAS 1969; Paris 1970; FCO 1970; Second Secretary 1971; Second later First Secretary FCO 1973; First Secretary (Chancery) later First Secretary (Economic/Commercial/Agriculture) Canberra 1978; First Secretary FCO 1982; Counsellor FCO 1986; Minister Madrid 1989; Chargé d'Affaires and HM Consul-General later HM Ambassador Belgrade 1994; On loan to St Antony's College, Oxford 1997; m 1974 Elizabeth Bray Bernard Smith (2s 1976, 1979; 1d 1982).

Roberts, Michael John Wyn; Head of Division Cabinet Office (European Secretariat) since September 1999; born 04/07/60; Second Secretary FCO 1984; Second later First Secretary (Chancery) Athens 1987; First Secretary FCO 1991; First Secretary (Institutions) Brussels (UKREP) 1995; Band D7; m 1985 Margaret Anne Ozanne (2d 1989, 1991; 1s 1993).

Roberts, Philip John Barclay; Counsellor FCO since June 1999; born 04/12/49; FCO 1973; Third later Second Secretary Islamabad 1977; First Secretary FCO 1980; Head of Chancery and Consul Hanoi 1982; First Secretary Tokyo 1984; First Secretary FCO 1987; First Secretary (Chancery) later Counsellor Lisbon 1991; Counsellor Bogotá 1994; Counsellor FCO 1995; Counsellor Vienna 1997; m 1996 Amparo Jimenez Avilan (1d 1997).

Roberts, Trevor Martin; FCO since October 1995; born 12/07/55; FCO 1974; Geneva (UKMIS) 1978; Floater Duties 1982; Kuwait 1984; Second Secretary FCO 1986; Second Secretary (Commercial) Madrid 1992.

Roberts-Gurr, Anne Catherine; FCO since November 1997; born 07/05/63; FCO 1985; Bucharest 1988; FCO 1990; Floater Duties 1991; FCO 1993; Athens 1995; Band B3; m 2001 Andrew William George Gurr.

Robertson, Brian; Resident Acting High Commissioner St Vincent and The Grenadines since May 1996; born 24/07/45; FO 1963; Cairo 1967; Washington 1968; Castries 1969; Warsaw 1974; FCO 1976; Gaborone 1979; Second Secretary Maseru 1982; First Secretary and Head of Chancery Asunción 1985; First Secretary FCO 1989; First Secretary (Management and HM Consul) Copenhagen 1991; m 1967 Ellen Roberts.

Robertson, Corin Jean Stella (née Leatherbarrow); Second Secretary (Trade Policy) Tokyo since September 1997; born 15/01/72; FCO 1994; Full-Time Language Training 1995; Band C4; m 1996 James Francis Robertson.

Robertson, Emma Jane; Third Secretary (Economic) Damascus since January 2000; born 25/12/71; FCO 1997; Band B3.

Robertson, Henry Macloskie; Second Secretary FCO since January 1987 (First Secretary 1995); born 10/10/41; ECGD 1960; CRO 1961; Zomba 1964; DSAO (later FCO) 1968; Freetown 1970; Tripoli 1972; Vientiane 1974; Kuala Lumpur 1975; FCO 1979; Sana'a 1981; Second Secretary Bridgetown 1985; m 1966 Audrey Lucy Dut (2s 1967, 1970).

Robertson, William Smellie; Third Secretary (Aid/Information) Harare since February 1996; born 05/03/66; FCO 1984; Dublin 1986; Riyadh 1989; On loan to the ODA 1992; Band B3; m 1986 Catherine Elizabeth McGregor (1d 1992; 2s 1995, 2002).

Robins, Terence Frederick; Second Secretary (Chancery) Strasbourg since May 1999; born 15/10/66; FCO 1989; Vice-Consul Algiers 1991; Victoria 1995; Band C4; m 1994 Wassila Kerri.

Robinson, David John, MBE (2002); FCO since January 1988; born 27/02/45; Army 1962-85; Moscow 1985; Baghdad 1986; Band B3; m 1976 Pauline Reed.

Robinson, Deborah; Tel Aviv since February 1996; born 20/04/58; FCO 1989; Maputo 1990; Algiers 1994; Band A2.

Robinson, Janice Kathleen; Jerusalem since September 1999; born 28/09/56; FCO 1995; Bonn 1997; Band A2.

Robinson, Julia; New York (UKMIS) since January 2000; born 24/09/50; FCO 1995; The Hague 1996; Band A2.

Robinson, Julie Anne (née Whitehead); FCO since September 1995; born 02/08/63; FCO 1984; Washington 1985; Bahrain 1988; FCO 1991; SUPL 1993; Band B3.

Robinson, Michael John; Counsellor (Regional Affairs) Budapest since November 2000; born 19/12/46; Third Secretary FCO 1968; Language Training 1969; Third later Second Secretary Moscow 1970; Second later First Secretary (Information) Madrid 1972; First Secretary FCO 1977; Madrid (CSCE) 1980; First Secretary and Head of Chancery Madrid 1981; SUPL with OECD Paris 1982; Deputy Head of Delegation Paris (UKDEL UNESCO) 1985; First Secretary FCO 1986 (Counsellor 1990); Deputy Head of Mission and Consul-General Belgrade 1990; Counsellor on CDA at Chatham House 1994; Deputy Governor Gibraltar 1995; FCO 1999; m 1971 Anne Jamieson Scott (2d 1974, 1987; 2s 1977, 1983).

Robinson, Philip Andrew; First Secretary (Management) Beijing since July 2001; born 18/09/51; FCO 1970; Warsaw 1973; Jedda 1974; FCO 1977; Wellington 1978; Islamabad 1980; FCO 1982; Johannesburg 1985; Moscow 1987; (Second Secretary 1988); Second Secretary FCO 1991; HM Consul Hong Kong 1996; Band D6; m 1972 Elizabeth Andrina Mathieson Riding (2d 1976, 1980).

Robinson, Susan Patricia; Gibraltar since July 1995; born 06/11/47; FCO 1979; Paris 1980; Helsinki 1982; Bridgetown 1986; FCO 1989; Band B3.

Robinson, William; Dublin since February 2000; born 26/11/44; RAF Regiment 1962; Islamabad 1987; Moscow 1991; Pretoria 1992; Amman 1996; Band C4; m 1966 Cynthia Margaret Pugh (2s 1966, 1969).

Robson, Elizabeth Carol; Deputy Head of Mission Copenhagen since March 2002; born 14/01/55; FCO 1977; Latin America Floater 1981; FCO 1982; Moscow 1984; Second Secretary FCO 1985; Second later First Secretary (Chancery) Geneva (UKMIS) 1988; Counsellor FCO 1993; Counsellor (Political) Stockholm 1996.

Roche, Claire Louise; Floater Duties since August 1998; born 17/03/72; FCO 1991; Warsaw 1995; Band B3.

Roche, Shaun Martin; Nairobi since April 2001; born 23/01/68; FCO 1992; Band C4; m 2001 Rebecca Louise York.

Rock, Gail Denise (née Purvis); SUPL since June 1993; born 26/06/56; FCO 1978; Mexico 1979; Rome 1981; FCO 1984; Islamabad 1987; FCO 1988; Tokyo 1990; Band B3; m Dereck Anthony Rock.

Rodemark, Janet Mary; SUPL since July 1999; born 28/05/65; FCO 1988; Islamabad 1992; Second Secretary FCO 1996; Band C4; m 1993 Timothy John Colley (1s 1997; 2d 1999, 2002).

Roden, Joel Charles; FCO since April 2002; born 24/02/77; Band C4; m 2000 Camila Miranda.

Rodgers, Catherine Mary; FCO since November 1996; born 18/04/46; FCO 1965; Resigned 1968; FCO 1990; SUPL 1993; New York (UKMIS) 1995; SUPL 1997; Band A2; m 1968 James Patrick Rodgers (2d 1970, 1972; 1s 1975).

Roe, Kirstie Gordon; FCO since October 1997; born 25/08/46; WRNS 1965-73; FCO 1974; New Delhi 1976; Hanover 1979; Bonn 1980; FCO 1982; Colombo 1985; Bucharest 1988 (Second Secretary 1991); On secondment to MOD 1992; Full-Time Language Training; Deputy Head of Mission Riga 1994; T/D Belgrade 1997.

Rogan, Janet Elizabeth; Deputy Head of Mission Sarajevo since February 1998; born 19/12/62; FCO 1986; Language Training 1988; Language Training Hong Kong 1989; Second later First Secretary (Chancery) Peking 1991; On loan to Cabinet Office 1994; First Secretary FCO 1995.

Rogers, David Alan; Counsellor FCO since December 1996; born 16/05/49; FCO 1971; Copenhagen 1974; Second Secretary 1975; Second later First Secretary FCO 1978; Jakarta 1981; First Secretary Brunei 1983; First Secretary FCO 1985; First Secretary (Chancery) Islamabad 1988; First Secretary FCO 1991; First Secretary (Political) Muscat 1993; First Secretary (Chancery/Economic) Dubai 1995; m 1989 Julie Anne Gardiner (1d 1990; 2s 1992, 1994).

Rogers, Diana Caroline; SUPL since November 2001; born 30/07/74; FCO 1998; World Wide Floater Duties 2000; Band B3.

Rogers, Michael Roy; SUPL since August 2000; born 14/12/48; FCO 1967; Tunis 1973; Bridgetown 1975; Pretoria/Cape Town 1976; FCO 1978; Bahrain 1981; Wellington 1984; Resigned 1989; Reinstated 1990; Second Secretary FCO 1990; Second Secretary (Management) JMO New York 1995; m 1970 Elaine Anne Stewart (2s 1980, 1986).

Roissetter, Frederick Charles; FCO since June 1998; born 09/10/50; Army 1966-77; FCO 1978; Cabinet Office 1979-81; Paris 1982; FCO 1984; Third later Second Secretary Tel Aviv 1989; FCO 1992; Athens 1995; m 1979 Kay Jacqueline (2d 1981, 1984; 1s 1986).

Rolt, Colette; FCO since February 2001; born 10/08/71; FCO 1989; Washington 1997; Band C4.

Rooney, Kay (née Smith); SUPL since July 1998; born 01/07/68; FCO 1990; Vienna 1993; Vice-Consul Frankfurt 1996; FCO 1996; Band B3; m 2000 Michael Rooney.

Rooney, Sean Michael; Düsseldorf since June 2000; born 17/02/72; FCO 1991; Vienna (UKDEL) 1995; Dhaka 1996; Band B3; m 2000 Kay Smith.

Roper, Martyn Keith; First Secretary (Economic) OECD Paris since July 1999; born 08/06/65; FCO 1984; Tehran 1986; Maputo 1988; Vice-Consul

Kuwait 1990; FCO 1993; Third Secretary (Political/Aid) Karachi 1993; Band D6; m 1989 Elisabeth Melanie Harman Watson (1s 1992; 1d 1995).

Roper, Neil Gregson; Second Secretary (Technical Management) Pretoria since August 2000; born 27/11/65; FCO 1987; Madrid 1993; FCO 1995; Band C4.

Roscoe, Helen Margaret; Second Secretary (Management) Berlin since March 2001; born 25/07/67; FCO 1987; Oslo 1989; Lagos 1992; FCO 1995; Band C4.

Rose, Philip Edmond; First Secretary FCO since January 1994; born 12/12/63; FCO 1987; Language Training 1988; Language Training Hong Kong 1989; Second Secretary (Commercial) Peking 1991.

Roskilly, Karen Elizabeth; Second Secretary (Management) Madrid since September 2001; born 18/10/65; FCO 1990; Amsterdam 1991; Gibraltar 1994; SUPL 1998; Band B3; m 1995 Antonio Gonzalez Saugar (1s 2000).

Ross, Barry Thomas; FCO since August 1994; born 22/08/65; FCO 1985; Tokyo 1987; FCO 1990; SUPL 1991; FCO 1993; SUPL 1993; Band B3.

Ross, Carne William; SUPL since June 2002; born 24/08/66; FCO 1989; Third later Second Secretary (Political) Bonn 1992; First Secretary FCO 1995; New York (UKMIS) 1997.

Ross, William Lawson; First Secretary (Commercial) Nicosia since June 2000; born 13/09/53; FCO 1973; New York (UKMIS) 1975; CG New York 1977; Tunis 1978; Kinshasa 1981; FCO 1984; Nassau 1985; Warsaw 1988; FCO 1991 (Second Secretary 1993); HM Consul and Second Secretary (Commercial) Al Khobar 1995; Full-Time Language Training 2000; Band C5; m 1978 Mary Margaret Delaney (1d 1980; 1s 1982).

Ross, Yolanda Marie; Bucharest since December 1998; born 16/05/69; FCO 1988; Buenos Aires 1993; FCO 1997; FCO 1998; Band A2.

Ross McDowell, Amanda (née Ross); Vice-Consul (Commercial) Sydney since June 1999; born 25/11/62; FCO 1981; 10 Downing St 1985; Cape Town 1988; Zurich 1991; Second Secretary FCO 1994; Second Secretary (Commercial) Addis Ababa 1997; m 1987 Christopher McDowell (1d 1990; 1s 1992).

Rossiter, Lynne; Copenhagen since July 2002; born 10/08/50; FCO 1990; Tel Aviv 1992; Floater Duties 1995; Band B3.

Rothery, James Peter; FCO since September 1985(Second Secretary 1993); born 15/04/51; FCO 1975; Masirah 1977; Washington 1982; Band D6; m 1996 Agnes Maria Smith.

Rous, Matthew James; Deputy Head of Mission Brussels since February 2002; born 29/06/64; FCO 1991; Full-Time Language Training SOAS 1992;

Full-Time Language Training Peking 1993; Second later First Secretary (Chancery) Peking 1994; First Secretary (Commercial) Tokyo 1998; m 1989 Beryl Ann Scott (2d 1992, 1998; 1s 1994).

Rouse, Philip Terence, MBE (1976); HM Ambassador Ulaanbaatar since December 2001; born 13/10/43; Ministry of Aviation 1960; MOD 1966; FO (later FCO) 1967; Bogotá 1969; Saigon 1973; Singapore 1973; FCO 1975; Bahrain 1979; Asunción 1981; Second Secretary FCO 1985; First Secretary, Resident Representative Castries 1990; First Secretary FCO 1995; Deputy Head of Mission Kampala 1997; m 1968 Janice Eileen Williamson (3s 1971, 1974, 1978).

Rousseau, Jenifer Lesley (née Hill); Paris since December 1986; born 09/07/60; FCO 1983; Kabul 1984; FCO 1986; Band A2; m 1988 Frank Stephane Frederick Rousseau.

Rowbottom, Major Kenneth John; Queen's Messenger 1988; born 04/03/47; HM Forces 1966-86.

Rowe, David Ian; FCO since November 1992; born 16/06/66; FCO 1985; Addis Ababa 1987; Bucharest 1991; Band C4; m 1993 Nancy Elizabeth Vince.

Rowe, Elizabeth Jane; Floater Duties since January 2001; born 19/01/71; FCO 1997; Sarajevo 1998; Band A2.

Rowe, Katherine Jane; FCO since April 2002; born 30/01/78; Band C4; ptnr, Robert Long.

Rowe, Victoria Helen (née Goodwin); Vice-Consul Geneva since July 2000; FCO 1995; Band C4; m 1996 Richard David Rowe.

Rowett, Caroline Sarah; FCO since September 1999; born 16/09/58; FCO 1990; Jakarta 1992; Paris 1996; Band C4; m 1992 Joseph Spurgeon (1d 1998).

Rowland, Keith Irving; Attaché (Management) Abuja since March 2001; born 09/11/46; Royal Navy 1963-88; Islamabad 1988; Moscow 1992; New York 1993; FCO 1996; Band B3; m 1971 Helena Sloan (1s 1972).

Rowlands, Jane Ellen; Third Secretary (Management) and Vice-Consul Ashgabat since August 2001; born 16/03/67; FCO 1987; Mexico City 1989; Seoul 1993; Third Secretary FCO 1997.

Rowlandson, Peter Roderick Saxby; FCO since January 1997; born 22/09/49; FCO 1970; Georgetown 1972; FCO 1976; Brussels 1978; Moscow 1981; FCO 1982; Brussels 1984; Madrid 1985; New Delhi 1988; FCO 1991; Dhaka 1995; Band B3; m (1) 1973 Nancy Lee Townsend (1d 1974); (2) 1989 Jillian Roberts (1s 1990; 1d 1992).

Rowney, Michael Ernest, MBE (1991); First Secretary Security Officer Moscow since June 1998; born 23/06/53; FCO 1972; Warsaw 1975; Kinshasa 1976; Hamilton 1979; Bahrain 1982;

FCO 1985; Vice-Consul Monrovia 1988; Lisbon 1991; FCO 1994.

Rowswell, Claire; FCO since October 1988; born 13/01/55; Quito 1979; FCO 1979; Brussels (UKREP) 1981; Moscow 1984; FCO 1985; Mexico City 1986; Band B3.

Rowton, Alastair Clifford; FCO since January 1998; born 28/11/46; FCO 1979; Gaborone 1981; FCO 1982; Darwin (BGWRS) 1984; FCO 1986; Second Secretary Budapest 1994; Band C4; m 1976 Jean Margaret Cowie (2d 1982, 1986).

Royal, Caroline Patricia; New York (UKMIS) since February 2001; born 22/01/57; MOD 1973; FCO 1990; Lisbon 1992; FCO 1995; Sana'a 1998; Band A2.

Royle, Catherine Jane; First Secretary (EU/Economic) Dublin since July 1997; born 17/08/63; FCO 1986; Third later Second Secretary (Chancery) Santiago 1988; First Secretary FCO 1991; m 1991 Marcelo Enrique Camprubi Valledor (1s 2000).

Rudge, Peter Alan; Second Secretary (Political) Rome since September 2001; born 05/09/73; Second Secretary FCO 1999; Band C4.

Runacres, Mark Alastair; Minister New Delhi since July 2002; born 19/05/59; FCO 1981; Third later Second Secretary New Delhi 1983; Second later First Secretary FCO 1986; First Secretary (Chancery) Paris 1991; First Secretary FCO 1995; On loan to the DTI 1998; Counsellor (Economic) New York (UKMIS) 1999; m 1989 Shawn Reid.

Ruse, Lynne Elaine (née Gerrish); FCO since October 1995; born 15/05/58; FCO 1988; Paris 1991; Band A2; m 1996 Howard Michael Ruse (1d 1998).

Russell, Andrew John; Second later First Secretary later Counsellor FCO since April 1987; born 12/08/48; FO (later FCO) 1967; Bonn 1972; Berlin 1973; FCO 1975; Second Secretary Vienna 1982; m 1972 Marilyn Elizabeth Turp (2d 1974, 1984; 1s 1982).

Russell, Gerard Simon Joseph, MBE (2002); Consul (Political) Jerusalem since September 1998; born 11/07/73; FCO 1995; Full-Time Language Training (Arabic) 1996; Cairo 1997; Band C4.

Russell, Joan; Kingston since January 2000; born 04/05/43; FCO 1986; Vienna (UKMIS) 1988; Lima 1992; Madrid 1995; Band B3.

Russell, Malcolm Arthur; Suva since November 1999; born 27/02/54; FCO 1973; Kuala Lumpur 1976; FCO 1980; Frankfurt 1983; Tehran 1985; Third Secretary Nuku'alofa 1988; Peking 1989; FCO 1992; Band C4; m 1982 Jean Frances Matthews (1d 1987; 1s 1992).

Russell, Neil; SUPL since April 2001; born 18/02/69; FCO 1989; Abu Dhabi 1992; Brasilia 1994; Third Secretary (Information) Warsaw 1998;

Full-Time Language Training 1998; Band B3; m 1993 Trudie Helen Denby (1d 1995).

Russell, Roger; Accra since November 2001; born 14/05/54; FCO 1970; Brussels 1983; FCO 1986; Canberra 1989; FCO 1999; Band C4; m 1983 Teresa Mary McGeough.

Rutherford, John; Regional Director, Invest in Britain Bureau Hong Kong since September 1998; born 02/01/59; FCO 1978; Nairobi 1980; Jedda (later Riyadh) 1983; Second Secretary Warsaw 1990 (Second Secretary 1988); Los Angeles 1994; m 1989 Karen Chapman (1s 1991).

Rutherford, Karen (née Chapman); SUPL since July 1992; born 19/02/59; FCO 1977; Rome 1979; Floater Duties 1982; FCO 1986; Warsaw 1990; Band B3; m 1989 John Rutherford (1s 1991).

Ryan, Elizabeth Jane Karen; Bratislava since November 1999; born 02/02/61; FCO 1998; Band B3; m 1993 Chaeil Ok-soon (1d 1994).

Ryan, Robert Christopher; Bucharest since January 2002; born 21/02/72; HCS 1991; FCO 1994; New Delhi 1997; FCO 2001; Band A2.

Rycroft, Matthew John; First Secretary (Political) Washington since September 1998; born 16/06/68; FCO 1989; Third Secretary Geneva (UKDIS) 1990; Third later Second Secretary (Chancery) Paris 1991; First Secretary FCO 1995; m 1997 (2d 1998, 2000).

Ryde, John; First Secretary FCO since August 1987; born 26/10/50; Third later Second Secretary FCO 1973; Language Training 1976; MECAS 1977; Second Secretary (Commercial) Sana'a 1978; First Secretary Tripoli 1980; FCO 1983; First Secretary (UN/Press) Geneva (UKMIS) 1986; Band D6; m 1974 Christine May Rydzewska (1s 1979).

Ryder, Michael; Special Representative for International Drugs Issues and Head of Drugs and International Crime Department FCO since September 1998; born 13/11/53; FCO 1984; Second later First Secretary BMG Berlin 1986; First Secretary FCO 1988; First Secretary Brussels (UKREP) 1993; First Secretary FCO 1996; Counsellor (Head of Security Policy Department) FCO 1997.

S

Sadler, Stuart Roger; Karachi since May 2001; born 22/12/70; FCO 1990; Pretoria 1994; Moscow 1998; Band B3.

Sagar, Rebecca Ann; Second Secretary (Political) Islamabad since May 2001; born 09/09/76; FCO 1999; Band C4.

Sage, Kelly Jane, MVO (1996); SUPL since April 2000; born 29/01/68; FCO 1989; The Hague 1992; Third Secretary (Visits/Information) Warsaw 1994; Third Secretary FCO 1996; Band B3.

Sainty, Christopher James; First Secretary (Political/EU) Madrid since March 2000; born 29/03/67; FCO 1989; Language Training 1991;

Third later Second Secretary (Chancery) New Delhi 1992; First Secretary FCO 1996; Language Training 1999; Band D6; m 1993 Sarah Helen Norris (1s 1996; 2d 1998, 2000).

Salkeld, Peter Charles; FCO since May 1993; born 31/08/53; FCO 1969; Bonn 1980; FCO 1983; New Delhi 1989; m 1978 Carol Elizabeth Anne Dent (2s 1985, 1988).

Salt, Richard André; On secondment to Petrofac UK Ltd since May 2000; born 30/07/62; FCO 1980; Brussels (UKREP) 1983; Algiers 1985; Banjul 1988; FCO 1990; New Delhi 1993; Second Secretary (Commercial) Damascus 1996; Band C4; m 1992 Karen Baden Davies (1s 1995).

Salter, Leigh Audra; SUPL since June 2002; born 16/03/69; FCO 1988; Wellington 1991; Windhoek 1994; Floater Duties 1998; Band B3.

Salvesen, Charles Hugh; FCO since August 2000; born 10/09/55; Second Secretary FCO 1982; First Secretary BMG Berlin 1984; First Secretary Bonn 1985; FCO 1988; Head of Political Section Buenos Aires 1993; Counsellor and Deputy High Commissioner Wellington 1996; m 1983 Emilie Maria Ingenhousz (2s twins 1987; 1d 1990 (dec'd 1995)).

Sambrook, Adam John; FCO since October 2001; born 01/02/78; Band C4.

Sambrook, Claire; Brussels (UKREP) since January 1999; born 26/01/66; FCO 1996; Kigali 1997; Band A2.

Sancar, Kim (née Neilson); SUPL since July 2002; born 30/09/71; FCO 1991; Islamabad 1995; Third Secretary (Immigration) Tehran 1998; Third Secretary (Commercial) and Vice-Consul Al Khobar 2001; Band B3; m 1997 Rizkul Oktay Sancar.

Sanderson, Michael John; First Secretary FCO since July 1995; born 21/01/48; FO 1967; Cairo 1972; FCO 1976; New York (UKMIS) 1979; Second Secretary (Chancery) Oslo 1984; Second Secretary FCO 1988; First Secretary Hong Kong 1993; Band C5; m 1976 Pauline Elizabeth Tippett (1d 1979; 1s 1982).

Sandover, William Geoffrey; Counsellor Paris since April 2002; born 07/04/55; FCO 1979; Third later Second Secretary Vienna (UKMIS) 1981; First Secretary FCO 1984; First Secretary (Chancery) Dublin 1986; First Secretary FCO 1987; First Secretary (Chancery) Buenos Aires 1992; First Secretary FCO 1996; Band D6; m (1) 1981 Sharman Winsome Knight (diss 1985); (2) 1992 Beatrice Martin.

Sargeant, Ian Charles; First Secretary and HM Consul Manila since November 1998; born 24/04/52; FCO 1971; Language Training SOAS 1974; Bangkok 1975; LA Floater 1979; FCO 1982; Manila 1986; Deputy Economic Adviser Berlin 1990; Vice-Consul (Commercial) Düsseldorf 1991; FCO 1995; m 1988 Mari Grace Eddun (diss 1999) (1d 1989).

Satheesan, Sujeevan; FCO since September 2001; born 25/03/77; Band C4.

Sattaur, Christopher; Amman since April 2000; born 25/04/71; FCO 1991; Athens 1996; Band A2.

Saunders, Caroline Ann; Deputy Consul-General Brisbane since October 2000; born 28/09/60; FCO 1983; New Delhi 1986; FCO 1988; Third Secretary (Chancery) Kuala Lumpur 1991; Second Secretary FCO 1995; Second Secretary British Trade International 1998; m 1989 Rhodri Christopher Kevin Meredith (1s 1993; 1d 1996).

Saunders, Kirsten Mary Margaret; Bangkok since January 1997; born 08/10/68; FCO 1995; Band A2.

Saunders, Liane; First Secretary (Chancery) Ankara since July 2000; born 24/10/68; FCO 1993; Full-Time Language Training 1994; Full-Time Language Training Cairo 1995; Second Secretary Kuwait 1996; Band D6; m 1994 Andrew Stewart Smith (1d 1998).

Saunderson, Lesley Margaret; On loan to DfID since June 1998; born 18/11/69; FCO 1991; New Delhi 1993; St Petersburg 1994; Dar es Salaam 1997.

Savage, Francis (Frank) Joseph, CMG (1996), OBE (1989), LVO (1986); Governor British Virgin Islands since July 1998; born 08/02/43; Passport Office 1961; FO 1966; Cairo 1967; Washington 1971; Vice-Consul Aden 1973; Second Secretary FCO 1975; Vice-Consul (Commercial) later Consul (Commercial) Düsseldorf 1978; First Secretary (Management) and HM Consul Peking 1982; First Secretary (Consular) Lagos and HM Consul Republic of Benin (non-resident) 1987; First Secretary later Counsellor FCO 1990; Governor Montserrat 1993; Counsellor FCO 1997 (Comprehensive Spending Review Team); m 1966 Veronica Mary McAleenan (2s 1969, 1971).

Savill, Margaret Ann; First Secretary FCO since April 1995; born 06/04/46; FCO 1968; Third Secretary Georgetown 1972; Second Secretary Rio de Janeiro 1975; Geneva 1975; FCO 1980; Second later First Secretary (Information) Berne 1984; First Secretary FCO 1989; First Secretary (Information/Management) Brussels (UKDEL NATO) 1993.

Saville, John Donald William; Deputy Head of Mission Havana since July 2000; born 29/06/60; FCO 1981; Third later Second Secretary Jakarta 1983; FCO 1985; Second later First Secretary (Information) Warsaw 1988; First Secretary FCO 1991; First Secretary (Political) Vienna 1995; FCO 1998; Full-Time Language Training 2000; Band D6; m 1992 Fabiola Moreno de Alboran (1d 1993).

Sawers, Robert John, CMG (1996); HM Ambassador Cairo since September 2001; born 26/07/55; FCO 1977; SUPL 1980; Sana'a 1980; Language Training 1981; Second Secretary Damascus 1982; First Secretary FCO 1984 (PS to Minister of State 1986); First Secretary

Pretoria/Cape Town 1988; Head of European
Union Department (Presidency) 1991; Principal
Private Secretary to the Secretary of State for
Foreign and Commonwealth Affairs 1993; Career
Development Attachment Harvard University
1995; Counsellor (Political/Military) Washington
1996; Foreign Affairs Private Secretary to the
Prime Minister 1999; m 1981 Avril Helen Shelley
Lamb (2s 1983, 1985; 1d 1987).

Say, Sarah Gillian; Brussels (UKREP) since
January 2000; born 02/04/59; FCO 1986; Paris
1988; Washington 1991; Havana 1993; FCO 1994;
Mexico City 1996; T/D Helsinki 1999; Band B3.

Sayle, Lorraine Mary; Luanda since August 2001;
born 22/09/72; FCO 1990; Brussels (UKDEL
NATO) 1994; Lilongwe 1996; SUPL 1998;
Lilongwe 1998; Band A2; (1s 1998).

Scaddan, Simon Mansfield; British High
Commissioner Port Moresby since February 2000;
born 22/01/44; FO 1962; Sofia 1966; Zomba
1967; Karachi 1970; Lahore 1971; Karachi 1972;
FCO 1974; Durban 1977; Second Secretary Kuala
Lumpur 1979; FCO 1982; Aden 1985; First
Secretary (Aid) Nairobi 1986; First Secretary
Islamabad 1988; First Secretary FCO 1992;
Deputy High Commissioner Calcutta 1996; m
1970 Frances Anne Barker (diss 2001) (1s 1972;
1d 1973); ptnr, Pablo Ganguli.

Scales, Martin Milner; Vice-Consul Oslo since
April 2001; born 31/01/65; FCO 1997; Band B3;
m 2001 Caroline Smyth.

Scanlon, Edward Joseph; Istanbul since November
1999; born 18/05/70; HCS 1990-93; FCO 1993;
Peking 1995; Band B3.

Scantlebury, Ian Patrick; Second Secretary Lima
since August 1997; born 12/09/60; FCO 1978;
Georgetown 1981; SE Asia Floater 1985; Calcutta
1987; FCO 1991; Third Secretary (Commercial)
Accra 1994.

Scarborough, Bryan David; Consul (Commercial)
Shanghai since May 1999; born 19/01/45; FCO
1973; Warsaw 1975; Douala 1976; Delhi 1979;
Freetown 1983; FCO 1985; Lilongwe 1988; Third
Secretary (Commercial) Jakarta 1991; FCO 1995;
m 1969 Kathleen Mary Johnston (1s 1980).

Scarborough, Vernon Marcus; Resident Deputy
High Commissioner Tarawa, Kiribati since March
2001; born 11/02/40; Passport Office 1958; CRO
1961; Dacca 1962; CRO 1964; Karachi 1965;
Vice-Consul Brussels 1969; Third Secretary
Banjul 1971; Second Secretary FCO 1977; Second
Secretary (Commercial) Muscat 1980; First
Secretary (Admin) Kuala Lumpur 1984; First
Secretary FCO 1987; Consul (Commercial)
Auckland 1990; Deputy Head of Mission Suva
and concurrently HM Ambassador (non-resident)
to Palau, Micronesia and the Marshall Islands
1995; T/D Suva 2000; m 1966 Jennifer Bernadette
Keane (3d 1970, 1972, 1980).

Scarratt, Claire Rebecca; Stockholm since
January 2000; born 07/02/75; HCS 1997; FCO
1999; Band A2.

Schofield, Nigel; Floater Duties since March
2000; born 17/04/70; FCO 1990; FCO 1993; Bonn
1993; Lagos 1994; On loan to DTI; Band B3; m
1994 Rebecca Imogen.

Scholes, Elizabeth Marian; First Secretary
(Chancery) Tel Aviv since September 1996; born
28/04/66; FCO 1987; Third later Second Secretary
(Chancery) Buenos Aires 1990; Second later First
Secretary FCO 1993; m 1998 Richard Wrigley.

Schroeder, Dominic Sebastian; First Secretary
(Commercial) Berlin since August 1997; born
13/11/65; FCO 1988; Third later Second Secretary
Kinshasa 1989; Second Secretary FCO 1992;
Second Secretary New York (UKMIS) 1993;
Second later First Secretary FCO 1994; m 1997
Susan Caroline Kerr (1s 2001).

Schroeder, Susan Caroline (née Kerr); On loan to
the DTI since December 1996; born 09/04/69;
FCO 1988; Prague 1990; Rabat 1992; FCO 1994;
Band B3; m 1997 Dominic Sebastian Schroeder
(1s 2001).

Schulz, Lynne; Pretoria since March 2002; born
16/11/66; HCS 1997; SUPL 1998; FCO 2000;
SUPL 2001; Band A2; m 1994 Sven Schulz (1s
1998; 1d 2001).

Schumann, Carol Ann (née Hill); Third Secretary
(Finance) Bonn since August 1997; born 18/07/46;
FCO 1976; Paris 1977; FCO 1980; Washington
1981; FCO 1987; The Hague 1988; Bonn 1991;
SUPL 1996; Band C4; m 1980 Jürgen Klaus
Dieter Schumann (2s 1981, 1983).

Scott, Gavin David; Private Secretary to the
Group Chief Executive British Trade International
since January 2002; born 26/06/60; FCO 1978;
Paris 1981; Beirut 1983; Washington 1985; FCO
1988; Third Secretary (Commercial) Bogotá 1991;
Bridgetown 1995; Third Secretary FCO 1995;
Band C4; m 1992 Julie Ann Owen.

Scott, George; Almaty since July 2002; born
11/10/56; FCO 1981; East Berlin 1982;
Luxembourg 1984; Lagos 1986; FCO 1991; Kigali
1995; Tirana 1999; Band C4.

Scott, Keith John; On loan to DTI since October
1999; born 19/02/69; FCO 1991; Abuja 1994;
Second Secretary FCO 1995; SUPL 1998; Band
C4.

Scott-Dunne, Naomi Anita; SUPL since April
2002; born 25/09/68; FCO 1990; Geneva
(UKMIS) 1995; SUPL 1997; FCO 2001; Band A2;
m 1997 John Richard Dunne.

Scroby, Gary Vance; Deputy Head of Mission
Managua since March 1999; born 15/07/69; FCO
1988; Brussels (UKREP) 1989; Floater Duties
1992; FCO 1994; Band B3; m 1999 Lisa Marie
Dowell (1d 2000).

Seaby, Paul Robert; Consul Tehran since April 1999; born 24/05/56; FCO 1975; Masirah 1978; Warsaw 1978; Ottawa 1979; Floater Duties 1982; Port Moresby 1984; FCO 1987; Third Secretary (Commercial) Muscat 1991; Lusaka 1994; m 1984 Lynette Margaret Heffernan.

Sealy, Amanda Sarah (née Franklin); FCO since September 1999; born 03/01/59; FCO 1980; Peking 1982; Pretoria/Cape Town 1984; Warsaw 1986; FCO 1988; Windhoek 1991; Jakarta 1995; Band C4; m 1989 Dominic John Sealy (1s 1992; 1d 1995).

Seaman, Michael William; First Secretary (Political) Tbilisi since May 2002; born 01/11/55; FCO 1975; Jakarta 1977; Bombay 1981; FCO 1984; Second Secretary (Chancery) The Hague 1988; Second Secretary FCO 1992; On loan to MOD 1992; First Secretary FCO 1994; Athens 1999; Full-Time Language Training 2001; Band C5; m 1978 Jane Lesley Stockwell (2d 1984, 1987).

Seaman, Stephen James, MBE (1991); First Secretary (Commercial) Caracas since October 2000; born 04/12/55; DOT 1975; Copenhagen 1979; DOT 1980; Salisbury 1980; FCO 1982; Vice-Consul Bucharest 1983; FCO 1986; Second Secretary and Deputy Head of Mission Monrovia 1988; Second Secretary (Commercial) Lilongwe 1991; Second Secretary (Management) Nicosia 1993; First Secretary FCO 1997; m (1) 1980 Katherine Ann Barker (dec'd 1996); (2) 2001 Magda Guillermina.

Seamer, Helen Maria; SUPL since October 1989; born 25/11/60; FCO 1981; Cairo 1985; SUPL 1988; Amsterdam 1989; Band B3; m (1) 1984 Timothy John Unsworth (diss); (2) Raymond Clive Seamer.

Searight, Pauline Mabel; Kuala Lumpur since May 1996; born 27/06/55; FCO 1988; Banjul 1990; Karachi 1993; Band A2; m 1991 Graham Kenneth Denham.

Seaton, Andrew James; Head of China Hong Kong Department FCO since November 2000; born 20/04/54; FCO 1977; Third later Second Secretary Dakar 1979; Trade Commissioner (China) BTC Hong Kong 1981; First Secretary FCO 1987; Trade Counsellor BTC later Deputy Consul-General and Trade Counsellor Hong Kong 1995; m 1983 Helen Elizabeth Pott (3s 1989, 1992, 1995).

Seddon, Christine; Floater Duties since October 2001; FCO 1988; Brasilia 1990; Wellington 1994; FCO 1998; Band A2.

Seddon, David William; First Secretary (Commercial) Harare since April 1999; born 30/05/48; FO (later FCO) 1966; Bonn 1970; FCO 1971; Port of Spain 1973; Vila 1977; FCO 1981; Milan 1983; Vice-Consul later Consul (Commercial/Admin/Consular) Douala 1987; Second Secretary FCO 1991; Kampala 1995; m

1972 Monica Elisabeth Josefina van Loon (1s 1976).

Seddon, Richard Charles Leslie; First Secretary Washington since April 1999; born 25/09/68; FCO 1992; Second Secretary (Political) New Delhi 1994; First Secretary FCO 1997; Band D6; m 1999 Alice Kim Fugate.

Sedwill, Mark Philip; FCO since December 1999; born 21/10/64; FCO 1989; Language Training 1990; Second Secretary Language Training Cairo 1991; Second Secretary (Political/External) Cairo 1992; First Secretary FCO 1994; First Secretary (Political) Nicosia 1998; m 1999 Sarah-Jane Lakeman.

Segar, Christopher Michael John; Head of Aviation, Maritime and Energy Dept FCO since January 2001; born 25/11/50; FCO 1973; Language Training MECAS 1974; Third later Second Secretary (Commercial) Dubai 1976; First Secretary FCO 1979; First Secretary (Commercial) and Head of Chancery Luanda 1984; First Secretary Paris (UKDEL) 1987; Counsellor, Consul-General and Deputy Head of Mission Baghdad 1990; On loan to MOD 1991; Counsellor (Commercial) Riyadh 1994; Counsellor (Commercial) Peking 1997.

Self, Andrew Paul; Second Secretary FCO since December 1998; born 02/04/64; FCO 1982; Hong Kong 1986; FCO 1988; Third Secretary (Information) Sana'a 1992; Third Secretary FCO 1993; Tehran 1996; Band C4; m (1) 1987 Michele Carmichael Crouch (diss 1995); (2) 1997 Andrea Louise Carter (1s 1998).

Selvadurai, Louise Mary (née McCallum); FCO since February 1999; born 26/04/69; FCO 1990; Vienna (UKDEL) 1992; Full-Time Language Training 1995; Third Secretary Moscow 1996; Band C4; m 2000 Samuel Selvadurai.

Selvadurai, Samuel Dayalan; Second Secretary (KHF) Moscow since August 1995; born 01/10/70; FCO 1993; Full-Time Language Training 1994; Band D6; m 2000 Louise McCallum.

Senior, Major Michael Roger; Queen's Messenger 1987; born 15/11/45; HM Forces 1964-87.

Setterfield, (James) Robert; Deputy Head of Mission Bratislava since October 2000; born 06/05/47; DSAO (later FCO) 1967; Bombay 1969; New Delhi 1971; FCO 1973; Second Secretary (Aid/Information) Rangoon 1976; Vice-Consul Stuttgart 1980; Assistant Secretary (Political) Vila 1980; Vice-Consul (Commercial) Düsseldorf 1982; First Secretary FCO 1985; First Secretary (Chancery) Wellington 1987; FCO 1992; First Secretary Helsinki 1995; Full-Time Language Training 2000; Band D6; m 1980 Margaret Jean McMahon (1s 1983; 1d 1985).

Seymour, Irene Frances (née McDonagh); SUPL since September 1995; born 02/12/64; FCO 1984; San José 1987; FCO 1990; Band A2; m 1991 Peter James Seymour.

Seymour, Peter James; First Secretary FCO since March 2001; born 10/02/62; FCO 1984; Second Secretary (Chancery/Information) and Vice-Consul San José 1987; Second Secretary FCO 1989; SUPL 1990; First Secretary FCO 1991; Berlin 1995; First Secretary Vienna 1999; Band D6; m 1991 Irene Frances McDonagh.

Shackell, Robin John; Quito since October 1999; born 04/02/63; HCS 1983; FCO 1985; Vienna 1987; T/D Munich 1989; Doha 1990; Management Officer/Vice-Consul La Paz 1991; FCO 1995; Band B3; m (1) 1991 Carol Plowman (diss); (2) 1994 Isabel Chavez-Bastos.

Shackleton, Richard David; Third Secretary (Commercial) Bogotá since May 1995; born 26/05/68; FCO 1990; Third Secretary (Political) New York (UKMIS) 1992; Band B3.

Shaikh, Farida; Second Secretary Accra since June 2002; born 16/10/65; FCO 1990; Third Secretary (Chancery/Information) Harare 1992; Third Secretary (Chancery) Singapore 1996.

Shakespeare, Karen Marie; FCO since July 1992; born 25/10/70; Band A2.

Shand, Ian, LVO (2000); Second Secretary (Press and Public Affairs) Milan since June 1999; born 17/01/54; FCO 1973; Accra 1975; Munich 1979; FCO 1982; Bonn 1985; Islamabad 1988; FCO 1991; Language Training 1994; Santiago 1995; m 1975 Lyndsey Elizabeth Hall (2d 1983, 1985).

Shanmuganathan, Krishna; First Secretary (Political) Athens since September 2000; born 14/02/74; FCO 1995; Second Secretary (Political) Pretoria 1998; FCO 2000; Band D6.

Shannon, Keith; First Secretary FCO since July 1999; born 17/09/66; FCO 1988; Third Secretary (Aid/Commercial) Maputo 1991; Second Secretary (Technology) Paris 1995.

Shapcott, William James; SUPL since October 1999 - Counsellor to Dr Javier Solana, EU High Representative for the CFSP, Brussels; born 25/07/61; HM Forces 1983-88; Second Secretary FCO 1988; Second Secretary Bonn 1990; First Secretary FCO 1993; First Secretary Washington 1995; (Counsellor 1999); m 1986 Shelley Mary Harrison (twin s 2001),

Shapland, Anthony Gregory; FCO since July 1992; born 17/12/49; PRO (Band D6) FCO 1979; On loan to the Cabinet Office 1990; m (1) 1973 Margaret Elizabeth Moriarty (diss); (2) 1982 Leonora Alexandra Hebden (1s 1983).

Sharma, Ajay; First Secretary (Economic) Moscow since February 2002; born 07/05/70; FCO 1995; Full-Time Language Training 1996; Second Secretary (Political/Information) Ankara 1997; Seconded to HM Treasury 2000; Full-Time Language Training 2001; m 2000 Evren Birdal

Sharp, David Stewart; Floater Duties since April 1995; born 19/01/71; FCO 1989; New York (UKMIS) 1992; Band A2.

Sharp, Gemma Goulding; Second Secretary (Political) Copenhagen since December 1998; born 07/08/72; Second Secretary FCO 1995; Band C4.

Sharp, James Frederick Bailey; New Delhi since October 2000; born 01/04/72; FCO 1994; SUPL 1998; Band A2.

Sharp, James Lyall; HM Ambassador Almaty and HM Ambassador (non-resident) Bishkek since October 2002; born 12/04/60; Second Secretary FCO 1987; Language Training Cairo 1988; Second Secretary Cairo 1989; First Secretary FCO 1992; First Secretary Vienna (UKDEL) 1996; FCO 1998; m 1992 Sara Essam el-Gammal.

Sharp, Janice Sarah; FCO since March 2001; born 11/08/66; FCO 1987; SUPL 1994; FCO 1995; Second Secretary (Immigration) Tehran 1998; Band C4.

Sharp, Jonathan Dinsdale; Second Secretary (Political) Lagos since August 2000; born 31/03/67; FCO 1988; Karachi 1990; Paris 1991; LA/Caribbean Floater 1994; Third Secretary (Political) Tunis 1997; FCO 1997; m 1995 Tracey Ennis.

Sharp, Paul John Gibson; Second Secretary FCO since April 1993; born 24/09/48; FCO 1967; New Delhi 1975; FCO 1976; Rome 1978; Attaché Ankara 1981; FCO 1981; FCO 1985; Attaché Moscow 1987; Second Secretary FCO 1989; Second Secretary Pretoria 1990; m (1) 1969 Anita Tsang (2s 1972, 1976) (diss 1986); (2) 1996 J Tuckey.

Sharp, Richard; First Secretary (Management) Ottawa since February 2002; born 08/03/49; FO (later FCO) 1967; Karachi 1971; Canberra 1972; Port Moresby 1974; Santiago 1975; Jakarta 1977; FCO 1980; Cairo 1984; Second Secretary (Admin) Moscow 1987; Second Secretary FCO 1990; Second Secretary and Vice-Consul Luanda 1993; First Secretary (Management) New Delhi 1997; m 1974 Patricia Anne Whitby (1s 1979; 1d 1983).

Sharpe, Jean Cynthia, OBE (1994); Trade Commissioner Hong Kong since October 1998; born 18/10/47; CO 1964; DSAO 1965; The Hague 1970; Kingston 1973; Dubai 1974; FCO 1974; FCO 1975; Freetown 1978; JAO Brussels 1981; Second Secretary FCO 1984; On loan to DTI 1986; Second Secretary (Commercial) Nairobi 1988; First Secretary and Consul Bangkok 1991; First Secretary FCO 1996.

Sharpe, Rosemary Helen; Counsellor Madrid since December 2000; born 11/03/56; Second Secretary FCO 1982; Second Secretary (Information) New Delhi 1985; First Secretary Brussels (UKREP) 1987; First Secretary FCO 1988; First Secretary (Economic) Berlin 1991; First Secretary FCO 1996.

Sharpless, Fiona Ure (née McGowan); Dhaka since April 2001; born 23/02/65; FCO 1988; Brussels (UKREP) 1989; SUPL 1992; Kathmandu

1993; SUPL 1994; Lagos 1998; SUPL 1999; Band B3; m 1990 Kristian Sharpless (1d 1993; 1s 1995).

Sharpless, Kristian; Second Secretary (Commercial/Press and Public Affairs) Dhaka since April 2001; born 17/06/67; Dept of Employment 1985; FCO 1987; Brussels 1989; Kathmandu 1992; FCO 1995; Lagos 1996; FCO 1999; Band C4; m 1990 Fiona Ure McGowan (1d 1993; 1s 1995).

Shaughnessy, Kevin John; Deputy Head of Mission Santo Domingo since January 2002; born 10/11/64; FCO 1983; Tehran 1986; Kingston 1988; Bonn 1991; Second Secretary FCO 1994; Second Secretary (Commercial) Bahrain 1998; m 1997 Elizabeth Ann Churchill (2d 1998, 2001).

Shaw, Alan John; Second Secretary (Political/Information) Dhaka since January 2002; born 09/06/66; FCO 1987; Washington 1989; Peking 1992; FCO 1995; Bangkok 1998; Prague 1999; Band B3; m 1989 Claire Louise Morgan.

Shaw, Andrew William; Harare since June 2002; born 31/03/50; FCO 1997; Band A2; m 1981 Ruth Heeps (2s 1984, 1989; 1d 1990).

Shaw, Claire Louise (née Morgan); FCO since May 1995; born 18/06/68; FCO 1987; Washington 1989; FCO 1992; Peking 1993; Band B3; m 1989 Alan John Shaw.

Shaw, Philip; First Secretary (Commercial) Paris since December 1999; born 22/05/45; CRO 1963; DSAO 1965; Khartoum 1966; Language Training 1969; Ulaanbaatar 1970; Nairobi 1973; FCO 1978; Seconded to DTI 1980; São Paulo 1982; Brussels 1985; FCO 1990; Lisbon 1991; First Secretary FCO 1997; m (1) 1970 Christine Goodwin (diss) (1d 1974; 1s 1976); (2) 1992 Marthe Vercammen.

Shaw, Samantha; Nicosia since October 2001; born 31/03/67; FCO 1999; Band A2.

Shaw, Sandra Heather; FCO since March 1992; born 07/09/43; Band A2.

Shaw, Sarah Elaine (née Gosling); SUPL since June 1997; born 29/07/69; FCO 1990; Bonn 1992; Tehran 1994; FCO 1994; FCO 1996; Band A2; m 1995 Andrew John Shaw.

Shead, Robert John; Second Secretary (Commercial) Shanghai since July 2002; born 14/04/50; FCO 1969; Bonn 1973; Seoul 1976; FCO 1977; Paris 1978; Damascus 1982; FCO 1985; Damascus 1986; FCO 1987; Nairobi 1988; Second Secretary Manila 1992; FCO 1997; Second Secretary Guangzhou 1998; m (1) 1981 Carol Ann Bostock (diss 1987); (2) 1987 Fayha Sultan (1s 1987).

Shearing, Sally Louise; FCO since August 1995; born 20/04/66; FCO 1985; Budapest 1988; FCO 1990; Sofia 1992; Band A2.

Shearman, Martin James; FCO since May 1999; born 07/02/65; Third later Second Secretary FCO 1989; Language Training 1991; Full-Time Language Training Tokyo 1992; Second Secretary

(Commercial) Tokyo 1993; First Secretary (Commercial) Tokyo 1994; On loan to the DTI 1996; On loan to the Cabinet Office 1998; NATO Secretariat 1999; m 1996 Miriam Elizabeth Pyburn.

Shearman, Miriam Elizabeth (née Pyburn); SUPL since June 2001; born 11/06/65; Full-Time Language Training 1990; FCO 1990; Tokyo 1992; APS/PUS 1996; FCO 2000; T/D Brussels (UKREP) 2000; Band D6; m 1996 Martin James Shearman.

Sheikh, Soraya Zia; Brussels since April 2000; born 03/07/72; FCO 1998; Band A2.

Sheinwald, Sir Nigel Elton, KCMG (2001), CMG (1999); Permanent Representative Brussels (UKREP) since September 2000; born 26/06/53; FCO 1976; Moscow 1978; Second later First Secretary FCO 1979; First Secretary (Chancery) Washington 1983; First Secretary later Counsellor FCO 1987; Counsellor and Head of Chancery Brussels (UKREP) 1993; Head of News Department FCO 1995; Director FCO (European Union) 1998; m 1980 Julia Dunne (3s 1984, 1985, 1987).

Shelly, Simon Richard; FCO since December 1998; born 05/07/60; HM Customs & Excise 1981-83; FCO 1983; Kabul 1986; Paris 1988; FCO 1991; Ankara 1995; m 1991 Monique Marie Renée Le Roux (1d 1995; 1s 1996).

Shepherd, Daniel James Owen; FCO since January 2001; born 05/11/71; FCO 1994; Language Training 1995; Language Training Hanoi 1996; Second Secretary Hanoi 1997; Band D6.

Shepherd, Sir John Alan, KCVO (2000), CMG (1989); HM Ambassador Rome since July 2000; born 27/04/43; Third Secretary CRO 1965; MECAS 1966; Second Secretary Amman 1968; Rome 1970; First Secretary FCO 1973; First Secretary (Economic) later Head of Chancery The Hague 1976; First Secretary later Counsellor and Head of Chancery Brussels (UKREP EC) 1980; Counsellor FCO 1985; HM Ambassador and Consul-General Bahrain 1988; Minister Bonn 1991; Director (Middle East/North Africa) FCO 1996; DUS (Non-Europe, Trade and Investment) 1997; m 1969 Jessica Mary Nichols (1d 1975).

Shepherd, Wendy Elizabeth; Peking since September 2000; born 03/07/71; OFFER 1993; FCO 1996; Port of Spain 1997; Band B3.

Sheppard, David Anthony; Second later First Secretary FCO since November 1995; born 06/07/51; HCS 1968; Hong Kong 1977; FCO 1980; Baghdad 1983; Tel Aviv 1986; FCO 1989 (Second Secretary 1992); Second Secretary Brussels 1993; Band D6; m 1988 Bonita Dorsman.

Sheppard, Jane Louise (née McMullin); Tel Aviv since April 2001; born 19/07/70; FCO 1997; Ottawa 1998; SUPL 2000; Band A2; m 1998 William John Crean.

Sheppard, Nicholas Ugo; First Secretary FCO since October 1998; born 02/06/56; DTI 1973; FCO 1974; Paris (UKDEL OECD) 1977; Islamabad 1980; FCO 1982; Aden 1983; Canberra 1986; Second Secretary FCO 1989; Second Secretary (Commercial) New Delhi 1992; Bucharest 1995.

Sherar, Paul Desmond; Second later First Secretary FCO since May 1995; born 24/02/53; FCO 1970; Brussels 1973; Africa Floater 1976; Georgetown 1978; FCO 1981; Vice-Consul (Commercial) New York (BTDO) 1986; Second Secretary (Commercial/Aid) Luanda 1991.

Sheriff, Philip Mark; FCO since April 2002; born 30/11/71; Band D6.

Sherman, Penelope Anne; Cape Town since March 2000; born 29/08/43; Tokyo 1971; Calcutta 1973; Jakarta 1975; Hanoi 1977; Rio de Janeiro 1978; FCO 1980; Algiers 1983; Nicosia 1987; FCO 1989; Harare 1990; New Delhi 1994; FCO 1998; Band B3.

Sherman, Sheila Ann (née Baker); FCO since April 1993; born 06/06/60; FCO 1984; Peking 1985; FCO 1988; Nicosia 1990; Band A2; m 1995 Christopher Sherman.

Sherrin, Barrie Robert; New Delhi since February 2000; born 20/07/44; Royal Marines 1961-84; Baghdad 1989; Moscow 1991; Lisbon 1992; Dublin 1996; Band B3; m 1967 Kathleen Mary.

Sherrington, Simon Richard; SUPL since June 2000; born 27/05/55; FCO 1980; Language Training Kamakura 1982; Tokyo 1983; Second Secretary (Chancery/Admin) Johannesburg 1987; Second Secretary FCO 1987; Second Secretary FCO 1989; First Secretary on loan to the DTI 1994; Deputy Consul-General Boston 1996; Band D6.

Shingler, Michael John; Consul (Commercial) Atlanta since September 1995 (First Secretary 1994); born 31/01/47; Post Office 1963; DSAO 1965; Manila 1969; Prague 1973; Dacca 1975; FCO 1979; Dar es Salaam 1981; Consul (Commercial) Casablanca 1984; FCO 1984; FCO 1988; Consul (Management) Istanbul 1991; m 1969 Katina Janet Wall (1d 1972; 1s 1975).

Shipster, Michael David, OBE (1990); First Secretary later Counsellor FCO since November 1994; born 17/03/51; Second later First Secretary FCO 1977; First Secretary (Chancery) Moscow 1981; First Secretary FCO 1983; New Delhi 1986; First Secretary (Chancery) Lusaka 1990; Consul Johannesburg 1991; m 1974 Jacquelynne Mann (2d 1981, 1982; 1s 1987).

Shivers, Marie Louise (née Stone); New York (UKMIS) since September 2002; born 27/08/74; FCO 1992; Singapore 1996; FCO 1999; Band A2; m 1999 Gavin John Shivers.

Shokat, Mohammed; FCO since October 2001; born 07/11/75; Band C4.

Short, James Walter; Dhaka since September 1999; born 19/10/66; FCO 1986; Calcutta 1989; Shanghai 1991; Third Secretary Tehran 1994; FCO 1997; Band B3; m 1990 Stephanie Sanjukta Ghosh (1s 1998).

Short, Roger Guy, MVO (1971); Consul-General and Director of Trade Promotion Istanbul since April 2001; born 09/12/44; Third Secretary Commonwealth Office (later FCO) 1967; Third later Second Secretary Ankara 1969; First Secretary FCO 1974; Consul (Commercial) Rio de Janeiro 1978; Head of Chancery Ankara 1981; Counsellor and Deputy Head of Permanent Under-Secretary's Department FCO 1984; Counsellor, Head of Chancery and Consul-General Oslo 1986; Counsellor FCO 1990; HM Ambassador Sofia 1994; Chief of Staff Sarajevo 1999; m 1971 Sally Victoria Taylor (2d 1978, 1982; 1s 1988).

Shorter, Hugo Benedict; FCO since August 2001; born 11/08/66; FCO 1990; Second Secretary on attachment to ENA Paris 1992; Second later First Secretary (Political) Brussels (UKDEL NATO) 1994; FCO 1998; Private Secretary to Minister of State 2000; m 2001 Laura M Lindon.

Shott, Philip Nicholas; Counsellor Pretoria since November 2001; born 27/11/54; FCO 1980 (Second Secretary 1980); First Secretary Lagos 1983; First Secretary FCO 1986; First Secretary (Chancery) Nicosia 1987; First Secretary FCO 1991; First Secretary (Political) Lusaka 1994; First Secretary FCO 1997; m 1981 Lesley Ann Marsh (1s 1986; 1d 1987).

Shute, Christopher David; First Secretary FCO since March 2000; born 08/10/49; HMIT 1968; FCO 1969; Middle East Floater 1972; Lagos 1974; Cairo 1975; FCO 1979; Rome 1983; Second Secretary FCO 1986; Second Secretary (Commercial) Warsaw 1987; Second Secretary FCO 1990; First Secretary (Chancery) Wellington 1995; FCO 1999; Band C5; m 1975 Peta Ann Dewhurst (2s 1987, 1990).

Sidnell, Gail Marilyn; SUPL since October 2001; born 09/04/53; FCO 1974; Addis Ababa 1975; Monrovia 1977; Gibraltar 1981; FCO 1982; Prague 1983; FCO 1985; Nairobi 1989; FCO 1993 (Second Secretary 1994); Second Secretary (Commercial) Jakarta 1996.

Silva, Ginny Anne (née Kesterton); Luxembourg since November 1994; born 09/07/64; Immigration Service, Heathrow 1985; FCO 1987; Seoul 1989; Band B3; m 1989 Ronie Silva.

Silverwood, Jane Mary; Muscat since April 1994; born 06/08/60; FCO 1985; Mexico City 1987; FCO 1991; T/D Montevideo 1993; Band B3.

Sime, Charles; First Secretary FCO since 1998; born 11/03/46; CO 1963; FCO 1965; Pretoria/Cape Town 1969; Warsaw 1972; Muscat 1974; FCO 1975; Kinshasa 1978; Perth 1981; FCO 1983; Second Secretary (Management) Dar es Salaam 1986; First Secretary FCO 1992; Istanbul 1995; m 1968 Edith Gregg.

Simmons, Ian Paul; Counsellor Nairobi since April 1999; born 05/09/55; FCO 1983; Second Secretary (Information) New Delhi 1987; First Secretary FCO 1989; First Secretary (Political) Hanoi 1992; Full-Time Language Training Point Cook, Melbourne 1992; First Secretary (Regional Affairs) Bangkok 1993; FCO 1996; m 1999 Elizabeth Jozina van de Ree (1d 2002).

Simmons, Timothy Michael John; Deputy Head of Mission Warsaw since November 2001; born 08/04/60; FCO 1982; Third later Second Secretary Warsaw 1985; First Secretary FCO 1987; First Secretary Geneva (UKMIS) 1993; Seconded to Price Waterhouse Coopers MCS 1997; Assistant Director FCO 1999; m 1989 Caroline Mary Radcliffe (2s 1990, 1993).

Simon, Susannah Kate; First Secretary (Political) Bonn since January 1999; born 07/06/64; FCO 1988; Third later Second Secretary Bonn 1989; Second Secretary Almaty 1992; FCO 1994; m 1994 Mikhail Mnaidarovich Kubekov (1s 1996).

Simpson, Beverley Jayne; New York (UKMIS) since July 2000; born 11/06/70; FCO 1989; Floater Training 1991; Floater Duties 1992; FCO 1993; Stanley 1994; T/D Mostar 1995; Madras 1997; Band B3.

Simpson, Brian; Vice-Consul Budapest since September 1999; born 08/05/67; FCO 1986; Warsaw 1988; Lagos 1991; FCO 1995; Band B3.

Simpson, Georgina Felicity (née Little); SUPL since March 1999; born 23/02/64; FCO 1986; Language Training 1987; Second Secretary Amman 1989; Second Secretary (Commercial/Economic/Political) Sana'a 1991; SUPL 1991; FCO 1994; m 1991 Dominic Mark Simpson.

Simpson, Gordon Grant; Deputy Consul-General and HM Consul (Commercial) San Francisco since September 1998; born 25/08/46; FO 1964; Peking 1968; Lisbon 1970; Ibadan 1972; FCO 1975; Bucharest 1978; Nairobi 1979; Lisbon 1982; Second Secretary FCO 1985; Second Secretary (Commercial) Luanda 1987; Second Secretary (Immigration) Islamabad 1990; First Secretary FCO 1992; Deputy Consul-General Rio de Janeiro 1994; m 1970 Jenny Frances Parker (1d 1974; 2s 1975, 1982).

Simpson, Karen Frances (née Thomas); T/D Accra since January 2002; born 25/08/54; FCO 1975; Islamabad 1976; FCO 1978; Brussels (UKREP) 1979; Cairo 1982; FCO 1985; Lagos 1987; SUPL 1990; Dhaka 1994; SUPL 1997; Lagos 1998; Band B3; m 1981 Kenneth Simpson (1s 1990; 1d 1994).

Simpson, Louise Jane; Kampala since November 1998; born 24/06/66; FCO 1986; Lima 1988; SUPL 1990; FCO 1992; Moscow 1993; FCO 1996; Band B3.

Simpson, Scott; Lima since May 1999; born 28/03/70; FCO 1991; Bangkok 1995; Band B3.

Simpson, Timothy John; FCO since September 1998; born 14/09/60; FCO 1988; Third Secretary (Political) Budapest 1994; Band B3; m 1985 Lise Margaret Finlay (3d 1986, 1992, 1995).

Sims, Christopher Julien Bouyer; Second Secretary (Political) Seoul since November 2001; born 08/05/78; FCO 1999; Full-Time Language Training 2000; Band C4.

Sims, Lynda; FCO since September 1977; born 10/11/50; MOD 1968; FCO 1970; Kuala Lumpur 1973; Bucharest 1976; Band B3; m 1981 Richard Ian Taylor.

Sinclair, Fiona Louise; Third Secretary (Political) Zagreb since May 2000; born 13/01/71; FCO 1993; Full-Time Language Training 1995; Third Secretary (Political) Strasbourg 1996; Band B3.

Sinclair, Rachel Elizabeth; FCO since August 1994; born 07/02/65; FCO 1984; Harare 1992; Band A2; m 1991 Alexander Field Douse.

Sinclair, Robert Nelson Gurney; On loan to DTI since November 1999; born 10/12/52; FCO 1972; Dacca 1975; Algiers 1978; East Berlin 1980; CG Berlin 1981; FCO 1984; Third later Second Secretary Jakarta 1987; FCO 1991; Second Secretary (KHF) Sofia 1996; Band C4; m 1975 Diana Sawyer (1s 1986).

Singh, Jatinder Jit; FCO since September 2001; born 08/09/75; Band C4.

Singh, Mala; Buenos Aires since June 2000; born 01/01/73; FCO 1996; Band A2.

Singh, Tracey Michelle (née Chapman); Third Secretary (Immigration) Accra since January 2001; born 30/10/68; FCO 1988; New Delhi 1990; FCO 1994; Dubai 1996; SUPL 1999; FCO 2000; Band B3; m 1995 Jasminder Singh (2d 1999, 2002).

Singleton, Jean Patricia; SUPL since January 1990; born 10/03/49; FCO 1987; Band A2.

Sinkinson, Philip Andrew; Deputy Head of Mission Kingston since September 2001; born 07/10/50; Inland Revenue 1967; FCO 1970; Warsaw 1973; FCO 1974; East Berlin 1974; Rome 1975; FCO 1976; Quito 1978; Rio de Janeiro 1978; Prague 1979; FCO 1981; Blantyre 1982; Lilongwe 1985; FCO 1986; Second Secretary (Commercial) São Paulo 1991; Olympic Attaché Atlanta 1995; First Secretary (Commercial) Lisbon 1996; m 1971 Clare Maria Catherine Jarvis (1s 1974).

Sinton, William Baldie, OBE (1999); HM Ambassador La Paz since October 2001; born 17/06/46; Third Secretary FCO 1968; Third later Second Secretary (Commercial) Prague 1970; Second later First Secretary Brussels (UKDEL NATO) 1973; First Secretary FCO 1977; First Secretary (Commercial) Algiers 1981; First Secretary FCO 1985; HM Ambassador Panama City 1996; HM Ambassador Algiers 1999; m 1995 Jane S B Aryee.

Sisum, Thomas George; FCO since September 1999; born 16/10/73; Band C4; m 2002 Sophie Katherine Devonshire.

Sizeland, Paul Raymond; Consul-General Shanghai since October 2000; born 19/02/52; FCO 1980; Brussels (UKDEL NATO) 1981; Doha 1985; Second Secretary FCO 1986; First Secretary (Chancery/Aid) Lagos 1988; First Secretary later Counsellor FCO 1991; Private Secretary to the Chairman of EC Conference on Yugoslavia 1991; Deputy Head of Mission Bangkok 1996; m 1976 Vasantha Jesudasan (2d 1981, 1982).

Skidmore, Jonathan Richard Llywelyn; Second Secretary Vienna (UKMIS) since October 2001; born 06/01/70; FCO 1998; Band C4.

Skilton, Christopher Paul; Deputy High Commissioner Kampala since January 2001; born 07/04/54; Bonn 1974; Santiago 1976; FCO 1980; Buenos Aires 1983; Madrid 1986; Resigned 1991; Reinstated 1993; FCO 1993; Madrid 1996; FCO 1998; m 1978 Kathleen Jane (1d 1982; 1s 1980).

Skingle, Diana; Deputy Head of Mission Addis Ababa since February 2001; born 03/05/47; Commonwealth Office (later FCO) 1966; Kampala 1970; FCO 1972; Abidjan 1974; Vila 1975; Prague 1977; Casablanca 1979; Second Secretary FCO 1982; Second Secretary (Aid/Commercial) Georgetown 1985; Second Secretary (Development) Bridgetown 1986; First Secretary (Information) Brussels (UKDEL NATO) 1988; First Secretary FCO 1993; ptnr, Christopher John Marshall Carrington.

Skinner, Dawn Emma; Bucharest since June 2002; born 18/05/65; FCO 1985; Prague 1987; Brussels (UKREP) 1989; Anguilla 1991; FCO 1993; World Wide Floater Duties 1995; SUPL 1996; Sarajevo 1997; FCO 1998; Band B3.

Skinner, Gillian (née Smith); FCO since November 1988 (Second Secretary 1992); born 09/01/57; FCO 1976; SUPL 1978; SUPL 1980; Beirut 1980; FCO 1982; Beirut 1982; Brussels 1983; FCO 1984; Kinshasa 1987; Band B3; m (1) 1978 Colin Wynn Crorkin (diss 1991) (2s 1985, 1992); (2) 1996 Graeme John Skinner.

Skyring, Andrea; Dar es Salaam since March 1999; born 01/08/66; FCO 1998; Band A2.

Slater, Angela (née Caldwell); SUPL since July 2002; born 09/03/67; FCO 1986; Washington 1988; Floater Duties 1992; FCO 1994; SUPL 1994; SUPL 1999; Second Secretary (Consular) New Delhi 2000; Band C4; m 1998 David John Slater (1d 1999).

Slater, David John; Consul (Commercial) Los Angeles since August 2002; born 02/03/68; FCO 1987; Abu Dhabi 1989; Accra 1991; FCO 1995; Second Secretary (Commercial) New Delhi 1999; Band C5; m 1998 Angela Caldwell (1d 1999).

Slater, Gina Michelle (née Lambert); Second Secretary FCO since March 1996; born 29/07/54; FCO 1974; Port Stanley 1976; SUPL 1978; Lisbon 1982; FCO 1986; Dhaka 1988; Harare 1992; m 1976 Gordon Slater (diss) (1d 1981).

Slater, Jacqueline (née Brewitt); SUPL since January 2002; born 02/08/65; FCO 1985; FCO 1989; Dublin 1989; Beirut 1992; Bonn 1996; Band B3; m 1997 Steven Haigh Slater.

Slater, Judith Mary; Assistant Director, Personnel Policy FCO since July 2001; born 26/06/64; FCO 1988; Third later Second Secretary (Political) Canberra 1989; New York (UKMIS) 1992; First Secretary FCO 1993; Private Secretary to Minister of State 1994; First Secretary (Press and Public Affairs) New Delhi 1997; m 1998 Philip Frederick de Waal (1d 2000).

Slater, Karen Elizabeth Sunley; Kiev since August 2002; born 03/07/70; FCO 1988; Lagos 1991; Anguilla 1995; Tunis 1999; Band B3.

Slaymaker, Caroline Frances (née Grigg); Belgrade since August 2001; born 14/10/64; FCO 1983; Düsseldorf 1986; Third Secretary (Aid) Khartoum 1988; FCO 1990; Vice-Consul Addis Ababa 1992; Third Secretary (Political/Information) Bratislava 1997; m 1996 Michael William Slaymaker.

Slinn, David Arthur, OBE (2000); T/D Skopje since June 2001; born 16/04/59; FCO 1981; Geneva (UKDIS) 1983; Language Training 1986; Second Secretary and Head of Chancery Ulaanbaatar 1987; Second Secretary (Information/Aid) Pretoria/Cape Town 1990; Second Secretary FCO 1993; Chargé d'Affaires T/D Tirana 1995; First Secretary (Commercial) later (Chancery) Belgrade 1996; Head of British Government Office Pristina 1999; On loan to MOD 2001; T/D Belgrade 2001; m 1982 Melody Sarah Hesford.

Sloan, Kevin Joseph Carnegie; Counsellor New Delhi since July 2001; born 31/08/58; FCO 1984; Second later First Secretary (Chancery) Islamabad 1987; First Secretary FCO 1990; First Secretary Phnom Penh 1992; First Secretary (Economic) Kuala Lumpur 1993; First Secretary FCO 1997; m 1991 Christine Ruth Lowson (2d 1993, 1994).

Slough, Christopher George James; FCO since July 1996; born 28/11/67; Band B3; m 1993 Angela (1s 1999).

Small, Susan Jane Rosemary; Prague since September 1999; born 23/01/49; FCO 1985; Banjul 1986; Brussels (UKDEL NATO) 1989; New York (UKMIS) 1992; FCO 1994; Brussels 1995; Band B3.

Smart, Christopher David Russell; Second Secretary (Commercial) Nairobi since March 1998; born 22/05/52; FCO 1971; Paris (UKDEL OECD) 1974; Bridgetown 1977; Lilongwe 1980; Third Secretary FCO 1983; Port Moresby 1987; Kingston 1991; Second Secretary FCO 1995; m 1980 Patricia Margaret King (2 adopted d 1993, 1998).

Smart, Stephen Brian; Third Secretary (Consular) Karachi since July 1998; born 21/03/58; FCO 1975; Brussels (UKREP) 1978; Seoul 1980; Karachi 1983; FCO 1985; Warsaw 1988; FCO 1990; Cairo 1991; T/D Moscow 1994; FCO 1995; Band B3; m 1980 Catherine Jane Beard (1s 1986).

Smart, Timothy Spencer; Second Secretary (Political) Tel Aviv since August 2001; born 17/09/74; FCO 1999.

Smith, Andrew Dominic Charles; SUPL since January 2001; born 01/06/67; FCO 1990; Full-Time Language Training 1992; Bangkok 1992; Third Secretary (Economic) Warsaw 1993; Third Secretary (Political) Bonn 1996; Band C4.

Smith, Anne; Warsaw since November 1997; born 16/05/60; FCO 1989; Reykjavik 1991; Hong Kong 1994; Band B3; (1d 1998).

Smith, Anthony Donald Raymond; On loan to DflD since October 1996; born 08/11/58; FCO 1986; Second later First Secretary Madrid 1988; First Secretary FCO 1991; On loan to the ODA 1996; m 1996 Kerry Jane Rankine.

Smith, Carol Ann; SUPL since January 2000; born 11/11/63; FCO 1987; Cape Town 1989; Budapest 1992; Moscow 1995; Khartoum 1999; Band B3.

Smith, Carol Susan (née Woods); FCO since July 1997; born 27/04/47; FCO 1970; FCO 1971; Warsaw 1971; Cairo 1972; FCO 1975; Karachi 1977; Kampala 1980; Bahrain 1983; FCO 1987; New Delhi 1990; Singapore 1994; Band B3; m 1976 Raymond Peter Smith.

Smith, Claire Helen (née Stubbs); Counsellor (Political/Aid) Islamabad since May 1999; born 23/12/56; FCO 1979; Language Training Hong Kong 1981; Second Secretary Peking 1983; First Secretary FCO 1985; SUPL 1990; On secondment to German MFA Bonn 1994; Bonn 1997; m 1986 Michael Forbes Smith (1d 1989; 1s 1992).

Smith, Colin Anthony; On loan to DflD Sofia since September 1999; born 19/09/69; FCO 1995; Secondment to European Commission Brussels 1997; Second Secretary (Political) Sofia 1998; Second Secretary FCO 1998; Band C4; m 2000 Suzanne Hunnewell.

Smith, David Joseph; First Secretary (Commercial) Tokyo since June 1996; born 12/01/51; FCO 1969; Tokyo 1972; Kuwait 1977; Warsaw 1979; FCO 1981; Osaka 1984; Second later First Secretary (Assistant Trade Commissioner) BTC Hong Kong 1989; First Secretary FCO 1994; First Secretary to T/D Taiwan 1994; m 1975 Hitomi Takahashi (2d 1978, 1982).

Smith, David Leslie Darwin; FCO since December 1976; born 20/04/42; Band B3.

Smith, Deborah Ann (née Connor); SUPL since January 1999; born 10/02/64; FCO 1992; New Delhi 1994; Amman 1998; Band B3; m 1997 (1d 1987).

Smith, Derek Moir; Second Secretary Freetown since February 2001; born 12/09/67; Department of Employment 1986; FCO 1987; Riyadh 1989; Latin America/Caribbean Floater 1993; SUPL 1995; FCO 1996; Band C4.

Smith, Gerald Dominic; Bratislava since September 2002; born 04/04/70; FCO 1988; Islamabad 1992; Luanda 1996; FCO 1998; Band B3; m 1992 Penelope Jane Clifford (1d 1996; 1s 1999).

Smith, Guy William; Rio de Janeiro since July 1991; born 20/04/66; FCO 1985; Brussels (UKREP) 1987; Sofia 1989; Band A2.

Smith, Hugh Maxwell; New York since January 1992; born 04/04/59; FCO 1981; Brussels 1985; FCO 1988; Band B3.

Smith, James; FCO since August 1998; born 23/02/42; RAF 1962-67; Post Office 1967; FCO 1970; Amman 1972; SE Asia Floater 1977; Tehran 1979; FCO 1980; Kampala 1981; FCO 1982; Hanoi 1983; Atlanta 1984; FCO 1986; Bonn 1990; FCO 1993; T/D Zagreb 1993; Band B3.

Smith, Jason R; Second Secretary (Political) Abu Dhabi since December 2000; born 20/11/70; FCO 1989; Sofia 1991; Dar es Salaam 1993; FCO 1998; Band C4; m 1994 Andreana Vlaeva (1s 1994).

Smith, John Lawrence; Second Secretary FCO since June 1997; born 15/10/65; FCO 1988; Vice-Consul Chicago 1990; Third Secretary Nairobi 1993; m 1990 Gillian Monsen (2s 1993, 1997).

Smith, John Stephen; Head of South Asian Department FCO since February 2002; born 28/03/57; Third Secretary FCO 1979; Third later Second Secretary (Commercial) Seoul 1980; Second Secretary FCO 1985; Second later First Secretary (Chancery) New York (UKMIS) 1987; First Secretary FCO 1990; First Secretary (Political/Internal) Bonn 1994; Deputy Head of Mission Brussels Embassy 1999; m 1984 Wanda Won Min Kim.

Smith, Justine Mary (née Bunn); FCO since August 2002; born 02/10/64; FCO 1983; Budapest 1986; Doha 1987; FCO 1991; Bangkok 1995; Durban 1999; SUPL 2001; Durban 2002; Band C4; m 2000 Stephen Thomas Smith (1d 2001).

Smith, Katherine Jane; SUPL since April 1999; born 21/05/67; FCO 1990; Third Secretary (Information) Istanbul 1993; T/D Suva 1997; Band B3.

Smith, Katherine Lucy; FCO since September 2001; born 10/01/64; FCO 1987; Full-Time Language Training 1990; Second Secretary (Chancery/Inf) Athens 1991; First Secretary FCO 1994; New York (UKMIS) 1997.

Smith, Lloyd Barnaby, CMG (2002); HM Ambassador Bangkok since February 2000; born 21/07/45; Third Secretary FCO 1968; Third later Second Secretary (Chancery) Bangkok 1970; First Secretary FCO 1974; First Secretary

(Chancery/Information) Paris 1977; Head of Chancery Dublin 1978; ENA Paris 1981; First Secretary later Counsellor (Press) Brussels (UKREP) 1982; Deputy Head of Mission and Counsellor (Commercial) Bangkok 1987; Director (KHF) for Eastern Europe 1990; Counsellor FCO 1993; HM Ambassador Kathmandu 1995; FCO 1999; m (1) Nicola Mary Whitefield (diss 1982); (2) 1983 Mary Sumner (1d 1983; 1s 1985).

Smith, Lynne Marie; Istanbul since March 1999; born 17/02/63; FCO 1982; Peking 1984; Ankara 1987; FCO 1990; SUPL 1994; Band B3; m 1989 Ahmet Kalaycio Fglu.

Smith, Mairi (née Dyer); Helsinki since March 2001; born 03/03/71; FCO 1991; SUPL 1995; FCO 1996; Canberra 1997; Band A2; m 1997 Daniel Beaton Smith.

Smith, Michael Forbes; HM Ambassador Dushanbe since July 2002; born 04/06/48; Board of Trade 1966-68; Army 1971-78; FCO 1978; Second later First Secretary and Head of Chancery Addis Ababa 1979; Deputy to the Civil Commissioner and Political Adviser Port Stanley 1983; First Secretary FCO 1985; Consul (Commercial) Zurich 1990; First Secretary (Press/Information) Bonn 1994; Deputy High Commissioner Islamabad 1999; FCO 1999; m (1) 1974 Christian Joanna Kersley (Annulled 1983) (1d 1975); (2) 1986 Claire Helen Stubbs (1d 1989; 1s 1992).

Smith, Nicolette Jane; Beirut since July 2001; born 30/04/70; FCO 1989; Kuala Lumpur 1992; SUPL 1995; FCO 1997; Band B3.

Smith, Peter; First Secretary (Consular/Immigration) Moscow since November 2001; born 06/08/51; FCO 1971; Canberra 1974; East Berlin 1976; Khartoum 1978; FCO 1982; Dhaka 1983; Manila 1988; Washington 1989; FCO 1991 (Second Secretary 1994); New Delhi 1994; Muscat 1996; m 1974 Cynthia Angela Shearn (1d 1975).

Smith, Roland Berkeley; First Secretary (Commercial) Bandar Seri Begawan since 2002; born 06/07/55; FCO 1973; Bonn 1975; Karachi 1979; FCO 1981; Nicosia 1985; Manila 1987; Bombay 1991; FCO 1995; First Secretary (Management/Consul) Kiev 1998; m (1) 1978 Shirley Kathleen Sandford (diss 1993) (1s 1988); (2) 1994 Marites Enriquez Garlan (1s 1999).

Smith, Shirley Kathleen (née Sandford); Second Secretary (Commercial) Dublin since August 1994; born 05/01/56; FCO 1974; Bonn 1977; Karachi 1979; FCO 1981; Nicosia 1985; Manila 1987; Second Secretary FCO 1991; m 1978 Roland Berkeley Smith (1s 1988).

Smith, Simon John Meredith; Head of North East Asia and Pacific Dept FCO since July 2002; born 14/01/58; Department of Employment 1981; Second Secretary FCO 1986; Language Training/Kamakura 1987; Second later First Secretary (Economic) Tokyo 1989; FCO 1992;

Counsellor (Commercial/Economic/S&T) Moscow 1998; m 1984 Siân Rosemary Stickings (2d 1989, 1993).

Smith, Simon Richard; FCO since July 1988; born 03/10/57; FCO 1974; Peking 1982; FCO 1983; Third Secretary Bucharest 1986; Band B3.

Smith, Stephen Jeremy; SMO Kabul since May 2002; born 25/10/44; FO later DSAO 1964; Baghdad 1968; Sofia 1973; FCO 1974; Vice-Consul Sydney 1977; Assistant Parliamentary Clerk FCO 1982; Second Secretary (Admin) and HM Consul Algiers 1983; FCO 1986; On secondment to the Birmingham Chamber of Industry and Commerce 1989; Second Secretary (Commercial) Dar es Salaam 1991; Deputy Consul-General and Consul (Commercial) Shanghai 1994; First Secretary FCO 1998; m 1969 Delyth Morris (2d 1973, 1977; 2s 1975, 1978).

Smith, Stuart Harris; Kiev since September 1998; born 24/04/48; Nicosia 1989; Belgrade 1991; World Wide Floater Duties 1993; Moscow 1996; Band B3; m 1969 Carol Ann (1s 1971; 1d 1974).

Smith, Stuart Vaughan; Rio de Janeiro since June 2002; born 05/07/72; FCO 1991; New Delhi 1995; Rio de Janeiro 1999; Band A2.

Smith, Susan Lesley; FCO since January 2000; born 29/12/63; FCO 1983; New Delhi 1985; Belgrade 1988; Kathmandu 1989; FCO 1992; Pretoria 1996; T/D Casablanca 1999; Band B3.

Smith, William John; Karachi since April 2002; born 20/02/48; Royal Marines 1964-88; Bonn 1988; Floater Duties 1993; Sofia 1994; Peking 1998; Band B3; m 1971 Doreen (1s 1973; 2d 1971, 1976).

Smithson, David John; SUPL since November 1997; born 16/04/70; FCO 1988; New York (UKMIS) 1991; Peking 1994; Band A2; m 1993 Paula Louise Smith.

Smithson, Paula Louise (née Smith); Peking since June 1994; born 13/10/68; FCO 1987; New York (UKMIS) 1990; SUPL 1992; Band A2; m 1993 David John Smithson.

Smyth, Caroline Ann, MBE (1999); Cape Town since April 2002; born 02/06/61; FCO 1980; Moscow 1982; Strasbourg 1983; Peking 1987; FCO 1989; Washington 1993; Tripoli 1997; FCO 1998; Band C4; m 2001 Michael Scales.

Sneddon, Deborah Phillips; FCO since September 1992; born 20/12/63; FCO 1985; Geneva (UKMIS) 1987; Valletta 1990; Band A2.

Snee, Nicholas James Michael; Vice-Consul Moscow since June 2001; born 10/07/65; HM Forces Army 1982-94; FCO 1996; Windhoek 1998; Band B3; m 2000 Valerie Johr.

Snell, Arthur Gordon; Second Secretary (Political) Abuja since March 2001; born 30/10/75; FCO 1998; Second Secretary (Political/Economic) Harare 2000; Band C4.

Snell, Michael George, MVO (1980); Management Officer Muscat since August 2001; born 09/06/47; FCO 1972; Darwin 1973; FCO 1975; Rome 1978; Banjul 1981; FCO 1982; Sofia 1983; Second Secretary FCO 1985; Second Secretary Washington 1988; Jakarta 1994; FCO 1998; m (1) 1973 Diana Mary Powell-Williams (diss 1992) (2d 1977, 1979; 1s 1982); (2) Victoria B Curry (1s 1996).

Snook, Andrew John; Vice-Consul Rio de Janeiro since April 1998; born 18/07/72; FCO 1992; World Wide Floater Duties 1995; Full-Time Language Training 1997; m 1999 Priscila de Medeiros Ivo Santos (1d 2000).

Snowdon, Susan Carol; FCO since 2000; born 12/07/65; MOD 1983; FCO 1985; Brussels 1987; Manila 1989; FCO 1993; Accra 1997; Band B3.

Snoxell, David Raymond; High Commissioner Port Louis since September 2000; born 18/11/44; FCO 1969; Islamabad 1972; Geneva (UKMIS) 1976; Second later First Secretary FCO 1984; Executive Director and Consul (Information) New York (BIS) 1986; First Secretary FCO 1991; HM Ambassador Cape Verde, Dakar, Guinea, Guinea Bissau and Mali 1997; m 1971 Anne Carter (2s 1972, 1977; 1d 1973).

Sommerlad, Alistair Martin; First Secretary (Political) Sarajevo since July 2001; born 15/10/65; Lagos 1996; FCO 1996; First Secretary FCO 1999; Band D6.

Soothill, Deborah Jane; FCO since October 2001; born 22/05/69; FCO 1992; Full-Time Language Training Peking 1995; Second Secretary (Chancery/External) Peking 1996; Second Secretary FCO 1999; SUPL 2000; Band C4; m 1996 Brendan Paul Mahoney da Madariaga.

Soper, Andrew Keith; Deputy Head of Mission Brasilia since June 2001; born 06/07/60; FCO 1985; Second later First Secretary (Chancery) Mexico City 1987; First Secretary FCO 1990; First Secretary Washington 1995; FCO 1999; m 1987 Kathryn Garrett Stevens (1s 1991; 1d 1993).

Soutar, Samuel Ian; HM Ambassador Sofia since December 2001; born 02/06/45; On loan to the RCDS 1991; Third Secretary FCO 1968; Third later Second Secretary Brussels (UKDEL EC) 1970; Saigon 1972; First Secretary FCO 1974; Private Secretary to the Parliamentary Under-Secretary of State for Foreign and Commonwealth Affairs 1976; First Secretary Washington 1977; First Secretary FCO 1981; Deputy High Commissioner and Head of Chancery Wellington 1986; Counsellor FCO 1991; UK Permanent Representative to the Conference on Disarmament Geneva 1997; m 1968 Mary Isabella Boyle (1s 1971; 1d 1973).

Southcombe, Julie Ann; SUPL since December 1988; born 13/10/57; FCO 1982; Moscow 1983; Brussels (UKREP) 1984; FCO 1987; Band A2.

Southern, Thomas Andrew Oliver; Second Secretary (Political) Skopje since January 2002; born 15/01/75; FCO 2000; Band C4.

Sowerby, Karen Dorothy Howell; Luanda since October 2000; born 14/06/46; FCO 1991; La Paz 1993; Yaoundé 1997; Band A2.

Sowerby, Lynne; Geneva since June 2002; born 17/09/67; FCO 1988; East Berlin 1990; Ankara 1993; FCO 1997; Band B3.

Sparkes, Andrew James; Deputy High Commissioner Pretoria since September 2001; born 04/07/59; FCO 1982; Second Secretary (Chancery) Ankara 1985; First Secretary FCO 1988; First Secretary (Political) Bangkok 1992; First Secretary later Counsellor FCO 1995; On loan to the DTI 1997; Deputy Head of Mission Jakarta 1999; m 1985 Jean Mary Meakin (1s 1988; 1d 1992).

Sparrow, Rosalyn Louise (née Morris), MVO (1999); SUPL since June 2001; born 15/05/61; FCO 1983; Dhaka 1986; Brussels (UKDEL) 1989; Second Secretary (Economic) Brussels 1991; Second Secretary (Commercial) Singapore 1993; Second Secretary Seoul 1998; m (1) 1986 Richard John Bryant (diss) (1s 1991); (2) David John Sparrow.

Spearman, Richard David; First Secretary FCO since August 2001; born 30/08/60; FCO 1989; Consul Istanbul 1992; First Secretary FCO 1994; First Secretary (Political) Paris 1997; Band D6; m 1987 Caroline Jill Scoones (1s 1992; 2d 1995, 1998).

Speller, Paul Anthony; Deputy Head of Mission Jakarta since January 2002; born 21/01/54; FCO 1983; Second later First Secretary Bonn 1986; First Secretary FCO 1989 (Private Secretary to the Parliamentary Under Secretary of State 1991); First Secretary (External Relations) Brussels (UKREP) 1993; FCO 1996; Deputy Governor Gibraltar 1998; m 1998 Jane Hennessey.

Speller, Susan Barbara (née Arnold); FCO since October 2001; born 22/10/56; FCO 1984; Vice-Consul (Commercial) Munich 1987; Vice-Consul (Information) Düsseldorf 1988; FCO 1990; Second Secretary FCO 1992; On loan to ODA 1994; Second later First Secretary (PPA/Management) Bonn 1996; First Secretary (Public Relations) Berlin 1999.

Spellman, Antoinette Marie (née Mills); Islamabad since October 1999; born 24/05/65; FCO 1988; Brussels (UKDEL NATO) 1991; Abuja 1993; Kuwait 1996; Band A2; m 1990 Garry James Spellman (2s 1993, 1998).

Spencer, David Paul, MBE (1988); First Secretary FCO since July 2002; born 04/04/59; FCO 1978; Kuala Lumpur 1981; FCO 1983; Aden 1985; First Secretary FCO 1988; First Secretary (Political) Stockholm 1992; FCO 1996; First Secretary (Political) Dubai 1999; Band D6; m 1988 Patricia Anne McCullock (2s 1990, 1993).

Spencer, Elaine Joan; FCO since March 1976; born 24/03/49; DSAO 1966; FO 1966; FO (later FCO) 1967; Bonn 1972; Khartoum 1975; Band A2.

Spencer, Sarah; SUPL since November 1999; born 31/05/68; FCO 1988; Kathmandu 1990; FCO 1993; Bucharest 1995; Cairo 1999; Band B3; m 1997 Mark Anthony James Hamilton (1s 2000).

Spicer, Haden Richard; Consul (Commercial) Guangzhou since February 2002; born 18/06/62; FCO 1985; Abu Dhabi 1989; Moscow 1992; FCO 1995; Second Secretary (Commercial) Bandar Seri Begawan 1999; Band C4; m 1988 Carole E Pymble.

Spindler, Guy David St. John Kelso; Counsellor (Political) Warsaw since August 2002; born 09/06/62; Second Secretary FCO 1987; Second later First Secretary (Commercial) Moscow 1989; First Secretary FCO 1992; First Secretary (Political) Pretoria 1997; First Secretary FCO 2000; Band D6; m 1999 Laura Jane Brady (1d 2000; 1s 2001).

Spires, David Mark, MVO (1992); Second Secretary (Commercial) Beijing since November 2001; born 18/11/61; FCO 1980; Warsaw 1982; Lima 1985; FCO 1986; Islamabad 1987; Paris 1991; San Salvador 1993; Full-Time Language Training 1993; Belgrade 1997; Second Secretary (Management) Dublin 1999; Band C4; m 1987 (2s 1986, 1996; 1d 1990).

Spivey, Donald; Tokyo since September 1999; born 12/04/68; FCO 1989; Tokyo 1992; FCO 1995; Kamakura 1998; Band B3.

Spoor, Peter Logan; Second later First Secretary FCO since October 1999; born 04/11/68; FCO 1992; Full-Time Language Training 1994-96; Third Secretary (Commercial) Bangkok 1996; Band C4; m 1998 Joanna M Haydon.

Sprake, Anthony Douglas; Consul-General Melbourne since August 2001; born 16/07/44; Department of Employment 1968; First Secretary (Labour) Brussels 1977; FCO 1980; Deputy High Commissioner Freetown 1982; First Secretary later Counsellor FCO 1985; Counsellor (Commercial) The Hague 1990; Counsellor FCO 1994; Minister Peking 1996; FCO 2000; m 1977 Jane McNeill (2s 1980, 1982 (dec'd 1989)).

Sprod, Caroline; FCO since June 2002; born 02/03/71; FCO 1993; T/D Kiev 1995; Third Secretary Hong Kong 1996; Full-Time Language Training 2000; Madrid 2000; Band B3.

Sprunt, Patrick William; Counsellor (Political Affairs) Tokyo since October 1999; born 13/04/52; Third Secretary FCO 1975; Language Training SOAS 1976; Second later First Secretary Tokyo 1978; Brussels (UKREP) 1982; FCO 1982; First Secretary Bonn 1983; First Secretary FCO 1986; First Secretary Tokyo 1987; First Secretary (ECOSOC) New York (UKMIS) 1992; First Secretary FCO 1996; m 1979 Haang Ai-Yuan Wong (1s 1985; 1d 1989).

Squibb, Keith Norman; Cairo since October 1999; born 02/09/49; Prague 1989; Tel Aviv 1991; Warsaw 1993; Moscow 1995; Lagos 1998; Band B3; m 1974 Brigitte Pronier (3s 1974, 1978, 1984).

Squire, Richard James; First Secretary (Political) Kabul since April 2002; born 11/09/74; FCO 1996; Full-Time Language Training 1998; Band D6.

Squires, George Thomas; First Secretary (Management) Peking since March 1997; born 20/10/48; FCO 1968; Dacca 1971; Antigua 1973; Warsaw 1975; Jakarta 1976; FCO 1979 (Second Secretary 1983); Vice-Consul later Consul and Administration Officer Sydney 1985; First Secretary (Commercial/Development) Bangkok 1990; First Secretary FCO 1993; m 1979 Helen Mary Thomas (2s 1983, 1985).

Squires, Helen (née Thomas); Second Secretary (Management) Peking since August 1997; born 18/10/51; FCO 1973; Third Secretary (Commercial) Jakarta 1976; Third Secretary FCO 1979; SUPL 1983; Vice-Consul Bangkok 1990; FCO 1993; m 1979 George Thomas Squires (2s 1983, 1985).

Stacey, Christopher Robin; ECM Manila since September 2002; born 09/12/47; RAF 1965-74; FCO 1974; Islamabad 1976; Budapest 1980; Singapore 1983; FCO 1984; Manila 1988; Nicosia 1992; FCO 1995; New Delhi 1999; Band C4; m 1977 Coral Jane Chargé (2s 1981, 1987).

Stafford, Andrew Jeremy; Counsellor (Political) Stockholm since June 1999; born 01/02/53; Third Secretary FCO 1975; Stockholm 1977; Second Secretary Accra 1979; FCO 1979; Second later First Secretary FCO 1981; First Secretary and Consul Prague 1984; First Secretary FCO 1987; First Secretary (Chancery) Brussels 1991; FCO 1994; m (1) 1977 Felicity Joanna Maria Kelly; (2) 1983 Elizabeth Rosemary Kempston (2d 1985, 1992; 1s 1988).

Stafford, Nina Jeanne; SUPL since February 2001; born 28/09/71; FCO 1991; Buenos Aires 1997; The Hague 2000; Band A2.

Stagg, Charles Richard Vernon, CMG (2001); Director (Information) since October 2001; born 27/09/55; FCO 1977; Third later Second Secretary Sofia 1979; The Hague 1982; First Secretary FCO 1985; Brussels (UKREP) 1987; First Secretary FCO 1988; First Secretary (Information) Brussels (UKREP) 1991; First Secretary FCO 1993; HM Ambassador Republic of Bulgaria 1998; m 1982 Arabella Clare Faber (3s 1984, 1985, 1990; 2d 1992, 1997).

Standbrook, Timothy William; On loan to British Trade International since June 2000; born 08/06/63; FCO 1988; Language Training Seoul 1990; Third Secretary (Political) Seoul 1992; FCO 1994; Peking (ECO) 1995; FCO 1997; Karachi 1997; m 1997 Jia Lei (1d 2000).

Stanton, Karen Jane (née Owen); First Secretary (Commercial) Tokyo since July 1999; born

25/01/62; FCO 1984; Language Training Kamakura 1986; Vice-Consul Tokyo 1987; Third Secretary (Chancery) Rome 1991; Second Secretary FCO 1994; First Secretary FCO 1996; m 1990 Graham Stanton.

Stanton, Louise Jane; FCO since April 1999; born 14/08/68; FCO 1990; Language Training (Japanese) SOAS 1991; Third Secretary (Commercial) Tokyo 1993; Full-Time Language Training Kamakura 1993; World Wide Floater Duties 1997; Band C4.

Stanyer, Julie Grace (née Robins); FCO since February 1992; born 15/03/48; FCO 1984; Bridgetown 1985; Brussels (UKDEL NATO) 1989; Band B3; m 1988 Patrick Julian Serville.

Staples, Graham Raymond; Vice-Consul and Third Secretary Windhoek since December 1997; born 24/01/69; FCO 1988; Dublin 1989; Warsaw 1992; FCO 1994; Band B3; m 1994 Sarah Kathleen Paterson (1d 1998).

Starkey, Nicholas Andrew; Senior Management Officer Islamabad since September 1999; born 20/12/52; FCO 1972; SE Asia Floater 1975; Warsaw 1977; Bridgetown 1979; FCO 1981; Kuwait 1985; Second Secretary (Consular) Lagos 1989; Second Secretary FCO 1992; Second Secretary (Management) Bucharest 1995; Band C5; m 1981 Rhodora Corrales Maroto (2s 1983, 1999; 1d 1985).

Staunton, Andrew James; Second Secretary FCO since July 1997; born 07/08/67; FCO 1987; Peking 1989; Third Secretary (Chancery/Management) Strasbourg 1991; Third Secretary (Economic) Bucharest 1994; Band D6; m 1990 Rebecca Anne Nixon (1s 1991; 1d 1993).

Stead, Michael; Second Secretary (Commercial) Lisbon since December 1997; born 19/01/58; British Library 1976; FCO 1979; Jedda 1981; Riyadh 1982; LA Floater 1985; Rio de Janeiro 1988; FCO 1991; Second Secretary (Political) Addis Ababa 1994.

Steel, Diane Elizabeth; On loan to No.10 Downing Street since December 1999; born 02/08/60; FCO 1978; Brussels (UKREP) 1982; Dar es Salaam 1985; Doha 1989; St Petersburg 1992; FCO 1995; Band B3.

Steele, Christopher David; First Secretary (Financial) Paris since September 1998; born 24/06/64; FCO 1987; Second Secretary (Chancery) Moscow 1990; Second later First Secretary FCO 1993; Band D6; m 1990 Laura Katharine Hunt (2s 1996, 1998; 1d 2000).

Steen, Barry John; FCO since June 2002; born 10/12/75; Benefits Agency 1997; Inland Revenue 1998-02; Band A2.

Steeples, John Charles; Management Officer/Consul Oslo since June 2002; born 14/02/45; Army 1966-70, 1972-73; FCO 1973; Dacca 1976; Brussels (UKDEL NATO) 1978; FCO 1981; Prague 1981; Paris 1985; FCO 1987;

Brussels 1988; Vienna 1992; Second Secretary FCO 1995; m 1975 Jennifer Maureen Davis (1d 1977; 2s 1980, 1983).

Stein, Gordon; ECM Tunis since July 2002; born 20/02/69; FCO 1989; Geneva (UKMIS) 1991; Rabat 1994; Third Secretary Peking 1998; Band C4; m 1994 Deborah Anne Hooper.

Stephen, Ann (née Barbour); Tripoli since April 2002; born 02/04/66; FCO 1988; Paris 1991; Freetown 1993; Banjul 1998; Brussels (UKDEL NATO) 1999; Band A2; m 1992 Robert Stephen (1s 1995).

Stephens, Adrian Charles; Consul-General Ho Chi Minh City since January 2001; born 19/03/46; DSAO (later FCO) 1964; Karachi 1968; Colombo 1970; Budapest 1972; FCO 1974; Islamabad 1976; FCO 1978; (Second Secretary 1979); Bangkok 1982; Consul Berlin 1986; First Secretary FCO 1990; Seoul 1993; First Secretary (Commercial) Mexico City 1997; m 1968 Susan Jane Everitt (1d 1971; 1s 1973).

Stephenson, John Edmund; First Secretary FCO since March 1998; born 19/12/60; FCO 1986; Second later First Secretary (Information) Santiago 1989; First Secretary FCO 1992; First Secretary Havana 1994; Band D7; m 1986 Jacqueline Denise Clayton (3s 1990, 1992, 1993).

Sterling, Janice Aeyesha Odonna; New York (UKMIS) since August 2000; born 08/08/69; FCO 1997; Band A2; m 1994 Dwight Sterling.

Steven, John Young; Floater Duties since May 2000; born 21/05/68; FCO 1988; Moscow 1989; Washington 1992; FCO 1995; Band B3.

Stevens, Ian James; First Secretary (Management) Dublin since June 2002; born 15/05/66; FCO 1985; Brussels (UKDEL NATO) 1989; New Delhi 1992; FCO 1996; First Secretary (Management/Consul) Oslo 1998; Band C5; m 1987 Adele Oliver (1d 1989; 1s 1991).

Stevens, Jill Frances; FCO since December 1992 (Second Secretary 1996); born 10/03/57; FCO 1977; Damascus 1979; Bridgetown 1982; FCO 1984; Dar es Salaam 1987; FCO 1989; Moscow 1990; Band C4.

Stevens, Mark; Consul-General Alexandria since May 1999; born 05/07/49; DSAO 1966; FCO 1968; Georgetown 1970; Madrid 1973; East Berlin 1976; FCO 1978; Kingston 1982; New Delhi 1985; Second Secretary FCO 1988; Second Secretary (Management) and Vice-Consul Tunis 1992; FCO 1995; m 1970 Pauline Elaine Graber (2d 1973, 1976).

Stevens, Paul David; Second Secretary Los Angeles since August 1999; born 08/09/59; MOD 1977; FCO 1981; Geneva (UKMIS) 1983; Kampala 1985; Washington 1988; FCO 1991; Full-Time Language Training 1994; Band B3; m 1985 Faye Jaqueline Brand.

Stevenson, Helen Elizabeth (née Dewsnap); SUPL since January 1999; born 14/01/66; FCO 1985;

Rio de Janeiro 1990; FCO 1992; Paris 1993; FCO 1996; Band A2; m 1992 James Richard Stevenson.

Stevenson, William Michael; FCO since July 1997; born 04/09/51; FCO 1971; Brussels (UKDEL NATO) 1973; Luxembourg 1977; Addis Ababa 1979; Moscow 1983; FCO 1985; Khartoum 1988; Second Secretary Ankara 1993; Band C5; m 1982 Laura Birse Stirton (2s 1986, 1987).

Stew, Timothy David, MBE (1996); FCO since May 2000; born 08/10/66; FCO 1988; Language Training 1989; Language Training Cairo 1990; Third Secretary (Chancery) Riyadh 1991; Sarajevo 1995; Deputy High Commissioner Belmopan 1996; Band C4; m 1991 Michelle Louise Mealor (1d 1996; 1s 1998).

Stewart, Brian Edward; Deputy Head of Mission and Counsellor Kuwait since July 1998; born 04/02/50; Third Secretary FCO 1972; MECAS 1973; Third later Second Secretary Amman 1975; On loan to Cabinet Office 1978; First Secretary 1979; FCO 1980; First Secretary and Head of Chancery Singapore 1982; Head of Chancery Tunis 1986; First Secretary FCO 1989; Deputy Head of Mission Damascus 1993; Counsellor FCO 1996; m 1975 Anne Elizabeth Cockerill.

Stewart, Iain Jamieson; Full-Time Language Training (Bulgarian) since September 2002; born 03/12/71; Geneva (UKDIS) 1994; World Wide Floater Duties 1999; Band C4.

Stewart, Rachel Lovett; FCO since April 2002; born 09/02/79; Band C4.

Stewart, Roderick James Nugent; SUPL since July 2000; born 03/01/73; FCO 1995; Second Secretary (Economic) Jakarta 1997; Second Secretary British Embassy Office Banja Luka 1999; Band C4.

Still, Jean Margaret (née Wilton); First Secretary (Management) Kuala Lumpur since April 1995; born 16/12/46; FO (later FCO) 1965; Prague 1969; Rio de Janeiro 1971; Nicosia 1974; FCO 1975; Brasilia 1979; Second Secretary on loan to CAD Hanslope Park 1982; Second Secretary FCO 1983; Second Secretary New Delhi 1986; Second later First Secretary FCO 1990; m 1978 Anthony Gerald Still.

Stirling, Sonia Louise; SUPL since June 2000; born 17/06/74; FCO 1994; Paris 1996; Band A2.

Stitt, (Thomas) Clive Somerville; British Trade International since May 1999; born 01/01/48; Third Secretary FCO 1970; Kabul 1972; Language Training Tehran 1972; Third later Second Secretary New Delhi 1974; First Secretary FCO 1977; Geneva (UKMIS) 1982; First Secretary later Counsellor FCO 1986; Counsellor New York (UKMIS) 1992; m 1977 Margaret Ann Milward (2d 1982, 1984).

Stokes, Antony, LVO (1996); First Secretary (Political) Seoul since April 2000; born 21/01/65; FCO 1994; First Secretary and Head of Political Section Bangkok 1996; Full-Time Language Training 1999; Band D6.

Stokes, Karen Ann (née Chambers); Tel Aviv since April 1999; born 18/12/67; FCO 1987; Bonn 1989; FCO 1991; Vienna 1993; FCO 1996; m 1998 Paul Terence Stokes.

Stokes, Paul Terence; SUPL since February 1999; born 09/10/63; FCO 1984; Bonn 1988; FCO 1992; Vienna (UKMIS) 1993; FCO 1996; Band B3; m 1998 Karen Chambers.

Stokey, Tracey Joanne Tudor; Brussels (UKDEL) since September 2002; born 10/03/65; FCO 1988; Bonn 1990; Luxembourg 1993; Band A2; m 1988 Brendan Stokey (1s 1996).

Stokoe, Kay; FCO since 1997; born 23/06/69; FCO 1989; Madrid 1992; Floater Duties 1995; Band B3.

Stollery, Mark Thomas; First Secretary FCO since June 2002; born 08/10/60; Royal Navy 1978-88; Second Secretary FCO 1988; On loan to EU Commission 1989; Second Secretary (EC Affairs) Brussels 1990; First Secretary FCO 1993; First Secretary (Political) Islamabad 2002; Band D6; m 1990 Denise Jekyll (1s 1995; 1d 1998).

Stone, Jemma Catherine; Riyadh since March 2002; born 08/01/70; FCO 1991; Bonn 1994; Moscow 1998; Band A2.

Stone, Marie Louise; FCO since October 1992; born 27/08/74; Band A2.

Stones, Adrian; First Secretary later Counsellor Harare since October 2000; born 16/10/60; FCO 1986; Second later First Secretary (Information) New Delhi 1989; First Secretary FCO 1991; First Secretary (Chancery) Washington 1992; First Secretary FCO 1995; m 1990 Gillian Ruth Millman (2s 1992, 1994; 1d 1998).

Stonor, Ralph William Robert Thomas; FCO since March 2002; born 10/09/74; Band C4.

Storey, Neil William; First Secretary (Management) and HM Consul Lima since September 2000; born 10/09/61; FCO 1982; Third Secretary Brasilia 1994; FCO 1998; Band C4; m 1992 Oyami Azevedo.

Stott, Adam Paul; Geneva (UKMIS) since March 2000; born 26/03/71; FCO 1993; Band A2.

Stoves, Margaret; FCO since October 1999; born 03/07/45; FCO 1987; Lisbon 1990; Almaty 1992; Brussels (UKDEL NATO) 1995; Band A2.

Strain, Scott Robert; Consul-General Chongqing since March 2000; born 04/10/70; FCO 1989; Attaché Pretoria/Cape Town 1991; Attaché later Third Secretary Vice-Consul Peking 1995; Band C4; m 1995 Caroline Joanne Ewing (diss 2000).

Stubbings, Graham James; Johannesburg since January 1996; born 17/09/57; DHSS 1974; FCO 1976; New York (UKMIS) 1979; Kingston 1982; FCO 1986; New Delhi 1989; Band B3; m 1989 Kirsty Alexander (2s 1987, 1994).

Stubbins, Caroline Mary; FCO since April 1991; born 26/02/52; FCO 1972; Prague 1974; FCO 1976; New York 1978; FCO 1981; Canberra 1984; FCO 1987; Washington 1988; Band A2.

Stucley-Houghton, Nicholas John Knight; FCO since June 1996; born 03/10/54; Inland Revenue 1974; Santiago 1976; Mbabane 1979; Warsaw 1982; FCO 1983; Kathmandu 1986; FCO 1988; Copenhagen 1989; Johannesburg 1992; Band C4; m (1) 1976 Beatriz Elvira Sierra-Galindo (1s 1978; 1d 1980) (diss 1990); (2) 1993 Susanna Elisabeth Watkins-Pitchford (diss 1996).

Studham, Clare Nicola; Consul Tokyo since April 1996; born 29/06/58; FCO 1977; Washington 1979; FCO 1982; Floater Duties 1983; Brasilia 1984; FCO 1988; Second Secretary (ECOSOC) New York (UKMIS) 1994.

Sturgeon, Christopher Charles Alexander; Islamabad since November 1998; born 15/03/68; FCO 1988; Floater Duties 1990; Colombo 1993; Sana'a 1996.

Sturgeon, Mary Nicol; Brussels (UKDEL NATO) since September 2001; born 27/05/48; FCO 1973; Bangkok 1974; Kuwait 1976; Suva 1978; Khartoum 1980; FCO 1982; Resigned 1985; Reinstated 1988; Nicosia 1991; Amman 1994; FCO 1998; Band B3.

Sturgess, Neil; FCO since August 1994; born 13/05/62; FCO 1980; Helsinki 1991; Band C4; m 1988 Wendy Alison (1d 1995).

Styles, Graham Charles Trayton; FCO since August 1998; born 16/04/58; FCO 1977; SUPL 1978; FCO 1981; Port Louis 1985; Paris 1989; FCO 1992; Vienna (UKDEL) 1995; Band C4; m 1984 Rachael Jane Hopkins (2d 1989, 1991).

Styles, Rachael Jane (née Hopkins); FCO since February 2000; born 14/05/62; FCO 1980; Port Louis 1985; SUPL 1988; Band B3; m 1984 Graham Charles Trayton Styles (2d 1989, 1991).

Sullivan, Janet Ann; On loan to the DTI as Director since September 2002; born 15/02/58; FCO 1977; Kuala Lumpur 1980; Montevideo 1984; Tel Aviv 1988; Floater Duties 1992; FCO 1996; Floater Duties 1999; Band C4.

Summers, David; Abidjan since July 2001; born 13/11/64; FCO 1983; Islamabad 1985; Lisbon 1988; FCO 1991; Lagos 1994; Third Secretary (Management) Ankara 1997; Band C4; m 1987 Anita Cecilia Marsh (2d 1991, 1999).

Summers, Timothy Andrew; Consul Hong Kong since September 1997; born 17/02/72; FCO 1994; Full-Time Language Training 1995; Band C4.

Sundblad, Emma Louise; Second Secretary (Political/PPA) Stockholm since August 2001; born 28/10/75; FCO 1999; Band C4; m 1998 Morgan Sundblad (2s 1994, 1997).

Surman, Derek Malcolm; FCO since May 1999; born 20/06/47; Commonwealth Office/DSAO 1967; Kinshasa 1969; FCO 1970; Madrid 1971;

Dacca 1974; Stuttgart 1976; Beirut 1977; Durban 1978; Salisbury 1980; Khartoum 1982; FCO 1985; Canberra 1990; Second Secretary (Immigration) Bombay 1994; Prague 1999; m 1982 Frances Louise Stapelberg.

Sutcliffe, Nicholas Derek; First Secretary FCO since September 2001; born 09/12/57; FCO 1985; Second Secretary (Economic) Brasilia 1990; Second Secretary FCO 1993; First Secretary (Commercial) Havana 1998; Band D6; m 1985 Carole Ann Hunter (4s 1990, 1992, 1994 (twins)).

Sutherland, Elizabeth Victoria (née Myles); FCO since June 1987 (Second Secretary 1988); born 27/04/49; FCO 1971; Havana 1972; Sana'a 1974; FCO 1975; Paris 1984; Band C4; m 1988 Neil Sutherland.

Sutton, Alan Edward; Consul-General Tokyo since May 2000; born 21/03/43; FO (later FCO) 1967; Düsseldorf 1970; Istanbul 1972; FCO 1975; Islamabad 1978; FCO 1980; Georgetown 1981; FCO 1985; Second Secretary and Consul Riyadh 1987; Consul Berlin 1991; Second Secretary (Management) Bombay 1993; Band C4; m 1965 Jacqueline Anderson (1d 1966; 1s 1969).

Sutton, Janet (née Christie); FCO since May 1991; born 25/03/64; Department of Employment 1983; FCO 1984; Abidjan 1987; Paris 1990; Band B3; m 1986 Andrew Richard Sutton (2s 1987, 1995).

Sutton, Rebecca Claire; Second Secretary (Political) Pristina since August 2002; born 25/09/73; FCO 1999; Full-Time Language Training 2001; Band C4.

Swainson, Emma Mary Dillwyn; Full-Time Language Training since January 2002; born 28/12/75; FCO 2000; Band C4.

Sweeney, Carole Mary (née Crofts); FCO since October 1999; born 24/06/59; MOD 1985; FCO 1987; Second Secretary Bonn 1989; Second Secretary East Berlin 1990; Second later First Secretary FCO 1991; First Secretary (Economic) Oslo 1997; m 1988 Paul Martin Sweeney (1d 1990; 1s 1992).

Sweet, Kay (née Rose); Brussels (UKREP) since January 1997; born 11/11/63; FCO 1984; Budapest 1985; Paris 1987; Floater Duties 1991; Brussels (UKREP) 1993; Paris 1995; SUPL 1996; Band B3; m 1996 Jonathan Charles Sweet.

Sweid, Janice Ann Townsend (née Oldfield); First Secretary (Management) JMO Brussels since October 1998; born 13/06/50; FCO 1970; On loan to Cabinet Office 1973; FCO 1974; Accra 1977; FCO 1979; Washington 1984; Second Secretary (Management) Tel Aviv 1987; FCO 1992; m 1980 Youda Yomtob Sweid.

Swift, Elined Clare (née Evans); First Secretary FCO since April 2001; born 22/02/60; FCO 1988; Second later First Secretary (Economic) Buenos Aires 1990; First Secretary FCO 1993; First Secretary Geneva (UKDIS) 1997; First Secretary

(Regional Affairs) Washington 1999; Band D6; m 1999 Hans Eric Swift.

Swift, Hans Eric; First Secretary FCO since April 2001; born 14/05/58; FCO 1980; New Delhi 1982; Second Secretary FCO 1986; Second later First Secretary (Chancery) Stockholm 1988; FCO 1991; First Secretary (Political) Washington 1998; Band D6; m (1) 1981 Susan Mary Brown (diss 1995) (1d 1988; 1s 1991); (2) 1999 Elined Clare Evans.

Sykes, Graham Leslie; Sana'a since June 1999; born 20/09/60; FCO 1987; New Delhi 1992; Pretoria 1995; FCO 1995; Band B3; m 1995 Wei Li Ming.

Sykes, Roger Michael Spencer, OBE (2002); Deputy Head of Mission Karachi since February 2002; born 22/10/50; FCO 1968; Caracas 1971; Freetown 1972; Karachi 1976; Valletta 1978; Lagos 1982; Port Vila 1986; Second Secretary FCO 1990; Amman 1993; First Secretary and Head of British Trade Office Al Khobar 1997-2001; Band D6; m 1976 Anne Lesley Groves-Gidney (3s 1977, 1980, 1988).

Sylvester, Robert Anthony; Johannesburg since June 1999; born 29/12/56; FCO 1996; Band B3; m 1976 Jacqueline Lovely (1d 1986).

Syme, Avril; FCO since 2001; born 13/04/65; FCO 1987; Dublin 1989; Addis Ababa 1992; FCO 1993; Brussels 1994; FCO 1998; Ottawa 2000; Band B3; m 2001 Mr Mirrlees Chassels.

Symon, Terence Paul; Vice-Consul Guangzhou since April 2000; born 30/09/56; Army 1973-96; FCO 1997; Band B3; m 1977 Wendy Yuk Wah Leung (2d 1977, 1981).

Synnott, Sir Hilary Nicholas Hugh, KCMG (2002), CMG (1997); High Commissioner Islamabad since May 2000; born 20/03/45; Royal Navy 1962-73; Second Secretary FCO 1973; First Secretary Paris (UKDEL OECD) 1975; First Secretary Bonn 1978; FCO 1981; Counsellor, Consul-General and Head of Chancery Amman 1985; Counsellor, Head of Western European Department FCO 1989; Security Co-ordination Department 1991; Minister and Deputy High Commissioner New Delhi 1993; Director (South and South-East Asia) FCO 1996; Sabbatical at IISS 1999; m 1973 Anne Penelope Clarke.

Syposz, Shelley Liann (née Mayman); FCO since June 1995; born 02/05/70; FCO 1991; New Delhi 1993; Band A2; m 1996 Julian Jeremy Syposz.

Syrett, Mark Robert; Second Secretary FCO since June 2002; born 09/04/69; FCO 1993; Second Secretary (Political) Oslo 1998; Band C4.

Syrett, Nicholas Simon; First Secretary FCO since June 2000; born 07/12/60; FCO 1989; First Secretary (Political) Luanda 1993; First Secretary FCO 1996; First Secretary (Political) Bogotá 1998; Band D6; m 1993 Elena Fircks (1s, 1d 1997 (twins)).

T

Tandy, Arthur David; Second later First Secretary FCO since May 1989; born 16/08/49; HO 1974-85; FCO 1985; Second Secretary Riyadh 1987; Band C5; m 1973 Hilary Denise Watson (1s 1978; 1d 1982).

Tansley, Anthony James Nicholas; Counsellor and Deputy Head of Mission Muscat since November 1998; born 19/07/62; FCO 1984; Language Training 1986; Second Secretary (Chancery) Riyadh 1988; Second Secretary (Chancery) Baghdad 1989; First Secretary FCO 1991; Dublin 1994; m 1998 Blaithin Mary Curran (1s 2002).

Tarif, Pamela (née Neave); Second Secretary Yaoundé since June 2000; born 03/06/65; FCO 1985; Lagos 1988; Ottawa 1992; FCO 1994; Quito 1997; m 1988 Nacer Tarif (1d 1992; 1s 1995).

Tarry, Stephen Norman; Second Secretary (Political) Suva since July 2001; born 21/01/54; FCO 1971; Washington 1974; Damascus 1977; Brussels 1981; FCO 1983; Islamabad 1983; FCO 1988; Warsaw 1991; Dublin 1993; Vilnius 1997; Band C5; m (1) 1981 Julie Christine Lawrence (dec'd 1985) (1d (adopted) 1984); (2) 1992 Elzbieta Jaskaczek (1s 1997).

Tarshish, Daniel Morton; Second Secretary FCO since December 2000; born 14/10/69; FCO 1994; Second Secretary New York (UKMIS) 1998; Band C4; m 1999 Pamela Goddard (1d 1999).

Tatham, Michael Harry; Deputy Head of Mission Prague since July 2002; born 02/07/65; FCO 1987; Third later Second Secretary (Chancery) Prague 1990; First Secretary FCO 1993; Deputy Head of Mission and HM Consul Sofia 1997; On loan to 10 Downing Street 1999; Band D6.

Tauwhare, Richard David, MVO (1983); FCO since August 1999; born 01/11/59; FCO 1980; Third later Second Secretary (Chancery/Information) Nairobi 1982; Second later First Secretary Paris (UKDEL OECD) 1986; First Secretary FCO 1989; First Secretary Geneva (UKDIS) 1994; m 1985 Amanda Jane Grey.

Taylor, Andrea Lynn (née Reid); Asmara since April 2002; born 06/02/70; FCO 1989; Lagos 1992; Banjul 1995; Abuja 1999; Band B3; m 1996 Charles Richard Taylor.

Taylor, Duncan John Rushworth; Deputy Consul General and Director British Information Services - Press and Public Affairs New York since April 2000; born 17/10/58; FCO 1982; Third later Second Secretary Havana 1983; First Secretary FCO 1987; Language Training 1991; First Secretary (Commercial) Budapest 1992; Counsellor FCO 1997; On loan to Rolls Royce PLC 1997; m 1981 Marie Beatrice (Bébé) Terpougoff (3 step d 1972 (twins), 1973; 2s 1984, 1986).

Taylor, Eric Raymond; Third Secretary (Political) New Delhi since April 2001; born 09/01/69; FCO 1994; Vice-Consul and Third Secretary

(Management) BE Tripoli 1999; Vice-Consul and Deputy Head of BIS Tripoli 1999; Band B3; m 1998 Lynn Dudley.

Taylor, Francis; Nairobi since June 1983; born 26/07/56; FCO 1980; Band B3.

Taylor, Helen de Chaville; Strasbourg since 1994; born 15/02/48; FCO 1970; Santiago 1973; Singapore 1974; Second Secretary (Commercial) Paris 1978; First Secretary FCO 1984; First Secretary New York (UKMIS) 1986; FCO 1991; m 1987 Adrian George Ferguson Porter.

Taylor, Hugh Mackay; Consul (Commercial) Munich since November 1999; born 15/05/54; FCO 1972; Brussels (UKREP) 1975; Brunei 1978; FCO 1981; Munich 1985; Second Secretary (Chancery/Information) Lisbon 1988; Second Secretary FCO 1993; Warsaw 1996; m 1977 Christine Caggie.

Taylor, Ian Stewart; Mexico City since August 2001; born 27/01/70; FCO 1986; Cairo 1994; FCO 1998; Band C4; m 1998 Kim Catherine Higgins (1s 2001).

Taylor, Jeffrey; First Secretary (Commercial) Chicago since January 2002; born 15/08/57; FCO 1976; BMG Berlin 1979; Lusaka 1982; Moscow 1984; FCO 1985; Melbourne 1988; Canberra 1990; Second Secretary (Commercial) Helsinki 1992; Second Secretary FCO 1997; Second Secretary British Trade International 1999; m 1981 Janette Anne Hunt (2s 1987, 1990).

Taylor, Karen Ruth (née Nelms); FCO since July 2000; born 23/06/57; New Delhi 1978; FCO 1978; Peking 1982; Washington 1983; FCO 1985; Port Louis 1992; SUPL 1996; Band B3; m 1991 Nigel David Muir Taylor (1d 1994; 1s 1995).

Taylor, Kim Catherine (née Higgins); Mexico City since July 2002; born 14/10/66; FCO 1987; Lagos 1989; FCO 1993; Cairo 1994; FCO 1998; SUPL 2000; Band A2; m 1998 Ian Stewart Taylor (1s 2001).

Taylor, Louis Charles; Consul Oporto since January 2000; born 10/03/54; Home Office 1973; Dhaka 1980; Home Office 1984; Second Secretary Lagos 1990; FCO 1994; Second Secretary (Economic and Trade Policy) New Delhi 1996; Band C5; m 1977 Margaret Ann Price (2s 1984, 1987).

Taylor, Margaret Emily; FCO since September 1997; born 28/08/71; FCO 1994; Kathmandu 1995; Band A2; m 2000 Stuart Docherty.

Taylor, Mark Christopher; Second Secretary (Political) Damascus since October 2002; born 04/06/76; FCO 2000; Band C4.

Taylor, Nigel David Muir; Second Secretary FCO since November 1999; born 21/04/61; FCO 1981; Kaduna 1982; Africa/Middle East Floater 1986; FCO 1989; Port Louis 1992; Second Secretary Grand Turk 1996; Band C4; m 1991 Karen Ruth Nelms (1d 1993; 1s 1995).

Taylor, Robert James; SUPL since October 2000; born 07/04/57; HCS 1987; FCO 1989; Prague 1990; Havana 1992; FCO 1993; Buenos Aires 1996; Band A2.

Taylor, Stephen Andrew; Bangkok since January 2002; born 15/09/66; FCO 2000; Band B3.

Taylor-Tagg, Neil Kevin; SUPL since October 2000; born 29/12/55; FCO 1973; Resigned 1974; Reinstated 1977; Valletta 1978; Sofia 1981; FCO 1984; Third later Second Secretary Abu Dhabi 1988; Secretary FCO 1993; m 1977 Patricia Anne Lodge (diss 1994).

Teale, Ian Robert McKinnon; T/D Antigua since July 2000; born 28/02/71; FCO 1991; The Hague 1995; Kingston 1996; Sana'a 1999; Band B3.

Tebbit, Sir Kevin Reginald, KCMG (2002), CMG (1997); On secondment to the Ministry of Defence since July 1998; born 18/10/46; MOD 1969-79; UKDEL NATO 1979; First Secretary FCO 1982; First Secretary and Head of Chancery Ankara 1984; On secondment as Directeur du Cabinet, Cabinet of the Secretary-General of NATO, Brussels 1987; Counsellor (Political/Military) Washington 1988; Counsellor FCO 1992; m 1966 Alison Tinley (1d 1972; 1s 1975).

Teller, Linda Margaret (née Campbell); SUPL since June 1995; born 12/04/61; FCO 1991; Prague 1993; Band A2; m 1995 Nicholas Roy Richard Teller.

Temple, Tracey Joy; Helsinki since December 1998; born 09/08/65; FCO 1993; Buenos Aires 1995; Band A2.

Tench, Gavin Andrew; Second Secretary (Commercial) Kingston since April 1999; born 29/08/68; FCO 1995; Band B3.

Terrett, Nicola; Havana since September 1999; born 02/09/66; HCS 1985; FCO 1994; Band B3.

Terry, Raymond Frederick; Deputy Consul-General Melbourne since October 1998; born 18/10/44; MAFF 1961; DSAO (later FCO) 1966; Addis Ababa 1968; Peking 1971; FCO 1974; Islamabad 1976; Second Secretary (Admin) Amman 1980; Second Secretary FCO 1983; Second Secretary (Admin) and Vice-Consul Maputo 1984; Second Secretary (Commercial) Jakarta 1988; Second later First Secretary FCO 1993; m 1968 Lois Mary Jones Evans (2d 1970, 1973).

Tesoriere, Harcourt Andrew Pretorius; HM Ambassador Riga since March 2002; born 02/11/50; Royal Navy 1969-73; FCO 1974; Language Training SOAS and Iran 1975; Oriental Secretary Kabul 1976; Nairobi 1979; Second Secretary Abidjan 1981; FCO 1985; First Secretary and Head of Chancery, later Chargé d'Affaires a.i. BIS Damascus 1987; First Secretary FCO 1991; SUPL on secondment as UNOCHA Head of Field Operations (Afghanistan) 1994; HM Ambassador Tirana 1996; Head of UN Special Mission Afghanistan 1998; Chargé d'Affaires a.i.

Kabul 2001; Full-Time Language Training 2001; m 1987 Dr Alma Gloria Vasquez.

Thackstone, Tina; SUPL since April 1997; born 05/02/61; HM Treasury 1980; FCO 1982; Port Stanley 1983; Kingston 1984; Peking 1986; FCO 1989; Harare 1993; Band B3; m 1996 Jürgen Manfred Wicke.

Thain, Robert; Second Secretary FCO since October 1994; born 09/09/52; FCO 1975; Warsaw 1977; Rabat 1979; Zagreb 1982; FCO 1984; Canberra 1986; FCO 1990; Vice-Consul Helsinki 1992; m 1977 Susan Mary Nice.

The MacLaren of MacLaren, Donald; Consul-General and Deputy Head of Mission Kiev since November 2000; born 22/08/54; FCO 1978; Third later Second later First Secretary BMG Berlin 1980; Language Training 1983; First Secretary and Press Attaché Moscow 1984; First Secretary FCO 1987; Deputy Head of Mission Havana 1991; First Secretary FCO 1994; m 1978 Maida-Jane Aitchison (3s 1980, 1981, 1984; 2d 1987, 1994).

Thiel, Ann Bernadette; Second Secretary FCO since May 1997; born 02/08/52; FCO 1971; Moscow 1973; Kuwait 1975; Düsseldorf 1978; FCO 1981; Floater Duties 1984; Moscow 1986; FCO 1988; Second Secretary FCO 1991; HM Consul Johannesburg (later Pristina) 1995.

Thom, Dr Gordon; SUPL since September 1998; born 18/05/53; DOE 1978; FCO 1979; Second later First Secretary Tokyo 1981; FCO 1985; First Secretary (Commercial) New Delhi 1989; Counsellor (Economic) Tokyo 1994; m 1977 Margaret Pringle (1s 1982; 1d 1986).

Thomas, Dr Catherine Clare Mitchell; FCO since July 1987; born 03/02/58; Senior Research Officer (DS Band C4) later Principal Research Officer (Band D6); m 1989 Martin Brian Howe (2d 1990, 1994).

Thomas, Colin Ronald; Third Secretary FCO since October 1987; born 27/03/49; Board of Trade 1967; FCO 1969; Dacca 1971; Havana 1974; Maputo 1975; FCO 1979; Geneva 1984; Rio de Janeiro 1987.

Thomas, David Lloyd; Pretoria since July 2000; born 04/08/70; FCO 1996; Lagos 1997; Band C4.

Thomas, David Roger, CMG (2000); Consul-General San Francisco since July 2001; born 01/01/45; FCO 1968; Third Secretary Cairo 1971; Attaché later Second Secretary Brussels (UKREP) 1974; Ankara 1978; Second later First Secretary FCO 1982; Consul (Commercial) Frankfurt 1986; Consul-General Stuttgart 1990; First Secretary FCO 1993; HM Ambassador Baku 1997; m (1) (2d 1968, 1970) (diss 1977); (2) 1978 Fiona Lindsey Tyndall.

Thomas, Graeme Gordon; FCO since July 2001; born 26/09/48; FCO 1968; Africa Floater 1971; FCO 1972; Africa Floater 1973; Sana'a 1975; Jedda 1976; Far East Floater 1977; SE Asia Floater 1978; FCO 1980; Victoria 1982; FCO

1986; Second Secretary and Consul Warsaw 1987; Second Secretary FCO 1988; Second Secretary (Commercial) Riyadh 1992; Full-Time Language Training 1996; First Secretary (Commercial) Athens 1997; m 1981 Penelope Ann Richmond.

Thomas, Jeffrey, MBE (1995); HM Consul-General Madrid Embassy since March 1999; born 13/07/47; CO 1964; FO (later FCO) 1966; Manila 1969; Berlin 1973; FCO 1975; Ibadan 1978; Kaduna 1980; Second Secretary FCO 1984; Second Secretary (Admin/Consular) Muscat 1987; Consul Oporto 1991; First Secretary FCO 1996; m 1969 Lesley Anne Wishart (3s 1973, twins 1975).

Thomas, Penelope Ann (née Richmond); FCO since August 2001; born 17/02/50; FCO 1973; Brussels (UKREP) 1974; Caracas 1977; FCO 1979; Victoria 1982; SUPL 1987; FCO 1988; Riyadh 1992; FCO 1996; Athens 1997; SUPL 1997; Band B3; m 1981 Graeme Gordon Thomas.

Thomas, Peter James; FCO since January 2002; born 04/05/74; Band B3.

Thomas, Philip Lloyd, CMG (2001); High Commissioner Nigeria, Ambassador (Non-resident) Benin since March 2001; born 10/06/48; FCO 1972; Second Secretary Belgrade 1974; Second later First Secretary FCO 1977; First Secretary (Commercial) Madrid 1981; FCO 1984; First Secretary (Press) Brussels (UKREP) 1987; Counsellor on loan to the Cabinet Office 1989; Counsellor (Political/Military) Washington 1991; FCO 1996; Consul-General Düsseldorf 1999.

Thomas, Ryder Hugh; FCO since June 2002; born 24/05/73; Band B3.

Thomas, Simon D; Second Secretary (Political) Warsaw since November 1998; born 24/05/75; FCO 1997; Band C4.

Thompson, Christopher Colin; Port Moresby since November 2000; born 18/05/69; FCO 1989; Floater Duties 1992; Tokyo 1995; On loan to the Football Association 1999; Band B3.

Thompson, Clive Vincent; First Secretary FCO since January 1996; born 03/04/47; FCO 1973; MECAS 1975; Islamabad 1976; Tunis 1978; Stuttgart 1981; Second Secretary FCO 1983; Second Secretary (Consul) Moscow 1987; Consul later First Secretary (Commercial) Munich 1990; Second Secretary FCO 1990; m 1969 Carol Knight (2d 1973, 1974).

Thompson, Gillian Hazel; FCO since December 1993; born 08/06/53; FCO 1979; Rio de Janeiro 1980; FCO 1981; Belgrade 1982; FCO 1984; Lisbon 1986; FCO 1989; Berlin 1991; Band A2.

Thompson, Jan; FCO since March 2000; born 25/08/65; FCO 1990 (Second Secretary 1991); Second Secretary Bonn 1991; First Secretary FCO 1994; First Secretary New York (UKMIS) 1997.

Thompson, John, MBE (1975); HM Ambassador Luanda since February 2002; born 28/05/45; FO 1964; DSA 1965; Vice-Consul Düsseldorf 1966; Abu Dhabi 1969; Phnom Penh 1972; Management

Studies Polytechnic of Central London 1974; Second Secretary on loan to DOT 1975; FCO 1977; First Secretary and Head of Chancery Luanda 1979; Consul (Commercial) São Paulo 1981; First Secretary FCO 1985; High Commissioner Vila 1988; Counsellor and Director of Trade Promotion BTIO New York 1992; Counsellor FCO 1997; m 1966 Barbara Hopper (1d 1967).

Thompson, Lynne Diana; FCO since January 2000; born 20/08/59; FCO 1981; Warsaw 1982; Bandar Seri Begawan 1983; FCO 1986; Vienna 1987; FCO 1988; Istanbul 1996; Band B3.

Thompson, Philippa Ann (née Hadley); Second Secretary (PPA) Paris since August 1999; born 03/08/62; FCO 1980; Brussels 1983; Bridgetown 1985; FCO 1989; Ottawa 1991; Second Secretary Brussels (UKREP) 1994; FCO 1995; ENA Paris 1998; m 2000 Alphaeus Randolph Thompson (1s 2001).

Thompson, Richard Paul Reynier, OBE (2001); First Secretary FCO since January 2001; born 17/08/60; FCO 1989; Second later First Secretary Stockholm 1991; First Secretary FCO 1993; First Secretary Geneva (UKMIS) 1996; Band D6; m 1991 Louisa Halliday-Yates (1d 1992).

Thompson, Sarah Jane; FCO since April 1982; born 01/04/58; FCO 1979; Pretoria/Cape Town 1980; Band A2.

Thomson, Adam McClure; New York (UKMIS) since August 2002; born 01/07/55; FCO 1978; Third later Second Secretary Moscow 1981; Second later First Secretary Brussels (UKDEL NATO) 1983; FCO 1986; On loan to Cabinet Office 1989; First Secretary (Chancery) Washington 1991; Counsellor (Head of Chancery) New Delhi 1995; Counsellor FCO 1998; m 1984 Fariba Shirazi (2d 1991, 1993; 1s 1996).

Thomson, Andrew Robert Hay; Second Secretary (Political) Pristina since September 2000; born 23/06/75; FCO 1998; Band C4.

Thomson, Fergus Russell Cullen; First Secretary FCO since February 1995; born 16/05/44; DWS 1964; DSAO 1967; Peking 1969; Lagos 1972; Second Secretary FCO 1976; BTDO New York 1978; First Secretary (Commercial) Addis Ababa 1984; First Secretary FCO 1987; Deputy Head of Mission Lima 1991; m 1970 Jeanette Patricia Louis Mutton (1d 1977).

Thomson, Jonathan Hiroshi Stewart; FCO since June 2001; born 13/05/72; FCO 1996; Full-Time Language Training 1997; Second Secretary Tokyo 1998.

Thorne, Karen Ann (née Higgins); FCO since March 1984; born 09/03/57; FCO 1974; Lusaka 1978; Grand Turk 1983; Band A2; m 1978 Richard J Thorne (1d 1981).

Thorne, Nicholas Alan, CMG (2002); Counsellor (Financial) New York (UKMIS) since June 1995; born 31/03/48; FO (later FCO) 1965; Yaoundé

1971; Brussels (UKREP) 1974; Central London Polytechnic 1977; Second Secretary FCO 1977; FCO 1978; Second later First Secretary New York (UKMIS) 1980; First Secretary and Head of Chancery Manila 1983; First Secretary FCO 1987; On secondment to Thorn EMI 1989; Counsellor (Commercial) and Deputy Head of Mission Helsinki 1991; m 1974 Ann Margaret Boorman (1s 1978; 1d 1980).

Thornton, Daniel Vernon; Second Secretary FCO since September 1996; born 06/08/69; FCO 1991; Second Secretary (EU Affairs) Brussels 1995.

Thornton, James Sebastian; First Secretary (Chancery) Mexico City since January 2000; born 02/11/64; UKAEA 1986-89; FCO 1989; Second Secretary (Commercial/Information) Algiers 1992; Second later First Secretary FCO 1994; Band D6; m 1999 Anne Scrase.

Thornton, John Norris; Third Secretary Berlin since May 1996; born 06/07/59; FCO 1978; BGWRS Darwin 1980; FCO 1982; Beirut 1983; FCO 1984; Third Secretary Tehran 1986; FCO 1987; Third Secretary Geneva 1991; FCO 1993; Band C4; m 1980 Angela Dawn Clarke (1d 1989; 1s 1994).

Thornton, Patricia Ann; First Secretary Islamabad since January 2000; born 11/01/52; FCO 1971; Tehran 1973; Lima 1976; New Delhi 1979; FCO 1982; Guatemala City 1984; FCO 1987; Second Secretary (Commercial) Santiago 1988; Consul Johannesburg 1991; FCO 1995.

Thornton, Sarah; FCO since July 2000; born 05/06/72; FCO 1992; Rome 1995; SUPL 1999; Band A2.

Thorpe, Adrian Charles, CMG (1994); HM Ambassador Mexico City since January 1999; born 29/07/42; FO 1965; Language Training Tokyo 1965; Third later Second Secretary (Information) Tokyo 1968; FCO 1970; Seconded to HCS 1971; FCO 1972; First Secretary Beirut 1973; First Secretary and Head of Chancery Beirut 1975; First Secretary (Economic) Tokyo 1976; FCO 1976; First Secretary FCO 1981; Counsellor Head of Information Technology Dept 1982; Counsellor (Economic) Bonn 1985; Deputy High Commissioner Kuala Lumpur 1989; Minister Tokyo 1991; HM Ambassador Manila 1995; m 1968 Miyoko Kosugi.

Thorpe, Nigel James, CVO (1991); HM Ambassador Budapest since April 1998; born 03/10/45; Third Secretary FCO 1969; Third later Second Secretary Warsaw 1970; Second later First Secretary Dacca 1973; FCO 1975; First Secretary (Economic) Ottawa 1979; On loan to Department of Energy 1981; FCO 1982; Counsellor and Head of Chancery Warsaw 1985; Deputy High Commissioner Harare 1989; Counsellor FCO 1992; Senior Directing Staff at the Royal College of Defence Studies 1996.

Thurlow, John Robert; Second Secretary (Commercial/Industrial Relations) Rome since

January 2000; born 28/08/67; HCS 1984; FCO 1988; Algiers 1990; Bridgetown 1992; FCO 1995; On loan to the DTI 1998; Band C4; m 1992 Joanna Welch (1d 1988).

Thursfield, Martin Robert; First Secretary (Political) Vilnius since December 2000; born 08/06/67; FCO 1989; Full-Time Language Training Peking 1991; Second Secretary (Information) BTC Hong Kong 1993; First Secretary FCO 1995; Band D6; m 1996 Ingrid Katharina Corbyn Hale (1s 1997; 1d 2000).

Thurston, Brenda Pauline; Yaoundé since June 2002; born 09/11/49; DHSS 1980; FCO 1984; Damascus 1986; Port Louis 1987; Karachi 1990; Pretoria 1994; Abuja 1998; Band A2; m 1974 John Anthony Thurston.

Tibber, Peter Harris; On loan to British Trade International since September 2000 (Director of Business Group 2002); born 07/09/56; Second Secretary FCO 1984; Second later First Secretary Paris 1986; First Secretary FCO 1989; PS to the Minister of State 1990; Full-Time Language Training 1992; First Secretary (Political) Ankara 1993; Deputy Head of Mission Mexico City 1996; m 1983 Eve Levy-Huet (3s 1986, 1988, 1992).

Tiffin, Sarah Anne; Dublin since August 2001; born 05/11/65; FCO 1988; ENA Paris 1989; Third later Second Secretary Paris 1990; Second later First Secretary 1993; First Secretary (Political) New Delhi 1997; On secondment to the Irish Department of Foreign Affairs 2000; m 2000 Pádraig Francis.

Tillyard, Barbara Ann (née Levett); Washington since November 1997; born 27/01/46; FCO 1974; Brussels (UKREP) 1975; SUPL 1979; FCO 1979; FCO 1983; Washington 1985; FCO 1989; Abu Dhabi 1992; Band B3; m 1977 Brian William Tillyard.

Timsit, Milli (née Abbott); Consul/MO Munich August 2000; born 11/06/56; FCO 1975; Washington 1977; Africa/Middle East Floater 1981; FCO 1982; Islamabad 1984; Tokyo 1986; FCO 1988; Tel Aviv 1991; Casablanca 1995; Band C4; m 1992 Uzi Timsit (1s 1995; 1d 1997).

Tindell, Derek Graham; Second Secretary The Hague since April 2002; born 11/08/69; FCO 1987; Oslo 1989; Moscow 1992; FCO 1995; Band C4; m 1993 Gail Joyce Brodie (1s 1999).

Tiney, Michael Charles; Floater Duties since March 2002; born 12/09/66; HCS 1989-92; Bucharest 1993; Kampala 1996; Kathmandu 1998; Band B3.

Tinline, Robert John; Second Secretary Bogotá since July 1999; born 13/08/76; FCO 1997.

Tiscenko, Julie Maria (née Cooper); FCO since April 1996; born 31/01/65; FCO 1984; Harare 1986; SUPL 1990; Dhaka 1991; SUPL 1994; Band A2; m (1) 1987 Eric Robert Cooper (2s 1989, 1990); (2) Kenneth Victor Tiscenko.

Tissot, Philip Marius Arthur; Deputy High Commissioner Valletta since April 1999; born 10/02/60; FCO 1978; Africa Floater 1981; Lagos 1983; FCO 1986; Vice-Consul Toronto 1988 (Second Secretary 1989); Second Secretary (Chancery) New York (UKMIS) 1990; FCO 1994; m (1) 1985 Julie Anne Grant (1s 1989; 1d 1990) (diss 1999); (2) 2001 Caroline Agius.

Tivey, Wendy; Copenhagen since March 1997; born 20/07/61; FCO 1995; Band A2.

Tluczek, Karl Shaun Paul; Third Secretary Sofia since April 2002; born 05/01/72; FCO 1991; Prague 1998; Band B3.

Tluczek, Mark Joseph; Moscow since October 2001; born 22/03/67; HCS FCO 1987; FCO 1996; Abuja 1998; Band B3; m 1991 Joanne Lindley.

Tobin, Patrick Michael; Third Secretary (Political) Cairo since July 2002; born 21/04/71; FCO 2000; Full-Time Language Training 2001; Full-Time Language Training (Amman) 2002; Band B3.

Todd, Damian Roderic; HM Ambassador Bratislava since November 2001; born 29/08/59; FCO 1980; Third later Second Secretary Pretoria/Cape Town 1981; Second Secretary FCO 1984; First Secretary and Consul Prague 1987; First Secretary FCO 1989; First Secretary (Economic) Bonn 1991; HM Treasury 1995; FCO 1997; On secondment to HM Treasury as Head of EU Co-ordination and Strategy Team 1998; m 1987 Alison Mary Digby (1s 1989; 2d 1992, 1999).

Tolfree, Alison (née Oxenford); FCO since August 2002; born 17/02/66; FCO 1985; Belgrade 1992; FCO 1995; Lusaka 1999; Band A2; m 1991 Mark Tolfree (1d 1997; 1s 2000).

Tollyfield, Caroline Leslie (née Brewer); Second Secretary FCO since September 1998; born 20/06/61; FCO 1994; Second Secretary (Political) Vienna 1995; Band C4; m 1995 Andrew John Tollyfield (1s 2000).

Tomkins, Michael Paul; First Secretary (Management) Jakarta since August 2000; born 23/12/50; FCO 1970; Honiara 1972; Aden 1976; Kingston 1977; Wellington 1980; Warsaw 1982; FCO 1983; Dhaka 1986; Geneva (UKMIS) 1989; FCO 1992 (Second Secretary 1994); Second Secretary (Commercial) Dubai 1996; m 1979 Eleanor Michelle Ritch (1d 1986; 1s 1989).

Tomkins, Roger James; Moscow since May 1998; born 30/06/48; Royal Navy 1966-88; Prison Service 1988-90; Budapest 1990; Islamabad 1992; Lagos 1994; Band B3; m 1971 Pauline Bennett (1s 1974; 1d 1976).

Tomlinson, Deborah Jane, MVO (1996); SUPL since September 2000; born 16/02/63; FCO 1981; Islamabad 1984; Jakarta 1986; FCO 1990; Third Secretary (Visits) Brussels (UKREP) 1993; Third Secretary Belgrade 1996; Second Secretary (KHF) Sarajevo 1998; Band C4; m 1992 Mark Hyland.

Tomlinson, Jean Lesley; Brussels (UKREP) since July 1998; born 14/07/62; FCO 1989; Rabat 1991; FCO 1994; Band A2.

Tomlinson, Thomas Mark; Second Secretary (Science and Technology) New Delhi since August 2002; born 02/02/63; Third Secretary (Management) and Vice Consul Maputo 1995; Jedda 1998; Second Secretary (Chancery) Belgrade 2001; Band C4.

Tonge, Simon David; Jakarta since July 1989; born 18/09/69; FCO 1996; New York (UKMIS) 1997; Band D6.

Tonkin, Ramsey Harris; First Secretary (Management) Berlin since May 2001; born 17/04/44; FO 1964; Ankara 1966; Bonn 1969; FCO 1972; Tehran 1975; Second Secretary (Commercial) Port of Spain 1978; Second Secretary FCO 1982; Second later First Secretary (Admin/Consul) Bombay 1987; First Secretary (Management) Oslo 1989; First Secretary FCO 1995; First Secretary Bangkok 1997; Full-Time Language Training 2000; m 1966 Valerie Anne Duff (2d 1967, 1969).

Tonner, Janice Wight (née Taylor); SUPL since March 1995; born 06/11/64; FCO 1985; Rome 1987; Lilongwe 1990; Band A2; m 1987 Gary Campbell Tonner (1s 1993).

Toothe, Adrian Gerald; On secondment to the Home Office since August 2001; born 07/01/52; FCO 1972; Jedda 1976; Second Secretary FCO 1980; Geneva (UKMIS) 1985; Second later First Secretary FCO 1989; Band D7; m 1976 Diane Whitehead (2s 1982, 1985).

Topping, Dr Patrick Gilmer; First Secretary FCO since August 1998; born 05/09/59; FCO 1986; Second later First Secretary (Chancery) Kuala Lumpur 1990; First Secretary FCO 1991; Washington 1994; Band D6; m 1985 Indira Annick Coomaraswamy (1s 1992; 1d 1993).

Torlot, Timothy Achille; On loan to DTI since January 2002; born 17/09/57; FCO 1981; Muscat 1984; Second Secretary (Chancery) Wellington 1987; Second later First Secretary FCO 1992; First Secretary (Commercial) Santiago 1997; m 1986 Bridie Morton (1d 1990).

Torrance, David John Baillie; Seoul since December 2001; born 29/02/56; FCO 1975; Bangkok 1978; LA Floater 1982; Doha 1984; FCO 1987; Third Secretary and Vice-Consul San Salvador 1990; Third later Second Secretary FCO 1994; Second Secretary (Commercial) Muscat 1998; Band C4.

Torry, Peter James; HM Ambassador Madrid since October 1998; born 02/08/48; FCO 1970; Third Secretary Havana 1971; Second Secretary (Economic/Commercial) Jakarta 1974; First Secretary FCO 1977; First Secretary (Chancery) Bonn 1981; First Secretary later Counsellor FCO 1985; Counsellor Washington 1989; Counsellor later AUSS (Personel and Security) FCO 1993; m

1979 Angela Wakeling Wood (3d 1980, 1982, 1985).

Totty, Alastair Walton; Rangoon since October 2000; born 24/07/69; FCO 1988; Abu Dhabi 1991; Jerusalem 1994; SUPL 1997; FCO 1998; Band B3; m 1996 Lorraine Helen Fussey (2s 1997, 2001).

Towe, Sheila; Second Secretary (Commercial) Toronto since August 1999; born 26/07/62; FCO 1981; East Berlin 1983; FCO 1985; Baghdad 1987; FCO 1990; On loan to the DTI 1992; Vice-Consul Jedda 1994; On loan to the DTI 1996; Band B3.

Townend, Warren Dennis; HM Consul-General and Counsellor (Management) Washington since February 2001; born 15/11/45; FO 1964; DSAO 1965; FO (later FCO) 1967; Vice-Consul Hanoi 1969; Vice-Consul (Commercial) Hamburg 1970; Third later Second Secretary (Commercial) Dacca 1973; FCO 1976; Second later First Secretary Bonn 1979; First Secretary (Commercial) Bangkok 1984; First Secretary FCO 1987; Deputy Consul-General Düsseldorf and Deputy Director-General for Trade Investment Promotion in Germany 1991; HM Consul-General Shanghai 1996; m Ann Mary Riddle (1d 1977; 3s 1979 (twins), 1980).

Towner-Evans, Louise; Floater Duties since June 2001; born 12/08/71; FCO 1994; Jakarta 1996; FCO 2000; Band A2.

Townsend, David John; Second Secretary (Political) Vienna (UKDEL) since June 2001; born 31/05/57; ECGD 1984-89; FCO 1989; Vienna 1991; Language Training 1994; Vice-Consul Prague 1995; FCO 1997; Band C4; m 1993 Sarah Ann Garry.

Townsend, Stephen Thomas; Second Secretary (Commercial) Cairo since March 2002; born 10/07/61; FCO 1980; Caracas 1982; Kinshasa 1986; FCO 1990; Full-Time Language Training 1992; Madrid 1993; FCO 1997; Band C4; m 1996 Fiona Maria Kilpatrick.

Townson, Jennifer Caroline; FCO since April 1999; born 22/02/68; On loan to the ODA 1991; FCO 1989; Third Secretary (Chancery) Paris 1992; Vice-Consul Port Louis 1995; Band B3.

Towsey, Malcolm John; First Secretary (Commercial) Helsinki since July 1999; born 06/05/47; MOD 1963; FO (later FCO) 1965; Baghdad 1969; Warsaw 1972; Rabat 1973; Dacca 1976; FCO 1979; Maseru 1982; Second Secretary FCO 1984; Second Secretary (Commercial) Dublin 1986; Second Secretary FCO 1990; First Secretary (Management) Lagos 1991; First Secretary (Management/Consular) Abuja 1993; First Secretary FCO 1994; m 1976 Erica Pamela Filder (1s 1979; 1d 1981).

Traylor, Owen John; Consul Istanbul since August 2000; born 26/09/55; FCO 1977; Language Training Tokyo 1980; Second Secretary (Economic) Tokyo 1981; First Secretary FCO

1985; First Secretary (Chancery) Berlin 1990; First Secretary FCO 1994; Band D6; m (1) 1981 Angela Carmel Webb (1d 1985) (diss 1989); (2) 1991 Carola Wangerin.

Treadell, Alan; British Trade International since June 1999; born 08/11/51; FCO 1971; Stockholm 1973; Sana'a 1976; FCO 1977; Islamabad 1979; FCO 1983; Kuala Lumpur 1985; FCO 1990; Band C4; m 1985 Victoria Marguerite Jansz.

Treadell, Victoria Marguerite (née Jansz), MVO (1989); First Secretary British Trade International since March 1998; born 04/11/59; FCO 1978; Islamabad 1981; FCO 1983; Kuala Lumpur 1985; FCO 1990 (First Secretary 1998); Band B3; m 1985 Alan Treadell.

Treherne, Susan Elizabeth (née Morton); SUPL since April 1998; born 25/02/62; FCO 1986; First Secretary (Chancery) Peking 1992; First Secretary FCO 1995; m 1996 Simon Grant Treherne.

Trevelyan, Sarah Frances; FCO since May 1993; born 06/02/65; FCO 1983; Lisbon 1987; Kampala 1990; Band A2; m 1993 Darren Francis Forbes-Batey.

Trott, Angela; FCO since June 2002; FCO 1990; Manila 1999; Band C4; m 1996 Jannick Pierre Michel Charpentier.

Trott, Christopher John; First Secretary (Commercial) later First Secretary (Political) Tokyo since July 1996; born 14/02/66; FCO 1991 (Second Secretary 1992); Consul and Deputy Head of Mission Rangoon 1993; m 1992 Sunna Park.

Truelove, Andrew John; New Delhi since October 1997; born 03/04/64; FCO 1991; Band B3.

Truman, Gary Douglas; FCO since March 1994; born 15/10/63; Home Civil Service 1981; FCO 1990; Bonn 1993; Band A2.

Tucker, Andrew Victor Gunn; HM Ambassador Baku since November 2000; born 20/12/55; Joint Technical Language Service 1978-81; FCO 1981; Second Secretary Dar es Salaam 1982; First Secretary on loan to the Cabinet Office 1985; First Secretary and Press Attaché Moscow 1987; First Secretary FCO 1991; First Secretary on loan to the German Ministry of Foreign Affairs 1993; First Secretary Bonn 1994; Deputy High Commissioner Nairobi 1997; Full-Time Language Training 2000; m 1986 Judith Anne Gibson.

Tucker, Ernest; Amman since September 1999; born 16/03/45; Army 1963-91; Warsaw 1991; Moscow 1993; Lagos 1996; Band B3; m 1965 Ute Elli Wilkelmine (1s 1978).

Tucker, James Philip; First Secretary (Political) Islamabad since October 2001; born 10/01/66; FCO 1990; Second Secretary (Political) Prague 1993; Second Secretary (Political) Bratislava 1994; Second Secretary FCO 1996; Band D6; m 1991 Susie Elizabeth Betts (2d 1994, 1995).

Tucknott, John Anthony, MBE (1990); Counsellor Stockholm since March 2002; born 02/01/58; DOE 1975; FCO 1977; Rome 1980; Cairo 1982; FCO 1985; Second Secretary (Admin) later Deputy Head of Mission Beirut 1988; Second Secretary FCO 1993 (First Secretary 1994); First Secretary New York (UKMIS) 1995; FCO 1998; m (1) 1980 Susan Jayne Elliott (diss 1992); (2) 1992 Tania Amine Charaf (diss); (3) 2000 Riita-Leena Irmeli Lehtinen.

Tuhey, Claire Elizabeth; Second Secretary (Commercial) Mumbai since May 2002; born 07/02/57; FCO 1976; SUPL 1976; FCO 1979; Paris 1982; Africa/Middle East Floater 1985; Vice-Consul New York 1987; FCO 1991; Dublin 1994; On secondment to the Glencree Centre on temporary duty 1997; FCO 1998; Band C4.

Tuke, Sarah Frances; SUPL since August 2000; born 08/03/63; FCO 1982; Cape Town/Pretoria 1984; Jakarta 1987; Floater Duties 1990; Peking 1993; New York (UKMIS) 1996; SUPL 1999; FCO 2000; Band B3.

Tully, Colin Nigel; FCO since August 1997; born 15/07/58; FCO 1980; Amman 1982; FCO 1985; New Delhi 1987; FCO 1991; Buenos Aires 1995; Band C4; m 1983 Wendy Joyce Ogden (1s 1985; 1d 1989).

Tunn, Douglas Charles; Tehran since April 2000; born 18/02/68; FCO 1987; New York (UKMIS) 1989; Port Moresby 1992; Jakarta 1998; Band B3; m 1996 Cecilia Rosemary Tokilala.

Tunn, Rachel Elizabeth; Dublin since 1999; born 28/05/68; FCO 1989; Bucharest 1991; Hanoi 1993; New York (UKMIS) 1995; T/D Croatia 1996; FCO 1997; Band A2; m 1994 Paul Mease.

Tunney, Davina; Washington since June 1999; born 31/07/67; Home Civil Service 1987-89; FCO 1998; Band A2.

Tunnicliffe, Christopher John Robin; Second Secretary (Chancery) Port Louis since May 1999; born 11/11/69; FCO 1989; Prague 1991; FCO 1993; Full-Time Language Training 1994; Riyadh 1995; FCO 1995; Band C4; m (1) 1991 Veronica Mary Walters (1d 1989; 1s 1992) (diss 1995); (2) 1996 Zara Louise Chapman.

Turnbull, David Robert; Second Secretary (Finance) New York (UKMIS) since September 1997; born 25/08/55; MOD 1976; Ankara 1980; FCO 1983; Maputo 1984; The Hague 1988; Third later Second Secretary FCO 1991; Second Secretary (Commercial) Beirut 1995; m 1987 Eva Marianne Persson.

Turnbull, Nicholas Piers, MBE (1999); FCO since April 2002; born 23/09/62; Band D6.

Turner, Alan Roger; Caracas since June 1992; born 09/04/48; Royal Air Force 1965-68; Band C4; m 1974 Caroline Grace.

Turner, Andrew Williams; FCO since August 2001; born 08/12/63; FCO 1986; Language Training 1987; Third later Second Secretary

(Chancery) Muscat 1989; Second Secretary (Chancery) Damascus 1992; Second later First Secretary FCO 1994; First Secretary (Political) Pretoria 1998; Band D7; m 1992 Angeline Marie Biegler (1d 2001).

Turner, David Harvey; First Secretary FCO since October 1993; born 17/02/45; FO 1966; Bonn 1968; Lagos 1970; Brasilia 1973; FCO 1975; Maputo 1978; Vice-Consul São Paulo 1981; Second later First Secretary FCO 1985; First Secretary (Commercial) Lisbon 1989; m 1966 Janet Mary Field (1s; 1d 1975).

Turner, Mark Robin; First Secretary (Commercial) Lisbon since April 2001; born 23/08/55; FCO 1975; Budapest 1977; Maseru 1979; Islamabad 1982; FCO 1984; Los Angeles 1988; Second Secretary FCO 1991; Consul and Second Secretary (Management) Buenos Aires 1994; First Secretary FCO 1998; m 1981 Patricia Louise Brown (2d 1984, 1987).

Turner, Richard Patrick; First Secretary (Information) Moscow since June 2001; born 19/01/63; FCO 1981; Brussels (UKREP) 1984; Dar es Salaam 1986; Third Secretary (Admin) Strasbourg (UKDEL) 1988; FCO 1991 (Second Secretary 1993); São Paulo 1996; Full-Time Language Training 2000; Band C5.

Turner, Robert Leigh; SUPL since October 2002; born 13/03/58; Department of Transport 1979; PSA 1980; DOE 1981; HM Treasury 1982; FCO 1983; Second Secretary (Chancery) Vienna 1984; First Secretary FCO 1987; Language Training 1991; First Secretary (Economic) Moscow 1992; First Secretary FCO 1995; Counsellor FCO 1997; Counsellor (EU/Economic) Bonn (later Berlin) 1998; m 1992 Pamela Ann Major (1s 1992; 1d 1994).

Turner, Stephen Edward; Consul-General and Director Trade Development Auckland since April 2002; born 25/03/46; CRO 1963; DSAO 1965; Jakarta 1968; Third Secretary (Commercial) Kuala Lumpur 1972; DTI 1972; Second Secretary FCO 1976; Valletta 1978; Second Secretary (Commercial) Jakarta 1983; First Secretary (Economic) Jakarta 1986; First Secretary FCO 1988; Consul (Commercial) Seattle 1990; Deputy Head of Mission and Consul-General Hanoi 1995; Deputy High Commissioner and Commercial Counsellor Dhaka 1999; m 1966 Maureen Ann Dick (2s 1969, 1971; 2d 1973, 1982).

Turner-Lamb, Lesley; Gibraltar since February 1993; born 29/10/61; FCO 1982; Harare 1983; Rangoon 1986; Grand Turk 1988; FCO 1991; Band B3; m 1993 Ian Stuart Lamb.

Turney, Nicholas; FCO since September 1984; born 31/03/53; FCO 1971; Washington 1981; Band C4.

Turunc, Susan Kay (née Powell); Cairo since November 1999; born 27/03/49; FCO 1968; Peking 1970; FCO 1971; Resigned 1972; Home Civil Service 1975-79; Reinstated FCO 1989; Istanbul 1990; Seoul 1994; FCO 1997; Band B3; m 1991 Gokhan Turunc.

Turvill, Carol May (née Massingham); Accra since July 2000; born 17/06/66; FCO 1985; Pretoria/Cape Town 1988; Havana 1990; FCO 1992; Islamabad 1995; SUPL 1995; FCO 1998; Band B3; m 1994 Stuart Graham Turvill.

Turvill, Stuart Graham; Accra since July 2000; born 18/02/71; FCO 1991; Islamabad 1995; FCO 1998; Band B3; m 1994 Carol May Massingham.

Twigg, Mark Paul; Consul-General Stuttgart since October 2001; born 01/03/56; FCO 1975; Beirut 1979; FCO 1980; Harare 1981; Düsseldorf 1983; Tripoli 1987; FCO 1989 (Second Secretary 1991); Second Secretary (Commercial) Prague 1994; Full-Time Language Training 1994; First Secretary British Trade International 1999.

Twyman, Robin Edward; Second Secretary Geneva (UKMIS) since March 2001; born 27/08/68; FCO 1987; Harare 1989; Africa/Middle East Floater 1993; FCO 1996; Band C4.

Tylor, Paul Andrew; Third Secretary (Immigration later Management) Karachi since April 2002; born 22/09/64; RAF 1985-95; FCO 1995; Peking 1997; Band B3; m 1988 Yvonne Margaret Wilson.

U

Uden, Martin David; Director International Invest UK since July 2001; born 28/02/55; FCO 1977; Seoul 1978; Second later First Secretary FCO 1982; First Secretary Bonn 1986; First Secretary FCO 1990; Counsellor (Political) and Consul-General Seoul 1994; Counsellor (Trade/Economic) Ottawa 1997; m 1982 Fiona Jane Smith (2s 1986, 1990).

Underwood, Sheila Bridget; World Wide Floater Duties since September 1999; born 26/11/70; FCO 1995; HCS 1995; Band A2.

Upton, Michael John; HM Consul (Commercial) Seattle since April 1995; born 28/10/51; RAF 1970-76; FCO 1976; Havana 1978; FCO 1982; Aden 1982; Bogotá 1984; Second Secretary New York (UKMIS) 1986; Vice-Consul (Inward Investment) Los Angeles 1990; First Secretary FCO 1992; m 1978 Susan Marshall (1s 1981; 1d 1983).

Usher, Janet Clare; Cape Town since May 1999; born 23/04/65; FCO 1983; Washington 1986; Prague 1989; Floater Duties 1991; FCO 1994; On loan to the DTI 1996; Band C4.

Usher, Judith; FCO since June 1999; born 14/10/69; FCO 1988; Peking 1991; Zagreb 1993; Lagos 1995; Band A2.

Usher, Seifeldin; Accra since November 1999; born 27/06/69; FCO 1987; Vienna (UKMIS) 1989; New Delhi 1991; Khartoum 1994; FCO 1997; Band C4; m 1995 Nihad Elnujumi.

V

Van Der Plank, Ian Derek; Second Secretary Islamabad since February 1997; born 21/08/56; Royal Navy 1972-77; FCO 1981; Paris 1987; Third Secretary Lagos 1990; Third Secretary FCO 1992.

Vargas, Emlyn Barry; First Secretary (Technical Management) New Delhi since January 2000; born 02/02/46; HM Forces 1964-86; FCO 1986; Caracas 1989; Helsinki 1992; FCO 1997; Band C5; m 1991 Carmen Rafaela Velazquez.

Varney, Carol June; FCO since July 1995; born 24/11/43; FCO 1969; Budapest 1972; Dacca 1973; Frankfurt 1976; FCO 1978; Stockholm 1981; New Delhi 1984; FCO 1987; Brussels (UKDEL) 1991; Geneva (UKMIS) 1992; Band B3.

Vaygelt, Robin (née Maitland); FCO since June 2000; born 14/06/61; FCO 1984; Rio de Janeiro 1986; FCO 1988; Johannesburg 1993; Paris 1996; Band A2; m 1992 Marek Stephen Fernyhough Vaygelt.

Venn, Robert Lawrence; First Secretary FCO since August 2001; born 15/04/65; FCO 1992; Second Secretary (Economic) Jakarta 1994; First Secretary (Political) Peking 1997; Band D6; m 1990 Wendy Ann Wightman (1s 1994; 1d 1996).

Verma, Neeras; SUPL since April 2000; born 21/11/62; FCO 1982; Brussels (UKDEL NATO) 1984; Luanda 1988; FCO 1992; Vienna 1996; Düsseldorf 1999; Band B3; m 1985 Sarah-Jane Dodman (diss 1996).

Verma, Sarah-Jane (née Dodman); Third Secretary Bridgetown since December 1996; born 31/12/63; FCO 1983; Brussels (UKREP) 1985; Luanda 1988; FCO 1992; Band B3; m 1985 Neeras Verma (diss 1996).

Very, Donna (née Grant); FCO since January 1999; born 27/07/69; FCO 1988; SUPL 1992; FCO 1994; Tehran 1996; Band A2; m 1994 Steve Jason Very (1s 1997; 1d 1999).

Vickers, David Victor Edwin; Grand Turk since November 1999; born 01/05/53; FCO 1973; Lusaka 1976; Kathmandu 1979; Sofia 1983; FCO 1984; Islamabad 1985; Ankara 1989; FCO 1992; Deputy Head of Mission Tallinn 1996; Band C4; m 1983 Pamela Barron (née Scott).

Vidal, Ruben Joel; FCO since September 1989; born 07/03/41; Royal Marines 1967-72; FCO 1979; Damascus 1981; FCO 1985; Harare 1988; m 1975 Delores Annett (1d 1983).

Vineall, Katherine Patricia (née Jenkins); SUPL since January 1999; born 07/11/63; FCO 1987 (Second Secretary 1989); Second Secretary (Chancery) Madrid 1991; Second Secretary FCO 1992; First Secretary FCO 1995; SUPL 1995; m 1992 Nicholas Edward John Vineall (1s 1995).

Vir Singh, Doris Nefertiti; FCO since June 2002; born 03/02/64; FCO 1993; Geneva (UKMIS) 1996; Paris 2000; Band B3.

Virgoe, John; FCO since April 1999; born 01/09/69; FCO 1991; Full-Time Language Training 1994; Jakarta 1995; m 1999 Tuti Suwidjiningsih.

Voak, Susan; Lilongwe since April 2001; born 02/06/69; FCO 1999; Band A2.

Vosper, Alistair John; FCO since January 2000; born 09/04/70; FCO 1989; Islamabad 1992; Manila 1996; Band C4; m 1995 Lucy Jane Medforth (1s 2001).

Vowles, John Philip, MBE (1994); Havana since April 1999; born 13/08/47; Royal Marines 1962-87; Moscow 1987; Pretoria 1989; Tehran 1991; Kampala 1995; Band C4; m 1968 Maureen Cann.

W

Waddington, Jane Caroline; FCO since July 2001; born 12/10/64; HO 1988; FCO 1998; Stockholm 2000; Band A2.

Wade, Emma Lesley; Second Secretary (Political) August 1998; born 15/09/73; FCO 1995; Band D6.

Wadvani, Sanjay Mark; Deputy Consul-General and Head of Commercial Section Guangzhou since May 2002; born 06/12/66; FCO 1987; Peking 1989; Damascus 1991; FCO 1995; Santiago 1998; Band C5.

Wahab, Mohammed Toafiq; Third Secretary (Visa) Lagos since December 2001; born 02/04/75; HM Customs & Excise 1993-94; FCO 1997; Islamabad 1998; Band B3; m 1996 Rozmina Muhammad Anwar (2s 1998, 2000).

Wain, Geoffrey William; Second Secretary (Commercial) Manila since February 2000; born 10/05/65; FCO 1983; Islamabad 1986; Istanbul 1989; FCO 1992 (Second Secretary 1994); Maseru 1995; Band C4; m 1985 Kathleen Anne Lowe (1d 1992).

Wain, Kathleen Anne (née Lowe); Third Secretary (Immigration) Manila since February 2000; born 11/02/63; FCO 1982; Addis Ababa 1984; FCO 1985; Islamabad 1986; Istanbul 1989; FCO 1992; SUPL 1995; Band B3; m 1985 Geoffrey William Wain (1d 1992).

Waite, Timothy Matthew; MO/Consul/ECM St Petersburg since January 1999; born 21/07/62; PSA 1988-91; FCO 1991; Jedda 1994; Band C4.

Walder, Jacqueline Ann; FCO since October 1998; born 30/08/67; FCO 1989; Abidjan 1992; Almaty 1996; Band B3.

Wales, Lee Anne; Brussels since February 2002; born 07/01/67; FCO 1996; Canberra 1998; Band A2.

Walford, Thomas Alexander; Second later First Secretary (Management/Consular) Damascus since 1997; born 02/03/49; FCO 1968; Malta 1971; Belmopan 1974; Tunis 1975; FCO 1978; Canberra 1981; The Hague 1983; FCO 1986; Second Secretary and Deputy Head of Mission Panama

City 1989; Second Secretary FCO 1991; m 1974 Mary Thérésa Heafield (1s 1977; 1d 1979).

Walker, Alisdair James; FCO since March 1999; born 14/09/65; FCO 1989; Third Secretary (Chancery) Islamabad 1991; Assistant Management Officer Moscow 1995; FCO 1995; Band C4; m 1992 Susan Mary Ireland (1s 1996; 1d 1998).

Walker, Angela Ruth; On secondment to the MOD since October 1997; born 07/05/54; FCO 1980; The Hague 1983; Vice-Consul Rio de Janeiro 1986; FCO 1989; Band C4.

Walker, Derek Leonard; Second Secretary JMO Brussels since July 1999; born 28/11/44; FCO 1971; Tripoli 1974; Bucharest 1976; Ottawa 1978; FCO 1980; JAO Brussels 1984; Vice-Consul later Second Secretary (Immigration) Lagos 1988; FCO 1992; Tunis 1995; m 1965 Janice Ann Gamble-Beresford (2d 1968, 1970).

Walker, Helen Mary; First Secretary FCO since January 1999; born 23/07/69; FCO 1991; Full-Time Language Training 1993; Athens 1994.

Walker, John Frank; Budapest since January 1998; born 10/02/64; Royal Engineers 1980-85; FCO 1987; Buenos Aires 1991; Band C4; m 1990 Caroline Jane Masters (2s 1985, 1991).

Walker, John Ronald; FCO since March 1985; born 04/05/60; Senior Research Officer Band D6.

Walker, John Stanley; Vice-Consul Damascus since September 1999; born 20/10/66; FCO/HCS 1984; FCO 1988; Bucharest 1989; Doha 1991; FCO 1994; Hong Kong 1997; T/D Bombay 1999; Band C4.

Walker, June (née Erwin); FCO since June 1997; born 01/06/59; FCO 1992; Dar es Salaam 1996; Band A2; m 1996 Vincent Charles Walker (1s 1997).

Walker, Mary Elizabeth; SUPL since October 1991; born 24/06/68; FCO 1990; Band B3.

Walker, Neil; FCO since March 1997; born 29/04/63; Royal Navy 1979-89; Band A2; m 1992 Angela Seatter (2d 1995, 1997).

Walker, Patricia Arlow; SUPL since May 1997; born 29/09/63; FCO 1988; Berlin 1990; Ankara 1993; Band A2; m 1998 Paul A Bertrand.

Wall, Eric Simon Charles; Counsellor FCO since September 2001; born 04/09/57; Royal Navy 1976-86; Second Secretary FCO 1986; Second later First Secretary Geneva (UKMIS) 1988; First Secretary FCO 1991; First Secretary (Political) Kampala 1994; First Secretary FCO 1995; Counsellor Harare 1998; m 1983 Elizabeth Anne Gibson (2s 1988, 1990; 1d 1994).

Wall, Sir (John) Stephen, KCMG (1996), LVO (1983); On loan to the Cabinet Office since September 2000; born 10/01/47; Third Secretary FCO 1968; Third later Second Secretary Addis Ababa 1969; Private Secretary to the Ambassador Paris 1972; Second later First Secretary FCO

1974; On loan to No 10 Downing Street 1976; Assistant Private Secretary to the Secretary of State 1977; First Secretary (Chancery) Washington 1979; First Secretary FCO 1983; Counsellor FCO 1985; PPS to the Secretary of State 1988; On loan to the Cabinet Office (at No 10 as Foreign Affairs PS to the Prime Minister) 1991; HM Ambassador Lisbon 1993; UK Permanent Representative Brussels (UKREP) 1995; m 1975 Catharine Jane Reddaway (1s 1979).

Wallace, Euan; Second Secretary FCO since June 1999; born 15/06/63; FCO 1981; Paris 1984; Moscow 1986; Resigned 1988; Reinstated 1990; FCO 1990; New York (UKMIS) 1993; Vice-Consul New York 1994; Brussels (UKDEL) 1996; m 1987 Gillian Whittaker (1d 1996; 1s 2000).

Wallace, Gillian (née Whittaker); SUPL since November 1996; born 14/11/63; FCO 1983; Paris 1985; Moscow 1987; FCO 1988; New York (UKMIS) 1993; Band B3; m 1987 Euan Wallace (1d 1996; 1s 2000).

Wallace, Neil Douglas; Dublin since September 1994; born 05/11/69; FCO 1990; SUPL 1993; Band A2.

Waller, Mark; Third Secretary (Political) Almaty since July 1999; born 29/09/67; FCO 1987; Kingston 1989; FCO 1992; Abuja 1995; Band B3.

Walley, Martin; Second later First Secretary (Management) Moscow since March 1999; born 11/06/58; HMIT 1977; FCO 1978; Ankara 1980; Mexico City 1984; Budapest 1985; FCO 1985; Dhaka 1987; FCO 1990; Third Secretary (Commercial) Manila 1992; Bangkok 1995; Second Secretary FCO 1996; On loan to DfID 1997; m 1981 Dilek Sule (2s 1991, 1995).

Wallis, Victor Charles; First Secretary FCO since April 1999; born 06/02/47; CO 1963; Commonwealth Office (later FCO) 1966; Bermuda 1969; Accra 1972; FCO 1975; Second Secretary Helsinki 1979; Vice-Consul (Commercial) Sydney 1985; First Secretary FCO 1989; Deputy Consul-General Los Angeles 1994; m 1971 Jacqueline Wadhams (1s 1979).

Walmsley, Alan; FCO since July 1998; born 06/09/61; FCO 1981; Abu Dhabi 1984; FCO 1988; Washington 1996; Band C5; m 1992 C Richardson (1d 1999).

Walmsley, Mark Ronan; First Secretary (Commercial) Jakarta since October 2001; born 17/06/58; FCO (HCS) 1978; FCO 1980; Bucharest 1981; Africa/Middle East Floater 1983; FCO 1984; Nicosia 1987; Second Secretary (Consular) Bombay 1990; Second Secretary FCO 1994; Head of Inward Investment Section Taipei 1997; m 1986 Andrea Elizabeth (1s 1995; 1d 1997).

Walpole, The Hon Alice Louise; New York (UKMIS) since August 2001; born 01/09/63; FCO 1985; Third later Second Secretary (Developing Countries) Brussels (UKREP) 1987; Language Training 1990; Second Secretary Dar es Salaam 1991; First Secretary FCO 1994; First Secretary

UKDEL NATO 1998; SUPL 1999; Brussels (UKREP) 2000; m 1990 Angel Carro Castrillo (3d 1990 (twins), 1993; 3s 1996, 1999 (twins)).

Walsh, Nicola Jane; Bridgetown since March 1993; born 24/01/61; FCO 1980; Bahrain 1982; Bridgetown 1985; Kingston 1986; LA/Caribbean Floater 1988; Band C4.

Walsh, Paul Richard; Consul (Management) Calcutta since April 2002; born 15/03/69; DHSS 1987; FCO 1988; FCO 1990; Berlin 1990; Islamabad 1991; Third Secretary (Commercial) Warsaw 1995.

Walsh, Penelope Ruth (known as Penny); FCO since October 2000; born 19/12/66; FCO 1990; Third Secretary (UN) Geneva (UKMIS) 1991; Third Secretary Tirana 1994; Consul Naples 1996; T/D Rome (UKMIS) 1996; Consul and Second later First Secretary (Management) Sana'a 1998; Band C4; m 1998 Primo Grilli.

Walter, Emily Rose; SUPL since August 2001; born 18/05/67; FCO 1992; Second Secretary (Political) Buenos Aires 1995; First Secretary FCO 2000; Band D6; m 1996 Dominic William Martin (3d 1996, 1998, 2001).

Walters, Alison Jane (née Lund); SUPL since October 1991; born 28/08/57; FCO 1976; Yaoundé 1978; FCO 1982; Sofia 1985; Paris 1987; SUPL 1988; Third later Second Secretary (Information/Chancery) Islamabad 1989; m 1978 Robert Leslie Walters (2s 1987, 1994).

Walters, David Anthony, MVO (1985); Islamabad since March 2000; born 03/01/57; NSB 1975; FCO 1977; Tehran 1979; Bonn 1980; Port of Spain 1982; FCO 1986; Dhaka 1988; Vice-Consul Atlanta 1991; FCO 1994; T/D Bogotá 1998; T/D Abuja 1998; T/D Tirana 1999; Band C4; m 1980 Janis Anne McPhail (3s 1982, 1984, 1991).

Walters, Helen Elizabeth; FCO since September 2001; born 27/03/80; Band C4; ptnr, Andrew Coolen.

Walters, Jonathan Mark; Second Secretary (Political) Berlin since January 1998; born 28/07/67; FCO 1990; Full-Time Language Training 1992; Third Secretary (Commercial) Bangkok 1993; FCO 1996; Band B3; m 2001 Elizabeth Woehr.

Walters, Robert Leslie; SUPL since October 2000; born 23/01/50; FCO 1970; Havana 1972; Kaduna 1973; Valletta 1976; FCO 1977; Masirah 1977; Yaoundé 1978; FCO 1982; Sofia 1985; Paris 1987; Third Secretary (Commercial) Islamabad 1989; T/D Shanghai 1993; Second Secretary FCO 1993; Second Secretary FCO 1994; Vice-Consul (Commercial) Brisbane 1996; Band C4; m (1) 1973 Mary Elaine Lee (diss 1978); (2) 1978 Alison Jane Lund (2s 1987, 1994).

Walters, Simon Christopher; Second Secretary FCO since October 2001; born 03/07/71; FCO 1995; Full-Time Language Training 1997; Full-Time Language Training 1998; Second Secretary Riyadh 1999; Band C4.

Walters, Stephen Brett; FCO since January 1985; born 23/08/60; FCO 1981; Peking 1982; Kingston 1983; Band B3.

Walton, Derek Antony Ruffel; First Secretary (Legal) Geneva (UKMIS) since December 1997; born 21/07/66; Called to the Bar (Lincoln's Inn) 1989; Assistant Legal Adviser FCO 1991; m 1994 Claire Margaret Hughes (1s 1996; 1d 2000).

Walton, Gillian Mary (née Booth); First Secretary FCO since November 1994; born 16/08/54; FCO 1975; Second Secretary Moscow 1987; Second Secretary FCO 1989; First Secretary Oslo 1992; Band C5; m 1979 (diss 1986).

Walwyn, David Scott; SUPL since June 2001; born 14/04/59; FCO 1985; Second later First Secretary (Chancery) Bangkok 1987; First Secretary FCO 1990; Paris (UKDEL OECD) 1995; FCO 1999; m 1988 Fiona Cassels-Brown (1s 1997).

Ward, Anthony John; Port Louis since October 1998; born 08/05/47; Royal Marines 1964-88; Brussels (UKREP) 1988; Moscow 1991; Paris 1992; FCO 1995; Band B3; m 1996 Penelope Joan Walter (3s 1974, 1975, 1977).

Ward, Christine (née Gray); SUPL since May 1997; born 25/12/59; FCO 1978; Budapest 1980; Istanbul 1982; SUPL 1986; Paris 1988; Manila 1992; Band B3; m 1986 Michael John Ward.

Ward, Gareth Edward; Second Secretary (KHF) Moscow since November 1998; born 17/01/74; FCO 1996.

Ward, Katherine Georgina Louise (Cathy); FCO since September 2001; born 07/04/65; Research Officer FCO 1994; Senior Research Officer 1995; Second Secretary Havana 1998.

Ward, Michael David; FCO since June 1995; born 01/06/63; FCO 1983; New Delhi 1986; Band C4.

Ward, Michael John; Seconded to European Commission since July 2000; born 25/12/58; FCO 1982; Istanbul 1985; Third Secretary (Commercial) later Second Secretary (Science and Technology) Paris 1988; Second later First Secretary FCO 1993; First Secretary Brussels (UKREP) 1997; m 1986 Christine Gray (2d 1990, 1995; 1s 1991).

Wardle, Mark Thomas; Pretoria since June 2000; born 22/11/62; Royal Navy 1979-89; Police 1990-95; FCO 1995; Kuala Lumpur 1997; Band B3; m 1994 Julie Anne Russell (1d 1999; 1s 2001).

Wardle, Mark William; Second Secretary (Chancery) Vienna since May 2000; born 25/02/75; FCO 1997; Band C4.

Wardle, Sharon Anne; Secondment to Private Sector since August 2000; born 02/03/65; FCO 1985; Moscow 1987; FCO 1989; Ex-Floater Duties 1990; Vice-Consul Beirut 1991; On loan to the DTI then British Trade International 1996; Band C5.

Ware, Jillian Angela; SUPL since February 1999; born 17/12/62; FCO 1982; New York (UKMIS) 1984; Africa/Middle East Floater 1988; FCO 1990; Amman 1994; Band B3; m 1990 David Edward Ware (2d 1991, 1995).

Warr, Martyn John; Second Secretary (Commercial) Lisbon since October 1993; born 01/05/59; FCO 1981; Language Training 1983; Jedda 1984; FCO 1988 (Second Secretary 1989); Band D7; m 1992 Sarah Jane Thompson.

Warren, David Alexander; Director, Business Group, Trade Partners UK April 2000; born 11/08/52; Third Secretary FCO 1975; Language Training (Japanese) 1976-78; Second Secretary and Private Secretary to the Ambassador Tokyo 1978; Second later First Secretary (Economic) Tokyo 1979; First Secretary FCO 1981; Head of Chancery Nairobi 1987; FCO 1990; Counsellor on loan to the Cabinet Office (Science and Technology Secretariat, later Office of Science and Technology) 1991; Counsellor (Commercial) Tokyo 1993; FCO 1998; Head of Hong Kong Department, later China Hong Kong Department 1998; m 1992 Pamela Pritchard.

Warren-Gash, Haydon Boyd; HM Ambassador Rabat since July 2002; born 08/08/49; FCO 1971; Language Training London University 1972; Third Secretary Ankara 1973; Second later First Secretary (Chancery) Madrid 1977; First Secretary FCO 1981; First Secretary (Commercial) Paris 1985; First Secretary FCO 1989; Deputy High Commissioner Nairobi 1991; Counsellor FCO 1994; HM Ambassador Abidjan and HM Ambassador non-resident to Liberia, Niger and Burkina Faso 1997; FCO 2001; m 1973 Caroline Emma Bowring Leather (1s 1975; 1d 1977).

Warrington, Guy Murray; FCO since September 2001; born 23/09/63; FCO 1986; Third later Second Secretary (Economic/Information) Singapore 1988; Second Secretary New York (UKMIS) 1992; First Secretary FCO 1993; Geneva (UKMIS) 1997.

Warwick, Sharon Joy; FCO since August 1983; born 31/01/57; FCO 1979; Rangoon 1980; Kuala Lumpur 1982; Band B3; m 1983 Aiden Eustace Warwick.

Watchorn, Kenneth Graham; FCO since April 2000; born 20/09/54; FCO 1971; Washington 1979; FCO 1982; Vienna 1984; Riyadh 1987; FCO 1987; Second Secretary FCO 1992; Paris 1997; Band D6; m 1980 Rossalyn Keen (2s 1983, 1985).

Watchorn, Mark; Deputy Head of Mission Maseru since July 2002; born 28/07/65; FCO 1984; Cape Town/Pretoria 1987; Africa/Middle East Floater 1990; FCO 1992; On loan to DTI 1996; Band C4; m 1996 Christine Jacqueline Holding (1s 1998; 1d 2001).

Waterhouse, Christine; Athens since October 1998; born 15/09/67; FCO 1987; Nairobi 1991; FCO 1994; Band B3.

Waterhouse, Peter Laurance; FCO since July 1999; born 03/02/58; FCO 1975; Bonn 1987; FCO 1990; Nicosia 1991; FCO 1994; Warsaw 1996; Band C4; m 1985 Clare Rachel Dewar (1d 1993).

Waterton, James, LVO (1995); Deputy Head of Mission Montevideo since May 2002; born 25/04/49; FCO 1968; Havana 1970; Valletta 1972; Bonn 1974; FCO 1977; Wellington 1981; Second Secretary and Vice-Consul Montevideo 1984; Second Secretary FCO 1987; HM Consul later First Secretary Durban 1991; Deputy Consul-General Istanbul 1996; First Secretary FCO 1999; m 1994 Judith Kerwin.

Waterworth, Peter Andrew; First Secretary (Political) Rome since September 1996; born 15/04/57; Assistant later Senior Assistant FCO 1987; Legal Adviser Bonn 1990; First Secretary FCO 1994; Full-Time Language Training 1996; m (1) 1981 Hilary Young (diss 1991); (2) 1994 Catherine Finnigan.

Watkinson, Barry; FCO since April 2000; born 22/08/44; FCO 1984; Brussels 1988; FCO 1991; Moscow 1996; Band C4; m 1988 Patricia Rose.

Watson, David James; First Secretary FCO since August 1999; born 04/03/57; FCO 1988; Second later First Secretary Harare 1989; First Secretary FCO 1992; First Secretary (Political) Madrid 1996; Band D6; m 1989 Sheelah McKeown (2d 1989, 1991).

Watson, Gavin Christopher; Assistant Legal Adviser FCO since April 2000; born 21/07/70; Solicitor; Legal Assistant Home Office 1995.

Watson, James Spencer Kennedy; First Secretary FCO since October 2000; born 30/11/64; FCO 1988; Second Secretary (Economic) Kuwait 1991; Second Secretary FCO 1994; First Secretary (Political) Damascus 1997; Band D6.

Watson, Joel Aaron; Deputy High Commissioner Vila since February 2002; born 14/09/69; FCO 1989; Belmopan 1991; Islamabad 1994; FCO 1998; Band C4; m 1990 Victoria Jane Baxter (1s 1999).

Watson, Nicholas Henry Lewis; Second Secretary FCO since November 2001; born 12/06/71; FCO 1995; Full-Time Language Training 1997; Full-Time Language Training Cairo 1998; Second Secretary (Political) Amman 1999; Band C4; m 1997 Catriona Ann (1s 2000).

Watson, Robert Emmerson; FCO since January 2001; born 10/08/70; FCO 1996; Second Secretary Tel Aviv 1998; Band C4.

Watson, Stephen; Chairman DSTUS FCO since July 2001; born 18/06/57; HO 1975; FCO 1976; Jedda 1979; Hong Kong 1982; Brasilia 1986; FCO 1988; Band C5.

Watson, Terence Paul; Second Secretary (Technical Management) New Delhi since April 2001; born 07/12/48; HM Forces 1964-76; FCO 1988; Band C4; m 1969 Jennifer Margaret (2s 1970, 1972).

Watt, James Wilfrid, CVO; Head of Consular Division January 2000; born 05/11/51; FCO 1977; MECAS 1978; Second later First Secretary Abu Dhabi 1980; FCO 1983; First Secretary (Chancery) New York (UKMIS) 1985; First Secretary FCO 1989; Deputy Head of Mission Amman 1992; Deputy Head of Mission Islamabad 1996; SOAS 1999; m 1980 Elizabeth Ghislaine Villeneuvre (dec'd) (1s 1981; 1d 1986).

Wattam, John; Second Secretary (Political) Geneva (UKDIS) since August 1998; born 11/05/63; FCO 1982; Bonn 1984; Karachi 1987; FCO 1991; Third Secretary (Commercial) Lagos 1994; Third Secretary (Political/Information) Lagos 1995; Full-Time Language Training 1998; Band B3; m 1991 Anne Michelle Watson (2d 1993, 1998; 1s 1995).

Watts, Elizabeth Helen; Bucharest since September 2000; born 22/03/79; OFTEL 1997; FCO 1999; Band A2.

Waugh, Linda Alison; FCO since October 1999; born 20/03/65; MOD 1984; FCO 1992; Athens 1996; Band A2.

Waugh, Lisa Helen (née Maley); Director, Americas FCO since August 2000; born 28/08/67; FCO 1988; Brussels 1990; FCO 1992; Hong Kong 1993; Istanbul 1996; RMU Americas Command 1999; SUPL 2000; Band C5; m 1995 Graeme Stewart Waugh (1d 1998).

Way, Lawrence Sidney; Third later Second Secretary FCO since October 1984; born 01/12/49; FO (later FCO) 1967; Washington 1974; FCO 1977; Amman 1978; FCO 1981; Madrid 1982; m 1970 Patricia Margaret Allcock (1s 1975; 1d 1977).

Weale, William Anthony Peter; First Secretary FCO since April 1995; born 26/01/45; HM Forces 1964-70; FCO 1970; Dacca 1971; Jedda 1973; Lagos 1974; FCO 1976; Moscow 1977; FCO 1979; Hanoi 1980; Beirut 1983; Second Secretary FCO 1985; On loan to MOD 1993; Band D6; m 1977 Sheila Ellen Anderson (1d 1985).

Webb, Richard, MBE (1996); First Secretary (Commercial) Jakarta since September 1998; born 20/11/43; Inland Revenue 1962; FO 1965; Peking 1967; Rio de Janeiro 1968; Lagos 1972; FCO 1974; Far East Floater 1978; FCO 1980; Jedda 1981; Second Secretary FCO 1984; Vice-Consul (Commercial) Melbourne 1988; Second Secretary (Consular) Moscow 1993; Full-Time Language Training 1993; T/D Montserrat 1995; Second Secretary FCO 1996; m (1) 1966 Hilary Anne John (diss 1977) (1d 1970; 1s 1971); (2) 1983 Sandra Mai Williams (1d 1985).

Webb, Robert, OBE (2000); FCO since July 2000; born 06/06/50; Montserrat DSAO (later FCO)

1966; Singapore 1971; Guatemala City 1974; FCO 1978; Floater Duties 1982; Hanoi 1984; Second Secretary and Consul Mexico City 1985; Second Secretary FCO 1989; Deputy Head of Mission Georgetown 1993; First Secretary Plymouth 1997; m 1989 Maria Del Carmen Colin Irieta (1s 1994).

Webb, Sarah Jane; FCO since July 2002; born 02/12/66; FCO 1987; Budapest 1990; FCO 1992; Kuala Lumpur 1994; FCO 1997; Floater Duties 2000; Band A2.

Webber, Barbara Ann (née Leatherbarrow); FCO since July 1995; born 06/03/66; FCO 1987; Peking 1992; Band B3; m 1996 Martin George Webber.

Webber, Martin George; Third Secretary (Political) Berne since March 2002; born 19/10/60; HO 1979-81; FCO 1989; Geneva (UKMIS) 1990; FCO 1992; Peking 1993; FCO 1995; Third Secretary (Management) Quito 1998; Band B3; m 1996 Barbara Ann Leatherbarrow (1s 1998).

Webster, John Auld; Strasbourg since November 1999; born 06/09/68; FCO 1988; Nicosia 1990; FCO 1992; Port Louis 1996; Band B3.

Weeks, Alan Richard; Deputy Head of Mission Quito since June 1997; born 29/07/48; FCO 1965; Tripoli 1970; Sofia 1972; Beirut 1974; Innsbruck 1976; FCO 1979; Second Secretary (Development) New Delhi 1984; Second Secretary (Admin) and Consul East Berlin 1987; First Secretary FCO 1991; m 1971 Penelope Dibb (2s 1974, 1976).

Weeks, Sarah Marguerite; Second Secretary (Chancery) Wellington since July 2002; born 15/10/68; FCO 1987; Abidjan 1990; Floater Duties 1993; Paris 1995; FCO 1998; Band B3.

Weinrabe, Stephen Michael; First Secretary (Management) Brasilia since January 2001; born 13/06/50; FO (later FCO) 1967; Bucharest 1971; Paris 1972; Dublin 1973; Tehran 1975; FCO 1977; Nicosia 1981; Bangkok 1984; Second Secretary (Admin) Lagos 1988; Second Secretary FCO 1991; Second Secretary (Commercial) Sydney 1994; Second Secretary (Commercial) Canberra 1994; Assistant Personal Secretary to the Minister of State 1999; Full-Time Language Training 2000; Band C5; m 1973 Eugenia Del Transito Poppescov Lazo (2s 1975, 1995).

Weldin, Jonathan Michael; First Secretary FCO since December 2001; born 23/02/59; FCO 1982; Second later First Secretary (Chancery) Sana'a 1986; First Secretary FCO 1988; First Secretary (Chancery) Tunis 1990; First Secretary FCO 1993; First Secretary (External) Athens 1996; Band D6; m 1984 Fiona Jean Nesbitt (1s 1987; 1d 1989).

Weldon, Lawrence John, MVO (1980); Second Secretary Moscow since January 2002; born 06/03/50; FCO 1972; Attaché (Development) Bangkok 1975; Attaché (Commercial) Tunis 1978; FCO 1981; British Vice-Consul Johannesburg 1983; Second Secretary FCO 1986; Second Secretary (Commercial) Caracas 1989; SUPL

1992; Second Secretary FCO 1995; Convent Liaison Officer Gibraltar 1997; m 1984 Sarah Helen Burn (1d 1989; 2s 1991, 1999).

Weldon, Paul; Athens since August 2000; born 03/04/59; FCO 1975; Pretoria 1987; FCO 1989; Band C4; m 1986 Karen Louise Ritchie (2s 1988, 1992).

Wells, Andrew Justin; Second Secretary (Commercial) Prague since June 2002; born 08/03/68; FCO 1988; Floater Duties 1991; Zagreb 1993; FCO 1995; Language Training Cairo 1997; Third Secretary Amman 1998; Band C4; m 1994 Juliette Swain (2s 1996, 1999).

Wells, Colin Neil; Second Secretary (Political) Abuja since August 2001; born 29/09/67; FCO HCS 1987; DS 1990; Bridgetown 1992; Geneva (UKMIS) 1996 (Second Secretary 1997); FCO 1999; Band C4; m 1997 Rebekah Wells (2d 1993, 1995; 1s 1997).

Wells, Daniel; New Delhi since August 2000; born 21/07/70; FCO 1989; Bucharest 1992; FCO 1994; Lagos 1995; FCO 1998; Band C4.

Wells, David John; Deputy High Commissioner Nassau since September 2000; born 29/06/63; FCO 1982; New Delhi 1988; FCO 1990; Vice-Consul Moscow 1995; FCO 1998; Band C4; m 1994 Helen Paula McCarron.

Wells, Helen Paula (née McCarron); SUPL since September 2000; born 29/06/68; FCO 1986; New Delhi 1989; Geneva (UKMIS) 1992; Moscow 1995; SUPL 1996; FCO 1998; SUPL 1999; FCO 2000; Band B3; m 1994 David John Wells (1d 1996).

Wells, Juliette Elizabeth (née Swain); SUPL since August 1994; born 12/06/67; FCO 1986; Zagreb 1993; Band A2; m 1994 Andrew Justin Wells (2s 1996, 1999).

Welsh, Jolyon Rimmer; FCO since August 2002; born 22/12/67; FCO 1990; Second Secretary (Chancery/Information) Colombo 1992; First Secretary FCO 1995; New York (UKMIS) 1998.

Welsh, Patricia Angela (née Sherry); Oslo since January 2000; born 23/08/64; FCO 1985; Madrid 1989; FCO 1992; Brasilia 1994; SUPL 1997; FCO 1999; Band A2; m 1993 James Ormsby Welsh (2d 1996, 1998).

Welsh, Paul Anthony; Second Secretary (Commercial) Lisbon since March 2002; born 12/10/67; FCO 1986; Harare 1988; Floater Duties 1992; FCO 1994; Deputy Head of Mission Tbilisi 1998; Band C4; m (1) 1988 Ann McCoy (diss 1993); (2) 1994 Emel Elif Icbilen.

Welsted, David Curtis; First Secretary FCO since July 1995; born 17/10/52; FCO 1969; Attaché Warsaw 1975; FCO 1976; FCO 1978; Tehran 1978; Nairobi 1980; FCO 1983; Attaché Amman 1984; FCO 1987; Washington 1992; m 1974 Gillian Mary Harris (1s 1978; 1d 1982).

Wenban, Mark; Lima since July 2001; born 29/05/67; FCO 2000; Band A2.

West, Brian William; HM Consul Paris since January 2002; born 04/01/48; FCO 1968; Moscow 1971; Kampala 1972; Strasbourg 1975; FCO 1977; Port Louis 1980; Second Secretary (Commercial) Abidjan 1984; Second Secretary FCO 1988; T/D Athens 1990; Second Secretary (Commercial) Paris 1991; T/D New Delhi 1996; Second Secretary (Commercial) Beirut 1997; T/D Guangzhou 1997; m 1976 Marie-Odile Gilbert (2s 1977, 1980).

West, Peter Bernard; Deputy Head of Mission Bangkok since April 2000; born 29/06/58; FCO 1977; Ankara 1978; Buenos Aires 1980; Auckland 1984; Second later First Secretary FCO 1986; First Secretary (Political/Information) Copenhagen 1992; First Secretary FCO 1997; m 1980 Julia Anne Chandler (1d 1993; 2s twins 1995).

West, Veronica Frances Bailey; FCO since November 1997; born 16/06/46; FCO 1977; Amman 1978; FCO 1981; Colombo 1983; Kuwait 1987; Sofia 1991; FCO 1993; Bucharest 1995; Band B3.

Westcott, Nicholas James, CMG (1998); Head of IT Strategy Unit FCO since June 2002; born 20/07/56; Second Secretary FCO 1982; Seconded to European Commission, Brussels 1984; First Secretary (Agriculture/Finance) Brussels (UKREP) 1985; First Secretary FCO 1989; Deputy Head of Mission Dar es Salaam 1993; Counsellor FCO 1996; Minister-Counsellor for Trade and Transport Policy Washington 1999; m 1989 Miriam Pearson (1d 1996; 1s 2000).

Westgarth, Nicholas Philip; Counsellor Peking since August 1999; born 25/11/56; FCO 1980; Third Secretary (Economic) Athens 1981; Second Secretary FCO 1984; Language Training 1985; First Secretary Hong Kong 1986; First Secretary FCO 1989; First Secretary (Chancery) Nicosia 1991; First Secretary FCO 1995; m 1988 Kate Judith Sykes (2s 1989, 1992).

Westmacott, Peter John, CMG (2000), LVO; HM Ambassador Ankara since January 2002; born 23/12/50; FCO 1972; Third later Second Secretary Tehran 1974; FCO 1978; Seconded to EC Commission Brussels 1978; First Secretary Paris 1980; PS to Minister of State 1984; FCO 1984; Head of Chancery Ankara 1987; Counsellor on secondment to Buckingham Palace as Assistant Private Secretary to TRH the Prince and Princess of Wales 1990; Head of Chancery Washington 1993; Director (Americas) 1997; DUS (Wider World) 2000; m 1972 Angela Margaret Lugg (2s 1975, 1979; 1d 1977) (diss 1999).

Wetherell, Gordon Geoffrey; HM Ambassador and Consul-General Luxembourg since September 2000; born 11/11/48; FCO (concurrently Third Secretary Vice-Consul British Embassy, Chad) 1973; Third later Second Secretary East Berlin 1974; First Secretary FCO (concurrently First Secretary UKDEL CTB at Geneva) 1977; First

Secretary UKDEL CTB Geneva 1979; New Delhi
1980; First Secretary FCO 1983; On loan to HM
Treasury 1986; FCO 1987; Counsellor and Deputy
Head of Mission Warsaw 1988; Counsellor
(Political/Military) Bonn 1992; Counsellor FCO
1994; HM Ambassador Addis Ababa and (non-
resident) Djibouti and Asmara 1997; m 1981
Rosemary Anne Myles (4d 1982, 1985, 1987,
1989).

Whaanga-Jacques, Lorna (née Jacques); Muscat
since November 1999; born 15/09/59; FCO 1985;
Rangoon 1988; Vienna (UKDEL CSCE) 1988;
Phnom Penh 1992; SUPL 1993; FCO 1997; Band
A2; m 1994 Dean Tamaku Whaanga.

Whale, Geoffrey; Peking since April 1988; born
03/07/52; FCO 1983; Band C5; m 1985 Ingrid
Moore (1s 1987).

Whatley, Malcolm George; Second Secretary
(Commercial) Hong Kong since November 1999;
born 05/09/52; FCO 1973; Washington 1975;
Kuwait 1978; Budapest 1982; Dhaka 1984; FCO
1985; Muscat 1986; FCO 1989; Rio de Janeiro
1992 (Second Secretary 1995); Band C4; m 1975
Mary Elizabeth Niven (2s 1979, 1985; 1d 1983).

Wheeler, Bernadette; Kinshasa since April 2000;
born 13/02/68; MOD 1986; FCO 1988; Lisbon
1989; FCO 1992; Jakarta 1994; Bucharest 1998;
Band B3.

Wheeler, Fraser William; FCO since July 2000;
born 23/03/57; FCO 1980; Accra 1982; FCO
1984; Geneva (UKMIS) 1985; FCO 1988;
Language Training 1990 (Second Secretary 1991);
Second Secretary (Commercial) Moscow 1991;
Deputy Consul-General Vancouver 1994; SUPL
1999; Band B3; m 1988 Sarah Humphreys.

Whipp, Kathryn Sarah; SUPL since January 2001;
born 01/03/67; FCO 1988; Kiev 1992; FCO 1995;
New Delhi 1998; FCO 2000; Band A2.

Whitaker, Giles David Humphrey; FCO since
September 2000; born 05/03/62; HM Forces 1980-
88; Second Secretary FCO 1988; Second Secretary
(Chancery) Brussels (UKDEL NATO) 1990; First
Secretary FCO 1994; Deputy Head of Mission
Berlin 1998; First Secretary (Political) Berlin (on
attachment to Auswärtiges Amt) 1999; m 1990
Lucy Phyllida Whately Anderson (2s 1992, 1998;
2d 1994, 1996).

Whitby, John Benjamin; First Secretary Vienna
since August 2002; born 21/02/67; FCO 1990;
Language Training 1993; Second Secretary
(Political) Tokyo 1994; First Secretary FCO 1997;
Band D6; m 1992 Ruth Alexander (1s 1995; 1d
1997).

White, Anthony William; Bridgetown since
October 1999; born 29/12/54; FCO 1973; Peking
1980; FCO 1982; Lilongwe 1985; FCO 1988;
Third Secretary Kuala Lumpur 1993; FCO 1996;
Band C4; m 1996 Rahani Mat Tahir.

White, Benjamin Matthew; FCO since September
2001; born 02/01/79; Band C4.

White, (Charles) John (Branford); High
Commissioner Bridgetown since August 2001;
born 24/09/46; Government of Botswana 1968;
ODM 1971; Economic Advisers 1977; ODM
1982; CDA at UCL (London) 1983; FCO 1986;
First Secretary Lagos 1990; Counsellor, Consul-
General and Deputy Head of Mission Tel Aviv
1993; Commissioner for the British Antarctic
Territory, Commissioner for the British Indian
Ocean Territory and Counsellor FCO 1997; m
1975 Judy Margaret Lewis.

White, Debra; Paris since October 2001; born
28/05/75; FCO 1996; Band A2; m 1997 Lee
Marcus Crawford.

White, Jacqueline Denise (née Hill); Grand Turk
since July 2000; born 24/05/64; FCO 1987; Dar es
Salaam 1989; New York (UKMIS) 1993; FCO
1993; New York (UKMIS) 1996; SUPL 1996;
SUPL 1997; FCO 2000; Band B3; m 1990 Jerry
Lee White (2s 1996, 1998).

White, Kate Georgina; Taipei since August 2000;
born 24/01/73; FCO 1995; Hong Kong 1998;
Band C4.

White, Richard Michael, MBE (1983); Assistant
Director, Personnel Services May 2000; born
12/07/50; FCO 1969; UKDEL (later UKREP) EC
Brussels 1971; Language Training SOAS and Yazd
1974; Tehran 1975; APS to the Minister of State
1978; Second Secretary 1978; FCO 1979; APS to
the Lord Privy Seal 1979; Second Secretary
(Commercial/Admin) and Consul Dakar 1980;
First Secretary (Technology) Paris 1984; First
Secretary FCO 1988; Deputy High Commissioner
Valletta 1992; First Secretary FCO 1996;
Counsellor, Head of Migration and Visa Division
1997; m 1979 Deborah Anne Lewis (1s 1984; 1d
1986).

White, Tiffany Alexandra; Second Secretary
(Political) Rangoon since April 1996; born
10/06/71; FCO 1994; Full-Time Language
Training Cairo 1995.

Whitecross, Andrew Ronald; First Secretary FCO
since July 2001; born 14/04/49; Army 1964-76;
FCO 1976; Private Industry 1978; FCO 1980;
Sana'a 1981; Baghdad 1985; Second Secretary
FCO 1989; First Secretary (Political) Muscat
1998; Band C5; m 1980 Nancy-Jane Evans (dec'd
1994).

Whiteford, Kathryn Elizabeth; FCO since June
2002; born 05/08/78; Band A2.

Whitehead, Ian Richard; Counsellor
(Management) Paris since December 1999; born
21/07/43; FO 1960; Addis Ababa 1965; Brussels
(NATO) 1969; Dubai 1971; Casablanca 1972;
FCO 1975; Second Secretary (Commercial)
Bridgetown 1978; First Secretary (COCOM) Paris
1983; First Secretary FCO 1988; Deputy High
Commissioner Dar es Salaam 1991; Head of
Mission Skopje 1993; FCO 1994; High
Commissioner Georgetown 1998; m 1996 Pamela
Denise Mitchison (1d 1996).

Whitehead, Laurence Jeremy; First Secretary FCO since June 2002; born 17/04/61; FCO 1984; Second Secretary Jakarta 1987; Second later First Secretary FCO 1990; First Secretary (Political) Vienna 1995; First Secretary (Political) Tirana 1999; Band D6; m 1995 Marjella Djorghi.

Whitehead, Roger; Second Secretary (Commercial) Singapore since October 1997; born 22/05/54; FCO 1976; Lagos 1979; Kathmandu 1982; FCO 1984; Rangoon 1988; Third Secretary (Management/Consular/Commercial) Toronto 1991; Second Secretary FCO 1994; m 1979 Diane Mann (1s 1987; 1d 1989).

Whitehorn, Caroline Mary; Vice-Consul and Second Secretary (Management) Buenos Aires since March 2001; born 04/10/67; Mexico City 1992; FCO 1992; Second Secretary FCO 1997.

Whiten, Peter Frank, MBE (1991); FCO since August 1998; born 05/12/51; FCO 1974; SE Asia Floater 1976; Brussels (UKDEL NATO) 1978; Port of Spain 1981; Second Secretary FCO 1986; Second Secretary (Commercial) Madras 1991; Consul Chiang Mai 1995; m 1987 Antonia Ramsaroop (3s 1989, 1991, 1993; 1d 1994).

Whiteside, Andrew John; First Secretary (Political) Rome since February 2002; born 21/09/68; FCO 1991; Language Training 1994; Second Secretary (Political) Budapest 1995; First Secretary FCO 1997; Band D6; m 1994 Fiona Elizabeth Bradley (1d 1999; 1s 2001).

Whiteside, Bernard Gerrard, MBE (1994); HM Ambassador Chisinau since April 2002; born 03/10/54; FCO 1979; Moscow 1983; Geneva (UKDIS) 1986 (Second Secretary 1988); Second Secretary FCO 1989; Second Secretary (Chancery/Aid) Bogotá 1991; First Secretary FCO 1995; First Secretary on loan to DfID 1999.

Whiteway, Paul Robin; Counsellor and Deputy Head of Mission Santiago since February 2000; born 01/12/54; FCO 1977; Third later Second Secretary Dublin 1980; First Secretary FCO 1984; First Secretary Stanley 1986; First Secretary FCO 1987; Seconded to MOD (Navy) 1988; Deputy High Commissioner Kampala 1990; First Secretary FCO 1993; Counsellor and Deputy Head of Mission Damascus 1996; m 1996 Maha Georges Yannieh (1s 1998).

Whitford, Victoria; Full-Time Language Training (Japanese) since October 2000; born 06/06/74; First Secretary (External Relations) Brussels (UKREP) Head of Hong Kong Section 1999; Hong Kong Desk, CHKD FCO 1999; SUPL 2000; Band C4.

Whittaker, Andrew Mark; Consul (Political) Jerusalem since October 2001; born 22/06/76; FCO 1998; Full-Time Language Training (Arabic) 1999; Cairo 2000; Band C4.

Whitting, Ian Robert; First Secretary (Economic) FCO since July 1997; born 02/04/53; FCO 1972; Moscow 1975; Tunis 1976; Athens 1980; (Second Secretary 1981); FCO 1983; Second Secretary (Chancery) Moscow 1985; Second Secretary FCO 1988; Second Secretary (Chancery) Dublin 1990; m 1986 Tracy Anne Gallagher (2d 1990, 1994).

Whittingham, Stephen Arthur; FCO since September 1990; born 29/01/56; FCO 1972; Brussels 1981; FCO 1983; Hong Kong 1988; Band C4; m 1977 Christine Mary Ruth Hodgson (1d 1978).

Whittle, Lesley Elizabeth; SUPL since July 1999; born 04/07/58; FCO 1980; Amman 1981; Cairo 1984; FCO 1987; Paris 1990; Islamabad 1994; Band B3; m 1986 Simon FD Mallett (1s 1995).

Whomersley, Christopher Adrian; Legal Counsellor FCO since 1997; born 18/04/53; Assistant Legal Adviser FCO 1977; Legal Counsellor FCO 1991; Legal Secretariat to the Law Officers 1994; m 1977 Jeanette Diana Szostak (1s 1991; 2d 1993, 1998).

Whomsley, Deborah Jane; Vienna (UKDEL) since July 1993; born 25/04/67; FCO 1991; Band A2.

Wicke, Tina (née Thackstone); Third Secretary Harare since August 1999; born 05/02/61; HM Treasury 1980; FCO 1982; Stanley 1983; Kingston 1984; Peking 1986; FCO 1989; Harare 1993; SUPL 1997; Band B3; m 1996 Jürgen Manfred Wicke.

Wicks, Graham; Second Secretary (Aid) Khartoum since November 2000; born 02/07/55; FCO 1974; Islamabad 1976; Luxembourg 1976; Peking 1979; Karachi 1981; FCO 1983; Victoria 1986; Vice-Consul Sofia 1990; Third later Second Secretary FCO 1992; Second Secretary (Commercial) Bombay 1995; FCO 1997; m 1978 Genevieve Harriot-Jane McCrossan (2s 1988, 1989).

Wicks, Joanna Ruth (née Collett); Second Secretary FCO since November 1995; born 09/05/56; FCO 1978; Warsaw 1981; FCO 1982; SUPL 1984; Second Secretary FCO 1986; SUPL 1989; Second Secretary FCO 1992; SUPL 1994; Band C4; m 1984 Nigel Earl Wicks (2d 1989, 1994).

Wicks, Nigel Earl; SUPL since March 2000; born 21/03/56; HM Forces 1973-76; FCO 1980; Attaché Damascus 1984; FCO 1986; Lisbon 1989; FCO 1992 (Second Secretary 1994); Second Secretary (Commercial/Economic) Oslo 1995; Band C4; m 1984 Joanna Ruth Collett (2d 1989, 1994).

Wickstead, Myles Antony; HM Ambassador Addis Ababa since November 2000 (also HM Ambassador (non-resident) Djibouti); born 07/02/51; Ministry of Overseas Development 1976; APS to Lord Privy Seal FCO 1979; Assistant to UK Executive Director IMF/IBRD 1980; Principal ODA 1984; Private Secretary to Minister for Overseas Development 1988; Head of ODA European Community and Food Aid Development 1990; Head of British Development Division in East Africa (BDDEA) 1993; UK Alternate Executive Director World Bank and

Counsellor (Development) Washington 1997; m 1990 Shelagh Paterson (1s 1996; 1d 1999).

Wigginton, Christopher James; Second Secretary (Immigration/Consular) Bogotá since November 2000; born 23/05/60; FCO 1982; Tehran 1984; Language Training 1984; Stockholm 1988; FCO 1991 (Second Secretary 1992); Islamabad 1994; FCO 1997; Full-Time Language Training 2000; Band C4.

Wightman, Andrew Norman Scott; Deputy Head of Mission Rome since January 2002; born 17/07/61; FCO 1983; Full-Time Language Training 1984; Second Secretary Peking 1986; First Secretary FCO 1989; On loan to the Cabinet Office 1989; First Secretary FCO 1991; On secondment to Quai d'Orsay 1994; First Secretary Paris 1995; Assistant Director Personnel Policy 1998; m 1988 Anne Margaret Roberts (2d 1993, 1997).

Wilbourn, Lillian; Kuwait since August 2002; born 27/07/47; FCO 1985; Madrid 1987; Brasilia 1990; Maputo 1994; Buenos Aires 1998; Band A2.

Wilcox, Juliette Sarah (née Hannah); First Secretary JLG Hong Kong since July 1996; born 29/06/66; FCO 1988; Full-Time Language Training Taiwan 1991; Second Secretary (Chancery) Peking 1992; First Secretary FCO 1995; Band D6; m 1996 Wayne Philip Wilcox (1 step s 1984; 1s 1999).

Wildash, Elizabeth Jane (née Walmsley), MVO (1997); SUPL since September 2001; born 17/10/58; FCO 1978; East Berlin 1980; FCO 1981; Abidjan 1983; FCO 1984; SUPL 1987; FCO 1988; Harare 1989; FCO 1992; Third Secretary (Chancery) New Delhi 1994; SUPL 1998; Second Secretary (Economic) Kuala Lumpur 1999; m 1981 Richard James Wildash (2d 1987, 1996).

Wildash, Richard James, LVO (1997); High Commissioner Yaoundé since June 2002; born 24/12/55; FCO 1977; East Berlin 1979; Abidjan 1981; FCO 1984; FCO 1986; Language Training 1986; Harare 1988; FCO 1992; New Delhi 1994; Deputy High Commissioner Kuala Lumpur 1998; m 1981 Elizabeth Jane Walmsley (2d 1987, 1996).

Wildman, Richard Hugh; FCO since January 2002; born 18/08/54; FCO 1983; Bridgetown 1989; FCO 1992; Brasilia 1999; Band C4; m (1) 1989 Fay Dawn Reid (1d 1983); (2) 1994 S E Odle.

Wiles, Celia Imogen; First Secretary (Economic and Public Affairs) Canberra since November 2001; born 23/04/63; FCO 1986; Language Training Kamakura 1988; Third Secretary (Commercial) Tokyo 1989; SUPL 1993; FCO 1995; On loan to European Commission 1998; FCO 1999; SUPL 2000; FCO 2001; Band D6; (1s 2000).

Wilkie, Robert Andrew; FCO since January 1989; born 09/12/59; FCO 1979; Nairobi 1980; FCO 1983; Darwin 1987; Band B3; m 1986 Sarah Jane Abraham (1d 1987).

Wilkinson, Richard Denys, CVO (1992); Director (Americas) FCO since May 2000; born 11/05/46; FCO 1972; Second later First Secretary Madrid 1973; FCO 1977; First Secretary (Economic/Commercial) Ankara 1983; Counsellor and Head of Chancery Mexico City 1985; Counsellor (Info) Paris 1988; Counsellor FCO 1993; HM Ambassador Caracas 1997; m 1982 Maria Angela Morris (2s 1983, 1986; 1d 1991).

Wilks, Jonathan Paul; SUPL since October 1999; born 30/09/67; FCO 1989; Full-Time Language Training Cairo 1992; Second Secretary (Political/Information) Khartoum 1993; First Secretary (Economic) Riyadh 1996; Band D6.

Willasey-Wilsey, Timothy Andrew; Counsellor FCO since April 2002; born 12/09/53; Second Secretary FCO 1981; First Secretary (Chancery) Luanda 1983; First Secretary, Head of Chancery (later Deputy Head of Mission) and Consul San José 1986; First Secretary FCO 1989; Counsellor Islamabad 1993; Counsellor FCO 1996; Counsellor (UN Affairs) Geneva (UKMIS) 1999; m 1983 Alison Middleton Mackie (3s 1986, 1988, 1989).

Williams, Alexander Patrick; Bangkok since July 1996; born 13/02/69; FCO 1986; Band B3.

Williams, Catrin Ceiros; FCO since January 1976; born 22/11/51; FCO 1972; Valletta 1974; Band A2.

Williams, David John; Deputy Head of Mission Yaoundé since September 2001; born 06/06/67; FCO 1986; Geneva (UKMIS) 1988; Bombay 1990; Second Secretary FCO 1995; m 1989 Denise Nowak (1d 1991; 1s 1995).

Williams, David Llewellyn; Sofia since March 1999; born 13/12/42; Royal Marines 1961-83; Baghdad 1984; Warsaw 1985; Islamabad 1986; Paris 1987; Peking 1990; Kampala 1991; Kiev 1995; Band B3; m 1969 Gillian Myra James (3d 1961, 1963, 1971; 1s 1966).

Williams, Deborah Mary; FCO since August 2002; born 30/10/64; FCO 1985; Tokyo 1987; Buenos Aires 1990; FCO 1993; Vice-Consul Rome 1998; Band B3.

Williams, Douglas James; Second Secretary (Commercial) Madras since May 1998; born 09/02/55; FCO 1978; Suva 1981; Brussels (UKREP) 1984; New Delhi 1987; FCO 1991; Bridgetown 1994; Band B3; m 1981 Susan Anwen Jones (1s 1984; 1d 1986).

Williams, George (aka Rick), BEM (1975); New Delhi since October 2001; born 06/02/43; HM Forces 1962-84; Prague 1984; Singapore 1985; Moscow 1987; Washington 1988; Dhaka 1991; Colombo 1995; Lagos 1998; Band C4 (CSO); m 1965 Eileen (2s 1965, 1968).

Williams, Jenni; Istanbul since November 1999; born 21/12/70; FCO 1990; Peking 1995; SUPL 1999; FCO 1999; Band B3.

Williams, John; Second Secretary (Political) Gibraltar since September 1996; born 17/06/59;

FCO 1978; Moscow 1981; Rabat 1982; Masirah 1985; FCO 1985; LA Floater 1986; FCO 1988; Vice-Consul Johannesburg 1992; m (1) 1981 Jacqueline Peplow (diss 1987); (2) 1994 Cheryl Ann Sim.

Williams, Karen Lesley, MBE (2001); Second Secretary (Commercial) Beirut since August 2002; born 28/06/63; FCO 1987; Riyadh 1988; New York (UKMIS) 1991; World Wide Floater Duties 1993; FCO 1995; Rangoon 1999; Band C4.

Williams, Laura Kate Elizabeth; Second Secretary (Political/Information) Addis Ababa since April 2001; born 03/04/74; FCO 1998; First Secretary Paris Embassy 1999; T/D Second Secretary (Political) Brussels (UKREP) 2000; Full-Time Language Training 2000; First Secretary Brussels (UKREP) 2000; Band C4.

Williams, Paul; First Secretary (Political) Berlin since October 2001; born 25/11/48; Immigration Service 1969; Islamabad 1977; Dhaka 1982; Lagos 1987; Second later First Secretary Muscat 1996; First Secretary Houston 1998; m 1969 Barbara Jane Briggs (2s 1975, 1979).

Williams, Paula Jean; SUPL since August 1994; born 22/10/54; Brussels (UKDEL NATO) 1976; Islamabad 1976; BMG Berlin 1979; Dakar 1980; Pretoria/Cape Town 1981; FCO 1984; Algiers 1990; Band B3; (1d 1991; 1s 1994).

Williams, Philip George; FCO since July 1988; born 26/07/54; FCO 1972; Nairobi 1985; Band D6; m 1987 Susan Traise McAlden.

Williams, Prue, RVM; SUPL since November 2001; Bonn 1978; Moscow 1980; FCO 1981; Port of Spain 1983; FCO 1985; Bangkok 1996 (State Visit); The Hague/Luxembourg (Presidency) 1997; FCO 1998; Band B3.

Williams, Dr Rhodri Huw; Counsellor Amman since November 2001; born 14/05/59; FCO 1990; First Secretary (Economic) Vienna 1992; First Secretary FCO 1996; m 1986 Hilary Clair Wakeham (1s, 1d (twins) 1991; 1s 1994).

Williams, Roger Gordon; Jakarta since 1999; born 28/07/48; Army 1963-89; Prague 1989; Washington 1991; Cairo 1993; Lagos 1997; Belgrade 1997; T/D Cairo 1997; Band B3; m 1974 Anne Elizabeth (1d 1974; 2s 1978, 1980).

Williams, Simon John; Casablanca since January 2002; born 22/08/60; FCO 1979; Manila 1981; Mbabane 1984; Kaduna 1986; FCO 1992; Third Secretary (Commercial) Riyadh 1995; Full-Time Language Training 1995; Second Secretary (Commercial) Doha 1998; Band C5; m 1987 Rosemarie Caguntas Williams (1s 1989).

Williams, Stephen Michael; Counsellor and Deputy Head of Mission Buenos Aires since July 2001; born 20/07/59; FCO 1981; Third later Second Secretary Sofia 1984; Second later First Secretary FCO 1987; On loan to Barclays Bank 1990; First Secretary (Commercial/Economic) Oslo 1991; First Secretary (External Relations)

Brussels (UKREP) 1995; Counsellor FCO 1998; Full-Time Language Training 2001; m 1983 Fiona Michele Hume (2d 1986, 1989; 1s 1991).

Williams, Steven; Brussels since May 2000; born 30/04/69; FCO 1987; Band C4; m 2000 Leah Victoria Cox.

Williams, Tony Scott; Second Secretary (Management) Sofia since August 2000; born 12/09/62; FCO 1981; Brussels (UKDEL NATO) 1984; Prague 1986; Dhaka 1988; FCO 1989; Athens 1993; Third Secretary (Commercial) New Delhi 1996; m 1985 Denise Tilbrook (1s 1992).

Williamson, George Moray; FCO since September 2001; born 25/02/74; Band C4.

Williamson, Morven Jane; Jedda since October 1999; born 16/04/71; FCO 1991; Hanoi 1994; Band B3.

Willis, Iain Edward; Third Secretary (Political) Valletta since July 1999; born 25/05/71; FCO 1991; T/D Karachi 1995; Vice-Consul Tokyo 1996; Band B3.

Willmer, Nigel Stuart; FCO since September 2000; born 03/07/65; FCO 1983; Madrid 1990; FCO 1993; Lusaka 1997; m 1985 Jackie Mann (diss 2001) (1d 1986).

Willmott, Emily Margaret; Assistant Legal Adviser FCO since October 2001; born 02/11/72; Solicitor 1998; m 1999 Simon Nathan Willmott.

Willock, Oriel; San José since August 2001; born 23/04/68; FCO 1988; Amman 1990; Floater Duties 1994; FCO 1997; T/D Islamabad 1999; T/D Ekaterinburg 2000; Band B3.

Wills, Jane Stirling; First Secretary and Deputy Head of Mission Bratislava since April 1999; born 12/12/46; Commonwealth Office (later FCO) 1964; Prague 1969; Copenhagen 1971; Vienna (UKDEL MBFR) 1973; Bombay 1976; FCO 1980; Prague 1983; Ankara 1986; Second Secretary FCO 1989; Deputy Head of Mission Reykjavik 1995.

Wills, Ruth Margaret; Second later First Secretary FCO since December 1991; born 07/11/54; FCO 1977; Rio de Janeiro 1980; Paris 1984; Second Secretary (Press/Information) Bonn 1989.

Willsher, Ian Robert; First Secretary Brussels since September 1998; born 14/04/47; Washington 1974; Vienna 1977; FCO 1979; Accra 1982; Geneva 1985; FCO 1988; Nairobi 1990; FCO 1994; British Forces Germany 1996; m 1976 Amanda Jane (2s 1978, 1979; 1d 1985).

Wilmshurst, Elizabeth Susan, CMG (1999); FCO since September 2001; born 28/08/48; Solicitor 1972; Assistant Legal Adviser FCO 1974; First Secretary later Counsellor on loan to Attorney-General's Chambers 1986; Legal Counsellor FCO 1991; Counsellor (Legal Adviser) New York (UKMIS) 1994; Legal Counsellor FCO 1998; Deputy Legal Adviser FCO 1999; SUPL 2001.

Wilson, Allan Richard James; Mexico City since August 2001; born 11/05/77; FCO 1999; Band A2.

Wilson, Caroline Melanie Cherry (née Meath); FCO since July 1999; born 16/09/69; FCO 1990; Canberra 1992; Moscow 1995; SUPL 1998; Band B3; m 1993 James Jeffrey Wilson.

Wilson, Elizabeth Claire; Second Secretary (Political) Peking since November 2002; born 20/09/74; FCO 1998; Full-Time Language Training 2000; Full-Time Language Training Peking 2001; Band C4.

Wilson, Fraser Andrew, MBE (1980); High Commissioner Victoria (Seychelles) since April 2002; born 06/05/49; Commonwealth Office (later FCO) 1967; Havana 1970; SE Asia Floater 1971; Seoul 1973; Salisbury 1977; Second Secretary FCO 1980; Language Training 1983; Second Secretary (Commercial) Moscow 1984; Second Secretary (Commercial) and Vice-Consul (later First Secretary (Commercial)) Rangoon 1986; First Secretary FCO 1990; Deputy Consul-General São Paulo 1994; HM Ambassador Turkmenistan 1998; Full-Time Language Training 1998; m 1981 Janet Phillips (2s 1982, 1985).

Wilson, Gillian Grace; Third Secretary (Chancery) Nairobi since April 1995; born 19/04/65; ODA 1981; FCO 1989; Accra 1991; T/D Dhaka 1991; Band C4.

Wilson, Harry Kenneth, BEM (1991); Madrid since November 1999; born 07/05/52; RAF 1971-97; FCO 1998; Band A2; m 1979 Elaine Patrick (1s 1981; 1d 1983).

Wilson, Ian Laurence; HM Consul Beijing since July 2001; born 19/06/44; FO 1962; Moscow 1966; Colombo 1967; FCO 1971; Brussels (UKDEL NATO) 1974; Banjul 1977; FCO 1981; Canberra 1983; Second Secretary (Consular/Admin) Calcutta 1987; FCO 1987; Second Secretary (Management) Bucharest 1992; First Secretary FCO 1995; Consul and First Secretary (Management) Tehran 1997; HM Consul Riyadh 2000; Band C5; m (1) 1970 (1d 1974; 1s 1976) (diss 1999); (2) 1999 Monica Dorri (1s 2000).

Wilson, James Jeffrey (Jeff); FCO since October 1999; born 07/08/67; FCO 1988; Canberra 1992; Moscow 1995; Vice-Consul Ekaterinburg 1997; Band C4; m 1993 Caroline Melanie Meath.

Wilson, Keith Edward; FCO since April 1990; born 18/06/46; CRO (later FCO) 1963; Islamabad 1970; Lagos 1974; Dacca 1977; FCO 1980; Tehran 1983; Johannesburg 1988; Band B3; m 1984 Christine Maria Theresia del Negro (1d 1985; 1s 1988).

Wilson, Peter Michael Alexander; SUPL since March 1999; born 31/03/68; FCO 1992; Full-Time Language Training 1993; Full-Time Language Training Peking 1994; Peking 1995; Band C4.

Wilson, Robert Thomas Osborne; FCO since January 2002; born 28/01/52; Senior Research Officer FCO 1982; First Secretary and Head of Chancery Abu Dhabi 1989; Principal Research Officer FCO 1993; Deputy Head of Mission, HM Consul Bahrain 1998; m 1979 Susan Ann Watson (2d 1985, 1988).

Wilson, Roy Andrew; Deputy Head of Mission Yerevan since September 2002; born 03/12/59; HCS 1978; FCO 1979; Karachi 1982; Seoul 1985; FCO 1987; Bombay 1990; Zurich 1994; First Secretary Banja Luka 2000; Band C4.

Wilson, Simon Charles Hartley; Deputy Head of Mission and Head of Political Section Bahrain since November 2001; born 09/08/57; FCO 1975; Johannesburg 1978; Helsinki 1981; FCO 1984; Riyadh 1987; Tehran 1987; Second Secretary (Chancery/Information) Lisbon 1992; Second later First Secretary FCO 1997; m 1984 Heather Graine Richardson (2s 1990, 1994).

Wilson, Simon Jules, OBE (1996); First Secretary Budapest since February 2002; born 13/03/66; FCO 1988; Third later Second Secretary (Economic) Athens 1991; Second later First Secretary (Political) Zagreb 1993; First Secretary FCO 1996; First Secretary New York (UKMIS) 1999; FCO 2000; Band D6.

Wilson, Susan Jean; New Delhi since January 2002; born 01/02/70; FCO 1989; Bangkok 1994; Istanbul 1997; Band B3.

Wilton, Christopher Edward John; HM Ambassador Kuwait since September 2002; born 16/12/51; FCO 1977; MECAS 1978; Second later First Secretary Bahrain 1979; FCO 1981; First Secretary (Chancery) Tokyo 1984; On loan to Cabinet Office 1988; Counsellor (Commercial) Riyadh 1990; Consul-General Dubai 1994; Counsellor FCO 1998; m 1975 Dianne Hodgkinson (1d 1981; 1s 1984).

Wiltshire, Terence Keith; Second Secretary (Technical Management) Budapest since February 2001; born 24/12/57; FCO 1981; New Delhi 1983; FCO 1987; Lagos 1994; FCO 1997; Band C4.

Windle, William James; Counsellor Washington since August 2002; born 03/07/52; On loan to MOD 1975; FCO 1972; FCO 1977; Second Secretary (Commercial) Muscat 1980; Second later First Secretary FCO 1984; First Secretary (Chancery) Washington 1989; First Secretary later Counsellor FCO 1992; Band C5; m 1974 June Constance Grimmond (3s 1980, 1982, 1985).

Windsor, Dallas Frederick; FCO since September 2001; born 24/04/74; Band C4; m 2001 Kiyoe Higashi.

Winnington-Ingram, Charles Pepys; FCO since 2000; born 06/10/55; Barrister 1977; Export Credits Guarantee Department 1979; FCO 1980; Third Secretary (Commercial) Tokyo 1981; Second Secretary FCO 1985; Second Secretary (Chancery/Information) Oslo 1989; HM Consul (Commercial) and Deputy Head of Mission St Petersburg 1995; HM Consul and Deputy Head of Mission Jerusalem 1996.

Winsley, Marcus Justin; First Secretary (Political) Washington since June 2002; born 01/09/67; ODA

1993; First Secretary Moscow 1996; FCO 2000; Band D6; m 1996 Claire Underwood.

Winter, Douglas; Second Secretary (Consular/Management) Sarajevo since April 1999; born 21/01/51; FCO 1969; Mogadishu 1972; Antigua 1974; FCO 1978; Bangkok 1981; Zagreb 1984; Warsaw 1985; Second Secretary FCO 1987; Second Secretary (Commercial) Abu Dhabi 1990; FCO 1994; m 1972 Linda Margaret Harmer (1s 1975; 1d 1978).

Winter, Simon; ECO Accra since November 2000; born 10/04/68; FCO 1990; Tokyo 1995; Budapest 1999; Band A2; m 1993 Alyson Barnett (1s 1994; 2d 1997, 2001).

Winterburn, Christine Catherine (née Lowrie); Second Secretary (Political/PPA) Sofia since August 1999; born 20/04/67; FCO 1986; Copenhagen 1987; FCO 1989; Kaduna/Abuja 1992; Lima 1996; Band C4; m 1989 John Winterburn (2s 1995, 2000).

Wise, Graeme Michael; SUPL since October 1999; born 17/06/64; FCO 1984; Addis Ababa 1985; Lagos 1988; Floater Duties 1991; FCO 1992; Second Secretary (Commercial) Buenos Aires 1997; Band C5.

Wise, Patricia (née Donnelly); Nicosia since March 2000; born 24/02/58; FCO 1982; Lusaka 1983; Port Stanley 1983; Rome 1987; Cape Town/Pretoria 1990; FCO 1993; Helsinki 1994; SUPL 1994; SUPL 1996; FCO 1997; Band B3; m (1) 1985 Edward Meredith Leighton (diss 1991); (2) 1992 David Wise (dec'd 1999) (1d 1994).

Wisker, Rita; FCO since January 1996; born 15/09/51; FCO 1972; Tokyo 1973; FCO 1975; Washington 1977; Brussels (UKREP) 1980; BMG Berlin 1983; New York (UKMIS) 1984; FCO 1985; Brussels (UKDEL) 1992; Band B3.

Withers, John Walter Charles; FCO since August 1994; born 24/11/47; FCO 1975; Moscow 1979; Lagos 1982; FCO 1982; FCO 1985; Ottawa 1986; New York 1987; FCO 1989; Third later Second Secretary Bucharest 1991; m 1970 Vivienne Chater (1d 1976; 1s 1986).

Withers, Matthew Robert; Third Secretary (Political) Buenos Aires since January 2001; born 14/10/67; FCO 1987; Kuala Lumpur 1988; Kathmandu 1992; Lagos 1994; FCO 1998; Band B3; m 1992 Leigh Cooper (2d 1994, 1996).

Witting, Lisa Marie; Vienna (UKMIS) since January 2000; born 22/02/69; FCO 1988; Dublin 1989; FCO 1993; Berlin 1995; Band A2.

Wolstenholme, Jonathan David; Second Secretary (Chancery) Wellington since August 1998; born 15/01/60; FCO 1980; Baghdad 1982; Moscow 1984; Harare 1986; FCO 1990; (Second Secretary 1992); Second Secretary (Management) Brussels (UKREP) 1994; m 1986 Karen Suzanne Vivian (2d 1989, 1994; 1s 1992).

Wolstenholme, Karen Suzanne (née Vivian); Wellington since August 1998; born 16/10/62;

FCO 1980; Language Training 1983; Moscow 1984; FCO 1984; Harare 1986; Second Secretary FCO 1990; SUPL 1992; Second Secretary FCO 1993; Brussels (UKREP) 1994; m 1986 Jonathan David Wolstenholme (2d 1989, 1994; 1s 1992).

Wong, Josephine; FCO since September 2001; born 17/12/72; Band D6.

Wong, Lillian Paterson (née Walker); FCO since February 1976; born 16/02/44; Senior Principal Research Officer FCO 1970; Second Secretary (Information/Aid) Yaoundé 1973; Band D6; m 1979 Robert Puck Keong Wong.

Wood, Christopher Terence; On loan to the Department of Environment since January 1992; born 19/01/59; FCO 1981; SOAS 1982; Language Training Hong Kong 1983; On secondment to Hong Kong Government as Assistant Political Adviser 1984; First Secretary FCO 1987.

Wood, Ian David; SUPL since August 2001; born 14/09/69; FCO 1992; Third later Second Secretary UKDEL OECD 1994; UKDEL NATO 1996; Second Secretary (Political) New Delhi 1996; FCO 1998.

Wood, James Sebastian Lamin, CMG (2002); Counsellor Washington since July 2001; born 06/04/61; FCO 1983; Language Training 1984; Second Secretary Bangkok 1986; Second later First Secretary FCO 1989; Full-Time Language Training Taiwan 1991; First Secretary and Consul for Macau BTC Hong Kong 1992; First Secretary UKREP JLG Hong Kong 1994; FCO 1996; On loan to the Cabinet Office 1998; Seconded to Harvard 2000; m 1990 Sirihat Penguam (3d 1992, 1993, 1995).

Wood, Michael Charles, CMG (1995); Legal Adviser FCO since December 1999; born 05/02/47; Called to the Bar, Grays Inn 1968; Assistant Legal Adviser FCO 1970; Legal Adviser Bonn 1981; Legal Adviser later Legal Counsellor FCO 1984; Counsellor (Legal) New York (UKMIS) 1991; Legal Counsellor FCO 1994; Deputy Legal Adviser 1996.

Wood, Michael John Hemsley; Counsellor (Regional Affairs) Accra since June 2002; born 16/09/48; FCO 1972; Third later Second Secretary Athens 1974; FCO 1976; First Secretary Harare 1980; Language Training 1983; First Secretary and Head of Chancery and Consul Hanoi 1984; First Secretary FCO 1987; Counsellor (Political) Helsinki 1993; Counsellor FCO 1997; Counsellor Lusaka 2000; m (1) 1975 Susan Christine Langford; (2) 1983 Wendy Mary Smith.

Wood, Dr Peter Gilruth; Counsellor Peking since September 2002; born 02/11/53; FCO 1982; Language Training 1983 (Taiwan 1984); First Secretary (Economic) Peking 1986; First Secretary FCO 1989; Kuala Lumpur 1995; Counsellor FCO 1998; m 1998 Pamela Sue Shookman.

Wood, Richard John; First Secretary (Economic) New York (UKMIS) since August 2002; born

27/08/67; FCO 1991; Cape Town/Pretoria 1993; First Secretary FCO 1998.

Wood, Richard Lewis; Third Secretary (Commercial) Johannesburg since February 1996; born 07/06/61; FCO 1982; Sofia 1984; Bandar Seri Begawan 1986; FCO 1989; Vice-Consul Riyadh 1992; m 1994 Frances Anne Curley (2s 1995, 1998).

Woodcock, Andrew; Third Secretary (Economic/Political) Mexico City since July 1996; born 18/09/65; FCO 1988; Vice-Consul Baghdad 1990; AMO/Vice-Consul Brasilia 1991; Third Secretary (Science and Technology) Bonn 1995; Band B3.

Woodham, Mark John; Bangkok since August 1998; born 18/11/67; FCO 1988; Helsinki 1991; Islamabad 1994; Band B3; m 1993 Sari Hannele Hakkarainen.

Woodier, Daniel Robert; FCO since July 1996; born 02/09/65; Band B3; m 1989 Sarah Harmer.

Woodrow, John Peter Gayford; Second Secretary (Consular) Helsinki since June 1997; born 21/11/47; FCO 1972; Barcelona 1975; Quito 1976; FCO 1979; La Paz 1983; Consul Istanbul 1988; FCO 1992; Consul Oslo 1995; m 1977 Yvonne Leffmann.

Woodruff Thomson, Helen; SUPL since January 1994; born 03/08/63; FCO 1985; Washington 1987; Harare 1989; FCO 1992; Band A2; m 1993 Captain Robert John Thomson.

Woodruffe, John Michael; Shanghai since September 1998; born 26/06/57; FCO 1986; Dublin 1989; Amman 1992; FCO 1995; Band C4; m 1989 Marian Barrett.

Woods, David John; Counsellor (Global Issues) Berlin since August 2002; born 04/08/51; Third later Second Secretary FCO 1976; Second later First Secretary (UNIDO & IAEA) Vienna 1978; First Secretary (Economic) Bucharest 1981; FCO 1981; First Secretary FCO 1985; Counsellor Harare 1992; Counsellor FCO 1995; Counsellor (Political) Pretoria 1997; m 1972 Rachel Haydon White (1s 1977; 1d 1979).

Woods, Harvey John; First Secretary Islamabad since March 2002; born 29/10/70; FCO 1999; Full-Time Language Training 2001; Band D6.

Woods, Ian Alexander; Counsellor FCO since September 1998; born 10/06/51; Third Secretary FCO 1976; Second Secretary New York (UKMIS) 1977; First Secretary FCO 1980; BMG Berlin 1984; Bonn 1986; First Secretary later Counsellor FCO 1989; Warsaw 1995; m 1978 Stephanie Flett (2s 1982, 1986).

Woodward, Amanda Jane; Rome since June 2002; born 29/04/56; FCO 1978; Brasilia 1979; New Delhi 1982; Moscow 1985; FCO 1988; Lisbon 1989; FCO 1991; Kuala Lumpur 1993; Muscat 1997; Band B3.

Woodward, Barbara Janet; Second Secretary Moscow since October 1994; born 29/05/61; FCO 1991.

Woodward, Emma Jane; BCG Jerusalem since May 2000; born 06/06/70; FCO 1996; BTCO Taipei 1997; Band A2.

Woodward, Gillian Yvonne (née Aplin); SUPL since November 1996; born 20/12/46; DSAO (later FCO) 1966; Paris (UKDEL OECD) 1969; Yaoundé 1972; FCO 1974; Lagos 1979; SUPL 1981; Helsinki 1984; FCO 1987; Mexico City 1990; FCO 1993; Band B3; m 1977 Roger Charles Woodward.

Woodward, Roger Charles; First Secretary (Management) Helsinki since October 2001; born 15/03/48; Commonwealth Office (later FCO) 1967; Dacca 1970; Caribbean Floater 1972; Doha 1973; FCO 1976; Lagos 1979; Helsinki 1982 (Second Secretary 1984); FCO 1987; Second Secretary (Commercial) Mexico City 1990; Second Secretary FCO 1993; First Secretary (Management) Paris 1997; m 1977 Gillian Yvonne Aplin.

Woolley, Lesley Ann; Islamabad since July 1986; born 27/04/64; FCO 1984; Band A2; m 1984 Samuel Patrick David Woolley.

Wooten, Sarah Elisabeth; Consul (Commercial and Investment) Nagoya since August 1999; born 04/02/68; FCO 1989; Third Secretary (Consular) Valletta 1992; Full-Time Language Training 1994; Full-Time Language Training Tokyo 1995; Osaka 1996; Band C4.

Wootton, Adam Nicholas; FCO since September 1996; born 19/05/60; FCO 1983; Baghdad 1985; FCO 1988; Nairobi 1993; Band C4; m 1984 Adele Wright (2s 1991).

Wordsworth, Ellyse Nichole (née Mingins); SUPL since July 1989; born 12/08/54; FCO 1975; Brussels (UKREP) 1977; Moscow 1980; FCO 1981; Second Secretary (Commercial) Lagos 1984; FCO 1986; m 1981 Stephen John Wordsworth (1s 1987).

Wordsworth, Stephen John, LVO (1992); Head of Eastern Adriatic Dept FCO since August 1999; born 17/05/55; FCO 1977; Third later Second Secretary Moscow 1979; FCO 1981; First Secretary (Economic/Commercial) Lagos 1983; On loan to Cabinet Office 1986; First Secretary FCO 1988; First Secretary (Political) Bonn 1990; Counsellor (Deputy International Affairs Adviser) SHAPE Mons 1994; m 1981 Ellyse Nichole Mingins (1s 1987).

Worham, Paul Andrew; Moscow since June 1999; born 15/12/66; HCS 1988; FCO 1997; Band A2; m 1999 Elizabeth Mary Smith.

Workman, Daniel John; FCO since September 2000; born 11/09/78; Band C4.

Worster, Paul Anthony; Third Secretary (Consular) Singapore since May 1999; born 14/05/62; FCO 1983; Warsaw 1985; Washington

1986; Helsinki 1989; FCO 1992; Tehran 1996; Band B3.

Worthington, Ian Alan, OBE (1999); First Secretary (Commercial) Berlin since October 2001; born 09/08/58; FCO 1977; Language Training 1978; Moscow 1980; Lusaka 1982; Second Secretary FCO 1985; Second Secretary (Commercial) Seoul 1988; Second Secretary (Chancery) Kingston 1992; Head BETO later Consul-General Ekaterinburg 1995; FCO 1998; Band D6.

Wotton, Rosaleen Mary (née McManus); ECO Nicosia since June 2000; born 15/01/62; FCO 1987; Oslo 1988; Brussels 1991; FCO 1992; Berne 1993; T/D Geneva 1993; FCO 1996; SUPL 1998; Band B3; m 1997 Alan Leslie Wotton (1s 1998).

Wragg, Ann Desson (née Traill); FCO since August 1992; born 20/03/65; FCO 1983; Paris 1985; FCO 1988; New York (UKMIS) 1989; Band B3; m 1988 John Wragg.

Wraight, Dr Christopher David; FCO since October 2001; born 19/11/75; Band C4.

Wright, Carol; Third Secretary (Management) Baku since August 2001; born 27/06/62; FCO 1988; Pretoria 1992; Johannesburg 1993; FCO 1996; Band B3.

Wright, Clive David; First Secretary Vienna (UKDEL OSCE) since May 1996; born 14/01/58; Royal Marines 1976; FCO 1977; Ankara 1980; Tripoli 1983; FCO 1984; Doha 1986 (Second Secretary 1989); Vice-Consul (Political/Admin) Johannesburg 1989; Second later First Secretary FCO 1993; m 1982 Christine Bernadette Caldwell (2d 1986, 1989).

Wright, David Alan, OBE (1984); HM Ambassador Doha since June 1997; born 27/05/42; FO 1965; APS to Minister of State FO 1966; MECAS 1968; Baghdad 1971; Second Secretary (Commercial) and Vice-Consul Doha 1973; On loan to DHSS 1976; Second later First Secretary FCO 1978; Consul and Head of Post Durban 1980; First Secretary (Commercial) Baghdad 1984; First Secretary later Counsellor FCO 1987; HM Consul-General Atlanta 1992; m 1966 Gail Karol Mesling (4s 1966, 1968, 1971, 1983; 1d 1978).

Wright, Sir David (John), GCMG (2002), KCMG (1996), LVO (1990), Grand Cordon of the Rising Sun (1998); Group Chief Executive (Permanent Secretary) British Trade International (Trade Partners UK and Invest UK) since June 1999; born 16/06/44; Third later Second Secretary Tokyo 1966; Diplomatic Service 1966; Second later First Secretary FCO 1972; ENA Paris 1975; First Secretary Paris 1976; Private Secretary to Secretary of Cabinet 1980; Counsellor (Economic) Tokyo 1982; Head of Personnel Services Department FCO 1985; On secondment to Buckingham Palace as Deputy Private Secretary to HRH The Prince of Wales 1988; HM Ambassador

Seoul (and Commissioner General, UK Pavillion Taejon EXPO 93) 1990; DUSS (Asia/Americas/Africa/Trade Promotion) 1994; FCO Non-Executive Director, AEA Technology 1994; HM Ambassador Tokyo 1996; m 1968 Sally Ann Dodkin (1s 1970; 1d 1973).

Wright, David Stephen; First Secretary (Political) Bogotá since February 2000; born 04/02/63; FCO 1989; Second Secretary (Chancery) Mexico City 1991; First Secretary FCO 1993; Band D6; m 1992 Tania Victoria Gessinger (2d 1999, 2001).

Wright, Julia Helen; Second Secretary (Political) Lisbon since April 2002; born 06/02/65; FCO 1991; Full-Time Language Training 1993; Amsterdam 1994; Third later Second Secretary (Chancery) Oslo 1997.

Wright, Nicola (née Daubney); FCO since February 1999; born 31/01/70; FCO 1989; Peking 1992; FCO 1993; Zagreb 1996; Band B3; m 1998 Alan David Wright.

Wright, Stephen John Leadbetter, CMG (1997); Deputy Under-Secretary FCO since October 2000; born 07/12/46; Third Secretary FCO 1968; Havana 1969; Second Secretary FCO 1972 (First Secretary 1975); Director of Policy and Reference Division and Consul (Information) New York (BIS) 1975; Brussels (UKREP) 1980; First Secretary FCO 1984; Counsellor 1985; On loan to Cabinet Office 1985; Counsellor and Head of Chancery New Delhi 1988; Counsellor (External Relations) Brussels (UKREP) 1991; Director (EU Affairs) FCO 1994; Minister Washington 1997; Director (Wider Europe) FCO 1999; m 1970 Georgina Susan Butler (diss 2000) (1d 1977; 1s 1979).

Wurr, Adam; Second Secretary FCO since January 2002; born 14/12/71; Second Secretary FCO 1995; Second Secretary Geneva (UKMIS) 2000; Band C4.

Wyatt, David; Deputy High Commissioner Lagos since October 2001; born 18/04/46; National Defence Course Latimer 1980; DSAO 1965; Lusaka 1968; SOAS 1971; Bangkok 1972 (Second Secretary 1975); Second Secretary Yaoundé 1976; Second later First Secretary FCO 1977 (First Secretary 1979); First Secretary (Commercial) Athens 1981; First Secretary and Head of Chancery Bangkok 1984; First Secretary FCO 1988; Deputy High Commissioner Accra 1994; FCO 1998; Counsellor (Commercial) Bangkok 1999; m 1969 Rosemary Elizabeth Clarke (1s 1972; 1d 1974).

Wye, Roderick Francis; FCO since 1999; born 13/09/50; Research Officer FCO 1973; PRO 1983; Peking 1985; First Secretary FCO 1988; First Secretary (Chancery) Peking 1995; m 1989 Katelin Rebecca Teller (1s 1994).

Wyithe, Philip Leslie; Second Secretary (Commercial) Ho Chi Minh City since March 2002; born 30/12/64; FCO 1983; Moscow 1987; Floater Duties 1990; Third Secretary (Consular) Sana'a 1992; Third Secretary (Immigration)

Biographical List

Valletta 1994; FCO 1995; Second Secretary (Management/Consular) Seoul 1997; Band B3; m 1992 Gina Olofernes Daniel (1d 1994).

Wylde, Richard Norman Gordon; First Secretary FCO since October 2000; born 18/10/58; FCO 1985; Second later First Secretary (Chancery) and Deputy Permanent Representative ESCAP Bangkok 1989; First Secretary FCO 1992; First Secretary (Political) Rome 1996; Band D6; m 1987 Lesley Tennison (1d 1991; 1s 1995).

Wynburne, Mark Barry; Second later First Secretary FCO since June 1981; born 29/03/45; Army 1963-64; FO 1966; Prague 1967; FCO 1968; Islamabad 1974; FCO 1978; Second Secretary and Vice-Consul Hanoi 1980; Band C5.

Wyver, Wendy Anne; Second Secretary (Political) Tokyo since September 1996; born 26/10/64; FCO 1993; Full-Time Language Training 1994; m 1995 Jakob Windfield Lund (1s 2001).

Y

Yaghmourian, Paul Barkef; Consul-General Rio de Janeiro since March 2002; born 14/02/58; FCO 1984; Second later First Secretary Lisbon 1986; First Secretary FCO 1989; First Secretary (Political) Brasilia 1993; Secondment to British Aerospace 1997; Counsellor and Deputy Head of Mission Copenhagen 1997.

Yapp, John William; FCO since October 2002; born 14/01/51; FCO 1971; Islamabad 1973; Kuala Lumpur (Consular) 1975; APS to Minister of State FCO 1978; Dubai (Commercial) 1980; Second Secretary (Economic/Commercial) The Hague 1984; First Secretary FCO 1988; First Secretary (Information/Political) Wellington 1991; Deputy Head of North America Department FCO 1995; High Commissioner Victoria (Seychelles) 1998; m (1) 1973 (1d 1975); (2) 1979 (1s 1981; 2d 1983, 1987); (3) 1997 Petra Jodelis (1d 1998).

Yarounina, Maggie; FCO since March 2000; born 08/07/72; Band B3; m 1999 Alexandre (Sasha) V Yarounine.

Yarrow, Jon William; Third later Second Secretary (Political/Information) Dubai since July 1998; born 29/01/69; FCO 1987; Washington 1989; Berne 1992; FCO 1995; m (1) 1989 Helen Mugridge (1d 1992; 1s 1995) (diss 1995); (2) 1999 Katherine Anne Short.

Yarrow, Katherine Anne (née Short); SUPL since October 1998; born 19/02/70; FCO 1992; Berne 1994; FCO 1996; Band A2.

Yeadon, Joanne Mary; Budapest since October 1996; born 01/08/65; FCO 1983; Washington 1986; Gibraltar 1989; FCO 1992; Full-Time Language Training 1996; Band B3.

Yearsley, Sara Elizabeth; FCO since June 2002; born 16/02/76; Band A2.

York, Jennifer Ann; Second Secretary (Management) December 1995; born 01/11/60; FCO 1980; BMG Berlin 1982; Africa/Middle East Floater 1985; Mogadishu 1988; FCO 1989; Vice-Consul Durban 1992; Band B3; m 1988 Murray Rex Clarkin (diss 1996).

Young, Amanda Elizabeth (née Mitchell); Dubai since September 1999; born 03/06/59; FCO 1977; Paris 1979; Cayman Islands 1982; FCO 1986; Riyadh 1987; Muscat 1989; FCO 1994; SUPL 1995; Band B3; m 2000 Murray Andrew James Young.

Young, Andrew John; SUPL since February 2000; born 02/04/60; Solicitor 1988 (Northern Ireland) and 1990 (England and Wales); Assistant Legal Adviser FCO 1990; Seconded to Hong Kong Government as Deputy Principal Crown Counsel 1994; Assistant Legal Adviser FCO 1997; Legal Counsellor FCO 1999; m (1) 1991 Lucy Stojak (diss 1996); (2) 1997 Annette Lee (1d 1997).

Young, Helena; FCO since September 1982 (First Secretary 1989); born 08/10/60; Band D6.

Young, Sir (John) Rob(ertson), KCMG (1999), CMG (1991); High Commissioner New Delhi since January 1999; born 21/02/45; Third Secretary FO 1967; MECAS 1968; Third later Second Secretary Cairo 1970; Second later First Secretary FCO 1973; Private Secretary to Parliamentary Under-Secretary later Minister of State FCO 1975; Paris 1977; ENA Paris 1977; FCO 1981; Acting Head of WED FCO 1983; Counsellor and Head of Chancery Damascus 1984; Counsellor FCO 1987; Minister Paris 1991; DUS (ME/FSU/EE) 1994; Chief Clerk 1995; m 1967 Catherine Houssait (2d 1969, 1978; 1s 1971).

Young, Sarah Louise (née Boxall); Second Secretary (Consular) Kampala since June 2002; born 16/09/63; FCO 1984; Lisbon 1987; FCO 1989; Cape Town 1997; Band B3; m 1990 Alan Young (2d 1991, 1992) (diss 1995).

Young, Thomas Nesbitt; High Commissioner Lusaka since January 1998; born 24/07/43; FO (later FCO) 1966; Ankara 1969; Madrid 1973; Second Secretary FCO 1977; Ankara 1978; First Secretary and Head of Chancery Ankara 1979; First Secretary Washington 1981; Deputy Director BTDO New York 1981; First Secretary FCO 1984; Deputy High Commissioner Accra 1987; Counsellor and Director of Trade Promotion Canberra 1990; HM Ambassador Baku 1993; m 1971 Elisabeth Hick (1d 1973; 1s 1975).

Young, Thomas Richard; FCO since September 2001; born 26/04/77; Band C4.

Younger, Alexander William; First Secretary (Political) Dubai since August 2002; born 04/07/63; Second Secretary FCO 1991; First Secretary (IAEA) Vienna (UKMIS) 1995; First Secretary FCO 1998; Band D6; m 1993 Sarah Hopkins (1d 1994; 2s 1996, 1998).

Younis, Fouzia; Islamabad since September 2001; born 08/07/78; FCO 2000; Band B3; m 2001 Haroon Suleman.

Z

Ziaullah, Suman Rafique; Second Secretary
(Political/Economic) Jakarta since October 2001;
born 27/10/76; FCO 1999; Band C4.

Printed in the United Kingdom by The Stationery Office
131710   C27   03/03   19585   824688